THE
ST.
JAMES

FILM DIRECTORS

ENCYCLOPEDIA

also from visible ink press

St. James Fashion Encyclopedia: A Survey of Style from 1945 to the Present Edited by Richard Martin, Curator of the Costume Institute of the Metropolitan Museum of Art, this is the most thorough survey of the contemporary world of fashion to date. It covers more than 200 famous and fledgling artists and houses from all over the world, including clothing designers, milliners, footwear designers and textile houses.

ISBN 0-7876-1036-4 • 7" x 9" • 438 pages • 100 photographs

St. James Modern Masterpieces: The Best of Art, Architecture, Photography and Design since 1945 Edited by Udo Kultermann, Professor Emeritus of Architecture at Washington University, St. Louis, this is an intriguing overview of the very best in contemporary art. *St. James Modern Masterpieces* is an essential and reasonably priced source for everyone who appreciates great art and design. It is international in scope and features 200 works created since 1945 that have achieved the status of "classic" or "masterpiece."

ISBN 1-57859-023-X • 7" x 9" • 450 pages • 200 photographs

St. James Opera Encyclopedia: A Guide to People and Works The history of opera, in all its drama and pageantry, is thoroughly explored in this lavishly illustrated book. Covering the art from its beginnings to the present day, *The St. James Opera Encyclopedia* presents 500 in-depth entries on operas, composers and performers.

ISBN 0-7876-1035-6 • 7" x 9" • 958 pages • 94 photographs

THE ST. JAMES

FILM DIRECTORS

ENCYCLOPEDIA

Andrew Sarris,
Editor

VISIBLE
INK
PRESS

DETROIT • NEW YORK • TORONTO • LONDON

The St. James Film Directors Encyclopedia

Edited by Andrew Sarris

Copyright © 1998 Visible Ink Press™
Visible Ink Press is a division of Gale Research
835 Penobscot Building
Detroit, MI 48226

Most Visible Ink Press™ books are available at special quantity discounts when purchased in bulk by corporations, organizations, or groups. Customized printings, special imprints, messages, and excerpts can be produced to meet your needs. For more information, contact Special Markets Manager, Gale Research, 835 Penobscot Bldg., Detroit, MI 48226. Or call 1-800-776-6265.

Cover Photo: Clint Eastwood on the set of *Unforgiven,* 1995. Courtesy of the Kobal Collection.
Cover Design: Pamela A. E. Galbreath

Library of Congress Cataloging-in-Publication Data

The St. James film directors encyclopedia / edited by Andrew Sarris
    p. cm.
  Includes filmographies and indexes.
  ISBN 1-57859-028-0
    1. Motion picture producers and directors—Biography—Dictionaries.
  I. Sarris, Andrew.

PN1998.2.S68 1997   97-26984
791.43'0233'0922—dc21   CIP

ISBN 1-57859-028-0
Printed in the United States of America
All rights reserved
10 9 8 7 6 5 4 3 2

about the editor

Andrew Sarris popularized the *auteur* theory of directing in the United States during the early 1960s. This theory became more widely accepted upon the publication of Sarris's *The American Cinema: Directors and Directions 1929-1968,* wherein Sarris used his theories to categorize and evaluate American directors. Sarris was the film critic for the *Village Voice* from 1960-1989 and an associate professor of cinema at Columbia University. He is the author or editor of nine books on film, including *The Primal Screen: Essays on Film and Related Subjects; Confessions of a Cultist: On the Cinema, 1955-1969; Politics and Cinema;* and *The John Ford Movie Mystery.*

contents

FILM DIRECTORS

contents

introduction

FILM DIRECTORS

When I was asked by Michael J. Tyrkus, editor at St. James Press, to winnow out two hundred or so directors from a previously compiled list of five hundred to include in the volume you now hold in your hands, it seemed an easy enough task, at least at first. After all, *The American Cinema,* which I first conceived back in 1962, contained material on 198 directors, and I had written critical comments on all of them, many not particularly favorable. How hard could it be then to accept and reject directors as if they were oranges on a pushcart? Only gradually did I realize the sheer size of the project. Actually, I was being asked to select the worthiest directorial careers from the motion picture industries of five continents over a hundred years of film history. The first hundred or so jumped out at me from the printed page, but by then I had exhausted my supply of personal favorites, other people's favorites, award winners, and the subjects of biographies and book-length critical studies. Indeed, many directors had burst into prominence during the thirty years since *The American Cinema* was published. It was no longer a question of who I liked, or who Mr. Tyrkus liked, or who all the people at St. James Press liked. It was more a question of what we and the many contributors to the encyclopedia remembered well enough to describe with conviction. What exactly had survived in someone's memory after thousands and thousands of movies had been screened throughout the world during this century?

Should we go back as far as Edwin S. Porter and D. W. Griffith in America or Louis Lumière and Georges Méliès in France? Should we flash forward to Quentin Tarantino and Tim Burton? Should we include documentarians besides Robert Flaherty? What about animators from Winsor McCay to Tex Avery? There were no fully satisfactory answers to these questions. We had to stop looking over our shoulders for naysayers to our final choices which begin alphabetically with Chantal Akerman and end with Fred Zinnemann. Undeniably many people will at least be partially unhappy with our choices, and why shouldn't they be when we are not entirely happy ourselves?

People still stop me in the street to argue with me over directors I allegedly either underrated or overrated three or four decades ago. The estimable David Thomson was recently criticized for omitting Dorothy Dandridge from his own excellent film reference book. The sifting of the sands of time for traces of talent and genius is an endless cultural activity. Where film is uniquely bothersome in this respect is in the realm perhaps less of creation than of consumption. Too many people have seen too many movies for any final pronouncements to be made. Also, though thousands of films from the silent era have been lost irretrievably, many hundreds more have been restored and recirculated. Happily, these are the best of times, technologically speaking, to catch up with old movie classics clustered around their directors, writers, actors, cinematographers, set designers, and all the other artists and technicians involved in the still liveliest art of them all.

No, I am not now, and have never been an unmodulated and uninflected auteurist. I insisted from the beginning of my discourses that directorial auteurism was the first step rather than the last stop of film scholarship. Yet, if what I wrote had not been maliciously misinterpreted and distorted, I would not today be considered worthy of saying thumbs up or thumbs down on five hundred directors through the ages. The choices speak for themselves as projections of time-tested tastes in film. And now, always, the director remains the center of cinematic creativity. Like the vain rooster in Edmond Rostand's *Chantecler,* I don't make the sun rise on the screen, but I am one of many critics and historians who herald its arrival in ambitious enterprises such as the *St. James Film Directors Encyclopedia.*

Andrew Sarris

chronology of film history

1829
Joseph Antoine Ferdinand Plateau develops and markets the Phenakistiscope, a small toy that provides the illusion of moving pictures

1884
George Eastman begins experimenting with celluloid roll film

1889
William Kennedy Laurie Dickson develops the Kinetophonograph while working for Thomas Alva Edison

1890-91
The earliest whole film on record at the Library of Congress, *Fred Ott's Sneeze*, is shot; Edison applies for patents for the Kinetograph (his motion picture camera) and the Kinetoscope (his peephole viewer)

1893
Edison's machines debut at the Chicago World's Fair

1894
Auguste Marie Louis Nicolas Lumière and Louis Jean Lumière develop the Cinématographe, a portable, crank operated camera

1895
The Lumière brothers shoot their first film, *Workers Leaving the Lumière Factory*; the first movie theatre opens in Paris on 28 December, and the Lumières show several films there

1896
The first public showing of a motion picture to a paying audience occurs on 23 April in New York, featuring Edison and Thomas Armat's Vitascope

1902
Georges Méliès shoots *A Trip to the Moon,* marking the first significant use of both narrative and special effects in a film

1903
Edwin S. Porter shoots *The Great Train Robbery,* which features the infamous sequence of a train racing towards the camera which causes viewers to believe that the train is actually coming off the screen towards them

1905
Cecil Hepworth shoots *Rescued by Rover*

1908
The major American motion picture companies form the Motion Picture Patents Company and usher in the Trust War; by 1915 the company will no longer exist and smaller studios will be the main producers of motion pictures; the National Board of Censorship is founded; D. W. Griffith begins directing films for Biograph; the French film company Film d'Art begins producing films; Charles Urban patents a color photographic process called Kinemacolor

1912
Mack Sennett begins producing comedic shorts for the Keystone Company

1913
Cecil B. De Mille begins making films

1914-15

Griffith shoots *The Birth of a Nation*; Charlie Chaplin begins working at Keystone

1917

The Technicolor Corporation is founded in the United States and begins experimenting with color film

1919

The Cabinet of Doctor Caligari is released, bringing the German Expressionist movement to film; Lev Kuleshov helps found the Moscow Film School, which eventually leads to the development of the *montage*; United Artists is formed by D. W. Griffith, Charlie Chaplin, Mary Pickford, and Douglas Fairbanks; Louis Delluc and Ricciotto Canudo found the first of many French societies for the preservation and presentation of the great films of the past, and the notion of the *cinéaste* (devotee of film) is born

1920s

Harold Lloyd, Buster Keaton, Harry Langdon, and Laurel and Hardy begin making films as the Golden Age of Comedy begins

1921

Chaplin shoots *The Kid*

1922

Will H. Hays becomes president of the Motion Picture Producers and Distributors of America; Robert Flaherty shoots *Nanook of the North*; F. W. Murnau's *Nosferatu* is released

1924

Erich von Stroheim's *Greed* is released: von Stroheim's original 7-plus hour version is cut down to 2½ that contain only one-quarter of footage shot by von Stroheim; John Ford makes his first western; Murnau's *The Last Laugh* is released

1925

Sergei M. Eisenstein shoots *Potemkin*; Chaplin shoots *The Gold Rush*; Alfred Hitchcock directs his first film, *The Pleasure Garden*

1926

Fritz Lang's *Metropolis* is released; Keaton shoots *The General*

1927

The Sound Era begins when *The Jazz Singer* opens on 6 October featuring a synchronized soundtrack on its musical numbers; Abel Gance's *Napoléon* is released at 270 minutes (the film is later restored to its original 5-hour length and re-released in 1981)

1928

The first all-talking film, *The Lights of New York,* is released; Walt Disney's *Steamboat Willie* is released; Carl-Theodor Dreyer's *The Passion of Joan of Arc* is released

1929

The First Academy Awards presentation is held on 16 May; Luis Buñuel and Salvador Dali release *Un Chien andalou*; the Marx Brothers make their first movie, *Cocoanuts*

1930s

Mae West and W. C. Fields begin making popular comedies

1930

The Hollywood Production Code is drafted by Martin Quigley and Daniel Lord, S.J., and is put into use; the Studio Era (1930-1945) begins in Hollywood; the Era of the French Film (1930-1940) begins; Josef von Sternberg's *The Blue Angel* is released

1931

Tod Browning's *Dracula* is released; René Clair's *A Nous la liberté* is released; Ernst Lubitsch's *Trouble in Paradise* is released

1932

George Cukor begins directing films for MGM and RKO

1933

Merian C. Cooper and Ernest Schoedsack make *King Kong*

mid-1930s

The television is introduced and the movies declare war

1935

Ford has his first major hit with *The Informer*; Hitchcock's *The 39 Steps* is released

1937

Jean Renoir's *Grand Illusion* is released

1938

Disney's first feature film, *Snow White and the Seven Dwarfs,* is released

1939

Hitchcock relocates to America; Victor Fleming's *Gone with the Wind* and *The Wizard of Oz* are released

1940

Ford shoots *The Grapes of Wrath*

1941

Orson Welles makes *Citizen Kane*; John Huston shoots *The Maltese Falcon*; Disney releases *Fantasia*

1943-45

Marcel Carné's *Les Enfants du paradis* is released

1945

Roberto Rossellini's *Roma, Città Aperta* is released, beginning the Neorealist Movement; the Motion Picture Export Association of America is founded to introduce American films in the global market

1946

Ford's *My Darling Clementine* is released; Frank Capra's *It's a Wonderful Life* is released; Jean Cocteau's *Beauty and the Beast* is released

1947

The first hearings of the House Un-American Activities Committee (HUAC) investigating Communist infiltration in the motion picture industry begin; the Czech film school, the F.A.M.U., is founded; Satyajit Ray helps found the first film society in India, the Calcutta Film Society

1948

Howard Hawks's *Red River* is released; Vittorio DeSica's *The Bicycle Thief* is released; Max Ophüls's *Letter from an Unknown Woman* is released; the Polish Lodz Film School is founded in Poland

1950s

Hollywood converts to color film; the Studio System collapses, necessitating that the director function as a producer as well—resulting in the increased production of teenage exploitation films to insure that monies spent are recouped; the drive-in becomes a popular place to view a movie; several types of films gain prominence, including the gangster, western, musical (which would fade by the mid-1950s), and science fiction film, as well as those labelled *film noir*; "trash" films are shot in France, such as the films of Joseph E. Levine, dubbed into English, then mass released in American theaters

1950

Buñuel's *Los olvidados* is released; Billy Wilder's *Sunset Boulevard* is released; Ophüls's *La Ronde* is released; Robert Bresson's *Diary of a Country Priest* is released; Akira Kurosawa's *Rashomon* is released and sparks intense popularity of films from the East in the West, beginning Japan's richest cinematic era (1950s)

1951

The second HUAC hearings begin, resulting in the Hollywood Black Lists; when ruling on the "Miracle" case (Burstyn v. Wilson, named "Miracle" after the Rossellini film *The Miracle*) the Supreme Court declares that motion pictures are part of the nation's press and are therefore guaranteed freedom of speech; Christian Nyby's *The Thing* is released; Paramount establishes a television-producing division, Screen Gems; Elia Kazan's *A Streetcar Named Desire* is released; Robert Wise's *The Day the Earth Stood Still* is released; Vincente Minnelli's *An American in Paris* is released

1952

Hollywood begins producing 3-D movies en masse in an attempt to compete with television; the Cinerama process is introduced to filmgoers; Chaplin's *Limelight* is released, becoming his last film produced in America; Fred Zinnemann's *High Noon* is released; Stanley Donen and Gene Kelly release *Singin' in the Rain*

1953

CinemaScope becomes a popular technique for recording motion pictures when the first CinemaScope feature, *The Robe*, is released; war is declared against the Production Code when Otto Preminger's *The Moon Is Blue* is released without approval; Laslo Benedek's *The Wild One* is released, ushering in an age of rebellious youth films; Samuel Fuller's *Pickup on South Street* is released; Kenji Mizoguchi's *Ugetsu monogatari* (*Ugetsu*) is released

1954

Cukor's *A Star Is Born* is released; Kazan's *On the Waterfront* is released; Hitchcock's *Rear Window* is released; Federico Fellini's *La Strada* is released; Kurosawa's *Shichinin no samurai* (*Seven samurai*) is released

1955

Satyajit Ray's *Pather Panchali* (*Father Panchali*) is released and leads to the short-lived Era of the Indian Cinema; Nicholas Ray's *Rebel without a Cause* is released; Henri-Georges Clouzot's *Les Diaboliques* is released; *Godzilla* is released in Japan, sparking the mutant monster movie genre; the Era of the Polish Cinema begins (1955-1964)

1956

Hollywood sells its first film to television, effectively ending its long-standing war with the small box; Don Siegel's *Invasion of the Body Snatchers* is released; Ford's *The Searchers* is released; Roger Vadim's *Et...Dieu créa la femme* is released; Satyajit Ray's *Aparajito* (*The Unvanquished*) is released

1957

Hitchcock's *Vertigo* is released; Ingmar Bergman's *Det sjunde inseglet* (*The Seventh Seal*) and *Smultronstället* (*Wild Strawberries*) are released; David Lean's *The Bridge on the River Kwai* is released; Kurosawa's *Kumonosu-jo* (*The Throne of Blood*) is released

1958

Bergman's *Ansiktet* (*The Magician*) is released; Andrzej Wajda's *Popiół i diament* (*Ashes and Diamonds*) is released

1959

Wilder's *Some Like it Hot* is released; at the suggestion of Rossellini, *Cahiers du cinéma* critics François Truffaut, Jean-Luc Godard, and Claude Chabrol begin seriously making films and the "New Wave" begins; Truffaut's *Les Quatre cents coups* (*The 400 Blows*) is released; Godard's *A bout de souffle* (*Breathless*) is released; Alain Resnais's *Hiroshima mon amour* is released; Jack Clayton's *Room at the Top* is released and becomes an international breakthrough for working-class British films; Satyajit Ray's *Apur Sansar* (*The World of Apu*) is released

late 1950s–early 1960s

The "auteur theory" of directorial control is simultaneously developed in America by Andrew Sarris and in France by François Truffaut; Sarris later solidifies his views with the publication of *The American Cinema: Directors and Directions 1929-1968* in 1968

1960

Hitchcock shoots *Psycho*; Kurosawa's *Yojimbo* (*The Bodyguard*) is released

1961

Truffaut's *Jules et Jim* is released; Buñuel's *Viridiana* is released

1962

Lean's *Lawrence of Arabia* is released

1963

The Czech New Wave (1963-1969) begins; Fellini's *8½* is released; Stanley Kubrick's *Dr. Strangelove: Or, How I Learned to Stop Worrying and Love the Bomb* is released

1964

Sergio Leone makes his first "spaghetti western," *A Fistful of Dollars*, with Clint Eastwood; Richard Lester directs the Beatles in *A Hard Day's Night*; Roman Polanksi's *Repulsion* is released

1965

Godard's *Alphaville* is released; Lean's *Doctor Zhivago* is released; Milos Forman's *Lásky jedné plavovlásky* (*Loves of a Blonde*) is released

1966

Michelangelo Antonioni's *Blow Up* is released; Bergman's *Persona* is released; Jan Nemec's *O slavnosti a hostech* (*Report on the Party and the Guests*) is released; Jirí Menzel's *Ostre sledované vlaky* (*Closely Watched Trains*) is released

1967

Arthur Penn's *Bonnie and Clyde* is released, defining the Hollywood Renaissance and bringing prominence to the independent American cinema; Jacques Tati's *Playtime* is released; Mike Nichols' *The Graduate* is released

1968

The war against the Production Code ends when the Code and Rating Administration replaces the Production Code Administration and the maturity rating system is established, including the ratings G for general audiences and M for mature audiences; Kubrick's *2001: A Space Odyssey* is released

1969

John Schlesinger's *Midnight Cowboy* is released; Sam Peckinpah's *The Wild Bunch* is released

late 1960s

Werner Herzog, Rainer Werner Fassbinder, and Wim Wenders enjoy critical, and some popular, success as the German cinema enjoys a renaissance

1970s

The Motion Picture Rating System is developed and replaces the maturity rating system—the new ratings include G for general audiences, PG which suggests parental guidance, R for restricted to those over 18, and X which was left over from the maturity rating system and was eventually adopted by the pornography industry and discarded by the Motion Picture Rating System for use on general release films

1971

Nicholas Roeg's *Walkabout* is released and brings attention to the Australian cinema; Louis Malle's

Le Souffle au coeur is released; Peter Bogdanovich's *The Last Picture Show* is released

1972

Francis Ford Coppola's *The Godfather* is released and a renewed fascination with the romanticism of crime begins

1974

Roman Polanksi's *Chinatown* is released; Coppola's *The Godfather, Part II* is released; Fassbinder's *Angst essen Seele auf (Ali: Fear Eats the Soul)* is released

1975

Steven Spielberg's *Jaws* is released and begins the era of the blockbuster film; Robert Altman's *Nashville* is released

1976

Martin Scorsese releases *Taxi Driver*; Bernardo Bertolucci's *1900* is released

1977

George Lucas's *Star Wars* is released; Woody Allen's *Annie Hall* is released; Pier Paolo Pasolini's *Salo* is released; Spielberg's *Close Encounters of the Third Kind* is released

1978

Michael Cimino's *The Deer Hunter* is released

1979

Allen's *Manhattan* is released; Coppola's *Apocalypse Now* is released; Scorsese shoots *Raging Bull*

late 1970s

Several advancements in moviemaking, such as the Dolby system, and constant advancements in the field of special effects, succeed in making seeing a movie an event again and, when added to the popularity of the blockbuster film, give rise to the Hollywood years

1980

The Hollywood years begin, characterized by several sub-genres of films that are aimed at a very specific demographic and designed to turn a profit, such as the *Friday the 13th* movies parts 1-9, and the rest of the slasher film genre

1981

István Szabó's *Mephisto* is released

1983

Shohei Imamura's *Narayama bushi-ko* (*The Ballad of Narayama*) is released

1984

Spielberg's *Indiana Jones and the Temple of Doom* is released and results in a new rating of PG-13 (not recommended for children under 13)

1986

David Lynch's *Blue Velvet* is released; Spielberg's *The Color Purple* is released

late 1980s

Rapid growth of cable television, pay-per-view premium channels, and home video once again threatens movie attendance

1990s

The major studios respond to the persistent threat of television by either purchasing or, once again, launching their own networks

1990

The first studio-released NC-17 movie is shown, disallowing anyone under 17

1993

Spielberg's *Jurassic Park* and *Schindler's List* are released, *Jurassic Park* becomes the highest grossing movie of all time and *Schindler's List* gives Spielberg his first Oscars, for Best Director and Best Picture

1994

The Motion Picture Export Association of America changes its name to the Motion Picture Association

1995

Quentin Tarantino's *Pulp Fiction* is released and signals the *cinemaphile modernist* movement, which is characterized by movies made by filmmakers who were raised on movies and consequently make extensive use of filmic allusions in their own films

1997

Five independent films are nominated for Best Picture at the 1996 Academy Awards

picture acknowledgments

Photographs in the *St. James Film Directors Encyclopedia* have been used with the permission of the following organizations:

British Film Institute, Department of Stills, Posters and Designs: Robert Altman, Lindsay Anderson, Gillian Armstrong, Alexandre Astruc, Ingmar Bergman, Bertrand Blier, Peter Bogdanovich, Tod Browning, Frank Capra, John Cassavetes, Charlie Chaplin, Jean Cocteau, Joel Coen, David Cronenberg, Cecil B. De Mille, Jonathan Demme, Carl Theodor Dreyer, Sergei Eisenstein, Federico Fellini, Robert Flaherty, Milos Forman, Samuel Fuller, Jean-Luc Godard, Jean Grémillon, D.W. Griffith, Howard Hawks, John Huston, James Ivory, Elia Kazan, Buster Keaton, Krzysztof Kieślowski, Stanley Kubrick, Akira Kurosawa, Fritz Lang, Alberto Lattuada, Spike Lee, Richard Lester, Albert Lewin, Joseph H. Lewis, Sidney Lumet, Louis Lumière, David Lynch, Louis Malle, Chris Marker, Albert and David Paul Maysles, Jonas Mekas, F.W. Murnau, Mikio Naruse, Mike Nichols, Marcel Ophuls, Max Ophüls, Sam Peckinpah, Maurice Pialat, Roman Polanski, Michael Powell and Emeric Pressburger, Otto Preminger, Nicholas Ray, Satyajit Ray, Jean Renoir, Nicolas Roeg, Roberto Rossellini, Jean Rouch, John Sayles, John Schlesinger, Martin Scorsese, Mack Sennett, Steven Spielberg, Mauritz Stiller, Preston Sturges, Maurice Tourneur, François Truffaut, Luchino Visconti, Margarethe Von Trotta

The Kobal Collection: Chantal Akerman, Robert Aldrich, Woody Allen, Theodoros Angelopoulos, Michelangelo Antonioni, Claude Autant-Lara, Jacques Becker, Robert Benton, Busby Berkeley, Bernardo Bertolucci, Budd Boetticher, John Boorman, Frank Borzage, Robert Bresson, Luis Buñuel, Tim Burton, James Cameron, Jane Campion, Marcel Carné, Claude Chabrol, Chen Kaige, René Clair, Jack Clayton, René Clement, Henri-Georges Clouzot, Francis Ford Coppola, Constantin Costa-Gavras, George Cukor, Michael Curtiz, Jules Dassin, Terence Davies, Jacques Demy, Vittorio De Sica, Alexander Dovzhenko, Marguerite Duras, Clint Eastwood, Blake Edwards, Victor Erice, Rainer Werner Fassbinder, John Ford, Bill Forsyth, Georges Franju, John Frankenheimer, Abel Gance, Peter

Greenaway, Sacha Guitry, Hal Hartley, Werner Herzog, Alfred Hitchcock, Kon Ichikawa, Jim Jarmusch, Aki Kaurismaki, Alexander Korda, Emir Kusturica, Gregory La Cava, David Lean, Patrice Leconte, Sergio Leone, Barry Levinson, Ken Loach, Joseph Losey, Ernst Lubitsch, George Lucas, Alexander Mackendrick, Dušan Makavejev, Terrence Malick, Rouben Mamoulian, Joseph L. Mankiewicz, Anthony Mann, Paul Mazursky, Leo McCarey, Georges Méliès, Jean-Pierre Melville, Vincente Minnelli, Kenji Mizoguchi, Robert Mulligan, Ermanno Olmi, Yasujiro Ozu, G.W. Pabst, Marcel Pagnol, Alan J. Pakula, Sergei Paradzhanov, Pier Paolo Pasolini, Arthur Penn, Sydney Pollack, Vsevolod Pudovkin, Carol Reed, Alain Resnais, Leni Riefenstahl, Jacques Rivette, Eric Rohmer, Francesco Rosi, Robert Rossen, Ken Russell, Claude Sautet, Volker Schlöndorff, Paul Schrader, Don Siegel, Robert Siodmak, Douglas Sirk, Alf Sjöberg, Victor Sjöström, Jerzy Skolimowski, Steven Soderbergh, John M. Stahl, George Stevens, Oliver Stone, Alain Tanner, Quentin Tarantino, Andrei Tarkovsky, Frank Tashlin, Jacques Tati, Bertrand Tavernier, Jacques Tourneur, Edgar Ulmer, Agnès Varda, King Vidor, Jean Vigo, Josef Von Sternberg, Erich Von Stroheim, Raoul Walsh, Charles Walters, Orson Welles, William Wellman, Wim Wenders, James Whale, Billy Wilder, Frederick Wiseman, William Wyler, Zhang Yi-Mou, Fred Zinnemann

THE
ST.
JAMES

FILM DIRECTORS

ENCYCLOPEDIA

Akerman, Chantal

Nationality *Belgian.* **Born** *Brussels, 6 June 1950.* **Education** *INSAS film school, Brussels, 1967-68; studied at Université Internationale du Théâtre, Paris, 1968-69.* **Career** *Saute ma vie entered in Oberhausen festival, 1971; lived in New York, 1972; returned to France, 1973; instructor, Harvard University, 1997.*

Films as Director: 1968: *Saute ma vie* (*Blow up My Town*). **1971:** *L'Enfant aimé* (*The Beloved Child*). **1972:** *Hotel Monterey; La Chambre.* **1973:** *Le 15/18* (co-d); *Hanging Out Yonkers* (unfinished). **1974:** *Je tu il elle* (+sc, role as Julie). **1975:** *Jeanne Dielman, 23 Quai du Commerce, 1080 Bruxelles* (+sc, voice of neighbor). **1977:** *News from Home* (+sc, voice). **1978:** *Les Rendez-vous d'Anna* (+sc). **1980:** *Dis-moi* (*Tell Me*). **1982:** *Toute une nuit* (*All Night Long*) (+sc). **1983:** *Les Années 80* (*The Golden Eighties*) (+co-sc); *Un jour Pina m'a demandé* (*One Day Pina Asked Me*). **1984:** *L'Homme à la valise* (*The Man with the Suitcase*); *J'ai faim, j'ai froid* (*I'm Hungry, I'm Cold*) (episode in *Paris vu par . . . 20 ans après*) (+co-sc); *Family Business; New York, New York Bis; Lettre d'un cinéaste* (*Letter from a Filmmaker*). **1986:** *La Paresse* (*The Sloth*); *Le Marteau* (*The Hammer*); *Mallet-Stevens; Letters Home.* **1987:** *Seven Women, Seven Sins* (co-d). **1988:** *Histoires d'Amérique: Food, Family and Philosophy/ American Stories.* **1989:** *Trois strophes sur la nom de Sacher* (*Three Stanzas on the Name Sacher*); *Les Trois dernières sonates de Franz Schubert* (*Franz Schubert's Last Three Sonatas*). **1991:** *Nuit et jour* (*Night and Day*) (+co-sc). **1992:** *Contre l'oubli* (*Against Oblivion*). **1993:** *D'est* (*From the East*) (+sc); *Le Déménagement* (*Moving In*). **1994:** *Portrait d'une jeune fille de la fin des années 60 á Bruxelles* (*Portrait of a Young Girl at the End of the 1960s in Brussels*) (+sc). **1996:** *Un Divan á New York* (*A Couch in New York*) (+co-sc).

Other Films: 1985: *Elle á passe tant d'heures sous les sunlights* (role as self).

At the age of fifteen Chantal Akerman saw Godard's *Pierrot le fou* and realized that filmmaking could be experimental and personal. She dropped in and out of film school and has since created short and feature films for viewers who appreciate the opportunity her works provide to think about sounds and images. Her films are often shot in real time, and in space that is part of the characters' identity.

During a self-administered apprenticeship in New York (1972-73) shooting short films on very low budgets, Akerman notes that she learned much from the work of innovators Michael

Chantal Akerman.
Photograph by Babette Mangolte.

Snow and Stan Brakhage. She was encouraged to explore organic techniques for her personal subject matter. In her deliberately paced films there are long takes, scenes shot with stationary camera, and a play of light in relation to subjects and their space. (In *Jeanne Dielman, 23 Quai du Commerce, 1080 Bruxelles,* as Jeanne rides up or down in the elevator, diagonals of light from each floor cut across her face in a regular rhythm.) Her films feature vistas down long corridors, acting with characters' backs to the camera, and scenes concluded with several seconds of darkness. In Akerman films there are hotels and journeys, little conversation. Windows are opened and sounds let in, doors opened and closed; we hear a doorbell, a radio, voices on the telephone answering machine, footsteps, city noises. Each frame is carefully composed, each gesture the precise result of Akerman's directions. A frequent collaborator is her sensitive cameraperson, Babette Mangolte, who has worked with Akerman on such works as *Jeanne Dielman, 23 Quai du Commerce, 1080 Bruxelles, News from Home,* and *Toute une nuit.* Mangolte has also worked with avant guardists Yvonne Rainer, Marcel Hanoun, and Michael Snow.

Plotting is minimal or non-existent in Akerman films. Old welfare clients come and go amid the impressive architecture of a once splendid hotel on New York's Upper West Side in *Hotel Monterey.* New York City plays its busy, noisy self for the camera as Akerman's voice on the sound track reads concerned letters from her mother in Belgium in *News from Home.* A young filmmaker travels to Germany to appear at a screening of her latest film, meets people who distress her, and her mother who delights her, and returns home in *Les Rendez-vous d'Anna.* Jeanne Dielman, super-efficient housewife, earns money as a prostitute to support herself and her son. Her routine breaks down by chance, and she murders one of her customers.

The films (some of which are semi-autobiographical) are not dramatic in the conventional sense, nor are they glamorized or eroticized; the excitement is inside the characters. In a film which Akerman has called a love letter to her mother, Jeanne Dielman is seen facing the steady camera as members of a cooking class might see her, and she prepares a meatloaf—in real time. Later she gives herself a thorough scrubbing in the bathtub; only her head and the motion of her arms are visible. Her straightening and arranging and smoothing are seen as a child would see and remember them.

In *Toute une nuit* Akerman displays her precision and control as she stages the separate, audience-involving adventures of a huge cast of all ages that wanders out into Brussels byways on a hot, stormy night. In this film, reminiscent of Wim Wenders and his wanderers and Marguerite Duras's inventive sound tracks, choreography, and sense of place, Akerman continues to explore her medium using no conventional plot, few spoken words, many sounds, people who leave the frame to a lingering camera, and appealing images. A little girl asks a man to dance with her, and he does. The filmmaker's feeling for the child and the child's independence can't be mistaken.

Akerman's *Moving In,* meanwhile, centers on a monologue delivered by a man who has just moved into a modern apartment. A film of "memory and loss," according to *Film Comment,* he has left behind "a melancholy space of relations, relations dominated by his former neighbors, a trio of female 'social science students.'"—LILLIAN SCHIFF

Aldrich, Robert

Nationality *American.* **Born** *Cranston, Rhode Island, 9 August 1918.* **Education** *Moses Brown School, Providence, and University of Virginia, graduated (law and economics) 1941.* **Family** *Married 1) Harriet Foster, 1941 (divorced 1965); children: Adell, William, Alida, and Kelly; 2) fashion model Sibylle Siegfried, 1966.* **Career** *Worked for RKO studios, 1941-44; under contract to Enterprise studios, 1945-48; TV director, from 1952; founded "Associates and Aldrich Company," 1955; signed contract for Columbia Pictures, then fired after refusing to "soften" script of* The Garment Jungle; *after five year period working abroad, returned to Hollywood, 1962; after* The Dirty Dozen, *established Aldrich Studios, 1967, but forced to sell, 1973; elected president of the Directors Guild, 1975; "Aldrich Company" reorganised, 1976.* **Awards** *Silver Prize, Venice Festival, for* The Big Knife, *1955; Silver Bear Award for Best Direction, Berlin Festival, for* Autumn Leaves, *1956; Italian Critics Award, Venice Festival, for* Attack!, *1956.* **Died** *In Los Angeles, of kidney failure, 5 December 1983.*

Films as Director: 1953: *The Big Leaguer.* **1954:** *World for Ransom* (+co-pr); *Apache; Vera Cruz.* **1955:** *Kiss Me Deadly* (+pr); *The Big Knife* (+pr). **1956:** *Autumn Leaves; Attack!* (+pr). **1957:** *The Garment Jungle* (un-credited). **1959:** *The Angry Hills; Ten Seconds to Hell* (+co-sc). **1961:** *The Last Sunset.* **1962:** *Sodoma e Gomorra* (*Sodom and Gomorrah*); *Whatever Happened to Baby Jane?* (+pr). **1963:** *Four for Texas* (+co-pr, co-sc). **1964:** *Hush . . . Hush, Sweet Charlotte* (+pr). **1966:** *Flight of the Phoenix* (+pr). **1967:** *The Dirty Dozen.* **1968:** *The Legend of Lylah Clare* (+pr); *The Killing of Sister George* (+pr). **1969:** *Too Late the Hero* (+pr, co-sc). **1971:** *The Grissom Gang* (+pr). **1972:** *Ulzana's Raid.* **1973:** *Emperor of the North* (*The Emperor of the North Pole*). **1974:** *The Longest Yard* (*The Mean Machine*). **1975:** *Hustle* (+ co-pr). **1977:** *Twilight's Last Gleaming; The Choirboys.* **1979:** *The Frisco Kid.* **1981:** *All the Marbles* (*California Dolls*).

Other Films: 1945: *The Southerner* (Renoir) (1st asst-d). **1946:** *The Story of G.I. Joe* (Wellman) (1st asst-d); *Pardon My Past* (Fenton) (1st asst-d); *The Strange Love of Martha Ivers* (Milestone) (1st asst-d). **1947:** *The Private Affairs of Bel Ami* (Lewin) (1st asst-d); *Body and Soul* (Rossen) (1st asst-d). **1948:** *Arch of Triumph* (Milestone) (1st asst-d); *So This Is New York* (Fleischer) (1st asst-d); *No Minor Vices* (Milestone) (1st asst-d). **1949:** *Force of Evil* (Polonsky) (1st asst-d); *The Red Pony* (Milestone) (1st asst-d); *A Kiss for Corliss* (Wallace) (1st asst-d). **1950:** *The White Tower* (Tetzlaff) (1st asst-d); *Teresa* (Zinnemann) (pre-production work). **1951:** *The Prowler* (Losey) (1st asst-d); *M* (Losey) (1st asst-d); *Of Men and Music* (Reis) (1st asst-d); *New Mexico* (Reis) (1st asst-d). **1952:** *Abbott and Costello Meet Captain Kidd* (Lamont) (1st asst-d); *Limelight* (Chaplin) (1st asst-d); *The Trio: Rubinstein, Heifetz and Piatigorsky* (*Million Dollar Trio*) (Dassin) (1st asst-d); *The Steel Trap* (Stone) (pr supervision). **1957:** *The Ride Back* (pr). **1969:** *Whatever Happened to Aunt Alice?* (pr).

Robert Aldrich

Despite a commercially respectable career both within the studio system and as an independent producer-director, Robert Aldrich remains an ill-appreciated, if not entirely bothersome presence for most American critics. Andrew Sarris did praise Aldrich in 1968 as "one of the most strikingly personal directors of the past two decades"; yet, for the most part, it has remained to the French and the English to attempt to unravel the defiant quirkiness of Aldrich's career. Only the otherworldly *Kiss Me Deadly,* which Paul Schrader unequivocably dubbed "the masterpiece of film noir," has received anything like the attention it deserves on this side of the Atlantic; yet the film is quite indicative of the bitter ironies, bizarre stylistics, and scathing nihilism characteristic of most of Aldrich's work.

In bringing Mickey Spillane's neo-fascist hero Mike Hammer to the screen, *Kiss Me Deadly* plays havoc with the conventions of the hardboiled detective, turning the existential avenger into a narcissistic materialist who exploits those around him for the benefit of his plush lifestyle. In an outrageous alteration of the novel's plot, Hammer becomes a modern neanderthal whose individualism is revealed as insanity when it causes him to botch a case involving a box of pure nuclear energy and thus the fate of the world. The result is a final shot of a mushroom cloud rising from a California beachhouse, consuming both Hammer and the bad guys. Only at this extreme and this distance in time has Aldrich's acute sense of irony impressed itself upon a liberal critical establishment whose repugnance to the surfaces of his films has usually served as an excuse for ignoring their savage, multi-layered critiques of Hollywood genres and American ideology.

The extremity of Aldrich's reinterpretations of the Western in *Ulzana's Raid,* of the war movie in *Attack!,* of the cop film in *The Choirboys,* and of the women's melodrama in *Autumn Leaves* betrays a cynicism so bitter that it could only arise from a liberal sensibility utterly disillusioned by an age in which morality has become a cruel joke. In fact, the shattering of illusions is central to Aldrich's work, and it is a powerfully self-destructive process, given the sweetness of the illusions and the anger of his iconoclasm. In *Whatever Happened to Baby Jane?,* a gothic horror film whose terms are explicitly the hideous realities hidden beneath the sugar-coating of the entertainment industry, Aldrich virtually defines the genre of camp, offering derisive laughter as the only alternative to an unbearably absurd cosmos. This sense of black comedy (which Aldrich shares with, and developed at the same time as, Hollywood contemporary Stanley Kubrick) has frequently been responsible for the volatile relationship his films have had with popular audiences. Given the context of a life-and-death prison football game in *The Longest Yard,* Aldrich was able to enlist the audience in the hero's bitter laughter in the face of a triumphant totalitarian authority. But when he adopted the same black humor toward the scandalous chicanery of the marginally psychotic cops in *The Choirboys,* he angered almost everybody, not the least of whom was the novel's author, Joseph Wambaugh.

Turned in an introspective direction, Aldrich's acid sensibility resulted in an intensely discomforting, stylistically alienated version of Clifford Odets's Hollywood-hating *The Big Knife* and the madly ambitious *The Legend of Lylah Clare,* an *8-1/2* cum *Vertigo* far too complex by any Hollywood standard. When turned outward toward the world at large, that same sensibility was responsible for a downbeat, disheartening masterpiece like the much-maligned *Hustle,* a film which succeeds better than almost any other in summing up the moral displacement and emotional anguish of the whole decade of the 1970s.

At his most skillful, Aldrich could juggle ideologically volatile issues so well that his most popular film, *The Dirty Dozen,* made during the politically turbulent period of the Vietnam War, played equally well to hawks and doves. Its story of death row prisoners exploited by the military bureaucracy into participation in a suicide raid, where they are to attack a chateau, slaughtering both German officers and civilians, seemed explicitly antiwar in its equation of heroism and criminality and its critique of the body-count mentality of a morally corrupt system. Yet, *The Dirty Dozen* still managed to emerge as a gung-ho war movie in the best Hollywood tradition. The multiple contradictions of the film's stance are nowhere clearer than in its climactic scene, where Aldrich has black athlete Jim Brown re-create one of his famous touchdown runs in order to set off an underground holocaust explicitly parallelled to Auschwitz.

In a far less popular film, the revisionist western *Ulzana's Raid,* Aldrich does confront the horrors of Vietnam with a nearly intolerable accuracy via the properly bloody metaphor of a cavalry company using West Point tactics to fight a band of Apache guerilla warriors. The film relentlessly refuses to diminish the brutality of the red man; even as it demonstrates the poverty of the white man's Christian idealism. The result is perhaps the first western ever to cast America's doctrine of Manifest Destiny in explicitly colonial terms.

More than any other mainstream director, Aldrich insisted on presenting the radical contradictions of American ideology. If we adopt a stance not nearly as cynical as his own in most of his films, we might observe that his capacity to do so has frequently resulted in sizable profits. Yet it is also important to remember that, while Stanley Kubrick (whose 1950s films bear striking stylistic and thematic similarities to those of Aldrich) found it necessary to retreat to England, reducing his output to two or three films a decade, Aldrich chose to fight it out in Hollywood, where his capacity for money-making allowed him the space to vent his own personal anger at the compromises we all must make.—ED LOWRY

Allen, Woody

Nationality American. *Born* Allen Stewart Konigsberg in Brooklyn, New York, 1 December 1935. *Education* Attended Midwood High School, Brooklyn; New York University, 1953; City College (now City College of the City University of New York), 1953. *Family* Married 1) Harlene Rosen, 1954 (divorced); 2) Louise Lasser, 1966 (divorced); one son, Satchel, by actress Mia Farrow, with whom Allen maintained a thirteen-year relationship, 1979-92; legally adopted two of Farrow's thirteen adopted children (one son, Moses; one daughter, Dylan), 1991. *Career* Began writing jokes for columnists and television

Woody Allen on the set of *Radio Days*. *Photograph by Brian Hamill.*

celebrities while still in high school; joined staff of National Broadcasting Company, 1952, writing for such television comedy stars as Sid Caesar, Herb Shriner, Buddy Hackett, Art Carney, Carol Channing, and Jack Paar; also wrote for The Tonight Show *and* The Garry Moore Show; *began performing as stand-up comedian on television and in nightclubs, 1961; hired by producer Charles Feldman to write* What's New, Pussycat?, *1964; production of his play* Don't Drink the Water *opened on Broadway, 1966; wrote and starred in Broadway run of* Play it Again, Sam, *1969-70 (filmed 1972); began collaboration with writer Marshall Brickman, 1976; wrote play* The Floating Light Bulb, *produced at Lincoln Center, New York, 1981.* **Awards** *Sylvania Award, 1957, for script of* The Sid Caesar Show; *Academy Awards (Oscars) from the Academy of Motion Picture Arts and Sciences for Best Director and Best Original Screenplay (co-recipient), New York Film Critics Circle Award, and National Society of Film Critics Award, all 1977, all for* Annie Hall; *British Academy Award and New York Film Critics Award, 1979, for* Manhattan; *Academy Award for Best Original Screenplay, New York Film Critics Award, and Los Angeles Film Critics Award, all 1986, all for* Hannah and Her Sisters. **Agent** *Rollins and Joffe, 130 W. 57th Street, New York, NY 10009, U.S.A.* **Address** *930 Fifth Avenue, New York, New York 10021, U.S.A.*

Films as Director, Scriptwriter, and Actor: 1969: *Take the Money and Run.* **1971:** *Bananas* (co-sc). **1972:** *Everything You Always Wanted to Know about Sex but Were Afraid to Ask.* **1973:** *Sleeper.* **1975:** *Love and Death.* **1977:** *Annie Hall* (co-sc). **1978:** *Interiors* (d, sc only). **1979:** *Manhattan* (co-sc). **1980:** *Stardust Memories.* **1982:** *A Midsummer Night's Sex Comedy.* **1983:** *Zelig.* **1984:** *Broadway Danny Rose.* **1985:** *The Purple Rose of Cairo* (d, sc only). **1986:** *Hannah and Her Sisters.* **1987:** *Radio Days* (role as narrator). **1988:** *September* (d, sc only); *Another Woman* (d, sc only). **1989:** *Crimes and Misdemeanors;* "Oedipus Wrecks" episode in *New York Stories.* **1990:** *Alice* (d, sc only). **1992:** *Shadows* and Fog; Husbands and Wives. **1993:** Manhattan Murder Mystery. **1994:** Bullets over Broadway (d, co-sc only); Don't Drink the Water (for TV). **1995:** Mighty Aphrodite. **1996:** Everyone Says I Love You. **1997:** Deconstructing Harry.

Other Films: 1965: What's New, Pussycat? (sc, role). **1966:** What's Up, Tiger Lily? (co-sc, assoc pr, role as host/narrator); Don't Drink the Water (play basis). **1967:** Casino Royale (Huston and others) (role). **1972:** Play It Again, Sam (Ross) (sc, role). **1976:** The Front (Ritt) (role). **1987:** King Lear (Godard) (role). **1991:** Scenes from a Mall (Mazursky) (role). **1998:** Ants (voice).

Woody Allen's roots in American popular culture are broad and laced with a variety of European literary and filmic influences, some of them paid explicit homage within his films (Ingmar Bergman and Dostoevsky, for example), others more subtly woven into the fabric of his work from a wide range of earlier comic traditions. Allen's genuinely original voice in the cinema recalls writer-directors like Buster Keaton, Charlie Chaplin, and Preston Sturges, who dissect their portions of the American landscape primarily through comedy. In his creative virtuosity Allen also resembles Orson Welles, whose visual and verbal wit, though contained in seemingly non-comic genres, in fact exposes the American character to satirical scrutiny.

Allen generally appears in his own films, resembling the great silent-screen clowns who created, then developed, an ongoing screen presence. However, Allen's film persona depends upon *heard* dialogue and especially thrives as an updated, urbanly hip, explicitly Jewish amalgam of personality traits and delivery methods associated with comic artists who reached their pinnacle in radio and film in the 1930s and 1940s. The key figures Allen plays in his own films puncture the dangerous absurdities of their universe and guard themselves against them by maintaining a cynical, even misogynistic verbal offense in the manner of Groucho Marx and W. C. Fields, but alternating it with incessant displays of self-deprecation, in the manner of the cowardly, unhandsome persona established by Bob Hope in, for example, his *Road* series.

Allen's early films emerge logically from the sharp, pointedly exaggerated jokes and sketches he wrote for others, then delivered himself as a stand-up comic in clubs and on television. Like the early films of Buster Keaton, most of these early films depend upon explicit parody of recognizable film genres. Even the films of this pre-*Annie Hall* period which do not formally rely upon a particular film genre incorporate references to various films and directors as commentary on the specific targets of social, political, or literary satire: political turbulence of the 1960s via television news coverage in *Bananas*; the pursuit by intellectuals of large religious and philosophical questions via the methods of Tolstoy and Dostoevsky in *Love and Death*; American sexual repression via the self-discovery guarantees offered by sex manuals in *Everything You Always Wanted to Know about Sex*.

All these issues will reappear in Allen's later, increasingly mature work—and they will persist in revealing an anomaly: Allen's comedy is cerebral in nature, dependent even in its occasional sophomoric moments upon an educated audience that responds to his brand of self-reflexive, literary, political, and sexual humor. But Allen distrusts and satirizes formal education and institutionalized discourse, which in his films lead repeatedly to humorless intellectual preening. "Those who can't do, teach, and those who can't teach, teach gym," declares Alvy Singer in *Annie Hall*. No character in that film is treated with greater disdain than the Columbia professor who smugly pontificates on Fellini while standing in line waiting to see *The Sorrow and the Pity*; Allen inflicts swift, cinematically appropriate justice. Yale, a university professor of English, bears the brunt of *Manhattan*'s moral condemnation as a self-rationalizing cheat who is far "too easy" on himself.

In *Annie Hall,* his Oscar-winning breakthrough film, Allen the writer (with Marshall Brickman) recapitulates and expands emerging Allen topics but removes them from the highly exaggerated apparatus of his earlier parodies. Alvy Singer (Allen) and Annie Hall (Diane Keaton in her most important of several roles in Allen's films) enact an urban-neurotic variation on the mismatched lovers of screwball comedy, now oriented away from farce and toward character analysis set against a realistic New York City *mise-en-scène.*

Annie Hall makes indelible the Woody Allen onscreen persona—a figure somehow involved in show business or the arts and obsessive about women, his parents, his childhood, his values, his terror of illness and death; perpetually and hilariously taking the mental temperature of himself and everyone around him. Part whiner, part *nebbish,* part hypochondriac, this figure is also brilliantly astute and consciously funny, miraculously irresistible to women—for a while—particularly (as in *Annie Hall* and *Manhattan*) when he can serve as their teacher. This developing figure in Allen's work is both comic victim and witty victimizer, a moral voice in an amoral age who repeatedly discovers that the only true gods in a Godless universe are cultural and artistic—movies, music, art, architecture—a perception pleasurably reinforced visually and aurally throughout his best films. With rare exception—*Hannah* is a notable one—this figure at the film's fadeout appears destined to remain alone, by implication enabling him to continue to function as a sardonically detached observer of human imperfection, including his own. In *Annie Hall,* this characterization, despite its suffusion in *angst,* remains purely comic but Allen becomes progressively darker—and harder on himself—as variants of this figure emerge in the later films.

Comedy, even comedy that aims for a laughter of recognition based on credibility of character and situation, depends heavily upon exaggeration. In *Zelig,* the tallest of Woody Allen's cinematic tall tales, the film's central figure is a human chameleon who satisfies his overwhelming desire for conformity by physically transforming himself into the people he meets. Zelig's bizarre behavior is made even more visually believable by stunning shots that appear to place the character of Leonard Zelig (Allen) alongside famous historical figures within actual newsreel footage of the 1920s and 1930s.

Shot in Panavision and velvety black-and-white, and featuring a Gershwin score dominated by "Rhapsody in Blue," *Manhattan* reiterates key concerns of *Annie Hall* but enlarges the circle of participants in a sexual *la ronde* that increases Allen's ambivalence toward the moral terrain occupied by his characters—especially by Ike Davis (Allen), a forty-two-year-old man justifying a relationship with a seventeen-year-old girl. By film's end she has become an eighteen-year-old woman who has outgrown him, just as Annie Hall outgrew Alvy Singer. The film (like *Hannah and Her Sisters* later) is, above all, a celebration of New York City, which Ike, like Allen, "idolize[s] all out of proportion."

In the Pirandellian *Purple Rose of Cairo,* the fourth Allen film to star Mia Farrow, a character in a black-and-white film within the color film leaps literally out of the frame into the heroine's local movie theatre. Here film itself—in this case the movies of the 1930s—both distorts reality (by setting dangerously high, incongruous expectations) and makes it more bearable (by permitting Cecilia, Allen's heroine, to escape from her dismal Depression existence). Like *Manhattan* before it, and *Hannah and Her Sisters* and *Radio Days* after it, *Purple Rose of Cairo* examines the healing power of popular art.

Arguably Allen's finest film to date, *Hannah and Her Sisters* shifts his own figure further away from the center of the story than he has ever been before, treating him as one of nine prominent characters in the action. Allen's screenplay weaves an ingenious tapestry around three sisters, their parents, assorted mates, lovers, and friends (including Allen as Hannah's ex-husband Mickey Sachs). A Chekhovian exploration of the upper-middle-class world of a group of New Yorkers a decade after *Annie Hall,* Hannah is deliberately episodic in structure, its sequences separated by Brechtian title cards that suggest thematic elements of each succeeding segment. Yet it is an extraordinarily seamless film, unified by the family at its center; three Thanksgiving dinner scenes at key intervals; an exquisite color celebration of an idyllic New York City; and music by Cole Porter, Rodgers and Hart, and Puccini (among others) that italicizes the genuinely romantic nature of the film's tone. The most optimistic of Allen's major films, *Hannah* restores its inhabitants to a world of pure comedy, their futures epitomized by the fate of Mickey Sachs. For once, the Allen figure is a man who will live happily ever after, a man formerly sterile, now apparently fertile, as is comedy's magical way.

Crimes and Misdemeanors further marginalizes—and significantly darkens—the figure Woody Allen invites audiences to confuse with his offscreen self. The self-reflexive plight of filmmaker Cliff Stern (Allen) alternates with the central dilemma confronted by ophthalmologist Judah Rosenthal, a medical pillar of society who bears primary, if indirect, responsibility for the murder of his mistress. Religious and philosophical issues present in Allen's films since *Love and Death* achieve a new and serious resonance, particularly through the additional presence of a faith-retaining rabbi gradually (in one of numerous Oedipal references in Allen's work) losing his sight, and a Holocaust survivor-philosopher who preaches the gospel of endurance—then commits suicide by (as his note prosaically puts it) "going out the window." In its pessimism diametrically opposed to the joyous *Hannah and Her Sisters, Crimes and Misdemeanors* posits a universe utterly devoid of poetic justice. The picture's genuinely comic sequences, usually involving Cliff and his fatuous producer brother-in-law ("Comedy is tragedy plus time!") do not contradict the fact that it is Allen's most somber major film, a family comedy-melodrama that in its final sequence crosses the brink to the level of domestic tragedy. Here, the Allen figure is not only alone, as he has been in the past, but alone and *in despair.*

In entirely contrasting visual ways, *Alice* and *Shadows and Fog* exhibit immediately recognizable Allen concerns in highly original fashion. A glossy, airy, gently satiric modern fairy tale, *Alice* implicitly functions as Allen's most open love letter to Mia Farrow. Her idealized title character searches for meaning in a Yuppified New York City. Eventually, she finds it by leaving her husband, meeting Mother Theresa, and, especially, by discovering that her two children offer her the only genuine vehicle for romance in this romantic comedy *manque.* The film's final shot displays a glowing Alice joyfully pushing them on playground swings as two former women friends, in voice-over dialogue, bemoan her self-selected maidless and nannyless condition, one which the film clearly intends us to embrace.

In *Shadows and Fog,* Allen employs a specific film genre more directly than at any time since the 1970s. His homage to German Expressionism, *Shadows and Fog* is shot in black and white in a manner deliberately reminiscent of the films of Pabst, Lang, and Murnau. That visual style and the placement at the film's center of a distinctly Kafkaesque hero (played by Allen) combine to make *Shadows and Fog* Allen's most explicitly "European," most wryly metaphysical film since *Interiors* fourteen years earlier. Not surprisingly, *Shadows and Fog* was greeted by critics much more favorably in Europe than in the United States.

As Chekhov's forgiving spirit energizes the comic tone of *Hannah and Her Sisters,* so the playwright August Strindberg's hostility controls the dark marital terrain of *Husbands and Wives.* Strindbergian gender battles frequently appear in earlier Allen films, but they are more typically rescued back from the precipice into a healing world of comedy. Allen's partial attempt to attribute comic closure to *Husbands and Wives* pleases but inadequately convinces. While the film (which might have been more accurately titled *Husbands, Wives, and Lovers*) is often extremely funny, its portrait of two deteriorating marriages is as corrosive as anything in the Allen canon. *Husbands and Wives* contains other elements long present in Allen's films: multiple story-lines, a deliberately episodic structure covering a period of about a year (as in *Hannah* and *Crimes and Misdemeanors*), and the involvement of a central character, Gabe Roth (played by Allen), with a woman young enough to be his daughter. Unlike Ike Davis's relationship with Tracy in *Manhattan,* however, this one is consummated—and concluded—with only a kiss.

Despite the presence of familiar material, *Husbands and Wives* shows Allen continuing to break new ground, particularly in the film's visual virtuosity. The frequent use of a hand-held camera reinforces the neurotic, darting, unpredictable behavior of key characters. Moving beyond his use of title cards to provide Brechtian distancing in *Hannah and Her Sisters,* Allen here employs a documentary technique to punctuate the main action of the film. The central characters and a minor one (the ex-husband of Judy Roth, the woman played by Mia Farrow) are individually interviewed by an off-screen male voice, which appears to function simultaneously as documentary recorder of their woeful tales *and* as therapist to their psyches. These sequences are inserted periodically throughout the film, as the interviewees speak directly to the camera— and therefore to *us,* thus forcing the audience to participate in the filmmaker-interviewer's role as therapist.

Husbands and Wives deserves a place alongside *Hannah and Her Sisters* and *Crimes and Misdemeanors* to represent Allen's most textured and mature work to date. But the film's visual and thematic pleasures have been obscured by audience desires to see in *Husbands and Wives* the spectacle of art imitating life with a vengeance; and, in fact, *Husbands and Wives* does contain uncanny links to the Allen-Farrow breakup even though the film was completed before their relationship came to a dramatic and highly visible end.

The type of ethical dilemma which occupies such a central place in the Allen canon (and which usually finds its most articulate definition in the mouths of characters played by Allen himself) appeared to have tumbled out of an Allen movie and onto worldwide front pages. ("Life doesn't imitate art; it imitates bad television," says Allen's Gabe Roth in *Husbands and Wives.*) In 1992, shortly before the release of *Husbands and Wives,* Allen's romantic relationship with Soon-Yi Previn, Mia Farrow's twenty-one-year-old adopted daughter, was discovered by her mother, who made the fact public. Furious and ugly charges and countercharges ensued and led to Allen's loss of custody of his three children a year later.

Allen has made several films since *Husbands and Wives* was released, all of them reverting to the explicit world of comedy: *Don't Drink the Water,* adapted from his early Broadway play and first shown in America on network television; *Manhattan Murder Mystery,* a comedy-mystery in the manner of *The Thin Man* films and the *Mr. and Mrs. North* radio and television series (with Diane Keaton replacing Mia Farrow, who was originally scheduled to play Allen's wife); *Bullets over Broadway,* in which John Cusack plays a younger Allen stand-in, a playwright grappling with his first Broadway production; and *Mighty Aphrodite,* which again tempts audiences to see elements of Allen's life reflected in the central plot issue of child adoption. But with its parodies of Greek tragedy and its broadly satiric array of characters, *Mighty Aphrodite* rarely strays from its identification as genuine Allen *comedy*. These 1990s films reveal yet again why so many actors want to work with Allen: Dianne Wiest won her second supporting actress Oscar for her role in an Allen film for *Bullets over Broadway* (her first was for *Hannah*); and Mira Sorvino won the same award for *Mighty Aphrodite* the following year.

Allen's primary response to the tarnish on his personal reputation has been to keep making films. He has always denied that his film persona is related to his own, although it is often justifiably difficult for us to believe that. "Is it over? Can I go now?" asks Gabe Roth of the off-screen interviewer in the final shot of *Husbands and Wives*. Divorced from his wife, Gabe is now alone, but he *chooses* be to alone. Gabe may not be happy—rarely is any character played by Woody Allen ever actually *happy*—but, unlike Clifford Stern at the end of *Crimes and Misdemeanors*, Gabe is decidedly *not* in despair. As the comic spirit of Allen's recent films suggests, that fact would appear to bode extremely well for Allen's future work and, especially, for those who love his films.—MARK W. ESTRIN

Altman, Robert

Nationality *American.* **Born** *Kansas City, Missouri, 20 February 1925.* **Education** *Attended University of Missouri, Columbia (three years).* **Military Service** *Bomber pilot, U.S. Air Force, 1943-47.* **Family** *Married 1) La Vonne Elmer, 1946, one daughter; 2) Lotus Corelli, 1954, divorced 1957, two sons; 3) Kathryn Reed, two sons.* **Career** *Directed industrial films for Calvin Company, Kansas City, 1947; wrote, produced, and directed first feature,* The Delinquents, *1955; TV director, 1957-63; co-founder of TV production company, 1963; founder, Lion's Gate production company (named after his own 8-track sound system), 1970, Westwood Editorial Services, 1974, and Sandcastle 5 Productions; made* Tanner '88 *for TV during American Presidential Campaign, 1988; directed* McTeague *for Chicago Lyric Opera.* **Awards** *Palme d'Or, Cannes Festival, and Academy Award nominations for Best Film and Best Director for* M*A*S*H, *1970; New York Film Critics' Circle Award, D.W. Griffith Award (National Board of Review), and National Society of Film Critics Award, all for Best Director, for* Nashville, *1975; Golden Bear, Berlin Festival, for* Buffalo Bill and the Indians, *1976; Academy Award nomination for Best Director, New York Film Critics Circle Award for Best Film and Best Director, for* The Player, *1992; Academy Award nomination for Best Director, for* Short Cuts. **Agent** *Johnny Planco, William Morris Agency, 1325 Avenue of the Americas, New York, New York 10019.* **Address** *Sandcastle 5 Productions, 502 Park Avenue, Suite 15G, New York, New York 10022-1108.*

Films as Director: 1954: *The Builders* (medium length publicity film). **1955:** *The Delinquents,* sc). **1957:** *The James Dean Story* (co-d, +co-pr, co-ed). **1964:** *The Party* (short); *Nightmare in Chicago* (*Once Upon a Savage Night*) (for TV). **1965:** *Pot au Feu* (short); *The Katherine Reed Story* (short). **1967:** *Countdown* (moon-landing sequence uncred by William Conrad). **1969:** *That Cold Day in the Park.* **1970:** *M*A*S*H; Brewster McCloud* (+pr). **1971:** *McCabe and Mrs. Miller* (+co-sc). **1972:** *Images* (+pr, sc). **1973:** *The Long Goodbye.* **1974:** *Thieves Like Us* (+co-sc); *California Split* (+co-pr). **1975:** *Nashville* (+co-pr, co-songwriter: "The Day I Looked Jesus in the Eye"). **1976:** *Buffalo Bill and the Indians, or Sitting Bull's History Lesson* (+pr, co-sc). **1977:** *Three Women* (+pr, sc). **1978:** *A Wedding* (+pr, co-sc). **1979:** *Quintet* (+pr, co-sc); *A Perfect Couple* (+pr, co-sc); *Health* (+pr, sc). **1980:** *Popeye.* **1981:** *The*

Robert Altman

Easter Egg Hunt. **1982:** *Come Back to the Five and Dime, Jimmy Dean, Jimmy Dean; Two by South* ("Rattlesnake in a Cooler" and "Precious Blood") (for TV) (+pr). **1983:** *Streamers* (+pr); *O.C. and Stiggs* (+pr) (released 1987). **1984:** *Secret Honor* (*Secret Honor: The Political Testament of Richard M. Nixon; Secret Honor: A Political Myth*) (+pr). **1985:** *The Laundromat* (for TV). **1986:** *Fool for Love.* **1987:** "Les Boreades" in *Aria; Beyond Therapy* (+co-sc); *The Room* (for TV); *The Dumb Waiter* (for TV). **1988:** *Tanner '88; The Caine Mutiny Court-Martial* (+pr). **1990:** *Vincent and Theo.* **1992:** *The Player.* **1993:** *Short Cuts.* **1994:** *The Real McTeague* (for TV, opera); *Ready to Wear* (*Pret a Porter*). **1996:** *Kansas City* (+pr, co-sc); *Jazz '34.* **1997:** *The Gingerbread Man; Gun* (co-d, +co-pr).

Other Films: 1948: *Bodyguard* (co-story). **1951:** *Corn's-A-Poppin'* (co-sc). **1976:** *Welcome to L.A.* (Rudolph) (pr). **1977:** *The Late Show* (Benton) (pr). **1978:** *Remember My Name* (Rudolph) (pr). **1979:** *Rich Kids* (Young) (pr). **1994:** *Mrs. Parker and the Vicious Circle* (pr). **1997:** *Afterglow* (pr).

The American 1970s may have been dominated by a "New Wave" of younger, auteurist-inspired filmmakers including George Lucas, Peter Bogdanovich, Steven Spielberg, Martin Scorsese, and Francis Ford Coppola, all contemporaries as well as sometime colleagues. It is, however, an outsider to this group, the older Robert Altman, perhaps that decade's most consistent chronicler of human behavior, who could be characterized as the artistic rebel most committed to an unswerving personal vision. If the generation of whiz kids tends to admire the American cinema as well as its structures of production, Altman tends to regard the American cinema critically and to view the production establishment more as an adversary to be cunningly exploited on the way to an almost European ambiguity.

Although Altman has worked consistently within American genres, his work can instructively be seen as anti-genre: *McCabe and Mrs. Miller* is a kind of anti-western, exposing the myth of the heroic westerner (as described by Robert Warshow and executed by John Wayne and John Ford) and replacing it with an almost Marxist view of the Westerner as financier, spreading capitalism and corruption with opportunism and good cheer. *The Long Goodbye* sets itself in opposition to certain aspects of the hard-boiled detective genre, as Elliott Gould's Philip Marlowe reflects a moral stance decidedly more ambiguous than that of Raymond Chandler's conventional lonely moralist. Similarly, *Countdown* can be seen in relationship to the science-fiction film; *Thieves Like Us* (based on *They Live by Night*) in relationship to the bandit-gangster film; *That Cold Day in the Park* in relationship to the psychological horror film inaugurated by Alfred Hitchcock's *Psycho*; and *California Split* in relationship to that generic phenomenon so common to the 1970s, the "buddy film." Even *Nashville,* Altman's complex bicentennial musical released in 1975, can be seen in relationship to a generic tradition with roots in *Grand Hotel* and branches in *Earthquake,* for it is a kind of disaster film about the American dream.

Aside from his generic preoccupations, Altman seems especially interested in people. His films characteristically contain perceptive observations, telling exchanges, and moments of crystal clear revelation of human folly. Altman's comments are made most persuasively in relationship to a grand social organization: that of the upper classes and *nouveaux riches* in *A Wedding*; health faddists and, metaphorically, the American political process, in *Health*; and so forth. Certainly, Altman's films offer a continuous critique of American society: people are constantly using and exploiting others, though often with the tacit permission of those being exploited. One thinks of the country-western singers' exploitation by the politician's p.r. man in *Nashville,* for instance, or the spinster in *That Cold Day in the Park*. Violence is often the climax of an Altman film—almost as if the tensions among the characters must ultimately explode. Notable examples include the fiery deaths and subsequent "surprise ending" in *A Wedding,* or the climactic assassination in *Nashville*.

Another recurring interest for Altman in his preoccupation with the psychopathology of women: one thinks of the subtly encroaching madness of Sandy Dennis's sexually repressed spinster in *That Cold Day in the Park,* an underrated, early Altman film; the disturbing instability of Ronee Blakley in *Nashville*; the relationships among the unbalanced subjects of *Three Women,* based on one of Altman's own dreams; and the real/surreal visions of Susannah York in the virtual horror film, *Images*. Because almost all of Altman's characters tend to be hypocritical, psychotic, weak, or morally flawed in some way, with very few coming to a happy end, Altman has often been attacked for a kind of trendy cynicism. The director's cynicism, however, seems a result of his genuine attempt to avoid the conventional myth-making of the American cinema. Altman imbues as many of his characters as possible with that sloppy imperfection associated with human beings as they are, with life as it is lived.

Performers enjoy working with Altman in part because he provides them with the freedom to develop their characters and often alter the script through improvisation and collaboration.

Like Bergman, Altman has worked often with a stock company of performers who appear in one role after another, among them Elliott Gould, Sally Kellerman, Rene Auberjonois, Keith Carradine, Shelley Duvall, Michael Murphy, Bert Remsen, and Henry Gibson.

Altman's distinctive style transforms whatever subject he approaches. He often takes advantage of widescreen compositions in which the frame is filled with a number of subjects and details that compete for the spectator's attention. Working with cinematographer Vilmos Zsigmond, he has achieved films that are visually distinguished and tend toward the atmospheric. Especially notable are the use of the zoom lens in the smoky cinematography of *McCabe and Mrs. Miller*; the reds, whites, and blues of *Nashville*; the constantly mobile camera, specially mounted, of *The Long Goodbye,* which so effortlessly reflects the hazy moral center of the world the film presents; and the pastel prettiness of *A Wedding,* particularly the first appearance of that icon of the American cinema, Lillian Gish, whose subsequent filmic death propels the narrative.

Altman's use of multi-track sound is also incredibly complex: sounds are layered upon one another, often emanating from different speakers in such a way that the audience member must also decide what to listen for. Indeed, watching and listening to an Altman film inevitably requires an active participant: events unroll with a Bazinian ambiguity. Altman's Korean War comedy *M*A*S*H* was the director's first public success with this kind of soundtrack. One of his more extreme uses of this technique can be found in *McCabe and Mrs. Miller,* generally thought to be among the director's finest achievements.

Nashville, Altman's most universally acclaimed work, provides a panoramic view of the American experience and society as it follows the interrelated experiences of twenty-four characters in the country-western music capital. In its almost three-hour length, *Nashville* accumulates a power of the whole even greater than the vivid individual parts which themselves resonate in the memory: the incredibly controlled debut performance of Lily Tomlin and the sensitive performances of at least a dozen others; the lesson on sexual politics Altman delivers when he photographs several women listening to a song by Keith Carradine; the vulnerability of Ronee Blakley, who suffers a painful breakdown in front of her surprisingly fickle fans; the expressions on the faces of the men who watch Gwen Welles's painfully humiliating striptease; and the final cathartic song of Barbara Harris, as Altman suddenly reveals the conventional "Star is Born" myth in his apparent anti-musical, like a magician stunning us with an unexpected trick.

Overall, Altman's career itself has been rather weird. His output since *M*A*S*H* has been prodigious indeed, especially in light of the fact that a great number of his films have been financial and/or critical failures. In fact, several of his films, among them *A Perfect Couple* and *Quintet* (with Paul Newman) barely got a national release; and *Health* (which starred Glenda Jackson, Carol Burnett, James Garner, and Lauren Bacall) languished on the shelf for years before achieving even a limited release in New York City. The most amazing thing about Altman's *Popeye,* which was relatively successful with critics and the public (though not the blockbuster that Hollywood had counted on), was that Altman managed to secure the assignment at all. The film that emerged was one of the most cynical and ultimately disturbing of children's films, in line with Altman's consistent vision of human beings and social organization.

Altman's career in the 1980s veered sharply away from mainstream film, dominated instead by a number of film adaptations of theatre pieces, including *Come Back to the Five & Dime, Jimmy Dean, Jimmy Dean; Streamers; The Laundromat; Secret Honor; Beyond Therapy;* and *Fool for Love.* Although many of these works are fascinating and contain incredibly modulated performances and surprisingly evocative cinematography (particularly *Jimmy Dean*), these films have not been particularly influential or financially successful. But they allowed Altman to continue to make notable films in a Spielberg-dominated era that was otherwise largely hostile to his provocative filmmaking.

Vincent and Theo, one of the few Altman films in this period which did not start out as a play, received much positive notice. Altman's decision to preface his film with documentary footage of a present-day auction in which millions of dollars are offered for a single Van Gogh painting was particularly stunning in a Brechtian way. He then begins his narrative story of Van Gogh's lifetime financial failure, trying to remain true to his painter's vision. Certainly, it is the parallels between Van Gogh and Altman which incite the director's interest. *Tanner '88,* a mock documentary about the 1988 American presidential campaign which many critics consider among Altman's master works, was even more amazing. It was a cult hit which marked Altman's return to the kind of satire with which he had already excelled. Unfortunately, its distribution on cable TV prevented this work from reaching a wide audience.

The most stunning development in Altman's career is the total critical and financial comeback he made with 1992's *The Player,* a film that appeared long after most Hollywood executives had written him off. The most insightful and scathing satire about Hollywood and filmmaking today, *The Player* hilariously skewered one target after another (the pitch, the Hollywood restaurant, the Hollywood party, the dispensable writer), in the process winning the New York Film Critics Circle awards for Best Film and Best Director. Contributing to the film's popular success were the dozens of stars who took cameos as themselves in order to support Altman, whom they have always admired.

The success of *The Player* allowed Robert Altman to go forward with his most ambitious project since *Nashville,* another panoramic narrative featuring dozens of characters, this time set in contemporary Los Angeles and based on a group of interlocking stories by Raymond Carver. The result, *Short Cuts,* seems unquestionably a masterpiece, one of those rare contemporary American films which truly attempts to examine American values (or what passes for them) and dissect life as it is being lived today. The film is memorable in many respects, from its opening images of helicopters sweeping over Los Angeles to spray for the Med-fly infestation to its depictions of phone sex, urban violence, and earthquake; from its depiction of Angelenos struggling to connect with each other to their debilitating failures; from its overwhelmingly rich soundtrack and striking cinematography to its complex narrative structure and brilliant perform- ances. *Short Cuts* is a key Altman film which will undoubtedly come to be regarded as a masterpiece of the American cinema as well.

In 1994 Altman took on the fashion industry in *Ready to Wear (Pret a Porter).* Critics and the public were much less kind in their regard for this panoramic satire, but the film was nevertheless witty and controlled, more subtle and light-hearted than had been anticipated. The film's finale—whereby a group of models parade naked—marked the witty and appropriate conclusion of Altman's satire on the political and ideological implications of fashion and its capacity to demean our values.

As a postscript on Altman, one should add that he, more than any other director, should never be counted out as an important force in American film culture. If his work is sometimes uneven, the fact that he continues to work on projects which are political, ideological, and personal—refusing to compromise his own artistic vision—is a sign that he remains, even in his seventies, the United States' single most ambitious *auteur*. His own future agenda includes two films based on the two plays comprising Tony Kushner's award-winning panorama *Angels in America*, widely praised as the most important American piece of theatre since Arthur Miller's *Death of a Salesman*. Although Altman might seem to be the perfect director, in a culminating masterpiece, to deal with AIDS, racism, homophobia, McCarthyism, Ethel Rosenberg, Mormon fundamentalism, the fall of Communism, the nature of capitalism, and God's culpability for problems in contemporary America, Altman's peripatetic popularity with Hollywood backers suggests that realization of these interlocking projects is by no means a sure thing, no matter how eagerly anticipated the results.—CHARLES DERRY

Anderson, Lindsay

Nationality British. *Born* Lindsay Gordon Anderson in Bangalore, South India, 17 April 1923. *Education* Attended Cheltenham College and Wadham College, Oxford. *Military Service* Member of Army Intelligence Corps during World War II. *Career* Editor, Sequence *magazine, 1947-52; helped organize first Free Cinema program, National Film Theatre, 1956; directed first feature,* This Sporting Life, *1963; associate artistic director, Royal Court Theatre, 1971-75; also directed TV plays and commercials. *Awards* Oscar for Best Short Subject, for* Thursday's Children, *1955; Palme d'Or, Cannes Festival, for* If. . . , *1969. *Died* Of a heart attack while vacationing in the Dordagne region of France, 30 August 1994.*

Films as Director: 1948: *Meet the Pioneers* (+sc, co-ed, narration). **1949:** *Idlers That Work* (+sc, narration). **1952:** *Three Installations* (+sc, narration); *Trunk Conveyor* (+sc, narration); *Wakefield Express* (+sc). **1953:** *Thursday's Children* (co-d, +co-sc); *O Dreamland* (+sc). **1955:** *Green and Pleasant Land* (+sc); *Henry* (+sc, role); *The Children Upstairs* (+sc); *A Hundred Thousand Children* (+sc); *£20 a Ton* (+sc); *Energy First* (+sc); *Foot and Mouth* (+sc, narration). **1957:** *Every Day Except Christmas* (+sc). **1963:** *This Sporting Life.* **1967:** *The White Bus*; *Raz, dwa, trzy* (*The Singing Lesson*) (+sc). **1969:** *If. . .* (+pr). **1972:** *O Lucky Man!* (+co-pr). **1974:** *In Celebration.* **1982:** *Britannia Hospital.* **1985:** *Wish You Were There* (*Foreign Skies*). **1986:** *The Whales of August.* **1988:** *Glory! Glory!.* **1993:** *Is That All There Is?* (+sc, role).

Other Films: 1949: *Out of Season* (Brendon) (narrator). **1952:** *The Pleasure Garden* (Broughton) (pr, role). **1956:** *Together* (Mazzetti) (supervising ed). **1958:** *March to Aldermaston* (supervising ed). **1960:** *Let My People Go* (Krish) (sponsor). **1962:** *The Story of Private Pooley* (Alsen) (English-language version of *Der Schwur des Soldaten Pooley*) (narrator). **1965:** *The Threatening Sky* (Ivens) (English-language version of *Le Ciel, la terre*) (narrator). **1966:** *Mucednici lásky* (*Martyrs of Love*) (Nemec) (role). **1967:** *About ''The White Bus''* (Fletcher) (role as himself). **1968:** *Abel Gance—The Charm of Dynamite* (Brownlow) (for TV) (narrator); *Inadmissable Evidence* (Page) (role). **1969:** *The Parachute* (Page) (for TV) (role). **1970:** *Hetty King—Performer* (Robinson) (narrator). **1971:** *A Mirror from India* (Sarabhai) (narrator). **1981:** *Chariots of Fire* (Hudson) (role as schoolmaster). **1991:** *Prisoner of Honor* (for TV) (role as war minister). **1992:** *Blame It on the Bellboy* (role as Mr. Marshall). **1994:** *Lucky Man* (role as himself).

In a 1958 essay entitled "Get Out and Push," Lindsay Anderson expressed his approach to working in the cinema. The way Anderson, the individual, approached working in the cinema paralleled the world view he put forth in feature films: the individual must examine the basis of the system within which he finds himself, "the motives that sustain it and the interests that it serves." It is the responsibility of the individual to actively seek a new self-definition beyond the confines of the established system; the individual cannot look for change to come from or through any outside authority—political, social, or spiritual. This theme is consistently present in Anderson's feature films.

In *This Sporting Life,* Anderson approaches the repression of a traditionally structured society through the personal, subjective story of Frank Machin and Margaret Hammond. The setting of *This Sporting Life,* an industrial northern city, is an environment divided into economic classes, a division which serves to emphasize the central problem of the film—the division within Frank Machin. Machin finds himself limited to the realm of the physical, and constantly attempts to connect with others on an emotional level. Despite his attempts, he is only seen in terms of his physical qualities; he is valued only when he is participating in the physical act of playing rugby.

Frank Machin is aware of his limitations but does not know how to change; he lacks direction. He tries to make others responsible for his happiness: Margaret Hammond, the rugby team, and even the elites of society who populate the world of Mr. and Mrs. Weaver, owners of the rugby team. Machin constantly attempts to break into the established system, seemingly unaware that it is this same system which controls and restrains him.

Lindsay Anderson
© **Roger Mayne**

Mick Travis, the protagonist of Anderson's second feature film, *If. . .,* struggles instead to break out of the established system. Mick takes on the responsibility of action, and although his revolution is not complete, he does not remain trapped like Frank. The environment in *If. . .,* the English public school system, is a metaphor for the "separation of intellect from imagination," according to Elizabeth Sussex. The environment of College House does not allow for the creative development of the individual. It encourages separation and fragmentation of the self.

Film technique in *If. . .* also serves to reveal the narrative theme of the division of the self. The chapter headings physically divide the film into rigidly ordered sections, reflecting the separation of intellect and imagination encouraged by the nature of the tradition of College House. These chapter headings, along with the alternation between black and white and color film, function as distancing devices, making the viewer more aware of the medium.

A narrative technique Anderson used to illustrate the process that leads to Mick's eventual break from the system is the establishment of verbal language as an essential part of the structure of College House. When Mick expresses his disdain for College House through words, they are simply absorbed by the system. There is no change in Mick's situation until he initiates action by bayoneting the college chaplain. After this point, Mick no longer recites revolutionary rhetoric; in fact, he rarely speaks. He is no longer existing within the structure of College House. Totally free of the system, Mick launches into the destruction of the established order. Mick is no longer acted upon but is the creator of action; in this respect, he triumphs where Frank Machin fails.

In *O Lucky Man!*, the thematic sequel to *If. . . ,* the medium of film itself becomes one of the narrative themes, and self-reflexive film techniques serve to reveal not only the narrative theme of self-definition, but also the process of filmmaking. The titles used in *O Lucky Man!* announce the different sections of the film but do not impose order; on the contrary, their abrupt appearance and brevity tend to interrupt the order of the narrative. It is as if the medium of film itself breaks through to remind the viewer of its existence. Indeed the medium, specifically the energy the medium generates, is one of the themes of *O Lucky Man!* The process of creation in the medium far exceeds anything Mick accomplishes in the narrative until the two meet in the final sequence.

Mick Travis, the character, confronts Lindsay Anderson, the director, at an audition for the film *O Lucky Man!* Mick obediently projects the different emotions Anderson demands of him until he is asked to smile. It is at this point that Mick finally takes action and rejects a direct order: "What is there to smile about?" he asks. Mick is looking outside himself for motivation, as he has done throughout the film, before he will take action. Anderson, exasperated, strikes Mick with a script. After receiving the blow, Mick is able to smile. He soon finds that he is one of the actors in the film; he too is capable of creating action.

Britannia Hospital, the final work in the series begun by *If. . . ,* presents a much darker vision than Anderson's previous films. As in *If. . . ,* the physical environment of the film—the hospital—is a metaphor for a static, repressive system. Unlike *If. . . ,* this film contains little hope for change or progress, not for the individual and certainly not within the system itself. Mick Travis appears in this film as an investigative reporter who has achieved success by selling "something the people want," a reference to his former position in *O Lucky Man!* and a description of his motives as a news reporter. He is attempting to expose the questionable experiments of Britannia Hospital staff member Dr. Millar, the same unethical researcher from *O Lucky Man!* Although Mick puts up a fight, the system finally overwhelms him in this film.

Glory! Glory!, a Home Box Office production, is somewhat of a synthesis of Anderson's previous work in both theme and technique. The institution that stands as metaphor in this case is one peculiar to the United States, a television evangelism empire—The Church of the Companions of Christ. Like the school in *If. . . ,* this institution has a verbal language essential to its structure, the use of which sanctions just about any action. Throughout the film people have "revelations" or "visions" in which God makes key decisions for them, removing all personal responsibility. Any action is justifiable—deception, fraud, blackmail—as long as it is done in "a holy cause" or "for the church."

The film techniques Anderson uses in *Glory! Glory!* are related to his earlier works. The medium is present throughout the narrative in the form of chapter headings and blackouts between chapters. Music is important to the narrative, as it is in *O Lucky Man!*, but in the later film it is integrated into the narrative structure rather than used as a distancing device.

The theme of personal responsibility for self-definition is clearly seen in the character of Ruth. She struggles throughout the film with the idea of who she wants to be and with the identities others want to impose on her. She reaches a key point in her personal progression when she admits that she has always needed some kind of crutch—sex, drugs, God. Not long after realizing that she has been looking outside herself for an identity, Ruth reveals that she finally understands God. In essence, she has created her own god, her own mythology. Ruth remains within the system, but for the first time actually believes in what she is "selling" because she has defined for herself the "authority" and the basis for the system.

Anderson's other features, *In Celebration* and *The Whales of August,* contain more subjective narratives but still explore the theme of the individual's responsibility for self-definition. In his last film, *Is That All There Is?,* an autobiographical documentary made for the BBC, Anderson presents himself as such an individual: an independent artist who actively sought a self-definition beyond the confines of the established system.—MARIE SAELI

Angelopoulos, Theodoros

*Nationality (Surname also spelled "Anghelopoulos") Greek. **Born** Athens, 27 April 1935.* ***Education*** *Studied in Athens, 1953-59, Sorbonne, Paris, 1961-64, and at IDHEC, Paris, 1962-63.* ***Military Service*** *1959-60.* ***Career*** *Film critic for left-wing journal* Dimoktatiki Allaghi *until its suppression in 1967 coup; worked as lawyer until 1969; began association with cinematographer Giorgios Arvanitis on* Reconstruction, *1970; taught at Stavrakou Film School in 1970s.* ***Awards*** *Georges Sadoul Award, 1971; FIPRESCI Award, 1973, for* Days of '36; *FIPRESCI Grand Prix, Golden Age Award, B.F.I. Best Film, Interfilm Award, for* The Travelling Players; *Golden Hugo Award, for* The Hunters; *Golden Lion Award, Venice, 1980; Chevalier des Arts et des Lettres.*

Films as Director and Scriptwriter: 1968: *Ekpombi* (*The Broadcast; L'Emission*). **1970:** *Anaparastassi* (*Reconstruction; Reconstitution*) (+ro). **1972:** *Mères tou 36* (*Days of '36; Jours de 36*). **1975:** *O Thiasos* (*The Travelling Players; Le Voyage des comédiens*) (+co-sc). **1977:** *I Kynighi* (*The Hunters*) (+co-pr). **1980:** *O Megalexandros* (*Alexander the Great*) (+co-sc). **1982:** *Athens* (doc). **1984:** *Taxidi sta Kithira* (*Voyage to Cythera*) (+pr, co-sc). **1986:** *O Melissokomos* (*The Beekeeper*) (+co-pr, co-sc). **1988:** *Topio stia Omichli* (*Landscape in the Mist*) (+co-sc). **1991:** *To Meteoro Vima tou Pelargou* (*The Suspended Step of the Stork*) (+co-pr, co-sc). **1995:** *To Vlemma tou Odyssea* (*Ulysses' Gaze, The Gaze of Odysseus*) (+co-sc); *Lumière et compagnie* (*Lumière and Company*).

Other Films: 1968: *Kieron* (role).

Theodoros Angelopoulos's considerable achievements in cinema during the 1970s and 1980s have made him not only the most important Greek filmmaker to date, but one of the truly creative and original artists of his time. In 1970 he convinced producer George Papalios to finance his first film, *Anaparastassi.* The story follows the pattern of a crime tale à la James Cain. A Greek peasant is killed by his wife and her lover on his return from Germany, where he had gone to find work. A judge tries to reconstruct the circumstances of the murder, but finds himself unable to communicate with the accused, who belong to a totally different culture. To shoot this Pirandellian story of misunderstanding, Angelopoulos adopted an austere style featuring long camera movements that show a bleak and desolate Greek landscape far removed from the tourist leaflets. Reminiscent of Visconti's *Ossessione,* this is a film noir that opens the way to more daring aesthetic ventures.

Angelopoulos's trilogy of *Days of '36, The Travelling Players,* and *The Hunters* can be seen as an exploration of contemporary Greek history. If his style shows some influences—particularly Jancsó's one reel-one take methodology and Antonioni's slow, meditative mood—Angelopoulos has nevertheless created an authentic epic cinema akin to Brecht's theatre in

Theodoros Angelopoulos

which aesthetic emotion is counterbalanced by a reflexive approach that questions the surfaces of reality. The audience is not allowed to identify with a central character, nor to follow a dramatic development, nor given a reassuring morality. The director boldly goes from the present to the past within the same shot, and in *The Hunters* broadens his investigation by including the fantasies of his characters. The sweep of a movie like *Travelling Players,* which includes songs and dances, is breathtaking. Its tale of an actors group circulating through Greece from 1939 to 1952 performing a pastoral play is transformed into a four-hour earth odyssey.

Angelopoulos's masterpiece was preceded by the haunting *Days of '36.* This political thriller about a murder in a prison proved a prelude to events of national importance. It is the director's most radical use of off-screen space and off-screen sound, of the dialectic between the seen and the unseen. With its closed doors, whispering voices in corridors, and silhouettes running to and fro, it evokes the mystery that surrounds the exercise of power.

Angelopoulos's fifth film, *Alexander the Great,* breaks new ground: it deals with myth and develops the exploration of the popular unconscious already present in *Travelling Players* and *The Hunters.* At the turn of the twentieth century, a bandit is seen as the reincarnation of the Macedonian king. He kidnaps some English residents in Greece and leads them to the mountains. The kidnapper tries to blackmail the British government but ends up killing his hostages. Angelopoulos opposes several groups: the foreigners, the outlaws, some Italian anarchists who have taken refuge in Greece, and village people who try to establish a utopian community. The director's indictment of hero-worship and his portrayal of diverse forms of political failure reveal a growing pessimism in his works. But his style is as masterful as ever, reaching a kind of austere grandeur reminiscent of Byzantine mosaics. Few have blended political investigation with a search for new forms of expression with such satisfying results.—MICHEL CIMENT

Antonioni, Michelangelo

*Nationality Italian. **Born** Ferrara, Italy, 29 September 1912. **Education** Studied at University of Bologna, 1931-35, and at Centro Sperimentale di Cinematografica, Rome, 1940-41. **Career** Journalist and bank teller, 1935-39; moved to Rome, 1939; film critic for* Cinema *(Rome) and others, 1940-49; assistant director on* I due Foscari *(Fulchignoni), 1942; wrote screenplays for Rossellini, Fellini, and others, 1942-52; directed first film,*

Gente del Po, *1943 (released 1947).* **Family** *Married Enrica Antonioni in 1986.* **Awards** *Special Jury Prize, Cannes Festival, for* L'avventura, *1960, and* L'eclisse, *1962; FIPRESCI Award from Venice Festival, for* Il deserto Rosso, *1964; Best Director Award, National Society of Film Critics, for* Blow-Up, *1966; Palme d'Or, Cannes Festival, for* Blow-Up, *1967.* **Address** *Via Vicenzo Tiberio 18, Rome, Italy.*

Films as Director: 1950: *Cronaca di un amore* (*Story of a Love Affair*) (+co-sc). 1952: *I Vinti* (*I nostri figli; The Vanquished*) (+co-sc). 1953: *La signora senza camelie* (*Camille without Camelias*) (+co-sc); "Tentato suicidio" episode of *L'Amore in città* (*Love in the City*)(+sc). 1955: *Le amiche* (*The Girlfriends*) (+co-sc). 1957: *Il grido* (*The Outcry*) (+co-sc). 1959: *L'avventura* (*The Adventure*) (+co-sc). 1960: *La notte* (*The Night*) (+co-sc). 1962: *L'eclisse* (*The Eclipse*) (+co-sc). 1964: *Deserto rosso* (*Red Desert*) (+co-sc). 1965: "Prefizione" episode of *Tre Volti* (*Three Faces of a Woman*) (+sc). 1966: *Blow-Up* (+co-sc). 1970: *Zabriskie Point* (+co-sc). 1972: *Chung Kuo* (*China; La cina*) (+co-sc). 1975: *Professione: Reporter* (*The Passenger*) (+co-sc, co-ed). 1979: *Il mistero di Oberwald* (*The Oberwald Mystery*) (+co-sc, co-ed). 1982: *Identificazione di una donna* (*Indentification of a Woman*)(+sc, ed). 1989: *Kumbha Mela; Roma '90.* 1992: *Noto—Mandorli—Vulcano—Stromboli—Carnevale.* 1995: *Par-delà les nuages* (*Beyond the Clouds*) (co-d, +co-sc, co-ed). 1997: *Just to Be Together* (co-d, +sc).

Short Films as Director and Scriptwriter: 1947: *Gente del Po.* 1948: *N.U.* (*Nettezza urbana*); *Roma—Montevideo; Oltre l'oblio.* 1949: *L'amorosa menzogna; Bomarzo; Superstizione; Ragazze in bianco.* 1950: *Sette canne e un vestito; La villa dei mostri; La funivia del Faloria; Uomini in più.*

Other Films: 1984: *Chambre 666* (role as himself). 1995: *Making a Film for Me Is Living* (role as himself).

Antonioni's cinema is one of non-identification and displacement. In almost all of his films shots can be found whose striking emphasis on visual structure works in opposition to the spectator's desire to identify, as in classical Hollywood cinema, with either a protagonist's existential situation or with anything like a seamless narrative continuity—the "impression of reality" so often evoked in conjunction with the effect of fiction films on the spectator.

Since his first feature, *Cronaca di un amore,* Antonioni's introduction of utterly autonomous, graphically stunning shots into the film's narrative flow has gradually expanded to the point where, in *Professione: Reporter,* but even more emphatically in *Il mistero di Oberwald* and *Identificazione di una donna,* the unsettling effect of these discrete moments in the narrative continuity of the earlier work has taken over entirely. If these graphically autonomous shots of Antonioni's films of the fifties and sixties functioned as striking "figures" which unsettled the "ground" of narrative continuity, his latest films undo altogether this opposition between form and content, technique and substance, in order to spread the strangeness of the previously isolated figure across the entirety of the film which will thus emphatically establish itself as a "text."

That which might at first seem to mark a simple inversion of this opposition—where narrative substance would take a back seat to formal technique—instead works to question, in a broad manner, the ways in which films establish themselves as fictions. Antonioni's cinema strains the traditional conventions defining fiction films to the breaking point where, beginning at least as early as *Professione: Reporter,* those aspects always presumed to define what is "given" or "specific" or "proper" to film (which are commonly grouped together under the general heading of "technique") find themselves explicitly incorporated into the overall fabric of the film's narration; technique finds itself drawn into that which it supposedly presents neutrally, namely, the film's fictional universe. One might name this strategy the fictionalization of technique.

Michelangelo Antonioni:
Blow-Up

Such a strategy, however, is anything but self-reflexive, nor does it bear upon the thematics of Antonioni's films. In even those films where the protagonist has something to do with producing images, narratives, or other works of art (the filmmaker of *La signora senza camelie,* the architect of *L'avventura,* the novelist of *La notte,* the photographer of *Blow-up,* the television reporter of *Professione: Reporter,* the poet of *Il mistero di Oberwald,* and the film director of *Identificazione di una donna*), their professions remain important only on the level of the film's drama, never in terms of its technique. It is as though the image of the artist were trapped in a world where self-reflection is impossible. Indeed, one common strand linking the thematics of all of Antonioni's films—the impossibility for men to communicate with women—might be seen to illustrate, on the level of drama, the kind of communicational impasse to be found on the level of "technique" in his cinema. Though his films are far from "experimental" in the sense of the work of Hollis Frampton, Michael Snow, or Andy Warhol, Antonioni's fictional narratives always feel flattened or, to borrow a term from Roland Barthes, they seem curiously *mat,* as if the spectator's ability to gain immediate access to the fiction were being impeded by something.

Antonioni's films, then, are not simply "about" the cinema, but rather, in attempting to make films which always side-step the commonplace or the conventional (modes responsible for spectatorial identification and the "impression of reality"), they call into question what is taken to be a "language" of cinema by constructing a kind of textual idiolect which defies comparison with any other film, even Antonioni's other films. This may at least in part account for the formidable strangeness and difficulty of Antonioni's work, not just for general audiences but for mainstream critics as well. One constantly has the impression that the complexity of his films requires years in the cellar of critical speculation before it is ready to be understood; a film that is initially described as sour and flat ends up ten years later, as in the case of *L'avventura,* being proclaimed one of the ten best films of all time ("International Critics Poll," *Sight and Sound*). To judge from the reception in the United States of his most recent work, it appears that we are still at least ten years behind Antonioni.

As Antonioni has himself stressed repeatedly, the dramatic or the narrative aspect of his films—telling a story in the manner of literary narrative—comes to be of less and less importance; frequently, this is manifested by an absurd and complete absence of dramatic plausibility (*Zabriskie Point, Professione: Reporter, Il mistero di Oberwald*). The nonverbal logic of what remain narrative films depends, Antonioni says, upon neither a conceptual nor emotional organization: "Some people believe I make films with my head; a few others think they come from the heart; for my part, I feel as though I make them with my stomach."—KIMBALL LOCKHART

Armstrong, Gillian

Nationality Australian. *Born* Melbourne, 18 December 1950. *Education* Swinburne College, studied filmmaking at Melbourne and Australian Film and Television School, Sydney. *Family* Married, one daughter. *Career* Worked as production assistant, editor, art director, and assistant designer, and directed several short films; directed first feature, My Brilliant Career, 1979; directed first American film, Mrs. Soffel, 1984; returned to Australia to direct High Tide, 1987; has since made films both in Australia and the United States; also director of documentaries and commercials. *Awards* Best Short Fiction Film, Sydney Festival, for The Singer and the Dancer, 1976; British Critics' Award and Best Film and Best Director, Australian Film Institute Awards, for My Brilliant Career, 1979. *Agent* Judy Scott-Fox, William Morris Agency, 151 El Camino Drive, Beverly Hills, California 90212.

Films as Director: 1970: *Old Man and Dog* (short). **1971:** *Roof Needs Mowing* (short). **1973:** *Gretel; Satdee Night; One Hundred a Day* (shorts). **1975:** *Smokes and Lollies* (doc). **1976:** *The Singer and the Dancer* (+pr, sc). **1979:** *My Brilliant Career.* **1980:** *Fourteen's Good, Eighteen's Better* (doc) (+pr); *Touch Wood* (doc). **1982:** *Starstruck.* **1983:** *Having a Go* (doc). **1984:** *Mrs. Soffel.* **1986:** *Hard to Handle: Bob Dylan with Tom Petty and the Heartbreakers.* **1987:** *High Tide.* **1988:** *Bingo, Bridesmaids and Braces* (+pr). **1991:** *Fires Within.* **1992:** *The Last Days of Chez Nous.* **1994:** *Little Women.* **1996:** *Not Fourteen Again* (+sc, co-pr). **1997:** *Oscar & Lucinda.*

While women directors in film industries around the world are still seen as anomalous (if mainstream) or marginalized as avant garde, the Antipodes have been home to an impressive cadre of female filmmakers who negotiate and transcend such notions.

Before the promising debuts of Ann Turner (*Celia*) and Jane Campion (*Sweetie*), Gillian Armstrong blazed a trail with *My Brilliant Career,* launching a brilliant career of her own as an international director. Like Turner and Campion, Armstrong makes films that resist easy categorization as either "women's films" or Australian ones. Her films mix and intermingle genres in ways which undermine and illuminate afresh, if not openly subvert, filmic conventions—as much as the films of her male compatriots, like Peter Weir, Bruce Beresford, or Paul Cox. Formally, however, the pleasures of her films are traditional ones, such as sensitive and delicate cinematography (often by Russell Boyd), fluid editing, an evocative feel for setting and costume, and most importantly, a commitment to solid character development and acting. All in all, her work reminds one of the best of classical Hollywood cinema, and the question of whether her aim is parody or homage is often left pleasingly ambiguous.

Although Armstrong has often spoken in interviews about her discomfort at being confined to the category of woman filmmaker of women's films, and has articulated her desire to reach an audience of both genders and all nationalities, her work continually addresses sexual politics and family tensions. Escape from and struggle with traditional sex roles and the pitfalls and triumphs therein are themes frequently addressed in her films—from *One Hundred a Day,* her final-year project at the Australian Film and Television School, through *My Brilliant Career,* her first and best-known feature, to *High Tide.* Even one of her earliest films at Swinburne

Gillian Armstrong

College, the short *Roof Needs Mowing*, obliquely tackled this theme, using a typical student filmmaker's pastiche of advertising and surrealism. Like most maturing filmmakers with an eye on wider distribution, Armstrong dropped the "sur" from surrealism in her later work, so that by *One Hundred a Day*—an adaptation of an Alan Marshall story about a shoe-factory employee getting a back-street abortion in the 1930s—she developed a more naturalistic handling of material, while her use of soundtrack and fast editing remained highly stylized and effective.

Made on a tiny budget and heavily subsidized by the Australian Film Commission, the award-winning *The Singer and the Dancer* was a precocious study of the toll men take on women's lives that marked the onset of Armstrong's mature style. On the strength of this and *One Hundred a Day*, producer Margaret Fink offered Armstrong the direction of *My Brilliant Career*. Daunted at first by the scale of the project and a lack of confidence in her own abilities, she accepted because she "thought it could be bungled by a lot of men."

While *The Singer and the Dancer* had been chastised by feminist critics for its downbeat ending, in which the heroine returns to her philandering lover after a half-hearted escape attempt, *My Brilliant Career* was widely celebrated for its feminist fairy-tale story as well as its employment of women crew members. Adapted from Miles Franklin's semi-autobiographical novel, *My Brilliant Career*, with its turn-of-the-century setting in the Australian outback, works like *Jane Eyre* in reverse (she does not marry him), while retaining the romantic allure of such a story and all the glossy production values of a period setting that Australian cinema had been known for up until then. Distinguished by an astonishing central performance by the then-unknown Judy Davis (fresh from playing Juliet to Mel Gibson's Romeo on the drama-school stage), the film managed to present a positive model of feminine independence without belying the time in which it was set. Like Armstrong's later *Mrs. Soffel*, *My Brilliant Career* potently evokes smothered sensuality and conveys sexual tension by small, telling details, as in the boating scene.

Sadly, few of Armstrong's later films have been awarded commensurate critical praise or been as widely successful, possibly because of her refusal to conform to expectations and churn out more upbeat costume dramas. Her next feature, *Starstruck*, although it too features a spunky, ambitious heroine, was a rock musical set in the present and displaying a veritable rattle bag of influences—including Judy Garland-Mickey Rooney "let's-put-on-a-show" films, Richard Lester editing techniques, new wave pop videos, and even Sternberg's *Blond Venus*, when the heroine sheds her kangaroo suit to sing her "torch song" à la Marlene Dietrich. Despite a witty script and fine bit characters, the music is somewhat monotonous, and the film was only mildly successful.

Armstrong's first film to be financed and filmed in America was *Mrs. Soffel.* Based on a true story and set at the turn of the century, it delineated the tragic story of the eponymous warden's wife who falls in love with a convict, helps him escape, and finally runs off with him. The bleak, monochrome cinematography is powerfully atmospheric but was not to all reviewers' tastes, especially in America. For Armstrong, the restricted palette was quite deliberate, so that the penultimate images of blood on snow would be all the more striking and effective. A sadly under-rated film, it features some unexpectedly fine performances from Diane Keaton in the title role, Mel Gibson as her paramour (a fair impersonation of young Henry Fonda), and the young Matthew Modine as his kid brother. At its best, it recalls, if not *McCabe and Mrs. Miller,* then at least *Bonnie and Clyde.*

High Tide returns to Australia for its setting in a coastal caravan park, and comes up trumps as an unabashedly sentimental weepie, and none the worse for it. It features three generations of women: Lilli (Judy Davis again), backup singer to an Elvis impersonator and drifter; Ally (Claudia Karvan), the pubescent daughter she left behind; and mother-in-law Bet (Jan Adele), who vies with Lilli for Ally's affections. In terms of camera work, it is Armstrong's most restless film, utilizing nervous zip pans, fast tracking, and boomshots, and then resting for quiet, intense close-ups on surfboards, legs being shaved, and shower nozzles, all highly motivated by the characters' perspectives. Like *Mrs. Soffel, High Tide* uses colors symbolically to contrast the gentle tones of the seaside's natural landscape with the garish buildings of the town called Eden.

Armstrong wears her feminist credentials lightly, never on her sleeve. Nevertheless, her fiction films—like her documentaries, which have followed three women from the ages of fourteen to twenty-five—can be seen as charting over the years the trajectory of the women's movement: *My Brilliant Career* in the 1970s celebrated women's independence, as Sybylla rejects the roles of wife and mother; *Mrs. Soffel* in the mid-1980s reopens negotiations with men (with tragic results); and finally *High Tide* returns to the rejected motherhood role, with all its attendant joys and anxieties.

Fires Within is a well-meaning but insipid tale of a Cuban political prisoner and his encounter with his family in Miami. A fiasco, Armstrong lost control of the project during post-production. The filmmaker bounced back strongly, however, with two impressive films centering on the relationships between female siblings.

The Last Days of Chez Nous, which Armstrong directed back in Australia, is a thoughtful, well-acted drama focusing on the emotional plight of a pair of sisters. One (Lisa Harrow) is a bossy, forty-something writer, and the other (Kerry Fox) has just emerged from an unhappy love affair. The scenario centers on events that take place after the latter becomes romantically involved with the former's husband (Bruno Ganz). The film's major strength is the depth and richness of its female characters. Its theme, consistent with Armstrong's best previous work, is the utter necessity of women's self-sufficiency.

Little Women, based on Louisa May Alcott's venerable 1868 novel of four devoted sisters coming of age in Concord, Massachusetts, during the Civil War, was Armstrong's first successful American-made film. It may be linked to *My Brilliant Career* as a story of feminine independence set in a previous era. Alcott's book had been filmed a number of times before: a silent version, made in 1918; most enjoyably by George Cukor, with Katharine Hepburn, in 1933; far less successfully, with a young Elizabeth Taylor (among others), in 1949; and in a made-for-TV movie in 1978. Armstrong's version is every bit as fine as the Cukor-Hepburn classic. Her cast is just about perfect, with Wynona Ryder deservedly earning an Academy Award nomination as the headstrong Jo March. Ryder is ably supported by Trini Alvarado, Claire Danes, Samantha Mathis, and Kirsten Dunst, and Susan Sarandon offers her usual solid performance as Marmee, the March girls' mother. If the film has one fault, it is the contemporary-sounding feminist rhetoric that Marmee spouts: the dialogue is completely out of sync with the spirit and reality of the times. But this is just a quibble. This new *Little Women* is a fine film, at once literate and extremely enjoyable.—LESLIE FELPERIN and ROB EDELMAN

Astruc, Alexandre

Nationality French. *Born* Paris, 13 July 1923. *Education* Saint-Germain-en-Laye, and at Polytechnique. *Family* Married Elyette Helies, 1983. *Career* Literary and film critic, since 1945; published novel Les Vacances, 1945; assistant to Marcel Achard and Marc Allegret, 1946-47; made two short films, 1948-49; began series of six feature-length films with Mauvaises rencontres, 1955; TV reporter for Radio Luxembourg, 1969-72. *Awards* Chevalier de la Légion d'honneur; Officier de l'Ordre du Mérite; Officier des Arts et des Lettres. *Address* 168 rue de Grenelle, 75007 Paris, France.

Films as Director: 1948: *Aller et retour* (*Aller-retour*) (+sc). **1949:** *Ulysse ou Les Mauvaises rencontres* (+sc). **1953:** *Le Rideau cramoisi* (*The Crimson Curtain*) (+sc). **1955:** *Les Mauvaises rencontres* (+co-sc). **1958:** *Une Vie* (*End of Desire*) (+co-sc). **1960:** *La Proie pour l'ombre* (+co-sc). **1962:** *L'Education sentimentale* (*Lessons in Love*) (+sc). **1963:** *Le Puits et le pendule* (*The Pit and the Pendulum*) (for TV)

Alexandre Astruc

(+sc). **1965:** *Evariste Galois* (+sc). **1966:** *La Longue Marche* (+co-sc). **1968:** *Flammes sur l'Adriatique* (+co-sc). **1976:** *Sartre par lui-même* (co-d).

Other Films: 1948: *Jean de la Lune* (Achard) (co-sc). **1949:** *La P . . . respecteuse* (Pagliero) (co-sc); *La Valse de Paris* (Achard) (role). **1950:** *L'Affaire Manet* (Aurel) (commentary). **1954:** *Le Vicomte de Bragelonne* (Cerchio) (co-sc). **1964:** *Bassae* (Pollet) (sc). **1974:** *La Jeune Fille assassinee* (role as Publisher). **1993:** *François Truffaut: Stolen Portraits* (role as himself).

Alexandre Astruc was the embodiment of the revolutionary hopes of a renewed cinema after the war. True, Clément, Bresson, and Melville were already making films in a new way, but making them in the age-old industry. Astruc represented a new, arrogant sensibility. He had grown up on the ideas of Sartre and was one of the youthful literati surrounding the philosopher in the St. Germain-des-Prés cafes. There he talked of a new French culture being born, one that demanded new representations in fiction and film.

His personal aspirations were great and grew even greater when his novel *Les Vacances* was published by the prestigious N.R.F., almost winning an important prize. While writing essays on art and culture for *Combat* and *L'Ecran français* he became convinced that the cinema must replace the novel.

But first the cinema must become more like the novel. In his crucial essay "Le Caméra stylo," written the same year as Sartre's "Situation of the Writer in 1948," he called for an end to institutional cinema and for a new style that would be both personal and malleable. He wanted cinema to be able to treat diverse ideas and a range of expressions. He, like Sartre, wanted to become ethical.

This was the first loud clarion cry of the New Wave and it provoked attention in its own day. Astruc found himself linked with Bazin, Cocteau, Marker, and Tacchella against the Stalinists at *L'Ecran français,* led by Louis Daquin. Banding together to form "Objectif 48," these men created a new atmosphere for cinema, attracting the young Truffaut and Godard to their screenings.

Everyone looked to Astruc to begin turning out short films, but his 16mm efforts ran aground. Soon he began writing scripts for acceptable standard directors like Marc Allégret. Finally in 1952 he was able to make *Le Rideau cramoisi* in his own way. It was a remarkable way: this nineteenth-century mystery tale was reduced to a set of unforgettable images and a soundtrack that contained no dialogue whatsoever. Pushing the voice-over discoveries of Bresson and Melville to the limit, Astruc's narrational device places the film somewhere between dream and memory. This coincides perfectly with the haunting night photography and Anouk Aimée's inscrutably romantic performance.

There followed more adaptations, not because Astruc had joined the industry's penchant for such quality material, but because he always believed in the overriding import of style, seeing plots as pretexts only. The color photography in *Une Vie,* for example, explores the painterly concerns of the impressionists. But since the plot comes from a Maupassant tale written in the same era, the result is unpretentious.

In his older age Astruc has renounced this obsession with style. The themes that possess him now, crises in marriage and love, can actually be seen in all his earlier work as well. Now he can explore these issues in television, the medium that seems perfectly suited to his early ideas. Only now his ideas have changed and so has his following. Alexandre Astruc must always be mentioned in any chronicle of modern French cinema, but his career can only be thought of as disappointing.—DUDLEY ANDREW

Autant-Lara, Claude

Nationality *French.* **Born** *Luzarches (Seine-et-Oise), 5 August 1903.* **Education** *Lycée Janson-de-Sailly, Paris, at Ecole nationale supérieure des arts décoratifs, at Ecole des Beaux Arts, and at Mill Hill School, London.* **Family** *Married Ghislain Auboin (deceased).* **Career** *Art director on L'Herbier's Le Carnaval des vérités, 1925; made several avant-garde films, and worked as assistant to René Clair, 1923-25; made French versions of American films in Hollywood, 1930-32; returned to France and directed first feature, 1933; president of Syndicat des techniciens du cinéma, 1948-55; president of Fédération nationale du spectacle, 1957-63.* **Awards** *Grand prix du Cinema français, 1954; Prix Europa, Rome, 1974; Chevalier de la Légion d'honneur; Commandeur des Arts et des Lettres.* **Address** *66 rue Lepic, 75018 Paris, France.*

Films as Director: 1923: *Faits divers.* **1926:** *Construire un feu; Vittel.* **1930:** *Buster se marie* (d of French version of American film *Parlor, Bedroom and Bath* [Sedgwick]). **1931:** *Le Plumbier amoureux* (d of French version of American film *The Passionate Plumber* [Sedgwick]); *Le Fils du Rajah* (d of French version of American film *Son of India* [Feyder]); *La Pente* (d of French version of American film); *Pur Sang* (d of French version of American film). **1932:** *L'Athlète incomplet* (d of French version of American film); *Le Gendarme est sans pitié; Un Client sérieux; Monsieur le Duc; La Peur des coups; Invite Monsieur à dîner.* **1933:** *Ciboulette* (+co-sc, co-costume des). **1936:** *My Partner Mr. Davis* (*The Mysterious Mr. Davis*) (+co-sc). **1937:** *L'Affaire du courrier de Lyon* (*The Courier of Lyon*) (co-d). **1938:** *Le Ruisseau* (co-d). **1939:** *Fric-Frac* (co-d). **1942:** *Le Mariage de Chiffon; Lettres d'amour.* **1943:** *Douce* (*Love Story*). **1944:** *Sylvie et le fantôme* (*Sylvie and the Phantom*). **1947:** *Le Diable au corps* (*Devil in the Flesh*). **1949:** *Occupe-toi d'Amélie* (*Oh Amelia!*). **1951:** *L'Auberge rouge* (*The Red Inn*) (+co-sc). **1952:** "L'Orgueil" ("Pride") episode of *Les 7 Péchés capitaux* (*The Seven Deadly Sins*) (+co-sc). **1953:** *Le Bon Dieu sans confession* (+co-sc); *Le Blé en herbe* (*The Game of Love*) (+co-sc). **1954:** *Le Rouge et le noir* (*The Red and the Black*) (+co-sc). **1956:** *Marguerite de la nuit; La Traversée de Paris* (*Four Bags Full*). **1958:** *En Cas de malheur* (*Love Is My Profession*); *Le Joueur.* **1959:** *La Jument verte* (*The Green Mare*) (+pr). **1960:** *Les Régates de San Francisco; Le Bois des amants.* **1961:** *Tu ne tueras point* (*Non uccidere; Thou Shalt Not Kill*) (+co-pr); *Le Comte de Monte Cristo* (*The Story of the Count of Monte Cristo*). **1962:** *Vive Henri IV . . . Vive l'amour!.* **1963:** *Le Meurtrier* (*Enough Rope*). **1964:** *Le Magot de Joséfa* (+co-sc); "La Fourmi" episode of *Humour noir.* **1965:** *Le Journal d'une femme en blanc* (*A Woman in White*). **1966:** *Le Nouveau Journal d'une femme en blanc* (*Une Femme en blanc se révolte*). **1967:** "Aujourd'hui" ("Paris Today") episode of *Le Plus Vieux Métier du monde* (*The Oldest Profession*); *Le Franciscain de Bourges.* **1969:** *Les Patates* (+co-sc). **1971:** *Le Rouge et le blanc.* **1973:** *Lucien Leuwen* (for TV). **1977:** *Gloria* (+co-sc).

Other Films: 1919: *Le Carnaval des vérités* (L'Herbier) (art d, costume des); *L'Ex-voto* (L'Herbier) (art d, costume des). **1920:** *L'Homme du large* (L'Herbier) (art d, costume des). **1921:** *Villa Destin* (L'Herbier) (art d, costume des); *Eldorado* (L'Herbier) (co-art d, costume des). **1922:** *Don Juan et Faust* (L'Herbier) (art d, costume des). **1923:** *L'Inhumaine* (L'Herbier) (co-art d, costume des); *Le Marchand de plaisir* (Catelain) (co-art d, costume des); *Nana* (Renoir) (co-art d, co-costume des). **1927:** *Le Diable au coeur* (L'Herbier) (art d, costume des).

Claude Autant-Lara is best known for his post-World War II films in the French "tradition of quality." His earliest work in the industry was more closely related to the avant-garde movements of the 1920s than to the mainstream commercial cinema with which he was later identified. He began as a set designer in the 1920s, serving as art director for several of Marcel

L'Herbier's films, including *L'Inhumaine,* and for Jean Renoir's *Nana;* he also assisted René Clair on a number of his early shorts. After directing several films, he worked on an early wide-screen experiment, *Construire un feu,* using the Hypergonar system designed by Henri Chretien. On the basis of his work in this format, he was brought to Hollywood and ended up directing French-language versions of American films for several years. He returned to France and directed his first feature of note, *Ciboulette,* in 1933.

During the war Autant-Lara exercised greater control in his choice of projects and started working with scenarists Jean Aurenche and Pierre Bost, who would continue to be among his most consistent collaborators. He also started assembling a basic crew that worked with him through the 1960s: composer René Cloerec, designer Max Douy, editor Madeleine Gug, and cameraman Jacques Natteau. Autant-Lara rapidly established his reputation as a studio director in

Claude Autant-Lara.
Photograph by C.S. Bull.

the tradition of quality. For many, the names Aurenche, Bost, and Autant-Lara are synonymous with this movement. Their films are characterized by an emphasis on scripting and dialogue, a high proportion of literary adaptations, a solemn "academic" visual style, and general theatricality (due largely to the emphasis on dialogue and its careful delivery to create a cinematic world determined by psychological realism). They frequently attack or ridicule social groups and institutions.

Autant-Lara's first major postwar film, *Le Diable au corps,* was adapted from a novel by Raymond Radiguet. Set during World War I, it tells the story of an adolescent's affair with a young married woman whose husband is away at war. While the film was considered scandalous by many for its valorization of adultery and tacit condemnation of war, it was also seen to express the cynical mood of postwar youth. Autant-Lara's films seem to revel in irreverent depictions of established authority and institutions. *L'Auberge rouge* is a black comedy involving murderous innkeepers, a group of insipid travellers (representing a cross-section of classes), and a monk trapped by the vows of confession.

Throughout the 1950s Autant-Lara was extremely active. His successes of the period include *Le Rouge et le noir,* adapted from Stendhal; *La Traversée de Paris,* a comedy about black-market trading in occupied France; and *En cas de malheur,* a melodrama involving a middle-aged lawyer, his young client, and her student lover. At the same time Autant-Lara was an active spokesman for the French film industry. As head of several film trade unions and other groups promoting French film, he criticized (often harshly) the Centre National du cinéma française (CNC) for its inadequate support of the industry; the American film industry for its stultifying presence in the French market; and government censorship policies for limiting freedom of expression.

Autant-Lara's prominence was effectively eclipsed with the emergence of the French New Wave, although he continued directing films. In the 1950s he, along with Aurenche and Bost, had been subject to frequent critical attacks, most notably by François Truffaut. In the wake of the success of the new generation of directors, Autant-Lara's work is often seen as no more than the "stale" French cinema of the 1950s which was successfully displaced by the more vital films of the New Wave. Yet in spite of, indeed owing to, their "armchair" criticism of authority, bleak representation of human nature, and slow-paced academic style, they possess a peculiarly appealing, insolent sensibility.—M.B. WHITE

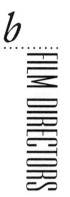

FILM DIRECTORS

Becker, Jacques

Nationality *French*. **Born** *Paris, 15 September 1906*. **Education** *Lycée Condorcet, and Schola Cantorum, Paris*. **Family** *Married actress Françoise Fabian, a son, Jean, and daughter*. **Career** *Became assistant to Jean Renoir, 1932; made first short film,* Le Commissaire . . . , *1935; German prisoner of war, 1941-42; directed first feature,* Le Dernier Atout, *1942; son and assistant Jean Becker completed* Le Trou *following his death.* **Died** *1960*.

Films as Director: 1935: *Le Commissaire est bon enfant, le gendarme est sans pitie* (co-d, co-sc with Pierre Prevert); *Tête de turc* (*Une Tête qui rapporte*) (+co-sc). **1938:** short documentary on Communist Party Congress at Arles. **1939:** *L'Or du Cristobal* (co-d, uncredited). **1942:** *Le Dernier Atout* (+co-pr, co-sc). **1943:** *Goupi Mains rouges* (*It Happened at the Inn*) (+co-sc). **1945:** *Falbalas* (*Paris Frills*) (+co-sc). **1947:** *Antoine et Antoinette* (+co-sc). **1949:** *Rendez-vous de Juillet* (+co-sc). **1951:** *Édouard et Caroline* (+co-sc). **1952:** *Casque d'Or* (+co-sc). **1953:** *Rue de l'Estrapade*. **1954:** *Touchez pas au Grisbi* (*Grisbi*) (+co-sc); *Ali Baba et les quarante voleurs* (*Ali Baba*) (+co-sc). **1956:** *Les Aventures d'Arsène Lupin* (*The Adventures of Arsène Lupin*) (+co-sc). **1957:** *Montparnasse 19* (*Modigliani of Montparnasse*) (+co-sc). **1960:** *Le Trou* (*The Night Watch, The Hole*) (+co-d, co-sc).

Other Films: 1929: *Le Bled* (Renoir) (role); *Le Rendez-vous de Cannes* (Petrossian—documentary) (appearance). **1932:** *Boudu sauvé des eaux* (Renoir) (asst, role); *La Nuit du carrefour* (Renoir) (asst). **1933:** *Chotard & Compagnie* (Renoir) (asst). **1934:** *Madame Bovary* (uncredited, asst). **1935:** *Le Crime de Monsieur Lange* (Renoir) (asst); *Toni* (Renoir) (asst). **1936:** *Les Bas-Fonds* (Renoir) (asst, role); *Une Partie de campagne* (Renoir) (asst, role); *La Vie est à nous* (Renoir) (asst, role). **1938:** *La Grande Illusion* (Renoir) (asst, role); *La Marseillaise* (Renoir) (asst); *La Bête humaine* (Renoir) (asst). **1939:** *Le Règle du jeu* (Renoir) (asst); *L'Héritier des Montdésir* (Valentin) (asst).

Next to Jean Grémillon, Jacques Becker is surely the most neglected of France's great directors. Known in France for *Goupi Mains rouges* and *Antoine et Antoinette,* his only film to reach an international critical audience was *Casque d'Or.* But from 1942 to 1959 Becker fashioned thirteen films, none of which could be called a failure and each of which merits respect and attention.

Jacques Becker: *Casque d'Or*

Tied to Jean Renoir through a youthful friendship (their families were both close to the Cézannes), Becker began assisting Renoir in 1932. For eight years he helped put together some of the greatest films ever made, allowing the generous genius of Renoir to roam, unconcerned over the details he had already prearranged. Becker gave Renoir the kind of grounding and order which kept his films from flying into thin air. His fastidiousness and precision made him the perfect assistant. Many of his friends, however, doubted that such a sensibility could ever command the energy needed to finish a film.

Nevertheless, film direction was Becker's ambition from the beginning of his career. It was he who developed the idea for *Le Crime de M. Lang,* and when the producer insisted that Renoir take over, it cost them their friendship for a time. Soon Becker was directing a cheap anarchist subject, *Le Commissaire est bon enfant,* with the Octobre groupe company of actors. He wasn't to be held back.

Like so many others, Becker was given his chance with the Occupation. A producer handed Becker the reins of a detective comedy, *Le Dernier Atout,* which he brought in under budget and to a good box office response. This opened his career, permitting him to film the unforgettable *Goupi.* Georges Sadoul claims that after the war an American firm bought up the film and had it destroyed so that it wouldn't compete with American products as *Open City* had done. Whether this is true or not, the film remains impressive in the clarity of its partly cynical, partly mysterious tone. In addition, the work shows Becker to be a brilliant director of actors.

The sureness of touch in each of Becker's films derives from a precision some link to craftsmanship; but Becker was striving for far more than competence, veneer, or "quality." He was first and always interested in rhythm. A musician, he was obsessed with jazz and ragtime. No other standard director spent so much time collaborating with his editor (Marguerite Renoir).

Goupi is only the first of a host of Becker films whose subjects are difficult to define. Becker seems to have gone out of his way to set himself problems. Many of his films are about groups of characters, most notably his final work, *Le Trou*. Others feature widely diverse settings: *Antoine et Antoinette* captures the working class quarters of Paris; *Rendez-vous de Juillet* must be the first film anywhere to explicitly bring out the youth culture of postwar Europe; *Falbalas* evokes the world of high fashion as only someone raised in such a world could know it; and, of course, *Casque d'Or* makes the turn-of-the century Parisian underworld come to life with a kind of grim romanticism.

Becker stated that his fastidious attention to milieu was the only way he could approach his characters. Bazin goes further, claiming that only through the exactitude of social particularity could the universality of his characters and their situations come to life. For Bazin, *Edouard et Caroline* is, if not his greatest film, at least his most revealing one. This brilliant farce in the style of Marivaux is virtually plotless. Becker was able, via the minuteness of his *découpage* and the sympathy he had for his actors, to build a serious moral comedy from literally nothing. *Edouard et Caroline,* along with *Le Trou,* shows him working at his best, working without plots and without the luxury of breadth. Both films take place in prison cells, *Le Trou* in an actual prison, *Edouard et Caroline* in the dingy apartment they share and the more menacing jail of her uncle's mansion.

Becker has been called "the mechanic" of cinema, for he took a delight in its workings, and he went about his own job with such order and method. This separates him further from such "quality" directors as Autant-Lara, Cayatte, and Delannoy, whose themes may seem grander. Becker was interested in what the cinema could do just as he was interested in what men and women do. Never searching for the extraordinary, he would go to endless lengths to bring out not some abstract rhythm in the lives of people (as René Clair did) but the true style and rhythm of their sensibilities.

In 1956 Max Ophuls bequeathed to Becker his project on the life of Modigliani. While the resultant film, *Montparnasse 19,* is one of his least successful, its style is illustrative Within weeks after Becker assumed control of the project, both the scriptwriter (Henri Jeanson) and the set designer (Annenkov) left in outrage, for Becker refused to let them show off with words and drapery. His was always a reduced idea of cinema, even when, as in *Falbalas*, his subject was fashion. Nor did he ever choose name actors, except perhaps Gérard Philipe as Modigliani. He had a sureness of taste, backed up by scrupulous reflection. Becker viewed filmmaking as an endless series of choices, each of which could founder the project.

Truffaut once claimed that Becker had his own pace of living; he would linger over meals, but race his car. He would spend hours of film over minor incidents in the lives of his characters, while whipping through the core of the intrigue that brought those characters together. Perhaps this is why *Le Trou* is a fitting finale to his career. For here the intrigue is given in advance and in a sense is without interest: five men struggling to escape from jail. For two and a half hours we observe the minutiae of their efforts and the silent camaraderie that develops among them. This is, for Becker, the state of life on earth: despite the ingenuity we bring to our struggle for freedom, we are doomed to failure; but in the effort we come upon another value, greater even than liberty, an awareness that our struggle is shared and of the friendship and respect that shared effort confers. If *Casque d'Or* is destined to remain his most popular and most acclaimed film (it was his personal favorite), it will not betray these sentiments, for the character of Manda gives up not only liberty, but also life with Marie-Casque d'Or, in order to be true to his friend. The stunning scene at the guillotine which ends that film evokes a set of emotions as contradictory as life itself. Jacques Becker was uniquely able to express such contradictions.—DUDLEY ANDREW

Benton, Robert

Nationality American. *Born* Robert Douglas Benton in Waxahachie, Texas, 29 September 1932. *Education* University of Texas, and at Columbia University, New York City. *Military Service* Served in U.S. Army, 1954-56. *Family* Married Sally Rendigs, 1964, one son. *Career* Art Director of Esquire magazine, New York, 1957-61 (consulting editor, 1962-); began screenwriting partnership with David Newman, on Bonnie and Clyde, 1967; directed first feature, Bad Company, 1972. *Awards* National Society of Film Critics Award, New York Film Critics Award, Writers Guild of America Award and Oscar nomination, Best Screenplay, for Bonnie and Clyde, 1967; Oscar nomination, Best Screenplay, for The Late Show, 1977; Oscars and Los Angeles Film Critics Association Awards for Best Screenplay and Best Director, Golden Globe Award for Best Screenplay, Writers Guild of America Award and Best Director, National Society of Film Critics and Directors Guild of America, for Kramer vs Kramer, 1979; Oscar for Best Screenplay, for Places in the Heart, 1984; Oscar nomination for Best Screenplay, for Nobody's Fool, 1994. *Address* c/o Sam Cohn, International Creative Management, 40 W. 57th Street, New York, New York 10019, U.S.A.

Robert Benton on the set of *Places in the Heart.*

Films as Director and Co-Scriptwriter: 1972: *Bad Company.* **1977:** *The Late Show* (sc). **1979:** *Kramer vs. Kramer.* **1982:** *Still of the Night.* **1984:** *Places in the Heart* (*The Texas Project*). **1987:** *Nadine.* **1991:** *Billy Bathgate.* **1994:** *Nobody's Fool.* **1997:** *The Magic Hour.*

Films as Scriptwriter Only (with David Newman except as indicated): 1967: *Bonnie and Clyde* (Penn). **1970:** *There Was a Crooked Man* (J. Mankiewicz). **1972:** *Oh! Calcutta!* (co-sc, with others); *What's Up Doc?* (Bogdanovich) (co-sc with Newman and Buck Henry). **1978:** *Superman* (Donner) (co-sc with David Newman, Mario Puzo, and Leslie Newman).

Other Films: 1988: *The House on Carroll Street* (Yates) (co-exec pr).

There were many ways to make it as a bigtime Hollywood director in the 1970s. Robert Benton's experience provides a common mode: a successful screenwriter turned director. Benton teamed with another aspiring author, David Newman, to pen the script of Arthur Penn's wildly successful, highly influential *Bonnie and Clyde* (1967), a film that showed Hollywood how to meld comedy, melodrama, and social commentary. The story of how Benton and Newman came to write *Bonnie and Clyde* is the stuff of Hollywood legend. In 1964 they were working for *Esquire* magazine, developing the magazine's annual college issue. As they were crafting the magazine's infamous Dubious Achievement Awards, they became caught up with the art cinema of Ingmar Bergman, Federico Fellini, and Akira Kurosawa. They decided to attempt an American version of Jean-Luc Godard's *Breathless* through the story of two desperados of the 1930s, Bonnie Parker and Clyde Barrow.

Benton and Newman wrote a seventy-page treatment in which they tried to make their film feel like an Hitchcock thriller, but with the comic violent tone of François Truffaut's *Shoot the Piano Player.* First they sent the *Bonnie and Clyde* script to Truffaut, who passed on it, as did Jean-Luc Godard. Warren Beatty rescued the project, agreed to produce it, and Arthur Penn became the director. Here were the first members of the film generation of the 1960s making what in some ways came to represent the most influential film of the decade, for it captured the restlessness of an age as well as the era's ethical ambiguity. *Bonnie and Clyde* at once demonstrated that Hollywood films could successfully incorporate the stylistic flourishes of the French New Wave into Classic Hollywood genre material.

The *Bonnie and Clyde* script won numerous awards, and the duo went on to co-script *There Was a Crooked Man* (1970), *What's Up Doc?* (1972), and *Superman* (1978). The latter two proved Benton and Newman were able to make movies that made money. *What's Up Doc?* finished in the top ten earners for 1971; *Superman* generated more than 100 million dollars worldwide. But Benton aspired to be his own director, and he worked single-mindedly at that goal during the 1970s.

Success came with *Kramer vs. Kramer* (1979), Benton's third directorial effort. Based on his screenplay, *Kramer vs. Kramer* won the Oscar for Best Picture, Best Actor (Dustin Hoffman), Best Screenplay, Best Director, and Best Supporting Actress (Meryl Streep), a sweep rarely accomplished in Hollywood history. More importantly for Benton's future, *Kramer vs. Kramer* finished atop the domestic box-office rankings for the year. Robert Benton had reached his goal; he was as hot a property as there was in Hollywood as the 1980s opened.

But thereafter Benton's filmmaking successes were limited. Benton did reach another peak in 1984 with *Places in the Heart.* The film, which featured Benton's award-winning screenplay, was one man's affectionate look at life in his hometown of Waxahachie, Texas, during the hard days of the great depression. On the other hand, Benton's *Nadine* (1987) was also set in Texas, but this comedy failed to capture either the fancy of the critics or the public.

As Benton moved into the 1990s, many saw him as the principle case of the power of the screenwriter as auteur. Perhaps this is so, but continuing success at the top—a Hollywood prerequisite if one wants to control one's movies—seemed to have sucked the life from Benton's story-telling ability. Some speculated that Benton, who had crafted fine stories of outsiders from Bonnie Parker to the aging detective of *The Late Show,* had difficulty functioning as a member of the Hollywood establishment.

Benton's most recent films have been set in the environs of upstate New York. *Billy Bathgate,* based on the E.L. Doctorow novel about a young man's involvement with mobster Dutch Schultz, has much going for it, beginning with a talented cast (headed by Dustin Hoffman and Nicole Kidman) and superlative production design. But the shoot was troubled, resulting in acrimony between Benton and Hoffman and a curiously emotionless and eminently forgettable film, despite the presence of the always watchable Hoffman (cast as Schultz—a character altogether different from his Ted Kramer character).

Nobody's Fool, based on a novel by Richard Russo, is far more successful. The characters are less flamboyant than those found in *Billy Bathgate*; as an evocation of time and place, and a portrait of small-town American life, the film is closer in spirit to *Places in the Heart.* Paul Newman is nothing short of superb as Donald "Sully" Sullivan, an aging, out-of-work construction worker. The film follows events when Sullivan, long estranged from his family, is forced to deal with his son and grandson. Also central to the story are Sullivan's relationships with various townsfolk, including his landlady (Jessica Tandy), who once was his eighth-grade teacher, his sometime employer (Bruce Willis), and the latter's neglected wife (Melanie Griffith). *Nobody's Fool* works best as a film of moods and feelings; ultimately, it is a knowing, entertaining blend of poignancy and humor. As in his earlier films, Benton draws fine performances from his cast. While one would expect exceptional acting from Newman and Tandy, the filmmaker elicits solid work from Griffith and Willis, who rarely have been better on screen.

—DOUGLAS GOMERY and ROB EDELMAN

Bergman, Ingmar

Nationality Swedish. *Born* Ernst Ingmar Bergman in Uppsala, Sweden, 14 July 1918. *Education* Palmgrens School, Stockholm, and Stockholm University, 1938-40. *Family* Married 1) Else Fisher, 1943 (divorced 1945), one daughter; 2) Ellen Lundström, 1945 (divorced 1950), two sons, two daughters; 3) Gun Grut, 1951, one son; 4) Käbi Laretei, 1959 (separated 1965; divorced), one son; 5) Ingrid von Rosen, 1971. Also one daughter by actress Liv Ullmann. *Career* Joined Svensk Filmindustri as scriptwriter, 1943; director of Helsingborg City Theatre, 1944; directed first film, Kris, 1946; began association with producer Lorens Marmstedt, and with Gothenburg Civic Theatre, 1946; began association with cinematographer Gunnar Fischer, 1948; director, Municipal Theatre, Malmo, 1952-58; began associations with Bibi Andersson and Max von Sydow, 1955; began association with cinematographer Sven Nykvist, 1959; became artistic advisor at Svensk Filmindustri, 1961; head of Royal Dramatic Theatre, Stockholm, 1963-66; settled on island of Faro,

Ingmar Bergman

1966; established Cinematograph production company, 1968; moved to Munich, follow-
ing arrest on alleged tax offences and subsequent breakdown, 1976; formed Personafilm
production company, 1977; director at Munich Residenzteater, 1977-82; returned to
Sweden, 1978; announced retirement from filmmaking, following Fanny and Alexander,
1982; directed These Blessed Two *for Swedish television, 1985; concentrated on directing*
for the theater, 1985; Film Society of Lincoln Center presented a retrospective of almost all
of Bergman's films as director, 1995; Brooklyn Academy of Music honored Bergman with
a four-month-long Bergman Festival, 1995; The Museum of Television & Radio honored
Bergman with a retrospective titled "Ingmar Bergman In Close-Up: The Television Work,"
1995. **Awards** *Golden Bear, Berlin Festival, for* Wild Strawberries, *1958; Gold Plaque,*
Swedish Film Academy, 1958; Oscars for Best Foreign Language Film, The Virgin Spring
(1961), Through a Glass Darkly *(1962), and* Fanny and Alexander *(1983); Oscar*
nominations, Best Director, for Cries and Whispers *(1973),* Face to Face *(1976), and*
Fanny and Alexander *(1983); Oscar nominations, Best Screenplay, for* Wild Strawberries
(1958), Through a Glass Darkly *(1962),* Cries and Whispers *(1973),* Face to Face *(1976),*
and Fanny and Alexander *(1983); co-winner of International Critics Prize, Venice Film*
Festival, for Fanny and Alexander; *Erasmus Prize (shared with Charles Chaplin), Nether-*
lands, 1965; Irving G. Thalberg Memorial Award, 1970; Order of the Yugoslav Flag, 1971;
Luigi Pirandello International Theatre Prize, 1971; honorary doctorate of philosophy,
Stockholm University, 1975; Gold Medal of Swedish Academy, 1977; European Film
Award, 1988; Le Prix Sonning, 1989; Praemium Imperiale Prize, 1991.

Films as Director: 1946: *Kris* (*Crisis*) (+sc); *Det regnar på vår kärlek* (*It Rains on Our Love; The Man with an Umbrella*) (+co-sc). **1947:** *Skepp till Indialand* (*A Ship Bound for India; The Land of Desire*) (+sc). **1948:** *Musik i mörker* (*Music in Darkness; Night Is My Future*); *Hamnstad* (*Port of Call*) (+co-sc). **1949:** *Fängelse* (*Prison; The Devil's Wanton*) (+sc); *Törst* (*Thirst; Three Strange Loves*). **1950:** *Till glädje* (*To Joy*) (+sc); *Sånt händer inte här* (*High Tension; This Doesn't Happen Here*). **1951:** *Sommarlek* (*Summer Interlude; Illicit Interlude*) (+co-sc). **1952:** *Kvinnors väntan* (*Secrets of Women; Waiting Women*) (+sc). **1953:** *Sommaren med Monika* (*Monika; Summer with Monika*) (+co-sc); *Gycklarnas afton* (*The Naked Night; Sawdust and Tinsel*) (+sc). **1954:** *En lektion i kärlek* (*A Lesson in Love*) (+sc). **1955:** *Kvinnodröm* (*Dreams; Journey into Autumn*) (+sc); *Sommarnattens leende* (*Smiles of a Summer Night*) (+sc). **1957:** *Det sjunde inseglet* (*The Seventh Seal*) (+sc); *Smultronstället* (*Wild Strawberries*) (+sc). **1958:** *Nära livet* (*Brink of Life; So Close to Life*) (+co-sc); *Ansiktet* (*The Magician; The Face*) (+sc). **1960:** *Jungfrukällen* (*The Virgin Spring*); *Djävulens öga* (*The Devil's Eye*) (+sc). **1961:** *Såsom i en spegel* (*Through a Glass Darkly*) (+sc). **1963:** *Nattvardsgästerna* (*Winter Light*) (+sc); *Tystnaden* (*The Silence*) (+sc). **1964:** *För att inte tala om alla dessa kvinnor* (*All These Women; Now About These Women*) (+co-sc under pseudonym "Buntel Eriksson"). **1966:** *Persona* (+sc). **1967:** **"Daniel" episode of** *Stimulantia* (+sc, ph). **1968:** *Vargtimmen* (*Hour of the Wolf*) (+sc); *Skammen* (*Shame; The Shame*) (+sc). **1969:** *Riten* (*The Ritual; The Rite*) (+sc); *En passion* (*The Passion of Anna; A Passion*) (+sc); *Fårö-dokument* (*The Fårö Document*) (+sc). **1971:** *Beröringen* (*The Touch*) (+sc). **1973:** *Viskningar och rop* (*Cries and Whispers*) (+sc); *Scener ur ett äktenskap* (*Scenes from a Marriage*) (+sc, narration, voice of the photographer) in six episodes: "Oskuld och panik (Innocence and Panic)"; "Kunsten att sopa unter mattan (The Art of Papering Over Cracks)"; "Paula"; "Tåredalen (The Vale of Tears)"; "Analfabeterna (The Illiterates)"; "Mitt i natten i ett mörkt hus någonstans i världen (In the Middle of the Night in a Dark House Somewhere in the World)" (shown theatrically in shortened version of 168 minutes). **1977:** *Das Schlangenei* (*The Serpent's Egg; Ormens ägg*) (+sc). **1978:** *Herbstsonate* (*Autumn Sonata; Höstsonaten*) (+sc). **1979:** *Fårö-dokument 1979* (*Fårö 1979*) (+sc, narration). **1980:** *Aus dem Leben der Marionetten* (*From the Life of the Marionettes*) (+sc). **1982:** *Fanny och Alexander* (*Fanny and Alexander*) (+sc). **1983:** *Efter Repetitioner* (*After the Rehearsal*) (+sc). **1985:** *Karin's Face* (short).

Other Films: 1944: *Hets* (*Torment; Frenzy*) (Sjöberg) (sc). **1947:** *Kvinna utan ansikte* (*Woman Without a Face*) (Molander) (sc). **1948:** *Eva* (Molander) (co-sc). **1950:** *Medan staden sover* (*While the City Sleeps*) (Kjellgren) (synopsis). **1951:** *Frånskild* (*Divorced*) (Molander) (sc). **1956:** *Sista paret ut* (*Last Couple Out*) (Sjöberg) (sc). **1961:** *Lustgården* (*The Pleasure Garden*) (Kjellin) (co-sc under pseudonym "Buntel Eriksson"). **1974:** *Kallelsen* (*The Vocation*) (Nykvist) (pr). **1975:** *Trollflöjten* (*The Magic Flute*) (for TV) (+sc). **1976:** *Ansikte mot ansikte* (*Face to Face*) (+co-pr, sc) (for TV, originally broadcast in serial form); *Paradistorg* (*Summer Paradise*) (Lindblom) (pr). **1977:** *A Look at Liv* (Kaplan) (role as interviewee). **1986:** *Dokument: Fanny och Alexander* (Carlsson) (subject). **1992:** *Den Goda Viljan* (*The Best Intentions*) (sc); *Sondagsbarn* (*Sunday's Children*) (sc).

Ingmar Bergman's unique international status as a filmmaker would seem assured on many grounds. His reputation can be traced to such diverse factors as his prolific output of largely notable work (40 features from 1946 through 1982); the profoundly personal nature of his best films since the 1950s; the innovative nature of his technique combined with its essential simplicity, even when employing surrealistic and dream-like treatments (as, for example, in *Wild Strawberries* and *Persona*); his creative sensitivity in relation to his players; and his extraordinary capacity to evoke distinguished acting from his regular interpreters, notably Gunnar Björnstrand, Max von Sydow, Bibi Andersson, Ingrid Thulin, and Liv Ullmann.

After an initial period of derivative, melodramatic filmmaking largely concerned with bitter man-woman relationships ("I just grabbed helplessly at any form that might save me, because I hadn't any of my own," he confesses in *Bergman on Bergman*), Bergman reached an initial maturity of style in *Summer Interlude* and *Summer with Monika,* romantic studies of adolescent love and subsequent disillusionment. In *The Naked Night* he used a derelict travelling circus—its proprietor paired with a faithless young mistress and its clown with a faithless middle-aged wife—as a symbol of human suffering through misplaced love and to portray the ultimate loneliness of the human condition, a theme common to much of his work. Not that Bergman's films are all gloom and disillusionment. He has a recurrent, if veiled, sense of humour. His comedies, such as *A Lesson in Love* and *Smiles of a Summer Night,* are ironically effective ("You're a gynecologist who knows nothing about women," says a man's mistress in *A Lesson in Love*), and even in *Wild Strawberries* the aged professor's relations with his housekeeper offer comic relief. Bergman's later comedies, the Shavian *The Devil's Eye* and *Now About All These Women,* are both sharp and fantastic.

"To me, religious problems are continuously alive ... not ... on the emotional level, but on an intellectual one," wrote Bergman at the time of *Wild Strawberries. The Seventh Seal, The Virgin Spring, Through a Glass Darkly, Winter Light,* and *The Silence* lead progressively to the rejection of religious belief, leaving only the conviction that human life is haunted by "a virulent, active evil." The crusading knight of *The Seventh Seal* who cannot face death once his faith is lost survives only to witness the cruelty of religious persecution. In Bergman's view, faith belongs to the simple-minded and innocent. *The Virgin Spring* exposes the violence of vengeance in a period of primitive Christianity.

Bergman no longer likes these films, considering them "bogus"; nevertheless, they are excellently made in his highly professional style. Disillusionment with Lutheran denial of love is deep in *Winter Light.* "In *Winter Light* I swept my house clean," Bergman has said. Other Bergman films reflect his views on religion as well: the mad girl in *Through a Glass Darkly* perceives God as a spider, while the ailing sister in *The Silence* faces death with a loneliness that passes all understanding as a result of the frigid silence of God in the face of her sufferings. In *The*

Face, however, Bergman takes sardonic delight in letting the rationalistic miracle-man suspect in the end that his bogus miracles are in fact genuine.

With *Wild Strawberries,* Bergman turned increasingly to psychological dilemmas and ethical issues in human and social relations once religion has proved a failure. Above all else, the films suggest, love, understanding, and common humanity seem lacking. The aged medical professor in *Wild Strawberries* comes through a succession of dreams to realize the truth about his cold and loveless nature. In *Persona,* the most psychologically puzzling, controversial, yet significant of all Bergman's films—with its Brechtian alienation technique and surreal treatment of dual personality—the self-imposed silence of the actress stems from her failure to love her husband and son, though she responds with horror to the self-destructive violence of the world around her. This latter theme is carried still further in *The Shame,* in which an egocentric musician attempts non-involvement in his country's war only to collapse into irrational acts of violence himself through sheer panic. *The Shame* and *Hour of the Wolf* are concerned with artists who are too self-centered to care about the larger issues of the society in which they live.

"It wasn't until *A Passion* that I really got to grips with the man-woman relationship," says Bergman. *A Passion* deals with "the dark, destructive forces" in human nature which sexual urges can inspire. Bergman's later films reflect, he claims, his "ceaseless fascination with the whole race of women," adding that "the film ... should communicate psychic states." The love and understanding needed by women is too often denied them, suggests Bergman. Witness the case of the various women about to give birth in *Brink of Life* and the fearful, haunted, loveless family relationships in *Cries and Whispers.* The latter, with *The Shame* and *The Serpent's Egg,* is surely among the most terrifying of Bergman's films, though photographed in exquisite color by Sven Nykvist, his principal cinematographer.

Man-woman relationships are successively and uncompromisingly examined in a series of Bergman films. *The Touch* shows a married woman driven out of her emotional depth in an extra-marital affair; *Face to Face,* one of Bergman's most moving films, concerns the nervous breakdown of a cold-natured woman analyst and the hallucinations she suffers; and a film made as a series for television (but reissued more effectively in a shortened, re-edited form for the cinema, *Scenes from A Marriage*) concerns the troubled, long-term love of a professional couple who are divorced but unable to endure separation. Supreme performances were given by Bibi Andersson in *Persona* and *The Touch,* and by Liv Ullmann in *Cries and Whispers, Scenes from a Marriage* and *Face to Face.*

Bergman's later films, made in Sweden or during his period of self-imposed exile, are more miscellaneous. *The Magic Flute* is one of the best, most delightful of opera-films. *The Serpent's Egg* is a savage study in the sadistic origins of Nazism, while *Autumn Sonata* explores the case of a mother who cannot love. Bergman declared his filmmaking at an end with his brilliant, German-made misanthropic study of a fatal marriage, *From the Life of the Marionettes,* and the semi-autobiographical television series *Fanny and Alexander.* Swedish-produced, the latter work was released in a re-edited version for the cinema. Set in 1907, *Fanny and Alexander* is the gentle, poetic story of two years in the lives of characters who are meant to be Bergman's maternal grandparents.

After *Fanny and Alexander,* Bergman directed *After the Rehearsal,* a small-scale drama which reflected his growing preoccupation with working in the theater. It features three characters: an aging, womanizing stage director mounting a version of Strindberg's *The Dream*

Play; the attractive, determined young actress who is his leading lady; and his former lover, once a great star but now an alcoholic has-been, who accepts a humiliating bit role in the production.

After the Rehearsal was not Bergman's cinematic swan song. He went on to author two scripts which are autobiographical outgrowths of *Fanny and Alexander*. *The Best Intentions*, directed by Bille August, is a compassionate chronicle of ten years in the tempestuous courtship and early marriage of Bergman's parents. His father starts out as an impoverished theology student who is unyielding in his views. His mother is spirited but pampered, the product of an upper-class upbringing. The film also is noteworthy for the casting of Max von Sydow as the filmmaker's maternal grandfather. The actor's presence is most fitting, given the roots of the scenario and his working relationship with Bergman, which dates back to the 1950s.

The Best Intentions was followed by *Sunday's Children*, directed by Bergman's son Daniel. The film is a deeply personal story of a ten-year-old boy named Pu, who is supposed to represent the young Ingmar Bergman. Pu is growing up in the Swedish countryside during the 1920s. The scenario focuses on his relationship to his minister father and other family members; also depicted is the adult Pu's unsettling connection to his elderly dad.—ROGER MANVELL and ROB EDELMAN

Berkeley, Busby

Nationality *American.* **Born** *Busby Berkeley William Enos in Los Angeles, 29 November 1895.* **Education** *Mohegan Military Academy, Peekskill, New York, 1907-14.* **Military Service** *Organized marching drills and touring stage shows for U.S. and French armies, and served as aerial observer in U.S. Air Corps, 1917-19.* **Family** *Married six times.* **Career** *Actor, stage manager, and choreographer, 1919-27; director of* A Night in Venice *on Broadway, 1928; director of dance numbers in* Whoopee *for Samuel Goldwyn, 1930; worked for Warner Bros., 1933-39; hired as dance advisor and director by MGM, 1939; returned to Warner Bros., 1943; released from Warner Bros. contract, returned to Broadway, 1944; directed last film,* Take Me Out to the Ball Game, *1949.* **Died** *14 March 1976.*

Films as Director: 1933: *She Had to Say Yes* (co-d, ch). **1935:** *Gold Diggers of 1935* (+ch); *Bright Lights* (+ch); *I Live for Love* (+ch). **1936:** *Stage Struck* (+ch). **1937:** *The Go-Getter* (+ch); *Hollywood Hotel* (+ch). **1938:** *Men Are Such Fools* (+ch); *Garden of the Moon* (+ch); *Comet Over Broadway* (+ch). **1939:** *They Made Me a Criminal* (+ch); *Babes in Arms* (+ch); *Fast and Furious* (+ch). **1940:** *Strike Up the Band* (+ch); *Forty Little Mothers* (+ch). **1941:** *Blonde Inspiration* (+ch); *Babes on Broadway* (+ch). **1942:** *For Me and My Gal* (+ch). **1943:** *The Gang's All Here* (+ch). **1946:** *Cinderella Jones* (+ch). **1949:** *Take Me Out to the Ball Game* (+ch).

Other Films: 1930: *Whoopee* (ch). **1931:** *Palmy Days* (ch); *Flying High* (ch). **1932:** *Night World* (ch); *Bird of Paradise* (ch); *The Kid from Spain* (ch). **1933:** *42nd Street* (ch); *Gold Diggers of 1933* (ch); *Footlight Parade* (ch); *Roman Scandals* (ch). **1934:** *Wonder Bar* (ch); *Fashions of 1934* (ch); *Dames* (ch). **1935:** *Go Into Your Dance* (ch); *In Caliente* (ch); *Stars Over Broadway* (ch). **1937:** *Gold Diggers of 1937* (ch); *The Singing Marine* (ch); *Varsity Show* (ch). **1938:** *Gold Diggers in Paris* (ch). **1939:** *Broadway Serenade* (ch). **1941:** *Ziegfield Girl* (ch); *Lady Be Good* (ch); *Born to Sing* (ch). **1943:** *Girl Crazy* (ch). **1950:** *Two Weeks with Love* (ch). **1951:** *Call Me Mister* (ch); *Two Tickets to Broadway* (ch). **1952:** *Million Dollar Mermaid* (ch). **1953:** *Small Town Girl* (ch); *Easy to Love* (ch). **1954:** *Rose Marie* (ch). **1962:** *Jumbo* (ch). **1970:** *The Phynx* (role in cameo appearance).

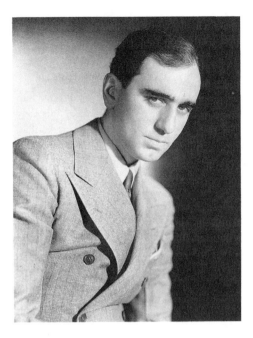

Busby Berkeley

No American film director of his time explored the possibilities of the mobile camera more fully or ingeniously than Busby Berkeley. He was the Méliès of the musical, the corollary of Vertov in the exploration of the possibilities of cinematic movement. His influence has since been felt in a wide array of filmmaking sectors, from movie musicals to television commercials.

Certain aspects of Berkeley's personal history are obvious in their importance to a discussion of his cinematic work, most specifically his World War I service and his work in the theatre. Born to a theatrical family, Berkeley learned early of the demands of the theatrical profession: when his father died, his mother refused to take the night off, instilling in Busby the work ethic of "the show must go on." Throughout most of his career, Gertrude Berkeley and her ethic reigned, no wife successfully displacing her as spiritual guide and confidante until after her death in 1948. Even then, Berkeley drove himself at the expense of his many marriages.

Berkeley's World War I service was significant for the images he created in his musical sequences. He designed parade drills for both the French and U.S. armies, and his later service as an aerial observer with the Air Corps formed the basis of an aesthetic which incorporated images of order and symmetry often seen from the peculiar vantage of an overhead position. In addition, that training developed his approach to economical direction. Berkeley often used storyboarding to effect his editing-in-the-camera approach, and provided instruction to chorus girls on a blackboard, which he used to illustrate the formations they were to achieve.

Returning from war, Berkeley found work as a stage actor. His first role was directed by John Cromwell, with Gertrude serving as his dramatic coach. He soon graduated to direction and choreography, and in 1929 he became the first man on Broadway to direct a musical for which he also staged the dance numbers, setting a precedent for such talents as Jerome Robbins, Gower Champion, Bob Fosse, and Tommy Tune. When Samuel Goldwyn invited him to Hollywood in 1930 as a dance director, however, that Broadway division of labor remained in effect. Berkeley had to wait until *Gold Diggers of 1935* before being allowed to do both jobs on the same film.

From 1933 through 1939 Berkeley worked for Warner Bros., where he created a series of dance numbers which individually and collectively represent much of the best Hollywood product of the time. An examination of his work in this period in relation to the Production Code and the developing conventions of the musical genre illustrates his unique contribution to cinema.

Boy/girl romance and the success story were standard narrative ingredients of 1930s musicals, and Berkeley's work contributed significantly to the formulation of these conventions.

Where he was unique was in his visualization of the onstage as opposed to the backstage segments of these dramas. Relying on his war service, he began to fashion onstage spectacles which had been impossible to perform on the Broadway stage. In his films he was able to explode any notion of the limitations of a proscenium and the relationship of the theatre spectator to it: the fixed perspective of that audience was abandoned for one which lacked defined spatial or temporal coordinates. His camera was regularly mounted on a crane (or on the monorail he invented) and swooped over and around or toward and away from performers in a style of choreography for camera which was more elaborate than that mapped out for the dancers. Amusingly, he generally reversed this procedure in his direction of non-musical scenes; he typically made the backstage dramas appear confined within a stage space and bound to the traditions of theatrical staging and dialogue.

As Berkeley created the illusion of theatre in his musical numbers, so too he created the illusion of dance. Having never studied dance, he rarely relied on trained dancers. Instead, he preferred to create movement through cinematic rather than choreographic means. Occasionally, when he included sophisticated dance routines, such as in the Lullaby of Broadway number from *Gold Diggers of 1935,* he highlighted the dancers' virtuosity in a series of shots which preserved the integrity of their movement without infringing on the stylistic nuances of his camerawork.

The virtuosity of Berkeley's camera movement remains important not only for a discussion of aesthetics, but also for understanding the meaning he brought to the depiction of sexual fantasy and spectacle in a period of Hollywood history when the Production Code Administration was keeping close watch over screen morality. Throughout the 1930s, Berkeley's camera caressed as if involved in foreplay, penetrated space as if seeking sexual gratification, and soared in an approximation of sexual ecstasy. Whether tracking through the legs of a line of chorus girls in *42nd Street,* swooping over an undulating vagina-shaped construction of pianos in *Gold Diggers of 1935,* or caressing gigantic bananas manipulated by scantily clad chorines in *The Gang's All Here,* his sexual innuendos were titillating in both their obviousness and seeming naiveté. Berkeley's ability to inject such visual excitement meant that he was often called upon to rescue a troubled picture by adding one or more extravagantly staged musical numbers.

After leaving Warner Bros. in 1939, Berkeley returned to MGM where, although generally less innovative, his work set precedents for the genre: he directed the first Judy Garland/Mickey Rooney musical, the first Garland/Gene Kelly film, and with his last effort as a director, introduced the team of Gene Kelly and Stanley Donen. Undoubtedly the master director of American musicals in the first decade of sound film and a huge influence on many of the musical talents of succeeding decades, Berkeley worked only occasionally through the 1950s, staging musical numbers for various studios. The last of these was the 1962 MGM film *Jumbo.*

With the nostalgia craze of the late 1960s, Berkeley's aesthetic was resurrected. In 1971 he triumphantly returned to the Broadway stage, where he directed a revival of the 1920s hit *No, No, Nanette,* starring his leading lady of the 1930s, Ruby Keeler, herself in retirement for thirty years. That moment was surely the fulfillment of all the success stories he had directed over his long career.—DOUG TOMLINSON

Bertolucci, Bernardo

Nationality *Italian.* **Born** *Parma, Italy, 16 March 1940.* **Education** *Attended University of Rome, 1960-62.* **Family** *Married Clare Peploe, 1978.* **Career** *Assistant director on Accattone (Pasolini), 1961; directed first feature, La commare secca, 1962; joined Italian Communist Party (PCI), late 1960s.* **Awards** *Special Award, Cannes Festival, for* Prima della revoluzione, *1964; Best Director Award, National Society of Film Critics, for* Il conformista, *1971; Oscars for Best Director and Best Screenplay, and Directors Guild of America Award for Outstanding Feature Film Achievement, for* The Last Emperor, *1987.* **Address** *via della Lungara 3, Rome 00165, Italy.*

Films as Director: **1962:** *La commare secca* (*The Grim Reaper*) (+sc). **1964:** *Prima della rivoluzione* (*Before the Revolution*) (+co-sc). **1965-66:** *La vie del Petrolio* (+sc); *Il canale* (+sc). **1966-67:** *Ballata de un milliardo* (+co-sc). **1967:** **"Il fico infruttuoso" episode of** *Amore e rabbia* (*Vangelo '70; Love and Anger*) (+sc). **1968:** *Partner* (+co-sc). **1969:** *La strategia del ragno* (*The Spider's Stratagem*) (+co-sc). **1970:** *Il conformista* (*The Conformist*) (+sc). **1971:** *La saluta e malato o I poveri muorioro prima* (*La Sante est malade ou Les Pauvres meurent les premiers*) (+sc); *L'inchiesa* (+co-sc). **1972:** *Last Tango in Paris* (*Le Dernier Tango à Paris; Ultimo tango a Parigi*) (+co-sc). **1976:** *1900* (*Novecento*) (presented in two parts in Italy: *Novecento atto I* and *Novecento atto II*) (+co-sc). **1979:** *La luna* (+co-sc). **1981:** *La tragedia di un uomo ridicolo* (*La Tragedie d'un homme ridicule; The Tragedy of a Ridiculous Man*) (+sc). **1987:** *The Last Emperor* (+co-sc). **1990:** *The Sheltering Sky* (+co-sc). **1994:** *Little Buddha* (+co-sc). **1996:** *Stealing Beauty* (+co-sc).

Other Films: **1961:** *Accattone* (Pasolini) (asst-d). **1967:** *C'era una volta il West* (*Once Upon a Time in the West*) (Leone) (co-sc).

Bernardo Bertolucci with Liv Tyler and Roberto Zibetti on the set of *Stealing Beauty*.

At the age of twenty-one, Bernardo Bertolucci established himself as a major artist in two distinct art forms, winning a prestigious award in poetry and receiving high critical acclaim for his initial film, *La commare secca*. This combination of talents is evident in all of his films, which have a lyric but exceptionally concrete style. His father, Attilio Bertolucci, was famous in his own right as a critic, professor, and poet, and in 1961 introduced Bernardo to Pier Paolo Pasolini, an esteemed literary figure. This friendship led both writers, ironically, away from poetry and into the cinema. Serving as the assistant director on Pasolini's inaugural film, *Accattone,* Bertolucci was very quickly entrusted with the full direction of Pasolini's next project, *La commare secca,* based on a story by the writer.

La commare secca is an auspicious debut; as both screenwriter and director, Bertolucci found at once the high visual style and narrative complexity which distinguish his later films. The sex murder of a prostitute is its central narrative event. As the probable witnesses and suspects are brought in for questioning, a series of lives are unraveled, with each sad story winding toward the city park where the murder occurred. Formally, the film is an ambitious amalgam of a film noir atmosphere and narrative style with a neorealist concentration on behavioral detail and realistic settings.

In *Before the Revolution,* Bertolucci first presents the theme that was to become foremost in his work: the conflict between freedom and conformity. Fabrizio, the leading character, is obliged to decide between radical political commitment and an alluring marriage into the bourgeoisie. In this reworking of Stendhal's *The Charterhouse of Parma,* Bertolucci expressly delineates the connection between politics and sexuality. The film also establishes the Freudian theme of the totemic father, which will recur throughout Bertolucci's work, here emblematized in the figure of Fabrizio's communist mentor, whom Fabrizio must renounce as a precondition to his entry into moneyed society.

Bertolucci diverged from the style of his first two critically successful films with *The Partner,* a complex, experimental work based on Dostoevski's *The Double*. Heavily influenced by the films of Godard and the events of May 1968, it eschews narrative exposition, developing instead a critique of literary consumerism, academic pacifism, and the student left, through a series of polemical debates between a bookish student and his radical double. For the most part *The Partner* is an anomalous film, which conveys very little of the heightened lyricism of his major works.

With *The Spider's Stratagem,* originally made for television in 1969, and *The Conformist,* Bertolucci combines an experimental narrative technique with lavish visual design, achieving in *The Conformist* an unprecedented commercial and critical triumph. Sexuality is here explicitly posited as the motor of political allegiance, as Marcello, the lead character in *The Conformist,* becomes a Fascist in order to suppress his growing recognition of his homosexuality. The character performs an outlandishly deviant act—killing his former professor, now a member of the Resistance, in order to declare his own conventionality and membership in the Fascist order. Conformity and rebellion are thus folded together, not only in the psyche of Marcello, but in the culture as a whole, as Bertolucci examines the interpenetrating structures, the twin pathologies, of family and politics. Bertolucci here unveils the full range of stylistic features—the elaborate tracking shots, the opulent color photography (realized by the virtuoso cinematographer Vittorio Storara), the odd, surrealistic visual incongruities—that give his work such a distinctive surface. It is here, also, that Bertolucci connects most directly with the general evolution of the postwar Italian cinema. Beginning with Visconti, and continuing with Antonioni and Bellocchio, an increasing emphasis is placed on the psychology of transgression, a motif which links politics and the libido. The inner life of the alienated protagonist becomes the lens displaying the spectrum of social forces, as the politics of the state are viewed in the mimetic behavior of disturbed individuals.

Last Tango in Paris depicts the last week in the life of Paul, played by Marlon Brando, as a man who is both geographically and spiritually in exile. His orbit crosses that of "the girl," played by Maria Schneider. The raw sexual encounters which ensue serve as a kind of purgation for the Brando character, who retaliates against the hypocrisy of cultural institutions such as family, church, and state through the medium of Jeanne's body. Sex is used as a weapon and symbolic cure, as the libidinal rage of the character is focused on the entire apparatus of social constraints. The outsized human passion Bertolucci depicts, chiefly through the threatening figure of Marlon Brando, seems to literalize the filmmaker's comment that "films are animal events." In addition to the players, the music by Gatto Barbieri and the cinematography of Vittorio Storaro contribute to the febrile intensity of the work.

The world acclaim brought by *Last Tango* assured Bertolucci of the financial resources to complete the long-planned Marxian epic, *1900*. Setting the film in the rural areas of Parma, a few miles from his childhood home, Bertolucci set out to compose a paean to a way of life that was passing—the "culture of the land" of the peasant farmers, seen as a native and pure form of communism. The film depicts the cruel historical awakening of the farmers of the region, part of an entire class that has been regularly brutalized, first by aristocratic landowners, and then by the Fascist regime. Bertolucci localizes this conflict in the twin destinies of two characters born on the same day in *1900*—Olmo, who becomes a peasant leader, and Alfredo, the scion of the feudal estate in which the film takes place.

The controversial work was released in a six-hour form in Europe, and shortened to three hours for American release. Bertolucci had complete control of the cutting of the film, and considers the shorter version a more finished work. The epic sweep remains, as do the contradictions—for the film amalgamates the most divergent elements: a Marxian epic, it is furnished with an international star cast; a portrait of the indigenous peasantry, its principle language is English. Intentionally fashioned for wide commercial appeal, it nonetheless broaches untried subject matter. The film keeps these elements in suspension, never dissolving these differences into an ideological portrait of life "after the revolution." The film's ending seems instead to return to the customary balance and tension between historical forces and class interests.

In *Luna,* Bertolucci turns to a much more intimate subject: the relation between mother and son. The work has a diminutive scale but a passionate focus, a quality crystallized in the opera scenes in which the mother, Caterina, performs. The reconciliation of mother, son, and father occurs during a rehearsal in which the mother reveals, through song, the identity of father and son. This cathartic and bravura scene plays in high relief the characteristic patterns of Bertolucci's cinema, in which the family drama is played against the backdrop of a ritualized art form, opera in this case, dance in *Last Tango,* and theater (the *Macbeth* scene in *Before the Revolution*).

With *Tragedy of a Ridiculous Man,* Bertolucci continues his inquiry into the relations between politics and family life, here framing the ambivalent bond between father and son with the correlative conflict between capitalism and political terror.

Bertolucci returned to the wide canvas of the historical film with *The Last Emperor* in 1987. Frustrated by his inability to acquire financing for a film of the Dashiell Hammett story *Red Harvest,* and unhappy with the state of filmmaking in Italy, the director turned to the autobiography of Pu Yi, China's last emperor, and had the privilege not only of filming in China but also of filming in the Forbidden City in Beijing, the first time such access had been allowed.

The story of Pu Yi illustrates a striking change in the political focus of Bertolucci's filmmaking. The relationship between individual psychology and the political and historical forces that mold it remains, as before, the central subject of the film, linking it to works such as *Before the Revolution, The Conformist,* and *1900.* But the resolution of the film seems to take place outside the political and historical context. The transformation of Pu Yi, in Bertolucci's words, from "a dragon to a butterfly," occurs only in the context of individual friendship. In depicting the rise and fall of imperialism, republicanism, and fascism, and ending the film with a portrayal of the harsh excesses of the Cultural Revolution, Bertolucci depicts a sequence of destructive political "solutions" that somehow clear the way for the journey of the main character from "darkness to light."

Following *The Last Emperor,* Bertolucci continued his exploration of non-Western cultures with *The Sheltering Sky* and *Little Buddha,* opening his work to existential and philosophical themes that would almost seem to defy dramatic expression. In *The Sheltering Sky,* Bertolucci fashions a disturbing portrait of a consciousness in search of its own annihilation. Drawn from the Paul Bowles novel of the same title, the film, in its first half, focuses on the pathos of a couple who adore each other but cannot be happy, on the difficulty of romantic love. The work centers on the willful isolation and self-loathing of the character Porter, who has traveled to Morocco in 1947 with his wife Kit and a friend, Tunner, in order to escape the bitter sense of his own emptiness and artistic impotence. Like the character Paul in *Last Tango in Paris,* Porter is a dangerous and mesmerizing character whose self-absorption creates a kind of vortex which draws others down with him. As the two main characters, Porter and Kit, push deeper into the Sahara, the physical hardships they encounter seem more and more like rites of purgation, as if only the heat and dirt of the desert could wear down the various masks and poses that they continually display to each other. Porter dies a horrifying death from typhus, revealing the depths of his love for Kit only as the curtain descends. Kit, cast adrift deep in Morocco, hitches up with a caravan of Tuareg nomads and allows the remains of her Western identity to dissolve; she becomes the lover of the leader of the caravan, her Western clothes are buried in the desert, and she enters his harem disguised as a boy, dressed in the indigo robes, turban, and sword of a Tuareg tribesman. In a sense, Kit becomes possessed by Porter's spirit, his taste for uncharted experience, without, however, assuming his arrogance or corrosive unhappiness. Kit's story, which Bertolucci poetically links with the phases of the moon and nocturnal shades of blue, becomes dream-like, a carnal utopia of full and expressive passion in which she submerges her identity and becomes whole, albeit temporarily.

The Sheltering Sky has much in common with Bertolucci's earlier films, particularly *Last Tango in Paris;* as Bertolucci says in an interview, "Isn't the empty flat of *Last Tango* a kind of desert and isn't the desert an empty flat?" By filming in North Africa, however, Bertolucci allows the landscape to provide a kind of silent commentary on the doomed protagonists, whose profound unhappiness is made more piercing by the almost cosmic scale of the environment. The film abounds in visual ideas, finding in the mountain overlooks, wind-blown expanses, and fly-infested outposts a kind of encompassing dimension comparable to the role played by history in other Bertolucci films. Here, cinematographer Vittorio Storaro composes scenes around the division of color temperatures associated with the two main characters, red and blue, in ways that accentuate their irreconcilability. Exceptional acting by John Malkovich and Debra Winger gives *The Sheltering Sky* a sense of emotional truth that stays with the spectator, like the tattoos on fingers and feet that Kit receives in the deepest Sahara.

Little Buddha, released in 1994, completes what Bertolucci has called his Eastern trilogy. Although it shares the exoticism and the chromatic richness of *The Last Emperor* and *The Sheltering Sky, Little Buddha* is a sharp departure from its predecessors. It is, Bertolucci has said, a story without dramatic conflicts, a story in which the dualism and division that animates his other films is resolved into a kind of harmonious unity. Weaving together the ancient tale of Siddartha and his quest for enlightenment with a contemporary story of an eight-year-old American boy who may be the reincarnation of a famous Buddhist master, the film aims for a simplicity of tone and address that could be understood and appreciated by children: indeed, Bertolucci has called *Little Buddha* a film for children, arguing that when it comes to Buddhism, everyone in the Western world is a child.

Little Buddha features a striking visual style, marked by heightened color abstraction. Vittorio Storaro, Bertolucci's cinematographer for all his films except one, has said in an interview that *Little Buddha* represents the culmination of his exploration into light, and that it may be a film that is "impossible to go beyond." The painterly style of *Little Buddha* is keyed not only to the contrast between the blue tonality of Seattle and the red and gold of the Siddartha story, but also to the four elements and the movement of the celestial spheres. When Siddartha achieves enlightenment under the banyan tree after staving off temptation and fear, harmony and balance are signified by the simultaneous appearance of the sun and the moon in the sky, and by the balanced color temperature of the sequence. In his career-long work with Bertolucci, Storaro has progressed from an exploration of light and shadow, to an exploration of the contrast of colors within light, to an exploration of the harmony within the spectrum.

The fascinating sequences of Siddartha's journey to enlightenment have a distinctly magical, storybook quality, a tone that is achieved partly by filming these scenes in 65 millimeter. The precision and detail that sets these sequences apart gives them the quality of an illuminated manuscript, or of a dazzling storybook of hand-colored pages. Also important here is the acting of Keanu Reeves, who embodies the part of a beautiful youth determined to find the true value of life. The slightly unformed, open innocence of Reeves' Siddartha is perfectly attuned to the enchanted vision of this benevolent film, which discovers in a tale of reincarnation a kind of dispensation from the drama of political and sexual conflict that had defined Bertolucci's filmmaking to this point.—ROBERT BURGOYNE

Blier, Bertrand

Nationality *French.* **Born** *Paris, 14 March 1939.* **Career** *Assistant director on films of Lautner, Christian-Jaque, Delannoy, and others, 1960-63; directed first feature,* Hitler? Connais pas!, *1963.* **Awards** *Oscar for Best Foreign Language Film, for* Preparez vos mouchoirs, *1978; Cesar for the screenplay of* Buffet froid, *1979; Special Jury Prize, Cannes Film Festival, for* Trop belle pour toi (Too Beautiful for You), *1989.* **Address** *c/o Chez Artmedia, 10 avenue George-V, 75008 Paris, France.*

Films as Director: 1963: *Hitler? Connais pas!* (+sc). **1966:** *La Grimace* (+sc). **1967:** *Si j'etais un espion* (*Breakdown; If I Were a Spy*) (+co-sc). **1973:** *Les Valseuses* (*Going Places*) (+sc). **1975:** *Calmos* (*Femmes Fatales*) (+co-sc). **1977:** *Preparez vos mouchoirs* (*Get Out Your Handkerchiefs*) (+sc). **1979:** *Buffet froid* (+sc). **1981:** *Beau-père* (+sc). **1982:** *La Femme de mon pote* (*My Best Friend's Girl*) (+co-sc). **1984:** *Notre Histoire* (*Our Story*) (+sc). **1986:** *Tenue de soirée* (*Menage*) (+sc). **1989:** *Trop belle pour toi* (*Too Beautiful for You*) (+sc). **1991:** *Merci la vie* (*Thanks, Life*) (+sc, pr). **1993:** *Un deux trois soleil* (*One Two Three Sun*) (+sc). **1996:** *Mon homme* (+sc).

Other Films: 1970: *Laisse aller, c'est une valse* (Lautner) (sc). **1992:** *Patrick Dewaere* (role as himself).

Bertrand Blier directs erotic buddy movies featuring men who are exasperated by the opposite sex, who perceive of themselves as macho but are incapable of satisfying the women in their lives. In actuality, his heroes are terrified of feminism, of the "new woman" who demands her right to experience and enjoy orgasm. But Blier's females are in no way villainesses. They are just elusive—and so alienated that they can only find fulfillment from oddballs or young boys.

Going Places (Les Valseuses, which in French is slang for testicles), based on Blier's best-selling novel, was a box office smash in France. Gérard Depardieu and Patrick Dewaere both achieved stardom as a couple of outsiders, adult juvenile delinquents, whose sexual and sadistic adventures are chronicled as they travel across France. They are both unable to bring to orgasm a young beautician (played by Miou-Miou) they pick up and take on as a sexual partner. They then attempt to please an older woman (Jeanne Moreau), who has just spent ten years in prison. After a night together, she attempts suicide by shooting herself in the vagina. Eventually, Miou-Miou is sexually satisfied by a crazy, physically unattractive ex-con.

In *Femmes Fatales* middle-aged Jean-Pierre Marielle and Jean Rochefort, one a gynaecologist and the other a pimp, decide to abandon wives and mistresses for the countryside, but end up pursued by an army of women intent on enslaving them as studs. Again, men cannot escape women's sexual demands: here, the latter come after the former with tanks and guns. And in *Get Out Your Handkerchiefs,* driving instructor Depardieu is so anxious to please bored, depressed wife Carol Laure that he finds her a lover. Both the husband and the stranger, a playground instructor (Dewaere), feel that she will be happy if she can only have a child. She in her own way does this, finding a substitute for them in a precocious young boy barely into his teens. *Handkerchiefs* is a prelude of sorts to *Beau-Père,* which features only one male lead (as does the later *Trop Belle Pour Toi,* in which Depardieu is at the centre of a love triangle). Here, a struggling pianist, played by Dewaere, is seduced by the refreshingly self-confident 14-year-old daughter of his recently de-ceased lover. The teenager's feelings are deep and pure, while the "adult" is imma-ture, too self-conscious and self-absorbed to accept her.

Bertrand Blier

In Blier's films, men do not understand women. "Maybe one day I'll do *Camille,*" the filmmaker says. "But I won't do *An Unmarried Woman,* because I don't feel I have the right to do it. I don't know what goes on in a woman's head. I believe I know what certain men think, but not women." As a result, the sexual barriers between the sexes seem irrevocable in Blier's movies. His men are more at ease talking among themselves about women than with actually being with wives or lovers; their relationships with each other are for them more meaningful than their contacts with the opposite sex. There are alternatives to women, such as turning to homosexual relationships (the characters in *Going Places* sleep with each other when they are lonely or celibate).

Another Blier film, *Buffet Froid,* is also about male bonding: Depardieu, as a psychopathic killer, becomes involved with a mass murderer (Jean Carmet) and a homicidal cop (the director's father, the distinguished character actor Bernard Blier). However, *Buffet Froid* is mostly a study of alienation in urban society, and the acceptance of random, irrational violence. It is thematically more closely related to Jules Feiffer's *Little Murders* than *Going Places* or *Get Out Your Handkerchiefs.*

Blier's most recent films have added little luster to his career. However, the film maker seems to have tired of making films about men. Beginning with *Trop belle pour toi (Too Beautiful for You),* the most accessible of his latter-career works, his primary characters have been women. *Trop belle pour toi* does feature a clever take on extramarital relationships. Blier regular Gerard Depardieu plays a car dealer whose wife is beautiful and intelligent; nonetheless, he cheats on her with his otherwise ordinary, chubby temporary receptionist. Despite this intriguing premise and recognition with a Cannes Film Festival Special Jury Prize, the film lacks the spark and outrageousness of his earlier work.

The director's other features include *Merci la vie (Thanks, Life),* a feminist take on *Going Places* that sparked controversy upon its opening in France. It is a road movie which chronicles the sexual exploits of two young women, one sluttish and the other naive. *Un deux trois soliel (One Two Three Sun)* focuses on the plight of a young girl, growing up in a public housing project in Marseilles, who adores her alcoholic father and is mortified by her mother's affectations.

Bertrand Blier best explains what he attempts to communicate in his films: "The relations between men and women are constantly evolving and it's interesting to show people leading the lifestyle of tomorrow."—ROB EDELMAN

Boetticher, Budd

Nationality American. *Born* Oscar Boetticher, Jr., in Chicago, 29 July 1916. *Education* Ohio State University. *Military Service* Made propaganda films, 1946-47. *Career* Football star at Ohio State, early 1930s; after recuperating from football injury in Mexico, became professional matador, 1940; technical advisor on Mamoulian's Blood and Sand, 1940; messenger boy at Hal Roach studios, 1941-43; assistant to William Seiter, George Stevens, and Charles Vidor, 1943-44; made cycle of Westerns for Ranown production company, 1956-60; left Hollywood to make documentary on matador Carlos Arruza, 1960; after many setbacks, returned to Hollywood, 1967.

Budd Boetticher: *Comanche Station*

Films as Director: (as Oscar Boetticher) 1944: *One Mysterious Night; The Missing Juror; Youth on Trial.* **1945:** *A Guy, a Gal and a Pal; Escape on the Fog.* **1946:** *The Fleet That Came to Stay* (and other propaganda films). **1948:** *Assigned to Danger; Behind Locked Doors.* **1949:** *Black Midnight; Wolf Hunters.* **1950:** *Killer Shark.*

(As Budd Boetticher): 1951: *The Bullfighter and the Lady* (+co-story); *The Sword of D'Artagnan; The Cimarron Kid.* **1952:** *Bronco Buster; Red Ball Express; Horizons West.* **1953:** *City Beneath the Sea; Seminole; The Man from the Alamo; Wings of the Hawk; East of Sumatra.* **1955:** *The Magnificent Matador* (+story); *The Killer is Loose.* **1956:** *Seven Men from Now.* **1957:** *The Tall T; Decision at Sundown.* **1958:** *Buchanan Rides Alone.* **1959:** *Ride Lonesome* (+pr); *Westbound.* **1960:** *Comanche Station* (+co-pr); *The Rise and Fall of Legs Diamond.* **1971:** *Arruza* (+pr, co-sc; production completed 1968); *A Time for Dying* (+sc; production completed 1969). **1985:** *My Kingdom for. . .* (+sc).

Other Films: 1970: *Two Mules for Sister Sara* (Siegel) (sc).

Budd Boetticher will be remembered as a director of Westerns, although his bullfight films have their fervent admirers, as does his *Scarface*-variant, *The Rise and Fall of Legs Diamond.* Since Boetticher's Westerns are so variable in quality, it is tempting to overcredit Burt Kennedy, the scriptwriter for all of the finest. But Kennedy's own efforts as director (*Return of the Seven, Hannie Caulder, The War Wagon,* etc.) are tediously paced dramas or failed comedies. Clearly the Boetticher/Kennedy team clicked to make Westerns significantly superior to what either could create on their own. Indeed, *The Tall T, Seven Men from Now,* and (on a slightly lower level) *Ride Lonesome* look now like the finest work in the genre during the 1950s, less pretentious and more tightly controlled than even those of Anthony Mann or John Ford.

Jim Kitses's still-essential *Horizons West* rightly locates Boetticher's significant Westerns in the "Ranown" cycle (a production company name taken from producer Harry Joe Brown and his partner Randolph Scott). But the non-Kennedy entries in the cycle have, despite Scott's key presence, only passing interest. One might have attributed the black comedy in the series to Kennedy without the burlesque *Buchanan Rides Alone,* which wanders into an episodic narrative opposite to the taut, unified action of the others; *Decision at Sundown* is notable only for its remarkably bitter finale and a morally pointless showdown, as if it were a cynic's answer to *High Noon.*

The Tall T's narrative is typical of the best Boetticher/Kennedy: it moves from a humanizing comedy so rare in the genre into a harsh and convincing savagery. Boetticher's villains are relentlessly cruel, yet morally shaded. In *The Tall T,* he toys with the redeemable qualities of Richard Boone, while deftly characterizing the other two (Henry Silva asks, "I've never shot me a woman, have I Frank?"). Equally memorable are Lee Marvin (in *Seven Men from Now*) and Lee Van Cleef (*Ride Lonesome*).

Randolph Scott is the third essential collaborator in the cycle. He is generally presented by Boetticher as a loner not by principle or habit but by an obscure terror in his past (often a wife murdered). Thus, he's not an asexual cowpoke so much as one who, temporarily at least, is beyond fears and yearnings. There's a Pinteresque sexual confrontation in *Seven Men from Now* among Scott, a pioneer couple, and an insinuating Lee Marvin when the four are confined in a wagon. And, indeed, the typical Boetticher landscape—smooth, rounded, and yet impassible boulders—match Scott's deceptively complex character as much as the majestic Monument Valley towers match Wayne in Ford's Westerns, or the harsh cliffs match James Stewart in Mann's.

Clearly the Westerns of the sixties and seventies owe more to Boetticher than Ford. Even such very minor works as *Horizons West, The Wings of the Hawk,* and *The Man from the Alamo* have the tensions of Spaghetti Westerns (without the iciness), as well as the Peckinpah fantasy of American expertise combining with Mexican peasant vitality. If Peckinpah and Leone are the masters of the post-"classic" Western, then it's worth noting how *The Wings of the Hawk* anticipates *The Wild Bunch,* and how *Once Upon a Time in the West* opens like *Seven Men from Now* and closes like *Ride Lonesome.* Boetticher's films are the final great achievement of the traditional Western, before the explosion of the genre.—SCOTT SIMMON

Bogdanovich, Peter

Nationality American. Born Kingston, New York, 30 July 1939. Education Collegiate School, New York; studied acting at Stella Adler's Theatre Studio. Family Married 1) Polly Platt, 1962 (divorced 1970), two daughters; 2) Louise Stratten (Hoogstraten), 1988. Career Actor in American and New York Shakespeare Festivals, 1956-58; first play as producer, The Big Knife, off-Broadway, 1959; film critic for Esquire, New York Times, and Cahiers du Cinéma, among others, from 1961; moved to Hollywood, 1964; 2nd unit director on The Wild Angels (Corman), 1966; directed first film, Targets (produced by Corman), 1968; Paramount formed and financed The Directors Company, independent unit partnership of Bogdanovich, Francis Ford Coppola, and William Friedkin, 1973; formed Copa de Oro production company, 1975; owner, Crescent Moon Productions, Inc., from 1986. Awards New York Film Critics Award and British Academy Award for Best Screenplay, for The Last Picture Show, 1971; Writer's Guild of America Award for Best

Peter Bogdanovich directing *The Last Picture Show.*

Screenplay, for What's Up, Doc?, *1972; Critics Prize, Venice Festival, for* Saint Jack, *1979.* **Address** *c/o William Peiffer, 2040 Avenue of the Stars, Century City, California 90067, U.S.A.*

Films as Director: 1967: *Targets* (+co-sc, pr, ed, role as Sammy Michaels). **1971:** *Directed by John Ford* (+sc); *The Last Picture Show* (+co-sc). **1972:** *What's Up, Doc?* (+pr, co-sc). **1973:** *Paper Moon* (+pr). **1974:** *Daisy Miller* (+pr). **1975:** *At Long Last Love* (+pr, sc, co-songwriter: "Poor Young Millionaire"). **1976:** *Nickelodeon* (+co-sc). **1979:** *Saint Jack* (+co-sc, role as Eddie Schuman). **1983:** *They All Laughed* (+sc). **1984:** *Mask.* **1987:** *Illegally Yours* (+co-pr). **1990:** *Texasville* (+co-pr, co-sc). **1992:** *Noises Off* (+exec pr). **1993:** *The Thing Called Love.* **1996:** *To Sir with Love 2.*

Other Films: 1966: *The Wild Angels* (Corman) (co-sc, 2nd unit d, all uncredited, +bit role, voice); *Voyage to the Planet of the Prehistoric Women* (*Gill-Women of Venus*) (from Russian science fiction film by Pavel Klushantsev, *Planeta Burg* [*Cosmonauts on Venus; Storm Clouds of Venus*], dubbed and re-edited for American Int'l Pictures) (supervising ed, d of add'l scenes under pseudonym Derek Thomas and/or Peter Stewart). **1967:** *The Trip* (Corman) (role). **1969:** *Lion's Love* (Varda) (guest star role). **1970:** *The Other Side of the Wind* (Welles, unreleased) (role as Higgam). **1973:** *F for Fake* (Welles) (voice-over). **1975:** *Diaries, Notes & Sketches* volume 1, reels 1-6: *Lost Lost Lost* (Jonas Mekas) (appearance in reel 3); *The Gentleman Tramp* (Patterson) ("special thanks" credit for supervising scenes shot at Charles Chaplin's home in Switzerland). **1978:** *Opening Night* (Cassavetes) (guest star role).

Of all trades ancillary to the cinema, few offer worse preparation for a directing career than criticism. Bogdanovich's background as Hollywood historian and profiler of its legendary figures inevitably invited comparisons between his movies and those of directors like Ford, Hawks, and Dwan, whom he had deified. That he should have occasionally created films which deserve such comparison argues for his skill and resilience.

He first attracted attention with *Targets,* a flashy exercise with an ailing Boris Karloff playing straight man to Bogdanovich's film-buff director and a psychotic sniper menacing the audience at a drive-in cinema. The documentary *Directed by John Ford* likewise exploited Hollywood history, but with uncertain scholarship and even less certain taste. Yet in his first major fiction feature, based on Larry McMurtry's rural nocturne *The Last Picture Show,* Bogdanovich created a precise and moving chronicle of small-town values eroded by selfishness and disloyalty. He also showed a flair for casting in his choice of underrated veterans and fresh newcomers. Ben Johnson, Cloris Leachman, and Ellen Burstyn earned new respect, while Timothy Bottoms, Jeff Bridges, and Cybill Shepherd received boosts to nascent careers— though Shepherd, via her relationship with the director, was to prove a troublesome protegée.

What's Up, Doc? and *Paper Moon* are among the shapeliest comedies of the 1970s, trading on nostalgia but undercutting it with sly character-playing and dead-pan wit. Ryan and Tatum O'Neal achieve a stylish ensemble performance in the latter as 1930s con-man and unwanted orphan auxiliary; in the former, O'Neal makes a creditable attempt at playing Cary Grant to Barbra Streisand's Hepburn, backed up by a typically rich character cast—notably Austin Pendleton, Kenneth Mars, and the ululating Madeline Kahn.

Daisy Miller, a period vehicle for Shepherd more redolent of Henry King than Henry James, inaugurated Bogdanovich's decline. An attempt at a 1930s Cole Porter musical, *At Long Last Love* likewise flopped, as did *Nickelodeon,* an unexpectedly leaden tribute to pioneer moviemaking. He returned to form with a low-budget adaptation of Paul Theroux's *Saint Jack,* dignified by Ben Gazzara's performance as the ironic man of honor coping with Occidental venality and Asian corruption. And the Manhattan comedy *They All Laughed,* though widely disliked, showed a truer synthesis of screwball humour and sentimentality than other equivalent films, and marked a return by Bogdanovich to the spirit of the classical directors he admires.

Bogdanovich worked little in the 1980s, apparently traumatised by the murder of his lover Dorothy Stratten shortly after her acting debut in *They All Laughed.* At decade's end, in a twin return to his roots that offered some hope for his future, he married Stratten's sister and directed *Texasville,* a *Last Picture Show* sequel with many of the original cast.

Texasville, like most sequels, fails because what made the original interesting and valuable cannot be repeated. Like Bogdanovich himself, then at the beginning of his career, the characters in *The Last Picture Show* were embarked, with tragi-comic results, on the painful journey into adulthood; the loss of childhood certainties was mirrored by the film's detailed mise-en-scène, a small Texas town that loses its heart and soul when a benevolent patriarch dies suddenly. Grown up, they are no longer connected by the irresistible force of adolescence, and Bogdanovich's film—though based on novelist Larry McMurtry's often poignant continuation— wanders in search of a plot, boring the spectator with childish antics meant to signify the onset of a collective life crisis. The story goes on, but without much interest or direction.

Much the same might be said of his career in the 1990s, which has continued but not prospered. *The Thing Called Love* tries to recapture Bogdanovich's earlier success with coming-of-age stories (not only *The Last Picture Show* but also *Paper Moon*). However, this overly predictable and slow-moving saga of young adults trying to make it big in the highly competitive world of country music deservedly failed to find much of an audience. *Noises Off,* based on Michael Frayn's hugely successful play, has moments that recall Bogdanovich's earlier success with fast-paced farce (the delightful *What's Up, Doc?*), but lacks a firm sense of directorial control; a fine cast—including Michael Caine and Carol Burnett—never becomes an effective ensemble, and the film's only virtues derive from Frayn's play, whose commercial productions are far superior to this screen version.—JOHN BAXTER and R. BARTON PALMER

Boorman, John

Nationality British. *Born* Shepperton, Middlesex, 18 January 1933. *Education* Salesian College. *Military Service* Sergeant in British Army, 1951-53. *Family* Married Christel Kruse, 1957, one son (actor Charley Boorman), three daughters. *Career* Film critic for *BBC Radio* and for Manchester Guardian, 1950-54; film editor, Independent Television News, 1955-58; head of documentaries, BBC Television, 1960-64; directed first feature, Catch Us If You Can, 1965; moved to United States to make Point Blank, 1967; chairor, National Film Studios of Ireland, 1975-85; governor, British Film institute, from 1985; founder and co-editor of Projections, published annually in London since 1992. *Awards* Best Director Award, Cannes Festival, for Leo the Last, 1970; Chevalier de l'Ordre des Arts et Lettres, 1985; New York Film Critics Circle Awards for Best Director and Best Screenplay, for Hope and Glory, 1987. *Agent* Edgar Gross, International Business Management, 1801 Century Park E., Suite 1132, Los Angeles, California 90067, U.S.A. *Address* The Glebe, Annamoe, County Wicklow, Ireland.

Films as Director: 1965: *Catch Us If You Can* (*Having a Wild Weekend*). **1967:** *Point Blank.* **1968:** *Hell in the Pacific.* **1970:** *Leo the Last* (+sc). **1972:** *Deliverance* (+pr). **1973:** *Zardoz* (+sc, pr). **1977:** *Exorcist II: The Heretic* (+pr). **1981:** *Excalibur* (+pr, co-sc). **1985:** *The Emerald Forest* (+pr). **1987:** *Hope and Glory* (+pr, sc). **1990:** *Where the Heart Is* (+sc, pr). **1991:** *I Dreamt I Woke Up* (+sc, role). **1995:** *Two Nudes Bathing* (+sc, pr); *Beyond Rangoon* (+pr); *Lumière et compagnie* (*Lumière and Company*) (co-d). **1997:** *A Simple Plan.*

Other Films: 1976: *Target of an Assassin* (*The Long Shot*) (role). **1982:** *Dream One* (pr).

"Film making is the process of turning money into light and then back into money again." John Boorman's neat epigram will probably haunt him for the rest of his filmmaking days, not simply because it is so tidy a formulation, but because the tensions it articulates have played such a prominent part in his own career.

Boorman has always been much concerned with the look of his films. In both *Deliverance* and *Point Blank* (shot, incidentally, in exquisite 'scope) he went to unusual lengths to control colour tones; *Zardoz* and *Exorcist II: The Heretic* are remarkable for their pictorial inventiveness; the images of the Irish countryside in *Excalibur* and of the Brazilian rain forest in *The Emerald Forest* are carefully imbued with a luminous, almost magical quality; and the extraordinary street of housing built for *Hope and Glory* (one of the largest sets constructed in Britain since the heyday of the studio system) speaks volumes for Boorman's commitment to a cinema of distinctively visual qualities.

Boorman has certainly proven himself able to turn money into light. Turning it back into money, however, has not always proved so easy, and the commercial weakness of *Zardoz* and the near total box-office disaster of *Exorcist II* were no help to him in trying to develop his ambitious projects of the 1980s. After all, an Irish-based adaptation of Malory's *Morte d'Arthur* (*Excalibur*), a "green" allegory scheduled for location filming in South America (*Emerald*

John Boorman on the set of *Deliverance*.

Forest), and an autobiographical evocation of his wartime childhood (*Hope and Glory*) are hardly the most obviously marketable ideas, even from a thoroughly bankable director. Yet sell them he did, and if *The Emerald Forest* doesn't come off as well as either *Excalibur* or *Hope and Glory,* two out of three is no mean record for an independent-minded filmmaker with a taste for startling visuals and unusual stories.

Boorman's is a high-risk approach. When it goes wrong, it goes wrong with a vengeance, and both *Exorcist II* and *The Emerald Forest* sacrifice narrative conviction in the cause of pictorial splendour and some risible metaphysics. But when his approach goes right, the results are sufficient to justify his reputation as one of the most courageous and imaginative filmmakers still working in the commercial mainstream.

At its best (in *Point Blank, Deliverance, Excalibur,* and *Hope and Glory*) Boorman's cinema is rich and subtle, his fascination with images matched by taut story-telling and a nice sense of the opacity of people's motives, his characters constantly made aware of the complex and unanticipated consequences of their actions. In many of his films, strong-willed individualists find themselves embroiled in a clash between established order and disorder, a context within which they appear as representative figures caught up in near mythical confrontations. In *Hell in the Pacific,* for instance, Lee Marvin and Toshiro Mifune play two enemy soldiers stranded on an island. As they continue to conduct the war their roles become emblematic, and they play out the tensions between conditioned aggression and common humanity.

In *Point Blank,* perhaps Boorman's most elegantly realised film, the force for disorder is Walker (Lee Marvin), a man obsessed by what he considers to be his just desserts. Double-crossed in a robbery, he wants only his share of the spoils, a goal he pursues step by step up the hierarchy of a criminal syndicate. The film leaves us little choice but to identify with Walker who is, like Sean Connery in *Zardoz,* an absolute individualist, a man who cannot be restrained by the hierarchical order on which he impinges so forcefully.

Yet *Point Blank* somehow transcends the conventional morality of assertive individualism. Walker is ruthless and violent, certainly, but it is his symbolic force to which we respond. The movie creates a paradox in which this unlovely figure comes to represent a more human spirit than that embodied in the syndicate's bureaucratic order. As ever, Boorman provides no easy solutions. After much death and violence it emerges that Walker, too, has been manipulated. Sharing his perspective as we do, we are left with a pervasive sense of impotence in the face of larger impersonal forces.

Deliverance, too, shows us order and certainty revealed as precarious fabrications. It concerns four men on a canoe trip through the wilderness who are forced to recognise that their ideas about morality and their belief in the social niceties are ineffectual constructs in the face of adverse and unintelligible circumstances. After killing a man who had buggered one of their party at gunpoint, they find that the action leads them down a path of lies and death. "There's no end to it," one character observes, close to despair.

Excalibur, perhaps inevitably given its source in Arthurian myth, tells of the imposition of order onto chaos and of the terrible price to be paid when that order is not firmly based. Human frailty destroys Camelot when Arthur finds Guinevere and Lancelot asleep together in the forest; in another of Boorman's inspired cinematic images, Arthur plunges the sword Excalibur into the ground between them. The despairing Guinevere is left curled naked around the sword while the land falls into pestilence and war.

In these three films Boorman ensures that we appreciate how difficult it is to make judgments of good and evil, how tangled the threads of motivation can be. But he does so not only as a pessimistic observer of human failings; he also has hope. There is a lovely scene in *Hope and Glory,* his most romantic of films, when young Bill (Boorman himself, for the film is autobiographical) has the "googly" explained to him by his father. When he realises what it involves (bowling a cricket ball so that it turns one way but with a bowling action which suggests that it will turn in the opposite direction) he is both horrified and fascinated. "That's like telling fibs," he says, a child's term for lying which is as accurate to the period as it is precise in its childish evocation of acceptable untruth. In Bill's (and Boorman's) world, people are forever telling fibs; like the googly, things are not always what they seem. But, also like the googly, that complexity can be a matter as much for celebration as for concern.—ANDREW TUDOR

Borzage, Frank

Nationality American. **Born** Salt Lake City, Utah, 23 April 1893. **Family** Married 1) Rena Rogers (divorced 1945); 2) Edna Marie Stillwell, 1945 (divorced 1949); 3) Juanita Borzage. **Career** Joined theatrical touring company as prop boy, 1906; moved to California, 1912; actor in many Ince Westerns and Mutual Comedies, 1913-15; began directing for Universal, 1916; signed to MGM, 1935-42; joined Republic Pictures as producer-director, 1945. **Awards** Oscar for Best Director, for Seventh Heaven, 1927-28, and Bad Girls, 1931-32. **Died** Of cancer in Los Angeles, 19 June 1962.

Films as Director: 1916: *That Gal of Burke's* (+role); *Mammy's Rose* (co-d, role); *Life's Harmony* (co-d, role); *The Silken Spider* (+role); *The Code of Honor* (+role); *Nell Dale's Men Folks* (+role); *The Forgotten Prayer* (+role); *The Courtin' of Calliope Clew* (+role); *Nugget Jim's Pardner* (+role); *The Demon of Fear* (+role); *Land o' Lizards* (*Silent Shelby*) (+role); *Immediate Lee* (*Hair Trigger Casey*) (+role); *Enchantment* (+sc, role); *The Pride and the Man* (+sc, role); *Dollars of Dross* (+sc). **1917:** *Wee Lady Betty* (co-d, role); *Flying Colors; Until They Get Me.* **1918:** *The Atom* (+role); *The Gun Woman* (+role); *Shoes That Danced; Innocent's Progress; An Honest Man; Society for Sale; Who Is to Blame?; The Ghost Flower; The Curse of Iku* (+role). **1919:** *Toton; Prudence of Broadway; Whom the Gods Destroy; Ashes of Desire.* **1920:** *Humoresque.* **1921:** *The Duke of Chimney Butte; Get-Rich-Quick Wallingford.* **1922:** *Back Pay; Billy Jim; The Good Provider; Hair Trigger Casey* (re-ed version); *Silent Shelby* (reissue of *Land o'Lizards*); *The Valley of Silent Men; The Pride of Palomar.* **1923:** *The Nth Commandment; Children of the Dust; Age of Desire.* **1924:** *Secrets.* **1925:** *The Lady; Daddy's Gone A-Hunting; Lazybones; Wages for Wives; The Circle.* **1926:** *The First Year; The Dixie Merchant; Early to Wed;*

Marriage License?. 1927: Seventh Heaven. 1928: Street Angel. 1929: The River; Lucky Star; They Had to See Paris. 1930: Son o' My Heart; Liliom. 1931: Doctors' Wives; Young as You Feel; Bad Girl. 1932: After Tomorrow; Young America; A Farewell to Arms. 1933: Secrets (remake of 1924 film); Man's Castle. 1934: No Greater Glory; Little Man What Now? (+pr); Flirtation Walk (+pr). 1935: Living on Velvet; Stranded; Shipmates Forever. 1936: Desire; Hearts Divided. 1937: Green Light; History Is Made at Night; Big City. 1938: Mannequin; Three Comrades; The Shining Hour. 1939: Disputed Passage (+co-pr). 1940: Strange Cargo; The Mortal Storm (+co-pr). 1941: Flight Command; Smilin' Through. 1942: The Vanishing Virginian; Seven Sweethearts. 1943: Stage Door Canteen; His Butler's Sister (+co-pr). 1944: Till We Meet Again (+pr). 1945: The Spanish Main. 1946: I've Always Loved You (+pr); Magnificent Doll. 1947: That's My Man (+pr). 1948: Moonrise. 1958: China Doll (+pr). 1959: The Big Fisherman.

Frank Borzage had a rare gift of taking characters, even those who were children of violence, and fashioning a treatment of them abundant with lyrical romanticism and tenderness, even a spirituality that reformed them and their story.

Borzage arrived in Hollywood in 1913, and Thomas H. Ince gave him his first small roles as a film actor, gradually promoting him to lead roles and providing him with his first opportunities to direct. He usually played the romantic lead in westerns and romantic melodramas with such Triangle players as Sessue Hayakawa (*The Typhoon* and *Wrath of the Gods,* both 1914) and Olive Thomas (*Toton,* 1919). The first really important feature he directed was *Humoresque,* written by Frances Marion from a Fannie Hurst story. It had all the elements which were later to stamp a picture as a Borzage film—hope, love, and faith in oneself and others in a world that was poverty-stricken and could be cruel. It won *Photoplay Magazine*'s award as Best Picture of the year.

Borzage insisted that "real art is simple, but simplicity requires the greatest art," adding that "naturalness is the primary requisite of good acting. I like my players to perform as though there were no camera on the set."

Frank Borzage.
Photograph by Frank Tanner.

Borzage did exceedingly well at Paramount's Cosmopolitan and at First National, where he directed two Norma Talmadge favorites, *Secrets* and *The Lady.* He then moved over to Fox, where, with the 1927 release of *Seventh Heaven,* he established himself as one of the best in the business. He directed two others with Janet Gaynor and Charles Farrell, *Street Angel* and *Lucky Star.* His *The River* of 1928, starring Farrell, is a virtual cinematic poem. In 1929 Borzage directed his first all-talking feature, *They Had to See Paris,* which starred Will Rogers, Fox's number one box-office star.

The year 1933 was probably Borzage's finest as a director, for he made three films which still rate as superb examples of the romantic cinema: *A Farewell to Arms,* from the Hemingway novel, with Gary Cooper and Helen Hayes; Mary Pickford's final and very best film, a re-make of the silent-era *Secrets,* which had originally starred Norma Talmadge; and *Man's Castle,* with Spencer Tracy and Loretta Young, a very moving romance.

There was a lasting tenderness about Borzage's treatment of a love story, and during the days of the Depression and the rise of Fascism, his pictures were ennobling melodramas about the power of love to create a heaven on earth. Penelope Gilliatt has remarked that Borzage "had a tenderness rare in melodrama and absolute pitch about period. He understood adversity." Outside of Griffith, there has never been another director in the business who could so effectively triumph over sentimentality, using true sentiment with an honest touch.

Borzage made four films with Margaret Sullavan that clearly indicated that she was the quintessential heroine for Borzage films: *Little Man, What Now?,* a study of love in the midst of deprivation and the growing terror in Germany; *Three Comrades,* in which Sullavan played an ill-fated tubercular wife; *The Shining Hour,* which featured her as a self-sacrificing woman; and *The Mortal Storm,* a moving film of the imminent battle with the Nazi forces.

Borzage also directed three other films during this time of stress that were extraordinary departures for him: *Desire,* a sleek romance in the Lubitsch tradition, starring Marlene Dietrich and Gary Cooper; *Mannequin,* co-starring Joan Crawford with Spencer Tracy, one of their best; and a drama that combined romance with effective disaster, *History Is Made at Night,* with Jean Arthur and Charles Boyer as lovers trapped in a Titanic-like explosion of violence. While in the case of *Desire* Ernst Lubitsch was producer, the picture features touches that are just as indicative of Borzage as they are of Lubitsch, for both were masters of cinematic subtlety. In the post-war period, it began to be clear that Borzage's career was on the wane. His best picture during this era was *Moonrise.*—DeWITT BODEEN

Bresson, Robert

Nationality *French.* **Born** *Bromont-Lamothe (Puy-de-Dome), France, 25 September 1907.* **Education** *Lycée Lakanal à Sceaux, Paris.* **Family** *Married 1) Leidia van der Zee, 1926 (deceased); 2) Myline van der Mersch.* **Career** *Attempted career as painter, to 1933; directed first film,* Affaires publiques, *1934; German prisoner of war, 1940-41; directed first major film,* Les Anges du péché, *1943; elected President d'honneur de la Société des réalisateurs de films, 1968.* **Awards** *International Prize, Venice Film Festival, for* Journal d'un curé campagne, *1951; Best Director Award, Cannes Festival, for* Un Condamné a mort s'est échappé, *1957; Special Jury Prize, Cannes Festival, for* Procès de Jeanne d'Arc, *1962; Ours d'Argent, Berlin, for* Le Diable probablement, *1977; Grand Prix national des Arts et des Lettres (Cinéma), France, 1978; Grand Prize, Cannes Festival, for* L'Argent, *1984; National Order of Merit, Commandeur of Arts and Letters of the Légion d'honneur; Lion d'Or, Venice, 1989; Felix Européen, Berlin, 1993.* **Address** *49 Quai de Bourbon, 75004 Paris, France.*

Films as Director: **1934:** *Affaires publiques* (+sc). **1943:** *Les Anges du péché (Angels of the Streets)* (+sc). **1945:** *Les Dames du Bois de Boulogne (The Ladies of the Bois de Boulogne)* (+sc). **1950:** *Journal d'un curé de campagne (Diary of a Country Priest)* (+sc). **1956:** *Un Condamné a mort s'est échappé (Le Vent souffle où il veut; A Condemned Man Escapes)* (+sc). **1959:** *Pickpocket* (+sc). **1962:** *Procès de*

Jeanne d'Arc (*The Trial of Joan of Arc*) (+sc). **1966:** *Au hasard Balthazar* (*Balthazar*) (+sc). **1967:** *Mouchette* (+sc). **1969:** *Une Femme douce* (+sc). **1971:** *Quatre Nuits d'un rêveur* (*Four Nights of a Dreamer*) (+sc). **1974:** *Lancelot du Luc* (*Le Graal; Lancelot of the Lake*) (+sc). **1977:** *Le Diable probablement* (+sc). **1983:** *L'Argent* (+sc).

Other Films: 1933: *C'était un musicien* (Zelnick and Gleize) (dialogue). **1936:** *Les Jumeaux de Brighton* (Heymann) (co-sc); *Courrier Sud* (Billon) (co-adaptation).

Robert Bresson began and quickly gave up a career as a painter, turning to cinema in 1934. The short film he made that year, *Affaires publiques,* is never shown. His next work, *Les Anges du péché,* was his first feature film, followed by *Les Dames du Bois du Boulogne* and *Journal d'un curé de campagne,* which firmly established his reputation as one of the world's most rigorous and demanding filmmakers. In the next fifteen years he made only four films: *Un Condamné à mort s'est échappé, Pickpocket, Procès de Jeanne d'Arc,* and *Au hasard Balthazar,* each a work of masterful originality and unlike the others. Since then he has made films with more frequency and somewhat less intensity. In 1975 Gallimard published his gnomic *Notes sur le cinématographe.*

As a whole Bresson's oeuvre constitutes a crucial investigation of the nature of cinematic narration. All three films of the 1950s are variations on the notion of a written diary transposed to a voice-over commentary on the visualized action. More indirectly, *Procès de Jeanne d'Arc* proposes yet another variant through the medium of the written transcript of the trial; *Une Femme douce* is told through the voice of the husband as he keeps a vigil for his suicidal wife; and in *Quatre nuits d'un rêveur* both of the principal characters narrate their previous histories to each other. In all of these instances Bresson allows the tension between the continuity of written and spoken language and the fragmentation of shots in a film to become an important thematic concern. His narrators tell themselves (and us) stories in order to find meaning in what has happened to them. The elusiveness of that meaning is reflected in the elliptical style of Bresson's editing.

For the most part, Bresson employs only amateur actors. He avoids histrionics and seldom permits his "models" (as he calls them, drawing a metaphor from painting) to give a traditional performance. The emotional tensions of the films derive from the elaborate interchange of glances, subtle camera movements, offscreen sounds, carefully placed bits of baroque and classical music, and rhythmical editing.

The Bressonian hero is often defined by what he or she sees. We come to understand the sexual tensions of Ambricourt from a few shots seen from the country priest's perspective; the fierce desire to escape helps the condemned man to see the most ordinary objects as tools for his purpose; the risk the pickpocket initially takes to prove his moral superiority to himself leads him to see

Robert Bresson.
Photograph by Bob Hawkins.

thefts where we might only notice people jostling one another: the film initiates its viewers into his privileged perspective. Only at the end does he realize that this obsessive mode of seeing has blinded him to a love which he ecstatically embraces.

Conversely, Mouchette kills herself suddenly when she sees the death of a hare (with which she identified herself); the heroine of *Une Femme douce* kills herself because she can see no value in things, while her pawnbroker husband sees nothing but the monetary worth of everything he handles. The most elaborate form this concentration on seeing takes in Bresson's cinema is the structure of *Au hasard Balthazar,* where the range of human vices is seen through the eyes of a donkey as he passes through a series of owners.

The intricate shot-countershot of Bresson's films reinforces his emphasis on seeing, as does his careful use of camera movement. Often he reframes within a shot to bring together two different objects of attention. The cumulative effect of this meticulous and often obsessive concentration on details is the sense of a transcendent and fateful presence guiding the actions of characters who come to see only at the end, if at all, the pattern and goal of their lives.

Only in *Un Condamné, Pickpocket,* and *Quatre Nuits* does the protagonist survive the end of the film. A dominant theme of his cinema is dying with grace. In *Mouchette, Une Femme douce,* and *Le Diable probablement* the protagonists commit suicide. In *Les Anges* and *L'Argent* they give themselves up as murderers. Clearly Bresson, who is the most prominent of Catholic filmmakers, does not reflect the Church's condemnation of suicide. Death, as he represents it, comes as the acceptance of one's fate. The three suicides emphasize the enigma of human will; they seem insufficiently motivated, but are pure acts of accepting death.—P. ADAMS SITNEY

Browning, Tod

*Nationality American. **Born** Charles Albert Browning in Louisville, Kentucky, 12 July 1880. **Education** Attended school in Churchill Downs. **Family** Married Alice Houghton (actress Alice Wilson), 1918. **Career** Ran away from home to join a carnival, 1898; worked carnival circuit, then Vaudeville and Burlesque shows; joined Biograph film studio as comedic actor, 1913; directed first film,* The Lucky Transfer, *1915; joined Universal Studios, began association with Lon Chaney, 1919; signed by MGM, 1925. **Award** Honorary Life Membership, Directors Guild of America. **Died** 6 October 1962.*

Films as Director: 1915: *The Lucky Transfer; The Slave Girl; The Highbinders; The Living Death; The Burned Hand; The Woman from Warren's; Little Marie; The Story of a Story; The Spell of the Poppy; The Electric Alarm.* **1916:** *Puppets; Everybody's Doing It; The Deadly Glass of Beer (The Fatal Glass of Beer).* **1917:** *Jim Bludso* (co-d, co-sc); *Peggy, The Will o' th' Wisp; The Jury of Fate; A Love Sublime* (co-d); *Hands Up!* (co-d). **1918:** *The Eyes of Mystery; The Legion of Death; Revenge; Which Woman; The Deciding Kiss; The Brazen Beauty; Set Free* (+sc). **1919:** *The Wicked Darling; The Exquisite Thief; The Unpainted Woman; A Petal on the Current; Bonnie, Bonnie Lassie* (+sc). **1920:** *The Virgin of Stamboul* (+sc). **1921:** *Outside the Law* (+co-sc); *No Woman Knows* (+co-sc). **1922:** *The Wise Kid; Under Two Flags* (+co-sc); *Man Under Cover.* **1923:** *Drifting* (+co-sc); *White Tiger* (+co-sc); *Day of Faith.* **1924:** *The Dangerous Flirt; Silk Stocking Girl (Silk Stocking Sal).* **1925:** *The Unholy Three* (+co-sc); *The Mystic* (+co-sc); *Dollar Down.* **1926:** *The Black Bird* (+co-sc); *The Road to Mandalay* (+co-sc). **1927:** *London After Midnight* (+co-sc); *The Show; The Unknown* (+co-sc). **1928:** *The Big City* (+co-sc); *West of Zanzibar.* **1929:** *Where East is East* (+co-sc); *The Thirteenth Chair.* **1930:** *Outside the Law* (+co-sc). **1931:** *Dracula* (+co-sc); *The Iron Man.* **1932:** *Freaks.* **1933:** *Fast Workers.* **1935:** *Mark of the Vampire* (+sc). **1936:** *The Devil-Doll* (+co-sc). **1939:** *Miracles for Sale.*

Other Films: 1913: *Scenting a Terrible Crime* (role); *A Fallen Hero* (role). **1914:** *A Race for a Bride* (role); *The Man in the Couch* (role); *An Exciting Courtship* (role); *The Last Drink of Whiskey* (role); *Hubby to the Rescue* (role); *The Deceivers* (role); *The White Slave Catchers* (role); *Wrong All Around* (role); *Leave It to Smiley* (role); *The Wild Girl* (role); *Ethel's Teacher* (role); *A Physical Culture Romance* (role); *The Mascot* (role); *Foiled Again* (role); *The Million Dollar Bride* (role); *Dizzy Joe's Career* (role); *Casey's Vendetta* (role); *Out Again—In Again* (role); *A Corner in Hats* (role); *The Housebreakers* (role); *The Record Breakers* (role). **1914-15:** Mr. Hadley in "Bill" series through no. 17; *Ethel Gets Consent* (role). **1915:** *The Queen of the Band* (Myers) (story); *Cupid and the Pest* (role); *Music Hath Its Charms* (role); *A Costly Exchange* (role). **1916:** *Sunshine Dad* (Dillon) (co-story); *The Mystery of the Leaping Fish* (Emerson) (story); *Atta Boy's Last Race* (Seligmann) (sc); *Intolerance* (Griffith) (role, asst d for crowd scenes). **1919:** *The Pointing Finger* (Kull) (supervisor). **1921:** *Society Secrets* (McCarey) (supervisor). **1928:** *Old Age Handicap* (Mattison) (story under pseudonym Tod Underwood). **1946:** *Inside Job* (Yarborough) (story).

Although his namesake was the poet Robert Browning, Tod Browning became recognized as a major Hollywood cult director whose work bore some resemblance to the sensibilities of a much different writer: Edgar Allen Poe. However, unlike Poe, Tod Browning was, by all accounts, a quiet and gentle man who could nonetheless rise to sarcasm and sardonic remarks when necessary to bring out the best from his players or to ward off interference from the front office.

Browning came to Hollywood as an actor after working circus and vaudeville circuits. Browning tapped into this background in supplying elements of many of his films, notably *The Unholy Three, The Show,* and *Freaks.* He worked in the film industry as an actor until D.W. Griffith (for whom Browning had worked on *Intolerance* as both a performer and assistant director) gave him the chance to direct at the Fine Arts Company. Browning directed a few films for Metro, but came to fame at Universal with a series of features starring Priscilla Dean.

Although *The Virgin of Stamboul* was admired by critics, it was his next film, *Outside the Law,* which has more historical significance, marking the first time that Browning directed Lon Chaney. (Browning remade the feature as a talkie.)

These Universal productions were little more than pretentious romantic melodramas, but they paved the way for a series of classic MGM horror films starring Lon Chaney, from *The Unholy Three* in 1925 through *Where East Is East* in 1929. These films were notable for the range of Chaney's performances—a little old lady, a cripple, an armless circus performer, a gangster, and so on—and for displaying Browning's penchant for the macabre. All were stylish productions, well directed, but all left the viewer with a sense of disappointment, of unfulfilled climaxes. Aside from directing, Tod Browning also wrote most of his films. He once explained that the

Tod Browning

plots of these works were secondary to the characterizations, a viewpoint that perhaps explains the dismal, unexciting endings to many of his features.

Tod Browning made an easy transition to sound films, although surprisingly he did not direct the 1930 remake of *The Unholy Three*. Instead, he directed the atmospheric *Dracula,* a skillful blend of comedy and horror that made a legend of the actor Bela Lugosi. A year later, Browning directed another classic horror talkie, *Freaks,* a realistic and at times offensive melodrama about the physically deformed members of a circus troupe. The film includes the marriage of midget Harry Earles to a trapeze artiste (Olga Baclanova).

Browning ended his career with *The Mark of the Vampire,* a remake of the Chaney feature *London After Midnight; The Devil Doll,* in which Lionel Barrymore appears as an old lady, a similar disguise to that adopted by Chaney in *The Unholy Three;* and *Miracles for Sale,* a mystery drama involving professional magicians. Tod Browning will, of course, be best remembered for his horror films, but it should also be recalled that during the first half of his directorial career he stuck almost exclusively to romantic melodramas.—ANTHONY SLIDE

Buñuel, Luis

Nationality Spanish. *Born* Calanda, province of Teruel, Spain, 22 February 1900. *Education* Jesuit schools in Zaragosa, 1906-15, Residencia de Estudiantes, Madrid, 1917-20, and University of Madrid, graduated 1924. *Family* Married Jeanne Rucar, 1933, two sons. *Career* Assistant to Jean Epstein in Paris, 1925; joined Surrealist group, and directed first film, Un Chien andalou, 1929; worked for Paramount in Paris, 1933;

Executive Producer for Filmofono, Madrid, 1935; served Republican government in Spain, 1936-39; worked at Museum of Modern Art, New York, 1939-42; produced Spanish versions of Warners films, Hollywood, 1944; moved to Mexico, 1946; returned to Spain to make Viridiana, *1961 (film suppressed).* **Awards** *Best Director Award and International Critics Prize, Cannes Festival, for* Los olvidados, *1951; Gold Medal, Cannes Festival, for* Nazarin, *1959, and* Viridiana, *1961; Golden Lion, Venice Festival, for* Belle de jour, *1967.* **Died** *In Mexico City, 29 July 1983.*

Films as Director: 1929: *Un Chien andalou (Andalusian Dog)*(+pr, co-sc, ed, role as Man with razor). **1930:** *L'Age d'or* (+co-sc, ed, mu). **1932:** *Las Hurdes—Tierra sin pan (Land without Bread)* (+sc, ed). **1935:** *Don Quintin el amargao* (Marquina) (co-d uncredited, +pr, co-sc); *La hija de Juan Simón* (Sáenz de Heredia) (co-d uncredited, +pr, co-sc). **1936:** *Centinella alerta!* (Grémillon) (co-d uncredited, +pr, co-sc). **1940:** *El Vaticano de Pío XII (The History of the Vatican)* (short, special issue of *March of Time* series). **1947:** *Gran Casino (Tampico)*. **1949:** *El gran calavera*. **1950:** *Los olvidados (The Forgotten; The Young and the Damned)* (+co-sc); *Susana (Demonio y carne)* (+co-sc). **1951:** *La hija del engaño (Don Quintín el amargao)*; *Cuando los hijos nos juzgan (Una mujer sin amor)*; *Subida al cielo* (+sc). **1952:** *El Bruto* (+co-sc); *Las aventuras de Robinson Crusoe (Adventures of Robinson Crusoe)* (+co-sc); *El* (+co-sc). **1953:** *Abismos de pasión (Cumbres borrascoses)* (+co-sc); *La ilusión viaja en tranvía* (+co-sc). **1954:** *El río y la muerte* (+co-sc). **1955:** *Ensayo de un crimen (La Vida Criminal de Archibaldo de La Cruz; The Criminal Life of Archibaldo de la Cruz)* (+co-sc); *Cela s'appelle l'Aurore* (+co-sc). **1956:** *La Mort en ce jardin (La muerte en este jardin)* (+co-sc). **1958:** *Nazarín* (+co-sc). **1959:** *La Fièvre monte à El Pao (Los Ambiciosos)* (+co-sc). **1960:** *The Young One (La Joven; La Jeune Fille)* (+co-sc). **1961:** *Viridiana* (+co-sc, story). **1962:** *El ángel exterminador (The Exterminating Angel)* (+co-sc, story). **1963:** *Le Journal d'une femme de chambre* (+co-sc). **1965:** *Simon del desierto* (+co-sc). **1966:** *Belle de jour* (+co-sc). **1969:** *La Voie lactée (The Milky Way; La via lattea)* (+co-sc, mu). **1970:** *Tristana* (+co-sc). **1972:** *Le Charme discret de la bourgeoisie (The Discreet Charm of the Bourgeoisie)* (+co-sc). **1974:** *Le Fantôme de la liberté (The Phantom of Liberty)* (+sc, sound effects). **1977:** *Cet obscur objet du desir (That Obscure Object of Desire)* (+co-sc).

Other Films: 1926: *Mauprat* (Epstein) (asst d, role as monk). **1927:** *La Sirène des tropiques* (Etiévant and Nalpas) (asst d). **1928:** *La Chute de la maison Usher* (Epstein) (asst d). **1936:** *Quién me quiere a mi?* (Sáenz de Heredia) (pr, co-sc, ed). **1937:** *Espagne 1937/España leal en armas!* (compilation, ed). **1940:** *Triumph of Will* (supervising ed, commentary, edited compilation of Riefenstahl's *Triumph des Willens* and Hans Bertram's *Feuertaufe*). **1950:** *Si usted no puede, yo sí* (Soler) (co-story). **1964:** *Llanto por un bandido (Lament for a Bandit)* (Saura) (role as the executioner; tech advisor on arms and munitions); *En este pueblo no hay ladrones* (Isaac) (role). **1972:** *Le Moine* (Kyrou) (co-sc). **1973:** *La Chute d'un corps* (Polac) (role).

For all the critical attention (and furious critical controversy) his work occasioned over half a century, Luis Buñuel resisted our best taxonomical efforts. To begin with, while no artist of this century strikes one as more quintessentially Spanish than Buñuel, how can one apply the term "Spanish filmmaker" to a man whose *oeuvre* is far more nearly identified with France and Mexico than with the land of his birth? By the same token, can one speak of any film as "typical" of the man who made both *L'Age d'or* and *Nazarín,* both *Los olvidados* and *Belle de jour,* both *Land Without Bread* and *Le Charme discret de la bourgeoisie?* Nonetheless, from *Un Chien andalou* to *Cet obscur objet du désir,* a Buñuel film is always (albeit, as in many of the Mexican pieces of the 1940s and 1950s, only sporadically), a Buñuel film.

Perhaps the easiest way to deal with Buñuel's career is to suggest that certain avatars of Luis Buñuel may be identified at different (if sometimes slightly overlapping) historical periods. The first Luis Buñuel is the surrealist: the man who slit eyeballs (*Un Chien andalou*), the man to whom blasphemy was less a matter of specific utterances and gestures than a controlling style out of which might emerge new modes of feeling and of expression (*L'Age d'or*), the man who documentarized the unimaginable (*Land Without Bread*) and finally, the man who demonstrated more clearly than any other that surrealist perspectives demanded cinematographic realism. The second Luis Buñuel (and the saddest, and much the least identifiable, now as then) is the all-but-anonymous journeyman film professional: the collaborator, often unbilled and almost always unremarked, on Spanish films which to this day remain unknown to any but the most dogged researchers; the archivist and adapter and functionary in New York and Hollywood; the long-term absentee from the world's attention. The third is the Mexican director, the man who achieved a few works that at the time attracted varying degrees of notice outside the sphere of Latin American commercial distribution (*Los olvidados, Él, Archibaldo de la Cruz, Robinson Crusoe*) but also of others that at the time attracted no notice at all. The fourth is the Luis Buñuel who gradually made his way back to Europe by way of a few French films made in alternation with films in Mexico; and who then, with *Viridiana,* returned to appall, and so to reclaim, his native land; and who thenceforth, and no matter where or under what conditions he operated, persuasively reasserted himself as a figure of unmistakable moment in world cinema. The last Luis Buñuel, following his emergence in the mid-1960s, was the past master, at once awesome and beloved, as serene in his command of his medium as he was cheerfully intrepid in his pursuit of whatever of value might be mined from the depths of the previously unexplored.

Each of the Buñuels of the preceding catalogue, except for the obscure and essentially uncreative second one, is manifest, or at least implicit, in the others. Even in his Mexican work, which included some otherwise less than exalted assignments (and Buñuel himself, unlike certain of his more indiscriminate adulators, was perfectly willing to acknowledge that much of his Mexican work was shoddy or aborted or simply dull), the scion of surrealism showed his hand. There are several astonishing dream sequences, of course: the vision of slabs of raw meat hanging from the racks of a Mexico City streetcar (*La ilusión viaja en tranvía*), the incongruous verticality of the skeletal skyscrapers rising from the Mexico City slums (*Los olvidados*), and the necrophiliac ragings at the end of the Buñuel version of *Wuthering Heights* (*Abismos de pasión*). At the same time, it was in his Mexican studio movies, with their often absurdly brief shooting schedules, that Buñuel developed the unobtrusive but sovereign sway over narrative continuity and visual construction that so exhilarates admirers of such later works as *Le Journal d'une femme de chambre* or *Cet obscur objet du désir*. (According to Francisco Aranda, Alfred Hitchcock in 1972 called Buñuel "the best director in the world.")

Similarly, one may recognize in *Tristana* that same merciless anatomy of a specific social milieu, and in *The Exterminating Angel* that same theme of inexplicable entrapment, that one first encountered in *Land Without Bread*. In *El rio y la muerte* a man, all of him save his head imprisoned in an iron lung, submits to a round of face-slapping. We recognize in the image (and in the gasp of laughter it provokes) something of the merciless attack on our pieties of Buñuel's early surrealist works and something of the more offhand wicked humor of, say, *Le Charme discret*. When such a recognition is reached, we know that the variety of styles and accents in which Buñuel addressed us over the years is almost irrelevant. The political and social (or anti-social) canons of early surrealism could not contain him, nor could the foolish melodramatic conventions of some of his Mexican films stifle his humor, nor could the elegant actors and luxurious color cinematography of some of the later French films finally seduce him. Against all odds, his vision sufficed to transcend any and all stylistic diversions.

"Vision," perhaps the most exhausted word in the critical vocabulary, struggles back to life when applied to Buñuel and his camera. In the consistent clarity of its perception, in its refusal to distinguish between something called "reality" and something called "hallucination," Buñuel's camera always acts in the service of a fundamental surrealist principle, one of the few principles of any kind that Buñuel was never tempted to call into question. Whether focused on the tragic earthly destiny of an inept would-be saint (*Nazarín*) or on the bizarre obsessions of an inept would-be sinner (the uncle in *Viridiana,* among a good many others), Buñuel's camera is the instrument of the most rigorous denotation, invoking nothing beyond that which it so plainly and patiently registers. The uncertainties and ambivalences we may feel as we watch a Buñuel film arise not from the camera's capacity to mediate but from the camera's capacity to record: our responses are inherent in the subjects Buñuel selects, in those extremes of human experiences that we recognize as his special domain.—E. RUBINSTEIN

Burnett, Charles

Nationality American. **Born** Vicksburg, Mississippi, 1944. **Education** Studied electronics at Los Angeles Community College, and theater, film, writing, arts, and languages at the University of Southern California, Los Angeles. **Career** Directed first feature film, Killer of Sheep, 1977. **Awards** Guggenheim Foundation Fellowship, 1981; Critics Prize, Berlin Festival, and First Prize, U.S. Festival, 1981, for Killer of Sheep; National Endowment for the Arts grant, MacArthur Foundation Fellowship, and Rockefeller Foundation Fellowship, 1988; Best Director and Best Screenplay, Independent Spirit Awards, Independent Feature Project/West, Best Film, Los Angeles Film Critics Association, and Best Film, National Society of Film Critics, 1990, for To Sleep with Anger. **Agent** Triad Artists, Los Angeles.

Films as Director: **1969:** *Several Friends* (short). **1973:** *The House* (short). **1977:** *Killer of Sheep* (+sc, pr, ph, ed). **1983:** *My Brother's Wedding* (+sc, pr, ph). **1989:** *Guests of Hotel Astoria* (+ph). **1990:** *To Sleep with Anger* (+sc). **1994:** *The Glass Shield* (+sc). **1995:** *When It Rains* (short). **1996:** *Nightjohn.*

Other Films: **1983:** *Bless Their Little Hearts* (Woodbury) (sc, ph). **1985:** *The Crocodile Conspiracy* (ph). **1987:** *I Fresh* (sc).

Prior to the release of *To Sleep with Anger* in 1990, Charles Burnett had for two decades been writing and directing low-budget, little-known, but critically praised films that examined life and relationships among contemporary African Americans. *Killer of Sheep,* his first feature, is a searing depiction of ghetto life; *My Brother's Wedding* knowingly examines the relationship between two siblings on vastly different life tracks; *Bless Their Little Hearts* (directed by Billy Woodbury, but scripted and photographed by Burnett) is a poignant portrait of a black family. But how many had even heard of these films, let alone seen them? Thanks to the emergence in the 1980s of the prolific Spike Lee as a potent box office (as well as critical) force, however, a generation of African-American moviemakers have had their films not only produced but more widely distributed.

Such was the case with *To Sleep with Anger,* released theatrically by the Samuel Goldwyn Company. The film, like Burnett's earlier work, is an evocative, character-driven drama about relationships between family members and the fabric of domestic life among contemporary African Americans. It is the story of Harry Mention (Danny Glover), a meddlesome trickster who arrives in Los Angeles at the doorstep of his old friend Gideon (Paul Butler). The film details the manner in which Harry abuses the hospitality of Gideon, and his effect on Gideon's family. First there is the older generation: Gideon and his wife Suzie (Mary Alice), who cling to the traditions of their Deep South roots. Gideon has attempted to pass on his folklore, and his sense of values, to his two sons. One, Junior (Carl Lumbly), accepts this. But the other, Babe Brother (Richard Brooks), is on the economic fast track—and in conflict with his family.

While set within an African-American milieu, *To Sleep with Anger* transcends the ethnic identities of its characters; it also deals in a generic way with the cultural differences between parents and children, the manner in which individuals learn (or don't learn) from experience, and the need to push aside those who only know how to cause violence and strife. As such, it becomes a film that deals with universal issues.

The Glass Shield is a departure for Burnett in that his scenario is not set within an African-American universe. Instead, he places his characters in a hostile white world. *The Glass Shield* is a thinking person's cop film. Burnett's hero is a young black officer fresh out of the police academy, JJ Johnson (Michael Boatman), who becomes the first African American assigned to a corruption-laden, all-white sheriff's station in Los Angeles. Johnson is treated roughly by the station's commanding officer and some of the veteran cops. Superficially, it seems as if he is being dealt with in such a manner solely because he is an inexperienced rookie, in need of toughening and educating to the ways of the streets. But the racial lines clearly are drawn when one of his senior officers tells him, "You're one of us. You're not a brother." Johnson, who always has wanted to be a cop, desires only to do well and fit in. And so he stands by idly as black citizens are casually stopped and harassed by his fellow officers. Even more telling, with distressing regularity, blacks seem to have died under mysterious circumstances while in custody within the confines of the precinct.

As the film progresses, Burnett creates the feeling that a bomb is about to explode. And it does, when Johnson becomes involved in the arrest of a black man, framed on a murder charge, and readily agrees to lie in court to protect a fellow officer. Burnett's ultimate point is that in contemporary America it is impossible for a black man to cast aside his racial identity as he seeks his own personal destiny. First and foremost, he is an African American, existing within a society in which all of the power is in the hands of a white male elite. But African Americans are not the sole powerless entity in *The Glass Shield*. Johnson befriends his station's first female officer (Lori Petty), who must deal with sexism within the confines of her precinct house as much as on the streets. Together, this pair becomes united in a struggle against a white male-dominated system in which everyday corruption and hypocrisy are the rule.

Burnett's themes—African-American identity within the family unit and, subsequently, African-American identity within the community at large—are provocative and meaningful. It seems certain that he will never direct a film that is anything short of insightful in its content.—ROB EDELMAN

Burton, Tim

Nationality American. *Born* Burbank, California, 25 August 1958. *Education* California Institute of Arts, B.A., 1981. *Family* Married Lena Gieseke, 1989. *Career* Cartoonist since grade school in Burbank; animator, Walt Disney Studios, Hollywood, California, 1981-85; director and producer of feature films, 1985—; executive producer, Batman:

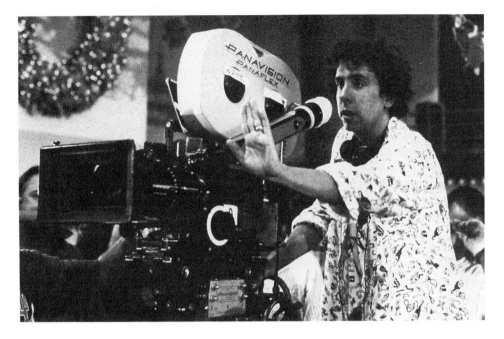

Tim Burton directing *Batman Returns*.

The Animated Series, *1992; executive producer,* Family Dog, *1993.****Awards*** *Chicago Film Festival Award, 1982, for* Vincent; *Director of the Year, National Association of Theatre Owners.* **Agent** *Creative Artists Agency, 9830 Wilshire Blvd., Beverly Hills, California, 90212.*

Films as Director: 1982: *Vincent* (animated short); *Frankenweenie* (live-action short). **1985:** *Pee-Wee's Big Adventure.* **1988:** *Beetlejuice.* **1989:** *Batman.* **1990:** *Edward Scissorhands* (+co-sc, pr). **1992:** *Batman Returns* (+co-pr). **1994:** *Ed Wood* (+co-pr). **1996:** *Mars Attacks!* (co-pr, co-sc). **1998:** *Superman Lives.*

Other Films: 1992: *Singles* (role). **1993:** *Tim Burton's The Nightmare before Christmas* (sc, co-pr). **1994:** *Cabin Boy* (co-pr). **1995:** *Batman Forever* (exec pr). **1996:** *James and the Giant Peach* (co-pr).

Although in the last resort I find his work more distinctive than distinguished, Tim Burton compels interest and attention by the way in which he has established within the Hollywood mainstream a cinema that is, to say the least, highly eccentric, idiosyncratic, and personal.

Burton's cinema is centered firmly on the figure of what I shall call (for want of a better term, and knowing that this one is now "politically incorrect") the freak. I define this as a person existing quite outside the bounds of the conventional notion of normality, usually (but not exclusively, as I include Burton's *Ed Wood* in this) because of some extreme physical peculiarity. Every one of the films, without exception, is built around at least one freak. One must then subdivide them into two categories: the "positive" freaks, who at least mean well, and the "negative" freaks, who are openly malignant. In the former category, in order of appearance: Pee-Wee Herman (*Pee-Wee's Big Adventure*), Edward Scissorhands, Catwoman (*Batman Returns*), Jack (*The Nightmare before Christmas*), Ed Wood; in the latter, the Joker (*Batman*) and the Penguin (*Batman Returns*). Beetlejuice (or "Betelgeuse") belongs ambiguously to both categories, though predominantly to the latter; to which one might also add, without stretching things too far, Riddler and Two-Face from *Batman Forever*—watered-down Burton, produced by him but written and directed by others, still owing a great deal to his influence. If one leaves aside *Pee-Wee's Big Adventure* and *The Nightmare before Christmas* (which Burton conceived and produced but did not direct), this gives us an alternative but exactly parallel division: three films with Michael Keaton, two with Johnny Depp (who might well have played Jack in *The Nightmare before Christmas* had Burton opted to make it as a live-action film).

Of the malignant freaks, Danny de Vito's Penguin is at once the most grotesque (to the verge of unwatchability) and the only one with an excuse for his malignancy: unlike the others he was *born* a freak, cast out and presumed to die by his parents, surviving by chance. The Joker and (if one permits the inclusion) Two-Face are physical freaks because of disfigurement, but this has merely intensified a malignancy already there. They are colorful and vivid, but not especially interesting: they merely embody a somewhat simplistic notion of evil, the worked-up energy of the over-the-top performances a means of concealing the essential emptiness at the conceptual level.

The benign freaks are more interesting. They are invariably associated with creativity: Pee-Wee, Edward Scissorhands, and Ed Wood are all artists, of a kind every bit as idiosyncratic as their creator's. This is set, obviously, against the determined destructiveness of the malignant freaks, who include in this respect Beetlejuice: the film's sympathetic characters (notably Winona Ryder) may find him necessary at times, but his dominant characteristic is a delight in destruction for its own sake. What gives the positive freaks (especially those played by Johnny Depp) an extra dimension is their extreme fragileness and vulnerability (the negative freaks always regard themselves, however misguidedly, as invincible).

Credit must be given to Burton's originality and inventiveness: he is an authentic artist in the sense that he is so clearly personally involved in and committed to his peculiar vision and its realization in film. What equally demands to be questioned is the degree of real intelligence underlying these qualities. The inventiveness is all on the surface, in the art direction, makeup, special effects. The conceptual level of the films does not bear very close scrutiny. The problem is there already, and in a magnified form, in *Beetlejuice:* the proliferation of invention is too grotesque and ugly to be funny, too wild, arbitrary, and unselfcritical to reward any serious analysis. The two *Batman* movies are distinguished by the remarkably dark vision (in a film one might expect to be "family entertainment") of contemporary urban/industrial civilization. But Michael Keaton's Batman, while unusually and mercifully restrained, fails to make any strong impression, and one is thrown back on the freaks who, with one notable exception, quickly outstay their welcome. The exception is Michelle Pfeiffer's Catwoman (in *Batman Returns*), and that is due primarily to one of the great screen presences of our time. Burton's overall project (in his work as a whole) seems to be to set his freaks (both positive and negative) against "normality" in order to show that normality, today, is every bit as weird: a laudable enough project, most evident in *Edward Scissorhands*. But the depiction of normality in that film (here, small-town suburbia) amounts to no more than amiable, simple-minded parody (despite the charm of Dianne Wiest's Avon Lady, but her role dwindles as the film proceeds). For all the grotesquerie of his monsters, Burton's cinema is ultimately too soft-centered, lacking in rigor and real *thinking*.

Ed Wood, however, may be taken as evidence that Burton is beginning to transcend the limitations of his previous work: it is far and away his most satisfying film to date. Here is surely

one of cinema's most touching celebrations of the sheer joy of creativity with the irony, of course, that it is manifested in an "artist" of no talent whatever. Johnny Depp, in what is surely, with Pfeiffer's Catwoman, one of the two most complex and fully realized incarnations in Burton's work, magically conveys his character's absolute belief in the value of his own creations and his own personal joy and excitement in creating them, never realizing that they will indeed go down in film history as topping everyone's list of the worst films ever made. Yet his Ed Wood never strikes us as merely stupid: simply as a man completely caught up in his own delight in creative activity—always longing for recognition, but never self-serving or mercenary. This self-delusion, at once marvelous and pathetic, goes hand in hand with his growing compassion for and commitment to the decrepit and drug-addicted Bela Lugosi (Martin Landau, in a performance that, for once, fully deserved its Oscar), and his equally delusory conviction that Lugosi is still a great star. One's expectations of Burton's future work mount considerably after this film.
—ROBIN WOOD

Cameron, James

Nationality *Canadian.* **Born** *Kapuskasing, Ontario, Canada, 16 August 1954; moved to United States in 1971.* **Education** *Majored in physics, California State University, Fullerton.* **Family** *Married 1) producer Gale Ann Hurd; 2) director Kathryn Bigelow in 1989; 3) actress Linda Hamilton.* **Career** *Truck driver; art director, process-projection supervisor, and miniature-set builder on Roger Corman's* Battle Beyond the Stars, *1980; directorial debut with* Piranha II: The Spawning, *1981; scriptwriter; founded Digital Domain special-effects company, Venice, California, 1993; founded Lightstorm Entertainment production company.*

Films as Director: 1981: *Piranha II: The Spawning (Piranha II: Flying Killers).* **1984:** *The Terminator* (+sc). **1986:** *Aliens* (+sc). **1989:** *The Abyss* (+sc). **1991:** *Terminator 2: Judgment Day (T2)* (+sc, pr). **1994:** *True Lies* (+sc, pr). **1996:** *Terminator 2: 3-D (T2 3-D: Battle Across Time).* **1997:** *Titanic* (+sc, pr).

Other Films: 1980: *Battle Beyond the Stars* (art director). **1981:** *Escape from New York* (special effects photograpy, matte artwork); *Galaxy of Terror* (pr designer). **1982:** *Android* (design consultant). **1985:** *Rambo: First Blood Part II* (sc). **1991:** *Point Break* (pr, sc uncredited). **1995:** *Strange Days* (pr, story).

In a career spanning almost two decades, James Cameron has strategically positioned himself as the "guru" of high-tech, muscular, blockbuster dramas that rely heavily (some would say solely) on state-of-the-art special effects. Depending on which side of the critical fence you're on, he has either salvaged the popular science-fiction/action genre with a thoughtful layer of human-interest narrative (e.g., *The Terminator*), or has strangled the humanity of his pictures with an excess of dazzling but superfluous computer-generated imaging (e.g., *The Abyss*). What is beyond dispute is the fact that Cameron has a talent for staying one step ahead of cutting-edge technology and generating big profits despite stratospheric costs.

As a boy, Cameron's fantasies were fueled by sci-fi comics and astronomy books (*The Abyss* is said to have been adapted from a story he wrote when he was twelve). But it wasn't until he saw *Star Wars* in 1977 that he realized what he had been visualizing in his head could actually

James Cameron directing *True Lies*. Photograph by Zade Rosenthal.

be transferred to the screen. "That's what turned me into a filmmaker," he told the *Los Angeles Times Magazine* (24 March 1996). "All the things I'd been imagining were now being done."

Given his beginnings in process work and as an art director for Roger Corman and John Carpenter, it does not seem unusual that Cameron developed a penchant for special effects. Even when well into his career as a director, he continued to be involved with the nuts and bolts of technical effects, creating the design for the queen alien in *Aliens,* for example. "Dream with your eyes open," is the axiom at Digital Domain, Cameron's special-effects company, which, in addition to creating effects for CD-ROMs, theme parks, television commercials, and films like *Apollo 13,* serves as his movie backlot.

Today, Cameron holds fast to the belief that digital effects are more than just wild rides. He considers applying the latest computer technology to a good story an exercise in overcoming cultural barriers around the world through the medium of film. Never mind that, at the same time, audiences are being homogenized and conditioned to accept no less than total (virtual) "reality" via this technology, and the effort by filmmakers like Cameron to keep up with (and spend buckets of money on) the latest trend is, in the minds of some critics, usually at the direct expense of any viable plot-line. Cameron believes that good storytelling endures, and special effects simply allow for getting it all out of our heads and onto the screen.

Cameron made his directorial debut with *Piranha II: The Spawning*—not a notable picture, but a chance for him to test and refine his skills. His first popular breakthrough was with *The Terminator*—for which he also wrote the screenplay. Here was a raw and resonating, mythic action-thriller with an ideally cast Arnold Schwarzenegger in the title role as the ultimate humanoid. The movie became one of those "sleeper" successes, and launched Cameron's career into high-orbit overnight.

Youthful moviegoers especially get their money's worth of a high-tech ride with Cameron's pictures, but many critics note that, since *The Terminator,* his films have been primarily overlong, under-written attempts to simply maintain his box-office returns—and desperate drives to justify his record-setting expenses—minus any allegorical poetry. *Aliens, The Abyss, Terminator 2: Judgment Day,* and *True Lies*—all of which he wrote and directed— had the adolescent-audience appeal factor working for them, but their costs (*Terminator 2* came in at a then-record-setting $90M, *True Lies* at $100M) created a lot of pressure for Cameron to recoup money for the studios. Cameron argues that the price of cutting-edge visual effects is justified because they increase profits. However, *Terminator 2* never matched the success of the original, and *The Abyss* and *True Lies* missed the expected mark both critically and at the box office.

Ironically, just under the surface, many of Cameron's trademark techniques reflect a loss of humanity via our modern embracing of all things technological. Modern technology is the ultimate villain even as it is being utilized to create a frenzied cinematic experience. Frequent sequences in which a video monitor is the perspective of the camera also create a feeling of claustrophobia—the notion that we are trapped inside of our own invention. T-800's infrared viewpoint in *The Terminator* and *Terminator 2* is one example, as are the helmet cameras in *Aliens,* "little geek" exploring the submarine in *The Abyss,* and the surveillance cameras in *True Lies.* This feeling of inescapability is further enhanced by Cameron's use of action cutaways— numerous close-up shots of feet trampling and wheels running over things. For critical fight scenes, he likes to bring the camera in uncomfortably close, and often the fighters are drenched in deep blues, or battling beneath the strobing of split-second flashes of light. As a counterpoint, chaotic background scenes of huge explosions, crashes, nuclear wars, and/or gun battles point up an impending Armageddon between forces of good and evil.

Cameron has long had a reputation as a difficult director: he is said to have nixed bathroom breaks while filming *True Lies,* threatening to fire anyone leaving the set. Impatience is, in Cameron's eyes, a director's prerogative when spending the kind of money he does, and he is notorious for expecting cast and crew to rise to his standard 16-hour-day work schedule. At the same time, his devotion to his projects is also legendary (again, some would say obsessive). He made, for example, while in pre-production for *Titanic,* over a dozen visits to the actual wreckage site, necessitating a three-hour drop to the ocean-floor in a tiny bathysphere with two other crew members, resulting in footage from inside Titanic that had previously never been seen.

"We do spectacle," Cameron told *Time* (25 November 1996) while on the set of *Titanic.* "Spectacle costs money." Not surprisingly, *Titanic* came in a half-year overdue and as the most expensive film ever made ($200M-plus for production and marketing). Costs were so lavish that the film was financed by both Fox and Paramount, and Hollywood insiders were openly skeptical whether it would ever make a profit (as of February 1998, *Titanic* had grossed over $300M domestically). Ever the perfectionist, Cameron insists on taking no shortcuts in getting his vision to the screen. For *Titanic,* he commissioned a 90-percent scale replica of the ship (complete with a hydraulic stern to simulate the climactic sinking) as well as historically accurate artwork and decor for the interior of the ship. When filming on *Titanic* began, some of the technology eventually used to create the film's effects did not yet exist. Digital Domain had to create much of the software that, for instance, allows the camera to stay with a character's face on deck while pulling back to reveal the entire ship—without any distracting cuts. While Cameron's detractors continue to insist that his obsession with effects over storyline will eventually "break the bank" for his career, the critical and popular success that has met

Titanic (winning 3 Golden Globe Awards and being nominated for a record 14 Academy Awards) all but assures that Cameron's career is anything but dead in the water. As the director told the *LA Times Magazine* (24 March 1996), "you can't sell the same car radio to people you could ten years ago . . . it's the same with movies."—JEROME SZYMCZAK

Campion, Jane

Nationality New Zealander. Born Wellington, 30 April 1954. Education Victoria University, Wellington, B.A. in structural arts; Chelsea School of Arts, London, diploma in fine arts (completed at Sydney College of the Arts); Australian Film and Television School, diploma in direction. Family Parents are opera/theater director Richard Campion and actress/writer Edith Campion; married television producer/director Colin Englert. Career Became interested in filmmaking and began making short films, late 1970s; short film, Tissues, *led to her acceptance into the Australian Film and Television School, 1981; took job with Australia's Women's Film Unit, 1984; directed an episode of the television drama* Dancing Daze, *1986; short films* Peel, Passionless Moments, *and* Girls Own Story *released theatrically in the United States, 1989-90. Awards Diploma of Merit, Melbourne Festival, and Palme d'Or, Best Short Film, Cannes Film Festival, for* Peel, *1983-86; Unique Artist Merit, Melbourne Festival, Best Experimental Film, Australian Film Institute, and Most Popular Short Film, Sydney Festival, for* Passionless Moments, *1984-85; Rouben Mamoulian Award, Best Overall Short Film, Unique Artist Merit, Melbourne Festival, Best Direction and Screenplay, Australian Film Institute Awards, and First Prize, Cinestud Amsterdam Festival, for* Girls Own Story, *1984-85; X. L. Elders Award and Best Short Fiction, Melbourne Festival, for* After Hours, *1985; Golden Plaque, Chicago Festival, and Best Director and Best TV Film, Australian Film Institute, for* 2 Friends, *1987; Georges Sadoul Prize, Best Foreign Film, Best Film, and Best Director, Australian Critics Awards, New Generation Award, Los Angeles Film Critics Association, and Best Foreign Film, Independent Spirit Award, for* Sweetie, *1989-90; Byron Kennedy Award, Special Jury Prize, Annual Elvira Notari Award, Si Presci Award, O.C.I.C. Award, Best Film for Young People, Cinema & Ragazzi, Otto Debelius Prize, Berlin Festival, Critics Award, Toronto Festival, and Best Foreign Film, Independent Spirit Award, for* An Angel at My Table, *1990; Academy Award, Best Screenplay, Academy Award nomination, Best Director and Screenplay, New York Film Critics Circle, Best Director and Screenplay, Los Angeles Film Critics Association, Best Director and Screenplay, Australian Film Institute Awards, Best Director and Screenplay, Australian Film Critics, Best Director, Guild of Regional Film Writers, and Best Screenplay, Chicago Film Critics, for* The Piano, *1993. Address Hilary Linstead & Associates, Level 18, Plaza II, 500 Oxford Street, Bondi Junction, NSW 2022, Australia.*

Films as Director: 1982: *Peel* (short) (+sc). **1984:** *Mishaps of Seduction and Conquest* (video short) (+sc); *Passionless Moments* (short) (co-d, co-sc); *Girls Own Story* (short) (+sc); *After Hours* (short) (+sc). **1985:** *2 Friends* (for Australian TV). **1989:** *Sweetie* (co-sc). **1990:** *An Angel at My Table* (for Australian TV; edited version released theatrically). **1993:** *The Piano* (+sc). **1996:** *Portrait of a Lady.*

Whatever their quality, all of Jane Campion's feature films have remained consistent in theme. They depict the lives of girls and women who are in one way or another separate from the mainstream, because of physical appearance (if not outright physical disability) or personality quirk, and she spotlights the manner in which they relate to and function within their respective societies.

Campion began directing features after making several highly acclaimed, award-winning short films which were extensively screened on the international film festival circuit. Her first two features are alike in that they focus on the relationships between two young women, and how they are affected by the adults who control their world. Her debut, *2 Friends,* was made for Australian television in 1985 and did not have its American theatrical premiere until 1996. It is a depiction of the connection between a pair of adolescents, focusing on the changes in their

Jane Campion

friendship and how they are influenced by adult authority figures. The narrative is told in reverse time: at the outset, the girls are a bit older, and their developing personalities have separated them; as the film continues, they become younger and closer.

Sweetie, Campion's initial theatrical feature, is a pitch-black comedy about a young woman who is overweight, overemotional, and even downright crazy, with the scenario charting the manner in which she relates to her parents and her skinny, shy, easily manipulated sister. The film was controversial in that critics and viewers either raved about it or were turned off by its quirky nature. While not without inspired moments, both *Sweetie* and *2 Friends* lack the assurance of Campion's future work.

The filmmaker's unequivocal breakthrough as a world-class talent came in 1990 with *An Angel at My Table.* The theatrical version of the film is 158 minutes long and is taken from a three-part mini-series made for New Zealand television. *An Angel at My Table* did not benefit from the media hype surrounding *The Piano,* Campion's 1993 international art house hit, but it is as equally fine a work. It is an uncommonly literate portrait of Janet Frame, a plump, repressed child who was destined to become one of New Zealand's most renowned writers. Prior to her fame, however, she was falsely diagnosed as a schizophrenic, passed eight years in a mental hospital, and received over 200 electric shock treatments.

Campion evocatively depicts the different stages of Frame's life; the filmmaker elicits a dynamic performance from Kerry Fox as the adult Janet and, in visual terms, she perfectly captures the essence of the writer's inner being. At the same time, Campion bitingly satirizes the manner in which society patronizes those who sincerely dedicate their lives to the creation of art. She depicts pseudo-artists who would not know a poem from a Harlequin Romance, and publishers who think that for Frame to truly be a success she must have a best-seller and ride around in a Rolls Royce.

If *An Angel at My Table* spotlights the evolution of a woman as an intellectual being, Campion's next work, *The Piano,* depicts a woman's development on a sexual and erotic level. *The Piano,* like *The Crying Game* before it and *Pulp Fiction* later on, became the cinematic cause celebre of its year. It is a deceptively simple story, beautifully told, of Ada (Holly Hunter, in an Academy Award-winning performance), a Scottish widow and mute who arrives with her nine-year-old daughter (Anna Paquin, who also won an Oscar) in remote New Zealand during the 1850s. Ada is to be the bride in an arranged marriage with a stern, hesitant farmer (Sam Neill). But she becomes sexually and romantically involved with Baines (Harvey Keitel), her illiterate, vulnerable neighbor to whom she gives piano lessons: an arrangement described by Campion as an "erotic pact."

Campion succeeds in creating a story about the development of love, from the initial eroticism between the two characters to something deeper and more romantic. Ada has a symbolic relationship with the piano, which is both her refuge and way of self-expression. *The Piano* is an intensely haunting tale of exploding passion and deep, raw emotion, and it put its maker at the forefront of contemporary, world-class cinema. Campion's most recent project was a period piece, *Portrait of a Lady,* based on a Henry James novel.—ROB EDELMAN

Capra, Frank

Nationality *American.* **Born** *Bisaquino, Sicily, 18 May 1897; emigrated with family to Los Angeles, 1903.* **Education** *Manual Arts High School, Los Angeles; studied chemical engineering at California Institute of Technology, Pasadena, graduated 1918.* **Family** *Married 1) Helen Howell, 1924 (divorced 1938); 2) Lucille Reyburn, 1932, two sons, one daughter.* **Military Service** *Ballistics teacher, U.S. Army, 1918-19.* **Career** *Lab assistant for Walter Bell, 1922-23; prop man, editor for Bob Eddy, writer for Hal Roach and Mack Sennett, 1923-25; hired by Columbia Pictures, 1928; began to work with Robert Riskin, 1931; elected President of Academy, 1935; elected President of Screen Directors' Guild, 1938; formed Frank Capra Productions with writer Robert Riskin, 1939; Major in Signal Corps, 1942-45; formed Liberty Films with Sam Briskin, William Wyler, and George Stevens, 1945 (sold to Paramount, 1948).* **Awards** *Oscar for Best Director, for* It Happened One Night, *1934, for* Mr. Deeds Goes to Town, *1936, and* You Can't Take It With You, *1938; Distinguished Service Medal, U.S. Armed Forces, 1945; D.W. Griffith Award, Directors Guild of America, 1958; Honorary Doctorates, Temple University, Philadelphia, 1971, and Carthage College, Wisconsin, 1972.* **Died** *3 September 1991.*

Films as Director: 1922: *Fultah Fisher's Boarding House.* **1926:** *The Strong Man* (+co-sc). **1927:** *Long Pants; For the Love of Mike.* **1928:** *That Certain Thing; So This Is Love; The Matinee Idol; The Way of the Strong; Say It With Sables* (+co-story); *Submarine; The Power of the Press; The Swim Princess; The Burglar* (*Smith's Burglar*). **1929:** *The Younger Generation; The Donovan Affair; Flight* (+dialogue). **1930:** *Ladies of Leisure; Rain or Shine.* **1931:** *Dirigible; The Miracle Woman; Platinum Blonde.* **1932:** *Forbidden* (+sc); *American Madness.* **1933:** *The Bitter Tea of General Yen* (+pr); *Lady for a Day.* **1934:** *It Happened One Night; Broadway Bill.* **1936:** *Mr. Deeds Goes to Town* (+pr). **1937:** *Lost Horizon* (+pr). **1938:** *You Can't Take It With You* (+pr). **1939:** *Mr. Smith Goes to Washington* (+pr). **1941:** *Meet John*

Frank Capra

Doe (+pr). **1942:** *Why We Fight* (Part 1): *Prelude to War* (+pr). **1943:** *Why We Fight* (Part 2): *The Nazis Strike* (co-d, pr); *Why We Fight* (Part 3): *Divide and Conquer* (co-d, pr). **1944:** *Why We Fight* (Part 6): *The Battle of China* (co-d, pr); *Tunisian Victory* (co-d, pr); *Arsenic and Old Lace* (+pr) (filmed in 1942). **1945:** *Know Your Enemy: Japan* (co-d, pr); *Two Down, One to Go* (+pr). **1946:** *It's a Wonderful Life* (+pr, co-sc). **1948:** *State of the Union* (+pr). **1950:** *Riding High* (+pr). **1951:** *Here Comes the Groom* (+pr). **1956:** *Our Mr. Sun* (+pr, sc) (Bell System Science Series Numbers 1 to 4). **1957:** *Hemo the Magnificent* (+pr, sc); *The Strange Case of the Cosmic Rays* (+pr, co-sc). **1958:** *The Unchained Goddess* (+pr, co-sc). **1959:** *A Hole in the Head* (+pr). **1961:** *Pocketful of Miracles* (+pr).

Other Films: 1924: (as co-sc with Arthur Ripley on films featuring Harry Longdon): *Picking Peaches; Smile Please; Shanghaied Lovers; Flickering Youth; The Cat's Meow; His New Mama; The First Hundred Years; The Luck o' the Foolish; The Hansom Cabman; All Night Long; Feet of Mud.* **1925:** (as co-sc with Arthur Ripley on films featuring Harry Langdon): *The Sea Squawk; Boobs in the Woods; His Marriage Wow; Plain Clothes; Remember When?; Horace Greeley, Jr.; The White Wing's Bride; Lucky Stars; There He Goes; Saturday Afternoon.* **1926:** (as co-sc with Arthur Ripley on films featuring Harry Langdon): *Fiddlesticks; The Soldier Man; Tramp, Tramp, Tramp.* **1943:** *Why We Fight* (Part 4): *The Battle of Britain* (pr). **1944:** *The Negro Soldier* (pr); *Why We Fight* (Part 5): *The Battle of Russia* (pr); *Know Your Ally: Britain* (pr). **1945:** *Why We Fight* (Part 7): *War Comes to America* (pr); *Know Your Enemy: Germany* (pr). **1950:** *Westward the Women* (story).

The critical stock of Frank Capra has fluctuated perhaps more wildly than that of any other major director. During his peak years, the 1930s, he was adored by the press, by the industry and, of course, by audiences. In 1934 *It Happened One Night* won nearly all the Oscars, and through the rest of the decade a film of Frank Capra was either the winner or the strong contender for that honor. Long before the formulation of the *auteur* theory, the Capra signature on a film was recognized. But after World War II his career went into serious decline. His first post-war film, *It's a Wonderful Life,* was not received with the enthusiasm he thought it deserved (although it has gone on to become one of his most-revered films). Of his last five films, two are remakes of material he treated in the thirties. Many contemporary critics are repelled by what they deem indigestible "Capracorn" and have even less tolerance for an ideology characterized as dangerously simplistic in its populism, its patriotism, its celebration of all-American values.

Indeed, many of Capra's most famous films can be read as excessively sentimental and politically naive. These readings, however, tend to neglect the basis for Capra's success—his skill as a director of actors, the complexity of his staging configurations, his narrative economy and energy, and most of all, his understanding of the importance of the spoken word in sound film. Capra captured the American voice in cinematic space. The words often serve the cause of apple pie, mom, the little man and other greeting card clichés (indeed, the hero of *Mr. Deeds Goes to Town* writes verse for greeting cards). But often in the sound of the voice we hear uncertainties about those very clichés.

Capra's career began in the pre-talkie era, when he directed silent comic Harry Langdon in two successful films. His action films of the early thirties are not characteristic of his later work, yet already, in the films he made with Barbara Stanwyck, his individual gift can be discerned. The narrative pretext of *The Miracle Woman* is the urgency of Stanwyck's voice, its ability to move an audience, to persuade listeners of its sincerity. Capra exploited the raw energy of Stanwyck in this and other roles, where her qualities of fervor and near-hysterical conviction are just as essential to her persona as her hard-as-nails implacability would be in the forties. Stanwyck's voice is theatricalized, spatialized in her revivalist circus-tent in *The Miracle Woman* and on the hero's suicide tower in *Meet John Doe,* where her feverish pleadings are the only possible tenor for the film's unresolved ambiguities about society and the individual.

John Doe is portrayed by Gary Cooper, another American voice with particular resonance in the films of Capra. A star who seems to have invented the "strong, silent" type, Cooper first plays Mr. Deeds, whose platitudinous doggerel comes from a simple, do-gooder heart, but who enacts a crisis of communication in his long silence at the film's climax, a sanity hearing. When Mr. Deeds finally speaks it is a sign that the community (if not sanity) is restored—the usual resolution of a Capra film. As John Doe, Cooper is given words to voice by reporter Stanwyck, and he delivers them with such conviction that the whole nation listens. The vocal/dramatic center of the film is located in a rain-drenched ball park filled with John Doe's "people." The hero's effort to speak the truth, to reveal his own imposture and expose the fascistic intentions of his sponsor, is stymied when the lines of communication are literally cut between microphone and loudspeaker. The Capra narrative so often hinges on the protagonist's ability to speak and be heard, on the drama of sound and audition.

The bank run in *American Madness* is initiated by a montage of telephone voices and images, of mouths spreading a rumor. The panic is quelled by the speech of the bank president (Walter Huston), a situation repeated in more modest physical surroundings in *It's a Wonderful Life*. The most extended speech in the films of Capra occurs in *Mr. Smith Goes to Washington*. The whole film is a test of the hero's voice, and it culminates in a filibuster, a speech that, by definition, cannot be interrupted. The climax of *State of the Union* involves a different kind of audience and audition. There, the hero confesses his political dishonesty and his love for his wife on television.

The visual contexts, both simple and complex, never detract from the sound of Capra's films. They enhance it. The director's most elaborately designed film, *The Bitter Tea of General Yen* (recalling the style of Josef von Sternberg in its chiaroscuro lighting and its exoticism) expresses the opposition of cultural values in its visual elements, to be sure, but also in the voices of Stanwyck and Nils Asther, a Swedish actor who impersonates a Chinese war lord. Less unusual but not less significant harmonies are sounded in *It Happened One Night*, where a society girl (Claudette Colbert) learns "real" American speech from a fast-talking reporter (Clark Gable). The love scenes in *Mr. Deeds* are for Gary Cooper and Jean Arthur, another quintessential Capra heroine, whose vocal personality is at least as memorable as her physical one. In James Stewart Capra finds his most disquieting voice, ranging in *Mr. Smith* from ingenuousness to hysterical desperation and in *It's a Wonderful Life* to an even higher pitch of hysteria when the hero loses his identity.

The sounds and sights of Capra's films bear the authority of a director whose autobiography is called *The Name above the Title*. With that authority comes an unsettling belief in authorial power, the power dramatized in his major films, the persuasiveness exercised in political and social contexts. That persuasion reflects back on the director's own power to engage the viewer in his fiction, to call upon a degree of belief in the fiction—even when we reject the meaning of the fable.—CHARLES AFFRON

Carné, Marcel

Nationality French. *Born* Batignolles, Paris, 18 August 1909. *Career* Worked as insurance clerk, mid-1920s; assistant to cameraman Georges Périnal on Les Nouveaux Messieurs, *1928; worked as film critic, and made short film, 1929; assistant to René Clair*

on Sous les toits de Paris, *1930; editor-in-chief,* Hebdo-Films *journal, and member, "October" group, early 1930's; assistant to Jacques Feyder, 1933-35; directed first feature,* Jenny, *1936.* **Award** *Special Mention, Venice Festival, for* Quai des brumes, *1938.* **Died** *31 October 1996 in Clamart, France.*

Films as Director: 1929: *Nogent, Eldorado du dimanche.* **1936:** *Jenny.* **1937:** *Drôle de drame (Bizarre Bizarre).* **1938:** *Quai des brumes (Port of Shadows); Hotel du Nord.* **1939:** *Le Jour se lève (Daybreak); École communale* (abandoned due to war). **1942:** *Les Visiteurs du soir (The Devil's Envoys).* **1945:** *Les Enfants du paradis (Children of Paradise).* **1946:** *Les Portes de la nuit (Gates of the Night).* **1947:** *La Fleur de l'âge* (not completed). **1949:** *La Marie du port* (+co-sc). **1951:** *Juliette ou la Clé des songes* (+co-sc). **1953:** *Thérèse Raquin (The Adulteress)* (+co-sc). **1954:** *L'Air de Paris* (+co-sc). **1956:** *Le Pays d'où je viens* (+co-sc). **1958:** *Les Tricheurs (The Cheaters)* (+co-sc). **1960:** *Terrain vague* (+co-sc). **1962:** *Du mouron pour les petits oiseaux* (+co-sc). **1965:** *Trois Chambres à Manhattan* (+co-sc). **1967:** *Les Jeunes Loups (The Young Wolves)* (+co-sc). **1971:** *Les Assassins de l'ordre* (+co-sc). **1974:** *La Merveilleuse Visite* (+co-sc). **1976:** *La Bible* (feature doc for TV and theatrical release).

Other Films: 1935: *La Kermesse héroïque (Carnival in Flanders)* (asst d).

At a time when film schools were non-existent and training in filmmaking was acquired through assistantship, no one could have been better prepared for a brilliant career than Marcel Carné. He worked as assistant to René Clair on the first important French sound film, *Sous les toits de Paris,* and to Jacques Feyder on the latter's three great films of 1934-35. Though he had also made a successful personal documentary, *Nogent, Eldorado du dimanche,* and a number of publicity shorts, it was only thanks to the support of Feyder and his wife, the actress Françoise Rosay, that Carné was able to make his debut as a feature filmmaker with *Jenny* in 1936. If this was a routine melodrama, Carné was able in the next three years to establish himself as one of Europe's leading film directors.

During the period up to the outbreak of war in 1939 Carné established what was to be a ten-year collaboration with the poet and screenwriter Jacques Prévert, and gradually built up a team of collaborators—including the designer Alexandre Trauner and composer Maurice Jaubert—which was unsurpassed at this period. In quick succession Carné made the comedy *Drole de drame,* which owes more to Prévert's taste for systematic absurdity and surreal gags than to the director's professionalism, and a trio of fatalistic romantic melodramas, *Quai des brumes, Hotel du nord* and *Le Jour se lève.*

These are perfect examples of the mode of French filmmaking that had been established by Jacques Feyder: a concern with visual style and a studio-created realism, a reliance on detailed scripts with structure and dialogue separately elaborated, and a foregrounding of star performers to whom

Marcel Carné

all elements of decor and photography are subordinate. Though the forces shaping a character's destiny may be outside his or her control, the story focuses on social behavior and the script offers set-piece scenes and confrontations and witty or trenchant dialogue that enables the stars to display their particular talents to the full.

The various advocates of either Prévert or Carné have sought to make exclusive claims as to which brought poetry to the nebulous and ill-defined "poetic realism" that these films are said to exemplify. In retrospect, however, these arguments seem over-personalized, since the pair seem remarkably well-matched. The actual differences seem less in artistic approach than in attitude to production. From the first, Carné, heir to a particular mode of quality filmmaking, was concerned with an industry, a technique, a career. Prévert, by contrast, though he is a perfect example of the archetypal 1930s screenwriter, able to create striking star roles and write dazzling and memorable dialogue, is not limited to this role and has a quite separate identity as surrealist, humorist and poet.

The pair share a certain fantastic conception of realism, with film seen as a studio construct in which fidelity to life is balanced by attention to a certain poetic atmosphere. Carné's coldly formal command of technique is matched by Prévert's sense of the logic of a tightly woven narrative. If it is Prévert's imagination that allows him to conceive both the *amour fou* that unites the lovers and the grotesque villains who threaten it, it is Carné's masterly direction of actors that turns Jean Gabin and Michèle Morgan into the 1930s ideal couple and draws such memorable performances from Michel Simon, Jules Berry and Arletty.

The collaboration of Prévert and Carné was sustained during the very different circum-stances of the German Occupation, when they together made two films that rank among the most significant of the period. Since films in the mode of 1930s poetic realism were now banned, it is hardly surprising that Carné and Prévert should have found the need to adopt a radically new style. Remaining within the concept of the studio-made film, but leaving behind the contempo-rary urban gloom of *Le Jour se lève,* they opted for a style of elaborate and theatrical period spectacle. The medieval fable of *Les Visiteurs du soir* was an enormous contemporary success but it has not worn well. Working with very limited resources the filmmakers—assisted clandestinely by Trauner and the composer Joseph Kosma—succeeded in making an obvious prestige film, a work in which Frenchmen could take pride at a dark moment of history. But despite the presence of such players as Arletty and Jules Berry, the overall effect is ponderous and stilted.

Carné's masterpiece is *Les Enfants du paradis,* shot during the war years but released only after the Liberation. Running for over three hours and comprising two parts, each of which is of full feature length, *Les Enfants du paradis* is one of the most ambitious films ever undertaken in France. Set in the twin worlds of theatre and crime in nineteenth century Paris, this all-star film is both a theatrical spectacle in its own right and a reflection on the nature of spectacle. The script is one of Prévert's richest, abounding in wit and aphorism, and Carné's handling of individual actors and crowd scenes is masterly. The sustained vitality and dynamism of the work as it moves seemingly effortlessly from farce to tragedy, from delicate love scenes to outrageous buffoonery, is exemplary, and its impact is undimmed by the years.

Marcel Carné was still only thirty-six and at the height of his fame when the war ended. Younger than most of those who now came to the fore, he had already made masterly films in two quite different contexts and it seemed inevitable that he would continue to be a dominant force in French cinema despite the changed circumstances of the postwar era. But in fact the first post-war Carné-Prévert film, *Les Portes de la nuit,* was an expensive flop. When a subsequent film, *La Fleur de l'âge,* was abandoned shortly after production had begun, one of the most fruitful partnerships in French cinema came to an end. Carné directed a dozen more films, from *La Marie du port* in 1950 to *La Merveilleuse Visite* in 1973, but he was no longer a major force in French filmmaking.

Marcel Carné was an unfashionable figure long before his directing career came to an end. Scorned by a new generation of filmmakers, Carné grew more and more out of touch with contemporary developments, despite an eagerness to explore new subjects and use young performers. His failure is a measure of the gulf that separates 1950s and 1960s conceptions of cinema from the studio era of the war and immediate prewar years. He was, however, the epitome of this French studio style, its unquestioned master, even if—unlike Renoir—he was unable to transcend its limitations. While future critics are unlikely to find much to salvage from the latter part of his career, films like *Drôle de drame* and *Quai des brumes, Le Jour se lève* and *Les Enfants du paradis,* remain rich and complex monuments to a decade of filmmaking that will reward fresh and unbiased critical attention.—ROY ARMES

Cassavetes, John

*Nationality American. **Born** New York City, 9 December 1929. **Education** Mohawk College, Colgate University, and New York Academy of Dramatic Arts, graduated 1950. **Family** Married actress Gena Rowlands, 1958, two sons, one daughter. **Career** Title*

John Cassavetes (left) with Peter Falk and Ben Gazzara in *Husbands.*

character in TV series Johnny Staccato, 1959-60; directed first film, Shadows, 1960; hired by Paramount, then by Stanley Kramer, 1961; worked as independent filmmaker, from 1964. **Awards** *Critics Award, Venice Festival, for Shadows, 1960; Best Screenplay, National Society of Film Critics, and five awards from Venice Festival, for Faces, 1968; Golden Lion, Venice Festival, for Gloria, 1980; Golden Bear, Berlin Festival, for Love Streams, 1984; Los Angeles Film Critics Career Achievement Award, 1986.* **Died** *Of cirrhosis of the liver, in Los Angeles, 3 February 1989.*

Films as Director: 1960: *Shadows* (+sc). **1961:** *Too Late Blues* (+sc, pr). **1962:** *A Child is Waiting.* **1968:** *Faces* (+sc). **1970:** *Husbands* (+sc, role as Gus). **1971:** *Minnie and Moskowitz* (+sc, role as Husband). **1974:** *A Woman Under the Influence* (+sc). **1976:** *The Killing of a Chinese Bookie* (+sc). **1977/78:** *Opening Night* (+sc). **1980:** *Gloria.* **1984:** *Love Streams* (+role as Robert Harmon). **1986:** *Big Trouble.*

Other Films: 1951: *Fourteen Hours* (Hathaway) (role as extra). **1953:** *Taxi* (Ratoff) (role). **1955:** *The Night Holds Terror* (Stone) (role). **1956:** *Crime in the Streets* (Siegel) (role). **1957:** *Edge of the City* (Ritt) (role). **1958:** *Saddle the Wind* (Parrish) (role); *Virgin Island* (P. Jackson) (role). **1962:** *The Webster Boy* (Chaffey) (role). **1964:** *The Killers* (Siegel) (role as Johnny North). **1967:** *The Dirty Dozen* (Aldrich) (role as Victor Franko); *Devil's Angels* (Haller) (role). **1968:** *Rosemary's Baby* (Polanski) (role as Rosemary's husband); *Gli Intoccabili* (*Machine Gun McCain*) (Montaldo) (role). **1969:** *Roma coma Chicago* (*Bandits in Rome*) (De Martino) (role); *If It's Tuesday, This Must Be Belgium* (M. Stuart) (cameo role). **1976:** *Two-Minute Warning* (Pearce) (role); *Mikey and Nicky* (May) (role). **1978:** *The Fury* (De Palma) (role). **1982:** *The Tempest* (Mazursky) (role). **1983:** *Marvin and Tige* (Weston) (role).

As perhaps the most influential of the independently produced feature films of its era (1958-67), *Shadows* came to be seen as a virtual breakthrough for American alternative cinema. The film and its fledgling writer-director had put a group of young, independent filmmakers on the movie map, together with their more intellectual, less technically polished, decidedly less commercial, low-budget alternatives to Hollywood features.

Begun as an improvisational exercise in the method-acting workshop that actor Cassavetes was teaching, and partly financed by his earnings from the *Johnny Staccato* television series, *Shadows* was a loosely plotted, heavily improvised work of cinema verité immediacy which explored human relationships and racial identity against the background of the beat atmosphere of the late 1950s, given coherence by the jazz score of Charles Mingus.

The origins and style of *Shadows* were to characterize John Cassavetes's work throughout his directorial career, once he got the studio-financed production bug out of his system—and his system out of theirs.

The five prizes garnered by *Shadows,* including the prestigious Critics Award at the 1960 Venice Film Festival, led to Cassavetes's unhappy and resentful experience directing two studio-molded productions (*Too Late Blues, A Child is Waiting*), both of which failed critically and commercially. Thereafter, he returned to independent filmmaking, although he continued to act in mainstream movies such as *The Dirty Dozen, Rosemary's Baby,* and *Two Minute Warning.* He continued directing feature films, however, in his characteristic, controversial style.

That style centers around a freedom afforded his actors to share in the creative process. Cassavetes's scripts serve as sketchy blueprints for the performers' introspective explorations and emotional embellishments. Consequently, camera movements, at the command of the actors' intuitive behavior, are of necessity spontaneous.

The amalgam of improvisational acting, hand-held camera work, grainy stock, loose editing, and threadbare plot give his films a texture of recreated rather than heightened reality, often imbuing them with a feeling of astonishing psychodramatic intensity as characters confront each other and lay bare their souls. Detractors, however, see Cassavetes as too dedicated to the performers' art and too trusting of the actor's self-discipline. They charge that the result is too often a mild form of aesthetic anarchy.

At worst Cassavetes's films are admittedly formless and self-indulgent. Scenes are stretched excruciatingly far beyond their climactic moments, lines are delivered falteringly, dialogue is repetitious. But, paradoxically, these same blemishes seem to make possible the several lucid, provocative, and moving moments of transcendent human revelation that a Cassavetes film almost inevitably delivers.

As his career progressed, Cassavetes changed his thematic concerns, upgraded his technical production values, and, not surprisingly, attracted a wider audience—but without overhauling his actor-as-auteur approach.

Faces represented Cassavetes's return to his favored semi-documentary style, complete with the seemingly obligatory excesses and gaffes. But the film also contained moments of truth and exemplary acting. Not only did this highly charged drama about the disintegration of a middle-class marriage in affluent Southern California find favor with the critical and filmmaking communities, it broke through as one of the first independent films to find a sizable audience among the general moviegoing public.

In *Husbands,* Cassavetes continued his exploration of marital manners, morals, and sexual identity by focusing on a trio of middle-class husbands—played by Cassavetes, Ben Gazzara, and Peter Falk—who confront their own mortality when a friend dies. Director Cassavetes's doubled-edged trademark—brilliant moments of intense acting amid the banal debris of over-indulgence—had never been in bolder relief.

Minnie and Moskowitz was Cassavetes's demonstration of a lighter touch, an amusing and touching interlude prior to his most ambitious and commercially successful film. The film starred Gena Rowlands (Cassavetes's wife) and Seymour Cassel as a pair of dissimilar but similarly lonely people ensnared in a manic romance. Cassavetes again examined miscommunication in *Minnie and Moskowitz,* but in a much more playful vein.

A Woman Under the Influence was by far Cassavetes's most polished, accessible, gripping, and technically proficient film. For this effort, Cassavetes departed from his accustomed style of working by writing a fully detailed script during pre-production. Starring Gena Rowlands in a magnificent performance as a lower-middle class housewife coming apart at the seams, and the reliable Peter Falk as the hardhat husband who is ill-equipped to deal with his wife's mental breakdown, *Woman* offered a more palatable balance of Cassavetes's strengths and weaknesses. The over-long scenes and overindulgent acting jags are there, but in lesser doses, while the privileged moments and bursts of virtuoso screen acting seem more abundant than usual.

Financed by Falk and Cassavetes, the film's crew and cast (including many family members) worked on deferred salaries. Promoted via a tour undertaken by the nucleus of the virtual repertory company (Cassavetes, Rowland, Falk) and booked without a major distributor,

Woman collected generally ecstatic reviews, Academy Award nominations for Cassavetes and Rowlands, and impressive box office returns.

Cassavetes's next two films (*The Killing of a Chinese Bookie, Opening Night*) feature a return to his earlier structure (or lack thereof)—inaccessible, interminable, and insufferable for all but diehard buffs. However, *Gloria,* which showcased Rowlands as a former gangster's moll, while uneven in tone and erratic in pace, represented a concession by Cassavetes to filmgoers seeking heightened cinematic energy and narrative momentum.

"People who are making films today are too concerned with mechanics—technical things instead of feeling," Cassavetes told an interviewer in 1980. "Execution is about eight percent to me. The technical quality of a film doesn't have much to do with whether it's a good film."—BILL WINE

Chabrol, Claude

Nationality *French.* **Born** *Paris, 24 June 1930.* **Education** *University of Paris, Ecole Libre des Sciences Politiques.* **Family** *Married 1) Agnes Goute, 1952 (divorced), two sons; 2) actress Stephane Audran, 1964 (divorced), one son; 3) Aurore Pajot.* **Career** *Film critic for* Arts *and for* Cahiers du Cinéma, *Paris, 1953-57 (under own name and as "Charles Eitel" and "Jean-Yves Goute"); Head of production company AJYM, 1956-61; directed first film,* Le Beau Serge, *1958; director,* Macbeth, *Théâtre Recamier, Paris, 1967; director, French TV, 1970s.* **Awards** *Golden Bear, Berlin Festival, for* Les Cousins, *1959; D. W. Griffith Award, National Board of Review, and New York Film Critics Circle Award for Best*

Claude Chabrol (left) directing *Story of Women.*

Foreign Film, for Story of Women, *1989.* **Agent** *c/o VMA, 40 rue Francois 1er, 75008 Paris, France.* **Address** *15 Quai Conti, 75006 Paris, France.*

Films as Director: 1958: *Le Beau Serge (Bitter Reunion)* (+pr, sc, bit role). **1959:** *Les Cousins (The Cousins)* (+pr, sc); *A Double Tour (Web of Passion; Leda)* (+bit role). **1960:** *Les Bonnes Femmes* (+adapt, bit role). **1961:** *Les Godelureaux* (+co-adapt, bit role); "L'Avarice" episode of *Les Sept Péchés capitaux (The Seven Deadly Sins)* (+bit role). **1962:** *L'Œil du malin (The Third Lover)* (+sc); *Ophélia* (+co-sc). **1963:** *Landru (Bluebeard)* (+co-sc). **1964:** "L'Homme qui vendit la tour Eiffel" episode of *Les Plus Belles Escroqueries du monde (The Beautiful Swindlers)*; *Le Tigre aime la chair fraîche (The Tiger Likes Fresh Blood; Code Name: Tiger)*; *La Chance et l'amour* (Tavernier, Schlumberger, Bitsch, and Berry) (d linking sequences only). **1965:** "La Muette" episode of *Paris vu par . . . (Six in Paris)* (+sc, role); *Marie-Chantal contre le Docteur Kha* (+co-sc, bit role); *Le Tigre se parfume à la dynamite (An Orchid for the Tiger)* (+bit role). **1966:** *La Ligne de démarcation (Line of Demarcation)* (+co-sc). **1967:** *Le Scandale (The Champagne Murders)*; *La Route de Corinthe (Who's Got the Black Box?; The Road to Corinth)* (+role). **1968:** *Les Biches (The Does; The Girlfriends; Bad Girls)* (+co-sc, role). **1969:** *La Femme infidèle (Unfaithful Wife)* (+co-sc): *Que la bête meure (This Man Must Die; The Beast Must Die)*. **1970:** *Le Boucher (The Butcher)* (+sc); *La Rupture (Le Jour des parques; The Breakup)* (+sc, bit role). **1971:** *Juste avant la nuit (Just Before Nightfall)* (+sc). **1972:** *La Piège à loup; La Décade prodigieuse (Ten Days' Wonder)* (+co-sc); *Docteur Popaul (High Heels; Scoundrel in White)* (+co-song); *De Grey— Le Banc de Desolation (for TV)*. **1973:** *Les Noces rouges (Wedding in Blood)* (+sc). **1974:** *Nada (The NADA Gang)*; *Histoires insolites* (series of 4 TV films); *Une Invitation à la chasse (for TV)*. **1975:** *Une Partie de plaisir (A Piece of Pleasure; Pleasure Party)*; *Les Innocents aux mains sales (Dirty Hands; Innocents with Dirty Hands)* (+sc); *Les Magiciens (Initiation à la mort; Death Rite Profezia di un delitto)*. **1976:** *Folies bourgeoises (The Twist)* (+co-sc). **1977:** *Alice ou La Dernière Fugue (Alice or the Last Escapade)* (+sc). **1978:** *Les Liens de sang (Blood Relatives)* (+co-sc); *Violette Nozière (Violette)*. **1980:** *Le Cheval d'Orgueil (The Horse of Pride; The Proud Ones)*. **1981:** *Les Affinités électives (for TV)*. **1982:** *Les Fantômes du chapelier (The Hatter's Ghost)*. **1983:** *Le Sang des autres (The Blood of Others)* (for TV). **1984:** *Poulet au vinaigre (Cop au Vin)* (+co-sc). **1985:** *Inspecteur Lavardin* (+co-sc). **1986:** *Masques* (+co-sc). **1987:** *Le cri du hibou (The Cry of the Owl)*. **1989:** *Une Affaire des femmes (Story of Women)* (+sc). **1990:** *Jours tranquilles a Clichy (Quiet Days in Clichy)* (+sc); *Docteur M (Club Extinction)* (+sc). **1991:** *Madame Bovary* (+sc). **1993:** *Bette* (+sc); *L'oeil de Vichy (The Eye of Vichy)* (doc). **1994:** *L'enfer (Hell; Jealousy)*. **1995:** *La ceremonie (A Judgment in Stone)* (+sc). **1997:** *Rien ne va plus* (+sc).

Other Films: 1956: *Le Coup de berger* (Rivette) (co-sc, uncred co-mu, role). **1959:** *A bout de souffle* (Godard) (tech adv); *Les Jeux de l'amour* (de Broca) (role). **1960:** *Paris nour appartient* (Rivette) (role); *Saint-Tropez blues* (Moussy) (role); *Les Distractions* (Dupont) (role). **1961:** *Ples v dezju (Dance in the Rain)* (Hladnik) (supervisor); *Les Menteurs* (Greville) (role). **1964:** *Les Durs à cuire* (Pinoteau) (role). **1965:** *Brigitte et Brigitte* (Moullet) (role). **1966:** *Happening* (Bokanowski) (tech adv); *Zoe bonne* (Deval) (role). **1968:** *La Femme ecarlate* (Valere) (role). **1969:** *Et crac!* (Douchet) (role); *Version latine* (Detre) (role); *Le Travail* (Detre) (role). **1970:** *Sortie de secours* (Kahane) (role). **1971:** *Eglantine* (Brialy) (tech adv); *Aussi loin que l'amour* (Rossif) (role). **1972:** *Piège à pucelles* (Leroi) (tech adv); *Un Meurtre est un meurtre* (Périer) (role). **1973:** *Le Flipping* (Volatron) (role as interviewee). **1987:** *Sale destin!* (Sylvain Madigan) (role). **1992:** *Sam Suffit* (role as Mr. Denis) *Music for the Movies: Bernard Herrmann* (role). **1993:** *Jean Renoir* (role); *François Truffaut: Portraits volés.* **1997:** *Cannes . . . les 400 coups* (for TV).

If Jean-Luc Godard appeals to critics because of his extreme interest in politics and film theory and if François Truffaut appeals to the popular audience because of his humanism and sentimentality, it is Claude Chabrol—film critic, filmmaker, philosopher—whose work consistently offers the opportunity for the most balanced appeal. His partisans find especially notable the subtle tone of Chabrol's cinema: his films are apparently cold and objective portraits of profoundly psychological situations; and yet that coldness never approaches the kind of fashionable cynicism, say, of a Stanley Kubrick, but suggests, rather, something closer to the viewpoint of a god who, with compassion but without sentiment, observes the follies of his creations.

Chabrol's work can perhaps best be seen as a cross between the unassuming and popular genre film and the pretentious and elitist art film: Chabrol's films tend to be thrillers with an incredibly self-conscious, self-assured style—that is, pretentious melodrama, aware of its importance. For some, however, the hybrid character of Chabrol's work is itself a problem: indeed, just as elitist critics sometimes find Chabrol's subject matter beneath them, so too do popular audiences sometimes find Chabrol's style and incredibly slow pace alienating.

Chabrol's films are filled with allusions and references to myth (as in *La Rupture,* which begins with an epigraph from Racine's *Phaedra*: "What an utter darkness suddenly surrounds me!"). The narratives of his films are developed through a sensuousness of decor, a gradual accumulation of psychological insight, an absolute mastery of camera movement, and the inclusion of objects and images—beautiful and evocative, like the river in *Le Boucher* or the lighthouse in *Dirty Hands*—which are imbued with symbolic intensity. Like Balzac, whom he admires, Chabrol attempts, within a popular form, to present a portrait of his society in microcosm.

Chabrol began his career as a critic for *Cahiers du cinéma*. With Eric Rohmer, he wrote a groundbreaking book-length study of Alfred Hitchcock, and with his friends (Truffaut, Godard, Rohmer, Jacques Rivette, and others) he attempted to turn topsy-turvy the entire cinematic value system. That their theories of authorship remain today a basic premise (albeit modified and continuously examined) certainly indicates the success of their endeavor. Before long, Chabrol found himself functioning as financial consultant and producer for a variety of films inaugurating the directorial careers of his fellow critics who, like himself, were no longer content merely to theorize.

Chabrol's career can perhaps be divided into five semi-discrete periods: 1) the early personal films, beginning with *Le Beau Serge* in 1958 and continuing through *Landru* in 1962; 2) the commercial assignments, beginning with *The Tiger Likes Fresh Blood* in 1964 and continuing through *The Road to Corinth* in 1967; 3) the mature cycle of masterpieces, beginning with *Les Biches* in 1968 and continuing through *Wedding in Blood* in 1973, almost all starring his wife Stephane Audran, and produced by Andre Genoves; 4) the more diverse (and uneven) accumulations of films from 1974 to the present, which have tended neither to garner automatic international release nor to feature Audran in a central role; and 5) the more recent films of higher quality, if sometimes uneven still, produced in the 1980s and 1990s by Marin Karmitz's company MK2 and including a new set of regular collaborators.

If Hitchcock's *Shadow of a Doubt,* as analyzed by Chabrol and Rohmer, is constructed upon an exchange of guilt, Chabrol's first film, *Le Beau Serge,* modeled after it, is constructed upon an exchange of redemption. Chabrol followed *Le Beau Serge,* in which a city-dweller visits a country friend, with *Les Cousins,* in which a country-dweller visits a city friend. Most notably, *Les Cousins* offers Chabrol's first "Charles" and "Paul," the names Chabrol would continue to use throughout much of his career—Charles to represent the more serious bourgeois man, Paul the more hedonistic id-figure. *A double tour,* Chabrol's first color film, is especially notable for its striking cinematography, its complex narrative structure, and the exuberance of its flamboyant style; it represents Chabrol's first studied attempt to examine and criticize the moral values of the bourgeoisie as well as to dissect the sociopsychological causes of the violence which inevitably erupts as the social and family structures prove inadequate. Perhaps the most wholly successful film of this period is the infrequently screened *L'Œil du malin,* which presents the most typical Chabrol situation: a triangle consisting of a bourgeois married couple—Hélène and her stolid husband—and the outsider whose involvement with the couple ultimately leads to violence and tragedy. Here can be found Chabrol's first "Hélène," the recurring beautiful and slightly aloof woman, generally played by Stephane Audran.

When these and other personal films failed to ignite the box office, despite often positive critical responses, Chabrol embarked on a series of primarily commercial assignments (such as *Marie-Chantal contre le Docteur Kha*), during which his career went into a considerable critical eclipse. Today, however, even these fairly inconsequential films seem to reflect a fetching style and some typically quirky Chabrolian concerns.

Chabrol's breakthrough occurred in 1968 with the release of *Les Biches,* an elegant thriller in which an outsider, Paul, disrupts the lesbian relationship between two women. All of Chabrol's films in this period are slow psychological thrillers which tend basically to represent variations upon the same theme: an outsider affecting a central relationship until violence results. In *La Femme infidèle,* one of Chabrol's most self-assured films, the marriage of Hélène and Charles is disrupted when Charles kills Hélène's lover. In the Jansenist *Que la bête meure,* Charles tracks down the unremittingly evil hit-and-run killer of his young son, and while doing so disrupts the relationship between the killer, Paul, and his sister-in-law Hélène. In *Le Boucher,* the butcher Popaul, who is perhaps a homicidal killer, attempts a relationship with a cool and frigid schoolteacher, Hélène, who has displaced her sexual energies onto her teaching of her young pupils, particularly onto one who is conspicuously given the name Charles.

In the extravagantly expressive *La Rupture,* the outsider Paul attempts a plot against Hélène in order to secure a better divorce settlement, desired by the rich parents of her husband Charles, who has turned to drug addiction to escape his repressive bourgeois existence. In *Juste avant la nuit,* it is Charles who has taken a lover, and Charles's wife Hélène who must ultimately resort to an act of calculated violence in order to keep the bourgeois surface intact. In the detective variation *Ten Days' Wonder,* the relationship between Charles and Hélène is disrupted by the intervention of a character named Théo (*Theos,* representing God), whose false image must be unmasked by the outsider Paul. Finally, in *Wedding in Blood,* based on factual material, it is the wife and her lover who team together to plot against her husband.

Jean Renoir said that all great directors make the same film over and over; perhaps no one has taken this dictum as seriously as Chabrol; indeed, all these films represent a kind of formal geometry as Charles, Hélène, and Paul play out their fated roles in a universe strongly influenced by Fritz Lang, the structures of their bourgeois existence unable to contain their previously repressed passions. Noteworthy too is the consistency of collaboration on these films: usually with Stephane Audran, Michel Bouquet, and Jean Yanne as performers; Jean Rabier as cinematographer; Paul Gégauff as co-scriptwriter; André Génovès as producer; Guy Littaye as art director; Pierre Jansen as composer; Jacques Gaillard as editor; Guy Chichignoud on sound.

In the late 1970s and 1980s, Chabrol has increasingly explored different kinds of financing, making television films as well as international co-productions. Some of these interesting films seem quite unusual from what he has attempted before, perhaps the most surprising being *Le Cheval d'Orgueil,* an ethnographic drama chronicling the simplicity and terrible harshness of peasant life in Brittany prior to World War I with a straightforwardness and lack of sentimentality which is often riveting. Indeed, the film seems so different from much of Chabrol's work that it forces a kind of re-evaluation of his career, making him seem less an emulator of Hitchcock and more an emulator of Balzac, attempting to create his own *Comedie humaine* in a panoramic account of the society about him.

Meanwhile, without his regular collaborators, most notably Stephane Audran, Chabrol has had to establish a new "team"—now including his son, Matthieu Chabrol, as the composer, replacing the superior Pierre Jansen. Although the series of films directed for producer Marin Karmitz seems laudable and superior to Chabrol's non-Karmitz films of the 1980s and 1990s, with a few exceptions they do not quite match the unity or quality of Chabrol's earlier masterpieces.

One of the exceptions is *Une affaire des femmes,* starring Isabelle Huppert, who had previously starred in *Violette Noziere*. The story of an abortionist who ends up the last female guillotined in France (by the Vichy government), *Une Affaire des femmes,* unlike other recent Chabrol films, received international distribution as well as a variety of awards and critical recognition. Chabrol's achievement here is extraordinary: offering a complex three-dimensional portrait of a woman who is not really very likeable, *Une Affaire des femmes* turns out, by its end, to be the most fair, progressive, and passionate film ever made about abortion, dissecting the sexual politics of the "crime"—without ever resorting to polemics; and Chabrol's unswerving gaze becomes the regard of an all-knowing God. *Madame Bovary,* again with Huppert, is perhaps one notch below in quality: is it surprising that Chabrol turns *Madame Bovary* into one of his tragic bourgeois love triangles—only this time, with the protagonist called Emma, rather than Hélène? The success of these two films, as well as the earlier *Violette Noziere* and Chabrol's recent film *La Ceremonie* (all four starring Isabelle Huppert), may indicate that Chabrol's films—so cold as an inherent result of the director's personality and formal interests—may absolutely require an extraordinary, talented, and expressive female presence in order to contribute a human, empathic dimension—else they seem slow, tedious exercises. Clearly, Stephane Audran's contributions to Chabrol's earlier masterpieces—both as fellow artist and muse—may have been seriously underestimated.

More typical of Chabrol's recent career are films like *Les Fantômes du Chapelier, Poulet au vinaigre, Inspecteur Lavardin, Masques,* and *Le cri du hibou,* which, although worthy of note, by no means measure up to Chabrol's greatest and are therefore disappointing. What becomes increasingly clear is that Chabrol is one of the most uneven great directors; and without a producer like Andre Genoves and forceful, talented collaborators on the same wavelength, Chabrol can sometimes make bad or very odd movies. The 1976 *Folies bourgeoises,* for instance, is all but unwatchable, and while *Docteur M* and *Betty* may have interesting concepts, one is a dreary re-interpretation of Fritz Lang, and the other a lifeless adaptation of a Simenon novel, containing a wooden performance by Marie Trintignant. *L'enfer* (directed in 1994) is certainly better, if still minor—a smoldering tale of growing jealousy based on the unproduced script of a master director with a somewhat kindred soul, Henri-Georges Clouzot. Nevertheless, the true cinephile loves Chabrol despite his failures—because in the midst of his overprodigious output, he can change gears and make a fascinating documentary (such as his 1993 *L'Œil de Vichy*) or can surprise everyone with a major, narrative film of startling ideas, unity, and performance (such as his 1995 *La Ceremonie,* which was nominated for a Cesar), suddenly again at the very top of his form, a New Wave exemplar for filmmakers everywhere.—CHARLES DERRY

Chaplin, Charlie (Sir Charles Chaplin)

Nationality *British.* **Born** *Charles Spencer Chaplin in London, 16 April 1889.* **Family** *Married 1) Mildred Harris, 1918 (divorced 1920); 2) Lita Grey, 1924 (divorced 1927), two sons; 3) Paulette Goddard, 1936 (divorced 1941); 4) Oona O'Neill, 1943, eight children.* **Career** *Music-Hall Performer in London and provincial theatres, from 1898; engaged by Fred Karno troupe, 1907; toured United States with Karno, 1910 and 1912; signed to Keystone and moved to Hollywood, 1913; after acting in eleven Keystone comedies, began directing (thirty-five films for Keystone), 1914; signed with Essanay (fourteen films), 1915; signed with Mutual (eleven films), 1916; signed with First National (nine films), 1917; joint-founder, with Griffith, Pickford, and Fairbanks, of United Artists, 1919; left United States to visit London, reentry permit rescinded en route, 1952; moved to Vevey, on Lake Geneva, Switzerland, 1953.* **Awards** *Best Actor, New York Film Critics, for* The Great Dictator, *1940 (award refused); Honorary Oscar, "for the incalculable effect he has had in making motion pictures the art form of the country," 1971; Medallion Award, Writers Guild of America, 1971; Oscar for Best Original Dramatic Score (shared) for* Limelight, *1972; Knighted, 1975.* **Died** *In Vevey, Switzerland, 25 December 1977.*

Films as Director, Actor and Scriptwriter: 1914: *Caught in a Cabaret (Jazz Waiter; Faking with Society)* (co-d, co-sc); *Caught in the Rain (Who Got Stung?; At It Again); A Busy Day (Lady Charlie; Militant Suffragette); The Fatal Mallet (The Pile Driver; The Rival Suitors; Hit Him Again)* (co-d, co-sc); *Her Friend the Bandit (Mabel's Flirtation; A Thief Catcher)* (co-d, co-sc); *Mabel's Busy Day (Charlie and the Sausages; Love and Lunch; Hot Dogs); Mabel's Married Life (When You're Married; The Squarehead)* (co-d, co-sc); *Laughing Gas (Tuning His Ivories; The Dentist); The Property*

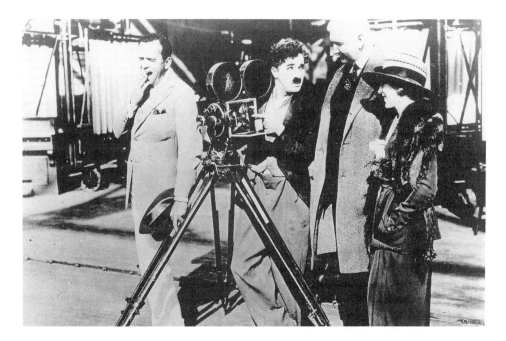

Man (*Getting His Goat*; *The Roustabout*; *Vamping Venus*); *The Face on the Bar-Room Floor* (*The Ham Artist*); *Recreation* (*Spring Fever*); *The Masquerader* (*Putting One Over*; *The Female Impersonator*); *His New Profession* (*The Good-for-Nothing*; *Helping Himself*); *The Rounders* (*Two of a Kind*; *Oh, What a Night!*); *The New Janitor* (*The Porter*; *The Blundering Boob*); *Those Love Pangs* (*The Rival Mashers*; *Busted Hearts*); *Dough and Dynamite* (*The Doughnut Designer*; *The Cook*); *Gentlemen of Nerve* (*Some Nerve*; *Charlie at the Races*); *His Musical Career* (*The Piano Movers*; *Musical Tramps*); *His Trysting Place* (*Family Home*); *Getting Acquainted* (*A Fair Exchange*; *Hullo Everybody*); *His Prehistoric Past* (*A Dream*; *King Charlie*; *The Caveman*). **1915:** (for Essanay): *His New Job*; *A Night Out* (*Champagne Charlie*); *The Champion* (*Battling Charlie*); *In the Park* (*Charlie on the Spree*); *A Jitney Elopement* (*Married in Haste*); *The Tramp* (*Charlie the Hobo*); *By the Sea* (*Charlie's Day Out*); *Work* (*The Paper Hanger*; *The Plumber*); *A Woman* (*The Perfect Lady*); *The Bank*; *Shanghaied* (*Charlie the Sailor*; *Charlie on the Ocean*); *A Night in the Show*. **1916:** (for Essanay): *Carmen* (*Charlie Chaplin's Burlesque on Carmen*); *Police!* (*Charlie the Burglar*); (for Mutual): *The Floorwalker* (*The Store*); *The Fireman*; *The Vagabond*; *One A.M.*; *The Count*; *The Pawnshop*; *Behind the Screen*; *The Rink*. **1917:** (for Mutual): *Easy Street*; *The Cure*; *The Immigrant*; *The Adventurer*. **1918:** (for First National): *A Dog's Life*; (for Liberty Loan Committee): *The Bond*; *Triple Trouble* (compiled from 1915 footage plus additional non-Chaplin film by Essanay after he left); (for First National): *Shoulder Arms*. **1919:** (for First National): *Sunnyside*; *A Day's Pleasure*. **1921:** *The Kid*; (+pr); *The Idle Class* (+pr). **1922:** *Pay Day* (+pr); *Nice and Friendly* (+pr) (made privately and unreleased). **1923:** *The Pilgrim* (+pr); *A Woman of Paris* (+pr). **1925:** *The Gold Rush* (+pr, narration, mus for sound reissue). **1926:** *A Woman of the Sea* (*The Sea Gull*) (von Sternberg) (unreleased) (pr, d additional scenes). **1927:** *The Circus* (+pr, mus, song for sound reissue). **1931:** *City Lights* (+pr, mus). **1936:** *Modern Times* (+pr, mus). **1940:** *The Great Dictator* (+pr, mus). **1947:** *Monsieur Verdoux* (+pr, mus); *Limelight* (+pr, mus, co-choreographer). **1957:** *A King in New York* (+pr, mus). **1959:** *The Chaplin Revue* (+pr, mus) (comprising *A Dog's Life*, *Shoulder Arms*, and *The Pilgrim*, with commentary and music). **1967:** *A Countess from Hong Kong* (+mus).

Other Films: 1914: *Making a Living* (*A Busted Johnny*; *Troubles*; *Doing His Best*) (Lehrman) (role as reporter); *Kid Auto Races at Venice* (*The Kid Auto Race*) (Lehrman) (role as Charlie); *Mabel's Strange Predicament* (*Hotel Mixup*) (Lehrman and Sennett) (role as Charlie); *Between Showers* (*The Flirts*; *Charlie and the Umbrella*; *In Wrong*) (Lehrman) (role as Charlie); *A Film Johnnie* (*Movie Nut*; *Million Dollar Job*; *Charlie at the Studio*) (Sennett) (role as Charlie); *Tango Tangles* (*Charlie's Recreation*; *Music Hall*) (Sennett) (role as Charlie); *His Favorite Pastime* (*The Bonehead*; *His Reckless Fling*) (Nichols) (role as Charlie); *Cruel, Cruel Love* (Sennett) (role as Charlie); *The Star Boarder* (*The Hash-House Hero*) (Sennett) (role as Charlie); *Mabel at the Wheel* (*His Daredevil Queen*; *Hot Finish*) (Normand and Sennett) (role as Charlie); *Twenty Minutes of Love* (*He Loved Her So*; *Cops and Watches*) (Sennett) (role as Charlie, +sc); *The Knock Out* (*Counted Out*; *The Pugilist*) (Arbuckle) (role as Charlie); *Tillie's Punctured Romance* (*Tillie's Nightmare*; *For the Love of Tillie*; *Marie's Millions*) (Sennett) (role as Charlie); *His Regeneration* (Anderson) (guest appearance). **1921:** *The Nut* (Reed) (guest appearance). **1923:** *Souls for Sale* (Hughes) (guest appearance). **1928:** *Show People* (King Vidor) (guest appearance).

Charles Chaplin was the first and the greatest international star of the American silent comic cinema. He was also the twentieth century's first media "superstar," the first artistic creator and popularized creature of our global culture. His face, onscreen antics, and offscreen scandals were disseminated around the globe by new media which knew no geographical or linguistic boundaries. But more than this, Chaplin was the first acknowledged artistic genius of the cinema, recognized as such by a young and influential generation of writers and artists including George Bernard Shaw, H.G. Wells, Bertolt Brecht, Pablo Picasso, James Joyce, Samuel Beckett, and the surrealist painters and poets of both Paris and Berlin. Chaplin may be the one cinema artist who might truly be called a seminal figure of the century—if only because of his influence on virtually every other recognized seminal figure of the century.

Chaplin was born in London into a theatrical family; his mother and father alternated between periods of separation and union, activities onstage and difficulties offstage (his father was an alcoholic, his mother fell victim to insanity). The young Chaplin spent his early life on the

London streets and in a London workhouse, but by the age of eight he was earning his living on the stage.

Chaplin's career, like that of Buster Keaton and Stan Laurel, indicates that gifted physical comedians often develop their talents as children (as do concert pianists and ballet dancers) or never really develop them at all. By the time he was twenty years old, Chaplin had become the star attraction of the Fred Karno Pantomime Troupe, an internationally acclaimed English music-hall act, and it was on his second tour of America that a representative of the Keystone comedy film company (either Mack Sennett, comedienne Mabel Normand, or co-owner Charles Bauman) saw Chaplin. In 1913 he was offered a job at Keystone. Chaplin went to work at the Keystone lot in Burbank, California, in January 1914.

To some extent, the story of Chaplin's popular success and artistic evolution is evident from even a cursory examination of the sheer volume of Chaplin's works (and the compensation he received). In 1914 at Keystone, Chaplin appeared in thirty-five one- and two-reel films (as well as the six-reeler *Tillie's Punctured Romance*), about half of which he directed himself, for the yearly salary of $7,800. The following year, Chaplin made fourteen one- and two-reel films for the Essanay Film Company—all of which he wrote and directed himself—for a salary of $67,000. In 1916-17, Chaplin wrote, directed and starred in twelve two-reel films for the Mutual Film company, and then signed a million-dollar contract with First National Corporation to write, direct, produce, and star in twelve more two-reel films. The contract allowed him to build his own studio, which he alone used until 1952 (it is now the studio for A&M Records), but his developing artistic consciousness kept him from completing the contract until 1923 with nine films of lengths ranging from two to six reels. Finally, in 1919, Chaplin became one of the founders of United Artists (along with Mary Pickford, Douglas Fairbanks, and D.W. Griffith), through which Chaplin released eight feature films, made between 1923-52, after which he sold his interest in the company.

In his early one- and two-reel films Chaplin evolved the comic tools and means that would lead to his future success. His character of the Tramp, the "little fellow," a figure invariably garbed with derby, cane, floppy shoes, baggy pants, and tight jacket, debuted in his second Keystone film, *Kid Auto Races at Venice*. Because the tramp was a little guy, he made an easy target for the larger and tougher characters who loomed over him, but his quick thinking, agile body, and surprising ingenuity in converting ordinary objects into extraordinary physical allies helped him more than hold his own in a big, mean world. Although he was capable of lechery (*The Masquerader, Dough and Dynamite*) he could also selflessly aid the innocent woman under attack (*The New Janitor, The Tramp, The Bank*). Although he deserved her affection as a reward, he was frequently rejected for his social or sexual inadequacies (*The Tramp, The Bank, The Vagabond, The Adventurer*). Many of his early films combined his dexterous games with physical objects with deliberate attempts at emotional pathos (*The Tramp, The Vagabond, The Pawnshop*) or with social commentary on the corruption of the police, the brutality of the slums, or the selfishness of the rich (*Police, Easy Street, The Adventurer*).

Prior to Chaplin, no one had demonstrated that physical comedy could be simultaneously hilariously funny, emotionally passionate, and pointedly intellectual. While his cinema technique tended to be invisible—emphasizing the actor and his actions—he gradually evolved a principle of cinema based on framing: finding the exact way to frame a shot to reveal its motion and meaning completely, thus avoiding disturbing cuts.

Chaplin's later films evolved and featured increasingly complicated or ironic situations in which to explore the Tramp's character and the moral paradoxes of his existence. His friend and ally is a mongrel dog in *A Dog's Life*; he becomes a doughboy in *Shoulder Arms*; acquires a child in *The Kid*; becomes a preacher in *The Pilgrim*; and explores the decadent Parisian high life in *A Woman of Paris,* a comedy-melodrama of subtle visual techniques in which the Tramp does not appear.

Chaplin's four feature films between 1925-36 might be called his "marriage group," in which he explores the circumstances by which the tramp might acquire a sexual-romantic mate. In *The Gold Rush* the Tramp succeeds in winning the dance-hall gal who previously rejected him, because she now appreciates his kindness and his new-found wealth. The happy ending is as improbable as the Tramp's sudden riches—perhaps a comment that kindness helps but money gets the girl. But in *The Circus,* Charlie turns his beloved over to the romantic high-wire daredevil Rex; the girl rejects him not because of Charlie's kindness or poverty but because he cannot fulfill the woman's image of male sexual attractiveness. *City Lights* builds upon this problem as it rises to a final question, deliberately and poignantly left unanswered: can the blind flower seller, whose vision has been restored by Charlie's kindness, love him for his kindness alone since her vision now reveals him to look so painfully different from the rich and handsome man she imagined and expected? And in *Modern Times,* Charlie successfully finds a mate, a social outcast and child of nature like himself; unfortunately, their marriage can find no sanctification or existence within contemporary industrial society. So the two of them take to the road together, walking away from society toward who knows where—the Tramp's final departure from the Chaplin world.

Although both *City Lights* and *Modern Times* used orchestral music and cleverly comic sound effects (especially *Modern Times*), Chaplin's final three American films were talking films—*The Great Dictator,* in which Chaplin burlesques Hitler and Nazism, *Monsieur Verdoux,* in which Chaplin portrays a dapper mass murderer, and *Limelight,* Chaplin's nostalgic farewell to the silent art of pantomime which nurtured him. In this film, in which Buster Keaton also plays a major role, Chaplin bids farewell not only to a dead movie tradition—silent comedy—but to a two-hundred-year tradition of physical comedy on both stage and screen, the tradition out of which both Keaton and Chaplin came, which would produce no clowns of the future.

Chaplin's later years were scarred by personal and political difficulties produced by his many marriages and divorces, his supposed sexual philanderings, his difficulties with the Internal Revenue Service, his outspoken defence of liberal political causes, and his refusal to become an American citizen. Although he was never called to testify before the House Un-American Activities Committee, Chaplin's films were picketed and boycotted by right-wing activist groups. When Chaplin left for a trip abroad in 1952, the State Department summarily revoked his automatic re-entry permit. Chaplin sent his young wife Oona O'Neill, daughter of the playwright Eugene O'Neill, back to America to settle their business affairs.

Chaplin established his family in Switzerland and conveyed his outrage against his former country by not returning to America for twenty years and by refusing to let any of his films circulate in America for two decades. In 1957 he made a very uneven, often embarrassing satire of American democracy, *A King in New York*. This film, like *A Countess from Hong Kong,* made ten years later, was a commercial and artistic disappointment, perhaps in part because Chaplin was cut off from the familiar studio, the experienced production team, and the painstakingly slow production methods he had been using for over three decades. In 1971 he enjoyed a triumphant return to Hollywood to accept an honorary Academy Award for a lifetime of cinematic achievement.—GERALD MAST

Chen Kaige

Nationality Chinese. *Born* Beijing, 12 August 1952; son of film director Chen Huai'ai. *Education* Sent to work in Rubber plantation in Yunnan province to "learn from the people," as part of Cultural Revolution, 1967. *Military Service* Served in Army. *Career* Worked in film processing lab, Beijing, 1975-78, then studied at Beijing Film Academy, 1978-82; assigned to Beijing Film Studio, assistant to Huang Jianzhong; transferred (with Zhang Yimou and He Qun) to Guangxi Film Studios, and directed first feature, Huang Tudi', 1984. *Award* Best Film, Berlin Film Festival, for Yellow Earth, 1984.

Films as Director: **1984:** *Huang Tudi' (Yellow Earth)* (+sc); *Qiangxing Qifei (Forced Take-Off)* (for TV). **1985:** *Da Yuebing (The Big Parade)* (released in 1987). **1987:** *Haizi Wang (King of the Children).* **1991:** *Bian Zou Bian Chang (Life on a String)* (+sc); *Ba Wang Bie Ji (Farewell My Concubine).* **1995:** *Feng Yue (Temptress Moon)* (+story).

Chen Kaige is, with Zhang Yimou, the leading voice among the Fifth Generation of Chinese filmmakers, the first group of students to have graduated following the reopening of the Beijing Film Academy in 1978 after the depredations of the Cultural Revolution. As both a participant in (as a Red Guard he denounced his own father) and a victim of the Cultural Revolution (his secondary education was curtailed and, like the protagonist of *King of the*

Chen Kaige: Ba Wang Bie Ji

Children, he was sent to the country to "learn from the peasants"), Chen is particularly well-placed to voice concerns about history and identity.

His films so far constitute an intelligent and powerfully felt meditation on recent Chinese history, within which, for him, the Cultural Revolution remains a defining moment. "It made," he has said, "cultural hooligans of us." He has a reputation within China as a philosophical director, and his style is indeed marked by a laconic handling of narrative and a classical reticence. This is largely deceptive: underneath is an unyielding anger and unflinching integrity.

Chen in interviews has stressed the complementary nature of his first three films. *Yellow Earth* examines the relationship of "man and the land," *The Big Parade* looks at "the individual and the group," and *King of the Children* considers "man and culture." *Yellow Earth* seems to adopt the structure of the folk ballads that provide a focus for its narrative, with its long held shots and almost lapidary editing. *The Big Parade* alternates static parade ground shots with the chaos of barrack room life, while the third film mobilises a more rhetorical style of poetic realism. Together the films act as a triple rebuttal of any heroic reading of Maoism and the revolution, precisely by taking up subjects much used in propagandist art—the arrival of the People's Liberation Army in a village, the training of new recruits, the fate of the teacher sent to the country—and by refuting their simplifications and obfuscations, shot for shot, with quite trenchant deliberation. Attention in *Yellow Earth* is focused not on the Communist Army whose soldier arrives at the village collecting songs, but on the barren plateau from which the peasantry attempts to wring a meagre existence. In the process the account of Yenan which sees it as the birthplace of Communism is marginalised. *King of the Children* banishes the bright-eyed pupils and spotless classrooms of propaganda in favour of a run-down school room, graffitied and in disrepair, from which the social fabric seems to have fallen away. Likewise *The Big Parade* banishes heroics and exemplary characters in favour of a clear-eyed look at the cost of moulding the individual into the collective.

In Chen's films what is unsaid is as important as that which is said; indeed the act of silence becomes a potent force. The voiceless appear everywhere—the almost mute brother in *Yellow Earth,* the girl's unspoken fears for her marriage ("voiced" in song), the mute cowherd in *King of the Children.* In *Yellow Earth* the girl's voice is silenced by the force of nature as she drowns singing an anthem about the Communist Party. It is almost better, Chen implies, not to speak at all, than—as he suggests in *King of the Children*—to copy, to repeat, to "shout to make it right."

Life on a String, a leisurely allegory whose protagonists are an elderly blind musician and his young acolyte, has as tangible a sense of physical terrain as *Yellow Earth.* It also has an icy twist. Dedicatedly following his own master's instructions all his life, the old man finds himself, in the end, to have been duped. The film, fitting no fashionable niche, was largely ignored. With *Farewell My Concubine* Chen seems, superficially, to have taken a leaf from his rival Zhang Yimou's book. The film has lavish studio sets and costumes and features Zhang's favourite performer, Gong Li. Funded by Hong Kong actress Hsu Feng's Tomson Films and based on a melodramatic novel by Lilian Lee, the film traces the relationship between a young boy, Deiyi, sold by his prostitute mother into the brutal regime of the Peking Opera School in 1920s China, and an older, tougher boy. Deiyi is destined to play female roles, and before he is accepted he undergoes a symbolic castration. The title is taken from the title of the opera in which they make their names—set during the last days of the reign of King Chu. The film follows their fortunes up to 1977, the end of the Cultural Revolution, and closes on a note of betrayal and sacrifice.

Scrupulously performed, finely filmed, the subject allows its director scope to investigate the tortuous intersection of performance, identity, self, gender, and history.

Unsurprisingly Chen's films have met with varying degrees of disapproval from the official regime. *Yellow Earth* was criticised in an anti-elitist policy. *The Big Parade* had its final sequence cut and ends with sounds of the eponymous parade in Tianenmen Square over an empty shot. *Life on a String* is banned. *Farewell My Concubine* was shown, withdrawn, then shown again. To young filmmakers in China Chen's work, and that of other Fifth Generation directors, can seem academic or irrelevant. To the rest of us, the care with which Chen Kaige observes his protagonists' struggles for integrity amid lethally shifting political tides makes for a perennially relevant body of work.—VERINA GLAESSNER

Clair, René

*Nationality French. **Born** René Chomette in Paris, 11 November 1898. **Education** Lycée Montaigne, and Lycée Louis-le-Grand, Paris, 1913-17. **Military Service** Served in Ambulance Corps, 1917. **Family** Married Bronya Perlmutter, 1926, one son. **Career** Retired to Dominican monastery, 1918; began acting at Gaumont studios, 1920; as René Clair, became film editor of* Le Théâtre et comoedia illustré, *Paris, 1922; directed first film,* Paris qui dort, *1923; directed for Alexander Korda in Britain, 1935-38; emigrated to United States and signed to Universal, 1940; returned to Paris, 1946. **Awards** Honorary doctorate, Cambridge University, 1956; elected to Academie Française, 1960; Doctor*

René Clair (right) with Joseph Paternak and Marlene Dietrich at a script conference for *The Flame of New Orleans*.

Honoris Causa, *Royal College of Arts, London, 1967; Commander of the Legion of Honour; Commander of Arts and Letters; Commander of the Italian Order of Merit.* **Died** *In Neuilly, France, 15 March 1981.*

Films as Director: **1923:** *Paris qui dort* (+sc, ed). **1924:** *Entr'acte; Le Fantôme du Moulin Rouge* (+sc). **1925:** *Le Voyage imaginaire* (+sc). **1926:** *La Proie du vent* (+sc). **1927:** *Un Chapeau de paille d'Italie* (+sc). **1928:** *La Tour* (+sc); *Les Deux Timides* (+sc). **1930:** *Sous les toits de Paris* (+sc). **1931:** *Le Million* (+sc); *A Nous la liberté* (+sc). **1932:** *Quatorze Juillet* (+sc). **1934:** *Le Dernier Milliardaire* (+sc). **1935:** *The Ghost Goes West* (+co-sc). **1937:** *Break the News* (+co-sc). **1939:** *Air pur* (+sc) (uncompleted). **1940:** *The Flame of New Orleans* (+co-sc). **1942:** Sketch featuring Ida Lupino in *Forever and a Day* (Lloyd) (+sc); *I Married a Witch* (+co-sc, pr). **1943:** *It Happened Tomorrow* (+co-sc). **1945:** *And Then There Were None* (+co-sc, pr). **1947:** *Le Silence est d'or* (+pr, sc). **1949:** *La Beauté du diable* (+co-sc, pr). **1952:** *Les Belles-de-nuit* (+sc, pr). **1955:** *Les Grandes Manoeuvres* (+co-sc, pr). **1957:** *Porte des Lilas* (+co-sc, pr). **1960:** "Le Mariage" episode of *La Française et l'amour* (+sc). **1961:** *Tout l'or du monde* (+co-sc, pr). **1962:** "Les Deux Pigeons" episode of *Les Quatres vérités* (+sc). **1965:** *Les Fêtes galantes* (+pr, sc).

Other Films: **1920:** *Le Lys de la Vie* (Fuller) (role); *Les Deux Gamines* (Feuillade—serial) (role). **1921:** *Le Sens de la mort* (Protozanoff) (role); *L'Orpheline* (Feuillade) (role); *Parisette* (Feuillade—serial) (role). **1930:** *Prix de beauté* (*Miss Europe*) (Genina) (sc contribution). **1939:** *Un Village dans Paris* (co-pr). **1959:** *La Grande Époque* (French version of Robert Youngson's *The Golden Age of Comedy*) (narrator).

During the 1930s, when the French cinema reigned intellectually preeminent, René Clair ranked with Renoir and Carné as one of its greatest directors—perhaps the most archetypally French of them all. His reputation has since fallen (as has Carné's), and comparison with Renoir may suggest why. Clair's work, though witty, stylish, charming, and technically accomplished, seems to lack a dimension when compared with the work of Renoir; there is a certain over-simplification, a fastidious turning away from the messier, more complex aspects of life. (Throughout nearly the whole of his career, Clair rejected location shooting, preferring the controllable artifice of the studio.) Critics have alleged that his films are superficial and emotionally detached. Yet, at their best, Clair's films have much of the quality of champagne— given so much sparkle and exhilaration, it would seem churlish to demand nourishment as well.

At the outset of his career, Clair directed one of the classic documents of surrealist cinema, *Entr'acte,* and this grounding in surrealism underlies much of his comedy work. The surrealists' love of sight gags (Magritte's cloud-baguettes, Duchamp's urinal) and mocking contempt for bourgeois respectability can be detected in the satiric farce of *Un Chapeau de paille d'Italie,* Clair's masterpiece of the silent era. Dream imagery, another surrealist preoccupation, recurs constantly throughout his career, from *Le Voyage imaginaire* to *Les Belles-de-nuit,* often transmuted into fantasy—touchingly poetic at its best, though in weaker moments declining into fey whimsicality.

The key films in Clair's early career, and those which made him internationally famous, were his first four sound pictures: *Sous les toits de Paris, Le Million, A Nous la liberté,* and *Quatorze Juillet.* Initially sceptical of the value of sound—"an unnatural creation"—he rapidly changed his opinion when he recognized the creative, non-realistic possibilities which the soundtrack offered. Sound effects, music, even dialogue could be used imaginatively to counterpoint and comment on the image, or to suggest a new perspective on the action. Words and pictures, Clair showed, need not, and in fact should not, be tied together in a manner that clumsily duplicates information. Dialogue need not always be audible; and even in a sound picture, silence could claim a validity of its own.

In these four films, Clair created a wholly individual cinematic world, a distinctive blend of fantasy, romance, social satire, and operetta. Song and dance are introduced into the action with no pretence at literal realism, characters are drawn largely from stock, and the elaborate sets are explored with an effortless fluidity of camera movement which would be impossible in real locations. These qualities, together with the pioneering use of sound and Clair's knack for effective pacing and brilliant visual gags, resulted in films of exceptional appeal, full of charm, gaiety, and an ironic wit which at times—notably in the satire on mechanised greed in *A Nous la liberté*—darkened towards an underlying pessimism.

As always, Clair wrote his own scripts, working closely on all four films with designer Lazare Meerson and cinematographer Georges Périnal. Of the four, *Le Million* most effectively integrated its various elements, and is generally rated Clair's finest film. But all were successful, especially outside France, and highly influential: both Chaplin (*Modern Times*) and the Marx Brothers (*A Night at the Opera*) borrowed from them.

In some quarters, though, Clair was criticized for lack of social relevance. Ill-advisedly, he attempted to respond to such criticisms; *Le Dernier Milliardaire* proved a resounding flop. This led to Clair's long exile. For thirteen years he made no films in France other than the abortive *Air pur,* and his six English-language pictures—two in Britain, four in America—have an uneasy feel about them, the fantasy strained and unconvincing. By the time Clair finally returned to France in 1946, both he and the world had changed.

The films that Clair made after World War II rarely recapture the lighthearted gaiety of his early work. In its place, the best of them display a new-found maturity and emotional depth, while preserving the characteristic elegance and wit of his previous films. The prevailing mood is an autumnal melancholy that at times, as in the elegiac close of *Les Grandes Manoeuvres,* comes near to tragedy. Characters are no longer the stock puppets of the pre-war satires, but rounded individuals, capable of feeling and suffering. More serious subjects are confronted, their edges only slightly softened by their context: *Porte des Lilas* ends with a murder, *La Beauté du diable* with a vision of the atomic holocaust. Nearest in mood to the earlier films is the erotic fantasy of *Les Belles-de-nuit,* but even this is darkly underscored with intimations of suicide.

In the late 1950s Clair came under attack from the writers of *Cahiers du cinéma,* François Truffaut in particular, who regarded him as the embodiment of the "Old Guard," the ossified *cinéma de papa* against which they were in revolt. To what he saw as Clair's emotionless, studio-bound artifice, Truffaut proposed an alternative, more "truly French" cinematic tradition, the lyrical freedom of Renoir and Jean Vigo. Clair's reputation never fully recovered from these onslaughts, nor from the lukewarm reception which met his last two films, *Tout l'or du monde* and *Les Fêtes galantes.*

Although Clair no longer commands a place among the very first rank of directors, he remains undoubtedly one of the most original and distinctive stylists of the cinema. His explorations of sound, movement, and narrative technique, liberating at the time, still appear fresh and inventive. For all his limitations, which he readily acknowledged—"a director's intelligence," he once wrote, "can be judged partly by his renunciations"—Clair succeeded in creating a uniquely personal vision of the world, which in his best films still retains the power to exhilarate and delight.—PHILIP KEMP

Clayton, Jack

*Nationality British. **Born** Brighton, Sussex, 1 March 1921. **Family** Married 1) actress Christine Norden; 2) Kathleen Kath; 3) Haya Haraneet. **Career** Trained as racing ice skater. Third assistant director, assistant director, then editor, London Films, 1935-40; served in Royal Air Force Film Unit, finally Commanding Officer, 1940-46; associate producer, Romulus Films, 1950s; directed first feature,* Room at the Top, *1958. **Awards** Best Screenplay Oscar, Special Prize, Venice Festival, for* The Bespoke Overcoat, *1956; Best Director Award, British Academy, for* Room at the Top, *1959. **Died** 26 February 1995 of heart and liver problems.*

Films as Director: 1944: *Naples Is a Battlefield* (+sc, co-ph—uncredited). **1955:** *The Bespoke Overcoat* (+pr). **1958:** *Room at the Top.* **1961:** *The Innocents* (+pr). **1964:** *The Pumpkin Eater.* **1967:** *Our Mother's House.* **1974:** *The Great Gatsby.* **1983:** *Something Wicked this Way Comes.* **1988:** *The Lonely Passion of Judith Hearne.* **1992:** *Memento Mori* (for TV).

Other Films: 1948: *Bond Street* (Parry) (2nd unit d); *An Ideal Husband* (A. Korda) (pr mgr); *The Queen of Spades* (Dickinson) (assoc pr). **1951:** *Flesh and Blood* (Kimmins) (assoc pr). **1952:** *Moulin Rouge* (Huston) (assoc pr). **1953:** *Beat the Devil* (Huston) (assoc pr). **1954:** *The Good Die Young* (Gilbert) (assoc pr). **1955:** *I Am a Camera* (Cornelius) (assoc pr). **1956:** *Sailor Beware!* (*Panic in the Parlor*) (Parry) (pr); *Dry Rot* (Elvey) (pr); *Three Men in a Boat* (Annakin) (pr). **1957:** *The Story of Esther Costello* (Miller) (assoc pr, 2nd unit d). **1958:** *The Whole Truth* (Guillermin) (pr).

Though nearly forty before directing his first feature, Clayton had a solid professional grounding as Associate Producer. His credits, though few, have been mostly major productions. Though he disclaims consciously *auteurial* choices, his films evince a heavily recognisable temperament. True, his approach is national-generational, insofar as his heavy, faintly expressionistic, blocking-in of a basic mood perpetuates the lyrical emphasis conspicuous in such "quality" films of the 1940s as *Brief Encounter, Odd Man Out,* and *Dead of Night.* His penchant for themes of melancholy, frustration, obsession, hallucination, and hauntings are also amply evident.

Clayton attracted much critical praise, and an Academy Award, with *The Bespoke Overcoat,* a "long short" brought in for £5000; writer Wolf Mankowitz adapted Gogol's tale of a haunted tailor to London's East End. Clayton's first feature was *Room at the Top,* from John Braine's novel. Laurence Harvey played the ambitious young Northerner who sacrifices his true love, played by Simone Signoret, to a cynical career-move, impregnating an industrialist's innocent daughter. Its sexual frankness (as the first "quality" film to carry the new X certificate) and its class-consciousness (its use of brand-names being as snobbery-conscious as James Bond's—though lower-class) elicited powerful audience self-recognition. It marked a major breakthrough for British cinema, opening it to other "angry young men" with their "kitchen-sink realism" and social indignation (though politically more disparate than legend has it).

Clayton kept his distance from such trends, turning down both *Saturday Night and Sunday Morning* and *The L-Shaped Room,* to select a very "literary," Victorian, ghost story, *The Innocents,* from Henry James's *The Turn of the Screw.* Deborah Kerr played the children's governess who sees ghosts by sunlight while battling to save her charges from possession by the souls of two evil, and very sexual, servants. Is the lonely governess imagining everything, or projecting her own evil? *The Pumpkin-Eater* adapted Penelope Mortimer's novel about a mother of eight (Anne Bancroft) whose new husband, a film scriptwriter, bullies her into having a

Jack Clayton directing
The Innocents.

hysterectomy. In *Our Mother's House,* a family of children conceal their mother's death from the authorities to continue living as a family—until their scapegrace father (Dirk Bogarde) returns and takes over, introducing, not so much "reality," as *his,* disreputable, reality.

The three films are all but a trilogy, brooding with "haunted realism" over the psychic chaos between parental—especially mother—figures and children caught in half-knowledge of sexuality, death, and individuality. Atmospheres sluggish or turbulent, strained or cavernous, envelope women or child-women enmeshed in tangles of family closeness and loneliness. If *The Innocents* arraigns Victorian fears of childhood sexuality, it acknowledges also the evil in children. *The Pumpkin Eater* balances assumptions of "excessive" maternal instinct being a neurotic defence by raising the question of whether modern superficiality is brutally intolerant of maternal desire. *Our Mother's House* concerns a "lost tribe" of children, caught between the modern, "small-family" world, infantile over-severity (with dangers of a *Lord of the Flies* situation) and adult dissipation (with Dirk Bogarde somewhat reminiscent of *The Servant*). Its echoes of other films may do it injustice.

Several years and aborted projects later came *The Great Gatsby,* an ultra-lavish version of Scott Fitzgerald's tale of the lost love of a bootlegger turned socialite. It's a 1920s yuppie story, but its glitzy surfaces and characters even wispier than their originals acquire an icy, sarcophagal air. Almost as expensive, *Something Wicked This Way Comes,* from Ray Bradbury, about an eerie carnival touring lonely prairie towns to snare unsatisfied souls, evokes children's storybook illustrations, but proved a heavy commercial failure. *The Lonely Passion of Judith Hearne* reverted to more intimate and lacerating material—Brian Moore's novel of a genteel but alcoholic spinster (Maggie Smith) courted by an opportunist (Bob Hoskins) for the money he mistakenly thinks she has.

Clayton's "family trilogy" achieves a strange osmosis of 1940s "lyrical realism" and a more "calligraphic" sensitivity, of strong material and complicated interactions between profoundly different people. The resultant tensions between a central subjectivity and "the others," emphasise the dark, confused, painful gaps between minds. If the films border on the "absurdist" experience (Pinter adapted the Mortimer), they retain the richness of "traditional" themes and forms. Critics (and collaborators) keenly discussed shifts between Mortimer's first person narration and the camera as third person, and the relegation of Fitzgerald's narrator to onlooker status. Even in the lesser films, "shifting emphases" (between gloss and core in *Gatsby,* space and emotion in *Wicked*) repay re-seeing, and Clayton's combinations of fine literary material with a troubling temperament make powerful testimony to their time and to abiding human problems.—RAYMOND DURGNAT

Clément, René

Nationality *French.* **Born** *Bordeaux, 18 March 1913.* **Education** *Educated in architecture at Ecole des Beaux-Arts.* **Career** *Made animated film,* Cesar chez les Gaulois, *while a student, early 1930s; directed first live-action film,* Soigne ton gauche *(with Jacques Tati), 1936; made documentaries in Arabia and North Africa, 1936-39; technical consultant on Cocteau's* La Belle et la bête, *1946.* **Awards** *Best Director Award, Cannes festival, for* La Bataille du rail, *1946, and* Au-dela des grilles, *1949; Academy Awards, Best Foreign Film, for* Au delà des grilles Le Mura di Malapaga *(1949) and* Jeux interdits *(1951).* **Died** *17 March 1996.*

Films as Director: 1936: *Soigne ton gauche* (short). **1937:** *L'Arabie interdite* (short). **1938:** *La Grande Chartreuse* (short). **1939:** *La Bièvre, fille perdue* (short). **1940:** *Le Triage* (short). **1942:** *Ceux du rail* (short). **1943:** *La Grande Pastorale* (short). **1944:** *Chefs de demain* (short). **1945:** *La Bataille du rail* (*Battle of the Rails*) (+sc). **1946:** *Le Père tranquille* (*Mr. Orchid*). **1947:** *Les Maudits* (*The Damned*) (+co-adapt). **1948:** *Au-delà des grilles Le Mura di Malapaga* (*The Walls of Malapaga*). **1950:** *Le Chateau de verre* (+co-sc). **1951:** *Les Jeux interdits* (*Forbidden Games*) (+co-sc). **1954:** *Monsieur Ripois* (*Knave of Hearts*); *Lovers, Happy Lovers* (+co-sc). **1956:** *Gervais.* **1958:** *Barrage contre le Pacifique* (*La Diga sul Pacifico*); *This Angry Age; The Sea Wall* (+co-sc). **1959:** *Plein soleil* (*Purple Noon; Lust for Evil*) (+co-sc). **1961:** *Che gioia vivere* (*Quelle joie de vivre*) (+co-sc). **1962:** *Le Jour et l'heure* (*The Day and the Hour*) (+co-sc). **1964:** *Les Félins* (*Joy House*); *The Love Cage* (+co-sc). **1966:** *Paris brûle-t-il?* (*Is Paris Burning?*). **1969:** *Le Passager de la pluie* (*Rider on the Rain*). **1971:** *La Maison sous les arbres* (*The Deadly Trap*). **1972:** *La Course du lièvre à travers les champs* (*And Hope To Die*). **1975:** *Jeune fille libre et soir* (*The Babysitter*).

René Clément was the most promising filmmaker to emerge in France at the end of World War II. He became the most technically adroit and interesting of the makers of "quality" films during the 1950s, only to see his career begin to disappoint the critics. In the years of the New Wave it was Clément, above all, who tied the older generation to the younger, especially through a film like *Purple Noon*. In a more recent phase he was associated with grand-scale dramas (*Is Paris Burning?*) and with small, personal, lyric films (*Rider on the Rain*).

Clément began his career auspiciously, helping Cocteau with *Beauty and the Beast* and directing France's only great resistance film, *La Bataille du rail*. These films showed the world his wide range. The first is a classic of fantasy while the second exhibits what can only be termed a "neo-realist" style. Because *La Bataille du rail* was shot on location with non-actors, and because its episodic story was drawn from the chronicle of everyday life, Clément, at the end of the war, was championed as France's answer to the powerful Italian school of the liberation.

For a time Clément seemed anxious to live up to this reputation. He associated himself with the progressive journal *L'Ecran francais* and sought other realist topics for his films. In *Les Maudits* he observed the plight of a group of Germans and refugees aboard a submarine. Evidently he was more concerned with the technical problems of filming in small spaces than with the moral dimensions of his plot, and this film was not a great success. But with *The Walls of Malapaga* Clément recovered his audience. This film, which won the Academy Award for best foreign film, was in fact a Franco-Italian co-production and brought together on the screen the

René Clement.
Photograph Stephane Fefer.

most popular star of each country: Jean Gabin and Isa Miranda. The plot and style returned Clément to the poetic-realist films of pre-war France and continued to exhibit that tension of realism and abstraction that characterized all his work.

Unquestionably he was, along with Claude Autant-Lara, the most important figure in the French film industry during the 1950s. His *Forbidden Games* remains a classic today and is notable both for the ingenuous performances of his child actors against a natural location and for the moral incisiveness of its witty plot and dialogue, scripted by the team of Aurenche and Bost. Doubtless because he had begun working with these writers, Truffaut condemned Clément in his notorious 1954 essay, "A Certain Tendency in French Cinema," but Bazin, commenting on this essay, found Truffaut to have been too harsh in Clément's case. Indeed Bazin lobbied to have the Cannes Film Festival award its Golden Palm to Clément's next feature, *Monsieur Ripois*. Starring Gérard Philipe, this film makes extensive use of subjective camera and voice over. Shot on location in London, it is clearly an experimental project.

But Clément's experiments are always limited. Technical problems continue to interest him, but he has never relinquished his belief that a film must be well-crafted in the traditional sense of that term. This is what must always distinguish him from the New Wave filmmakers with whom he otherwise has something in common. His all-knowing pessimism, and his literary good taste, finally put him in the camp of the "quality" directors.

Clément, then, must be thought of as consummately French. His technical mastery sits well with his advanced political and moral ideas. He is cultured and trained. He makes excellent films both on a grand scale and on a smaller, more personal one. But finally there is something impersonal about even these small films, for, before representing himself, René Clément represents the institution of filmmaking in France. He is a good representative, perhaps the best it had after the war right up through the New Wave.—DUDLEY ANDREW

Clouzot, Henri-Georges

Nationality French. *Born* Niort, 20 November 1907. *Education* Ecole Navale, Brest. *Family* Married Vera Amado Gibson, 1950 (died 1960). *Career* As reporter for Paris-Midi, offered job in film industry while interviewing Adolphe Osso, 1930; assistant to Carmine Gallone, Anatole Litvak, and others, 1930-34; contracted pleurisy, confined to sanatoriums, 1934-38; reentered film industry as writer, 1938; directed first film,

L'Assassin habite au 21, *1942.* **Awards** *Best Director, Venice Festival, for* Quai des Orfèvres, *1947; Grand Prix, Cannes Festival, for* Le Salaire de la peur, *1953; Prix Louis Delluc, for* Les Diaboliques, *1955; Jury Prize, Cannes Festival, for* Le Mystère Picasso, *1956; Oscar for Best Foreign Film, for* La Vérité, *1960.* **Died** *12 January 1977.*

Films as Director: 1931: *La Terreur des Batignolles* (short). **1942:** *L'Assassin habite au vingt-et-un* (+co-sc). **1943:** *Le Corbeau* (+co-sc). **1947:** *Quai des Orfèvres* (+co-sc). **1948:** *Manon* (+co-sc). **1949:** "Le Retour de Jean" in *Retour à la vie* (+co-sc); *Miquette et sa mère* (+co-sc). **1952:** *Le Salaire de la peur* (+sc). **1954:** *Les Diaboliques* (+co-sc). **1955:** *Les Espions* (+co-sc). **1956:** *Le Mystère Picasso.* **1960:** *La Vérité* (+sc). **1968:** *La Prisonnière* (+sc).

Other Films: 1931: *Ma Cousine de Varsovie* (Gallone) (co-sc); *Un Soir de Rafle* (Gallone) (adaptation); *Je serai seule après minuit* (de Baroncelli) (co-sc): *Le Chanteur inconnu* (Tourjansky) (co-adapt). **1932:** *Le Roi des palaces* (Gallone) (co-sc); *Le Dernier Choc* (de Baroncelli) (co-sc); *La Chanson d'une nuit* (French language version of Anatole Litvak's *Das Lied einer Nacht*) (co-adapt, dialogue); *Faut-il les marier?* (French version of Carl Lamac's *Die grausame Freundin*, co-d with Pierre Billon) (adapt, dialogue). **1933:** *Caprice de princesse* (French version of Karl Hartl's *Ihre Durchlacht, die Verkäuferin*) (adapt, assoc d, ed, sc); *Chateau de rêve* (French version of Geza von Bolvary's *Das Schloss im Süden*) (sc, adapt, assoc d, ed); *Tout pour l'amour* (French version of Joe May's *Ein Lied für dich*) (sc, adapt, co-dialogue, lyrics, assoc d). **1934:** *Itto d'Afrique* (Benoit-Lévy) (lyrics). **1938:** *Le Révolté* (Mathot) (co-sc, lyrics, dialogue). **1939:** *Le Duel* (Fresnay) (co-sc, lyrics, dialogue); *Le Monde tremblera* (*La Révolté des vivants*) (Pottier) (co-sc, lyrics, dialogue). **1941:** *Le Dernier des six* (Lacombe) (lyrics, dialogue); *Les Inconnus dans la maison* (Decoin) (co-adapt, lyrics, dialogue). **1955:** *Si tous les gars du monde . . .* (Christian-Jaque) (co-adapt).

In a country like France where good taste is so admired, Henri-Georges Clouzot has been a shocking director. A film critic during the age of surrealism, Clouzot was always eager to assault his audience with his style and concerns.

Henri-Georges Clouzot: *Les Diaboliques*

Like so many others, Clouzot found his chance to move from scriptwriting to directing during the Occupation, a time when there was a paucity of directors in France. His first effort, *L'Assassin habite au 21,* was a safe film. Its script followed two similar films he had written which had been well-received by audiences. These witty police dramas were exercises in style and cleverness, befitting the epoch. *Le Corbeau,* made the next year, was in contrast a shattering film, unquestionably hitting hard at the society of the war years. Retaining all the conventions of the thriller, Clouzot systematically exposed the physical and psychological grotesqueries of every character in the film. A grim picture of small-town mores, *Le Corbeau* was condemned by the Nazis and French patriots alike.

When the war ended Clouzot found himself barred from the industry for two years by the "purification committee," an industry-appointed watchdog group that self-righteously judged complicity with the Germans. Clouzot's crime was to have made films for a German-financed company, though he was officially arraigned on charges of having maligned the French character and having demoralized the country during its dark hours. But even at this time many critics claimed that *Le Corbeau* was the only authentically engaged film made during the entire Occupation.

When he did resume his career, Clouzot's grim view of life had not improved. Both *Quai des Orfèvres* and his 1948 adaptation of *Manon* emulated American film noir with their lowlife settings. Both are extremely well acted, but ultimately small works.

Clouzot's fame in the United States came in the mid-1950s when *The Wages of Fear* and *Diabolique* gave him a reputation as a French Hitchcock, interested in the mechanics of suspense. In France, however, these films, especially *Diabolique,* were seen as only well-made studio products. His 1960 *La Vérité,* starring Brigitte Bardot, was designed to win him favor in the youth culture of the time, which was obsessed by New Wave life and movies. While the film outgrossed its New Wave competition, its cloyingly paternalistic style showed how far Clouzot was from the spontaneity of the New Wave. The cafe scenes in the film are insincere, and the inevitable indictment of society rings false.

All of Clouzot's films, even up to the 1968 *La Prisonnière* were financial successes, but in the end he ceased being the instrumental force in the film industry he had been twenty years earlier.—DUDLEY ANDREW

Cocteau, Jean

Nationality French. *Born* Maisons-Lafitte, near Paris, 5 July 1889. *Education* Lycée Condorcet and Fenelon, Paris. *Career* Actor, playwright, poet, librettist, novelist, painter and graphic artist in 1920s and throughout career. Directed first film, Le Sang d'un poète, 1930; became manager of boxer Al Brown, 1937; remained in Paris during the Occupation, 1940. *Awards* Chevalier de la Légion d'honneur, 1949; member, Academie Royale de Belgique, 1955; member, Academie Française, 1955; honorary doctorate, Oxford University, 1956. *Died* In Milly-la-Foret, France, 11 October 1963.

Films as Director: **1925:** *Jean Cocteau fait du cinéma* (+sc) (neg lost?). **1930:** *Le Sang d'un poète* (originally *La Vie d'un poète*) (+ed, sc, voice-over). **1946:** *La Belle et la bête* (+sc). **1947:** *L'Aigle à deux têtes* (+sc). **1948:** *Les Parent terribles* (+sc, voice-over). **1950:** *Orphée* (+sc); *Coriolan* (+sc, role); a 1914 "dramatic scene" by Cocteau included in *Ce siècle a cinquante ans* (Tual) (+sc). **1952:** *La Villa Santo-Sospir* (+sc). **1960:** *Le Testament d'Orphée* (*Ne me demandez pas pourquoi*) (+sc, role as le poète).

Other Films: 1940: *La Comedie du bonheur* (L'Herbier) (co-sc). **1942:** *Le Baron fantôme* (de Poligny) (sc, role as Le Baron). **1943:** *L'Eternel Retour* (Delannoy) (sc); *La Malibran* (Guitry) (narration + role as Alfred de Musset). **1945:** *Les Dames du Bois de Boulogne* (Bresson) (co-sc). **1946:** *L'Amitie noire* (Villiers and Krull) (role and narration). **1947:** *Ruy Blas* (Billon) (sc). **1948:** *La Voix humaine* (Rossellini, from Cocteau's play); *Les Noces de sable* (Zvoboda) (sc, voice-over); *La Légende de Sainte Ursule* (Emmer) (role and narration). **1949:** *Tennis* (Martin) (role +narration). **1950:** *Les Enfants terribles* (Melville) (sc); *Colette* (Bellon) (role +narration); *Venise et ses amants* (Emmer and Gras) (role +narration). **1951:** *Desordre* (Baratier) (role +narration). **1952:** *La Couronne noire* (Saslavski) (co-sc); *8x8* (Richter) (role +narration). **1953:** *Le Rouge est mis* (Barrère and Knapp) (role +narration). **1956:** *A l'aube d'un monde* (Lucot) (role +narration); *Pantomimes* (Lucot) (role +narration). **1957:** *Le Bel indifferent* (Demy, from Cocteau's play). **1958:** *Django Reinhardt* (Paviot) (role +narration); *Le Musée Grevin* (Demy and Masson) (role +narration). **1959:** *Charlotte et son Jules* (Godard, from same play as Demy 1957 film). **1961:** *La Princesse de Cleves* (Delannoy) (co-sc). **1963:** *Anna la bonne* (Jutra, from song by Cocteau). **1965:** *Thomas l'imposteur* (Franju) (co-sc). **1970:** *La Voix humaine* (Delouche, from Poulenc and Cocteau opera).

Jean Cocteau's contribution to cinema is as eclectic as one would expect from a man who fulfilled on occasion the roles of poet and novelist, dramatist and graphic artist, and dabbled in such diverse media as ballet and sculpture. In addition to his directorial efforts, Cocteau also wrote scripts and dialogue, made acting appearances, and realized amateur films. His work in other media has inspired adaptations by a number of filmmakers ranging from Rossellini to Franju and Demy, and he himself published several collections of eclectic and stimulating thoughts on the film medium.

Though Cocteau took his first real steps as a filmmaker at the very beginning of the sound era, his period of greatest involvement was in the 1940s, when he contributed to the scripts of a half-dozen films, at times dominating his director (as in *L'Eternel Retour*), at other times submitting to the discipline of contributing to another's vision (as in his dialogue for Bresson's *Les Dames du Bois de Boulogne*). In addition, he directed his own adaptations of such diverse works as the fairy tale *La Belle et la bête,* his own period melodrama *L'Aigle à deux têtes,* and his intense domestic drama, *Les Parents terribles.*

But Cocteau's essential work in cinema is contained in just three wholly original films in which he explores his personal myth of the poet as Orpheus: *Le Sang d'un poète, Orphée,* and *Le Testament d'Orphée.* Though made over a period of thirty years, these three works have a remarkable unity of inspiration. They are works of fascination in a double sense. They convey Cocteau's fascination with poetry and his own creative processes, and at the same time display his

Jean Cocteau

openness to all the ways of fascinating an audience, utilizing stars and trickery, found material and sheer fantasy. The tone is characterized by a unique mixture of reality and dream, and his definition of *Le Sang d'un pòete* as "a realistic documentary of unreal events" is a suitable description of all his finest work.

Crucial to the lasting quality of Cocteau's work, which at times seems so light and fragile, is the combination of artistic seriousness and persistent, but unemphatic, self-mockery. For this reason his enclosed universe, with its curiously idyllic preoccupation with death, is never oppressive or constricting; instead, it allows the spectator a freedom rare in mainstream cinema of the 1930s and 1940s. In technical terms Cocteau displays a similar ability to cope with the contributions of totally professional collaborators, while still retaining a disarming air of ingenuousness, which has sometimes been wrongly characterized as amateurism.

Reviled by the Surrealists as a literary poseur in the 1920s and 1930s and distrusted as an amateur in the 1940s, Cocteau nonetheless produced films of lasting quality. In retrospect he is to be admired for the freedom with which he expressed a wholly personal vision and for his indifference to the given rules of a certain period of French "quality" filmmaking. He was one of the few French filmmakers of the past to whom the directors of the New Wave could turn for inspiration, and it is totally fitting that Cocteau's farewell to cinema, *Le Testament d'Orphée*, should have been produced by one of the most talented of these newcomers, François Truffaut.—ROY ARMES

Coen, Joel

Nationality American. Born Minneapolis, 1955. Education Attended Simon's Rock College, Massachusetts, and New York University. Family Married actress Frances McDormand. Career Worked as an assistant film editor on Fear No Evil *and* Evil Dead; *collaborated on screenplays with brother Ethan Coen (b. 1958); with Ethan produced first film,* Blood Simple, *1984. Awards Grand Jury Prize, U.S. Film Festival, for* Blood Simple, *1984; Best Director Award, Cannes Film Festival, for* Barton Fink, *1991; Best Screenplay Oscar, for* Fargo, *1996. Address c/o UTA, 9560 Wilshire Blvd., Suite 500, Beverly Hills, California 90212, U.S.A.*

Films as Director and Co-scriptwriter (All co-written and produced by brother, Ethan Coen):
1984: *Blood Simple* (+ed as Roderick Jaynes). **1987:** *Raising Arizona.* **1990:** *Miller's Crossing.* **1991:** *Barton Fink* (+ed as Roderick Jaynes). **1994:** *The Hudsucker Proxy.* **1996:** *Fargo* (+ed as Roderick Jaynes). **1997:** *The Big Lebowski.*

Other Films: 1981: *Fear No Evil* (asst ed). **1982:** *The Evil Dead* (*Into the Woods; Book of the Dead*) (asst ed). **1985:** *Crimewave* (*Broken Hearts and Noses; The XYZ Murders*) (sc).

Although Joel Coen had worked as an assistant film editor on commercial projects and had made valuable contacts within the industry (particularly director Sam Raimi), he and brother Ethan decided to produce their first feature film independently, raising $750,000 to shoot their jointly written script for *Blood Simple,* a neo-noir thriller with a Dashiell Hammett title and a script full of homages to Jim Thompson. Though Joel received screen credit for direction and Ethan for the script, this distinction is somewhat artificial both here and in their subsequent productions. Joel and Ethan co-write their scripts and meticulously prepare storyboards in a collaborative effort unusual for the American cinema (the closest analogy perhaps comes from abroad with the British team of Powell and Pressburger).

Blood Simple was hardly the first film the brothers Coen made together. Addicted to TV and movies at an early age, they spent a good deal of their childhood writing films and then shooting them on a Super-8 camera. Movie brats in the Spielberg tradition, Ethan and Joel desired commercial success but were determined to retain control over what they produced. Hence their initial decision to make an independent film rather than continue working in an industry where Joel was already beginning to be established.

A hit with many on the art film/independent circuit but also a commercial success in art house and cable release, *Blood Simple* was the perfect choice to achieve this aim. Here was a film that succeeded because of its individual, even quirky vision. Using the film noir conventions popular with American audiences for half a century, the Coens offer a clear narrative, solidly

Joel (right) and Ethan Coen

two-dimensional characters, and the requisite amount of riveting violent spectacle (including one scene that pictures a dying man buried alive and another featuring close-ups of a white-gloved hand suddenly impaled by a knife). *Blood Simple,* however, is by no means an ordinary thriller. The plot turns expertly and unexpectedly on a number of dramatic ironies (no character knows what the spectator does, and even the spectator is sometimes taken by surprise). Unlike hardboiled narrative à la Raymond Chandler, the narrative delights in its Aristotelian neatness, in its depiction of experiences that make perfect sense, climaxing in a poetic justice that the main character and narrator, a venal private detective, finds humorous even as it destroys him. Thematically, the Coens offer a compelling analysis of *mauvaise foi* in the Sartrean vein as they develop characters doomed by bad intentions or a failure to trust and communicate (an existentialist theme that results perhaps from the fact that Ethan majored in philosophy at Princeton). *Blood Simple*'s most notable feature, however, is an expressive stylization of both sound and image that creates an experiential correlative for the viewer of the characters' confusion and disorientation. These effects are achieved by a Wellesian repertoire of tricks (wide-angle lenses, tracking set-ups, unusual framings, an artfully selected score of popular music, etc.). The film noir genre naturalizes this stylization to some degree, but *Blood Simple* exudes a riotous self-consciousness, a delight in the creation of an exciting cinema that offers moments of pure visceral or visual pleasure.

Though some critics thought *Blood Simple* a kind of pointless film-school exercise, audiences were impressed—as were the major studios who competed for releasing rights to the brothers' next project. The Coens' subsequent films have all been made with substantial commercial backing; but these films continue to be independent in the sense that none fits into the routine categories of contemporary Hollywood production. In fact, the art cinema tradition of the seventies has been kept alive by the Coens and the few other mavericks (e.g., Quentin Tarantino) who have emerged to prominence.

The least successful of these films—*Miller's Crossing*—is the most traditional. A "realistic" drama (though the scenes of violence are highly stylized) with a well-developed plot line, this saga of Prohibition-era mobsters, like Scorsese's *Goodfellas* (released the year before), aims to debunk the romantic tradition of the gangster film most tellingly exemplified by *The Godfather* (1972). The central character, a "good guy" high up in the organization, confusingly seems more a victim of his poor circumstances than a force to be reckoned with. The plot is otherwise dependent upon unbelievable characters and unlikely twists and turns. Some elements of parody are present, but are not well integrated into the film's structure, indicating that the Coens were uncertain about how to proceed, whether to make a gangster film or send up the conventions of the genre.

The other films share a different representational regime, a magical realism that does not demand verisimilitude or logical closure, but has the virtue—for the Coens—of permitting more stylization, more moments of pure cinema. *Raising Arizona* and *The Hudsucker Proxy* offer postmodern versions of the traditional Hollywood madcap comedy; in both films, a series of zany adventures climax in romantic happiness for the male and female leads. *Raising Arizona* concerns the ultimately unsuccessful attempt of a zany and childless couple to kidnap a baby; *The Hudsucker Proxy* sends up, in mock Capra-corn style, the triumph of the virtuous, if obtuse, hero over the evil system that attempts to use him for its own purposes. *Barton Fink,* in contrast, is a darker story, heavily indebted to German Expressionism (an influence to be noted as well in the elaborately artificial sets and unnaturalistic acting of *The Hudsucker Proxy*). The film's main character is a thirties stereotype, a left-wing Jewish playwright committed to representing the miseries of what he calls "the common man." Hired away from Broadway by a Hollywood studio, he embarks unwittingly on a penitential journey that lays bare the forces of the id both in the apparently common man he meets (a salesman who is actually a serial killer) and in himself (abandoning his writing responsibility, he finds himself at film's end at the beach with the beautiful woman whose picture he first saw in a calendar).

All three of these films abound in bravura stylizations. A man dives out a skyscraper window and the camera traces the stages of his fall (*Hudsucker*); a baby's meanderings across the floor are captured by a camera literally at floor level (an elaborate mirror shot in *Arizona*); wallpaper peels off a hotel room wall revealing something warm and gooey like human flesh underneath (*Barton Fink*); exaggerated sounds—a mosquito's flight, a noisy bed, a whirling fan—perfectly express the main character's self-absorption and anxiety (*Barton Fink* again).

With *Fargo,* their 1996 release, the Coen brothers return to the crime drama. Set primarily in Minnesota, the film follows an immensely likable and very pregnant sheriff (played by Frances McDormand, Joel Coen's wife) as she pursues a couple of dimwitted and cold-blooded kidnappers. A macabre thriller veined with moments of comedy, *Fargo* features the Coen brothers' trademark cinematic flair (though the landscape mutes this somewhat) and intelligent narrative focus.

The Coens appear to have abandoned for good the stylized realism and Aristotelian narrative that made *Blood Simple* such a success. But in an era that has witnessed the commercial success of cartoonish anti-naturalism (*Dick Tracy,* the Batman films), their concern with striking visual and aural effects may provide the basis for a long career, though difficult films like *Barton Fink,* despite critical acclaim, will never gain a wide audience.—R. BARTON PALMER

Coppola, Francis Ford

Nationality American. *Born* Detroit, Michigan, 7 April 1939. *Education* Hofstra University, B.A., 1959; University of California, Los Angeles, M.F.A. in cinema, 1967. *Family* Married Eleanor Neil, 1963; children: Sophia, Giancarlo (died, 1987), Roman. *Career* Worked in various capacities for Roger Corman at American International, 1962-64; director for Seven Arts, 1964-68; founder, American Zoetrope production organization, San Francisco, 1969; director for American Conservatory Theatre and San Francisco Opera Company, 1971-72; founder, with Peter Bogdanovich and William Friedkin, Directors Company, 1972; publisher, City magazine, 1975-76; opened Zoëtrope Studios, San Francisco, 1980. *Awards* Oscar for Best Screenplay (with Edmund H. North), for Patton, 1970; Oscar for Best Screenplay (with Mario Puzo), and Best Director Award, Directors Guild of America, for The Godfather, 1973; Palme d'or, Cannes Festival, for The Conversation, 1974; Oscars for Best Director and Best Screenplay (with Puzo) for The Godfather, Part II, 1975; Palme d'or and FIPRESCI Prize, Cannes Festival, 1979, for Apocalypse Now, 1979. *Address* Zoëtrope Studios, 916 Kearny Street, San Francisco, California 94133, U.S.A.

Films as Director and Scriptwriter: **1962:** *The Playgirls and the Bellboy* (co-d, co-sc); *Tonight for Sure* (+pr); **1963:** *The Terror* (*Lady of the Shadows*) (co-d, +assoc pr); *Dementia 13* (*The Haunted and*

the Hunted) (co-sc). **1966:** *You're a Big Boy Now.* **1968:** *Finian's Rainbow* (d only). **1969:** *The Rain People.* **1972:** *The Godfather* (co-sc). **1974:** *The Conversation* (+pr); *The Godfather, Part II* (co-sc, +co-pr). **1979:** *Apocalypse Now* (co-sc, +pr, role, co-mus). **1982:** *One from the Heart* (co-sc, +pr). **1983:** *The Outsiders* (+pr); *Rumble Fish* (co-sc, +pr). **1984:** *The Cotton Club* (co-sc). **1986:** *Peggy Sue Got Married* (+pr); *Captain Eo.* **1987:** *Gardens of Stone* (+pr). **1988:** *Tucker: The Man and His Dream* (+pr). **1989:** episode 2 in *New York Stories.* **1991:** *The Godfather, Part III.* **1992:** *Bram Stoker's Dracula* (+co-pr). **1996:** *Jack* (+pr). **1997:** *The Rainmaker.* **1998:** *On the Road* (d only).

Other Films: 1962: *The Premature Burial* (Corman) (asst-d); *Tower of London* (dialogue d); *The Magic Voyage of Sinbad* (adaptor). **1963:** *The Young Racers* (Corman) (sound, 2nd unit ph—uncredited); *Battle Beyond the Sun* (Corman) (sc). **1966:** *This Property Is Condemned* (Pollack) (co-sc); *Is Paris Burning?* (*Paris brûle-t-il?*) (Clément) (co-sc). **1967:** *Reflections in a Golden Eye* (Huston) (sc). **1970:** *Patton* (Schaffner) (co-sc). **1971:** *THX 1138* (Lucas) (exec pr). **1973:** *American Graffiti* (Lucas) (exec pr). **1974:** *The Great Gatsby* (Clayton) (sc). **1979:** *The Black Stallion* (Ballard) (exec pr). **1982:** *Hammett* (Wenders) (exec pr); *The Escape Artist* (Deschanel) (exec pr). **1983:** *The Black Stallion Returns* (Dalva) (exec pr). **1985:** *Mishima: A Life in Four Chapters* (Schrader) (exec pr). **1987:** *Tough Guys Don't Dance* (Mailer) (exec pr). **1992:** *Wind* (exec pr). **1993:** *The Secret Garden* (exec pr). **1994:** *Mary Shelley's Frankenstein* (co-pr). **1995:** *My Family, Mi Familia* (exec pr); *Haunted* (exec pr); *Don Juan DeMarco* (pr). **1996:** *Dark Angel* (exec pr) (for TV); *Marlon Brando: The Wild One* (role) (for TV). **1997:** *Buddy* (exec pr); *The Odyssey* (exec pr) (for TV).

Francis Ford Coppola became the first major American film director to emerge from a university degree program in filmmaking. He received his Master of Cinema degree from UCLA in 1968, after submitting his first film of consequence, *You're a Big Boy Now* (1967), a free-wheeling comedy about a young man on the brink of manhood, to the university as his master's thesis.

The Rain People (1969), based on an original scenario of his own, followed in due course. The plot of this tragic drama concerns a depressed housewife who impulsively decides to walk out on her family one rainy morning to make a cross-country trek in her station wagon, in the hope of getting some perspective on her life. For the first time Coppola's overriding theme, which centers on the importance of the role of a family spirit in people's lives, is clearly delineated in one of his films.

Coppola's preoccupation with the importance of family in modern society is brought into relief in his *Godfather* films, which depict an American family over a period of more than seventy years. Indeed, the thing that most attracted him to the project in the first place was the fact that the best-selling book on which the films are based is really the story of a family. It is about "this father and his sons," he says, "and questions of power and succession." In essence, *The Godfather* (1972) offers a chilling depiction of the way in which young Michael Corleone's loyalty to his flesh-and-blood family gradually turns into an allegiance to the larger Mafia family to which they in turn belong—a devotion that in the end renders him a cruel and ruthless mass murderer. With this film Coppola definitely hit his stride as a filmmaker, and the picture was an enormous critical and popular success.

The Godfather II (1974) treats events that happened before and after the action covered in the first film. The second *Godfather* movie not only chronicles Michael's subsequent career as head of the "family business," but also presents, in flashback, the early life of his father in Sicily, as well as his rise to power in the Mafia in New York City's Little Italy. *The Godfather II,* like *The Godfather,* was a success both with the critics and the public, and Coppola won Oscars for directing the film, co-authoring the screenplay, and co-producing the best picture of the year. In

1990 he made his third *Godfather* film. This trilogy of movies, taken together, represents one of the supreme achievements of the cinematic art.

In contrast to epic films like the *Godfather* series, *The Outsiders* was conceived on a smaller scale; it revolves around a gang of underprivileged teenage boys growing up in Tulsa, Oklahoma, in the 1960s. *The Outsiders* was a box-office hit, as was *Peggy Sue Got Married,* a remarkable fantasy. The title character is a woman approaching middle age who passes out at a high-school reunion and wakes up back in high school in 1960. But she brings with her on her trip down memory lane a forty-two-year-old mind, and hence views things from a more mature perspective than she possessed the first time around.

Francis Ford Coppola on the set of *Jack*. Photograph by Merrick Morton.

Coppola has made two films about the Vietnam War. *Apocalypse Now,* the first major motion picture about the war, is a king-sized epic shot on location in the Philippines; and it contains some of the most extraordinary combat footage ever filmed. But there are no such stunning battle sequences in its companion film, *Gardens of Stone,* since it takes place state-side, and is concerned with the homefront during the same period.

His next subject was a biographical film about Preston Tucker, a maverick automobile designer, entitled *Tucker: The Man and His Dream.* Coppola contends that Tucker developed plans for a car that was way ahead of its time in terms of engineering; yet the auto industry at large stubbornly resisted his ideas. Unfortunately, Coppola comments, creative people do not always get a chance to exercise their creativity.

Coppola demonstrated once more that he had mastered his craft in making *Bram Stoker's Dracula*. In it he created a more faithful rendering of the Stoker novel than had been the case with previous film versions of the celebrated horror tale, and the film turned out to be a huge critical and popular success.

Francis Coppola is one creative person who has continued to exercise his considerable talent throughout his career. Admittedly, he has had his occasional failure, such as the off-center teen movie *Rumble Fish* (1983). But the majority of the films he has directed over the years have demonstrated that he is one of the most gifted directors to come across the Hollywood horizon since Stanley Kubrick.

Coppola himself observes that he looks upon the movies he has directed in the past as providing him with the sort of experience that will help him to make better films in the future. So the only thing for a filmmaker to do, he concludes, is to just keep going.—GENE D. PHILLIPS

Costa-Gavras, Constantin

Nationality *French.* **Born** *Konstantinos Gavras in Athens, Greece, on February 13, 1933 (naturalized French citizen, 1956).* **Education** *Sorbonne, Paris, and Institut des Hautes Etudes Cinématographiques.* **Family** *Married Michèle Ray, 1968, one son, one daughter.* **Career** *Ballet dancer in Greece, then moved to Paris, 1952; assistant to Yves Allegret, René Clair, René Clément, Henri Verneuil, and Jacques Demy, 1958-65; directed first film,* Compartiment tueurs, *1966; became president of the Cinematheque Francais, 1982.* **Awards** *Moscow Film Festival Prize for* Un Homme de trop; *Best Director, New York Film Critics Award, and Jury Prize, Cannes Festival, for* Z, *1970; Oscar nominations for Best Director and Best Screenplay, for* Z, *1970; Louis Delluc Prize for* State of Siege, *1973; Best Director Award, Cannes Festival, for* Special Section, *1975; Palme d'or, Cannes Festival, 1982, and Oscar for Best Screenplay (with Donald Stewart), for* Missing, *1983; ACLUF Award for* Betrayed, *1988.* **Agent** *John Ptak, William Morris Agency, 151 El Camino Drive, Beverly Hills, California 90212, U.S.A.*

Films as Director and Scriptwriter: 1966: *Compartiment tueurs* (*The Sleeping Car Murders*). **1968:** *Un Homme de trop* (*Shock Troops*). **1969:** *Z* (co-sc). **1970:** *L'Aveu* (*The Confession*). **1973:** *Etat de siège* (*State of Siege*) (co-sc). **1975:** *Section speciale* (*Special Section*) (co-sc). **1979:** *Clair de femme* (*Womanlight; Die Liebe einer Frau*). **1982:** *Missing* (co-sc). **1983:** *Hanna K* (co-sc, +pr). **1985:** *Le Conseil de famille* (*Family Business*). **1988:** *Summer Lightning* (*Sundown*); *Betrayed* (d only). **1990:** *Music Box* (d only). **1991:** *Contre l'oubli* (*Against Oblivion*). **1993:** *La Petite Apocalypse* (*The Minor Apocalypse*) (co-sc). **1995:** *Les kankobals,* episode in *A propos de Nice, la suite; Lumière et compagnie* (*Lumière and Company*). **1997:** *Mad City.*

Other Films: 1977: *La Vie devant soi* (*Madame Rosa*) (Mizrahi) (role as Ramon). **1985:** *Spies Like Us* (Landis) (role as Tadzhik); *Thé au harem d'Archimede* (*Tea in the Harem*) (sc).

The films of Constantin Costa-Gavras are exciting, enthralling, superior examples of dramatic moviemaking, but the filmmaker is far from being solely concerned with keeping the viewer in suspense. A Greek exile when he made *Z,* set in the country of his birth, Costa-Gavras is most interested in the motivations and misuses of power: politically, he may be best described as an anti-fascist, a humanist. As such, his films are as overtly political as any above-ground, internationally popular and respected filmmaker in history.

Costa-Gavras's scenarios are often based on actual events in which citizens are deprived of human rights and expose the hypocrisies of governments to both the left and right of center. In *Z,* Greek pacifist leader Yves Montand is killed by a speeding truck, a death ruled accidental by the police. Journalist Jean-Louis Trintignant's investigation leads to a right-wing reign of terror against witnesses and friends of the deceased, and to revelations of a government scandal. *The Confession* is the story of a Communist bureaucrat (Montand) who is unjustifiably tortured and coerced into giving false testimony against other guiltless comrades. *State of Siege* is based on the political kidnapping of a United States official in Latin America (Montand); the revolutionaries slowly discover the discreetly hidden function of this "special advisor"—to train native police in the intricacies of torture. In *Special Section,* a quartet of young Frenchmen are tried and condemned by an opportunistic Vichy government for the killing of a German naval officer in occupied Paris. In *Missing,* an idealistic young American writer (John Shea) is arrested, tortured, and killed in a fascist takeover of a Latin American country. His father, salt-of-the-earth businessman Jack Lemmon, first feels it's all a simple misunderstanding. After he realizes that he has been manipulated and lied to by the American embassy, he applies enough pressure and embarrasses enough people so that he can finally bring home the body of his son.

Despite these sobering, decidedly non-commercial storylines, Costa-Gavras has received popular as well as critical success, particularly with *Z* and *Missing,* because the filmmaker does not bore his audience by structuring his films in a manner that will appeal only to intellectuals. Instead, he casts popular actors with significant box office appeal. Apart from a collective message—that fascism and corruption may occur in any society anywhere in the world—Costa-Gavras's films also work as mysteries and thrillers. He has realized that he must first entertain in order to bring his point of view to a wider, more diversified audience, as well as exist and even thrive within the boundaries of motion picture economics in the West-

Constantin Costa-Gavras on the set of *Hanna K.*

ern world. As Pauline Kael so aptly noted, *Z* is "something very unusual in European films—a political film with a purpose and, at the same time, a thoroughly commercial film." Costa-Gavras, however, is not without controversy: *State of Siege* caused a furor when it was cancelled for political reasons from the opening program of the American Film Institute theater in Washington.

Not all of Costa-Gavras's features are "political": *The Sleeping Car Murders* is a well-made, atmospheric murder mystery, while *Clair de femme* is the dreary tale of a widower and a woman scarred by the death of her young daughter. Both of these films star Yves Montand. But while Costa-Gavras's most characteristic works do indeed condemn governments that control other governments or suppress human rights, his concerns as a filmmaker have perhaps shifted towards the more personal. The two features made with scriptwriter Joe Eszterhaus, *Betrayed* and *Music Box,* focused on the relationship between the central female character and a man (a lover in *Betrayed,* a father in *Music Box*) who is subsequently revealed as a fascist.

On further review, both *Betrayed* and *Music Box* prove to be deeply flawed films. Both are set in America, and spotlight quintessentially American characters: an all-American farmer and an up-by-the-bootstraps immigrant. Yet both reveal deeply prejudicial, preconceived notions about the essence of the American character.

Betrayed covers a difficult, explosive topic: Racism and white supremacy in mainstream America. Gary Simmons (Tom Berenger) is a Vietnam war hero and widowed farmer who, outwardly at least, is a likable, salt-of-the-earth American. His mother is the type whose apple pies win blue ribbons at county fairs. His two kids, a boy and a girl, are fine, well-behaved youngsters. On the Fourth of July, this family joins with its neighbors for an afternoon of picnicking and an evening of fireworks.

Yet underneath this picture-perfect view of Main Street lies something warped and sinister. Through changing times and economic realities beyond their understanding and control, Gary and those like him have been losing their farms and their way of life. This powerlessness has been translated into a violent, horrific extremism. Gary—and, it is implied, thousands of others like him—has become a clandestine terrorist. He spouts the gospel that "the Jews are running the country." He claims that blacks are not human, but rather "mud people." In a sequence that is among the most jarring of any movie of the late 1980s, he and his cronies hunt down and kill a black man strictly for sport. Most disturbing of all, Gary's sweet, cuddly daughter repeats what she's learned from her father. On to the scene comes a government investigator (Debra Winger), posing as an itinerant farm laborer. Before she is certain of his true nature, she finds herself becoming involved with him sexually and romantically.

Betrayed is ultimately an outsider's view of the American heartland and the Vietnam veteran. While Gary and his ilk objectify blacks, Jews, Asians, and gays, Costa-Gavras and screenwriter Joe Eszterhaus are equally as guilty of objectifying white midwesterners. The film would lead you to believe that every last American farmer is a closet cross-burner. And Gary Simmons, a psycho in sheep's clothing, is yet one more superficial celluloid Vietnam veteran.

In *Music Box,* Armin Mueller-Stahl takes on the Berenger role: a Hungarian-immigrant father accused of horrible war crimes and thus faces deportation. Jessica Lange plays his devoted attorney daughter who defends him in a high-profile trial. Of course, the sweet old man eventually is shown to be guilty as charged. The generalization here is that all working-class immigrants hold equally sinister views, and equally clandestine pasts.

La Petite Apocalypse (The Minor Apocalypse), is a decidedly minor affair, a satire of 1960s radicals, capitalist greed, the demise of communism, and an overzealous media. It premiered in New York in 1995 not on a theatrical run, but as the opening film in the Sixth Annual Human Rights Watch International Film Festival.

Costa-Gavras was one of 40 filmmakers who took part in *Lumière and Company,* a collaborative project that celebrated the 100th anniversary of film. The actual movie camera first developed by the Lumière brothers, the Cinematograph, was restored and each of the directors used it to film tiny vignettes, constrained mostly by the capabilities of the machine. Filming was comprised of a single shot that could not exceed 52 seconds; only three takes were allowed; and no artificial lighting or synchronous soundtrack could be used. These were interspersed with segments of interviews with the various directors. Costa-Gavras's contribution captures the delight and amazement of people on the street as they peer into the humble wooden box with its crank handle. It is an apt reminder of the power of cinema.—ROB EDELMAN

Cronenberg, David

Nationality Canadian. Born Toronto, 15 May 1943. Education University of Toronto, B.A., 1967. Career After making two short films, made first feature, Stereo, 1969; travelled to France, directed filler material for Canadian TV, 1971. Award Special Jury Prize, Cannes, 1996, for Crash. Address David Cronenberg Productions, 217 Avenue Road, Toronto M5R 2J3, Canada. Agent John Burnham, William Morris Agency, 151 El Camino Drive, Beverly Hills, California 90212, U.S.A.

Films as Director and Scriptwriter: 1966: *Transfer* (short) (+ph, ed). **1967:** *From the Drain* (short) (+ph, ed). **1969:** *Stereo* (+pr, ph, ed). **1970:** *Crimes of the Future* (+pr, ph). **1975:** *Shivers* (*They Came from Within*; *The Parasite Murders*; *Frissons*). **1976:** *Rabid* (*Rage*). **1978:** *Fast Company* (d only); *The Brood*. **1979:** *Scanners*. **1982:** *Videodrome*. **1983:** *The Dead Zone* (d only). **1986:** *The Fly* (co-sc, +role as gynecologist). **1988:** *Dead Ringers* (*Twins*) (co-sc, +pr). **1991:** *Naked Lunch*. **1992/3:** *M. Butterfly* (d only). **1996:** *Crash* (+voice of auto wreck salesman).

Other Films: 1985: *Into the Night* (Landis) (role). **1989:** *Nightbreed* (Barker) (role). **1992:** *Blue* (McKellar) (role). **1994:** *Trial by Jury* (Gould) (role); *Henry and Verlin* (role). **1995:** *To Die For* (Van Sant) (role); *Blood and Donuts* (role). **1996:** *The Stupids* (Landis) (role); *Extreme Measures* (role).

Following the box-office success of his first major film, *Shivers,* David Cronenberg was critically confined by an assortment of directorial titles, including the "Baron of Blood" and the "King of Venereal Horror." Indeed, Cronenberg was pigeonholed as a horror/sci-fi director throughout the 1970s and well into the 1980s. While these generalizations and classifications adequately describe certain aspects of Cronenberg's earlier work that were obsessed with visually documenting the loss of control over and the decay of the human body, they fail to recognize the creative metamorphosis Cronenberg has undergone, as well as the overlying politic that governs his films. Therefore, before discussing David Cronenberg and his films, the strain of discourse that runs from his earliest films to the controversial *Crash* must be identified and approached in conjunction with Cronenberg's growth as a filmmaker.

Until recently, Cronenberg's films have all fallen neatly into what has been referred to by fans and critics as the Cronenberg project. With the release of *Crash,* however, that term has become obsolete. In the aforementioned film, the character of Vaughan is obsessed with the "modification of the human body through the use of technology," and refers to this endeavor as his *project.* Such an undertaking is most assuredly at the heart of the Cronenberg project as well,

David Cronenberg (right) directing Jeremy Irons in *Dead Ringers* courtesy of The Rank Organization Plc.

since the importance of the body and the mind, in addition to their reactions to external stimuli, have been the center of the project since the beginning. From the parasites imposing a new world order in *Shivers,* to the reprogramming of the human mind in *Videodrome,* to the gene-splicing of *The Fly,* and finally the body modifications of *Crash,* Cronenberg has been interested in the functionality and physical importance of the mind and body. Unfortunately, the fact that Cronenberg signals awareness of the critical theory governing the project corrupts its critical notion. As a result, it has become less emphatically vital and the acknowledgement of its existence in *Crash* indicates that the project has reached some kind of conclusion and has become something else. The Cronenberg project has transcended a merely physical definition and is now something more of a philosophy, or a politic. The Cronenberg politic then has replaced the concept of the project.

The Cronenberg politic (which takes its name from, among other things, a Clive Barker short-story called "The Body Politic," wherein human body parts revolt against their keepers) is, like the project, concerned with the notion of the mind and body and the revolutions that plague them. The difference between the two resides in the politic being the solution to the problem proposed by the project. We can then consequently divide Cronenberg's films to date into four filmic periods by referring to Cronenberg's development as a filmmaker and not necessarily to the progressive development of the politic as a philosophy since the elements of the politic are strewn throughout the Cronenberg canon. As a result, all of these films show the presence and construction of the politic.

Cronenberg's early obsessions, as his first filmic period can be labelled, include *Transfer, From the Drain, Stereo,* and *Crimes of the Future.* Although the films are all relatively short subjects, they showcase Cronenberg's eye for disturbing visuals (such as the make-up and nail polish worn by the men in *Crimes of the Future*). Present in this first group of films are the foundations of what will become the politic. All four films involve, to some degree, the mind and body relationship. In *Transfer,* the psychiatrist's control of his patients is indicative of this. *From the Drain* takes the concept even further and gives a glimpse of the second phase of Cronenberg's filmography when a phallic plant creature emerges from the drain and disposes of its victim. *Stereo* and *Crimes of the Future,* with their secretive medical practices and cold, emotionless hospitals exerting their will upon a hapless society, set the stage for the films in Cronenberg's second period.

The second period of Cronenberg's filmic development is marked by an obsession with venereal disease, an obsession which, in the early 1970s earned him the nickname the King of Venereal Horror. The two major films of this period, *Shivers* and *Rabid,* serve as the nucleus for the politic. Whereas Cronenberg's early obsessions can be found, upon reflection, throughout the films of the politic it is with these two films that Cronenberg's filmic sensibilities begin to gestate and grow, much like one of the venereal parasites from *Shivers.* In both films, an out-of-control disease threatens the established society. In *Shivers,* the appropriately phallic sex parasites threaten society with its reconstruction into a more sexually unrepressed one. And in *Rabid,* the mutated form of rabies that spreads through society displays the same kind of unrepressed emotion, although in its disease form it now has no sexual connotations. Present in these films for the first time is the concept of the Cronenberg hero. He is usually the odd-man-out, the one trying to come to terms with the bizarre evolution that is overtaking mind and body, an especially good example of which is in *Shivers* in the guise of Dr. Roger St. Luc who is so much the opposite of those infested with the sex slug that he becomes almost unlikable, thereby making the parasites' conquest of him at the end of the film an act of salvation.

The third group in Cronenberg's filmography encompasses two decades and includes his films from 1978's *Fast Company* to *The Fly* in 1986. These films all concern themselves to varying degrees with the relationship between the mind and the body, a concept which is solidified in *Videodrome* with the introduction of the term the "new flesh" to the Cronenberg canon. The "new flesh" is instrumental here in that it gives a concrete designation to the previously referred to revolution of the body. Although this relationship was present in Cronenberg's earlier works it was in this period that he began to examine it with full interest. Even a seemingly non-Cronenbergian film like *Fast Company* succeeds in addressing the politic by examining the mind/body relationship by suggesting that technology can be used to facilitate and foster the relationship by serving as a type of *flesh,* an idea that would be expounded upon to a greater degree, and more successfully, in *Crash.* For Cronenberg, the relationship between mind and body is not necessarily a cooperative or civil one; it is usually a violently destructive battle. For example, in *Scanners* (incidentally, the only Cronenberg film where the good guys actually win), the politic is represented in that Cameron Vale ultimately loses the battle for his own body. Although it could be said that he surrenders his physical presence for the noble motive of defeating his brother and assuming his, Vale displays little control throughout the film over his destiny. In fact, he is the victim of manipulation throughout the film and his final victory over Revok, although heroic, is belittled by the fact that he has only performed the function for which his father has rescued him from the gutter to do. His biology has succeeded in controlling his destiny. It is this biological control of destiny that now emerges as a major concern of the Cronenberg film and politic. In his next films, *Videodrome, The Dead Zone,* and *The Fly,* Cronenberg will explore with great detail this relationship. In *Videodrome,* Max Renn is the pawn in a predestined plot of political assassination and apparent global domination. In *The Dead Zone,* Johnny Smith is apparently chosen to rid the world of the next Hitler. And in *The Fly,* Seth Brundle cannot escape the transformation that will eventually cost him both his mind and his body.

The notion of control and the idea that biology is destiny is carried over into the final Cronenberg period. In *Dead Ringers,* this idea is given substantial recognition when the twins cannot hope to escape their biological connections and must die. In *Naked Lunch,* Bill Lee is unable to escape the control that drugs and the accidental murder of his wife have over him. In *M. Butterfly,* René Gallimard also cannot fight his biological destiny when he takes his own life, becoming a symbolic Madame Butterfly. And, in *Crash,* the complacent marriage of James and Catherine Ballard cannot escape the predetermined path that must inevitably end in death. The nature of control in these films is ultimately the tragedy in each of them—the characters cannot possibly hope to escape control, as is perfectly illustrated in *Dead Ringers.* The tragedy of that film erupts from the concept that biology is destiny. Cronenberg succeeds in questioning this theory while at the same time subscribing to it by suggesting that the concept of free will is the destructor of destiny. That is, while the brothers in *Dead Ringers* functioning as gynecologists allows them to control biology to a certain degree, it is death that ultimately triumphs, although they still maintain a certain amount of control over that.

To equate the new Cronenberg film with dramatic tragedy however, is ultimately a simplistic method of characterizing Cronenberg's development as a filmmaker. Although the four Cronenberg films following *The Fly* have displayed the traits of a classical tragedy (indeed, each film ends with a death or, in the case of *Crash*, the expectation of certain death), it is difficult to label them as anything other than Cronenberg films and subscribers to the politic. In *Dead Ringers,* Cronenberg first displayed concerns for the biological control of destiny and the usurpation of that control in a more cerebral and suspenseful method than he had in previous films. In *Naked Lunch,* he would further explore this relationship using drug dependency and Burroughs' writing as framework. Even *M. Butterfly,* which could easily be dismissed by those unfamiliar with the Cronenberg politic as being highly un-Cronenbergian, belongs to the politic by showing how two people can be controlled not only by their physical bodies but by their mental states as well. The new Cronenberg filmic period then culminates in *Crash,* which is in many ways an old Cronenberg movie, by using technology and its relationship with human biology to examine the concerns of the Cronenberg politic. While it is true that the films since and including *Dead Ringers* have had roots grounded more in genres other than sci-fi, as did his earlier films to a lesser extent, it is also the case that the classification of a David Cronenberg film as anything other than just that is ultimately futile.—MICHAEL J. TYRKUS

Cukor, George

Nationality American. *Born* George Dewey Cukor in New York, 7 July 1899. *Education* DeWitt Clinton High School, New York. *Military Service* Served in U.S. armed forces; directed film for the Signal Corps., 1943. *Career* Stage manager on Broadway, 1919-24; manager, stock company in Rochester, New York, and director, New York City, 1924-26; stage director, New York, 1926-29; co-director for Paramount in Hollywood, 1929-32;

George Cukor (left) with John Howard, Katharine Hepburn, and Cary Grant on the set of *The Philadelphia Story.*
Photograph by James Stewart.

joined RKO, began association with Katharine Hepburn, 1932; began association with writers Ruth Gordon and Garson Kanin, 1947. **Awards** *Oscar for Best Director, and Directors Guild of America Award, for* My Fair Lady, *1964; Honorary doctorates, University of Southern California, 1968, and Loyola University, Chicago, 1976; D.W. Griffith Award, Directors Guild of America, 1981; Golden Lion, Venice Festival, 1982.* **Died** *24 January 1983.*

Films as Director: 1930: *Grumpy* (co-d); *The Virtuous Sin* (co-d); *The Royal Family of Broadway* (co-d). **1931:** *Tarnished Lady; Girls About Town.* **1932:** *What Price Hollywood?; A Bill of Divorcement; Rockabye; One Hour with You* (co-d with Lubitsch, uncredited, +dialogue director); *The Animal Kingdom* (co-d, uncredited). **1933:** *Our Betters; Dinner at Eight; Little Women; David Copperfield (The Personal History, Adventures, Experience, and Observations of David Copperfield, the Younger); No More Ladies* (co-d, uncredited). **1936:** *Sylvia Scarlett; Romeo and Juliet.* **1937:** *Camille.* **1938:** *Holiday.* **1939:** *Zaza; The Women; Gone with the Wind* (co-d, uncredited). **1940:** *Susan and God; The Philadelphia Story.* **1941:** *A Woman's Face; Two-Faced Woman.* **1942:** *Her Cardboard Lover.* **1943:** *Keeper of the Flame.* **1944:** *Gaslight; Winged Victory.* **1945:** *I'll Be Seeing You* (co-d, uncredited). **1947:** *A Double Life; Desire Me* (co-d, uncredited). **1949:** *Edward My Son; Adam's Rib.* **1950:** *A Life of Her Own; Born Yesterday.* **1951:** *The Model and the Marriage Broker.* **1952:** *The Marrying Kind; Pat and Mike.* **1953:** *The Actress.* **1954:** *It Should Happen to You; A Star Is Born.* **1956:** *Bhowani Junction.* **1957:** *Les Girls; Wild Is the Wind.* **1958:** *Hot Spell* (co-d, uncredited). **1960:** *Heller in Pink Tights; Let's Make Love; Song without End* (co-d, uncredited). **1962:** *The Chapman Report.* **1964:** *My Fair Lady.* **1969:** *Justine.* **1972:** *Travels with My Aunt.* **1975:** *Love among the Ruins* (for TV). **1976:** *The Bluebird.* **1979:** *The Corn Is Green* (for TV). **1981:** *Rich and Famous.*

Other Films: 1929: *River of Romance* (Wallace) (dialogue d). **1930:** *All Quiet on the Western Front* (Milestone) (dialogue d).

George Cukor's films range from classics like Greta Garbo's *Camille,* to *Adam's Rib* with Spencer Tracy and Katharine Hepburn, to the Judy Garland musical *A Star Is Born.* Throughout the years he managed to "weather the changes in public taste and the pressures of the Hollywood studio system without compromising his style, his taste, or his ethical standards," as his honorary degree from Loyola University of Chicago is inscribed. Indeed, Cukor informed each of the stories he brought to the screen with his affectionately critical view of humanity. In film after film he sought to prod the mass audience to reconsider their cherished illusions in order to gain fresh insights into the problems that confront everyone. "When a director has provided tasteful entertainment of a high order consistently," noted Andrew Sarris, "it is clear that he is much more than a mere entertainer, he is a genuine artist."

Although most of Cukor's films are adaptations of preexisting novels and plays, he has always chosen material that has been consistent with his view of reality. Most often he has explored the conflict between illusion and reality in peoples' lives. The chief characters in his films are frequently actors and actresses, for they, more than anyone, run the risk of allowing the world of illusion with which they are constantly involved to become their reality. This theme is obvious in many of Cukor's best films and appears in some of his earliest work, including *The Royal Family of Broadway,* which he co-directed. In it he portrays a family of troupers, based on the Barrymores, who are wedded to their world of fantasy in a way that makes a shambles of their private lives.

The attempt of individuals to reconcile their cherished dreams with the sober realities of life continues in films as superficially different as *Dinner at Eight, The Philadelphia Story,* and *A Double Life.* Ronald Colman earned an Academy Award in the latter as an actor who becomes so identified with the parts he plays that, while enacting Othello, he develops a murderous streak of jealousy which eventually destroys him.

While it is true that Cukor was often drawn to stories about show people, his films also suggest that everyone leads a double life that moves between illusion and reality, and that everyone must seek to sort out fantasy from fact if they are to cope realistically with their problems—something Cukor's characters frequently fail to do. *Les Girls* is the most explicit of all Cukor's films in treating this theme. Here the same events are told from four different points of view at a libel trial, each version differing markedly from the others. Because Cukor allows each narrator "equal time," he is sympathetic to the way each of them has subconsciously revised their common experiences in a manner that enables him or her to live with the past in the present. As Andrew Sarris remarks, Cukor does not imply that people necessarily are liars, but rather that they tell the truth in their own fashion.

Though Cukor must have harbored some degree of affection and sympathy for the world of romantic illusion—for there is always a hint of regret in his films when actuality inevitably asserts itself in the life of one of his dreamers—his movies nonetheless remain firmly rooted in, and committed to, the workaday world of reality.

Directing his last film, *Rich and Famous,* merited Cukor the distinction of being one of the oldest filmmakers ever to direct a major motion picture. His work on that film likewise marked him as a man who had enjoyed the longest continuous career of any director in film or television. Some of the satisfaction which he derived from his long career was grounded in the fact that few directors have commanded such a large portion of the mass audience. "His movies," Richard Schickel has noted, "can be appreciated—no, liked—at one level or another by just about everyone."

For his part, Cukor once reflected that "I look upon every picture that I make as the first one I've ever done—and the last. I love each film I have directed, and I try to make each one as good as I possibly can. Mind you, making movies is no bed of roses. Every day isn't Christmas. It's been a hard life, but also a joyous one."—GENE D. PHILLIPS

Curtiz, Michael

Nationality Hungarian. *Born* Born Mihály Kertész in Budapest, 24 December 1888. Also known as Michael Courtice. *Education* Markoszy University and Royal Academy of Theatre and Art, Budapest. *Military Service* Served in Hungarian infantry, 1914-15. *Family* Married 1) actress Lucy Dorraine, 1915 (divorced 1923); 2) Bess Meredyth. *Career* Stage actor, 1906-12; directed first Hungarian feature film, Az utolsó bohém, 1912; studied filmmaking at Nordisk Studios in Denmark, 1912-14; managing director, Phönix Studios, Hungary, 1917; left Hungary, worked in Swedish, French, and German film industries, 1918; director for Sascha Films, Austria, 1919; signed by Jack Warner, directed first Hollywood film, The 3rd Degree, 1926. *Award* Oscar for Best Director for Casablanca, 1943. *Died* 11 April 1962.

Films as Director: (In Hungary, as Mihály Kertész) **1912:** *Az utolsó bohém (The Last Bohemian); Ma es holnap (Today and Tomorrow)* (+role). **1913:** *Rablélek (Captive Soul); Hazasodik az uram (My Husband Lies).* **1914:** *A hercegnö Pongyolaban (Princess Pongyola); Az éjszaka rabjai (Slaves of the*

Night) (+role); *A Kölcsönkért csecsemök (Borrowed Babies); Bánk bán; A tolonc (The Vagrant); Aranyáso (The Golden Shovel).* **1915:** *Akit ketten szeretnek (Loved By Two)* (+role). **1916:** *Az ezust kecske (The Silver Goat)* (+co-sc); *A medikus (The Apothecary); Doktor ur (The Doctor); Farkas (The Wolf); A fekete szivarvany (The Black Rainbow); Makkbetes (Seven of Clubs); Karthauzi (The Carthusian); A Magyar föld ereje (The Strength of the Hungarian Soil).* **1917:** *Arendás zsidó (John, the Tenant); Az ezredes (The Colonel); A föld embere (The Man of the Soil); Halálcsengö (The Death Bell); A kuruzslo (The Charlatan); A Szentjóbi erdö titka (The Secret of St. Job Forest); A senki fia (Nobody's Son); Tavasz a télben (Spring in Wintertime); Zoárd Mester (Master Zoard); Tatárjárás (Invasion); A béke ut ja (The Road to Peace); A vörös Sámson (The Red Samson); Az utolsó hajnal (The Last Dawn); Egy krajcár története (The Story of a Penny).* **1918:** *Kilencvenkilenc (99); Judás; Lulu; Az ördog (The Devil); A napraforgós hölgy (The Lady with Sunflowers); Alraune (co-d); Vig özvegy (The Merry Widow)* (+sc); *Varázskeringö (Magic Waltz); Lu, a kokott (Lu, the Cocotte); A Wellingtoni rejtély (The Wellington Mystery); Szamárbör (The Donkey Skin); A csunya fiu (The Ugly Boy); A skorpió (The Scorpion).* **1919:** *Jön az öcsem (John the Younger Brother); Liliom* (unfinished).

(In Austria, as Michael Kertesz) 1919: *Die Dame mit dem schwarzen Handschuh (The Lady with the Black Glove).* **1920:** *Der Stern von Damaskus; Die Dame mit den Sonnenblum* (+sc); *Herzogin Satanella; Boccaccio* (+pr); *Die Gottesgeisel.* **1921:** *Cherchez la femme; Dorothys Bekenntnis (Frau Dorothys Bekenntnis); Wege des Schreckens (Labyrinth des Grauens); Miss Tutti Frutti.* **1922:** *Sodom und Gomorrah: Part 1. Die Sünde (Die Legende von Sünde und Strafe)* (+co-sc). **1923:** *Sodom und Gomorrah: Part II. Die Strafe (Die Legende von Sünde und Strafe)* (+co-sc); *Samson und Dalila* (co-d); *Der Lawine (Avalanche); Der junge Medardus; Namenlos (Der Scharlatan; Der falsche Arzt).* **1924:** *Ein Spiel ums Leben; Harun al Raschid; Die Slavenkönigin (Moon of Israel).* **1925:** *Celimene, Poupee de Montmartre (Das Spielzeug von Paris; Red Heels).* **1926:** *Der goldene Schmetterling (The Road to Happiness); Fiaker Nr. 13 (Einspänner Nr. 13).*

(In United States, as Michael Curtiz) 1926: *The Third Degree.* **1927:** *A Million Bid; Good Time Charley; A Desired Woman.* **1928:** *Tenderloin.* **1929:** *Noah's Ark; The Glad Rag Doll; Madonna of Avenue A; Hearts in Exile; The Gamblers.* **1930:** *Mammy; Under a Texas Moon; The Matrimonial Bed (A Matrimonial Problem); Bright Lights; A Soldier's Plaything (A Soldier's Pay); River's End.* **1931:** *Dämon des Meeres* (German language version of Lloyd Bacon's *Moby Dick*); *God's Gift to Women (Too Many Women); The Mad Genius.* **1932:** *The Woman from Monte Carlo; Alias the Doctor; The Strange Love of Molly Louvain; Doctor X; Cabin in the Cotton.* **1933:** *Twenty Thousand Years in Sing Sing; The Mystery of the Wax Museum; The Keyhole; Private Detective 62; Goodbye Again; The Kennel Murder Case; Female.* **1934:** *Mandalay; British Agent; Jimmy the Gent; The Key.* **1935:** *Black Fury; The Case of the Curious Bride; Front Page Woman; Little Big Shot; Captain Blood.* **1936:** *The Walking Dead; Stolen Holiday; Charge of the Light Brigade.* **1937:** *Kid Galahad; Mountain Justice; The Perfect Specimen.* **1938:** *Gold is Where You Find It; The Adventures of Robin Hood* (co-d); *Four Daughters; Four's a Crowd; Angels with Dirty Faces.* **1939:** *Dodge City; Sons of Liberty; The Private Lives of Elizabeth and Essex; Four Wives; Daughters Courageous.* **1940:** *Virginia City; The Sea Hawk; Santa Fe Trail.* **1941:** *The Sea Wolf; Dive Bomber.* **1942:** *Captains of the Clouds; Yankee Doodle Dandy; Casablanca.* **1943:** *Mission to Moscow; This is the Army.* **1944:** *Passage to Marseille; Janie.* **1945:** *Roughly Speaking; Mildred Pierce.* **1946:** *Night and Day.* **1947:** *Life with Father; The Unsuspected.* **1948:** *Romance on the High Seas (It's Magic).* **1949:** *My Dream is Yours* (+pr); *Flamingo Road* (+exec pr); *The Lady Takes a Sailor.* **1950:** *Young Man with a Horn (Young Man of Music); Bright Leaf; Breaking Point.* **1951:** *Jim Thorpe—All American (Man of Bronze); Force of Arms.* **1952:** *I'll See You in My Dreams; The Story of Will Rogers.* **1953:** *The Jazz Singer; Trouble Along the Way.* **1954:** *The Boy from Oklahoma; The Egyptian; White Christmas.* **1955:** *We're No Angels.* **1956:** *The Scarlet Hour* (+pr); *The Vagabond King; The Best Things in Life are Free.* **1957:** *The Helen Morgan Story (Both Ends of the Candle).* **1958:** *The Proud Rebel; King Creole.* **1959:** *The Hangman; The Man in the Net.* **1960:** *The Adventures of Huckleberry Finn; A Breath of Scandal (Olympia).* **1961:** *Francis of Assisi.* **1962:** *The Comancheros.*

Other Films: 1913: *Atlantis* (Blom) (asst d, role).

The films of Michael Curtiz have come to symbolize Warner Brothers Studios of the 1930s and 1940s. Curtiz directed many favorites from that era, including *Captain Blood, The Charge of the Light Brigade, The Sea Hawk, Yankee Doodle Dandy, 20,000 Years in Sing Sing,* and *Mildred*

Michael Curtiz

Pierce. He helped guide Bette Davis as her popularity rose in the 1930s, and helped establish Errol Flynn as the symbol of the swashbuckling hero. James Cagney (*Yankee Doodle Dandy*) and Joan Crawford (*Mildred Pierce*) both won Oscars under Curtiz's direction. His long career and directorial strengths benefitted from the constant work available in the studios of the 1930s and 1940s. Most observers, however, note a precipitous decline in the quality of Curtiz's films after World War II.

Surely Curtiz's most famous creation for today's audience is *Casablanca,* the only film for which he received an Oscar for Best Director. This cult favorite now has achieved a life of its own and established Bogart and Bergman as modern folk heroes. Conversely, director Curtiz has been lost in the shuffle with the passage of time. The anti-auteurist argument seems to be that this particular film represents a happy "accident" of the studio system, and that its enduring popularity should not be credited to its director. What is lost in this analysis is the fact that *Casablanca* was a major hit of 1943 (finishing among the top grossing films of the year), won three Academy Awards (Best Picture, Director, and Screenplay), and earned Curtiz several awards as the year's best director. Critics of the day recognized Curtiz's input. Certainly today we should give proper credit to the director of a film that was popular upon release, continues to be popular today, and has influenced countless other works.

Curtiz has been difficult for film historians to deal with because of the length and breadth of his career. Usually overlooked is the time he spent in Europe; Curtiz did not begin with Warner Brothers until he came to the United States at the age of thirty-eight. His career began in Hungary, where he participated in the beginning of the Hungarian film industry, usually receiving credit for directing that country's first feature film.

Curtiz remained active until the outbreak of the First World War. After the war he moved to Vienna where he directed several important films, including the epic *Sodom and Gomorrah*. Scholars know little else about this part of Curtiz's career, however. Accounts of other activities lead only to contradictions; no wholly reliable list of credits exists. Sadly, historians have written off the first two decades of Curtiz's career. We know a great deal of the work of other emigrés, such as Fritz Lang and F.W. Murnau, but virtually nothing of Curtiz.

Not unexpectedly there exist several versions of why and how Warner Brothers contacted Curtiz and brought him to the United States. Regardless, from 1926 Curtiz became intertwined with all the innovations of the Warner Brothers studio. In the mid-1920s he was thrust into Warner attempts to innovate sound. His *Tenderloin* and *Noah's Ark* were two-part talkies which achieved considerable popularity and garnered millions in box-office revenues. In a key transitional year, 1930, Curtiz directed no less than six Warner Brothers talkies. In that same year

Warner Brothers tried to introduce color, but with none of the success associated with the studio's efforts with sound. Curtiz's *Mammy,* one of Jolson's follow-ups to *The Jazz Singer* and *The Singing Fool,* had color sequences. In 1933 he directed the well-regarded, all-color, horror film, *The Mystery of the Wax Museum.*

Curtiz's record during the transition to sound elevated him to the top echelon of contract directors at Warner Brothers. Unlike others, Curtiz seemed not to utilize this success to push for greater freedom and independence. Instead, he seemed content to take what was assigned, executing his work in a classic style. He produced crisp flowing narratives, seeking efficiency of method. He was a conservative director, adapting, borrowing, and ultimately utilizing all the dominant codes of the Hollywood system. Stylistic innovations were left to others. Today critics praise the film noir look of *Mildred Pierce,* but this film was never thought of as one of the forerunners of that style when it was initially released. After *Mildred Pierce,* Curtiz moved on to *Night and Day,* the fictionalized life of Cole Porter starring Cary Grant, and *Life With Father,* a nostalgic, light family romance starring William Powell and Irene Dunne. Both of these latter features took in a great deal of money and earned considerable critical praise, once again demonstrating how well Curtiz could operate when called upon by his employer.

If there is a way to get a handle on the enormous output of Curtiz's career, it is through genre analysis. In the early 1930s Curtiz stuck to formula melodramas. His limited participation in Warner Brothers's social realism cycles came with films like *Black Fury,* which looked at strikebreaking. Curtiz seemed to hit his stride with Warner Brothers's Errol Flynn pirate cycle of the late 1930s. *Captain Blood* and *The Sea Hawk* stand as lasting symbols of Hollywood's ability to capture the sweep of romantic adventure. Warner Brothers also sent director Curtiz and star Flynn to the Old West in *Dodge City* and *Virginia City.*

In the early 1940s the Warner studio returned to the musical, establishing its niche with the biographical film. Curtiz participated, directing *Yankee Doodle Dandy* (which depicted George M. Cohan's life), *This Is the Army* (Irving Berlin), and the aforementioned *Night and Day* (Cole Porter). *Yankee Doodle Dandy* demonstrated how well this European emigré had taken to the United States. Curtiz would continue to deal with Americana in his films during the 1940s. For example, he touched deep American ideological strains with *Casablanca,* while *Mildred Pierce* examined the dark side of the American family. Feminist critics have noted how the portrait of a strong woman in the latter film mirrors the freedom women achieved during World War II—a freedom withdrawn after the war when the men returned home. The family in *Mildred Pierce* is constructed in an odd, bitter way, contrasting with Curtiz's affectionate portrait in *Life with Father.*

Genre analysis is helpful, but in the end it still tells us too little of what we want to know about this important director. As critics and historians continue to go through his films and utilize the records now available at the University of Wisconsin, University of Southern California, and Princeton, more insights will come to light about Curtiz's participation in the Hollywood studio system. In the meantime, Curtiz's films will live on for the fans with continual re-screenings of *Casablanca, Mildred Pierce,* and *The Adventures of Robin Hood.*—DOUGLAS GOMERY

Dassin, Jules

Nationality *American.* **Born** *Middletown, Connecticut, 12 December 1911.* **Education** *Morris High School, the Bronx, New York.* **Family** *Married 1) Beatrice Launer, 1933 (divorced 1962), one son, two daughters; 2) actress Melina Mercouri, 1966.* **Career** *Member of Artef Players (Jewish socialist theatre collective), 1936; directed first Broadway production,* Medicine Show, *1939; contracted to RKO (moved to MGM after eight months), Hollywood, 1940; left MGM and worked with producer Mark Hellinger, 1946; named by Edward Dmytryk and Frank Tuttle in HUAC testimony as member of Hollywood "Communist faction," 1951; subpoenaed by HUAC, 1952; moved to Europe, 1953.* **Award** *Best Director Award (shared), Cannes Festival, for* Rififi, *1955.* **Address** *25 Anagnostopoulou St., Athens, Greece.*

Films as Director: 1941: *The Tell-Tale Heart* (short). **1942:** *Nazi Agent; The Affairs of Martha (Once Upon a Thursday); Reunion (Reunion in France; Mademoiselle France).* **1943:** *Young Ideas.* **1944:** *The Canterville Ghost.* **1946:** *A Letter for Evie, Two Smart People.* **1947:** *Brute Force.* **1948:** *The Naked City.* **1949:** *Thieves' Highway.* **1950:** *Night and the City.* **1955:** *Du Rififi chez les hommes (Rififi)* (+co-sc, role as jewel thief under pseudonym Perlo Vita). **1958:** *Celui qui doit mourir (He Who Must Die)* (+co-sc). **1959:** *La legge (La Loi)* (released in U.S. 1960 as *Where the Hot Winds Blow*) (+sc). **1960:** *Pote tin kyriaki (Never on Sunday)* (+pr, sc, role). **1962:** *Phaedra* (+pr, co-sc). **1964:** *Topkapi* (+pr). **1966:** *10:30 p.m. Summer* (+co-pr, sc, bit role). **1967:** *Survival 67* (+co-pr, appearance) (documentary). **1968:** *Uptight!* (+pr, co-sc). **1971:** *La Promesse de l'aube (Promise at Dawn)* (+pr, sc, role as Ivan Mozhukhin under pseudonym Perlo Vita). **1974:** *The Rehearsal* (+sc). **1978:** *A Dream of Passion* (+pr, sc). **1980:** *Circle of Two (Obsession)* (released in USA 1982).

Between the mid-1940s and the late 1950s, Jules Dassin directed some of the better realistic, hard-bitten, fast-paced crime dramas produced in America, before his blacklisting and subsequent move to Europe. However, while he has made some very impressive films, his career as a whole is lacking in artistic cohesion.

Dassin's films are occasionally innovative: *The Naked City* is one of the first police dramas shot on location, on the streets of New York; *Rififi* is a forerunner of detailed jewelry heist dramas, highlighted by a thirty-five-minute sequence chronicling the break-in, shot without a word of dialogue or note of music; *Never on Sunday,* starring his wife Melina Mercouri as a happy hooker, made the actress an international star, won her an Academy Award nomination, and popularized in America the Greek *bouzouki* music. *The Naked City* and *Rififi* are particularly exciting, as well as trend-setting, while *Brute Force* remains a striking, naturalistic prison drama, with Burt Lancaster in one of his most memorable early performances and Hume Cronyn wonderfully despicable as a Hitlerish guard captain. *Thieves' Highway,* also shot on location, is a vivid drama of truck driver Richard Conte taking on racketeer Lee J. Cobb. *Topkapi* is a *Rififi* remake, with a delightful touch of comedy.

Jules Dassin on the set of *Never on Sunday.*

Many of Dassin's later films, such as *Brute Force* and *Thieves' Highway,* attempt to observe human nature: they focus on the individual fighting his own demons while trying to survive within a chaotic society. For example, in *A Dream of Passion,* an updating of Sophocles' *Medea,* an American woman is jailed in Greece for the murder of her three children; *Up Tight,* the filmmaker's first American-made release after the McCarthy hysteria, is a remake of *The Informer* set in a black ghetto. Unfortunately, they are all generally flawed: with the exception of *Never on Sunday* and *Topkapi,* his collaborations with Melina Mercouri (from *He Who Must Die* to *A Dream of Passion*) are disappointing, while *Up Tight* pales beside the original. *Circle of Two,* with teenager Tatum O'Neal baring her breasts for aging Richard Burton, had a limited release. Dassin's early triumphs have been obscured by his more recent fiascos, and as a result his critical reputation is now irrevocably tarnished.

The villain in his career is the blacklist, which tragically clipped his wings just as he was starting to fly. Indeed, he could not find work in Europe for five years, as producers felt American distributors would automatically ban any film with his signature. When *Rififi* opened, critics wrote about Dassin as if he were European. The *New York Herald Tribune* reported in 1961, "At one ceremony, when the award to *Rififi* was announced, (Dassin) was called to the dais, and a French flag was raised above him. 'It should have been a moment of triumph but I feel awful. They were honoring my work and I'm an American. It should have been the American flag raised in honor.'" The blacklist thus denied Jules Dassin his roots. In 1958, it was announced that he was planning to adapt James T. Farrell's *Studs Lonigan,* a project that was eventually shelved. It is one more tragedy of the blacklist that Dassin was not allowed to follow up *Brute Force, The Naked City,* and *Thieves' Highway* with *Studs Lonigan.*—ROB EDELMAN

Davies, Terence

Nationality British. *Born* Liverpool, 1945. *Education* Studied at drama school in Coventry, 1971-73, and at National Film School, Beaconsfield, late 1970s. *Career* Clerk and accountant in a shipping office, 1960-71; directed first film, Children, 1974. *Award* International Critics' Prize, Cannes Film Festival, for Distant Voices, Still Lives, 1988.

Films as Director and Scriptwriter: 1974: *Children.* **1980:** *Madonna and Child.* **1983:** *Death and Transfiguration.* **1984:** *Terence Davies Trilogy* (comprising three previous films). **1988:** *Distant Voices, Still Lives.* **1992:** *The Long Day Closes.* **1995:** *The Neon Bible.*

"I make films to come to terms with my family history. . . . If there had been no suffering, there would have been no films." Hardly the most unusual of artistic subjects, but for Terence Davies it has been the source of perhaps the most emotionally and technically distinctive films in recent British film history. *The Terence Davies Trilogy* and *Distant Voices, Still Lives* chart what some might think unremarkable territory—working class life in northern England after the war—but do so with an artistic seriousness more usually seen as the exclusive preserve of "European" cinema.

Born in Liverpool in 1945, the youngest of ten children (seven of whom survived infancy), Davies's early life was overshadowed by the mute malevolence and tyrannical violence of his father, for whom he still feels undiminished hatred. In a house where domesticity would cut violently to the most extreme brutality, Davies developed a sensitivity to mood and detail that was to prove intrinsic to his later filmmaking. "I have a very retentive memory, and can remember things, even atmospheres on particular days. And I think it's these details, particularly about people's behaviour, that reveal the greater truth. As a child, up to the point when my father died, because you had to gauge whether he was in a good mood or not, all my nerve endings were exposed. And when you're a child, you're like an animal, you smell things, so that now that instinct is absolutely there." When young Davies was eight his father died of a stomach cancer that was perhaps accelerated by drinking disinfectant in an effort to avoid military service.

The next few years of Davies's childhood, until his secondary school, were relatively happy, particularly because of his discovery of American musicals. Davies left school at the age of 15 and began working as a clerk and an accountant, spending his spare moments writing for the stage and radio. By the age of 26 he was shopping a script that was rejected by various television companies. It was after leaving drama school in Coventry that he applied for and received a grant from the British Film Institute Production Board to direct. *Children* received critical acclaim, including the bronze Hugo at the Chicago Film Festival. He then won a place at the National Film School, where he began his second film.

Children, Madonna and Child, and *Death and Transfiguration* took ten years for the director to complete, in part because they required three different sources of funding (including the Greater London Arts Association). His critical reputation began to build during this time. His trilogy showing the three stages in the life of Robert Tucker—from being bullied at school through a loveless middle age of masochistic homosexual fantasy to death—constituted an expiation of sexual and religious guilt. "Not having come to terms with being gay, I had prayed for forgiveness until my knees were literally raw, and I just thought, that's it. I was so angry, it seemed that even if there was a God he was just inhumane. . . . Although I had rejected Catholicism before I made the films, in the making of the trilogy I worked out my precise reasons for doing so." The autobiographical basis of the films, however, indicated a startling emotional maturity on the part of the filmmaker, for he explores the bleak potential future of Davies's life—a lonely death (and transfiguration) in a geriatric ward on Christmas Day.

Davies's subject matter was not to everyone's taste. Religious groups in America protested at its sexual content. And according to one critic, "It makes Ingmar Bergman look like Jerry Lewis." But its thoughtful handling of non-linear narrative and "spare and beautiful" black and white photography picked up an array of prizes.

Distant Voices, Still Lives, again made in parts with a variety of funds, confirmed the legitimacy of previous critical accolades. The film, which dealt with his family's history rather than his own, achieved a deepened emotional range and presented considerable technical innovation, winning major prizes at Cannes, Locarno, and Toronto. The des-

Terence Davies directing
Distant Voices, Still Lives.

perate groping by critics to find appropriate language to describe the work underscored the originality of his achievement. "If you can readily imagine a musical version of *Coronation Street* directed by Robert Bresson, with additional dialogue by Sigmund Freud and Tommy Handley, you might know what to expect from Terence Davies;" "A proletarian Proust;" "A musical, albeit a brutal, Proustian one." Whilst 1950s revivals were not uncommon at this time, this was unmistakably something new. As Davies put it, "I remember the 1950s which have now become very fashionable and unreal, with films like *Absolute Beginners* and all those television commercials. . . . It was not romantic, and that's why I chose to shoot the film in that particular shade of brown, because I didn't want it to look like 'The Good Old Days.'" This colouring was achieved through a "Bleach By-Pass" operation in the laboratory and careful suppression of primary colours on the set, apart from the red of lipstick and nail-varnish. The effect is stunning. In set pieces that look like tinted photographs it captures the romance and sterility of a culture bound in working-class patriarchy, but glazed with Hollywood escapism. The father's brutality—cutting from him gently filling the children's Christmas stockings to demolishing the dinner table—is contrasted by the love songs tripping off the girls' lips, and a soundtrack featuring such songs as "Taking A Chance On Love." Scenes are overlapped through the music, and static holds are animated by sound (the incantationary Home Service Shipping Forecast in the opening shot).

Such qualities have marked Davies as the most promising director in British cinema. He shows a passionate concern with film *craft,* lamenting what he sees as the British instinct to use film as a medium for recorded theatre; primarily verbal, sentimental, and in the tight bodice of traditional narrative. His films are remarkably effective in disturbing collective memories—and myths—of British cultural life with such cinematic ingenuity.—SAUL FRAMPTON

De Mille, Cecil B.

Nationality American. *Born* Cecil Blount De Mille in Ashfield, Massachusetts, 12 August 1881. *Education* Pennsylvania Military Academy, Chester, 1896-98; American Academy of Dramatic Arts, New York, 1898-1900. *Family* Married Constance Adams, 16 August 1902, two sons, two daughters. *Career* Actor, playwright, stage producer, and associate with mother in De Mille Play Co. (theatrical agency), to 1913; co-founder, then Director-General, of Jesse L. Lasky Feature Play Co., 1913 (which became Paramount Pictures Corp. after merger, 1918); directed first film, The Squaw Man, 1914; founder, Mercury Aviation Co., 1919; established De Mille Pictures Corp., 1924; joined MGM as producer-director, 1928; co-founder, Screen Directors Guild, 1931; independent producer for Paramount, 1932; producer, Lux Radio Theater of the Air, 1936-45. *Awards* Outstanding Service Award, War Agencies of the Government of the U.S.; Special Oscar "for 37 years of brilliant showmanship," 1949; Irving Thalberg Award, Academy, 1952; Milestone Award, Screen Producers' Guild, 1956; Chevalier de Légion d'honneur, France; Honorary doctorate, University of Southern California. *Died* 21 January 1959.

Films as Director: 1914: *The Squaw Man* (*The White Man*) (co-d, sc, bit role); *The Call of the North* (+sc, introductory appearance); *The Virginian* (+sc, co-ed); *What's His Name* (+sc, ed): *The Man from Home* (+sc, ed); *Rose of the Rancho* (+sc, ed): *Brewster's Millions* (co-d, uncredited, sc); *The Master Mind* (co-d, uncredited, sc); *The Man on the Box* (co-d, uncredited, sc); *The Only Son* (co-d, uncredited, sc); *The Ghost Breaker* (co-d, uncredited, co-sc). **1915:** *The Girl of the Golden West* (+sc, ed); *The Warrens of Virginia* (+sc, ed); *The Unafraid* (+sc, ed); *The Captive* (+co-sc, ed); *The Wild Goose Chase* (+co-sc, ed); *The Arab* (+co-sc, ed); *Chimmie Fadden* (+co-sc, ed): *Kindling* (+sc, ed); *Carmen* (+sc, ed); *Chimmie Fadden Out West* (+co-sc, ed); *The Cheat* (+sc, ed); *The Golden Chance* (+co-sc, ed); *The Goose Girl* (co-d with Thompson, uncredited, co-sc). **1916:** *Temptation* (+co-story, ed); *The Trail of the Lonesome Pine* (+sc, ed); *The Heart of Nora Flynn* (+ed); *Maria Rosa* (+ed); *The Dream Girl* (+ed). **1917:** *Joan the Woman* (+ed); *A Romance of the Redwoods* (+co-sc, ed); *The Little American* (+co-sc, ed); *The Woman God Forgot* (+ed); *The Devil Stone* (+ed); *Nan of Music Mountain* (co-d with Melford, uncredited); *Lost and Won*. **1918:** *The Whispering Chorus* (+ed); *Old Wives for New* (+ed); *We Can't Have Everything* (+co-ed); *Till I Come Back to You*; *The Squaw Man*. **1919:** *Don't Change Your Husband; For Better, For Worse; Male and Female* (*The Admirable Crichton*). **1920:** *Why Change Your Wife?; Something to Think About.* **1921:** *Forbidden Fruit* (+pr); *The Affairs of Anatol* (*A Prodigal Knight*); *Fool's Paradise.* **1922:** *Saturday Night; Manslaughter; Don't Tell Everything* (co-d with Wood, uncredited) (incorporates two reel unused *The Affairs of Anatol* footage). **1923:** *Adam's Rib; The Ten Commandments.* **1924:** *Triumph* (+pr); *Feet of Clay.* **1925:** *The Golden Bed; The Road to Yesterday.* **1926:** *The Volga Boatman.* **1927:** *The King of Kings.* **1929:** *The Godless Girl; Dynamite* (+pr). **1930:** *Madame Satan* (+pr). **1931:** *The Squaw Man* (+pr). **1932:** *The Sign of the Cross* (+pr) (re-released 1944 with add'l footage). **1933:** *This Day and Age* (+pr). **1934:** *Four Frightened People* (+pr); *Cleopatra* (+pr). **1935:** *The Crusades* (+pr). **1937:** *The Plainsman* (+pr). **1938:** *The Buccaneer* (+pr). **1939:** *Union Pacific* (+pr). **1940:** *North West Mounted Police* (+pr, prologue narration). **1942:** *Reap the Wild Wind* (+pr, prologue narration). **1944:** *The Story of Dr. Wassell* (+pr). **1947:** *Unconquered* (+pr). **1949:** *Samson and Delilah* (+pr, prologue narration). **1952:** *The Greatest Show on Earth* (+pr, narration, introductory appearance). **1956:** *The Ten Commandments* (+pr, prologue narration).

Other Films: 1914: *Ready Money* (Apfel) (co-sc); *The Circus Man* (Apfel) (co-sc); *Cameo Kirby* (Apfel) (co-sc). **1915:** *The Country Boy* (Thompson) (co-sc); *A Gentleman of Leisure* (Melford) (sc); *The Governor's Lady* (Melford) (co-sc); *Snobs* (Apfel) (co-sc). **1916:** *The Love Mask* (Reicher) (co-sc). **1917:** *Betty to the Rescue* (Reicher) (co-sc, supervisor). **1923:** *Hollywood* (Cruze) (guest appearance). **1930:** *Free and Easy* (Sedgwick) (guest appearance). **1935:** *The Hollywood You Never See* (short) (seen directing *Cleopatra*); *Hollywood Extra Girl* (Moulton) (seen directing *The Crusades*). **1942:** *Star Spangled Rhythm* (Marshall) (guest appearance). **1947:** *Variety Girl* (Marshall) (guest appearance);

Jens Mansson i Amerika (Jens Mansson in America) (Janzon) (guest appearance); *Aid to the Nation* (short) (appearance). **1950:** *Sunset Boulevard* (Wilder) (role as himself). **1952:** *Son of Paleface* (Tashlin) (guest appearance). **1956:** *The Buster Keaton Story* (Sheldon) (guest appearance). **1957:** *The Heart of Show Business* (Staub) (narrator). **1958:** *The Buccaneer* (pr, supervisor, introductory appearance).

For much of his forty-year career, the public and the critics associated Cecil B. De Mille with a single kind of film, the epic. He certainly made a great many of them: *The Sign of the Cross, The Crusades, King of Kings,* two versions of *The Ten Commandments, The Greatest Show on Earth,* and others. As a result, De Mille became a symbol of Hollywood during its "Golden Age." He represented that which was larger than life, often too elaborate, but always entertaining. By having such a strong public personality, however, De Mille came to be neglected as a director, even though many of his films— not just the epics—stand out as extraordinary.

Cecil B. De Mille

Although he made films until 1956, De Mille's masterpiece may well have come in 1915 with *The Cheat.* Even this early in his career, we can locate some of the motifs that turn up again and again in De Mille's work: a faltering upper-class marriage, the allure and exoticism of the Far East, and sexual attraction equated with hypnotic control. He also made a major aesthetic advancement in the use of editing in *The Cheat* that soon became a part of the repertoire of most filmmakers.

For the cinema's first twenty years, editing was based primarily on following action. During a chase, when actors exited screen right, the next shot had them entering screen left; or, a director might cut from a person being chased to those characters doing the chasing. In either case, the logic of the action controls the editing, which in turn gives us a sense of the physical space of a scene. But in *The Cheat,* De Mille used his editing to create a sense of psychological space. Richard Hardy, a wealthy businessman, confronts his wife with her extravagant bills, but Mrs. Hardy can think only of her lover, Haka, who is equally obsessed with her. De Mille provides a shot/counter-shot here, but the scene does not cut from Mr. Hardy to his wife, even though the logic of the action and the dialogue seems to indicate that it should. Instead, the shots alternate between Mrs. Hardy and Haka, even though the two lovers are miles apart. This sort of editing, which follows thoughts rather than actions, may seem routine today, but in 1915 it was a major development in the method of constructing a sequence.

As a visual stylist, however, De Mille became known more for his wit than for his editing innovations. At the beginning of *The Affairs of Anatol,* for instance, our first view of the title character, Anatol DeWitt Spencer, is of his feet. He taps them nervously while he waits for his wife to make breakfast. Our first view of Mrs. Spencer is also of her feet—a maid gives them a pedicure. In just seconds, and with only two shots, De Mille lets us know that this couple is in trouble. Mrs. Spencer's toenails must dry before Anatol can eat. Also from these opening shots, the viewers realize that they have been placed firmly within the realm of romantic comedy. Such closeups have no place within a melodrama.

One normally does not think of De Mille in terms of pairs of shots. Instead, one thinks on a large scale, and remembers the crowd scenes (the lions versus Christians extravaganza in *The Sign of the Cross*), the huge upper-crust social functions (the charity gala in *The Cheat*), the orgiastic parties (one of which takes place in a dirigible in *Dynamite*), and the bathrooms that De Mille turns into colossal marble shrines.

De Mille began directing in the grand style quite early in his career. In 1915, with opera star Geraldine Farrar in the lead role, he made one of the best film versions of *Carmen,* and two years later, again with Farrar, he directed *Joan the Woman*. Again and again, De Mille would refer to history as a foundation to support the believability of his stories, as if his most obvious excesses could be justified if they were at least remotely based on real-life incidents. A quick look at his filmography shows many films based on historical events (often so far back in the past that accuracy hardly becomes an issue): *The Sign of the Cross, The Crusades, Union Pacific, Northwest Mounted Police,* and others. When history was inconvenient, De Mille made use of a literary text to give his films a high gloss of acceptability and veracity. In the opening credits of *The Affairs of Anatol,* for instance, De Mille stresses that the story derives from the play by Schnitzler.

In both his silent and sound films, De Mille mixes Victorian morality with sizable doses of sex and violence. The intertitles of *Why Change Your Wife?,* for example, rail against divorce as strongly as any nineteenth century marital tract, but the rest of the film deals openly with sexual obsession, and shows two women in actual physical combat over one man. Similarly, all of De Mille's religious epics extol the Christian virtues while at the same time reveling in scenes depicting all of the deadly sins. Though it is tension between extremes that makes De Mille's films so intriguing, critics have often made this aspect of his work seem laughable. Even today De Mille rarely receives the serious recognition and study that he deserves.—ERIC SMOODIN

Demme, Jonathan

Nationality American. Born Baldwin, New York, 1944. Education University of Miami. Military Service U.S. Air Force, 1966. Family Married director Evelyn Purcell. Career Publicity writer for United Artists, Avco Embassy, and Pathe Contemporary Films, early 1960s; writer on Film Daily, *1968-69; worked in London, 1969; unit publicist, then writer for Roger Corman, 1970; directed first film,* Caged Heat, *1974; also director of TV films, commercials, and music videos for recording artists Chrissie Hynde, New Order, Suzanne Vega, and others. Awards Best Picture and Best Director Academy Awards, for* The Silence of the Lambs, *1991.*

Films as Director: 1974: *Caged Heat* (+sc). **1975:** *Crazy Mama.* **1976:** *Fighting Mad* (+sc). **1977:** *Citizen's Band* (*Handle With Care*). **1979:** *Last Embrace.* **1980:** *Melvin and Howard.* **1981:** *Who Am I This Time?* (for TV). **1983:** *Swing Shift* (co-d). **1984:** *Stop Making Sense* (doc). **1986:** *Something Wild* (+co-pr). **1987:** *Swimming to Cambodia.* **1988:** *Married to the Mob; Famous All Over Town.* **1991:** *The Silence of the Lambs; Cousin Bobby* (doc). **1993:** *Philadelphia* (+co-pr). **1998:** *Beloved.*

Other Films: 1970: *Sudden Terror* (*Eyewitness*) (Irwin Allen) (music coordinator). **1972:** *Angels Hard as They Come* (Viola) (pr, co-sc); *The Hot Box* (Viola) (pr, co-sc). **1973:** *Black Mama, White Mama* (Romero) (co-story). **1985:** *Into the Night* (Landis) (role). **1990:** *Miami Blues* (pr). **1993:** *Household Saints* (Savoca) (exec pr); *Amos and Andrew* (exec pr). **1995:** *Devil in a Blue Dress* (C. Franklin) (exec pr). **1996:** *That Thing You Do!* (Hanks) (pr, role); *Mandela* (A. Gibson, Menell) (pr).

Jonathan Demme has proven himself to be one of the more acute observers of the inner life of America during the course of a directorial career that began in the early 1970s, though he began as just another protégé of the Roger Corman apprentice school of filmmaking. Demme's concern with character—focused particularly through the observation of telling eccentricities— is perhaps his trademark, combined with a vitality and willingness to use the frameworks of various genres to their fullest extent. A film such as *Something Wild,* for example, combines a tale of character and relationship development in an exhilarating movie which successfully mixes classic screwball comedy (you could imagine Hepburn and Tracy in the leads) with a very real menace in the closing stages that extends earlier comic confusion into the deadlier paranoia of the thriller.

Perhaps inspired by the "anything goes" aura of his Corman days, Demme has never been afraid to experiment with mood and subject matter in his films: Hitchcockian suspense in *The Last Embrace,* the possibilities of monologue in *Swimming To Cambodia,* romantic comedy in *Swing Shift,* horror in *The Silence of the Lambs,* and gangster conventions in *Married To The Mob.*

Even his earliest films—*Caged Heat* and *Fighting Mad* (which he also wrote)—showed Demme exploiting the possibilities offered by the sex-and-violence format (rampaging girl-gangs in the first, rampaging rednecks in the second) for original and highly distinctive exploration of subjects and style.

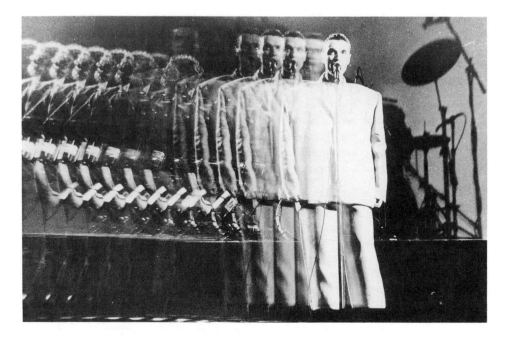

Jonathan Demme: *Stop Making Sense*

Caged Heat also gave early signs of Demme's concern with those struggling to take control of their lives—particularly, but not exclusively, women. This examination of self-determination has remained a theme throughout his work, from the women prisoners of *Caged Heat* and the munitions worker (Goldie Hawn) in *Swing Shift* to the central characters in *Something Wild* (Melanie Griffith) and *Married To The Mob* (Michelle Pfeiffer), and contributed to his reputation as a feminist filmmaker. Their struggle to establish themselves against patriarchal attitudes epitomizes, for Demme, the struggles of the underdog, which he has called "heroic." This real concern for his characters is clear in the (usually affectionate) intensity with which they—and their lives—are portrayed, and Demme recently described his films as "a little old-fashioned, at the same time as we try to make them modern."

Demme is concerned with entertaining a mass audience, and it is probably unwise to consider the low-key mood of the earlier critically-adored films *Citizen's Band* (a black comedy that explores lack of communication through a small town's obsession with CB-radio) and *Melvin And Howard* (an offbeat comedy based on a true story of a working-class man who gave a lift to a hobo Howard Hughes in the Nevada desert) as being necessarily closest to his own heart. Both films, however good they may be, were also conscious reactions to the over-the-top nature of earlier Corman-inspired work.

Misjudgment of Demme's concerns is nothing new for the filmmaker. His much-noted focus on the everyday kitsch of Americana, for example, is driven more by an understanding of its importance as a yardstick by which America consumer society measures itself ("it's our kind of fetishism") than with being a desire to be "hip." For Demme, observing kitsch is simply a form of realism in a country where the bizarre is often real.

Though much concerned with achieving an honest view of character, Demme is not uncaring about stylish direction. A sequence such as the series of out-takes used for the final credits of *Married To The Mob* is one mark of a freewheeling approach to filmmaking that has roots in the knowing wit of the French New Wave (Demme cites Truffaut as an early influence), while his pared-down vision of a Talking Heads concert in *Stop Making Sense* is a distinctive, classy example of the rock film which pointedly eschews the tacky visual trappings too often associated with the genre.

Ultimately, though, his concern is with character rather than style—content over form. Demme is concerned more with exploring humanity than with proving himself an auteur for film critics. His own description of *Married To The Mob* offers an excellent insight into what he has sought in his work. "It was intelligent fun, it didn't patronise the characters or the audience, it was good-hearted. Those are tough commodities to come by."

Since his late 1980s work, Demme has gone on to make two of the higher-profile films of the 1990s. *The Silence of the Lambs,* based on the Thomas Harris bestseller, was a film about a young FBI trainee (Jodie Foster) who locks horns with Hannibal Lecter (Anthony Hopkins), a psychopathic, cannibalistic murderer. The film, which featured fine performances and excellent direction, earned Oscars for Best Picture, Director, Actor, Actress and Adapted Screenplay— quite a haul for what is essentially a big-budget splatter film.

In quite a change of pace, Demme next directed *Philadelphia,* a film that stars Tom Hanks as Andrew Beckett, an AIDS-afflicted lawyer who fights the system after being fired from a prestigious Philadelphia law firm. Upon the film's release, gay activists complained—sometimes bitterly—that the film soft-pedals its subject. However, *Philadelphia* was not produced for those who already are highly politicized and need no introduction to the reality of AIDS. The film was made for the masses who do not live in urban gay enclaves, and who have never met—or think they have never met—a homosexual, let alone a person with AIDS. As a drama, *Philadelphia* is not without flaws. The members of Beckett's family are unfailingly supportive and understanding, a much-too-simplistic ideal in a world in which many gays and lesbians are shunned by their relatives. It also is difficult to accept the subtle changes that occur within Joe Miller (Denzel Washington), the homophobic lawyer who takes Beckett's case. But *Philadelphia* does succeed in showing that homosexuals are human beings, people who deserve to be treated fairly and civilly. It enjoyed a mainstream success with audiences who normally might be turned off by a more radical, politically loaded (let alone sexually frank) film about gays or AIDS.—NORMAN MILLER and ROB EDELMAN

Demy, Jacques

Nationality *French.* **Born** *Pontchâteau (Loire-Atlantique), 5 June 1931.* **Education** *Ecole des Beaux-Arts, Nantes; Ecole Technique de Photographie et de Cinématographiques, Paris.* **Family** *Married director Agnes Varda, 1962; children: Mathieu and Rosalie.* **Career** *Assistant to animator Paul Grimault, 1952; assistant to Georges Rouquier, 1954; made first short film,* Le Sabotier du Val de Loire, *began association with editor Anne-Marie Cotret, 1955; directed first feature,* Lola, *1961.* **Died** *27 October, 1990, of a brain hemorrhage resulting from leukemia.*

Films as Director and Scriptwriter: 1956: *Le Sabotier du Val de Loire.* **1957:** *Le Bel Indifférent.* **1958:** *Le Musée Grévin.* **1959:** *La Mère et l'infant* (co-d); *Ars.* **1961:** *Lola.* **1962:** "La Luxure" (Lust) episode of *Les Sept Péchés capitaux* (*Seven Deadly Sins*). **1963:** *La Baie des Anges* (*Bay of the Angels*). **1964:** *Les Parapluies de Cherbourg* (*The Umbrellas of Cherbourg*). **1967:** *Les Demoiselles de Rochefort* (*The Young Girls of Rochefort*). **1969:** *The Model Shop* (+pr). **1971:** *Peau d'ane* (*Donkey Skin*). **1972:** *The Pied Piper of Hamelin* (*The Pied Piper*). **1973:** *L'Évènement le plus important depuis que l'homme a marché sur la lune* (*A Slightly Pregnant Man*). **1978:** *Lady Oscar.* **1982:** *Une Chambre en ville* (*A Room in Town*). **1985:** *Parking.* **1988:** *Trois Places pour le 26* (*Three Places for the 26th*).

Other Films: 1954: *Lourdes et ses miracles* (Rouquier) (asst d). **1955:** *Arthur Honegger* (Rouquier) (asst d). **1956:** *S.O.S. Noronha* (Rouquier) (asst d). **1959:** *Les Quatre Cents Coups* (Truffaut) (role as policeman). **1960:** *Paris nous appartient* (Rivette) (role as guest at party). **1991:** *Jacquot de Nantes* (role as himself).

Jacques Demy's first feature film, *Lola,* is among the early distinguished products of the New Wave and is dedicated to Max Ophüls. These two facts in conjunction define its particular character. It proved to be the first in a series of loosely interlinked films (the intertextuality is rather more than a charming gimmick, relating as it does to certain thematic preoccupations already established in *Lola* itself); arguably, it remains the richest and most satisfying work so far in Demy's erratic, frustrating, but also somewhat underrated career.

The name and character of Lola (Anouk Aimée) herself can be traced to two previous celebrated female protagonists: the Lola Montès of Max Ophüls's film of that name, and the Lola-Lola (Marlene Dietrich) of von Sternberg's *The Blue Angel*, to which Demy pays homage in a number performed by Aimée in a top hat. The explicit philosophy of Lola Montès ("For me, life is movement") is enacted in Demy's film by the constant comings and goings, arrivals and departures, and intricate intercrossings of the characters. Ophüls's work has often been linked to concepts of fate; at the same time the auteurs of the early New Wave were preoccupied with establishing Freedom—as a metaphysical principle, to be enacted in their professional methodology. The tension between fate and freedom is there throughout Demy's work. *Lola*'s credit sequence alternates the improvisatory freedom of jazz with the slow movement of Beethoven's 7th Symphony. The latter musical work is explicitly associated with destiny in the form of the huge white American car that brings back Michel, Lola's lover and father of her child, who, like his predecessors in innumerable folk songs, has left her for seven years to make his fortune. No film is more intricately and obsessively patterned, with all the characters interlinked: the middle-aged woman used to be Lola (or someone like her), her teenage daughter may become Lola (or someone like her). Yet neither resembles Lola as she is in the film: everyone is different, yet everyone is interchangeable.

Two subsequent Demy films relate closely to *Lola*. In *Les Parapluies de Cherbourg,* Roland, Lola's rejected lover, recounts his brief liaison with Lola to the visual accompaniment of a flashback to the arcade that was one of their meeting-places. In addition, Lola herself reappears in *The Model Shop.* Two other films are bound in to the series as well. *Les Demoiselles de Rochefort* is linked by means of a certain cheating on the part of Demy—Lola has been found murdered and dismembered in a laundry basket, but the corpse is a different Lola. Especially poignant, as the series continues, is the treatment of the abrupt, unpredictable, seemingly fortuitous happy ending. At the end of *Lola,* Lola drives off with Michel and their child (as Roland of *Parapluies,* discarded and embittered, departs on his diamond-smuggling trip to South Africa). At the conclusion of *Le Baie des Anges*—a film that, at the time, revealed no connection with *Lola*—Jackie (Jeanne Moreau), a compulsive gambler, manages to leave the casino to follow her lover *before* she knows the result of her bet: two happy endings which are exhilarating precisely because they are so arbitrary. Then, several films later, in *Model Shop,* Lola recounts how her great love Michel abandoned her to run off with a compulsive gambler called Jackie. Thus both happy endings are reversed in a single blow.

It is not so much that Demy doesn't believe in happy endings: he simply doesn't believe in *permanent* ones (as "life is movement"). The ambivalent, bittersweet "feel" of Demy is perhaps best summed up in the end of *Les Parapluies de Cherbourg,* where the lovers, now both married to others, accidentally meet, implicitly acknowledge their love, and return with acceptance to the relationships to which they are committed.

Outside the *Lola* series, Demy's touch has been uncertain. His two fairy-tale films, *Peau d'ane* and *The Pied Piper,* unfortunately tend to confirm the common judgment that he is more a decorator than a creator. But he should not be discounted. *A Room in Town,* a return to the *Lola* mode if not to the *Lola* characters, was favorably received.

Demy's final two credits, *Parking* and *Three Places for the 26th,* are musicals which disappointed in that they were unable to capture the spark of his earlier work. Agnes Varda, his wife of almost three decades, then directed a film about Demy titled *Jacquot de Nantes,* which was released a year after his death. The film is a poignant, straight-from-the-heart record of the measure of a man's life, with Varda shifting between interviews with Demy (tenderly shot in extreme close-up), sequences from his films, and a narrative which details the youth of Demy in Nantes during the 1940s and relates how he cultivated a love of the movies. The film works best, however, as a beautiful and poignantly composed love letter. Its essence is summed up in one of its opening shots: the camera pans the content of a watercolor, focusing first on a nude woman, then on a nude man, and finally on their interlocking hands.

Jacquot de Nantes is obviously a very personal film. But it was not meant to be a tribute; rather, it was conceived and filmed when Demy was still alive. "Jacques would speak about his childhood, which he loved," Varda explained at a New York Film Festival press conference. "His memories were very vivid. I told him, 'Why don't you write about them?' So he did, and he let me read the pages. The more he wrote the more he remembered—even the names of the children who sat next to him in school. Most children do not know what they want to do when they grow up. But Jacques did, from the time he was 12. He had an incredible will. So I said, 'This [material] would make a good film.' I wrote the script, and I tried to capture the spirit of Jacques and his family, and the way people spoke and acted in [the 1940s]. We shot the film in the exact [locations] in which he grew up. I also filmed an interview with him. It's just Jacques speaking about his childhood. It's not a documentary about Jacques Demy. It's just him saying, 'Yes, this is true. This is my life.'

Jacques Demy with Agnès Varda

"He saw most of the final [version]. When Jacques 'went away,' I had to finish the film. It was difficult, but that's the only thing I know. I think the film makes Jacques very alive."

Demy was the subject of two follow-ups to *Jacquot de Nantes,* also directed by Varda: *The Young Girls Turn 25,* a sentimental reminiscence of the filming of *The Young Girls of Rochefort* and *The World of Jacques Demy,* an intensely intimate documentary-biography which includes clips from his films and interviews with those who worked with and respected him.—ROBIN WOOD and ROB EDELMAN

De Sica, Vittorio

Nationality *Italian/French (became French citizen in order to marry second wife, 1968.)* **Born** *Sora (near Rome), 7 July 1902.* **Education** *Institut Superieur de Commerce, Rome, and University of Rome.* **Family** *Married 1) Giuditta Rissone (divorced 1968); 2) Maria Mercader, 1968, two sons.* **Career** *Actor in Tatiana Pavlova's Stage Company, 1923; formed own stage company with actress-wife, late 1920s; leading film actor, from 1931; directed first film,* Rose scarlatte, *1940.* **Died** *In Paris, 13 November 1974.*

Films as Director: 1940: *Rose scarlatte* (co-d, role as The Engineer). **1941:** *Maddelena zero in condotta* (+dialogue, role as Carlo Hartman); *Teresa Venerdi* (+co-sc, role). **1942:** *Un garibaldino al convento* (+co-sc, role as Nino Bixio). **1943:** *I bambini ci guardano* (+co-sc). **1946:** *La porta del cielo* (+co-sc, completed 1944); *Sciuscia* (*Shoeshine*) (+co-sc). **1948:** *Ladri di biciclette* (*The Bicycle Thief*) (+pr, co-sc). **1950:** *Miracolo a Milano* (*Miracle in Milan*) (+co-sc). **1952:** *Umberto D* (+pr, co-sc).

1953: *Stazione Termini* (*Indiscretion of an American Wife; Indiscretion*) (+co-pr). **1954:** *L'oro di Napoli* (*Gold of Naples*) (+co-sc, role). **1956:** *Il tetto* (*The Roof*) (+pr). **1960:** *La ciociara* (*Two Women*). **1961:** *Il giudizio universale* (+role). **1962:** "La Riffa (The Raffle)" episode of *Boccaccio '70; I sequestrati di Altona* (*The Condemned of Altona*). **1963:** *Il boom; Ieri, oggi, domani* (*Yesterday, Today and Tomorrow*). **1964:** *Matrimonio all'italiana* (*Marriage, Italian Style*). **1965:** *Un Monde nouveau* (*Un Monde jeune; Un mondo nuovo; A Young World*). **1966:** *Caccia alla volpe* (*After the Fox*) (+guest role); "Un sera come le altre (A Night Like Any Other)" episode of *Le streghe* (*The Witches*). **1967:** *Woman Times Seven* (*Sept fois femmes*). **1968:** *Amanti* (*A Place for Lovers*) (+co-sc). **1970:** *I girasoli* (*Sunflower*); *Il giardino dei Finzi Contini* (*The Garden of the Finzi-Continis*); "Il leone" episode of *Le coppie* (*The Couples*). **1972:** *Lo chiameremo Andrea*. **1973:** *Una breve vacanza* (*A Brief Vacation*). **1974:** *Il viaggio* (*The Journey; The Voyage*).

Other Films: **1918:** *Il processo Clémenceau* (*L'Affaire Clemenceau*) (Bencivenga) (role). **1926:** *La bellezza del mondo* (Almirante) (role). **1928:** *La compagnia dei matti* (*La compagnie des fous*) (Almirante) (role). **1932:** *La vecchia signora* (Palermi) (role); *La segretaria per tutti* (Palermi) (role); *Due cuori felici* (Negroni) (role); *Gli uomini che mascalzoni!* (Camerini) (role). **1933:** *Un cattivo soggetto* (Bragaglia) (role); *Il signore desidera?* (Righelli) (role); *La canzone del sole* (German version: *Das Lied der Sonne*) (Neufeld) (role as The Secretary); *Lisetta* (Boese) (role). **1934:** *Tempo massimo* (Mattoli) (role). **1935:** *Darò un millione* (Camerini) (role as The Millionaire); *Amo te sola* (Mattòli) (role). **1936:** *Lohengrin* (Malasomma) (role); *Ma non è una cosa seria!* (Camerini) (role); *Non ti conosco più* (Malasomma) (role); *L'uomo che sorride* (Mattoli) (role). **1937:** *Hanno rapito un uomo* (Righelli) (role); *Il signor Max* (Camerini) (role); *Questi ragazzi* (Mattoli) (role). **1938:** *Napoli d'altri tempi* (Palermi) (role); *L'orologio a cucù* (Mastrocinque) (role); *Partire* (Palermi) (role); *Ai vostri ordini, signora!* (Mattòli) (role); *La mazurka di papà* (Biancoli) (role); *Le due madri* (Palermi) (role); *Castelli in aria* (German version: *Ins blaue Leben*, 1939) (Genina) (role). **1939:** *Grandi magazzini* (Camerini) (role); *Finisce sempre cosí* (Susini) (role); *Napoli che non muore* (Palermi) (role). **1940:** *La peccatrice* (Palermi) (role); *Pazza di gioia* (Bragaglia) (role); *Manon Lescaut* (Gallone) (role). **1941:** *L'avventuriera del piano di sopra* (Matarazzo) (role). **1942:** *Se io fossi onesto!* (Bragaglia) (role, co-sc); *La guardia del corpo* (Bragaglia) (role, co-sc). **1943:** *I nostri sogni* (Cottafavi) (role, co-sc); *Non sono superstizioso, ma. . .!* (Bragaglia) (role, co-sc); *L'ippocampo* (Rosmino) (role, co-sc); *Dieci minuti di vita* (Longanesi) (unfinished; another version made 1944 with different cast) (role); *Nessuno torna indietro* (Blasetti) (role). **1945:** *Lo sbaglio di essere vivo* (Bragagalia) (role); *Il mondo vuole cosí* (Bianchi) (role). **1946:** *Roma città libera* (co-sc); *Il marito povero* (Amara) (co-sc); *Abbasso la ricchezza!* (Righelli) (role, co-sc). **1947:** *Sperduti nel buio* (Mastrocinque) (role as Nanzio, co-sc); *Natale al campo 119* (Francisci) (supervisor, role as The Noble Neopolitan). **1948:** *Lo sconosciuto di San Marino* (Waszinsky) (role as The Proprietor); *Cuore* (Coletti) (co-sc, role as The Landlord). **1950:** *Domani è troppo tardi* (Moguy) (role as Professor Landi). **1951:** *Cameriera bella presenza offresi* (Pastina) (role as The Actor); "Il processo di Frine" episode of *Altri tempi* (Blasetti) (role as the Barrister); *Gli uomini non guardano il cielo* (Scarpelli) (role). **1952:** *Buongiorno elefante!* (*Sabú principe ladro*) (Franciolini) (co-sc, role as Garetti); "Scena all'aperto" (role as Count) and "Don Corradino" (role as Don Corradino) episodes of *Tempi nostri* (Blasetti). **1953:** *Madame De . . .* (Ophuls) (role as Fabrizio Donati); *Pane, amore e fantasia* (Comencini) (role as Marshal Carotenuto); "Pendolin" episode of *Cento anni d'amore* (De Felice) (role); "Incidente a Villa Borghese" episode of *Villa Borghese* (Franciolini) (role); *Il matrimonio* (Petrucci) (role); "Il fine dicitore" episode of *Gran varietà* (Paolella) (role); "Le Divorce (Il divorzio)" episode of *Secrets d'alcôve* (*Il letto*) (Franciolini) (role). **1954:** *Vergine moderna* (Pagliero) (role as The Banker); *L'Allegro Squadrone* (Moffa) (role as The General); *Pane, amore e gelosia* (Comencini) (role); *Peccato che sia una canaglia* (Blasetti) (role as Mr. Stroppiani). **1955:** *Il segno di Venere* (Risi) (role as Alessio Spano, the Poet); *Gli ultimi cinque minuti* (*The Last Five Minutes*) (Amato) (role as Carlo); *La bella mugnaia* (Camerini) (role as The Governor); *Pane, amore e . . .* (Risi) (role as Carotenuto); *Racconti romani* (Franciolini) (role); *Il bigamo* (Emmer) (role as The Barrister). **1956:** *Mio figlio Nerone* (*Nero's Weekend*) (Steno) (role as Sénèquel); *Tempo di villegiatura* (Racioppi) (role as The Celebrity); *The Monte Carlo Story* (*Montecarlo*) (Taylor) (role as Count Dino Giocondo Della Fiaba); *I giorni più belli* (*I nostri anni più belli, Gli anni più belli*) (Mattòli) (role as The Banker); *Noi siamo le colonne* (D'Amico) (role as Celimontani).

1957: *Padri e figli* (Monicelli) (role as the tailor Corallo); *I colpevoli* (Vasile) (role as the barrister Vasari); *Souvenir d'Italie* (*It Happened in Rome*) (Pietrangeli) (role as The Count); *La donna che venne del mare*

(De Robertis) (role as Bordigin); *Vacanze a Ischia* (Camerini) (role as Occhipinti); *I conte Max* (Bianchi) (role as Count Max Orsini Baraldo); *Amore e chiacchiere* (Blasetti) (role as Bonelli); *Il medico e lo stregone* (Monicelli) (role as Locoratolo); *Totò, Vittorio e la dottoressa* (Mastrocinque) (role as the sick nobleman); *Casino de Paris* (Hunebelle) (role as Alexandre Gordy). **1958:** *A Farewell to Arms* (Vidor) (role as Count Alessandro Rinaldi); *Domenica è sempre domenica* (Mastrocinque) (role as Mr. Guastaldi); *Ballerina e buon Dio* (Leonviola) (roles as the policeman, the taxi driver, and the costume porter); *Kanonenserenade* (*Pezzo, capopezzo e capitano*) (Staudte) (role as Count Ernesto De Rossi); *Anna di Brooklyn* (Denham and Lastricati) (supervisor, co-music, role as Don Luigino); *La ragazza di Piazza S. Pietro* (Costa) (role as Armando Conforti); *Gli zitelloni* (Bianchi) (role as Professor Landi); *Pane, amore e Andalusia* (Setò) (role as Carotenuto); *La prima notte* (Cavalcanti) (role as Alfredo). **1959:** *Nel blu dipinto di blu* (*Volare*) (Tellini) (role as Spartaco); *Il nemico di mia moglie* (Puccini) (role as The Husband); *Vacanze d'inverno* (Mastrocinque) (role as Manrizie); *Il moralista* (Bianchi) (role as The President); *Il Generale Della Rovere* (Rossellini) (role as Giovanni Bertone); *Il mondo dei miracoli* (Capuano) (role as Pietro Giordani); *Uomini e nobiluomini* (Bianchi) (role as Marquis Nicolas Peccoli); *Ferdinando I, re di Napoli* (Franciolini) (role as Ceccano); *Gastone* (Bonnard) (role as The Prince); *Les trois etc . . . du colonel* (*Le tre eccetera del colonello*) (Boissol) (role as Colonel Belalcazar).

1960: *Il vigile* (Zampa) (role as The Trustee); *Le pillole di Ercole* (Salce) (role as Colonel Pietro Cuocolo); *Austerlitz* (Gance) (role as Pope Pius VII); *The Angel Wore Red* (*La sposa bella*) (Johnson) (role as General Clave); *The Millionairess* (Asquith) (role as Joe); *It Started in Naples* (Shavelson) (role as Mario Vitale); *Gli incensurati* (Giaculli) (role as comic actor); *Un amore a Roma* (Risi) (role). **1961:** *Gli attendenti* (Bianchi) (role as Colonel Bitossi); *I due marescialli* (Corbucci) (role as Antonio Cotone); *Le meraviglie di Aladino* (*The Wonders of Aladdin*) (Bava and Levin) (role as The Genie); *L'onorata società* (Pazzaglia) (role as The Chef); *La Fayette* (*La Fayette, una spada per due bandiere*) (Dréville) (role as Bancroft). **1962:** *Vive Henry IV, vive l'amour* (Autant-Lara) (role as Don Pedro). **1965:** *The Amorous Adventures of Moll Flanders* (T. Young) (role as The Count). **1966:** *Io, io, io . . . e gli altri* (Blasetti) (role as Count Trepossi). **1967:** *Gli altri, gli altri e noi* (Arena) (role as man on pension); *Un italiano in America* (Sordi) (role as Giuseppe's Father); *The Biggest Bundle of Them All* (Annakin) (role as Cesare Celli); *Caroline Cherie* (de la Patelliere) (role as Count de Bièvres). **1968:** *The Shoes of the Fisherman* (*Les Souliers de Saint-Pierre*) (M. Anderson) (role as Cardinal Rinaldi). **1969:** *If It's Tuesday, This Must Be Belgium* (M. Stuart) (role as The Shoemaker); *Una su tredici* (*12 + 1*) (Gessner and Lucignani) (role as Di Seta). **1970:** *Cose di Cosa Nostra* (Steno) (role as The Lawyer); *L'Odeur des fauves* (Balducci) (role as Milord). **1971:** *Trastevere* (Tozzi) (role as Enrico Formichi); *Io non vedo, tu non parli, lui non sente* (Camerini) (role as Count at the Casino). **1972:** *Pinocchio* (Comencini) (for TV) (role as The Judge); *Snow Job* (*The Ski Raiders*) (Englund) (role as Dolphi); *Ettore lo fusto* (Castellari) (role as Giove); *Siamo tutti in libertà provvisoria* (Scarpelli) (role). **1973:** *Storia de fratelli e de cortelli* (Amendola) (role as The Marshal); *Il delitto Matteotti* (Vancini) (role as Mauro del Giudice). **1974:** *Andy Warhol's Dracula* (*Dracula cerca sangue di vergine e . . . morì di sete!!, Blood for Dracula*) (Morrissey) (role as Marquis di Fiori); *C'eravamo tanto amati* (Scola) (role as himself); *Vittorio De Sica, il Regista, l'attore, l'uomo* (Gragadze) (role).

The films of Vittorio De Sica are among the most enduring of the Italian post-war period. His career suggests an openness to form and a versatility uncommon among Italian directors. De Sica began acting on stage as a teenager and played his first film role in 1918. In the 1920s his handsome features and talent made him something of a matinee idol, and from the mid-1930s he appeared in a number of films by Mario Camerini, including *Gli uomini che mascalzoni!, Darò un milione,* and *Grandi magazzine.*

During his lifetime, De Sica acted in over one hundred films in Italy and abroad, using this means to finance his own directorial efforts. He specialized in breezy comic heroes, men of great self-assurance or confidence men (as in Rossellini's *Generale della Rovere*). The influence of his tenure as actor cannot be overestimated in his directorial work, where the expressivity of the actor in carefully written roles was one of his foremost technical implements. In this vein De Sica

Vittorio De Sica

has continually mentioned the influence on his work of Charlie Chaplin. The tensive continuity between tragic and comic, the deployment of a detailed yet poetic gestural language, and a humanist philosophy without recourse to the politically radical are all elements of De Sica's work that are paralleled in the silent star's films.

De Sica's directorial debuts, *Rose scarlatte* and *Maddalena, zero in condotta,* were both attempts to bring theater pieces to the screen with suitable roles for himself. In 1943, with *I bambini ci guardano,* De Sica teamed with Cesare Zavattini, who was to become his major collaborator for the next three decades. Together they began to demonstrate elements of the post-war realist aesthetic which, more than any other director except Visconti and Rossellini, De Sica helped shape and determine. Despite the overt melodrama of the misogynistic story (a young mother destroys her family by deserting them), the filmmaker refused to narrow the perspective through an overwrought Hollywoodian mise-en-scène, preferring instead a refreshing simplicity of composition and a subdued editing style. Much of the film's original flavor can be traced to the clear, subjective mediation of a child, as promised in the title.

De Sica's intense feeling for children's sensibilities led him to imagine how children viewed the failing adult reconstruction of society after the war. *Sciuscia,* a realistic look at the street and prison life of poor, abandoned children, was the result. It is the story of how the lasting friendship of two homeless boys, who make their living shining shoes for the American G.I.'s, is betrayed by their contact with adults. At the end of the film one boy inadvertently causes the other's death. Although Zavattini insists that his creative role was minimal in this instance, the presence of his poetic imagination is evident in the figure of a beautiful white horse. This horse serves to cement the boys' mutual bond and their hope for a future. Though a miserable failure in Italy, *Sciuscia* marked De Sica's entry into international prominence; the film won a special Oscar in 1947.

For the balance of the neorealist period De Sica fought an uphill battle to finance his films through friends and acting salaries. *Ladri di biciclette* anchors searching social documentation in metaphor and a non-traditional but highly structured narrative. Workman Ricci's desperate search for his bicycle is an odyssey that enables us to witness a varied collection of characters and situations among the poor and working class of Rome. Each episode propels the narrative toward a sublimely Chaplinesque but insufficiently socially critical ending in which Ricci is defeated in his search and therefore in his attempts to provide for his family. Reduced to thievery himself, he takes his son's hand and disappears into the crowd. Like De Sica's other neorealist films, *Ladri di biciclette* gives the impression of technical nonchalance only to the indiscriminate eye, for De Sica planned his work with attention to minute details of characterization, mise-en-scène, and camera technique. During this period he preferred the non-professional actor for his or her ability to accept direction without the mediation of learned acting technique.

The story of Toto the Good in *Miracolo a Milano* remains one of the outstanding stylistic contradictions of the neorealist period (there are many), yet one which sheds an enormous amount of light on the intentions and future of the De Sica-Zavattini team. The cinematography and setting, markedly neorealist in this fable about the struggle to found a shanty town for the homeless, is undercut at every moment with unabashed clowning both in performance and in cinematic technique. Moreover, the film moves toward a problematic fairy tale ending in which the poor, no longer able to defend their happy, make-shift village from the voracious appetite of capitalist entrepreneurs, take to the skies on magic broomsticks. (The film has more special effects than anyone would ever associate with neorealism; could De Sica have left his mark on Steven Spielberg?) Still, Zavattini, who had wanted to make the film for a number of years, and De Sica defend it as the natural burlesque transformation of themes evident in their earlier work together.

By this time De Sica's films were the subject of a good deal of controversy in Italy, and generally the lines were drawn between Catholic and Communist critics. The latter had an especially acute fear (one which surfaced again with Fellini's *La Strada*) that the hard-won traits of neorealism had begun to backslide into those of the so-called "calligraphic" films of the Fascist era. These were based on an ahistorical, formal concern for aesthetic, compositional qualities and the nuances of clever storytelling. However, it was their next film, *Umberto D*, that comes closest to realizing Zavattini's ideas on the absolute responsibility of the camera eye to observe life as it is lived without the traditional compromises of entertaining narratives. The sequence of the film in which the maid wakes up and makes the morning coffee has been praised many times for its day-in-the-life directness and simplicity. *Il Tetto*, about a curious attempt to erect a small house on municipal property, is generally recognized as the last neorealist film of this original period.

Continually wooed by Hollywood, De Sica finally acquiesced to make *Stazione termini* in 1953, produced by Selznick and filmed in Rome with Jennifer Jones and Montgomery Clift. Unfortunately, neorealist representation formed only an insignificant background to this typically American star vehicle. A similar style is employed in *La ciociara,* which was created from a Moravia story about the relationship of a mother and daughter uprooted by the war. De Sica attempted to reconstruct reality in the studio during the making of this work, making use of a somewhat unsuccessful stylized lighting technique. But as usual, he obtains excellent performances in an engaging dramatic vehicle (Sophia Loren won an Oscar).

The filmmakers returned to comedic vehicles in 1954 in *L'oro di Napoli*. Human comedy emerges from the rich diversity and liveliness of Neapolitan life. Though still within the confines of realism, the film foreshadows the director's entrance into the popular Italian market for sexual satire and farce. The exactitude with which he sculpts his characters and his reluctance to reduce the scenario to a mere bunch of gags demonstrates his intention to fuse comedy and drama, putting De Sica at the top of his class in this respect—among Risi, Comencini, and Monicelli. Often with Zavattini but also with Eduardo De Filippo, Tonino Guerra, and even Neil Simon (*After the Fox*), De Sica turned out about eight such films for the lucrative international market between 1961 and 1968, the best of which are: *Il giudizio universale,* which featured an all-star cast of international comedians; *Ieri, oggi, domani* and *Matrimonio all'Italiana,* both with Loren and Mastroianni; and *Sette volte donna.*

Il giardino dei Finzi Contini, based on a Bassani novel about the incarceration of Italian Jews during the war, shows a strong Viscontian influence in its lavish setting and thematics (the film deals with the dissolution of the bourgeois family). *Una breve vacanza,* an examination of a woman who has managed to break out of the confines of an oppressive marriage during a sanitorium stay, reinstitutes the tensive relationship between comedy and tragedy of the earlier films. De Sica's last film, *Il viaggio,* is from a Pirandello novel.—JOEL KANOFF

Dovzhenko, Alexander

Nationality *Ukrainian.* **Born** *Sosnytsia, Chernigov province of Ukraine, 12 September 1894.* **Education** *Hlukhiv Teachers' Institute, 1911-14; Kiev University, 1917-18; Academy of Fine Arts, Kiev, 1919.* **Military Service** *1919-20.* **Family** *Married 1) Barbara Krylova, 1920 (divorced 1926); 2) Julia Solntseva, 1927.* **Career** *Teacher, 1914-19; chargé d'affaires, Ukrainian embassy, Warsaw, 1921; attached to Ukrainian embassy, Berlin; studied painting with Erich Heckel, 1922; returned to Kiev, expelled from Communist Party, became cartoonist, 1923; co-founder, VAPLITE (Free Academy of Proletarian Literature), 1925; joined Odessa Film Studios, directed first film,* Vasya-reformator, *1926; moved to Kiev Film Studios, 1928; Solntseva began as his assistant, 1929; lectured at State Cinema Institute (VGIK), Moscow, 1932; assigned to Mosfilm by Stalin, 1933; artistic supervisor, Kiev Studio, 1940; front-line correspondent for Red Army and* Izvestia *in the Ukraine, 1942-43; denounced as "bourgeois nationalist," transferred to Mosfilm, 1944; theatre director, 1945-47; settled in Kakhiva, 1952. Julia Solntseva directed five films based on Dovzhenko's writings, 1958-69.* **Awards** *Lenin Prize, 1935; Honored Art Worker of the Ukrainian SSR, 1939; 1st Degree Stalin Prize for* Shchors, *1941; Order of the Red Flag, 1943; Order of the Red Labor Flag, 1955.* **Died** *In Moscow, 26 November 1956.*

Films as Director: 1926: *Vasya-reformator* (*Vasya the Reformer*) (co-d, sc); *Yahidka kokhannya* (*Love's Berry, Yagodko lyubvi*) (+sc). **1927:** *Teka dypkuryera* (*The Diplomatic Pouch; Sumka dipkuryera*) (+revised sc, role). **1928:** *Zvenyhora* (*Zvenigora*) (+revised sc). **1929:** *Arsenal* (+sc). **1930:** *Zemlya* (*Earth*) (+sc). **1932:** *Ivan* (+sc). **1935:** *Aerograd* (*Air City, Frontier*) (+sc). **1939:** *Shchors* (co-d, co-sc). **1940:** *Osvobozhdenie* (*Liberation*) (co-d, ed, sc). **1945:** *Pobeda na pravoberezhnoi Ukraine i izgnanie Nemetskikh zakhvatchikov za predeli Ukrainskikh Sovetskikh zemel* (*Victory in Right-Bank Ukraine and the Expulsion of the Germans from the Boundaries of the Ukrainian Soviet Earth*) (co-d, commentary). **1948:** *Michurin* (co-d, pr, sc).

Other Films: 1940: *Bukovyna-Zemlya Ukrayinska* (*Bucovina-Ukrainian Land*) (Solntseva) (artistic spvr). **1941:** *Bohdan Khmelnytsky* (Savchenko) (artistic spvr). **1942:** *Alexander Parkhomenko* (Lukov) (artistic spvr). **1943:** *Bytva za nashu Radyansku Ukrayinu* (*The Battle for Our Soviet Ukraine*) (Solntseva and Avdiyenko) (artistic spvr, narration). **1946:** *Strana rodnaya* (*Native Land; Our Country*) (co-ed uncredited, narration).

(Films directed by Julia Solntseva, prepared or written by Dovzhenko or based on his writings): 1958: *Poema o more* (*Poem of an Inland Sea*). **1961:** *Povest plamennykh let* (*Story of the Turbulent Years; The Flaming Years; Chronicle of Flaming Years*). **1965:** *Zacharovannaya Desna* (*The*

Enchanted Desna). **1968:** *Nezabivaemoe (The Unforgettable; Ukraine in Flames).* **1969:** *Zolotye vorota (The Golden Gates).*

Unlike many other Soviet filmmakers, whose works are boldly and aggressively didactic, Alexander Dovzhenko's cinematic output is personal and fervently private. His films are clearly political, yet at the same time he is the first Russian director whose art is so emotional, so vividly his own. His best films, *Arsenal, Earth,* and *Ivan,* are all no less than poetry on celluloid. Their emotional and poetic expression, almost melancholy simplicity, and celebration of life ultimately obliterate any external event in their scenarios. His images—most specifically, farmers, animals, and crops drenched in sunlight—are penetratingly, delicately real. With Eisenstein and Pudovkin, Dovzhenko is one of the great inventors and masters of the Russian cinema.

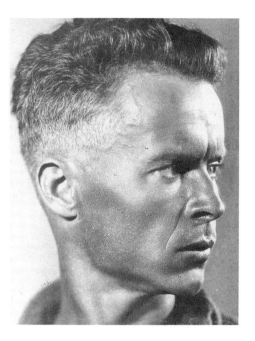

Alexander Dovzhenko

As evidenced by his very early credits, Dovzhenko might have become a journeyman director and scenarist, an adequate technician at best: *Vasya the Reformer,* his first script, is a forgettable comedy about an overly curious boy; *The Diplomatic Pouch* is a silly tale of secret agents and murder. But in *Zvenigora,* his fourth film, he includes scenes of life in rural Russia for the first time. This complex and confusing film proved to be the forerunner of *Arsenal, Earth,* and *Ivan,* a trio of classics released within four years of each other, all of which honor the lives and struggles of peasants.

In *Arsenal,* set in the Ukraine in a period between the final year of World War I and the repression of a workers' rebellion in Kiev, Dovzhenko does not bombard the viewer with harsh, unrealistically visionary images. Despite the subject matter, the film is as lyrical as it is piercing and pointed; the filmmaker manages to transcend the time and place of his story. While he was not the first Soviet director to unite pieces of film with unrelated content to communicate a feeling, his *Arsenal* is the first feature in which the totality of its content rises to the height of pure poetry. In fact, according to John Howard Lawson, "no film artist has ever surpassed Dovzhenko in establishing an intimate human connection between images that have no plot relationship."

The storyline of *Earth,* Dovzhenko's next—and greatest—film, is deceptively simple: a peasant leader is killed by a landowner after the farmers in a small Ukrainian village band together and obtain a tractor. But these events serve as the framework for what is a tremendously moving panorama of rustic life and the almost tranquil admission of life's greatest inevitability: death. Without doubt, *Earth* is one of the cinema's few authentic masterpieces.

Finally, *Ivan* is an abundantly eloquent examination of man's connection to nature. Also set in the Ukraine, the film chronicles the story of an illiterate peasant boy whose political consciousness is raised during the building of the Dnieper River dam. This is Dovzhenko's initial sound film: he effectively utilizes his soundtrack to help convey a fascinating combination of contrasting states of mind.

None of Dovzhenko's subsequent films approach the greatness of *Arsenal, Earth,* and *Ivan.* Stalin suggested that he direct *Shchors,* which he shot with his wife, Julia Solntseva. Filmed over a three-year period under the ever-watchful eye of Stalin and his deputies, the scenario details the revolutionary activity of a Ukrainian intellectual, Nikolai Shchors. The result, while unmistakably a Dovzhenko film, still suffers from rhetorical excess when compared to his earlier work.

Eventually, Dovzhenko headed the film studio at Kiev, wrote stories, and made documentaries. His final credit, *Michurin,* about the life of a famed horticulturist, was based on a play he wrote during World War II. After *Muchurin,* the filmmaker spent several years putting together a trilogy set in the Ukraine, chronicling the development of a village from 1930 on. He was set to commence shooting when he died, and Solntseva completed the projects.

It is unfortunate that Dovzhenko never got to direct these last features. He was back on familiar ground: perhaps he might have been able to recapture the beauty and poetry of his earlier work. Still, *Arsenal, Ivan,* and especially *Earth* are more than ample accomplishments for any filmmaker's lifetime.—ROB EDELMAN

Dreyer, Carl Theodor

Nationality Danish. Born Copenhagen, 3 February 1889. Family Married Ebba Larsen, 1911, two sons. Career Journalist in Copenhagen, 1909-13; after writing scripts for

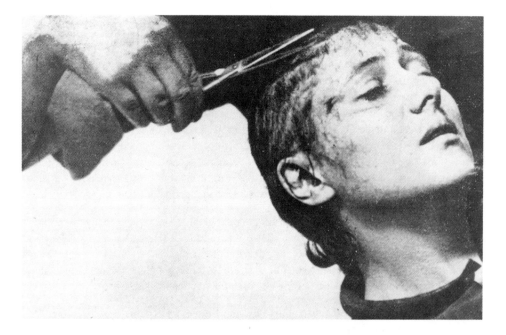

Carl Theodor Dreyer: Maria Falconetti in *La Passion de Jeanne d'Arc*.

Scandinavisk-Russiske Handelshus, joined Nordisk Films Kompagni, 1913; directed first film, Praesidenten, *1919; moved to Berlin, worked for Primusfilm, 1921; joined Ufa, 1924; returned to Copenhagen, 1925; hired by Société Generale de Films, Paris, 1926; left film industry, returned to journalism in Denmark, 1932; returned to filmmaking with documentary* Good Mothers, *1942; awarded managership of a film theatre by Danish government, 1952; worked on film project on the life of Jesus, 1964-68. **Award** Golden Lion Award, Venice Festival, for* Ordet, *1955. **Died** In Copenhagen, 20 March 1968.*

Films as Director: 1919: *Praesidenten* (*The President*) (+sc, co-art d). **1920:** *Prästänkan* (*The Parson's Widow; The Witch Woman; The Fourth Marriage of Dame Margaret*) (+sc). **1921:** *Blade af Satans Bog* (*Leaves from Satan's Book*) (+co-sc, co-art d) (shot in 1919). **1922:** *Die Gezeichneten* (*The Stigmatized One; Love One Another*) (+sc); *Der Var Engang* (*Once Upon a Time*) (+co-sc, ed). **1924:** *Michael* (+co-sc). **1925:** *Du Skal Aere Din Hustru* (*Thou Shalt Honor Thy Wife; The Master of the House*) (+co-sc, art d). **1926:** *Glomdalsbruden* (*The Bride of Glomdal*) (+sc, art d). **1928:** *La Passion de Jeanne d'Arc* (+co-sc). **1932:** *Vampyr* (*The Dream of David Gray*) (+co-sc, pr). **1942:** *Mødrehjaelpen* (*Good Mothers*). **1943:** *Vredens Dag* (*Day of Wrath*) (+co-sc). **1945:** *Två Manniskor* (*Two People*) (+co-sc, ed). **1946:** *Vandet Pa Låndet* (*Water from the Land*) (never finished) (+sc). **1947:** *Landsbykirken* (*The Danish Village Church*) (+co-sc); *Kampen Mod Kraeften* (*The Struggle Against Cancer*) (+co-sc). **1948:** *De Naaede Faergen* (*They Caught the Ferry*) (+sc). **1949:** *Thorvaldsen* (+co-sc). **1950:** *Storstrømsbroen* (*The Bridge of Storstrøm*) (+sc). **1954:** *Et Slot I Et Slot* (*Castle within a Castle*) (+sc). **1955:** *Ordet* (*The Word*) (+sc). **1964:** *Gertrud* (+sc).

Other Films: 1912: *Bryggerens Datter* (*The Brewer's Daughter*) (Ottesen) (co-sc). **1913:** *Ballonek-splosionen* (*The Balloon Explosion*) (sc); *Krigs-korrespondenten* (*The War Correspondent*) (Glückstadt) (sc); *Hans og Grethe* (*Hans and Grethe*) (sc); *Elskovs Opfindsomhed* (*Inventive Love*) (Wolder) (sc); *Chatollets Hemmelighed, eller Det gamle chatol* (*The Secret of the Writing Desk; The Old Writing Desk*) (Davidsen) (sc). **1914:** *Ned Med Vabnene* (*Lay Down Your Arms*) (Holger-Madsen) (sc). **1915:** *Juvelerernes Skrœck, eller Skelethaanden, eller Skelethaandens sidste bedrift* (*The Jeweller's Terror; The Skeleton's Hand; The Last Adventure of the Skeleton's Hand*) (Christian) (sc). **1916:** *Penge* (*Money*) (Mantzius) (sc); *Den Hvide Djœvel, eller Djœvelens Protege* (*The White Devil; The Devil's Protegé*) (Holger-Madsen) (sc); *Den Skonne Evelyn* (*Evelyn the Beautiful*) (Sandberg) (sc); *Rovedderkoppen, eller Den røde Enke* (*The Robber Spider; The White Widow*) (Blom) (sc); *En Forbryders Liv og Levned, eller En Forbryders Memoirer* (*The Life and Times of a Criminal; The Memoirs of a Criminal*) (Christian) (sc); *Guldets Gift, eller Lerhjertet* (*The Poison of Gold; The Clay Heart*) (Holger-Madsen) (sc); *Pavillonens Hemmelighed* (*The Secret of the Pavilion*) (Mantzius) (sc). **1917:** *Den Mystiske Selskabsdame, eller Legationens Gidsel* (*The Mysterious Lady's Companion; The Hostage of the Embassy*) (Blom) (sc); *Hans Rigtige Kone* (*His Real Wife*) (Holger-Madsen) (sc); *Fange Nr. 113* (*Prisoner No. 113*) (Holger-Madsen) (sc); *Hotel Paradis* (*Hotel Paradiso*) (Dinesen) (sc). **1918:** *Lydia* (Holger-Madsen) (sc); *Glaedens Dag, eller Miskendt* (*Day of Joy; Neglected*) (Christian) (sc). **1919:** *Gillekop* (Blom) (sc); *Grevindens Aere* (*The Countess' Honor*) (Blom) (sc). **1947:** *De Gamle* (*The Seventh Age*) (sc). **1949:** *Radioens Barndom* (ed). **1950:** *Shakespeare og Kronborg* (*Hamlet's Castle*) (Roos) (sc). **1954:** *Rønnes og Nexøs Genophygning* (*The Rebuilding of Ronne and Nexø*) (sc).

Carl Theodor Dreyer is the greatest filmmaker in the Danish cinema, where he was always a solitary personality. But he is also among the few international directors who turned films into an art and made them a new means of expression for the artistic genius. Of Dreyer's feature films, seven were produced in Denmark, three in Germany, two in France, two in Sweden, and one in Norway.

If one tries to understand the special nature of Dreyer's art, one can delve into his early life to find the roots of his never failing contempt for pretentions and his hatred of bourgeois respectability, as well as his preoccupation with suffering and martyrdom. In his biography of Dreyer, M. Drouzy revealed the fate of Dreyer's biological mother, who died in the most cruel way following an attempted abortion. Dreyer, who was adopted by a Copenhagen family, learned about the circumstances of her death when he was eighteen years old, and Drouzy's psychoanalytical study finds the victimized woman in all of Dreyer's films. But of what value is the biographical approach to the understanding of a great artist? The work of an artist need not be the illumination of his private life. This may afford some explanation when we are inquiring into the fundamental point of departure for an artist, but Dreyer's personality is expressed very clearly and graphically in his films. We can therefore well admire the consistency which has always characterized his outlook on life.

Like many great artists, Dreyer is characterized by the relatively few themes that he constantly played upon. One of the keynotes in Dreyer's work is suffering, and his world is filled with martyrs. Yet suffering and martyrdom are surely not the fundamentals. They are merely manifestations, the results of something else. Suffering and martyrdom are the consequences of wickedness, and it is malice and its influence upon people that his films are concerned about. As early in his career as the 1921 film, *Leaves From Satan's Book,* Dreyer tackled this theme of the power of evil over the human mind. He returned to examine this theme again and again.

If the popular verdict is that Dreyer's films are heavy and gloomy, naturally the idea is suggested by the subjects which he handled. Dreyer never tried to make us believe that life is a bed of roses. There is much suffering, wickedness, death, and torment in his films, but they often conclude in an optimistic conviction in the victory of spirit over matter. With death comes deliverance. It is beyond the reach of malice.

In his delineation of suffering man, devoid of any hope before the arrival of death, Dreyer was never philosophically abstract. Though his films were often enacted on a supersensible plane, and are concerned with religious problems, his method as an artist was one of psychological realism, and his object was always the individual. Dreyer's masterly depiction of milieu has always been greatly admired; his keen perception of the characteristic detail is simply dazzling. But this authenticity in settings has never been a means towards a meticulous naturalism. He always sought to transcend naturalism so as to reach a kind of purified, or classically simplified, realism.

Though Dreyer occupied himself with the processes of the soul, he always preserved an impartiality when portraying them. One might say that he maintained a high degree of objectivity in his description of the subjective. This can be sensed in his films as a kind of presentation rather than forceful advocacy. Dreyer himself, when describing his method in *La Passion de Jeanne d'Arc,* once employed the expression "realized mysticism." The phrase indicates quite precisely his endeavours to render understandable things that are difficult to comprehend, to make the irrational appear intelligible. The meaning behind life lies in just this recognition of the necessity to suffer in order to arrive at deliverance. The characters nearly always suffered defeat in the outward world because Dreyer considered defeat or victory in the human world to be of no significance. For him the triumph of the soul over life was what was most important.

There are those who wish to demonstrate a line of development in Dreyer's production, but there is no development in the customary sense. Dreyer's world seemed established at an early period of his life, and his films merely changed in their way of viewing the world. There was a complete congruity between his ideas and his style, and it was typical of him to have said: "The soul is revealed in the style, which is the artist's expression of the way he regards his material." For Dreyer the image was always the important thing, so important that there is some justification in describing him as first and foremost the great artist of the silent film. On the other hand, his last great films were concerned with the effort to create a harmony between image and sound, and to that end he was constantly experimenting.

Dreyer's pictorial style has been characterized by his extensive and careful employment of the close-up. His films are filled with faces. In this way he was able to let his characters unfold themselves, for he was chiefly interested in the expressions that appear as the result of spiritual conflicts. Emphasis has often been given to the slow lingering rhythm in Dreyer's films. It is obvious that this dilatoriness springs from the wish to endow the action with a stamp of monumentality, though it could lead dangerously close to empty solemnity, to the formalistic.

Dreyer quickly realized the inadequacy of the montage technique, which had been regarded as the foundation of film for so many years. His films became more and more based on long uncut sequences. By the end of his career his calm, elaborating style was quite in conformity with the newer trends in the cinema.—IB MONTY

Duras, Marguerite

Nationality French. *Born* Marguerite Donnadieu in Giadinh, French Indo-China, 1914. *Education* Educated in mathematics, law and political science at the Sorbonne, Paris. *Career* Published first novel, Les Impudents, 1943; subsequently novelist, journalist and playwright; directed first film, La Musica, 1966. *Awards* Prix Goncourt for novel L'Amant, 1984, Ritz Paris Hemingway, Paris, 1986. *Died* March 1996.

Films as Director: 1966: *La Musica* (co-d, sc). **1969:** *Détruire, dit-elle* (*Destroy She Said*) (+sc). **1971:** *Jaune le soleil* (+pr, co-ed, sc, from her novel *Abahn, Sabana, David*). **1972:** *Nathalie Granger* (+sc,

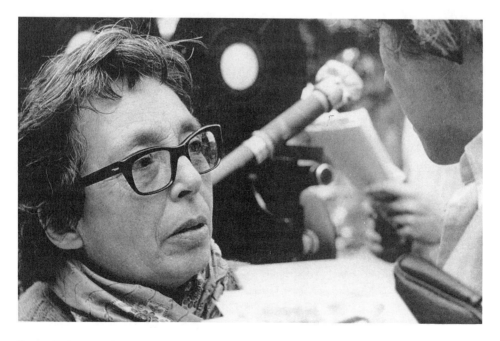

Marguerite Duras on the set of *Détruire, dit-elle*.

music). **1974:** *La Femme du Ganges* (+sc). **1975:** *India Song* (+sc, voice). **1976:** *Des journées entières dans les arbres* (*Days in the Trees*) (+sc); *Son Nom de Venises dans Calcutta desert* (+sc). **1977:** *Baxter, Vera Baxter* (+sc); *Le Camion* (+sc, role). **1978:** *Le Navire Night* (+sc). **1978/79:** *Aurelia Steiner* (4-film series): *Cesarée* (1978) (+sc); *Les Mains négatives* (1978) (+sc); *Aurelia Steiner—Melbourne* (1979) (+sc); *Aurelia Steiner—Vancouver* (1979) (+sc). **1981:** *Agatha et les lectures illimitées* (*Agatha*) (+sc). **1985:** *Les Enfants* (*The Children*).

Other Films: 1959: *Hiroshima mon amour* (Resnais) (sc). **1960:** *Moderato Cantabile* (Brook) (sc, co-adapt from her novel). **1961:** *Une Aussi longue absence* (*The Long Absence*) (Colpi) (co-sc from her novel). **1964:** *Nuit noire, Calcutta* (Karmitz) (short) (sc). **1965:** "Les rideaux blancs" (Franju) episode of *Der Augenblick des Friedens* (*Un Instant de la paix*) (for W.German TV) (sc). **1966:** *10:30 P.M. Summer* (*Dix heures et demie du soir en été*); (Dassin) (co-sc uncredited, from her novel) *La Voleuse* (Chapot) (sc, dialogue).

As a writer, Marguerite Duras's work is identified, along with that of such authors as Alain Robbe-Grillet and Jean Cayrol, with the tradition of the New Novel. Duras began working in film as a screenwriter, with an original script for Alain Resnais's first feature, *Hiroshima mon amour*. She subsequently wrote a number of film adaptations from her novels. She directed her first film, *La Musica*, in 1966. If *Hiroshima mon amour* remains her best known work in cinema, her later films have won widespread praise for the profound challenge they offer to conventional dramatic narrative.

The nature of narrative and the potential contained in a single text are major concerns of Duras's films. Many of her works have appeared in several forms, as novels, plays, and films. This not only involves adaptations of a particular work, but also extends to cross-referential networks that run through her texts. The film *Woman of the Ganges* combines elements from three novels—*The Ravishing of Lol V. Stein*, *The Vice-Consul*, and *L'Amour*. *India Song* was initially written as a play, taking characters from *The Vice-Consul* and elaborating on the structure of external voices developed in *Woman of the Ganges*. *India Song* was made as a film in 1975, and its verbal track was used to generate a second film, *Son Nom de Venises dans Calcutta desert*.

This process of transformation suggests that all works are "in progress," inherently subject to being reconstructed. This is partly because Duras's works are more concerned with the quality or intensity of experience than with events *per se*. The films present narrative rather than a linear, unambiguous sequence of events. In *Le Camion*, two characters, played by Gerard Depardieu and Duras, sit in a room as the woman describes a movie about a woman who hitches a ride with a truck driver and talks with him for an hour and twenty minutes. This conversation is intercut with scenes of a truck driving around Paris, and stopping for a female hitchhiker (with Depardieu as the driver, and Duras as the hitchhiker). Thus, the verbal description of a potential film is juxtaposed by images of what that film might be.

An emphasis on the soundtrack is also a crucial aspect of Duras's films; her verbal texts are lyrical and are as important as the images. In *India Song*, sound and image function contrapuntally, and the audience must actively assess the relation between them, reading across the body of the film, noting continuities and disjunctions. The verbal text often refers in past tense to events and characters on screen, as the viewer is challenged to figure out the chronology of events described and depicted—which name on the soundtrack corresponds to which actor, whether the voices belong to on- or off-screen characters, and so forth. In this way the audience participates in the search for a story, constructing possible narratives.

As minimal as they are, Duras's narratives are partially derived from melodrama, focusing on relations between men and women, the nature or structure of desire, and colonialism and imperialism in both literal and metaphoric terms. In pursuing these issues through non-conventional narrative forms, and shifting the burden of discovering meaning to the audience, Duras's films provide an alternative to conventional ways of watching movies. Her work is seen as exemplifying a feminine writing practice that challenges the patriarchal domination of classical narrative cinema. In an interview, Duras said, "I think the future belongs to women. Men have been completely dethroned. Their rhetoric is stale, used up. We must move on to the rhetoric of women, one that is anchored in the organism, in the body." It is this new rhetoric, a new way of communicating, that Duras sought through her films.—M.B. WHITE

d FILM DIRECTORS

Eastwood, Clint

Nationality *American.* **Born** *31 May 1930 in San Francisco, California.* **Education** *Oakland Technical High School; Los Angeles City College, 1953-54.* **Military Service** *Drafted into the U.S. Army, 1950.* **Family** *Married Maggie Johnson, 1953 (divorced, 1980); one son, one daughter.* **Career** *Under contract with Universal, 1954-55; sporadic work in film, late 1950s; played Rowdy Yates in TV series* Rawhide, *1959-65; went to Europe to make three highly successful westerns with Sergio Leone, 1965; returned to U.S., 1967; formed Malpaso production company and directed first film,* Play Misty for Me, *1971; first effort as producer,* Firefox, *1982; mayor of Carmel, California, 1986-88.* **Awards** *Chevaliers des Lettres, France, 1985; Academy Awards, Best Director and Best Picture, for* Unforgiven, *1992; Fellowship of the British Film Institute, 1993.* **Address** *Malpaso Productions, 4000 Warner Boulevard, Burbank, California 91522, USA.*

Films as Director: 1971: *Play Misty for Me* (+role). **1972:** *High Plains Drifter* (+role). **1973:** *Breezy.* **1975:** *The Eiger Sanction* (+role). **1976:** *The Outlaw Josey Wales* (+role). **1977:** *The Gauntlet* (+role). **1980:** *Bronco Billy* (+role, song composer). **1982:** *Firefox* (+role, pr); *Honkytonk Man* (+role, pr). **1983:** *Sudden Impact* (+role, pr). **1985:** *Pale Rider* (+role, pr). **1986:** *Heartbreak Ridge* (+role, pr, song composer). **1987:** *Bird* (+pr). **1990:** *The Rookie* (+role); *White Hunter, Black Heart* (+role, pr). **1992:** *Unforgiven* (+role, pr, music). **1993:** *A Perfect World* (+role, pr). **1995:** *The Bridges of Madison County* (+role, pr). **1997:** *Absolute Power* (+role, pr).

Other Films: 1955: *Francis in the Navy* (role); *Lady Godiva* (role); *Revenge of the Creature* (role); *Tarantula* (role). **1956:** *The First Travelling Saleslady* (role); *Never Say Goodbye* (role); *Star in the Dust* (role). **1957:** *Escapade in Japan* (role). **1958:** *Ambush at Cimarron Pass* (role); *Lafayette Escradille* (role). **1964:** *A Fistful of Dollars* (role). **1965:** *For a Few Dollars More* (role). **1966:** *Il Buono, il brutto, il cattivo* (*The Good, the Bad, and the Ugly* (Leone) (role); *Le Streghe* (role). **1967:** *Hang 'em High* (role). **1968:** *Coogan's Bluff* (role). **1969:** *Paint Your Wagon* (role); *Where Eagles Dare* (role). **1970:** *Kelly's Heroes* (role); *Two Mules for Sister Sara* (role). **1971:** *The Beguiled* (role); *Dirty Harry* (role). **1972:** *Joe Kidd* (role). **1973:** *Magnum Force* (role). **1974:** *Thunderbolt and Lightfoot* (role). **1976:** *The Enforcer* (role). **1978:** *Every Which Way but Loose* (role). **1979:** *Escape from Alcatraz* (role). **1980:** *Any Which Way You Can* (role, song composer). **1984:** *City Heat* (role); *Tightrope* (role, pr). **1988:** *The Dead Pool* (role, pr); *Thelonius Monk: Straight No Chaser* (exec pr). **1989:** *Pink Cadillac* (role). **1993:** *In the Line of Fire* (role).

In 1992, after almost forty years in the business, Clint Eastwood finally received Oscar recognition. *Unforgiven* brought him the awards for Best Achievement in Directing and for Best Picture, along with a nomination for Best Actor. Indeed, this strikingly powerful Western was nominated for no less than nine Academy Awards, Gene Hackman collecting Best Supporting Actor for his performance as the movie's ruthless marshall, "Little Bill" Daggett, and Joel Cox taking the Oscar for editing. It seems appropriate, therefore, that this film, which brought him such recognition, should end with the inscription "Dedicated to Sergio and Don." For without the intervention and influence of his two "mentors," directors Sergio Leone and Don Siegel, it is difficult to imagine Eastwood achieving his present respectability, let alone emerging as the only major star of the modern era who has become a better director than he ever was an actor.

That is not to belittle Eastwood, who has always been generous in crediting Leone and Siegel, and who is certainly far more than a passive inheritor of their directorial visions. Even in his *Rawhide* days of the 1950s and early 1960s he wanted to direct; more than once Eastwood has told of his attempts to persuade that series' producers to let him shoot some of the action rather more ambitiously than was the TV norm. Not surprisingly, they were reluctant, but they did in the end allow him to make trailers for upcoming episodes. He was not to take on a full-fledged directorial chall nge until 1971 with *Play Misty for Me,* but in the intervening years he had become a massive box-office attraction as an actor, first with Leone in Europe in the three famous and founding "spaghetti westerns," and then in a series of films with Siegel back in the United States, most significantly *Dirty Harry.*

It is not easy to untangle the respective influences of his mentors. In general terms, because they both contributed to the formation of Eastwood's distinctive screen persona, they helped him to crystallise an image which, as a director, he would so often use as a foil. The Italian Westerns' "man with no name," and his more anguished urban equivalent given expression in *Dirty Harry*'s eponymous anti-hero, have provided Eastwood with well-established and economical starting characters for so many of his performances. In directing himself, furthermore, he has used that persona with a degree of irony and distance. Sometimes, especially in his Westerns, that has meant leaning toward stylization and almost operatic exaggeration (*High Plains Drifter, Pale Rider,* the last section of *Unforgiven*), though rarely reaching Leone's extremes of delirious overstatement. On other occasions, it has seen him play on the tension between the seemingly assertive masculinity of the Eastwood image and the strong female characters who are so often featured in his films (*Play Misty for Me, The Gauntlet, Heartbreak Ridge* and, in part at least, *The Bridges of Madison County*). It is, of course, notoriously difficult to both direct and star in a movie. Where Eastwood has succeeded in that combination (not always the case) it has depended significantly on his inventive building on the Eastwood persona.

It is important to give Eastwood full credit for this inventiveness in any attempt to assess his work. His better films as a director have a richness to them, not just stylistically—though in those respects he has learned well from Leone's concern with lighting and composition and from Siegel's way with in-frame movement, editing, and tight narration—but also a moral complexity which belies the one-dimensionality of the Eastwood image. The protagonists in his better films, like Josey Wales in *The Outlaw Josey Wales,* Highway in *Heartbreak Ridge,* Munny in *Unforgiven,* even Charlie Parker in the flawed *Bird,* are not simple men in either their virtues or their failings. Eastwood's fondness for narratives of revenge and redemption, furthermore, allows him to draw

Clint Eastwood

upon a rich generic vein in American cinema, a tradition with a built-in potential for character development and for evoking human complexity without giving way to art-film portentousness.

In these respects Eastwood is the modern inheritor of traditional Hollywood directorial values, once epitomised in the transparent style of a John Ford, Howard Hawks, or John Huston (himself the subject of Eastwood's *White Hunter, Black Heart*), and passed on to Eastwood by that next-generation carrier of the tradition, Don Siegel. For these filmmakers, as for Eastwood, the action movie, the Western, the thriller were opportunities to explore character, motivation, and human frailty within a framework of accessible entertainment. Of course, all of them were also capable of "quieter" films, harnessing the same commitment to craft, the same attention to detail, in the service of less action-driven narratives, just as Eastwood has done most recently with *The Bridges of Madison County*. But in the end their and Eastwood's real art was to draw upon Hollywood's genre traditions and make of them unique and perceptive studies of human beings under stress. Though his directorial career has been uneven, at his best Eastwood has proved a more than worthy carrier of this flame.—ANDREW TUDOR

Edwards, Blake

Nationality *American.* ***Born*** *William Blake McEdwards in Tulsa, Oklahoma, 26 July 1922.* ***Military Service*** *Served in the U.S. Coast Guard, 1944-45.* ***Family*** *Married 1) Patricia Walker, 1953, one son, one daughter; 2) actress Julie Andrews, 1969, two adopted daughters.* ***Career*** *Created NBC radio series,* Richard Diamond, Private Detective, *for Dick Powell, 1949; as writer/director for Columbia B-picture Unit, directed first feature* Bring Your Smile Along, *1955; directed first A-picture,* Mister Cory, *1957; creator,* Peter Gunn, *1958,* Mr. Lucky, *1959, and* Dante's Inferno, *1960, for TV; after dispute over* The Carey Treatment, *moved to Europe; signed three-picture deal with Orion, 1978, agreement terminated after 10, 1979; directed Julie Andrews on Broadway in a stage adaptation of* Victor/Victoria, *1995; lives in Gstaad, Switzerland.* ***Award*** *Writers Guild of America Award, Best-Written Comedy Adapted from Another Medium, for* The Pink Panther Strikes Again *(co-authored with Frank Waldman), 1976.*

Films as Director: 1955: *Bring Your Smile Along* (+sc). **1956:** *He Laughed Last* (+sc). **1957:** *Mister Cory* (+sc). **1958:** *This Happy Feeling* (+sc). **1959:** *The Perfect Furlough* (*Strictly for Pleasure*) (+sc); *Operation Petticoat* (+sc). **1960:** *High Time* (+sc). **1961:** *Breakfast at Tiffany's.* **1962:** *Experiment in*

Terror (*The Grip of Fear*) (+pr, sc); *Days of Wine and Roses; Walk on the Wild Side* (Dmytryk) (d add'l scenes, uncredited). **1963:** *The Pink Panther* (+co-sc). **1964:** *A Shot in the Dark* (+sc). **1965:** *The Great Race* (+sc, co-story, bit role as troublemaker); *What Did You Do in the War, Daddy?* (+sc, co-story, pr). **1967:** *Gunn* (+co-sc). **1968:** *The Party* (+co-sc, pr). **1970:** *Darling Lili* (+co-sc, co-pr). **1971:** *The Wild Rovers* (+co-pr, sc). **1972:** *The Carey Treatment* (*Emergency Ward*). **1974:** *The Tamarind Seed* (+sc); *The Return of the Pink Panther* (+co-sc, pr). **1976:** *The Pink Panther Strikes Again* (+co-sc, pr). **1978:** *Revenge of the Pink Panther* (+co-sc, pr). **1979:** *10* (+sc, pr). **1981:** *S.O.B.* (+sc, pr). **1982:** *Victor/ Victoria* (+co-pr, sc); *Trail of the Pink Panther* (+pr, co-sc). **1983:** *Curse of the Pink Panther* (+pr, sc); *The Man Who Loved Women* (+pr, co-sc). **1984:** *Micki and Maude* (+pr). **1986:** *A Fine Mess* (*The Music Box*) (+sc); *That's Life* (*Crisis*) (+co-sc). **1987:** *Blind Date.* **1988:** *Sunset* (+sc); *Justin Case* (for TV). **1989:** *Skin Deep* (+sc); *Peter Gunn* (for TV) (+sc, ex pr). **1991:** *Switch* (+sc). **1992:** *Julie* (TV series) (+ex pr). **1993:** *Son of the Pink Panther* (+sc).

Other Films: **1941:** *Panhandle* (Selander) (role). **1942:** *Ten Gentlemen from West Point* (Hathaway) (role); *Lucky Legs* (Barton) (role). **1943:** *A Guy Named Joe* (Fleming) (role). **1944:** *In the Meantime, Darling* (Preminger) (role); *Marshal of Reno* (Grissell) (role); *See Here, Private Hargrove* (Ruggles) (role); *Ladies Courageous* (Rawlins) (role); *The Eve of St. Mark* (Stahl) (role); *Marine Raiders* (Schuster) (role); *Wing and a Prayer* (Hathaway) (role); *My Buddy* (Sekely) (role); *The Unwritten Code* (Rotsten) (role); *Thirty Seconds over Tokyo* (LeRoy) (role); *She's a Sweetheart* (Lord) (role). **1945:** *This Man's Navy* (Wellman) (role); *A Guy, a Gal, and a Pal* (Boetticher) (role); *Gangs of the Waterfront* (Blair) (role); *What Next, Corporal Hargrove?* (Thorpe) (role); *They Were Expendable* (Ford) (role); *Tokyo Rose* (Landers) (role); *Strangler of the Swamp* (Wisbar) (major role). **1946:** *The Strange Love of Martha Ivers* (Milestone) (role); *Till the End of Time* (Dmytryk) (role); *The Best Years of Our Lives* (Wyler) (role). **1947:** *The Beginning or the End* (Taurog) (role); *Panhandle* (co-sc, co-pr, role). **1948:** *Leather Gloves* (*Loser Take All*) (Quine and Asher) (sc, role). **1949:** *Stampede* (Selander) (co-sc, pr). **1952:** *Sound Off* (Quine) (sc); *Rainbow Round My Shoulder* (Quine) (sc). **1953:** *All Ashore* (Quine) (sc); *Cruisin' Down the River* (Quine) (sc). **1954:** *Drive a Crooked Road* (Quine) (sc); *The Atomic Kid* (Martinson) (story, sc). **1955:** *My Sister Eileen* (Quine) (sc). **1956:** *Operation Mad Ball* (Quine) (co-sc). **1961:** *The Couch* (Crump) (co-story). **1962:** *The Notorious Landlady* (Quine) (co-sc). **1963:** *Soldier in the Rain* (Nelson) (co-sc, pr). **1967:** *Inspector Clouseau* (Yorkin) (sc). **1969:** *The Monk* (McCowan) (for TV) (co-story). **1987:** *City Heat* (Benjamin) (co-sc as Sam O. Brown, story). **1992:** *Alan & Naomi* (Van Wagenen) (role); *Stompin' at the Savoy* (Allen) (role).

Blake Edwards is one of the few filmmakers from the late classical period of American movies (the late 1940s and 1950s) to survive and prosper through the 1980s. If anything, Edwards's work has deepened with the passing decades, though it no longer bears much resemblance to the norms and styles of contemporary Hollywood. Edwards is an isolated figure, but a vital one.

Edwards's critical and box office reputation first peaked in the early 1960s with such films as *Operation Petticoat, Breakfast at Tiffany's, Days of Wine and Roses,* and *The Pink Panther.* But as the new, post-studio Hollywood moved away from his brand of classicism, Edwards had a string of commercial disappointments—*What Did You Do in the War, Daddy?, Gunn, The Party*—leading up to the total failure of the multi-million dollar musical *Darling Lili.* In the early 1970s, Edwards was barely visible, issuing occasional programmers—*The Wild Rovers, The Carey Treatment, The Tamarind Seed*—until he decided to revive the Inspector Clouseau character for *The Return of the Pink Panther.*

The mordant slapstick of the Panther films was back in style, and Edwards rode the success of *Return* through three more sequels, with the promise (despite the death of Clouseau's interpreter, Peter Sellers) of more to come. The success of the Panther films allowed Edwards to capitalize more personal projects, one of which—the 1979 *10*—became a sleeper hit. In his sixties, he again became a brand name, with his own production company (Blake Edwards Entertainment) and a measure of security.

Blake Edwards

For all his artistic independence, Edwards has always chosen to work within well-defined, traditional genres—the musical, the melodrama, the slapstick farce, the thriller. There is little continuity in tone between a film like *The Tamarind Seed* (a transcendent love story) and *S.O.B.* (a frenzied black farce), yet there are the more important continuities of personality. Edwards has no particular commitment to any single genre (though his greatest successes have been comedies); he varies his choices as a painter varies the colors of his palette, to alter the tonal mix. The single stylistic constant has been Edwards's use of Panavision; with very few exceptions, his films have used the widescreen format as the basic unit of organization and expression.

At their most elemental level, Edwards's films are about space—crossing it, filling it, transcending it. In his comedies, the widescreen space becomes a vortex fraught with perils—hidden traps, aggressive objects, spaces that abruptly open onto other, unexpected spaces. Edwards extends the principles of silent comedy into modern technology and modern absurdism; his comic heroes are isolated in the hostile widescreen space, unable to conquer it as Chaplin and Keaton could conquer the more manageable dimensions of the silent frame. (Though the Panther films employ this principle, Edwards's masterpiece in this vein is the relatively unknown 1968 film, *The Party.*)

Visually, Edwards's thrillers appear to be more dense, more furnished, more confining than his comedies (and two of the best of them, *Gunn* and *Experiment in Terror,* were photographed in the standard screen ratio); the threat comes not from empty space, but from the crowding of objects, colors, surfaces—the hard, cold *thingness* of things. This deathly solidity gives way, when the surfaces dissolve, to a more deathly chaos. In the romances, that operative space is the space between the characters; it must be collapsed, transformed, overcome. In *Darling Lili,* a room full of red roses is an emblem of love; it is not the trite symbolism of the flowers that gives the image its power, but the complete filling in of the widescreen space, its emotional conquest. In *The Tamarind Seed,* the lovers' conquest of space entails, as it does in the sublime 1930s romances of Frank Borzage, a conquest of death.

With *10* and *Victor/Victoria,* Edwards managed to blend the styles and assumptions of his comedies and romances. The strict genre divisions that once ruled his work are broken down, and with their dissolution a new humanism appears. Edwards's *10* uses its long lenses trained on Bo Derek's face (as perfect a blank, deathly surface as any in Edwards's films) to create looming, overlarge images of romantic fantasy. But when Dudley Moore finds his way back to Julie Andrews, Edwards shifts to balanced wide-screen compositions—two lovers occupying the same stable space—which convey images of a realistic, responsible romanticism. *Victor/*

Victoria, with its theatrical metaphors, builds small proscenium spaces for each of its role-playing characters; as the constricting roles are cast off, these isolating spaces give way to an overall openness and warmth. The widescreen space is no longer inherently hostile, but contains the promise of closeness and comfort.

With the exception of *That's Life*—a clever domestic comedy co-scripted with his analyst—Edwards' recent output has been disappointing. For the post part, he has attempted—and failed—to recycle old material and stale comic formulas.

A perfect case-in-point is *Switch,* a poor variation of *Victor/Victoria,* in which a womanizing male is killed by a vengeful conquest and comes back to earth as a member of the opposite sex. *Blind Date* (about a yuppie on a blind date) and *Sunset* (in which Tom Mix and Wyatt Earp come together to solve a mystery) featured Bruce Willis in two of his weakest screen roles. *Skin Deep* is an erratic comedy about a hedonistic writer. Finally, *Son of the Pink Panther,* with popular Italian comedian Roberto Benigni replacing the late Peter Sellers, was a dreadful picture that quickly vanished after its theatrical release.—DAVE KEHR and AUDREY E. KUPFERBERG

Eisenstein, Sergei

Nationality *Russian.* **Born** *Sergei Mikhailovich Eisenstein in Riga, Latvia, 23 January 1898.* **Education** *Educated in St. Petersburg and at gymnasium in Riga; Institute of Civil Engineering, St. Petersburg (studied architecture), 1914-17; studied Japanese at General Staff Academy, Moscow, 1920.* **Family** *Married Peta Attasheva.* **Career** *Sent for officer training, 1917; poster artist on front at Minsk, then demobilized, 1920; scenic artist, then co-director of Proletkult Theatre, Moscow, 1920; designer for Vsevolod Meyerhold's "directors' workshop," 1922; directed* Stachka, *1925; made professor at State Institute for Cinema, 1926; with Grigori Alexandrov and Edouard Tisse, travelled to Hollywood, 1929; signed for Paramount, but after work on various scripts, contract broken, 1930; refused a work permit by State Department, went to Mexico to work on* Que Viva Mexico!; *refused reentry permit to United States, after financier Upton Sinclair halts shooting and keeps uncut film; returned to U.S.S.R., 1932; began teaching at Moscow Film Institute, 1933;* Behzin Meadow *project denounced, production halted, 1937; worked on Pushkin film project, named Artistic Director of Mosfilm Studios, 1940; after finishing* Ivan the Terrible, *suffered heart attack, 1946; prepared a third part to* Ivan, *to have been made in color, 1947.* **Awards** *Gold Medal, Exposition Internationale des Arts Décoratifs, Paris, for* Strike!, *1925; Order of Lenin, 1939; Stalin Prize, 1st Class, for* Ivan the Terrible, Part I, *1946.* **Died** *In Moscow, 11 February 1948.*

Films as Director: 1923: *Kinodnevik Glumova* (*Glumov's Film Diary*) (short film inserted in production of Ostrovsky's *Enough Simplicity in Every Wise Man,* Proletkult Theater, Moscow) (+sc). **1925:** *Stachka* (*The Strike*) (+co-sc, ed); *Bronenosets Potemkin* (*The Battleship Potemkin*) (+sc, ed). **1928:** *Oktiabr* (*October, Ten Days That Shook the World*) (co-d, co-sc). **1929:** *Staroe i novoe* (*Old and New*) [film produced as *Generalnaia linia* (*The General Line*), title changed before release] (co-d, co-sc). **1930:** *Romance sentimentale* (co-d, sc). **1933:** *Thunder Over Mexico* (unauthorized, produced by Sol Lesser from *Que Viva Mexico!* footage, seen by Eisenstein in 1947 and disowned); *Death Day* and *Eisenstein in Mexico* (also unauthorized productions by Sol Lesser from *Que Viva Mexico!* footage). **1938:** *Aleksandr Nevskii* (*Alexander Nevsky*) (+co-sc, set des, costume des, ed). **1939:** *Time in the Sun*

Sergei Eisenstein

(produced by Marie Seton from *Que Viva Mexico!* footage); *The Ferghana Canal* (short documentary out of footage from abandoned feature subject on same subject) (+sc). **1941:** shorts edited by William Kruse for Bell and Howell from *Que Viva Mexico!* footage: *Mexico Marches*; *Conquering Cross*; *Idol of Hope*; *Land and Freedom*; *Spaniard and Indian*; *Mexican Symphony* (feature combining previous five titles); *Zapotecan Village*. **1944:** *Ivan Groznyi* (*Ivan the Terrible, Part I*) (+sc, set des, costume des, ed). **1958:** *Ivan Groznyi II: Boyarskii zagovor* (*Ivan the Terrible, Part II: The Boyars' Plot*) (+sc) (completed 1946); *Eisenstein's Mexican Project* (+sc) (unedited sequences of *Que Viva Mexico!* assembled by Jay Leyda). **1966:** *Bezhin Lug* (*Bezhin Meadow*) (+sc) (25 minute montage of stills from original film assembled by Naum Kleiman, with music by Prokofiev).

Other Films: 1924: *Doktor Mabuze—Igrok* (co-ed) (Russian version of Lang's *Dr. Mabuse der Spieler*). **1929:** *Everyday* (Hans Richter) (role as London policeman).

Sergei Eisenstein is generally considered to be one of the most important figures—perhaps *the* most important figure—in the history of cinema. But he was not only the leading director and theorist of Soviet cinema in his own lifetime, he was also a theatre and opera director, scriptwriter, graphic artist, teacher, and critic. His contemporaries called him quite simply "the Master."

Eisenstein's reputation as a filmmaker rests on only seven completed feature films, but among them *The Battleship Potemkin* has consistently been regarded as one of the greatest films ever made. The pivotal scene in the film—the massacre on the Odessa Steps—has become the most famous sequence in film history and a paradigm of the montage techniques that were central to Eisenstein's theories of filmmaking.

Like many early Soviet filmmakers, Eisenstein came to cinema by a circuitous route. Born in Riga, then a largely German-speaking provincial city of the Russian Empire, he saw his first film on a visit to Paris with his parents when he was only eight: *Les 400 farces du diable* by Méliès. He was educated at a technical grammar school so that he would follow his father's career as an engineer. Despite, or perhaps because of, his artistic bent, he was consistently given low marks at school for his drawing. Conversely, he consistently did his best in the subject of religious knowledge. In 1909 his parents separated and his mother went to live in St. Petersburg. On various visits to her, Eisenstein was entranced by his first taste of the circus and intrigued by his clandestine reading of her copies of *Venus in Furs* by Sacher-Masoch and Mirabeau's *The Torture Garden*. Reflections of this can be detected in his later work.

In 1915 Eisenstein entered the Institute for Civil Engineering in Petrograd, where he saw his first Meyerhold productions in the theatre. After the Revolution he abandoned his courses and joined the Red Army. He was assigned to a theatrical troupe, where he worked as a director, designer, and actor. In 1920 he was demobilised to Moscow and rapidly became head of design at the First Proletkult Workers Theatre. His first sets were for a production of *The Mexican*, written by Jack London, Lenin's favorite writer. In 1921 he joined Meyerhold's theatre workshop (he was later to describe Meyerhold as his "spiritual father") and worked on designs for *Puss in Boots*.

Eisenstein's first stage production, a version of Ostrovsky's *Enough Simplicity for Every Wise Man* in 1923, included his first venture into cinema, *Glumov's Diary*. This was inspired by the use of a short film in the Kozintsev and Trauberg production of Gogol's *The Wedding*, which he had seen the year before. His production of Tretyakov's *Gas Masks* in 1924 staged in the Moscow gasworks was an attempt to bridge the gap between stage "realism" and the reality of everyday life. It failed and, as Eisenstein himself put it, he "fell into cinema."

Eisenstein had already worked with Esfir Shub re-editing Fritz Lang's *Dr. Mabuse* for Soviet audiences in 1923, but he made his first full-length film—*The Strike,* set in 1905—in 1925. In this film he applied to cinema the theory of the "montage of attractions" that he had first developed in *Enough Simplicity for Every Wise Man.* Eisenstein was not the first to develop the notion of montage as the essence of cinema specificity: that honour belonged to Lev Kuleshov in 1917. Unlike Kuleshov, however, Eisenstein thought that montage depended on a *conflict* between different elements from which a new synthesis would arise. This notion developed partly from his study of Japanese ideograms and partly from his own partial understanding of the Marxist dialectic. It followed from the primacy accorded to montage in this theory that the actor's role was diminished while the director's was enhanced. Eisenstein's view of the primacy of the director was to cause him serious problems on both sides of the Atlantic.

In his silent films Eisenstein used amateur actors who were the right physical types for the part, a practice he called "typage": hence an unknown worker, Nikandrov, played the role of Lenin in *October,* released in 1927. Most of the parts in his second full-length film, *The Battleship Potemkin,* released in 1926, were played by amateurs. Even the local actors who appeared in the Odessa Steps sequence were chosen not for their professional training, but because they looked right for the parts. It was *Potemkin* that secured Eisenstein's reputation both at home and abroad, especially in Germany, where it was a spectacular commercial success and attracted far greater audiences than in the USSR itself. *Potemkin* put Soviet cinema on the world map.

After *Potemkin* Eisenstein started work on a film about collectivisation, *The General Line,* but broke off to make *October* for the tenth anniversary of the October Revolution. It was with this film that his serious problems with the authorities began. Critics were divided about the film. Some enthused about the birth of a new "intellectual cinema," based on "intellectual montage," which, like Brecht's "alienation effect," stimulated audiences to think rather than to react solely with their emotions. Other critics were troubled by what they saw as an overabundance of abstract symbolism that was, in the (officially inspired) catch-phrase of the times, "unintelligible to the millions."

When Eisenstein returned to *The General Line* and completed it in 1929, the Party's general line on agriculture had changed and Trotsky had fallen from grace: the film therefore had to be re-edited to reflect these developments, and it was finally released under the title of *The Old and the New.* The political problems Eisenstein encountered with this project were to recur in all his subsequent film work in the Soviet Union.

In 1929 Eisenstein went abroad with his assistants Alexandrov and Tisse, ostensibly to study the new medium of sound film. In his "Statement on Sound," published in the summer of 1928, he had warned against the dangers of purely illustrative sound, as in the "talkies," and argued for the application of the techniques of the montage of attractions to produce what he called "orchestral counterpoint." It was to be another ten years before he had the chance to put these ideas into effect.

Eisenstein first visited Western Europe and then travelled to Hollywood to work for Paramount. From the outset he was subjected to a hostile press campaign characterizing him as a "red dog" and a Bolshevik. After rejecting several of his film projects, Paramount cancelled his contract. He went on to start filming *Que Viva Mexico!* with funds provided by the Socialist millionaire novelist Upton Sinclair. Eisenstein spent most of 1931 working on the film, but Sinclair was not satisfied either with the pace of progress or the escalating cost. Material for three-quarters of the Mexican film had, however, been shot when the project collapsed in acrimonious exchanges. Eisenstein returned to the Soviet Union in May 1932. He had accepted assurances from Sinclair that the raw footage would be shipped to Moscow so that he could edit it, but this assurance was never honoured.

The Soviet Union that Eisenstein returned to was significantly different from the country he had left three years earlier. The political and economic changes associated with the first Five-Year Plan had led to concomitant changes in Soviet cinema, which was now run by an Old Bolshevik, Boris Shumyatsky, who was determined to create a "cinema for the millions." After several abortive projects, including *Moscow,* a history of the capital, *The Black Consul,* which would have starred Paul Robeson, and a film version of Karl Marx's *Das Kapital,* Eisenstein began making his first sound feature, *Bezhin Meadow,* in 1935. The film focused on the generational conflict engendered by the collectivization program, but it too was dogged with problems and was eventually stopped on the orders of Shumyatsky in March 1937. Eisenstein was forced to confess his alleged errors in public. This submission, together with the dismissal of Shumyatsky in January 1938, enabled him to start filming again.

The result was Eisenstein's most popular film, *Alexander Nevsky,* made in record time and released in 1938, but it was also the film that he regarded as his least successful. Nevertheless, it contains the best, and most famous, illustration of his technique of "orchestral counterpoint" in the sequence of the Battle on the Ice. On the other hand, *Nevsky* to some extent gave Eisenstein the reputation of "court filmmaker," particularly after he was awarded the Order of Lenin. It was because of this that, after the signature of the Nazi-Soviet Pact—and the subsequent withdrawal of *Nevsky* from distribution—Eisenstein was asked to direct a new production of Wagner's *Die Walküre* at the Bolshoi Theatre.

When not filming, Eisenstein taught at the State Institute of Cinema, where he had been head of the directing department since his return to the Soviet Union and where he was made professor in January 1937, shortly before the final crisis with *Bezhin Meadow.* He also devoted an increasing amount of time and energy to his theoretical writings, but his magnum opus on *Direction,* like his other works on *Mise-en-Scène* and the theory of montage, remained unfinished at his death.

Eisenstein's last film, arguably his masterpiece of masterpieces, was also unfinished: filming of the first part of *Ivan the Terrible* was begun in 1943 in Alma-Ata, where the Moscow studios had been evacuated because of the war, and released in 1945. The film was an instant success and earned Eisenstein and his associates the Stalin Prize. While celebrating this award in February 1946, Eisenstein suffered a heart attack, a development that encouraged his premonitions of an early death at the age of fifty. He threw himself into a flurry of frenzied activity, completing his memoirs and Part 2 of *Ivan* and starting on Part 3. In Part 2, however, the historical parallels between Ivan and Stalin became too obvious and, although completed, the film was not shown until 1958.

Eisenstein died of a second, massive heart attack in February 1948, just past his fiftieth birthday. He died very much under a cloud in his own country, but has since been universally acknowledged as one of cinema's greatest creative geniuses and a towering figure in the culture of the twentieth century. Some of his most important theoretical texts are only now being properly assembled and published, both in the Soviet Union and abroad.—RICHARD TAYLOR

Erice, Victor

Nationality *Spanish.* **Born** *San Sebastian, Basque, Spain, 1940.* **Education** *Studied economics and political science at the University of Madrid; attended the Escuela Oficial de Cinematografia, also in Madrid.* **Career** *Directed shorts while in film school; was film critic at the Spanish journals* Nuestro Cine *and* Cuadernos de Arte y Pensamiento; *earned international acclaim with his first full-length feature,* The Spirit of the Beehive, *1973.* **Address** *Ministry of Culture, Motion Picture Division, San Marcos 40, Madrid, Spain 28004.*

Films as Director and Screenwriter: 1968: *Los Desafíos* (*The Challenges*) (segment). **1973:** *El espíritu de la colmena* (*The Spirit of the Beehive*). **1982:** *El Sur* (*The South*). **1992:** *El Sol del Membrillo* (*The Dream of Light; The Quince Tree Sun*).

Other Films: 1967: *Oscuros sueños eróticos de agosto* (Picazo) (co-sc).

Such is the power of the press that a reviewer for an influential publication can laud a heretofore little-known film by an obscure director and thereby thrust that work into the international spotlight. Back in 1976, *New York Times* critic Richard Eder authored an article in praise of what was then a three-year-old film. The title of the piece was "A Great Film We May Never See." The film in question is *The Spirit of the Beehive,* directed by Victor Erice. According to Eder, it had played in Spain ("where it did not so much evade the censorship as envelop it") and on the film-festival circuit, and had been screened at the Museum of Modern Art. But it had not earned a commercial U.S. distributor. Eder discovered the film at the Telluride Festival, where his piece was filed. "It is one of the two or three most haunting films about children ever

made," Eder wrote. "It is perhaps one of the two dozen best pictures made anywhere in the past half-dozen years," he added, before going on to describe it as a film "whose power to move and astonish comes in quite original and magical ways."

The Spirit of the Beehive unfolds in a Castillan village in 1940, just after the end of the Spanish Civil War. While the town has not been a battleground, its young men are nowhere to be seen as they all have gone off to fight. The focus is on two children, eight-year-old Ana and her sister, ten-year-old Isabel. They see a print of James Whale's *Frankenstein,* at which point little Ana becomes obsessed with the image of the Frankenstein monster—especially the sequence in which a small girl picks a flower and hands it to the creature. Ana asks her wiser older sister if the story is true. Isabel says yes. And so Ana sets out in and around her village in search of the monster's spirit.

Victor Erice

Its existence is authenticated for her when she finds and helps an escaped prisoner who has found refuge in a barn, prior to his being found and shot by the police.

Much of the film's allure derives from the poignancy and simplicity of its sequences, especially those focusing on Ana, which are graceful unions of image and sound. *The Spirit of the Beehive* works as a fable of childhood, an ode to the wonders of youthful imagination and the magic of the moving image, and a subtly telling portrait of life in Spain under the repressive regime of Franco. At the film's core are the constraints on Spanish society under Franco, from the time in which it is set all the way through the time in which it was made. Franco's Spain is depicted as being in a state of inertia, with the only spark of life coming from Ana's imagination. Out of necessity, so as not to incur the fury of local censors, this commentary is ever-so-subtly drawn.

Prior to making *The Spirit of the Beehive,* Erice directed the last segment of *Los Desafios,* a three-part film, each episode of which deals with the experiences of Americans in Spain. Since then, he has worked infrequently. *El Sur,* made a full decade after *The Spirit of the Beehive,* is similar to its predecessor in that it too centers around an imaginative young girl—this one growing up in the 1950s—who fantasizes about her father. The documentary *El Sol del Membrillo* spotlights the inner workings of the creative process as it records the elaborate manner in which Spanish artist Antonio Lopez goes about painting a quince tree. A parallel exists between Lopez's exacting artistic method and Erice's, given the filmmaker's minute output over the past quarter-century.—ROB EDELMAN

Fassbinder, Rainer Werner

Nationality *German.* **Born** *Bad Wörishofen, Bavaria, 31 May 1946.* **Education** *Rudolf Steiner School and secondary schools in Augsburg and Munich until 1964; studied acting at Fridl-Leonhard Studio, Munich.* **Family** *Married Ingrid Caven, 1970 (divorced).* **Career** *Worked as decorator and in archives of* Süddeutsche Zeitung, *Munich, 1964-66; failed entrance exam to West Berlin Film and Television Academy, 1965; joined* action-theater, *Munich, with Hanna Schygulla, 1967; first original play produced* (Katzelmacher), action-theater *closed in May, co-founded* anti-theater, *1968; began making films with members of* anti-theater, *1969; worked in German theatre and radio, and as actor, 1969-82; founder, Tango Film, independent company, 1971; with Kurt Raab and Roland Petri, took over Theater am Turm (TAT), Frankfurt, 1974; TAT project failed, returned to Munich to concentrate on film work, 1975.* **Award** *Golden Bear, Berlin Festival, for* Die Sehnsucht der Veronika Voss, *1982.* **Died** *In Munich, 10 June 1982.*

Films as Director (under pseudonym Franz Walsch): 1965: *Der Stadtstreicher* (*The City Tramp*) (+sc, ed, uncredited pr, role). **1966:** *Das kleine Chaos* (*The Little Chaos*) (+sc, ed, role, uncredited pr). **1969:** *Liebe ist kälter als der Tod* (*Love Is Colder than Death*) (+sc, ed, role as Franz, uncredited pr); *Katzelmacher* (+sc, ed, art d, role as Jorgos, uncredited pr); *Götter der Pest* (*Gods of the Plague*) (+sc, ed, role as Porno Buyer, uncredited pr); *Warum läuft Herr R amok?* (*Why Does Herr R Run Amok?*) (co-d, co-sc, co-ed, uncredited pr). **1970:** *Rio das Mortes* (+sc, role as Discotheque-goer); *Whity* (+sc, co-ed, role as Guest in Saloon, uncredited pr); *Die Niklashauser Fahrt* (*The Niklashausen Journey*) (co-d, co-sc, co-ed, role as Black Monk, uncredited pr); *Der amerikanische Soldat* (*The American Soldier*) (sc, song, role as Franz); *Warnung vor einer heiligen Nutte* (*Beware of a Holy Whore*) (+co-ed, sc, role as Sascha, uncredited pr)

(Under real name): 1971: *Pioniere in Ingolstadt* (*Pioneers in Ingolstadt*) (+sc, uncredited pr); *Das Kaffeehaus* (*The Coffee House*) (for television) (+sc, uncredited pr); *Der Händler der vier Jahreszeiten* (*The Merchant of the Four Seasons*) (+sc, role as Zucker, uncredited pr). **1972:** *Die bitteren Tränen der Petra von Kant* (*The Bitter Tears of Petra von Kant*) (+sc, des, uncredited pr); *Wildwechsel* (*Wild Game*) (+sc, uncredited pr); *Acht Stunden sind kein Tag* (*Eight Hours Don't Make a Day*) (+sc, uncredited pr) (shown on German television in five monthly segments); *Bremer Freiheit* (*Bremen Freedom*) (for

television) (+sc, uncredited pr). **1973:** *Welt am Draht* (*World on a Wire*) (in two parts) (+co-sc, uncredited pr); *Angst essen Seele auf* (*Fear Eats the Soul*) (+sc, des, uncredited pr); *Martha* (+sc, uncredited pr); *Nora Helmer* (for television) (+sc, uncredited pr). **1974:** *Fontane Effi Briest* (*Effi Briest*) (+sc, role as narrator, uncredited pr); *Faustrecht der Freiheit* (*Fox*) (+co-sc, role as Franz Biberkopf— 'Fox,' uncredited pr); *Wie ein Vogel auf dem Draht* (*Like a Bird on a Wire*) (for television) (+sc, uncredited pr). **1975:** *Mutter Küsters Fahrt zum Himmel* (*Mother Küster's Trip to Heaven*) (+co-sc, uncredited pr); *Angst vor der Angst* (*Fear of Fear*) (+sc, uncredited pr). **1976:** *Ich will doch nur, dass Ihr mich liebt* (*I Only Want You to Love Me*) (+sc, uncredited pr); *Satansbraten* (*Satan's Brew*) (+sc, uncredited pr); *Chinesisches Roulette* (*Chinese Roulette*) (+sc, co-pr). **1977:** *Bolwieser* (+sc, uncredited pr); *Frauen in New York* (*Women in New York*); *Eine Reise ins Licht* (*Despair*). **1978:** Episode of *Deutschland im Herbst* (*Germany in Autumn*) (+sc, role, uncredited pr); *Die Ehe der Maria Braun* (*The Marriage of Maria Braun*) (+story); *In einem Jahr mit dreizehn Monden* (*In a Year with Thirteen Moons*) (+sc, ph, uncredited pr). **1979:** *Die dritte Generation* (*The Third Generation*) (+sc, ph, uncredited pr). **1980:** *Berlin Alexanderplatz* (for television, thirteen episodes with epilogue) (+sc, ph, role as himself in dream sequence, uncredited pr); *Lili Marleen* (+sc, ph, uncredited pr). **1981:** *Lola*

Rainer Werner Fassbinder on the set of *Querelle*.

(+sc, ph, uncredited pr); *Theater in Trance* (TV documentary) (+commentary). **1982:** *Die Sehnsucht der Veronika Voss* (Veronika Voss) (+sc, uncredited pr, ph); *Querelle* (+sc, ph, uncredited pr).

Other Films: 1967: *Tony Freunde* (Vasil) (role as Mallard). **1968:** *Der Bräutigam, die Komödiantin und der Zuhalter* (*The Bridegroom, the Comedienne and the Pimp*) (Straub) (role as the pimp). **1969:** *Fernes Jamaica* (*Distant Jamaica*) (Moland) (sc); *Alarm* (Lemmel) (role as the man in uniform); *Al Capone im deutschen Wald* (Wirth) (role as Heini); *Baal* (Schlöndorff) (role as Baal); *Frei bis zum nächsten Mal* (Köberle) (role as the mechanic). **1970:** *Matthias Kneissl* (Hauff) (role as Flecklbauer); *Der plötzliche Reichtum der armen Leute von Kombach* (Schlöndorff) (role as a peasant); *Supergirl* (Thome) (role as man who looks through window). **1973:** *Zärtlichkeit der Wölfe* (Lommel) (role as Wittkowski). **1974:** *1 Berlin-Harlem* (Lambert) (role as himself). **1976:** *Schatten der Engel* (*Shadow of Angels*) (Schmid) (sc, role as Raoul, the pimp). **1978:** *Bourbon Street Blues* (Sirk, Schonherr, and Tilman) (role). **1980:** *Lili Marleen* (Weisenborn) (role).

Rainer Werner Fassbinder was the leading member of a group of second-generation, alternative filmmakers in West Germany. The first generation consisted of Alexander Kluge and others who in 1962 drafted the Oberhausen Manifesto, initiating what has come to be called the "New German Cinema." Fassbinder's most distinguishing trait within the tradition of "counter-cinema," aside from his reputation for rendering fragments of the new left ideology of the 1960s on film, was his modification of the conventions of political cinema initiated in the 1920s and subsequent tailoring of these conventions to modern conditions of Hollywood cinema. He did this to a greater degree than Godard, who is credited with using these principles as content for filmic essays on narrative.

In an interview in 1971 Fassbinder asserted what has come to represent his most convincing justification for his innovative attachment to story: "The American cinema is the only one I can take really seriously, because it's the only one that has really reached an audience. German cinema used to do so, before 1933, and of course there are individual directors in other countries who are in touch with their audiences. But American cinema has generally had the happiest relationship with its audience, and that is because it doesn't try to be 'art.' Its narrative style is not so complicated or artificial. Well, of course it's artificial, but not 'artistic.'"

This concern with narrative and popular expression (some of his productions recall the good storytelling habits of Renoir) was evident early in the theatrical beginnings of Fassbinder's career, when he forged an aesthetic that could safely be labeled a creative synthesis of Brecht and Artaud oriented toward the persuasion of larger audiences.

This aesthetic began to form with Fassbinder's turn to the stage in 1967. He had finished his secondary school training in 1964 in Augsburg and Munich. He joined the Action-Theater in Munich with Hanna Schygulla, whom he had met in acting school. After producing his first original play in 1968, the Action-Theater was closed by the police in May of that year. Fassbinder then founded the "anti-theater," a venture loosely organized around the tenets of Brechtian theater translated into terms alluring for contemporary audiences. Although the 1969 *Liebe ist kälter als der Tod* marks the effective beginning of his feature film career (*Der Stadtsreicher* and *Das kleine Chaos* constituting minor efforts), he was to maintain an intermittent foothold in the theater over the years until his premature death, working in various productions throughout Germany and producing a number of radio plays in the early 1970s. The stint with "anti-theater" was followed by the assumption of directorial control, with Kurt Raab and Roland Petri, over the Theater am Turm (TAT) of Frankfurt in 1974, and the founding of Albatross Productions for coproductions in 1975.

When TAT failed, Fassbinder became less involved in the theater, but a trace of his interest always remained and was manifested in his frequent appearances in his own films. In fact, out of the more than forty feature films produced during his lifetime, there have only been a handful or so in which Fassbinder did not appear in one way or another. Indeed, he has had a major role in at least ten of these films.

Fassbinder's mixing together of Hollywood and avant-garde forms took a variety of turns throughout his brief career. In the films made during the peak of 1960s activism in Germany— specifically *Katzelmacher, Liebe ist kälter als der Tod, Götter der Pest,* and *Warum läuft Herr R. Amok?*—theatrical conventions, principally those derived from his Brechtian training, join forces with a "minimalist" aesthetic and the indigenous energies of the *Heimatfilm* to portray such sensitive issues as the foreign worker problem, contradictions within supposedly revolutionary youth culture, and concerns of national identity. These early "filmed theater" pieces, inevitably conforming to a static, long-take style because of a dearth of funding, tended to resemble parables or fables in their brevity and moral, didactic structuring. As funding from the government increased in proportion to his success, the popular forms of filmmaking associated with Hollywood became his models. His output from 1970 through the apocalyptic events of October 1977 (a series of terrorist actions culminated in Hans-Martin Schleyer's death, etc.) is an exploration of the forms of melodrama and the family romance as a way to place social issues within the frame of sexual politics. *Whity, Der Händler der vier Jahreszeiten, Die bitteren Tränen der Petra von Kant, Martha, Faustrecht der Freiheit,* and *Frauen in New York* are perhaps the most prominent examples. A self-reflexive pastiche of the gangster film is evident as well in *Der amerikanische Soldat.* This attention to the mediation of other forms ultimately began to assume the direction of a critique of the "art film": *Warnung vor einer heiligen Nutte,* an update of *8 1/2*; *Satansbraten,* a comment on aesthetics and politics centered around the figure of Stephen George; and *Chinesisches Roulette,* a parody concerning an inbred aristocracy.

The concern with the continuation of fascism into the present day received some attention in this period (specifically in *Wildwechsel, Despair,* and *Bolwieser*), but it became the dominant structuring motivation in the final period (1977-82) of Fassbinder's career. Here there is a kind of epic recombination of all earlier innovations in service of an understanding of fascism and its implications for the immediate postwar generation. Fassbinder's segment in *Deutschland im Herbst* (a collective endeavor of many German intellectuals and filmmakers) inaugurates this period. It and *Die Ehe der Maria Braun, Lili Marleen, Lola,* and *Die Sehnsucht der Veronika Voss* may be seen as a portrayal of the consolidation of German society to conform to the "American Model" of social and economic development. *In einem Jahr mit 13 Monden, Berlin Alexanderplatz,* and *Querelle* are depictions of the crisis in sexual identity, and the criminal and counter-cultural worlds associated with that process, in relation to "capitalism in crisis." *Die dritte Generation* is a kind of cynical summation of the German new left in the wake of a decade of terrorist activities.

This final phase, perhaps Fassbinder's most brilliant cinematically, will be the one given the greatest critical attention in future years. It is the one which evinces the keenest awareness of the intellectual spaces traversed in Germany since the years of fascism (and especially since the mid-1960s), and the one which reveals the most effective assimilation of the heritage of forms associated with art and political cinema.—JOHN O'KANE

Fellini, Federico

Nationality *Italian.* **Born** *Rimini, Italy, 20 January 1920.* **Education** *Catholic schools in Rimini, until 1938.* **Family** *Married Giulietta Masina in Rome, 30 October 1943, one son (died).* **Career** *Worked on 420 and* Avventuroso *magazines in Florence, 1938; caricature artist and writer in Rome, from 1939; through friend Aldo Fabrizi, worked as screenwriter, from 1941; worked on Rossellini's* Rome, Open City, *1944; screenwriter and assistant director, 1946-52; formed Capitolium production company with Alberto Lattuada for* Variety Lights, *1950; formed Federiz production company with Angelo Rizzoli (subsequently taken over by Clemente Fracazzi), 1961.* **Awards** *Grand Prize, Venice Festival, 1954, New York Film Critics Circle Award, 1956, Screen Directors Guild Award, 1956, and Oscar for Best Foreign Film, 1956, for* La strada; *Oscar for Best Foreign Film, for* La notti di Cabiria, *1957; Oscar for Best Foreign Film, 1960, Palme d'or, Cannes Festival, 1960, and New York Critics Circle Award, 1961, for* La dolce vita; *Oscar for Best Foreign Film, for* 8 1/2, *1963; Oscar for Best Foreign Film, and New York Film Critics Circle Award, for* Amarcord, *1974; Special Prize, Cannes Festival, 1987; Special Oscar, honoring the body of his work, 1993; Honorary Doctor of Humane Letters, Columbia University, New York, 1970.* **Died** *Italy, 31 October 1993.*

Films as Director and Scriptwriter: 1950: *Luci del varieta* (co-d, +co-pr). **1951:** *Lo Sceicco Bianco.* **1953:** *I Vitelloni;* "Un'agenzia matrimoniale" in *Amore in citta* (Zavattini). **1954:** *La strada.* **1955:** *Il bidone.* **1956:** *La notti di Cabiria* (*Nights of Cabiria*). **1960:** *La dolce vita.* **1962:** "Le tentazioni del dottor Antonio" in *Boccaccio '70* (Zavattini). **1963:** *Otto e mezzo* (*8 1/2*). **1965:** *Giulietta degli spiriti* (*Juliet of the Spirits*). **1968:** "Toby Dammit" (Il ne faut jamais parier sa tête contre le diable) in *Histoires*

extraordinaires/Tre passi nel delirio (anthology film). **1969:** Block-notes di un regista (Fellini: A Director's Notebook) (for TV) (+narration, role); Satyricon (Fellini Satyricon). **1970:** I clowns (The Clowns). **1972:** Roma (Fellini Roma) (+role). **1974:** Amarcord. **1976:** Casanova (Il Casanova di Federico Fellini). **1978:** Prova d'orchestra (Orchestra Rehearsal) (for TV). **1980:** La città delle donne (City of Women). **1983:** E la nave va (And the Ship Sailed On). **1986:** Ginger and Fred (+co-sc). **1987:** Intervista (The Interview) (+role). **1990:** La voce della luna (The Voice of the Moon).

Other Films: 1939: Lo vedi come . . . lo vedi come sei?! (Mattòli) (gagman). **1940:** Non me lo dire! (Mattòli) (gagman); Il pirata sono io! (Mattòli) (gagman). **1941:** Documento Z3 (Guarini) (sc/co-sc, uncredited). **1942:** Avanti, c'e posto (Bonnard) (sc/co-sc, uncredited); Chi l'ha visto? (Alessandrini) (sc/co-sc); Quarta pagina (Manzari and Gambino) (sc/co-sc). **1943:** Apparizione (de Limur) (sc/co-sc, uncredited); Campo dei fiori (Bonnard) (sc/co-sc); Tutta la città canta (Freda) (sc/co-sc); L'ultima carrozzella (Mattòli) (sc/co-sc). **1945:** Roma, città aperta (Rossellini) (asst d, co-sc). **1946:** Paisà (Rossellini) (asst d, co-sc). **1947:** Il delitto di Giovanni Episcopo (Lattuada) (co-sc); Il passatore (Coletti) (co-sc); La fumeria d'oppio (Ritorna Za-la-mort) (Matarazzo) (co-sc); L'ebreo errante (Alessandrini) (co-sc). **1948:** "Il miracolo" episode of L'amore (Rossellini) (asst d, co-sc, role as stranger mistaken for St. Joseph); Il mulino del Po (Lattuada) (co-sc); In nome della legge (Germi) (co-sc); Senza pietà (Lattuada) (co-sc); La città dolente (Bonnard) (co-sc). **1949:** Francesco, giullare di Dio (Rossellini) (co-sc, asst d). **1950:** Il cammino della speranza (Germi) (co-sc); Persiane chiuse (Comencini) (co-sc). **1951:** La città si difende (Germi) (co-sc); Cameriera bella presenza offresi (Pastina) (co-sc). **1952:** Il brigante di Tacca del Lupo (Germi) (co-sc); Europa '51 (Rossellini) (co-sc, uncredited). **1958:** Fortunella (De Filippo) (co-sc). **1970:** Alex in Wonderland (Mazursky) (role as himself). **1974:** C'eravamo tanto amati (Scola) (guest appearance).

Federico Fellini is one of the most controversial figures in the recent history of Italian cinema. Though his successes have been spectacular, as in the cases of *La strada, La dolce vita,* and *Otto e mezzo,* his failures have been equally flamboyant. This has caused considerable doubt in some quarters as to the validity of his ranking as a major force in contemporary cinema, and made it somewhat difficult for him to achieve sufficient financial backing to support his highly personalized film efforts in his last years. Certainly, few directors in any country could equal Fellini's interest in the history of the cinema or share his certainty regarding the appropriate place for the body of his work within the larger film canon. Consequently, he has molded each of his film projects in such a way that any discussion of their individual merits is inseparable from the autobiographical details of his personal legend.

Fellini's early film *La sceicco bianco* gave a clear indication of the autobiographical nature of the works to follow, for it drew upon his experience as a journalist and merged it with many of the conceits he had developed in his early motion picture career as a gag writer and script writer. However, he was also an instrumental part of the development of the neorealistic film in the 1940s, writing parts of the screenplays of Roberto Rossellini's *Roma città aperta* and *Paisà,* and his reshaping of that tradition toward an autobiographical mode of expression in *La sceicco bianco* troubled a number of his former collaborators. But on his part, Fellini was seemingly just as critical of the brand of neorealism practiced by Rossellini, with its penchant for overt melodrama.

In a succeeding film, *La strada,* Fellini took his autobiographical parallels a step farther, casting his wife, Giulietta Masina, in the major female role. This highly symbolic work was variously interpreted as a manifesto on human rights, or at least a treatise on women's liberation. In these contexts, however, it roused the ire of strict neorealists who regarded it as containing too much justification for political oppression. Yet as a highly metaphorical personal parable about the relationship between a man and a woman it was a critical success and a confirmation of the validity of Fellini's autobiographical instincts. This gave him the confidence to indulge in a subtle criticism of the neorealistic style in his next film, *Il bidone*. The film served, in effect, a tongue-in-cheek criticism of the form's sentimental aspects.

In the films of Fellini's middle period, beginning in 1959 with *La dolce vita,* Fellini became increasingly preoccupied with his role as an international "auteur." As a result, the autobiographical manifestations in his films became more introspective and extended to less tangible areas of his psyche than anything that he had previously brought to the screen. *La dolce vita* is a relatively straightforward psychological extension of what might have become of Moraldo, the director's earlier biographical persona (*I vitelloni*), after forsaking his village for the decadence of Rome. But its successors increasingly explored the areas of its creator's fears, nightmares, and fantasies.

After establishing actor Marcello Mastroianni as his alter ego in *La dolce vita,* Fellini again employed him in his masterpiece, *Otto e mezzo (8 1/2),* as a vehicle for his analysis of the complex nature of artistic inspiration. Then, in a sequel of sorts, he examined the other side of the coin. In *Giulietta degli spiriti (Juliet of the Spirits),* he casts his wife as the intaglio of the Guido figure in *8 1/2*. Both films, therefore, explored the same problems from different sexual perspectives while, on the deeper, ever-present autobiographical plane, the two characters became corresponding sides of Fellini's mythic ego.

Subsequent films continued the rich, flamboyant imagery that became a Fellini trademark, but with the exception of the imaginative fantasy *Fellini Satyricon,* they have, for the most part, returned to the vantage point of direct experience that characterized his earlier works. Finally, in 1980's *La città delle donne,* which again featured Mastroianni, he returned to the larger than life examination of his psyche. In fact, a number of critics regarded the film as the ultimate statement in an ideological trilogy (begun with *8 1/2* and continued in *Juliet of the Spirits*) in which he finally attempts a rapprochement with his inner sexual and creative conflicts. Unfortunately, *City of Women* is too highly derivative of the earlier work. Consequently, it does not resolve the issues raised in the earlier two films.

Several of Fellini's films are masterpieces by anyone's standards. Yet in no other director's body of films does each work identifiably relate a specific image of the creator that he wishes to present to the world and to posterity. Whether any of the films are truly autobiographical in any traditional sense is open to debate. They definitely do not interlock to provide a history of a man, and yet each is a deliberately crafted building block in the construction of a larger than life Fellini legend which may eventually come to be regarded as the "journey of a psyche."

While the final credits on Fellini's filmography are far from his best works, they nonetheless are fitting conclusions to what is one of the legendary careers in the history of world cinema. *And the Ship Sails On* is the wildly preposterous but uniquely Felliniesque tale of the miscellaneous luminaries who come together for an ocean cruise in which they will bid farewell to a just-deceased opera performer. *Ginger and Fred* is a sweetly nostalgic film because of its union of two of Fellini's then-aging but still vibrant stars of the past, Giulietta Masina and Marcello Mastroianni. *The Voice of the Moon,* Fellini's last feature—which did not earn a U.S. distributor—works as a summation of the cinematic subjects which had concerned the film maker for the previous quarter century.

The most outstanding and revealing late-career Fellini is *Intervista,* an illuminating film (and characteristic Fellini union of reality and fantasy) about the production by a Japanese television crew of a documentary about the director. Fellini himself appears on screen, where he is shown to be shooting an adaptation of Kafka's *Amerika,* a film that appears to be a typically Felliniesque extravaganza-in-the-making, complete with eccentric extras, surreal images, and autobiographical touches. We watch the filmmaker as he casts *Amerika.* We meet his various associates and underlings, from producers to actors, from casting director to assistant director. We see how Fellini directs his performers and the steps he takes to inspire feelings and attitudes within them. And we are privy to the various crises, big and small, which are standard fare during the filmmaking process. Finally, Marcello Mastroianni and Anita Ekberg, who over thirty years before had co-starred in *La dolce vita,* appear as themselves. Mastroianni's entrance is especially magical; the sequence in which he and Ekberg (whom, he remarks, he has not seen since making *La dolce vita*) observe their younger selves in some famous clips from the film is wonderful nostalgia.

However, *Intervista* is primarily an homage to Cinecitta, the studio where Fellini shot his films. Revealingly, the filmmaker describes the studio as "a fortress, or perhaps an alibi." Fellini first came to Cinecitta in 1940, when he was a young journalist. His assignment was to interview an actress for a magazine profile. This event is dramatized in *Intervista*; at various points in the film, the narrative drifts from images of the real Fellini, an artist in the twilight of a much-honored career, to a recreation of young Federico (played by Sergio Rubini) and his initiation into the world of Cinecitta.To fully appreciate this very personal movie about the movie-making process, you must be familiar with—and an admirer of—Fellini and his work.—STEPHEN L. HANSON and ROB EDELMAN

Feuillade, Louis

Nationality *French.* **Born** *Lunel, France, 19 February 1873.* **Education** *Institut de Brignac and at the Petit Séminaire, Carcassonne.* **Military Service** *Served with French Army, 1891-95, and 1915.* **Family** *Married Jeanne-Léontine Janjou, 1895 (daughter married to filmmaker Maurice Champreux).* **Career** *Worked in publishing in Paris, 1898; founder of satirical journal* La Tomate, *1903; hired as writer by Alice Guy at Gaumont Studios, 1905; replaced Guy as Director of Gaumont Productions, 1907; began series of "ciné-romans" (serials) with* Judex, *1916; first President of the Societé des Auteurs de Films, 1917-18; moved, with Gaumont, to Nice, 1918.* **Died** *In Nice, 26 February 1925.*

Films as Director (Feuillade wrote and directed an estimated eight hundred films; this partial listing includes all series titles and known non-series titles): **1906:** *Le billet de banque; C'est Papa qui prend la purge; Les deux Gosses; La Porteuse de pain; Mireille* (co-d); *N'te promène donc pas toute nue.* **1907:** *Un accident d'auto; La course des belles-mères; Un facteur trop ferré; L'homme aimanté; La légende de la fileuse; Un paquet embarrassant; La sirène; Le thé chez la concierge; Vive le sabotage.* **1908:** *Les agents tels qu'on nous les présente; Une dame vraiment bien; La grève des apaches; Nettoyage par le vide; Une nuit agitée; Prométhé; Le récit du colonel; Le roman de Sœur Louise; Un tic.* **1909:** *L'aveugle de Jerusalem; La chatte métamorphosée en femme; La cigale et la fourmi; Le collier de la reine; Les filles du cantonnier; Les heures; Histoire de puce; Le huguenot; Judith et Holopherne; Fra Vincenti; La légende des phares; La mère du moine; La mort de Mozart; La mort; La possession de l'enfant; Le savetier et le financier; Le printemps; Vainqueur de la course pédestre.* **1910:** *Benvenuto Cellini; Le Christ en croix; Esther; L'Exode; Le festin de Balthazar; La fille de Jephté; Mil huit cent quatorze; Mater dolorosa; Maudite soit la guerre; Le pater; Le roi de Thulé.* **1910/11:** "Le Film Esthétique" series: (1910: *Les sept péchés capitaux, La nativité;* 1911: *La vierge d'Argos*). **1910/13:** "Bébé" series (74 films, from 88 to 321 meters length) (series begins with *Bébé fume* in 1910; final title is *Bébé en vacances* in 1913). **1911:** *L'aventurière, dame de compagnie; Aux lions les chrétiens; Dans la vie; Les doigts qui voient; Fidélité romaine; Le fils de la sunamité; Le fils de Locuste; Les petites apprenties; Quand les feuilles tombent; Sans le joug; Le trafiquant.* **1911/13:** "La vie telle qu'elle est" series: (1911: *Les vipères, Le mariage de l'aînée, Le roi Lear au village, En grève, Le bas de laine [Le Trésor], La tare, Le poison, La souris blanche, Le trust [Les batailles de l'argent], Le chef-lieu de Canton, Le destin des mères, Tant que vous serez heureux;* 1912: *L'accident, Les braves gens, Le nain, Le pont sur l'Abîme;* 1913: *S'affranchir*).

1912: *Amour d'automne; Androclès; L'anneau fatal; L'attrait du bouge; Au pays des lions; L'Aventurière; La cassette de l'émigrée; Le chateau de la peur; Les cloches de Paques; Le cœur et l'argent; La course aux millions; Dans la brousse; La demoiselle du notaire; La fille du margrave; La hantise; Haut les mains!; L'homme de proie; La maison des lions; Le maléfice; Le mort vivant; Les noces siciliennes; Le Noël de Francesca; Préméditation; La prison sur le gouffre; Le témoin; Le tourment; Tyrtée; La vertu de Lucette; La vie ou la mort; Les yeux qui meurent.* **1912/16:** "Bout-de-Zan" series (53 films, from 79 to 425 meters length) [series begins with *Bout-de-Zan revient du cirque* (1912); final title is *Bout-de-Zan et la torpille* (1916)]. **1912/13:** "Le Détective Dervieux" series (1912: *Le Proscrit, L'oubliette;* 1913: *Le guet-apens, L'écrin du rajah*). **1913:** *L'agonie de Byzance; L'angoisse; Les audaces du cœur; Bonne année; Le bon propriétaire; Le browning; Les chasseurs de lions; La conversion d'Irma; Un drame au pays basque; L'effroi; Erreur tragique; La gardienne du feu; Au gré des flots; L'intruse; La marche des rois; Le mariage de miss Nelly; Le ménestrel de la reine Anne; La mort de Lucrèce; La petite danseuse; Le revenant; La rose blanche; Un scandale au village; Le secret du forçat; La vengeance du sergent de ville; Les yeux ouverts.* **1913/14:** "Fantômas" series: (1913: *Fantômas, Juve contre Fantômas, La mort qui tue;* 1914: *Fantômas contre Fantômas, Le faux magistrat*). **1913/16:** "La vie drôle" series (35 films, of which 26 are preserved) [series begins with *Les millions de la bonne* (1913), and includes *L'Illustre Machefer* (1914), *Le colonel Bontemps* (1915), and *Lagourdette, gentleman cambrioleur* (1916)].

1914: *Le calvaire; Le coffret de Tolède; Le diamant du Sénéchal; L'enfant de la roulotte; L'épreuve; Les fiancés de 1914; Les fiancés de Séville; Le gendarme est sans culotte; La gitanella; L'hôtel de la gare; Les lettres; Manon de Montmartre; La neuvaine; Paques rouges; La petite Andalouse; La rencontre; Severo Torelli.* **1915:** *L'angoisse au foyer; La barrière; Le blason; Celui qui reste; Le collier de perles; Le coup du fakir; La course a l'abîme; Deux Françaises; L'escapade de Filoche; L'expiation; Le fer a cheval; Fifi tambour; Le furoncle; Les noces d'argent; Le Noël du poilu; Le sosie; Union sacrée.* **1915/16:** "Les vampires" series (1915: *La tête coupée; La bague qui tue; Le cryptogramme rouge;* 1916: *Le spectre; L'évasion du mort; Les yeux qui fascinent; Satanas; Le maître de la foudre; L'homme des poisons; Les noces sanglantes*). **1916:** *L'aventure des millions; C'est le printemps; Le double jeu; Les fiançailles d'Agénor; Les fourberies de Pingouin; Le malheur qui passe; Un mariage de raison; Les mariés d'un jour; Notre pauvre cœur; Le poète et sa folle amante; La peine du talion; Le retour de Manivel; Si vous ne m'aimez pas; Judex* (serial in a prologue and twelve episodes). **1917:** *L'autre; Le bandeau sur les yeux; Débrouille-toi; Déserteuse; La femme fatale; La fugue de Lily; Herr Doktor; Mon oncle; La nouvelle mission de Judex* (serial in twelve episodes); *Le passé de Monique.* **1918:** *Aide-toi; Les petites marionnettes; Tih Minh* (serial in twelve episodes); *Vendémiaire.* **1919:** *Barrabas* (serial in twelve episodes); *L'engrenage; L'énigme* (*Le mot de l'*); *L'homme sans visage; Le nocturne.* **1920:** *Les deux Gamines* (serial in twelve episodes). **1921:** *L'Orpheline* (serial in twelve episodes); *Parisette* (serial in twelve episodes). **1921/22:** "Belle humeur" series (1921: *Gustave est médium, Marjolin ou la fille manquée, Saturnin ou le bon allumeur, Séraphin ou les jambes nues, Zidore ou les métamorphoses;* 1922: *Gaétan ou le commis audacieux, Lahire ou le valet de cœur*). **1922:** *Le fils du flibustier* (serial in twelve episodes). **1923:** *Le gamin de Paris; La gosseline; L'orphelin de Paris* (serial in six episodes); *Vindicta* (film released in five parts). **1924:** *La fille bien gardée; Lucette; Pierrot Pierrette; Le stigmate* (serial in six episodes).

Other Films: 1905: *Le coup de vent* (*Le chapeau*) (sc). **1906:** *La course au potiron* (sc).

Louis Feuillade was one of the most solid and dependable talents in French cinema during the early twentieth century. He succeeded Alice Guy as head of production at Gaumont in 1906 and worked virtually without a break—aside from a period of war service—until his death in 1925. He produced some eight hundred films of every conceivable kind: comedies and contemporary melodramas, biblical epics and historical dramas, sketches and series with numerous episodes adding up to many hours of running time. Although most of these films were made from his own scripts, Feuillade was not an innovator. The years of his apprenticeship in the craft of filmmaking were those in which French producers reigned supreme, and he worked uncomplainingly in a context in which commercial criteria were paramount. For Feuillade—as for so many of his successors in the heyday of Hollywood—aesthetic strategies not rooted in sound commercial practices were inconceivable, and a filmmaker's only viable ambition was to reach the widest possible audience.

Most of Feuillade's output forms part of a series of some kind and he clearly saw films in generic terms rather than as individually sculpted works. Though not an originator in terms of the forms or styles he adopted, he made films which are among the finest examples of the various popular genres he successively explored. Before 1914 his work is enormously diverse. It included thirty comic films in the series of *La Vie drôle,* a group of seriously intended dramas in which a concern with the quality of the pictorial image is apparent (marketed under the banner of the *Film esthétique*), and a number of contemporary dramas, *La Vie telle qu'elle est,* with somewhat ambiguous claims to realism. In addition, he made some seventy-six films with a four-year-old child star, Bébé, and another fifty or so with the urchin Bout-de-Zan.

But the richest vein of Feuillade's work is the series of crime melodramas that extended from *Fantômas* in 1913-14 to *Barrabas* in 1920. Starting with his celebration of Fantômas, master criminal and master of disguise, who triumphs effortlessly over the dogged ordinariness of his opponent Inspector Juve, Feuillade went on to make his wildest success with *Les Vampires.* Made to rival the imported American serials, this series reflects the chaotic wartime state of French production. It is marked by improvised stories refusing all logic, bewildering changes of casting (necessary as actors were summoned to the war effort), economical use of real locations, and dazzling moments of total incongruity.

Les Vampires reached a level that Feuillade was never able to duplicate. Subsequent works like *Judex* and especially *La Nouvelle Mission de Judex* are marked by a new tone of moralising, with the emphasis placed on the caped avenger rather than the feckless criminals. If the later serials, *Tih Minh* and *Barrabas,* contain sequences able to rank with the director's best, Feuillade's subsequent work in the 1920s lacks the earlier forcefulness.

It was the films' supreme lack of logic, the disregard for hallowed bourgeois values—so appropriate at a time when the old social order of Europe was crumbling under the impact of World War I—which led the surrealists such as André Breton and Louis Aragon to hail *Fantômas* and *Les Vampires,* and most of Feuillade's subsequent advocates have similarly celebrated the films' anarchistic poetry. But this should not lead us to see Feuillade as any sort of frustrated artist or poet of cinema, suffocating in a world dominated by business decisions. On the contrary, the director was an archetypal middle class family man who prided himself on the commercial success of his work and conducted his personal life in accord with strictly ordered bourgeois principles.—ROY AARMES

Flaherty, Robert

Nationality American. *Born* Robert Joseph Flaherty in Iron Mountain, Michigan, 16 February 1884. *Education* Upper Canada College, Toronto, and Michigan College of Mines. *Family* Married Frances Hubbard, 1914. *Career* Explorer, surveyor and prospec-

tor for Canadian Grand Trunk Railway and Canadian Mining Syndicates, 1900s; worked for industrial entrepreneur William MacKenzie, searching for iron ore deposits along Hudson Bay, 1910-16; made first travelogue film, 1915; made first feature, Nanook of the North, *1922; made* Moana *with backing of Paramount (then Famous Players-Lasky), 1923-25; invited to work for Irving Thalberg at MGM, quit and formed company with F.W. Murnau to produce* Tabu, *1928; made* Industrial Britain *for John Grierson's Empire Marketing Board, 1931; moved to Aran Islands and made* Man of Aran, *1932-34; made* The Land *for U.S. government, 1939-41; hired by Frank Capra to work in U.S. Army orientation film unit, 1942; made* Louisiana Story, *sponsored by Standard Oil, 1946-48. Robert Flaherty Foundation (later renamed International Film Seminars Inc.) established, 1953.* **Award** *International Prize, Venice Festival, for* Louisiana Story, *1948.* **Died** *23 July 1951.*

Films as Director: 1922: *Nanook of the North* (+ph, ed, sc). **1925:** *The Potterymaker* (*Story of a Potter*) (short) (+ph, sc). **1926:** *Moana* (*Moana: A Romance of the Golden Age. Moana: The Love Life of a South Sea Siren*) (+co-sc, co-ph, co-ed). **1927:** *The Twenty-Four-Dollar Island* (short) (+sc, ph). **1931:** *Tabu* (co-d, co-sc, uncredited co-ph). **1933:** *Industrial Britain* (co-d, co-ph); *The English Potter* (short) (+ph) (edited by Marion Grierson from footage shot for *Industrial Britain*); *The Glassmakers of England* (short) (+ph) (edited from *Industrial Britain* footage); *Art of the English Craftsman* (short) (+ph) (from *Industrial Britain* footage). **1934:** *Man of Aran* (+sc, co-ph). **1937:** *Elephant Boy* (co-d). **1942:** *The Land* (+sc, co-ph, narration). **1948:** *Louisiana Story* (+co-sc, co-ph, pr). **1949:** *The Titan* (+sc, ph). **1967:** *Studies for Louisiana Story* (+sc, ph) (fifteen hours of outtakes from *Louisiana Story* edited by Nick Cominos).

Other Films: 1945: *What's Happened to Sugar* (David Flaherty) (pr). **1949:** *The Story of Michelangelo* (co-pr). **1950:** *Green Mountain Land* (short) (David Flaherty) (pr). **1951:** *St. Matthew's Passion* (ed, narration) (reedited version of Ernst Marischka's 1949 *Matthaus-Passion*).

Robert Flaherty was already thirty-six years old when he set out to make a film, *Nanook of the North*. Before that he had established himself as a prospector, surveyor, and explorer, having made several expeditions to the sub-Arctic regions of the Hudson Bay. He had shot motion picture footage on two of these occasions, but before *Nanook,* filmmaking was only a sideline.

Yet these years in the wilderness were to have a profound effect on Flaherty's development as a filmmaker. First, the expeditions brought Flaherty into intimate contact with the Eskimo culture. Second, they enhanced his knowledge about the human condition in a natural setting. Third, the numerous evenings that he spent in isolation encouraged him to contemplate the day's events by writing in his diaries, from which he developed highly skilled powers of observation which sharpened his sense of photographic imagery and detail. Also a violinist and an accomplished storyteller, Flaherty had clearly cultivated an artistic sensibility before becoming a film director. Filmmaking became a compelling mechanism for expressing this sensibility.

Flaherty turned to filmmaking not only as a means of creation but also to communicate to the outside world his impressions of Eskimo culture. He held a profound admiration for these people, who lived close to nature and whose daily existence was an unrelenting struggle to survive. The struggle ennobled this proud race. Flaherty sought to portray their existence in a manner that would illustrate the purity and nobility of their lives, a purpose underlying each of his films.

Flaherty developed a method of working that was fairly consistent from film to film. The films about the people of Hudson Bay, Samoa, the Aran Islands, and the Louisiana Bayou demonstrate a more or less constant concern with people who live in natural settings. These geographical locations are incidental; others would have done just as well. Eskimo culture was the only one in which he was deeply versed. Nevertheless, the locations were chosen because they represented societies on the verge of change. Indeed, Flaherty has often been criticized for presenting his subjects as they existed years ago, not as he found them. But Flaherty saw his projects as the last opportunity to capture a way of life on film.

Another consistent feature of Flaherty's technique was the selection of a "cast." Although he pioneered the use of real people to re-enact their own everyday lives before the camera lens, he deliberately chose ideal types on the basis of physical appearance and even created artificial families to act before the camera.

Robert Flaherty: *Man of Aran*

Flaherty worked without a plot or script, allowing for a maximum of improvisation. The Flaherty method entailed total immersion in these cultures in order to discover the basic patterns of life. *Nanook* represented the least difficulty because of his thorough familiarity with Eskimo culture. However, *Moana* and *Man of Aran* represented unfamiliar territory. Flaherty had to become steeped in strange cultures. His search for struggle and conflict in Savaii misled him and he later abandoned it. Struggle was more readily apparent in the Aran Islands, in terms of conflict between man and the sea; the hunt for the basking shark which he portrayed, abandoned in practice some years earlier, helps the audience to visualize this conflict.

Flaherty's technical facility also served him well. Generally he carried projectors and film printers and developing equipment to these far off places so that he could view his rushes on a daily basis. Flaherty, a perfectionist, shot enormous quantities of footage for his films; the lack of a script or scenario contributed to this. He went to great lengths to achieve photographic excellence, often shooting when shadows were longest. In *Moana* he used the new panchromatic film stock, which was much more sensitive to color than orthochromatic film. He pioneered the use of long lenses for close-up work, a method that allowed him an intimacy with his subjects that was novel for its time.

Flaherty's films were generally well received in the popular press and magazines as well as in the more serious critical literature. *Nanook* was praised for its authenticity and its documentary value as well as its pictorial qualities. John Grierson was the first to use the term "documentary" to describe a film when he reviewed *Moana*. Subsequently, Grierson, through his filmmaking activities and writings, began to formulate a documentary aesthetic dealing with social problems and public policy, subjects that Flaherty (except for *The Land*) tried to avoid. Nevertheless, Grierson's writings, which were to influence the development of the modern sponsored film, had their foundations in Flaherty's work. Their purposes were ultimately quite different, but Grierson gave due credit to Flaherty for working with real people, shaping the story from the material, and bringing a sense of drama to the documentary film.

Man of Aran aroused the most critical responses to Flaherty's work. It was released at a time when the world was beset with enormous political, social, and economic problems, and many enthusiasts of documentary film believed it was irresponsible and archaic of Flaherty to produce a documentary that made no reference to these problems or concealed them from public view. *Louisiana Story,* on the other hand, was greeted as the culminating work of a master filmmaker. Recognized for its skillful interweaving of sound and image, one critic described the film as an audiovisual symphony. However, in today's world of pollution and oil spills it is much more difficult to accept the film's picture of the oil industry as a benign presence in the bayou.

Although Flaherty made a relatively small number of films in his long career, one would be hard pressed to find a more influential body of work. He always operated outside the mainstream of the documentary movement. Both he and Grierson, despite their contradictory purposes, can be credited with the development of a new genre and a documentary sensibility; Flaherty by his films, Grierson by his writing. Watching today's 16mm distribution prints and video cassettes, it is often difficult to appreciate the photographic excellence of Flaherty's work. Nevertheless, the clean lines are there, as well as an internal rhythm created by the deft editing touch of Helen Van Dongen. Although his films were improvised, the final product was never haphazard. It showed a point of view which he wished to share.—WILLIAM T. MURPHY

Ford, John

Nationality American. *Born* Sean Aloysius O'Feeney (or John Augustine Feeney) in Cape Elizabeth, Maine, 1 February 1895. *Education* Portland High School, Maine; University of Maine, 1913 or 1914 (for three weeks). *Military Service* Lieutenant-Commander, U.S. Marine Corps, 1942-45 (wounded at Battle of Midway); in U.S. Naval Reserve, given rank of Admiral by President Nixon. *Family* Married Mary McBryde Smith, 1920, one son, one daughter. *Career* Joined brother Francis (director for Universal) in Hollywood, 1914; actor, stuntman and special effects man for Universal, 1914-17; assumes name "Jack Ford," 1916; contract director for Universal, 1917-21; signed to Fox Film Corp., 1921; began collaboration with screenwriter Dudley Nichols on Men without Women, 1930; assembled film crew that became Field Photographic Branch of U.S. Office of Strategic Services, 1940. *Awards* Oscar for Best Director, and Best Direction Award, New York Film Critics, for The Informer, 1935; Best Direction Award, New York Film Critics, for Stagecoach, 1939; Oscar for Best Director, for Grapes of Wrath, 1940; Oscar for Best Director and Best Direction Award, New York Film Critics, for How Green Was My Valley, 1941; Oscar for Best Documentary, for Battle of Midway, 1942; Legion of Merit and Purple Heart; Annual Award, Directors Guild of America, 1952; Grand Lion Award, Venice Festival, 1971; Lifetime Achievement Award, American Film Institute, 1973. *Died* In Palm Desert, California, 31 August 1973.

Films as Director: **1917:** *The Tornado* (+sc, role); *The Trail of Hate* (may have been directed by Francis Ford); *The Scrapper* (+sc, role); *The Soul Herder; Cheyenne's Pal* (+story); *Straight Shooting; The*

John Ford

Secret Man; A Marked Man (+story); *Bucking Broadway*. **1918:** *The Phantom Riders; Wild Woman; Thieves' Gold; The Scarlet Drop* (+story); *Hell Bent* (+co-sc); *A Woman's Fool; Three Mounted Men*. **1919:** *Roped; The Fighting Brothers; A Fight for Love; By Indian Post; The Rustlers; Bare Fists; Gun Law; The Gun Packer* (*The Gun Pusher*); *Riders of Vengeance* (+co-sc); *The Last Outlaw; The Outcasts of Poker Flat; The Ace of the Saddle; The Rider of the Law; A Gun Fightin' Gentleman* (+co-story); *Marked Men*. **1920:** *The Prince of Avenue A; The Girl in Number 29; Hitchin' Posts; Just Pals; The Big Punch* (+co-sc). **1921:** *The Freeze Out; Desperate Trails; Action; Sure Fire, Jackie*. **1922:** *The Wallop; Little Miss Smiles; The Village Blacksmith; Silver Wings* (Carewe) (d prologue only). **1923:** *The Face on the Barroom Floor; Three Jumps Ahead* (+sc); *Cameo Kirby; North of Hudson Bay; Hoodman Blind*. **1924:** *The Iron Horse; Hearts of Oak*. **1925:** *Lightnin'; Kentucky Pride; The Fighting Heart; Thank You*. **1926:** *The Shamrock Handicap; Three Bad Men; The Blue Eagle*. **1927:** *Upstream*. **1928:** *Mother Machree; Four Sons; Hangman's House; Napoleon's Barber; Riley the Cop*. **1929:** *Strong Boy; Salute; The Black Watch*. **1930:** *Men Without Women* (+co-story); *Born Reckless; Up the River* (+co-sc, uncredited). **1931:** *Seas Beneath; The Brat; Arrowsmith; Flesh*. **1933:** *Pilgrimage, Dr. Bull*. **1934:** *The Lost Patrol; The World Moves On; Judge Priest*. **1935:** *The Whole Town's Talking; The Informer; Steamboat Round the Bend*. **1936:** *The Prisoner of Shark Island; Mary of Scotland; The Plough and the Stars*. **1937:** *Wee Willie Winkie; The Hurricane*. **1938:** *Four Men and a Prayer; Submarine Patrol*. **1939:** *Stagecoach; Drums Along the Mohawk; Young Mr. Lincoln*. **1940:** *The Grapes of Wrath; The Long Voyage Home*. **1941:** *Tobacco Road; Sex Hygiene; How Green Was My Valley*. **1942:** *The Battle of Midway* (+co-ph); *Torpedo Squadron*. **1943:** *December Seventh* (co-d); *We Sail at Midnight*. **1945:** *They Were Expendable*. **1946:** *My Darling Clementine*. **1947:** *The Fugitive* (+co-pr). **1948:** *Fort Apache* (+co-pr); *Three Godfathers* (+co-pr). **1949:** *She Wore a Yellow Ribbon* (+co-pr). **1950:** *When Willie Comes Marching Home, Wagonmaster* (+co-pr); *Rio Grande* (+co-pr). **1951:** *This is Korea!*. **1952:** *What Price Glory; The Quiet Man* (+co-pr). **1953:** *The Sun Shines Bright; Mogambo*. **1955:** *The Long Gray Line; Mister Roberts* (co-d); *Rookie of the Year* (episode for *Screen Directors Playhouse* TV series); *The Bamboo Cross* (episode for *Fireside Theater* TV series). **1956:** *The Searchers*. **1957:** *The Wings of Eagles; The Rising of the Moon*. **1958:** *The Last Hurrah*. **1959:** *Gideon of Scotland Yard* (*Gideon's Day*); *Korea; The Horse Soldiers*. **1960:** *The Colter Craven Story* (episode for *Wagon Train* TV series); *Sergeant Rutledge*. **1961:** *Two Rode Together*. **1962:** *The Man Who Shot Liberty Valance, Flashing Spikes* (episode for Alcoa Premiere TV series); *How the West Was Won* (directed "The Civil War" segment). **1963:** *Donovan's Reef* (+pr). **1964:** *Cheyenne Autumn*. **1965:** *Young Cassidy* (+co-d). **1966:** *Seven Women*. **1970:** *Chesty: A Tribute to a Legend*.

Other Films: 1914: *Lucille Love, the Girl of Mystery* (fifteen-episode serial) (Francis Ford) (role); *The Mysterious Rose* (Francis Ford) (role). **1915:** *The Birth of a Nation* (Griffith) (role); *Three Bad Men and a Girl* (Francis Ford) (role); *The Hidden City* (Francis Ford) (role); *The Doorway of Destruction* (Francis Ford) (asst d, role); *The Broken Coin* (twenty-two-episode serial) (Francis Ford) (role). **1916:** *The Lumber Yard Gang* (Francis Ford) (role); *Peg o' the Ring* (fifteen-episode serial) (Francis Ford and Jacques Jaccard) (role); *Chicken-Hearted Jim* (Francis Ford) (role); *The Bandit's Wager* (Francis Ford) (role). **1929:** *Big Time* (Kenneth Hawks) (role as himself). **1971:** *Vietnam! Vietnam!* (Beck, for USIA) (exec pr).

John Ford has no peers in the annals of cinema. This is not to place him above criticism, merely above comparison. His faults were unique, as was his art, which he pursued with a single-minded and single-hearted stubbornness for sixty years and 112 films. Ford grew up with the American cinema. That he should have begun his career as an extra in the Ku Klux Klan sequences of *The Birth of a Nation* and ended it supervising the documentary *Vietnam! Vietnam!* conveys the remarkable breadth of his contribution to film, and the narrowness of its concerns.

Ford's subject was his life and his times. Immigrant, Catholic, Republican, he spoke for the generations that created the modern United States between the Civil and Great Wars. Like Walt Whitman, Ford chronicled the society of that half century, expansionist by design, mystical and religious by conviction, hierarchical by agreement; an association of equals within a structure of command, with practical, patriotic, and devout qualities. Ford portrayed the society Whitman celebrated as "something in the doings of man that corresponds with the broadcast doings of night and day."

Mythologizing the armed services and the church as paradigms of structural integrity, Ford adapts their rules to his private world. All may speak in Ford's films, but when divine order is invoked, the faithful fall silent, to fight and die as decreed by a general, a president, or some other member of a God-anointed elite.

In Ford's hierarchy, Native and African Americans share the lowest rung, women the next. Businessmen, uniformly corrupt in his world, hover below the honest and unimaginative citizenry of the United States. Above them are Ford's elite, within which members of the armed forces occupy a privileged position. In authority over them is an officer class of career military men and priests, culminating in a few near-saintly figures of which Abraham Lincoln is the most notable, while over all rules a retributory, partial, and jealous God.

The consistency of Ford's work lies in his fidelity to the morality implicit in this structure. *Mary of Scotland*'s Mary Queen of Scots, the retiring Nathan Brittles in *She Wore a Yellow Ribbon* and outgoing mayor Frank Skeffington in *The Last Hurrah* all face the decline in their powers with a moral strength drawn from a belief in the essential order of their lives. Mary goes triumphantly to the scaffold, affirming Catholicism and the divine right of kings. Duty to his companions of the 7th Cavalry transcending all, Brittles returns to rejoin them in danger. Skeffington prefers to lose rather than succumb to modern vote-getting devices such as television.

"I make westerns," Ford announced on one well-publicized occasion. Like most of his generalizations, it was untrue. Only a third of his films are westerns, and of those a number are rural comedies with perfunctory frontier settings: *Doctor Bull, Judge Priest, Steamboat Round the Bend, The Sun Shines Bright.* Many of his family films, like *Four Men and a Prayer* and *Pilgrimage,* belong with the stories of military life, of which he made a score. A disciple of the U.S. Navy, from which he retired with the emeritus rank of Rear Admiral, Ford found in its command structure a perfect metaphor for moral order. In *They Were Expendable,* he chose to falsify every fact of the Pacific War to celebrate the moral superiority of men trained in its rigid disciplines—men who obey, affirm, keep faith.

Acts, not words, convey the truths of men's lives; public affirmations of this dictum dominate Ford's films. Dances and fights signify in their vigor a powerful sense of community; singing and eating and getting drunk together are the great acts of Fordian union. A film like *The Searchers,* perhaps his masterpiece, makes clear its care for family life and tradition in a series of significant actions that need no words. Ward Bond turns away from the revelation of a woman's love for her brother-in-law, exposed in her reverent handling of his cloak; his turn away is the instinctive act of a natural gentleman. Barred from the family life which his anger and independence make alien to his character, John Wayne clutches his arm in a gesture borrowed from Ford's first star, Harry Carey; in a memorable final image, the door closes on him, a symbol of the rejection of the eternal clan-less wanderer.

Ford spent his filmmaking years in a cloud of critical misunderstanding, with each new film unfavorably compared to earlier works. *The Iron Horse* established him as an epic westerner in the mold of Raoul Walsh, *The Informer* as a Langian master of expressionism, the cavalry pictures as Honest John Ford, a New England primitive whose work, in Lindsay Anderson's words, was "unsophisticated and direct." When, in his last decades of work, he returned to reexamine earlier films in a series of revealing remakes, the skeptical saw not a moving reiteration of values but a decline into self-plagiarism. Yet it is *The Man Who Shot Liberty Valance,* in which he deals with the issues raised in *Stagecoach,* showing his beloved populist west destroyed by law and literacy, that stands today among his most important films.

Belligerent, grandiose, deceitful, and arrogant in real life, Ford seldom let these traits spill over into his films. They express at their best a guarded serenity, a skeptical satisfaction in the beauty of the American landscape, muted always by an understanding of the dangers implicit in the land, and a sense of the responsibility of all men to protect the common heritage. In every Ford film there is a gun behind the door, a conviction behind the joke, a challenge in every toast. Ford belongs in the tradition of American narrative art where telling a story and drawing a moral are twin aspects of public utterance. He saw that we live in history, and that history embodies lessons we must learn. When Fordian man speaks, the audience is meant to listen—and listen all the harder for the restraint and circumspection of the man who speaks. One hears the authentic Fordian voice nowhere more powerfully than in Ward Bond's preamble to the celebrating enlisted men in *They Were Expendable* as they toast the retirement of a comrade. "I'm not going to make a speech," he states. "I've just got something to say."—JOHN BAXTER

Forman, Milos

Nationality Czech. *Born* Tomas Jan Forman, Kaslov, Czechoslovakia, 18 February 1932, became U.S. citizen, 1975. *Education* Academy of Music and Dramatic Art, Prague, and at Film Academy (FAMU), Prague, 1951-56. *Family* Married 1) Jana

Milos Forman: *Hoří, má panenko*

Brejchová (divorced); 2) Vera Kresadlova (divorced). **Career** *Collaborated on screenplay for Frič's* Leave It to Me, *1956; theatre director for Laterna Magika, Prague, 1958-62; directed first feature,* Black Peter, *1963; moved to New York, 1969, after collapse of Dubcek government in Czechoslovakia; co-director of Columbia University Film Division, from 1975: became American citizen, 1975.* **Awards** *Czechoslovak Film Critics' Prize, for* Black Peter, *1963; Grand Prix Locarno, for* Black Peter, *1964; Czechoslovak State Prize, 1967; Oscar for Best Director, and Best Director Award, Directors Guild of America, for* One Flew Over the Cuckoo's Nest, *1975; Oscar for Best Director, for* Amadeus, *1984.* **Agent** *Robert Lantz, 888 Seventh Ave., New York, NY 10106, U.S.A.*

Films as Director: 1963: *Cerný Petr* (*Black Peter; Peter and Pavla*); (+co-sc); *Konkurs* (*Talent Competition*) (+co-sc); *Kdyby ty muziky nebyly.* **1965:** *Lásky jedné plavovlásky* (*Loves of a Blonde; A Blonde In Love*) (+co-sc); *Dobře placená procházka* (*A Well Paid Stroll*) (+co-sc). **1967:** *Hoří, má panenko* (*The Firemen's Ball; Like a House on Fire*) (+co-sc). **1971:** *Taking Off* (+co-sc). **1972:** "Decathlon" segment of *Visions of Eight* (+co-sc). **1975:** *One Flew Over the Cuckoo's Nest.* **1979:** *Hair.* **1981:** *Ragtime.* **1983:** *Amadeus.* **1989:** *Valmont.* **1996:** *The People vs. Larry Flynt.*

Other Films: 1955: *Nechte to na mně* (*Leave It to Me*) (Frič) (co-sc); *Dědeček automobil* (*Old Man Motorcar*) (Radok) (asst d, role). **1957:** *Stěnata* (*The Puppies*) (co-sc, asst dir). **1962:** *Tam za lesem* (*Beyond the Forest*) (Blumenfeld) (asst d, role as the physician). **1968:** *La Pine à ongles* (Carrière) (co-sc). **1975:** *Le Mâle du siècle* (Berri) (story). **1981:** *Chytilová Venus Forman* (Chytilová) (role). **1986:** *Heartburn* (Nichols) (role). **1989:** *New Year's Day* (Jaglom) (role). **1990:** *Dreams of Love* (pr). **1991:** *Why Havel?* (Jasny) (narrator). **1992:** *L'Envers du d'ecor: Portrait de Pierre Guffroy* (*Behind the Scenes: A Portrait of Pierre Guffroy*) (Salis) (role). **1997:** *Cannes. . .les 400 coups* (Nadeau) (for TV) (role).

In the context of Czechoslovak cinema in the early 1960s, Milos Forman's first films (*Black Peter* and *Talent Competition*) amounted to a revolution. Influenced by Czech novelists who revolted against the establishment's aesthetic dogmas in the late 1950s rather than by Western cinema (though the mark of late neorealism, in particular Ermanno Olmi, is visible), Forman introduced to the cinema after 1948 (the year of the Communist coup) portrayals of working-class life untainted by the formulae of socialist realism.

Though Forman was fiercely attacked by Stalinist reviewers initially, the more liberal faction of the Communist party, then in ascendancy, appropriated Forman's movies as expressions of the new concept of "socialist" art. Together with great box office success and an excellent reputation gained at international festivals, these circumstances transformed Forman into the undisputed star of the Czech New Wave. His style was characterized by a sensitive use of non-actors (usually coupled with professionals); refreshing, natural-sounding, semi-improvised dialogue which reflected Forman's intimate knowledge of the milieu he was capturing on the screen; and an unerring ear for the nuances of Czech folk-rock and music in general.

All these characteristic features of Forman's first two films are even more prominent in *Loves of a Blonde,* and especially in *The Firemen's Ball.* The latter film works equally well on one level as a realistic, humorous story and on an allegorical level that points to the aftermath of the Communist Party's decision to reveal some of the political crimes committed in the 1950s (the Slánský trial). In all these films—developed, except for *Black Peter,* from Forman's original ideas—he closely collaborated with scriptwriters Ivan Passer and Jaroslav Papousek, who later became directors in their own right.

Shortly after the Soviet invasion of Czechoslovakia in 1968, *The Firemen's Ball* was banned and Forman decided to remain in the West, where he was working on the script for what was to become the only film in which he would apply the principles of his aesthetic method and vision to indigenous American material, *Taking Off*. It is also his only American movie developed from his original idea; the rest are adaptations.

Traces of the pre-American Forman are easily recognizable in his most successful U.S. film, *One Flew Over the Cuckoo's Nest*, which radically changed Ken Kesey's story and—just as in the case of Papousek's novel *Black Peter*—brought it close to the director's own objective and comical vision. The work received an Oscar in 1975. In that year Forman became an American citizen.

The Forman touch is much less evident in his reworking of the musical *Hair*, and almost—though not entirely—absent from his version of E.L. Doctorow's novel *Ragtime*. The same is true of the box-office smash hit and multiple Oscar winner *Amadeus*, and his later adaptation, *Valmont*. Of marginal importance are the two remaining parts of Forman's oeuvre, *The Well-Paid Stroll*, a jazz opera adapted from the stage for Prague TV, and *Decathlon*, his contribution to the 1972 Olympic documentary *Visions of Eight*.

Forman is a merciless observer of the *comedie humaine* and has often been accused of cynicism, both in Czechoslovakia and in the West. To such criticisms he answers with the words of Chekhov, pointing out that what is cruel in the first place is life itself. But apart from such arguments, the rich texture of acutely observed life and the sensitive portrayal of and apparent sympathy for people as victims—often ridiculous—of circumstances over which they wield no power, render such critical statements null and void. Forman's vision is deeply rooted in the anti-ideological, realistic, and humanist tradition of such "cynics" of Czech literature as Jaroslav Hasek (*The Good Soldier Svejk*), Bohumil Hrabal (*Closely Watched Trains*) or Josef Skvorecký (whose novel *The Cowards* Forman was prevented from filming by the invasion of 1968).

Although the influence of Forman's filmmaking methods may be felt even in some North American films, his lasting importance will, very probably, rest with his three Czech movies. *Taking Off*, a valiant attempt to show America to Americans through the eyes of a sensitive, if caustic, foreign observer, should be added to this list as well. After the mixed reception of this film, however, Forman turned to adaptations of best sellers and stage hits.

In recent years, Forman has been inactive as a director. *Valmont* attempted to capture the spirit of his smash hit *Amadeus*. But *Valmont* suffers by comparison. Moreover, it was released after Stephen Frears' superior *Dangerous Liaisons*, adapted from the same Choderlos de Laclos novel. Forman remains an outstanding craftsman and a first-class actors' director; however, in the context of American cinema he does not represent the innovative force he was in Prague.

Forman has been more involved in the academic world in recent years, accepting a position as professor of film and co-chair of the film division at Columbia University's School of the Arts, although he did successfully return to directing in 1996 with *The People vs. Larry Flynt*. He also appeared onscreen in a small role as Catherine O'Hara's husband in Mike Nichols' *Heartburn*, in which he was reunited with his *One Flew Over the Cuckoo's Nest* star, Jack Nicholson. He also played, oddly enough, an apartment house janitor in Henry Jaglom's *New Years' Day.*—JOSEF SKVORECKÝ and ROB EDELMAN

Forsyth, Bill

Nationality Scottish. ***Born*** *William David Forsyth, in Glasgow, 29 July 1946.* ***Education*** *Studied at National Film School, Beaconsfield, Buckinghamshire, for three months, 1971.* ***Family*** *One son, one daughter.* ***Career*** *Left school at age sixteen and worked for documentary filmmaker Stanley Russell; set up Tree Films with Charles Gormley, 1972; producer of documentaries, 1970s; began working with Glasgow Youth Theatre, 1977; directed first feature,* That Sinking Feeling, *1979.* ***Awards*** *British Academy Award for Best Screenplay, for* Gregory's Girl, *1981; BAFTA Award for Best Screenplay, 1983; Honorary Doctorate, University of Glasgow, 1983.*

Films as Director and Scriptwriter: 1979: *That Sinking Feeling* (+pr). **1981:** *Gregory's Girl.* **1983:** *Local Hero.* **1984:** *Comfort and Joy.* **1987:** *Housekeeping* (*Sylvie's Ark*). **1989:** *Breaking In.* **1990:** *Rebecca's Daughter.* **1993:** *Being Human.*

For a while during the early 1980s Scottish cinema was virtually synonymous with Bill Forsyth. Today his work remains among the most original and distinctive to have emerged not only from Scotland but from Britain as a whole. The Forsyth oeuvre is rooted in a gentle and extremely charming offbeat view of the world which has affinities with a variety of comic traditions including Ealing comedy, Frank Capra, Jacques Tati, and Ermanno Olmi (*Il Posto* is practically a blueprint in tone and feel of *Gregory's Girl*), but which maintains its own individuality and character. Forsyth's choice of comedy as his mode of expression was partly dictated by the fact that his first two films were made on tiny budgets. In characteristically modest fashion he regarded comedy as more appropriate, being less self-indulgent and more fun to do

Bill Forsyth on the set of *Housekeeping.*

for everyone involved. Crucially, the comic character of these films gave them a vitality which helped them transcend their budgetary limitations and, in the case of *Gregory's Girl,* find a sizable audience outside Scotland.

Forsyth's charm lies in his attention to detail, particularly the various quirks and idiosyncrasies of his characters, which are conveyed equally effectively through both image and dialogue. These characters are often marginalised individuals caught up in circumstances they are ill equipped to deal with. Forsyth finds a great deal of humour in their predicaments but he does so in a wry and generous manner which is never at the expense of the characters. Instead, his approach amounts to a celebration of the human spirit with all its foibles and shortcomings.

Forsyth's acute perception of human behaviour gives his films a depth which transcends their initial charm as quirky comedies. *Gregory's Girl,* for example, is populated by dreamers lost in their various obsessions. The film centre is the first stirrings of sexuality in rather awkward male adolescents. Gregory is obsessed with the enigmatic and ultimately unobtainable Dorothy (a situation repeated in *Local Hero* with the unrequited love that Danny and McIntyre feel for Marina and Stella, respectively). But Forsyth also uncovers a variety of obsessions, ranging from a fascination with numbers to useless facts and cookery, that serve as expressions of the problems and confusions associated with adolescence; these obsession are presented as, in essence, a redirection of sexual energy.

Although equally obsessed with boys, the girls in the film are more knowing and sophisticated (Gregory constantly seeks advice on matters of the heart from his eleven-year-old sister) and wield greater control over their own destinies—Dorothy overcomes the sexist opposition of the coach to earn a place in the football team, while Susan ingeniously uses her friends to divert Gregory's romantic attentions away from Dorothy and towards herself. Forsyth obviously has a great empathy with the female point of view, and it is no coincidence that *Housekeeping,* his most mature and accomplished work, concentrates totally on the relationship between two young girls and their rather eccentric aunt.

Despite the generally upbeat ambience, Forsyth's cinema has its darker side. There are poignant moments of irony in *That Sinking Feeling,* a film which, despite its quirkiness and innocence, features a group of teenagers attempting to cope with the problems of unemployment. The film is set against a bleak and crumbling urban landscape. *Local Hero* has a rather subdued ending, which compensates for the cozy and contrived resolution reached between beachcomber Ben Knox and Happer the oil tycoon; McIntyre resumes a life in Texas that he has come to regard as shallow and meaningless.

Comfort and Joy is darker than its predecessors not only in theme but in visual style. It concentrates on one solitary character, charting his development from morbid introspection (after his girlfriend leaves him at Christmas) to fascination with the absurdities of the world around him. Despite Forsyth's intention to make a gloomier film, *Comfort and Joy* appears rather whimsical when compared to the brutality of the real Glasgow "Ice Cream Wars" which occurred at about the same time.

But Forsyth's most serious effort by far is *Housekeeping,* his first adaptation and the first film that he shot outside Scotland. In exploring the dilemma of whether to conform to social expectations or opt out altogether, it successfully mixes very real moments of tragedy and grief (it is the only Bill Forsyth film to provoke real anxiety and even tears) with lighter and more familiar Forsythian observations and character traits. *Housekeeping* marks a major development in Forsyth's career, demonstrating a greater emotional complexity and directorial assuredness. It opens out his cinema from its provincial Scottish roots while retaining the charm and warmth of his earlier work.

Since *Housekeeping,* though, Forsyth has not made any films that rival the work of his early career. *Breaking In,* a comedy which charts the relationship between a young thief (Casey Siemaszko) and his aging mentor (Burt Reynolds), was a dud. *Being Human* is an oddity—and a box office disaster—featuring Robin Williams as five separate characters from different eras of history, each of whom are laboring to attain satisfaction in their lives. *Being Human* is an adventuresome and well-intentioned project, to be sure. But the result is maddeningly uneven, and one hopes that Forsyth will be able to recapture the spirit of his first features.—DUNCAN J. PETRIE and ROB EDELMAN

Franju, Georges

Nationality French. *Born* Fougères, Brittany, 12 April 1912. *Education* Religious school in Fougères. *Military Service* In Algeria, 1928-32. *Career* Set builder for Folies Bergères and the Casino de Paris, 1932-33; began Cercle du Cinéma programme with Henri Langlois, and directed Le Metro, 1934; co-founder, with Langlois, of Cinémathèque Française and Cinématographe magazine, 1937; executive secretary of La Fedération Internationale des Archives du Film (FIAF), from 1938; Secretary-General of the Institut de Cinématographie Scientifique, 1945-54; founder, L'Academie du Cinéma, 1946; directed first feature-length film, 1958; director for French television (including Chroniques de France), from 1965. *Awards* Chevalier de la Légion d'honneur; Officier de l'ordre national du Mérite et des Arts et des Lettres. *Died* 5 November 1987.

Films as Director: 1934: Le Metro (co-d, sc) (short). **1949:** Le Sang des bêtes (+sc) (short). **1950:** En passant par la Lorraine (+sc) (short). **1951:** Hôtel des Invalides (+sc) (short). **1952:** Le Grand Méliès (+sc) (short). **1953:** Monsieur et Madame Curie (+sc) (short). **1954:** Les Poussières (+sc) (short); Navigation marchande (Marine marchande) (+sc) (short; disowned by Franju). **1955:** A propos d'une rivière (Le Saumon Atlantique) (+sc) (short); Mon chien (+sc) (short). **1956:** Le Théâtre National Populaire (Le T.N.P.) (+sc) (short); Sur le Pont d'Avignon (+sc) (short). **1957:** Notre Dame, cathédrale de Paris (+sc) (short). **1958:** La Première nuit (+sc) (short); La Tête contre les murs (The Keepers). **1959:** Les Yeuxs sans visage (+co-adapt). **1960:** Pleins feux sur l'assassin (Spotlight on Murder). **1962:** Thérèse Desqueyroux (+co-sc). **1963:** Judex. **1964:** Thomas l'imposteur (Thomas the Imposter) (+co-sc). **1970:** La Faute de l'Abbé Mouret (The Demise of Father Mouret) (+co-sc). **1974:** Nuits rouges (L'Homme sans visage; Shadowman) (+co-mus).

Other Film: 1956: Décembre, mois des enfants (Storck) (co-sc).

Franju's career falls clearly into two parts, marked by the format of the films: the early period of documentary shorts, and a subsequent period of fictional features. The parts are connected by many links of theme, imagery, attitude, and iconography. Critical attention has focused primarily on the shorts, and there is some justice in this. While it is difficult to accept Noel Burch's assertion that "the magic that is so much a part of his nonfiction work no longer survives in his fiction features," it is true that nothing in the later work surpasses *Le Sang des bêtes* and *Hôtel des Invalides,* and the intensity and poetic concentration of those early masterpieces are recaptured only in intermittent moments. It is necessary to define the *kind* of documentary

Georges Franju

Franju made (it is highly idiosyncratic, and I can think of no close parallels; though Resnais's documentaries are often linked with his, the differences seem more important than the similarities).

The traditional documentary has three main modes: the factual, the lyrical, and the politically tendentious. It is the peculiar distinction of Franju's documentaries that they correspond to none of these modes. The kind of organization that structures them is essentially poetic, built upon imagery and juxtaposition, rather than on overt statement or clear-cut symbolism. *Hôtel des Invalides* might well have been expected, from its genesis, to correspond to either the second or third type of documentary (or an amalgamation of the two, a quite common phenomenon). It was commissioned by an organization called Forces et Voix de France, and the intention was to celebrate a national monument-institution: the Musée de L'Armée, home of Napoleon's tomb, an edifice dedicated to the glory of France and of war. Franju seized upon and made central to his film the fact that the building also houses the *victims* of war and "glory": the veterans' hospital of the film's title, peopled with the shell-shocked, the crippled, the mutilated. These wounded soldiers continue to carry military banners, wear their medals, and attend the religious ceremonies that constitute an aspect of their oppression. Beyond the skillful use of purely cinematic codes (lighting, camera movement, editing, etc.) and Maurice Jarre's music, Franju adds nothing extraneous to his raw material. The introductory commentary (spoken by Michel Simon), locating the museum in place and history, is rigorously factual and unemotional. Once inside, we have only the "authentic" commentary of the museum guides. Yet the application of cinematic codes to this material transforms its meaning totally, producing a continuous irony that modulates back and forth between the violent and the subtle: the emblems of military glory and national pride become sinister, monstrous, terrifying.

A politically tendentious documentary after all, then? Certainly not in any simple or clear-cut way. Ultimately, *Hôtel des Invalides* is no more an anti-war movie than *Le Sang des bêtes* is an appeal for vegetarianism—though those meanings can and will be read by many viewers. The film's elements of rage and protest are finally subordinated to an overriding sense of irredeemable insanity, an intimation of a world and a species so fundamentally crazy that protest is almost superfluous. The supreme irony Franju produces out of his material involves the museum's very status as a national monument: here, at the heart of civilization, regarded with pride, admiration and wonderment, stands what amounts to a monument to pain, cruelty, ugliness, death—and no one notices.

The basic problem with Franju's feature films is that he does not seem greatly interested in narrative. He has usually relied on the support of a pre-existent literary work, whose structure, characters, and movement he recreates with a generally scrupulous fidelity, delicacy, and discretion, the changes being mainly of emphasis and omission. The curious feat of *Thérèse Desqueyroux* has often been noted: a faithful, almost literal translation of a novel by a famous Catholic writer (Mauriac) that never violates the integrity of Franju's atheism. Cocteau singled out Franju as the director to whom he would most confidently entrust his work, and Franju justified that confidence fully with his version of *Thomas l'imposteur*. Nonetheless, these films are discernibly Franju's: the directorial reticence should not be mistaken for abdication. The clearest way to demonstrate the continuity of the director's work is to show how the Franjuesque iconography that is already fully developed in the documentaries recurs in the features, producing those moments of poetic density and resonance that are the films' chief distinction.

If *Les Yeux sans visage* remains the finest of Franju's feature films, it is because it is the one that permits the greatest concentration of poetry created out of the association of these elements.—ROBIN WOOD

Frankenheimer, John

Nationality American. *Born* Malba, New York, 19 February 1930. *Education* La Salle Military Academy, graduated 1947; Williams College, B.A., 1951. *Military Service* Served in newly-formed Film Squadron, U.S. Air Force, 1951-53. *Family* Married Carolyn Miller, 1954 (divorced, 1961), two daughters; remarried, 1964. *Career* Assistant director, later director, CBS-TV, New York, 1953; television director, Danger, Climax!, Playhouse 90, Hollywood, from 1950; directed first feature, The Young Stranger, 1957; formed John Frankenheimer Productions, 1963; directed episode of Tales from the Crypt, 1989. *Awards* Christopher Award, 1954; Grand Prize for best film direction, Locarno Film Festival, 1955; Emmy Award for Directing for a Miniseries Or a Special, The Burning Season, 1994. *Address* c/o John Frankenheimer Productions, 2800 Olympic Blvd., Suite 201, Santa Monica, CA 90404, U.S.A.

Films as Director: 1957: *The Young Stranger; The Comedian* (for TV). **1958:** *Days of Wine and Roses* (for TV). **1959:** *The Turn of the Screw.* **1961:** *The Young Savages.* **1962:** *The Manchurian Candidate* (+co-pr, co-sc); *All Fall Down; Birdman of Alcatraz.* **1964:** *Seven Days in May.* **1965:** *The Train.* **1966:** *Grand Prix; Seconds.* **1968:** *The Fixer.* **1969:** *The Extraordinary Seaman; The Gypsy Moths.* **1970:** *I Walk the Line; The Horsemen.* **1973:** *L'Impossible Objet* (*Impossible Object; Story of a Love Story*); *The Iceman Cometh.* **1974:** *99 44/100% Dead* (retitled *Call Harry Crown* for general release in U.K.). **1975:** *French Connection II.* **1977:** *Black Sunday* (+bit role as TV controller). **1979:** *Prophecy.* **1982:** *The Challenge* (*Sword of the Ninja*). **1985:** *The Holcroft Covenant.* **1986:** *52 Pick-Up.* **1987:** *Across the River and Into the Trees; Riviera* (for TV) (as Alan Smithee). **1989:** *Dead Bang; The Fourth War.* **1991:** *Year of the Gun.* **1994:** *Against the Wall* (for TV). **1994:** *The Burning Season* (for TV) (+co-pr). **1996:** *Andersonville* (for TV) (+ex pr); *The Island of Dr. Moreau.* **1997:** *George Wallace* (for TV) (+pr).

The seven feature films John Frankenheimer directed between 1961 and 1964 stand as a career foundation unique in American cinema. In a single talent, film had found a perfect bridge between television and Hollywood drama, between the old and new visual technologies, between the cinema of personality and that of the corporation and the computer.

John Frankenheimer

Frankenheimer's delight in monochrome photography, his instinct for new light cameras, fast stocks, and lens systems like Panavision informed *The Manchurian Candidate, Seven Days in May,* and *Seconds* with a flashing technological intelligence. No less skillful with the interior drama he had mastered as a director of live television, he turned *All Fall Down* and *The Young Savages* into striking personal explorations of familial disquiet and social violence. He seemed unerring. Even *Birdman of Alcatraz* and *The Train,* troubled projects taken over at the last minute from Charles Crichton and Arthur Penn, respectively, emerged with the stamp of his forceful technique.

Frankenheimer's career began to sour with *Seconds,* a film that was arguably too self-conscious with its fish-eye sequences and rampant paranoia. *Grand Prix,* an impressive technical feat in Super Panavision, showed less virtuosity in the performances. His choices thereafter were erratic: heavy-handed comedy, rural melodrama, a further unsuccessful attempt at spectacle in *The Horsemen,* which was shot in Afghanistan. Frankenheimer relocated in Europe, no doubt mortified that Penn, Lumet, and Delbert Mann, lesser lights of live TV drama, had succeeded where he failed.

Despite a career revival with the 1975 *French Connection II,* a sequel which equalled its model in force and skill, Frankenheimer has not hit his stride since. The director's choices remain variable in intelligence, though by staying within the area of violent melodrama he has at least ceased to dissipate his talent in the pursuit of production values. *Black Sunday* is a superior terrorist thriller, *Prophecy* a failed but worthy horror film with environmental overtones, and *The Challenge* a stylish Japanese romp in the style of *The Yakuza.* Unfortunately, new directors who grew up with the Frankenheimer work as benchmarks do such material better.

Frankenheimer's late 1980s and early 1990s features—*Dead Bang, The Fourth War,* and *Year of the Gun*—did nothing to resuscitate his career, and were quickly forgotten as they made their way to video store oblivion. Only the 1987 theatrical re-release of *The Manchurian Candidate,* after decades of unavailability, earned Frankenheimer high critical praise. Indeed, the film was atop many critics' lists as among the best to come to movie houses that year. Additionally, the emergence of the high-tech thriller genre, so popular in the 1990s, has been critically traced back to *The Train.*

In 1994 Frankenheimer returned to his roots in television by directing *Against the Wall* and *The Burning Season,* two above-average made-for-TV movies. The former is a solid prison drama which retraces the events surrounding the 1971 Attica prison riots. The latter is even better: an outstanding, politically savvy account of the life of activist Chico Mendes, who battled against the exploitation of those who toil in the Amazon rain forests of Brazil and paid for his valor with his life.—JOHN BAXTER and ROB EDELMAN

Fuller, Samuel

f. FILM DIRECTORS

Nationality American. ***Born*** *Samuel Michael Fuller in Worcester, Massachusetts, 12 August 1911.* ***Military Service*** *Served in 16th regiment of U.S. Army 1st Division, 1942-45, awarded Bronze Star, Silver Star, and Purple Heart.* ***Family*** *Married actress Christa Lang, 1965.* ***Career*** *Copy-boy and journalist*, New York Journal, *from 1924; crime reporter, from 1928; screenwriter in Hollywood, from 1936; screenwriter at Warner Bros., 1946-48; directed first feature, 1948; signed to 20th Century-Fox, 1951-57; TV director, 1960s.*

Films as Director: 1949: *I Shot Jesse James* (+sc). **1950:** *The Baron of Arizona* (+sc); *The Steel Helmet* (+sc, co-pr). **1951:** *Fixed Bayonets* (+sc). **1952:** *Park Row* (+sc, co-pr). **1953:** *Pickup on South Street* (+sc) [remade in 1968 as *Cape Town Affair* (Webb)]. **1954:** *Hell and High Water* (+co-sc). **1955:** *The House of Bamboo* (+co-sc, role as Japanese policeman). **1957:** *Run of the Arrow* (*Hot Lead*) (+pr, sc); *China Gate* (+pr, sc); *Forty Guns* (+pr, sc). **1958:** *Verboten!* (+pr, sc). **1959:** *The Crimson Kimono* (+pr, sc). **1961:** *Underworld USA* (+pr, sc). **1962:** *Merrill's Marauders* (+co-sc). **1963:** *Shock Corridor* (+pr, sc). **1964:** *The Naked Kiss* (*The Iron Kiss*) (+co-pr, sc). **1967:** *Caine* (+sc); *The Meanest Men in the World* (for TV) (+sc). **1970:** *Sahrk!* (*Maneater*) (+sc). **1972:** *Tatort—Tote Taubein der Beethovenstrasse* (*Dead Pigeon on Beethoven Street* (+sc, role as United States Senator). **1980:** *The Big Red One* (+sc, role). **1982:** *White Dog* (+co-sc, role). **1983:** *Les voleurs de la nuit* (*Thieves After Dark*) (+co-sc, role). **1989:** *Sans espoir de retour* (*Street of No Return*) (+co-sc). **1990:** *The Day of Reckoning* (for TV) (+co-sc).

Other Films: 1936: *Hats Off* (Petroff) (sc). **1937:** *It Happened in Hollywood* (Lachman) (sc). **1938:** *Gangs of New York* (Cruze) (remade in 1945 as *Gangs of the Waterfront* (Blair) (sc); *Adventure in Sahara* (Lederman) (sc); *Federal Man-Hunt* (Grinde) (sc). **1941:** *Bowery Boy* (Morgan) (sc); *Confirm or Deny* (Lang, Mayo) (sc). **1943:** *Power of the Press* (Landers) (sc). **1949:** *Shockproof* (Sirk) (sc). **1951:** *The Tanks Are Coming* (Seiler) (sc). **1952:** *Scandal Sheet* (*The Dark Page*) (Karlson) (sc). **1953:** *The Command* (Butler) (sc). **1965:** *Pierrot le fou* (Godard) (role as himself). **1966:** *Brigitte et Brigitte* (Moullet) (role as himself). **1971:** *The Last Movie* (Hopper) (role as himself). **1973:** *The Deadly Trackers* (Shear) (role). **1974:** *The Klansman* (*The Burning Cross; KKK*) (Young) (sc). **1977:** *Der Amerikanische Freund* (*The American Friend*) (Wenders) (role as The American). **1979:** *1941* (Spielberg) (small role). **1982:** *Der stand der dinge* (Wenders) (role). **1983:** *Hammett* (Wenders) (role). **1984:** *Slapstick (Of Another Kind)* (Paul) (role); *Les sang des autres* (*The Blood of Others*) (Chabrol) (role). **1987:** *A Return to Salem's Lot* (Cohen) (role); *Helsinki Napoli All Night Long* (Mika Kaurismäki) (role). **1989:** *Sons* (Rockwell) (role). **1992:** *La vie de boème* (*Bohemian Life*) (Aki Kaurismäki); *Missä on Musette?* (*Where is Musette?*) (Nieminen and Vesteri) (role); *Golem, l'esprit de l'exil* (*Golem, The Spirit of the Exile*) (Gitai) (role). **1994:** *Girls in Prison* (for TV) (co-sc); *Tigrero: A Film That Was Never Made* (Mika Kaurismäki) (role); *Somebody to Love* (Rockwell) (role). **1995:** *Anything for John* (Cazenave and Headline) (role). **1996:** *The Typewriter, The Rifle and the Movie Camera* (Simon) (role). **1997:** *The End of Violence* (Wenders) (role).

Sam Fuller's narratives investigate the ways that belonging to a social group simultaneously functions to sustain and nurture individual identity and, conversely, to pose all sorts of emotional and ideological threats to that identity. Fuller's characters are caught between a solitude that is both liberating and debilitating, and a communality that is both supportive and oppressive. Unlike Howard Hawks, whose films suggest the triumph of the group over egoism, Fuller is more cynical and shows that neither isolation nor group membership is without its hardships and tensions.

Many of the films touch upon a broad kind of belonging, as in membership in a nation—specifically the United States (although *China Gate* comments on several other nationalities)—as a driving idea and ideal, national identity becoming a reflection of personal identity. For example, in Fuller films about the building of the West, such as *Forty Guns, The Baron of Arizona,* or *Run of the Arrow,* the central characters initially understand their own quests as necessarily divergent from the quest of America for its own place in the world. Even though the course of the films suggests the moral and emotional losses that such divergence leads to, the films also imply that there is something inadequate in the American quest itself, in the ways such a quest undercuts its own purity by finding strength in a malevolent violence (the readiness of "ordinary" people in *The Baron of Arizona* to lynch at a moment's notice), in mistrust and prejudice (unbridled racism in *Run of the Arrow*), or in political corruption.

Similarly, in films such as *House of Bamboo, Underworld USA,* and *Pickup on South Street,* about criminal organizations infiltrated by revenging outsiders, the narrative trajectory will begin

by suggesting the moral separation of good guys and bad guys, but will then continue to demonstrate their parallelism, their interweaving, even their blurring. For example, in *Underworld USA*, the criminals and crimefighters resemble each other in their methods, in their cold calculation and determination, and in their bureaucratic organization. Tolly, the film's central character, may agree to map his own desire for revenge onto the crimefighters' desire to eliminate a criminal element, but the film resolutely refuses to unambiguously propagandize the public good over personal motives.

At a narrower level of group concern, Fuller's films examine the family as a force that can be nurturing but is often stifling and riddled with contradictions. Not accidentally, many of Fuller's films concentrate on childless or parentless figures: the family here is not given but something that one loses or that one has to grope towards. Often, the families that do exist are, for Fuller, like the nation-state, initially presenting an aura of innocent respectability but ultimately revealing a corruption and rotted perversity. Indeed, *The Naked Kiss* connects questions of political value to family value in its story of a woman discovering that her fiancé, the town's benefactor and a model citizen, is actually a child molester. Similarly, *Verboten!* maps the story of postwar America's self-image as benefactor to the world onto an anti-love love story. A German woman initially marrys a G.I. for financial support and then finds she really loves him, only to discover that he no longer loves her.

Love, to be sure, is a redemptive promise in Fuller's films but it is run through by doubt, anger, mistrust, deception. Any reciprocity or sharing that Fuller's characters achieve comes at a great price, ranging from mental and physical pain to death. For example, in *Underworld USA*, Tolly is able to drop his obsessional quest and give himself emotionally to the ex-gangster's moll, Cuddles, only when he is at a point of no return that will lead him to his death. Against the possibility of love (which, if it ever comes, comes so miraculously as to call its own efficacy into doubt), Fuller's films emphasize a world where everyone is potentially an outsider and therefore a mystery and even a menace. No scene in Fuller's cinema encapsulates this better than the opening of *Pickup on South Street* where a filled subway car becomes the site of intrigued and intriguing glances as a group of strangers warily survey each other as potential victims and victimizers. Echoing the double-entendre of the title (the pickup is political—the passing on of a secret microfilm—as well as sexual), the opening scene shows a blending of sexual desire and aggression as a sexual come-on reveals itself to be a cover for theft, and passive passengers reveal themselves to be government agents.

In a world of distrust, where love can easily betray, the Fuller character survives either by fighting for the last vestiges of an honest, uncorrupted love (in the most optimistic of the films) or, in the more cynical cases, by displacing emotional attachment from people to ideas; to myths of masculine power in *Forty Guns*; to obsessions (for example, Johnny Barratt's desire in *Shock Corridor* to win the Pulitzer Prize even if that desire leads him to madness); to mercenary self-interest; to political or social ideals; and ultimately, to a professionalism that finally means doing nothing other than doing your job right without thinking about it. This is especially the case in Fuller's war films, which show characters driven to survive for survival's sake, existence being defined in *Merrill's Marauders* as "put(ting) one foot in front of the other."

Fuller's style, too, is one based on tensions: a conflict of techniques that one can read as an enactment for the spectator of Fuller themes. Fuller is both a director of rapid, abrupt, shocking montage, as in the alternating close-ups of robber and victim in *I Shot Jesse James,* and a director who uses extremely long takes incorporating a complex mix of camera movement and character action. Fuller's style is the opposite of graceful; his style seems to suggest that in a world where grace provides little redemption, its utilization would be a kind of lie. Thus, a stereotypically beautiful shot like the balanced image of Mount Fujiyama in *House of Bamboo* might seem a textbook example of the well-composed nature shot but for the fact that the mountain is framed through the outstretched legs of a murdered soldier.—DANA B. POLAN

Gance, Abel

Nationality *French.* **Born** *Paris, 25 October 1889.* **Education** *Collège de Chantilly; Collège Chaptal, Paris, baccalaureate 1906. Served with Service Cinématographique et Photographique de l'Armée, 1917.* **Family** *Married (second wife) actress Odette Vérité, 1933. Daughter: Clarisse (Mme. Jacques Raynaud).* **Career** *Actor at Théâtre du Parc, Brussels, 1908-09; began selling screenplays to Gaumont, 1909; formed production company, Le Film Français, 1911; artistic director of Le Film d'Art, 1917; after death of first wife, travelled to United States, 1921; patented widescreen "Polyvision" process, 1926; patented "Perspective Sonore," stereophonic sound process, 1929; directed* Marie Tudor *for television, 1965; lived in Nice, worked on screenplay for* Christophe Colomb *project, first begun in 1939, 1970s; reassembled* Napoléon *premiered in New York, 1981.* **Awards** *Gold Medal, Union Française des Inventeurs, and Cinérama Gold Medal, Société des Auteurs, 1952; Théâtre de l'Empire named for Gance, Paris, 1961; Grand prix national de Cinéma, 1974; César Award, 1980; Commandeur de la Légion d'honneur; Grand officier de l'ordre national du Merité, et des Arts et des Lettres.* **Died** *In Paris, 10 November 1981.*

Films as Director: 1911: *La Digue, ou Pour sauver la Hollande* (+sc). **1912:** *Le Nègre blanc* (+sc, role); *Il y a des pieds au plafond* (+sc); *Le Masque d'horreur* (+sc). **1915:** *Un drame au Château d'Acre* (*Les Morts reviennent-ils?*) (+sc); *Ecce Homo* (+sc) (unfinished). **1916:** *La Folie du Docteur Tube* (+sc); *L'Enigme de dix heures* (+sc); *Le Fleur des ruines* (+sc); *L'Heroïsme de Paddy* (+sc); *Fioritures* (*La Source de beauté*) (+sc); *Le Fou de la falaise* (+sc); *Ce que les flots racontent* (+sc); *Le Périscope* (+sc): *Barberousse* (+sc); *Les Gaz mortels* (*Le Brouillard sur la ville*) (+sc); *Strass et compagnie* (+sc). **1917:** *Le Droit à la vie* (+sc); *La Zone de la mort* (+sc); *Mater Dolorosa* (+sc). **1918:** *La Dixième Symphonie* (+sc); *Le Soleil noir* (+sc) (unfinished). **1919:** *J'Accuse* (+sc). **1923:** *La Roué* (+sc); *Au secours!* (+sc). **1927:** *Napoléon* (*Napoléon vu par Abel Gance*) (+sc). **1928:** *Marines et Cristeaux* (+sc) (experimental footage for "Polyvision"). **1931:** *La Fin du monde* (+sc). **1932:** *Mater Dolorosa* (+sc). **1934:** *Poliche* (+sc); *La Dame aux Camélias* (+sc); *Napoléon Bonaparte* (+sc) (sound version, with additional footage). **1935:** *Le Roman d'un jeune homme pauvre* (+sc); *Lucrèce Borgia*. **1936:** *Un Grand Amour de Beethoven* (*The Life and Loves of Beethoven*) (+sc); *Jérome Perreau, héro des barricades* (*The Queen and the Cardinal*); *Le Voleur de femmes* (+sc). **1937:** *J'accuse* (*That They May Live*) (+sc). **1939:** *Louise* (+co-sc); *Le Paradis* perdu (*Four Flights to Love*) (+co-sc). **1941:** *La Vénus aveugle* (+sc). **1942:** *Le Capitaine Fracasse* (+co-sc). **1944:** *Manolete* (+sc) (unfinished). **1954:** *Quatorze Juillet* (+sc); *La Tour de Nesle* (+sc). **1956:** *Magirama* (+sc, co-pr) (demonstration of "Polyvision" in color). **1960:** *Austerlitz* (co-d, +co-sc). **1964:** *Cyrano et d'Artagnan* (+co-sc). **1971:** *Bonaparte et la révolution* (+sc, co-pr).

Other Films: 1909: *Le Portrait de Mireille* (Perret) (sc); *Le Glas du Père Césaire* (+sc); *La Légende de l'arc-en-ciel* (sc); *Molière* (Perret) (role). **1909/10:** Some Max Linder short comedies (role as Max's brother). **1910:** *Paganini* (sc); *La Fin de Paganini* (sc); *Le Crime de Grand-père* (Perret) (sc); *Le Roi des parfums* (sc); *L'Aluminité* (sc); *L'Auberge rouge* (sc); *Le Tragique Amour de Mona Lisa* (Capellani) (sc). **1911:** *Cyrano et D'Assoucy* (Capellani) (sc); *Un Clair de lune sous Richelieu* (Capellani) (sc); *L'Électrocuté* (Morlhon) (sc). **1912:** *Une Vengeance d'Edgar Poe* (Capellani) (sc); *La Mort du Duc d'Enghien* (Capellani) (sc); *La Conspiration des drapeaux* (sc); *La Pierre philosophe* (sc). **1914:** *L'Infirmière* (Pouctal) (sc). **1920:** *L'Atre* (Boudrioz) (pr). **1929:** *Napoléon auf St. Helena* (*Napoléon à Saint-Hélène*) (Pick) (sc). **1933:** *Le Maître de forges* (Rivers) (sc, supervisor). **1953:** *Lumière et l'invention du cinématographe* (*Louis Lumière*) (Paviot) (commentary, narration). **1954:** *La Reine Margot* (Dréville) (sc).

Abel Gance's career as a director was long and flamboyant. He wrote his first scripts in 1909, turning to directing a couple of years later, and made his last feature, *Cyrano et d'Artagnan,* in 1964. As late as 1971 he re-edited a four-hour version of his Napoleon footage to make *Bonaparte et la révolution,* and he lived long enough to see his work again reach wide audiences.

Gance's original aspirations were as a playwright, and throughout his life he treasured the manuscript of his verse tragedy *La Victoire de Samothrace,* written for Sarah Bernhardt and on the brink of production when the war broke out in 1914. If Gance's beginnings in the film industry he then despised were unremarkable, he showed his characteristic audacity and urge for experimentation with an early work, the unreleased *La Folie du Docteur Tube,* which made great use of distorting lenses, in 1916. He learned his craft in a dozen or more films during 1916 and 1917—the best remembered of which are *Les Gaz mortels, Barberousse,* and *Mater dolorosa.* He reached fresh heights with a somewhat pretentious and melodramatic study of a great and suffering composer, *La Dixième Symphonie.* Even more significant was his ambitious and eloquent antiwar drama, *J'Accuse,* released in 1919. These films established him as the leading French director of his generation and gave him a preeminence he was not to lose until the coming of sound.

The 1920s saw the release of just three Gance films. If *Au secours!,* a comedy starring his friend Max Linder, is something of a lighthearted interlude, the other two are towering landmarks of silent cinema. *La Roue* began as a simple melodramatic tale, but in the course of six months scripting and a year's location shooting, the project took on quite a new dimension. In the central figure of Sisif, Gance seems to have struggled to create an amalgam of Oedipus, Sisyphus, and Lear. Meanwhile portions of the film that were eventually cut apparently developed a social satire of such ferocity that the railway unions demanded its excision. The most expensive film as yet made in France, its production was again delayed when the death of Gance's wife caused him to abandon work and take a five month trip to the United States.

Like his previous work, *La Roue* had been conceived and shot in the pre-1914 style of French cinema, which was based on a conception of film as a series of long takes, each containing a significant section of the action, rather than as a succession of scenes made up of intercut shots of different lengths, taken from varying distances. But in Hollywood, where he met D.W. Griffith, Gance came into contact with the new American style of editing. Upon his return to France, Gance spent a whole year reediting his film. On its release in 1923 *La Roue* proved to be one of the stunning films of the decade. Even in its shortened version—comprising a prologue and four parts—the film had a combined running time of nearly eight hours.

Gance's imagination and energy at this period seemed limitless. Almost immediately he plunged into an even vaster project whose title clearly reflects his personal approach, *Napoléon va par Abel Gance*. If *La Roue* was particularly remarkable for its editing (certain sequences are classic moments of French 1920s avant-garde experimentation), *Napoléon* attracted immediate attention for its incredibly mobile camerawork, created by a team under the direction of Jules Kruger. *Napoléon* thus emerges as a key masterpiece of French cinema at a time when visual experimentation took precedence over narrative and the disorganization of production offered filmmakers the chance to produce extravagant and ambitious personal works within the heart of the commercial industry.

Abel Gance

Gance's conception of himself as visionary filmmaker and of Napoleon as a master of his destiny points to the roots of Gance's style in the nineteenth century and his romantic view of the artist as hero. The scope of Gance's film, bursting into triple screen effects at the moment of Napoleon's climactic entry into Italy, remains staggering even today.

The 1920s in France was a period of considerable creative freedom. Given this atmosphere, a widespread urge to experiment with the full potential of the medium was apparent. If the freedom came from the lack of a tightly controlled studio system, the desire to explore new forms of filmic expression can be traced to a reaction against the situation imposed by Pathé and Gaumont before 1914, when film was seen as a purely commercial product, underfinanced and devoid of artistic or personal expression. This had been the cinema in which Gance had made his debut, and he was one of those striving most forcefully in the 1920s both to increase the possibilities for personal expressiveness and to widen the technical scope of cinema. He pioneered new styles of cutting and camerawork, as well as widescreen and multiscreen techniques.

It is ironic, then, that the advent of the greatest technical innovation of the period left Gance stranded. The explanation for this lies less in the irrelevance of sound to his personal vision of the medium—he was pioneering a new stereophonic system with *La Fin du monde* as early as 1929—than the fact that new forms of tighter production control were implemented as a result of the greater costs associated with sound filmmaking.

The 1930s emerge as a sad era for a man accustomed to being in the forefront of the French film industry. Gance, whose mind had always teemed with new and original projects, was now reduced to remaking his old successes: sound versions of *Mater dolorosa* in 1932, *Napoléon Bonaparte* in 1934, and *J'accuse* in 1937. Otherwise, the projects he was allowed to make were largely adaptations of fashionable stage dramas or popular novels: *Le Maître de forges, Poliche, La Dame aux camélias,* and *Le Roman d'un jeune homme pauvre.* In the late 1930s he was able to treat subjects in which his taste for grandly heroic figures is again apparent: Savonarola in *Lucrèce Borgia* and the great composer—played by Harry Baur—in *Un Grand Amour de Beethoven,* but by 1942, when he made *Le Capitaine Fracasse,* Gance's career seemed to have come to an end.

Though a dozen years were to pass before he directed another feature film, Gance maintained his incredible level of energy. Refusing to be beaten, he continued his experiments with "polyvision" which were to culminate in his *Magirama* spectacle. He eventually made three further features, all historical dramas in which his zest, if not the old towering imagination, is still apparent: *La Tour de Nesle, Austerlitz,* and *Cyrano et d'Artagnan.*

The French 1920s cinema of which Gance is the major figure has consistently been undervalued by film historians, largely because its rich experimentation with visual style and expressiveness was not accompanied by an similar concern with the development of film narrative. Gance's roots were in the nineteenth century romantic tradition, and despite his literary background, he, like his contemporaries, was willing to accept virtually any melodramatic story that would allow him to pursue his visual interests. For this reason French 1920s work has been marginalized in accounts of film history that see the growth of storytelling techniques as the central unifying factor. The rediscovery of Gance's *Napoléon* in the 1980s, though—thanks largely to twenty years of effort by Kevin Brownlow—has made clear to the most skeptical the force and mastery achieved in the years preceding the advent of sound, and restored Gance's reputation as a master of world cinema.—ROY ARMES

Godard, Jean-Luc

Nationality French. *Born* Paris, 3 December 1930, became citizen of Switzerland. *Education* Nyon, Switzerland; Lycée Buffon, Paris; Sorbonne, 1947-49, certificate in ethnology 1950. *Family* Married 1) Anna Karina, 1960 (divorced); 2) Anne Wiamzensky, 1967 (divorced). *Career* Delivery boy, cameraman, assistant editor for Zurich television, construction worker, and gossip columnist (for Les Temps de Paris), in Switzerland and Paris, 1949-56; founded short-lived Gazette du cinéma, writing as "Hans Lucas," 1950-51; critic for Cahiers du cinéma, from 1952; directed first film, Opération Béton, 1954; worked as film editor, 1956; worked in publicity department, 20th Century-Fox, Paris, with producer Georges de Beauregard, 1957; working for Beauregard, directed first feature, A bout de souffle, 1959; formed Anoucka films with Anna Karina, 1964; led protests over firing of Henri Langlois, director of Cinémathèque, instigated shut down of Cannes Festival, 1968; began collaboration with Jean-Pierre Gorin, editor of Cahiers marxistes-léninistes, 1969 (partnership terminated 1973); "reclaimed" work from 1969-72 as that of the Dziga Vertov group; established Sonimage film and video studio in Grenoble with Anne-Marie Miéville, 1974-75; moved to the Swiss town of Rolle, 1978; began the second stage of his directorial career, 1980; directed jeans advertisement, 1987. *Awards* Best Direction Award, Berlin Festival, for A bout de souffle, 1960; Prix Pasinetti, 1962; Golden Lion, Venice Film Festival, for Prenom: Carmen, 1983; Honorary César,

1986; Lifetime Achievement Award, New York Film Critics' Circle, 1994. **Address** *15 rue du Nord, 1180 Roulle, Switzerland.*

Films as Director: 1954: *Opération Béton* (+pr, sc, ed, narrator) (released 1958). **1955:** *Une Femme coquette* (d as 'Hans Lucas,' +sc pr, ph, ed, bit role as man visiting prostitute). **1957:** *Tous les garçons s'appellent Patrick* (*Charlotte et Véronique; All the Boys are Called Patrick*) (+sc). **1958:** *Une Histoire d'eau* (co-d: actual shooting by Truffaut, +co-sc, ed, role) (released 1961); *Charlotte et son Jules* (*Charlotte and Her Jules*) (+sc, ed, dubbed voice of Jean-Paul Belmondo) (released 1961). **1959:** *A bout de souffle* (*Breathless*) (+sc, role as passerby who points out Belmondo to police). **1961:** *Une Femme est une femme* (*Woman Is a Woman*) (+sc). **1962:** "La Paresse" episode of *Les Sept Péchés capitaux* (*The Seven Deadly Sins; The Seven Capital Sins*) (+sc); *Vivre sa vie* (*My Life to Live*) (+sc, dubbed voice of Peter Kassowitz), "Il nuovo mondo (Le Nouveau Monde)" in *RoGoPaG* (*Laviamoci il cervello; Let's Have a Brainwash*) (+sc, bit role). **1963:** *Le Petit Soldat* (*The Little Soldier*) (+sc, bit role as man at railway station) (completed 1960); *Les Carabiniers* (+sc); *Le Mépris* (*Contempt*) (+sc, role). **1964:** "Le Grand Escroc" in *Les Plus Belles Escroqueries du monde* (*The Beautiful Swindlers; World's Greatest Swindles; The World's Most Beautiful Swindlers*) (+sc, narration, bit role as man wearing Moroccan chéchia); *Bande à part* (*Band of Outsiders*) (+sc, narrator); *La Femme mariée* (*Une Femme mariée; A Married Woman*) (+sc, role); *Reportage sur Orly* (+sc) (short). **1965:** "Montparnasse—Levallois" in *Paris vu par . . .* (*Six in Paris*) (+sc); *Alphaville, Alphaville, une étrange aventure de Lemmy Caution* (+sc); *Une Étrange aventure de Lemmy Caution* (+sc); *Pierrot le fou* (+sc). **1966:** *Masculin-féminin* (*Masculin féminin: quinze faits précis*) (+sc); *Made in U.S.A.* (+sc, voice on tape recorder). **1967:** *Deux ou trois choses que je sais d'elle* (*Two or Three Things I Know About Her*) (+sc, narrator); "Anticipation" episode of *Le Plus Vieux Métier du monde* (*The Oldest Profession*) (+sc); *La Chinoise ou Plutôt à la*

chinoise (+sc); "Caméra-oeil" in *Loin du Viêt-Nam* (*Far from Vietnam*) (+sc, appearance); *Le Weekend* (*Weekend*) (+sc). **1968:** *Le Gai Savoir* (*The Joy of Knowledge; Joyful Wisdom*) (+sc); *Cinétracts* (+sc) (series of untitled, creditless newsreels); *Un Film comme les autres* (*A Film Like Any Other*) (+sc, ph, ed, voice); *One Plus One* (*Sympathy for the Devil*) (+sc, voice); *One A.M.* (*One American Movie*) (+sc) (unfinished). **1969:** *British Sounds* (*See You at Mao*) (co-d, co-sc); *Pravda* (+sc) (collective credit to Groupe Dziga-Vertov); *Lotte in Italia* (*Luttes en Italie*) (+sc) (collective credit to Groupe Dziga-Vertov); "L'amore" episode of *Amore e rabbia* (+sc) (completed 1967: festival showings as "Andante e ritorno dei figli prodighi" episode of *Vangelo 70*); *Vent d'est* (*East Wind* (+sc); *Wind from the East*) (co-d, co-sc, ed). **1970:** *Jusqu'à la victoire* (*Till Victory*) (co-d, +sc) (unfinished). **1971:** *Vladimir et Rosa* (*Vladimir and Rosa*) (+sc, ph, collective credit to Groupe Dziga-Vertov, role as U.S. policeman, appearance, narration). **1972:** *Tout va bien* (co-d, +co-sc, pr); *A Letter to Jane or Investigation About a Still* (*Lettre à Jane*) (co-d, +co-sc, co-pr, narration). **1975:** *Numéro deux* (+co-sc, co-pr, appearance). **1976:** *Ici et ailleurs* (co-d, +co-sc) (includes footage from *Jusqu'à la victoire*); *Comment ça va* (co-d, +co-sc). **1977:** *6 x 2: sur et sous la communication* (co-d, +co-sc, ed) (for TV); "*France/tour/detour/deux/enfants*" (for TV) (co-d with Miéville, co-sc). **1980:** *Sauve qui peut* (*La vie; Every Man for Himself; Slow Motion*) (+co-sc, co-ed, pr, ed). **1982:** *Passion* (+sc, ed, role). **1983:** *Prenom: Carmen* (*First Name: Carmen*) (+ed, role). **1985:** *Je vous salue, Marie* (*Hail Mary; The Book of Mary*) (+sc); *Detective* (+sc). **1986:** *Grandeur et Decadence d'un Petit Commerce du Cinema* (*The Rise and Fall of a Little Film Company*) (for TV) (+sc). **1987:** *Soigne ta droite* (*Keep Up Your Right*) (+sc, ed, role); episode in *Aria* (+ed); *King Lear* (+sc, ed, role). **1990:** *Nouvelle Vague* (*New Wave*) (+sc, ed); *Visages Suisse* (*Faces of Switzerland*) (co-d). **1991:** *Contre l'oubli* (*Against Oblivion*); *Allemagne Neuf Zero* (*Germany Nine Zero*) (+sc). **1993:** *Helas Pour Moi* (*Oh, Woe Is Me*) (+sc, ed). **1994:** *JLG/JLG—Autoportrait de Decembre* (*JLG/JLG—Self-Portrait in December*) (+sc, pr, ed, appearance). **1995:** *Deux fois cinquante ans de cinema Francais* (*2 x 50 Years of French Cinema*) (co-d, +co-sc, co-ed, appearance); *Les enfants jouent a la Russie* (*The Kids Play Russian*) (+sc, ed, appearance). **1996:** *Forever Mozart* (+sc, ed). **1997:** "*Histoires du cinéma*" (for TV).

Other Films: **1950:** *Quadrille* (Rivette) (pr, role). **1951:** *Présentation ou Charlotte et son steack* (Rohmer) (role). **1956:** *Kreutzer Sonata* (Rohmer) (pr); *Le Coup du berger* (Rivette) (role). **1958:** *Paris nous appartient* (Rivette) (Godard's silhouette). **1959:** *Le Signe du lion* (Rohmer) (role). **1961:** *Cléo de cinq à sept* (Varda) (role with Anna Karina in comic sequence); *Le Soleil dans l'oeil* (Bourdon) (role); *The Connection* (Clarke) (role). **1963:** *Schehérézade* (Gaspard-Huit) (role); *The Directors* (pr: Greenblatt) (appearance); *Paparazzi* (Rozier) (appearance); *Begegnung mit Fritz Lang* (Fleischmann) (appearance); *Petit Jour* (Pierre) (appearance). **1964:** *Bardot et Godard* (*Le parti des choses*) (Rozier) (appearance). **1965:** *Tentazioni proibite* (Civirani) (appearance). **1966:** *L'Espion* (*The Defector*) (Levy) (role). **1971:** *One P.M.* (*One Parallel Movie*) (Pennebaker) (includes footage from abandoned *One A.M.* and documentary footage of its making) (role). **1976:** *Der kleine Godard an das Kuratorium junger deutscher Film* (*The Little Godard to the Production Board for Young German Film*) (Costard) (appearance). **1982:** *Chamber 666* (for TV) (Wenders) (appearance). **1997:** *Nous sommes tous encore ici* (Miéville) (role).

If influence on the development of world cinema is the criterion, then Jean-Luc Godard is certainly the most important filmmaker of the past thirty years; he is also one of the most problematic.

Godard's career so far falls roughly into three periods: the early works from *About de souffle* to *Weekend* (1959-1968), a period whose end is marked decisively by the latter film's final caption, "Fin de Cinéma"; the period of intense politicization, during which Godard collaborated (mainly though not exclusively) with Jean-Pierre Gorin and the Dziga Vertov group (1968-1972); and the subsequent work, divided between attempts to renew communication with a wider, more "mainstream" cinema audience and explorations of the potentialities of video (in collaboration with Anne-Marie Miéville). One might also separate the films from *Masculin-Féminin* to *Weekend* as representing a transitional phase from the first to the Dziga Vertov period, although in a sense all Godard's work is transitional.

What marks the middle period off from its neighbours is above all the difference in intended audience: the Dziga Vertov films were never meant to reach the general public. They were instead aimed at already committed Marxist or leftist groups, campus student groups, and so on, to stimulate discussion of revolutionary politics and aesthetics, and, crucially, the relationship between the two.

Godard's importance lies in his development of an authentic modernist cinema in opposition to (though, during the early period, at the same time *within*) mainstream cinema; it is with his work that film becomes central to our century's major aesthetic debate, the controversy developed through such figures as Lukács, Brecht, Benjamin, and Adorno as to whether realism or modernism is the more progressive form. As ex-*Cahiers du Cinéma* critic and New Wave filmmaker, Godard was initially linked with Truffaut and Chabrol in a kind of revolutionary triumvirate; it is easy, in retrospect, to see that Godard was from the start the truly radical figure, the "revolution" of his colleagues operating purely on the aesthetic level and easily assimilable into the mainstream.

A simple way of demonstrating the essential thrust of Godard's work is to juxtapose his first feature, *Breathless,* with the excellent American remake. Jim McBride's film follows the original fairly closely, with the fundamental difference that in it all other elements are subordinated to the narrative and the characters. In Godard's film, on the contrary, this traditional relationship between signifier and signified shows a continuous tendency to come adrift, so that the *process of narration* (which mainstream cinema strives everywhere to conceal) becomes foregrounded; *A bout de souffle* is "about" a story and characters, certainly, but it is also about the cinema, about film techniques, about Jean Seberg, etc.

This foregrounding of the process—and the means—of narration is developed much further in subsequent films, in which Godard systematically breaks down the traditional barrier between fiction/documentary, actor/character, narrative film/experimental film to create freer, "open" forms. Persons appear as themselves in works of fiction, actors address the camera/ audience in monologues or as if being interviewed, materiality of film is made explicit (the switches from positive to negative in *Une Femme mariée,* the turning on and off of the soundtrack in *Deux ou trois choses que je sais d'elle,* the showing of the clapper-board in *La Chinoise*). The initial motivation for this seems to have been the assertion of personal freedom: the filmmaker shatters the bonds of traditional realism in order to be able to say and do whatever he wants, creating films spontaneously. (*Pierrot le fou*—significantly, one of Godard's most popular films—is the most extreme expression of this impulse.) Gradually, however, a political motivation (connected especially with the influence of Brecht) takes over. There is a marked sociological interest in the early films (especially *Vivre sa vie* and *Une Femme mariée*), but the turning-point is *Masculin- féminin* with its two male protagonists, one seeking fulfillment through personal relations, the other a political activist. The former's suicide at the end of the film can be read as marking a decisive choice: from here on, Godard increasingly listens to the voice of revolutionary politics and eventually (in the Dziga Vertov films) adopts it as his own voice.

The films of the Dziga Vertov group (named after the great Russian documentarist who anticipated their work in making films that foreground the means of production and are continuously self-reflexive) were the direct consequence of the events of May 1968. More than ever before the films are directly concerned with their own process, so that the ostensible subjects—the political scene in Czechoslovakia (*Pravda*) or Italy (*Lotte in Italia*), the trial of the Chicago Eight (*Vladimir and Rosa*)—become secondary to the urgent, actual subject: how does one make a revolutionary film? It was at this time that Godard distinguished between making political films (i.e. films on political subjects: Costa-Gavras's *Z* is a typical example) and making films politically, the basic assumption being that one cannot put radical content into traditional form without seriously compromising, perhaps negating, it. Hence the attack on realism initiated at the outset of Godard's career manifests its full political significance: realism is a bourgeois art form, the means whereby the bourgeoisie endlessly reassures itself, validating its own ideology as "true," "natural," "real"; its power must be destroyed. Of the films from this period, *Vent d'est* (the occasion for Peter Wollen's seminal essay on "Counter-Cinema" in *After Image*) most fully realized this aesthetic: the original pretext (the pastiche of a Western) recedes into the background, and the film becomes a discussion about itself—about the relationship between sound and image, the materiality of film, the destruction of bourgeois forms, the necessity for continuous self-criticism and self-awareness.

The assumption behind the Dziga Vertov films is clearly that the revolutionary impetus of May 1968 would be sustained, and it has not been easy for Godard to adjust to its collapse. That difficulty is the subject of one of his finest works, *Tout va bien* (again in collaboration with Gorin), an attempt to return to commercial filmmaking without abandoning the principles (both aesthetic and political) of the preceding years. Beginning by foregrounding Godard's own problem (how does a radical make a film within the capitalist production system?), the film is strongest in its complex use of Yves Montand and Jane Fonda (simultaneously fictional characters/personalities/star images) and its exploration of the issues to which they are central. These issues include the relationship of intellectuals to the class struggle; the relationship between professional work, personal commitment, and political position; and the problem of sustaining a radical impulse in a non-revolutionary age. *Tout va bien* is Godard's most authentically Brechtian film, achieving radical force and analytical clarity without sacrificing pleasure and a degree of emotional involvement.

Godard's relationship to Brecht has not always been so clear-cut. While the justification for Brecht's distanciation principles was always the communication of clarity, Godard's films often leave the spectator in a state of confusion and frustration. He continues to seem by temperament more anarchist than Marxist. One is troubled by the continuity between the criminal drop-outs of the earlier films and the political activists of the later. The insistent intellectualism of the films is often offset by a wilful abeyance of systematic thinking, the abeyance, precisely, of that self-awareness and self-criticism the political works advocate. Even in *Tout va bien,* what emerges from the political analysis as the film's own position is an irresponsible and ultimately desperate belief in spontaneity. Desperation, indeed, is never far from the Godardian surface, and seems closely related to the treatment of heterosexual relations: even through the apparent feminist awareness of the recent work runs a strain of unwitting misogyny (most evident, perhaps, in *Sauve qui peut*). The central task of Godard criticism, in fact, is to sort out the remarkable and salutary nature of the positive achievement from the temperamental limitations that flaw it.

From 1980 on, Godard commenced the second phase of his directorial career. Unfortunately, far too many of his films have become increasingly inaccessible to the audiences who had championed him in his heyday during the 1960s. *Sauve qui peut (La Vie) (Every Man for Himself),* Godard's comeback film, portended his future work. It is an awkward account of three characters whose lives become entwined: a man who has left his wife for a woman; the woman, who is in the process of leaving the man for a rural life; and a country girl who has become a prostitute.

In fact, several of Godard's works might best be described as anti-movies. *Passion,* for example, features characters named Isabelle, Michel, Hanna, Laszlo and Jerzy (played respectively by Isabelle Huppert, Michel Piccoli, Hanna Schygulla, Laszlo Szabo, and Jerzy Radziwilowicz), who are involved in the shooting of a movie titled *Passion.* The latter appears to be not so much a structured narrative as a series of scenes which are visions of a Renaissance painting. The film serves as a cynical condemnation of the business of moviemaking-for-profit, as the extras are poorly treated and the art of cinema is stained by commercial considerations.

Prenom: Carmen (First Name: Carmen) is Godard's best latter-career effort, a delightfully subversive though no less pessimistic mirror of the filmmaker's disenchantment with the cinema. His Carmen is a character straight out of his earlier work: a combination seductress/terrorist/wannabe movie maker. Her uncle, played by Godard, is a once-celebrated but now weary and faded film director named, not surprisingly, Jean-Luc Godard.

It seemed that Godard had simply set out to shock in *Hail, Mary,* a redo of the birth of Christ set in contemporary France. His Mary is a young student and gas station attendant; even though she has never had sex with Joseph, her taxi-driving boyfriend, she discovers she is pregnant. Along with Scorsese's *The Last Temptation of Christ,* this became a cause celebre among Catholics and even was censured by the Pope. However, the film is eminently forgettable; far superior is *The Book of Mary,* a perceptive short about a girl and her constantly quarrelling parents. It accompanied showings of *Hail, Mary,* and is directed by long-time Godard colleague Anne-Marie Miéville.

Detective, dedicated to auteur heroes John Cassavetes, Edgar G. Ulmer, and Clint Eastwood, is a verbose, muddled film noir. Despite its title, *Nouvelle Vague (New Wave),* an observance of the lives of a wealthy and influential couple, only makes one yearn for the days of the real "Nouvelle Vague." The narrative, which focuses on the sexual and political issues that are constants in Godard's films, is barely discernable; the dialogue—including such lines as "Love doesn't die, it leaves you," "One man isn't enough for a woman—or too much," "A critic is a soldier who fires at his own regiment," "Have you ever been stung by a dead bee?"—is superficially profound.

King Lear, an excessive, grotesque updating of Shakespeare, is of note for its oddball, once-in-a-lifetime cast: Godard; Woody Allen; Norman and Kate Mailer; stage director Peter Sellars; Burgess Meredith; and Molly Ringwald. The political thriller *Allemagne Neuf Zero (Germany Nine Zero),* although as confusing as any latter-day Godard film, works as nostalgia because of the presence of Eddie Constantine. He is recast as private eye Lemmy Caution, who last appeared in *Alphaville.* Here, he encounters various characters in a reunified Germany.

Helas Pour Moi (Oh, Woe Is Me), based on the Greek legend of Alcmene and Amphitryon and a text penned by the Italian poet Leopardi, is a long-winded bore about a God who wants to perceive human feeling; those intrigued by the subject matter would be advised to see Wim Wenders' *Wings of Desire* and *Faraway, So Close. JLG/JLG—Autoportrait de Decembre (JLG/JLG—Self-Portrait in December),* filmed in and near Godard's Swiss home, is a semi-abstract biography of the filmmaker. Its structure is appropriate, given the development of Godard's cinematic style. Ultimately, it is of interest mostly to those still concerned with Godard's life and career.—ROBIN WOOD and ROB EDELMAN

Greenaway, Peter

Nationality British. *Born* London, 5 April 1942. *Education* Studied painting. *Career* First exhibition of paintings, London, 1964; worked as a film editor for Central Office of Information, 1965-76; made first film, Train, 1966; made first feature, The Falls, 1980; A TV Dante broadcast, 1990. *Awards* Special Award, British Film Institute, for The Falls, 1980; Best Short Film, Melbourne Festival, for Act of God, 1981; Best Artistic Contribution, Cannes Festival, for Drowning by Numbers, 1988; two prizes, Festival International du Nouveau Cinema et de la Video, for A TV Dante, 1990.

Films as Director and Screenwriter: 1966: *Train; Tree.* **1967:** *Revolution; Five Postcards from Capital Cities.* **1969:** *Intervals.* **1971:** *Erosion.* **1973:** *H is for House* (+ph, ed, narration). **1975:** *Windows* (+ph, ed, narration); *Water.* **1976:** *Goole by Numbers; Vertical Features Remake* (+ed, ph). **1977:** *Dear Phone* (+ph, ed). **1978:** *1-100; A Walk Through H* (*The Re-Incarnation of an Ornithologist*); *Water Wrackets* (+ph, ed). **1980:** *The Falls* (+ed, narration); *Act of God* (for TV). **1979:** *Zandra Rhodes.* **1982:** *The Draughtsman's Contract.* **1983:** *Four American Composers.* **1984:** *Making a Splash.* **1985:** *26 Bathrooms; A Zed and Two Noughts* (*Zoo*) (+pr). **1987:** *The Belly of an Architect; Drowning by Numbers.* **1988:** *Fear of Drowning* (+narration); *Death in the Seine.* **1989:** *The Cook, the Thief, His Wife and Her Lover; A TV Dante, I-VIII* (for TV); *Hubert Bals Handshake.* **1991:** *Prospero's Books; M is for Man, Music, Mozart.* **1992:** *Rosa.* **1993:** *The Baby of Macon; Darwin* (for TV). **1995:** *Stairs 1 Geneva* (+narration); *The Pillow Book* (+ed); *Lumière et compagnie* (*Lumière and Company*).

Other Films: 1968: *Love Love Love* (Nyman) (ed).

An ancient Chinese encyclopedia, according to Borges, divides animals into "(a) those that belong to the Emperor, (b) embalmed ones, (c) those that are trained, (d) suckling pigs, (e) mermaids, (f) fabulous ones, (g) stray dogs, (h) those that are included in this classification, (i) those that tremble as if they are mad, (j) innumerable ones, (k) those drawn with a very fine camel's hair brush, (l) others, (m) those that have just broken a flower vase, (n) those that resemble flies from a distance." One is tempted to add, (o) those featured in Peter Greenaway's films. The inclusion would seem appropriate for a filmmaker who has constantly displayed a fascination for the organic and the classificatory in a body of films that have themselves retained an art-house individuality within the broader criteria of popular success.

Greenaway's biography implies a deeper integration between life and his art than some critics might suggest. He grew up in post-war Essex, his father was an ornithologist—perhaps the quintessential English hobby—and the petit-bourgeois world of public respectability and private eccentricity seems to have left him with a taste for the contradictory that hallmarks his work ("The black humour, irony, distancing, a quality of being in control, an interest in landscape, treating the world as equal with an image, these are very English qualities. I can't imagine myself living abroad"). He trained as a painter rather than a filmmaker, but his first exhibition, "Eisenstein at the Winter Palace," indicated an interest that led him into film editing at the Central Office of Information, the government department responsible for informing the public in the unique "home-counties" voice of domestic propaganda.

These years also saw Greenaway developing a crop of his own absurdist works—films, art, novels, illustrated books, drawings—with titles such as *Goole by Numbers* and *Dear Phone,* as well as directing (non-absurdist) Party Political Broadcasts for the Labour Party. They also saw the introduction of his fictional alter ego, Tulse Luper, archivist, cartographer, ornithologist extraordinaire ("He's me at about 65. A know-all, a Buckminster Fuller, a McLuhan, a John Cage,

Peter Greenaway.
Photograph by Julie Colour.

a pain"). Nomenclature means a lot to Greenaway in determining where one would be filed in the unfortunate event of a statistically (im)probable end. *The Falls* is a catalogue of victims of V.U.E. (Violent Unknown Event), with characters such as Mashanter Fallack, Carlos Fallanty, Raskado Fallcastle, and Hearty Fallparco. The epitome of absurdity was perhaps reached in *Act of God,* a film based around interviews with people who'd been struck by lightning in an attempt to find out what led to such an unpredictable event.

But perhaps the most tickling piece of absurdity for Greenaway came in the commercial success of *The Draughtsman's Contract,* his first film made on a reasonable budget. It made an uncharacteristic concession to plot, characterization, and scenic coherence. A stylish, lavish, and enigmatic puzzle revolving around murder in a stately seventeenth-century English home, it soon became the subject of a mythical French film conference that discussed its title for five days, and gained popular fame as everyone asked what was it all about. But it made Greenaway's name, and briefly contested box office ratings with the likes of *E.T.* and *Gandhi,* although Greenaway's intended length was four hours—"one suspects it was originally closer to *Tristram Shandy* than *Murder at the Vicarage,*" as one critic remarked.

Greenaway's ideas tend to work in twos. *A Zed and Two Noughts* took Siamese twins separated at birth and saw them cope with their grief at the death of their wives in a study in the decomposition of zoo animals. *Belly of an Architect* silhouetted the visceral mortality of Stourley Kracklite against his plans for an exhibition on a visionary eighteenth-century architect, Etiénne-Louis Boullée. But the dialectic seems more important than the ideas themselves, as Greenaway hints: "The important thing about Boullée—and this is where he's very like a filmmaker, who tends to spend much more time on uncompleted projects than completed ones—is that very few of his buildings were constructed. I've taken that up in Kracklite's fear of committal, being prepared to go half-way and no further, which is Kracklite's position and maybe my position as well."

In this position Greenaway has always been most successful when casting strong leading actors. He secured Brian Dennehy as Kracklite, for instance, and the cast of arguably his most successful film, *The Cook, The Thief, His Wife and Her Lover,* included Michael Gambon (the Thief) and Helen Mirren (his Wife).

Greenaway's ideas are always sufficiently ambiguous to resist trivialisation, but invariably involve death: Death and Landscape, Death and Animals, Death and Architecture, Death and Sex, Death and Food (cannibalism). But there are factors which make them more palatable. One of them is a taste for sumptuous framing (helped by cinematographer Sacha Vierney), in which he envisages an aesthetic complexity similar to that of the golden age of Dutch art, "where those amazing manifestations of the real world that we find in Vermeer and Rembrandt are enriched by a fantastic metaphorical language." The other is his close collaboration with the composer Michael Nyman, whose insistent scores lend an inexorable quality to Greenaway's sometimes spatial fabric of ideas.

The films of Peter Greenaway continue to be consistently outrageous and challenging. *Drowning by Numbers* is a bizarre, erotic concoction about three generations of women, each named Cissie Colpitts (and played by Joan Plowright, Juliet Stevenson, and Joely Richardson). Each Cissie is saddled with a husband who is lecherous or inattentive. And each one decides to murder her mate by drowning him. Madgett the coroner (Bernard Hill), who lusts after these women, agrees to list the deaths as natural. But the heroines hold the upper hand in the story, and Madgett's fate proves to be beyond his control.

Prospero's Books is an original, daring adaptation of Shakespeare's *The Tempest,* with almost all of the dialogue spoken by 87-year-old Sir John Gielgud (cast as Prospero, a role he played many times on stage). The other actors are little more than extras and, as in many of Greenaway's works, there is a mind-boggling amount of nudity. Purist defenders of the Bard may find much to fault in *Prospero's Books.* But the film remains noteworthy both for Gielgud's splendid reading of the text and its exquisitely layered imagery and production design.

Finally, *The Baby of Macon,* which featured Julia Ormond and Ralph Fiennes prior to their ascension to stardom, is a demanding drama. It is set in the 17th century and presented as a play being performed on a vast stage. The play depicts the birth and life of a saint-like baby. In typical Greenaway fashion, there is luminous cinematography (by the filmmaker's frequent collaborator, Sacha Vierny) and production design. Some will find *The Baby of Macon* stimulating; others will think it overblown; and still others will be perplexed by it all.

There are contradictions in Greenaway's works, a fact that seems to openly provoke divided opinion. Some would suggest that the fecundity of his vision, his intellectual rigor, is the stuff of great cinema; others, while admitting his originality, would still look for evidence of a deeper engagement with film as a medium, rather than as a vehicle for ideas. Lauded in Europe, under-distributed in the United States, loved and reviled in his own country, Greenaway is, nevertheless, in an enviable position for a filmmaker.—SAUL FRAMPTON and ROB EDELMAN

Grémillon, Jean

Nationality *French.* **Born** *Bayeux, Normandy, 3 October 1901.* **Education** *l'Ecole Communale de Saint-Lô, Lycée de Brest, and Ecole des Cordeliers, Dinan; Schola Cantorum, Paris (studied with Vincent d'Indy), 1920.* **Military Service** *1920-22.* **Family** *Married Christiane (Grémillon).* **Career** *Film titler, editor, and director of short films, from 1923; worked in Spain and Germany, 1935-38; war cinematographer, from 1939; elected president of Cinémathèque Française, 1944; president of C.G.T., film technicians union, 1946-50.* **Died** *25 November 1959.*

Films as Director: 1923: *Chartres (Le Cathédrale de Chartres)* (+ed); *Le Revêtement des routes* (+ed). **1924:** *La Fabrication du fil* (+ed); *Du fil à l'aiguille* (+ed); *La Fabrication du ciment artificiel* (+ed); *La Bière* (+ed); *Le Roulement à billes* (+ed); *Les Parfums* (+ed); *L'Étirage des ampoules électriques* (+ed); *La*

Photogénie mécanique (+ed). **1925:** *L'Education professionelle des conducteurs de tramway* (six short films) (+ed); *L'Electrification de la ligne Paris-Vierzon* (+ed); *L'Auvergne* (+ed); *La Naissance des cigognes* (+ed); *Les Aciéries de la marine et d'Homécourt* (+ed). **1926:** *La Vie des travailleurs italiens en France* (+ed); *La Croisière de L'Atalante* (+ed); *Un Tour au large* (+ed, sc, music—recorded on piano rolls). **1927:** *Maldone* (+ed, co-music); *Gratuités* (+ed). **1928:** *Bobs* (+ed). **1929:** *Gardiens de phare* (+ed). **1930:** *La Petite Lise* (+ed). **1931:** *Dainah la métisse* (+ed) (disowned due to unauthorized reediting); *Pour un sou d'amour* (no d credit on film; +ed). **1932:** *Le Petit Babouin* (+ed, music). **1933:** *Gonzague ou L'Accordeur* (+sc). **1934:** *La Dolorosa.* **1935:** *La Valse royale* (French version of Herbert Maisch's *Königswalzer*). **1936:** *Centinella alerta!* (not completed by Grémillon); *Pattes de mouches* (+co-sc). **1937:** *Gueule d'amour.* **1938:** *L'Etrange Monsieur Victor.* **1941:** *Remorques.* **1943:** *Lumière d'été.* **1944:** *Le Ciel est à vous.* **1945:** *Le Six Juin à l'aube* (*Sixth of June at Dawn*) (+sc, music). **1949:** *Pattes blanches* (+co-dialogue); *Les Charmes de l'existence* (co-d, co-sc, co-commentary, music advisor). **1951:** *L'Etrange Madame X.* **1952:** *Astrologie ou Le Miroir de la vie* (+sc, co-music); "Alchimie" episode of *L'Encyclopédie filmée—Alchimie, Azur, Absence* (+sc). **1954:** *L'Amour d'une femme* (+sc, dubbed actor Paolo Stoppa); *Au cœur de l'Ile de France* (+sc, co-music). **1955:** *La Maison aux images* (+sc, music). **1956:** *Haute Lisse* (+sc, music adapt). **1958:** *André Masson et les quatre éléments* (+sc, music).

Other Film: 1951: *Désastres de la guerre* (Kast) (commentary and co-music).

Jean Grémillon is finally beginning to enjoy the international reputation most French film scholars always bestowed upon him. Although Americans have until recently been able to see only one or two of his dozen important works, he has generally been placed only slightly below Renoir, Clair, and Carné in the hierarchy of French classical cinema.

Evidently, no one was more versatile than Grémillon. A musician, he composed many of his own scores and supervised all aspects of his productions scrupulously. Along with the search for a romantic unity of feeling and consistency of rhythm, his films also display an attention to details and locations that derives from his earliest documentaries.

No one was more prepared than Grémillon for the poetic realist sensibility that dominated French cinema in the 1930s. Even in the silent period his *Maldone* and *Gardiens de phare* reveal a heightening of strange objects as they take on fatal proportions in these tense and dark melodramas. *La Petite Lise* displayed these same qualities, along with an incredibly imaginative and rigorous use of sound. It should be called the first poetic realist film, anticipating Carné's work in particular.

After a few years of obscurity, Grémillon re-emerged with *Gueule d'amour,* a Foreign Legion love story with Jean Gabin. Then came a series of truly wonderful films: *L'Étrange M. Victor, Remorques, Le Ciel est à vous,* and *Lumière d'été.* Spanning the period of French subjugation by the Nazis, these

Jean Grémillon

films capture the sensibility of the times with their wistful romanticism, the fatality of their conclusions, and their attention to social classes.

Le Ciel est à vous must be singled out as a key film of the Occupation. Enormously popular, this tale of a small-town couple obsessed with aviation has been variously interpreted as a work promoting Vichy morality (family, small-town virtues, hard work) and as a representation of the indomitable French spirit, ready to soar beyond the temporary political restraints of the Occupation. Charles Vanel and Madeleine Renaud give unforgettable performances.

Grémillon often sought mythic locations (mysterious villages in the Alps or Normandy, the evocative southern cities of Orange and Toulon) where his quiet heroes and heroines played out their destinies of passion and crime. Unique is the prominent place women hold in his dramas. From the wealthy femme fatale murdered by Gabin in *Gueule d'amour* to the independent professional woman who refuses to give up her medical career, even for love (*L'Amour d'une femme*), women are shown to be far more prepossessed than the passionate but childish men who pursue them.

It is perhaps the greatest tragedy of French cinema that Grémillon's career after World War II was derailed by the conditions of the industry. His *Sixth of June at Dawn* shows how even a documentary project could in his hands take on poetic proportions and become a personal project. Yet the final years before his death in 1959 (when he was only fifty-seven) were spent in teaching and preparing unfinanced scripts. This is a sad end for the man some people claim to have been the most versatile cinematic genius ever to work in France.—DUDLEY ANDREW

Griffith, D.W.

*Nationality American. **Born** David Wark Griffith on Oldham County Farm, near Centerfield, Kentucky, 23 January 1875. **Education** District schools in Oldham County, Shelby County, and Louisville, Kentucky. **Family** Married 1) Linda Arvidson, 1906 (divorced 1936); 2) Evelyn Baldwin, 1936 (divorced 1947). **Career** As "Lawrence Griffith," "Alfred Lawrence," "Lawrence Brayington," and "Thomas Griffith," actor in regional stock companies, 1895-99; actor in New York and in touring companies, 1899-1906; actor for Edison Company and Biograph Pictures, also sold scenarios to Biograph and American Mutascope, 1907; director and scriptwriter for Biograph (approximately 485 one- and two-reelers), 1908-13; began association with cameraman G.W. (Billy) Bitzer, and with actress Mary Pickford, 1909; supervised Mack Sennett's first films, 1910; made first film with Lillian and Dorothy Gish,* An Unseen Enemy, *1912; joined Reliance Majestic (affiliated with Mutual), 1913; became partner in Triangle Pictures, 1915; travelled to Britain to aid war effort, 1917; engaged by Paramount, 1918; with Pickford, Fairbanks, and Chaplin, formed United Artists, 1919; built own studio at Mamaroneck, New York, 1920; directed three pictures for Paramount, 1925-26; returned to United Artists, 1927 (through 1931); directed his first talking picture,* Abraham Lincoln, *1930; resigned as head of his own production company, resigned from United Artists Board and sold UA stock, 1932-33; returned to Hollywood to work on* One Million B.C., *1939. **Awards** Director of the Year, 1931, and Special Award, 1936, from Academy of Motion*

Picture Arts and Sciences; Honorary Doctorate, University of Louisville, 1945. **Died** In Los Angeles, 23 July 1948.

Films as Director and Scriptwriter: (at Biograph): 1908: *The Adventures of Dolly; The Redman and the Child; The Tavern Keeper's Daughter; The Bandit's Waterloo; A Calamitous Elopement; The Greaser's Gauntlet; The Man and the Woman; For Love of Gold; The Fatal Hour; For a Wife's Honor; Balked at the Altar; The Girl and the Outlaw; The Red Girl; Betrayed by a Hand Print; Monday Morning in a Coney Island Police Court; Behind the Scenes; The Heart of Oyama; Where the Breakers Roar; The Stolen Jewels; A Smoked Husband; The Zulu's Heart; The Vaquaro's Vow; Father Gets in the Game; The Barbarian, Ingomar; The Planter's Wife; The Devil; Romance of a Jewess; The Call of the Wild; After Many Years; Mr. Jones at the Ball; Concealing a Burglar; Taming of the Shrew; The Ingrate; A Woman's Way; The Pirate's Gold; The Guerrilla; The Curtain Pole; The Song of the Shirt; The Clubman and the Tramp; Money Mad; Mrs. Jones Entertains; The Feud and the Turkey; The Test of Friendship; The Reckoning; One Touch of Nature; An Awful Moment; The Helping Hand; The Maniac Cook; The Christmas Burglars; A Wreath in Time; The Honor of Thieves; The Criminal Hypnotist; The Sacrifice; The Welcome Burglar; A Rural Elopement; Mr. Jones Has a Card Party; The Hindoo Dagger; The Salvation Army Lass; Love Finds a Way; Tragic Love; The Girls and a Daddy.*

1909: *Those Boys; The Cord of Life; Trying to Get Arrested; The Fascinating Mrs. Frances; Those Awful Hats; Jones and the Lady Book Agent; The Drive for Life; The Brahma Diamond; Politician's Love Story; The Jones Have Amateur Theatricals; Edgar Allen Poe; The Roué's Heart; His Wife's Mother; The Golden Louis; His Ward's Love; At the Altar; The Prussian Spy; The Medicine Bottle; The Deception; The Lure of the Gown; Lady Helen's Escapade; A Fool's Revenge; The Wooden Leg; I Did It, Mama; The Voice of the Violin; And a Little Child Shall Lead Them; The French Duel; Jones and His New Neighbors; A Drunkard's Reformation; The Winning Coat; A Rude Hostess; The Road to the Heart; The Eavesdropper; Schneider's Anti-Noise Crusade; Twin Brothers; Confidence; The Note in the Shoe; Lucky Jim; A Sound Sleeper; A Troublesome Satchel; Tis an Ill Wind That Blows No Good; The Suicide Club; Resurrection; One Busy Hour; A Baby's Shoe; Eloping with Auntie; The Cricket on the Hearth; The Jilt; Eradicating Auntie; What Drink Did; Her First Biscuits; The Violin Maker of Cremona; Two Memories; The Lonely*

D.W. Griffith

Villa; The Peach Basket Hat; The Son's Return; His Duty; A New Trick; The Necklace; The Way of Man; The Faded Lilies; The Message; The Friend of the Family; Was Justice Served?; Mrs. Jones' Lover or "I Want My Hat!"; The Mexican Sweethearts; The Country Doctor; Jealousy and the Man; The Renunciation; The Cardinal's Conspiracy; The Seventh Day; Tender Hearts; A Convict's Sacrifice; A Strange Meeting; Sweet and Twenty; The Slave; They Would Elope; Mrs. Jones' Burglar; The Mended Lute; The Indian Runner's Romance; With Her Card; The Better Way; His Wife's Visitor; The Mills of the Gods; Franks; Oh, Uncle; The Sealed Room; 1776 or The Hessian Renegades; The Little Darling; In Old Kentucky; The Children's Friend; Comata, the Sioux; Getting Even; The Broken Locket; A Fair Exchange; The Awakening; Pippa Passes; Leather Stockings; Fools of Fate; Wanted, a Child; The Little Teacher; A Change of Heart; His Lost Love; Lines of White on the Sullen Sea; The Gibson Goddess; In the Watches of the Night; The Expiation; What's Your Hurry; The Restoration; Nursing a Viper; Two Women and a Man; The Light that Came; A Midnight Adventure; The Open Gate; Sweet Revenge; The Mountaineer's Honor; In the Window Recess; The Trick That Failed; The Death Disc; Through the Breakers; In a Hempen Bag; A Corner in Wheat; The Redman's View; The Test; A Trap for Santa Claus; In Little Italy; To Save Her Soul; Choosing a Husband; The Rocky Road; The Dancing Girl of Butte; Her Terrible Ordeal; The Call; The Honor of His Family; On the Reef; The Last Deal; One Night, and Then—; The Cloister's Touch; The Woman from Mellon's; The Duke's Plan; The Englishman and the Girl.

1910: *The Final Settlement; His Last Burglary; Taming a Husband; The Newlyweds; The Thread of Destiny; In Old California; The Man; The Converts; Faithful; The Twisted Trail; Gold is Not All; As It Is in Life; A Rich Revenge; A Romance of the Western Hills; Thou Shalt Not; The Way of the World; The Unchanging Sea; The Gold Seekers; Love Among the Roses; The Two Brothers; Unexpected Help; An Affair of Hearts; Romona; Over Silent Paths; The Implement; In the Season of Buds; A Child of the Ghetto; In the Border States; A Victim of Jealousy; The Face at the Window; A Child's Impulse; The Marked Time-table; Muggsy's First Sweetheart; The Purgation; A Midnight Cupid; What the Daisy Said; A Child's Faith; The Call to Arms; Serious Sixteen; A Flash of Light; As the Bells Rang Out; An Arcadian Maid; The House with the Closed Shutters; Her Father's Pride; A Salutary Lesson; The Usurer; The Sorrows of the Unfaithful; In Life's Cycle; Wilful Peggy; A Summer Idyll; The Modern Prodigal; Rose o' Salem Town; Little Angels of Luck; A Mohawk's Way; The Oath and the Man; The Iconoclast; Examination Day at School; That Chink at Golden Gulch; The Broken Doll; The Banker's Daughters; The Message of the Violin; Two Little Waifs; Waiter No. Five; The Fugitive; Simple Charity; The Song of the Wildwood Flute; A Child's Strategem; Sunshine Sue; A Plain Song; His Sister-in-law; The Golden Supper; The Lesson; When a Man Loves; Winning Back His Love; His Trust; His Trust Fulfilled; A Wreath of Orange Blossoms; The Italian Barber; The Two Paths; Conscience; Three Sisters; A Decree of Destiny; Fate's Turning; What Shall We Do with Our Old?; The Diamond Star; The Lily of the Tenements; Heart Beats of Long Ago.*

1911: *Fisher Folks; His Daughter; The Lonedale Operator; Was He a Coward?; Teaching Dad to Like Her; The Spanish Gypsy; The Broken Cross; The Chief's Daughter; A Knight of the Road; Madame Rex; His Mother's Scarf; How She Triumphed; In the Days of '49; The Two Sides; The New Dress; Enoch Arden, Part I; Enoch Arden, Part II; The White Rose of the Wilds; The Crooked Road; A Romany Tragedy; A Smile of a Child; The Primal Call; The Jealous Husband; The Indian Brothers; The Thief and the Girl; Her Sacrifice; The Blind Princess and the Poet; Fighting Blood; The Last Drop of Water; Robby the Coward; A Country Cupid; The Ruling Passion; The Rose of Kentucky; The Sorrowful Example; Swords and Hearts; The Stuff Heroes Are Made Of; The Old Confectioner's Mistake; The Unveiling; The Eternal Mother; Dan the Dandy; The Revue Man and the Girl; The Squaw's Love; Italian Blood; The Making of a Man; Her Awakening; The Adventures of Billy; The Long Road; The Battle; Love in the Hills; The Trail of the Books; Through Darkened Vales; Saved from Himself; A Woman Scorned; The Miser's Heart; The Failure; Sunshine Through the Dark; As in a Looking Glass; A Terrible Discovery; A Tale of the Wilderness; The Voice of the Child; The Baby and the Stork; The Old Bookkeeper; A Sister's Love; For His Son; The Transformation of Mike; A Blot on the 'Scutcheon; Billy's Strategem; The Sunbeam; A String of Pearls; The Root of Evil.*

1912: *The Mender of the Nets; Under Burning Skies; A Siren of Impulse; Iola's Promise; The Goddess of Sagebrush Gulch; The Girl and Her Trust; The Punishment; Fate's Interception; The Female of the Species; Just Like a Woman; One Is Business, the Other Crime; The Lesser Evil; The Old Actor; A Lodging for the Night; His Lesson; When Kings Were the Law; A Beast at Bay; An Outcast Among Outcasts; Home*

Folks; A Temporary Truce; The Spirit Awakened; Lena and the Geese; An Indian Summer; The Schoolteacher and the Waif; Man's Lust for Gold; Man's Genesis; Heaven Avenges; A Pueblo Legend; The Sands of Dee; Black Sheep; The Narrow Road; A Child's Remorse; The Inner Circle; A Change of Spirit; An Unseen Enemy; Two Daughters of Eve; Friends; So Near, Yet So Far; A Feud in the Kentucky Hills; In the Aisles of the Wild; The One She Loved; The Painted Lady; The Musketeers of Pig Alley; Heredity; Gold and Glitter; My Baby; The Informer; The Unwelcome Guest; Pirate Gold; Brutality; The New York Hat; The Massacre; My Hero; Oil and Water; The Burglar's Dilemma; A Cry for Help; The God Within; Three Friends; The Telephone Girl and the Lady; Fate; An Adventure in the Autumn Woods; A Chance Deception; The Tender Hearted Boy; A Misappropriated Turkey; Brothers; Drink's Lure; Love in an Apartment Hotel

1913: *Broken Ways; A Girl's Strategem; Near to Earth; A Welcome Intruder; The Sheriff's Baby; The Hero of Little Italy; The Perfidy of Mary; A Misunderstood Boy; The Little Tease; The Lady and the Mouse; The Wanderer; The House of Darkness; Olaf—An Atom; Just Gold; His Mother's Son; The Yaqui Cur; The Ranchero's Revenge; A Timely Interception; Death's Marathon; The Sorrowful Shore; The Mistake; The Mothering Heart; Her Mother's Oath; During the Round-up; The Coming of Angelo; An Indian's Loyalty; Two Men of the Desert; The Reformers* or *The Lost Art of Minding One's Business; The Battle at Elderbush Gulch* (released 1914); *In Prehistoric Days* (*Wars of the Primal Tribes; Brute Force*); *Judith of Bethulia* (+sc) (released 1914).

Films as Director: (after quitting Biograph): 1914: *The Battle of the Sexes; The Escape; Home, Sweet Home; The Avenging Conscience.* **1915:** *The Birth of a Nation* (+co-sc, co-music). **1916:** *Intolerance* (+co-music). **1918:** *Hearts of the World* (+sc under pseudonyms, co-music arranger); *The Great Love* (+co-sc); *The Greatest Thing in Life* (+co-sc). **1919:** *A Romance of Happy Valley* (+sc); *The Girl Who Stayed at Home; True-Heart Susie; Scarlet Days; Broken Blossoms* (+sc, co-music arranger); *The Greatest Question.* **1920:** *The Idol Dancer; The Love Flower; Way Down East.* **1921:** *Dream Street* (+sc); *Orphans of the Storm.* **1922:** *One Exciting Night* (+sc). **1923:** *The White Rose* (+sc). **1924:** *America: Isn't Life Wonderful* (+sc). **1925:** *Sally of the Sawdust.* **1926:** *That Royle Girl; The Sorrows of Satan.* **1928:** *Drums of Love; The Battle of the Sexes.* **1929:** *Lady of the Pavements.* **1930:** *Abraham Lincoln.* **1931:** *The Struggle* (+pr, co-music arranger).

Perhaps no other director has generated such a broad range of critical reaction as D.W. Griffith. For students of the motion picture, Griffith's is the most familiar name in film history. Generally acknowledged as America's most influential director (and certainly one of the most prolific), he is also perceived as being among the most limited. Praise for his mastery of film technique is matched by repeated indictments of his moral, artistic, and intellectual inadequacies. At one extreme, Kevin Brownlow has characterized him as "the only director in America creative enough to be called a genius." At the other, Paul Rotha calls his contribution to the advance of film "negligible" and Susan Sontag complains of his "supreme vulgarity and even inanity"; his work "reeks of a fervid moralizing about sexuality and violence" and his energy comes "from suppressed voluptuousness."

Griffith started his directing career in 1908, and in the following five years made some 485 films, almost all of which have been preserved. These films, one or two reels in length, have customarily been regarded as apprentice works, films in which, to quote Stephen Zito, "Griffith borrowed, invented, and perfected the forms and techniques that he later used to such memorable effect in *The Birth of a Nation, Intolerance, Broken Blossoms,* and *Way Down East.*" These early "Biographs" (named after the studio at which Griffith worked) have usually been studied for their stylistic features, notably parallel editing, camera placement, and treatment of light and shadow. Their most famous structuring devices are the last-minute rescue and the cross-cut.

In recent years, however, the Biographs have assumed higher status in film history. Many historians and critics rank them with the most accomplished work in Griffith's career. Vlada

Petric, for instance, calls them "masterpieces of early cinema, fascinating lyrical films which can still affect audiences today, conveying the content in a cinematic manner often more powerful than that of Griffith's later feature films." Scholars have begun studying them for their characters, images, narrative patterns, themes, and ideological values, finding in them a distinctive signature based on Griffith's deep-seated faith in the values of the woman-centered home. Certain notable Biographs—*The Musketeers of Pig Alley, The Painted Lady, A Corner in Wheat, The Girl and Her Trust, The Battle of Elderbush Gulch, The Unseen Enemy,* and *A Feud in the Kentucky Hills*—have been singled out for individual study.

Griffith reached the peak of his popularity and influence in the five years between 1915 and 1920, when he released *The Birth of a Nation, Intolerance, Broken Blossoms,* and *Way Down East.* He also directed *Hearts of the World* during this period, a film that incorporates newsreel and faked documentary footage into an epic fictional narrative. A First World War propaganda epic, *Hearts of the World,* alone among his early spectacles, is ignored today. But in 1918 it was the most popular war film of its time, and rivalled *The Birth of a Nation* as the most profitable of all Griffith's features. Today, it is usually studied as an example of World War I hysteria or as a pioneering effort at government-sponsored mass entertainment.

Although Griffith's epics are generally grouped together, Paul Goodman points out that his films are neither so ideologically uniform nor so consistent as recent writers have generally assumed. With equal fervor Griffith could argue white supremacy and make pleas for toleration, play the liberal crusader and the reactionary conservative, appear tradition-bound yet remain open to experimentation, saturate his work in Victorian codes while struggling against a Victorian morality. Frustrated by his inability to find consistent ideological threads in Griffith's work, Norman Silverstein has called Griffith the father of anarchy in American films because his luminous movements in these epics never appear to sustain a unified whole.

Yet, as Robert Lang observes, the epics do share broad formal characteristics, using history as a chaotic background for a fictional drama that stresses separation and reunification. Whether set in the French Revolution (*Orphans of the Storm*), the American Revolution (*America*), the Civil War (*Birth of a Nation*), or in the various epochs of *Intolerance,* the Griffith epic is an action-centered spectacle that manipulates viewer curiosity with powerfully propulsive, intrinsically developmental scenes culminating in a sensational denouement.

Griffith also made a much different sort of feature during these years—the pastoral romance. These have only recently received serious critical attention. In these films, which are stripped of spectacle and historical surroundings, the cast of principal characters does not exceed two or three, the action is confined in time and space, and the story is intimate. Here, in films like *Romance of Happy Valley, True-heart Susie,* and *The Greatest Question,* Griffith experiments with alternative narrative possibilities, whereby he extends the techniques of exposition to the length of a feature film. Strictly narrative scenes in these films are suspended or submerged to convey the illusion of near-plotlessness. The main figures, Griffith implied (usually played by Lillian Gish and Bobby Harron), would emerge independent of fable; atmosphere would dominate over story line.

From the start, critics and reviewers found the near absence of action sequences and overt physical struggle noteworthy in the Griffith pastorals, but differed widely in their evaluation of it. Most of the original commentators assumed they had found a critical shortcoming, and complained about the thinness of plot, padded exposition, and frequent repetition of shots.

Even Kenneth MacGowan, who alone among his contemporaries preferred Griffith's pastorals to his epics, scored the empty storyline of *The Romance of Happy Valley* for its "loose ends and dangling characters." More recent critics, on the other hand—notably Jean Mitry, John Belton, and Rene Kerdyk—have found transcendental virtues in the forswearing of event-centered plots. Ascribing to Griffith's technique a liberating moral purpose, Mitry called *True-heart Susie* "a narrative which follows characters without entrapping them, allowing them complete freedom of action and event." For John Belton, *True-heart Susie* is one of Griffith's "purest and most immediate films" because, "lacking a 'great story' there is nothing between us and the characters." Equating absence of action sequences with the elimination of formal structure, Belton concludes that "it is through the characters not plot that Griffith expresses and defines the nature of the characters' separation."

If these judgments appear critically naive (plainly these films have plots and structures even if these are less complex than in *Intolerance* and *Birth*), they raise important questions Griffith scholars continue to debate: how does Griffith create the impression that characters exist independent of action, and, in a temporal medium, how does Griffith create the impression of narrative immobility?

By and large, Griffith's films of the mid- and late-1920s have not fared well critically, although they have their defenders. The customary view—that Griffith's work became dull and undistinguished when he lost his personal studio at Mamaroneck in 1924—continues to prevail, despite calls from John Dorr, Arthur Lennig, and Richard Roud for re-evaluation. The eight films he made as a contract director for Paramount and United Artists are usually studied (if at all) as examples of late 1920s studio style. What critics find startling about them—particularly the United Artists features—is not the lack of quality, but the absence of any identifiable Griffith traits. Only *Abraham Lincoln* and *The Struggle* (Griffith's two sound films) are recognizable as his work, and they are usually treated as early 1930s oddities.—RUSSELL MERRITT

Guitry, Sacha

Nationality *French.* **Born** *Alexandre-Georges Pierre Guitry in St. Petersburg, Russia, 21 February 1885.* **Education** *Lycée Jeanson-de-Sailly, St. Petersburg, 1894, then at twelve different schools until 1902.* **Family** *Married 1) Charlotte Lysès, 1907 (divorced); 2) Yvonne Printemps, 1919 (divorced); 3) Jacqueline Delubac, 1935 (divorced); 4) Geneviève de Séréville, 1942 (divorced); 5) Lana Marconi, 1949.* **Career** *Debut as actor, with father Lucien Guitry, 1904; playwright and stage actor, through 1930s; directed first feature, Bonne Chance, 1935; arrested for collaborating with the Nazis, released after two months, 1944; officially cleared of charges, ban on work lifted, 1947.* **Awards** *Chevalier de la Légion d'Honneur, 1923; Commander of the Légion d'Honneur, 1936; elected to the Goncourt Academy, 1939; Grande Médaille d'Or de la Société des Auteurs, 1955.* **Died** *In Paris, 24 July 1957.*

Films as Director: 1915: *Ceux de chez nous* (+sc, ph). **1935:** *Pasteur* (co-d, +sc, role as Pasteur); *Bonne chance* (+sc, role as Claude). **1936:** *Le Nouveau Testament* (+sc, role as Jean Marcelin); *Le Roman d'un tricheur* (*The Story of a Cheat*) (+sc, role as the cheat); *Mon Père avait raison* (+sc, role as Charles Bellanger); *Faisons un rêve* (+sc, role as He). **1937:** *Le Mot de Cambronne* (+sc, role as Cambronne); *Les Perles de la couronne* (*Pearls of the Crown*) (+sc, role as François I, Barras, Napoleon

III, Jean Martin); *Désiré* (+sc, role as Désiré Tronchais). **1938:** *Quadrille* (+sc, role as Philippe de Moranes); *Remontons les Champs-Elysées* (+sc, role as the teacher, Louis XV, Ludovic at 54 years of age, Jean-Louis at 54, Napoleon III). **1939:** *Ils étaient neuf célibataires* (+sc, role as Jea Lécuyer). **1942:** *Le Destin fabuleux de Desirée Clary* (+sc, role as Napoleon I). **1943:** *Donne-moi tes yeux* (+sc, role as François Bressoles). **1944:** *La Malibran* (+sc, role as M. Malibran). **1948:** *Le Comédien* (+sc, role as Lucien Guitry at 40). **1949:** *Le Diable boiteux* (+sc, role as Talleyrand); *Aux deux colombes* (+sc, role as Jean-Pierre Walter); *Toâ* (+sc, role as Michel Desnoyers). **1950:** *Le Trésor de Cantenac* (+sc, role as Baron de Cantenac); *Tu m'as sauvé la vie* (+sc, role as Baron de Saint-Rambert). **1951:** *Deburau* (+sc, role as Jean-Gaspard Deburau); *La Poison* (+sc). **1952:** *Je l'ai été trois fois* (+sc, role as Jean Renneval). **1953:** *La Vie d'un honnête homme* (+sc). **1954:** *Si Versailles m'etait conté* (+sc, role as Louis XIV). **1955:** *Napoléon* (+sc, role as Talleyrand). **1956:** *Si Paris nous était conté* (+sc). **1957:** *Assassins et voleurs* (+sc); *Les Trois font la paire* (+sc).

Other Films: 1918: *Un Roman d'amour . . . et d'aventures* (Hervil and Mercanton) (role). **1931:** *Le Blanc et le noir* (sc). **1935:** *Les Deux coverts* (sc). **1938:** *L'Accroche-coeur* (sc); *Bluebeard's Eighth Wife* (Lubitsch) (guest appearance as man leaving hotel with girl on arm). **1951:** *Adhemar* or *Le Jouet de la fatalité* (sc). **1958:** *La Vie à deux* (sc).

Values change and time plays tricks on one's memory of how it really was. Back in the early 1930s, when talking pictures were gaining a foothold in this country and all foreign nations were exhibiting their product in America, it seemed as if there was nobody in films as charming, witty, and multi-talented as Sacha Guitry. His films, made in France, appeared at all the best art houses; he was a delightful actor, a director with a Lubitsch-like wit, and a writer of amusing sophisticated comedy. Seeing his films today in revival, however, they do not seem that funny. His features appear old-fashioned and are often dull, while his preoccupation with sex is too often mere lechery. Only two films are still diamond-bright: *Les Perles de la couronne,* which he co-directed with Christian-Jaque, and *Le Roman d'un tricheur.*

Sacha Guitry as he appeared in *Le Roman d'un tricheur.*

The first of the above-mentioned films has a narrative device that enables Guitry to skip back and forth from one century to another and from one country to another, and still keep the story clear and funny. In *Les Perles de la couronne* Guitry plays tricks with actual events and people. The comedy has a nice bite, and Guitry pulls off a narrative resolution that is masterly in its irony. *Le Roman d'un tricheur,* meanwhile, is a razor-sharp treatise on the rewards of dishonesty. It involves a hero who as a young boy is sent to bed without dinner as punishment for a lie he has told. Because he does not eat the meal that has been prepared, he lives while all other members of his family perish, having consumed a dish prepared from toad-stools rather than fresh mushrooms.

Sacha Guitry was once the toast of Paris. One season he had as many as three plays running simultaneously. When he turned his talents to talking pictures, the medium seemed to have been invented expressly for his convenience. His father, Lucien Guitry, was France's greatest actor, and in time his talented son wrote two plays that his father turned into pure gold—*Pasteur* and *Mon Père avait raison.* In all, Sacha Guitry wrote more than a hundred plays; his films were often adaptations of these. Most were boudoir farces, remarkable in that they always seemed to work thanks to skillful construction, though they were also generally feather light and too often highly forgettable.

Guitry married five actresses who all rose to prominence in roles he wrote before he divorced them. The one who became a star in her own right was Yvonne Printemps, the second actress he married; she finally divorced him to marry her leading man, handsome Pierre Fresnay, while Guitry that same year married a new leading lady, the beautiful Jacqueline Delubac.

In World War Two Guitry was trapped in Paris, and he was not permitted by the Nazis to act on the Parisian stage. After four years, when the Germans were forced to quit Paris, Guitry was arrested by a ridiculous quirk of fate on a charge of having collaborated with the enemy; he was released after two months, exonerated, and freed to go on with his career.—DeWITT BODEEN

Hartley, Hal

Nationality American. ***Born*** *3 November 1959, in Lindenhurst, New York.* ***Education***
Attended Massachusetts College of Art, late 1970s; State University of New York at Purchase
Film School, graduated with honors, 1984. ***Career*** *Free-lance production assistant, mid-*
1980s; worked for Action Productions (public service announcements), whose president
sponsored Hartley's first feature, The Unbelievable Truth, *1989; this film's success at the*
Toronto Film Festival led to its commercial release by Miramax, 1990. ***Address*** *c/o True*
Fiction Pictures, 12 W. 27th St., New York, NY 10001, U.S.A.

Films as Director: 1984: *Kid* (short, student thesis film) (+sc, ed, pr). **1987:** *Dogs* (short) (+pr); *The Cartographer's Girlfriend* (short) (+ed, pr). **1990:** *The Unbelievable Truth* (+sc, ed, pr). **1991:** *Trust* (+sc); *Theory of Achievement* (short, for TV) (+sc, mus); *Surviving Desire* (for TV) (+sc, ed, mus); *Ambition* (short, for TV) (+sc). **1992:** *Simple Men* (+sc, co-pr, mus). **1994:** *Amateur* (+sc, pr, mus). **1995:** *Flirt* (+sc, mus, role).

Well known in Europe, but more of a cult favorite than a box-office draw in his native United States, Hal Hartley has been held in high critical esteem for his quirky feature films and shorts and, incidentally, for putting Long Island on the map of famed cinematic locales. Writing his own screenplays, punctuating the dramas with his own sparse music, and working regularly with the same actors and technicians, Hartley is a model of the resolutely independent film artist.

Hartley's screenplays are among the most distinctive features of his cinema. Reminiscent of both David Mamet (perhaps the film *House of Games* as well as certain plays) and Harold Pinter (chiefly the period of *The Homecoming*), Hartley's dialogue tends toward the laconic and the absurd: occasionally downright hilarious and almost always droll, especially when spoken by mostly humorless characters. Of the actors whom Hartley has used a number of times, Martin Donovan is supreme in his deadpan delivery of lines, with exactly the right amount of dry irony, anger, or cluelessness, as the moment calls for.

Of cinematic influences, Jean-Luc Godard has constantly been singled out. Occasionally Hartley appears to be doing a conscious homage, as in the sudden burst into dance in *Surviving*

Desire, a nod to *Bande à part* (*Band of Outsiders*)—but a dance scene in *Simple Men,* similarly unexpected but more elaborately choreographed and integrated into the story world, seems altogether original. The stylization of violence in *Amateur* also recalls Godard, though the shoving matches of most of the earlier films seem pure Hartley. Perhaps more subtly Godardian, *Weekend* vintage, are the vacant landscapes of "Long Island" (actually Texas, for the most part) in *Simple Men,* where characters more or less stumble through their peculiar lives.

The Unbelievable Truth already has Hartley's unmistakable style and tone. With a plot suited for either soap opera or film noir in its melodrama and romantic entanglements—an ex-con returns to the town where he caused the deaths of two people, and where he is shunned by most but loved by a rebellious young woman—the film is instead a black comedy with a bent toward

Hal Hartley.
Photograph by Stephane Fefer.

real romance, all centered around the question of trusting people enough to accept their versions of "the true story." Hartley's hometown of Lindenhurst, a rather ramshackle-looking small town half metamorphosed into a commuter suburb, seems the perfect pale backdrop for his oddball characters.

Trust superficially resembles *The Unbelievable Truth,* with Adrienne Shelley again as a rebellious youth and Lindenhurst as locus of American family dysfunction. It also has much of the same droll comedy as *The Unbelievable Truth,* yet a considerably darker tone overall, with its brutal parents, severely asocial hero (Martin Donovan), and unexpected violence—as in the liquor store clerk's attack upon the Shelley character. In its confident handling of mixed moods it may be Hartley's most impressive feature to date.

Simple Men, set on a more rural Long Island after a brief stop in Lindenhurst, has a wilder plot and if anything more outrageous comedy, as two sons—a criminal and a college student— follow clues in search of their long-missing father, a reputed terrorist bomber. The cynical Bill, who notes that "you don't need an ideology to knock over a liquor store," has been betrayed in love, and so is determined to seduce women by appearing to be "mysterious, thoughtful, deep, but modest" and then "throw them away." Of course he falls for a woman who claims to find him all of those things (she manages to use all four adjectives in a short conversation), although the words seem to apply much more to her. The less-experienced Dennis falls for an eccentric Rumanian who turns out to be his father's new girlfriend. When he points out that his father is a womanizer—a married man who has also stood her up—she tells him he should be more respectful. Including two actors from *The Unbelievable Truth* who essentially reprise their roles as garage mechanic and assistant—and featuring a nun who answers a question about a medallion with, "It's the Holy Blessed Virgin, you idiot," before wrestling the man to the ground—*Simple Men* often crosses the border into farce, then withdraws to a dryer detachment. Again issues of truth and reliability are central, though this film is in addition more directly concerned with masculine values and behavior than any of the others. The story is almost always focused upon the two brothers and their attitudes toward their father, or their confusion about women; the women are rarely seen apart from men observing them; the talk is very often macho, though at one point the two couples and another would-be lover preposterously launch into a discourse about Madonna and modern women's "control over the exploitation of their own bodies."

Amateur, more or less commissioned by Isabel Huppert, who stars in it, is yet more melodramatic, featuring an amnesiac (Donovan again), evidently a sadistic criminal in his "former life," who is befriended by an ex-nun who wants to write pornography (Huppert)—the pair of them having to flee various crazed and criminal types. Here the themes of trust and the knowability of a mysterious person's past are developed through the most lurid situations. *Flirt* is also concerned with issues of love and betrayal, but is also an experiment in structure: Hartley's fifth feature is actually a trilogy of short films, each using some of the same dialogue and following the same dramatic trajectory, but with different settings (New York-Berlin-Tokyo) and gender relations (according to whether the flirt is straight or gay, male or female).

All of Hartley's films call attention to their own artifice through the stylized dialogue and the actors' deliveries of it, and through the eccentric plots. *Flirt* moves to a new level of self-reflexivity in that the director plays a character named "Hal" who carries around a can of a film called "Flirt." It will be interesting to see how Hartley continues to balance artifice and dramatic passions, cool wit and melodrama, in films to come.—JOSEPH MILICIA

Hawks, Howard

Nationality American. *Born* Howard Winchester Hawks in Goshen, Indiana, 30 May 1896. *Education* Pasadena High School, California, 1908-13; Phillips Exeter Academy, New Hampshire, 1914-16; Cornell University, New York, degree in mechanical engineering, 1917. *Military Service* Served in U.S. Army Air Corps, 1917-19. *Family* Married 1) Athole (Hawks), 1924 (divorced 1941); 2) Nancy Raye Gross, 1941 (divorced), one daughter; 3) Mary (Dee) Hartford (divorced), two sons, two daughters. *Career* Worked in property dept. of Famous Players-Lasky during vacations, Hollywood, 1916-17; designer in airplane factory, 1919-22; worked in independent production as editor, writer, and assistant director, from 1922; in charge of story dept. at Paramount, 1924-25; signed as director for Fox, 1925-29; directed first feature, Road to Glory, 1926; formed Motion Picture Alliance for the Preservation of American Ideals, with Borden Chase, 1944. *Awards* Quarterly Award, Directors Guild of America, for Red River, 1948/49; Honorary Oscar for "A master American filmmaker whose creative efforts hold a distinguished place in world cinema," 1974. *Died* In Palm Springs, California, 26 December 1977.

Films as Director: **1926:** The Road to Glory (+story); Fig Leaves (+story). **1927:** The Cradle Snatchers; Paid to Love; Fazil. **1928:** A Girl in Every Port (+co-sc); The Air Circus (co-d). **1929:** Trent's Last Case. **1930:** The Dawn Patrol. **1931:** The Criminal Code. **1932:** The Crowd Roars (+story); Tiger Shark; Scarface: The Shame of a Nation (+pr, bit role as man on bed). **1933:** Today We Live; The Prizefighter and the Lady (Everywoman's Man) (Van Dyke; d parts of film, claim disputed). **1934:** Viva Villa!

(Conway; d begun by Hawks); *Twentieth Century*. **1935:** *Barbary Coast; Ceiling Zero*. **1936:** *The Road to Glory; Come and Get It* (co-d). **1938:** *Bringing Up Baby*. **1939:** *Only Angels Have Wings*. **1940:** *His Girl Friday*. **1941:** *The Outlaw* (Hughes; d begun by Hawks); *Sergeant York; Ball of Fire*. **1943:** *Air Force*. **1944:** *To Have and Have Not*. **1946:** *The Big Sleep*. **1947:** *A Song is Born* (remake of *Ball of Fire*). **1948:** *Red River* (+pr). **1949:** *I Was a Male War Bride* (*You Can't Sleep Here*). **1952:** *The Big Sky* (+pr); "The Ransom of Red Chief" episode of *O. Henry's Full House* (episode cut from some copies) (+pr); *Monkey Business*. **1953:** *Gentlemen Prefer Blondes*. **1955:** *Land of the Pharaohs* (+pr). **1959:** *Rio Bravo* (+pr). **1962:** *Hatari!* (+pr). **1963:** *Man's Favorite Sport* (+pr). **1965:** *Red Line 7000* (+story, pr). **1966:** *El Dorado* (+pr). **1970:** *Rio Lobo* (+pr).

Other Films: 1917: *A Little Princess* (Neilan) (d some scenes, uncredited; prop boy). **1923:** *Quicksands* (Conway) (story, sc, pr). **1924:** *Tiger Love* (Melford) (sc). **1925:** *The Dressmaker from Paris* (Bern) (co-story, sc). **1926:** *Honesty—the Best Policy* (Bennett and Neill) (story, sc); *Underworld* (von Sternberg) (co-sc, uncredited). **1932:** *Red Dust* (Fleming) (co-sc, uncredited). **1936:** *Sutter's Gold* (Cruze) (co-sc, uncredited). **1937:** *Captains Courageous* (Fleming) (co-sc, uncredited). **1938:** *Test Pilot* (Fleming) (co-sc, uncredited). **1939:** *Gone with the Wind* (Fleming) (add'l dialogue, uncredited); *Gunga Din* (Stevens) (co-sc, uncredited). **1943:** *Corvette K-225* (*The Nelson Touch*) (Rosson) (pr). **1951:** *The Thing* (*The Thing from Another World*) (Nyby) (pr).

Howard Hawks was perhaps the greatest director of American genre films. Hawks made films in almost every American genre, and each of these films could well serve as one of the very best examples and artistic embodiments of the type: gangster (*Scarface*), private eye (*The Big Sleep*), western (*Red River, Rio Bravo*), screwball comedy (*Bringing Up Baby*), newspaper reporter (*His Girl Friday*), prison picture (*The Criminal Code*), science fiction (*The Thing*), musical (*Gentlemen Prefer Blondes*), race-car drivers (*The Crowd Roars, Red Line 7000*), and air pilots (*Only Angels Have Wings*). But into each of these narratives of generic expectations Hawks infused his particular themes, motifs, and techniques.

Born in the Midwest at almost the same time that the movies themselves were born in America, Hawks migrated with his family to southern California when the movies did; he spent his formative years working on films, learning to fly, and studying engineering at Cornell University. His initial work in silent films as a writer and producer would serve him well in his later years as a director, when he would produce and, if not write, then control the writing of his films as well. Although Hawks' work has been consistently discussed as exemplary of the Hollywood studio style, Hawks himself did not work for a single studio on a long-term contract. Instead, he was an independent producer who sold his projects to every Hollywood studio.

Whatever the genre of a Hawks film, it bore traits that made it unmistakably a Hawks film. The narrative was always elegantly and symmetrically structured and patterned. This quality was a sign of Hawks' sharp sense of storytelling as well as his sensible efforts to work closely with very talented writers: Ben Hecht, William Faulkner, and Jules Furthman being the most notable among them. Hawks' films were devoted to characters who were professionals with fervent vocational commitments. The men in Hawks' films were good at what they did, whether flying the mail, driving race cars, driving cattle, or reporting the news. These vocational commitments were usually fulfilled by the union of two apparently opposite physical types who were spiritually one: either the union of the harder, tougher, older male and a softer, younger, prettier male (John Wayne and Montgomery Clift in *Red River,* Wayne and Ricky Nelson in *Rio Bravo*), or by a sharp, tough male and an equally sharp, tough female (Cary Grant and Rosalind Russell in *His Girl Friday,* Bogart and Bacall in *To Have and Have Not* and *The Big Sleep,* John Barrymore and Carole Lombard in *Twentieth Century*). This spiritual alliance of physical opposites revealed Hawks' unwillingness to accept the cultural stereotype that those who are able to accomplish

Howard Hawks

difficult tasks are those who appear able to accomplish them.

This tension between appearance and ability, surface and essence in Hawks' films led to several other themes and techniques. Characters talk very tersely in Hawks' films, refusing to put their thoughts and feelings into explicit speeches which would either sentimentalize or vulgarize those internal abstractions. Instead, Hawks' characters reveal their feelings through their actions, not by what they say. Hawks deflects his portrayal of the inner life from explicit speeches to symbolic physical objects—concrete visual images of things that convey the intentions of the person who handles, uses, or controls the piece of physical matter. One of those physical objects—the coin which George Raft nervously flips in *Scarface*—has become a mythic icon of American culture itself, symbolic in itself of American gangsters and American gangster movies (and used as such in both *Singin' in the Rain* and *Some Like It Hot*). Another of Hawks' favorite actions, the lighting of cigarettes, became his subtextual way of showing who cares about whom without recourse to dialogue.

Consistent with his narratives, Hawks' visual style was one of dead-pan understatement, never proclaiming its trickiness or brilliance but effortlessly communicating the values of the stories and the characters. Hawks was a master of point-of-view, knowledgeable about which camera perspective would precisely convey the necessary psychological and moral information. That point of view could either confine us to the perceptions of a single character (Marlowe in *The Big Sleep*), ally us with the more vital of two competing life styles (with the vitality of Oscar Jaffe in *Twentieth Century,* Susan Vance in *Bringing Up Baby,* Walter Burns in *His Girl Friday*), or withdraw to a scientific detachment that allows the viewer to weigh the paradoxes and ironies of a love battle between two equals (between the two army partners in *I Was a Male War Bride,* the husband and wife in *Monkey Business,* or the older and younger cowboy in *Red River*). Hawks' films are also masterful in their atmospheric lighting; the hanging electric or kerosene lamp that dangles into the top of a Hawks frame became almost as much his signature as the lighting of cigarettes.

Hawks' view of character in film narrative was that actor and character were inseparable. As a result, his films were very improvisatory. He allowed actors to add, interpret, or alter lines as they wished, rather than force them to stick to the script. This trait not only led to the energetic spontaneity of many Hawks films, but also contributed to the creation or shaping of the human archetypes that several stars came to represent in our culture. John Barrymore, John Wayne, Humphrey Bogart, and Cary Grant all refined or established their essential personae under Hawks' direction, while many actors who would become stars were either discovered by Hawks or given their first chance to play a major role in one of his films. Among Hawks' most important discoveries were Paul Muni, George Raft, Carole Lombard, Angie Dickinson, Montgomery Clift, and his Galatea, Lauren Bacall.

Although Hawks continued to make films until he was almost seventy-five, there is disagreement about the artistic energy and cinematic value of the films he made after 1950. For some, Hawks' artistic decline in the 1950s and 1960s was both a symptom and an effect of the overall decline of the movie industry and the studio system itself. For others, Hawks' later films—slower, longer, less energetically brilliant than his studio-era films—were more probing and personal explorations of the themes and genres he had charted for the three previous decades.—GERALD MAST

Herzog, Werner

Nationality *German.* **Born** *Werner Stipetic in Sachrang, 5 September 1942.* **Education** *Classical Gymnasium, Munich, until 1961; University of Munich, early 1960s.* **Family** *Married journalist Martje Grohmann, one son.* **Career** *Worked as a welder in a steel factory for U.S. National Aeronautics and Space Administration; founded Werner Herzog Filmproduktion, 1966; walked from Munich to Paris to visit film historian Lotte Eisner, 1974.* **Awards** *Bundesfilmpreis, and Silver Bear, Berlinale, for* Signs of Life, *1968; Bundespreis, and Special Jury Prize, Cannes Festival, for* Every Man for Himself and God against All, *1975; Best Director, Cannes Festival, for* Fitzcarraldo, *1982.* **Address** *Turkenstr. 91, D-80799 Münich, Germany.*

Werner Herzog on the set of *Fitzcarraldo*.

Films as Director (beginning 1966, films are produced or co-produced by Werner Herzog Filmproduktion) **1962:** *Herakles* (+pr, sc). **1964:** *Spiel im Sand* (*Game in the Sand*) (unreleased) (+pr, sc). **1966:** *Die beispiellose Verteidigung der Festung Deutschkreuz* (*The Unprecedented Defense of the Fortress of Deutschkreuz*) (+pr, sc). **1967:** *Lebenszeichen* (*Signs of Life*) (+sc, pr). **1968:** *Letzte Worte* (*Last Words*) (+pr, sc); *Massnahmen gegen Fanatiker* (*Precautions against Fanatics*) (+pr, sc). **1969:** *Die fliegenden Ärzte von Ostafrika* (*The Flying Doctors of East Africa*) (for TV) (+pr, sc); *Fata Morgana* (*Mirage*) (+sc, pr). **1970:** *Auch Zwerge haben klein angefangen* (*Even Dwarfs Started Small*) (+pr, sc, mu arrangements); *Behinderte Zukunft* (*Handicapped Future*) (for TV) (+pr, sc). **1971:** *Land des Schweigens und der Dunkelheit* (*Land of Silence and Darkness*) (+pr, sc). **1972:** *Aguirre, der Zorn Gottes* (*Aguirre, the Wrath of God*) (+pr, sc). **1974:** *Die grosse Ekstase des Bildschnitzers Steiner* (*The Great Ecstasy of the Sculptor Steiner*) (+pr, sc); *Jeder für sich und Gott gegen alle* (*Every Man for Himself and God Against All*; *The Enigma of Kaspar Hauser*) (+pr, sc). **1976:** *How Much Wood Would a Woodchuck Chuck* (+pr, sc); *Mit mir will keiner spielen* (*No One Will Play with Me*) (+pr, sc); *Herz aus Glas* (*Heart of Glass*) (+pr, co-sc, bit role as glass carrier). **1977:** *La Soufrière* (+pr, sc, narration, appearance). **1978:** *Stroszek* (+pr, sc). **1979:** *Nosferatu—Phantom der Nacht* (*Nosferatu, the Vampyre*) (+pr, sc, bit role as monk). **1980:** *Woyzeck* (+pr, sc); *Glaube und Währung* (*Creed and Currency*) (for TV); *God's Angry Man* (for TV); *Huies predigt* (*Huie's Sermon*) (for TV). **1981:** *Fitzcarraldo* (+pr, sc). **1983:** *Where the Green Ants Dream* (*Wo Die Grünen Ameisen Traümen*) (+sc). **1984:** *Ballade vom Kleinen Soldaten* (*Ballad of the Little Soldier*) (for TV); *Gasherbrum—Der leuchtende Berg* (*Gasherbrum—The Dark Glow of the Mountains*) (for TV). **1987:** *Cobra Verde* (*Slave Coast*) (+sc). **1988:** *Wodaabe—Die Hirten der Sonne* (*Herdsmen of the Sun*) (for TV); *Les Gaulois* (*The French*). **1989:** *Es ist nicht leicht ein Gott zu sein* (*It Isn't Easy Being God*). **1990:** *Echos aus Einem Dustern Reich* (*Echoes from a Somber Kingdom*). **1991:** *Schrie aus Stein* (*Scream of Stone*); *Jag Mandir: Das excentrische privattheated des Maharadscha von Udaipur* (*The Eccentric Private Theatre of the Maharajah of Udaipur*) (for TV). **1992:** *Lektionen in Finsternis* (*Lessons of Darkness*). **1993:** *Bells from the Deep: Faith and Superstition in Russia* (*Glocken aus der Tiefe*). **1994:** *Die Verwandlung der Welt in Musik* (*The Transformation of the World into Music*) (for TV). **1995:** *Tod für fünf Stimmen* (*Death for Five Voices*) (for TV) (+sc).

Other Films: **1970:** *Geschichten von Kübelkind* (Reitz and Stoeckl) (role). **1980:** *Werner Herzog Eats His Shoe* (Blank and Gosling) (role); *Garlic Is As Good As Ten Mothers* (Blank and Gosling) (role). **1982:** *Chambre 666* (Wenders) (appearance); *Burden of Dreams* (Blank) (role). **1983:** *Man of Flowers* (Cox) (role). **1988:** *Gekauttes Glück* (Odermatt) (role). **1989:** *Es ist nicht leicht ein Gott zu sein* (*Hard to Be a God*) (Fleischmann) (role). **1995:** *Brennedes Herz* (*Burning Heart*) (Patzak) (role).

Werner Herzog, more than any director of his generation, has through his films embodied German history, character, and cultural richness. While references to verbal and other visual arts would be out of place in treating most film directors, they are key to understanding Herzog. For his techniques he reaches back into the early part of the twentieth century to the Expressionist painters and filmmakers; back to the Romantic painters and writers for the luminance and allegorization of landscape and the human figure; even further beyond into sixteenth-century Mannerist extremes of Mathias Grünwald; and throughout his nation's heritage for that peculiarly Germanic grotesque. In all these technical and expressive veins, one finds the qualities of exaggeration, distortion, and the sublimation of the ugly.

More than any, "grotesque" presents itself as a useful term to define Herzog's work. His use of an actor like Klaus Kinski, whose singularly ugly face is sublimated by Herzog's camera, can best be described by such a term. Persons with physical defects like deafness and blindness, and dwarfs, are given a type of grandeur in Herzog's artistic vision. Herzog, as a contemporary German living in the shadow of remembered Nazi atrocities, demonstrates a penchant for probing the darker aspects of human behavior. Herzog's vision renders the ugly and horrible sublime, while the beautiful is omitted and, when included, destroyed or made to vanish (like the beautiful Spanish noblewoman in *Aguirre*).

Closely related to the grotesque in Herzog's films is the influence of German expressionism on him. Two of Herzog's favorite actors, Klaus Kinski and Bruno S., have been compared to Conrad Veidt and Fritz Kortner, prototypical actors of German expressionistic dramas and films during the teens and 1920s. Herzog's actors make highly stylized, indeed often stock, gestures; in close-ups, their faces are set in exaggerated grimaces.

The characters of Herzog's films often seem deprived of free will, merely reacting to an absurd universe. Any exertion of free will in action leads ineluctably to destruction, death, or at best frustration by the unexpected. The director is a satirist who demonstrates what is wrong with the world but, as yet, seems unable or unwilling to articulate the ways to make it right; indeed, one is at a loss to find in his world view any hope, let alone prescription, for improvement.

Herzog's mode of presentation has been termed by some critics as romantic and by others as realistic. This seeming contradiction can be resolved by an approach that compares him with those Romantic artists who first articulated elements of the later realistic approach. Critics have found in the quasi-photographic paintings of Caspar David Friedrich an analogue for Herzog's super-realism. As with these artists, there is an aura of unreality in Herzog's realism. Everything is seen through a camera that rarely goes out of intense, hard focus. Often it is as if his camera is deprived of the normal range of human vision, able only to perceive part of the whole through a telescope or a microscope.

In this strange blend of romanticism and realism lies the paradoxical quality of Herzog's talent: he, unlike Godard, Resnais, or Altman, has not made great innovations in film language; if his style is to be defined at all it is as an eclectic one; and yet, his films do have a distinctive stylistic quality. He renders the surface reality of things with such an intensity that the viewer has an uncanny sense of seeing the essence beyond. *Aguirre,* for example, is unrelenting in its concentration on filth, disease, and brutality; and yet it is also an allegory which can be read on several levels: in terms of Germany under the Nazis, America in Vietnam, and more generally on the bestiality that lingers beneath the facade of civilized conventions. In one of Herzog's romantic tricks within his otherwise realistic vision, he shows a young Spanish noblewoman wearing an ever-pristine velvet dress amid mud and squalor; further, only she of all the rest is not shown dying through violence and is allowed to disappear almost mystically into the dense vegetation of the forest: clearly, she represents that transcendent quality in human nature that incorruptibly endures. This figure is dropped like a hint to remind us to look beyond mere surface.

One finds, however, in *Fitzcarraldo,* Herzog's supreme apotheosis of the spiritual dimensions of the rain forest. As much in the production as in the substance of the film, the Western Imperialist will to reshape the wilderness is again and again met with reversals that render that will meaningless. The protagonist's titanic effort to get a riverboat over a hill from one river to another is achieved only to be thwarted by the natives who cut the ropes, sending it careening downstream through the rapids in a sacrifice to their river deity. The boat ends up uselessly back where it began: a massive symbol of human futility. Only the old gramophone shown playing records of Caruso throughout the jungle voyage offers—like the Spanish noblewoman in *Aguirre*—Herzog's vision of beauty that rarely escapes being rendered meaningless by an otherwise absurd universe.

Herzog's Australian film *Where Green Ants Dream* does penance for any taint of Western Imperialism that *Fitzcarraldo* might have given him. The director comes down hard against the modern way of life. This film is saved from tendentiousness by movements of human comedy through which a very sympathetic hero learns from the Native Australians, and by Herzog's much-loved 360-degree pans over the flatness of the Outback. This technique is also used by Herzog to convey the sense of flat immensity of sub-Saharan Africa in *Herdsmen of the Sun,* a lyrical celebration of the Wodaabe tribesmen, who bend Western gender expectations by having the men and women reverse roles in courtship. Here, too, Herzog evidences his German heritage by following in the African footsteps of his greatest—if most problematic—filmmaking compatriot: Leni Riefenstahl, whose last work was a documentary of a sub-Saharan tribe to the east of the Wodaabe.—RODNEY FARNSWORTH

Hitchcock, Alfred

*Nationality British. **Born** Alfred Joseph Hitchcock in Leytonstone, London, 13 August 1899, became U.S. citizen, 1955. **Education** Salesian College, Battersea, London, 1908; St. Ignatius College, Stamford Hill, London, 1908-13; School of Engineering and Navigation, 1914; attended drawing and design classes under E.J. Sullivan, London University, 1917. **Family** Married Alma Reville, 2 December 1926, daughter Patricia born 1928. **Career** Technical clerk, W.T. Henley Telegraph Co., 1914-19; title-card designer for Famous Players-Lasky at Islington studio, 1919; scriptwriter and assistant director, from 1922; directed two films for producer Michael Balcon in Germany, 1925; signed with British International Pictures as director, 1927; directed first British film to use synchronized sound, Blackmail, 1929; signed with Gaumont-British Studios, 1933; moved to America to direct Rebecca for Selznick International Studios, decided to remain, 1939; returned to Britain to make short films for Ministry of Information, 1944; directed first film in color, Rope, 1948; producer and host, Alfred Hitchcock Presents (The Alfred Hitchcock Hour from 1962), for TV, 1955-65. **Awards** Irving Thalberg Academy Award, 1968; Chevalier de la Légion d'Honneur, 1971; Commander of the Order of Arts and Letters, France, 1976; Life Achievement Award, American Film Institute, 1979; Honorary Doctorate, University of Southern California; Knight of the Legion of Honour of the Cinémathèque Français; knighted, 1980. **Died** Of kidney failure, in Los Angeles, 29 April 1980.*

Films as Director: 1922: *Number Thirteen* (or *Mrs. Peabody*) (incomplete). **1923:** *Always Tell Your Wife* (Croise; completed d). **1926:** *The Pleasure Garden* (*Irrgarten der Leidenschaft*); *The Mountain Eagle* (*Der Bergadler, Fear o' God*); *The Lodger, A Story of the London Fog* (*The Case of Jonathan Drew*) (+co-sc, bit role as man in newsroom, and onlooker during Novello's arrest). **1927:** *Downhill* (*When Boys Leave Home*); *Easy Virtue; The Ring* (+sc). **1928:** *The Farmer's Wife* (+sc); *Champagne* (+adapt); *The Manxman.* **1929:** *Blackmail* (+adapt, bit role as passenger on "tube") (silent version also made); *Juno and the Paycock* (*The Shame of Mary Boyle*). **1930:** *Elstree Calling* (Brunel; d after Brunel dismissed, credit for "sketches and other interpolated items"); *Murder* (*Mary, Sir John greift ein!*) (+co-adapt, bit role as passerby) *An Elastic Affair* (short). **1931:** *The Skin Game* (+co-sc). **1932:** *Rich and Strange* (*East of Shanghai*) (+co-sc): *Number Seventeen* (+co-sc). **1933:** *Waltzes from Vienna* (*Strauss's Great Waltz; The Great Waltz*). **1934:** *The Man Who Knew Too Much.* **1935:** *The Thirty-Nine Steps* (+bit role as passerby). **1936:** *Secret Agent; Sabotage* (*The Woman Alone*). **1937:** *Young and Innocent* (*The Girl Was Young*) (+bit as photographer outside courthouse). **1938:** *The Lady Vanishes* (+bit role as man at railway station). **1939:** *Jamaica Inn.* **1940:** *Rebecca* (+bit role as man outside phone

Alfred Hitchcock

booth); *Foreign Correspondent* (+bit role as man reading newspaper). **1941:** *Mr. and Mrs. Smith* (+bit role as passerby); *Suspicion.* **1942:** *Saboteur* (+bit role as man by newsstand). **1943:** *Shadow of a Doubt* (+bit role as man playing cards on train). **1944:** *Life Boat* (+bit role as man in "Reduco" advertisement); *Bon Voyage* (short); *Aventure Malgache* (*The Malgache Adventure*) (short). **1945:** *Spellbound* (+bit role as man in elevator). **1946:** *Notorious* (+story, bit role as man drinking champagne). **1947:** *The Paradine Case* (+bit role as man with cello). **1948:** *Rope* (+bit role as man crossing street). **1949:** *Under Capricorn*; *Stage Fright* (+bit role as passerby). **1951:** *Strangers on a Train* (+bit role as man boarding train with cello). **1953:** *I Confess* (+bit role as man crossing top of flight of steps). **1954:** *Dial M for Murder* (+bit role as man in school reunion dinner photo); *Rear Window* (+bit role as man winding clock); *To Catch a Thief* (+bit role as man at back of bus); *The Trouble with Harry* (+bit role as man walking past exhibition). **1955:** *The Man Who Knew Too Much* (+bit role as man watching acrobats). **1956:** *The Wrong Man* (+intro appearance). **1957:** *Vertigo* (+bit role as passerby). **1959:** *North by Northwest* (+bit role as man who misses bus). **1960:** *Psycho* (+bit role as man outside realtor's office). **1963:** *The Birds* (+bit role as man with two terriers). **1964:** *Marnie* (+bit role as man in hotel corridor). **1966:** *Torn Curtain* (+bit role as man in hotel lounge with infant). **1969:** *Topaz* (+bit role as man getting out of wheelchair). **1972:** *Frenzy* (+bit role as man in crowd listening to speech). **1976:** *Family Plot* (+bit role as silhouette on office window).

Other Films: **1920:** *The Great Day* (Ford) (inter-titles des); *The Call of Youth* (Ford) (inter-titles des). **1921:** *The Princess of New York* (Crisp) (inter-titles des); *Appearances* (Crisp) (inter-titles des); *Dangerous Lies* (Powell) (inter-titles des); *The Mystery Road* (Powell) (inter-titles des); *Beside the Bonnie Brier Bush* (*The Bonnie Brier Bush*) (Crisp) (inter-titles des). **1922:** *Three Live Ghosts* (Fitzmaurice) (inter-titles des); *Perpetua* (*Love's Boomerang*) (Robertson and Geraghty) (inter-titles des); *The Man from Home* (Fitzmaurice) (inter-titles des); *Spanish Jade* (Robertson and Geraghty) (inter-titles des); *Tell Your Children* (Crisp) (inter-titles des). **1923:** *Woman to Woman* (Cutts) (co-sc, asst-d, art-d, ed); *The White Shadow* (*White Shadows*) (Cutts) (art-d, ed). **1924:** *The Passionate Adventure* (Cutts) (co-sc, asst-d, art-d); *The Prude's Fall* (Cutts) (asst-d, art-d). **1925:** *The Blackguard* (*Die Prinzessin und der Geiger*) (Cutts) (asst-d, art-d). **1932:** *Lord Camber's Ladies* (Levy) (pr). **1940:** *The House Across the Bay* (Mayo) (d add'l scenes); *Men of the Lightship* (MacDonald, short) (reediting, dubbing of U.S. version). **1941:** *Target for Tonight* (Watt) (supervised reediting of U.S. version). **1960:** *The Gazebo* (Marshall) (voice on telephone telling Glenn Ford how to dispose of corpse). **1963:** *The Directors* (pr: Greenblatt) (appearance). **1970:** *Makin' It* (Hartog) (documentary appearance from early thirties). **1977:** *Once Upon a Time . . . Is Now* (Billington, for TV) (role as interviewee).

In a career spanning just over fifty years (1925-1976), Hitchcock completed fifty-three feature films, twenty-three in the British period, thirty in the American. Through the early British films we can trace the evolution of his professional/artistic image, the development of both the Hitchcock style and the Hitchcock thematic. His third film (and first big commercial success), *The Lodger,* was crucial in establishing him as a maker of thrillers, but it was not until the mid-1930s that his name became consistently identified with that genre. In the meantime, he assimilated the two aesthetic influences that were major determinants in the formation of his mature style: German Expressionism and Soviet montage theory. The former, with its aim of expressing emotional states through a deformation of external reality, is discernible in his work from the beginning (not surprisingly, as he has acknowledged Lang's *Die müde Tod* as his first important cinematic experience, and as some of his earliest films were shot in German studios). Out of his later contact with the Soviet films of the 1920s evolved his elaborate editing techniques: he particularly acknowledged the significance for him of the Kuleshov experiment, from which he derived his fondness for the point-of-view shot and for building sequences by cross-cutting between person seeing/thing seen.

The extreme peculiarity of Hitchcock's art (if his films do not seem very odd it is only because they are so familiar) can be partly accounted for by the way in which these aesthetic influences from high art and revolutionary socialism were pressed into the service of British middle-class popular entertainment. Combined with Hitchcock's all-pervasive scepticism ("Everything's perverted in a different way, isn't it?"), this process resulted in an art that at once endorsed (superficially) and undermined (profoundly) the value system of the culture within which it was produced, be that culture British or American.

During the British period the characteristic plot structures that recur throughout Hitchcock's work are also established. I want here to single out three examples of his work, not because they account for *all* of the films, but because they link the British to the American period, because their recurrence is particularly obstinate, and because they seem, taken in conjunction, central to the thematic complex of Hitchcock's total *oeuvre*.

The first Hitchcock theme is the story about *the accused man*: this is already established in *The Lodger* (in which the male protagonist is suspected of being Jack the Ripper); it often takes the form of the "double chase," in which the hero is pursued by the police and in turn pursues (or seeks to unmask) the actual villains. Examples in the British period are *The 39 Steps* and *Young and Innocent*. In the American period it becomes the commonest of all Hitchcock plot structures: *Saboteur, Spellbound, Strangers on a Train, I Confess, To Catch a Thief, The Wrong Man, North by Northwest,* and *Frenzy* are all based on it.

A second Hitchcock plot device is the story about *the guilty woman*: although there are guilty women in earlier films, the structure is definitively established in *Blackmail,* Hitchcock's (and Britain's) first sound film. We may also add *Sabotage* from the British period, but it is in the American period that examples proliferate: *Rebecca* (Hitchcock's first Hollywood film), *Notorious, Under Capricorn, The Paradine Case, Vertigo, Psycho* (the first third), *The Birds,* and *Marnie* are all variations on the original structure.

It is striking to observe that the opposition of the two themes discussed above is almost complete; there are very few Hitchcock films in which the accused man turns out to be guilty after all (*Shadow of a Doubt* and *Stage Fright* are the obvious exceptions; *Suspicion* would have been a third if Hitchcock had been permitted to carry out his original intentions), and no Hitchcock film features an accused woman who turns out to be innocent (*Dial M for Murder* comes closest, but even there, although the heroine is innocent of murder, she is guilty of adultery). Second, it should be noticed that while the falsely accused man is usually (not quite always) the central consciousness of type one, it is less habitually the case that the guilty woman is the central consciousness of type two: frequently, she is the object of the male protagonist's investigation. Third, the outcome of the guilty woman films (and this may be dictated as much by the Motion Picture Production Code as by Hitchcock's personal morality) is dependent upon the *degree* of guilt: the woman can sometimes be "saved" by the male protagonist (*Blackmail, Notorious, Marnie*), but not if she is guilty of murder or an accomplice to it (*The Paradine Case, Vertigo*).

Other differences between the two types of films are also evident. One should note the function of the opposite sex in the two types, for example. The heroine of the falsely accused man films is, typically, hostile to the hero at first, believing him guilty; she subsequently learns to trust him, and takes his side in establishing his innocence. The function of the male protagonist in the guilty woman films, on the other hand, is either to save the heroine or to be destroyed (at least morally and spiritually) by her. It is important to recognize that the true nature of the guilt is always sexual, and that the falsely accused man is usually seen to be contaminated by this (though innocent of the specific crime, typically murder, of which he is accused). Richard

Hannay in *The 39 Steps* can stand as the prototype of this: when he allows himself to be picked up by the woman in the music hall, it is in expectation of a sexual encounter, the notion of sexual disorder being displaced on to "espionage," and the film systematically moves from this towards the construction of the "good" (i.e. socially approved) couple. The very title of *Young and Innocent*, with its play on the connotations of the last word, exemplifies the same point, and it is noteworthy that in that film the hero's *sexual* innocence remains in doubt (we only have his own word for it that he was not the murdered woman's gigolo). Finally, the essential Hitchcockian dialectic can be read from the alternation, throughout his career, of these two series. On the whole, it is the guilty woman films that are the more disturbing, that leave the most jarring dissonances: here, the potentially threatening and subversive female sexuality, precariously contained within social norms in the falsely accused man films, erupts to demand recognition and is answered by an appalling violence (both emotional and physical); the cost of its destruction or containment leaves that "nasty taste" often noted as the dominant characteristic of Hitchcock's work.

It is within this context that the third plot structure takes on its full significance: the story about the *psychopath*. Frequently, this structure occurs in combination with the falsely accused man plot (see, for example, *Young and Innocent, Strangers on a Train, Frenzy,*) with a parallel established between the hero and his perverse and sinister adversary, who becomes a kind of shadowy alter ego. Only two Hitchcock films have the psychopath as their indisputably central figure, but they (*Shadow of a Doubt, Psycho*) are among his most famous and disturbing. The Hitchcock villain has a number of characteristics which are not necessarily common to all but unite in various combinations: a) Sexual "perversity" or ambiguity: a number are more or less explicitly coded as gay (the transvestite killer in *Murder!,* Philip in *Rope,* Bruno Anthony in *Strangers on a Train*); others have marked mother-fixations (Uncle Charlie in *Shadow of a Doubt,* Anthony Perkins in *Psycho,* Bob Rusk in *Frenzy*), seen as a source of their psychic disorder; (b) Fascist connotations: this becomes politically explicit in the U-boat commander of *Lifeboat,* but is plain enough in, for example, *Shadow of a Doubt* and *Rope;* (c) The subtle associations of the villain with the devil: Uncle Charlie and Smoke in *Shadow of a Doubt,* Bruno Anthony in the paddle-boat named Pluto in *Strangers on a Train,* Norman Bates' remark to Marion Crane that "no one ever comes here unless they've gotten off the main highway" in *Psycho;* (d) Closely connected with these characteristics is a striking and ambiguous fusion of power and impotence operating on both the sexual and non-sexual levels. What is crucially significant here is that this feature is by no means restricted to the villains. It is shared, strikingly, by the male protagonists of what are perhaps Hitchcock's two supreme masterpieces, *Rear Window* and *Vertigo*.

The latter aspect of Hitchcock works also relates closely to the obsession with control (and the fear of losing it) that characterized Hitchcock's own methods of filmmaking: his preoccupation with a totally finalized and story-boarded shooting script, his domination of actors and shooting conditions. Finally, it's notable that the psychopath/villain is invariably the most fascinating and seductive character of the film, and its chief source of energy. His inevitable destruction leaves behind an essentially empty world.

If one adds together all these factors, one readily sees why Hitchcock is so much more than the skillful entertainer and master craftsman he was once taken for. His films represent an incomparable exposure of the sexual tensions and anxieties (especially *male* anxieties) that characterize a culture built upon repression, sexual inequality, and the drive to domination.—ROBIN WOOD

Huston, John

Nationality *Irish/American.* **Born** *John Marcellus Huston, son of actor Walter, in Nevada, Missouri, 5 August 1906, became Irish citizen, 1964.* **Education** *Attended boarding school in Los Angeles and at Lincoln High School, Los Angeles, 1923-24.* **Military Service** *Served in Signal Corps, Army Pictorial Service, 1942-45, discharged at rank of major.* **Family** *Married 1) Dorothy Jeanne Harvey, 1926 (divorced 1933); 2) Leslie Black, 1937 (divorced 1944); 3) Evelyn Keyes, 1946 (divorced 1950), one adopted son; 4) Ricki Soma, 1950 (died 1969), one son, two daughters including actress Anjelica; also son Daniel by Zoë Sallis; 5) Celeste Shane, 1972 (divorced 1977).* **Career** *Doctors in St. Paul, Minnesota, diagnose Huston with enlarged heart and kidney disease; taken to California for cure, 1916; boxer in California, 1920s; actor in New York, 1924; competition horseman, Mexico, 1927; journalist in New York, 1928-30; scriptwriter and actor in Hollywood, 1930; worked for Gaumont-British, London, 1932; moved to Paris with intention of studying painting, 1933; returned to New York, editor* Midweek Pictorial, *stage actor, 1934; writer for Warner Bros., Hollywood, 1936; directed first film,* The Maltese Falcon, *1941; with William Wyler and Philip Dunne, formed Committee for the 1st Amendment to counteract HUAC investigation, 1947; formed Horizon Pictures with Sam Spiegel, 1948; formed John Huston Productions for unrealized project* Matador, *1952; moved to Ireland, 1955; narrator for TV, from mid-1960s; moved to Mexico, 1972.* **Awards** *Legion of Merit, U.S. Armed Services, 1944; Oscar for Best Direction, for* Treasure of the Sierra Madre, *1947.* **Died** *Of pneumonia, in Newport, Rhode Island, 28 August 1987.*

Films as Director: 1941: *The Maltese Falcon* (+sc). **1942:** *In This Our Life* (+co-sc, uncredited); *Across the Pacific* (co-d). **1943:** *Report from the Aleutians* (+sc); *Tunisian Victory* (Capra and Boulting; d some replacement scenes when footage lost, +co-commentary). **1945:** *San Pietro* (*The Battle of San Pietro*) (+sc, co-ph, narration). **1946:** *Let There Be Light* (unreleased) (+co-sc, co-ph); *A Miracle Can Happen* (*On Our Merry Way*) (King Vidor and Fenton; d some Henry Fonda/James Stewart sequences, uncredited). **1948:** *The Treasure of the Sierra Madre* (+sc, bit role as man in white suit); *Key Largo* (+co-sc). **1949:** *We Were Strangers* (+co-sc, bit role as bank clerk). **1950:** *The Asphalt Jungle* (+co-sc). **1951:** *The Red Badge of Courage* (+sc). **1952:** *The African Queen* (+co-sc). **1953:** *Moulin Rouge* (+pr, co-sc). **1954:** *Beat the Devil* (+co-pr, co-sc). **1956:** *Moby Dick* (+pr, co-sc). **1957:** *Heaven Knows, Mr. Allison* (+co-sc); *A Farewell to Arms* (Charles Vidor; d begun by Huston). **1958:** *The Barbarian and the Geisha*; *The Roots of Heaven.*

1960: *The Unforgiven.* **1961:** *The Misfits.* **1963:** *Freud* (*Freud: The Secret Passion*) (+narration); *The List of Adrian Messenger* (+bit role as Lord Ashton). **1964:** *The Night of the Iguana* (+co-pr, co-sc). **1965:** *La bibbia* (*The Bible*) (+role, narration). **1967:** *Casino Royale* (co-d, role); *Reflections in a Golden Eye* (+voice heard at film's beginning). **1969:** *Sinful Davey; A Walk with Love and Death* (+role); *De Sade* (Enfield; d uncredited) (+role as the Abbe). **1970:** *The Kremlin Letter* (+co-sc, role). **1971:** *The Last Run* (Fleischer; d begun by Huston). **1972:** *Fat City* (+co-pr); *The Life and Times of Judge Roy Bean* (+role as Grizzly Adams). **1973:** *The Mackintosh Man.* **1975:** *The Man Who Would Be King* (+co-sc). **1976:** *Independence* (short). **1979:** *Wise Blood* (+role). **1980:** *Phobia.* **1981:** *Victory* (*Escape to Victory*). **1982:** *Annie.* **1984:** *Under the Volcano.* **1985:** *Prizzi's Honor.* **1987:** *The Dead.*

Other Films: 1929: *The Shakedown* (Wyler) (small role); *Hell's Heroes* (Wyler) (small role). **1930:** *The Storm* (Wyler) (small role). **1931:** *A House Divided* (Wyler) (dialogue, sc). **1932:** *Murders in the Rue Morgue* (Florey) (dialogue, sc). **1935:** *It Started in Paris* (Robert Wyler) (co-adapt, sc); *Death Drives Through* (Cahn) (co-story, sc). **1938:** *Jezebel* (Wyler) (co-sc); *The Amazing Dr. Clitterhouse* (Litvak) (co-sc). **1939:** *Juarez* (Dieterle) (co-sc). **1940:** *The Story of Dr. Ehrlich's Magic Bullet* (*Dr. Ehrlich's Magic Bullet*) (Dieterle) (co-sc). **1941:** *High Sierra* (Walsh) (co-sc); *Sergeant York* (Hawks) (co-sc). **1946:** *The Killers* (Siodmak) (sc, uncredited); *The Stranger* (Welles) (co-sc, uncredited); *Three Strangers* (Negulesco) (co-sc). **1951:** *Quo Vadis* (LeRoy) (pre-production work). **1963:** *The Cardinal* (Preminger) (role as Cardinal Glennon); *The Directors* (pr: Greenblatt, short) (appearance). **1968:** *Candy* (Marquand) (role as Dr. Dunlap); *The Rocky Road to Dublin* (Lennon) (role as interviewee).

1970: *Myra Breckenridge* (Sarne) (role as Buck Loner). **1971:** *The Bridge in the Jungle* (Kohner) (role as Sleigh); *The Deserter* (Kennedy) (role as General Miles); *Man in the Wilderness* (Sarafian) (role as Captain Henry). **1974:** *Battle for the Planet of the Apes* (Thompson) (role as Lawgiver); *Chinatown* (Polanski) (role as Noah Cross). **1975:** *Breakout* (Gries) (role as Harris); *The Wind and the Lion* (Milius) (role as John Hay). **1976:** *Sherlock Holmes in New York* (Sagal) (role as Professor Moriarty). **1977:** *Tentacles* (Hellman) (role as Ned Turner); *Il grande attacco* (*La battaglia di Mareth*; *The Biggest Battle*) (Lenzi) (role); *El triangulo diabolico de la Bermudas* (*Triangle: The Bermuda Mystery*; *The Mystery of the Bermuda Triangle*) (Cardona) (role); *Angela* (Sagal) (role). **1978:** *Il visitatore* (*The Visitor*) (Paradisi) (role). **1979:** *Jaguar Lives* (Pintoff) (role); *Winter Kills* (Richert) (role). **1980:** *Head On* (Grant) (role); *Agee* (Spears) (role as interviewee). **1981:** *To the Western World* (Kinmonth) (narrator). **1982:** *Cannery Row* (Ward) (narrator). **1983:** *Lovesick* (Brickman) (role as psychiatrist).

Few directors have been as interested in the relationship of film to painting as has John Huston and, perhaps, none has been given as little credit for this interest. This lack of recognition is not completely surprising. Criticism of film, despite the form's visual nature, has tended to be derived primarily from literature and not from painting or, as might be more reasonable, a combination of the traditions of literature, painting, theater, and the unique forms of film itself.

In a 1931 profile in the *American Mercury* that accompanied a short story by John Huston, the future director said that he wanted to write a book on the lives of French painters. The following year, unable to or dissatisfied with work as a film writer in London, Huston moved to Paris to become a painter. He studied for a year and a half, making money by painting portraits on street corners and singing for pennies. Even after he became an established film director, Huston's continued to indulge his interest in painting, "retiring" from filmmaking from time to time to concentrate on his painting.

Each of Huston's films has reflected this prime interest in the image, the moving portrait and the use of color—as well as the poetic possibilities of natural dialogue. Each film has been a moving canvas on which Huston explores his main subject: the effect of the individual ego on the group and the possibility of the individual's survival.

Huston began exploring his style of framing in his first film, *The Maltese Falcon*. Following his sketches, he set up shots like the canvases of paintings he had studied. Specifically, Huston showed an interest in characters appearing in the foreground of a shot, with their faces often covering half the screen. Frequently, too, the person whose face half fills the screen is not talking, but listening. The person reacting thus becomes more important than the one speaking or moving.

Huston's first film as a director presented situations he would return to again and again. Spade is the obsessed professional, a man who will adhere to pride and dedication, to principle unto death. Women are a threat, temptations that can only sway the hero from his professional commitment. They may be willfully trying to deceive, as with Brigid and Iva, or they may, as in later Huston films, be the unwitting cause of the protagonist's defeat or near-defeat. In *The Asphalt Jungle,* for example, the women in the film are not evil; it is the men's obsession with them that causes disaster.

Even with changes and cuts, a film like *The Red Badge of Courage* reflects Huston's thematic and visual interests. Again, the film features a group with a quest that may result in death. These soldiers argue, support each other, pretend they are not frightened, brag, and, in some cases, die. In the course of the action, both the youth and the audience discover that the taking of an isolated field is not as important as the ability of the young men to face death without fear. Also, as in other Huston films, the two central figures in *The Red Badge of Courage,* the youth and Wilson, lie about their attitudes. Their friendship solidifies only when both confess that they have been afraid during the battle and have fled.

John Huston

Visually, Huston continued to explore an important aspect of his style: the placement of characters in a frame so that their size and position reflect what they are saying and doing. He developed this technique with Bogart, Holt, and Walter Huston in *The Treasure of the Sierra Madre* and Audie Murphy and Bill Mauldin in *The Red Badge of Courage.*

Early in *The African Queen,* for instance, after Rosie's brother dies, there is a scene in which Rosie is seated on the front porch of the mission. Charlie, in the foreground, dominates the screen while Rosie, in the background, is small. As Charlie takes control of the situation and tells Rosie what must be done, he raises his hand to the rail and his arm covers our view of her. Charlie is in command.

Thematically, *Moulin Rouge* was a return to Huston's pessimism and exploration of futility. The director identified with the character of Lautrec who, like Huston, was given to late hours, ironic views of himself, performing for others, sardonic wit, and a frequent bitterness toward women. Lautrec, like Huston, loved horses, and frequently painted pictures of them.

The narrative as developed by Huston and Ray Bradbury in *Moby Dick* is in keeping with the director's preoccupation with failed quests. Only one man, Ishmael, survives. All the other men of the *Pequod* go down in Ahab's futile attempt to destroy the whale. But Huston sees Ahab in his actions and his final gesture as a noble creature who has chosen to go down fighting.

The Roots of Heaven is yet another example of Huston's exploration of an apparently doomed quest by a group of vastly different people, led by a man obsessed. In spite of the odds, the group persists in its mission and some of its members die. As in many Huston films, the quest is not a total failure; there is the likelihood of continuation, if not success, but the price that must be paid in human lives is high.

Huston's *The Misfits* again featured a group on a sad and fruitless quest. The group, on a search for horses, find far fewer than they had expected. The expedition becomes a bust and the trio of friends are at odds over a woman, Roslyn (Marilyn Monroe), who opposes the killing and capturing of the horses.

With the exception of Guido, the characters represent the least masked or disguised group in Huston's films. Perhaps it is this very element of never-penetrated disguise in Guido that upset Huston and drove him to push for a motivation scene, an emotional unmasking of the character.

As a Huston film, *Freud* has some particular interests: Huston serves as a narrator, displaying an omnipotence and almost Biblical detachment that establishes Freud as a kind of savior and messiah. The film opens with Huston's description of Freud as a kind of hero or God on a quest for mankind. "This is the story of Freud's descent into a region as black as hell, man's unconscious, and how he let in the light," Huston says in his narration. The bearded, thin look of Freud, who stands alone, denounced before the tribunal of his own people, also suggests a parallel with Christ. Freud brings a message of salvation which is rejected, and he is reluctantly denounced by his chief defender, Breuer.

Of all Huston's films, *The List of Adrian Messenger* is the one that deals most literally with people in disguise. George, who describes himself as unexcused evil, hides behind a romantic or heroic mask that falls away when he is forced to face the detective, who functions very much like Freud. The detective penetrates the masks, revealing the evil, and the evil is destroyed.

Huston's touch was evident in *The Night of the Iguana* in a variety of ways. First, he again took a group of losers and put them together in an isolated location. The protagonist, Shannon, once a minister, has been reduced to guiding tourists in Mexico. At the furthest reaches of despair and far from civilization, the quest for meaning ends and the protagonist is forced to face himself. Religion is an important theme. The film opens with Richard Burton preaching a sermon to his congregation. It is a startling contrast to Father Mapple's sermon in *Moby Dick*. Shannon is lost, confused, his speech is gibberish, an almost nonsensical confession about being unable to control his appetites and emotions. The congregation turns away from him.

This choice between the practical and the fantastic is a constant theme in Huston's life and films. There is also a choice between illusion and reality, a choice Huston finds difficult to make. Religion is seen as part of the fantasy world, a dangerous fantasy that his characters must overcome if they are not to be destroyed or absorbed by it. This theme is present in *The Bible, Wise Blood,* and *Night of the Iguana*.

Huston's negative religious attitude is also strong in *A Walk with Love and Death,* which includes three encounters with the clergy. In the first, Heron is almost killed by a group of ascetic monks who demand that he renounce the memory of Claudia and "repent his knowledge of women." The young man barely escapes with his life. These religious zealots counsel a move away from the pleasure of the world and human love, a world that Huston believes in.

There are clearly constants in Huston's works—man's ability to find solace in animals and nature, the need to challenge oneself—but his world is unpredictable, governed by a whimsical God or no God at all. Each of Huston's characters seeks a way of coming to terms with that unpredictability, establishing rules of behavior by which he can live.

The Huston character, like Cain or Adam, is often weak, and frequently his best intentions are not sufficient to carry him through to success or even survival. The more a man thinks in a

Huston film, the more dangerous it is for his survival. Conversely, however, his films suggest that those who are carried away by emotion, or too much introspection, are doomed. Since the line between loss of control and rigidity is difficult to walk, many Huston protagonists do not survive. It takes a Sam Spade, Sergeant Allison, or Abraham, very rare men indeed, to remain alive in this director's world.

Reflections in a Golden Eye raised many questions about the sexuality inherent in many of the themes that most attracted Huston: riding horses, hunting, boxing, and militarism. The honesty with which the director handles homosexuality is characteristic of his willingness to face what he finds antithetical to his own nature. In the film, the equation of Leonora and her horse is presented as definitely sexual, and at one point Penderton actually beats the horse in a fury because he himself is impotent. Huston also includes a boxing match in the film which is not in the novel. The immorally provocative Leonora watches the match, but Penderton watches another spectator, Williams. *Reflections* becomes an almost comic labyrinth of voyeurism, with characters spying on other characters.

Huston's protagonists often represent extremes. They are either ignorant, pathetic, and doomed by their lack of self-understanding (Tully and Ernie in *Fat City,* Dobbs in *The Treasure of the Sierra Madre,* Peachy and Danny in *The Man Who Would Be King*) or intelligent, arrogant, but equally doomed by their lack of self-understanding (Penderton in *Reflections in a Golden Eye* and Ahab in *Moby Dick*). Between these extremes is the cool, intelligent protagonist who will sacrifice everything for self-understanding and independence (Sam Spade in *The Maltese Falcon,* and Freud). Huston always finds the first group pathetic, the second tragic, and the third heroic. He reserves his greatest respect for the man who retains his dignity in spite of pain and disaster.

Many of Huston's films can de divided between those involving group quests that fail and those involving a pair of potential lovers who must face a hostile world. Generally, Huston's films about such lovers end in the union of the couple or, at least, their survival. In that sense, *A Walk with Love and Death,* starring his own daughter, proved to be the most pessimistic of his love stories, and *Annie,* his most commercial venture, proved to be his most optimistic.—STUART M. KAMINSKY

Ichikawa, Kon

Nationality *Japanese.* **Born** *Uji Yamada in Ise, Mie Prefecture, 20 November 1915.*
Education *Ichioka Commercial School, Osaka.* **Family** *Married scriptwriter Natto Wada,*
1948. **Career** *Worked in animation dept. of J.O. Studios, Kyoto, from 1933; assistant*
director on feature-filmmaking staff, late 1930s; transferred to Tokyo when J.O. became
part of Toho company, early 1940s; collaborated on scripts with wife, 1948-56; used pen
name "Shitei Kuri" (after Japanese rendering of Agatha Christie), from 1957; writer and
director for TV, 1958-66. **Award** *San Giorgio Prize, Venice Festival, for* Harp of Burma,
1956.

Films as Director: 1946: *Musume Dojoji (A Girl at Dojo Temple)* (+co-sc). **1947:** *Toho senichi-ya*
(1001 Nights with Toho) (responsible for some footage only). **1948:** *Hana hiraku (A Flower Blooms)*;
Sanbyaku rokujugo-ya (365 Nights). **1949:** *Ningen moyo (Human Patterns; Design of a Human*
Being); *Hateshinaki jonetsu (Passion without End; The Endless Passion).* **1950:** *Ginza Sanshiro*
(Sanshiro of Ginza); *Netsudeichi (Heat and Mud; The Hot Marshland)* (+co-sc): *Akatsuki no tsuiseki*
(Pursuit at Dawn). **1951:** *Ieraishan (Nightshade Flower)* (+co-sc): *Koibito (The Lover)* (+co-sc);
Mukokuseki-sha (The Man without a Nationality); *Nusumareta koi (Stolen Love)* (+co-sc); *Bungawan*
Solo (River Solo Flows) (+co-sc); *Kekkon koshinkyoku (Wedding March)* (+co-sc). **1952:** *Rakkii-san*
(Mr. Lucky); *Wakai hito (Young People, Young Generation)* (+co-sc); *Ashi ni sawatta onna (The*
Woman Who Touched Legs) (+co-sc); *Ano te kono te (This Way, That Way)* (+co-sc). **1953:** *Puu-san*
(Mr. Pu) (+co-sc); *Aoiro kakumei (The Blue Revolution)*; *Seishun Zenigata Heiji (The Youth of Heiji*
Zenigata) (+co-sc); *Ai-jin (The Lover).* **1954:** *Watashi no subete o (All of Myself)* (+co-sc); *Okuman*
choja (A Billionaire) (+co-sc); *Josei ni kansuru juni-sho (Twelve Chapters on Women).* **1955:** *Seishun*
kaidan (Ghost Story of Youth); *Kokoro (The Heart).* **1956:** *Biruma no tategoto (The Burmese Harp;*
Harp of Burma); *Shokei no heya (Punishment Room)*; *Nihonbashi (Bridge of Japan).* **1957:** *Manin*
densha (The Crowded Streetcar) (+co-sc); *Tohoku no zummu-tachi (The Men of Tohoku)* (+sc); *Ana*
(The Pit; The Hole) (+sc). **1958:** *Enjo (Conflagration).* **1959:** *Sayonara, konnichiwa (Goodbye, Hello)*
(+co-sc); *Kagi (The Key; Odd Obsession* (+co-sc); *Nobi (Fires on the Plain)*; *Jokyo II: Mono o takaku*
uritsukeru onna (A Woman's Testament, Part 2: Women Who Sell Things at High Prices).

1960: *Bonchi* (+co-sc); *Ototo (Her Brother).* **1961:** *Kuroijunin no onna (Ten Dark Women).* **1962:**
Hakai (The Outcast; The Broken Commandment); *Watashi wa nisai (I Am Two; Being Two Isn't Easy).*

1963: *Yukinojo henge* (*An Actor's Revenge; The Revenge of Yukinojo*); *Taiheiyo hitoribotchi* (*My Enemy, the Sea; Alone on the Pacific*). **1964:** *Zeni no odori* (*The Money Dance; Money Talks*) (+sc). **1965:** *Tokyo Orimpikku* (*Tokyo Olympiad*) (+co-sc). **1967:** *Toppo Jijo no botan senso* (*Toppo Gigio and the Missile War*) (+co-sc). **1969:** *Kyoto* (+sc). **1970:** *Nihon to Nihonjin* (*Japan and the Japanese*) (+sc). **1972:** *Ai futatabi* (*To Love Again*). **1973:** *Matatabi* (*The Wanderers*) (+pr, co-sc); "The Fastest" episode of *Visions of Eight*. **1975:** *Wagahai wa neko de aru* (*I Am a Cat*). **1976:** *Tsuma to onna no aida* (*Between Women and Wives*) (co-d); *Inugami-ke no ichizoku* (*The Inugami Family*) (+co-sc). **1977:** *Akuma no temari-uta* (*A Rhyme of Vengeance; The Devil's Bouncing Ball Song*) (+sc); *Gokumonto* (*The Devil's Island; Island of Horrors*) (+co-sc). **1978:** *Jo-bachi* (*Queen Bee*) (+co-sc). **1980:** *Koto* (*Ancient City*) (+co-sc); *Hi no tori* (*The Phoenix*) (+co-sc). **1982:** *Kofuku* (*Lonely Hearts, Happiness*) (+co-sc). **1983:** *Sasame Yuki* (*The Makioka sisters; Fine Snow*). **1985:** *Ohan; Biruma no tategoto* (*The Burmese Harp*). **1987:** *Eiga Joyu* (*The Actress*); *Taketori Monogatari* (*Princess from the Moon*). **1991:** *Tenkawa Densetsu Satsujin Jiken.* **1993:** *Fusa* (+sc). **1994:** *47 Ronin.*

Other Film: 1970: *Dodes'ka-den* (Kurosawa) (pr).

Kon Ichikawa is noted for a wry humor that often resembles black comedy, for his grim psychological studies—often of misfits and outsiders—and for the visual beauty of his films. He is noted as one of Japan's foremost cinematic stylists, and has commented, "I began as a painter and I think like one."

His early films show a perverse sense of humor as they reveal human foibles and present an objective view of corruption. In *Mr. Pu,* a projector breaks down while showing scenes of an atomic explosion. In *A Billionaire,* a family dies from eating radioactive tuna, leaving only a lazy elder son and a sympathetic tax collector. In *The Key,* a group of rather selfish, despicable people are poisoned inadvertently by a senile old maid, who becomes the only survivor. The film is a study of an old man who becomes obsessed with sex to compensate for his fears of impotency. He becomes a voyeur, and through the manipulation of the camera, we come to share in this activity. Slowly, however, he emerges as being sympathetic while the other characters are revealed in their true light.

Throughout his career Ichikawa has proven himself a consistent critic of Japanese society, treating such themes as the rebirth of militarism (*Mr. Pu*), the harshness and inhumanity of military feudalism (*Fires on the Plain*), the abuse of the individual within the family (*Bonchi* and *Her Brother*), as well as familial claustrophobia and the tendency of repression to result in perversion and outbreaks of violence (*The Key*). His films usually refuse a happy ending, and Ichikawa has been frequently criticized for an unabashed pessimism, bordering on nihilism.

Two of his most important films, *Harp of Burma* and *Fires on the Plain,* deal with the tragedies of war. The former concerns a soldier who adopts Buddhist robes and dedi-

Kon Ichikawa

cates himself to burying the countless Japanese dead on Burma; the latter is about a group of demoralized soldiers who turn to cannibalism. A third work, *Tokyo Olympiad,* provided a new approach to sports films, giving as much attention to human emotions and spectator reactions as to athletic feats.

Ichikawa is a master of the wide screen and possesses a strong sense of composition, creating enormous depth with his use of diagonal and overhead shots. Often he utilizes black backgrounds to isolate images within the frame, or a form of theatrical lighting, or he blocks out portions of the screen to alter the format and ratio.

Ichikawa remains fascinated with experimental techniques. His excellent use of the freeze frame in *Kagi* reflects his case study approach to characterization. He has also done much in the way of color experimentation. *Kagi* is bathed in blues, which bleach skin tones to white, thus creating corpse-like subjects. *Her Brother* is so filtered that it resembles a black and white print with dull pinks and reds. On most of his films, Ichikawa has used cameramen Kazuo Miyagawa or Setsuo Kobayashi.

After *Tokyo Olympiad* Ichikawa encountered many studio difficulties. His projects since then include a twenty-six-part serialization of *The Tale of Genji* and *The Wanderers,* a parody of gangster films with a nod to *Easy Rider,* plus a dozen documentaries and fiction features, among which *The Inugami Family,* a suspense thriller, proved to be the biggest box office success in Japanese film history.—PATRICIA ERENES

Ivory, James

*Nationality American. **Born** Berkeley, California, 7 June 1928. **Education** Educated in architecture and fine arts, University of Oregon; studied filmmaking at University of Southern California, M.A. 1956. **Military Service** Corporal in U.S. Army Special Services, 1953-55. **Career** Founder and partner, Merchant-Ivory Productions, New York, 1961; directed first feature, also began collaboration with writer Ruth Prawer Jhabvala, on* The Householder, *1963. **Awards** Best Foreign Film, French Academie du Cinema, and prize at Berlin Festival, for* Shakespeare Wallah, *1968; Guggenheim Fellow, 1973; Oscar nomination, Best Director and Directors Guild nomination, for* A Room with a View, *1987; Silver Lion, Venice Festival, for* Maurice, *1987; Oscar nomination, Best Director, for* Howards End, *1992; John Cassavetes Award, Independent Spirit Award, Independent Feature Project/West, 1993. **Address** c/o Merchant-Ivory Productions, Ltd., 250 W. 57th St., Suite 1913-A, New York, New York 10107, U.S.A.*

Films as Director: 1957: *Venice: Themes and Variations* (doc) (+sc, ph). 1959: *The Sword and the Flute* (doc) (+sc, ph, ed). 1963: *The Householder.* 1964: *The Delhi Way* (doc) (+sc). 1965: *Shakespeare Wallah* (+co-sc). 1968: *The Guru* (+co-sc). 1970: *Bombay Talkie* (+co-sc). 1971: *Adventures of a Brown Man in Search of Civilization* (doc). 1972: *Savages* (+pr, sc). 1974: *The Wild Party.* 1975: *Autobiography of a Princess.* 1977: *Roseland.* 1979: *Hullabaloo over Georgie and Bonnie's Pictures; The Europeans* (+pr, co-sc, role as man in warehouse). 1980: *Jane Austen in Manhattan.* 1981: *Quartet* (+co-sc). 1982: *Courtesans of Bombay* (doc) (+co-sc). 1983: *Heat and Dust.* 1984: *The Bostonians.* 1986: *A Room with a View.* 1987: *Maurice* (+co-sc). 1989: *Slaves of New York.* 1990: *Mr. and Mrs. Bridge.* 1992: *Howards End.* 1993: *The Remains of the Day.* 1995: *Jefferson in Paris.* 1996: *Surviving Picasso.* 1998: *A Soldier's Daughter Never Cries* (+co-sc).

The work of James Ivory was a fixture in independent filmmaking of the late 1960s and 1970s. *Roseland,* for example, Ivory's omnibus film about the habitués of a decaying New York dance palace, garnered a standing ovation at its premiere at the New York Film Festival in 1977, and received much critical attention afterward. However, it was not until *A Room with a View,* his stately adaptation of E. M. Forster's novel, that Ivory gained full international recognition. The name-making films Ivory directed earlier in the 1980s—which included adaptations of two Forster works and two Henry James novels among them—linked him inextricably with the contemporary British cinema's tradition of urbane, even ultra-genteel, costume-dramas.

Ivory's independence, his influential involvement with English film, and his sustained collaborative partnership with producer Ismail Merchant invite comparisons

James Ivory

with an earlier pairing in British cinema, Michael Powell and Emeric Pressburger. Both teams have found themselves attracted to material dealing with the effects of sexual repression or with the clash of differing cultures, as in, for example, *Black Narcissus* (Powell/Pressburger, 1947) or *The Europeans* (Ivory/Merchant, 1979). But while Powell and Pressburger worked with various forms of visual experimentation, employing heightened colors, frequently moving cameras, and various forms of cinematographic juxtaposition to achieve an opulent, metaphorical visual texture, Ivory's work represents a distinct retrenchment, a withdrawal from visual hyperbole, a comparative conservatism of visual style. An example of one of Ivory's few attempts at visual expressionism (a moment in his work that seems directly inspired by Powell, in fact) illustrates this point. In *The Bostonians,* Ivory attempts to express Olive Chancellor's hysteria by using stylized colors and superimposition in isolated dream sequences. Because the film's style is deeply rooted in naturalism, unlike that of Powell, the sequences look stilted and awkward, remarkably out of place in the context of the film.

The naturalism of Ivory's style often perfectly complements the director's interest in the dynamics of isolated communities: the drama troupe in *Shakespeare Wallah,* for example, or the dancers in *Roseland,* or the members of the New York downtown-punk scene in *Slaves of New York.* Ivory's films characteristically trace the formation of community around a common interest—or, more often, a common flaw or a shared loss—and his powers of observation are enlivened by attention to minute details of gesture and a keen sympathy for marginal characters. It is this sympathy that attracts him to works such as Evan Connell's novels *Mrs. Bridge* and *Mr. Bridge.* Ivory thus provides a densely ironic but ultimately sympathetic account of the quietly desperate middle-class lives of the Bridges in Kansas City. This sympathy accounts as well for Ivory's handling of characters such as Charlotte Bartlett in *Room with a View.* In Forster's novel, Miss Bartlett is lampooned tirelessly, emerging as one of the novel's chief examples of English hypocrisy and Forster's conception of high culture as the poison of the spirit (this is in spite of a half-hearted reprieve for the character in the novel's last pages). In the film, Maggie Smith's agile, witty performance makes the character far more appealing, and Ivory's treatment of the character (he cuts from the lovers' final union to shots of Miss Bartlett's soundless, unbending loneliness) shows that he clearly interprets her as a fully sympathetic character of great pathos.

Ivory's two Forster adaptations, *Room with a View* and *Maurice,* may well prove to be the high-water mark of his career. These two films do more than demonstrate Ivory's often bracingly literary sensibility (most of Ivory's films are adaptations that doggedly strive for extreme "faithfulness" to their source material): In the Forster adaptations, this "faithfulness" co-exists with crucial shifts of emphasis that provide, simultaneously, modern interpretations of the texts.

An example of this occurs in the scene of the murder in the square in *Room with a View.* In its use of hand-held cameras, graphic matches, and rhythmic editing, which provides mercurial shifts in the tone of the sequence from gravity to exultation, the sequence becomes one of the film's set-pieces, supplying the complexities that Forster largely avoids in his comparatively laconic treatment of the scene.

The work of Ivory, Merchant, and Jhabvala has become even more distinguished as they have aged. Upon its theatrical release, *Howards End* (directed by Ivory, produced by Merchant and scripted by Prawer Jhabvala) was justifiably hailed as the best film ever in their long and distinguished careers. This stylish work is yet another adaptation of an E. M. Forster novel. Its scenario examines a popular Ivory theme, exploring the repercussions when social classes come together at a specific point in recent history (in this case, at the close of the Edwardian era in England). Emma Thompson is altogether brilliant in the role that solidified her career. She plays a cheeky and individualistic young woman who does not come from a monied background, and who is slyly charmed by a prosperous gentleman (Anthony Hopkins) whose upper class facade hides a deceitful and heartless disposition.

The Remains of the Day is nearly as fine a film as *Howards End.* Based on the acclaimed novel by Kazuo Ishiguro, the scenario dissects the personality of an ideal servant: Stevens (Hopkins), a reserved British butler who is singlemindedly dedicated to his employer, Lord Darlington (James Fox). The time is between the World Wars. No matter that the misguided Darlington is perilously flirting with Nazism. No matter that Miss Kenton (Thompson), the new housekeeper, might be a potential romantic partner. Stevens is steadfastly absorbed in his professional role, to the exclusion of all else. He knows only to suppress his needs, feelings, and desires, all in the name of service to his master. *The Remains of the Day* essentially is a character study of Stevens, who is superbly played by the ever-reliable Hopkins. It is yet one more in a line of Ivory's meticulous period dramas.

The period drama *Jefferson in Paris* concerns the American Thomas Jefferson, one of America's founding fathers, shown here as the U.S. Ambassador to France. However, the film is several shades below the best of the previous Ivory-Merchant-Jhabvala collaborations. While *Jefferson in Paris* captures a time and place with exquisite detail, the level of detail included in the film renders the narrative all too episodic in quality. Still, Ivory offers a full-bodied portrayal of Jefferson (Nick Nolte), while depicting a large range of his personal and political involvements. Most intriguing of all is the paradox of Jefferson's disgust with the overindulgences of the French aristocracy combined with his agonized collusion in keeping the status quo with regard to the maintenance of slavery as an American "institution." In *Jefferson in Paris,* Ivory yet again depicts his theme of class differences, exploring the invisible walls that separate those classes. Only here, class is measured by the color of one's skin. Even though individuals share the same bloodlines because of sexual liaisons between master and slave, those with black skin are enslaved by those with white skin. Ivory portrays the widowed Jefferson as a man who falls in love with a married woman (Greta Scacchi), and has a sexual tryst with Sally Hemings (Thandie Newton), a teenaged slave girl. It remains uncertain if the latter affair ever happened. For this reason, *Jefferson in Paris* was the subject of debate and controversy among Jeffersonian scholars.—JAMES MORRISON and ROB EDELMAN

Jarmusch, Jim

Nationality American. *Born* Akron, Ohio, 1953. *Education* Columbia University, New York, graduated 1975; New York University Graduate Film School, 1976-79, as teaching assistant to Nicholas Ray. *Career* With help of Ray, completed first film, Permanent Vacation, for $10,000, 1980; made New World *with 30 minutes of leftover film, 1982; added another hour's worth of film to it to make* Stranger Than Paradise, *1984; recording artist with "The Del-Byzanteens." *Awards* Golden Leopard, Locarno Festival, Best Film Award, National Society of Film Critics, and Camera d'Or for Best New Director, Cannes Festival, for* Stranger Than Paradise, *1984; Palme d'Or, Cannes Festival, for* Coffee and Cigarettes (Somewhere in California), *1993. *Address* Lives in the Bowery, New York.*

Films as Director and Scriptwriter: 1980: *Permanent Vacation* (+sc, ed, mus). **1982:** *The New World* (*Stranger Than Paradise, Part One*) (short). **1984:** *Stranger Than Paradise.* **1986:** *Down by Law.* **1987:** *Coffee and Cigarettes.* **1989:** *Mystery Train.* **1989:** *Coffee and Cigarettes (Memphis Version).* **1992:** *Night on Earth* (+pr). **1993:** *Coffee and Cigarettes (Somewhere in California).* **1995:** *Dead Man.* **1997:** *Year of the Horse.*

Other Films: 1979: *Red Italy* (Mitchel) (role). **1980:** *Lightning Over Water* (*Nick's Movie*) (Wenders and Ray) (prod asst); *Underground U.S.A.* (Mitchell) (sound recordist). **1981:** *Only You* (Vogel) (role); *You Are Not I* (Driver) (ph). **1982:** *Burroughs* (Brookner) (sound recordist); *The State of Things* (Wenders) (featured songs by The Del-Byzanteens). **1983:** *Fraulein Berlin* (Lambert) (role as Mr. Dade). **1984:** *Sleepwalk* (Driver) (ph); *American Autobahn* (Degas) (role). **1986:** *Straight to Hell* (Cox) (role). **1987:** *Candy Mountain* (Wurlitzer, Frank) (role). **1988:** *Helsinki Napoli All Night Long* (role). **1989:** *Leningrad Cowboys Go America* (Kaurismaki) (role). **1990:** *Golden Boat* (Ruiz) (role). **1992:** *In the Soup* (Rockwell) (role). **1994:** *Tigrero: A Film That Was Never Made* (Kaurismaki) (role); *Iron Horsemen* (role as Silver Rider). **1995:** *Blue in the Face* (Wang, Auster) (role as Bob). **1996:** *Sling Blade* (role as Frosty Freeze Boy).

Jim Jarmusch has risen quickly to the forefront of young, independent American filmmakers. Recognition has been his from the very beginning with the release of his first film, *Stranger Than Paradise,* a work that won a Camera d'Or at the 1984 Cannes Film Festival (for best "first film") and "Best Picture" from the National Society of Film Critics. The key to Jarmusch's success is a well-defined and thoughtfully conceived stylistic approach and a coherent circle of interests.

The focal point of all Jarmusch's work is the apparent contradiction that exists between the popular perception of the American Dream and what that dream actually holds for the individual who doesn't quite fit in. This contradiction is explored through the interaction of a characteristic ensemble of characters. Each of Jarmusch's films is built around a trio of characters, although *Mystery Train* varies that slightly by using three separate stories to explore this central theme.

Jim Jarmusch

The characters are all decidedly off-beat, but all seem to have a vision or aspiration which echoes a popular perception of America. The central characters—Tom Waits' down and out disc jockey in *Down by Law,* or John Lurie's small-time pimp in the same film—are forced to confront their misconceptions and misguided dreams when they are thrown together by fate with a foreigner who views this dream as an observer. In *Down by Law,* for example, the two central characters find themselves in jail with an Italian immigrant who has murdered someone for cheating at cards. The character carries a small notebook of American slang expressions from which he quotes dutifully and incorrectly. He refers to this notebook as "everything I know about America." It is this kind of character situation that Jarmusch uses to scoff at an America he sees as misguided and woefully out of touch with itself.

Stylistically, Jarmusch's work echoes the work of the French "New Wave" filmmakers, in particular the Godard of films like *Breathless* and *Weekend.* Jump-cuts are frequently used to disconnect characters from sublime and rational passages of time and space. A sense of disenfranchisement is created in this way, separating characters from the continuity of space and time which surrounds them. In *Down by Law,* for example, Tom Waits sits in his cell, then lays on the floor, then lays across his bed, but what seems like "a day in the life" editing approach actually concludes with days having passed, not hours. Jarmusch also uses moving-camera a great deal, but unlike his predecessors in other traditions, his fluid camera style is not functional. Camera movements in films like *Down by Law* and *Mystery Train* create a visual world that is always in transition. *Down by Law* opens with camera movement first right to left down a street in a small town, then left to right. As a result, the audience is introduced, through a visual metaphor, to the collision course that is central to the film's themes.

Night on Earth, Jarmusch's most mature film to date, is an exhilarating five-part slice-of-life, each of which unravels at the same point in time in Los Angeles, New York, Paris, Rome, and Helsinki. All are set in taxis, and spotlight brief but poignant exchanges between cab driver and passenger. The best of many highlights: the sequence in which a black Brooklynite (Giancarlo Esposito) and an East German refugee (Armin Mueller-Stahl) reveal their names to each other. Jarmusch's point is that people are people, whether black or white, American or French or Finnish.

Jarmusch also is not averse to working in the short film format. In 1987 he made *Coffee and Cigarettes,* in which an American (Steven Wright) and an Italian (Roberto Benigni) meet in a cafe and converse over coffee and cigarettes. Jarmusch reworked the film's concept and structure twice more: *Coffee and Cigarettes (Memphis Version),* made two years later, in which an argument between twins Joie and Cinque Lee is intruded on by an overly earnest waiter (Steve Buscemi); and *Coffee and Cigarettes (Somewhere in California),* made four years after that, this time featuring a barroom conversation between Iggy Pop and Tom Waits.

Jarmusch's cool style and strangers-in-a-strange-land subject matter have influenced other filmmakers. *Cold Fever,* a likable 1995 Icelandic feature co-produced and co-scripted by Jarmusch colleague Jim Stark and directed by Fridrik Thor Fridriksson, chronicles a Japanese businessman's odyssey across Iceland to perform a memorial ritual at the spot where his parents had died seven years earlier.

Like other young filmmakers of his generation, such as Spike Lee, Jim Jarmusch approaches the American way of life with a sense of hip cynicism. A product of contemporary American film school savvy, Jarmusch incorporates a sense of film history, style, and awareness in his filmmaking approach. The tradition which he has chosen to follow, the one which offers him the most freedom, is that established by filmmakers such as Chabrol, Godard, and Truffaut in the 1950s and 1960s.—ROB WINNING and ROB EDELMAN

Kaurismaki, Aki

Nationality *Finnish.* **Born** *Finland, 4 April 1957.* **Career** *Began working as co-scenarist and assistant director with his older brother, Mika Kaurismaki, 1980; co-directed* Saimaa Ilmio *with Mika, 1981; directed first feature on his own,* Crime and Punishment, *1983; directed the music videos* Rocky VI, Thru the Wire, *and* L.A. Woman, *1986; with Mika, runs own production company, Villealfa Film Productions, in Helsinki, operates art movie houses in Helsinki, and organized the Midnight Sun Film Festival.* **Awards** *Jussi Award, Best First Film and Script, and diplomas from FILMEX, Nordische Filmtage, and Karlovy Vary Festival, 1983, for* Crime and Punishment; *Special Award, Hong Kong Festival, 1985, for* Calimari Union; *Jussi Award, Best Finnish Film, 1986, for* Shadows in Paradise. **Address** *Villealfa Filmproductions Oy, Vainamoisenkatu 19 A, SF-00100 Helsinki, Finland.*

Films as Director: 1981: *Saimma Ilmio* (*The Saimma Gesture*) (co-dir). **1983:** *Rikos ja Pangaistus* (*Crime and Punishment*) (+co-sc). **1985:** *Calimari Union* (+sc). **1986:** *Varjoja Paratiisissa* (*Shadows in Paradise*) (+sc). **1987:** *Hamlet Liikemaailmassa* (*Hamlet Goes Business*) (+sc, pr). **1988:** *Ariel* (+sc, pr). **1989:** *Leningrad Cowboys Go America* (+sc). **1990:** *I Hired a Contract Killer* (+sc, pr); *Tulitikkutehtaan Tytto* (*The Match Factory Girl*) (+sc, pr). **1991:** *Those Were the Days* (short) (+sc, ed). **1992:** *La Vie de Boheme* (*The Bohemian Life*) (+sc, pr). **1993:** *These Boots* (short) (+sc, pr, ed). **1994:** *Leningrad Cowboys Meet Moses* (+sc, pr, ed). **1994:** *Total Balalaika Show* (doc) (+pr); *Pida huivsta kiinnim Tatjana* (*Take Care of Your Scarf, Tatiana*) (+pr, co-sc).

Other Films: (as co-scenarist and assistant director to brother Mika Kaurismaki) **1980:** *The Liar* (+role). **1982:** *Arvottomat* (*The Worthless*) (+role). **1984:** *Klanni—tarina sammokoitten* (*The Clan—Tale of the Frogs*). **1985:** *Rosso.*

(As producer) 1993: *The Prodigal Son* (Aaltonen). **1994:** *Iron Horsemen* (Charmant) (+role).

The cinema of Aki Kaurismaki is a cinema of the absurd. He and his brother, director Mika Kaurismaki, have become two of the world's most prolific and uniquely impudent movie-makers. At first, they were far outside the Finnish establishment, in that their parodies and farces lampooned the conventions of their society. Nevertheless, as they became known and respected on the international film scene, they quickly came to be regarded as the leading talents of their country's minuscule motion picture industry. Certainly, the Kaurismaki brothers' success helped educate cineastes to the fact that Scandinavian films do not only come from Sweden and Norway.

Aki and Mika Kaurismaki began collaborating in the early 1980s, but Aki was the one who initially established himself internationally. In 1990 alone, seven of his films were screened in various venues in New York City. His films are linked in that they are straightforward, serio-comic studies infused with a unique sense of the ridiculous. His characters are far removed from the mainstream, in some cases to the point of being isolated and completely alone; occasionally, they are on the road, roaming across landscapes in which they will be eternal outsiders. But their feelings of alienation or despondency rarely become the principal force at work on screen. Rather, Kaurismaki elicits a poignancy as he charts his characters' lives, with a special emphasis on the humor which symbolizes the utter absurdity of their situations.

A number of Kaurismaki's heros are dejected blue-collar loners driven to desperate acts and outrageous behavior by a repressive society. Such is the case in *Ariel,* a comical, existential road movie about a mine worker (Turo Pajala) who loses his job and sets out on an odyssey across Finland. *Ariel* offers a textbook example of the manner in which Kaurismaki drolly observes the life of a character whose very existence is outwardly depressing. In a similar vein is *The Match Factory Girl,* a sharply drawn black comedy about a dreary, oppressed young woman (Kati Outinen). Her job is tiresome, her life is going nowhere, and then she becomes involved with a man who is destined to drop her. He expects her to meekly squirm back into her shell, but her response—and her revenge—is way out of character.

Aki Kaurismaki

Retaliation also is a prominent theme in the first film Kaurismaki directed by himself, *Crime and Punishment,* a reworking of the Dostoyevsky novel. *Crime and Punishment* is set in 1980s Helsinki, and the hero, Rahikaainen (Markku Toikka), murders a powerful businessman who was responsible for the hit-and-run death of his fiancee. By far, *Crime and Punishment* is Kaurismaki's most somber film. On the other end of the emotional scale is *I Hired a Contract Killer,* in which he brings his alienated hero to an outlandishly comic extreme. Here, he tells the story of a nebbish (Jean-Pierre Leaud) with nothing to live for who haplessly fails to kill himself. He hires a pro to do the job but changes his mind after unexpectedly falling in love, and then must hurriedly attempt to cancel the contract.

Another Kaurismaki concern is the creative lifestyle. He examines this issue in *La Vie de Boheme,* an affectionate comedy about what it means to single-mindedly devote one's life to art, regardless of the consequences and sacrifices. The film is a slice-of-life about three men, a writer (Andre Wilms), a painter (Matti Pellonpaa), and a composer-musician (Kari Vaanenen). Each is aging, has little or no money, and has not earned any kind of commercial or critical recognition. Indeed, there are no undiscovered Hemingways, Picassos, or Mozarts in the group; it would not be unfair to judge each a mediocre talent. But all three remain steadfastly committed to their work and ideals. The women in their lives remain secondary figures; each values his library, piano, and paint above everything else.

One of Kaurismaki's zaniest films is *Leningrad Cowboys Go America,* which also features characters with warped senses of their talents. But here, they revel in their awfulness as they proudly hold the mantle as "the worst rock 'n' roll band in the world." *Leningrad Cowboys* is a loopy farce that lampoons the manner in which the tackiest aspects of American pop culture have impacted on even the farthest reaches of Finland. His "cowboys" are a deadpan, perfectly dreadful band of rock musicians from the Finnish tundra, who embark on a "world tour" which will take them not to Madison Square Garden but across a vast small-town American wasteland.

Kaurismaki had only begun to mine the Leningrad Cowboys' comic possibilities. He followed *Leningrad Cowboys Go America* with two short films featuring the Cowboys in renditions of hit pop songs: *Those Were the Days,* a six-minute mini-saga of a lonesome cowpoke rambling through the streets of the Big City in the company of his donkey; and *These Boots,* a five-minute history of Finland between 1950 and 1969 as seen from the viewpoint of the Cowboys. Next came the feature-length *Leningrad Cowboys Meet Moses,* in which the Cowboys actually have a top-ten hit to their credit. They start out in Mexico, make their way through Coney Island, and end up back in Europe; their manager (Matti Pellonpaa) professes that he is Moses, and pledges to guide the boys home to the Promised Land of Siberia. Finally, in the documentary *Total Balalaika Show,* Kaurismaki presents the Leningrad Cowboys in concert before fifty thousand fans in Helsinki's Senate Square with none other than Russia's Alexandrov Red Army Chorus and Dance Ensemble—described by a *Variety* critic as "the most incongruous—and inspired—crosscultural pairing since Nureyev danced with Miss Piggy."—ROB EDELMAN

Kazan, Elia

Nationality American. *Born* Elia Kazanjoglou in Constantinople (now Istanbul), Turkey, 7 September 1909; moved with family to New York, 1913. *Education* Mayfair School; New Rochelle High School, New York; Williams College, Massachusetts, B.A. 1930;

Yale Drama School, 1930-32. **Family** *Married 1) Molly Day Thatcher, 1932 (died 1963), two sons, two daughters; 2) actress Barbara Loden, 1967 (died 1980), one son; 3) Frances Rudge, 1982.* **Career** *Actor, property manager, then director, Group Theatre, New York, from 1933; stage director, including plays by Tennessee Williams and Arthur Miller, 1935 through 1960s; co-founder, with Cheryl Crawford, Actors' Studio, New York, 1948; appeared voluntarily before HUAC, admitting membership of Communist Party, 1934-36, and naming fellow members, 1952; began career as novelist, 1961; left Actors' Studio to direct newly-formed Lincoln Center Repertory Company, 1962-64.* **Awards** *Many awards for theatre work; Academy Award for Best Director, and Best Direction Award, New York Film Critics, for* Gentleman's Agreement, *1947; International Prize, Venice Festival, for* Panic in the Streets, *1950; Special Jury Prize, Venice Festival, for* A Streetcar Named Desire, *1951; Oscar for Best Director, and Most Outstanding Directorial Achievement, Directors Guild of America, for* On the Waterfront, *1954; Honorary doctorates from Wesleyan University, Carnegie Institute of Technology, and Williams College.* **Address** *c/o 432 W. 44th St., New York, New York 10036, U.S.A.*

Films as Director: 1937: *The People of the Cumberlands* (+sc) (short). **1941:** *It's Up to You.* **1945:** *A Tree Grows in Brooklyn.* **1947:** *The Sea of Grass; Boomerang; Gentleman's Agreement.* **1949:** *Pinky.* **1950:** *Panic in the Streets.* **1952:** *A Streetcar Named Desire; Viva Zapata!, Man on a Tightrope.* **1954:** *On the Waterfront.* **1955:** *East of Eden* (+pr). **1956:** *Baby Doll* (+pr, co-sc). **1957:** *A Face in the Crowd* (+pr). **1960:** *Wild River* (+pr). **1961:** *Splendour in the Grass* (+pr). **1964:** *America, America* (+sc, pr). **1969:** *The Arrangement* (+pr, sc). **1972:** *The Visitors.* **1976:** *The Last Tycoon.* **1978:** *Acts of Love* (+pr). **1982:** *The Anatolian* (+pr). **1989:** *Beyond the Aegean.*

Other Films: 1934: *Pie in the Sky* (Steiner) (short) (role). **1940:** *City for Conquest* (Litvak) (role as Googie, a gangster). **1941:** *Blues in the Night* (Litvak) (role as a clarinetist).

Elia Kazan (right) directing *On the Waterfront.*

Elia Kazan's career has spanned more than four decades of enormous change in the American film industry. Often he has been a catalyst for these changes. He became a director in Hollywood at a time when studios were interested in producing the kind of serious, mature, and socially conscious stories Kazan had been putting on the stage since his Group Theatre days. During the late 1940s and mid-1950s, initially under the influence of Italian neorealism and then the pressure of American television, he was a leading force in developing the aesthetic possibilities of location shooting (*Boomerang, Panic in the Streets, On the Waterfront*) and CinemaScope (*East of Eden, Wild River*). At the height of his success, Kazan formed his own production unit and moved back east to become a pioneer in the new era of independent, "personal" filmmaking that emerged during the 1960s and contributed to revolutionary upheavals within the old Hollywood system. As an archetypal *auteur,* he progressed from working on routine assignments to developing more personal themes, producing his own pictures, and ultimately directing his own scripts. At his peak during a period (1950-65) of anxiety, gimmickry, and entropy in Hollywood, Kazan remained among the few American directors who continued to believe in the cinema as a medium for artistic expression and who brought forth films that consistently reflected his own creative vision.

Despite these achievements and his considerable influence on a younger generation of New York-based filmmakers, including Sidney Lumet, John Cassavetes, Arthur Penn, Martin Scorsese, and even Woody Allen, Kazan's critical reputation in America has ebbed. The turning point both for Kazan's own work and the critics' reception of it was almost certainly his decision to become a friendly witness before the House Un-American Activities Committee in 1952. While "naming names" cost Kazan the respect of many liberal friends and colleagues (Arthur Miller most prominent among them), it ironically ushered in the decade of his most inspired filmmaking. If Abraham Polonsky, himself blacklisted during the 1950s, is right in claiming that Kazan's post-HUAC movies have been "marked by bad conscience," perhaps he overlooks how that very quality of uncertainty may be what makes films like *On the Waterfront, East of Eden,* and *America America* so much more compelling than Kazan's previous studio work.

His apprenticeship in the Group Theater and his great success as a Broadway director had a natural influence on Kazan's films, particularly reflected in his respect for the written script, his careful blocking of scenes, and, pre-eminently, his employment of Method Acting on the screen. While with the Group, which he has described as "the best thing professionally that ever happened to me," Kazan acquired from its leaders, Harold Clurman and Lee Strasberg, a fundamentally artistic attitude toward his work. Studying Marx led him to see art as an instrument of social change, and from Stanislavski he learned to seek a play's "spine" and emphasize the characters' psychological motivation. Although he developed a lyrical quality that informs many later films, Kazan generally employs the social realist mode he learned from the Group. Thus, he prefers location shooting over studio sets, relatively unfamiliar actors over stars, long shots and long takes over editing, and naturalistic forms over genre conventions. *On the Waterfront* and *Wild River,* though radically different in style, both reflect the Group's quest, in Kazan's words, "to get poetry out of the common things of life." And while one may debate the ultimate ideology of *Gentleman's Agreement, Pinky, Viva Zapata!* and *The Visitors,* one may still agree with the premise they all share, that art should illuminate society's problems and the possibility of their solution.

Above all else, however, it is Kazan's skill in directing actors that has secured his place in the history of American cinema. Twenty-one of his performers have been nominated for

Academy Awards; nine have won. He was instrumental in launching the film careers of Marlon Brando, Julie Harris, James Dean, Carroll Baker, Warren Beatty, and Lee Remick. Moreover, he elicited from such undervalued Hollywood players as Dorothy McGuire, James Dunn, Eva Marie Saint, and Natalie Wood perhaps the best performances of their careers. For all the long decline in critical appreciation, Kazan's reputation among actors has hardly wavered. The Method, which became so identified with Kazan's and Lee Strasberg's teaching at the Actors Studio, was once simplistically defined by Kazan himself as "turning psychology into behavior." An obvious example from *Boomerang* would be the suspect Waldron's gesture of covering his mouth whenever he lies to the authorities. But when Terry first chats with Edie in the park in *On the Waterfront,* unconsciously putting on one of the white gloves she has dropped as he sits in a swing, such behavior becomes not merely psychological but symbolic and poetic. Here Method acting transcends Kazan's own mundane definition.

His films have been most consistently concerned with the theme of power, expressed as either the restless yearning of the alienated or the uneasy arrangements of the strong. The struggle for power is generally manifested through wealth, sexuality, or, most often, violence. Perhaps because every Kazan film except *A Tree Grows in Brooklyn* and *The Last Tycoon* (excluding a one-punch knockout of the drunken protagonist) contains at least one violent scene, some critics have complained about the director's "horrid vulgarity" (Lindsay Anderson) and "unremitting stridency" (Robin Wood), yet even his most "overheated" work contains striking examples of restrained yet resonant interludes: the rooftop scenes of Terry and his pigeons in *On the Waterfront,* the tentative reunion of Bud and Deanie at the end of *Splendor in the Grass,* the sequence in which Stavros tells his betrothed not to trust him in *America, America.* Each of these scenes could be regarded not simply as a necessary lull in the drama, but as a privileged, lyrical moment in which the ambivalence underlying Kazan's attitude toward his most pervasive themes seems to crystallize. Only then can one fully realize how Terry in the rooftop scene is both confined by the *mise-en-scène* (seen within the pigeon coop) and free on the roof to be himself; how Bud and Deanie are simultaneously reconciled and estranged; how Stavros becomes honest only when he confesses to how deeply he has been compromised.—LLOYD MICHAELS

Keaton, Buster

Nationality *American.* **Born** *Joseph Francis Keaton in Piqua, Kansas, 4 October 1895.* **Military Service** *Served in U.S. Army, France, 1918.* **Family** *Married 1) Natalie Talmadge, 1921 (divorced 1932), two sons; 2) Mae Scribbens, 1933 (divorced 1935); 3) Eleanor Norris, 1940.* **Career** *Part of parents' vaudeville act, The Three Keatons, from 1898; when family act broke up, became actor for Comique Film Corp., moved to California, 1917; appeared in 15 two-reelers for Comique, 1917-19; offered own production company with Metro Pictures by Joseph Schenk, 1919, produced 19 two-reelers, 1920-23; directed ten features, 1923-28; dissolved production company, signed to MGM, 1928; announced retirement from the screen, 1933; starred in 16 comedies for Educational Pictures, 1934-39; worked intermittently as gag writer for MGM, 1937-50; appeared in 10 two-reelers for Columbia, 1939-41; appeared on TV and in commercials,* *from 1949; Cinémathèque Française Keaton retrospective, 1962.* **Died** *Of lung cancer, in Woodland Hills, California, 1 February 1966.*

Films as Director and Actor: 1920: *One Week* (co-d, co-sc with Eddie Cline); *Convict Thirteen* (co-d, co-sc with Cline); *The Scarecrow* (co-d, co-sc with Cline). **1921:** *Neighbors* (co-d, co-sc with Cline); *The Haunted House* (co-d, co-sc with Cline); *Hard Luck* (co-d, co-sc with Cline) *The High Sign* (co-d, co-sc with Cline); *The Goat* (co-d, co-sc with Mal St. Clair); *The Playhouse* (co-d, co-sc with Cline); *The Boat* (co-d, co-sc with Cline). **1922:** *The Paleface* (co-d, co-sc with Cline); *Cops* (co-d, co-sc with Cline); *My Wife's Relations* (co-d, co-sc with Cline); *The Blacksmith* (co-d, co-sc with Mal St. Clair); *The Frozen North* (co-d, co-sc with Cline); *Day Dreams* (co-d, co-sc with Cline); *The Electric House* (co-d, co-sc with Cline). **1923:** *The Balloonatic* (co-d, co-sc with Cline); *The Love Nest* (co-d, co-sc with Cline); *The Three Ages; Our Hospitality* (co-d). **1924:** *Sherlock Jr.* (co-d); *The Navigator* (co-d). **1925:** *Seven Chances; Go West* (+story). **1926:** *Battling Butler; The General* (co-d, co-sc). **1927:** *College* (no d credit). **1928:** *Steamboat Bill, Jr.* (no d credit); *The Cameraman* (no d credit, pr). **1929:** *Spite Marriage* (no d credit). **1938:** *Life in Sometown, U.S.A.; Hollywood Handicap; Streamlined Swing.*

Other Films: 1917: *The Butcher Boy* (Fatty Arbuckle comedy) (role as village pest); *A Reckless Romeo* (Arbuckle) (role as a rival); *The Rough House* (Arbuckle) (role); *His Wedding Night* (Arbuckle) (role); *Oh, Doctor!* (Arbuckle) (role); *Fatty at Coney Island* (Coney Island) (Arbuckle) (role as husband touring Coney Island with his wife); *A Country Hero* (Arbuckle) (role). **1918:** *Out West* (Arbuckle) (role as a dude gambler); *The Bell Boy* (Arbuckle) (role as a village pest); *Moonshine* (Arbuckle) (role as an assistant revenue agent); *Good Night, Nurse!* (Arbuckle) (role as the doctor and a visitor); *The Cook* (Arbuckle) (role as the waiter and helper). **1919:** *Back Stage* (Arbuckle) (role as a stagehand); *The Hayseed* (Arbuckle) (role as a helper). **1920:** *The Garage* (Arbuckle) (role as a garage mechanic); *The Round Up* (role as an Indian); *The Saphead* (role as Bertie "the Lamb" Van Alstyne). **1922:** *Screen Snapshots, No. 3* (role). **1929:** *The Hollywood Revue* (role as an Oriental dancer). **1930:** *Free & Easy* (*Easy Go*) (role as Elmer Butts); *Doughboys* (pr, role as Elmer Stuyvesant). **1931:** *Parlor, Bedroom & Bath* (pr, role as Reginald Irving); *Sidewalks of New York* (pr, role as Tine Harmon). **1932:** *The Passionate Plumber* (pr, role as Elmer Tuttle); *Speak Easily* (role as Professor Timoleon Zanders Post). **1933:** *What! No Beer!* (role as Elmer J. Butts). **1934:** *The Gold Ghost* (role as Wally); *Allez Oop* (role as Elmer); *Le Roi des Champs Elysees* (role as Buster Garnier and Jim le Balafre). **1935:** *The Invader* (*The Intruder*) (role as Leander Proudfoot); *Palookah from Paducah* (role as Jim); *One Run Elmer* (role as Elmer); *Hayseed Romance* (role as Elmer); *Tars & Stripes* (role as Elmer); *The E-Flat Man* (role as Elmer); *The Timid Young Man* (role as Elmer). **1936:** *Three On a Limb* (role as Elmer); *Grand Slam Opera* (role as Elmer); *La Fiesta de Santa Barbara* (role as one of several stars); *Blue Blazes* (role as Elmer); *The Chemist* (role as Elmer); *Mixed Magic* (role as Elmer). **1937:** *Jail Bait* (role as Elmer); *Ditto* (role as Elmer); *Love Nest on Wheels* (last apearance as Elmer). **1939:** *The Jones Family in Hollywood* (co-sc): *The Jones Family in Quick Millions* (co-sc); *Pest from the West* (role as a traveler in Mexico); *Mooching through Georgia* (role as a Civil War veteran); *Hollywood Cavalcade* (role).

1940: *Nothing but Pleasure* (role as a vacationer); *Pardon My Berth Marks* (role as a reporter); *The Taming of the Snood* (role as an innocent accomplice); *The Spook Speaks* (role as a magician's housekeeper); *The Villain Still Pursued Her* (role); *Li'l Abner* (role as Lonesome Polecat); *His Ex Marks the Spot* (role). **1941:** *So You Won't Squawk* (role); *She's Oil Mine* (role); *General Nuisance* (role). **1943:** *Forever and a Day* (role as a plumber). **1944:** *San Diego, I Love You* (role as a bus driver). **1945:** *That's the Spirit* (role as L.M.); *That Night with You* (role). **1946:** *God's Country* (role); *El Moderno Barba azul* (role as a prisoner of Mexicans who is sent to moon). **1949:** *The Loveable Cheat* (role as a suitor); *In the Good Old Summertime* (role as Hickey); *You're My Everything* (role as butler). **1950:** *Un Duel a mort* (role as a comic duellist); *Sunset Boulevard* (Wilder) (role as a bridge player). **1952:** *Limelight* (Chaplin) (role as the piano accompanist in a music hall sketch); *L'incantevole nemica* (role in a brief sketch); *Paradise for Buster* (role). **1955:** *The Misadventures of Buster Keaton* (role). **1956:** *Around the World in Eighty Days* (role as a train conductor). **1960:** *When Comedy was King* (role in a clip from *Cops*); *The Adventures of Huckleberry Finn* (Curtiz) (role as a lion tamer). **1963:** *Thirty Years of Fun* (appearance in clips); *The Triumph of Lester Snapwell* (role as Lester); *It's a Mad, Mad, Mad, Mad World* (Kramer) (role as Jimmy the Crook). **1964:** *Pajama Party* (role as an Indian chief). **1965:** *Beach Blanket Bingo* (role as a would-be surfer); *Film* (role as Object/Eye); *How to Stuff a Wild Bikini* (role as Bwana); *Sergeant Deadhead* (Taurog) (role as Private Blinken); *The Rail-rodder* (role); *Buster Keaton Rides*

Again (role). **1966:** *The Scribe* (role); *A Funny Thing Happened on the Way to the Forum* (Lester) (role as Erronius). **1967:** *Due Marines e un Generale* (*War, Italian Style*) (role as the German general). **1970:** *The Great Stone Face* (role).

Buster Keaton is the only creator-star of American silent comedies who equals Chaplin as one of the artistic giants of the cinema. He is perhaps the only silent clown whose reputation is far higher today than it was in the 1920s, when he made his greatest films. Like Chaplin, Keaton came from a theatrical family and served his apprenticeship on stage in the family's vaudeville act. Unlike Chaplin, however, Keaton's childhood and family life were less troubled, more serene, lacking the darkness of Chaplin's youth that would lead to the later darkness of his films. Keaton's films were more blithely athletic and optimistic, more committed to audacious physical stunts and cinema tricks, far less interested in exploring moral paradoxes and emotional resonances. Keaton's most famous comic trademark, his "great stone face," itself reflects the commitment to a comedy of the surface, but attached to that face was one of the most resiliently able and acrobatic bodies in the history of cinema. Keaton's comedy was based on the conflict between that imperviously dead-pan face, his tiny but almost superhuman physical instrument, and the immensity of the physical universe that surrounded them.

After an apprenticeship in the late 1910s making two-reel comedies that starred his friend Fatty Arbuckle, and after service in France in 1918, Keaton starred in a series of his own two-reel comedies beginning in 1920. Those films displayed Keaton's comic and visual inventiveness: the delight in bizarrely complicated mechanical gadgets (*The Scarecrow, The Haunted House*); the realization that the cinema itself was an intriguing mechanical toy (his use of split-screen in *The Playhouse* of 1921 allows Buster to play all members of the orchestra and audience, as well as all nine members of a minstrel troupe); the games with framing and composition (*The Balloonatic* is a comic disquisition on the surprises one can generate merely by entering, falling out of, or suppressing information in the frame); the breathtaking physical stunts and chases (*Daydreams, Cops*); and the underlying fatalism when his exuberant efforts produce ultimately disastrous results (*Cops, One Week, The Boat*).

In 1923 Keaton's producer, Joseph M. Schenck, decided to launch the comic star in a series of feature films, to replace a previously slated series of features starring Schenck's other comic star, the now scandal-ruined Fatty Arbuckle. Between 1923 and 1929, Keaton made an even dozen feature films on a regular schedule of two a year—always leaving Keaton free in the early autumn to travel east for the World Series. This regular pattern of Keaton's work—as opposed to Chaplin's lengthy laboring and devoted concentration on each individual project—reveals the way Keaton saw his film work. He was not making artistic masterpieces but knocking out everyday entertainment, like the vaudevillian playing the

Buster Keaton

two-a-day. Despite the casualness of this regular routine (which would be echoed decades later by Woody Allen's regular one-a-year rhythm), many of those dozen silent features are comic masterpieces, ranking alongside the best of Chaplin's comic work.

Most of those films begin with a parodic premise—the desire to parody some serious and familiar form of stage or screen melodrama, such as the Civil War romance (*The General*), the mountain feud (*Our Hospitality*), the Sherlock Holmes detective story (*Sherlock, Jr.*), the Mississippi riverboat race (*Steamboat Bill, Jr.*), or the western (*Go West*). Two of the features were built around athletics (boxing in *Battling Butler* and every sport but football in *College*), and one was built around the business of motion picture photography itself (*The Cameraman*). The narrative lines of these films were thin but fast-paced, usually based on the Keaton character's desire to satisfy the demands of his highly conventional lady love. The film's narrative primarily served to allow the film to build to its extended comic sequences, which, in Keaton's films, continue to amaze with their cinematic ingenuity, their dazzling physical stunts, and their hypnotic visual rhythms. Those sequences usually forced the tiny but dexterous Keaton into combat with immense and elemental antagonists—a rockslide in *Seven Chances*; an entire ocean liner in *The Navigator*; a herd of cattle in *Go West*; a waterfall in *Our Hospitality*. Perhaps the cleverest and most astonishing of his elemental foes appears in *Sherlock, Jr.* when the enemy becomes cinema itself—or, rather, cinematic time and space. Buster, a dreaming movie projectionist, becomes imprisoned in the film he is projecting, subject to its inexplicable laws of montage, of shifting spaces and times, as opposed to the expected continuity of space and time in the natural universe. Perhaps Keaton's most satisfyingly whole film is *The General*, virtually an extended chase from start to finish, as the Keaton character chases north, in pursuit of his stolen locomotive, then races back south with it, fleeing his Union pursuers. The film combines comic narrative, the rhythms of the chase, Keaton's physical stunts, and his fondness for mechanical gadgets into what may be the greatest comic epic of the cinema.

Unlike Chaplin, Keaton's stardom and comic brilliance did not survive Hollywood's conversion to synchronized sound. It was not simply a case of a voice's failing to suit the demands of both physical comedy and the microphone. Keaton's personal life was in shreds, after a bitter divorce from Natalie Talmadge. Always a heavy social drinker, Keaton's drinking increased in direct proportion to his personal troubles. Neither a comic spirit nor an acrobatic physical instrument could survive so much alcoholic abuse. In addition, Keaton's contract had been sold by Joseph Schenck to MGM (conveniently controlled by his brother, Nicholas Schenck, head of Loew's Inc., MGM's parent company). Between 1929 and 1933, MGM assigned Keaton to a series of dreary situation comedies—in many of them as Jimmy Durante's co-star and straight man. For the next two decades, Keaton survived on cheap two-reel sound comedies and occasional public appearances, until his major role in Chaplin's *Limelight* led to a comeback. Keaton remarried, went on the wagon, and made stage, television, and film appearances in featured roles. In 1965 he played the embodiment of existential consciousness in Samuel Beckett's only film work, *Film*, followed shortly by his final screen appearance in Richard Lester's *A Funny Thing Happened on the Way to the Forum.*—GERALD MAST

Kieślowski, Krzysztof

Nationality Polish. *Born* Warsaw, 27 June 1941. *Education* School of Cinema and Theatre, Lodz, graduated 1969. *Career* Worked as director of documentaries and fiction *films for TV, from 1969; directed first feature for cinema,* Blizna, *1976; vice-president of the Union of Polish Cinematographers, 1978-81; member of faculty of Radio and Television, University of Silesia, 1979-82; made* Dekalog, *series of short films for Polish TV, 1988-89, then gained financing to make longer versions of two episodes for cinematic release.* **Awards** *First Prize, Mannheim Festival, for* Personel, *1975; FIPRESCI Prize, Moscow Festival, for* Amator, *1979; Diploma from the Polish Ministry of Foreign Affairs, 1979; Special Jury Prize, Cannes Film Festival, and Academy Award for Best Foreign Feature Film, for* A Short Film about Killing, *1988.* **Died** *Of a heart attack, 13 March 1996.*

Films as Director: (Documentary shorts, unless otherwise stated) **1967:** *Urząd* (*The Job*). **1968:** *Zdjęcie* (*The Photograph*) (for TV). **1969:** *Z miasta Łodzi* (*From the City of Lodz*). **1970:** *Byłem żołnierzem* (*I Was a Soldier*); *Przed rajdem* (*Before the Rally*); *Fabryka* (*Factory*). **1972:** *Gospordaze* (*Workers*) (co-d); *Miedzy Wrocławiem a Zieloną Górą* (*Between Wroclaw and Zielona Gora*); *Podstawy BHP w kopalni miedzi* (*The Degree of Hygiene and Safety in a Copper Mine*); *Robotnicy 71 nic o nas bez nas* (*Workers 71*) (co-d); *Refren* (*Refrain*). **1973:** *Murarz* (*Bricklayer*); *Dziecko* (*Child*); *Pierwsza miłość* (*First Love*) (for TV); *Prześwietlenie* (*X-Ray*); *Przajście podziemne* (*Pedestrian Subway*) (feature for TV). **1975:** *Życiorys* (*Life Story*); *Personel* (*Personnel*) (feature for TV). **1976:** *Klaps* (*Slate*); *Szpital* (*Hospital*); *Spokój* (*Stillness*) (feature for TV); *Blizna* (*The Scar*) (feature). **1977:** *Nie wiem* (*I Don't Know*); *Z punktu widzenia nocnego portiera* (*Night Porter's Point of View*). **1978:** *Siedem kobiet w różnym wieku* (*Seven Women of Various Ages*). **1979:** *Amator* (*Camera Buff*) (feature). **1980:** *Dworzec* (*The Station*); *Gadajace głowy* (*Talking Heads*). **1981:** *Krótki dzień pracy* (*A Short Working Day*) (feature for TV); *Przypadek* (*Blind Chance*) (feature, released 1987). **1984:** *Bez końca* (*No End*) (feature). **1988:** *Krótki film o zabijaniu* (*A Short Film about Killing*) (feature); *Krótki film o miłości* (*A Short Film about Love*) (feature). **1989:** *Dekalog* (*Decalogue*) (10 episodes for TV). **1990:** *City Life* (*Episode in Netherlands*) (feature). **1991:** *Podwójne życie Weroniky* (*La Double vie de Véronique; The Double Life of Véronique*) (feature) (+sc). **1993:** *Trois couleurs Bleu* (*Three Colours: Blue*) (feature)

Krzysztof Kieślowski

(+sc); *Trois couleurs Blanc* (*Three Colours: White*) (feature) (+sc); *Trois couleurs Rouge* (*Three Colours: Red*) (feature) (+sc).

In the late 1970s, when the conflict between the State and the citizens of Poland was imminent, a new trend emerged in cinematography—the "cinema of moral unrest." All the films in this trend have one common denominator: an unusually cutting critical view of the state of the society and its morals, human relationships in the work process, public and private life. It is more than logical that Krzysztof Kieślowski would have belonged to this trend; he had long been concerned with the moral problems of the society, and paid attention to them throughout his film career with increasing urgency. The direction of his artistic course was anticipated by his graduation film *From the City of Lodz,* in which he sketched the problems of workers, and by his participation in the stormy protest meeting of young filmmakers in Cracow in 1971, who warned against a total devaluation of basic human values.

A broad scale of problems can be found in the documentary films Kieślowski made between shooting feature films: disintegration of the economic structure, criticism of executive work, and the relationship of institutions and individuals. These documentaries are not a mere recording of events, phenomena, or a description of people and their behaviour, but always attempt instead to look underneath the surface. The director often used non-traditional means. Sometimes the word dominates the image, or he may have borrowed the stylistics of slapstick or satire, or he interfered with the reality in front of the camera by a staged element. Kieślowski did not emphasize the aesthetic function of the image, but stressed its real and literal meaning.

His feature films have a similar orientation: he concentrated on the explication of an individual's situation in the society and politics, on the outer and inner bonds of man with the objectively existing world, and on the search for connections between the individual and the general. He often placed his heroes in situations where they have to make a vital decision (in his TV films *The Staff* and *The Calm,* and in his films for theatrical release).

The Amateur is the synthesis of his attitudes and artistic search of the 1970s, and is also one of the most significant films of the "cinema of moral unrest." In the story of a man who buys a camera to follow the growth of a newborn daughter, and who gradually, thanks to this film instrument, begins to realize his responsibility for what is happening around him, the director placed a profound importance on the role of the artist in the world, on his morality, courage, and active approach to life. Here Kieślowski surpassed, to a large extent, the formulaic restrictions of the "cinema of moral unrest" resulting from the outside-the-art essence of this trend. These restrictions are also eliminated in his following films. In *The Accident* (made in 1981, released in 1987) he extended his exploration of man and his actions by introducing the category of the accidental. The hero experiences the same events (Poland in 1981) three times, and therefore is given three destinies, but each time on a different side. Two destinies are more or less given by accident, the third one he chooses himself, but even this choice is affected by the accidental element. The transcendental factor appears in *No End* (a dead man intervenes in worldly events), but the film is not an exploration of supernatural phenomena so much as a ruthless revelation of the tragic period after the declaration of the state of emergency in December 1981, and a demonstration of the professed truth that private life cannot be lived in isolation from the public sphere.

In the 1980s Kieślowski's work culminated in a TV cycle and two films with subjects from the Ten Commandments. *A Short Film about Killing* is based on the fifth commandment (Thou shalt not kill), while *A Short Film about Love* comes from the sixth. Both films and the TV cycle are anchored in the present and express the necessity of a moral revival, both of the individual and the society, in a world which may be determined by accidentality, but which does not deliver us from the right and duty of moral choice.

After the fall of communism when, as a consequence of changes in economic conditions, the production of films experienced a sharp fall in all of Eastern Europe, some Polish directors sought a solution to the ensuing crisis in work for foreign studios and in co-productions. This was the road taken by Kieślowski, and so all his films made in the 1990s were created with the participation of French producers: *The Double Life of Véronique* and the trilogy *Three Colours: Blue, Three Colours: White, Three Colours: Red*—loosely linked to the noble motto of the French Revolution: liberty, equality, fraternity. In these films Kieślowski followed up on his films from the 1980s, in which his heroes struggle with the duality of reason and feelings, haphazardness and necessity, reality and mystery. Even in these films made abroad we can also trace certain irony and sarcasm which first appeared in his films made in the 1970s in Poland.—BLAŽENA URGOŠÍKOVÁ

Korda, Alexander

Nationality *Hungarian/British.* **Born** *Sándor László Kellner in Puszta Turpósztó, Hungary, 16 September 1893; adopted surname Korda, from journalistic pseudonym "Sursum Corda" (meaning "lift up your hearts"), 1910.* **Education** *Attended schools in Kisújszállás, Mezötúr, and Budapest, until 1909.* **Family** *Married 1) Maria Farkas (actress Maria Corda), 1919 (divorced 1930), one son; 2) Merle Oberon, 1939 (divorced 1945); 3) Alexander Boycun, 1953.* **Career** *Worked at Pathé studios, Paris, 1911; title writer and secretary, Pictograph films, Budapest, and founder of film journal* Pesti mozi, *1912; directed first film, 1914; formed Corvin production company with Miklós Pásztory, built studio near Budapest, 1917; arrested under Horthy regime, fled to Vienna, 1919; formed Corda Film Consortium, 1920 (dissolved 1922); formed Korda-Films, Berlin, 1923; with wife, contracted to First National, Hollywood, 1927; hired by Paramount French subsidiary, 1930; moved to British Paramount, London, 1931; founder, London Films, 1932; built Denham Studios, also made partner in United Artists, 1935 (sold interest, 1944); lost control of Denham Studios, 1938; formed Alexander Korda Productions, retained position as head of London Films, 1939; based in Hollywood, 1940-43; entered partnership with MGM, 1943 (dissolved, 1946); reorganized London Films, bought controlling interest in British Lion (distributors), 1946; founder, British Film Academy (now British Academy of Film and Television Arts), 1947.* **Award** *Knighthood, 1942.* **Died** *In London, 23 January 1956.*

Films as Director: 1914: *A becsapott újságíró* (*The Duped Journalist*) (co-d); *Tutyu és Totyo* (*Tutyu and Totyo*) (co-d)**1915:** *Lyon Lea* (*Lea Lyon*) (co-d); *A tiszti kardbojt* (*The Officer's Swordknot*) (+sc). **1916:** *Fehér éjszakák* (*White Nights*) or *Fedora* (+sc); *A nagymama* (*The Grandmother*) (+sc); *Mesék az írógépről* (*Tales of the Typewriter*) (+sc); *A kétszívű férfi* (*The Man with Two Hearts*); *Az egymillió fontos bankó* (*The One Million Pound Note*) (+sc); *Ciklámen* (*Cyclamen*); *Vergödő szívek* (*Struggling Hearts*); *A nevető Szaszkia* (*The Laughing Saskia*); *Mágnás Miska* (*Miska the Magnate*). **1917:** *Szent Péter esernyője* (*St. Peter's Umbrella*) (+pr); *A gólyakalifa* (*The Stork Caliph*) (+pr); *Mágia* (*Magic*) (+pr);

Harrison és Barrison (Harrison and Barrison) (+pr). **1918:** *Faun* (+pr); *Az aranyember (The Man with the Golden Touch)* (+pr); *Mary Ann* (+pr). **1919:** *Ave Caesar!* (+pr); *Fehér rózsa (White Rose)* (+pr); *Yamata* (+pr); *Se ki, se be (Neither In Nor Out)* (+pr); *A 111-es (Number 111)* (+pr). **1920:** *Seine Majestät das Bettelkind (Prinz und Bettelknabe, The Prince and the Pauper)*. **1922:** *Heeren der Meere (Masters of the Sea)*; *Eine Versunkene Welt (Die Tragödie eines Verschollenen Fürstensohnes) (A Vanished World)*; *Samson und Delilah (Samson and Delilah)* (+pr). **1923:** *Das unbekannte Morgen (The Unknown Tomorrow)* (+pr). **1924:** *Jedermanns Frau (Jedermanns Weib) (Everybody's Woman)* (+pr); *Tragödie im Hause Habsburg (Das Drama von Mayerling) (Tragedy in the House of Hapsburg)* (+pr). **1925:** *Der Tänzer meiner Frau (Dancing Mad)*. **1926:** *Madame wünscht keine Kinder (Madame Wants No Children)*. **1927:** *Eine Dubarry von heute (A Modern Dubarry)*; *The Stolen Bride; The Private Life of Helen of Troy*. **1928:** *Yellow Lily; Night Watch*. **1929:** *Love and the Devil; The Squall; Her Private Life*. **1930:** *Lilies of the Field; Women Everywhere; The Princess and the Plumber*. **1931:** *Die Manner um Lucie* (+pr); *Rive Gauche* (French version of *Die Manner um Lucie*) (+pr); *Marius; Zum Goldenen Anker* (German version of *Marius*). **1932:** *Service for Ladies (Reserved for Ladies)* (+pr). **1933:** *Wedding Rehearsal* (+pr); *The Private Life of Henry VIII* (+pr); *The Girl from Maxim's* (+co-pr). **1934:** *La Dame de Chez Maxim* (French version) (+pr); *The Private Life of Don Juan* (+pr). **1936:** *Rembrandt* (+pr). **1941:** *That Hamilton Woman (Lady Hamilton)* (+pr). **1945:** *Perfect Strangers (Vacation from Marriage)* (+pr). **1947:** *An Ideal Husband* (+pr).

Alexander Korda may be Britain's most controversial film figure, but there is no doubt that his name stands everywhere for the most splendid vision of cinema as it could be, if one had money and power. Both of these Korda had, although several times he was close to bankruptcy, living on pure Hungarian charm and know-how. He at least had a dream that came near reality on several occasions.

Korda had two younger brothers, Zoltan, who worked with him as a director, and Vincent, who was an art director; both were outstanding in their fields. Alexander worked as a journalist and film magazine editor before he directed his first film in Hungary in 1914. He had labored long in the cinematic fields of Vienna and Berlin when finally in 1926 his film production of *A Modern Dubarry* earned him a contract in Hollywood with First National, where his initial film was the extravagantly beautiful *The Private Life of Helen of Troy,* starring his wife Maria Corda as Helen. It brought him instant recognition. He directed four features starring Billie Dove (who should have played Helen of Troy for him): *The Stolen Bride, The Night Watch, The Yellow Lily,* and *Her Private Life,* a remake of Zoë Akins's play, which Corinne Griffith had filmed earlier under its stage title, *Declassé.* Korda also directed a sound feature starring Griffith, *Lilies of the Field.* Alexander Korda could soon write his own ticket.

He did just that in 1931, leaving Hollywood to return to England where he set up his own production company, London Film Productions. There he was almost fully occu-

Alexander Korda

pied with production details, and only directed eight of the many films which his company produced. It was an exciting era for an ambitious producer like Korda. His company's product was so lavish that he seemed in a fair way not only to rival Hollywood but to surpass it. His first big success was *The Private Life of Henry VIII,* starring Charles Laughton as Henry and with Merle Oberon making her debut as the unfortunate Anne Boleyn. Korda then married Oberon and started to set the stage for her stardom. Hers was not the only career Korda established, for he had much to do with the film careers of Laurence Olivier, Vivian Leigh, Robert Donat, and Leslie Howard, among others. He was the power behind it all who set up financial deals for pictures that starred these actors.

While the pictures he directed, like *Rembrandt, That Hamilton Woman,* and *Vacation from Marriage,* were done in exquisite taste, Korda was also involved in the production of such pictures as *Catherine the Great, The Scarlet Pimpernel, Elephant Boy, The Ghost Goes West, Drums, The Four Feathers, The Thief of Bagdad, The Fallen Idol,* and *The Third Man.*

Three times Korda built and rebuilt his company, and the third time it was with national aid. Even after the Korda empire collapsed he was able to secure new financial alliances which allowed him to keep producing until his death in 1956. His name stood for glory, and when, after 1947, his name ceased to appear as part of the film credits, the lustre surrounding a London Films production vanished.—DeWITT BODEEN

Kubrick, Stanley

Nationality American. *Born* New York, 26 July 1928. *Education* Attended New York City public schools; attended evening classes at City College of the City University of New York, 1945. *Family* Married 1) Toba Metz, 1947 (divorced, 1952); 2) dancer Ruth Sobotka, 1952 (divorced), one daughter; 3) actress Suzanne Christiane Harlan, 1958, two daughters. *Career* Apprentice photographer, Look magazine, New York, 1946; made first film, 1950; formed Harris-Kubrick Productions with James Harris, 1955 (dissolved 1962); worked on One-Eyed Jacks with Marlon Brando, 1958; planned film on Napoléon, 1969; moved to England, 1974. *Awards* Best Direction, New York Film Critics Award, and Best Written American Comedy (screenplay) Award (with Peter George and Terry Southern), Writers Guild of America, for Dr. Strangelove, 1964; Oscar for Special Visual Effects, for 2001, 1968; Best Direction, New York Film Critics, for A Clockwork Orange, 1971; Best Direction, British Academy Award, for Barry Lyndon, 1975; Luchino Visconti Award, 1988. *Address* P.O. Box 123, Borehamwood, Hertfordshire, England.

Films as Director: 1952: *Day of the Fight* (doc) (+pr, sc, ph, ed); *Flying Padre* (doc) (+sc, ph). **1953:** *The Seafarers* (+ph); *Fear and Desire* (+pr, co-sc, ph, ed). **1955:** *Killer's Kiss* (+co-pr, co-sc, ph, ed). **1956:** *The Killing* (+co-pr, sc). **1957:** *Paths of Glory* (+co-pr, co-sc). **1960:** *Spartacus.* **1962:** *Lolita.* **1964:** *Dr. Strangelove: Or, How I Learned to Stop Worrying and Love the Bomb* (+pr, co-sc). **1968:** *2001: A Space Odyssey* (+pr, co-sc, special effects designer). **1971:** *A Clockwork Orange* (+pr, sc). **1975:** *Barry Lyndon* (+pr, sc). **1980:** *The Shining* (+pr, co-sc). **1987:** *Full Metal Jacket* (+pr, co-sc). **1998:** *Eyes Wide Shut* (+pr, co-sc).

Few American directors have been able to work within the studio system of the American film industry with the independence that Stanley Kubrick has achieved. By steadily building a reputation as a filmmaker of international importance, he has gained full artistic control over his

Stanley Kubrick

films, guiding the production of each of them from the earliest stages of planning and scripting through post-production. Kubrick has been able to capitalize on the wide artistic freedom that the major studios have accorded him because he learned the business of filmmaking from the ground up.

In the early 1950s Kubrick turned out two documentary shorts for RKO; he was then able to secure financing for two low-budget features which he says today were "crucial in helping me to learn my craft," but which he would otherwise prefer to forget. He made both films almost singlehandedly, doing his own camerawork, sound, and editing, besides directing the films.

Then, in 1955, he met James Harris, an aspiring producer; together they made *The Killing,* about a group of small-time crooks who rob a race track. *The Killing* not only turned a modest profit but prompted the now-legendary remark of *Time* magazine that Kubrick "has shown more imagination with dialogue and camera than Hollywood has seen since the obstreperous Orson Welles went riding out of town."

Kubrick next acquired the rights to Humphrey Cobb's 1935 novel *The Paths of Glory,* and in 1957 turned it into one of the most uncompromising antiwar films ever made. Peter Cowie is cited in *Major Film Directors of the American and British Cinema* as saying that Kubrick uses his camera in the film "unflinchingly, like a weapon," as it sweeps across the slopes to record the wholesale slaughter of a division.

Spartacus, a spectacle about slavery in pre-Christian Rome, Kubrick recalls as "the only film over which I did not have absolute control," because the star, Kirk Douglas, was also the movie's producer. Although *Spartacus* turned out to be one of the better spear-and-sandal epics, Kubrick vowed never to make another film unless he was assured of total artistic freedom, and he never has.

Lolita, about a middle-aged man's obsessive infatuation with his pre-teen step-daughter, was the director's first comedy. "The surprising thing about *Lolita,*" Pauline Kael wrote in *For Keeps,* "is how enjoyable it is. It's the first new American comedy since those great days in the 1940s when Preston Sturges re-created comedy with verbal slapstick. *Lolita* is black slapstick and at times it's so far out that you gasp as you laugh."

For those who appreciate the dark humor of *Lolita,* it is not hard to see that it was just a short step from that film to Kubrick's masterpiece in that genre, *Dr. Strangelove: Or How I Learned to Stop Worrying and Love the Bomb,* concerning a lunatic American general's decision to launch an attack inside Russia. The theme implicit in the film is man's final capitulation to his own machines of destruction. Kubrick further examined his dark vision of man in a mechanistic age in *2001: A Space Odyssey.*

Kubrick's view of life, as it is reflected in *2001,* seems to be somewhat more optimistic than it was in his previous pictures. *2001* holds out hope for the progress of mankind through man's creative encounters with the universe. In *A Clockwork Orange,* however, the future appears to be less promising than it did in *2001;* in the earlier film Kubrick showed (in the "person" of the talking computer, Hal) the machine becoming human, whereas in *A Clockwork Orange* he shows man becoming a machine through brainwashing and thought control.

Ultimately, however, the latter film only reiterates in somewhat darker terms a repeated theme in all of Kubrick's previous work: man must retain his humanity if he is to survive in a dehumanized, highly mechanized world. Moreover, *A Clockwork Orange* echoes the warning of *Dr. Strangelove* and *2001* that man must strive to gain mastery over himself if he is to master the machines of his own invention.

After a trio of films set in the future, Kubrick reached back into the past and adapted Thackeray's historical novel *Barry Lyndon* to the screen in 1975. Kubrick has portrayed Barry, an eighteenth-century rogue, and his times in the same critical fashion as Thackeray did before him. The film echoes a theme which appears in much of the director's best work, that through human error the best-laid plans often go awry; and hence man is often thwarted in his efforts to achieve his goals. The central character in *Lolita* fails to possess a nymphet exclusively; the "balance of terror" between nations designed to halt the nuclear arms race in *Dr. Strangelove* does not succeed in averting global destruction; and modern technology turns against its human instigators in *Dr. Strangelove, 2001,* and *A Clockwork Orange.* In this list of films about human failure the story of *Barry Lyndon* easily finds a place, for its hero's lifelong schemes to become a rich nobleman in the end come to nothing. And the same can be said for the frustrated writing aspirations of the emotionally disturbed hero of Kubrick's provocative "thinking man's thriller," *The Shining,* derived from the horror novel by Stephen King.

It is clear, therefore, that Kubrick can make any source material fit comfortably into the fabric of his work as a whole, whether it be a remote and almost forgotten Thackeray novel, or a disturbing story about the Vietnam war by a contemporary writer, as with *Full Metal Jacket,* based on the book by Gustav Hasford. Furthermore, it is equally evident that Kubrick wants to continue to create films that will stimulate his audience to think about serious human problems, as his pictures have done from the beginning. Because of the success of his movies in the past, Kubrick can go on making films in the way he wants to, proving in the future, as he has in the past, that he values the artistic freedom which he has worked so hard to win and he has used so well.—GENE D. PHILLIPS

Kurosawa, Akira

Nationality Japanese. *Born* Tokyo, 23 March 1910. *Education* Kuroda Primary School, Edogawa; Keika High School; studied at Doshusha School of Western Painting, 1927. *Family* Married Yoko Yaguchi, 1945, one son (producer Hisao Kurosawa), one daughter. *Career* Painter, illustrator, and member, Japan Proletariat Artists' Group, from late 1920s; assistant director, P.C.L. Studios (Photo-Chemical Laboratory, later Toho Motion

Akira Kurosawa

Picture Co.), studying in Kajiro Yamamoto's production group, from 1936; also scriptwriter, from late 1930s; directed first film, Sugata Sanshiro, *1943; began association with actor Toshiro Mifune on* Yoidore tenshi, *and founder, with Yamamoto and others, Motion Picture Artists Association (Eiga Gei jutsuka Kyokai), 1948; formed Kurosawa Productions, 1959; signed contract with producer Joseph E. Levine to work in United States, 1966 (engaged in several aborted projects through 1968); with directors Keisuke Kinoshita, Kon Ichikawa, and Masaki Kobayashi, formed Yonki no Kai production company, 1971.*

Awards *Oscar for Best Foreign Language Film, and Grand Prix, Venice Festival, for* Rashomon, *1951; Golden Bear Award for Best Direction and International Critics Prize, Berlin Festival, for* The Hidden Fortress, *1959; Oscar for Best Foreign Language Film, for* Dersu Uzala, *1976; European Film Academy Award, for "humanistic contribution to society in film production," 1978; Best Director, British Academy Award, and Palme d'Or, Cannes Festival, for* Kagemusha, *1980; Order of Culture of Japan, 1985; British Film Institute Fellowship, 1986; Honorary Academy Award, 1989.*

Films as Director: 1943: *Sugata Sanshiro* (*Sanshiro Sugata, Judo Saga*) (remade as same title by Shigeo Tanaka, 1955, and by Seiichiro Uchikawa, 1965, and edited by Kurosawa) (+sc). **1944:** *Ichiban utsukushiku* (*The Most Beautiful*) (+sc). **1945:** *Zoku Sugata Sanshiro* (*Sanshiro Sugata—Part 2; Judo Saga—II*) (+sc); *Tora no o o fumu otokotachi* (*Men Who Tread on the Tiger's Tail*) (+sc). **1946:** *Asu o tsukuru hitobito* (*Those Who Make Tomorrow*); *Waga seishun ni kuinashi* (*No Regrets for Our Youth*) (+co-sc). **1947:** *Subarashiki nichiyobi* (*One Wonderful Sunday*) (+co-sc). **1948:** *Yoidore tenshi* (*Drunken Angel*) (+co-sc). **1949:** *Shizukanaru ketto* (*A Silent Duel*) (+co-sc); *Nora inu* (*Stray Dog*) (+co-sc). **1950:** *Shubun* (*Scandal*) (+co-sc); *Rashomon* (+co-sc). **1951:** *Hakuchi* (*The Idiot*) (+co-sc). **1952:** *Ikiru* (*To Live, Doomed*) (+co-sc). **1954:** *Shichinin no samurai* (*Seven Samurai*) (+co-sc). **1955:** *Ikimono no kiroku* (*Record of a Living Being; I Live in Fear; What the Birds Knew*) (+co-sc). **1957:** *Kumonosu-jo* (*The Throne of Blood; The Castle of the Spider's Web*) (+co-sc, co-pr); *Donzoko* (*The Lower Depths*) (+co-sc, co-pr). **1958:** *Kakushi toride no san-akunin* (*The Hidden Fortress; Three Bad Men in a Hidden Fortress*) (+co-sc, co-pr). **1960:** *Warui yatsu hodo yoku nemuru* (*The Worse You Are the Better You Sleep; The Rose in the Mud*) (+co-sc, co-pr); *Yojimbo* (*The Bodyguard*) (+co-sc). **1962:** *Sanjuro* (+co-sc). **1963:** *Tengoku to jigoku* (*High and Low; Heaven and Hell; The Ransom*) (+co-sc). **1965:** *Akahige* (*Red Beard*) (+co-sc). **1970:** *Dodesukaden* (*Dodeskaden*) (+co-sc, co-pr). **1975:** *Dersu Uzala* (+co-sc). **1980:** *Kagemusha* (*The Shadow Warrior*) (+co-sc, co-pr). **1985:** *Ran* (+sc). **1990:** *Dreams* (*Akira Kurosawa's Dreams*) (+sc). **1991:** *Hachigatsu No Kyohshikyoku* (*Rhapsody in August*) (+sc). **1993:** *Madadayo* (+sc, ed).

Other Films: 1937: *Sengoku gunto den* (*Sage of the Vagabond*) (sc, asst dir). **1941:** *Uma* (*Horses*) (Yamamoto) (co-sc). **1942:** *Seishun no kiryu* (*Currents of Youth*) (Fushimizi) (sc); *Tsubasa no gaika* (*A Triumph of Wings*) (Yamamoto) (sc). **1944:** *Dohyo-matsuri* (*Wrestling-Ring Festival*) (Marune) (sc). **1945:** *Appare Isshin Tasuke* (*Bravo, Tasuke Isshin!*) (Saeki) (sc). **1947:** *Ginrei no hate* (*To the End of the Silver Mountains*) (Taniguchi) (co-sc); *Hatsukoi* (*First Love*) segment of *Yottsu no koi no monogatari* (*Four Love Stories*) (Toyoda) (sc). **1948:** *Shozo* (*The Portrait*) (Kinoshita) (sc). **1949:** *Yakoman to Tetsu* (*Yakoman and Tetsu*) (Taniguchi) (sc); *Jigoku no kifujin* (*The Lady from Hell*) (Oda) (sc). **1950:** *Akatsuki no dasso* (*Escape at Dawn*) (Taniguchi) (sc); *Jiruba no Tetsu* (*Tetsu 'Jilba'*) (Kosugi) (sc); *Tateshi danpei* (*Fencing Master*) (Makino) (sc). **1951:** *Ai to nikushimi no kanata e* (*Beyond Love and Hate*) (Taniguchi) (sc); *Kedamono no yado* (*The Den of Beasts*) (Osone) (sc); *Ketto Kagiya no tsuji* (*The Duel at Kagiya Corner*) (Mori) (sc). **1957:** *Tekichu odan sanbyakuri* (*Three Hundred Miles through Enemy Lines*) (Mori) (sc). **1960:** *Sengoku guntoden* (*The Saga of the Vagabond*) (Sugie) (sc).

Unquestionably Japan's best-known film director, Akira Kurosawa introduced his country's cinema to the world with his 1951 Venice Festival Grand Prize winner, *Rashomon*. His international reputation has broadened over the years with numerous citations, and when 20th

Century-Fox distributed his 1980 Cannes Grand Prize winner, *Kagemusha,* it was the first time a Japanese film achieved worldwide circulation through a major Hollywood studio.

At the time *Rashomon* took the world by surprise, Kurosawa was already a well-established director in his own country. He had received his six-year assistant director's training at the Toho Studios under the redoubtable Kajiro Yamamoto, director of both low-budget comedies and vast war epics such as *The War at Sea from Hawaii to Malaya.* Yamamoto described Kurosawa as more than fully prepared to direct when he first grasped the megaphone for his own screenplay, *Sanshiro Sugata,* in 1943. This film, based on a best-selling novel about the founding of judo, launched lead actor Susumu Fujita as a star and director Kurosawa as a powerful new force in the film world.

Despite numerous battles with wartime censors, Kurosawa managed to get production approval for three more of his scripts before the Pacific War ended in 1945. By this time he was fully established with his studio and his audience as a writer-director. His films were so successful commercially that he would, until late in his career, receive a free creative hand from his producers, ever-increasing budgets, and extended schedules. In addition, he was never subjected to a project that was not of his own initiation and his own writing.

In the pro-documentary, female emancipation atmosphere that reigned briefly under the Allied Occupation of Japan, Kurosawa created his strongest woman protagonist and produced his most explicit pro-left message in *No Regrets for Our Youth.* But internal political struggles at Toho left bitterness and creative disarray in the wake of a series of strikes. As a result, Kurosawa's 1947 *One Wonderful Sunday* is perhaps his weakest film, an innocuous and sentimental story of a young couple who are too poor to get married.

The mature Kurosawa appears in the 1948 *Drunken Angel.* Here he displays not only a full command of black-and-white filmmaking technique with his characteristic variety of pacing, lighting, and camera angles for maximum editorial effect, but his first use of sound-image counterpoints in the "Cuckoo Waltz" scene, where lively music contrasts with the dying gangster's dark mood. Here too is the full-blown appearance of the typical Kurosawan master-disciple relationship first suggested in *Sanshiro Sugata,* as well as an overriding humanitarian message despite the story's tragic outcome. The master-disciple roles assume great depth in Takashi Shimura's portrayal of the blustery alcoholic doctor and Toshiro Mifune's characteriza-tion of the vain, hotheaded young gangster. The film's tension is generated by Shimura's questionable worthiness as a mentor and Mifune's violent unwillingness as a pupil. These two actors would recreate similar testy relationships in numerous Kurosawa films from the late 1940s through the mid-1950s, including the noir police drama *Stray Dog,* the doctor dilemma film *Quiet Duel,* and the all-time classic *Seven Samurai.* In the 1960s Yuzo Kayama would assume the disciple role to Mifune's master in the feudal comedy *Sanjuro* and in *Red Beard,* a work about humanity's struggle to modernize.

Kurosawa's films of the 1990s have been minor asterisks to the career of this formidable, legendary director. *Dreams (Akira Kurosawa's Dreams)* is a disappointingly uneven recreation of eight of the director's dreams; *Hachigatsu No Kyohshikyoku (Rhapsody in August)* is a slight account of the recollection of a grandmother who remembers the bombing of Nagasaki.

These films are linked to *Madadayo,* Kurosawa's most recent film to date, in that all are deeply personal and reflective. *Madadayo,* released when Kurosawa was 83 years old, is an account of 17 years in the retirement of a beloved teacher who is respected by the generations of his former students. As he ages into a "genuine old man," he remains as feisty and vigorous as ever; his favorite phrase is the film's title, the English translation of which is "not yet." But he is as equally vulnerable to the ravages of time and life's losses, as illustrated by his grieving upon the disappearance of his pet cat. *Madadayo* is a flawed film, if only because one-too-many sequences ramble. While it most decidedly is the work of an old man, it and his other latter-period work do not negate the vitality of Kurosawa's many all-time classics.

Part of Kurosawa's characteristic technique throughout his career has involved the typical Japanese studio practice of using the same crew or "group" on each production. He consistently worked with cinematographer Asakazu Nakai and composer Fumio Hayasaka, for example. Kurosawa's group became a kind of family that extended to actors as well. Mifune and Shimura were the most prominent names of the virtual private repertory company that, through lifetime studio contracts, could survive protracted months of production on a Kurosawa film and fill in with more normal four-to-eight-week shoots in between. Kurosawa was thus assured of getting the performance he wanted every time.

Kurosawa's own studio contract and consistent box-office record enabled him to exercise creativity never permitted lesser talents in Japan. He was responsible for numerous technical innovations as a result. He pioneered the use of long lenses and multiple cameras in the famous final battle scenes in the driving rain and splashing mud of *Seven Samurai*. He introduced the first use of widescreen in Japan in the 1958 samurai entertainment classic *Hidden Fortress*. To the dismay of leftist critics and the delight of audiences, he invented realistic portrayals of swordfighting and other violence in such extravagant confrontations as those of *Yojimbo,* which spawned the entire Clint Eastwood spaghetti western genre in Italy. Kurosawa further experimented with long lenses on the set in *Red Beard,* and accomplished breathtaking work with his first color film *Dodeskaden,* now no longer restorable. A firm believer in the importance of motion picture science, Kurosawa pioneered the use of Panavision and multi-track Dolby sound in Japan with *Kagemusha.* His only reactionary practice is his editing, which he does entirely himself on an antique Moviola, better and faster than anyone else in the world.

Western critics have most often chastised Kurosawa for using symphonic music in his films. His reply to this is to point out that he and his entire generation grew up on music that was more Western in quality than native Japanese. As a result, native Japanese music can sound artificially exotic to a contemporary audience. Nevertheless, he has succeeded in his films in adapting not only boleros and elements of Beethoven, but snatches of Japanese popular songs and musical instrumentation from Noh theater and folk song.

Perhaps most startling of Kurosawa's achievements in a Japanese context, however, have been his innate grasp of a story-telling technique that is not culture bound, and his flair for adapting Western classical literature to the screen. No other Japanese director would have dared to set Dostoevski's *Idiot,* Gorki's *Lower Depths,* or Shakespeare's *Macbeth (Throne of Blood)* and *King Lear (Ran)* in Japan. But he also adapted works from the Japanese Kabuki theater (*Men Who Tread on the Tiger's Tail*) and used Noh staging techniques and music in both *Throne of Blood* and *Kagemusha.* Like his counterparts and most admired models, Jean Renoir, John Ford, and Kenji Mizoguchi, Kurosawa has taken his cinematic inspirations from the full store of world film, literature, and music. And yet the completely original screenplays of his two greatest films, *Ikiru,* the story of a bureaucrat dying of cancer who at last finds purpose in life, and *Seven Samurai,* the saga of seven hungry warriors who pit their wits and lives against marauding bandits in the defense of a poor farming village, reveal that his natural storytelling ability and humanistic convictions transcend all limitations of genre, period, and nationality.—AUDIE BOCK and ROB EDELMAN

Kusturica, Emir

*Nationality Yugoslavian (Bosnia-Herzegovina). **Born** Sarajevo, Yugoslavia, 24 November 1955. **Education** Studied film direction at FAMU (Prague Film School) in Czechoslovakia. **Career** Produced amateur films while attending secondary school; moved to Czechoslovakia to study film, 1973; directed* Guernica, *his diploma film, 1978; directed two television films and played guitar in a rock band, late 1970s; directed first feature,* Do You Remember Dolly Bell?, *1981; earned international acclaim with* When Father Was Away on Business, *1985; came to the United States and began teaching a film directing course at Columbia University, 1988. **Awards** Golden Lion, Venice Festival, 1981, for* Do You Remember Dolly Bell?; *Palme d'Or and co-winner, International Critics Prize, Cannes Festival, and Oscar nomination, Best Foreign Language Film, 1985, for* When Father Was Away on Business; *Best Director, Cannes Festival, and Roberto Rossellini Career Achievement Award, 1988, for* Time of the Gypsies; *Palme d'Or, Cannes Festival, 1995, for* Underground. ***Agent** CAA, 9830 Wilshire Blvd., Beverly Hills, California 90212.*

Films as Director: 1978: *Guernica; Nevjeste dolaze (The Brides Are Coming)* (for TV). **1980:** *Bife Titanic (The Titanic Bar)* (for TV) (+sc). **1981:** *Sjecas li se Dolly Bell? (Do You Remember Dolly Bell?).* **1985:** *Otac na sluzbenob putu (When Father Was Away on Business).* **1988:** *Dom za vesanje (Time of the Gypsies)* (+co-sc). **1993:** *Arizona Dream.* **1995:** *Underground* (+co-sc, role). **1997:** *Chat noir, chat blanc.*

Other Film: 1987: *Strategija svrake (The Magpie Strategy)* (sc); *Zivot Radina* (sc).

Emir Kusturica's films are concerned with a universal humanism. While they come out of a specific part of the world—in which the political situation plays no small role in affecting his characters' lives—they are timeless stories in that they deal with basic human needs, wants, desires, feelings, and experiences.

Do You Remember Dolly Bell?, Kusturica's first feature, is an insightful, bittersweet comedy about Dino (Slavko Stimac), an adolescent who goes about losing his virginity and experiencing first love. There may be political and social implications within the story: Dino's father is a Muslim-Marxist who fervently believes in a communist utopia despite the fact that he and his family reside in one crowded room; and the scenario is rife with jabs at Communist Party bureaucracy. During the course of the story Dino's father dies, which symbolically mirrors Kusturica's conviction that the failure of communism to improve peoples' lives is irrevocable. Still, the film mainly is a coming-of-age comedy not dissimilar to scores of other cinematic rite-of-passage chronicles. Undoubtedly, its gently ironic style was influenced by Kusturica's having attended the Prague Film School, where he studied with Jiri Menzel.

Kusturica was to emerge as a force on the international film scene with his next feature, *When Father Was Away on Business,* which won him a Cannes Film Festival Palme d'Or. It is the fresh, winning account of what happens when a philandering, indiscreet Yugoslavian man, Mesha Malkoc (Miki Manojlovic), is sent into exile for three years, with the scenario unravelling through the eyes and perceptions of Malik (Moreno D'E Bartolli), his six-year-old son. Politics and history impact on the story, which is set in the early 1950s after Marshal Tito, Yugoslavia's ruler, had split with Stalin. This resulted in the country's expulsion from the Soviet Socialist Bloc. In Yugoslavia, individual loyalties were harshly divided between Tito and Stalin, leading to mass denunciations and betrayals which often had nothing to do with political leanings. Such is the case with the father in *When Father Was Away on Business.* The spitefulness of one of Mesha's girlfriends, along with that of his brother-in-law, results in his arrest during a family party. But all Malik knows is that his father has been whisked away from the family, and his mother is left to struggle along as a seamstress in order to feed and clothe her children.

The scenario eventually takes Malik and his family to the salt mine where Mesha is being held. The camp is filled with prisoners who, like Mesha, have been incarcerated for reasons having nothing to do with political ideology. There, Malik also comes of age, but in an altogether different manner than depicted in *Do You Remember Dolly Bell?* Primarily, his maturation results from his interaction with an incurably ill young girl. *When Father Was Away on Business* is a major work, one of the finest films of the 1980s.

Emir Kusturica.
Photograph by Stephane Fefer.

Kusturica's next feature, *Time of the Gypsies,* is another coming-of-age story as well as a flavorful account of gypsy life. It tells of an innocent young boy (Davor Dujmovic) who wishes to make a better life for himself, but finds he can only accomplish this by becoming involved in a criminal lifestyle. In telling his story, Kusturica offers a bitter condemnation of a society's exploitation of children. *Arizona Dream,* Kusturica's first American film, was a major disappointment. It features Johnny Depp as a recently orphaned young man who returns to his Arizona hometown for the wedding of his uncle (Jerry Lewis). The movie only received a limited theatrical distribution in the United States.

The civil war that has bitterly divided his homeland was bound to influence Kusturica's work. In 1995 he won a second Cannes Palme d'Or for *Underground,* a French-German-Hungarian-produced allegorical epic of Yugoslavia between 1941 and 1992. As he charts the camaraderie and conflict between two Belgrade men, Marko and Blacky, Kusturica bitterly censures both the postwar communist domination of his homeland and the bloody present-day civil war in which, in his view, all sides are culpable.—ROB EDELMAN

FILM DIRECTORS *1*

La Cava, Gregory

Nationality *American.* **Born** *Towanda, Pennsylvania, 10 March 1892.* **Education** *Educated in Rochester, New York; Art Institute of Chicago; Art Students League and National Academy of Design, New York.* **Family** *Married (second time) Grace Carland, 1941, one son.* **Career** *Cartoonist for American Press Association, New York, then head of animated cartoon unit, Hearst Enterprises, 1917; worked on* Mutt and Jeff *series, then* Torchy *stories for Johnny Hines, from 1921; director, from 1922, then writer and director for Paramount, from 1924 (moved to Hollywood 1929); director for First National, 1929, then Pathé, 1930; signed with 20th Century Pictures, 1933, then freelance, from 1934; hired by Mary Pickford company to direct* One Touch of Venus, *then left set after dispute, 1948.* **Award** *New York Film Critics Circle Award, for* Stage Door, *1937.* **Died** *In 1952.*

Films as Director: (partial list) 1917: *Der Kaptain Discovers the North Pole* ("Katzenjammer Kids" series) (co-d) (animated short). **1919:** *How Could William Tell?* ("Jerry on the Job" series) (animated short). **1920:** *Smokey Smokes (and) Lampoons* ("Judge Rummy Cartoons" series) (animated short); *Judge Rummy in Bear Facts* (animated short); *Kats Is Kats* ("Krazy Kat Cartoon") (animated short). **1922:** *His Nibs* (5 reels); *Faint Heart* (2 reels); *A Social Error* (2 reels). **1923:** *The Four Orphans* (2 reels); *The Life of Reilly* (2 reels); *The Busybody* (2 reels); *The Pill Pounder* (2 reels); *So This Is Hamlet?* (2 reels); *Helpful Hogan* (2 reels); *Wild and Wicked* (2 reels); *Beware of the Dog* (2 reels); *The Fiddling Fool* (2 reels). **1924:** *The New School Teacher* (+co-sc); *Restless Wives.* **1925:** *Womanhandled.* **1926:** *Let's Get Married; So's Your Old Man; Say It Again.* **1927:** *Paradise for Two* (+pr); *Running Wild; Tell It to Sweeney* (+pr); *The Gay Defender* (+pr). **1928:** *Feel My Pulse* (+pr); *Half a Bride.* **1929:** *Saturday's Children; Big News.* **1930:** *His First Command* (+co-sc). **1931:** *Laugh and Get Rich* (+sc, co-dialogue); *Smart Woman.* **1932:** *Symphony of Six Million; Age of Consent; The Half Naked Truth* (+co-sc). **1933:** *Gabriel over the White House; Bed of Roses* (+co-dialogue); *Gallant Lady.* **1934:** *Affairs of Cellini; What Every Woman Knows* (+pr). **1935:** *Private Worlds* (+co-sc); *She Married Her Boss.* **1936:** *My Man Godfrey* (+pr, co-sc). **1937:** *Stage Door.* **1939:** *Fifth Avenue Girl* (+pr). **1940:** *Primrose Path* (+pr, co-sc). **1941:** *Unfinished Business* (+pr). **1942:** *Lady in a Jam* (+pr). **1947:** *Living in a Big Way* (+story, co-sc).

Although many of his individual films are periodically reviewed and reassessed by film scholars, Gregory La Cava remains today a relatively under-appreciated director of some of the best "screwball comedies" of the 1930s. Perhaps his apparent inability to transcend the screwball form or his failure with a number of straight dramas contributed to this lack of critical recognition. Yet, at his best, he imposed a vitality and sparkle on his screen comedies that overcame their often weak scripts and some occasionally pedestrian performances from his actors.

The great majority of La Cava's films reflect an instinctive comic sense undoubtedly gained during his early years as a newspaper cartoonist and as an animator with Walter Lantz on such fast and furious cartoons as those in "The Katzenjammer Kids" and "Mutt and Jeff" series. La Cava subsequently became one of the few directors capable of transferring many of these techniques of animated comedy to films involving real actors. His ability to slam a visual gag home quickly sustained such comedies as W.C. Fields's *So's Your Old Man* and *Running Wild*. Yet his real forte emerged in the sound period when the swiftly paced sight gags were replaced by equally quick verbal repartee.

La Cava's "screwball comedies" of the 1930s were characterized by improbable plots and brilliantly foolish dialogue but also by a dichotomous social view that seemed to delight in establishing satirical contrasts between the views of themselves held by the rich and by the poor. Although treated in varying degrees in *Fifth Avenue Girl, She Married Her Boss,* and *Stage Door,* La Cava's classic treatment of this subject remains *My Man Godfrey*. Made during the depths of the Depression, it juxtaposes the world of the rich and frivolous with the plight of the real victims of the economic disaster through the sharply satiric device of a scavenger hunt. When one of the hunt's objectives turns out to be "a forgotten man," in this case a hobo named Godfrey Parke

Gregory La Cava with Irene Dunne on the set of *Unfinished Business*. Photograph by Roman Freulich.

(William Powell), it provides a platform for one of the Depression's victims to lash out at the upper class as being composed of frivolous "nitwits." The film seemingly pulls its punches at the end, however, when one socialite, Irene Bullock (Carole Lombard), achieves some realization of the plight of the less fortunate, and the hobo Godfrey turns out to be a formerly wealthy Harvard man who actually renews his fortune through his association with her, although he has been somewhat tempered by his experience with the hoboes.

La Cava, perhaps more than other directors working in the screwball genre, was able, by virtue of doing much of the writing on his scripts, to impose his philosophical imprint upon the majority of his films. While he was often required to keep a foot in both the conservative and the liberal camps, his films do not suffer. On the contrary, they maintain an objectivity that has allowed them to grow in stature with the passage of years. *My Man Godfrey, Stage Door,* and *Gabriel over the White House,* which is only now being recognized as a political fantasy of great merit, give overwhelming evidence that critical recognition of Gregory La Cava is considerably overdue.—STEPHEN L. HANSON

Lang, Fritz

Nationality German/American. *Born* Vienna, 5 December 1890, became U.S. citizen, 1935. *Education* Studied engineering at the Technische Hochschule, Vienna. *Family* Married (second time) writer Thea von Harbou, 1924 (separated 1933). *Career* Cartoonist, fashion designer, and painter in Paris, 1913; returned to Vienna, served in army, 1914-16; after discharge, worked as scriptwriter and actor, then moved to Berlin, 1918; reader and story editor for Decla, then wrote and directed first film, Halbblut, 1919; worked with von Harbou, from 1920; visited Hollywood, 1924; Das Testament des Dr. Mabuse banned by Nazis, 1933; offered post as supervisor of Nazi film productions by Goebbels, but fled Germany; after working in Paris and London, went to Hollywood, 1934; signed with Paramount, 1940; co-founder, then president, Diana Productions, 1945; quit Hollywood, citing continuing disputes with producers, 1956; directed two films in India, 1958-59, before last film, directed in Germany, 1960. *Award* Officier d'Art et des Lettres, France. *Died* In Beverly Hills, 2 August 1976.

Films as Director: 1919: *Halbblut* (*Half Caste*) (+sc); *Der Herr der Liebe* (*The Master of Love*) (+role); *Hara-Kiri; Die Spinnen* (*The Spiders*) Part I: *Der Goldene See* (*The Golden Lake*) (+sc). **1920:** *Die Spinnen* (*The Spiders*) Part II: *Das Brillantenschiff* (*The Diamond Ship*) (+sc); *Das Wandernde Bild* (*The Wandering Image*) (+co-sc); *Kämpfende Herzen* (*Die Vier um die Frau; Four around a Woman*) (+co-sc). **1921:** *Der müde Tod: Ein Deutsches Volkslied in Sechs Versen* (*The Weary Death; Between Two Worlds; Beyond the Wall; Destiny*) (+co-sc). **1921/22:** *Dr. Mabuse, der Spieler* (*Dr. Mabuse, the Gambler; The Fatal Passions*) in two parts: *Ein Bild der Zeit* (*Spieler aus Leidenschaft; A Picture of the Time*) and *Inferno—Menschen der Zeit* (*Inferno des Verbrechens; Inferno—Men of the Time*) (+co-sc). **1924:** *Die Nibelungen* in two parts: *Siegfrieds Tod* (*Death of Siegfried*) and *Kriemhilds Rache* (*Kriemhild's Revenge*) (+co-sc, uncredited). **1927:** *Metropolis* (+co-sc, uncredited). **1928:** *Spione* (*Spies*) (+pr, co-sc, uncredited). **1929:** *Die Frau im Mond* (*By Rocket to the Moon; The Girl in the Moon*) (+pr, co-sc, uncredited). **1931:** *M, Mörder unter Uns* (*M*) (+co-sc, uncredited). **1933:** *Das Testament des Dr. Mabuse* (*The Testament of Dr. Mabuse; The Last Will of Dr. Mabuse*) (+co-sc, uncredited) (German and French versions). **1934:** *Liliom* (+co-sc, uncredited). **1936:** *Fury* (+co-sc). **1937:** *You Only Live Once.* **1938:** *You and Me* (+pr). **1940:** *The Return of Frank James.* **1941:** *Western Union; Man Hunt; Confirm or Deny* (co-d, uncredited). **1942:** *Moontide* (co-d, uncredited). **1943:** *Hangmen Also*

Fritz Lang (center) directing *Human Desire*.

Die! (+pr, co-sc). **1944:** *Ministry of Fear; The Woman in the Window.* **1945:** *Scarlet Street* (+pr). **1946:** *Cloak and Dagger.* **1948:** *Secret Beyond the Door* (+co-pr). **1950:** *House by the River; An American Guerrilla in the Philippines.* **1952:** *Rancho Notorious; Clash by Night.* **1953:** *The Blue Gardenia; The Big Heat.* **1954:** *Human Desire.* **1955:** *Moonfleet.* **1956:** *While the City Sleeps; Beyond a Reasonable Doubt.* **1959:** *Der Tiger von Eschnapur* (*The Tiger of Bengal*) and *Das Indische Grabmal* (*The Hindu Tomb*) (+co-sc) (released in cut version as *Journey to the Lost City*). **1960:** *Die Tausend Augen des Dr. Mabuse* (*The Thousand Eyes of Dr. Mabuse*) (+pr, co-sc).

Other Films: 1917: *Die Hochzeit im Ekzentrik Klub* (*The Wedding in the Eccentric Club*) (May) (sc); *Hilde Warren und der Tod* (*Hilde Warren and Death*) (May) (sc, four roles); *Joe Debbs* (series) (sc). **1918:** *Die Rache ist mein* (*Revenge Is Mine*) (Neub) (sc); *Herrin der Welt* (*Men of the World*) (May) (asst d); *Bettler GmbH* (sc). **1919:** *Wolkenbau und Flimmerstern* (*Castles in the Sky and Rhinestones*) (d unknown, co-sc); *Totentanz* (*Dance of Death*) (Rippert) (sc); *Die Pest in Florenz* (*Plague in Florence*) (Rippert) (sc); *Die Frau mit den Orchiden* (*The Woman with the Orchid*) (Rippert) (sc); *Lilith und Ly* (sc). **1921:** *Das Indische Grabmal* (in 2 parts: *Die Sendung des Yoghi* and *Der Tiger von Eschnapur*) (co-sc). **1963:** *Le Mépris* (*Contempt*) (Godard) (role as himself).

Fritz Lang's career can be divided conveniently into three parts: the first German period, 1919-33, from *Halbblut* to the second Mabuse film, *Das Testament des Dr. Mabuse*; the American period, 1936-56, from *Fury* to *Beyond a Reasonable Doubt*; and the second German period, 1959-60, which includes the two films made in India and his last film, *Die tausend Augen des Dr. Mabuse.*

Lang's apprentice years as a scriptwriter and director were spent in the studios in Berlin where he adopted certain elements of expressionism and was imbued with the artistic seriousness with which the Germans went about making their films. In Hollywood this seriousness would earn Lang a reputation for unnecessary perfectionism, a criticism also thrown at fellow émigrés von Stroheim and von Sternberg. Except for several films for Twentieth Century-Fox, Lang never worked long for a single studio in the United States, and he often preferred to work on underbudgeted projects which he could produce, and therefore control, himself. The rather radical dissimilarities between the two studio worlds within which Lang spent most of his creative years not surprisingly resulted in products which look quite different from one another, and it is the difference in look or image which has produced the critical confusion most often associated with an assessment of Lang's films.

One critical approach to Lang's work, most recently articulated by Gavin Lambert, argues that Lang produced very little of artistic interest after he left Germany; the *Cahiers du cinéma* auteurists argue the opposite, namely that Lang's films made in America are superior to his European films because the former were clogged with self-conscious artistry and romantic didacticism which the leanness of his American studio work eliminated. A third approach, suggested by Robin Wood and others, examines Lang's films as a whole, avoiding the German-American division by looking at characteristic thematic and visual motifs. Lang's films can be discussed as exhibiting certain distinguishing features—economy, functional precision, detachment—and as containing basic motifs such as the trap, a suppressed underworld, the revenge motive, and the abuse of power. Investigating the films from this perspective reveals a more consistent development of Lang as a creative artist and helps to minimize the superficial anomalies shaped by his career.

In spite of the narrowness of examining only half of a filmmaker's creative output, the sheer number of Lang's German movies which have received substantial critical attention as "classic" films has tended to submerge the critical attempt at breadth and comprehensiveness. Not only did these earlier films form an important intellectual center for the German film industry during the years between the wars, as Siegfried Kracauer later pointed out, but they had a wide international impact as well and were extensively reviewed in the Anglo-American press. Lang's reputation preceded him to America, and although it had little effect ultimately on his working relationship, such as it was, with the Hollywood moguls, it has affected Lang's subsequent treatment by film critics.

If Lang is a "flawed genius," as one critic has described him, it is less a wonder that he is "flawed" than that his genius had a chance to develop at all. The working conditions Lang survived after his defection would have daunted a less dedicated director. Lang, however, not only survived but flourished, producing films of undisputed quality: the four war movies, *Man Hunt, Hangmen Also Die!, Ministry of Fear,* and *Cloak and Dagger,* and the urban crime films of the 1950s, *Clash by Night, The Blue Gardenia, The Big Heat, Human Desire,* and *While the City Sleeps.*

These American films reflect a more mature director, tighter mise-en-scène, and more control as a result of Lang's American experience. The films also reveal continuity. As Robin Wood has written, the formal symmetry of his individual films is mirrored in the symmetry of his career, beginning and ending in Germany. All through his life, Lang adjusted his talent to meet the changes in his environment, and in so doing produced a body of creative work of unquestionable importance in the development of the history of cinema.—CHARLES L.P. SILET

Lattuada, Alberto

Nationality *Italian.* **Born** *Milan, 13 November 1914.* **Education** *Studied architecture.* **Family** *Married Carla Del Poggio, 1945 (divorced).* **Career** *Co-founder of avant-garde journal* Camminare, *1933; helped found* Corrente; *with Mario Ferreri and Luigi Comencini, founder of Cineteca Italiana, Italian film archive, 1940; directed first film, 1942; opera director, from 1970.* **Address** *Via N. Paganini, 7 Rome, Italy.*

Films as Director and Co-Scriptwriter: 1942: *Giacomo l'idealista.* **1945:** *La freccia nel fianco; La nostra guerra* (documentary). **1946:** *Il bandito.* **1947:** *Il delitto di Giovanni Episcopo (Flesh Will Surrender).* **1948:** *Senza pietà (Without Pity).* **1949:** *Il mulino del Po (The Mill on the Po).* **1950:** *Luci del varietà (Variety Lights)* (co-d, co-pr). **1952:** *Anna; Il cappotto (The Overcoat).* **1953:** *La lupa (The She-Wolf);* "Gli italiani si voltano" episode of *Amore in città (Love in the City).* **1954:** *La spiaggia (The Beach); Scuola elementare.* **1956:** *Guendalina.* **1958:** *La tempesta (Tempest).* **1960:** *I dolci inganni; Lettere di una novizia (Rita).* **1961:** *L'imprevisto.* **1962:** *Mafioso; La steppa.* **1965:** *La mandragola (The Love Root).* **1966:** *Matchless.* **1967:** *Don Giovanni in Sicilia* (+co-pr). **1968:** *Fräulein Doktor.* **1969:** *L'amica.* **1970:** *Venga a prendere il caffe . . . da noi (Come Have Coffee With Us).* **1971:** *Bianco, rosso e . . . (White Sister).* **1973:** *Sono stato io.* **1974:** *Le farò da padre . . . (Bambina).* **1976:** *Cuore di cane; Bruciati da cocente passione (Oh Serafina!).* **1978:** *Così come sei.* **1980:** *La cicala.* **1983:** *Cristoforo Colombo (Christopher Columbus).* **1987:** *Una spina nel cuore* (+sc). **1988:** *Fratelli.*

Other Films: 1935: *Il museo dell'amore* (asst d). **1936:** *La danza delle lancette* (collaborator on experimental short). **1941:** *Piccolo mondo antico* (Soldati) (asst d). **1942:** *Si signora* (asst d, co-sc). **1958:** *Un eroe dei nostri tempi* (Monicelli) (role). **1994:** *Il toro* (Colombani) (role).

One of the most consistently commercially successful directors in Italy, Lattuada has continued to enjoy a freedom of subject matter and style despite ideological shifts and methodological changes. His main films during the neorealist period, which he claims never to have taken part in, succeeded in further establishing the Italian cinema in the international

Alberto Lattuada

market and, unlike many of his colleagues' works, also proved popular in the domestic market. *Il bandito* and *Il mulino del Po,* for example, combined progressive ideology, realistic detail (due to location shooting and attention to quotidian activities), and tight narrative structure through careful attention to editing. In fact, Lattuada's entire career has demonstrated an on-going interest in editing, which he considers more fundamental than the script and which gives his films a strictly controlled rhythm with no wasted footage. He shoots brief scenes that, he claims, are more attractive to an audience and that can be easily manipulated at the editing stage.

Lattuada's background stressed the arts, and his films display a sophisticated cultural appreciation. As a boy, he took an active interest in his father's musicianship in the orchestra of La Scala in Milan. As a young man, Lattuada worked as a film critic, wrote essays on contemporary painters, co-founded cultural magazines, and worked as an assistant director and scriptwriter. Lattuada co-scripts most of his films and occasionally produces them. He also co-founded what became the Milan film archive, the Cineteca Italiana.

As a director, Lattuada is often called eclectic because of his openness to projects and his ability to handle a wide variety of subject matter. His major commercial successes have been *Bianco, rosso e . . . ,* which he wrote especially for Sophia Loren; *Matchless,* a parody of the spy genre; *Anna,* the first Italian film to gross over one billion lire in its national distribution; *La spiaggia,* a bitter satire of bourgeois realism; and *Mafioso,* starring Alberto Sordi and filmed in New York, Sicily, and Milan.

Lattuada has also filmed many adaptations of literary works that remain faithful to the original but are never simply static reenactments. These range from the comically grotesque *Venga a prendere . . .*; a version of Brancati's satirical *Don Giovanni in Sicilia*; the horror film *Cuore di cane,* taken from a Bulgakov novel; the spectacular big-budget *La tempesta,* from two Pushkin stories; and Chekhov's metaphorical journey in *La steppa.* His 1952 version of *The Overcoat* is considered his masterpiece for its portrayal of psychological states and the excellence of Renato Rascel's performance. Lattuada is famous for his handling of actors, and has launched the career of many an actress, including Catherine Spaak, Giulietta Masina and Nastassia Kinski.

Notwithstanding the diversity of subject matter he has directed, Lattuada's main interest has been pubescent sexuality, the passage of a girl into womanhood, and the sexual relationship of a couple as the primary attraction they have for each other. Thus, his films deal with eroticism as a central theme and he chooses actresses whose physical beauty and sensuousness are immediately apparent. This motif appeared in Lattuada's work as early as his second feature and has been his main preoccupation in his films since 1974.

His films have been critically well-received in Italy, although rarely given the attention enjoyed by some of his contemporaries. In France, however, his work is highly acclaimed; *Il bandito* and *Il cappotto* received much praise at the Cannes festivals when they were shown. With a few exceptions, his more recent work is little known in Britain and the United States, although when *Come Have Coffee with Us* was released commercially in the U.S. ten years after it was made, it enjoyed a fair success at the box office and highly favorable reviews.—ELAINE MANCINI

Lean, David

Nationality *British.* **Born** *Croydon, Surrey, 25 March 1908.* **Education** *Leighton Park Quaker School, Reading.* **Family** *Married 1) Kay Walsh, 1940 (divorced 1949); 2) Ann Todd, 1949 (divorced 1957); 3) Leila Matkar, 1960 (divorced 1978); 4) Sandra Hotz, 1981 (marriage dissolved 1985).* **Career** *Clapperboard boy at Lime Grove Studios under Maurice Elvey, 1926; camera assistant, then cutting room assistant, 1928; chief editor for Gaumont-British Sound News, 1930, then for British Movietone News, from 1931; editor for British Paramount, from 1934; invited by Noel Coward to co-direct* In Which We Serve, *1942; co-founder, with Ronald Neame and Anthony Havelock-Allan, Cineguild, 1943 (dissolved 1950); began association with producer Sam Spiegel, 1956; returned to filmmaking after fourteen-year absence to make* A Passage to India, *1984.* **Awards** *British Film Academy Award for* The Sound Barrier, *1952; Commander Order of the British Empire, 1953; Best Direction, New York Film Critics, 1955; Oscar for Best Director, and Best Direction, New York Film Critics, for* The Bridge on the River Kwai, *1957; Oscars for Best Director and Best Film, for* Lawrence of Arabia, *1962; Officier des Arts et des Lettres, France, 1968; Fellow of the British Film Institute, 1983; Fellow of the American Film Institute, 1989.* **Died** *In London, 16 April 1991.*

Films as Director: 1942: *In Which We Serve* (co-d). **1944:** *This Happy Breed* (+co-adapt). **1945:** *Blithe Spirit* (+co-adapt); *Brief Encounter* (+co-sc). **1946:** *Great Expectations* (+co-sc). **1948:** *Oliver Twist* (+co-sc). **1949:** *The Passionate Friends* (*One Woman's Story*) (+co-adapt). **1950:** *Madeleine.* **1952:** *The Sound Barrier* (*Breaking the Sound Barrier*) (+pr). **1954:** *Hobson's Choice* (+pr, co-sc). **1955:** *Summertime* (*Summer Madness*) (+co-sc). **1957:** *The Bridge on the River Kwai.* **1962:** *Lawrence of Arabia.* **1965:** *Doctor Zhivago; The Greatest Story Ever Told* (uncredited). **1970:** *Ryan's Daughter.* **1984:** *A Passage to India.*

Other Films: 1933: *Money for Speed* (ed). **1935:** *Escape Me Never* (Czinner) (ed). **1936:** *As You Like It* (Czinner) (ed). **1937:** *Dreaming Lips* (Czinner) (ed); *The Last Adventurers* (ed). **1938:** *Pygmalion* (Asquith and Howard) (ed). **1939:** *French Without Tears* (Asquith) (ed). **1941:** *Major Barbara* (Pascal) (ed). **1942:** *49th Parallel* (Powell) (ed); *One of Our Aircraft Is Missing* (Powell) (ed).

There is a trajectory that emerges from the shape of David Lean's career, and it is a misleading one. Lean first achieved fame as a director of seemingly intimate films, closely based on plays of Noel Coward. His first directorial credit was shared with Coward, for *In Which We Serve*. In the 1960s he was responsible for extraordinarily ambitious projects, for an epic cinema of grandiose effects, difficult location shooting, and high cultural, even literary, pretention. But, in fact, Lean's essential approach to the movies never changed. All of his films, no matter how

David Lean

small or large their dimensions, demonstrate an obsessive cultivation of craft, a fastidious concern with production detail that defines the "quality" postwar British cinema. That craft and concern are as hyperbolic in their devices as is the medium itself. Viewers surprised at the attention to detail and composition in *Ryan's Daughter,* a work whose scope would appear to call for a more modest approach, had really not paid attention to the truly enormous dimensions of *Brief Encounter,* a film that defines, for many, intimist cinema.

Lean learned about the movies during long years of apprenticeship, gaining particularly important experience as an editor. It is clear, even in the first films he directed with (and then for) Coward, that his vision was not bound to the playwright's West End proscenium. *This Happy Breed,* a lower class version of *Cavalcade,* makes full use of the modest terraced house that is the film's prime locus. The nearly palpable patterns of the mise-en-scène are animated by the highly professional acting characteristic of Lean's early films. Watching the working out of those patterns created by the relationship between camera, decor, and actor is like watching choreography at the ballet, where the audience is made aware of the abstract forms of placement on the stage even as that placement is vitalized by the individual quality of the dancer. The grief of Celia Johnson and Robert Newton is first expressed by the empty room that they are about to enter, then by the way the camera's oblique backward movement respects their silence.

It is in *Brief Encounter* that the fullness of the director's talent becomes clear. This story of chance meeting, love, and renunciation is as apparently mediocre, conventional, and echoless as Flaubert's *Madame Bovary.* What could be more boringly middle-class than the romantic longing of a nineteenth-century French provincial housewife or the oh-so-tasteful near adultery of two "decent" Britishers? In both cases, the authorial interventions are massive. Lean conveys the film's passion through the juxtaposition of the trite situation against the expressionistic violence of passing express trains and the wrenching departure of locals, against the decadent romanticism of the Rachmaninoff score, and most emphatically against one of the most grandiose and hyperbolic exposures of an actress in the history of film. The size of Celia Johnson's eyes finally becomes the measure of *Brief Encounter,* eyes whose scope is no less expansive than Lawrence's desert or Zhivago's tundra.

Lean's next two successes were his adaptations (with Ronald Neame) of Charles Dickens novels, *Great Expectations* and *Oliver Twist.* Again, intimacy on the screen becomes the moment of gigantic display. The greatness of Pip's expectations are set by the magnitude of his frightful encounter with an escaped convict who, when he emerges into the frame, reminds us all what it is like to be a small child in a world of oversized, menacing adults. A variation of this scale is also seen in Pip's meeting with mad Miss Havisham, in all her gothic splendor.

Lean's next few films seem to have more modest ambitions, but they continue to demonstrate the director's concern with expressive placement. Of his three films with his then-wife Ann Todd, *Madeleine* most fully exploits her cool blond beauty.

A significant change then took place in the development of his career. Lean's reputation as a "location" director with a taste for the picturesque was made by *Summertime,* an adaptation of the play *The Time of the Cuckoo,* in which the city of Venice vies with Katharine Hepburn for the viewer's attention. It is from this point that Lean must be identified as an international rather than an English director. The subsequent international packages that resulted perhaps explain the widespread (and unjust) opinion that Lean is more of an executive than a creator with a personal vision.

The personality of Lean is in his compulsive drive to the perfectly composed shot, whatever the cost in time, energy, and money. In this there is some affinity between the director and his heroes. The Colonel (Alec Guinness) in *The Bridge on the River Kwai* must drive his men to build a good bridge, even if it is for the enemy. Lawrence (Peter O'Toole) crosses desert after desert in his quest for a self purified through physical ordeal, and viewers must wonder about the ordeals suffered by the filmmakers to photograph those deserts. The same wonder is elicited by the snowy trek of Dr. Zhivago (Omar Sharif) and the representation of life in early twentieth-century Russia.

That perfectly composed shot is emblemized by the principal advertising image used for *Ryan's Daughter*—an umbrella floating in air, suspended over an oceanside cliff. This is a celebration of composition per se, composition that holds unlikely elements in likely array. Composition is an expressive tension, accessible to viewers as it simultaneously captures the familiar and the unfamiliar. It is the combination that makes so many viewers sensitive to *Brief Encounter,* where middle-class lives (the lives of filmgoers) are filled with overwhelming passion and overwhelming style. Laura and Alex fall in love when they go to the movies.—CHARLES AFFRON

Leconte, Patrice

Nationality French. *Born* Paris, France, 12 November 1947. *Education* Studied at the Institute des Hautes Etudes Cinematographiques. *Career* Directed first feature, *Les veces etaient fermes de l'interieur, 1976; often worked with producer Christian Fechner, and actors from the Cafe Splendide, the famed Parisian comedy cafe theater; cemented his international reputation with* Monsieur Hire, *1989; has directed many commercials for French television, including ads for Peugeot and Carlsberg beer. *Address* French Film Office, 745 Fifth Avenue, New York, New York 10151.*

Films as Director and Screenwriter: **1976:** *Les vécés étaient fermés d'interieur.* **1978:** *Les bronzés.* **1979:** *Les bronzés font du ski.* **1981:** *Viens chez moi, j'habite chez une copine (Come to My Place, I'm Living at My Girlfriend's).* **1982:** *Ma femme s'appelle reviens (Singles).* **1983:** *Circulez y a rien a voir (Move Along, There's Nothing to See).* **1985:** *Les Specialistes (The Specialists).* **1986:** *Tandem.* **1989:** *Monsieur Hire.* **1990:** *Le mari de la coiffeuse (The Hairdresser's Husband).* **1991:** *Contre l'oubli (Against Oblivion)* (co-d). **1992:** *Le batteur du bolero.* **1993:** *Le tango (Tango); Le parfum d'Yvonne*

(*Yvonne's Perfume*). **1995:** *Lumiere et compagnie* (*Lumiere and Company*) (short Lumiere film). **1996:** *Les grands ducs; Ridicule.* **1997:** *Half a Chance.*

Other Films: 1984: *Moi vouloir toi* (*Me Want You*) (Dewolf) (co-sc). **1994:** *The Son of Gascogne* (role).

In 1989 Patrice Leconte earned international acclaim upon the release of *Monsieur Hire,* a sharp, clever thriller. Yet for almost a decade and a half, he had been thriving as a director of light, strictly commercial satires—smashingly successful at home but little-known outside France—which were crammed with physical slapstick, plays-on-words, and other assorted shenanigans. These films were amusing and nonsensical, with his casts including Josiane Balasko, Michel Blanc, Bernard Giraudeau, and other prominent actors from the French theater and cinema. A typical Leconte film of this period is *Les bronzés,* a farce which chides Club Med-style vacation villages by contrasting two single males. One (Blanc) is hopelessly unsuccessful with the opposite sex, even in such ready-made surroundings. The other (Thierry Lhermitte) is a stud who finds it all-too-easy to seduce women.

So it seemed astonishing when Leconte directed *Monsieur Hire,* a film that was anything but funny. It is a psychological thriller, based on the same Georges Simenon novel that inspired Duvivier's *Panique,* in which Blanc appears as the title character—a bald, eccentric, middle-aged loner. The film is a revealing portrait of French-style provincialism in that M. Hire resides in a Parisian suburb where the status quo reigns, and where anyone who is different is viewed with suspicion. And M. Hire is different indeed. So he is the logical suspect after a young girl is brutally murdered, and is summarily and mercilessly hounded by the cop on the case. *Monsieur Hire* may be linked to a film like *Les bronzés* in that both deal with men who obsess over women, seeing them not as human beings but as objects. Here, M. Hire has a voyeuristic obsession with

Patrice Leconte directing *The Hairdresser's Husband.*

Alice (Sandrine Bonnaire), his pretty young neighbor. But M. Hire is no comically inept male; rather, he is a lonely, affection-starved soul who eventually strikes up a friendship with the free-spirited Alice. Of course, M. Hire is not the kind of man to attract such a woman. Because he is blinded by his feelings for Alice and oblivious to her true nature, he ends up being manipulated and victimized.

Leconte's follow-up, *The Hairdresser's Husband,* works as a companion piece to *Monsieur Hire.* It is the deceptively simple story of Antoine, who as a young boy on the edge of puberty does not spend his time with other kids, riding bicycles or indulging in sports. Instead, he is constantly at the town barbershop, where he is smitten with the buxom haircutter. As a middle-aged man, Antoine (Jean Rochefort) can describe the woman in minute detail. Back when he was a boy, he decided that his sole goal in life would be to marry a hairdresser. And so he does. He proposes to the beautiful Mathilde (Anna Galiena) while she cuts his hair for the first time. She accepts, and they are wed. Both are content and the days pass, one after the other, as if in a dream. If all of this sounds slight, it is not. The film, as it focuses on Antoine and Mathilde's love and their attempt to shelter themselves from all that is bad in life, is crammed with profoundly deep layers of emotion. Like *Monsieur Hire,* it is a concise, knowing allegory about romantic obsession and how a man can be fascinated by a woman. The difference between the two films is that, here, love brings him peace. But how fragile is that peace? All lovers are destined to be separated by death, if not by cruel fate. In *Monsieur Hire,* a man is thwarted in his attempt to find his idealized love, to the point where his life becomes enveloped by tragedy. While a different (yet not dissimilar) man does find love in *The Hairdresser's Husband,* Leconte is worldly enough to know that, because of the very nature of human existence, such happiness is fated to be only temporary.

In *Tango,* a third Leconte feature, the filmmaker returned to his comic roots, but with a devilish twist. *Tango* is the story of a woman-hater (Philippe Noiret) who believes that "wife-killing isn't really murder." Via blackmail, he coerces another man (Richard Bohringer), who had killed his own wife and her lover, into murdering the mate of his nephew (Thierry Lhermitte), who is tired of married life and wants the freedom to play around. What sounds like a thriller actually is a freewheeling, ingeniously structured, pitch-black comedy about the manner in which men are endlessly fascinated by women but dislike being tied down by them. In this regard, *Tango* is an extension of the characters and themes explored in *Monsieur Hire* and *The Hairdresser's Husband.* These three films are evidence that Leconte has matured as a filmmaker, and that his days making frivolous farces are forever past.—ROB EDELMAN

Lee, Spike

Nationality American. ***Born*** *Shelton Jackson Lee in Atlanta, Georgia, 20 March 1957; son of jazz musician Bill Lee.* ***Education*** *Morehouse College, B.A., 1979; New York University, M.A. in Filmmaking; studying with Martin Scorsese.* ***Family*** *Married lawyer Tonya Linette Lewis, 1993; one son, Satchel.* ***Career*** *Set up production company 40 Acres and a Mule; directed first feature,* She's Gotta Have It, *1986; also directs music videos and commercials for Nike/Air Jordan; Trustee of Morehouse College, 1992.* ***Awards*** *Student Directors Academy Award, for* Joe's Bed-Stuy Barbershop: We Cut Heads, *1980; U.S. Independent Spirit Award for First Film, New Generation Award, Los Angeles Film Critics*

Association, and Prix de Jeunesse, Cannes Film Festival, all for She's Gotta Have It, *1986; U.S. Independent Spirit Award, Best Picture, L.A. Film Critics, and Best Picture, Chicago Film Festival, all for* Do the Right Thing, *1989; Essence Award, 1994.* **Address** *40 Acres and a Mule, 124 Dekalb Avenue, Suite 2, Brooklyn, New York 11217-1201.*

Films as Director, Scriptwriter, and Editor: 1977: *Last Hustle in Brooklyn* (Super-8 short). **1980:** *The Answer* (short). **1981:** *Sarah* (short). **1982:** *Joe's Bed-Stuy Barbershop: We Cut Heads* (+role). **1986:** *She's Gotta Have It* (+role as Mars Blackmon). **1988:** *School Daze* (+role as Half Pint). **1989:** *Do the Right Thing* (+role as Mookie). **1990:** *Mo' Better Blues* (+role as Giant). **1991:** *Jungle Fever* (+role as Cyrus). **1992:** *Malcolm X* (+role as Shorty). **1994:** *Crooklyn* (+role as Snuffy). **1995:** *Clockers* (+role as Chucky). **1996:** *Girl 6* (+role as Jimmy); *Get on the Bus.*

Other Films: 1993: *The Last Party* (*Youth for Truth*) (doc) (appearance); *Seven Songs for Malcolm X* (doc) (appearance); *Hoop Dreams* (doc) (appearance). **1994:** *DROP Squad* (exec pr, appearance). **1995:** *New Jersey Drive* (exec pr); *Tales from the Hood* (exec pr). **1996:** *When We Were Kings* (appearance).

Spike Lee is the most famous African-American to have succeeded in breaking through the Hollywood establishment to create a notable career for himself as a major director. What makes this all the more notable is that he is not a comedian—the one role in which Hollywood has usually allowed blacks to excel—but a prodigious, creative, multifaceted talent who writes, directs, edits, and acts, a filmmaker who invites comparisons with American titans like Woody Allen, John Cassavetes, and Orson Welles.

His films, which deal with different facets of the black experience, are innovative and controversial even within the black community. Spike Lee refuses to be content with presenting blacks in their "acceptable" stereotypes: noble Poitiers demonstrating simple moral righteousness are nowhere to be found. Lee's characters are three-dimensional and often vulnerable to

moral criticism. His first feature film, *She's Gotta Have It,* dealt with black sexuality, unapologetically supporting the heroine's promiscuity. His second film, *School Daze,* drawing heavily upon Lee's own experiences at Morehouse College, examined the black university experience and dealt with discrimination within the black community based on relative skin colors. His third film, *Do the Right Thing,* dealt with urban racial tensions and violence. His fourth film, *Mo' Better Blues,* dealt with black jazz and its milieu. His fifth film, *Jungle Fever,* dealt with interracial sexual relationships and their political implications, by no means taking the traditional, white liberal position that love should be color blind. His sixth film, *Malcolm X,* attempted no less than a panoramic portrait of the entire racial struggle in the United States, as seen through the life story of the controversial activist. Not until his seventh film, *Crooklyn,* primarily an autobiographical family remembrance of growing up in Brooklyn, did Spike Lee take a breath to deal with a simpler subject and theme.

Lee's breakthrough feature was *She's Gotta Have It,* an independent film budgeted at $175,000 and a striking box-office success: a film made by blacks for blacks which also attracted white audiences. *She's Gotta Have It* reflects the sensibilities of an already sophisticated filmmaker and harkens back to the early French New Wave in its exuberant embracing of bravura technique—intertitles, black-and-white cinematography, a sense of improvisation, characters directly addressing the camera—all wedded nevertheless to serious philosophical/sociological examination. The considerable comedy in *She's Gotta Have It* caused many critics to call Spike Lee the "black Woody Allen," a label which would increasingly reveal itself as a rather simplistic, muddle-headed approbation, particularly as Lee's career developed. (Indeed, in his work's energy, style, eclecticism, and social commitment, he more resembles Martin Scorsese, a Lee mentor at the NYU film school.) Even to categorize Spike Lee as a black filmmaker is to denigrate his talent, since there are today virtually no American filmmakers (except Allen) with the ambitiousness and talent to write, direct, and perform in their own films. And Lee edits as well.

Do the Right Thing, Lee's third full-length feature, is one of the director's most daring and controversial achievements, presenting one sweltering day which culminates in a riot in the Bedford Stuyvesant section of Brooklyn. From its first images—assailing jump cuts of a woman dancing frenetically to the rap "Fight the Power" while colored lights stylistically flash on a location ghetto block upon which Lee has constructed his set—we know we are about to witness something deeply disturbing. The film's sound design is incredibly dense and complex, and the volume alarmingly high, as the film continues to assail us with tight close-ups, extreme angles, moving camera, colored lights, distorting lenses, and individual scenes directed like high operatic arias.

Impressive, too, is the well-constructed screenplay, particularly the perceptively drawn Italian family at the center of the film who feel so besieged by the changing, predominantly black neighborhood around them. A variety of ethnic characters are drawn sympathetically, if unsentimentally; perhaps never in American cinema has a director so accurately presented the relationships among the American urban underclasses. Particularly shocking and honest is a scene in which catalogs of racial and ethnic epithets are shouted directly into the camera. The key scene in *Do the Right Thing* has the character of Mookie, played by Spike Lee, throwing a garbage can through a pizzeria window as a moral gesture which works to make the riot inevitable. The film ends with two quotations: one from Martin Luther King Jr., eschewing violence; the other from Malcolm X, rationalizing violence in certain circumstances.

Do the Right Thing was one of the most controversial films of the last twenty years. Politically conservative commentators denounced the film, fearful it would incite inner-city violence. Despite widespread acclaim the film was snubbed at the Cannes Film Festival, outraging certain Cannes judges; despite the accolades of many critics' groups, the film was also largely snubbed by the Motion Picture Academy, receiving a nomination only for Spike Lee's screenplay and Danny Aiello's performance as the pizzeria owner.

Both *Mo' Better Blues* and the much underrated *Crooklyn* owe a lot to Spike Lee's appreciation of music, particularly as handed down to him by his father, the musician Bill Lee. *Crooklyn* is by far the gentler film, presenting Lee's and his siblings' memories of growing up with Bill Lee and his mother. Typical of Spike Lee, the vision in *Crooklyn* is by no means a sentimental one, and the father comes across as a proud, if weak, man; talented, if failing in his musical career; loving his children, if not always strong enough to do the right thing for them. The mother, played masterfully by Alfre Woodard, is the stronger of the two personalities; and the film—ending as it does with grief—seems Spike Lee's version of Fellini's *Amarcord*. For a white audience, *Crooklyn* came as a revelation: the sight of black children watching cartoons, eating Trix cereal, playing hopscotch, and singing along with the Partridge family, seemed strange—because the American cinema had so rarely (if ever?) shown a struggling black family so rooted in popular-culture iconography all Americans could relate to. Scene after scene is filled with humanity, such as the little girl stealing groceries rather than be embarrassed by using her mother's food stamps. *Crooklyn*'s soundtrack, like so many other Spike Lee films, is unusually cacophonous, with everyone talking at once, and its improvisational style suggests Cassavetes or Scorsese. Lee's 1995 film, *Clockers,* which deals with drug dealing, disadvantage, and the young "gangsta," was actually produced in conjunction with Scorsese, whose own work, particularly the seminal *Meanstreets,* Lee's work often recalls.

Another underrated film from Lee is *Jungle Fever* (from 1991). Taken for granted is how well the film communicates the African-American experience; more surprising is how persuasively and perceptively the film communicates the Italian-American experience, particularly working-class attitudes. Indeed, one looks in vain in the Hollywood cinema for an American director with a European background who presents blacks with as many insights as Lee presents his Italians. And certainly unforgettable, filmed expressively with nightmarish imagery, is the film's set-piece in which we enter a crack house and come to understand profoundly and horrifically the tremendous damage being done to a component of the African-American community by this plague. *Jungle Fever,* like *Do the Right Thing,* basically culminates in images of Ruby Dee screaming in horror and pain, a metaphor for black martyrdom and suffering.

Nevertheless, the most important film in the Spike Lee *oeuvre* (if not his best) is probably *Malcolm X*—important because Lee himself campaigned for the film when it seemed it would be given to a white director, creating then an epic with the sweep and majesty of a David Lean and a clear political message of black empowerment. If the film on the whole seems less interesting than many of Lee's films (because there is less Lee there), the most typical Lee touches (such as the triumphant coda which enlists South African President Nelson Mandela to play himself and teach young blacks about racism and their future) seem among the film's most inspired and creative scenes. If more cautious and conservative, in some ways the film is also Lee's most ambitious: with dozens of characters, historical reconstructions, and the biggest budget in his entire career. *Malcolm X* proved definitively to fiscally conservative Hollywood studio executives that an African-American director could be trusted to direct a high-budget "A film." The success of *Malcolm X,* coupled with the publicity machine supporting Spike Lee, helped a variety of young black directors—like John Singleton, the Wayans brothers, and Mario Van Peebles—all break through into mainstream Hollywood features.

And indeed, Lee seems often to be virtually everywhere. On television interview shows he is called upon to comment on every issue relevant to black America: from the O. J. Simpson verdict to Louis Farrakhan and the Million Man March. In bookstores, his name can be found on a variety of published books on the making of his films, books created by his own public relations arm particularly so that others can read about the process, become empowered, find their own voices, and follow in Lee's filmic footsteps. On the basketball court, Lee can be found very publicly attending the New York Knicks' games. On MTV, he can be found in notable commercials for Nike basketball shoes. On college campuses, he can be found making highly publicized speeches on the issues of the day. And on the street, his influence can be seen even in fashion trends—such as the ubiquitous "X" on a variety of clothing the year of *Malcolm X's* release. There may be no other American filmmaker working today who is so willing to take on all comers, so politically committed to make films which are consistently and unapologetically in-your-face. Striking, too, is that instead of taking his inspiration from other movies, as do the gaggle of Spielberg imitators, Lee takes his inspiration from real life—whether the Howard Beach or Yusuf Hawkins incidents, in which white racists killed blacks, or his own autobiographical memories of growing up black in Brooklyn.

As Spike Lee has become a leading commentator on the cultural scene, there has been an explosion of Lee scholarship, not all of it laudatory: increasing voices attack Lee and his films for either homophobia, sexism, or anti-Semitism. Lee defends both his films and himself, pointing out that because characters espouse some of these values does not imply that he himself does, only that realistic portrayal of the world *as it is* has no place for political correctness. Still, some of the accusers point to examples which give pause: Lee's insistence on talking only to black journalists for stories about *Malcolm X,* but refusing to meet with a black journalist who was gay; the totally cartoonish portrait of the homosexual neighbor in *Crooklyn,* one of the few characters in that film who is given no positive traits to leaven the harsh criticism implied by Lee's treatment or to make him seem three-dimensional. Similar points have been made regarding Lee's attitudes toward Jews (particularly in *Mo' Better Blues*) and women. At one point, Lee even felt the need to defend himself in the *New York Times* in a letter to the editor entitled, "Why I Am Not an Anti-Semite."

Interesting, almost as an aside, is Lee's canny ability to use certain catch phrases in his films which help both to attract and delight audiences. In *She's Gotta Have It,* there was the constant refrain uttered by Spike Lee as Mars Blackmon, "Please baby, please baby, please baby, baby, baby, please. . . ."; in *Do the Right Thing,* the disc jockey's "And that's the truth, Ruth." Lee's fusion of popular forms and audience-pleasing entertainment with significant cultural commentary is particularly impressive coming from a filmmaker still so young. Notable also is the director's assembly—in the style of Bergman and Chabrol and Woody Allen in their prime—of a consistent stable of very talented collaborators, including his father, Bill Lee, as musical composer, production designer Wynn Thomas, producer Monty Ross, and cinematographer Ernest Dickerson, among others. He has also used many of the same actors from one film to another, including Wesley Snipes, Denzel Washington, his sister Joie Lee, John Turturro, Samuel L. Jackson, Ossie Davis, and Ruby Dee, helping to create a climate which propelled several to stardom and inspired a new wave of high-level attention to a variety of breakout African-American performers.—CHARLES DERRY

Leone, Sergio

Nationality *Italian.* **Born** *Rome, 3 January 1929.* **Education** *Attended law school, Rome.* **Family** *Son of director Vincenzo Leone; married Carla (Leone), 1960, three daughters.* **Career** *Assistant to, then second unit director for, Italian filmmakers and American directors working in Italy, such as LeRoy, Walsh, and Wyler, 1947-56; scriptwriter, from late 1950s; directed first feature, Il colosso di Rodi, 1961; headed own production company, Rafran Cinematografica, 1970s.* **Died** *In Rome, April 1989.*

Films as Director: 1961: *Il colosso di Rodi* (*The Colossus of Rhodes*) (+co-sc). **1964:** *Per un pugno di dollari* (*A Fistful of Dollars*) (+co-sc). **1965:** *Per qualche dollaro in più* (*For a Few Dollars More*) (+co-sc). **1966:** *Il buono il brutto il cattivo* (*The Good, the Bad, and the Ugly*) (+co-sc). **1968:** *C'era una volta il West* (*Once upon a Time in the West*) (+co-sc). **1972:** *Giù la testa* (*Duck, You Sucker; Il était une fois la révolution*) (+co-sc). **1975:** *Un genio due compari e un pollo.* **1984:** *Once upon a Time in America* (+co-sc).

Other Films: 1958: *Nel segno di Roma* (*Sign of the Gladiator*) (co-sc). **1959:** *Gli ultimi giorni di Pompeii* (*The Last Days of Pompeii*) (Bonnard) (co-sc, uncredited co-d). **1961:** *Sodoma e Gommorra* (*Sodom and Gomorrah*) (Aldrich) (2nd unit d, co-d according to some sources). **1973:** *My Name Is Nobody* (story idea). **1978:** *Il gatto* (pr).

Not since Franz Kafka's *America* has a European artist turned himself with such intensity to the meaning of American culture and mythology. Sergio Leone's career is remarkable in its unrelenting attention to both America and American genre film. In France, Truffaut, Godard, and Chabrol have used American film as a touchstone for their own vision, but Leone, an Italian, a Roman who began to learn English only after five films about the United States, devoted most of his creative life to this examination.

Leone's films are not realistic or naturalistic visions of the American nightmare or fairy tale, but comic nightmares about existence. The feeling of unreality is central to Leone's work. His is a world of magic and horror. Religion is meaningless, a sham which hides honest emotions; civilization is an extension of man's need to dominate and survive by exploiting others. The Leone world, while not womanless, is set up as one in which men face the horror of existence. In this, Leone is very like Howard Hawks: as in Hawks's films, death erases a man. A man who dies is a loser, and the measure of a man is his ability to survive, to laugh or sneer at death. This is not a bitter point in Leone films. There are few lingering deaths and very little blood. Even the death of Ramon (Gian Maria Volonte) in *Fistful of Dollars* takes place rather quickly and with far less blood than the comparable death in *Yojimbo.* A man's death is less important than how he faces it. The only thing worth preserving in Leone's world is the family—and his world of American violence is such a terrible place that few families survive. In *Fistful of Dollars,* Clint Eastwood's primary emotional reaction is to attempt to destroy the family of the woman Ramon has taken. In the later films, *The Good, the Bad, and the Ugly* and *Once upon a Time in the West, Duck, You Sucker* and *Once upon a Time in America,* family life is minimal and destroyed by self-serving evil, not out of hatred but by a cold, passionless commitment to self-interest. Leone's visual obsessions contribute to his thematic interests. Many directors could work with and develop the same themes and characters, but Leone's forte lies in the development of these themes and characters in a personal world. No director, with the possible exception of Sam Fuller, makes as extensive use of the close-up as does Leone, and Leone's close-ups often show only a portion of the face, usually the eyes of one of the main characters. It is the eyes of these men that reveal what they are feeling—if they are feeling anything.

Such characters almost never define their actions in words. Plot is of minimal interest to Leone. What is important is examination of the characters, watching how they react, what makes them tick. It appears almost as if everything is, indeed, happening randomly, as if we are watching with curiosity the responses of different types of people, trying to read meaning in the slightest flick of an eyelid. The visual impact of water dripping on Woody Strode's hat, or Jack Elam's annoyed reaction to a fly, is of greater interest to Leone than the gunfight in which the two appear in *Once upon a Time in the West.*

Sergio Leone

The use of the pan in Leone films is also remarkable. The pan from the firing squad past the church and to the poster of the governor, behind which Rod Steiger watches in bewilderment through the eyes of the governor's image, is a prime example in *Duck, You Sucker.* The shot ties the execution to the indifferent church, to the non-seeing poster, and to Steiger's reaction in one movement.

The apparent joy and even comedy of destruction and battle in Leone films is often followed immediately by some intimate horror, some personal touch that underlines the real meaning of the horror which moments before had been amusing. The death of Dominick and his final words, "I slipped," in *Once upon a Time in America* undercut the comedy and zest for battle. There is little dialogue; the vision of the youthful dead dominates as it does in the cave scene in *Duck, You Sucker,* in which Juan's family lies massacred.

At the same time, Leone's fascination with spontaneous living, his zeal for existence in the midst of his morality films, can be seen in his handling of details. For example, food in his films is always colorful and appetizing and people eat it ravenously.

The obsession of Leone protagonists and villains, major and minor, with the attainment of wealth can be seen as growing out of a dominant strain within American genres, particularly western and gangster films. The desire for wealth and power turns men into ruthless creatures who violate land and family.

Leone's films are explorations of the mythic America he created. Unlike many directors, he did not simply repeat the same convention in a variety of ways. Each successive film takes the same characters and explores them in greater depth, and Leone's involvement with this exploration is intense.—STUART M. KAMINSKY

Lester, Richard

Nationality *American.* **Born** *Philadelphia, 19 January 1932.* **Education** *William Penn Charter School, Germanstown, Pennsylvania; University of Pennsylvania, B.S. in Clinical Psychology, 1951.* **Family** *Married dancer and choreographer Deirdre Vivian Smith, 1956, one son, one daughter.* **Career** *Music editor, assistant director, then director, CBS-TV, Philadelphia, 1951-54; director and composer, ITV, London, 1955-57, then producer, 1958; director, Courtyard Films, Ltd., from 1967; also composer, musician, and, from 1960, director of TV commercials.* **Awards** *Palme d'Or, Cannes Festival, for* The Knack, *1965; Gandhi Peace Prize, Berlin Festival, for* The Bed Sitting Room, *1969.* **Address** *c/o Twickenham Studios, St. Margarets, Middlesex, England.*

Films as Director: 1959: *The Running, Jumping and Standing Still Film* (+ph, mu, co-ed). **1962:** *It's Trad, Dad* (*Ring-a-Ding Rhythm*). **1963:** *The Mouse on the Moon.* **1964:** *A Hard Day's Night.* **1965:** *The Knack—and How to Get It*; *Help!.* **1966:** *A Funny Thing Happened on the Way to the Forum.* **1967:** *Mondo Teeno* (*Teenage Rebellion*) (doc) (co-d); *How I Won the War* (+pr). **1968:** *Petulia.* **1969:** *The Bed Sitting Room* (+co-pr). **1974:** *The Three Musketeers* (*The Queen's Diamonds*); *Juggernaut.* **1975:** *The Four Musketeers* (*The Revenge of Milady*); *Royal Flash.* **1976:** *Robin and Marian* (+co-pr); *The Ritz.* **1979:** *Butch and Sundance: The Early Days*; *Cuba.* **1980:** *Superman II* (U.S. release 1981). **1983:** *Superman III.* **1984:** *Finders Keepers* (+exec pr). **1989:** *Return of the Musketeers.* **1991:** *Get Back* (doc).

It is ironic that *A Hard Day's Night,* the one film guaranteed to ensure Richard Lester his place in cinema history, should in many ways reflect his weaknesses rather than his strengths. If the film successfully captures the socio-historical phenomenon that was the Beatles at the beginning of their superstardom, it is as much due to Alun Owen's "day in the life" style script, which provides the ideal complement to (and restraint on) Lester's anarchic mixture of absurd/surreal humour, accelerated motion, and cinema verité, to name but a few ingredients. Lester made a mark on cinema through his innovative utilisation of the techniques of television advertisements and pop shows. His inability to entirely dispense with these methods, regardless of the subject matter to which they were applied, wrecked too many of his later projects.

The Knack stands as a supreme example of style (or styles) obliterating content. Bleached imagery, choruses of schoolboys reciting the litany of the "knack," disapproving members of the older generation talking straight to the camera, seem randomly assembled to no apparent end. Worse is the lack of taste. Can the sight of Rita Tushingham running down a street crying "rape" to an assortment of indifferent individuals have ever seemed funny? *How I Won the War* fails along similar lines. Realistic battlefields and bloodshed clash with a ridiculous plot (soldiers sent to construct a cricket pitch on enemy territory) and characters who are peculiar rather than likeable. One does not doubt Lester's sincerity in his aim of making his audience ashamed of watching men die for their entertainment, but his lack of judgement is disconcerting. Even the more controlled *Petulia* is afflicted by a surfeit of flashbacks and flashforwards, its often intriguing examination of unhappy relationships in an out-of-control society weighed down by a relentless determination to Say Something Important. All this is a far cry from the skillfully orchestrated physical comedy of *A Funny Thing Happened on the Way to the Forum* or the opening section of *Superman III,* both free from a desire to preach.

Where Lester's major strength as a director lies is in his ability to produce personal works within the confines of an established genre, such as the swashbuckler (*The Three Musketeers/The Four Musketeers*), the western (*Butch and Sundance: The Early Days*), and the fantasy

(*Superman II*). If we wish to seek out underlying themes in his work these later films provide fertile ground (the mythical hero surrendering his power for human love in *Superman II,* Robin Hood attempting to regain his heroic status in a world no longer interested in heroes in *Robin and Marian*) while avoiding the collapse into uneasy self-importance or significance suffered by earlier work. Occasional lapses into heavy-handedness (the priest blessing the cannons for use in a religious war while muttering to himself in Latin in *The Four Musketeers,* the overly bloody beating inflicted on the mortal Clark Kent in *Superman II*) can be discounted as minor flaws.

Richard Lester

It is this talent for creating something original out of conventional material that gives Lester his distinction, rather than his misguided, if bold attempts at "serious" comedy (with all the accompanying cinematic tricks which ultimately produce only weariness in the viewer). Though it may seem paradoxical, Lester is a director who needs a firm foundation to work from before his imagination can be let loose. Sadly, he has had little opportunity to demonstrate this since the high-profile Superman films, following the misfiring farce *Finders Keepers* with two slightly threadbare attempts at recapturing former glories. *Return of the Musketeers* appears to have been ill-fated from the start, with the accidental death of Lester regular Roy Kinnear during filming. Moments of inspired action and slapstick could not disguise an overall feeling of deja vu (the film went straight to cable television in the United States). *Get Back* amounts to little more than an adequate, if staid record of Paul McCartney's 1989-90 world tour, though Lester's use of footage from the Beatles' heyday serves as a poignant reminder of both the overall 1960s cultural explosion and his own emergence as one of the cinema's most outlandish frontrunners.—DANIEL O'BRIEN

Levinson, Barry

*Nationality American. **Born** Baltimore, Maryland, 1942. **Education** Studied Broadcast Journalism, American University, Washington, D.C. **Family** Married 1) screenwriter and actress Valerie Curtin (divorced, 1982); 2) Diana Mona; three sons, one daughter. **Career** Comedy performer and writer, Los Angeles, from mid-1960s; writer for TV, including "Carol Burnett Show" and "Marty Feldman Show," winning three Emmy awards, from 1970; directed first feature,* Diner, *1982. **Award** Oscar for Best Director, for* Rain Man, *1988.*

Films as Director and Scriptwriter: 1982: *Diner.* **1984:** *The Natural.* **1985:** *Young Sherlock Holmes.* **1987:** *Tin Men; Good Morning, Vietnam.* **1988:** *Rain Man.* **1990:** *Avalon.* **1991:** *Bugsy* (+pr). **1992:** *Toys* (+pr). **1993:** *Homicide: Life on the Street* (TV pilot) (+exec pr). **1994:** *Jimmy Hollywood* (+pr, role); *Disclosure* (+pr). **1996:** *Sleepers* (+pr). **1997:** *Sphere* (+pr). **1998:** *Wag the Dog.*

Other Films: 1974: *Street Girls* (Miller) (co-sc, asst ph). **1976:** *Silent Movie* (Brooks) (co-sc, role as executive). **1978:** *High Anxiety* (Brooks) (co-sc, role as bellhop). **1979:** *. . . And Justice For All* (Jewison) (co-sc). **1980:** *Inside Moves* (Donner) (co-sc). **1981:** *History of the World, Part 1* (Brooks) (role as column salesman). **1982:** *Best Friends* (Jewison) (co-sc). **1984:** *Unfaithfully Yours* (Zieff) (co-sc). **1993:** *Wilder Napalm* (pr). **1994:** *Quiz Show* (Redford) (role as Dave Garroway). **1997:** *Donnie Brasco* (pr); *Home Fries* (pr).

Although his most lucrative Oscar-winning film, *Rain Man,* was set in conservative Cincinnati, Los Angeles, Las Vegas, and several points in between, Barry Levinson has never forgotten his roots and is still regarded by Marylanders as the ultimate Baltimore filmmaker. *Diner,* the film that launched his directing career in 1982, was based in the Baltimore suburb of Forest Park, where he grew up. So was *Tin Men,* made five years later. And in 1989, at the age of forty-seven, following the success of *Rain Man* and *Good Morning, Vietnam,* Levinson was back again in Baltimore, to the delight of the Maryland Film Commission, shooting *Avalon.*

It could not have been otherwise, since *Avalon* is based upon Levinson's own family immigrating to Baltimore from Russia in 1914. Baltimore is his city and his most personal films have focussed upon ordinary people he might have met there growing up during the 1940s and 1950s—the youngsters of *Diner,* the aluminum siding hucksters of *Tin Men.* Levinson has internalized the values of middle-America and has succeeded most brilliantly when filming stories about characters who live by those values.

If some of the critics were disturbed that Robert Redford's Roy Hobbs was not as seriously flawed as the original character in Bernard Malamud's *The Natural,* it is perhaps because Levinson's interpretation of the character is governed by assumptions different from Malamud's and because Levinson's orientation is decidedly more optimistic. The fidelity of Levinson's *The Natural* can be and has been challenged on pedantic grounds. The film might better be regarded not as an adaptation, but as an interpretation that will stand on its own, regardless of its source.

Levinson told the *New York Times Magazine* that he does not consider himself as a writer or a "writer-director." As Alex Ward rightly suggested, however, Levinson can be considered an American *auteur* who will leave his personal imprint on any project he touches, through sentimental touches (in *The Natural* or *Tin Men,* for example), quirky casting, or inspired comedic improvisation. He has an unfailing sense of what might constitute the right touch in a given dramatic situation. "I don't like other people directing what I write," Levinson told Ward, "but I don't mind directing something somebody else wrote."

In fact, after moving to the West Coast from American University in Washington, D.C., Levinson worked for over two years as a writer for Mel Brooks on two pictures, *Silent Movie* and *High Anxiety* (also making his screen debut as an insane bellhop in the *Psycho* parody scene). While working with Brooks on *High Anxiety* he first met Mark Johnson, who later became the Executive Producer of *Diner.* At that point Levinson had already won three Emmy Awards for his network television writing with the "Tim Conway Show" and "Carol Burnett Show."

Levinson collaborated with Valerie Curtin (whom he met at the Comedy Store in Los Angeles) on two feature film scripts, *. . . And Justice for All* (for Norman Jewison) and *Inside Moves* (for Richard Donner), before writing the script for *Diner.* His debut film as director is about young men "hanging out" in Baltimore over Christmas of 1959, one of them (Steve Guttenberg) enjoying his last days of bachelorhood before getting married. Mel Brooks told him that the script idea resembled *I vitelloni,* but Levinson had not even seen Fellini's film. Levinson told Stephen Farber of the *New York Times* that the Guttenberg character was based upon his cousin Eddie, who "loved fried bologna sandwiches" and "slept until 2:30 in the afternoon." The cast also featured Mickey Rourke and talented newcomers Kevin Bacon and Ellen Barkin. It was the lowest-budgeted "sleeper" produced by MGM that year. It started slowly after being reviewed in *Rolling Stone* and the *New Yorker,* then gradually built a following and staying power. (The president for distribution at MGM/UA referred to it as "Lazarus.") Vincent Canby in the *New York Times* called it the "happiest surprise of the year to date," and Levinson was "discovered."

Barry Levinson

Levinson also collaborated with Valerie Curtin in writing *Best Friends* (starring Burt Reynolds and Goldie Hawn) and a remake of the Preston Sturges classic *Unfaithfully Yours.* The screenplay for *... And Justice for All,* meanwhile, was nominated for an Academy Award, demonstrating the quality of the Levinson-Curtin team. Levinson also directed the high-spirited fantasy *Young Sherlock Holmes,* but aside, perhaps, from *Rain Man* and *The Natural,* Levinson will best be remembered for his Baltimore pictures, drawn from his own experience and marked with his own special brand of compassionate humor and nostalgia. As a personal filmmaker he is perhaps the nearest American equivalent to François Truffaut.

During the 1990s Levinson scored a popular and critical success working with author James Toback on *Bugsy,* starring Warren Beatty as larger-than-life gangster Benjamin (Bugsy) Siegel and Annette Bening as Virginia Hill. The film was much admired for its snappy dialogue and named best picture of 1991 by the Los Angeles Film Critics, who also voted Levinson Best Director and Toback Best Screenwriter. *Bugsy* later earned ten Academy Award nominations, including Best Picture and Best Director.

In 1992 Levinson misfired with *Toys,* an odd antiwar fable written by Levinson and Valerie Curtin, starring Robin Williams, Joan Cusack, and Michael Gambon. Levinson had the project in mind for years and was able to direct it after the success of *Bugsy.* The idea that children can be conditioned by the kinds of toys they are given was workable, but the fantasy was too bizarre to be taken seriously. Levinson also misfired in 1994 with *Jimmy Hollywood,* starring Joe Pesci as a loser and hustler, which was described in *Variety* as "an oddball attempt to mix offbeat comedy with social commentary."

In 1994 Levinson reclaimed his Hollywood clout with his expert direction of *Disclosure,* starring Michael Douglas and Demi Moore and adapted by Paul Attanasio from the popular novel by Michael Crichton, who also worked with Levinson as producer. The controversial novel, concerning sexual harassment in the workplace, helped to generate interest in the film. But a far more important collaboration between Levinson and Paul Attanasio started in 1993 on the NBC television police series *Homicide: Life on the Street,* adapted from *Baltimore Sun* reporter David Simon's published memoir about policework in Levinson's hometown. The series was hailed by critics as the best police drama on television, giving it prominence over the flashier yet more conventional *NYPD Blue.* As executive producer of the series Levinson also directed the pilot in 1993 and the season finale in 1995, thus helping *Homicide* to establish and maintain its quality and authenticity as an outstanding reality-based detective drama. Arguably, the series represents the director's best work since *Avalon* while setting a new standard for television drama.—JAMES M. WELSH

Lewin, Albert

Nationality *American.* **Born** *Brooklyn, New York, 23 September 1894; grew up in Newark, New Jersey.* **Education** *New York University, B.A. in English; Harvard University, M.A. in English; attended Columbia University.* **Military Service** *U.S. Army, 1918.* **Family** *Married Mildred Mindlin, 17 August 1918; no children.* **Career** *English instructor, University of Missouri, 1916-18; assistant national director, American Jewish Relief Committee, 1918-22; drama and film critic,* The Jewish Tribune, *1921-22; entered films as a New York-based reader for Samuel Goldwyn, 1921; moved to Culver City, continued as a reader, then trained as script clerk with King Vidor and Victor Sjöström and worked unofficially as an assistant editor, 1922-23; hired as writer by Metro Pictures, 1924; promoted to head of Metro-Goldwyn-Mayer (MGM) story department, 1927; promoted to production supervisor, 1929; after death of mentor, Irving Thalberg, moved to Paramount as producer, 1937-40; quit Paramount, founded independent production company with David Loew, 1940; Loew-Lewin released its second production, and Lewin's first as director,* The Moon and Sixpence, *after which Lewin returned to MGM as a director, 1942; quit MGM after release of his second directorial film,* The Picture of Dorian Gray, *and revived Loew-Lewin, 1945; dissolved Loew-Lewin again, after one film, Lewin's third as director,* The Private Affairs of Bel Ami, *and returned to MGM as an executive, 1948; wrote and directed* Pandora and the Flying Dutchman *while on sabbatical from MGM, 1950-51; retired from films after a near-fatal heart attack, 1959.* **Award** *As producer, received best picture Academy Award for* Mutiny on the Bounty, *1935.* **Died** *In New York City, 9 May 1968, of pneumonia.*

Films as Director: 1942: *The Moon and Sixpence* (+co-exec pr, sc). **1945:** *The Picture of Dorian Gray* (+sc). **1947:** *The Private Affairs of Bel-Ami* (+co-exec pr, sc). **1951:** *Pandora and the Flying Dutchman* (+co-pr, sc). **1954:** *Saadia* (+pr, sc). **1957:** *The Living Idol* (+co-pr, sc).

Other Films: 1924: *Bread* (continuity). **1925:** *The Fate of a Flirt* (continuity). **1926:** *Ladies of Leisure* (story, continuity); *Blarney* (co-scenarist); *Tin Hats* (continuity). **1927:** *A Little Journey* (scenarist); *Altars of Desire* (continuity); *Spring Fever* (co-scenarist); *Quality Street* (co-scenarist, co-adapter). **1928:** *The Actress* (co-scenarist). **1929:** *The Kiss* (production supervisor, uncredited); *Devil-May-Care* (production supervisor, uncredited). **1931:** *The Guardsman* (production supervisor, uncredited); *The Cuban Love Song* (production supervisor, uncredited). **1932:** *Red-Headed Woman* (production supervisor, uncredited); *Smilin' Through* (production supervisor, uncredited). **1934:** *What Every Woman Knows* (production supervisor, uncredited). **1935:** *China Seas* (assoc pr); *Mutiny on the Bounty* (assoc pr). **1937:** *The Good Earth* (assoc pr); *True Confession* (pr). **1938:** *Spawn of the North* (pr). **1939:** *Zaza* (pr). **1940:** *So Ends Our Night* (co-exec pr).

A genuine Hollywood highbrow, Albert Lewin trod the line between the commercially viable and the artistically daring in his own inimitable way. Friends with the likes of writers Djuna Barnes and Robert Graves, artist Man Ray and director Jean Renoir, Lewin had given up a nascent career as scholar and critic to pursue the grail of movies. Impressed especially by the most stylized and fantastic aspects of silent cinema, from Sjöström to Stroheim, Caligari to Keaton, Lewin left New York for Hollywood in 1922 and—just prior to Sam Goldwyn and Louis B. Mayer—joined Metro Pictures early in 1924. He impressed Irving Thalberg with his combination of erudition and sense and soon made himself indispensable at the Metro-Goldwyn-Mayer (MGM) story department, where he came to be known as Thalberg's story brain. He thrived first as a writer, then a producer at MGM until Thalberg's death. After a brief and unhappy stint as a producer at Paramount, he embarked upon his career as a director, he claimed, out of financial necessity. Lewin and his college fraternity brother, David Loew, had founded their own independent production company, and Loew urged Lewin to direct his own adaptation of W. Somerset Maugham's *The Moon and Sixpence* (1942) as an economic measure.

The result was a commercial and critical success. Lewin's adaptation of Maugham's strange novel about a milquetoast English stockbroker and family man turned passionate painter and fierce misanthrope (his protagonist, Charles Strickland, was based on the French painter Paul Gauguin) was made on the cheap, but includes several original turns and stylistic and thematic signatures that would return faithfully in Lewin's films, particularly his next two, more lavish productions: *The Picture of Dorian Gray* (1945) and *The Private Affairs of Bel Ami* (1947). All three films feature suave, cynical George Sanders, who clearly represented a kind of ego ideal for Lewin, in variations on what would become his standard film persona.

The three black-and-white films from the 1940s are united not only by Sanders and their fin-de-siècle European settings, but also by the fact that all are essentially morality plays—albeit rather perverse and ambiguous ones—in which art, decadence, and sexual thrall are viewed through the prism of a very pictorial, complex, and studied mise-en-scène. *The Picture of Dorian Gray,* the most elaborate of the three, is a film of stunning self-consciousness and density—a psychosexual horror film, enacted with choreographic precision in exquisite and mannered late-Victorian interiors. Hurd Hatfield plays the eponymous protagonist with chilling circumspection and Sanders is persuasive uttering the Wildean epigrams of Lord Henry Wotton. Harry Stradling's cinematography won the film's only Academy Award; it along with the sets and costumes realizes Lewin's Beardsleyesque visual conception perfectly, while Herbert Stothart's score employs Chopin's Twenty-fourth Prelude evocatively.

The musical score, this time by Darius Milhaud, was also a strength of Lewin's next film, *The Private Affairs of Bel Ami,* based on Guy de Maupassant's novel *Bel-Ami*. This story of a narcissistic and calculating Parisian bounder whose successes are achieved through a series of sexual liaisons secured Lewin's reputation, according to the *Times,* for achieving "censor-proof depravity." Subtly feminist, this film revolves around a (rather wooden) male object of female desire (Sanders, again, as Georges Duroy, a.k.a. *bel ami*) and features impressive performances from its female cast, including Ann Dvorak, Angela Lansbury, and Katherine Emery. Russell

Albert Lewin

Metty's cinematography and Gordon Wiles's set design contribute to *Bel Ami's* measured, almost anaesthetic contemplation of desire and duplicity. Here, as in *Dorian Gray,* the characters move—or are moved—around on patterned floors like chessmen on a checkerboard. The metaphysical implications of this trope are reiterated in *Bel Ami* by a host of symbols: Punch and Judy, dolls and games, and by a somewhat heavy-handed moral coda.

Notably, these films each include the revelation in color insert of a painting. In the original prints of *The Moon and Sixpence* black-and-white photography changed to sepia when the scene changed from Europe to Tahiti and then, momentarily, to color when the painter Strickland's "masterpiece" (in fact a mediocre Gauguinesque pastiche) was revealed near the end. In *Bel Ami* it is a shockingly anachronistic painting of *The Temptation of St. Anthony* by Surrealist Max Ernst that erupts from the screen in color. The technique is put more in the service of the narrative in *The Picture of Dorian Gray,* where Technicolor enhances the vivid senescence and putrefaction of Ivan Albright's rendition of the titular portrait.

Lewin continued to highlight art works in his color films of the 1950s, including in what is arguably his masterpiece, the singular *Pandora and the Flying Dutchman* (1951), a heady melange of Greek myth, German legend, Shakespearean and Jacobean drama, Romantic poetry, and Surrealist imagery, all spiced up with bullfighting, flamenco dancing, jazz combos, and speed-racing! From an original story, this dazzling film, often deliberately Surrealist and sometimes inadvertently camp, was shot on Spain's Costa Brava and features Ava Gardner (divinely beautiful as costumed by Beatrice Dawson and photographed by Jack Cardiff) and James Mason in the title roles. Its uneven reception—most Anglo-American critics cringed, while the French swooned—is a testimony to its audacity.

Lewin's last two films, made under considerable budget and casting restraints by MGM, were almost unanimously (and fairly) deemed failures. *Saadia* (1954), based on a minor French novel of colonial Morocco, despite the authenticity and beauty of its location ambience, is an awkward blend of romantic cliché and intellectual speculation. *The Living Idol* (1957), from an original script, like Lewin's later novel *The Unaltered Cat,* is an even uneasier synthesis of formulaic romance, sensational supernaturalism, and almost laughable pedantry, in which the plot seems a flimsy armature upon which its director's pet intellectual obsessions are top-heavily disposed.

Albert Lewin was a dilettante in the fullest sense of the word. His profound enthusiasms for the other arts are manifest in his films, several of which have artist-protagonists and all of which incorporate literary allusion, scenes of song and dance (e.g., Tahitian, Indonesian,

Parisian, Andalusian, Moroccan, and Mexican), and manifold art objects. But Lewin's (real and anticipated) battles with the Hays Office and his sense of popular taste seem to have led him to add, as sops to the censors and the box office, plot elements and characters for their strictly comedic, sentimental, or moralizing values. Even his best films are thus occasionally weakened by an anomalous scene or banal figure. And, especially in his original scripts, his literary and dilettantish impulses were wont to run amok. But his efforts resulted in a few films of real distinction, of proto-Godardian reflexivity, visual intricacy, and literary pith. In the United States, where critics and audiences are often alienated by such qualities, Lewin's reputation has languored, while in Europe, where his influence on directors like Godard and Antonioni has been claimed, it has borne up rather better.—SUSAN FELLEMAN

Lewis, Joseph H.

Nationality American. **Born** New York, 6 April 1907 (other sources say 1900). **Education** De Witt Clinton High School. **Military Service** Served in U.S. Army Signal Corps, 1943-44. **Career** Camera boy at MGM, 1926; editor and director of title sequences at Mascot studio (became Republic, 1935), 1930s; director, from 1937; director in charge of second units at Universal and Republic, 1940s; TV director, from late 1950s; subject of retrospective, Edinburgh Film Festival, 1980.

Films as Director: 1937: Navy Spy (co-d); Courage of the West; Singing Outlaw. **1938:** The Spy Ring (International Spy); Border Wolves; Last Stand. **1939:** Two Fisted Rangers (Forestalled). **1940:** Blazing Six Shooters (Stolen Wealth); The Man from Tumbleweeds; Texas Stagecoach (Two Roads); The Return of Wild Bill (False Evidence); Boys of the City; That Gang of Mine; Pride of the Bowery (Here We Go Again). **1941:** Invisible Ghost; Criminals Within; Arizona Cyclone; The Mad Doctor of Market Street. **1942:** Bombs Over Burma (+co-sc); The Silver Bullet; Boss of Hangtown Mesa. **1943:** Secret of a Co-ed (Silent Witness). **1944:** Minstrel Man. **1945:** The Falcon in San Francisco; My Name Is Julia Ross. **1946:** So Dark the Night. **1947:** The Swordsman. **1948:** The Return of October (Date with Destiny). **1949:** Undercover Man; Gun Crazy (Deadly as the Female). **1950:** A Lady without Passport. **1952:** Retreat, Hell!; Desperate Search. **1953:** Cry of the Hunted. **1954:** The Big Combo. **1955:** Man on a Bus; A Lawless Street. **1956:** 7th Cavalry. **1957:** The Halliday Brand. **1958:** Terror in a Texas Town.

Other Films: 1934: In Old Santa Fe (Howard) (sup ed). **1935:** Behind the Green Lights (Cabanne) (ed); The Miracle Rider (Eason and Shaefer) (ed); One Frightened Night (Cabanne) (ed); The Headline Woman (The Woman in the Case) (Nigh) (ed); Ladies Crave Excitement (Grindé) (ed); The Adventures of Rex and Rinty (Eason and Beebe); Harmony Lane (Santley) (sup ed); Streamline Express (Fields) (ed); Waterfront Lady (Santley) (sup ed); Confidential (Cahn) (sup ed); $1000 a Minute (Scotto) (sup ed). **1936:** Hitch Hike Lady (Eventful Journey) (Scotto) (sup ed); The Leavenworth Case (Collins) (sup ed); Darkest Africa (Hidden City) (Eason and Kane) (sup ed); The House of a Thousand Candles (Lubin) (sup ed); Laughing Irish Eyes (Santley) (sup ed); The Harvester (Santley) (sup ed); Undersea Kingdom (Eason and Kane) (sup ed); The Devil on Horseback (Wilbur) (ed). **1946:** The Jolson Story (Green) (d production numbers). **1953:** The Naked Jungle (Haskin) (begun by Lewis).

Joseph H. Lewis simultaneously supports and confounds the critical methodology of authorship. His forty-one features in twenty-one years provide enough examples of strong visual creativity, originality, and intelligence under the severe budgetary constraints of B film production to warrant bestowing the title "auteur." Yet, banal scripts, meager production values, and unaccomplished actors seem to deny him the opportunity to articulate a "consistent world view," reducing Lewis to a "metteur en scene." This dichotomy between a recognizable (if

Joseph H. Lewis

inconsistent) personal style and a lack of personally revealing (or expressive) thematic content forms the core of the Lewis debate.

Lewis labored for many studios, adapting to many genres, but began his best work while at Columbia after World War II. In 1945 and 1946, he directed *My Name Is Julia Ross* and *So Dark the Night, films noir* that precipitated his first important critical recognition. Until 1955, with a few exceptions, he continued surveying *film noir,* directing *Undercover Man, A Lady without Passport,* and the *noir*-influenced *Desperate Search* and *Cry of the Hunted,* culminating his fluency in the genre with two "undisputed masterpieces," *Gun Crazy* and *The Big Combo.* The critical favor awarded these films, and their eventual cult status, pushes Lewis into an intimate association with *film noir,* even though he directed many more Westerns.

His *films noir,* like his other films, were co-features or B movies slotted for the second half of a double bill. They were typically based on weak scripts with witless dialogue, ran under 90 minutes (many under 75), and received little distribution marketing. They were shot in less than two or three weeks, with miniscule budgets, on inexpensive black and white film stock, without stars or accomplished actors, using a few minimal sets or locations, and without rehearsed crowd scenes. These limitations functioned as a catalyst for his ingenuity. Improvising practical solutions to production limitations, Lewis devised a complex and unique visual style—a combination of Bresson and Ophuls—upon which his reputation and signature rest. His films emphasize images, employing low key lighting, high contrast, location shooting, long takes, camera movement, great depth of focus with dominating foreground objects, choreographed violence and sexuality, montage, off-screen action, sound manipulation, and a reduction of dialogue to a minimum. Each aspect ultimately accommodates a dual purpose, economic and aesthetic.

The use of low-key lighting served three practical economic purposes associated with B movie making: it cost less than high key lighting; it allowed the construction of only partial sets; and it concealed meager production values. It also served a vital aesthetic purpose by providing a striking visual style differentiating film noir from other genres. High contrast images resulted from the use of cheap black and white film stocks, yet underscored the visual play of blinding light cutting through opaque darkness. Location shooting reduced the dependence on sets and sound stage work while evoking a gritty urban realism. The combination of exceptionally long takes, great depth of focus with dominating foreground objects, and camera movement reduced shooting schedules and post-production expenses. They also added a documentary "time" and "atmosphere" to the realism of the films. The depiction of violence and sexuality through montage, off-screen space, and sound manipulation intensified their effect on the spectator while requiring neither complete performance nor extensive set construction and circumventing the Production Code. The reduction of dialogue hid the limited acting skills of his performers and returned the emphasis of his films to the visual. Examples of the combined utilization of these techniques include: the celebrated 4-minute Hampton robbery one-take and the robbery sequence in *Gun Crazy*; the torture by hearing-aid, the "kissing" shot, and the climax in *The Big Combo*; the report of the girl's death in *So Dark the Night*; and Rocco's assassination in *Undercover Man*. In other words, due to economic factors, Lewis's *films noir* represent the genre reduced to its visual essence.

Lewis's visual style stands without question. Whether or not this textual surface supports a consistent thematic content initiates a heated debate. Is he, as Richard Combs claims, "a stylistic authority operating in a vacuum," or as Richard Sattin explains, someone with visual intelligence and style who doesn't recognize the need for theme? Or is he, as Andrew Sarris states in Lewis's description under "Expressive Esoterica," a "somber personality revealed through a complex visual style?" Traditional analyses see his films betraying efforts to construct thematic coherence because their pleasure exists only as complex textual surfaces. More recent approaches can note the pleasure of his films' complex textual surfaces precisely activating the thematic concerns of *film noir* as well as inaugurating a disturbing and fascinating exploration of Existentialism.

The primacy of textual surface derived from the economic limitations of B movie making denies Lewis the luxury of psychologizing characters, character motivation, and events. Consequently, behavior finds its truest and clearest (and only) expression in action. Action is readily observable and objectively presentable as "pure" textuality. The accent on action as textual surface offers no judgement on or explanation of existence, only description. The world described is Existential, devoid of logic, justice, and order.

Lewis approached these Existential themes by eliding individual identity with social action. These themes find their sharpest focus in Lewis's masterpieces, *Gun Crazy* and *The Big Combo,* but appear in all his *films noir* and his late Westerns (*A Lawless Street, The Halliday Brand,* and *Terror in a Texas Town*).

Lewis's film career ended in 1958, coinciding with the death of "classical" *film noir*. His intensification and fusing of textuality and Existentialism within the genre pushed *film noir* to its logical extreme. His work, however, influenced a budding French movement, the *Nouvelle Vague* (a comparison between *Gun Crazy* and its focus on *l'amour fou* and Godard's *A bout de souffle* and *Pierrot le fou* would prove an interesting study), and may even stand as the base for today's technologically driven and production design oriented action-adventure films.—GREG S. FALLER

Loach, Ken

*Nationality British. **Born** Kenneth Loach in Nuneaton, Warwickshire, 17 June 1937. **Education** Read law at Oxford University. **Military Service** Two years in the Royal Air Force. **Family** Married Lesley Ashton (Loach), three sons (one deceased), two daughters. **Career** Actor with repertory company, Birmingham, then joined BBC, 1961; director of Z Cars for TV, 1962; directed Wednesday Play for TV, 1965; first collaboration with producer Tony Garnett was Up the Junction, 1965; with Garnett, set up Kestrel Films* *production company, 1969; freelanced, though working mainly for Central TV, from 1970s. Lives in London.* **Awards** *TV Director of the Year Award, British TV Guild, 1965; Special Jury Prize, Cannes Festival, for* Hidden Agenda, *1990; Felix Award, 1992, for* Riff-Raff; *International Critics Prize, FIPRESCI, 1995, for* Land and Freedom.

Films as Director and Co-Scriptwriter: 1967: *Poor Cow.* **1969:** *Kes.* **1971:** *The Save the Children Fund Film* (short); *Family Life.* **1979:** *Black Jack.* **1981:** *Looks and Smiles.* **1986:** *Fatherland* (*Singing the Blues in Red*). **1990:** *Hidden Agenda.* **1991:** *Riff Raff.* **1993:** *Raining Stones.* **1994:** *Ladybird Ladybird.* **1995:** *Land and Freedom.* **1996:** *Carla's Song.*

Films for Television: 1964: *Catherine; Profit By Their Example; The Whole Truth; The Diary of a Young Man.* **1965:** *Tap on the Shoulder; Wear a Very Big Hat; Three Clear Sundays; Up the Junction; The End of Arthur's Marriage; The Coming Out Party.* **1966:** *Cathy Come Home.* **1967:** *In Two Minds.* **1968:** *The Golden Vision.* **1969:** *The Big Flame; In Black and White* (not transmitted). **1971:** *The Rank and File; After a Lifetime.* **1973:** *A Misfortune.* **1976:** *Days of Hope* (in four parts). **1977:** *The Price of Coal.* **1979:** *The Gamekeeper.* **1980:** *Auditions.* **1981:** *A Question of Leadership.* **1983:** *The Red and the Blue; Questions of Leadership* (in four parts, not transmitted). **1984:** *Which Side Are You On?.* **1985:** *Diverse Reports: We Should Have Won.* **1989:** *Split Screen: Peace in Northern Ireland.*

Ken Loach is not only Britain's most political filmmaker, he is also its most censored—and the two are not entirely unconnected. Loach's career illustrates all too clearly the immense difficulties facing the radical filmmaker in Britain today: the broadcasting organisations' position within the state makes them extraordinarily sensitive sites from which to tackle certain fundamental political questions (about labour relations, "national security," or Northern Ireland, for example), while the film industry, though less subject to political interference and self-censorship, simply finds Loach's projects too "uncommercial," thanks to its habitually poverty-stricken state. And what other filmmaker, British or otherwise, has found one of his films the

Ken Loach directing *Ladybird Ladybird.*

subject of vitriolic attacks by sections of his own country's press at a major international film festival—as happened at Cannes in 1990 with *Hidden Agenda?*

For all the obvious *political* differences with Grierson, Loach is the chief standard bearer of the British cinematic tradition that started with the documentary movement in the 1930s. His quintessentially naturalistic approach was apparent even in his earliest works (in his contributions to the seminal BBC police series *Z Cars,* for instance) but really came to the fore with *Up the Junction* and *Cathy Come Home.* In the days when television drama was still finding its way beyond the proscenium arch and out from under the blanket of middle-brow, middle-class, literary-based classics, *Cathy's* portrayal of a homeless family hounded by the forces of a pitiless bureaucracy caused a sensation and led directly to the founding of the housing charity Shelter. Indeed, one critic described it as "effecting massive, visceral change in millions of viewers in a single evening." Typically, however, Loach himself has been far more circumspect, arguing that the film was *socially* as opposed to *politically* conscious, that it made people aware of a problem without giving them any indication of what they might do about it. He concludes that "ideally I should have liked *Cathy* to lead to the nationalisation of the building industry and home ownership. Only political action can do anything in the end"—a point of view to which he has remained faithful throughout his career.

Accordingly, in *The Big Flame, The Rank and File,* and the four-part series *Days of Hope,* Loach turned to more directly political subjects. It is in these dramas that Loach begins his project of giving voice to the politically silenced and marginalised. As he put it, "I think it's a very important function to let people speak who are usually disqualified from speaking or who've become non-persons—activists, militants, or people who really have any developed political ideas. One after the other in different industries, there have been people who've developed very coherent political analyses, who are really just excluded. They're vilified—called extremists and then put beyond the pale."

Such views made enemies across the spectrum of political ideologies but, typically, Loach's critics cloaked what were basically *political* objections in apparently *aesthetic* rhetoric. In particular, Loach was dragged into the much-rehearsed argument that the "documentary-drama" form dishonestly and misleadingly blurs the line between fact and fiction and, in particular, presents the latter as the former. Loach himself dismisses such criticisms as "ludicrous" and a "smokescreen," citing the numerous uncontroversial disinterrings of Churchill, Edward VII, and others and concluding that "It's an argument that's always dragged out selectively when there's a view of history, a view of events, that the Establishment doesn't agree with—it's not really the form which worries them at all. It's such an intellectual fraud that it doesn't bear serious consideration."

Loach's work, especially *Days of Hope,* was also drawn into a more serious debate which raged at one time in the pages of *Screen* about whether films with "progressive" political content can be truly "progressive" if they utilise the allegedly outworn and ideologically dubious conventions of realism. Loach's response was to accuse such critics of "not seeing the woods for the trees. The big issue which we tried to make plain to ordinary folks who aren't film critics was that the Labour leadership had betrayed them fifty years ago and were about to do so again. That's the important thing to tell people. It surprised me that critics didn't take the political point, but a rather abstruse cinematic point. . . . Even the more serious critics always avoid confronting the content of the film and deciding if they think it is truthful. They'll skirt around it by talking about realism and the Function of Film or they'll do a little paragraph while devoting all their space to some commercial film they pretend to dislike.''

With the coming of the 1980s Loach began to shift increasingly into documentary proper, abandoning dramatic devices altogether. This was partly a result of the increasing difficulty, both economic and political, that he had in making the kind of films in which he was most interested, but was also related to the advent of Thatcherism in 1979. As he himself explained, "There were things we wanted to say head on and not wrapped up in fiction, things that should be said as directly as one can say them. Thatcherism just felt so urgent that I thought that doing a fictional piece for TV, which would take a year just to get commissioned and at least another year to make, was just too slow. Documentaries can tackle things head on, and you can make them faster than dramas too—though with hindsight it's just as hard, if not harder, to get them transmitted.''

Indeed, Loach had major problems with his analysis of the relationship between trade union leaders and the rank and file in *A Question of Leadership* and the series *Questions of Leadership,* the first of which was cut in order to include a final "balancing" discussion and broadcast in only one ITV region, while the second was never broadcast at all after numerous legal wrangles over alleged defamation. Similarly, Loach's coal dispute film, *Which Side Are You On?,* was banned by the company (London Weekend Television) which commissioned it. It was finally televised, but only after it could be "balanced" by a programme less sympathetic to the striking miners than Loach's. It says a great deal about the system of film and television programme making in Britain that one of the country's most experienced and politically conscious directors was, and remains, unable to produce a full-scale work about one of the most momentous political events in the country's recent history.

Exactly the same could be said about Loach and Northern Ireland. Revealingly, the initial idea for what was to become *Hidden Agenda* came from David Puttnam when he was studio boss at Columbia, after two of Loach's long-cherished Irish projects, one with the BBC and the other with Channel 4, had foundered. However, Loach has borne his treatment at the hands of the British establishment with remarkable fortitude. With his particular political outlook he would presumably be surprised if things were otherwise. Nor does he have an inflated view of the role of film and the filmmaker. As his remarks about *Cathy* clearly testify, Loach is a great believer in the primacy of the political. And, as he himself concludes, "filmmakers have a very soft life really, in comparison to people who have to work for a living. And so it's easy to be a radical filmmaker. The people who really are on the front line aren't filmmakers. We're in a very privileged position, very free and good wages—if you can keep working.''

As Ken Loach ages, his films remain consistently provocative and politically savvy, with a deep respect for and understanding of his struggling, working class characters. *Riff Raff* features a prototypical Loach hero: an unemployed blue collar worker who comes to London and lands a job on a construction site. However, the film is no dry, pedantic political tract. While it is never less than pointed in its depiction of the never-ending conflict between the classes, it also is piercingly funny. Comic asides also highlight *Raining Stones,* an otherwise intense drama depicting the efforts of an out-of-work laborer to scrape together funds to feed his family. He is a proud man, who will not accept charity; however, trouble comes when he unwittingly borrows money from a loan shark to pay for his daughter's communion dress. With vivid irony, Loach graphically depicts the sense of hopelessness of honorable laborers who desire nothing more than the right to a suitable job, for suitable pay.

Loach's concerns are not solely with the male working class. *Ladybird Ladybird* is a trenchant, based-on-fact drama about a profoundly distressed single mother with a sad history of being exploited by men. He also is interested in the impact of history on the individual; in *Land and Freedom,* he abandons his usual British working class setting to tell the story of a jobless but passionate Liverpudlian Communist who treks to Barcelona during the Spanish Civil War to do battle for "land and freedom." The film works best as a potent look at political idealism in the face of the reality of a heartless, brutal enemy.—JULIAN PETLEY and ROB EDELMAN

Losey, Joseph

Nationality American. *Born* La Crosse, Wisconsin, 14 January 1909. *Education* Dartmouth College, New Hampshire, B.A., 1929; Harvard University, M.A. in English literature, 1930. *Career* Stage director, New York, 1932-34; attended Eisenstein film classes, Moscow, 1935; staged Living Newspaper productions and other plays for Federal Theater Project, New York, 1947; hired by Dory Schary for RKO, 1948; blacklisted, moved to London, 1951; began collaboration with writer Harold Pinter and actor Dirk Bogarde, 1963; directed Boris Godunov, *Paris, Opera, 1980. Awards* Chevalier de l'Ordre des Arts et des Lettres, 1957; International Critics Award, Cannes Festival, for Accident, 1967; Palme d'Or, Cannes Festival, for The Go-Between, 1971; Honorary Doctorate, Dartmouth College, 1973. *Died* In London, 22 June 1984.

Films as Director: 1939: *Pete Roleum and His Cousins* (short) (+p, sc). **1941:** *A Child Went Forth* (short) (+co-p, sc); *Youth Gets a Break* (short) (+sc). **1945:** *A Gun in His Hand* (short). **1949:** *The Boy*

Joseph Losey on the set of ***The Go-Between.***

with Green Hair. **1950:** The Lawless. **1951:** The Prowler, M; The Big Night (+co-sc). **1952:** Stranger on the Prowl (Encounter) (d as "Andrea Forzano"). **1954:** The Sleeping Tiger (d as "Victor Hanbury"). **1955:** A Man on the Beach. **1956:** The Intimate Stranger (Finger of Guilt) (d as "Joseph Walton"). **1957:** Time without Pity. **1958:** The Gypsy and the Gentleman. **1959:** Blind Date (Chance Meeting). **1960:** The Criminal (The Concrete Jungle). **1962:** Eve. **1963:** The Damned (These Are the Damned); The Servant (+co-p). **1964:** King and Country (+co-p). **1966:** Modesty Blaise. **1967:** Accident (+co-p). **1968:** Boom!; Secret Ceremony. **1970:** Figures in a Landscape; The Go-Between. **1972:** The Assassination of Trotsky (+co-p). **1973:** A Doll's House. **1975:** Galileo (+co-sc); The Romantic Englishwoman. **1977:** Mr. Klein. **1979:** Don Giovanni. **1982:** The Trout. **1985:** Steaming.

Joseph Losey's career spanned five decades and included work in both theater and film. Latterly an American expatriate living in Europe, the early years of his life as a director were spent in the very different milieus of New Deal political theater projects and the paranoia of the Hollywood studio system during the McCarthy era. He was blacklisted in 1951 and left America for England where he continued making films, at first under a variety of pseudonyms. His work is both controversial and critically acclaimed, and Losey has long been recognized as a director with a distinctive and highly personal cinematic style.

Although Losey rarely wrote his own screenplays, preferring instead to work closely with other authors, there are nevertheless several distinct thematic concerns which recur throughout his work. It is his emphasis on human interaction and the complexity of interior thought and emotion that makes a Losey film an intellectual challenge, and his interest has always lain with detailed character studies rather than with so-called "action" pictures. Losey's domain is interior action and his depiction of the physical world centers on those events which are an outgrowth or reflection of his characters' inner lives. From The Boy with Green Hair to The Trout, his films focus on individuals and their relationships to themselves, to those around them, and to their society as a whole.

One of Losey's frequent subjects is the intruder who enters a pre-existing situation and irrevocably alters its patterns. In his earlier films, this situation often takes the form of a community reacting with violence to an individual its members perceive as a threat. The "boy with green hair" is ostracized and finally forced to shave his head by the inhabitants of the town in which he lives; the young Mexican-American in The Lawless becomes the object of a vicious manhunt after a racially motivated fight; and the child-murderer in Losey's 1951 version of M inspires a lynch mob mentality in the community he has been terrorizing. In each of these cases, the social outsider who, for good or evil, does not conform to the standards of the community evokes a response of mass rage and suspicion. And as the members of the group forsake their individuality and rational behavior in favor of mob rule, they also forfeit any hope of future self-deception regarding their own capacity for unthinking brutality.

In Losey's later films, the scope of the "intruder" theme is often narrowed to explore the effect of a newcomer on the relationship of a husband and wife. The Sleeping Tiger, Eve, Accident, The Romantic Englishwoman, and The Trout all feature married couples whose lives are disrupted and whose relationships are shattered or redefined by the arrival of a third figure. In each of these films, either the husband or the wife is strongly attracted to the outsider. In The Sleeping Tiger, Eve, and The Trout, this attraction leads to tragedy and death for one of the partners, while the couples in Accident and The Romantic Englishwoman are forced to confront a serious rift in a seemingly untroubled relationship. A further level of conflict is added by the fact that the intruder in all of the films is either of a different social class (The Sleeping Tiger, Eve, The

Trout) or a different nationality (*Accident, The Romantic Englishwoman*) than the couple, representing not only a sexual threat but a threat to the bourgeois status quo as well.

This underlying theme of class conflict is one which runs throughout Losey's work, emerging as an essential part of the framework of films as different as *The Lawless, The Servant,* and *The Go-Between*. Losey's consistent use of film as a means of social criticism has its roots in his theatrical work of the 1930s and his association with Bertolt Brecht. The two collaborated on the 1947 staging of Brecht's *Galileo Galilei,* starring Charles Laughton—a play which twenty-seven years later Losey would bring to the screen—and Brecht's influence on Losey's own career is enormous. In addition to his interest in utilizing film as an expression of social and political opinions, Losey has adapted many of Brecht's theatrical devices to the medium as well. The sense of distance and reserve in Brechtian theatre is a keynote to Losey's filmic style, and Brecht's use of a heightened dramatic reality is also present in Losey's work. The characters in a Losey film are very much of the "real" world, but their depiction is never achieved through a documentary-style approach. We are always aware that it is a drama that is unfolding, as Losey makes use of carefully chosen music on the soundtrack, or photography that borders on expressionism, or deliberately evokes an atmosphere of memory to comment on the characters and their state of mind. It is this approach to the intellect rather than the emotions of the viewer that ties Losey's work so closely to Brecht.

Losey's films are also an examination of illusion and reality, with the true nature of people or events often bearing little resemblance to their outer appearances. The friendly community that gives way to mob violence, the "happy" marriage that unravels when one thread is plucked; these images of actual versus surface reality abound in Losey's work. One aspect of this theme manifests itself in Losey's fascination with characters who discover themselves through a relationship which poses a potential threat to their position in society. Tyvian, in *Eve,* can only acknowledge through his affair with a high-class prostitute that his fame as a writer is actually the result of plagiarism, while Marian, in *The Go-Between,* finds her true sexual nature, which her class and breeding urge her to repress, in her affair with a local farmer.

Several of Losey's films carry this theme a step further, offering characters who find their own sense of identity becoming inextricably bound up in someone else. In *The Servant,* the complex, enigmatic relationship between Tony and his manservant, Barrett, becomes both a class struggle and a battle of wills as the idle young aristocrat slowly loses control of his life to the ambitious Barrett. This is an idea Losey pursues in both *Secret Ceremony* and *Mr. Klein*. In the former, a wealthy, unbalanced young girl draws a prostitute into a destructive fantasy in which the two are mother and daughter, and the prostitute finds her initial desire for money becoming a desperate need to believe the fantasy. Alain Delon in *Mr. Klein* portrays a man in occupied France who becomes obsessed with finding a hunted Jew who shares his name. At the film's conclusion, he boards a train bound for the death camps rather than abandon his search, in effect becoming the other *Mr. Klein*. Losey emphasizes his characters' identity confusion cinematically, frequently showing them reflected in mirrors, their images fragmented, prism-like, or only partially revealed.

Losey's choice of subject led to his successful collaboration with playwright Harold Pinter on *The Servant, Accident,* and *The Go-Between,* and Losey once hoped to film Pinter's screenplay of Proust's *Remembrance of Things Past*. Their parallel dramatic interests served both men well, and their work together is among the finest in their careers. Yet if Losey found his most nearly perfect voice in Pinter's screenplays, his films with a wide variety of other writers have still resulted in a body of work remarkably consistent in theme and purpose. His absorbing, sometimes difficult films represent a unique and uncompromising approach to cinema, and guarantee Losey's place among the world's most intriguing directors.—JANET E. LORENZ

Lubitsch, Ernst

Nationality German/American. *Born* Berlin, 28 January 1892; became U.S. citizen, 1936. *Education* Attended the Sophien Gymnasium. *Family* Married 1) Irni (Helene) Kraus, 1922 (divorced 1930); 2) Sania Bezencenet (Vivian Gaye), 1935 (divorced 1943), one daughter. *Career* Taken into Max Reinhardt Theater Company, 1911; actor, writer, then director of short films, from 1913; member of Adolph Zukor's Europäischen Film-Allianz (Efa), 1921; joined Warner Brothers, Hollywood, 1923; began association with Paramount, 1928; began collaboration with writer Ernest Vajda, 1930; head of production at Paramount, 1935 (relieved of post after a year); left Paramount for three-year contract with 20th Century-Fox, 1938; suffered massive heart attack, 1943. *Award* Special Academy Award (for accomplishments in the industry), 1947. *Died* In Hollywood, 29 November 1947.

Films as Director: 1914: *Fräulein Seifenschaum* (+role); *Blindkuh* (+role); *Aufs Eis geführt* (+role). **1915:** *Zucker und Zimt* (co-d, co-sc, role). **1916:** *Wo ist mein Schatz?* (+role); *Schuhpalast Pinkus* (+role as Sally Pinkus); *Der gemischte Frauenchor* (+role); *Der G.m.b.H. Tenor* (+role); *Der Kraftmeier* (+role); *Leutnant auf Befehl* (+role); *Das schönste Geschenk* (+role); *Seine neue Nase* (+role). **1917:** *Wenn vier dasselbe Tun* (+co-sc, role); *Der Blusenkönig* (+role); *Ossis Tagebuch*. **1918:** *Prinz Sami* (+role); *Ein fideles Gefängnis*; *Der Fall Rosentopf* (+role); *Der Rodelkavalier* (+co-sc); *Die Augen der Mumie Mâ*; *Das Mädel vom Ballett*; *Carmen*. **1919:** *Meine Frau, die Filmschauspielerin*; *Meyer aus Berlin* (+role as apprentice); *Das Schwabemädle*; *Die Austernprinzessin*; *Rausch*; *Madame DuBarry*; *Der lustige Ehemann* (+sc); *Die Puppe* (+co-sc). **1920:** *Ich möchte kein Mann sein!* (+co-sc); *Kohlhiesels Töchter* (+co-sc); *Romeo und Julia im Schnee* (+co-sc); *Sumurun* (+co-sc); *Anna Boleyn*. **1921:** *Die Bergkatze* (+co-sc). **1922:** *Das Weib des Pharao*. **1923:** *Die Flamme; Rosita*. **1924:** *The Marriage Circle; Three Women; Forbidden Paradise* (+co-sc). **1925:** *Kiss Me Again* (+pr); *Lady Windermere's Fan* (+pr). **1926:** *So This Is Paris* (+pr). **1927:** *The Student Prince in Old Heidelberg* (+pr). **1928:** *The Patriot* (+pr). **1929:** *Eternal Love* (+pr); *The Love Parade* (+pr). **1930:** *Paramount on Parade* (anthology film); *Monte Carlo* (+pr). **1931:** *The Smiling Lieutenant* (+pr). **1932:** *The Man I Killed* (*Broken Lullaby*) (+pr); *One Hour with You* (+pr); *Trouble in Paradise* (+pr); *If I Had a Million* (anthology film). **1933:** *Design for Living* (+pr). **1934:** *The Merry Widow* (+pr). **1936:** *Desire* (co-d, pr). **1937:** *Angel* (+pr). **1938:** *Bluebeard's Eighth Wife* (+pr). **1939:** *Ninotchka* (+pr). **1940:** *The Shop Around the Corner* (+pr). **1941:** *That Uncertain Feeling* (+co-pr). **1942:** *To Be or Not to Be* (co-source, co-pr). **1943:** *Heaven Can Wait* (+pr). **1946:** *Cluny Brown* (+pr). **1948:** *That Lady in Ermine* (co-d).

Other Films: 1913: *Meyer auf der Alm* (role as Meyer). **1914:** *Die Firma Heiratet* (Wilhelm) (role as Moritz Abramowski); *Der Stolz der Firma* (Wilhelm) (role as Siegmund Lachmann); *Fräulein Piccolo* (Hofer) (role); *Arme Marie* (Mack) (role); *Bedingung—Kein Anhang!* (Rye) (role); *Die Ideale Gattin* (role); *Meyer als Soldat* (role as Meyer). **1915:** *Robert und Bertram* (Mack) (role); *Wie Ich Ermordet Wurde* (Ralph) (role); *Der Schwarze Moritz* (Taufstein and Berg) (role); *Doktor Satansohn* (Edel) (role as Dr. Satansohn); *Hans Trutz im Schlaraffenland* (Wegener) (role as Devil).

Ernst Lubitsch's varied career is often broken down into periods to emphasize the spectrum of his talents—from an actor in Max Reinhardt's Berlin Theater Company to head of production at Paramount. Each of these periods could well provide enough material for a sizeable book. It is probably most convenient to divide Lubitsch's output into three phases: his German films between 1913 and 1922; his Hollywood films from 1923 to 1934; and his

Hollywood productions from 1935 till his death in 1947.

During the first half of Lubitsch's filmmaking decade in Germany he completed about nineteen shorts. They were predominantly ethnic slapsticks in which he played a "Dummkopf" character by the name of Meyer. Only three of these one- to five-reelers still exist. He directed eighteen more films during his last five years in Germany, almost equally divided between comedies—some of which anticipate the concerns of his Hollywood works—and epic costume dramas. Pola Negri starred in most of these historical spectacles, and the strength of her performances together with the quality of Lubitsch's productions brought them both international acclaim. Their *Madame Dubarry* (retitled *Passion* in the United States) was not only one of the films responsible for breaking the American blockade on imported German films after World War I, but it also began the "invasion" of Hollywood by German talent.

Ernst Lubitsch.
Photograph by Robert Coburn.

Lubitsch came to Hollywood at Mary Pickford's invitation. He had hoped to direct her in *Faust,* but they finally agreed upon *Rosita,* a costume romance very similar to those he had done in Germany. After joining Warner Brothers, he directed five films that firmly established his thematic interests. The films were small in scale, dealt openly with sexual and psychological relationships in and out of marriage, refrained from offering conventional moral judgments, and demystified women. As Molly Haskell and Marjorie Rosen point out, Lubitsch created complex female characters who were aggressive, unsentimental, and able to express their sexual desires without suffering the usual pains of banishment or death. Even though Lubitsch provided a new and healthy perspective on sex and increased America's understanding of a woman's role in society, he did so only in a superficial way. His women ultimately affirmed the status quo. The most frequently cited film from this initial burst of creativity, *The Marriage Circle,* also exhibits the basic narrative motif found in most of Lubitsch's work—the third person catalyst. An essentially solid relationship is temporarily threatened by a sexual rival. The possibility of infidelity serves as the occasion for the original partners to reassess their relationship. They acquire a new self-awareness and understand the responsibilities they have towards each other. The lovers are left more intimately bound than before. This premise was consistently reworked until *The Merry Widow* in 1934.

The late 1920s were years of turmoil as every studio tried to adapt to sound recording. Lubitsch, apparently, was not troubled at all; he considered the sound booths nothing more than an inconvenience, something readily overcome. Seven of his ten films from 1929 to 1934 were musicals, but not of the proscenium-bound "all-singing, all-dancing" variety. Musicals were produced with such prolific abandon during this time (what better way to exploit the new technology?) that the public began avoiding them. Film histories tend to view the period from 1930 to 1933 as a musical void, yet it was the precise time that Lubitsch was making significant contributions to the genre. As Arthur Knight notes, "He was the first to be concerned with the 'natural' introduction of songs into the development of a musical-comedy plot." Starting with *The Love Parade,* Lubitsch eliminated the staginess that was characteristic of most musicals by employing a moving camera, clever editing, and the judicial use of integrated musical perform- ance, and in doing so constructed a seminal film musical format.

In 1932 Lubitsch directed his first non-musical sound comedy, *Trouble in Paradise.* Most critics consider this film to be, if not his best, then at least the complete embodiment of everything that has been associated with Lubitsch: sparkling dialogue, interesting plots, witty and sophisticated characters, and an air of urbanity—all part of the well-known "Lubitsch Touch." What constitutes the "Lubitsch Touch" is open to continual debate, the majority of the definitions being couched in poetic terms of idolization. Andrew Sarris comments that the "Lubitsch Touch" is a counterpoint of poignant sadness during a film's gayest moments. Leland A. Poague sees Lubitsch's style as being gracefully charming and fluid, with an "ingenious ability to suggest more than he showed. . . ." Observations like this last one earned Lubitsch the unfortunate moniker of "director of doors," since a number of his jokes relied on what unseen activity was being implied behind a closed door.

Regardless of which romantic description one chooses, the "Lubitsch Touch" can be most concretely seen as deriving from a standard narrative device of the silent film: interrupting the dramatic interchange by focusing on objects or small details that make a witty comment on or surprising revelation about the main action. Whatever the explanation, Lubitsch's style was exceptionally popular with critics and audiences alike. Ten years after arriving in the United States he had directed eighteen features, parts of two anthologies, and was recognized as one of Hollywood's top directors.

Lubitsch's final phase began when he was appointed head of production at Paramount in 1935, a position that lasted only one year. Accustomed to pouring all his energies into one project at a time, he was ineffective juggling numerous projects simultaneously. Accused of being out of step with the times, Lubitsch updated his themes in his first political satire, *Ninotchka,* today probably his most famous film. He continued using parody and satire in his blackest comedy, *To Be or Not to Be,* a film well liked by his contemporaries, and today receiving much reinvestiga- tion. If Lubitsch's greatest talent was his ability to make us laugh at the most serious events and anxieties, to use comedy to make us more aware of ourselves, then *To Be or Not to Be* might be considered the consummate work of his career.

Lubitsch, whom Gerald Mast terms the greatest technician in American cinema after Griffith, completed only two more films. At his funeral in 1947, Mervyn LeRoy presented a fitting eulogy: "he advanced the techniques of screen comedy as no one else has ever done. Suddenly the pratfall and the double-take were left behind and the sources of deep inner laughter were tapped."—GREG S. FALLER

Lucas, George

*Nationality American. **Born** Modesto, California, 14 May 1944. **Education** Attended Modesto Junior College; University of Southern California Film School, graduated 1966.*

Career Six-month internship at Warner Bros. spent as assistant to Francis Ford Coppola, 1967-68; co-founder, with Coppola, American Zoetrope, Northern California, 1969; directed first feature, THX-1138, 1971; established special effects company, Industrial Light and Magic, at San Rafael, California, 1976; formed production company Lucasfilm, Ltd., 1979; founded post production company Sprocket Systems, 1980; built Skywalker Ranch, and executive producer for Disneyland's 3-D music space adventure, Captain EO, 1980s. *Award* New York Film Critics Award for Best Screenwriting (with Gloria Katz and Willard Huyck), 1973. *Address* c/o Lucasfilm, Ltd., P.O. Box 2009, San Rafael, California 94912.

Films as Director and Scriptwriter: (Short student films) 1965-67: Look at Life; Freiheit; 1.42.08; Herbie (co-d); Anyone Lived in a Pretty How Town (co-sc); 6.18.67 (doc); The Emperor (doc); THX 1138:4EB. **1968:** Filmmaker (doc).

(Feature films) 1971: THX 1138 (co-sc). **1973:** American Graffiti (co-sc). **1977:** Star Wars (+exec pr).

Films as Executive Producer: 1979: More American Graffiti (Norton) (+story). **1980:** The Empire Strikes Back (Kershner) (+story); Kagemusha (The Shadow Warrior) (Kurosawa) (int'l version). **1981:** Raiders of the Lost Ark (Spielberg) (+story); Body Heat (Kasdan) (uncredited). **1982:** Twice upon a Time (Korty and Swenson). **1983:** Return of the Jedi (Marquand) (+co-sc, story). **1984:** Indiana Jones and the Temple of Doom (Spielberg) (+story). **1985:** Mishima (Schrader). **1986:** Howard the Duck (Huyck); Labyrinth (Henson); Captain EO (Coppola) (+sc). **1988:** Willow (Howard) (+story); Tucker: The Man and His Dream (Coppola); The Land Before Time. **1989:** Indiana Jones and the Last Crusade (Spielberg) (+story). **1994:** Radioland Murders (Mel Smith) (+story).

In whatever capacity George Lucas works—director, writer, producer—the films in which he is involved are a mixture of the familiar and the fantastic. Thematically, Lucas's work is often familiar, but the presentation of the material usually carries his unique mark. His earliest commercial science-fiction film, *THX 1138,* is not very different in plot from previous stories of futuristic totalitarian societies in which humans are subordinate to technology. What is distinctive about the film is its visual impact. The extreme close-ups, bleak sets, and crowds of "properly sedated" shaven-headed people moving mechanically through hallways effectively produce the physical environment of this cold, well-ordered society. The endless whiteness of the vast detention center without bars could not be more oppressive.

Although not a special effects film, *American Graffiti,* Lucas's second feature, does show his attention to detail and his interest in archetypal themes. Within the 24-hour period of the film, the hero potential is brought forth from within the main characters, either through courageous action or the making of courageous decisions. The film captures America on the verge of transition from the 1950s to the brave new world of the 1960s. Lucas does this visually by recreating the 1950s on screen down to the smallest detail, but he also communicates through his characters the feeling that their lives will never be the same again.

The combination of convention, archetype, and fantasy comes together fully in Lucas's subsequent films—the *Star Wars* and *Indiana Jones* series. On one level the *Star Wars* trilogy is a fairy tale set in outer space, as suggested in the opening title: "A long time ago in a galaxy far, far away. . . ." The basic plot conventions of the fairy tale are present: a princess in distress, a powerful evil ruler, and courageous knights. The trilogy is also a tale of the emergence of the hero within and the quest by which individuals realize their true selves, for the princess is really a Shaman, the evil ruler a self divided in need of healing, and the knights latent heroes who do not

**George Lucas on the set of *Willow*.
Photograph by Keith Hamshere.**

realize themselves as such at the beginning of the tale.

Scenes, especially from *Star Wars* and *The Empire Strikes Back,* look and sound like *Flash Gordon* episodes. Members of the Empire—the Emperor, Darth Vadar, the stormtroopers—are an easily identifiable evil in their dark, drab clothing and cloaked or helmeted faces. Their movements are accompanied by a menacing, martial film score of the type that ushered Ming the Merciless on screen. Another reference that associates the Empire with a great evil is that the stormtroopers in several scenes resemble the rows of assembled stormtroopers on review in *Triumph of the Will.* In contrast to these images of darkness, the rebel forces and their habitats are colorful and full of life.

The *Star Wars* trilogy is also very much science fiction. The special effects developed to realize Lucas's futuristic vision brought about technological advances in motion picture photography. The workshop formed for the production of *Star Wars,* Industrial Light and Magic, continues on as an independent special effects production company. While working on *Star Wars,* John Dykstra developed the Dykstraflex camera, for which he received an Academy Award. The camera was used in conjunction with a computer to achieve the accuracy necessary in photographing multiple-exposure visual effects. Another advancement in motion-control photography was developed for *The Empire Strikes Back*—Brian Edlund's Empireflex camera.

Lucas and Steven Spielberg then set out to make a film based on the romantic action/adventure movies of the 1940s. The successful result was *Raiders of the Lost Ark.* Indiana Jones, based on the rough-edged, worldly-wise screen heroes of those earlier adventure films, is set to such mythic tasks as the quest for the Ark of the Covenant and the quest for the Holy Grail. Jones's enemies on these quests (which occur in the first and the last films of the series), the Nazis, are representatives of the dark side of this universe and carry legendary status of their own. As in the *Star Wars* trilogy, the main characters, including the extraordinary Indiana, face challenges that will bring forth qualities and strengths they had not yet realized. The dialogue in *Indiana Jones and the Last Crusade* especially emphasizes the theme of the hero within. At one point the senior Jones tells Indiana that "The search for the cup of Christ is the search for the divine in all of us"; later in the film Indiana is challenged by the enemy as he is told, "It's time to ask yourself what you believe."

Radioland Murders is set in the world of live radio broadcasts of the late 1930s. All the conventional character types are here—from the inept director and his highly competent assistant to the golden-voiced booth announcer to the ever-creative sound-effects man. This romantic comedy/murder mystery was directed by Mel Smith, produced by Lucas, and based on an original story by Lucas. The narrative contains all the heroic challenges to spirit and character of more epic films condensed into a much smaller space and a much shorter time period. The action takes place within a few prime-time hours as a new radio network premieres. The broadcast carries on to a successful completion in spite of the murders of cast and crew, the police investigation, set breakdowns, and ego clashes. This universe of carefully contained chaos sometimes appears to be on the verge of spinning out of control, but it never does. The narrative, the broadcast, and the main characters persevere to the finish.

Lucas's films contain references to genre conventions and to earlier films. Also familiar in his work are the archetypal figures from myths and legends. At the same time, the films are fantastic and unfamiliar, filled with stunning visuals and exotic settings produced by innovative special effects.—MARIE SAELI

Lumet, Sidney

*Nationality American. **Born** Philadelphia, 25 June 1924. **Education** Professional Children's School, New York; Columbia University extension school. **Military Service** Served in Signal Corps, U.S. Army, 1942-46. **Family** Married 1) Rita Gam (divorced); 2) Gloria Vanderbilt, 1956 (divorced, 1963); 3) Gail Jones, 1963 (divorced, 1978); 4) Mary Gimbel, 1980; two daughters. **Career** Acting debut in Yiddish Theatre production, New York, 1928; Broadway debut in Dead End, 1935; film actor, from 1939; stage director, off-Broadway, from 1947; assistant director, then director, for TV, from 1950. **Awards***

Sidney Lumet (center) directing *The Deadly Affair*.

Directors Guild Awards for Twelve Angry Men, *1957, and* Long Day's Journey into Night, *1962. **Address** c/o LAH Film Corporation, 1775 Broadway, New York, NY 10019, U.S.A.*

Films as Director: 1957: *Twelve Angry Men.* **1958:** *Stage Struck.* **1959:** *That Kind of Woman.* **1960:** *The Fugitive Kind.* **1962:** *A View from the Bridge; Long Day's Journey into Night.* **1964:** *Fail Safe.* **1965:** *Pawnbroker; Up from the Beach; The Hill.* **1966:** *The Group* (+pr). **1967:** *The Deadly Affair* (+pr). **1968:** *Bye Bye Braverman* (+pr); *The Seagull* (+pr). **1969:** *Blood Kin* (doc) (co-d, co-pr). **1970:** *King: A Filmed Record . . . Montgomery to Memphis* (doc) (co-d, co-pr); *The Appointment; The Last of the Mobile Hot Shots.* **1971:** *The Anderson Tapes.* **1972:** *Child's Play.* **1973:** *The Offense; Serpico.* **1974:** *Lovin' Molly; Murder on the Orient Express.* **1975:** *Dog Day Afternoon.* **1977:** *Equus; Network.* **1978:** *The Wiz.* **1980:** *Just Tell Me What You Want* (+pr). **1981:** *Prince of the City.* **1982:** *Deathtrap; The Verdict.* **1983:** *Daniel.* **1984:** *Garbo Talks.* **1986:** *Power; The Morning After.* **1988:** *Running on Empty.* **1989:** *Family Business.* **1990:** *Q & A* (+sc). **1992:** *A Stranger Among Us.* **1993:** *Guilty as Sin.* **1997:** *Night Falls on Manhattan* (+sc); *Critical Care.*

Other Films: 1939: *One Third of a Nation* (Murphy) (role as Joey Rogers). **1940:** *Journey to Jerusalem* (role as youthful Jesus). **1990:** *Listen Up! The Lives of Quincy Jones* (role).

Although Sidney Lumet has applied his talents to a variety of genres (drama, comedy, satire, caper, romance, and even a musical), he has proven himself most comfortable and effective as a director of serious psychodramas and was most vulnerable when attempting light entertainments. His Academy Award nominations, for example, have all been for character studies of men in crisis, from his first film, *Twelve Angry Men,* to *The Verdict.*

Lumet was, literally, a child of the drama. At the age of four he was appearing in productions of the highly popular and acclaimed Yiddish Theatre in New York. He continued to act for the next two decades but increasingly gravitated toward directing. At twenty-six he was offered a position as an assistant director with CBS television. Along with John Frankenheimer, Robert Mulligan, Martin Ritt, Delbert Mann, George Roy Hill, Franklin Schaffner, and others, Lumet quickly won recognition as a competent and reliable director in a medium where many faltered under the pressures of producing live programs. It was in this environment that Lumet learned many of the skills that would serve him so well in his subsequent career in films: working closely with performers, rapid preparation for production, and working within tight schedules and budgets.

Because the quality of many of the television dramas was so impressive, several of them were adapted as motion pictures. Reginald Rose's *Twelve Angry Men* brought Lumet to the cinema. Although Lumet did not direct the television production, his expertise made him the ideal director for this low-budget film venture. *Twelve Angry Men* was an auspicious beginning for Lumet. It was a critical and commercial success and established him as a director skilled at adapting theatrical properties to motion pictures. Fully half of Lumet's complement of films have originated in the theater. Another precedent set by *Twelve Angry Men* was Lumet's career-long disdain for Hollywood.

Lumet prefers to work in contemporary urban settings, especially New York. Within this context, Lumet is consistently attracted to situations in which crime provides the occasion for a group of characters to come together. Typically these characters are caught in a vortex of events they can neither understand nor control but which they must work to resolve. *Twelve Angry Men* explores the interaction of a group of jurors debating the innocence or guilt of a man being tried for murder; *The Hill* concerns a rough group of military men who have been sentenced to prison; *The Deadly Affair* involves espionage in Britain; *The Anderson Tapes* revolves around the robbery of a luxury apartment building; *Child's Play,* about murder at a boy's school, conveys an almost supernatural atmosphere of menace; *Murder on the Orient Express, Dog Day Afternoon,* and *The Verdict* all involve attempts to find the solution to a crime, while *Serpico* and *Prince of the City* are probing examinations of men who have rejected graft practices as police officers.

Lumet's protagonists tend to be isolated, unexceptional men who oppose a group or institution. Whether the protagonist is a member of a jury or party to a bungled robbery, he follows his instincts and intuition in an effort to find solutions. Lumet's most important criterion is not whether the actions of these men are right or wrong but whether the actions are genuine. If these actions are justified by the individual's conscience, this gives his heroes uncommon strength and courage to endure the pressures, abuses, and injustices of others. Frank Serpico, for example, is the quintessential Lumet hero in his defiance of peer group authority and the assertion of his own code of moral values.

Nearly all the characters in Lumet's gallery are driven by obsessions or passions that range from the pursuit of justice, honesty, and truth to the clutches of jealousy, memory, or guilt. It is not so much the object of their fixations but the obsessive condition itself that intrigues Lumet. In films like *The Fugitive Kind, A View from the Bridge, Long Day's Journey into Night, The Pawnbroker, The Seagull, The Appointment, The Offense, Lovin' Molly, Network, Just Tell Me What You Want,* and many of the others, the protagonists, as a result of their complex fixations, are lonely, often disillusioned individuals. Consequently, most of Lumet's central characters are not likable or pleasant, and sometimes not admirable figures. And, typically, their fixations result in tragic or unhappy consequences.

Lumet's fortunes have been up and down at the box office. One explanation seems to be his own fixation with uncompromising studies of men in crisis. His most intense characters present a grim vision of idealists broken by realities. From Val in *A View from the Bridge* and Sol Nazerman in *The Pawnbroker* to Danny Ciello in *Prince of the City,* Lumet's introspective characters seek to penetrate the deepest regions of the psyche.

Lumet's memoir about his life in film, *Making Movies,* is extremely lighthearted and infectious in its enthusiasm for the craft of moviemaking itself. This stands in marked contrast to the tone and style of most of his films. Perhaps Lumet's signature as a director is his work with actors—and his exceptional ability to draw high-quality, sometimes extraordinary perform-ances from even the most unexpected quarters: Melanie Griffith's believable undercover policewoman in *A Stranger among Us* and Don Johnson's smooth-talking sociopath in *Guilty as Sin.* These two examples of the "Lumet touch" with actors demonstrate that he has not lost it.—STEPHEN E. BOWLES and JOHN McCARTY

Lumière, Louis

Nationality *French.* **Born** *Besançon, 5 October 1864.* **Education** *L'école de la Marti-nière, Besançon, degree 1880; attended Conservatoire de Lyon, 1880-81.* **Career** *Chemist and inventor, son of an industrialist specializing in photographic chemistry and the making of emulsions; after seeing the Edison Kinetoscope demonstrated in Paris, developed with brother Auguste Lumière (1862-1954) the "Cinématographe Lumière," incorporating invention of claw driven by eccentric gear for advancing film, 1894; projected first film, showing workers leaving the Lumière factory, 1895; projected first*

*program for a paying audience at Grand Café, Boulevard des Capucines, Paris, 28
December 1895; Société du Cinématographe Lumière formed, 1896; projected film onto
16 by 21 foot screen at Paris Exposition, 1900; company ceased film production, 1905;
subsequently invented and manufactured photographic equipment; worked on stereo
projection method, from 1921; première of "cinéma en relief" in Paris, 1936.* **Died** *In
Bandol, France, 6 June 1948.*

Films as Director: 1896-1900: Directed about 60 films and produced about 2000, mostly documentaries. **1894 or 95:** *La Sortie des usines* (version no. 1). **1895:** *La Sortie des usines* (version no. 2);
L'Arroseur arrosé (*Le Jardinier*); *Forgerons; Pompiers; Attaque du feu; Le Repas de bébé* (*Le Déjeuner de
bébé, Le Gouter de bébé*); *Pêche aux poissons rouges; La Voltige, Débarquement* (*Arrivée des congressistes à
Neuville-sur-Saône*); *Discussion de M. Janssen et de M. Lagrange; Saut à la couverture* (*Brimade dans
une caserne*); *Lyon, place des Cordeliers; Lyon, place Bellecour; Récréation à la Martinière; Charcuterie
mécanique; Le Maréchalferrant; Lancement d'un navire à La Ciotat; Baignade en mer; Ateliers de La
Ciotat; Barque sortant du port* (*La Sortie du port*); *Arrivée d'un train à La Ciotat; Partie d'écarté;
Assiettes tournantes; Chapeaux à transformations* (*Trewey: Under the Hat*); *Photographe; Démolition
d'un mur* (*Le Mur*); *Querelle enfantine, Aquarium; Bocal aux poissons-rouges; Partie de tric-trac; Le
Dejeuner du chat; Départ en voiture; Enfants aux jouets; Course en sac; Discussion.* **1896-97:** *Barque
en mer; Baignade en mer; Arrivée d'un bateau à vapeur; Concours de boules; Premiers pas de Bébé;
Embarquement pour le promenade; Retour d'une promenade en mer; Marché; Enfant et chien; Petit
frèree et petite soeur; Douche après le bain; Ronde enfantine; Enfants au bord de la mer; Bains en mer;
Touristes revenant d'une excursion; Scènes d'enfants; Laveuses; Repas en famille, Bal d'enfants; Leçon
de bicyclette; Menuisiers; Radeau avec baigneurs; Le Goûter de bébé.* **1900:** *Inauguration de
l'Exposition universelle, La Tour Eiffel; Le Pont d' Iéna; Danses espagnoles* and other films shown on
large screen at Paris Exposition 1900. **1936:** *Arrivée d'un train en gare de La Ciotat* and other films
presented in "cinéma en relief" program.

Few directors since Louis Lumière have enjoyed such total control over their films. As
inventor of the *cinématographe,* the first camera-cum-projector, he determined not only the
subjects but also the aesthetics of early cinema. A scientist devoted to the plastic arts, Lumière
initially specialized in outdoor photography. This experience, coupled with an appreciation of
framing, perspective, and light values in a composition, informed his pioneering films.

To promote the *cinématographe,* he made demonstration shorts which, because of the
camera's limited spool capacity, lasted less than a minute. If art refines itself through constraint,
Lumière's films are excellent models. He overcame the *cinématographe's* technical limitations to
achieve tightly structured views of contemporary life, both public and private.

Though Lumière's role in establishing the cinema has been dutifully recorded together
with the audience's thrilled disbelief at his moving images, his contribution to film practice
deserves more recognition. His first film, *La Sortie des usines,* pictures employees leaving his
photographic factory. Framed by the open gates, they disperse before the camera set at a
medium close-up distance, and with the closure of the gates the sequence ends. The film does
not result from a casual pointing of the camera at the chosen subject: all has been pre-planned,
from the placing of the hidden camera to the squaring of the action's duration with the available
footage.

Over the next two years or so, Lumière experimented with diverse subjects and filming
techniques. His themes reflect an unquestioning confidence in the permanence of contemporary political and social structures. Whether recording aspects of city life or the calmer pleasures
of the seaside, the work of the artisan, fireman, or soldier, more personal family subjects or
rehearsed comic episodes, his films imply a well-ordered, contented society where individuals

cheerfully perform their allotted roles. Images of social deprivation or discontent are noticeably absent.

Scenes featuring family or friends are often filmed in medium close-up, with the single framing here reinforcing the intimacy and denying a world outside. Immaculate children, invariably in white, are shown feeding (*Repas de bébé*), learning to walk (*Premiers pas de bébé*), playing with toys (*Enfants aux jouets*), arguing (*Querelle enfantine*), dancing (*Bal d'enfants*), or delightfully trying to catch goldfish (*Pêche aux poissons rouges*). In *Concert,* Madame Lumière plays a violin, while card games involve family friends (*Partie d'écarté* and *Partie de tric-trac*). A cat lapping milk (*Déjeûner du chat*) is filmed in close-up and in *Aquarium* the fish tank fills the frame to create the illusion of underwater photography.

Louis Lumière

In films such as *Place des Cordeliers* and *Place Bellecour* the atmosphere of public squares alive with horse-drawn carriages and bustling crowds is captured, while in films such as *Baignade en mer* the novelties of sea-bathing are recorded. Other films prefigure newsreels by documenting particular events. The first of these, *Débarquement,* records photographers arriving for their conference and was projected the next day. Similar events include a street sack race (*Course en sac*), the demolition of a wall (*Démolition d'un mur*), the launching of a ship (*Lancement d'un navire à La Ciotat*), and various arrivals or departures, such as *Touristes revenant d'une excursion,* or *Arrivée d'un bateau à vapeur.* An early triumph was *Barque sortant du port,* where glistening waves and a sudden swell rocking the boat impressed themselves on a public familiar only with static images. Sequences capturing movement were an immediate attraction.

Lumière's most celebrated arrival subject was the train entering La Ciotat station (*Arrivée d'un train à la Ciotat*). Here the dramatic resources of depth of field are exploited, with the platform and the track forming strong diagonals reaching into the distance. The train, first pictured in longshot, thrusts itself towards the camera to create a dynamic close-up. So powerful was the illusion of the train's immanence that the first audiences reportedly feared for their safety. The creative use of perspective was also fundamental to the depiction of plowing in *Labourage* and to the sack race in *Course en sac.*

Documentaries concerning artisans or the military reveal a studied composition. The camera is positioned to make actions comprehensible, whether in terms of shoeing horses (*Maréchal-ferrant*), shaping iron bars (*Forgerons*), or horsemanship (*Voltige*). Cooperation with the fire service produced a more substantial documentary. Recognizing the dramatic potential of his subject, Lumière portrayed a full-scale fire practice in four linked films: *Sortie de la Pompe, Mise en Batterie, Attaque du feu,* and *Sauvetage.*

Comic sketches required careful preparation. In *L'Arroseur arrosé* a young prankster soaks an unsuspecting gardener by interrupting, then releasing, the water supply to a hose. All is tightly organized in time and space to meet the limitations of the fixed camera. In *Photographe* the innocent subject is again drenched, while in *Charcuterie mécanique* (which ridicules American mechanization long before Tati's postman in *Jour de fête*) a pig is converted into sausages which then magically transform themselves into a pig again. Although Lumière renounced filmmaking, he extended his influence through trained operators, such as Promio, Mesguish, and Doublier. His impact on early cinema is evident in the way others, notably Méliès, imitated his subjects. His abiding presence in French film culture is witnessed in various homages: in *Les Mistons* Truffaut affectionately alludes to *L'Arroseur arrosé,* while in *Les Carabiniers* Godard parodies *L'Arrivée d'un train à la Ciotat* and *Le Repas de bébé.*

To celebrate the 100th anniversary of film, *Lumière et compagnie,* a filmed tribute to Lumière's contribution to the industry, brought together the work of 40 filmmakers who used the original Cinematograph, now restored, to film short vignettes (constrained by the limitations of the camera). These were interspersed with segments of interviews with the directors, among whom were Zhang Yi-Mou and Constantin Costa-Gavras.—R.F. COUSINS

Lynch, David

Nationality *American.* **Born** *Missoula, Montana, 20 January 1946.* **Education** *High school in Alexandria, Virginia; Corcoran School of Art, c. 1964; Boston Museum School, 1965; Pennsylvania Academy of Fine Art, 1965-69; American Film Institute Centre for Advanced Studies, studying under Frank Daniel, 1970.* **Family** *Married 1) Peggy Reavey, 1967 (divorced, 1974), one daughter, writer/director Jennifer Lynch; 2) Mary Fisk, 1977 (divorced, 1987), one son, Austin.* **Career** *Spent five years making* Eraserhead, *Los Angeles, 1971-76; worked as paperboy and shed-builder, late 1970s; invited by Mel Brooks to direct* The Elephant Man, *1980; with Mark Frost, made* Twin Peaks *for video (two-hour version) and as TV series, 1989.* **Awards** *National Society of Film Critics Awards for Best Film and Best Director, for* Blue Velvet, *1986; Palme d'Or, Cannes Festival, for* Wild at Heart, *1990.*

Films as Director and Scriptwriter: 1968: *The Alphabet* (short). **1970:** *The Grandmother* (short). **1978:** *Eraserhead.* **1980:** *The Elephant Man* (co-sc). **1984:** *Dune.* **1986:** *Blue Velvet.* **1988:** episode in *Les Français vus par . . . .* **1990:** *Wild at Heart.* **1992:** episodes of *On The Air* for TV (+pr); *Twin Peaks: Fire Walk with Me* (+co-pr, role as Gordon Cole). **1993:** episodes of *Hotel Room* for TV (+ex pr). **1996:** *Lost Highway* (+co-sc, sd ds).

Other Films: 1988: *Zelly and Me* (role as Willie). **1991:** *The Cabinet of Dr. Ramirez* (exec pr). **1994:** *Nadja* (exec pr, role as Morgue Attendant); *Crumb* (Zwigoff) (pr).

The undoubted perversity that runs throughout the works of David Lynch extends to his repeated and unexpected career turns: coming off the semi-underground *Eraserhead* to make the semi-respectable *The Elephant Man,* with a distinguished British cast; then bouncing into a Dino de Laurentiis mega-budget science-fiction fiasco, *Dune;* creeping back with the seductive and elusive small-town mystery of *Blue Velvet;* capping that by transferring his uncompromising vision of lurking sexual violence to American network television in *Twin Peaks;* and alienating the viewers of that bizarre soap with the rambling, intermittently stupefying, road movie *Wild at*

Heart. Although there are recognisable Lynchian elements, with both *Eraserhead* and *Blue Velvet*—his two most commercially and critically successful movies—leaking images and ideas into the pairs of movies that followed them up, Lynch has proved surprisingly difficult to pin down. Given one Lynch movie, it has been—until the slightly too self-plagiaristic *Wild at Heart*—almost impossible to predict the next step. A painter and animator—his first films are Svankmajer-style shorts *The Grandmother* and *Alphabet*—Lynch came into the film industry through the back door, converting his thesis movie into *Eraserhead* on a shooting schedule that stretched over some years and required the eternal soliciting of money from friends, like Sissy Spacek, who had gone on to do well.

Eraserhead is one of the rare cult movies that deserves its cult reputation, although it is a hard movie to sit still through for a

David Lynch

second time around. Set in a monochrome fantasy world that suggests the slums of Oz, it follows a pompadoured drudge, Henry (John Nance), through his awful life in a decaying apartment building, with occasional bursts of light relief from the fungus-cheeked songstress behind the radiator, and winds up with two extraordinarily bizarre and horrid fantasy sequences, one in which Henry's head falls off and is mined for indiarubber to be used in pencil erasers, and the other in which he cuts apart his skinned fetus of a mutant child and is deluged with a literal tide of excrement. Without really being profound, the film manages to worm its way into the hearts of the college crowd, cannily appealing—in one of Lynch's trademarks—to intellectuals who relish the multiple allusions and evasive "meanings" of the film, and to horror movie fans who just like to go along with the extreme imagery. With *The Elephant Man,* also in black and white and laden with the steamy industrial imagery of *Eraserhead,* Lynch, cued perhaps by the poignance of John Hurt's under-the-rubber performance and the presence of the sort of cast (Anthony Hopkins, John Gielgud, Freddie Jones, Michael Elphick) one would expect from some BBC-TV Masterpiece Theatre serial, opts for a more humanist approach, mellowing the sheer nastiness of the first film. In the finale, as the mutant John Merrick attends a lovingly recreated Victorian magic show, Lynch even pays homage to the gentle magician whose *The Man with the Indiarubber Head* might be cited as a precursor to *Eraserhead,* Georges Méliès.

Dune is a folly by anyone's standards, and the re-cut television version—which Lynch opted to sign with the Director's Guild pseudonym Allan Smithee—is no help in sorting out the multiple plot confusions of Frank Herbert's pretentious and unfilmable science-fiction epic. Hoping for a fusion of *Star Wars* and *Lawrence of Arabia,* De Laurentiis—who stuck by Lynch throughout the troubled $40 million production—wound up with a turgid mess, overloaded with talented performers in nothing roles, that only spottily seems to have engaged Lynch's interest, mostly when there are monsters on screen or when Kenneth McMillan is campily overdoing his perverse and evil emperor act. *Dune* landed Lynch in the doldrums, and his comeback movie, also for the forgiving De Laurentiis, was very carefully crafted to evoke the virtues and cult commercial appeal of *Eraserhead* without seeming a throwback. Drawing on *Shadow of a Doubt,* Lynch made a small-town mystery that deigns to work on a plot level, and then shot it through with his own cruel insights into the teeming, insectoid nightmare that exists beneath the red, white, and blue prettiness of the setting, coaxing sinister meaning out of resonant pop songs like "Blue Velvet" and "In Dreams," and establishing the core of a repertory company—Kyle MacLachlan of *Dune,* Isabella Rossellini, Laura Dern—who would recur in his next projects. *Blue Velvet,* far more than the muddy *Dune,* established Lynch as a master of colour in addition to his black and white skills, and also, through his handling of human monster Dennis Hopper's abuse of Rossellini, as a chronicler of extreme emotions, often combining sex and violence in one disturbing, yet undeniably appealing package.

Twin Peaks, a television series Lynch devised and for which he directed the pilot film, is a strange offshoot of *Blue Velvet,* set in a similar town and with MacLachlan again the odd investigator of a crime the nature of which is hard to define. Although it lacks the explicit tone of the earlier film, in which Dennis Hopper is given to basic outbursts like "baby wants to fuck!," *Twin Peaks* is also insidiously fascinating, using the labyrinthine plot convolutions of the typical soap opera—among other things, the show is a lineal descendant of *Peyton Place*—in addition to the puzzle-solving twists of the murder mystery to probe under the surface of a folksy America of junk food and picket fences. As a reaction to the eerie restraint of *Twin Peaks, Wild at Heart* is an undisciplined, half-satisfactory movie, a road film which evokes Elvis in Nicolas Cage's subtly overwrought performance and straggles along towards its *Wizard of Oz* finale, passing by the high points of Lynch's career (featuring players and jokes from all his earlier movies) as it plays out its couple-on-the-run storyline in a surprisingly straightforward and above-board manner. With Willem Dafoe's dirty-toothed monster replacing Dennis Hopper's gas-sniffing gangster, *Wild at Heart* echoes the violent and sexual excesses of *Blue Velvet,* including one exploding head stunt out of *The Evil Dead* and many heavy-metal-scored, heavy-duty sex scenes, but suffers perhaps from its relative predictability.

Both a genuine artist and a cunning commercial survivor, Lynch appeared—in the minds of many critics—to be one of the best hopes for cinema in the 1990s. However, Lynch's promise as a savior had yet to be fulfilled. Unable to get the ill-fated *Twin Peaks* out of his system after it went unceremoniously off the air without a resolution, Lynch launched a theatrical version of his TV show, *Twin Peaks: Fire Walk with Me.* Ironically, it turned out to be a prequel to the events portrayed in the series rather than a sequel, so to date we are still left without a resolution to the labyrinthine mysteries surrounding the puzzle of "who killed Laura Palmer?" Overlong and oddly underheated, it was a commercial bomb, even with hardcore *Peaks* fans.—KIM NEWMAN and JOHN McCARTY

Mackendrick, Alexander

Nationality *Scottish*. **Born** *Boston, 1912*. **Education** *Glasgow School of Art*. **Career** *Commercial artist, animator of advertising films, also worked in Holland with George Pal, 1930s; made short propaganda films for Ministry of Information, World War II; later head of documentary and newsreel department of Psychological Warfare Branch, Rome; joined Ealing Studios as scriptwriter, 1946; directed first feature,* Whisky Galore, *1946; signed contract with Hecht-Lancaster (Harold Hecht and Burt Lancaster) to make* Sweet Smell of Success *in U.S., 1956; Dean, Film Dept. of California Institute of the Arts, Valencia, from 1969; resigned Deanship, continued to teach at CalArts, from 1978.* **Died** *In Los Angeles, 22 Decmeber 1993, of pneumonia.*

Films as Director: 1949: *Whisky Galore (Tight Little Island)* (+co-sc). **1951:** *The Man in the White Suit* (+co-sc). **1952:** *Mandy (The Story of Mandy; Crash of Silence).* **1954:** *The Maggie (High and Dry)* (+story). **1955:** *The Ladykillers.* **1957:** *Sweet Smell of Success.* **1963:** *Sammy Going South (A Boy Ten Feet Tall).* **1965:** *A High Wind in Jamaica.* **1967:** *Oh Dad, Poor Dad, Mamma's Hung You in the Closet and I'm Feelin' So Sad* (Quine) (d add'l scenes); *Don't Make Waves.*

Other Films: 1950: *The Blue Lamp* (Dearden) (add'l dialogue).

In 1955 Alexander Mackendrick made *The Ladykillers,* the last of his four Ealing comedies. Two years later, in Hollywood, came his brilliantly acid study of corruption and betrayal, *Sweet Smell of Success.* At first glance, the gulf is prodigious. Yet on closer examination, it narrows considerably: the apparent contrast between the two films becomes little more than a matter of surface tone. For behind the comedies that Mackendrick made for Ealing can be detected a mordant humor, a pessimism, and even an instinct for cruelty that sets them apart from the gentle sentimentality of their stablemates (Hamer's *Kind Hearts and Coronets* always excepted). The mainstream of Ealing comedy, even including such classics as *Passport to Pimlico* and *The Lavender Hill Mob,* presents (as Charles Barr has pointed out) "a whimsical daydream of how things might be." There is little of that daydream about Mackendrick's films; at times—as in *The Ladykillers*—they edge closer to surrealist nightmare.

Alexander Mackendrick

In *Whisky Galore* the English outsider, Captain Waggett, is subjected by islanders to continual humiliation, unalleviated even in their triumph by the slightest friendly gesture. Similarly Marshall, the American tycoon in *The Maggie,* is abused, exploited, and physically assaulted by the Scots he encounters. Both workers and bosses in *The Man in the White Suit* turn violently upon Sidney Stratton, the idealistic inventor; and *The Ladykillers* culminates in a whole string of brutal murders. Not that this blackness detracts in the least from the effectiveness of the comedy. Rather, it lends the films a biting edge that makes them all the funnier, and may well explain why they have dated far less than most other Ealing movies.

A constant theme of Mackendrick's films is the clash between innocence and experience. Innocence connotes integrity, but also blindness to the interests of others; experience brings shrewdness, but also corruption. Generally, innocence is defeated, but not always: in *The Ladykillers* it is serenely innocent Mrs. Wilberforce who survives—as does Susan Hunsecker in *Sweet Smell of Success,* albeit at a price. Children feature prominently in Mackendrick's films—especially *Mandy, Sammy Going South, The Maggie*—and often embody the principle of innocence, though again not always. In *A High Wind in Jamaica,* against all audience expectations, it is the pirates, not the children they capture, who prove to be the innocents and who suffer death for it. As so often with Mackendrick's characters, they are doomed by their lack of perception; trapped, like the deaf heroine of *Mandy,* in a private world, they see only what they expect to see.

Mackendrick established a reputation as an exacting and perfectionist director, bringing to his films a visual acuteness and a flair for complex fluid composition to support the tight dramatic structure. After *Sweet Smell of Success,* though, the quality of his work is generally considered to have declined, and he made no films after 1967. A planned project on *Mary Queen of Scots* (intriguingly outlined by Mackendrick as "a sophisticated French lady landed in Boot Hill") never materialized. From 1969 to 1978 he headed an outstanding film department at the California Institute of the Arts; but the withdrawal of such a subtle and individual director from active filmmaking is greatly to be regretted.—PHILIP KEMP

Makavejev, Dušan

Nationality *Yugoslavian.* **Born** *Belgrade, 13 October 1932.* **Education** *Studied psychology at Belgrade University, graduated 1955; studied direction at the Academy for Theatre, Radio, Film, and Television, Belgrade.* **Military Service** *1959-60.* **Family**

Married Bojana Marijan, 1964. **Career** *Experimental filmmaker for Kino-Club, 1955-58; joined Zagreb Films, 1958; worked for Avala films, 1961; went to United States on Ford Foundation Grant, 1968; worked in United States, since 1974; instructor of film at various universities, including Columbia, Harvard, and New York.*

Films as Director: (Shorts and documentaries): 1953: *Jatagan Mala* (+sc). **1955:** *Pečat* (*The Seal*) (+sc). **1957:** *Antonijevo razbijeno ogledalo* (*Anthony's Broken Mirror*) (+sc). **1958:** *Spomenicima ne treba verovati* (*Don't Believe in Monuments*) (+sc); *Slikovnica pčelara* (*Beekeeper's Scrapbook*) (+sc); *Prokleti praznik* (*Damned Holiday*) (+sc); *Boje sanjaju* (*Colors Are Dreaming*) (+sc). **1959:** *Što je radnički savjet?* (*What Is a Workers' Council?*). **1961:** *Eci, pec, pec* (*One Potato, Two Potato . . .*) (+sc); *Pedagoška bajka* (*Educational Fairy Tale*) (+sc); *Osmjeh 61* (*Smile 61*) (+sc). **1962:** *Parada* (*Parade*) (+sc); *Dole plotovi* (*Down with the Fences*) (+sc); *Ljepotica 62* (*Miss Yugoslavia 62*) (+sc); *Film o knjizi A.B.C.* (*Film about the Book*) (+sc). **1964:** *Nova igračka* (*New Toy*) (+sc); *Nova domaća zivotinja* (*New Domestic Animal*) (+sc).

(Feature films): 1966: *Covek nije tica* (*Man Is Not a Bird*) (+sc). **1967:** *Ljubavni Slučaj, tragedija sluzbenice PTT* (*Love Affair, Switchboard Operator, An Affair of the Heart*) (+sc). **1968:** *Nevinost bez zaštite* (*Innocence Unprotected*) (+sc). **1971:** *WR—Misterije organizma* (*WR—Mysteries of the Organism*) (+sc). **1974:** *Sweet Movie* (+co-sc). **1981:** *Montenegro* (*Or Pigs and Pearls*) (+sc). **1985:** *The Coca-Cola Kid.* **1989:** *Manifesto* (*For a Night of Love*). **1993:** *The Gorilla Bathes at Noon.* **1995:** *A Hole in the Soul* (+sc, role as himself). **1996:** *Danske piger viser alt.*

Before making his first feature film, *Man Is Not a Bird,* Makavejev had developed his filmmaking skills and formulated his chief thematic and formal concerns by producing a number of 35mm experimental shorts and documentaries. His second feature, *Love Affair,* furthered Makavejev's reputation and situated him within a growing community of Eastern European filmmakers committed to exploring the potential of the film medium by opening it up to new subject matter and experimenting with non-conventional narrative forms. *Love Affair* deals with the romance between a Hungarian-born switchboard operator, Isabella, and Ahmed, an Arab sanitation engineer, and the breakdown of the relationship, Isabella's death, and Ahmed's arrest for her murder. However, this straightforward plot is only the skeleton which supports the rest of the film. Influenced by Eisenstein and Godard, Makavejev builds an elaborate, Brechtian amalgam of documentary-like examinations of rat extermination, interviews with a sexologist and criminologist, actual stock footage of the destruction of church spires during the October Revolution, as well as almost quaint digressions on how mattress stuffing is combed and how strudel is made. Makavejev questions the nature of sexual relationships in a changing, post-revolutionary, but still puritanical society by juxtaposing ostensibly unrelated images. For example, the razing of the church spires is intercut with and comments on Isabella's seduction of Ahmed and the destruction of his archaic sexual inhibitions.

Innocence Unprotected also manifests Makavejev's interest in the dialectics of montage, the ability to create new ideas by juxtaposing incongruous or contradictory images. In this film, Makavejev rescues a little bit of "unprotected innocence" from oblivion by incorporating the original *Innocence Unprotected,* the first Serbian "all-talking" feature, into a new cinematic context. This 1940s romance-adventure—filmed by a well-known local trongman-daredevil during the Nazi Occupation, censored by the occupation government, and ironically later denounced as being Nazi-inspired—is intercut with interviews Makavejev conducted with members of the original production crew as well as newsreel footage from the period of the occupation. Moreover, Makavejev hand-tints portions of the original film to contribute to the critical distance created by the archaic quality of the footage. Perhaps more than any of his other films, *Innocence Unprotected* shows Makavejev's loving interest in traditional Yugoslavian folk culture and humor.

WR—Mysteries of the Organism deals with the sexuality of politics and the politics of sexuality. A radical condemnation of both the sterility of Stalinism and the superficial commercialism of Western capitalism, *WR* is certainly a document of its time—of Yugoslavia attempting to follow its "other road" to socialism while America fights in Vietnam and Moscow invades Czechoslovakia. Makavejev looks to Wilhelm Reich (the "WR" of the title) for enlightenment. Reich was, early in his career, one of the first to recognize the profound interconnections between socio-political structure and the individual psyche. His radical sexual ideas alienated the psychoanalytic profession and his unorthodox medical theories and practices eventually led to his imprisonment in the United States.

Although elaborate cross-cutting blends the two sections of the film, roughly the first half of *WR* is devoted to a documentary study of Wilhelm Reich's life in the United States. Interviews with Reich's therapists, Reich's relatives, even people who knew him casually, including his barber, are intercut with an examination of American sexual mores circa 1970 via interviews with Jackie Curtis, Barbara Dobson, one of the editors of *Screw* magazine, and others. The second half of the film is primarily a fictional narrative set in Belgrade, which concerns the love affair between a young female admirer of Reich (Milena) and a rather priggish and prudish Soviet ice skater named Vladimir Ilyich. Freed of his inhibitions by Milena's persistence, Vladimir makes love to her and then, unable to deal with his sexuality, decapitates her with his ice skate. However, after death, Milena's severed head continues to speak. Vladimir sings a song with a lyric written by a Soviet citizen critical of his government. *WR* ends with a photo of the smiling Reich—a sign of hope, a contradictory indication of the possibility for change and new beginnings.

WR was never released in Yugoslavia, and Makavejev made his two subsequent films, *Sweet Movie* and *Montenegro,* in the United States and Europe. Like *WR, Sweet Movie* has two parts. In the first a beauty contestant, Miss World, is wedded to and violated by Mr. Kapital and, after other humiliations, ends up in Otto Muehl's radical therapy commune. Miss World is taken in and nurtured by actual commune members who engage in various types of infantile regressions (including carrying their excrement displayed on dinner plates) as therapy. The second part of the film is an allegorical commentary on the East. A ship, with a figurehead of Karl Marx, sails about under the command of Anna Planeta, who seduces and murders young men and boys, while providing for their rebirth out of a hold filled with white sugar and corpses.

Montenegro continues this development of allegory in favor of Makavejev's earlier documentary interests. Marilyn, an American-born Swedish housewife, is lured into a world peopled by earthy and sexually active Yugoslavian immigrants who run a club called Zanzibar as an almost anarchistic communal venture. Like the heroes and heroines of Makavejev's earlier films, Marilyn cannot deal with her newly acquired sexual freedom, and she—like Ahmed, Vladimir Ilyich, and Anna Planeta—kills her lovers. *Montenegro's* linear plot contrasts sharply with the convoluted narrative structure and elaborate montage techniques characteristic of Makavejev's earlier works. While being accused of making needlessly ambiguous films with scenes of gratuitous violence and sexuality, Makavejev has consistently explored the interrelationship of sexual life and socioeconomic structure while experimenting with narrative forms that challenge traditional notions of Hollywood filmmaking.

Makavejev's seventeen years as a "knapsack director," during his exile following *WR,* were echoed in films about displaced persons, immigrants, and "nowhere men in nowhere lands." As one of his characters says, "The place which is nowhere is a true home." Another character similarly notes, "Everyone has to come from somewhere," prompting a third to reply, "Not me! I come from here!" After *Sweet Movie,* several promising projects foundered in the choppy sea of international co-financing, until Swedish producer Bo Jonsson, visiting Makavejev at Harvard University, proposed a "high-quality comedy with a popular appeal and measured eroticism," in which the director could add his "little somethings." They soon grew into the rich ethnico-socio-political dimensions of *Montenegro (Or Pigs and Pearls).* The pearl necklace of its Swedish-American heroine (Susan Ansprach) symbolizes her ego and commodity fetishism; "pigs"

Dušan Makavejev

emblemize the funky, ego-despoiling, unbridled instincts of work-immigrants from Southeast Europe (promptly polluted by consumerism's *teasing* of real, biological, desire).

Makavejev's second comedy in the genre (comedy with psycho-political infill) came four years later, from Australia. *The Coca-Cola Kid, not* sponsored by that corporation's marketing division, concerns an enterprising young salesman who succeeds in opening a tiny regional market, a sort of "last valley," hitherto monopolized by a local dynast's soft drink; but himself succumbs to its values. Though ten years in preparation with Australian novelist Frank Moorhouse, its *Local Hero*-type story and backwoods setting inspired less intricate detail, and a thinner intellectual texture, than the culturally mixed settings of Makavejev's richest films.

His long exile ended with *Manifesto (For a Night of Love),* by far the best of the art-house films funded, through the good offices of American Zoetrope's Tom Luddy, by Cannon-Globus (others were by Godard and Norman Mailer). As Bolsheviks of different classes and ideologies fumble their Revolution in 1920 Ruritania, Makavejev hilariously re-explores his abiding subject matter, shared with the Yugoslavian *Praxis* group of Marxist-humanist writers. His characters can only steer erratically between the four cardinal points of a spiritual compass: True Socialism (which Marxist bureaucratic classes too easily make oppressive), individualism (which Western capitalism makes smilingly rapacious); man's bodily instincts (commonly selfish and barbaric, *pace* Wilhelm Reich); and idealism (which may only camouflage the cold, abstract logic of power). Whereas "idealistic" Freudians (whether bourgeois or radical, or, like Reich, both) claim love and sex are natural but deny egoism and power, Makavejev understands that *both* instinct and idealism may spread, not just love and desire, but terror and violence. And after all, Mother Nature, like Anna Planeta, is a serial murderess: whatever lives will be killed, by *something.* Similarly, biological instincts involve, as much as sex, *food;* whence much play on bodies and nourishment. In *WR,* egg yolks, transferred unbroken from hand to hand, suggest an optimum of "communal kindness"; but even food may be over-refined (like, in *Sweet Movie,* consumerist chocolate, and the white sugar of revolutionary purity). Hence political history weighs like a nightmare on the minds of the living. And subsequent "tribal" massacres, in the former Yugoslavia and around the world, corroborate Makavejev's pessimism. Though faint hopes, and pity for history's victims, remain, his "laughter" at "mankind's follies" is more wistful, bitter, and tragic than many spectators perceive.

In his largely German film, *The Gorilla Bathes at Noon,* a Red Army officer, storming Berlin in 1945, suddenly finds himself in the reunified city near a Lenin statue, which he loyally pickets, as it is marked for demolition with yellow paint, like the egg on Marxism's face. This fantasy gambit presages a return to the *Wit/Sweet Movie* genre of allegorical cinema, although the plot becomes uncertain where to go. The problem, perhaps, was topicality, for the consequences of political collapse were not yet clear enough to work on. And perhaps Makavejev's cultural background, a sort of Freudo-Marxist-Marcusian humanism, uneasily mixing economism and instinct theory, and concentrating on capitalism, cannot quite get to terms with the wider resurgence of nationalism, ethnicity, and "tribal" psychology. Though to these things the films' human stories are very sensitive.

Some spectators find that Makavejev's mixture of caricature and pessimism rather freeze their "rooting interest" in his characters, compared with his early dramas. It is a perennial problem in "serious satire." Nonetheless, Makavejev's sparkling and poetic inventions make him Eisenstein's true heir and the great reinvigorator of "intellectual cinema," integrating montage editing as one instrument in an entire orchestra, with "non-synch" sound, voice-over, music, colour, calligraphic camera, comic symbolism, dramatic fables, and visual sensuality, all weaving arguments so sophisticated that Eisenstein's look prehistoric. Where Godard faltered and fell, the Nowhere Man from ex-communist former Yugoslavia continues to blaze new trails of "philosophical cinema."—GINA MARCHETTI and RAYMOND DURGNAT

Malick, Terrence

Nationality American. Born Waco, Texas, 30 November 1943. Education Harvard University, B.A., 1966; Oxford University on Rhodes Scholarship; Center for Advanced Film Studies, American Film Institute, 1969. Career Journalist for Newsweek, Life, and the New Yorker, late 1960s; lecturer in philosophy, Massachusetts Institute of Technology, 1968; directed first feature, Badlands, 1973. Award Best Director Awards, National Society of Film Critics and New York Film Critics, 1978, and Cannes Festival, 1979, for Days of Heaven. Agent c/o Evarts Ziegler Associates, Inc., 9255 W. Sunset Boulevard, Los Angeles, California 90069.

Films as Director and Screenwriter: 1973: *Badlands* (+pr, role as architect). **1978:** *Days of Heaven.*

Other Films: 1969: *Lanton Mills* (short) (sc). **1972:** *Pocket Money* (Rosenberg) (sc). **1974:** *The Gravy Train* (co-sc, under pseudonym David Whitney). **1982:** *Deadhead Miles* (Zimmerman) (co-sc) (filmed 1970).

Though he has directed only two feature films, Terrence Malick has received the kind of critical attention normally reserved for more experienced and prolific filmmakers. His career reflects a commitment to quality instead of quantity—an unusual and not always profitable gamble in the film industry.

In 1972, Malick wrote the screenplay for *Pocket Money,* which starred Paul Newman and Lee Marvin, a film memorable more for character study than story. The following year, Malick made his first feature, *Badlands.* The film was an amazing debut. Based loosely on the sensational Starkweather-Furgate murder spree, *Badlands* concerns Kit Carruthers, a twenty-five-year-old James Dean look-alike, and Holly Sargis, his fifteen-year-old girlfriend. After murdering Holly's father, they begin a flight across the northeastern United States, killing five others along the way.

This disturbing and beautiful film is narrated by Holly (Sissy Spacek), who unemotionally describes the couple's actions

Terrence Malick (right) with Martin Sheen on the set of *Badlands*.

and feelings. Her partner in crime, Kit (Martin Sheen), is a likeable, unpredictable, and romantic killer who is so confident of his place in American history as a celebrity that he marks the spot where he is arrested, and gives away his possessions as souvenirs to police officers.

Days of Heaven, Malick's long-awaited second feature, was released five years later. The film was critically acclaimed in the United States, and Malick was named best director at the Cannes Film Festival. *Days of Heaven* is a homage to silent films (the director even includes a glimpse of Chaplin's work), with stunning visual images and little dialogue. Moving very slowly at first, the film's pace gradually accelerates as the tension heightens. Its plot and style elaborate on that of *Badlands:* the flight of two lovers following a murder, and the use of unemotional narration and off-beat characterizations.

Malick now lives in Paris, and as critics wait for his next endeavor, some wonder how the director will remain profitable to any studio with his lapses between projects, his aversion to interviews, and his refusal to help in the marketing of his films. Paramount, however, is confident of Malick's value, and has continued to send the director scripts plus a yearly stipend.

In the 1990s, Malick has not revived his career, perhaps because conditions within the industry would make it difficult for him to continue his attempts to create an American art cinema. Unlike Welles, whose lack of productivity must be traced in large measure to studio hostility to his methods and work, Malick cannot blame anyone but himself for a talent and interests that have been wasted now for almost two decades.—ALEXA FOREMAN and R. BARTON PALMER

Malle, Louis

Nationality *French.* **Born** *Thumeries, France, 30 October 1932.* **Education** *Collège des Carmes; Institut d'Études Politiques at the Sorbonne, Paris, 1951-53; Institut des Hautes Études Cinématographiques (IDHEC), 1953-54.* **Family** *Married 1) Anne-Marie Deschodt, one son, one daughter (divorced 1967); 2) actress Candice Bergen, 1980, one daughter.* **Career** *Assistant and cameraman to Jacques Cousteau, 1954-55; assistant to Robert Bresson on* Un Condamné à mort s'est échappé, *1956; cameraman on Tati's* Mon Oncle, *1957; directed first film, 1958; reported from Algeria, Vietnam, and Thailand for French Television, 1962-64; moved to India, 1968; moved to the United States, 1976; returned to France to make* Au revoir les enfants, *1987.* **Awards** *Palme d'Or, Cannes Festival, 1956, and Oscar for Best Documentary, 1957, for* The Silent World; *Prix Louis Delluc for*

Ascenseur pour l'échafaud, *1958; special jury prize, Venice Festival, for* Les Amants, *1958; special jury prize, Venice Festival, for* Le Feu follet, *1963; Italian Critics Association Best Film Award, for* The Fire Within, *1964; Grand Prix du Cinema Francais, 1965, and Czechoslovakian best film award, 1966, for* Viva Maria; *Grand Prize, Melbourne Film Festival, for* Calcutta, *1970; Prix Raoul Levy and Prix Méliès for* Lacombe, Lucien, *1974; five Academy Award nominations, including best picture and best director, for* Atlantic City, *1980; Golden Lion, Venice Festival, and Prix Louis Delluc, for* Au revoir les enfants, *1987; British Academy of Film and Television Arts Awards nomination, best director, and Felix Award, European Film Awards, for* Au revoir les enfants, *1988; elected Film Academy Fellow, British Academy of Film and Television Arts, 1991.* **Died** *Of lymphoma, in Beverly Hills, California, 23 November 1995.*

Films as Director: 1956: *Le Monde du silence* (*The Silent World*) (co-d, ph). **1958:** *Ascenseur pour l'échafaud* (*Elevator to the Gallows; Frantic*) (+pr, co-sc); *Les Amants* (*The Lovers*) (+pr, co-sc). **1960:** *Zazie dans le Métro* (*Zazie*) (+pr, co-sc). **1962:** *Vie privée* (*A Very Private Affair*) (+pr, co-sc). **1963:** *Le Feu follet* (*The Fire Within; A Time to Live, a Time to Die*) (+pr, sc). **1965:** *Viva Maria* (+co-pr, co-sc). **1967:** *Le Voleur* (*The Thief of Paris*) (+pr, co-sc). **1968:** "William Wilson" episode of *Histoires extraordinaires* (*Spirits of the Dead*) (+pr, sc). **1969:** *Calcutta* (+pr, sc); *L'Inde fantôme* (*Phantom India*) (+pr, sc) (six-hour feature presentation of TV documentary). **1971:** *Le Souffle au coeur* (*Murmur of the Heart*) (+pr, sc). **1972:** *Humain trop humain* (+pr, sc). **1973:** *Lacombe, Lucien* (+pr, co-sc). **1975:** *Black Moon* (+pr, co-sc). **1978:** *La Petite* (+pr, sc); *Pretty Baby* (+pr, co-story). **1980:** *Atlantic City* (+pr, sc). **1981:** *My Dinner with Andre* (+pr, sc). **1984:** *Crackers* (+pr, sc). **1985:** *Alamo Bay* (+pr, sc); *God's Country* (+pr, sc). **1986:** *And the Pursuit of Happiness* (+pr, sc). **1987:** *Au Revoir les enfants* (*Goodbye, Children*) (+pr, sc). **1990:** *Milou en Mai* (*May Fools*) (+pr, sc). **1992:** *Damage.* **1994:** *Vanya on 42nd Street.*

Other Films: 1969: *La Fiancée du pirate* (Kaplan) (role).

In the scramble for space and fame that became the *nouvelle vague,* Louis Malle began with more hard experience than Godard, Truffaut, or Chabrol, and he showed in *Ascenseur pour l'échafaud* that his instincts for themes and collaborators were faultless. Henri Decaë's low-light photography and Malle's use of Jeanne Moreau established him as emblematic of the new French cinema. But the *Cahiers* trio with their publicist background made artistic hay while Malle persisted in a more intimate voyage of discovery with his lovely star. As the cresting new wave battered at the restrictions of conventional narrative technique, Malle created a personal style, sexual and emotional, which was to sustain him while flashier colleagues failed. Of the new wave survivors, he is the most old-fashioned, the most erotic, and, arguably, the most widely successful.

Re-viewing reveals *Ascenseur* as clumsy and improbable, a failure redeemed only by the Moreau and Maurice Ronet performances. A flair for coaxing the unexpected from his stars had often saved Malle from the consequences of too-reverent respect for production values, a penchant for burnished low-lit interiors being his most galling stylistic weakness. But playing Bardot against type in *Vie privée* as a parody of the harried star, and using Moreau as one of a pair of comic Western trollops (in *Viva Maria*) provided an indication of the irony that was to make his name.

Thereafter Malle became a gleeful chronicler of the polymorphously perverse. Moreau's hand falling eloquently open on the sheet in *Les Amants* as she accepts the joy of cunnilingus is precisely echoed in her genuflection to fellate a yoked George Hamilton in *Viva Maria.* Incest in *Souffle au coeur,* child prostitution in *Pretty Baby,* and, in particular, the erotic and sadomasochistic overtones of Nazism in *Lacombe, Lucien* found in Malle a skillful, committed, and sensual celebrant.

Malle's Indian documentaries of 1969 belong more to the literature of the mid-life crisis than to film history. *Black Moon* likewise explores an arid emotional *couloir*. Malle returned to his richest sources with the U.S.-based films of the late 1970s and after. *Pretty Baby, Atlantic City, My Dinner with Andre,* and *Alamo Bay* delight in overturning the stones under which closed communities seethe in moist darkness. The ostensible source material of the first, Bellocq's New Orleans brothel photographs, receives short shrift in favour of a lingering interest in the pre-pubescent Brooke Shields. *Atlantic City* relishes the delights of post-climactic potency, giving Burt Lancaster one of his richest roles as the fading ex-strong-arm man, dubbed "Numb Nuts" by his derisive colleagues. He seizes a last chance for sexual passion and effective action as the friend and protector of Susan Sarandon's character, an ambitious nightclub croupier.

My Dinner with Andre focuses with equal originality on the social eroticism of urban intellectuals. A globe-trotting theatrical voluptuary reviews his thespian conquests to the grudging admiration of his stay-at-home colleague. An account of theatrical high-jinks in a Polish wood with Jerzy Grotowski and friends becomes in Andre Gregory's fruity re-telling, and with Malle's lingering attention, something very like an orgy. Again, production values intrude on, even dominate the action; mirrors, table settings, the intrusive old waiter, and even the food itself provide a rich, decorated background that adds considerably to the sense of occasion. Malle sends his audiences out of the cinema conscious of having taken part in an event as filling as a five-course meal.

Given this general richness, it may be by contrast that certain of Malle's quieter, less vivid works shine. *Zazie dans le Métro,* his fevered version of Queneau's farce, marked his first break with the stable pattern of the new wave. Compared with Godard's *Une Femme est une femme*, it shows Malle as the more skillful of the two at remaking the genre film. The terse *Le Feu follet,* a vehicle for Maurice Ronet adapted from F. Scott Fitzgerald's *Babylon Revisited,* showed Malle moving towards what had become by then the standard "new" French film, characterized by the work of the so-called "Left Bank" group of Resnais, Varda, Rivette, and Rohmer. But again Malle found in the character a plump, opulent self-regard that turned *Le Feu follet,* despite its black and white cinematography and solemn style, into a celebration of self-pity, with Ronet at one point caressing the gun with which he proposes to put an end to his life. Like the relish with which Belmondo's gentleman thief in *Le Voleur* savours the objects he steals, Malle's love of physicality, of weight and color and texture, seems so deeply rooted as to be almost religious. (And Malle did, after all, work as assistant to Bresson on *Un Condamné à mort s'est échappé.*)

The latter stages of Malle's career included one well-publicized fiasco and two very different but equally brilliant films. The former is *Damage,* a boring adaptation of Josephine Hart's best-seller, crammed with boring sex footage of Jeremy Irons (as a British politician) and Juliette Binoche (as his son's girlfriend, with whom he commences an affair). The film is of note only for the hubbub created when Malle was forced to edit footage to earn the film an R (rather than NC-17) rating, and for Miranda Richardson's brief but riveting presence as Irons' rejected wife.

Au revoir les enfants, on the other hand, is as fine a film as Malle ever has made. It is set at that point in time, if such a moment can be measured, in which childhood inevitably and irrevocably ends. The film is a heartbreaking autobiographical drama which tells the story of Julien Quentin, a universal 11-year-old: a spirited prankster who attends a rural Catholic boarding school in Occupied France. Julien senses something unusual about a new classmate, a sweet-faced, bushy-haired, exceptionally intelligent boy called Jean Bonnet. Jean really is a Jew, in hiding at Julien's school. And Julien is oblivious to what Jean knows all to well: In Occupied France, it's highly dangerous—and nearly always fatal—to be Jewish. The film, ultimately, is a story of heroes and villains, of those who will risk their all to shelter the needy and those who will collaborate with the enemy to fill their pockets or gain a false sense of power. Malle slowly, carefully introduces you to his characters, so the resulting impact of the unfolding events is that much more profound. One example of Malle's mastery: Julien and Jean become lost in a forest, and are come upon by German soldiers. Jean's sense of all-encompassing terror, revealed in a split second as he panics and runs, is explicitly real. Additionally, there is a sequence in which the students come together for some entertainment and laugh at Chaplin cavorting in *The Immigrant*. Here, Malle communicates how film can be a true universal language, how the genius of an artist such as Chaplin is timeless. In its overall setting and view of life and loyalty in Occupied France, *Au revoir les enfants* is related thematically to *Lacombe, Lucien*. Julien's feelings for his mother, as personified by his sniffing for her scent after reading one of her letters, mirrors the intense mother-son relationship in *Murmur of the Heart*.

Vanya on 42nd Street, which reunites Wallace Shawn and Andre Gregory, the entire cast of *My Dinner with Andre,* is as stunningly original as the earlier film. The setting is a crumbling theater in midtown Manhattan that once was home to the Ziegfeld Follies. The film opens with actors converging on the theater, where they will rehearse a stage production of an adaptation by David Mamet of Chekhov's *Uncle Vanya*. Gregory is the director, while Shawn plays the title role. As the rehearsal proceeds, *Vanya on 42nd Street* becomes at once a highly cinematic example of filmed theater and an intimate look at the illusion that is the theater.

Sensual and perverse, Malle is an unlikely artist to have sprung from the reconstructed film-buffs of the *nouvelle vague*. It is with his early mentors—Bresson, Cousteau, Tati—that he seems, artistically and spiritually, to belong, rather than with Melville, spiritual hero of the *Cahiers* group, and there is a strong flavour of essentially French autobiographical soul searching in his *Au revoir les enfants* and *Milou en mai*. If Truffaut turned into the René Clair of the new French cinema, Malle may yet become its Max Ophüls.—JOHN BAXTER and ROB EDELMAN

Mamoulian, Rouben

Nationality American. *Born* Tiflis, Caucasia, Russia, 8 October 1897; became U.S. citizen, 1930. *Education* Lycée Montaigne, Paris; gymnasium in Tiflis; University of Moscow; Vakhtangov Studio Theatre, Moscow. *Family* Married Azadia Newman, 1945. *Career* Stage director in London, from 1920; production director of Eastman Theater, Rochester, New York, 1923-26; directed Porgy on Broadway, 1927; signed to Paramount, directed first film, 1929; stage director, especially of musicals, through the 1940s. *Awards* Best Direction, New York Film Critics, for The Gay Desperado, 1936; Award of Excellence, Armenian American Bicentennial Celebration, 1976. *Died* In Los Angeles, 4 December 1987.

Films as Director: 1929: *Applause.* **1931:** *City Streets.* **1932:** *Dr. Jekyll and Mr. Hyde* (+pr); *Love Me Tonight* (+pr). **1933:** *Song of Songs* (+pr); *Queen Christina.* **1934:** *We Live Again.* **1935:** *Becky Sharp.* **1936:** *The Gay Desperado.* **1937:** *High, Wide and Handsome.* **1939:** *Golden Boy.* **1940:** *The Mark of Zorro.* **1941:** *Blood and Sand.* **1942:** *Rings on Her Fingers.* **1948:** *Summer Holiday.* **1957:** *Silk Stockings.*

Rouben Mamoulian is certainly one of the finest directors in American film history. While not considered strictly an *auteur* with a unifying theme running through his films, the importance of each of his movies on an individual basis is significant. Mamoulian did not have a large output, having completed only sixteen assignments in his twenty-year career in motion pictures, principally because he was also very active in the theater. His most famous stage successes were the highly innovative productions of Richard Rodgers and Oscar Hammerstein II's musicals *Oklahoma!* and *Carousel* in the mid-1940s.

Mamoulian's first film, *Applause,* is a poignant story of a third-rate vaudevillian played by the popular singer Helen Morgan. The first film to utilize two sound tracks instead of one to produce a better quality sound, *Applause* is also noteworthy for its innovative use of a moving camera.

Mamoulian's third film, *Dr. Jekyll and Mr. Hyde,* is still regarded by most historians as the definitive film version of the Robert Louis Stevenson novella, as well as being one of the best horror films of all time. Yet it would be doing the film a disservice to call it "just" a horror movie. The use of light and shadows, the depth of emotion expressed by the main character, and the evocation of the evil hidden in all men make it a classic. For the time it was a very sensual film. Miriam Hopkins as Ivy Pearson is not just a girl from the lower strata of society, as the character was in other versions. In Mamoulian's film she is deliberately sensual. Fredric March, in a truly

magnificent performance, is troubled by his desire for Ivy long before he turns into Hyde, which is especially evident in the erotic dream sequence. What Mamoulian was able to do in this film is show the simultaneous existence of good and evil in Jekyll before it erupts into the drug-induced schizophrenic manifestation of Mr. Hyde.

Becky Sharp, although not particularly noteworthy for its dramatic style, is today remembered as being the first film in the three-strip Technicolor process. Unusually for a director more closely associated with the stage than film, Mamoulian tried to learn and perfect virtually all of the techniques of filmmaking, and he could be accomplished in almost any genre: horror, musical, swashbuckler, or historical drama. Perhaps the only genre at which he was not successful was light comedy. His only real comedy, *Rings on Her Fingers,* is entertaining, but does not live up to the standards which he

Rouben Mamoulian

set in his other films. The three previous films, *Golden Boy, The Mark of Zorro,* and *Blood and Sand,* were all very successful films which are still applauded by critics and audiences alike.

Mamoulian's last film, *Silk Stockings,* was a very popular adaption of the musical play derived from *Ninotchka,* with a lively score by Cole Porter. The combination of Cyd Charisse and Fred Astaire in the lead roles was naturally responsible for a great part of the movie's success, and Mamoulian's direction and staging allowed their talents to be shown to their best advantage. *Silk Stockings* has a variety of delightful "specialty" numbers which do not detract from the main action, notably "Stereophonic Sound," as well as some charming character roles played by Peter Lorre, Jules Munshin, and George Tobias.

Rouben Mamoulian was one of the most talented, creative filmmakers of all time, and while his films are few, virtually every one is a tribute to his genius.—PATRICIA KING HANSON

Mankiewicz, Joseph L.

Nationality *American.* **Born** *Joseph Leo Mankiewicz in Wilkes-Barre, Pennsylvania, 11 February 1909.* **Education** *Stuyvesant High School, New York; Columbia University, B.A., 1928.* **Family** *Married 1) Elizabeth Young, 1934 (divorced 1937), one son; 2) Rosa Stradner, 1939 (died 1958), two sons; 3) Rosemary Matthews, 1962, one daughter.* **Career** *Reporter for* Chicago Tribune, *and stringer for* Variety *in Berlin, 1928; with help of brother Herman, became junior writer at Paramount, 1929; writer for MGM, 1933, then producer, from 1935; contract taken over by Twentieth Century-Fox, 1943; directed* La Bohème *for Metropolitan Opera, New York, 1952; formed Figaro Inc., independent production company, 1953.* **Awards** *Academy Awards for Best Director and Best Screenplay, for* A Letter to Three Wives, *1949, and for Best Director and Best Screenplay, for* All about Eve, *1950.* **Died** *5 February 1993.*

Films as Director: **1946:** *Dragonwyck* (+sc); *Somewhere in the Night* (+co-sc). **1947:** *The Late George Apley, The Ghost and Mrs. Muir.* **1948:** *Escape.* **1949:** *A Letter to Three Wives* (+sc); *House of Strangers* (+co-sc, uncredited). **1950:** *No Way Out* (+co-sc); *All about Eve* (+sc). **1951:** *People Will Talk* (+sc). **1952:** *Five Fingers* (+dialogue, uncredited). **1953:** *Julius Caesar* (+sc). **1954:** *The Barefoot Contessa* (+sc). **1955:** *Guys and Dolls* (+sc). **1958:** *The Quiet American* (+sc). **1959:** *Suddenly, Last Summer.* **1963:** *Cleopatra* (+co-sc). **1967:** *The Honey Pot* (+co-p, sc). **1970:** *There Was a Crooked Man . . .* (+pr). **1972:** *Sleuth.*

Other Films: **1929:** *Fast Company* (Sutherland) (sc, dialogue). **1930:** *Slightly Scarlet* (co-sc); *The Social Lion* (Sutherland) (sc, adaptation and dialogue); *Only Saps Work* (Gardner and Knopf) (sc, dialogue). **1931:** *The Gang Buster* (Sutherland) (sc, dialogue); *Finn and Hattie* (Taurog) (sc, dialogue); *June Moon* (Sutherland) (co-sc); *Skippy* (Taurog) (co-sc); *Newly Rich* (*Forbidden Adventure*) (co-sc); *Sooky* (Taurog) (co-sc). **1932:** *This Reckless Age* (sc); *Sky Bride* (co-sc); *Million Dollar Legs* (Cline) (co-sc); "Rollo and the Roadhogs" and "The Three Marines" sketches of *If I Had a Million* (sc). **1933:** *Diplomaniacs* (co-sc); *Emergency Call* (co-sc); *Too Much Harmony* (Sutherland) (sc); *Alice in Wonderland* (McLeod) (co-sc). **1934:** *Manhattan Melodrama* (Van Dyke, W.S.) (co-sc); *Our Daily Bread* (Vidor) (sc, dialogue); *Forsaking All Others* (Van Dyke, W.S.) (sc). **1935:** *I Live My Life* (Van Dyke, W.S.) (sc). **1936:** *Three Godfathers* (pr); *Fury* (Lang) (pr, co-story, uncredited); *The Gorgeous Hussy* (Brown) (pr); *Love on the Run* (Van Dyke, W.S.) (pr). **1937:** *The Bride Wore Red* (Arzner) (pr); *Double Wedding* (pr). **1938:** *Mannequin* (Borzage) (pr); *Three Comrades* (Borzage) (pr); *The Shopworn Angel* (pr); *The Shining Hour* (Borzage) (pr); *A Christmas Carol* (pr). **1939:** *The Adventures of Huckleberry Finn* (*Huckleberry Finn*) (pr). **1940:** *Strange Cargo* (Borzage) (pr); *The Philadelphia*

Joseph L. Mankiewicz

Story (Cukor) (pr). **1941:** *The Wild Man of Borneo* (pr); *The Feminine Touch* (Van Dyke, W.S.) (pr). **1942:** *Woman of the Year* (Stevens) (pr); *Cairo* (Van Dyke, W.S.) (pr); *Reunion in France* (pr). **1944:** *The Keys of the Kingdom* (Stahl) (pr, co-sc).

Few of Mankiewicz's contemporaries experimented so radically with narrative form. In *The Barefoot Contessa,* Mankiewicz (who wrote most of the films he directed) let a half-dozen voice-over narrators tell the Contessa's story, included flashbacks within flashbacks, and even showed one event twice (the slapping scene in the restaurant) from two different points of view. Multiple narrators tell the story in *All about Eve,* too, and in the non-narrated framing story for that film, Mankiewicz uses slow motion to make it seem as if the elapsed time between the beginning of the film and the end is only a few seconds. For much of the film, *The Quiet American* also has a narrator, and he seems almost totally omniscient. Apparently, he looks back at events with a firm understanding of their development and of the motivation of the people involved. But in the end, we find out that the narrator was wrong about practically everything, and so gave us an inaccurate account of things. *A Letter to Three Wives* is made up, primarily, of several lengthy flashbacks, and hallucinogenic flashback sequences provide the payoff to the story in Mankiewicz's adaption of the Tennessee Williams play *Suddenly Last Summer.*

Mankiewicz's films, then, stand out in part because of the way they tell their stories. But there are also thematic motifs that turn up again and again, and one of the most important is the impact of the dead upon the living. Frequently, a dead character is more important in a Mankiewicz film than any living one. *The Late George Apley,* of course, concerns someone who has already died. Understanding a mother's dead son is the key for the psychiatrist in *Suddenly Last Summer.* In *The Ghost and Mrs. Muir,* it is the presence of the non-corporeal sea captain that makes the film so entertaining. *The Barefoot Contessa* opens with the Contessa's funeral, and then various mourners tell us what they know about the woman who has just been buried. And, of course, a famous funeral scene forms the centerpiece of another Mankiewicz film: Mark Antony's oration in *Julius Caesar.* It is Antony's stirring performance as a eulogist that turns his countrymen against Brutus.

Indeed, Mankiewicz's films deal constantly with the notion of effective and highly theatrical performance. *All about Eve,* for instance, is all about performing, since it concerns people who work on the Broadway stage. The barefoot contessa goes from cabaret dancer to Hollywood star. In *The Honey Pot,* an aging man pretends to be dying, to see how it affects his mistress. And in *Sleuth,* one marvels at the number of disguises worn by one man in his attempt to gain revenge on another.

Perhaps because he began as a screenwriter, Mankiewicz has often been thought of as a scenarist first and a director only second. But not only was he an eloquent scriptwriter, he was also an elegant visual stylist whose talents as a director far exceeded his reputation. He is one of the few major American directors who was more appreciated during the early years of his career than during the later stages. He won consecutive Best Director Academy Awards in 1949 and 1950 (for *A Letter to Three Wives* and *All about Eve*), but after the 1963 disaster *Cleopatra*, Mankiewicz's standing as a filmmaker declined rapidly.—ERIC SMOODIN

Mann, Anthony

Nationality *American.* **Born** *Anton or Emil Bundsmann in Point Loma or San Diego, California, 1907.* **Education** *New York City public schools.* **Family** *Married 1) Mildred Kenyon, 1931 (divorced 1956), one son, one daughter; 2) Sarita Montiel, 1957 (marriage annulled 1963); 3) Anna (Mann), one son.* **Career** *Began work in theatre following father's death, 1923; production manager for Theater Guild, New York, from late 1920s, then director, 1933; director for Federal Theater Project, New York, 1936-38; talent scout for David Selznick, and casting director, Hollywood, 1938; assistant director at Paramount, 1939; signed to Republic Pictures, 1943, to R.K.O., 1945, then to MGM, 1949; withdrew from* Spartacus *after quarrelling with Kirk Douglas, 1960.* **Died** *During shooting of last film, in Germany, 29 April 1967.*

Films as Director: 1942: *Dr. Broadway; Moonlight in Havana.* **1943:** *Nobody's Darling.* **1944:** *My Best Gal; Strangers in the Night.* **1945:** *The Great Flamarion; Two O'Clock Courage; Sing Your Way Home.* **1946:** *Strange Impersonation; The Bamboo Blonde.* **1947:** *Desperate; Railroaded.* **1948:** *T-Men* (+co-sc, uncredited); *Raw Deal; He Walked by Night* (co-d, uncredited). **1949:** *Reign of Terror* (*The Black Book*); *Border Incident.* **1950:** *Side Street; Devil's Doorway; The Furies; Winchester '73.* **1951:** *The Tall Target.* **1952:** *Bend of the River.* **1953:** *The Naked Spur; Thunder Bay.* **1954:** *The Glenn Miller Story.* **1955:** *The Far Country; Strategic Air Command; The Man from Laramie; The Last Frontier.* **1956:** *Serenade.* **1957:** *Men in War; The Tin Star.* **1958:** *God's Little Acre; Man of the West.* **1961:** *Cimarron; El Cid.* **1964:** *The Fall of the Roman Empire.* **1965:** *The Heroes of Telemark.* **1968:** *A Dandy in Aspic* (co-d).

Though he incidentally directed films in various genres (the musical, the war movie, the spy drama), Anthony Mann's career falls into three clearly marked phases: the early period of low-budget, B-feature films noir; the central, most celebrated period of westerns, mostly with James Stewart; and his involvement in the epic (with Samuel Bronston as producer). All three periods produced distinguished work (in particular, *El Cid* has strong claims to be considered the finest of all the wide screen historical epics of the 1950s and 1960s, and the first half of *The Fall of the Roman Empire* matches it), but it is the body of work from the middle period in which Mann's achievement is most consistent and on which his reputation largely depends.

The first of the Stewart westerns, *Winchester '73*, contains most of the major components Mann was to develop in the series that followed. There is the characteristic use of landscape—never for the superficial beauty or mere pictorial effect that is a cliché of the genre, nor to ennoble the human figures through monumental grandeur and harmonious man-in-nature compositions, as in the classical westerns of Ford. In Mann, the function of landscape is primarily dramatic, and nature is felt as inhospitable, indifferent, or hostile. If there is a mountain, it will have to be climbed, arduously and painfully; barren rocks provide a favourite location for a

Anthony Mann

shoot-out, offering partial cover but also the continued danger of the ricochet. The preferred narrative structure of the films is the journey, and its stages are often marked by a symbolic progression in landscape, from fertile valley to bare rock or snow-covered peak, corresponding to a stripping-away of the trappings of civilization and civilized behavior. *Bend of the River* represents the most systematic treatment of this prior to *Man of the West*. *Winchester '73* also establishes the Mann hero ("protagonist" might be a better word): neurotic, obsessive, driven, usually motivated by a desire for revenge that reduces him emotionally and morally to a brutalized condition scarcely superior to that of the villain. Hero and villain, indeed, become mirror reflections of one another: in *Winchester '73* they are actually brothers (one has murdered the father, the other seeks revenge); in *Bend of the River,* both are ex-gunfighters, Stewart bearing the mark around his neck of the hangman's noose from which, at the beginning of the film, he saves Arthur Kennedy. Violence in Mann's westerns is never glorified: it is invariably represented as ugly, disturbing, and painful (emotionally as much as physically), and this is true as much when it is inflicted by the heroes as by the villains.

Mann's supreme achievement is certainly *Man of the West,* the culmination of the Stewart series despite the fact that the Stewart role is taken over by Gary Cooper. It remains one of the great American films and one of the great films *about* America. It carries to their fullest development all the components described above, offering a magnificently complete realization of their significance. Cooper plays Link Jones (the "link" between the old West and the new), a reformed outlaw stranded in the wilderness while on a mission to hire a teacher for the first school in the new township of Good Hope. Link is sucked back into involvement with his old gang of "brother," "cousins," and monstrous adoptive father Dock Tobin (Lee J. Cobb), and forced into more and more excessive violence, as he destroys his doubles in order finally to detach himself, drained and compromised, from his own roots.—ROBIN WOOD

Marker, Chris

Nationality *French.* **Born** *Christian François Bouche-Villeneuve in Neuilly sur Seine (one source says Ulan Bator, Mongolia), 29 July 1921.* **Military Service** *During World War II, resistance fighter, then joined American army.* **Career** *Novelist, poet, playwright, and journalist, from late 1940s; formed SLON film cooperative (Société pour le Lancement des Oeuvres Nouvelles), 1967.* **Awards** *Golden Bear, Berlin Festival, for* Description d'un combat, *1961; International Critics Prize, Cannes Festival, for* Le Joli Mai, *1963.*

Films as Director: 1952: _Olympia 52_ (+sc, co-ph). **1953:** _Les Statues meurent aussi_ (co-d, co-sc). **1956:** _Dimanche à Pekin_ (+sc, ph). **1958:** _Lettre de Sibérie_ (_Letter from Siberia_) (+sc). **1960:** _Description d'un combat_ (+sc); _Les Astronautes_ (co-d, sc). **1961:** _Cuba Si!_ (+sc, ph). **1963:** _Le Joli Mai_ (+sc). **1964:** _La Jetée_ (completed 1962) (+sc). **1965:** _Le Mystère Koumiko_ (_The Koumiko Mystery_) (+sc). **1966:** _Si j'avais quatre dromadaires_ (+sc). **1968:** _La Sixième Face du Pentagone_ (collaboration with Francois Reichenbach) (+sc). **1969:** _A bientôt j'espère_ (+sc). **1970:** _La Bataille des dix millions_ (_Cuba: Battle of the Ten Million_) (+sc); _Les Mots ont un sens_ (+sc). **1973:** _Le Train en marche_ (+sc). **1977:** _Le Fond de l'air est rouge_ (in 2 parts) (+sc). **1983:** _Sans soleil_ (_Sunless_). **1984:** _2084_ (+sc). **1985:** _A.K._ (_A.K.: The Making of Kurosawa's Ran_) (+sc). **1986:** _Hommage à Simone Signoret_ (+sc). **1989:** _L'Heritage de la Chouette_ (for TV, 13-part series) (+sc, pr). **1993:** _Le Dernier Bolchevik_ (_The Last Bolshevik_) (+sc). **1996:** _Level Five._

Other Films: 1957: _Le Mystère de l'atelier_ (commentary, collaborator on production). **1967:** _Loin du Vietnam_ (_Far from Vietnam_) (Resnais) (pr, ed). **1970:** _L'Aveu_ (_The Confession_) (Costa-Gavras) (asst ph). **1973:** _Kashima Paradise_ (commentary). **1975/76:** _La batalla de Chile_ (_The Battle of Chile_) (Guzmá) (co-pr). **1976:** _La Spirale_ (contributor). **1988:** _Les Pyramides bleues_ (artistic advisor).

Chris Marker's principal distinction may be to have developed a form of personal essay within the documentary mode. Aside from his work little is known about him; he is elusive bordering on mysterious. Born in a suburb of Paris, he has allowed a legend to grow up about his birth in a "far-off country." Marker is not his name; it is one of a half-dozen aliases he has used. He chose "Marker," it is thought, in reference to the Magic Marker pen.

He began his career as a writer (publishing poems, a novel, and various essays and translations) and journalist (whose travels took him all over the world). He is the writer of all his films and cinematographer on many of them. Their verbal and visual wit almost conceal the philosophical speculation and erudition they contain. Their commentaries are a kind of stream

Chris Marker

of consciousness; their poetry is about himself as well as about the subjects—his reactions to what he and we are seeing and hearing.

Marker is the foreign correspondent and inquiring reporter. He is especially interested in transitional societies, in "Life in the process of becoming history," as he has put it. His films are not only set in specific places, they are about the cultures of those places. Though he has tended to work in socialist countries more than most Western filmmakers, he is also fascinated by Japan. Concerned with leftist issues, he remains a member of the intellectual Left, politically committed but not doctrinaire. "Involved objectivity" is his own phrase for his approach.

In *Le Joli Mai,* for example, Marker interviews Parisians about their ambitions, their political views, their understanding of the society they live in. His sample is a cross section—a street-corner clothing salesman, a clerk, a house painter, a black student, a young couple wanting to get married, an Algerian worker—with a substantial working-class representation. The interviewees find that work offers no satisfaction. Its goal is money; what happiness money will bring is by no means certain. Marker insists to one interviewee who opts for material success that his view of life is "a trifle limited." "No interest in other things?" Marker asks.

This exchange is characteristic. Marker's tone is frequently ironical and implicitly judgmental. He engages in argument with the interviewees and makes known his disappointment in some of their answers. The interviews assume the form of a dialectic.

In the second half of *Le Joli Mai* Marker breaks away from individuals and interviews altogether. Instead he deals with news events—a police charge which crushed eight people to death in the Métro, the half-million mourners at their funeral, violent responses to the acquittal of General Salan (former commander-in-chief of French forces in Algeria), massive railroad and Renault strikes—intercut with nightclub revelry. The events refer back to those interviewed in the first half who felt themselves "unfree" to alter or even to question the social system.

The Koumiko Mystery, set amidst the 1964 Tokyo Olympics, begins but never stays with them for long. Its real subject is a young Japanese woman named Koumiko Moroaka, her city (Tokyo), her country, and the Far East as a whole. If, in a sense, Koumiko is protagonist, there is also an antagonist of sorts. The Western world and its influences are seen again and again in images on television screens, in the tastes evident in department store windows. Part of the film is photographed directly off black-and-white television screens. In this way the concerns and attitudes of the larger world are isolated. The rest of the film, which is in color, is wholly personal.

Marker's fascination with foreign, particularly Japanese, cultures is evident in the making of *Sans soleil* and *A.K.* The former is an idiosyncratic travelogue about Japan, narrated by a fictional cameraman, while the latter is a documentary about Akira Kurosawa's (arguably Japan's most renowned filmmaker) making of *Ran.* In both films, Marker's point of view remains that of an observer, a bystander. It is exactly through such deliberate distance and distanciation that the filmmaker contemplates issues that have dominated his work to date: How do various cultures perceive and sustain themselves and each other in the increasingly intermingled modern age? How, on the other hand, can one find the space of him/herself when time, place, and memory are obscured, constructed, and forgotten? In the case of *Sans soleil,* not only are images of Japan—purposefully inserted with those of Guinea Bissau, Ireland, Iceland, and elsewhere—robbed of any consistency and specificity, but memories and perceptions are also fictionalized and therefore called into ultimate question.

Following the failure of communism, as most brutally indicated by the disintegration of the former Soviet Union, comes "one of the most trenchant commentaries Marker has ever allowed himself," according to David Thomson, in his 1993 film *Le Dernier Bolchevik* (*The Last Bolshevik*). Although this film still maintains a sense of "involved objectivity" stylistically, it also may suggest a stark disillusionment of a sort in Marker, the Marxist-inspired documentarist. There is, however, no reason to stop anticipating further works by Marker that demonstrate the willingness to impose his own shaping intelligence and imagination on his materials. His films will continue to be most valued for what he perceives and understands about what he is observing, and for their whimsical juggling of forms, their tweaking of conventions and expectations, and their idiosyncratic style.—JACK C. ELLIS and GUO-JUIN HONG

Maysles, Albert and David Paul

ALBERT. Nationality *American.* **Born** *Brookline, Massachusetts, 26 November 1926.* **Education** *Brookline High School; Syracuse University, New York, degree in psychology; Boston University, M.A. in psychology.* **Military Service** *Served in U.S. Army Tank Corps, during World War II.* **Career** *Taught psychology at Boston University, from late 1940s, then travelled to Russia to make first film, 1955; worked as cameraman for Richard Leacock, 1960; worked as cameraman on one section of Godard's* Paris vu par.

DAVID PAUL. Nationality *American.* **Born** *Brookline, Massachusetts, 10 January 1932.* **Education** *Brookline High School; Boston University, degree in psychology.* **Military Service** *Served in the Army at Headquarters, Military Intelligence school, Oberammergau,*

Albert (left) and David Paul Maysles

Germany. **Family** *Married Judy (Maysles), one son, one daughter.* **Career** *Worked as production assistant on* Bus Stop *and* The Prince and the Showgirl, *1956; worked as reporter on* Adventures on the New Frontier *for TV, late 1950s and early 1960s.* **Died** *In New York, 3 January 1987.*

Career *(joint) They make first film together, 1957; formed production company together and made first film, 1962; and the brothers received Guggenheim Fellowship in experimental film, 1965; continued making full-length documentaries and industrial and corporate promotional films together, from 1970.* **Awards** *(joint) Academy Award nomination, Best Dramatic Short, for* Christo's Valley Curtain, *1972; Emmy Award, for* Horowitz Plays Mozart, *1987.*

Films as Directors: 1955: *Psychiatry in Russia* (Albert only). **1957:** *Youth in Poland.* **1960:** *Primary* (Albert only, co-d). **1962:** *Showman.* **1964:** *What's Happening: The Beatles in the USA* (*Yeah Yeah Yeah, The Beatles! The First U.S. Visit*). **1965:** *Meet Marlon Brando.* **1966:** *With Love From Truman.* **1969:** *Salesman* (co-d). **1970:** *Gimme Shelter* (co-d). **1972:** *Christo's Valley Curtain* (co-d). **1975:** *Grey Gardens* (co-d). **1977:** *Running Fence* (co-d). **1980:** *Muhammad and Larry.* **1984:** *Islands* (co-d). **1986:** *Vladimir Horowitz: the Last Romantic; Ozawa* (co-d). **1987:** *Horowitz Plays Mozart* (Albert only, co-d). **1989:** *Jessye Norman Sings Carmen* (Albert only, co-d). **1991:** *Christo in Paris* (Albert only). **1992:** *Baroque Diet* (Albert only); *Sports Illustrated: Swimsuit '92* (Albert only). **1993:** *Abortion: Desperate Choices* (Albert only, co-d). **1996:** *Umbrellas* (Albert only, co-d).

Shooting unobtrusively in sync sound with no instructions to the subject, the Maysles brothers made films in what they preferred to call "direct cinema." Albert, gifted photographer and director of all their projects, carried the lightweight, silent camera that he perfected on his shoulder, its accessories built in and ready for adjustment. Maysles characters, who occasionally talk to the filmmakers on screen, seem astonishingly unaware that strangers and apparatus are in the room.

David, the soundman, carried a sensitive directional mike and a Nagra recorder unattached to the camera. He was often involved in the editing and as producer had final say. During the shooting a story might become apparent, or a dominant character may surface. These elements may become clear only as the editors examine, cut, and structure the vast amounts of footage that they receive in the dailies.

In 1962, a time when Albert had acquired brief experience in documentary filmmaking and David had garnered a similar amount of experience in Hollywood feature films, they formed a partnership committed to direct cinema. Commercials and industrial filmmaking supported their preferred activity from time to time.

The company's production of two feature documentaries (which they distributed commercially), *Salesman,* a study of four bible salesmen, and *Grey Gardens,* an essay on two eccentric women, fed the constant discussions between documentarists and critics about whether objectivity is at all possible in documentaries. Both films were charged with dishonesty, exploitation, and tastelessness, but other quarters praised the Maysles' sensitivity, rapport with their subjects, and choice of situations that viewers could identify with.

The Maysles sought to answer the criticism and describe their philosophy and working methods at screenings of their films, in articles, and in letters to editors. Their instinct took them, they said, to situations related to closeness between human beings, and pointed out that they could not do films about people they dislike. They looked on their work as a discovery of how people really are, first spending time with them to get acquainted, then filming their lives as lived. All their subjects agreed to the project under consideration beforehand, and several have spoken of their satisfaction with the finished film and their good relationship with Albert and David, whom they trusted.

The Maysles did not deny that their choices affected their creation in some way. Their methodology, for example, meant that much footage must be discarded. They emphasized that nothing was staged, a structure that eventually emerges from the material. In their own work they saw a relationship to Truman Capote's concepts and methods for his "non-fiction novel": discarding preconceptions about their subjects, while concentrating on learning about them and understanding their motivations and feelings.

Albert and David Maysles have an important place in the history of the documentary for many reasons. They produced a large, varied, evocative body of work in their chosen style, as very active members of their own small company. Despite some severe criticism of their work, they are admired, and probably envied for qualities that Americans value. Directly influential or not on documentaries today, their work is certainly part of the flow of films that aim to show the truth about contemporary problems. While many other filmmakers' reports and studies embrace large communities, or even whole countries, Maysles productions are about individuals and their concerns, which often illuminate larger aspects of society as well as its general attitudes toward non-traditional behavior.

Since David Maysles' death, Albert has continued turning out documentaries, mostly collaborating with Susan Froemke, Charlotte Zwerin, and Deborah Dickson. His subjects are as varied as when he worked with his brother, ranging from classical music (*Horowitz Plays Mozart, Jessye Norman Sings Carmen*) to social issues (*Abortion: Desperate Choices,* which traces the history of abortion in America) to attempts by artists to realize their visions. One of these efforts, *Christo in Paris,* chronicles the artist Christo's efforts to wrap Paris' Pont-Neuf Bridge; two decades earlier, Albert and David had made *Christo's Valley Curtain,* in which the artist tried to hang an orange curtain over a valley.—LILLIAN SCHIFF and ROB EDELMAN

Mazursky, Paul

Nationality *American.* **Born** *Irwin Mazursky in Brooklyn, New York, 25 April 1930.* **Education** *Brooklyn College, degree 1951; studied acting with Paul Mann, Curt Conway, and Lee Strasberg.* **Family** *Married Betsy Purdey, 1953, two daughters.* **Career** *Nightclub comedian, actor, and director, off-Broadway, from 1954; joined Second City in Los Angeles, 1959; writer, with Larry Tucker, for* The Danny Kaye Show *for TV, 1964-67; co-creator of* The Monkees *for TV, 1965; directed first film,* Bob and Carol and Ted and Alice, *1969.* **Address** *c/o Telecote Productions, Inc., 280 South Beverly Drive, Suite 311, Beverly Hills, California 90212, U.S.A.*

Films as Director: 1969: *Bob and Carol and Ted and Alice* (+co-sc). **1970:** *Alex in Wonderland* (+co-sc, role as Hal Stern). **1973:** *Blume in Love* (+sc, pr, role as Hellman). **1974:** *Harry and Tonto* (+co-sc, pr). **1976:** *Next Stop Greenwich Village* (+sc, co-pr). **1978:** *An Unmarried Woman* (+sc, co-pr, role as Hal). **1980:** *Willie and Phil* (+sc). **1982:** *The Tempest* (+sc). **1984:** *Moscow on the Hudson* (+co-sc, pr, role). **1986:** *Down and Out in Beverly Hills* (+co-sc, pr, role). **1988:** *Moon Over Parador* (+co-sc, pr, role). **1989:** *Enemies: A Love Story* (+co-sc, pr, role as Leon Tortshiner). **1990:** *Scenes from a Mall* (+co-sc, pr, role as Dr. Hans Clava). **1993:** *The Pickle* (+sc, pr, role as Butch Levine). **1996:** *Faithful* (+role as Dr. Susskind).

Other Films: 1951: *Fear and Desire* (Kubrick) (role). **1955:** *Blackboard Jungle* (Brooks) (role as Emmanuel Stoken). **1966:** *Deathwatch* (Morrow) (role as petty thief). **1968:** *I Love You Alice B. Toklas* (Averback) (co-sc). **1976:** *A Star Is Born* (Pierson) (role as John Norman's manager). **1979:** *A Man, a Woman, and a Bank* (Black) (role). **1985:** *Into the Night* (Landis) (role). **1988:** *Punchline* (Seltzer) (role); *Scenes from the Class Struggle in Beverly Hills* (Bartel) (role). **1990:** *Taking Care of Business* (Hiller) (exec pr). **1992:** *Man Trouble* (role as Lee Mac Greevy). **1993:** *Carlito's Way* (role as Judge Feinstein). **1994:** *Love Affair* (role as Herb Stillman). **1995:** *Miami Rhapsody* (role as Vic). **1996:** *2 Days in the Valley* (role as Teddy Peppers).

It is no small irony that Paul Mazursky's best film is one he wrote (with Larry Tucker), but was not given the chance to direct. *I Love You Alice B. Toklas,* like most of Mazursky's work, stages a humorous, if somewhat predictable, encounter between deadening forms of everyday life (especially the monotonous regularity of heterosexual monogamy) and the bewildering, if attractive, otherness of nonconformity. Directed by Hy Averback (at the insistence of star Peter Sellers, who would not work with a novice), this film records the fall of its main character, seduced by free love and marijuana brownies, into a late 1960s California underworld of unlimited self-indulgence, social honesty, and brotherly tolerance. Recovering his desire for a comfortable working life and marriage to the right girl, the Sellers character almost decides to go straight, but refuses at the very end to choose between the extremes his culture offers, the discontents of which have been equally and mercilessly exposed.

The commercial and critical success of *Alice* gave Mazursky an entree into New Hollywood directing. Unlike the film school whiz-kids (Coppola, Scorsese, Lucas, Spielberg, and company) who came into prominence at this same time, Mazursky had spent many years in show business, developing not only an acting career (which he has continued, if in a more limited way, after turning to directing) but a fair reputation as a writer (among other credits he wrote, with Tucker, the pilot episode of *The Monkees*). Like the more famous talents of the Hollywood Renaissance, however, Mazursky has manifested an abiding interest not only in a critical social realism, but also in the European art film, which, through imitation and *hommage,* he has attempted to domesticate for the general American audience. His cinema, at the same time, favors the writer and the actor; not interested in or capable of an individual, arresting visual style, his films are based on literate scripts and afford excellent opportunities for affecting performance. And yet, unlike *Alice,* they usually retreat from the harsh conclusions which their initially penetrating analyses of contemporary life should require.

Bob and Carol and Ted and Alice, for example, offers an upwardly mobile California couple whose lives, following what appears to be a marathon Essalen encounter session, find a new direction. Taking the message of absolute honesty and non-stop self-expression to heart, they resolutely transform their social selves, experimenting with free love and attempting to loosen up their best friends, a more traditional couple who use up their energy in self-defeating games and manipulations. The foursome, now mixed, eventually winds up in a luxurious resort bed together, but are unable, presumably because of a residual conservatism, to consummate their contemplated new relationship. The film, however, offers this ideological dead-end as a triumph, as a happy ending whose import is hardly clear. Traditional marriage, with its jealousies and lies, has been mercilessly satirized, but open marriage, Mazursky seems to suggest, does not suit basic human needs. And yet Mazursky's relentless tenderness toward his characters, a sentimentality that surfaces as his desire to make the spectator identify with their predicament, blunts this critique by focussing attention on a relief-filled retreat from choice (the irony that the characters are set free to enjoy themselves in Las Vegas is not underlined).

Bob and Carol made a good deal of money during its initial release in 1969, perhaps because it dared to deal with some of the conflicts of the developing sexual revolution; it has not worn well. Most of Mazursky's subsequent films re-stage the same dramatic and ideological conflicts with mixed results. *Harry and Tonto* begins by challenging notions of ageing, but winds up confirming a whole range of social stereotypes: despite an occasional bitter note, the film exudes a warm, accepting humanism that trivializes its criticism of socially acceptable self-indulgence and mindless role-playing (the main character finds his niche as a lovably cantankerous septuagenarian who likes cats). *An Unmarried Woman* cuts its richly pampered Upper East Side heroine adrift from her cheat-

Paul Mazursky

ing husband only to enmesh her in a suitably vague conventional fantasy—having to choose between wonderful sex and a bohemian lifestyle with a handsome artist, on the one hand, and the self-fulfilling exploration of the world of work (whose details are deliberately left rather vague), on the other. *Alex in Wonderland* strikes an autobiographical note with its portrait of a director, naturally enamored of Fellini, in search of a powerful theme for his next project. Compared to Woody Allen's similar *hommage* (*Stardust Memories*), the film lacks biting humor and fails to find interesting reflexes for Fellini's modernist technique and intellectual seriousness. *Willie and Phil* cannot create American equivalents for Truffaut's cinema of interpersonal conflict and triumph, while *Down and Out in Beverly Hills,* based on a classic Renoir study of the venality and selfishness that cut across class lines, becomes an unintentional comedy of integration, constructing a cinematic world that sentimentalizes the inauthentic, the mindless, and the hypocritical. Like its director, the film's main character has his heart in the right place and is a reasonable success in his chosen field, even if he is unable to master the madness of the world around him without romanticizing its foibles and absurdities.

In the late 1980s and early 1990s, Mazursky has continued to find success with chronicles of contemporary American life that emphasize its contradictions and absurdities. Like *Down and Out in Beverly Hills, Scenes from a Mall* (with its deliberate Bergmanesque echoes) centers on marital problems among the haute bourgeoisie, in this case an upscale California two-career couple whose relationship disintegrates and reestablishes itself during a nightmarish odyssey through a suburban mall. The film is not only an homage to Bergman but, with its hyperconscious and motor-mouth main characters, an homage to Woody Allen, who plays the self-doubting but good-hearted husband he might have created himself. Though certainly funny and often inventive, *Scenes from a Mall* depends too heavily on its script (which bogs down in repetition halfway through) and the engaging style of Allen and Bette Midler. Mazursky does little more than stage their encounter, and except for brief moments never uses the mall inventively to create more of a cinematic experience. Though it suffered from a poor release, *The Pickle* offers Mazursky at his best, with a chronicle of the absurdities of contemporary filmmaking, especially its deal making and artistic compromises. Here the script is well constructed and allows Mazursky to do what he does best: direct the actors.

Mazursky's most memorable recent film, however, is his most untypical. *Enemies: A Love Story*, based on an Isaac Bashevis Singer story, offers a tragi-comic narrative of a man who, falling victim to circumstance and his own desires, winds up with two wives and a mistress he would like to marry. Set in a post-Shoah New York, the film offers the character's failure to settle down as, in part, the result of an entire culture's displacement and ruin (the deadly aspects of which have not ended, as one of his women kills herself, doing what the Nazis were never able to accomplish). Coaxing fine performances from a largely unknown ensemble cast (Ron Silver plays the lead), Mazursky successfully evokes a bygone era by using nicely detailed sets (camp in the Catskills, Brooklyn streets, a Coney Island diner) and a photographic style that emphasizes the human drama played out within them. *Enemies: A Love Story* deserves to be considered, like *The Godfather* and *Avalon,* one of the most engaging and penetrating cinematic interpretations of postwar America.—R. BARTON PALMER

McCarey, Leo

Nationality *American.* **Born** *Los Angeles, 3 October 1898.* **Education** *Los Angeles High School; University of Southern California Law School.* **Family** *Married Stella Martin, 1920, one daughter.* **Career** *Lawyer in San Francisco and Los Angeles, 1916-17; third assistant to Tod Browning, then script supervisor, at Universal, 1918-19; supervisor and director of about 300 comedy shorts for Hal Roach studios, 1923-28; gagman for Our Gang series, 1923-24; teamed Stan Laurel and Oliver Hardy, 1927; signed with Fox Studios, 1930; signed with Paramount, 1933; formed Rainbow Productions with Bing Crosby and others, 1946.* **Awards** *Oscar for Best Direction for* The Awful Truth, *1937; Oscars for Best Direction and Best Original Story for* Going My Way, *1944.* **Died** *5 July 1969.*

Films as Director: 1921: *Society Secrets* (+pr). **1924:** *Publicity Pays* (+co-sc); *Young Oldfield* (+co-sc); *Stolen Goods* (+co-sc); *Jeffries Jr.* (+co-sc); *Why Husbands Go Mad* (+co-sc); *A Ten Minutes Egg* (+co-sc); *Seeing Nellie Home* (+co-sc); *Sweet Daddy* (+co-sc); *Why Men Work* (+co-sc); *Outdoor Pajamas* (+co-sc); *Sittin' Pretty* (+co-sc); *Too Many Mamas* (+co-sc); *Bungalow Boobs* (+co-sc); *Accidental Accidents* (+co-sc); *All Wet* (+co-sc); *The Poor Fish* (+co-sc); *The Royal Razz* (+co-sc). **1925:** *Hello Baby* (+co-sc); *Fighting Fluid* (+co-sc); *The Family Entrance* (+co-sc); *Plain and Fancy Girls* (+co-sc); *Should Husbands Be Watched?* (+co-sc); *Hard Boiled* (+co-sc); *Is Marriage the Bunk?* (+co-sc); *Bad Boy* (+co-sc); *Big Red Riding Hood* (+co-sc); *Looking for Sally* (+co-sc); *What Price Goofy?* (+co-sc); *Isn't Life Terrible* (+co-sc); *Innocent Husbands* (+co-sc); *No Father to Guide Him* (+co-sc); *The Caretaker's Daughter* (+co-sc); *The Uneasy Three* (+co-sc); *His Wooden Wedding* (+co-sc). **1926:** *Charley My Boy* (+co-sc); *Mama Behave* (+co-sc); *Dog Shy* (+co-sc); *Mum's the Word* (+co-sc); *Long Live the King* (+co-sc); *Mighty Like a Moose* (+co-sc); *Crazy Like a Fox* (+co-sc); *Bromo and Juliet* (+co-sc); *Tell 'em Nothing* (+co-sc); *Be Your Age* (+co-sc). **1928:** *We Faw Down* (*We Slip Up*); *Should Married Men Go Home?* (+co-sc, supervisor); *Two Tars* (+story, supervisor); *Should Women Drive?* (+co-sc); *A Pair of Tights* (+co-sc); *Blow By Blow* (+co-sc); *The Boy Friend* (+co-sc); *Came the Dawn* (+co-sc); *Do Gentlemen Snore?* (+co-sc); *Dumb Daddies* (+co-sc); *Going Ga-ga* (+co-sc); *Pass the Gravy* (+co-sc); *Tell It to the Judge* (+co-sc); *That Night* (+co-sc). **1929:** *Liberty* (+co-sc); *Wrong*

Again (+co-sc); *Dad's Day* (+co-sc); *Freed 'em and Weep* (+co-sc); *Hurdy Gurdy* (+co-sc); *Madame Q* (+co-sc); *Sky Boy* (+co-sc); *The Unkissed Man* (+co-sc); *When Money Comes* (+co-sc); *Why Is Plumber* (+co-sc). **1929:** *The Sophomore* (+co-sc); *Red Hot Rhythm* (+co-sc). **1930:** *Wild Company; Part Time Wife* (+co-sc). **1931:** *Indiscreet.* **1932:** *The Kid from Spain.* **1933:** *Duck Soup.* **1934:** *Six of a Kind; Belle of the Nineties* (*It Ain't No Sin*); *Ruggles of Red Gap.* **1935:** *The Milky Way.* **1937:** *Make Way for Tomorrow* (*The Years Are So Long; When the Wind Blows*) (+pr); *The Awful Truth.* **1938:** *Love Affair.* **1940:** *My Favorite Wife* (+co-sc). **1942:** *Once upon a Honeymoon* (+pr). **1944:** *Going My Way* (+pr, story). **1945:** *The Bells of Saint Mary's* (+pr, story). **1948:** *Good Sam* (+pr, co-story). **1952:** *My Son John* (+pr, story, co-sc). **1957:** *An Affair to Remember* (+co-sc). **1958:** *Rally 'round the Flag, Boys!* (+pr, co-sc). **1961:** *Satan Never Sleeps* (*China Story*) (+pr, co-sc).

Other Films: **1927:** *Second Hundred Years* (story). **1938:** *The Cowboy and the Lady* (co-story).

Leo McCarey has always presented *auteur* criticism with one of its greatest challenges and one that has never been convincingly met. The failure to do so should be seen as casting doubt on the validity of *auteurism* (in its cruder and simpler forms) rather than on the value of the McCarey oeuvre. He worked consistently (and apparently quite uncomplainingly) within the dominant codes of shooting and editing that comprise the anonymous "classical Hollywood" style; the films that bear his name as director, ranging from *Duck Soup* to *The Bells of St. Mary's,* from Laurel and Hardy shorts to *My Son John,* from *The Awful Truth* to *Make Way for Tomorrow* (made the same year!), resist reduction to a coherent thematic interpretation. Yet his name is on some of the best—and best-loved—Hollywood films (as well as on some that embarrass many of even his most fervent defenders).

In fact, it might be argued that McCarey's work validates a more sophisticated and circumspect *auteur* approach: not the author as divinely inspired individual creative genius, but the author as the animating presence in a project within which multiple determinants—collaborative, generic, ideological—complexly interact. The only adequate approach to a McCarey film would involve the systematic analysis of that interaction. A few notes can be offered, however, towards defining the "animating presence."

McCarey's formative years as an artist were spent working with the great clowns of the late silent/early sound period: Harold Lloyd, Mae West, W.C. Fields, the Marx Brothers and (especially) Laurel and Hardy, for whom he was "supervising manager" for many years, personally directing two of their greatest shorts (*Liberty* and *Wrong Again*). His subsequent career spans (with equal success) the entire range of American comedy from screwball (*The Awful Truth*) to romantic (*An Affair to Remember*). The director's congenial characteristic seems to have been a commitment to a spontaneous, individualist anarchy which he never entirely abandoned, accompanied by a consistent

Leo McCarey directing *Make Way for Tomorrow.*

skepticism about institutions and restrictive forms of social organization, a skepticism which produces friction and contradiction even within the most seemingly innocuous, conservative projects. *Going My Way* and *The Bells of St. Mary's* are usually rejected outright by the intelligentsia as merely pious and sentimental, but their presentation of Catholicism is neither simple, straightforward, nor uncritical, and it is easy to mistake for sentimentality, in contexts where you expect to find it anyway (such as Hollywood movies about singing priests), qualities such as tenderness and generosity. The celebration of individualism is of course a mainspring of American ideology, yet, pushed far enough in certain directions, it can expose contradictions *within* that ideology: its oppressive response to many forms of individuality, for example.

Make Way for Tomorrow (which, understandably, remained McCarey's favorite among his own films) is exemplary in this respect. Taking as its starting point an apparently reformable social problem (with Lee Grant's *Tell Me a Riddle* it is one of the only important Hollywood films about the aged), and opening with an unassailably respectable Biblical text ("Honor thy father and thy mother"), it proceeds to elaborate what amounts to a systematic radical analysis of the constraints, oppression, and divisiveness produced by capitalist culture, lending itself to a thoroughgoing Marxist reading that would certainly have surprised its director. Typically, the film (merely very good for its first three-quarters) suddenly takes off into greatness at the moment when Victor Moore asks the ultimate anarchic question "Why not?", and proceeds to repudiate his family in favour of rediscovering the original relationship with his wife before they become absorbed into the norms of democratic-capitalist domesticity. The process is only completed when, in one of the Hollywood cinema's most poignant and subversive moments, he "unmarries" them as they say their last farewell at the train station: "It's been a pleasure knowing you, Miss Breckenridge."—ROBIN WOOD

Mekas, Jonas

Nationality *Lithuanian.* **Born** *Semeniskiai, 24 December 1922.* **Education** *Gymnasium, Birzai, Lithuania, graduated 1942; studied philosophy and literature, Johannes Gutenberg University, Mainz, and University of Tübingen.* **Family** *Married Hollis Melton, 1974; children: Oona and Sebastian.* **Career** *During German occupation, taken, with brother Adolfas, to forced labor camp near Hamburg, 1944; they escaped, 1945; lived in displaced persons camps, 1945-49; while studying in Germany, edited Lithuanian emigré literary magazine Zvilgsniai (Glimpses), and wrote collections of short stories and poetry; moved to New York, 1949; worked in factories and shops in various capacities, through 1950s; founded Film Culture magazine, 1955, remains editor-in-chief; began "Movie Journal" column for Village Voice, 1958; shot first film, Guns of the Trees, and helped organize New American Cinema Group, 1960; organized The Film-Makers Cooperative, 1961; organized the Film-Makers Cinematheque, arrested and charged with showing obscene film (Jack Smith's Flaming Creatures), given six-month suspended sentence, 1964; co-founder with P. Adams Sitney, then acting director, Anthology Film Archives, 1970.* **Award** *Documentary Award, Venice Festival, for The Brig, 1965.* **Address** *c/o Anthology Film Archives, 32 Second Avenue, New York, New York 10003, U.S.A.*

Films as Director: 1961: *Guns of the Trees.* **1963:** *Film Magazine of the Arts.* **1964:** *The Brig; Award Presentation to Andy Warhol.* **1966:** *Report from Millbrook; Hare Krishna; Notes on the Circus; Cassis.*

1968: *Walden (Diaries, Notes, and Sketches).* **1969:** *Time & Fortune Vietnam Newsreel.* **1972:** *Reminiscences of a Journey to Lithuania.* **1976:** *Lost, Lost, Lost.* **1978:** *In Between.* **1980:** *Paradise Not Yet Lost, or Oona's Fifth Year.* **1981:** *Notes for Jerome.* **1986:** *He Stands in the Desert Counting the Seconds of His Life.* **1990:** *Self Portrait; Scenes from the Life of Andy Warhol.*

Other Films: 1993: *Jonas in the Desert* (co-sc).

Born in Lithuania in 1922, Jonas Mekas was a poet and resistance worker against both the German and Soviet occupations during the Second World War. After some years in a German camp for displaced persons, he and his brother, Adolfas, also a filmmaker, immigrated to New York, where they later founded the journal *Film Culture.* Initially hostile to the American avant-garde, Mekas became its champion and spokesman in the 1960s. Throughout that decade he exerted great influence through *Film Culture,* his "Movie Journal" column in the *Village Voice,* and his founding of the Film-makers Cooperative (in 1962) to distribute independent films, and the Film-makers Cinematheque (in 1963) as a New York showcase.

His first film, *Guns of the Trees,* a 35-millimeter feature, describes aspects of Beat culture in New York through the lives of four fictional characters. It reflects his hopes, at that time, for the establishment of a feature-length narrative cinema on the model of the French and Polish "New Waves." By the time he made *The Brig* with his brother, directly filming Ken Brown's stage play in the Living Theatre Production as if it were a documentary, he had already shifted his energies to his ongoing cinematic diary. The diary had actually begun in the mid-1950s when he reached the United States, but it took the liberating inspiration of Stan Brakhage and Marie Menken for Mekas to acknowledge that his artistic talent was focused outside of the feature film tradition he had been espousing.

The first installment of his *Diaries, Notes, and Sketches,* the nearly three-hour-long *Walden,* records his life, with numerous por-traits of his friends and colleagues, in the mid-1960s. Its techniques are characteristic of the filmmaker's mature work: staccato, single-frame flashes, composed directly in the camera, are counterpointed to longer sketches of weddings, trips to the circus, meetings. Printed intertitles often occur. Long passages have musical accompaniment. The filmmaker repeatedly breaks in on the soundtrack to offer private reflections and aphorisms.

In 1976 Mekas released *Lost, Lost, Lost,* another three-hour section of the megadiary. This time, he went back to his initial experi-ments with the camera, in a more conven-tional and leisurely style, to document the aspirations and frustrations of his life as an exile dreaming of the re-establishment of an independent Lithuanian republic. Bits of this material had already appeared in his master-ly and moving *Reminiscences of a Journey to*

Jonas Mekas

Lithuania, a three-part film made with the help of German television. The middle section of that film describes the emotional reunion of both brothers with their mother, then almost ninety years old, when they returned home for their first visit since the war. The film opens with a summary of Mekas's initial experiences in America and ends with a recognition of the impossibility of recovering the past, as he joins a group of his friends, mostly artists, in Vienna.

That elegiac tone is sustained and refined in *Notes for Jerome,* the record of his visits to the estate of Jerome Hill, in Cassis, France, in the late 1960s, and edited after Hill's death in 1972. Mekas married Hollis Melton in 1974; their first child, Oona, was born the next year. *Paradise Not Yet Lost, or Oona's Fifth Year* deals with his family life, but continues the theme of lost childhood which permeates Mekas's vision. It is filmed in the style of *Walden,* as is *In Between,* which records the years between *Lost, Lost, Lost* and *Walden.*—P. ADAMS SITNEY

Mélies, Georges

Nationality French. Born Paris, 8 December 1861. Education the Lycée Imperial, Vanves, 1868-70; Lycée Louis-le-Grand, Paris, 1871-80. Family Married 1) Eugénie Genin, 1885, children: Georgette and André; 2) Fanny Manieux (born Charlotte-Stéphanie Faës, stage name Jahanne D'Arcy), 1925. Career Introduced to illusionism by English conjuror John Maskelyne, 1884; bought Théâtre Robert-Houdin, Paris, began to present performance of magic and illusionism, and began association with technician Eugène Calmels, 1888; attended première of Cinematographe Lumière, 1895; bought Animatographe projector in London, developed camera with Lucien Reulos, built first studio at Montreuil, began shooting first film Partie des cartes, "Star Film Company" begun, 1896; transformed theatre into cinema, 1897; brother Gaston Mélies opens Star Film branch in New York, 1903; second Montreuil studio built, 1905; studio closes temporarily due to American competition, 1909; returned to stage as magician, 1910 (last performance 1920); Mélies retrospective, Paris, after "rediscovery" by Leon Druhot, 1929; given an apartment at Chateau d'Orly by the Mutuelle du Cinéma, 1932. Award Legion of Honour, 1933. Died In Paris, 21 January 1938.

Films as Director, Producer, Scenarist, Art Director and Actor: 1896: (seventy-eight films, two extant): *Une Nuit terrible* (*A Terrible Night*); *Escamotage d'une dame chez Robert-Houdin* (*The Vanishing Lady*). **1897:** (fifty-two films, five extant): *Entre Calais et Douvres* (*Between Calais and Dover*); *L'Auberge ensorcelée* (*The Bewitched Inn*); *Aprés le bal* (*After the Ball*); *Danse au sérail* (*Dancing in a Harem*); *Combat naval en Grèce.* **1898:** (thirty films, eight extant: *Visite sous-marine du Maine* (*Divers at Work on the Wreck of the Maine*); *Panorama pris d'un train en marche* (*Panorama from Top of a Moving Train*); *Le Magicien*; *Illusions fantasmagoriques* (*The Famous Box Trick*); *La Lune à un mètre* (*The Astronomer's Dream*); *Un Homme de tête* (*The Four Troublesome Heads*); *La Tentation de Saint-Antoine* (*The Temptation of Saint Anthony*); *Salle à manger fantastique* (*A Dinner Under Difficulties*). **1899:** (thirty-four films, four extant): *Cléopâtre* (*Robbing Cleopatra's Tomb*); *L'Impressioniste fin de siècle* (*An Up-To-Date Conjurer*); *Le Portrait mystérieux* (*A Mysterious Portrait*); *L'Affaire Dreyfus* (*The Dreyfus Affair*). **1900:** (thirty-three films, seven extant): *Les Miracles de Brahmane* (*The Miracles of Brahmin*); *L'Exposition de 1900* (*Paris Exposition, 1900*); *L'Homme orchestre* (*The One-Man Band*); *Le Rêve de Noël* (*The Christmas Dream*); *Gens qui pleurent et gens qui rient* (*Crying and Laughing*); *Nouvelles Luttes extravagantes* (*The Wrestling Sextette*); *Le Malade hydrophobe* (*The Man with Wheels in His Head*). **1901:** (twenty-nine films, four extant): *Le Brahmane et le papillon* (*The Brahmin and the Butterfly*); *Dislocations mystérieuses* (*Extraordinary Illusions*); *Le*

Charlatan (*Painless Dentistry*); *Barbe-Bleue* (*Blue Beard*). **1902:** (twenty-three films, five extant): *L'Homme à la tête de caoutchouc* (*The Man with the Rubber Head. India Rubber Head*); *Eruption volcanique à la Martinique* (*The Eruption of Mount Pelée*); *Le Voyage dans la lune* (*A Trip to the Moon*); *Le Sacré d'Édouard VII* (*The Coronation of Edward VII*); *Les Trésors de Satan* (*The Treasures of Satan*).

1903: (twenty-nine films, twenty-eight extant): *La Corbeille enchantée* (*The Enchanted Basket*); *La Guirlande merveilleuse* (*The Marvellous Wreath*); *Les Filles du Diable* (*Beelzebub's Daughters*); *Un Malheur n'arrive jamais seul* (*Misfortune Never Comes Alone*); *Le Cake-walk infernal* (*The Infernal Cake Walk*); *La Boîte à malice* (*The Mysterious Box*); *Le Puits fantastique* (*The Enchanted Well*); *L'Auberge du bon repos* (*The Inn Where No Man Rests*); *La Statue animée* (*The Drawing Lesson*); *La Flamme merveilleuse* (*The Mystical Flame*); *Le Sorcier* (*The Witch's Revenge*); *L'Oracle de Delphes* (*The Oracle of Delphi*); *Le Portrait spirite* (*A Spiritualist Photographer*); *Le Mélomane* (*The Melomaniac*); *Le Monstre* (*The Monster*); *Le Royaume des Fées* (*The Kingdom of the Fairies*); *Le Chaudron infernal* (*The Infernal Cauldron*); *Le Revenant* (*The Apparition*); *Le Tonnerre de Jupiter* (*Jupiter's Thunderbolts*; *La Parapluie fantastique* (*Ten Ladies in One Umbrella*); *Tom Tight et Dum Dum* (*Jack Jaggs and Dum Dum*); *Bob Kick, l'enfant terrible* (*Bob Kick the Mischievous Kid*); *Illusions funambulesques* (*Extraordinary Illusions*); *L'Enchanteur Alcofrisbas* (*Alcofrisbas, the Master Magician*); *Jack et Jim*; *La Lanterne magique* (*The Magic Lantern*); *La Rêve du maître de ballet* (*The Ballet Master's Dream*); *Faust aux enfers* (*The Damnation of Faust*). **1904:** (thirty-five films, nineteen extant): *Le Bourreau turc* (*The Terrible Turkish Executioner*); *Au Clair de la lune ou Pierrot malheureux* (*A Moonlight Serenade, or The Miser Punished*); *Un Bonne Farce avec ma tête* (*Tit for Tat*); *Le Coffre enchanté* (*The Bewitched Trunk*); *Les Apparitions fugitives* (*Fugitive Apparitions*); *Le Roi du maquillage* (*Untamable Whiskers*); *La Rêve d'horloger* (*The Clockmaker's Dream*); *Les Transmutations imperceptibles* (*The Imperceptible Transformations*); *Un Miracle sous l'inquisition* (*A Miracle Under the Inquisition*); *Benvenutto Cellini ou une curieuse évasion* (*Benvenuto Cellini, or a Curious Evasion*); *La Damnation du Docteur Faust* (*Faust and Marguerite*); *Le Thaumaturge chinois* (*Tchin-Chao, the Chinese Conjurer*); *Le Merveilleux éventail vivant* (*The Wonderful Living Fan*); *Sorcellerie culinaire* (*The Cook in Trouble*); *La Sirène* (*The Mermaid*); *Le Rosier miraculeux* (*The Wonderful Rose Tree*); *Le Voyage à travers l'impossible* (*The Impossible Voyage*); *Le Juif errant* (*The Wandering Jew*); *La Cascade de Feu* (*The Firefall*).

1905: (twenty-two films, eleven extant): *Les Cartes vivants* (*The Living Playing Cards*); *Le Diable noir* (*The Black Imp*); *Le Menuet lilliputien* (*The Lilliputian Minuet*); *Le Bacquet de Mesmer* (*A Mesmerian Experiment*); *Le Palais des mille et une nuits* (*The Palace of the Arabian Nights*); *La Compositeur toqué* (*A Crazy Composer*); *La Chaise à porteurs enchantée* (*The Enchanted Sedan Chair*); *Le Raid Paris-Monte Carlo en deux heures* (*An Adventurous Automobile Trip*); *Un Feu d'artifice improvisé* (*Unexpected Fireworks*); *La Légende de Rip van Winkle* (*Rip's Dream*); *Le Tripot clandestin* (*The Scheming Gambler's Paradise*). **1906:** (eighteen films, ten extant): *Une Chute de cinq étages* (*A Mix-up in the Galley*); *La Cardeuse de Matelas* (*The Tramp and the Mattress-Makers*); *Les Affiches en goguette* (*The Hilarious Posters*); *Histoire d'un crime* (*A Desperate Crime*); *L'Anarchie chez Guignol* (*Punch and Judy*); *L'Hôtel des voyageurs de commerce* (*A Roadside Inn*); *Les Bulles de savon animées* (*Soap Bubbles*); *Les 400 Farces du Diable* (*The Merry Frolics of Satan*); *L'Alchimiste Prarafaragamus ou la Cornue infernale* (*The Mysterious Retort*); *La Fée caraboose ou le Poignard fatal* (*The Witch*). **1907:** (nineteen films, seven extant): *La Douche d'eau bouillante* (*Rogue's Tricks*); *Le Mariage de Victorine* (*How Bridget's Lover Escaped*); *Le Tunnel sous la manche ou Le Cauchemar franco-anglais* (*Tunnelling the English Channel*); *L'Eclipse du soleil en pleine lune* (*The Eclipse, or the Courtship of the Sun and the Moon*); *Pauvre John ou Les Aventures d'un buveur de whiskey* (*Sight-Seeing Through Whiskey*); *La Colle universelle* (*Good Glue Sticks*); *Ali Barbouyou et Ali Bouf à l'huile* (*Delirium in a Studio*). **1908:** (sixty-eight films, twenty-one extant): *Le Tambourin fantastique* (*The Knight of the Black Art*); *Il y a un dieu pour les ivrognes* (*The Good Luck of a Souse*); *La Génie de feu* (*The Genii of Fire*); *Why the Actor Was Late*; *Le Rêve d'un fumeur d'opium* (*The Dream of an Opium Fiend*); *La Photographie electrique à distance* (*Long Distance Wireless Photography*); *Salon de coiffure* (*In the Barber Shop*); *Le Nouveau Seigneur du village* (*The New Lord of the Village*); *Sideshow Wrestlers*; *Lulli ou le violon brisé* (*The Broken Violin*); *The Woes of Roller Skates*; *Le Fakir de Singapoure* (*The Indian Sorcerer*); *The Mischances of a Photographer*; *His First Job*; *French Cops Learning English*; *A Tricky Painter's Fate*; *Au patys des jouets* (*Grandmother's Story*); *Buncoed Stage Johnnie*; *Not Guilty*; *Hallucinations pharmaceutiques* (*Pharmaceutical Hallucinations*); *La Bonne Bergère et la méchante princesse* (*The Good Shepherdess and the Evil Princess*). **1909:** (nine films, none extant). **1910:** (thirteen films, three extant): *Hydrothérapie fantastique* (*The Doctor's Secret*); *Le Locataire diabolique* (*The Diabolic Tenant*); *Les Illusions fantaisistes* (*Whimsical Illusions*). **1911:** (two films, one extant): *Les Hallucinations du Baron Münchausen* (*Baron Münchausen's Dream*). **1912:** (four films, three extant): *La conquête du Pôle* (*The Conquest of the Pole*); *Cendrillon ou la pantoufle mystérieuse* (*Cinderella or the Glass Slipper*); *Le Chevalier des neiges* (*The Knight of the Snows*).

Georges Mélies, prestidigitator and master illusionist in the Parisian theatre of the late nineteenth century, turned to the cinema and made some five hundred films of every kind fashionable at the time between 1896 and 1912. Of these less than ninety survive, though working drawings (Mélies was a prolific and considerable graphic artist) remain to supplement his work.

Born in Paris in 1861, Mélies as a youth habitually attended the Théâtre Robert-Houdin, a first-floor establishment with two hundred seats and a stage carefully devised to present Jean-Eugène Robert-Houdin's technically advanced forms of conjuring and illusion. He was also influenced by visits to Maskelyne and Cooke's Egyptian Hall in London, where for a while his father, a wealthy bootmaker, sent him to work. Maskelyne presented spectacular dramatic shows involving illusions of the kind Mélies was himself to develop when, in 1888, after selling his share in his late father's business to his brothers, he was able to buy the Théâtre Robert-Houdin and take over as showman illusionist. In addition, he exhibited lantern-slide shows with an illusion of movement achieved by continuities of superimposition.

After seeing the celebrated Cinématographe Lumière in Paris in December 1895, Mélies could not rest until he had obtained equipment for himself. He acquired his first motion picture apparatus in 1896 from R.W. Paul in London, and presented his first film show at the Robert-

Georges Mélies (in vest)

Houdin on 4 April 1896, using Edison's kinetoscope loops; his own initial ventures into filmmaking—moving snapshots much like Lumière's—were exhibited in the fall.

In his first year Méliès made seventy-eight films, all but one running about one minute; the exception, *The Devil's Castle,* was a vampire film that was three minutes in length. Within a year, by March 1897, he had constructed a glass studio in the garden of his house in Montreuil, near Paris, its equipment modelled on that for the stage in the Théâtre Robert-Houdin. He then turned the theater over, in part at least, to screening programs made up exclusively of films. With his staff he built the sets, designed and made the costumes, photographed and processed the films, using cameras made mainly by Gaumont, Lumière, and Pathé. He sold the prints outright to fairground and music-hall showmen, initially in France and England. He worked at a furious pace and became known as a tough employer of both artists and technicians. At first he used non-professional players, often performing himself.

Although he was to try his hand at every kind of film, Méliès' more lasting reputation was for burlesque, magical pantomime, and stage-derived illusion. But like other producers of the era, he also made money from bogus newsreel reconstruction, theatrical melodrama, adaptions from literary sources, historical costume drama, and even so-called "stag" films (mild strip-teases) and advertising films. Among his staged newsreels were films that purported to provide coverage of the Greco-Turkish war (1897) and American involvement in Cuba and the Philippines (1898). He even reconstructed *The Eruption of Mount Pelée* on Martinique in 1902, using models, and *The Coronation of Edward VII* before the event even took place; the coronation was in any case postponed.

It is well-known that Méliès was an exponent of trick photography, inspired, according to Georges Sadoul, the French film historian, by the publication in 1897 of Albert Allis Hopkins' *Magic, Stage Illusions and Scientific Diversions, Including Trick Photography.* On the other hand, his most reliable biographer, Paul Hammond, claims Méliès would have been familiar with such devices long before. His standard techniques included duplex photography (through which a single man could appear as himself and a double in a single frame) and spirit (ghost) photography using multiple images. These techniques enabled him to make films projecting stage illusions like *The Vanishing Lady* and *The Astronomer's Dream*—dream films are recurrent in his catalogue—and *The Four Troublesome Heads,* in which a magician repeatedly removes his head. Méliès was to specialize in comic dismemberment of heads and limbs.

By the turn of the century Méliès was handling historical subjects, including *Joan of Arc.* He even made a pro-Dreyfus film of 13 minutes, *The Dreyfus Affair.* Méliès also pursued literary adaptions, such as *The Damnation of Faust,* and provided coverage (backed by phonograph recordings) of the comedian-singer Paulus in a series of films, using for the first time electric arc-lights. He even made *Christ Walking on the Water* as well as simple travel or view films, including panoramas of Paris for the 1900 World Fair. He also reproduced in modern form the past glories of celebrated ghost and skeleton exhibitions, such as *Pepper's Ghost* of London in 1862 and Robertson's *Fantasmagorie* of Paris in 1794. His mildly pornographic "stag" films included *After the Ball* and *The Bridegroom's Dilemma,* in which the actress Jahanne d'Arcy (Méliès' mistress, who became his second wife in 1925) appeared.

Most of Méliès' more celebrated films depended on illusion, comic burlesque, and pantomime. These films included *The Man with the Rubber Head,* in which Méliès' own head is seen expanding to giant size and exploding; the delightfully absurd *A Trip to the Moon,* with acrobats playing the Selenites and hand-waving dancing girls sitting on stars; *The Melomaniac,* in which Méliès conjures with numerous images of his own head, creating musical notes out of them; the space-travelling burlesque *The Impossible Voyage* (length twenty-four minutes); the pantomimic *The Merry Frolics of Satan,* with its animated, skeleton puppet horse; a ninety-one-minute version of *Hamlet; The Conquest of the Pole,* with its man-eating Giant of the Snows, a vast marionette; and *Cinderella and the Glass Slipper,* produced in association with Pathé and cut by his order from fifty-four to thirty-three minutes.

Until around 1909 Méliès remained a largely successful filmmaker. In 1900 he was elected president of the International Convention of Cinematograph Editors (a position he held until 1912), and in 1904 he became president of the Chambre Syndicale de la Prestidigitation. There were agencies for his Star Film company in Berlin, Barcelona, London, and New York. Some of his films were available at double or treble cost in hand-tinted color prints. But the introduction of the practice of renting films, advocated by Pathé and other well-financed producers, was finally to defeat Méliès. He began to turn his attention back to theatrical presentation, producing pantomimes in Paris.

His brother Gaston, based by this time in America, began to produce live-action films for Star, including Westerns in Texas and California, even for a while employing Francis Ford, John Ford's older brother, and later in 1912 touring the South Seas and Far East to make travelogues. (Gaston was to die of food poisoning in Algeria in 1914.) Georges Méliès ceased filmmaking in 1912, his kind of work outdated and unwanted, and by 1914, a widower in his sixties, he was forced to rent his properties or see them taken over for war purposes, though one of his studios was converted into a vaudeville theater and run from 1917 to 1923 by his daughter, Georgette. Méliès gave his last show in the Théâtre Robert-Houdin in 1920, by which time he was deeply in debt. Many of his negatives and prints were destroyed for scrap.

As an artist of stage and screen, Méliès was at once illusionist and pantomimist; in his films, human beings became comic creatures with fantastic costumes and make-up, liable to disintegrate or reshape into anything. Méliès' world was one of ceaseless change, a product partly of fairground magic and of costume tableaux vivants. Chaplin described him as an "alchemist of light." His sets, often beautifully painted in trompe-l'oeil with deceptive perspective, were essentially theatrical. His remarkable drawings, many happily preserved, show what a magnificent cartoon animator he could have become with his Protean imagination for the grotesque and the marvellous. As it was, adopting the cinema in the very year of its birth, he endowed it with the work of his highly individualist imagination, an imagination unlike that of any other filmmaker of his time. The best study of him in English is that by Paul Hammond, *Marvellous Méliès.*—ROGER MANVELL

Melville, Jean-Pierre

__Nationality__ French. __Born__ Jean-Pierre Grumbach in Paris, 20 October 1917. __Education__ The Lycées Condorcet and Charlemagne, Paris, and Michelet, Vanves. __Military Service__ Began military service, 1937; evacuated to England after Dunkirk, then served with Free French Forces in North Africa and Italy. __Career__ Founder, O.G.C. (Organisation générale cinématographique) as production company, 1945; built own studio, Paris, 1949 (de-

stroyed by fire, 1967). **Awards** *Prix René-Jeanne for* Le cercle rouge, *1970; Chevalier de la Légion d'honneur; Chevalier des Arts et des Lettres.* **Died** *In Paris, 2 August 1973.*

Films as Director: 1946: *Vingt quatre heures de la vie d'un clown* (+sc, pr). **1948:** *Le Silence de la mer* (+pr, sc). **1950:** *Les Enfants terribles* (+co-sc, pr, art d). **1953:** *Quand tu liras cette lettre* (+sc). **1956:** *Bob le flambeur* (+pr, co-art d, sc). **1959:** *Deux hommes dans Manhattan* (+pr, sc, role as Moreau). **1963:** *Léon Morin, prêtre* (+sc); *Le Doulos* (+sc); *L'Aîné des Ferchaux* (+sc). **1966:** *Le Deuxième Souffle* (+sc). **1967:** *Le Samourai* (+sc). **1969:** *L'Armée des ombres* (+sc). **1972:** *Le Cercle rouge* (+sc); *Un Flic* (+sc).

Other Films: 1948: *Les Dames du Bois de Boulogne* (Bresson) (role). **1949:** *Orphée* (Cocteau) (role as hotel director). **1957:** *Un Amour de poche* (role as police commissioner). **1960:** *A bout de souffle* (Godard) (role as the writer Parvulesco). **1962:** *Landru* (Chabrol) (role as Georges Mandel).

The career of Jean-Pierre Melville is one of the most independent in modern French cinema. The tone was set with his first feature film, *Le Silence de la mer,* made quite outside the confines of the French film industry. Without union recognition or even the rights to the novel by Vercors which he was adapting, Melville proceeded to make a film which, in its counterpointing of images and a spoken text, set the pattern for a whole area of French literary filmmaking extending from Bresson and Resnais down to Duras in the 1980s. *Les Enfants terribles,* made in close collaboration with Jean Cocteau, was an equally interesting amalgam of literature and film, but more influential was *Bob le flambeur,* a first variation on gangster film themes which emerged as a striking study of loyalty and betrayal.

But by the time that the New Wave directors were drawing from *Bob le flambeur* a set of stylistic lessons which were to be crucial to their own breakthrough—economical location shooting, use of natural light, improvisatory approaches, and use of character actors in place of stars—Melville himself had moved in quite a different direction. *Léon Morin, prêtre* marks

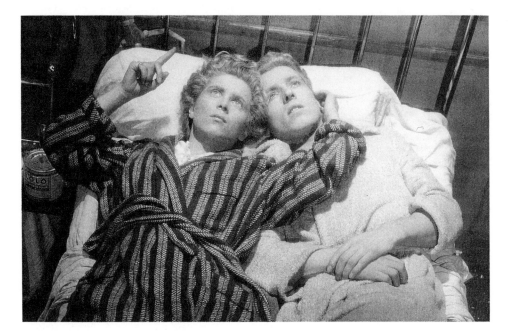

Jean-Pierre Melville: *Les Enfants terribles*

Melville's decision to leave this directly personal world of low-budget filmmaking for a mature style of solidly commercial genre filmmaking that used major stars and tightly wrought scripts to capture a wide audience.

This style is perfectly embodied in the trio of mid-1960s gangster films which constitute the core of Melville's achievement in cinema. Melville's concern with the film as a narrative spectacle is totally vindicated in these films, each of which was built around a star performance: Jean-Paul Belmondo in *Le Doulos,* Lino Ventura in *Le Deuxième Souffle,* and Alain Delon in *Le Samourai.* Drawing on his 1930s viewing and his adolescent reading of American thrillers, Melville manipulated the whole mythology of the gangster film, casting aside all pretence of offering a social study. His criminals are idealized figures, their appearance stylized with emphasis on the belted raincoat, soft hat, and ever-present handgun. Their behavior oddly blends violence and ritualized politeness, and lifts them out from their settings. Melville had no interest in the realistic portrayal of life. He disregarded both psychological depth and accuracy of location and costume. The director instead used his stars to portray timeless, tragic figures caught up in ambiguous conflicts and patterns of deceit, relying on the actor's personality and certainty of gesture to fill the intentional void.

Le Samourai, a perfect distillation of the cinematic myth of the gangster, remains Melville's masterpiece. Subsequent attempts to widen his range included an effort to transpose his characters into the world of Occupation and Resistance in *L'Armée des ombres,* as well as a film—*Le Cercle rouge*—that combined his particular gift for atmosphere with a *Rififi*-style presentation of the mechanics of a robbery. These films are interesting but flawed works. Melville's frustration and dissatisfaction was reflected in his last work, *Un Flic,* which completed the passage towards abstraction begun in the mid-1960s. It offers a derisory world lacking even the human warmth of loyalty and friendship which the director had earlier celebrated. In retrospect, it seems likely that Melville's reputation will rest largely on his ability, almost unique in French cinema, to contain deeply-felt personal attitudes within the tight confines of commercial genre production. Certainly his thrillers are unequalled in European cinema.—ROY ARMES

Minnelli, Vincente

Nationality American. **Born** Chicago, 28 February 1910. **Education** The Art Institute of Chicago, mid-1920s. **Family** Married 1) Judy Garland, 1945 (divorced 1951), daughter Liza; 2) Georgette Magnani, 1954 (divorced 1958), one daughter; 3) Denise Giganti, 1961 (divorced 1971); 4) Lee M. Anderson, 1982. **Career** Child actor, Minnelli Brothers Dramatic Tent Show, 1913-18; billboard painter, then window dresser, Marshall Field's department store, Chicago, 1929; assistant stage manager and costume designer, Balaban and Katz theatre chain, Chicago, then set and costume designer, Paramount Theater, New York, 1931-33; art director, Radio City Music Hall, New York, 1934; director of ballets and musicals for the stage, then signed as producer/director, Paramount Pictures, Hollywood, 1936; bought out contract after eight months and returned to New York as theatre director; joined MGM under auspices of Arthur Freed, 1940; directed sequences in Babes on Broadway, 1941, and Panama Hattie, 1942; directed first feature, Cabin in the Sky, 1942; returned to stage directing with Mata Hari, 1967, closed after two-week run.

Vincente Minnelli with Judy Garland on the set of *Meet Me in St. Louis*.

Awards *Academy Award for Best Director for* Gigi, *1958; Order of Arts and Letters, France, for contribution to French culture.* **Died** *In Beverly Hills, California, 25 July 1986.*

Films as Director: 1942: *Cabin in the Sky.* **1943:** *I Dood It* (*By Hook or By Crook*). **1944:** *Meet Me in St. Louis.* **1945:** *The Clock* (*Under the Clock*); *Yolanda and the Thief.* **1946:** *Ziegfeld Follies* (co-d); *Undercurrent.* **1947:** *Till the Clouds Roll By* (Whorf) (Judy Garland sequences only). **1948:** *The Pirate.* **1949:** *Madame Bovary.* **1950:** *Father of the Bride.* **1951:** *An American in Paris; Father's Little Dividend.* **1952:** *Lovely to Look At* (LeRoy) (fashion show sequence only). **1953:** "Mademoiselle" episode of *The Story of Three Loves; The Bad and the Beautiful; The Band Wagon.* **1954:** *The Long, Long Trailer; Brigadoon.* **1955:** *The Cobweb; Kismet.* **1956:** *Lust for Life; Tea and Sympathy.* **1957:** *Designing Woman; The Seventh Sin* (Neame; replaced Neame as director, refused credit). **1958:** *Gigi; The Reluctant Debutante.* **1959:** *Some Came Running.* **1960:** *Home from the Hill; Bells Are Ringing.* **1962:** *The Four Horsemen of the Apocalypse; Two Weeks in Another Town.* **1963:** *The Courtship of Eddie's Father.* **1964:** *Goodbye Charlie.* **1965:** *The Sandpiper.* **1970:** *On a Clear Day You Can See Forever.* **1976:** *A Matter of Time.*

Between 1942 and 1962, Vincente Minnelli directed twenty-nine films (and parts of several others) at Metro-Goldywn-Mayer, eventually becoming the studio's longest-tenured director. Brought to Hollywood following a tremendously successful career as a Broadway set designer and director of musicals, he was immediately placed at the helm of MGM's biggest musical productions, beginning with *Cabin in the Sky.* Over the next decade-and-a-half, he gained a reputation as the premiere director at work in the genre. This reputation was based on a remarkable series of productions, including *Meet Me in St. Louis, The Pirate, An American in Paris,* and *The Band Wagon,* and culminating with a Best Director's Academy Award for *Gigi.* Yet Minnelli's career was by no means restricted to musicals. During the same period he also directed a series of successful comedies and melodramas with flair and stylistic elegance.

If anything, Minnelli's accomplishments as a stylist, which were recognized from the beginning of his Hollywood career, worked against his being taken seriously as a director-auteur. By the late 1950s he had been dubbed (by critic Albert Johnson) "the master of the decorative image," which seemed, at the time, the highest compliment which might be paid a director of musicals. Indeed, Minnelli's films are impeccably crafted—filled with lushly stylized sets, clever and graceful performances, and a partiality for long tales. Minnelli also utilized a fluid mobile camera suited to the filming of dance, mounting and preserving performance spatially, even as the camera involves the audience in the choreographed movement. Yet it also informs the non-musical sequences of Minnelli's films with the same kind of liberal sensibility associated with contemporaries like Otto Preminger and Nicholas Ray, one that allows both the characters and the eyes of the audience a certain freedom of movement within a nearly seamless time and space. An accompanying theatricality (resulting from a tendency to shoot scenes from a fourth-wall position) blends with Minnelli's specifically cinematic flourishes in a clever realization of the themes of art and artificiality, themes which run throughout his films.

Stylization and artifice are necessarily addressed by musical films in general, and Minnelli's films do so with great verve—most thoroughly in the baroque otherworldliness of *Yolanda and the Thief,* and most brilliantly in the interplay of character and actor, stage and screen in *The Band Wagon.* But an equal concern with levels of unreality informs most of his films. This is perhaps most evident in the Pirandellian meditation on Hollywood, *The Bad and the Beautiful,* and its bizarre, Cinecitta-made quasi-sequel, *Two Weeks in Another Town.* This exploration surely reaches a kind of limit in Minnelli's last film, *A Matter of Time.* This story of an aspiring actress, played by Liza Minnelli, becomes an examination of his own daughter's talents and persona (haunted by the ghost of Judy Garland), making the film into the director's own *Vertigo,* a fitting conclusion to a career devoted to the interplay of various levels of fantasy.

Filmic fantasy is almost always present in Minnelli's films, even when they address the most mundane human problems in basically realistic settings. Virtually every Minnelli film contains a fantasy sequence, a moment in which the narrative recedes in order to allow a free play of symbols on an almost exclusively formal level. In Minnelli's musicals, this is invariably an extended "ballet." The most memorable of these ballets may be the twenty-minute number which concludes *An American in Paris,* but the most powerful example might be Judy Garland's erotic fantasy of Gene Kelly as "Mack the Black" in *The Pirate.* In *Meet Me in St. Louis,* the burst of pure style occurs in the non-musical, and surprisingly horrific, Halloween sequence. In the comedy *Father of the Bride,* it is a tour-de-force dream sequence in which all of Spencer Tracy's fatherly anxieties are unleashed. The position is filled by a hallucinatory chase through a carnival in *Some Came Running,* by fantastic visions of the title figures in *The Four Horsemen of the Apocalypse,* and by mad car rides in both *The Bad and the Beautiful* and *Two Weeks in Another Town.* Such extra-narrative sequences serve to condense and resolve plot elements on a visual/emotional plane, providing the only escape routes from the exigencies of a world which Minnelli otherwise depicts as emotionally frustrating, overly complex, and terribly delicate.

Indeed, Andrew Sarris quite rightly noted that "Minnelli had an unusual, sombre outlook for musical comedy," a fact which seems responsible for the unexpected depth of most of his films. Certainly one of the factors responsible for the continued interest in *Meet Me in St. Louis* is the overt morbidity of its nostalgic tone. Yet Minnelli's troubled perspective is probably most evident in the existential isolation of his characters, and in the humanistic, yet stoic, attitude he adopts in treating equally their petty jealousies and their moral fears. A genuinely pained sense of the virtual impossibility of meaningful human contact informs the machinations of such stylized melodramas as *Some Came Running, Home from the Hill,* and *The Four Horsemen.* And the tenuousness of love and power is nowhere more artfully rendered than in his generic masterpiece, *The Cobweb,* where an argument over drapes for the rec room of a mental hospital reveals a network of neuroses amongst the staff and their families that is as deep-seated as the disorders of the patients.

At worst, Minnelli has been cited as the epitome of Hollywood's "middlebrow" aspirations toward making art accessible to the mass audience. At best, he was championed by the British critics at *Movie* during the early 1960s as one of Hollywood's consummate auteurs. For one such critic, V. F. Perkins, Minnelli's films provided some of the best examples of classical narrative style, which naturalized meaning through understated flourishes of mise-en-scène. It is certainly this capacity which enabled Minnelli to employ a forty-foot trailer as an effortless metaphor for the marriage of newlyweds Lucille Ball and Desi Arnaz (*The Long, Long Trailer*), to critique the manipulations of parental love by consumer culture through depiction of an increasingly overblown wedding (*Father of the Bride*), and to displace a child's incapacity to deal with his mother's death onto his horror at the discovery of his dead goldfish (*The Courtship of Eddie's Father*).

We must certainly categorize Minnelli as something more than a decorative artist, for the stylistic devices of his films are informed with a remarkably resilient intelligence. Even if we are finally to conclude that, throughout his work, there is a dominance of style over theme, it ultimately serves only to confirm his contribution to the refinement of those techniques by which Hollywood translates meanings into style and presents both as entertainment.—ED LOWRY

Mizoguchi, Kenji

Nationality Japanese. Born Tokyo, 16 May 1898. Education Aobashi Western Painting Research Institute, Tokyo, enrolled 1914. Career Apprentice to textile designer, 1913; newspaper illustrator, Kobe, 1916; assistant director to Osamu Wakayama, 1922; direct-ed first film, 1923; began association with art director Hiroshi Mizutani on Gio matsuri, *1933; began collaboration with writer Yoshikata Yoda on* Naniwa ereji, *1936; member of Cabinet Film Committee, from 1940; elected president of Japanese directors association, 1949; signed to Daiei Company, 1952. Award International Prize, Venice Festival, for* The Life of Oharu, *1952. Died Of leukemia, in Kyoto, 24 August 1956.*

Films as Director: 1923: *Ai ni yomigaeru hi* (*The Resurrection of Love*); *Furusato* (*Hometown*) (+sc); *Seishun no yumeji* (*The Dream Path of Youth*) (+sc); *Joen no chimata* (*City of Desire*) (+sc); *Haizan no uta wa kanashi* (*Failure's Song is Sad*) (+sc); *813* (*813: The Adventures of Arsene Lupin*); *Kiri no minato* (*Foggy Harbor*); *Chi to rei* (*Blood and Soul*) (+sc); *Yoru* (*The Night*) (+sc); *Haikyo no naka* (*In the Ruins*). **1924:** *Toge no uta* (*The Song of the Mountain Pass*) (+sc); *Kanashiki hakuchi* (*The Sad Idiot*) (+story); *Gendai no joo* (*The Queen of Modern Times*); *Josei wa tsuyoshi* (*Women Are Strong*); *Jinkyo* (*This Dusty World*); *Shichimencho no yukue* (*Turkeys in a Row*); *Samidare zoshi* (*A Chronicle of May Rain*); *Musen fusen* (*No Money, No Fight*); *Kanraku no onna* (*A Woman of Pleasure*) (+story); *Akatsuki no shi* (*Death at Dawn*). **1925:** *Kyohubadan no joo* (*Queen of the Circus*); *Gakuso o idete* (*Out of College*) (+sc); *Shirayuri wa nageku* (*The White Lily Laments*); *Daichi wa hohoemu* (*The Earth Smiles*); *Akai yuhi ni terasarete* (*Shining in the Red Sunset*); *Furusato no uta* (*The Song of Home*); *Ningen* (*The Human Being*); *Gaijo no suketchi* (*Street Sketches*). **1926:** *Nogi Taisho to Kuma-san* (*General Nogi and Kuma-san*); *Doka o* (*The Copper Coin King*) (+story); *Kaminingyo haru no sayaki* (*A Paper Doll's Whisper of Spring*); *Shin ono ga tsumi* (*My Fault, New Version*); *Kyoren no onna shisho* (*The Passion of a Woman Teacher*); *Kaikoku danji* (*The Boy of the Sea*); *Kane* (*Money*) (+story). **1927:** *Ko-on* (*The Imperial Grace*); *Jihi shincho* (*The Cuckoo*). **1928:** *Hito no issho* (*A Man's Life*). **1929:** *Nihombashi* (+sc); *Tokyo koshinkyoku* (*Tokyo March*); *Asahi wa kagayaku* (*The Morning Sun Shines*); *Tokai kokyogaku* (*Metropolitan Symphony*). **1930:** *Furusato* (*Home Town*); *Tojin okichi* (*Mistress of a Foreigner*). **1931:** *Shikamo karera wa yuku* (*And Yet They Go*). **1932:** *Toki no ujigami* (*The Man of the Moment*); *Mammo Kenkoku no Reimei* (*The Dawn of Manchukuo and Mongolia*).

1933: *Taki no Shiraito* (*Taki no Shiraito, the Water Magician*); *Gion matsuri* (*Gion Festival*) (+sc); *Jimpuren* (*The Jimpu Group*) (+sc). **1934:** *Aizo toge* (*The Mountain Pass of Love and Hate*); *Orizuru osen* (*The Downfall of Osen*). **1935:** *Maria no Oyuki* (*Oyuki the Madonna*); *Gubijinso* (*Poppy*). **1936:** *Naniwa ereji* (*Osaka Elegy*) (+story); *Gion no shimai* (*Sisters of the Gion*) (+story). **1937:** *Aienkyo* (*The Straits of Love and Hate*). **1938:** *Aa furusato* (*Ah, My Home Town*); *Roei no uta* (*The Song of the Camp*). **1939:** *Zangiku monogatari* (*The Story of the Last Chrysanthemum*). **1944:** *Danjuro sandai* (*Three Generations of Danjuro*); *Miyamoto Musashi* (*Musashi Miyamoto*). **1945:** *Meito Bijomaru* (*The Famous Sword Bijomaru*); *Hisshoka* (*Victory Song*) (co-d). **1946:** *Josei no shori* (*The Victory of Women*); *Utamaro o meguru gonin no onna* (*Utamaro and His Five Women*). **1947:** *Joyu Sumako no koi* (*The Love of Sumako the Actress*). **1948:** *Yoru no onnatachi* (*Women of the Night*). **1949:** *Waga koi wa moenu* (*My Love Burns*). **1950:** *Yuki Fujin ezu* (*A Picture of Madame Yuki*). **1951:** *Oyu-sama* (*Miss Oyu*); *Musashino Fujin* (*Lady Musashino*). **1952:** *Saikaku ichidai onna* (*The Life of Oharu*). **1953:** *Ugetsu monogatari* (*Ugetsu*); *Gion bayashi* (*Gion Festival Music*). **1954:** *Sansho dayu* (*Sansho the Bailiff*); *Uwasa no onna* (*The Woman of the Rumor*); *Chikamatsu monogatari* (*A Story from Chikamatsu; Crucified Lovers*). **1955:** *Yokihi* (*The Princess Yang Kwei-fei*); *Shin Heike monogatari* (*New Tales of the Taira Clan*). **1956:** *Akasen chitai* (*Street of Shame*).

By any standard Kenji Mizoguchi must be considered among the world's greatest directors. Known in the West for the final half-dozen films which crowned his career, Mizoguchi considered himself a popular as well as a serious artist. He made eighty-five films during his career, evidence of that popularity. Like John Ford, Mizoguchi is one of the few directorial geniuses to play a key role in a major film industry. In fact, Mizoguchi once headed the vast union governing all production personnel in Japan, and was awarded more than once the industry's most coveted citations. But it is as a meticulous, passionate artist that Mizoguchi will be remembered. His temperament drove him to astounding lengths of research, rehearsal, and execution. Decade after decade he refined his approach while energizing the industry with both his consistency and his innovations.

Mizoguchi's obsessive concern with ill-treated women, and his maniacal pursuit of a lofty notion of art, stemmed from his upbringing. His obstinate father, unsuccessful in business, refused to send his older son beyond primary school. With the help of his sister, a onetime geisha who had become the mistress of a wealthy nobleman, Mizoguchi managed to enroll in a western-style art school. For a short time he did layout work

Kenji Mizoguchi

and wrote reviews for a newspaper, but his real education came through the countless books he read and the theater he attended almost daily. In 1920 he presented himself as an actor at Nikkatsu studio, where a number of his friends worked. He moved quickly into scriptwriting, then became an assistant director, and finally a director. Between 1922 and 1935, he made fifty-five films, mostly melodramas, detective stories, and adaptations. Only six of these are known to exist today.

Though these lost films might show the influences his work had on the development of other Japanese films, German expressionism, and American dramatic filmmaking (not to mention Japanese theatrical style and western painting and fiction), Mizoguchi himself dismissed his early efforts, claiming that his first real achievement as an artist came in 1936. Working for the first time with scriptwriter Yoshikata Yoda, who would be his collaborator on nearly all his subsequent films, he produced *Osaka Elegy* and *Sisters of the Gion,* stories of exploited women in contemporary Japan. Funded by Daiichi, a tiny independent company he helped set up to bypass big-studio strictures, these films were poorly distributed and had trouble with the censors on account of their dark realism and touchy subject. While these films effectively bankrupted Daiichi, they also caused a sensation among the critics and further secured Mizoguchi's reputation as a powerful, if renegade, force in the industry.

Acknowledged by the wartime culture as Japan's chief director, Mizoguchi busied himself during the war mainly with historical dramas which were ostensibly non-political, and thus acceptable to the wartime government. Under the Allied occupation Mizoguchi was encouraged to make films about women, in both modern and historical settings, as part of America's effort to democratize Japanese society. With Yoda as scriptwriter and with actress Kinuyo Tanaka as star, the next years were busy but debilitating for Mizoguchi. He began to be considered old-fashioned in technique, even if his subjects were of a volatile nature.

Ironically, it was the West which resuscitated this most oriental director. With his critical and box-office reputation on the decline, Mizoguchi decided to invest everything in *The Life of Oharu,* a classic seventeenth-century Japanese picaresque story, and in 1951 he finally secured sufficient financing to produce it himself. Expensive, long, and complex, *Oharu* was not a particular success in Japan, but it gained an international reputation for Mizoguchi when it won the grand prize at Venice. Daiei Films, a young company that took Japanese films and aimed them at the export market, then gave Mizoguchi virtual carte blanche in his filmmaking. Under such conditions, he was able to create his final string of masterpieces, beginning with *Ugetsu,* his most famous film.

Mizoguchi's fanatic attention to detail, his insistence on multiple rewritings of Yoda's scripts, and his calculated tyranny over actors are legendary, as he sought perfection demanded by few other film artists. He saw his later films as the culmination of many years' work, his style evolving from one in which a set of tableaux were photographed from an imperial distance and then cut together (one scene/one shot) to one in which the camera moves between two moments of balance, beginning with the movements of a character, then coming to rest at its own proper point.

It was this later style which hypnotized the French critics and through them the West in general. The most striking oppositions in his themes and dramas (innocence vs. guilt, good vs. bad) unroll like a seamless scroll until in the final camera flourish one feels the achievement of a majestic, stoic contemplation of life.

More recently Mizoguchi's early films have come under scrutiny, both for their radical stylistic innovations (such as the shared flashbacks of the 1935 *Downfall of Osen*) and for the radical political positions which they virtually shriek (in the final close-ups of *Sisters of the Gion* and *Osaka Elegy,* for instance). When charges of mysticism are levelled at Mizoguchi, it is good to recall that his final film, *Street of Shame,* certainly helped bring about the ban on prostitution in Japan in 1957.

A profound influence on the New Wave directors, Mizoguchi continues to fascinate those in the forefront of the art (Godard, Straub, Rivette). Complete retrospectives of his thirty-one extant films in Venice, London, and New York resulted in voluminous publications about Mizoguchi in the 1980s. A passionate but contemplative artist, struggling with issues crucial to cinema and society, Mizoguchi will continue to reward anyone who looks closely at his films. His awesome talent, self-discipline, and productivity guarantee this.—DUDLEY ANDREW

Moretti, Nanni

Nationality *Italian.* ***Born*** *Brunico, Bolzano, Italy, 19 August 1953.* ***Education*** *Self-taught.* ***Career*** *Made his first amateur film,* La sconfitta, *1973; directed additional amateur films* Pate de bourgeois, *1973, and* Come parli frate, *1974, shot on Super 8mm, which were screened in local cine-clubs and amateur festivals; directed first feature,* Sono un autarchico, *1976; started production company, Sacher Films, and an art house cinema, Nuovo Sacher, which screens independent films from across the globe.* ***Awards***

Special Jury Prize, Berlin Festival, for The Mass Is Ended, *1986; Best Director, Cannes Festival, for* Caro Diario, *1994.*

Films as Director, Screenwriter, and Actor: 1976: *Lo sono un autarchico (I Am Self-Sufficient)* (+pr). **1978:** *Ecce bombo.* **1981:** *Sogni d'oro (Sweet Dreams).* **1984:** *Bianca* (co-sc). **1985:** *La massa e finita (The Mass Is Ended)* (co-sc). **1989:** *Palombella rossa (Red Lob)* (co-sc). **1990:** *La cosa (The Thing)* (doc) (d and sc only). **1993:** *Isole.* **1994:** *Caro Diario (Dear Diary)* (+co-pr). **1997:** *Aprile.*

Other Films: 1988: *Domani accadra (It'll Happen Tomorrow)* (Luchetti) (pr). **1991:** *Il portaborse (The Factotum; The Yes Man)* (Luchetti) (co-pr, role). **1995:** *La seconda volta (The Second Time)* (Calopresti) (co-pr, role). **1996:** *Trois vies et une seule mort (Three Lives and Only One Death)* (Ruiz) (role).

Most Americans have never heard of Nanni Moretti, an Italian-born director-comedian who made his first film in 1973 at age twenty and has been a regular on the international film festival circuit since the early 1980s. This lack of recognition is not without irony, since his style of visually refined physical humor may be linked to the comic techniques of some of America's most beloved funnymen (including Buster Keaton, Charlie Chaplin, and the Marx Brothers). But Moretti's cinematic concerns involve much more than making his audiences laugh. He has been compared to Woody Allen in that both filmmakers have intellects, and both fill their work with philosophical deliberations.

Moretti is especially concerned with the political situation in his country, and the manner in which politics and politicians affect the lives of citizens. *Palombella rossa* is a typical Moretti film: both an off-the-wall satire and a pensive allegory about the choices, both personal and political, an individual makes in his life. It is the story of Michele, a character who often appears in Moretti's films in different guises (and is played by the filmmaker). By 1990s' standards, Michele is an anachronism in that he is a staunch communist. He also is a politician and a water-polo player. Much of the film is set during a water-polo match in which Michele constantly debates the merits of his politics with various individuals, from his teenaged daughter to journalists and political activists. All the while, the screen version of *Dr. Zhivago,* Boris Pasternak's contemplation of communism, airs on a nearby TV set. There also are flashbacks to Michele's youth. He is shown to be haunted by the more painful of his childhood memories, which adds insight into his present-day character.

Despite all this, Michele primarily is a comical creation. In his first appearance on screen, he drives his car and trades funny faces with some children in the back seat of the auto in front of him. This diversion results in his crashing into another car, causing a brief bout of amnesia that sets the stage for the goings-on during the water-polo match.

On one level, *Palombella rossa* serves as an examination of the state of communism in Italy; the athletic contest slowly degenerates into chaos, which may be seen as a reflection of the political state of Italy. But one thing is clear: Moretti is lampooning all political theorists and blowhards, those who are pro- or anti-communist/fascist/capitalist but who end up becoming tangled in their own rhetoric. And even more specifically, the film serves as his shout of despair for the collapse of communism and the corruption of the true, ideologically pure communist objective: a fair and equitable economic system in which all people, rather than certain individuals, might thrive.

Moretti also overtly deals with politics in his first feature, *I Am Self-Sufficient,* in which he spoofs the totalitarian ideal while chronicling the goings-on in a theater group; he also appears as an actor in Daniel Luchetti's *Il Portaborse,* an impassioned assault on corruption within Italy's Socialist party. In his other films, however, Moretti focuses on additional issues with which he is intrigued. In *The Mass Is Over,* a speculation on the meaning of love, he plays a young cleric whose sense of priestly duty is jarred by the fact that his predecessor had broken his vows.

Moretti further spotlights this theme in *Bianca,* in which he plays a high school mathematics teacher who is consumed by the idea of romantic love. In this film, Moretti also drolly scrutinizes Europeans' fixation with American pop culture, as his teacher is employed in the "Marilyn Monroe" alternative high school, where each classroom comes complete with a jukebox. In the autobiographical *Sweet Dreams,* he plays a filmmaker who shares a complex relationship with his mother. As he is lauded by those who desire to collaborate with him on future projects and censured as a fraud by those put off by his opinions, Moretti reflects on the varied manner in which he is viewed as a filmmaker.

Moretti's most widely distributed film to date is *Caro Diario.* It is divided into three distinctly personal sections, each of which mirrors the director's concerns about his culture and, ultimately, his own survival. In the first, Moretti rides around Rome on a Vespa and makes off-the-wall observations about what he sees and feels. He pronounces that he is obsessed with Jennifer Beals, of *Flashdance* fame. This plays itself out on screen with the sudden appearance of Beals, who just so happens to be on the same street as Moretti at that very moment; as a cinematic effect, this also coincides with the manner in which Woody Allen employed Marshall McLuhan in *Annie Hall.* Moretti also savages pompous film critics who know nothing of real life, and who extol such films as *Henry: Portrait of a Serial Killer,* and he ponders why he has never visited the spot where Pier Paolo Pasolini was murdered.

In Part 2, Moretti goes island-hopping in Southern Italy. Here, he spotlights the same concerns he had dealt with earlier in *Bianca,* and ponders a most relevant contemporary question: How long can a man exist without a television set? Part 3 is the most serious segment. Here, Moretti restages his own cancer treatment. A sequence he filmed as he readied himself for a real chemotherapy treatment precedes re-enactments of him enduring uncomfortable itches and visiting numerous doctors. Each one offers different diagnoses. Each one hands him prescriptions for different pills, and the poor guy ends up with so many that he could open his own drugstore. Once again, Moretti manages to joke about a most serious situation, and in doing so pulls off quite a feat: finding humor in his own mortality.—ROB EDELMAN

Mulligan, Robert

Nationality American. Born The Bronx, New York, 23 August 1925. Education Attended theological seminary; studied radio communications, Fordham University, New York. Military Service Marine radio operator, World War II. Career Worked in editorial department of the New York Times, late 1940s; began working in TV as messenger for CBS, then TV director on Suspense, TV Playhouse, Playhouse 90, and others, mid-1950s; directed first feature film, Fear Strikes Out, 1957; founded Pakula-Mulligan Productions with Alan J. Pakula, 1962 (dissolved 1969). Award Academy Award nomination for Best Director, for To Kill a Mockingbird, 1962. Agent Robert Stein, United Talent Agency, 9560

Wilshire Boulevard, 5th Floor, Beverly Hills, California 90210, U.S.A. **Address** *c/o J.V. Broffman, 5150 Wilshire Boulevard #505, Los Angeles, California 90036, U.S.A.*

Films as Director: 1957: *Fear Strikes Out.* **1960:** *The Rat Race.* **1961:** *The Great Imposter; Come September.* **1962:** *The Spiral Road; To Kill a Mockingbird.* **1963:** *Love with the Proper Stranger.* **1965:** *Baby the Rain Must Fall.* **1966:** *Inside Daisy Clover.* **1967:** *Up the Down Staircase.* **1968:** *The Stalking Moon.* **1971:** *The Pursuit of Happiness; Summer of '42.* **1972:** *The Other* (+pr). **1975:** *The Nickel Ride* (+pr). **1978:** *Blood Brothers.* **1979:** *Same Time, Next Year* (+co-pr). **1982:** *Kiss Me Goodbye* (+co-pr). **1988:** *Clara's Heart* (+co-pr). **1991:** *Man in the Moon.*

In an era in which consistent visual style seems perhaps too uniformly held as the prerequisite of the valorized auteur, one can all too easily understand why Robert Mulligan's work has failed to evince any passionate critical interest. His films all look so different; for instance, *To Kill a Mockingbird,* with its black-and-white measured pictorialism; *Up the Down Staircase,* photographed on location with a documentary graininess; *The Other,* with its heightened Gothic expressionism rather conventional to the horror genre, if not to Mulligan's previous work; and *The Summer of '42,* with a pastel prettiness which suffuses each image with the nostalgia of memory. If some would claim this visual eclecticism reflects the lack of a strong personality, others could claim that Mulligan has too much respect for his material to impose arbitrarily upon it some monolithic consistency and instead brings to his subjects the sensibility of a somewhat self-effacing Hollywood craftsman. Yet there are certainly some sequences in Mulligan's work which spring vividly to mind: the silent, final seduction in *The Summer of '42*; the almost surreal walk home by a child dressed as a ham in *To Kill a Mockingbird*; the high school dance in *Up the Down Staircase*; the climactic camera movement in *The Other,* from Niles to that empty space where Holland, were he not imaginary, would be sitting.

Robert Mulligan directing *Man in the Moon*. Photograph by Elliott Marks.

Even Mulligan's two biggest critical successes, *To Kill a Mockingbird* and *The Summer of '42*, both examples of the kind of respectable Hollywood filmmaking which garners Academy Award nominations, have not been greeted by any significant critical cult. And yet, if Mulligan's good taste has been steadfastly held against him, it must be noted that his films, albeit generally ignored, hold up remarkably well. Mulligan has a strong sense of narrative; and all his films are imbued with human values and a profound compassion which make for compelling audience identification with Mulligan's characteristic protagonists. Mulligan's tendency is to work in less familiar movie genres (such as Hollywood exposé, the family drama, the teacher film, the cinematic *Bildungsroman*), but to avoid—through sincerity and human insight—that emphasis on the purely formal which sometimes makes genre works "go dead" for their audiences upon repeated viewings. Perhaps it is American mistrust of male emotional expression which contributes to Mulligan's facile dismissal by many; certainly it appears that those critics who attacked as sentimental *The Summer of '42*, Mulligan's tasteful and bittersweet paean to lost virginity, failed to assess negatively those same qualities in so many of the French New Wave films, especially, for instance, the Antoine Doinel cycle by François Truffaut, which were instead praised for their lyrical and compassionate exploration of human interaction. Is nostalgia somehow more acceptable when it is French?

Certainly Mulligan seems especially interested in the deviant, the outsider, the loner: the mentally unbalanced Jimmy Peirsall in *Fear Strikes Out*; the enlightened attorney whose values put him in conflict with a bigoted community in *To Kill a Mockingbird*; the ex-convict trying to accustom himself to life outside the penitentiary in *Baby the Rain Must Fall*; the character of Ferdinand Demara, based on real life, who, in *The Great Imposter*, succeeds by the sheer force of his skillful impersonations in insinuating himself into a variety of environments in which he would otherwise never be accepted; the students in *Up the Down Staircase* who, psychologically stunted and economically deprived, may—even with a committed teacher's help—never fit into mainstream society. Like Truffaut, Mulligan has an extraordinary insight into the world of the child or adolescent and the secret rituals of that world. Mulligan's children never display that innocence conventionally associated with children, instead participating in often traumatic ceremonies of passage. One thinks of the child through whose eyes the innate racism of small-town America is seen in *To Kill a Mockingbird*; the precocious child-star in *Inside Daisy Clover*; the lost and often already jaded students in *Up the Down Staircase*; the pubescent adolescents who learn about sex and morality in *The Summer of '42*; and the irrevocably evil child, Niles, and his twin, Holland, in *The Other*.

Unfortunately, despite the high quality of Robert Mulligan's films, there has been not even a minor re-evaluation of the director as a significant artist who has a consistency of themes (such as his association of puberty with violence)—this neglect despite the fact that *To Kill a Mockingbird* remains one of the most well-respected and emotionally engaging films in the American cinema, a movie which continues to please audiences whether they remember it from their past or whether they see it today for the first time. Not even the consistently fine performances elicited by Mulligan from his players (Anthony Perkins in *Fear Strikes Out*, Gregory Peck and Mary Badham in *To Kill a Mockingbird*, Sandy Dennis in *Up the Down Staircase*, Jennifer O'Neil in *The Summer of '42*, Richard Gere in *Blood Brothers*, Neil Patrick Harris in *Clara's Heart*, and indeed, all the children and adolescents who populate Mulligan's world) have served to summon ongoing critical attention. Ultimately, Mulligan's taste may be too fine and his feelings too sentimental to attract contemporary regard in a culture which thrives on the sexy, profane conflicts of a *Pulp Fiction*. And certainly, even at Mulligan's best or near-best, one sensed a subtlety or indirection when he dealt with things sexual: such as the homosexual orientation of Robert Redford's character in the underrated and fascinating Hollywood exposé *Inside Daisy Clover*. One suspects that if Mulligan may have never really had the gusto to publicize himself in the Sammy Glick-style, he neither had the opportunism or hypocrisy to jump on any passing bandwagon.

In any case, his recent films, though laudable and interesting, are hardly the works that would attract critical or popular attention. In 1982's curiously unengaging *Kiss Me Goodbye,* a reworking of the Brazilian film *Donna Flor and Her Two Husbands,* Mulligan does not seem to be especially inspired by the romantic comedy form, despite the film dealing with typical Mulligan themes of loss and grief. *Clara's Heart,* in 1988, reprised Mulligan's coming-of-age theme and, like *To Kill a Mockingbird,* dealt with personal relationships between whites and blacks, in this case, the friendship of a young white boy and the black woman who becomes his nanny. Although the narrative develops with surprising turns, the film was unjustly ignored, with Whoopi Goldberg giving a sensitive, often surprising, performance. Ultimately, *Clara's Heart* had too much heart and not enough cynicism to be successful; even though it dealt (if gently) with violence, divorce, rape, and incest, *Clara's Heart* faded in the glare of more trendy and explicit contemporary films like *Do the Right Thing.* Mulligan's final film to date, *Man in the Moon,* which had a few ardent critical supporters in 1991, is once again a coming-of-age story imbued with feelings of hopefulness and loss, nostalgia and regret. Although beautifully photographed in an older, Hollywood style by Freddie Francis, *Man in the Moon*—though a period piece—seems almost purposely set in a cultural vacuum so that Mulligan can avoid dealing with a contemporary America from which he seems rather alienated. The result is a film which, despite good performances from everyone, particularly the adolescent leads, seems somewhat dead and unconnected, certainly not the film to ignite a critical re-evaluation of Mulligan's work.—CHARLES DERRY

Murnau, F.W.

Nationality *German.* **Born** *Friedrich Wilhelm Plumpe in Bielefeld, Germany, 28 December 1888.* **Education** *Educated in philology, University of Berlin; art history and literature, University of Heidelberg.* **Military Service** *Served in German army, from 1914; transferred to air force, interned in Switzerland following crash landing, 1917.* **Career** *Attended Max Reinhardt theater school, 1908, later joined company; founder, with other Reinhardt school colleagues, Murnau Veidt Filmgesellschaft, 1919; invited by William Fox to Hollywood, 1926; returned to Germany, 1927; sailed to Tahiti with Robert Flaherty to prepare* Tabu, *1929.* **Died** *In auto accident, California, 11 March 1931.*

Films as Director: 1919: *Der Knabe in Blau (Der Todessmaragd; The Boy in Blue).* **1920:** *Satanas; Sehnsucht (Bajazzo); Der Bucklige und die Tanzerin (The Hunchback and the Dancer); Der Januskopf (Schrecken; Janus-Faced); Abend . . . Nacht . . . Morgen.* **1921:** *Der Gang in die Nacht; Schloss Vogelöd (Haunted Castle); Nosferatu—Eine Symphonie des Grauens (Nosferatu the Vampire).* **1922:** *Marizza, genannt die Schmuggler-Madonna; Der Brennende Acker (Burning Soil); Phantom.* **1923:** *Die Austreibung (Driven from Home).* **1924:** *Die Finanzen des Grossherzogs (The Grand Duke's Finances); Der Letzte Mann (The Last Laugh).* **1926:** *Tartüff; Faust.* **1927:** *Sunrise (Sunrise: A Song of Two Humans).* **1928:** *Four Devils.* **1930:** *Die zwolfte Stunde—Eine Nacht des Grauens (Nosferatu the Vampire; Nosferatu)* (adapted for sound); *Our Daily Bread.* **1931:** *Tabu (+co-pr, co-sc).*

F.W. Murnau was studying with Max Reinhardt when the First World War began. He was called up for military service, and after achieving his lieutenancy, he was transferred to the air service, where he served as a combat pilot. But his plane was forced down in Switzerland, where he was interned for the duration. Through the German Embassy, however, he managed to direct several independent stage productions, and he began his lifelong dedication to the motion picture, compiling propaganda film materials and editing them. This experience made it possible for him to enter the reborn film industry after peace as a full-fledged director.

Murnau's first feature film as director was *The Boy in Blue,* produced in 1919, and he made twenty-one full-length features from that year until 1926, when Fox Studios brought him to Hollywood. Unfortunately, most of the pictures he made in his native country no longer exist except in fragmentary form. They are tempting to read about, especially items like *Janus-Faced,* a study of a Jekyll and Hyde personality, which he made in 1920 with Conrad Veidt and Bela Lugosi. Critics found it more artistic than the John Barrymore version of the story made at about the same time in Paramount's New York studios.

Extant today in a complete version is *Nosferatu,* which was subtitled "a symphony of horror." It was a more faithful version of Bram Stoker's *Dracula* than any made thereafter, and the film, starring the incredibly gaunt and frightening Max Schreck as the vampire, is still available.

The next Murnau film that is still viewable is *The Last Laugh,* which starred Emil Jannings. At the time of its release, it was noted as being a picture without subtitles, told almost completely in pantomime. Its real innovation was the moving camera, which Murnau used brilliantly. The camera went everywhere; it was never static. Audiences watched spellbound as the camera moved upstairs and down, indoors and out, although the film told only the simple story of a

F.W. Murnau (left) with cameraman Charles Rosher.

proud commissionaire reduced in his old age to menial work as a lavatory attendant. The camera records, nevertheless, a very real world in an impressionistic way. In fact, Murnau, because of his skill with the moving camera, was generally known as the Great Impressionist, for he gave a superb impression of actual reality.

That title fit Murnau even more aptly in his next two features, both of which also starred Emil Jannings. They are *Tartuffe,* a screen adaption of Moliere's black comedy, in which Lil Dagover and Werner Krauss were also featured. It is topped by what must be the most definitive film version of Goethe's *Faust.* The film starred Jannings as Mephistopheles, with the handsome Swedish favorite, Gosta Ekman, in the title role; Camilla Horn as Marguerite; the great Parisian star Yvette Guilbert as Marthe; and a young William Dieterle as Valentine. Again, the camera not only moved, it soared, especially in the sequence where Faust is shown the world which will be his if he sells his soul to the devil. Murnau was a master of light and shadow, and his work is always brilliantly choreographed as it moves from lightness to the dark.

It came as no surprise when in 1926 Murnau was invited to Hollywood, where the red carpet at Fox was unrolled for him. He was allowed to bring his cameraman, writers, and other craftsmen to work with him, and his initial feature was called *Sunrise,* subtitled "a song of two human beings." The two stars were Janet Gaynor and George O'Brien, playing a young farm couple who make their first trip to the big city, which was constructed on the Fox lot, so that Murnau and his camera could follow them everywhere indoors and out of doors and onto a moving streetcar. Again, the story was very simple, adapted from a Hermann Suderman novel, *A Trip to Tilsit,* and simply proved that real love will always be triumphant.

Sunrise was highly praised by all critics, and was one of three pictures which brought Janet Gaynor an Academy Award as Best Actress in the 1927-28 year. Quite naturally, awards also went to cinematographers Charles Rosher and Karl Struss and to interior decorator Harry Oliver, while *Sunrise* was given a special award for its Artistic Quality of Production, a category never again specified.

For all that, *Sunrise* was not a box-office success, and the studio moved in to supervise Murnau closely on his next two productions. *Four Devils* was a circus story of four young aerialists that gave Murnau's camera a chance to fly with them from one performing trapeze to another. All prints of *Four Devils* are unfortunately lost, which is a fate common to most of the last great silent films. Murnau began shooting on his final film at Fox, called *Our Daily Bread,* with Charles Farrell and Mary Duncan, but he was not allowed to finish the picture. The overwhelming popularity of the talking screen was allowed to flaw it, for the only version of it now shown is called *City Girl,* and is only effective when it is recognizably silent and all Murnau. As a part-talkie, the film is crude and not at all Murnau.

Murnau then allied himself with Robert Flaherty, and the two men journeyed to the South Seas to make *Tabu.* Flaherty, however, withdrew, and *Tabu* is pure Murnau; some praise it as his greatest film. Murnau returned to California and was on the eve of signing at Paramount, which treated directors like Mamoulian, Lubitsch, and von Sternberg very kindly in their talking debuts. Unfortunately, Murnau lost his life in a motor accident on the Pacific Coast highway. He was only forty-two years old at the time, and after the success of *Tabu,* a new fame might have been his.
—DeWITT BODEEN

Naruse, Mikio

Nationality Japanese. *Born* Tokyo, 1905. *Education* Educated in Tokyo technical school, 1918-20. *Family* Married actress Sachiko Chiba, 1937 (separated 1942), one child. *Career* Prop man for Shochiku film company at Tokyo Kamata studios, 1920; assistant to director Yoshinobu Ikeda, 1921-28; comedy writer under pen name "Chihan Miki"; joined staff of Heinosuke Gosho, 1929; directed first film (now lost), 1930; left Shochiku, joined P.C.L. studios (later Toho Company), 1934; left Toho to freelance, 1945. *Died* 1969.

Films as Director: 1930: *Chambara fufu* (*Mr. and Mrs. Swordplay*); *Junjo* (*Pure Love*); *Fukeiki jidai* (*Hard Times*) (+story); *Ai wa chikara da* (*Love Is Strength*); *Oshikiri shinkonki* (*A Record of Shameless Newlyweds*) (+story). **1931:** *Nee kofun shicha iya yo* (*Now Don't Get Excited*); *Nikai no himei* (*Screams from the Second Floor*) (+sc); *Koshiben gambare* (*Flunky, Work Hard!*) (+sc); *Uwaki wa kisha ni notte* (*Fickleness Gets on the Train*) (+sc); *Hige no chikara* (*The Strength of a Moustache*) (+sc); *Tonari no yane no shita* (*Under the Neighbors' Roof*). **1932:** *Onna wa tamoto o goyojin* (*Ladies, Be Careful of Your Sleeves*) (+sc); *Aozora ni naku* (*Crying to the Blue Sky*); *Eraku nare* (*Be Great!*) (+sc); *Mushibameru haru* (*Motheaten Spring*); *Chokoreito garu* (*Chocolate Girl*); *Nasanu naka* (*Not Blood Relations*). **1933:** *Kimi to wakarete* (*Apart from You*) (+sc); *Yogoto no yume* (*Every Night Dreams*) (+story); *Boku no marumage* (*A Man with a Married Woman's Hairdo*); *Sobo* (*Two Eyes*). **1934:** *Kagirinaki hodo* (*Street Without End*). **1935:** *Otome-gokoro sannin shimai* (*Three Sisters with Maiden Hearts*) (+sc); *Joyu to shijin* (*The Actress and the Poet*); *Tsuma yo bara no yo ni* (*Wife! Be Like a Rose*) (+sc); *Sakasu gonin-gumi* (*Five Men in the Circus*); *Uwasa no musume* (*The Girl in the Rumor*) (+sc). **1936:** *Tochuken Kumoemon* (*Kumoemon Tochuken*) (+sc); *Kimi to iku michi* (*The Road I Travel with You*) (+sc); *Asa no namikimichi* (*Morning's Tree-lined Street*) (+sc). **1937:** *Nyonin aishu* (*A Woman's Sorrows*) (+co-sc); *Nadare* (*Avalanche*) (+sc); *Kafuku I, II* (*Learn from Experience, Parts I, II*). **1938:** *Tsuruhachi tsurujiro* (*Tsuruhachi and Tsurujiro*) (+sc). **1939:** *Hataraku ikka* (*The Whole Family Works*) (+sc); *Magokoro* (*Sincerity*) (+sc). **1940:** *Tabi yakusha* (*Traveling Actors*) (+sc). **1941:** *Natsukashi no kao* (*A Face from the Past*) (+sc); *Shanhai no tsuki* (*Shanghai Moon*); *Kideko no shasho-san* (*Hideko the Bus Conductor*) (+sc). **1942:** *Haha wa shinazu* (*Mother Never Dies*). **1943:** *Uta andon* (*The Song Lantern*). **1944:** *Tanoshiki kana jinsei* (*This Happy Life*) (+co-sc); *Shibaido* (*The Way of Drama*). **1945:** *Shori no hi made* (*Until Victory Day*); *Sanjusangendo toshiya monogatari* (*A Tale of Archery at the Sanjusangendo*).

1946: *Urashima Taro no koei* (*The Descendants of Taro Urashima*); *Ore mo omae mo* (*Both You and I*) (+sc). 1947: *Yottsu no koi no monogatari, II: Wakare mo tanoshi* (*Four Love Stories, Part II: Even Parting Is Enjoyable*); *Haru no mezame* (*Spring Awakens*) (+co-sc). 1949: *Furyo shojo* (*Delinquent Girl*) (+sc); *Ishinaka sensei gyojoki* (*Conduct Report on Professor Ishinaka*); *Ikari no machi* (*The Angry Street*) (+co-sc); *Shiroi yaju* (*White Beast*) (+co-sc); *Bara gassen* (*The Battle of Roses*). 1951: *Ginza gesho* (*Ginza Cosmetics*); *Maihime* (*Dancing Girl*); *Meshi* (*Repast*). 1952: *Okuni to Gohei* (*Okuni and Gohei*); *Okasan* (*Mother*); *Inazuma* (*Lightning*). 1953: *Fufu* (*Husband and Wife*); *Tsuma* (*Wife*); *Ani imoto* (*Older Brother, Younger Sister*). 1954: *Yama no oto* (*Sound of the Mountain*); *Bangiku* (*Late Chrysanthemums*). 1955: *Ukigumo* (*Floating Clouds*); *Kuchizuke, III: Onna doshi* (*The Kiss, Part III: Women's Ways*). 1956: *Shu-u* (*Sudden Rain*); *Tsuma no kokoro* (*A Wife's Heart*); *Nagareru* (*Flowing*). 1957: *Arakure* (*Untamed*). 1958: *Anzukko* (+co-sc); *Iwashigumo* (*Herringbone Clouds*). 1959: *Kotan no kuchibue* (*Whistling in Kotan; A Whistle in My Heart*). 1960: *Onna ga kaidan o agaru toki* (*When a Woman Ascends the Stairs*); *Musume tsuma haha* (*Daughters, Wives and a Mother*); *Yoru no nagare* (*Evening Stream*) (co-d); *Aki tachinu* (*The Approach of Autumn*). 1961: *Tsuma toshite onna toshite* (*As a Wife, as a Woman; The Other Woman*). 1962: *Onna no za* (*Woman's Status*); *Horoki* (*A Wanderer's Notebook; Lonely Lane*). 1963: *Onna no rekishi* (*A Woman's Story*). 1964: *Midareru* (*Yearning*). 1966: *Onna no naka ni iru tanin* (*The Stranger within a Woman; The Thin Line*); *Hikinige* (*Hit and Run; Moment of Terror*). 1967: *Midaregumo* (*Scattered Clouds; Two in the Shadow*).

Mikio Naruse belongs in the second echelon of Japanese directors of his generation, along with Gosho, Ozu, and Kinoshita. This group ranks behind Mizoguchi, Kurosawa, Ichikawa, and Kobayashi, who broke out beyond the bounds of the conventions of the Japanese cinema, whereas Naruse and the others were mostly content to work within it. This is not to say that all of them did not tackle contemporary as well as historical subjects. And certainly Gosho, Ozu, Kinoshita, and Naruse were no less accomplished technically, though it might be noted that the last two did not respond to the challenge of the wide screen in as exciting a fashion as did Kurosawa and Kobayashi.

The homogeneity of Japanese cinema and the concomitant audience acceptance of remake after remake (at least while Naruse was working) enables us to categorize these directors: Naruse's domestic comedies share themes and situations with those of Gosho and Kinoshita, and his domestic dramas are not unlike those of middle-period Ozu, after he had lost the freshness and urgency of his early work, but before he had atrophied. But Naruse, although most of his (lost) silent films were simple slapsticks, was not later prolific in comedy. He was, however, occasionally drawn out into greater subjects, particularly towards the end of his career, and in rising to the occasion his career parallels that of Gosho, for both their filmographies contain some unexpected masterpieces. Most comments on Naruse emphasise that he was a pessimist because of his orphaned childhood, but most Japanese films tend to examine the shackles—rather than the joys—of family life or life in the geisha-house. His best films are suffused with a melancholy, with a desire for what might-have-been, which becomes, as art, warming and enlightening—and despairing rather than depressing.

It is true, however, that the few silent films made by Naruse that survive are chiefly tragedies of a not particularly high order. *Apart From You* (1933) and *Every Night Dreams* (1933) make it clear that the meek shall not inherit the earth. Naruse wrote the screenplay of the first, in which an adolescent geisha is determined that her younger sister will not follow her into that way of life; and he provided the story of the second, in which a barmaid is confronted with her useless husband, who had walked out on her some years previously. The men are weak but dangerous; the women are strong but compromised. Both are simple films, but *Street Without End* (1934) is of a richness and complexity rare for the period, despite the limitations of soap opera imposed by the newspaper serial on which it was based. It is one of the earliest surviving examples of a film

Mikio Naruse

that showcases the talents of a particular local star—usually female, as in this case—permitting audiences to sympathize to the ultimate with her difficulties. Naruse brings truth to this tale which, shot at an amazing number of urban locations, also includes an underlying theme concerning the survival of feudalism in modern city life.

For his first sound film Naruse adapted a novel by Yasunari Kawabata, *Three Sisters With Maiden Hearts* (1935). No better constructed than the works of Ozu and Mizoguchi at this point, Naruse used flashbacks within flashbacks to complicate matters, but also displayed an imaginative use of sound. *Wife! Be Like a Rose* (1935) concerns a girl's renewed relationship with her father, who had left his self-centred wife to live happily in the country with another woman. This elegant, subtle domestic drama, which contains more humor than hitherto, was Naruse's twenty-fifth film, one of the few to survive from this period. This was a transitional film for him, for it rejects melodrama entirely. This change in emphasis by Naruse can be seen again in *Tsuruhachi and Tsurujiro* (1938), which details the destructive relationship of a man-woman shamizen team, while *The Whole Family Works* (1939) makes Western domestic dramas of the period look horrendously melodramatic.

Indeed, Naruse's pictures over the next few years cannot escape a charge of monotony. The martial subjects demanded by the authorities during World War II did not interest him, nor, it would seem, did those taken on during the Occupation, after he had left Toho. With *Repast* (1951), the story of a failing marriage, he began a series of domestic dramas which were to constitute a compassionate body of work, more sustained than either Ozu or Gosho, also concentrating on *shomin-geki*. *Repast* was based on a novel by Fumiko Hayashi, and Naruse was to turn to her work again for four more of his best movies—*Lightning* (1952), *Late Chrysanthemums* (1954), *Floating Clouds* (1955), and the autobiographical *Lonely Lane* (1962). Hayashi was somewhat more optimistic than Naruse, but he finds in her work that life must go on, if imperfectly, and then asks why. The unanswerable questions, particularly in his studies of married life, bring him close to Bergman—though Bergman was considerably less interested in the banality of everyday existence.

It is interesting to compare Naruse's version of Saisei Muroo's novel *Older Brother Younger Sister* (1953) with those made in 1936 by Sotoji Kimura and in 1976 by Tadashi Imai. Each is of its period and each presents the riverside neighborhood vividly, but Naruse's film is by far the best, infused with an intensity and a sensitivity that the others lack.

As his peers accepted the challenge presented in the 1950s by the international reception of the Japanese cinema, so did Naruse, but the relatively minor *Mother* (1952) was the only one of his films then seen in the West. *Floating Clouds,* from Hayashi's novel about life in the immediate postwar period, is perhaps his richest and most compelling film, an example of a director at his most confident working on completely congenial material.

Perhaps an equally successful achievement is *Flowing* (1956), a haunting study of the disillusionments which come to aging geishas. Unlike his contemporaries, Naruse had not seemed interested in geishas or prostitutes, except as an escape from poverty. His marital dramas looked away from sex, which he seemed to think was more a preoccupation for the young, while many of his women look yearningly at other women, only because they might be preferable to men.

Towards the end of his career Naruse was to widen his range, perhaps in response to Ozu's restriction of his own. He took to color and the wide screen with *Herringbone Clouds* (1958), one of his rare rural dramas, about the break-up of feudal family rules under the pressure of modern times. Thereafter he worked chiefly in monochrome and wide screen, producing more rewarding work than some of his colleagues, for whom mere prettiness was enough. Some of them were content to turn out tear-jerkers with very popular stars, but while Naruse continued to work with his preferred actress, Hideko Takemine, he did so with a rigor which others could well have emulated. In *When a Woman Ascends the Stairs* (1960) she has a tough time managing a bar in the Ginza, not least because of amorous complications, and in *Yearning* (1964), again widowed, she is running a small grocer's shop in the face of the new competition, thrusting supermarkets. As films, both are schematic (as can happen with aging directors), but in *Yearning* a passion develops when Takemine refuses to submit to the romantic and sexual demands of her brother-in-law. As he pursues her to a small spa town, Naruse brings to the fore his mastery of the medium (locations, photography, acting, editing), delving into the mysteries and mixed motives of his two protagonists. In the telling a good film has become a great one.

Naruse made only three more films. The last two, *Hit and Run* (1966) and *Scattered Clouds* (1967), were both thrillers set among people much more affluent than we had been accustomed to from this director. It is exhilarating to see them, not only for the supremacy of what was for him a new form but because, like all great filmmakers, he could still surprise his admirers.—DAVID SHIPMAN

Nichols, Mike

Nationality American. *Born* Michael Igor Peschkowsky in Berlin, 6 November 1931; became U.S. citizen, 1944. *Education* University of Chicago, 1950-53; studied acting with Lee Strasberg, 1954. *Family* Married 1) Patricia Scott, 1957 (divorced), one daughter; 2) Margot Callas, 1974 (divorced); 3) Annabel (divorced), two children; 4) Diane Sawyer, 1988. *Career* Member of Compass Players improvisational theatre group, Chicago, 1955-57; partnership with Elaine May, 1957-61; director on Broadway, from 1963; produced The Family for TV, 1976. *Awards* 7 Tony Awards; Academy Award for Best Direction, for The Graduate, 1968. *Office* c/o Marvin B. Meyer, Rosenfeld, Meyer and Sussman, 9601 Wilshire Blvd., Beverly Hills, California 90210, U.S.A.

Films as Director: 1966: *Who's Afraid of Virginia Woolf?*. **1967:** *The Graduate*. **1970:** *Catch-22*. **1971:** *Carnal Knowledge* (+pr). **1973:** *The Day of the Dolphin*. **1975:** *The Fortune* (+co-pr). **1980:** *Gilda Live*. **1983:** *Silkwood* (+co-pr). **1986:** *Heartburn* (+co-pr). **1988:** *Biloxi Blues; Working Girl*.

1990: *Postcards from the Edge* (+co-pr). **1991:** *Regarding Henry* (+co-pr). **1994:** *Wolf.* **1996:** *The Birdcage* (+pr). **1997:** *Primary Colors.*

Other Films: **1993:** *The Remains of the Day* (co-pr). **1997:** *The Designated Mourner* (co-pr, role as Jack).

The films of Mike Nichols are guided by an eye and ear of a satirist whose professional gifts emerge from a style of liberal, improvisational comedy that originated in a Chicago theater club and developed into a performing partnership with Elaine May in the late 1950s and early 1960s. In clubs and recordings, on radio, television, and Broadway, Nichols and May routines gnawed hilariously close to the bone. Aimed at literate, self-aware audiences, their skits (sometimes anticipating key elements of Nichols's films) gleefully anatomized men and women dueling in post-Freudian combat, by turns straying from the marriage bond and clinging to it for dear life.

Before directing *Who's Afraid of Virginia Woolf?* for the screen in 1966, Nichols earned a reputation as a skillful Broadway director with particular flair for devising innovative stage business and eliciting unusually polished performances from his casts. That sure theatrical sense, honed by his subsequent direction of Broadway plays by writers as diverse as Neil Simon, Anton Chekhov, Lillian Hellman, David Rabe, and Tom Stoppard, combines in his best films with the sardonic attitude toward American life underlying even the gentlest of his collaborations with Elaine May.

Many of Nichols's major films begin as comedies and evolve into mordant, generically ambiguous dissections of the American psyche. Their central characters exist in isolation from the landscapes they inhabit, often manufacturing illusions to shield themselves against reality (George and Martha in *Virginia Woolf,* Sandy and Jonathan in *Carnal Knowledge*) or fleeing with mounting desperation societies whose values they alone perceive as neurotic (Benjamin in *The Graduate*) or murderous (Yossarian in *Catch-22*).

Martha and George, Edward Albee's Strindbergian couple, flail at each other on their New England campus and reveal a tormented relationship that concludes with a glimmer of hope but seems nevertheless to imply the futility of monogamy, a view reenforced by *Carnal Knowledge* and *The Graduate.* Until he dates Elaine Robinson, Ben Braddock is segregated by script and camera from the company of friends: in a packed airplane, on the Berkeley campus teeming with students, surrounded by his parents' partying guests, Ben is alone. His detachment, italicized by numerous shots within the film, permits him to function as the funnel for *The Graduate's* social satire. In this respect he is Nichols's surrogate, but the director complicates the viewer's empathetic response to Ben by scrutinizing him rather as an experimenting scientist scrutinizes a mouse darting about a maze, especially as he scampers in frantic pursuit of Elaine.

In Dustin Hoffman's memorable screen debut, Ben became the moralistic spokesman for a generation that mistrusted anyone over thirty and vowed never to go into plastics. But like some other Nichols heroes Ben may be himself more than a little crazy, the inevitable child of a Southern California lifestyle that leads him to anticipate instant gratification. Nichols, moreover, intentionally undermines the comic resolution toward which the film has been heading through ambivalent shots of Ben and Elaine on their departing bus, implicating them in mutual recognition of a colossal mistake. At film's end, Ben Braddock still has considerable cause to be "worried about [his] future."

For Yossarian, worrying about the future means literally staying alive. To survive a catch-22 universe he behaves like a lunatic, but the more bizarrely he acts the more sanely is he regarded according to the military chop-logic that drives him toward madness. In *Catch-22* time is fractured (in Buck Henry's screenplay) to retain the basic storytelling method of Joseph Heller's novel. Flashbacks occur within flashbacks. Conversations are inaudible (as in the opening scene), incidents only partially revealed (as in the first Snowden sequences), to be played later in the film with deleted elements restored.

Fond of foreground shooting, long takes, and distorting close-ups to intensify the sense of his characters' entrapment, Nichols also frequently employs overlapping sound and a spare, modernistic mise-en-scène (the latter at times reminiscent of Antonioni) to convey an aura of disorientation and sterility. In the underpraised and misunderstood *Carnal Knowledge,* Nichols uses whiteouts (also prominent in *Catch-22*) and Bergmanesque talking heads as structural and thematic devices to increase the viewer's

Mike Nichols

alienation from the two central characters and to ridicule notions of male sexual fantasy at the core of the film. Visually and textually (in Jules Feiffer's original screenplay) Jonathan and Sandy are the most isolated and self-deluded of Nichols's characters.

Things are seldom what they initially seem in this director's work. Like Nick and Honey, misled by George and Martha's pretense of hospitality in *Who's Afraid of Virginia Woolf?,* the viewer may be easily duped by a deceptively comic tone, enticing visual stylization, and innovative storytelling technique into misreading the bleak vision that the films usually harbor. *The Day of the Dolphin* is certainly more than just a story of talking dolphins. The film has mythic qualities, concerns good and evil, and has a painful ending. Even *The Fortune,* a farce in the screwball tradition, hinges on the attempted murder by the film's two heroes of its heroine, whose fate hangs in the balance at the final fadeout.

Nichols directs literate, intelligent scripts that pull few punches in their delineations of sexual subjects (*Virginia Woolf, The Graduate, Carnal Knowledge, Heartburn*) and political ones (*Catch-22, Day of the Dolphin, Silkwood, Working Girl*). While *The Graduate* continues to be regarded as an American classic, Nichols is sometimes undervalued for his film work because he prefers the New York theater and because his contributions to his pictures are periodically credited to their writers' screenplays (Buck Henry, Jules Feiffer) or their theatrical and literary sources (Edward Albee, Joseph Heller, Charles Webb). But Nichols is very much the auteur who works intimately with his collaborators on all aspects of his films, principally the writing. As with many auteurs, Nichols uses many of the same people over and over again, both in cast and on crew.

The films uphold Nichols's original reputation as a gifted director of actors: Hoffman in *The Graduate,* Elizabeth Taylor and Richard Burton in *Who's Afraid of Virginia Woolf?,* Jack

Nicholson in *Carnal Knowledge, The Fortune, Heartburn,* and *Wolf,* George C. Scott in *The Day of the Dolphin,* Alan Arkin in *Catch-22,* Meryl Streep in *Silkwood, Heartburn,* and *Postcards from the Edge.* They also reveal, even in their intermittent self-indulgence, a director of prodigious versatility and insight.

Nichols's films are purely fiction during the first phase of his film directing career, beginning with *Who's Afraid of Virginia Woolf?* in 1966, and including *The Graduate, Catch-22, Carnal Knowledge, The Day of the Dolphin,* and ending with *The Fortune* in 1975. After seven years, the second phase begins with *Silkwood* in 1983, and this and the next seven films are closer to reality. These films are also much more hopeful and optimistic, as the characters often shed their illusions, change for the better, and achieve inner peace. *Silkwood* is based on a real person, Karen Silkwood. In Nichols's adaptation of the nuclear plant worker's story, Karen (Meryl Streep) gains a new awareness and tries to help herself and her friends even though she dies. *Heartburn* was written by Nora Ephron and was influenced by her own experiences. Although Rachel (Meryl Streep) finds her illusions about her perfect marriage shattered, she and her children move on to try again. In *Biloxi Blues,* a grown up Eugene (Matthew Broderick) thinks that his army experiences were the happiest time of his life, and some may have been inspired by writer Neil Simon's time in the army. *Working Girl* is an incisive look into the contemporary subculture of working women in Manhattan. Tess (Melanie Griffith) achieves her move up in the business world even though she has far to go. *Postcards from the Edge,* about a daughter's relationship with her famous Hollywood mother, was written by Carrie Fisher, who is certainly familiar with the Hollywood scene and the daughter of Debbie Reynolds, although the film is not autobiographical. Suzanne Vale (Meryl Streep) gets stronger and stronger throughout the film as she is finally able to shed her illusions and understand reality. *Regarding Henry* may be partially related to an incident in Nichols's life, when he states that he gained a new appreciation of life after recovering from an illness. In the film, the character of Henry (Harrison Ford) is wounded in the head, and as he recovers, he also gains a new appreciation of life.

It seems no coincidence that in 1988 Nichols married Diane Sawyer, a television news personality who deals in reality images, since Nichols himself, as shown by the films in his second phase, was now concerned more with reality than illusion.

In 1994, Nichols directed *Wolf,* which may mark the beginning of a new phase of his work. Nichols in *Wolf* tackles profound questions about aging, death, and what lies beyond concrete knowledge. Elaine May, his old partner from his comedy days, helped with the script (uncredited). *Wolf* concerns a middle aged New York City book editor, Will Randall (Jack Nicholson), who is bitten by a wolf. Will's senses become more acute, he fights for and regains his job, he falls in love with the publishing company owner's daughter, Laura Alden (Michelle Pfeiffer), and slowly realizes that he is becoming a wolf. Nichols directs a film about transformation and possible immortality.

So from *Who's Afraid of Virginia Woolf?* to *Wolf,* and beyond Nichols has transformed from a great director to an even greater director, and has obtained a type of immortality himself, for many of his films are of such artistic merit that they will be preserved forever.—MARK W. ESTRIN and H. WAYNE SCHUTH

Olmi, Ermanno

Nationality Italian. *Born* Bergamo, 24 July 1931. *Education* Attended Accadémia d'Arte Drammatica, Milan. *Family* Married Loredana Detto, three children. *Career* Worked for electric company Edisonvolta S.p.A., Milan, from 1949; director and supervisor of over forty shorts and documentaries for, or sponsored by, Edisonvolta, 1952-61; directed first feature, semi-documentary Il tempo si è fermato, 1959; formed production company "22 December S.p.A." with Tullio Kezich and others, 1961; TV director, from 1964; co-founded Hypothesis Cinema, a school for aspiring directors; formed Ipotesi Cinema, a workshop for young filmmakers, at Bassano del Grappa, 1980s.

Films as Director: 1953: *La digi sul ghiaccio* (short/doc) (+spvr). **1954:** *La pattuglia di passo San Giacomo* (short/doc) (+spvr). **1955:** *Società Ovesticino-Dinamo* (short/doc) (+spvr); *Cantiere d'inverno* (short/doc) (+spvr); *La mia valle* (short/doc) (+spvr); *L'onda* (short/doc) (+spvr); *Buongiorno natura* (short/doc) (+spvr). **1956:** *Michelino la B* (short/doc) (+spvr); *Construzione meccaniche riva* (short/doc) (+spvr). **1958:** *Tre fili fino a Milano* (short/doc) (+spvr); *Giochi di Colonia* (short/doc) (+spvr); *Venezia città minore* (short/doc) (+spvr). **1959:** *Il tempo si è fermato* (*Time Has Stopped; Time Stood Still*) (+sc, spvr). **1960:** *Il grande paese d'Acciaio* (short/doc) (+spvr). **1961:** *Le grand barrage* (short/doc) (+spvr); *Un metro lungo cinque* (short/doc) (+spvr); *Il posto* (*The Sound of Trumpets; The Job*) (+sc). **1963:** *I fidanzati* (*The Fiancés; The Engagement*) (+pr, sc). **1965:** *. . . e venne un uomo* (*A Man Called John; And There Came a Man*) (+co-sc). **1968:** *Un certo giorno* (*One Fine Day*) (+sc, ed). **1969:** *I recuperanti* (*The Scavengers*) (+co-sc, ph) (for TV). **1971:** *Durante l'estate* (*During the Summer; In the Summertime*) (+co-sc, ph, ed) (for TV). **1974:** *La circostanza* (*The Circumstance*) (+pr, sc, ph, ed) (for TV). **1978:** *L'albero degli zoccoli* (*The Tree of the Wooden Clogs*) (+sc, ph, ed). **1983:** *Cammina, cammina* (*Keep Walking*). **1984:** *Milano '83* (doc). **1987:** *Lunga Vita alla Signora* (*Long Live the Lady!*) (+sc, co-ph). **1988:** *La leggenda del santo bevitore* (*The Legend of the Holy Drinker*) (+sc, ed). **1992:** *Lungo il fiume* (*Down the River*) (+sc, ed). **1993:** *Il segreto del bosco vecchio* (*The Secret of the Old Forest*) (+sc). **1994:** *Genesi: La creazione e il diluvio* (*Genesis: The Creation and the Flood*) (+sc).

Other Films: 1955: *La tesatura meccanica della linea a 220.000 volt* (short/doc) (spvr); *San Massenza (Cimego)* (short/doc) (spvr). **1956:** *Pantano d'avio* (short/doc) (spvr); *Peru—Istituto de Verano* (short/doc) (spvr); *Fertilizzanti complessi* (short/doc) (spvr). **1957:** *Fibre e civilta* (short/doc) (spvr); *Progresso in agricoltura* (short/doc) (spvr); *Campi sperimentali* (short/doc) (spvr). **1958:** *Colonie Sicedison* (short/doc) (spvr); *Bariri* (short/doc) (spvr); *Il frumento* (short/doc) (spvr). **1959:** *El frayle* (short/doc) (spvr); *Fertiluzzanti prodotti dalla Societa del Gruppo Edison* (short/doc) (spvr); *Cavo olio fludio 220.000 volt* (short/doc) (spvr); *Auto chiese* (short/doc) (spvr); *Natura e chimica* (short/doc) (spvr). **1961:** *Il pomodoro* (short/doc) (spvr); *Il sacco in Plypac* (short/doc) (spvr); *Po: forza 50.000* (short/doc) (pr). **1962:** *Una storia milanese* (E. Visconti) (role).

Ermanno Olmi, born in Bergamo in 1931, is the Italian filmmaker most committed to and identified with a regional heritage. His films are distinctly Lombardian; for the most part they describe life in Milan, the provincial capital (for example, *Il posto, Un certo giorno, Durante l'estate* and *La circonstanza*). He has also filmed in the Lombardian Alps (*Il tempo si è fermato*), and his native Bergamo (*L'albero degli zoccoli*), but even when he ventures to Sicily, it is to make a film of a Milanese worker temporarily assigned to the south who longs for home (*I fidanzati*), and when he makes a semi-documentary biography (*. . . e venne un uomo*), it is of the Lombardian Pope, John XXIII.

Furthermore, his work bears affinities to the central literary figure of the Lombardian tradition, Alessandro Manzoni, whose great historical novel, *I promessi sposi,* is variously reflected in at least three of Olmi's films: most directly in *I findanzati,* whose very title recasts the

1827 novel, but also in the idealization of a great ecclesiastic (. . . *e venne un uomo*), and in the vivid recreation of a past century (*L'albero degli zoccoli),* which portrays peasant life in the late nineteenth century rather than Manzoni's seventeenth. The most significant Manzonian characteristic of Olmi's cinema is its Catholicism: of all the major Italian filmmakers he has the least problematic relationship with the Church. He embodies the spirit of the "opening to the Left" which has characterized both religious and parliamentary politics in Italy since the early 1960s. For the most part, his films center upon an individual worker caught between employment and an individual quest to assert dignity through labor. Quite often this tension carries over from work to the conjugal or preconjugal love life of the protagonist.

Like Pasolini, Rosi, and Bertolucci, Olmi is a filmmaker nurtured by postwar neorealism. Like his great precursors, Rossellini, De Sica, and Visconti, he has worked extensively with amateur actors, chosen simplified naturalistic settings, eschewed elaborate artifices or lighting, and employed an ascetic camera style. What mobility his camera has comes largely from his extensive use of the zoom lens. In contrast, however, to the first generation of neorealists, he has a high tolerance for abstraction and ambiguity in his storytelling. Dramatic and emotional moments are consistently understated. Instead of a mobile camera, he has relied heavily upon montage (especially in the intercutting of scenes between Milan and Sicily in *I fidanzati)* and even more on the overlapping of sounds. In fact, Olmi's meticulous attention to sound, his isolation and manipulation of auditory details, tends to transform his realistically photographed scenes into psychologically inflected domains of space and time.

After *L'albero degli zoccoli,* the predominately latent religiosity in his cinema became more manifest. *Cammina, cammina* recounts a version of the story of the Three Wise Men seeking the Christ child. *La leggenda del santo bevitore* turns the last days of a Parisian clochard

Ermanno Olmi (right) with Rod Steiger on the set of *. . . e venne un uomo.*

into a parable of divine intervention. Its plot is perhaps more characteristic of Rohmer than Olmi, but the filmmaker uses it to reimagine the simple daily activities of proletarian life through the eyes of a drunkard bewildered by his sudden streak of good fortune. Similarly, in a wholly secular mode, *Lunga Vita alla Signora* returns to the topos of *Il tempo si e fermato* and *Il posto* after nearly thirty years to glimpse the intricacies of an affluent family reunion from the perspective of a naive adolescent in his first job as a busboy in an elegant Alpine hotel.

Olmi released two films in 1992, *Lunga il fiume,* a poetic documentary on the Po River, and *Il segreto del Bosco vecchio,* a fable adapted from Dino Buzzati, set in the Dolomites before the First World War, in which a sentient forest, with talking animals and winds, defeats the plans of a retired colonel for its commercial exploitation. Both films celebrate nature as a conduit of Divinity. The commentary of *Lunga il fiume* even allegorizes the outpouring of the river into the Adriatic as a type of Jesus's kenosis and death.

Throughout the 1980s Olmi directed a workshop for young filmmakers, Ipotesi Cinema, at Bassano del Grappa. In the face of radically reduced film production and the domination of television in Italy, Ipotesi Cinema was a utopian project for helping filmmakers find alternative modes of production and financing without compromising the originality of their ideas.—P. ADAMS SITNEY

Ophuls, Marcel

Nationality *French/American.* **Born** *Frankfurt-am-Main, Germany, 1 November 1927, son of director Max, became citizen of France, 1938, and of the U.S.A., 1950.* **Education** *Hollywood High School, graduated 1945; Occidental College; University of California at Berkeley; studied philosophy, the Sorbonne.* **Military Service** *Served with Occupation forces in Japan during World War II.* **Family** *Married Regina Ackermann, 1956, three daughters.* **Career** *Moved to France, 1932, and to Hollywood, 1941; performed with theater unit, Tokyo, 1946; 3rd assistant director, using name "Marcel Wall," Paris, from 1951; radio and TV story editor for Sudwestfunk, Baden-Baden, West Germany, also director for radio, stage and TV, 1956-59; returned to Paris, 1960; TV journalist and director of* Zoom, *TV news magazine, 1966-68; directed first major documentary, Munich, or Peace in Our Time, 1967; senior story editor at NDR TV, Hamburg, 1968-71; Senior Visiting Fellow, Council of the Humanities, Princeton University, 1973-74; staff producer at CBS News, then ABC News, 1975-78; returned to Europe, 1979; Secretary General, French Filmmakers' Society, and on Board of Directors, Societé des gens de lettres.* **Awards** *Prix de Dinard, Prix Georges Sadoul, British Film Academy Award, National Society of Film Critics Special Award, and Special Citation, New York Film Critics, for* The Sorrow and the Pity, *1971; Oscar for Best Documentary, for* Hotel Terminus, *1988.* **Address** *10 rue Ernest Deloison, Neuilly-sur-Seine, France.*

Films as Director: 1960: *Matisse, or The Talent for Happiness* (+sc). **1961:** German episode of *L'Amour à vingt ans* (*Love at Twenty*) (+sc). **1963:** *Peau de banane* (*Banana Skin/Banana Peel*) (+co-sc). **1964:** *Feu à volonté* (*Faites vos jeux; Fire at Will*) (+co-sc). **1966:** *Till Eulenspiegel* (co-d, co-sc, quit during filming) (in two parts, for German TV). **1967:** *Munich, ou La Paix pour cent ans* (*Munich, or Peace in Our Time*) (for French TV) (+sc). **1969:** *Le Chagrin et la pitié* (*The Sorrow and the Pity*) (for TV, in two parts, 4.5 hours long) (+sc). **1970:** *Clavigo* (for TV); *The Harvest of My Lai* (for TV) (+sc).

1971: *America Revisited* (for TV, in two parts) (+sc); *Zwei ganze tage* (*Two Whole Days*) (for TV). **1972:** *A Sense of Loss* (+sc). **1976:** *The Memory of Justice* (+sc). **1988:** *Hotel Terminus: The Life and Times of Klaus Barbie.* **1990:** *November Days: Voices and Choices* (for TV). **1994:** *Veillés d'armes* (*The Troubles We've Seen: A History of Journalism in Wartime*) (+sc).

Other Films: (partial list) 1953: *Moulin Rouge* (Huston) (asst d). **1954:** *Un Acte d'amour* (*Act of Love*) (Litvak) (asst d); *Marianne de ma jeunesse* (Duvivier) (asst d). **1955:** *Lola Montès* (Max Ophüls) (asst d).

Marcel Ophuls' 1976 film, *The Memory of Justice,* which examines war crimes by juxtaposing the Nuremburg Trials with the conflict in Vietnam, managed to please neither the critic Pauline Kael ("I feel a pang of guilt, because I think it's a very bad film—chaotic and plodding, and with an excess of self-consciousness which at times Ophuls seems to mistake for art") nor David Puttnam, one of its British producers, who claimed that the work was far too "personal" and who apparently urged Ophuls to be more "fascist" in his approach. Ophuls was not inclined to be seduced by Radical Chic: he refused to make glib parallels between Auschwitz and the My Lai massacre, and thus enraged his backers. The film was overlong (Ophuls had been contracted to make a four-hour, thirty-minute documentary and had come up with four hours and thirty-eight minutes), over-budget, and featured pubic hair in a sauna sequence which had the BBC, the project's co-sponsor, throwing up its arms in horror. Puttnam elbowed Ophuls off the production after a stormy meeting in the Ritz Bar and called in another director, Lutz Becker, to recut the footage. The film was "rescued" by an intrepid production assistant who stole a scratch print and smuggled it over to America, where it was watched in darkened Manhattan viewing rooms by Mike Nichols, Lillian Hellman, Susan Sontag, and other New York cultural luminaries. A wealthy backer bought back the negative. The movie was premiered in its intended form, acclaimed as a masterpiece by some, and savaged by Kael.

Ophuls is closely associated with polemical documentaries that court controversy and split the critics, so it seems surprising that his first feature was made in France under the aegis of François Truffaut. It starred Jeanne Moreau and Jean-Paul Belmondo, and had a title no more contentious than *Banana Skin.* One forgets that the filmmaker spent his school days at Hollywood High. Ophuls claims the two directors who really influenced him were his father, Max, and Truffaut. His grounding was in fiction. He worked for his father on *Lola Montès,* was on the crew of Huston's *Moulin Rouge,* and spent a three-year apprenticeship in the 1950s on 2nd Features. He has always taken a determinedly personal approach toward documentary, and is full of disdain for filmmakers who use it as a smokescreen behind which to hide their own lack of creative ability. *Hotel Terminus,* his 1988 investigation into the Klaus Barbie affair, was, he claims, structured along the lines of TV's *Columbo,* with Ophuls the interviewer casting himself as the detective in the dirty raincoat.

If the director's follow-up to *Banana Skin, Feu a Volonte* (1964), had not been such a failure, it is quite conceivable that Ophuls would have turned into a filmmaker along the lines of Chabrol and Rivette. As it was, he was lured away (or fled) into the world of TV journalism, working for *60 Minutes* in Germany and learning about reportage and interview techniques. *The Sorrow and the Pity,* the film which established his name, was originally intended for French TV. When French broadcasters refused to show it, however, the film found a new lease on life in the country's art houses.

As a documentary maker, Ophuls examines how the past is mediated and constructed by the present: he is interested in the past as fiction, not as actuality, in the "process of recollection, in things like choice, selective memory, rationalization." He does not try to maintain the charade of impartiality: he is an egotist who inserts himself, his character and feelings, into the films he makes. He is polite in his anger, willing to shake Barbie's hand or to listen to Albert Speer's side of the story. Often, the most startling information he garners is the incidental, the discursive: Klaus Barbie was kind to animals, for example, and was much liked by cats. Always with an eye on a profit, the Nazi tried to charge journalists for interviews when he was waiting to be extradited from Bolivia. Hannah Arendt's old cliche about the banality of evil finds new currency in Ophuls' work. Like Claud Lanzmann, he is loath to allow us the easy convenience of forgetting.

Marcel Ophuls

Ophuls' photography is often ramshackle and his work has been accused of lacking structure. Rather than employ commentary or voice-over, he allows his interviewees to tell their myriad different stories in their own voices. However, he is a consummate editor who believes that films are made in the cutting room. He is not above using editing to make his point and to caricature the opinions he disagrees with. For example, in his film about sectarian violence in Belfast, *A Sense of Loss,* he manages to make a whole galaxy of Protestant grotesques while his representations of Catholics are generally favourable. He is a quixotic director who will continue to infuriate critics by intruding into his documentaries when they feel he should be behind the camera, paring his fingernails.

A great admirer of the comedies of Ernst Lubitsch, in particular *To Be Or Not To Be,* Ophuls has lectured on Hollywood comedy at Princeton University and probably feels somewhat burdened by his reputation as the maker of grave, earnest, and very long films which go down well with the liberal intellectuals of Greenwich Village. (Woody Allen queues to see *The Sorrow and the Pity* in *Annie Hall.*) It seems to have eluded his critics that he too has a sense of humour.

Ophuls continued to tackle demanding subject matter in his documentaries in the late 1980s and 1990s. *Hotel Terminus: The Life and Times of Klaus Barbie,* his first film in twelve years, picks up where *The Sorrow and the Pity* leaves off, providing an investigation of the whos, hows, and whys of the Second World War. It is the provocative account of the life of, and four-decade-long manhunt for, the notorious Gestapo chief Klaus Barbie, known as the "Butcher of Lyon." Especially telling is the information Ophuls reveals regarding Barbie's post-war activities, and the manner in which his escape to South America was arranged by American counterintelligence officers.

The title tells all in Ophuls' latest documentary, *The Troubles We've Seen: A History of Journalism in Wartime,* in which he examines the politics and ethics of his subject. He especially is intrigued by the combination of fearlessness, egotism, and benevolence often found in the best war correspondents.—G.C. MACNAB and ROB EDELMAN

Ophüls, Max

Nationality French. *Born* Max Oppenheimer in Saarbrucken, Germany, 6 May 1902, became French citizen, 1938. *Family* Married actress Hilde Wall in 1926, one son, director Marcel Ophuls. *Career* Acting debut, 1919; began as stage director, 1924; began working at Burgtheater, Vienna, 1926; dialogue director to Anatole Litvak at UFA, 1929; directed first film, 1930; with family, left Germany, 1932; directed in France, Italy, and Holland, 1933-40; worked in Switzerland, 1940, then moved to Hollywood, 1941; "rediscovered" by Preston Sturges, 1944; returned to France, 1949; directed for German radio, mid-1950s. *Died* In Hamburg, 26 March 1957.

Films as Director: 1930: *Dann schon lieber Lebertran* (+co-adaptation). **1932:** *Die verliebte Firma*; *Die verkaufte Braut* (*The Bartered Bride*). **1933:** *Die lachende Erben* (produced 1931); *Liebelei*; *Une Histoire d'amour* (French version of *Liebelei*). **1934:** *On a volé un homme*; *La Signora di tutti* (+co-sc). **1935:** *Divine* (+co-sc). **1936:** *Komedie om Geld* (+co-sc); *Ave Maria* (short); *La Valse brillante* (short); *La Tendre Ennemie* (*The Tender Enemy*) (+co-sc). **1937:** *Yoshiwara* (+co-sc). **1938:** *Werther* (*Le Roman de Werther*) (+co-adaptation). **1940:** *Sans lendemain*; *De Mayerling à Sarajevo* (*Mayerling to Sarajevo*); *L'Ecole des femmes* (unfinished). **1946:** *Vendetta* (co-d, uncredited). **1947:** *The Exile.* **1948:** *Letter from an Unknown Woman.* **1949:** *Caught*; *The Reckless Moment.* **1950:** *La Ronde* (+co-sc). **1952:** *Le Plaisir* (*House of Pleasure*) (+co-sc). **1953:** *Madame de . . .* (*The Earrings of Madame De*) (+co-sc). **1955:** *Lola Montès* (*The Sins of Lola Montes*) (+co-sc).

Max Ophüls' work falls neatly into three periods, marked by geographical locations and diverse production conditions, yet linked by common thematic concerns and stylistic/formal procedures: the pre-Second World War European period (during which he made films in four countries and four languages); the four Hollywood films of the late 1940s (to which one might add the remarkable Howard Hughes-produced *Vendetta,* on which he worked extensively in its early pre-production phases and which bears many identifiable Ophülsian traces, both thematic and stylistic); and the four films made in France in the 1950s. It is these latter films on which Ophüls' current reputation chiefly rests, and in which certain stylistic traits (notably the long take with elaborately mobile camera) are carried to their logical culmination.

Critical estimation of Ophüls has soared during the past twenty years; prior to that, the prevailing attitude was disparaging (or at best condescending), and the reasons for this now seem highly significant, reflecting far more on the limitations of the critics than of the films. The general consensus was that Ophüls' work had distinctive qualities (indeed, this would be difficult to deny), but was overly preoccupied with "style" (regarded as a kind of spurious, slightly decadent ornamentation) and given over to trivial or frivolous subjects quite alien to the "social" concerns considered to characterize "serious" cinema. In those days, the oppression of women within the patriarchal order was not identified as a "social concern"—especially within the overwhelmingly male-dominated field of film criticism. Two developments have contributed to the revaluation of Ophüls: the growth of *auteur* criticism in the 1960s and of feminist awareness, and I shall consider his work in relation to these phenomena.

1. *Ophüls and auteurism.* One of the first aims of auteur criticism was to dethrone the "subject" as the prime guarantee of a film's quality, in favor of style, mise-en-scène, the discernible presence of a defined directorial "voice": in Andrew Sarris's terms, the "how" was given supremacy over the "what." "Subject," in fact, was effectively redefined as what the auteur's mise-en-scène created. Ophüls was a perfect rallying-point for such a reformulation of

critical theory. For a start, he offered one of the most highly developed and unmistakable styles in world cinema, consistent through all changes of time and place (though inevitably modified in the last two Hollywood melodramas, *Caught* and *The Reckless Moment*). Ophüls works were marked by elaborate tracking-and-craning camera movements, ornate décor, the glitter of glass and mirrors, objects intervening in the foreground of the image between characters and camera. His style can be read in itself as implying a meaning, a metaphysic of entrapment in movement, time, and destiny. Further, this style could be seen as developing, steadily gaining in assurance and definition, through the various changes in cultural background and circumstances of production—from, say, *Liebelei* through *Letter from an Unknown Woman* to *Madame de . . .* Ophüls could be claimed (with partial justice) as a major creative artist whose personal vision transcended the most extreme changes of time and place.

Max Ophüls

The stylistic consistency was underlined by an equally striking thematic consistency. For example, the same three films mentioned above, though adapted from works by fairly reputable literary figures (respectively, Arthur Schnitzler, Stefan Zweig, Louise de Vilmorin), all reveal strong affinities in narrative/thematic structure: all are centered on romantic love, which is at once celebrated and regarded with a certain irony. Similarly, all three works move towards a climactic duel in which the male lover is destroyed by an avenging patriarch, an offended husband. All three films also feature patriarchal authority embodied in military figures. Finally, style and theme were perceived as bound together by a complicated set of visual motifs recurring from period to period. The eponymous protagonist of Ophüls' last film, *Lola Montès,* declares "For me, life is movement"; throughout his work, key scenes take place in vehicles of travel and places of transition (carriages, trains, staircases, and railway stations figure prominently in many of the films). Even a superficially atypical work like *The Reckless Moment* (set in modern California rather than the preferred "Vienna, 1900" or its equivalent) contains crucial scenes on the staircase, in moving cars, on a ferry, at a bus station. Above all, the dance was recognized as a central Ophülsian motif, acquiring complex significance from film to film. The romantic/ironic waltz scene in *Letter from an Unknown Woman,* the fluid yet circumscribed dances of *Madame de . . .,* the hectic and claustrophobic *palais de danse* of *Le Plaisir,* the constricted modern dance floor of *Caught,* and the moment in *De Mayerling à Sarajevo* where the lovers are *prevented* from attending the ball: all of the above scenes are reminders that "life is movement" is not the simple proposition it may at first appear.

There is no doubt that the development of *auteur* theory enormously encouraged and extended the appreciation of Ophüls' work. In its pure form (the celebration of the individual artist), however, auteurism tends towards a dangerous imbalance in the evaluation of specific films: a tendency, for example, to prefer the "typical" but slight *La Ronde* (perhaps the film that most nearly corresponds to the "primitive" account of Ophüls) to a masterpiece like *The Reckless Moment,* in which Ophüls' engagement with the structural and thematic materials of the Hollywood melodrama results in an amazingly rich and radical investigation of ideological assumptions.

2. *Ophüls and Feminism.* Nearly all of Ophüls' films are centered on a female consciousness. Before the 1960s this tended merely to confirm the diagnosis of them as decorative, sentimental, and essentially frivolous: the social concerns with which "serious" cinema should be engaged were those which could be resolved within the patriarchal order, and more fundamental social concerns that threatened to undermine the order itself simply could not be recognized. The films belong, of course, to a period long before the eruption of what we now know as radical feminism; they do not (and could not be expected to) explicitly engage with a feminist politics, and they are certainly not free of a tendency to mythologize women. In retrospect, however, from the standpoint of the feminist theory and consciousness that evolved in the 1970s, they assume a quite extraordinary significance: an incomparably comprehensive, sensitive, and perceptive analysis of the position of women (subject to oppression) within patriarchal society. The films repeatedly present and examine the options traditionally available to women within our culture—marriage, prostitution (in both the literal and the looser sense), romantic love—and the relationship between those options. *Letter from an Unknown Woman,* for example, dramatizes marriage (Lisa's to von Stauffer, her mother's to the "military tailor") and prostitution ("modelling") as opposite cultural poles, then goes on to show that they really amount to the same thing: in both cases, the women are selling themselves (this opposition/parallel is brilliantly developed through the three episodes of *Le Plaisir*). Essentially, *Letter from an Unknown Woman* is an enquiry into the validity of romantic love as the only possible means of transcending this illusory dichotomy. Clearly, Ophüls is emotionally committed to Lisa and her vision; the extraordinary complexity and intelligence of the film lies in its simultaneous acknowledgement that romantic love can only exist as narcissistic fantasy and is ultimately both destructive and self-destructive.

Far from being incompatible, the auteurist and feminist approaches to Ophüls demand to be synthesized. The identification with a female consciousness and the female predicament is the supreme characteristic of the Ophülsian thematic; at the same time, the Ophüls style—the commitment to grace, beauty, sensitivity—amounts to a celebration of what our culture defines as "femininity," combined with the force of authority, the drive, the organizational (directorial) abilities construed as masculine. In short, the supreme achievement of Ophüls' work is its concrete and convincing embodiment of the collapsibility of our culture's barriers of sexual difference.—ROBIN WOOD

Ozu, Yasujiro

*Nationality Japanese. **Born** Tokyo, 12 December 1903. **Education** Uji-Yamada (now Ise) Middle School, Matsuzaka, graduated 1921. **Military Service** In China, 1937-39; interned for six months as British POW, 1945. **Career** Teacher, 1922-23; after introduction from uncle, began as assistant cameraman at Shochiku Motion Picture Co., 1923;*

assistant director, 1926; directed first film, 1927; made propaganda films in Singapore, 1943. **Died** *In Kamakura, 12 December 1963.*

Films as Director: 1927: *Zange no yaiba* (*The Sword of Penitence*). **1928:** *Wakodo no yume* (*The Dreams of Youth*) (+sc); *Nyobo funshitsu* (*Wife Lost*); *Kabocha* (*Pumpkin*); *Hikkoshi fufu* (*A Couple on the Move*); *Nikutai bi* (*Body Beautiful*) (+co-sc). **1929:** *Takara no yama* (*Treasure Mountain*) (+story); *Wakaki hi* (*Days of Youth*) (+co-sc); *Wasei kenka tomodachi* (*Fighting Friends, Japanese Style*); *Daigaku wa deta keredo* (*I Graduated, But . . .*); *Kaisha-in seikatsu* (*The Life of an Office Worker*); *Tokkan kozo* (*A Straightforward Boy*) (+co-story). **1930:** *Kekkon-gaku nyumon* (*An Introduction to Marriage*); *Hogaraka ni ayume* (*Walk Cheerfully*); *Rakudai wa shita keredo* (*I Flunked, But . . .*) (+story); *Sono yo no tsuma* (*That Night's Wife*); *Erogami no onryo* (*The Revengeful Spirit of Eros*); *Ashi ni sawatta koun* (*Lost Luck*); *Ojosan* (*Young Miss*). **1931:** *Shukujo to hige* (*The Lady and the Beard*); *Bijin aishu* (*Beauty's Sorrows*); *Tokyo no gassho* (*Tokyo Chorus*). **1932:** *Haru wa gofujin kara* (*Spring Comes from the Ladies*) (+story); *Umarete wa mita keredo* (*I Was Born, But . . .*) (+story); *Seishun no yume ima izuko* (*Where Now Are the Dreams of Youth?*); *Mata au hi made* (*Until the Day We Meet Again*). **1933:** *Tokyo no onna* (*A Tokyo Woman*) (+story); *Hijosen no onna* (*Dragnet Girl*) (+story); *Dekigokoro* (*Passing Fancy*) (+story). **1934:** *Haha o kowazu-ya* (*A Mother Should Be Loved*); *Ukigusa monogatari* (*A Story of Floating Weeds*). **1935:** *Hakoiri musume* (*An Innocent Maid*); *Tokyo no yado*. **1936:** *Daigaku yoi toko* (*College Is a Nice Place*) (+story); *Hitori musuko* (*The Only Son*) (+story). **1937:** *Shukujo wa nani o wasuretaka* (*What Did the Lady Forget?*) (+co-story). **1941:** *Toda-ke no kyodai* (*The Brothers and Sisters of the Toda Family*) (+co-sc). **1942:** *Chichi ariki* (*There Was a Father*) (+co-sc). **1947:** *Nagaya no shinshi roku* (*The Record of a Tenement Gentleman*) (+co-sc). **1948:** *Kaze no naka no mendori* (*A Hen in the Wind*) (+co-sc). **1949:** *Banshun* (*Late Spring*) (+co-sc with Kogo Noda). **1950:** *Munekata shimai* (*The Munekata Sisters*) (+co-sc with Kogo Noda). **1951:** *Bakushu* (*Early Summer*) (+co-sc with Kogo Noda). **1952:** *Ochazuke no aji* (*The Flavor of Green Tea over Rice*) (+co-sc with Kogo Noda). **1953:** *Tokyo monogatari* (*Tokyo Story*) (+co-sc with Kogo Noda). **1956:** *Soshun* (*Early Spring*) (+co-sc with Kogo Noda). **1957:** *Tokyo boshoku* (*Twilight in Tokyo*) (+co-sc with Kogo Noda). **1958:** *Higanbana* (*Equinox Flower*) (+co-sc with Kogo Noda). **1959:** *Ohayo* (+co-sc with Kogo Noda); *Ukigusa* (*Floating Weeds*) (+co-sc with Kogo Noda). **1960:** *Akibiyori* (*Late*

Yasujiro Ozu: *Tokyo boshoku*

Ozu

Autumn) (+co-sc with Kogo Noda). **1961:** *Kohayagawa-ke no aki* (*The End of Summer*) (+co-sc with Kogo Noda). **1962:** *Samma no aji* (*An Autumn Afternoon*) (+co-sc with Kogo Noda).

Throughout his career, Yasujiro Ozu worked in the mainstream film industry. Obedient to his role, loyal to his studio (the mighty Shochiku), he often compared himself to the tofu salesman, offering nourishing but supremely ordinary wares. For some critics, his greatness stems from his resulting closeness to the everyday realities of Japanese life. Yet since his death another critical perspective has emerged. This modest conservative has come to be recognized as one of the most formally intriguing filmmakers in the world, a director who extended the genre he worked within and developed a rich and unique cinematic style.

Ozu started his career within a well-established genre system, and he quickly proved himself versatile, handling college comedies, wistful tales of office workers, even gangster films. By 1936, however, he had started to specialize. The "home drama," a Shochiku specialty, focused on the trials and joys of middle-class or working-class life—raising children, finding a job, marrying off sons and daughters, settling marital disputes, making grandparents comfortable. It was this genre in which Ozu created his most famous films and to which he is said to have paid tribute on his deathbed: "After all, Mr. President, the home drama."

Ozu enriched this genre in several ways. He strengthened the pathos of family crisis by suggesting that many of them arose from causes beyond the control of the individual. In the 1930s works, this often led to strong criticism of social forces like industrialization, bureaucratization, and Japanese "paternalistic" capitalism. In later films, causes of domestic strife tended to be assigned to a mystical super-nature. This "metaphysical" slant ennobled the characters' tribulations by placing even the most trivial action in a grand scheme. The melancholy resignation that is so pronounced in *Tokyo Story* and *An Autumn Afternoon* constituted a recognition of a cycle of nature that society can never control.

To some extent, the grandiose implications of this process are qualified by a homely virtue: comedy. Few Ozu films wholly lack humor, and many involve outrageous sight gags. As a genre, the home drama invited a light touch, but Ozu proved able to extend it into fresh regions. There is often an unabashed vulgarity, running to jokes about eating, bodily functions, and sex. Even the generally sombre *Autumn Afternoon* can spare time for a gag about an elderly man run ragged by the sexual demands of a young wife. *Ohayo* is based upon equating talk, especially polite vacuities, with farting. Ozu also risked breathtaking shifts in tone: in *Passing Fancy,* after a tearful scene at a boy's sickbed, the father pettishly says that he wishes his son had died. The boy responds that the father was looking forward to a good meal at the funeral.

Ozu developed many narrative tendencies of the home drama. He exploited the family-plus-friends-and-neighbors cast by creating strict parallels among characters. If family A has a son of a certain type, family B will have a daughter of that type, or a son of a different sort. The father may encounter a younger or older man, whom he sees as representing himself at another point in his life. The extended-family format allowed Ozu to create dizzying permutations of comparisons. The sense is again of a vast cycle of life in which an individual occupies many positions at different times.

Ozu had one of the most distinctive visual styles in the cinema. Although critics have commonly attributed this to the influence of other directors or to traditions of Japanese art, these are insufficient to account for the rigor and precision of Ozu's technique. No other Japanese director exhibits Ozu's particular style, and the connections to Japanese aesthetics are general and often tenuous. (Ozu once remarked: "Whenever Westerners don't understand something, they simply think it's Zen.") There is, however, substantial evidence that Ozu built his unique style out of deliberate imitation of and action against Western cinema (especially the work of Chaplin and Lubitsch).

Ozu limited his use of certain technical variables, such as camera movement and variety of camera position. This can seem a willful asceticism, but it is perhaps best considered a ground-clearing that let him concentrate on exploring minute stylistic possibilities. For instance, it is commonly claimed that every Ozu shot places the camera about three feet off the ground, but this is false. What Ozu keeps constant is the perceived *ratio* of camera height to the subject. This permits a narrow but nuanced range of camera positions, making every subject occupy the same sector of each shot. Similarly, most of Ozu's films employ camera movements, but these are also systematized to a rare degree. Far from being an ascetic director, Ozu was quite virtuosic, but within self-imposed limits. His style revealed vast possibilities within a narrow compass.

Ozu's compositions relied on the fixed camera-subject relation, adopting angles that stand at multiples of 45 degrees. He employed sharp perspectival depth; the view down a corridor or street is common. Ozu enjoyed playing with the positions of objects within the frame, often rearranging props from shot to shot for the sake of minute shifts. In the color films, a shot will be enhanced by a fleck of bright and deep color, often red; this accent will migrate around the film, returning as an abstract motif in scene after scene.

Ozu's use of editing is no less idiosyncratic. In opposition to the 180-degree space of Hollywood cinema, Ozu employed a 360-degree approach to filming a scene. This "circular" shooting space yields a series of what Western cinema would consider incorrect matches of action and eyelines. While such devices crop up in the work of other Japanese filmmakers, only Ozu used them so rigorously—to undermine our understanding of the total space, to liken characters, and to create abstract graphic patterns. Ozu's shots of objects or empty locales extend the concept of the Western "cutaway": he will use them not for narrative information but for symbolic purposes or for temporal prolongation. Since Ozu early abjured the use of fades and dissolves, cutaways often stand in for such punctuations. And because of the unusually precise compositions and cutting, Ozu was able to create a sheerly graphic play with the screen surface, "matching" contours and regions of one shot with those of the next.

Ozu's work remains significant not only for its extraordinary richness and emotional power, but also because it suggests the extent to which a filmmaker working in popular mass-production filmmaking can cultivate a highly individual approach to film form and style.—DAVID BORDWELL

Pabst, G.W.

Nationality Austrian. ***Born*** *Georg Wilhelm Pabst in Raudnitz, Bohemia, 27 August 1885.* ***Education*** *Educated in engineering at technical school, Vienna, and at Academy of Decorative Arts, Vienna, 1904-06.* ***Military Service*** *Interned as prisoner of war, Brest, 1914-18.* ***Family*** *Married Gertrude (Pabst), one son.* ***Career*** *Actor, from 1906; travelled to United States with German language troupe, 1910; returned to Europe, prisoner of war, 1914-18; directed season of expressionist theatre in Prague, 1919; artistic director Neuen Wiener Bühne also joined Carl Froelich's film production company, 1920; directed first film, 1923; formed Volksverband für Filmkunst (Popular Association for Film Art) with Heinrich Mann, Erwin Piscator, and Karl Freund, 1928; studied sound film techniques in London, 1929; moved to Hollywood, 1933, returned to France, 1935; planned to emigrate to United States on outbreak of war, but illness forced him to remain in Austria; formed Pabst-Kiba Filmproduktion in Vienna, 1949; worked in Italy, 1950-53.* ***Awards*** *Légion d'honneur, 1931; Best Director, Venice Festival, for* Der Prozess, *1948.* ***Died*** *In Vienna, 29 May 1967.*

Films as Director: 1923: *Der Schatz* (*The Treasure*) (+co-sc). **1924:** *Gräfin Donelli* (*Countess Donelli*). **1925:** *Die freudlose Gasse* (*The Joyless Street*); *Geheimnisse einer Seele* (*Secrets of a Soul*). **1926:** *Man spielt nicht mit der Liebe* (*One Does Not Play with Love*). **1927:** *Die Liebe der Jeanne Ney* (*The Love of Jeanne Ney*). **1928:** *Abwege* (*Begierde*) [*Crisis* (*Desire*)]; *Die Büchse der Pandora* (*Pandora's Box*). **1929:** *Die weisse Hölle vom Pitz-Palu* (*The White Hell of Pitz-Palu*) (co-d); *Das Tagebuch einer Verlorenen* (*Diary of a Lost Girl*) (+pr). **1930:** *Westfront 1918*; *Skandal um Eva* (*Scandalous Eva*). **1931:** *Die Dreigroschenoper* (*The Threepenny Opera*); *Kameradschaft* (*Comradeship*). **1932:** *L'Atlantide* (*Die Herrin von Atlantis*). **1933:** *Don Quichotte*; *Du haut en bas* (*High and Low*). **1934:** *A Modern Hero*. **1936:** *Mademoiselle Docteur* (*Salonique, nid d'espions*). **1938:** *Le Drame de Shanghai*. **1939:** *Jeunes Filles en détresse*. **1941:** *Komödianten* (+co-sc). **1943:** *Paracelsus* (+co-sc). **1944:** *Der Fall Molander* (unfinished and believed destroyed). **1947:** *Der Prozess* (*The Trial*). **1949:** *Geheimnisvolle Tiefen* (+pr). **1952:** *La Voce del silenzio*. **1953:** *Cose da pazzi*. **1954:** *Das Bekenntnis der Ina Kahr*. **1955:** *Der Letzte Akt* (*The Last Ten Days*; *Ten Days to Die*); *Es geschah am 20 Juli* (*Jackboot Mutiny*). **1956:** *Rosen für Bettina*; *Durch die Wälder, durch die Auen*.

Other Films: 1921: *Im Banne der Kralle* (Frohlich) (role).

Bryher, writing in *Close Up* in 1927, noted that "it is the thought and feeling that line gesture that interest Mr. Pabst. And he has what few have, a consciousness of Europe. He sees psychologically and because of this, because in a flash he knows the sub-conscious impulse or hunger that prompted an apparently trivial action, his intense realism becomes, through its truth, poetry."

Pabst was enmeshed in the happenings of his time, which ultimately engulfed him. He is the chronicler of the churning maelstrom of social dreams and living neuroses, and it is this perception of his time which raises him above many of his contemporary filmmakers.

Like other German directors, Pabst drifted to the cinema through acting and scripting. His first film, *Der Schatz,* dealt with a search for hidden treasure and the passions it aroused. Expressionist in feeling and design, it echoed the current trend in German films, but in *Die freudlose Gasse* he brought clinical observation to the tragedy of his hungry postwar Europe. For Pabst the cinema and life grew closer together. In directing the young Greta Garbo and the more experienced Asta Nielsen, Pabst was beginning his gallery of portraits of women, to whom he would add Brigitte Helm, Louise Brooks, and Henny Porten.

Geheimnisse einer Seele carried Pabst's interest in the subconscious further, dealing with a Freudian subject of the dream and using all the potential virtues of the camera to illuminate the problems of his central character, played by Werner Krauss. *Die Liebe der Jeanne Ney,* based on a melodramatic story by Ilya Ehrenburg, reflected the upheavals and revolutionary ideas of the day. It also incorporated a love story that ranged from the Crimea to Paris. Through his sensitive awareness of character and environment Pabst raised the film to great heights of cinema. His

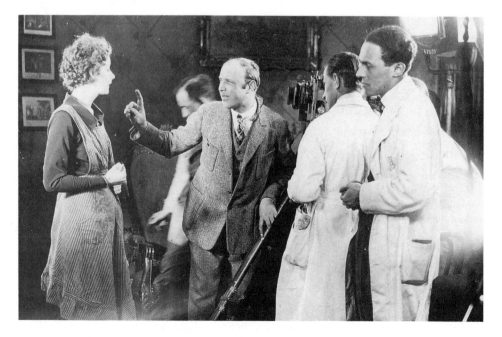

G.W. Pabst (center) with Greta Garbo on the set of *The Joyless Street.*

individual style of linking image to create a smoothly flowing pattern induced a rhythm which carried the spectator into the very heart of the matter.

Two Pabst films have a special significance. *Die Büchse der Pandora* and *Das Tagebuch einer Verlorenen* featured the American actress Louise Brooks, in whom Pabst found an ideal interpreter for his analysis of feminine sensuality.

Between the high spots of Pabst's career there were such films as *Grafin Donelli,* which brought more credit to its star, Henny Porten, than to Pabst. *Man spielt nicht mit der Liebe* featured Krauss and Lily Damita in a youth and age romance. *Abwege,* a more congenial picture that took as its subject a sexually frustrated woman, gave Pabst the opportunity to direct the beautiful and intelligent Brigitte Helm. His collaboration with Dr. Arnold Fanck on *Die weisse Hölle vom Pitz-Palu* resulted in the best of the mountain films, aided by Leni Riefenstahl and a team of virtuoso cameramen, Angst, Schneeberger, and Allgeier.

The coming of sound was a challenge met by Pabst. Not only did he enlarge the scope of filmmaking techniques, but he extended the range of his social commitments in his choice of subject matter. Hans Casparius, his distinguished stills cameraman and friend, has stressed the wonderful teamwork involved in a Pabst film. There were no divisions of labor; all were totally involved. *Westfront 1918, Die Dreigroschenoper,* and *Kameradschaft* were made in this manner when Pabst began to make sound films. Vajda the writer, cameraman Fritz Arno Wagner (who had filmed *Jeanne Ney)* and Ernö Metzner, another old colleague, worked out the mise-en-scène with Pabst, assuring the smooth, fluid process of cinema. With Pabst the cinema was still a wonder of movement and penetrating observation. The technical devices used to ensure this have been described by the designer Metzner.

Westfront 1918 was an uncompromising anti-war film which made *All Quiet on the Western Front* look contrived and artificial. Brecht's *Die Dreigroschenoper,* modified by Pabst, is still a stinging satire on the pretensions of capitalist society. *Kameradschaft,* a moving plea for international cooperation, shatters the boundaries that tend to isolate people. All these films were studio-made and technically stupendous, but the heart and human warmth of these features were given by G.W. Pabst.

When Germany was in the grip of growing Nazi domination, Pabst looked elsewhere to escape from that country, of which he had once been so much a part.

L'Atlantide was based on the Pierre Benoit novel of adventure in the Sahara. The former success of Jacques Feyder, Pabst's work featured Brigitte Helm as the mysterious Antinea. *Don Quixote* with Chaliapin did not fulfil its promise. *A Modern Hero,* made in Hollywood for Warner Brothers, had little of Pabst in it. On his return to France he handled with some competence *Mademoiselle Docteur, Le Drame de Shanghai,* and *Jeunes Filles en détresse.*

In 1941 circumstances compelled him to return to his estate in Austria. He was trapped, and if he was to make films, it had to be for the Nazi regime. *Komödianten* was a story of a troupe of players who succeed in establishing the first National Theatre at Weimar. Its leading player was Pabst's old friend Henny Porten, who gave an excellent performance. The film won an award at the then Fascist-controlled Venice Biennale. *Paracelsus,* again an historical film, showed Pabst had lost none of his power. For his somewhat reluctant collaboration with the Nazis, Pabst has been savagely attacked, but it is hard to believe that any sympathy could have ever existed from the man who made *Kameradschaft* for the narrow chauvinists who ruled his country.

After the war Pabst made *Der Prozess,* dealing with Jewish pogroms in nineteenth-century Hungary. It was a fine film. After some work in Italy he made *Der letze Akt,* about the last days of Hitler, and *Es geschah am 20 Juli,* about the generals' plot against Hitler. Both were films of distinction.

Pabst died in Vienna in 1967, having been a chronic invalid for the last ten years of his life. As Jean Renoir said of him in 1963: "He knows how to create a strange world, whose elements are borrowed from daily life. Beyond this precious gift, he knows how, better than anyone else, to direct actors. His characters emerge like his own children, created from fragments of his own heart and mind."—LIAM O'LEARY

Pagnol, Marcel

Nationality *French.* **Born** *Aubagne, near Marseilles, 25 (or 28) February 1895.* **Education** *Lycée Thiers, Marseilles; University of Montpellier, degree in letters.* **Military Service** *Served with French Infantry, 1914-17, and in 1940.* **Family** *Married Jacqueline Bouvier, 1945, two sons.* **Career** *Founded literary magazine* Fortunio, *1911; teacher of English, from 1912; appointed professor at Lycée Condorcet, Paris, 1922; resigned teaching position after success of play* Marius, *1929; created film company and founded magazine* Les Cahiers du film, *1931; opened studio at Marseilles, 1933; directed first film, 1934; President of Society of French Dramatic Authors and Composers, 1944-46.* **Awards** *Member, Academie française, 1947; Officer of the Légion d'honneur.* **Died** *18 April 1974.*

Films as Director: 1934: *Le Gendre de Monsieur Poirier* (+pr, sc); *Jofroi* (+pr, sc); *L'Article 330* (+pr, sc); *Angèle* (+pr, sc). **1935:** *Merlusse* (+pr, sc); *Cigalon* (+pr, sc). **1936:** *Topaze* (second version) (+pr, sc); *César* (+pr, sc). **1937:** *Regain* (+pr, sc). **1938:** *Le Schpountz* (+pr, sc); *La Femme du boulanger* (+pr, sc). **1940:** *La Fille du puisatier* (+pr, sc). **1945:** *Naïs* (+pr, sc). **1948:** *La Belle Meunière* (+pr, sc). **1951:** *Topaze* (third version) (+pr, sc). **1952:** *Manon des sources* (+pr, sc). **1954:** *Les Lettres de mon moulin* (+pr, sc). **1967:** *Le Curé de Cucugnan* (for television) (+pr, sc).

Other Films: 1931: *Marius* (Korda) (sc). **1932:** *Fanny* (Allégret) (co-pr, sc). **1933:** *Topaze* (Gasnier) (original play) (sc); *Un Direct au coeur* (Lion) (co-author of original play, sc); *L'Agonie des aigles* (Richebé) (co-pr, sc). **1934:** *Tartarin de Tarascon* (Bernand) (sc). **1939:** *Monsieur Brotonneau* (Esway) (pr, sc). **1950:** *Le Rosier de Madame Husson* (Boyer) (sc). **1953:** *Carnaval* (Verneuil) (pr, sc). **1962:** *La Dame aux camélias* (Gir) (sc). **1986:** *Jean de Florette* (Berri) (original story); *Manon des sources* (Berri) (original story).

"The art of the theatre is reborn under another form and will realize unprecedented prosperity. A new field is open to the dramatist enabling him to produce works that neither Sophocles, Racine, nor Molière had the means to attempt." With these words, Marcel Pagnol greeted the advent of synchronous sound to the motion picture, and announced his conversion to the new medium. The words also served to launch a debate, carried on for the most part with René Clair, in which Pagnol argued for the primacy of text over image in what he saw as the onset of a new age of filmed theater.

At the time Pagnol reigned supreme in the Parisian theater world. His plays, *Topaze* and *Marius,* both opened in the 1928-29 season to the unanimous acclaim of the critics and the

Marcel Pagnol

public. Their success vindicated the theories of a group of playwrights which had gathered around Paul Nivoix, the drama critic for *Comoedia*. They were determined to develop an alternative to the predictable theater of the boulevards and the impenetrable experiments of the surrealist avant-garde. The group pursued a dramatic ideal based on the well-made, naturalistic plays of Scribe and Dumas *fils*. The formula featured crisp dialogue, tight structures, and devastating irony. Its renewed popular appeal did not escape the notice of Bob Kane, the executive producer of the European branch of Paramount Pictures. Kane secured the rights for the screen versions of two plays, retaining Pagnol as writer for *Marius,* to be directed by Alexander Korda, but he then excluded him from any participation in the *Topaze* project. This neglect spurred the volatile young ex-schoolmaster from Provence to undertake his own productions.

With Pierre Braunberger and Roger Richebe, Pagnol produced and adapted his play *Fanny,* a sequel to *Marius,* and hired Marc Allégret to direct. Then, in 1933, he formed his own production company, modelled on United Artists, which would control the production and distribution of all his future projects. At the same time he founded *Les Cahiers du film,* dedicated to the propagation of "cinematurgie," Pagnol's theories of filmed theater.

Jofroi and *Angèle,* the first two projects over which Pagnol exercised complete artistic control, established the tone for much of his ensuing career. Adapted from stories by Jean Giono and set in Provence in the countryside surrounding Marseilles, where Pagnol was born and raised, the films treat the manners and lifestyle of the simple farmers and shopkeepers of the south and are executed with the precise principles of dramatic structure Pagnol had developed in his years with Nivoix. *Angèle* is especially notable because it was shot on location on a farm near Aubagne. The film established a precedent followed by Jean Renoir in making *Toni,* a film produced and distributed by Pagnol's company, regarded by many as a forerunner of Italian neorealism. This is the formula to which Pagnol would return with increasing success in *Regain* and *Le Femme du boulanger:* a story or novel by Giono honed by Pagnol into a taut drama, elaborating the myths and folkways of "le coeur meridonale" and pivoting on the redemptive power of woman; set on location in Provence; and peopled with the excellent repertory company Pagnol had assembled from the Marseille music halls (including Raimu, Fernandel, Fernand Charpin, Orane Dumazis, and Josette Day).

Even after a formal break with Giono in an ugly squabble over money in 1937, Pagnol continued to exploit the formula in *La Fille du puisatier* and his masterpiece, *Manon des sources.* Running three hours and more, these films, even more than before, reflected how the pace and flavor of the south colored Pagnol's approach to filmmaking. As Fernandel has put it: "With

Marcel Pagnol, making a film is first of all going to Marseille, then eating some bouillabaisse with a friend, talking about the rain or the beautiful weather, and finally if there is a spare moment, shooting. . . ." Along with Clair and Cocteau, Pagnol was inducted into the Academie Française. Every year his status grows among historians of cinema who once ridiculed his "canned theater."—DENNIS NASTAV

Pakula, Alan J.

*Nationality American. **Born** The Bronx, New York, 7 April 1928. **Education** Attended Bronx High School of Science; studied drama, Yale University, degree 1948. **Family** Married 1) actress Hope Lange (divorced 1969); 2) Hannah Cohn Boorstin, 1973, five stepchildren. **Career** Assistant, cartoon department, Warner Bros., also stage director at Circle Theatre, Los Angeles, 1948; apprentice to producer-director Don Hartman at MGM, then at Paramount, from 1950; as producer, founded Pakula-Mulligan Productions with director Robert Mulligan, 1962 (active through 1969). **Awards** Best Director, London Film Critics, 1971, for* Klute; *Best Direction, New York Film Critics, 1976, for* All the President's Men; *Eastman Award for Continued Excellence in Filmmaking, 1981. **Address** Pakula Productions, Inc., 330 W. 58th Street, New York, New York 10019, U.S.A.*

Films as Director: 1969: *The Sterile Cuckoo.* **1971:** *Klute* (+co-pr). **1972:** *Love and Pain and the Whole Damn Thing* (+pr). **1974:** *The Parallax View* (+pr). **1976:** *All the President's Men.* **1978:** *Comes a Horseman.* **1979:** *Starting Over* (+co-pr). **1981:** *Rollover.* **1982:** *Sophie's Choice* (+sc, co-pr). **1986:** *Dream Lover* (+co-pr). **1987:** *Orphans* (+pr). **1989:** *See You in the Morning* (+sc, pr). **1990:** *Presumed Innocent* (+co-sc). **1992:** *Consenting Adults* (+pr). **1993:** *The Pelican Brief* (+sc, pr). **1997:** *The Devil's Own.*

Other Films: 1957: *Fear Strikes Out* (Mulligan) (pr); *To Kill a Mockingbird* (Mulligan) (pr). **1963:** *Love with a Proper Stranger* (Mulligan) (pr). **1965:** *Baby the Rain Must Fall* (Mulligan) (pr). **1966:** *Inside Daisy Clover* (Mulligan) (pr). **1967:** *Up the Down Staircase* (Mulligan) (pr). **1968:** *The Stalking Moon* (Mulligan) (pr).

Now considered by many a major cinematic stylist, Alan J. Pakula began his career as a producer. The quality of his films is rather uneven, ranging from the acclaimed *Fear Strikes Out* and *To Kill a Mockingbird* to the universally panned *Inside Daisy Clover*. Critic Guy Flatley noted that Pakula is affectionately acknowledged within the film industry as an "actor's director," eliciting "richly textured performances" from Liza Minnelli in *The Sterile Cuckoo*; Maggie Smith in *Love and Pain and the Whole Damn Thing*; Warren Beatty in *The Parallax View*; Robert Redford, Dustin Hoffman, and Jason Robards, Jr. in *All the President's Men*; Jane Fonda, James Caan, and Robards in *Comes a Horseman*; and Burt Reynolds, Candice Bergen, and Jill Clayburgh in *Starting Over*. Many filmgoers are surprised upon discovering that it was Pakula who directed all these films.

Pakula's self-effacement is deliberate. In the Oscar-winning *Sophie's Choice* (for Meryl Streep as best actress), the director's name is less known than the actors who worked so effectively under his direction, and far less known than the tragic personal, social, and historical themes of the film. Pakula stresses the psychological dimension of his films. *Klute,* one of his most celebrated efforts, is highlighted by his use of taped conversation to both reveal character and heighten suspense. The film is noted for "visual claustrophobia" and unusual, effective mise-en-scène. For her performance, Jane Fonda received an Academy Award.

Alan J. Pakula.
Photograph by S. Karin Epstein.

Klute was Pakula's first "commercial and critical gold." As one critic writes, "the attention to fine, authentic detail in *Klute* reflected the careful research done by both the director and the actress in the Manhattan demimonde, and many of the shadings of the complex character of the prostitute were developed improvisationally during the filming by ... Fonda in collaboration with Pakula." Critical response to *Klute* is represented by such writers as Robin Wood, who said, "If it is too soon to be sure of Pakula's precise identity as an auteur, it remains true that *Klute* belongs, like any other great movie, to its director." Characteristically, Pakula believes that "the auteur theory is half-truth because filmmaking is very collaborative." Pakula's other films have had equal success: *All the President's Men,* for example, was the top-grossing film of 1976, and won four Academy Awards. It was nominated for best picture and best director, as well. Even the critic known as "Pakula's relentless nemesis," Stanley Kauffmann, "relented a little" concerning *All the President's Men.*

Alan J. Pakula is a filmmaker whose work most notably features tautness in both narrative and performance; he is a director of "moods," and is often "congratulated for the moods he sustains." He has described his approach to filmmaking as follows: "I am oblique. I think it has to do with my own nature. I like trying to do things which work on many levels, because I think it is terribly important to give an audience a lot of things they may not get as well as those they will, so that finally the film does take on a texture and is not just simplistic communication."

Although he has remained active in recent years, Pakula has not produced—with one exception—work of real significance since *Sophie's Choice* (itself more of an actors' than director's film). *See You in the Morning* attempts to recycle the melodramatic poignancy of *Klute* and *The Sterile Cuckoo,* but does not rediscover the stylistic finesse that made these earlier films so successful. *See You in the Morning*'s examination of family and personal breakdown is heavy-handed and hence strangely unaffecting.

The Pelican Brief, based on John Grisham's amateurish novel about the corrupt Washington establishment, makes no good sense, but is also strangely unexciting and unsuspenseful. Unlike Hitchcock, Pakula here proves unable to forge a masterful thriller from a marginal literary source; *The Pelican Brief,* it must be said, also fails to create the paranoid atmosphere that is the hallmark of Pakula's earlier, more successful forays into the political thriller (*The Parallax View* is the best of these). *Consenting Adults* is a domestic thriller centering on an unfaithful suburban husband who falls victim to a psychopath eager to perpetrate insurance fraud and steal his wife. The first part of this film offers a chilling version of contemporary upscale suburban life; but the film's second half descends into sub-Hitchcockian third-rate twists and turns that fail to engage or excite.

Only in *Presumed Innocent* does Pakula recapture some of his earlier success. Despite numerous plot inconsistencies (the legacy of Scott Turow's novel), *Presumed Innocent* is compelling viewing because Pakula takes pains to fashion a detailed setting (heightened by fine character performances); he also astutely directs Harrison Ford in the lead role.—DEBORAH H. HOLDSTEIN and R. BARTON PALMER

Paradzhanov, Sergei

Nationality *Soviet Georgian.* **Born** *Tiflis (Tbilisi), Soviet Georgia, 1924. Transliterations of name include "Paradjanov" and "Parajanov."* **Education** *Kiev Conservatory of Music, 1942-45; studied under Igor Savchenko at Moscow Film Institute (V.G.I.K.), graduated 1951.* **Family** *Married Svetlana (Paradzhanova), early 1950s (divorced after 2 years), one son.* **Career** *Began as director at Kiev Dovzhenko Studio, 1953; following international success of* Shadows of Our Forgotten Ancestors, *ten filmscripts rejected by authorities through 1974; indicted for a variety of crimes, convicted of trafficking in art objects, sentenced to six years hard labor, 1974; released after international and Russian protests to Supreme Soviet, 1978.* **Award** *British Film Academy Award for* Shadows of Our Forgotten Ancestors, *1966.* **Died** *In Yerevan, of cancer, 20 July 1990.*

Films as Director and Scriptwriter: **1951:** *Moldavskaia skazka (Moldavian Fairy Tale)* (short). **1954:** *Andriesh* (co-d). **1958:** *Pervyi paren (The First Lad).* **1961:** *Ukrainskaia rapsodiia (Ukrainian*

Sergei Paradzhanov: *Sayat nova*

Rhapsody). **1963:** Tsvetok no kamne (Flower on the Stone). **1964:** Dumka (The Ballad). **1965:** Teni zabytykh predkov (Shadows of Our Forgotten Ancestors) (co-sc). **1969:** Sayat nova (The Color of Pomegranates; The Blood of the Pomegranates) (released 1972). **1978:** Achraroumès (Retour à la vie). **1985:** Legenda o Suramskoj kreposti (The Legend of the Suram Fortress). **1986:** Arabeski na temu Pirosmani (doc). **1988:** Ashik kerib.

The cinema, like heaven, has many mansions, and the place occupied by Sergei Paradzhanov is a very rich one indeed. This dissident, highly individual film creator made films startling in their beauty, deeply imbued with ethnic consciousness, as unique in their style as, say, the work of Miklos Jancsó.

Paradzhanov was unmistakably a dissident. Not for him the systematic social realism of the authorities. Like his distinguished predecessors Eisenstein and Dovzhenko, it was the poetry of life that he sought. His films must be taken in their totality, for the cumulative effect is stunning. His beautiful images, created with the eye of a painter, while striking in themselves, progress with the steady tempo of tableaux vivants.

When Paradzhanov's *Teni zabytykh predkov (Shadows of Our Forgotten Ancestors)* burst upon world screens, it was quite evident that a major artist had appeared in Soviet cinema. This film, more flexible than his later stylized creations, revealed a powerful individuality. A tale of life in an ancient Carpathian village, it revealed also a sensitive feeling for nature and landscapes and an awareness of religious forces as it probed into the recesses of the inherited mind.

It was inevitable that Paradzhanov's work would not be appreciated by lesser men. He was uncompromising even when pressures and persecution pursued him. His personal lifestyle and his dogged pursuit of an ideal made him a marked man for bureaucratic tyranny, and after his *Sayat nova (The Colour of Pomegranates)* was completed in 1972 he was driven from the cinema. He was sentenced to six years in a labour camp for charges ranging from homosexuality and fraud to incitement to suicide. After several years under duress, world opinion forced the Soviet authorities to release him. He knew shame and beggary until with great determination he won his way back to making films once more.

The Colour of Pomegranates (or *The Blood of the Pomegranates*) evokes the life of the eighteenth-century Armenian poet Arution Sayadian. In it the images are almost an *embarras de richesses*. The bleeding pomegranates, the struggling fish, details of utensils and native crafts, the boy swinging from the bellrope, pages of hundreds of books blown in the wind, the stately horseman parading back and forth, and the blazing colours of textiles in the dye-works scene pile up in a series of unforgettable impressions.

More sombre in tone is the *Legenda o Suramskoj kreposti (The Legend of the Suram Fortress)*, made in 1984 when Paradzhanov returned to the Georgian Film Studio. It is again a series of episodes integrated in mood and feeling and characteristically poetic in approach. His last film, *Ashik kerib,* is suitably dedicated to Tarkovsky and tells the tale of a Turkish minstrel and his frustrated love. Again rich images prevail and the idiosyncratic style persists.

Paradzhanov was a poet of the Eastern Soviet Republics. A Georgian, born in Tiflis, he was steeped in the culture and traditions of his native region. His concern with its past was the source of his creative strength and his independence of mind. He lived, thankfully, to see repressive forces at least temporarily dissipated, bringing freedom to himself as an artist. Yet it is a great pity that in the West he is known by only a few, if important, key films. The future will no doubt bring a greater knowledge of his work.—LIAM O'LEARY

Pasolini, Pier Paolo

Nationality Italian. Born Bologna, 5 March 1922. Education School Reggio Emilia e Galvani, Bologna, until 1937; University of Bologna, until 1943. Military Service Conscripted, 1943; regiment taken prisoner by Germans following Italian surrender; escaped and took refuge with family in Casarsa. Career Formed "Academiuta di lenga furlana" with friends, publishing works in Friulian dialect, 1944; secretary of Communist Party cell in Casarsa, 1947; accused of corrupting minors, fired from teaching post, moved to Rome, 1949; teacher in Ciampino, suburb of Rome, early 1950s; following publication of Ragazzi di vita, indicted for obscenity, 1955; co-founder and editor of review Officina (Bologna); prosecuted for "vilification of the Church" for directing "La ricotta" episode of Rogopag, 1963. Award Special Jury Prize, Venice Festival, for Il vangelo secondo Matteo, 1964. Died Bludgeoned to death in Ostia, 2 November 1975; buried at Casarsa.

Films as Director: 1961: *Accattone* (+sc). **1962:** *Mamma Roma* (+sc). **1963:** "La ricotta" episode of *Rogopag* (+sc); *La rabbia* (part one) (+sc). **1964:** *Comizi d'amore* (+sc); *Sopralluoghi in Palestina* (+sc); *Il vangelo secondo Matteo* (*The Gospel According to Saint Matthew*) (+sc). **1966:** *Uccellacci e uccellini* (*The Hawks and the Sparrows*) (+sc); "La terra vista dalla luna" episode of *Le Streghe* (*The Witches*) (+sc). **1967:** "Che cosa sono le nuvole" episode of *Cappriccio all'italiana* (+sc); *Edipo re* (*Oedipus Rex*) (+sc). **1968:** *Teorema* (+sc); "La sequenza del fiore di carta" episode of *Amore e rabbia* (+sc). **1969:** *Appunti per un film indiano* (+sc); *Appunti per una Orestiade africana* (*Notes for an African Oresteia*) (+sc); *Porcile* (*Pigsty; Pigpen*) (+sc); *Medea* (+sc). **1971:** *Il decameron* (*The Decameron*) (+sc, role as Giotto). **1972:** *12 dicembre* (co-d, sc); *I racconti di Canterbury* (*The*

Pier Paolo Pasolini directing *Salò o le 120 giornate di Sodome*.

Canterbury Tales) (+sc, role). **1974:** Il fiore delle mille e una notte (A Thousand and One Nights) (+sc).
1975: Salò o le 120 giornate di Sodome (Salo—The 120 Days of Sodom) (+co-sc).

Other Films: 1954: La donna del fiume (co-sc). **1955:** Il prigioniero della montagna (co-sc). **1956:** Le
notti di Cabiria (Fellini) (co-sc). **1957:** Marisa la civetta (Bolognini) (co-sc). **1958:** Giovanni Mariti
(Bolognini) (co-sc). **1959:** La notte brava (Bolognini) (co-sc). **1960:** La canta delle marane (sc); Morte
di un amico (co-sc); Il bell' Antonio (Bolognini) (co-sc); La giornata balorda (Bolognini) (co-sc); La
lunga notte del '43 (co-sc); Il carro armato dell '8 settembre (co-sc); Il gobbo (role). **1961:** La ragazza
in vetrina (co-sc). **1962:** La commare secca (Bertolucci) (sc). **1966:** Requiescat (role). **1969:** Ostia (co-
sc). **1973:** Storie scellerate (co-sc).

Pier Paolo Pasolini, poet, novelist, philosopher, and filmmaker, came of age during the
reign of Italian Fascism, and his art is inextricably bound to his politics. Pasolini's films, like those
of his early apprentice Bernardo Bertolucci, began under the influence of neorealism. He also
did early scriptwriting with Bolognini and Fellini. Besides these roots in neorealism, Pasolini's
works show a unique blend of linguistic theory and Italian Marxism. But Pasolini began
transcending the neorealist tradition even in his first film, *Accattone* (which means "beggar").

The relationship between Pasolini's literary work and his films has often been observed,
and indeed Pasolini himself noted in an introduction to a paperback selection of his poetry that
"I made all these films as a poet." Pasolini was a great champion of modern linguistic theory and
often pointed to Roland Barthes and Erich Auerbach in discussing the films many years before
semiotics and structuralism became fashionable. His theories on the semiotics of cinema
centered on the idea that film was a kind of "real poetry" because it expressed reality with reality
itself and not with other semiotic codes, signs, or systems.

Pasolini's interest in linguistics can also be traced to his first book of poetry, *Poems of
Casarsa,* which is written in his native Friuli dialect. This early interest in native nationalism and
agrarian culture is also a central element in Pasolini's politics. His first major poem, "The Ashes of
Gramsci" (1954), pays tribute to Antonio Gramsci, the Italian Marxist who founded the Italian
Communist party. It created an uproar unknown in Italy since the time of D'Annunzio's poetry
and was read by artists, politicians, and the general public.

The ideas of Gramsci coincided with Pasolini's own feelings, especially concerning that
part of the working class known as the sub-proletariat, which Pasolini described as a
prehistorical, pre-Christian, and pre-bourgeois phenomenon, one which occurs for him in the
South of Italy (the Sud) and in the Third World.

This concern with "the little homelands," the indigenous cultures of specific regions, is a
theme linking all of Pasolini's films, from *Accattone* to his final black vision, *Salò.* These marginal
classes, known as *cafoni* (hicks or hillbillies), are among the main characters in Pasolini's novels
Ragazzi de vita (1955) and *A Violent Life* (1959), and appear as protagonists in many of his films,
notably *Accattone, Mamma Roma, Hawks and Sparrows,* and *The Gospel According to Saint
Matthew.* To quote Pasolini: "My view of the world is always at bottom of an epical-religious
nature: therefore even, in fact above all, in misery-ridden characters, characters who live outside
of a historical consciousness, these epical-religious elements play a very important part."

In *Accattone* and *The Gospel,* images of official culture are juxtaposed against those of a
more humble origin. The pimp of *Accattone* and the Christ of *The Gospel* are similar figures.
When Accattone is killed at the end of the film, a fellow thief is seen crossing himself in a strange
backward way, it is Pasolini's indictment of how Christianity has "contaminated" the subproletarian
world of Rome. Marxism is never far away in *The Gospel;* it is evident, for instance, in the scene

where Satan, dressed as a priest, tempts Christ. In *The Gospel,* Pasolini has put his special brand of Marxism even into camera angles and has, not ironically, created one of the most moving and literal interpretations of the story of Christ. A recurrent motif in Pasolini's filmmaking, and especially prominent in *Accattone* and *The Gospel,* is the treatment of individual camera shots as autonomous units; the cinematic equivalent of the poetic image. It should also be noted that *The Gospel According to Saint Matthew* was filmed entirely in southern Italy.

In the 1960s Pasolini's films became more concerned with ideology and myth, while continuing to develop his epical-religious theories. *Oedipus Rex* (which has never been distributed in the United States) and *Medea* reaffirm Pasolini's attachment to the marginal and pre-industrial peasant cultures. These two films indict capitalism as well as communism for the destruction of these cultures, and the creation of a world which has lost its sense of myth.

In *Teorema* ("theorem" in Italian), which is perhaps Pasolini's most experimental film, a mysterious stranger visits a typical middle class family, sexually seduces mother, father, daughter, and son, and destroys them. The peasant maid is the only character who is transformed because she is still attuned to the numinous quality of life which the middle class has lost. Pasolini has said about this film: "A member of the bourgeoisie, whatever he does, is always wrong."

Pigpen, which shares with *Teorema* the sulphurous volcanic location of Mount Etna, is a double film. The first half is the story or parable of a fifteenth-century cult of cannibals and their eventual destruction by the church. The second half concerns two former Nazis-turned-industrialists in a black comedy of rank perversion. It is the film closest in spirit to the dark vision of *Salò.*

In the 1970s Pasolini turned against his elite international audience of intellectuals and film buffs and embraced the mass market with his "Trilogy of Life": *Decameron, Canterbury Tales,* and *Arabian Nights.* The *Decameron* was his first major European box-office hit, due mainly to its explicit sexual content. All three films are a celebration of Pasolini's philosophy of "the ontology of reality, whose naked symbol is sex." Pasolini, an avowed homosexual, in *Decameron,* and especially *Arabian Nights,* celebrates the triumph of female heterosexuality as the epitome of the life principle. Pasolini himself appears in two of these films, most memorably in the *Decameron* as Giotto's best pupil, who on completion of a fresco for a small town cathedral says, "Why produce a work of art, when it's so much better just to dream about it."

As a result of his growing political pessimism Pasolini disowned the "Trilogy" and rejected most of its ideas. His final film, *Salò,* is an utterly clinical examination of the nature of fascism, which for Pasolini is synonymous with consumerism. Using a classical, unmoving camera, Pasolini explores the ultimate in human perversions in a static, repressive style. *Salò,* almost impossible to watch, is one of the most horrifying and beautiful visions ever created on film. Pasolini's tragic, if not ironic, death in 1975 ended a visionary career that almost certainly would have continued to evolve.—TONY D'ARPINO

Peckinpah, Sam

Nationality *American.* ***Born*** *David Samuel Peckinpah in Fresno, California, 21 February 1925.* ***Education*** *Fresno State College, B.A. in Drama 1949; University of Southern*

California, M.A. 1950. **Military Service** *Enlisted in Marine Corps, 1943.* **Family** *Married 1) Marie Selland, 1947, four children; 2) Begonia Palacios, 1964 (divorced), one child; 3) Joie Gould, 1972 (divorced).* **Career** *Director/producer in residence, Huntington Park Civic Theatre, California, 1950-51; propman and stagehand, KLAC-TV, Los Angeles, then assistant editor at CBS, 1951-53; assistant to Don Siegel, from 1954; writer for television, including "Gunsmoke" and "The Rifleman," late 1950s; worked on scripts at Walt Disney Productions, 1963.* **Died** *Of a heart attack, 28 December 1984.*

Films as Director: 1961: *The Deadly Companions* (*Trigger Happy*). **1962:** *Ride the High Country* (*Guns in the Afternoon*) (+co-sc, uncredited). **1965:** *Major Dundee* (+co-sc). **1966:** *Noon Wine* (+sc). **1969:** *The Wild Bunch* (+co-sc). **1970:** *The Ballad of Cable Hogue.* **1971:** *Straw Dogs* (+co-sc). **1972:** *Junior Bonner, The Getaway.* **1973:** *Pat Garrett and Billy the Kid.* **1974:** *Bring Me the Head of Alfredo Garcia* (+co-sc). **1975:** *The Killer Elite.* **1977:** *Cross of Iron.* **1978:** *Convoy.* **1983:** *The Osterman Weekend.*

Other Films: 1956: *Invasion of the Body Snatchers* (Siegel) (role as Charlie the meter reader). **1978:** *China 9 Liberty 37* (Hellmann) (role). **1980:** *Il Visitatore* (Paradise) (role).

It is as a director of westerns that Sam Peckinpah remains best known. This is not without justice. His non-western movies often lack the sense of complexity and resonance that he brings to western settings. He was adept at exploiting this richest of genres for his own purposes, explaining its ambiguities, pushing its values to uncomfortable limits. *Ride the High Country, Major Dundee,* and *The Wild Bunch* are the work of a filmmaker of high ambitions and rare talents. They convey a sense of important questions posed, yet finally left open and unanswered. At their best they have a visionary edge unparalleled in American cinema.

His non-westerns lose the additional dimensions that the genre brings, as in, for example, *Straw Dogs.* A polished and didactic parable about a besieged liberal academic who is forced by the relentless logic of events into extremes of violence, it is somehow too complete, its answers too pat, to reach beyond its own claustrophobic world. Though its drama is entirely compelling, it lacks the referential framework that carries Peckinpah's westerns far beyond the realm of tautly-directed action. Compared to *The Wild Bunch,* it is a one-dimensional film.

Nevertheless, *Straw Dogs* is immediately recognizable as a Peckinpah movie. If a distinctive style and common themes are the marks of an *auteur,* then Peckinpah's right to that label is indisputable. His concern with the horrors and the virtues of the male group was constant, as was his refusal to accept conventional movie morality. "My father says there's only Right and Wrong, Good and Evil, with nothing in between. But it's not that

Sam Peckinpah

simple, is it?" asks Elsa in *Ride the High Country.* Judd's reply could almost be Peckinpah's: "No. It should be, but it isn't".

In traditional westerns, of course, right and wrong are clearly distinguishable. The westerner, as Robert Warshow has characterised him, is the man with a code. In Peckinpah's westerns, as in some of his other movies such as *Cross of Iron,* it is the code itself that is rendered problematic. Peckinpah explores the ethic rather than taking it for granted, plays off its elements one against the other, and uses his characters as emblems of those internal conflicts. He presents a world whose moral certainty is collapsing, leaving behind doomed variations on assertive individualism. In some modern westerns that theme has been treated as elegy; in Peckinpah it veers nearer to tragedy. His is a harsh world, softened only rarely in movies like *The Ballad of Cable Hogue* and *Junior Bonner.*

Peckinpah's richest achievements remain the two monumental epics of the 1960s, *Major Dundee* and *The Wild Bunch.* In both, though *Major Dundee* was butchered by its producers both before and after shooting, there is ample evidence of Peckinpah's ability to marshall original cinematic means in the service of a morally and aesthetically complex vision. It has become commonplace to associate Peckinpah with the rise of explicit violence in modern cinema, and it is true that few directors have rendered violence with such horrific immediacy. But his cinema is far more than that: his reflections upon familiar western themes are technically sophisticated, elaborately constructed, and, at their best, genuinely profound.—ANDREW TUDOR

Penn, Arthur

Nationality American. *Born* Philadelphia, 27 September 1922. *Education* Black Mountain College, North Carolina, 1947-48; studied at Universities of Perugia and Florence, 1949-50; trained for the stage with Michael Chekhov. *Military Service* Enlisted in Army, 1943; joined Soldiers Show Company, Paris, 1945. *Family* Married actress Peggy Maurer, 1955, one son, one daughter. *Career* Assistant director on The Colgate Comedy Hour, 1951-52; TV director, from 1953, working on Gulf Playhouse: 1st Person (NBC), Philco Television Playhouse (NBC), and Playhouse 90 (CBS); directed first feature, The Left-Handed Gun, 1958; director on Broadway, from 1958. *Awards* Tony Award for stage version of The Miracle Worker; two Sylvania Awards. *Address* c/o 2 West 67th Street, New York, New York 10023, U.S.A.

Films as Director: 1958: *The Left-Handed Gun.* **1962:** *The Miracle Worker.* **1965:** *Mickey One* (+pr). **1966:** *The Chase.* **1967:** *Bonnie and Clyde.* **1969:** *Alice's Restaurant* (+co-sc). **1970:** *Little Big Man* (+pr). **1973:** "The Highest" in *Visions of 8.* **1975:** *Night Moves.* **1976:** *The Missouri Breaks.* **1981:** *Four Friends.* **1985:** *Target.* **1987:** *Dead of Winter.* **1989:** *Penn and Teller Get Killed* (+pr). **1993:** *The Portrait* (for TV). **1995:** *Lumière et Compagnie (Lumière and Company)* (co-d). **1996:** *Inside.*

Arthur Penn has often been classed—along with Robert Altman, Bob Rafelson, and Francis Coppola—among the more "European" American directors. Stylistically, this is true enough. Penn's films, especially after *Bonnie and Clyde,* tend to be technically experimental, and episodic in structure; their narrative line is elliptical, undermining audience expectations with abrupt shifts in mood and rhythm. Such features can be traced to the influence of the French New Wave, in particular the early films of François Truffaut and Jean-Luc Godard, which Penn greatly admired.

In terms of his thematic preoccupations, though, few directors are more utterly American. Repeatedly, throughout his work, Penn has been concerned with questioning and re-assessing the myths of his country. His films reveal a passionate, ironic, intense involvement with the American experience, and can be seen as an illuminating chart of the country's moral condition over the past thirty years. *Mickey One* is dark with the unfocused guilt and paranoia of the McCarthyite hangover, while the stunned horror of the Kennedy assassination reverberates through *The Chase*. The exhilaration, and the fatal flaws, of the 1960s anti-authoritarian revolt are reflected in *Bonnie and Clyde* and *Alice's Restaurant*. *Little Big Man* reworks the trauma of Vietnam, while *Night Moves* is steeped in the disillusioned malaise that pervaded the Watergate era.

As a focus for his perspective on America, Penn often chooses an outsider group and its relationship with mainstream society. The Indians in *Little Big Man*, the Barrow Gang in *Bonnie and Clyde*, the rustlers in *The Missouri Breaks*, the hippies in *Alice's Restaurant*, the outlaws in *The Left-Handed Gun*, are all sympathetically presented as attractive and vital figures, preferable in many ways to the conventional society which rejects them. But ultimately they suffer defeat, being infected by the flawed values of that same society. "A society," Penn has commented, "has its mirror in its outcasts."

An exceptionally intense, immediate physicality distinguishes Penn's work. Pain, in his films, unmistakably *hurts*, and tactile sensations are vividly communicated. Often, characters are conveyed primarily through their bodily actions: how they move, walk, hold themselves, or use their hands. Violence is a recurrent feature of his films—notably in *The Chase, Bonnie and Clyde*, and *The Missouri Breaks*—but it is seldom gratuitously introduced, and represents, in Penn's view, a deeply rooted element in the American character which has to be acknowledged.

Arthur Penn with Melanie Griffith on the set of *Night Moves*.

Penn established his reputation as a director with *Bonnie and Clyde,* one of the most significant and influential films of its decade. But since 1970 he has made only a handful of films, none of them successful at the box office. *Night Moves* and *The Missouri Breaks,* both poorly received on initial release, now rank among his most subtle and intriguing movies, and *Four Friends,* though uneven, remains constantly stimulating with its oblique, elliptical narrative structure.

But since then Penn seems to have lost his way. Neither *Target,* a routine spy thriller, nor *Dead of Winter,* a reworking of Joseph H. Lewis's cult B-movie *My Name Is Julia Ross,* offered material worthy of his distinctive talents. *Penn and Teller Get Killed,* a spoof psycho-killer vehicle for the bad-taste illusionist team, got few showings outside the festival circuit. His only recent directorial work is *The Portrait,* a solidly crafted adaptation for television of Tina Rowe's Broadway hit, *Painting Churches.*

"It's not that I've drifted away from film," Penn told Richard Combs in 1986. "I'm very drawn to film, but I'm not sure that film is drawn to me." Given the range, vitality, and sheer unpredictability of his earlier work, the estrangement is much to be regretted—especially if, as looks increasingly likely, it turns out to be permanent.—PHILIP KEMP

Pialat, Maurice

Nationality French. *Born* Puy de Dôme, 31 August 1925. *Education* Studied Art at Ecole des Arts Décoratifs and Ecole des Beaux Arts, Paris. *Career* Exhibited work at salons, 1945-47; actor and assistant stage director to Michel Vitold, from 1955; worked in TV, made films, from 1960; directed first feature, 1967. *Awards* Jean Vigo Prize, for L'enfance nue, 1967; Prix Louis Delluc, and César for Best Film, for A nos amours, 1983; Palme d'Or, Cannes Festival, for Sous le soleil de Satan, 1987.

Films as Director: 1960: *L'amour existe* (short). **1961:** *Janine* (for TV). **1962:** *Maitre Galip* (for TV). **1967:** *L'enfance nue* (+sc). **1971:** *La maison des bois* (for TV) (+role). **1972:** *Nous ne vieillirons pas ensemble* (+sc, pr). **1974:** *La gueule ouverte* (+sc, pr). **1979:** *Passe ton bac d'abord.* **1979:** *Loulou.* **1983:** *A nos amours* (*To Our Loves*). **1985:** *Police* (+co-sc). **1987:** *Sous le soleil de Satan* (*Under Satan's Sun*) (+co-sc, role). **1991:** *Van Gogh* (+sc). **1995:** *Le Garcu* (+co-sc). **1997:** *Les auto-stoppeuses.*

Other Films: 1969: *Que la bete meure* (Chabrol) (role). **1996:** *Enfants de salaud* (role).

Described by Alain Bergala in *Cahiers du Cinéma* as "Renoir's true heir today," Maurice Pialat is squarely in the tradition of French *auteur* cinema. Like Renoir, Feyder, and Grémillon in the 1930s, and Godard, Resnais, Varda, and a few others after the war, Pialat is an artisan who works both within and against the French film industry. He has often acknowledged his "debt" to Renoir, as well as to Pagnol, in terms of both working methods and a certain conception of realism. However, unlike the benign humanism of these two predecessors, Pialat's work is marked by harshness, violence, and conflict, both on and off screen.

From his first feature (*L'enfance nue,* on deprived childhood), Pialat's films have shown an almost ethnographic concern with unglamorous areas of French society: difficult adolescents (*Passe ton bac d'abord*), semi-hooligans (*Loulou*), the bitter breakdown of a couple (*Nous ne vieillirons pas ensemble*) and cancer (*La gueule ouverte*), combining a quasi *cinéma-vérité* approach with the reworking of deeply personal matters. Although Pialat has claimed to be "fed

Maurice Pialat

up with realism," and even though he has made forays into genre films with *Police* and *Sous le soleil de Satan,* his cinema is still within a realistic idiom, fusing the New Wave (and neo-realist) concern with location shooting and contemporary setting with the "intimate" realism of the central European cinema of the 1960s. His films draw on basic realist strategies such as the use of non-professional or little-known actors (sometimes alongside stars like Gérard Depardieu, and on occasion—Renoir-style—the charismatic Pialat himself), the frequent recourse to improvisation and colloquial language, hand-held camerawork, long takes, and shooting without a finished script. If these strategies traditionally produce a sense of immediacy and authenticity, they often combine, in Pialat's films, with a rare violence.

Pialat has earned a reputation as a "difficult" director. To some extent, this is an inherent part of the myth of *auteur* cinema which stresses the romantic pains of creation. Yet Pialat's career is littered with well-publicized working and personal conflicts: with actors Gérard Depardieu (*Loulou*) and Sophie Marceau (*Police*), with scriptwriter Catherine Breillat over *Police,* and with technicians on many occasions. But part of his method consists precisely of inscribing his own personal relationships within the fabric of his films, as epitomised in *A nos amours* by the Pialat/Bonnaire couple (on several professional and personal levels).

"Pialat le terrible," as he was dubbed by a French paper, sometimes makes headlines, and occasionally the courtrooms. This would be mere gossip if it did not echo the very subject matter of his films. In the same way as Sam Fuller defined cinema as "a battleground," Pialat's filmmaking might be described as belonging to the boxing ring. He has repeatedly stated his preference for situations where people have rows, where they clash, where "there is trouble," and this is borne out by all his films, where conflict is the preferred element, a type of conflict which moreover assumes a great physicality. In Pialat's cinema, contact is more likely to be made through violence than through tenderness, particularly within the family, where the boxing ring overlaps with the Oedipal stage. This is true both thematically (families and couples tearing each other apart) and in the way Pialat's films address their spectators. A predominance of indoor scenes shot in claustrophobic medium close-ups, and the deliberate inclusion of "flawed" episodes, of moments of rupture or tension in the films, are ways of capturing "the truth" of characters or situations, sometimes with little regard for narrative continuity. Pialat does not pull his punches, and his cinema, in the words of editor Yann Dedet, "tends more towards emotion than comprehension."

If Pialat's films, in their bleak examination of some of the least palatable aspects of contemporary French society and personal emotions, make for difficult viewing, their reward lies in an emotional and documentary power rare in French cinema today.—GINETTE VINCENDEAU

Polanski, Roman

Nationality *Polish.* ***Born*** *Paris, 18 August 1933.* ***Education*** *Krakow Liceum Sztuk Plastycznych (art school), 1950-53; State Film School, Lodz, 1954-59.* ***Family*** *Married 1) actress Barbara Kwiatkowska, 1959 (divorced 1961); 2) actress Sharon Tate, 1968 (died 1969); 3) actress Emmanuelle Seigner, 1989.* ***Career*** *Returned to Poland, 1936; actor on radio and in theatre, from 1945, and in films, from 1951; joined filmmaking group KAMERA as assistant to Andrzej Munk, 1959; directed first feature,* Knife in the Water, *1962, denounced by Polish Communist Party chief Gomulka, funding for subsequent films denied, moved to Paris, 1963; moved to London, 1964, then to Los Angeles, 1968; wife Sharon Tate and three friends murdered in Bel Air, California, home by members of Charles Manson cult, 1969; opera director, from 1974; convicted by his own plea of unlawful sexual intercourse in California, 1977; committed to a diagnostic facility, Department of Correction; upon completion of study, returned to Paris; also stage actor and director.* ***Awards*** *Silver Bear, Berlin Film Festival, for* Repulsion, *1965; Golden Bear, Berlin Festival, for* Cul-de-Sac, *1966; César Award, for* Tess, *1980.* ***Address*** *Lives in Paris.*

Roman Polanski

Films as Director and Scriptwriter: 1955/57: *Rower* (*The Bike*) (short). **1957/58:** *Morderstwo* (*The Crime*) (short). **1958:** *Rozbijemy zabawe* (*Break Up the Dance*) (short); *Dwaj ludzie z szasa* (*2 Men and a Wardrobe*) (short) (+role). **1959:** *Gdy spadaja anioly* (*When Angels Fall*) (short) (+role as old woman). **1961:** *Le Gros et le maigre* (*The Fat Man and the Thin Man*) (short) (co-sc, +role as servant). **1962:** *Ssaki* (*Mammals*) (short) (co-sc, +role); *Nóz w wodzie* (*Knife in the Water*) (co-sc). **1963:** "La Rivière de diamants" ("A River of Diamonds") episode of *Les Plus Belles Escroqueries du monde* (*The Most Beautiful Swindles in the World*) (co-sc). **1964:** *Repulsion* (co-sc). **1965:** *Cul-de-sac* (co-sc). **1967:** *The Fearless Vampire Killers* (*Pardon Me, But Your Teeth Are in My Neck; Dance of the Vampires*) (co-sc, +role as Alfred). **1968:** *Rosemary's Baby*. **1972:** *Macbeth* (co-sc). **1973:** *What?* (*Che?; Diary of Forbidden Dreams*) (co-sc, +role as Mosquito). **1974:** *Chinatown* (d only, +role as man with knife). **1976:** *Le Locataire* (*The Tenant*) (co-sc, +role as Trelkovsky). **1979:** *Tess* (co-sc). **1985:** *Pirates* (co-sc). **1988:** *Frantic* (co-sc). **1992:** *Lunes de fiel* (*Bitter Moon*) (co-sc, +pr). **1993:** *Death and the Maiden*. **1997:** *The Raft*.

Other Films: 1953: *Trzy opowiesci* (*Three Stories*) (Nalecki, Poleska, Petelski) (role as Maly). **1954:** *Pokolenie* (*A Generation*) (Wajda) (role as Mundek). **1955:** *Zaczárowany rower* (*The Enchanted Bicycle*) (Sternfeld) (role as Adas). **1956:** *Koniec wojny* (*End of the Night*) (Dziedzina, Komorowski, Uszycka) (role as Maly). **1957:** *Wraki* (*Wrecks*) (Petelski) (role). **1958:** *Zadzwoncie do mojej zony* (*Phone My Wife*) (Mach) (role). **1959:** *Lotna* (Wajda) (role as bandsman). **1960:** *Niewinni czarodzieje* (*Innocent Sorcerors*) (Wajda) (role as Dudzio); *Ostroznie yeti* (*The Abominable Snowman*) (Czekalski) (role); *Do Widzenia do Jutra* (*See You Tomorrow*) (Morgenstern) (role as Romek); *Zezowate szczescie* (*Bad Luck*) (Munk) (role). **1964:** *Do You Like Women?* (Léon) (co-sc). **1968:** *The Woman Opposite* (Simon) (co-sc). **1969:** *A Day at the Beach* (Hessera) (pr); *The Magic Christian* (McGrath) (role). **1972:** *Weekend of a Champion* (Simon) (pr, role as interviewer). **1974:** *Blood for Dracula* (Morrissey) (role as a villager). **1991:** *Back in the U.S.S.R.* (Serafian) (role as Kurilov). **1994:** *Gross Fatigue* (role as himself). **1995:** *A Simple Formality* (role as Inspector).

As a student at the Polish State Film School and later as a director working under government sponsorship, Roman Polanski learned to make films with few resources. Using only a few trained actors (there are but three characters in his first feature) and a hand-held camera (due to the unavailability of sophisticated equipment) Polanski managed to create several films which contributed to the international reputation of the burgeoning Polish cinema. These same limitations contributed to the development of a visual style which was well suited to the director's perspective on modern life: one which emphasized the sort of precarious, unstable world suggested by a hand-held camera, and the sense of isolation or removal from a larger society which follows the use of only small groupings of characters. In fact, Polanski's work might be seen as an attempt to map out the precise relationship between the contemporary world's instability and tendency to violence and the individual's increasing inability to overcome his isolation and locate some realm of meaning or value beyond himself.

What makes this concern with the individual and his psyche especially remarkable is Polanski's cultural background. As a product of a socialist state and its official film school at Lodz, he was expected to use his filmmaking skills to advance the appropriate social consciousness and ideology sanctioned by the government. However, Polanski's first feature, *Knife in the Water,* drew the ire of the Communist Party and was denounced at the Party Congress in 1964 for showing the negative aspects of Polish life. Although less an ideological statement than an examination of the various ways in which individual desires and powers determine our lives, *Knife in the Water* and the response it received seem to have precipitated Polanski's subsequent development into a truly international filmmaker. In a career that has taken him to France, England, Italy, and the United States in search of opportunities to write, direct, and act, he has consistently shown more interest in holding up a mirror to the individual impulses, unconscious urges, and the personal psychoses of human life than in dissecting the different social and political forces he has observed.

The various landscapes and geographies of Polanski's films certainly seem designed to enhance this focus, for they pointedly remove his characters from most of the normal structures of social life as well as from other people. The boat at sea in *Knife in the Water,* the oppressive flat and adjoining convent in *Repulsion,* the isolated castle and flooded causeway of *Cul-de-sac,* the prison-like apartments of *Rosemary's Baby* and *The Tenant,* and the empty fields and deserted manor house in *Tess* form a geography of isolation that is often symbolically transformed into a geography of the mind, haunted by doubts, fears, desires, or even madness. The very titles of films like *Cul-de-sac* and *Chinatown* are especially telling in this regard, for they point to the essential strangeness and isolation of Polanski's locales, as well as to the sense of alienation and entrapment which consequently afflicts his characters. Brought to such strange and oppressive environments by the conditions of their culture (*Chinatown*), their own misunderstood urges (*Repulsion*), or some inexplicable fate (*Macbeth*), Polanski's protagonists struggle to make the unnatural seem natural, to turn entrapment into an abode, although the result is typically tragic, as in the case of *Macbeth,* or absurd, as in *Cul-de-sac.*

Such situations have prompted numerous comparisons, especially of Polanski's early films, to the absurdist dramas of Samuel Beckett. As in many of Beckett's plays, language and its inadequacy play a significant role in Polanski's works, usually forming a commentary on the absence or failure of communication in modern society. The dramatic use of silence in *Knife in the Water* actually "speaks" more eloquently than much of the film's dialogue of the tensions and desires which drive its characters and operate just beneath the personalities they try to project. In the conversational clichés and banality which mark much of the dialogue in *Cul-de-sac,* we can discern how language often serves to cloak rather than communicate meaning. The problem, as the director most clearly shows in *Chinatown,* is that language often simply proves inadequate for capturing and conveying the complex and enigmatic nature of the human situation. Detective Jake Gittes's consternation when Evelyn Mulwray tries to explain that the girl he has been seeking is both her daughter and her sister—the result of an incestuous affair with her father—points out this linguistic inadequacy for communicating the most discomfiting truths. It is a point driven home at the film's end when, after Mrs. Mulwray is killed, Gittes is advised not to try to "say anything." His inability to articulate the horrors he has witnessed ultimately translates into the symptomatic lapse into silence also exhibited by the protagonists of *The Tenant* and *Tess,* as they find themselves increasingly bewildered by the powerful driving forces of their own psyches and the worlds they inhabit.

Prompting this tendency to silence, and often cloaked by a proclivity for a banal language, is a disturbing force of violence which all of Polanski's films seek to analyze—and for which they have frequently been criticized. Certainly, his own life has brought him all too close to this most disturbing impulse, for when he was only eight years old Polanski and his parents were interned in a German concentration camp where his mother died. In 1969 his wife Sharon Tate and several friends were brutally murdered by Charles Manson's followers. The cataclysmic violence in the decidedly bloody adaptation of *Macbeth,* which closely followed his wife's death, can be traced through all of the director's features, as Polanski has repeatedly tried to depict the various ways in which violence erupts from the human personality, and to confront in this specter the problem of evil in the world. The basic event of *Rosemary's Baby*—Rosemary's bearing the offspring of the devil, a baby whom she fears yet, because of the natural love of a mother for her own child, nurtures—might be seen as a paradigm of Polanski's vision of evil and its operation in our world. Typically, it is the innocent or unsuspecting individual, even one with the best of intentions, who unwittingly gives birth to and spreads the very evil or violence he most fears. The protagonist of *The Fearless Vampire Killers,* for example, sets about destroying the local vampire and saving his beloved from its unnatural hold. In the process, however, he himself becomes a vampire's prey and, as a concluding voice-over solemnly intones, assists in spreading this curse throughout the world.

It is a somber conclusion for a comedy, but a telling indication of the complex tone and perspective which mark Polanski's films. He is able to assume an ironic, even highly comic attitude towards the ultimate and, as he sees it, inevitable human problem—an abiding violence and evil nurtured even as we individually struggle against these forces. The absurdist stance of Polanski's short films, especially *Two Men and a Wardrobe* and *The Fat and the Lean,* represents one logical response to this paradox. That his narratives have grown richer, more complicated, and also more discomfiting in their examination of this situation attests to Polanski's ultimate commitment to understanding the human predicament and to rendering articulate that which seems to defy articulation. From his own isolated position—as a man effectively without a country—Polanski tries to confront the problems of isolation, violence, and evil, and to speak of them for an audience prone to their sway.

After a highly publicized 1977 sex scandal resulted in his flight from the United States and subsequent exile, Polanski surprised many by doing an apparent about face in terms of subject matter, and creating one of his most restrained and visually beautiful films: the aforementioned *Tess.* It was based on the classic Thomas Hardy novel of innocence destroyed, *Tess of the D'Urbervilles.* Polanski dedicated the movie to the memory of his murdered wife, Sharon Tate. *Tess* was followed by *Pirates,* a parody of the swashbuckling adventure films starring Errol Flynn that Polanski had enjoyed as a youth. Walter Matthau starred in the film as the comically villainous Captain Red, a role Polanski had written for Jack Nicholson. When *Pirates* failed at the box-office, Polanski returned to the cinema of fear with *Frantic,* a Hitchcock-style thriller with a Polanski touch, starring Harrison Ford. The story of a man inadvertently trapped in a nightmare situation in a foreign land, *Frantic* drew upon many of Polanski's favorite themes. But as a bid for critical and commercial success, it failed to repeat the performance of his earlier fear-films. The master of psychological suspense was not to be counted out yet, though. In 1992, Polanski bounced back with the film his fans had been clamoring for for years—a potent and powerful synthesis of all the absurdist comedies, parodies, thrillers, fear-films, and detective yarns Polanski had made in the past: *Bitter Moon.* He followed it up with the taut and well-reviewed but only modestly successful *Death and the Maiden.*

Roman Polanski's importance as a filmmaker hinges upon a uniquely unsettling point of view. All his characters try continually, however clumsily, to connect with other human beings, to break out of their isolation and to free themselves of their alienation. Could it be that his nightmarish films serve much the same purpose? Perhaps they too are the continuing efforts of a terrified young Jewish boy, adrift in a war-torn land, to connect with the rest of humanity—even after all these years.—J.P. TELOTTE and JOHN McCARTY

Pollack, Sydney

Nationality American. Born Lafayette, Indiana, 1 July 1934. Education South Bend Central High School; studied with Sanford Meisner, Neighborhood Playhouse, New York. Military Service U.S. Army, 1957-59. Family Married Claire Griswold, 1958, three children. Career Actor on Broadway and for TV, also acting instructor, from 1955; TV director in Los Angeles, from 1960; directed first film, 1965; also produced his own films, from 1975. Awards Emmy Award for The Game, *1966; Oscars for Best Film and Best Direction, for* Out of Africa, *1986.*

Films as Director: 1965: *The Slender Thread.* **1966:** *This Property Is Condemned.* **1968:** *The Swimmer* (Perry) (d one sequence only); *The Scalphunters.* **1969:** *Castle Keep; They Shoot Horses, Don't They?.* **1972:** *Jeremiah Johnson.* **1973:** *The Way We Were.* **1975:** *Three Days of the Condor; The Yakuza* (*Brotherhood of the Yakuza*) (+pr). **1976:** *Bobby Deerfield* (+pr). **1979:** *The Electric Horseman.* **1981:** *Absence of Malice* (+pr). **1982:** *Tootsie* (+co-pr, role as George Fields). **1985:** *Out of Africa* (+pr). **1990:** *Havana* (+co-pr). **1993:** *The Firm* (+pr). **1995:** *Sabrina* (+pr).

Other Films: 1961: *The Young Savages* (Frankenheimer) (dialogue coach). **1962:** *War Hunt* (Sanders) (role as Sergeant Van Horn). **1963:** *Il gattopardo* (*The Leopard*) (Visconti) (supervisor of dubbed American version). **1973:** *Scarecrow* (Schatzberg) (pr). **1980:** *Honeysuckle Rose* (Schatzberg) (exec pr). **1984:** *Songwriter* (Rudolph) (pr); *Sanford Meisner—The Theater's Best Kept Secret* (doc) (exec pr). **1988:** *Bright Lights, Big City* (Bridges) (pr). **1989:** *The Fabulous Baker Boys* (Kloves) (exec pr). **1990:** *Presumed Innocent* (Pakula) (pr); *White Palace* (Mandoki) (exec pr). **1992:** *The Player* (Altman) (role); *Death Becomes Her* (Zemeckis) (role); *Husbands and Wives* (Allen) (role). **1991:** *Dead Again* (Branagh) (exec pr); *King Ralph* (Ward) (exec pr). **1993:** *Flesh and Bone* (Kloves) (exec pr); *Searching for Bobby Fischer* (Zaillian) (exec pr). **1995:** *Sense and Sensibility* (Lee) (exec pr).

Sydney Pollack is especially noted for his ability to elicit fine performances from his actors and actresses and has worked with leading Hollywood stars, including Robert Redford (who has appeared in five Pollack films), Jane Fonda, Barbra Streisand, Dustin Hoffman, Paul Newman, and Burt Lancaster, among others. Though Pollack has treated a cross-section of Hollywood genres, the majority of his films divide into male-action dramas and female melodramas. Among the former are *The Scalphunters, Castle Keep, Jeremiah Johnson, Three Days of the Condor,* and *The Yakuza.* Among the latter are *The Slender Thread, This Property Is Condemned, The Way We Were,* and *Bobby Deerfield.*

The typical Pollack hero is a loner whose past interferes with his ability to function in the present. Throughout the course of the narrative, the hero comes to trust another individual and exchanges his isolation for a new relationship. For the most part, Pollack's heroines are intelligent women, often with careers, who possess moral strength, although in several cases they are victims of emotional weakness. Pollack is fond of portraying the attraction of opposites. The central issue in all of Pollack's work focuses on the conflict between cultural antagonists. This can be racial, as in *The Slender Thread, The Scalphunters,* or *Jeremiah Johnson* (black vs. white; white vs. Indian); religious, as in *The Way We Were* (Protestant vs. Jew); geographic, as in *This Property Is Condemned* and *The Electric Horseman* (city vs. town); nationalistic, as in *Castle Keep* (Europe vs. America; East vs. West); or based on gender differences, as in *Tootsie* (feminine vs. masculine).

Pollack's films do not possess a readily identifiable visual style. However, his works are generally noteworthy for their total visual effect, and he frequently utilizes the helicopter shot. Structurally the plots possess a circular form, often ending where they began. Visually this is

**Sydney Pollack on the set of *Sabrina*.
Photograph by Brian Hamill.**

echoed in the circular dance floor of *They Shoot Horses, Don't They?*, but is also apparent in *Jeremiah Johnson* and *The Way We Were*.

Along with Sidney Lumet, Pollack is one of Hollywood's foremost liberals. His work highlights social and political issues, exposing organized exploitation rather than individual villainy. Most prominent among the issues treated are racial discrimination (*The Scalphunters*), the destructiveness of war (*Castle Keep*), the Depression (*They Shoot Horses, Don't They?*), Hollywood blacklisting (*The Way We Were*), CIA activities (*Three Days of the Condor*), commercial exploitation (*The Electric Horseman*), media exploitation (*Absence of Malice*), and feminism (*Tootsie*). Although Pollack has often been attacked for using these themes as background, rather than delving deeply into their subtleties, the French critics, among others, hold his work in high esteem.

Over the years, Pollack's cache in the Hollywood community has steadily risen. Unlike Lumet, to whom his work and directorial approach bear many similarities, he is not a New York director who occasionally works in Hollywood, but a Hollywood insider. His films make money and score multiple Oscar nominations. He is instantly forgiven for a failure like *Havana,* his sweeping attempt to recall the filmmaking styles of the Old Hollywood and such pictures as *Casablanca.* Because of all this, an American Film Institute Life Achievement Award cannot be long in coming for him.

Pollack began his career as an actor and frequently appears, sometimes unbilled, in the films of other directors—though, ironically, not his own films a la Hitchcock (for whose legendary TV series Pollack both acted and directed). Woody Allen gave this former actor a particularly juicy part in *Husbands and Wives.*

But Pollack prefers to direct, and with his standing in the industry he is able to command big budgets and big stars—and choice properties—for his work. His *The Firm,* based on the runaway best-seller by lawyer turned novelist John Grisham, and starring Tom Cruise, was a sizable hit, the film's alteration of the book's ending not even a minus with Grisham fans. His latest, *Sabrina,* is, surprisingly, Pollack's first outright romantic comedy, a remake of the 1954 Billy Wilder gem, with Harrison Ford, Julia Ormond, and Greg Kinnear taking the respective roles of Humphrey Bogart, Audrey Hepburn, and William Holden.—PATRICIA ERENS and JOHN McCARTY

Polonsky, Abraham

Nationality American. *Born* Abraham Lincoln Polonsky in New York City, 5 December 1910. *Education* City College of New York; Columbia University, law degree. *Career* Lawyer with Manhattan firm, then quit to write; signed with Paramount, late 1930s; served in Europe with Office of Strategic Services (O.S.S.), World War II; moved to Enterprise Productions, 1947; directed first feature, 1948; spent year in France, 1949; signed with Twentieth Century-Fox, 1950; called to testify before House Un-American Activities Committee, invoked Fifth Amendment, 1951; blacklisted until 1968; also novelist.

Films as Director and Scriptwriter: 1948: *Force of Evil.* **1970:** *Tell Them Willie Boy Is Here.* **1971:** *Romance of a Horsethief.*

Other Films: 1947: *Golden Earrings* (Leisen) (sc); *Body and Soul* (Rossen) (sc). **1951:** *I Can Get It For You Wholesale* (Gordon) (sc). **1968:** *Madigan* (Siegel) (sc). **1979:** *Avalanche Express* (Robson) (sc). **1982:** *Monsignor* (sc). **1991:** *Guilty by Suspicion* (sc).

Abraham Lincoln Polonsky's filmography is quite thin: his second film as director, *Tell Them Willie Boy Is Here,* was released twenty-one years after his first, *Force of Evil.* "I was a left-winger," he told *Look* magazine in 1970. "I supported the Soviet Union. In the middle 1940s, we'd have meetings at my house to raise money for strikers and radical newspapers." For these crimes—and, equally, for the less-than-superficially patriotic qualities of his protagonists—a promising, perhaps even major, directorial career was squelched in its infancy by the insidious Hollywood blacklist.

A discussion of Polonsky would be incomplete without noting his collaborations with John Garfield, the American cinema's original anti-hero. Polonsky scripted *Body and Soul,* one of the best boxing films of all time, and both authored and directed *Force of Evil,* a "B film" ignored in its time, but now a cult classic highly regarded for its use of blank verse dialogue.

Garfield stars in *Force of Evil* as a lawyer immersed in the numbers racket. When his brother, a small-time gambler, is murdered by his gangster boss, he hunts the hood down and turns himself in to the police. In *Body and Soul,* the actor portrays a poor boy with a hard, knockout punch who rises in the fight game while alienating his family, friends, and the girl he loves. In the end he reforms, defying the mob by refusing to throw a fight. "What are you gonna do, kill me?" he chides the chief thug, "Everybody dies." With that, he walks off into the night with his girl. The final cut of *Body and Soul* is as much Polonsky's as it is director Robert Rossen's. Polonsky claimed to have prevented Rossen from altering the film's finale.

Both of Polonsky's protagonists become casualties of their desire for success. They seek out the all-American dream, but are corrupted in the process. They can only attain status by throwing fights, aligning themselves with lawbreakers. Fame and money, fancy hotels and snazzy suits, come not by hard work and honesty but by cheating, throwing the fight, fixing the books—the real American way.

Polonsky, and Garfield, were blacklisted as much for the tone of their films as their politics. Polonsky's heroes are cocky, cynical loner-losers, estranged from society's mainstream, who break the rules and cause others extreme sorrow—not the moral, honest, often comic-book caricatures of American manhood that dominated Hollywood cinema. In addition,

Polonsky created a character in *Body and Soul,* a washed-up boxer (lovingly played by Canada Lee), who was one of the earliest portraits of a black man as a human being with emotions and feelings, a man exploited. *Body and Soul* and *Force of Evil* played the nation's moviehouses in 1947 and 1948, when anything less than a positive vision of America was automatically suspect.

Polonsky's plight is particularly sad. His passport was revoked, and he could not escape to find work abroad. Years after others who had been blacklisted had returned to the good graces of the cinema establishment, he toiled in obscurity writing television shows and perhaps dozens of film scripts—some Academy Award winners—under assumed names. His first post-blacklist directorial credit, *Willie Boy,* is a spiritual cousin of his earlier work. It is the tale of a nonconformist Paiute Indian (Robert Blake, who played Garfield as a child in *Humoresque*), victimized by an insensitive society after he kills in self-defense. The parallels between Polonsky and his character's fate are clear.

Before the blacklist, Polonsky had hoped to film Thomas Mann's novella, *Mario and the Magician*; in 1971, he was again planning this project, among others. None was ever completed. But most significantly, the films that he might have made between 1948 and 1969—the prime years of his creative life—can now only be imagined.—ROB EDELMAN

Powell, Michael and Emeric Pressburger

*POWELL. **Nationality** British. **Born** Michael Latham Powell at Bekesbourne, near Canterbury, Kent, 30 September 1905. **Family** Married 1) Frances Reidy, 1943 (died 1983), two sons; 2) editor, Thelma Schoonmaker, 1984. **Career** Worked in various*

Michael Powell (left) and Emeric Pressburger

*capacities on films of Rex Ingram, Léonce Perret, Alfred Hitchcock, Lupu Pick, from 1922; director, from 1931; Senior Director in Residence, Zoetrope Studios, 1981. **Died** In Gloucestershire, 19 February 1990.*

***PRESSBURGER. Nationality** Hungarian/British. **Born** Imre Pressburger in Miskolc, Hungary, 5 December 1902. **Education** Studied at Universities of Prague and Stuttgart. **Career** Contract writer for UFA, Berlin, 1930, later in France and, from 1935, in England, for Alexander Korda's London Films. Powell and Pressburger began collaboration on The Spy in Black, 1939; formed "The Archers," as producing, directing, and writing team, 1942 (disbanded 1956); also set up Vega Productions Ltd. **Awards** (joint) British Film Institute Special Award, 1978; Fellowship, BAFTA, 1981; Fellowship, British Film Institute, 1983; (Powell) honorary doctorate, University of East Anglia, 1978; Golden Lion, Venice Festival, 1982. **Died** In Suffolk, 5 February 1988.*

Films by Powell and Pressburger: (Powell as director, Pressburger as scriptwriter) 1939: *The Spy in Black* (*U-Boat*). **1940:** *Contraband* (*Blackout*). **1941:** *49th Parallel* (*The Invaders*). **1942:** *One of Our Aircraft Is Missing*. **1972:** *The Boy Who Turned Yellow.*

(Produced, directed and scripted by "The Archers") 1943: *The Life and Death of Colonel Blimp; The Volunteer.* **1944:** *A Canterbury Tale.* **1945:** *I Know Where I'm Going.* **1946:** *A Matter of Life and Death* (*Stairway to Heaven*). **1947:** *Black Narcissus.* **1948:** *The Red Shoes.* **1949:** *The Small Back Room* (*Hour of Glory*). **1950:** *Gone to Earth* (*The Wild Heart*); *The Elusive Pimpernel* (*The Fighting Pimpernel*). **1951:** *The Tales of Hoffman.* **1955:** *Oh! Rosalinda* (*Fledermaus '55*). **1956:** *The Battle of the River Plate* (*Pursuit of the Graf Spee*); *Ill Met By Moonlight* (*Intelligence Service; Night Ambush*).

Other Films Directed by Powell: 1931: *Two Crowded Hours; My Friend the King; Rynox; The Rasp; The Star Reporter.* **1932:** *Hotel Splendide; C.O.D.; His Lordship; Born Lucky.* **1933:** *The Fire-Raisers* (+co-sc). **1934:** *The Night of the Party; Red Ensign* (+co-sc); *Something Always Happens; The Girl in the Crowd.* **1935:** *Lazybones; The Love Test; The Phantom Light; The Price of a Song; Someday.* **1936:** *The Man Behind the Mask; Crown Versus Stevens; Her Last Affair; The Brown Wallet.* **1937:** *Edge of the World* (+sc). **1939:** *The Lion Has Wings* (co-d). **1940:** *The Thief of Bagdad* (co-d). **1941:** *An Airman's Letter to His Mother* (short). **1955:** *The Sorceror's Apprentice* (short). **1956:** *Luna de miel* (*Honeymoon*) (+pr). **1960:** *Peeping Tom* (+pr, role). **1961:** *Queen's Guards* (+pr). **1964:** *Bluebeard's Castle.* **1966:** *They're a Weird Mob* (+pr). **1968:** *Sebastian* (Greene) (co-pr only). **1969:** *Age of Consent* (+pr). **1974:** *Trikimia* (*The Tempest*) (+pr, sc). **1978:** *Return of the Edge of the World* (doc for television) (+pr).

Other Films Written By Pressburger: 1953: *Twice Upon a Time* (+d, pr). **1957:** *Miracle in Soho* (Amyes) (+pr).

Between the years 1942 and 1957, English director Michael Powell and his Hungarian partner, Emeric Pressburger, formed one of the most remarkable partnerships in cinema. Under the collaborative pseudonym "The Archers," the two created a series of highly visual and imaginative treatments of romantic and supernatural themes that have defied easy categorization by film historians. Although both were listed jointly as director, screenwriter, and frequently as producer, and the extent of each one's participation on any given film is difficult to measure, it is probably most accurate to credit Powell with the actual visualization of the films, while Pressburger functioned primarily as a writer. The latter, in fact, had no background as a director before joining Powell. He had drifted through the Austrian, German, and French film industries as a screenwriter before traveling to England in 1936.

Many of the gothic, highly expressionistic characteristics of the films produced by the partnership seem to trace their origins to Powell's apprenticeship at Rex Ingram's studio in Nice in the 1920s. There he performed various roles on at least three of the visionary director's silent productions: *Mare Nostrum* (1926), *The Magician* (1926), and *The Garden of Allah* (1927). Working on these films and subsequently on his own features in the 1930s, Powell developed a penchant for expressionism that manifested itself in several rather unique ways. The most fundamental of these was in his use of the fantasy genre, as illustrated by *A Matter of Life and Death,* with its problematic juxtaposition of psychiatry and mysticism. Another manifestation was an almost philosophical sadism that permeated his later films, such as *Peeping Tom,* with a camera that impales its photographic subjects on bayonet-like legs. The mechanical camera itself, in fact, represents still another Powell motif: the use of machines and technology to create or heighten certain aspects of fantasy. For example, the camera obscura in *A Matter of Life and Death* and the German warship in the *Pursuit of the Graf Spee* (which is revealed through a slow camera scan along its eerie structure, causing it to turn into a metallic killer fish) effectively tie machines into each film's set of symbolic motifs. In doing so, a technological mythology is created in which these objects take on near-demonic proportions.

Finally, the use of color, which most critics cite as a trademark of the Powell-Pressburger partnership, is shaped into an expressionistic mode. Powell chose his hues from a broad visual palette, and brushed them onto the screen with a calculated extravagance that became integrated into the themes of the film as a whole. In the better films, the visual and technological aspects complement each other in a pattern of symbolism. The mechanical staircase which descends from the celestial vortex in *A Matter of Life and Death,* for example, blends technology and fantasy as no other image has. Similarly, when the camera replaces the young pilot's eye in the same film and the pink and violet lining of an eyelid descends over it, the effect is extravagant, even a bit bizarre, but it effectively serves notice that the viewer is closing his eyes to external reality and entering another world. The audience is left to decide whether that world is supernatural or psychological.

This world has been most palatable in popular Powell-Pressburger fantasies like *The Red Shoes,* a ballet film used as an allegory for the artist's unremitting dedication to his art; and *The Tales of Hoffman,* in which the moody eccentricities of style have been kept in bounds by the built-in circumscriptions of the fantasy genre. At least one critic, however, has noted a strange morbidity in *The Red Shoes* derived from the directors' use of certain peculiarities of color, a criticism that has been magnified when some of Powell's and Pressburger's fantastic techniques occur in more realistic films. Their appearance in otherwise veracious contexts usually upsets normal audience expectations. *Black Narcissus* and Powell's *Peeping Tom* both created some problems for critics, for both films went to extremes in the exaggeration of otherwise plausible storylines.

Thematically, Powell and Pressburger operate in a limbo somewhere between romance and realism. The former, characterized by technical effects, camera angles and movements, and the innovative use of color, often intrudes in the merest of details in fundamentally naturalistic films. In the eyes of some, this weakens the artistic commitment to realism. On the other hand, the psychological insights embodied in serious fantasies like *A Matter of Life and Death* are too often dismissed as simply entertainment. Most of the Powell-Pressburger efforts are, in fact, attempts at fundamental reconciliations between modern ideas and the irrational, between science and savagery, or between religion and eroticism. This dichotomy usually occurs in one character's mind—as with Peter Carter in *A Matter of Life and Death* or the sex-obsessed nun in *Black Narcissus*—and hinges upon a second character such as *A Matter of Life and Death*'s Dr.

Frank Reeves, who effects a degree of movement between the two sides of the dichotomy, particularly through his own death.

Although such mergings of reality and fantasy met with approval by the moviegoing public, Powell and Pressburger were less successful with the British film establishment. In a sense they were alienated from it through their exercise of a decidedly non-British flamboyance. To some degree, the Clive Candy character in *The Life and Death of Colonel Blimp* embodies the British film community during the period after the war. Powell and Pressburger's visual and thematic extravagances of style conflicted with the self-consciousness of the film industry's strivings for a rigid postwar realism not to be embellished by colorful and expressionistic ventures.

The team broke up in 1957 after *Ill Met by Moonlight,* and although Pressburger subsequently made some films by himself, they were not well received. Powell, though, continued in the vein established by his collaboration with the Hungarian director. *Luna de Miel* and *The Queen's Guards* pursue all of the philosophical concerns of his earlier efforts, while *Peeping Tom,* which is now regarded as his masterpiece, indicates a certain morbid refinement of his thematic interests. Unfortunately, the film was perhaps ahead of its time—a problem that plagued the director and his collaborator for most of their careers.—STEPHEN L. HANSON

Preminger, Otto

Nationality *American.* **Born** *Vienna, 5 December 1905, became U.S. citizen, 1943.* **Education** *University of Vienna, LL.D, 1926.* **Family** *Married 1) Marion Deutsch (stage name Marion Mill), 1932 (divorced); 2) Mary Gardner, 1951 (divorced 1959); 3) Hope (Preminger), 1960, two children; also one son by Gypsy Rose Lee.* **Career** *Actor with Max Reinhardt company, 1924; joined theater in der Josefstadt, 1928 (succeeding Reinhardt as director, 1933); invited to Hollywood by Joseph Schenck, 1935; contract with Fox broken, moved to New York, 1937; director on Broadway, 1938-41 (and later); returned to Hollywood as actor, 1942; signed seven-year contract with Fox, 1945; independent producer, from early 1950s.* **Died** *Of cancer, in New York City, 23 April 1986.*

Films as Director: **1931:** *Die grosse Liebe.* **1936:** *Under Your Spell.* **1937:** *Danger, Love at Work.* **1943:** *Margin for Error* (+role as Nazi consul Rudolf Forster). **1944:** *In the Meantime, Darling* (+pr); *Laura* (+pr). **1945:** *Royal Scandal; Fallen Angel* (+pr). **1946:** *Centennial Summer* (+pr). **1947:** *Forever Amber; Daisy Kenyon* (+pr). **1948:** *That Lady in Ermine.* **1949:** *The Fan (Lady Windermere's Fan)* (+pr); *Whirlpool* (+pr). **1950:** *Where the Sidewalk Ends* (+pr); *The Thirteenth Letter* (+pr). **1952:** *Angel Face.* **1953:** *The Moon Is Blue* (+co-pr). **1954:** *River of No Return; Carmen Jones* (+pr). **1955:** *The Man with the Golden Arm* (+pr); *The Court Martial of Billy Mitchell (One Man Mutiny).* **1957:** *Saint Joan* (+pr); *Bonjour Tristesse* (+pr). **1959:** *Porgy and Bess; Anatomy of a Murder* (+pr). **1960:** *Exodus* (+pr). **1962:** *Advise and Consent* (+pr). **1963:** *The Cardinal* (+pr). **1964:** *In Harm's Way* (+pr). **1965:** *Bunny Lake Is Missing* (+pr). **1966:** *Hurry Sundown* (+pr). **1968:** *Skidoo* (+pr). **1970:** *Tell Me That You Love Me, Junie Moon* (+pr). **1971:** *Such Good Friends* (+pr). **1975:** *Rosebud* (+pr). **1980:** *The Human Factor* (+pr).

Other Films: **1942:** *The Pied Piper* (role); *They Got Me Covered* (role). **1945:** *Where Do We Go from Here* (role). **1953:** *Stalag 17* (Wilder) (role as camp commandant). **1981:** *Unsere Leichen Leben Noch* (Von Prauheim) (role).

Otto Preminger

The public persona of Austrian-born Otto Preminger has epitomized for many the typical Hollywood movie director: an accented, autocratic, European-born disciplinarian who terrorized his actors, bullied his subordinates, and spent millions of dollars to ensure that his films be produced properly, although economically. Before the *Cahiers du Cinéma* critics began to praise Preminger, it may have been this public persona, more than anything else, which impeded an appreciation of Preminger's extraordinarily subtle style or thematic consistencies.

Preminger's career can be divided into two periods. Throughout the first period, Preminger worked as a studio director for Twentieth Century-Fox, where he had several well-publicized conflicts with Darryl F. Zanuck and found it difficult to conform to studio demands or to collaborate without retaining overall artistic control. His evocative and romantic mystery *Laura,* his breakthrough film, was produced during this period. Among the other eclectic assignments he directed at Fox, the most interesting include a series of film noir features in the late 1940s: *Whirlpool, Where the Sidewalk Ends, The Thirteenth Letter,* and *Angel Face.*

Throughout the second and far more interesting period of Preminger's career, Preminger worked as one of the first notable independent producer-directors, in the process successfully undermining the studio system in various ways. He fought against institutional censorship by releasing several films without the Motion Picture Association seal (for example, *The Moon is Blue*) and he explored controversial subjects the studios might have been hesitant to touch (such as criticism of the War Department in *The Court Martial of Billy Mitchell* or homosexuality in *Advise and Consent*). Preminger also championed the independent producers movement by exploiting the Paramount Divorcement Decree and aggressively marketing and arranging exhibition for his films

Preminger incorporated fresh and authentic backgrounds by promoting location shooting away from Hollywood. He worked diligently to discover new performers (such as Jean Seberg) and to develop properties (such as *Carmen Jones* and *Hurry Sundown*) which would allow the casting of Hollywood's under-used black performers. Finally, he even helped to break the studio blacklist by hiring and publicly crediting Dalton Trumbo as screenwriter on *Exodus.*

Preminger's tastes have always been as eclectic as the disparate sources from which his films have been adapted. Throughout the 1950s and 1960s, however, Preminger's films grew in pretention, displaying considerable interest in monolithic institutions (the military in *The Court Martial of Billy Mitchell* and *In Harms's Way*; the Senate in *Advise and Consent*; the Catholic Church in *The Cardinal*; the medical profession in *Such Good Friends*) as well as the examination of social and political problems (drug addiction in *The Man with the Golden Arm*;

Jewish repatriation in *Exodus*; racial prejudice in *Hurry, Sundown*; political terrorism in *Rosebud*). A consistent archetype in Preminger's films is the quest for truth; indeed, the director's recurring image is the courtroom.

What has especially fascinated Preminger's admirers is the subtlety of his mise-en-scène; his most typical effort is a widescreen film with long takes, no pyrotechnical montage, few reaction shots, fluid and simple camera movements, and careful yet unselfconscious compositions. Preminger's style, though apparently invisible, is one which forces the audience to examine, to discern, to arrive at some ultimate position. Several critics have written persuasively on the ambiguity associated with Preminger's apparent objectivity, including Andrew Sarris, who has characterized Preminger as a "director who sees all problems and issues as a single-take two-shot, the stylistic expression of the eternal conflict, not between right and wrong, but between the right-wrong on one side and the right-wrong on the other, a representation of the right-wrong in all of us as our share of the human condition."

If Preminger's formula floundered in the 1970s and 1980s, an era in which the American cinema seemed dominated by mainstream genre works and overt escapism, one cannot help but feel nostalgia and profound respect for Preminger's serious subjects and artistry. Indeed, his series of films beginning with *Bonjour, Tristesse* in 1957 and continuing through *Porgy and Bess, Anatomy of a Murder, Exodus, Advise and Consent, The Cardinal, In Harm's Way, Bunny Lake Is Missing*, and *Hurry, Sundown* in 1966, constitute one of the longest strings of ambitious, provocative films in American cinema.—CHARLES DERRY

Pudovkin, Vsevolod

Nationality *Russian.* **Born** *Vsevolod Illarionovitch Pudovkin in Penza, 16 February 1893.* **Education** *Educated in physics and chemistry, Moscow University; entered State Cinema School, 1920.* **Military Service** *Enlisted in artillery, 1914; wounded and taken prisoner, 1915; escaped and returned to Moscow, 1918.* **Family** *Married actress and journalist Anna Zemtsova, 1923.* **Career** *Worked as writer and chemist, 1919-20; worked on agit films, 1920-21; student at Lev Kuleshov's studio, from 1922; quit State Cinema Institute to join Kuleshov's Experimental Laboratory, 1923; began collaboration with cinematographer Anatoly Golovnia and scriptwriter Nathan Zarkhi, 1925; with Alexandrov, signed Eisenstein's "Manifesto on Audio-Visual Counterpoint," 1928; travelled to England and Holland, 1929; joined Communist Party, 1932; after car accident, taught theoretic studies at V.G.I.K., 1935; joined Mosfilm studios, 1938.* **Award** *Order of Lenin, 1935.* **Died** *In Riga, 30 June 1953.*

Films as Director: 1921: *Golod . . . golod . . . golod (Hunger . . . Hunger . . . Hunger)* (co-d, co-sc, role). **1925:** *Shakhmatnaya goryachka (Chess Fever)* (co-d). **1926:** *Mekhanikha golovnovo mozga (Mechanics of the Brain)* (+sc); *Mat (Mother).* **1927:** *Konyets Sankt-Peterburga (The End of St. Petersburg).* **1928:** *Potomok Chingis-khan (The Heir to Genghis-Khan; Storm Over Asia).* **1932:** *Prostoi sluchai (A Simple Case)* (revised version of *Otchen kharacho dzivioata (Life's Very Good)*; first screened in 1930). **1933:** *Dezertir (Deserter).* **1938:** *Pobeda (Victory)* (co-d). **1939:** *Minin i Pozharsky* (co-d). **1940:** *Kino za XX liet (Twenty Years of Cinema)* (co-d, co-ed). **1941:** *Suvorov* (co-d); *Pir v Girmunka (Feast at Zhirmunka)* (co-d) (for "Fighting Film Album"). **1942:** *Ubitzi vykhodyat na dorogu (Murderers Are on Their Way)* (co-d, co-sc). **1943:** *Vo imya rodini (In the Name of the Fatherland)* (co-d). **1946:** *Amiral Nakhimov* (*Admiral Nakhimov*). **1948:** *Tri vstrechi* (*Three Encounters*) (co-d). **1950:** *Yukovsky* (co-d). **1953:** *Vozvrachenia Vassilya Bortnikov* (*The Return of Vasili Bortnikov*).

Other Films: 1920: *V dni borbi* (*In the Days of Struggle*) (role). **1921:** *Serp i molot* (*Sickle and Hammer*) (asst d, role). **1923:** *Slesar i kantzler* (*Locksmith and Chancellor*) (co-sc). **1924:** *Neobychainye priklucheniya Mistera Vesta v stranye bolshevikov* (*Extraordinary Adventures of Mr. West in the Land of the Bolsheviks*) (Kuleshov) (co-sc, asst, role as the 'Count'). **1925:** *Luch smerti* (*The Death Ray*) (Kuleshov) (design, role); *Kirpitchiki* (*Little Bricks*) (role). **1928:** *Zhivoi trup* (*A Living Corpse*) (role as Feodor Protassov). **1929:** *Vessiolaia kanareika* (*The Cheerful Canary*) (role as the illusionist); *Novyi vavilon* (*The New Babylon*) (Kozintsev and Trauberg) (role as shop assistant). **1944:** *Ivan Grozny* (*Ivan the Terrible*) (Eisenstein) (role as Nikolai the fanatic).

Vsevolod Illarionovitch Pudovkin's major contribution to the cinema is as a theorist. He was fascinated by the efforts of his teacher, the filmmaker Lev Kuleshov, in exploring the effects of montage. As Pudovkin eventually did in his own work, Kuleshov often created highly emotional moments by rapidly intercutting shots of diverse content. Of course, the results could be manipulated. In *The End of St. Petersburg,* for instance, Pudovkin mixed together shots of stock market speculation with those depicting war casualties. Occasionally, Pudovkin's images are uninspired: the above sequence looks static, even simplistic, today. Nevertheless, while other filmmakers may have advanced this technique, Pudovkin was one of the first to utilize it in a narrative.

Pudovkin's essays on film theory, "The Film Scenario" and "Film Director and Film Material," remain just as valuable as any of his works; these texts have become primers in film technique. Pudovkin wrote that it is unnecessary for a film actor to overperform or overgesture as he might in the theater. He can underplay in a film because the director or editor, via montage, is able to communicate to the viewer the pervading feeling in the shots surrounding the actor. Meanwhile, the actor may concentrate on his or her internal emotions, transmitting the truths of the character in a more subtle manner.

Beyond this, contended Pudovkin, an actor on screen is at the mercy of his director. The performer could be directed to cry without knowing his character's motivations; the shots placed around him will pass along the cause of his grief. A non-actor could even be made to give a realistic performance as a result of perceptive editing. Pudovkin often integrated his casts with both actors and non-actors; the latter were utilized when he felt the need for realism was greater than the need for actors with the ability to perform. In *Chess Fever,* a two-reel comedy, Pudovkin even edited in shots of Jose Raoul Capablanca, a famous chess master, to make him seem an active participant in the scenario. As the filmmaker explained, "the foundation of film art is editing." He noted that "the film is not shot, but built up from separate strips of celluloid that are its raw material."

Pudovkin's first significant credit, *The Death Ray,* was directed by Kuleshov. But he designed the production, wrote the scenario, assisted his teacher, and acted in the film. Before the end of the 1920s, he completed his three great silent features, which remain his best-remembered films: *Mother, The End of St. Petersburg,* and *The Heir to Genghis-Khan*. While they were each concerned with various aspects of the Revolution, they are not totally propagandistic: each film deals with human involvements, conflicts, and the effect that ideas and actions have on the lives of those involved. This is illustrated perfectly in *Mother,* based on a Maxim Gorky novel. Set during the 1905 Revolution, the film chronicles the plight of the title character (Vera Baranovskaya), who accidentally causes her politically active worker son (Nikolai Batalov) to be sentenced to prison. Eventually, Batalov is shot during an escape attempt and Baranovskaya, whose political consciousness has been raised, is trampled to death by the cavalry attacking a workers' protest.

Baranovskaya also appears in *The End of St. Petersburg,* filmed to mark the tenth anniversary of the 1917 Revolution. The work centers on the political education of an inexperienced young peasant (Ivan Chuvelyov). This film is significant in that it is one of the first to satisfactorily blend a fictional scenario into a factual setting. Typically, Pudovkin cast real pre-Revolution stockbrokers and executives as stockbrokers and executives.

The Heir to Genghis-Khan (more commonly known as *Storm Over Asia*) is not as successful as the others, but is still worthy of note. The film, set in Central Asia, details the activities of partisan revolutionaries and the English army of occupation in Mongolia (called the White Russian army in foreign prints). It focuses on a young Mongol trapper (Valeri Inkizhinov) whose fate is not dissimilar to that of Pudovkin's other heroes and heroines: he is radicalized by unfolding events after he is cheated out of a prized fox fur by a European merchant.

Vsevolod Pudovkin.
Photograph by Bob Hawkins.

Pudovkin continued making films after the advent of sound. *A Simple Case,* revised from his silent *Life's Very Good,* was scheduled to be the Soviet cinema's first sound feature; instead, the honor went to Nikolai Ekk's *The Road to Life.* Pudovkin was not content to just add sound to his scenarios. His initial talkie was *Deserter,* in which he experimented with speech patterns: by editing in sound, he contrasted the conversational dialogue of different characters with crowd noises, traffic sounds, sirens, music, and even silence. But Pudovkin did not abandon his concern for visuals: *Deserter* contains approximately three thousand separate shots, an unusually high number for a feature film.

Pudovkin did make other sound films. His *Minin and Pozharsky,* released at the beginning of World War II, takes place in the seventeenth century, when Moscow was controlled by King Sigismund; it was the first major Soviet film to depict Poland as an invader. Nevertheless, his cinematic language is essentially one that is devoid of words, relying instead on visual components.—ROB EDELMAN

Ray, Nicholas

Nationality *American.* **Born** *Raymond Nicholas Kienzle in Galesville, Wisconsin, 7 August 1911.* **Education** *Educated in architecture and theater, University of Chicago.* **Family** *Married 1) Jean Evans, 1930 (divorced); 2) Gloria Grahame, 1948 (divorced 1952); 3) dancer Betty Schwab (divorced); 4) Susan (Ray), four children.* **Career** *Director, Frank Lloyd Wright's Taliesin Playhouse, early 1930s; in Theater of Action, 1935-37; joined John Houseman's Phoenix Theater, accident results in loss of sight in right eye, 1938; named War Information Radio Program Director by Houseman, 1942; director on Broadway, 1943; assistant to Elia Kazan in Hollywood, 1944; directed first film,* They Live By Night, *1948; walked off set of* 55 Days at Peking, *moved to Paris, 1962; teacher of filmmaking at State University of New York, Binghamton, 1971-73.* **Died** *In New York, 16 June 1979.*

Films as Director: 1948: *They Live By Night* (first released in Britain as *The Twisted Road*, U.S. release 1949); *A Woman's Secret.* **1949:** *Knock on Any Door.* **1950:** *In a Lonely Place; Born to Be Bad.* **1951:** *The Flying Leathernecks.* **1952:** *On Dangerous Ground; The Lusty Men.* **1954:** *Johnny Guitar.* **1955:** *Run for Cover; Rebel without a Cause* (+story). **1956:** *Hot Blood; Bigger Than Life.* **1957:** *The True Story of Jesse James; Bitter Victory* (+co-sc). **1958:** *Wind Across the Everglades; Party Girl.* **1959:** *The Savage Innocents* (+sc). **1961:** *King of Kings.* **1963:** *55 Days at Peking* (co-d). **1975:** *You Can't Go Home Again* (+sc, unfinished). **1981:** *Lightning over Water* (*Nick's Movie*) (co-d, role as himself).

Other Films: 1977: *Der Amerikanische Freund* (*The American Friend*) (Wenders) (role). **1979:** *Hair* (Forman) (role).

Godard's magisterial statement, "the cinema is Nicholas Ray," has come in for a good deal of ridicule, not by any means entirely undeserved. Yet it contains a core of truth, especially if taken in reverse. Nicholas Ray is cinema in the sense that his films work entirely (and perhaps only) as *movies,* arrangements of space and movement charged with dramatic tension. Few directors demonstrate more clearly that a film is something beyond the sum of its parts. Consider only the more literary components—dialogue, plot, characterisation—and a film like *Party Girl* is patently trash. But on the screen the visual turbulence of Ray's shooting style, the fractured intensity of his editing, fuse the elements into a valid emotional whole. The flaws are still apparent, but have become incidental.

Nor is Ray's cinematic style in any way extraneous, imposed upon his subjects. The nervous tension within the frame also informs his characters, vulnerable violent outsiders at odds with society and with themselves. The typical Ray hero is a loner, at once contemptuous of the complacent normal world and tormented with a longing to be reaccepted into it—to become (like Bowie and Keechie, the young lovers of *They Live by Night*) "like real people." James Dean in *Rebel without a Cause,* Robert Ryan in *On Dangerous Ground,* Robert Mitchum in *The Lusty Men,* all start by rejecting the constraints of the nuclear family, only to find themselves impelled to recreate it in substitute form, as though trying to fill an unacknowledged void. In one achingly elegiac scene in *The Lusty Men,* Mitchum prowls around the tumbledown shack that was his childhood home, "looking for something I thought I'd lost."

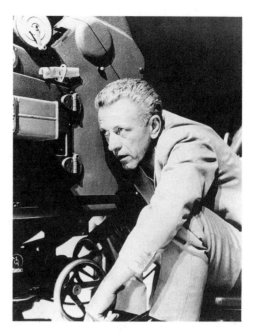

Nicholas Ray

Ray's grounding in architecture (he studied at Taliesin with Frank Lloyd Wright) reveals itself in an exceptionally acute sense of space, often deployed as an extension of states of mind. In his films the geometry of locations, and especially interiors, serves as a psychological terrain. Conflict can be played out, and tension expressed, in terms of spatial areas (upstairs and downstairs, for example, or the courtyards and levels of an apartment complex) pitted against each other. Ray also credited Wright with instilling in him "a love of the horizontal line"—and hence of the CinemaScope screen, for which he felt intuitive affinity. Unlike many of his contemporaries, who found it awkward and inhibiting, Ray avidly explores the format's potential, sometimes combining it with lateral tracking shots to convey lyrical movement, at other times angling his camera to create urgent diagonals, suggesting characters straining against the constrictions of the frame.

Equally idiosyncratic is Ray's expressionist use of colour, taken at times to heights of delirium that risk toppling into the ridiculous. In *Johnny Guitar,* perhaps the most flamboyantly baroque Western ever made, Joan Crawford is colour-coded red, white, or black according to which aspect of her character—whore, victim, or gunslinger—is uppermost in a given scene. Similarly, the contrast in *Bigger Than Life* between the hero's respectable job as a schoolteacher and his déclassé moonlighting for a taxi firm is signalled by an abrupt cut from the muted grey-browns of the school to a screenful of gaudy yellow cabs that hit the audience's eyes with a visual slap.

Nearly all Ray's finest films were made in the 1950s, their agonized romanticism cutting across the grain of that decade's brittle optimism. "The poet of American disenchantment" (in David Thomson's phrase), Ray viewed social conventions as a trap, from which violence or madness may be the only escape. In *Bigger Than Life,* James Mason's smalltown teacher, frustrated by his low social status, gains the feelings of power and superiority he aspires to from a nerve drug. Under its influence the character is transformed into a hideous parody of the dominant father-figure enjoined by society. Similarly—but working from the opposite perspective—*In a Lonely Place* subverts Bogart's tough-guy persona, revealing the anguish and insecurity that underlie it and, as V.F. Perkins puts it, making "violence the index of the character's weakness rather than strength."

"I'm a stranger here myself." Ray often quoted Sterling Hayden's line from *Johnny Guitar* as his personal motto. His career, as he himself was well aware, disconcertingly mirrored the fate of his own riven, alienated heroes. Unappreciated (or so he felt) in America, and increasingly irked by the constraints of the studio system, he nonetheless produced all his best work there. In Europe, where he was hailed as one of the world's greatest directors, his craft deserted him: after two ill-starred epics, the last sixteen years of his life trickled away in a mess of incoherent footage and abortive projects. Victim of his own legend, Ray finally took self-identification with his protagonists to its ultimate tortured conclusion—collaborating, in *Lightning Over Water,* in the filming of his own disintegration and death.—PHILIP KEMP

Ray, Satyajit

Nationality Indian. *Born* Calcutta, 2 May 1921. *Education* Attended Ballygunj Government School; Presidency College, University of Calcutta, B.A. in economics (with honors), 1940; studied painting at University of Santiniketan, 1940-43. *Family* Married

Bijoya Das, 1949; one son. **Career** Commercial artist for D. J. Keymer advertising agency, Calcutta, 1943; co-founder, Calcutta Film Society, 1947; met Jean Renoir making The River, 1950; completed first film, Pather Panchali, 1955; composed own music, from Teen Kanya (1961) on; made first film in Hindi (as opposed to Bengali), The Chess Players, 1977; editor and illustrator for children's magazine Sandesh, 1980s. **Awards** Grand Prize, Cannes Festival, 1956, Golden Gate Award, San Francisco International Film Festival, 1957, Film Critics Award, Stratford Festival, 1958, and President of India Gold Medal, all for Pather Panchali; Gold Lion, Venice Festival, 1957, Best Direction, San Francisco International Film Festival, 1958, and President of India Gold Medal, all for Aparajito; Selznick Award and Sutherland Trophy, 1960, for Apur Sansar; Silver Bear for Best Direction, Berlin Festival, for Mahanagar, 1964, and for Charulata, 1965; Special Award of Honour, Berlin Festival, 1966; Decorated Order Yugoslav Flag, 1971; Golden Bear Award, Berlin Film Festival, 1973, for Distant Thunder; D.Litt, Oxford University, 1978; Life Fellow, British Film Institute, 1983; Legion of Honour, France, 1989; Indian Awards, Best Picture and Best Director, 1991, for Agantuk; Academy Award for lifetime achievement in cinema, 1992. **Died** Of heart failure, 23 April 1992, in Calcutta.

Films as Director and Scriptwriter: 1955: Pather Panchali (Father Panchali) (+pr). **1956:** Aparajito (The Unvanquished) (+pr). **1957:** Parash Pathar (The Philosopher's Stone). **1958:** Jalsaghar (The Music Room) (+pr). **1959:** Apur Sansar (The World of Apu) (+pr). **1960:** Devi (The Goddess) (+pr, mus). **1961:** Teen Kanya (Two Daughters) (+pr); Rabindranath Tagore (doc). **1962:** Abhijan (Expedition); Kanchanjanga (+pr). **1963:** Mahanagar (The Big City). **1964:** Charulata (The Lonely Wife). **1965:** Kapurush-o-Mahapurush (The Coward and the Saint); Two (short). **1966:** Nayak (The Hero). **1967:** Chiriakhana (The Zoo). **1969:** Goopy Gyne Bagha Byne (The Adventures of Goopy and Bagha). **1970:** Pratidwandi (The Adversary); Aranyer Din Ratri (Days and Nights in the Forest). **1971:** Seemabaddha; Sikkim (doc). **1972:** The Inner Eye (doc). **1973:** Asani Sanket (Distant Thunder). **1974:** Sonar Kella (The Golden Fortress). **1975:** Jana Aranya (The Middleman). **1976:** Bala (doc). **1977:** Shatranj Ke Khilari (The Chess Players). **1978:** Joi Baba Felunath (The Elephant God). **1979:** Heerak Rajar Deshe (The Kingdom of Diamonds). **1981:** Sadgati (Deliverance) (for TV); Pikoo (short). **1984:** Ghare Bahire (The Home and the World) (+pr, mus). **1989:** Ganashatru (An Enemy of the People). **1990:** Shakha Proshakha (Branches of the Tree). **1991:** Agantuk (The Visitor).

From the beginning of his career as a filmmaker, Satyajit Ray was interested in finding ways to reveal the mind and thoughts of his characters. Because the range of his sympathy was wide, he has been accused of softening the presence of evil in his cinematic world. But a director who aims to represent the currents and cross-currents of feeling within people is likely to disclose to viewers the humanness even in reprehensible figures. In any case, from the first films of his early period, Ray devised strategies for rendering inner lives; he simplified the surface action of the film so that the viewer's attention travels to (1) the reaction of people to one another, or to their environments, (2) the mood expressed by natural scenery or objects, and (3) music as a clue to the state of mind of a character. In the *Apu Trilogy* the camera often stays with one of two characters after the other character exits the frame to see their silent response. Or else, after some significant event in the narrative, Ray presents correlatives of that event in the natural world. When the impoverished wife in *Pather Panchali* receives a postcard bearing happy news from her husband, the scene dissolves to water skates dancing on a pond. As for music, in his films Ray commissioned compositions from India's best classical musicians—Ravi Shankar, Vilayat Khan, Ali Akbar Khan—but since *Teen Kanya* composed his own music and progressed towards quieter indication through music of the emotional experience of his characters.

Ray's work can be divided into three periods on the basis of his cinematic practice: the early period, 1955-66, from *Pather Panchali* through *Nayak*; the middle period, 1969-77, from *Googy Gyne Bagha Byne* through *Shatranj Ke Khilari*; and the final period, from *Joy Baba Felunath* and through *Sadgati* and *Ghare Bahire*. The early period is characterized by thoroughgoing realism: the mise-en-scène are rendered in deep focus; long takes and slow camera movements prevail. The editing is subtle, following shifts of narrative interest and cutting on action in the Hollywood style. Ray's emphasis in the early period on capturing reality is obvious in *Kanchanjangha*, in which 100 minutes in the lives of characters are rendered in 100 minutes of film time. *The Apu Trilogy, Parash Pather, Jalsaghar,* and *Devi* all exemplify what Ray had learned from Hollywood's studio era, from Renoir's mise-en-scène, and from the use of classical music in Indian cinema. *Charulata* affords the archetypal example of Ray's early style, with the decor, the music, the long takes, the activation of various planes of depth within a composition, and the reaction shots all contributing significantly to a representation of the lonely wife's inner conflicts. The power of Ray's early films comes from his ability to suggest deep feeling by arranging the surface elements of his films unemphatically.

Ray's middle period is characterized by increasing complexity of style; to his skills at understatement Ray adds a sharp use of montage. The difference in effect between an early film and a middle film becomes apparent if one compares the early *Mahanagar* with the middle *Jana Aranya,* both films pertaining to life in Calcutta. In *Mahanagar,* the protagonist chooses to resign her job in order to protest the unjust dismissal of a colleague. The film affirms the rightness of her decision. In the closing sequence, the protagonist looks up at the tall towers of Calcutta and says to her husband so that we believe her, "What a big city! Full of jobs! There must be something somewhere for one of us!" Ten years later, in *Jana Aranya,* it is clear that there are no jobs and that there is precious little room to worry about niceties of justice and injustice. The darkness running under the pleasant facade of many of the middle films seems to derive from the turn in Indian politics after the death of Nehru. Within Bengal, many ardent young people joined a Maoist movement to destroy existing institutions, and more were themselves destroyed by a ruthless police force. Across India, politicians abandoned Nehru's commitment to a socialist democracy in favor of a scramble for personal power. In *Seemabaddha* or *Aranyer Din Ratri* Ray's editing is sharp but not startling. In *Shatranj Ke Khilari,* on the other hand, Ray's irony is barely restrained: he cuts from the blue haze of a Nawab's music room to a gambling scene in the city. In harsh daylight, commoners lay bets on fighting rams, as intent on their gambling as the Nawab was on his music.

Audiences in India who have responded warmly to Ray's early films have sometimes been troubled by the complexity of his middle films. A film like *Shatranj Ke Khilari* was expected by many viewers to reconstruct the splendors of Moghul India as the early *Jalsaghar* had reconstructed the sensitivity of Bengali feudal landlords and *Charulata* the decency of upper class Victorian Bengal. What the audience found instead was a stern examination of the sources of Indian decadence. According to Ray, the British seemed less to blame for their role than the Indians who demeaned themselves by colluding with the British or by ignoring the public good and plunging into private pleasures. Ray's point of view in *Shatranj* was not popular with distributors and so his first Hindi film was denied fair exhibition in many cities in India.

Ray's late style, most evident in the short features *Pikoo* and *Sadgati*, pays less attention than earlier to building a stable geography and a firm time scheme. The exposition of characters and situations is swift: the effect is of great concision. In *Pikoo,* a young boy is sent outside to sketch flowers so that his mother and her lover can pursue their affair indoors. The lover has brought along a drawing pad and colored pens to divert the boy. The boy has twelve colored pens in his packet with which he must represent on paper the wealth of colors in nature. In a key scene (lasting ten seconds) the boy looks at a flower, then down at his packet for a matching color. Through that action of the boy's looking to match the world with his means, Ray suggests the striving in his own work to render the depth and range of human experience.

In focussing on inner lives and on human relations as the ground of social and political systems, Ray continued the humanist tradition of Rabindranath Tagore. Ray studied at Santiniketan, the university founded by Tagore, and was close to the poet during his last years. Ray acknowledged his debt in a lyrical documentary about Tagore, and through the Tagore stories on which he has based his films *Teen Kanya*, *Charulata*, and *Ghare Bahire*. As the poet Tagore was his example, Ray has become an example to important younger filmmakers (such as Shyam Benegal, M. S. Sathyu, G. Aravindan), who have learned from him how to reveal in small domestic situations the working of larger political and cultural forces.—SATTI KHANNA

Reed, Carol

Nationality British. **Born** Putney, London, 30 December 1906, son of actor Herbert Beerbohm Tree. **Education** King's School, Canterbury. **Family** Married 1) Diana Wynyard (divorced); 2) actress Penelope Ward, two sons. **Career** Actor on London stage, from 1924; dramatic advisor to author Edgar Wallace, 1927; stage director, from 1929; dialogue director for Associated Talking Pictures, 1932; directed first feature, 1933; served

Carol Reed (right) with (l-r) Bernard Lee and Joseph Cotten on the set of *The Third Man*.

*in British Army Film Unit, World War II; began collaboration with writer Graham Greene, 1946. **Awards** Best British Film Award, British Film Academy, for Odd Man Out, 1947; Best British Film Award, British Film Academy, and Best Direction, New York Film Critics, for The Fallen Idol, 1948; Best British Film Award, British Film Academy, and Quarterly Award, Directors Guild of America, for The Third Man, 1949; Knighted, 1952; Oscar for Best Director, for Oliver!, 1968. **Died** In London, 1976.*

Films as Director: 1933: *Midshipman Easy (Men of the Sea).* **1936:** *Laburnum Grove; Talk of the Devil* (+story). **1937:** *Who's Your Lady Friend?.* **1938:** *Bank Holiday (Three on a Week-End); Penny Paradise.* **1939:** *Climbing High; A Girl Must Live; The Stars Look Down.* **1940:** *Night Train to Munich (Night Train); The Girl in the News.* **1941:** *Kipps (The Remarkable Mr. Kipps); A Letter from Home* (short documentary). **1942:** *The Young Mr. Pitt; The New Lot.* **1944:** *The Way Ahead.* **1945:** *The True Glory* (collaboration with Garson Kanin). **1947:** *Odd Man Out.* **1948:** *The Fallen Idol.* **1949:** *The Third Man.* **1951:** *Outcast of the Islands.* **1953:** *The Man Between.* **1955:** *A Kid for Two Farthings.* **1956:** *Trapeze.* **1958:** *The Key.* **1960:** *Our Man in Havana.* **1963:** *The Running Man* (+pr). **1965:** *The Agony and the Ecstasy* (+pr). **1968:** *Oliver!.* **1970:** *Flap.* **1972:** *Follow Me (The Public Eye).*

Other Film: 1937: *No Parking* (Raymond) (story).

Carol Reed came to films from the theater, where he worked as an assistant to Edgar Wallace. He served his apprenticeship in the film industry first as a dialogue director, and then graduated to the director's chair via a series of low-budget second features.

Reed's early films, such as *Midshipman Easy,* are not remarkable, but few British films before World War II were. In the 1920s and 1930s British distributors were more interested in importing films from abroad, especially from America, than in encouraging film production at home. As a result British films were, with rare exceptions, bargain-basement imitations of Hollywood movies. In 1938, however, the British government stipulated that producers must allocate sufficient funds for the making of domestic films in order to allow an adequate amount of time for preproduction preparation, shooting, and the final shaping of each picture. Directors like Carol Reed took advantage of this increased support of British production to produce films which, though still modestly made by Hollywood standards, demonstrated the artistry of which British filmmakers were capable. By the late 1930s, then, Reed had graduated to making films of considerable substance, like *Night Train to Munich.*

"For the first time," Arthur Knight has written, "there were English pictures which spoke of the British character, British institutions—even social problems such as unemployment and nationalization—with unexpected frankness and awareness." An outstanding example of this new trend in British film making was Reed's *The Stars Look Down,* an uncompromising picture of life in a mining community that brought the director serious critical attention on both sides of the Atlantic.

Reed went on to work on some of the best documentaries to come out of the war, such as the Academy Award-winning *The True Glory.* He also directed the documentary-like theatrical feature *The Way Ahead,* an unvarnished depiction of army life. The experience gained by Reed in making wartime documentaries not only influenced his direction of *The Way Ahead,* but also was reflected in his post-war cinematic style, enabling him to develop further in films like *Odd Man Out* the strong sense of realism which had first appeared in *The Stars Look Down.* The documentary approach that Reed used to tell the story of *Odd Man Out,* which concerns a group of anti-British insurgents in Northern Ireland, was one to which audiences were ready to respond. Wartime films, both documentary and fictional, had conditioned moviegoers in Britain and elsewhere to expect a greater degree of realism in post-war cinema, and Reed provided it.

The more enterprising British producers believed that films should be made to appeal primarily to the home market rather than to the elusive American market. Yet the films that Carol Reed and some others were creating in the post-war years—films which were wholly British in character and situation—were the first such movies to win wide popularity in the United States. Among these, of course, was *Odd Man Out,* the first film which Reed both produced and directed, a factor which guaranteed him a greater degree of creative freedom than he had enjoyed before the war.

For the first time, too, the theme that was to appear so often in Reed's work was perceptible in *Odd Man Out.* In depicting for us in this and other films a hunted, lonely hero caught in the middle of a crisis usually not of his own making, Reed implies that man can achieve maturity and self-mastery only by accepting the challenges that life puts in his way and by struggling with them as best he can.

The Fallen Idol was the first of a trio of masterful films which he made in collaboration with novelist-screenwriter Graham Greene, one of the most significant creative associations between a writer and a director in the history of film. The team followed *The Fallen Idol* with *The Third Man,* which dealt with the black market in post-war Vienna, and, a decade later, *Our Man in Havana.* Commenting on his collaboration with the director, Greene has written that the success of these films was due to Reed, "the only director I know with that particular warmth of human sympathy, the extraordinary feeling for the right face for the right part, the exactitude of cutting, and not the least important, the power of sympathizing with an author's worries and an ability to guide him."

Because most of the films which Reed directed in the next decade or so were not comparable to the post-war films mentioned above, it was thought that he had passed his peak for good. *Oliver!* in fact proved that Reed was back in top form. In her *New Yorker* review of the film, Pauline Kael paid Reed a tribute that sums up his entire career in the cinema: "I applaud the commercial heroism of a director who can steer a huge production and keep his sanity and perspective and decent human feelings as beautifully intact as they are in *Oliver!*"

A genuinely self-effacing man, Reed was never impressed by the awards and honors that he garnered throughout his career (he was knighted in 1952). Summarizing his own approach to filmmaking some time before his death at age sixty-nine in 1976, he said simply, "I give the public what *I* like, and hope they will like it too." More often than not, they did.—GENE D. PHILLIPS

Renoir, Jean

Nationality French/American. ***Born*** *Paris, 15 September 1894, son of painter Auguste Renoir, became citizen of United States (naturalized) in 1946, retained French citizenship.* ***Education*** *Collége de Sainte-Croix, Neuilly-sur-Seine, 1902; Ecole Sainte-Marie de Monceau, 1903; Ecole Massina, Nice, until 1912; University of Aix-en-Provence, degree in mathematics and philosophy, 1913.* ***Military Service*** *Served in French cavalry, 1914-15; transferred to French Flying Corps, 1916, demobilized 1918.* ***Family*** *Married 1) Andrée Madeleine Heuschling ("Dédée," took name Catherine Hessling following 1924* *appearance in* Catherine), *1920 (divorced 1930); 2) Dido Freire, 1944, one son.* **Career** *Worked as potter and ceramicist, 1920-23; directed first film,* La Fille de l'eau, *1924; joined Service Cinématographique de l'Armée,* La Règle du jeu *banned by French government as demoralizing, 1939; Robert Flaherty arranged Renoir's passage to United States, 1940; signed with 20th Century-Fox, 1941; signed with Universal, then terminated contract, 1942; re-established residence in Paris, retained home in Beverly Hills, 1951; active in theatre through 1950s; Compagnie Jean Renoir formed with Anna de Saint Phalle, 1958; taught theatre at University of California, Berkeley, 1960.* **Awards** *Prix Louis Delluc, for* Les Bas-Fonds, *1936; Chevalier de la Légion d'honneur, 1936; International Jury Cup, Venice Biennale, for* La Grande Illusion, *1937; New York Critics Award, for* Swamp Water, *1941; Best Film, Venice Festival, for* The Southerner, *1946; Grand Prix de l'Academie du Cinéma for* French Cancan, *1956; Prix Charles Blanc, Academie Française, for* Renoir, *biography of father, 1963; Honorary Doctorate in Fine Arts, University of California, Berkeley, 1963; Fellow of the American Academy of Arts and Sciences, 1964; Osella d'Oro, Venice Festival, 1968; Honorary Doctorate of Fine Arts, Royal College of Art, London, 1971; Special Oscar for Career Accomplishment, 1975.* **Died** *In Beverly Hills, California, 12 February 1979.*

Films as Director: **1925:** *La Fille de l'eau* (+pr). **1926:** *Nana* (+pr, adaptation). **1927:** *Catherine* (*Une vie sans joie; Backbiters*) (co-d, co-pr, sc, role as sub-prefect); *Sur un air de Charleston* (*Charleston-Parade*) (+pr, ed); *Marquitta* (+pr, adaptation). **1928:** *La Petite marchande d'allumettes* (*The Little Match Girl*) (co-d, co-pr, sc). **1928:** *Tire au flanc* (+co-sc); *Le Tournoi dans la cité* (*Le Tournoi*) (+adaptation). **1929:** *Le Bled.* **1931:** *On purge bébé* (+co-sc); *La Chienne* (+co-sc). **1932:** *La Nuit du carrefour* (*Night at the Crossroads*) (+sc); *Boudu sauvée des eaux* (*Boudu Saved from Drowning*) (+co-sc). **1933:** *Chotard et cie* (+co-sc). **1934:** *Madame Bovary* (+sc). **1935:** *Toni* (*Les Amours de Toni*) (+co-sc). **1936:** *Le Crime de Monsieur Lange* (*The Crime of Monsieur Lange*) (+co-sc); *La Vie est à nous* (*The People of France*) (co-d, co-sc); *Les Bas-Fonds* (*Underworld; The Lower Depths*) (+adaptation). **1937:** *La Grande Illusion* (*Grand Illusion*) (+co-sc). **1938:** *La Marseillaise* (+co-sc); *La Bête humaine* (*The Human Beast; Judas Was a Woman*) (+co-sc). **1939:** *La Règle du jeu* (*Rules of the Game*) (+co-sc, role as Octave). **1941:** *La Tosca* (*The Story of Tosca*) (co-d, co-sc); *Swamp Water.* **1943:** *This Land Is Mine* (+co-p, co-sc). **1944:** *Salute to France* (*Salut à France*) (co-d, co-sc). **1945:** *The Southerner* (+sc). **1946:** *Une Partie de campagne* (*A Day in the Country*) (+sc) (filmed in 1936); *The Diary of a Chambermaid* (+co-sc). **1947:** *The Woman on the Beach* (+co-sc). **1951:** *The River* (+co-sc). **1953:** *Le Carrosse d'or* (*The Golden Coach*) (+co-sc). **1955:** *French Cancan* (*Only the French Can*) (+sc). **1956:** *Elena et les hommes* (*Paris Does Strange Things*) (+sc). **1959:** *Le Testament du Docteur Cordelier* (*The Testament of Dr. Cordelier; Experiment in Evil*) (+sc); *Le Déjeuner sur l'herbe* (*Picnic on the Grass*) (+sc). **1962:** *Le Caporal épinglé* (*The Elusive Corporal; The Vanishing Corporal*) (co-d, co-sc). **1970:** *Le Petit Théâtre de Jean Renoir* (*The Little Theatre of Jean Renoir*) (+sc).

Other Films: **1927:** *Le Petit chaperon rouge* (Cavalcanti) (co-sc, role as the Wolf). **1930:** *Die Jagd nach dem Gluck* (Gliese) (role as Robert). **1937:** *The Spanish Earth* (Ivens) (wrote commentary and narration for French version). **1971:** *The Christian Licorice Store* (Frawley) (role as himself).

Jean Renoir's major work dates from between 1924 and 1939. Of his 21 films the first six are silent features that put forward cinematic problems that come to dominate the entire oeuvre. All study a detachment, whether of language and image, humans and nature, or social rules and real conduct. Optical effects are treated as problems coextensive with narrative. He shows people who are told to obey rules and conventions in situations and social frames that confine them. A sensuous world is placed before everyone's eyes, but access to it is confounded by cultural mores. In Renoir's work, nature, like a frame without borders, isolates the impoverished subjects within limits at once too vast and too constricting for them. Inherited since the Cartesian revolution, and the growth of the middle class after 1789, bourgeois codes of conduct do not fit individuals whose desires and passion know no end.

The patterns established in the films appear simple, and they are. Renoir joins optical to social contradictions in the sense that every one of his films stages dramas about those who cannot conform to the frame in which they live. For the same reason his work also studies the dynamics of love in cinematography that marks how the effect is undeniably "scopic"—grounded in an impulse to see and thus to hold. Sight conveys the human wish to contain whatever is viewed, and to will to control what knows no border. As love cannot be contained, it becomes tantamount to nature itself.

The director has often been quoted as saying that he spent his life making one film. Were it fashioned from all of his finished works—including those composed in the

Jean Renoir

1920s or 1940s or 1960s in France, America, or India—it would tell the story of a collective humanity whose sense of tradition is effectively gratuitous or fake. The social milieu of many of his films is defined by a scapegoat who is killed in order to make that tradition both firm and precarious. All of Renoir's central characters thus define the narratives and visual compositions in which they are found. Boudu (Michel Simon), who escapes the confinement of bourgeois ways in *Boudu sauvé des eaux,* is the opposite of Lestingois (Charles Granval), ensconced in a double-standard marriage *à la* Balzac. Boudu, a tramp, a trickster, and a refugee from *La Chienne* (1931), changes the imagination of his milieu by virtue of his passage through it. The effect he leaves resembles that of Amédée Lange (René Lefevre) in *Le Crime de Monsieur Lange,* who gives life to a collective venture—an emblem of Leon Blum's short-lived Popular Front government launched in 1936—that lives despite his delusions about the American West and the pulp he writes. Lange is the flip side of Jacques Lantier (Jean Gabin) of *La Bête humaine* (1938), a tragic hero whose suicide prefigures André Jurieux's (Roland Toutain's) passion of *La Règle du jeu* (1939).

Boudu floats through the frame in ways that the migrant laborers of *Toni* or the souls of *La Vie est à nous* cannot. The latter are bound to conventions of capital exploitation that incarcerate humanity. In these and other films the characters all "have their reasons," that is, they have many contradictory drives that cannot be socially reconciled but that are individually well founded and impeccably logical on their own terms. When Renoir casts his characters' plural "reasons" under an erotic aura, he offers superlative studies of love. His protagonists wish to find absolution for their passion at the vanishing points of the landscapes—both imaginary and real—in which they try to move. The latter are impossible constructs, but their allure is nonetheless tendered within the sensuous frame of deep-focus photography, long takes, and lateral reframing.

Rosenthal and Maréchal (Marcel Dalio and Gabin) seek an end to war when they tramp into the distance of a snowscape at the end of *La Grande Illusion*. Lange and Florelle (Valentine) wave goodbye as they walk into the flat horizon of Belgium. But Jurieux can imagine love only as a picture-postcard when he and Christine (Nora Grégor), he hopes in desperation, will rejoin his mother in snowy Alsace. Or Lantier can be imagined jumping from his speeding locomotive into a space where the two tracks of the railroad converge, at infinity, beyond the line between Paris and Le Havre. In *Une Partie de campagne*, Henri (Georges Darnoux), frustrated beyond end at the sight of melancholy Juliette (Sylvia Bataille) rowing upstream with her husband sitting behind her in their skiff, looks tearfully at the lush Marne riverside. Sitting on the trunk of a weeping willow arched over the current, he flicks his cigarette butt in the water, unable to express otherwise the fate he has been dealt.

These scenes are shot with an economy that underscores the pathos Renoir draws from figures trapped in situations too vast for their ken or their lives. If generalization can seek an emblem, Renoir's films appear to lead to a *serre,* the transparent closure of the greenhouse that serves as the site of the dénouement of *La Règle du jeu*. The "serre" is literally what constricts, or what has deceptive depth for its beholder. It is the scene where love is acted out and extinguished by the onlooker. The space typifies what Renoir called "the feeling of a frame too narrow for the content" of the dramas he selected from a literary heritage (*Madame Bovary, The Lower Depths*) or wrote himself, such as *Rules*.

Renoir's films have an added intensity and force when viewed in the 1990s. They manifest an urgent concern for the natural world and demonstrate that we are the "human beast" destroying it. Clearly opposed to the effects of capitalism, Renoir offers glimpses of sensuous worlds that seem to arch beyond history. A viewer of *La Fille de l'eau* (1924), *Boudu,* or *Toni* surmises that trees have far more elegance than the characters turning about them, or that, echoing Baudelaire's pronouncements in his *Salons* of 1859, landscapes lacking the human species are of enduring beauty. Renoir puts forth studies of the conflict of language and culture in physical worlds that possess an autonomy of their own. His characters are gauged according to the distance they gain from their environments or the codes that tell them how to act and to live. Inevitably, Renoir's characters are marked by writing. Boudu, a reincarnation of Pan and Nature itself, can only read "big letters." By contrast, Lantier is wedded to his locomotive, a sort of writing machine he calls "la lison." The urbane La Chesnaye (Dalio) in *Rules* cannot live without his writing, the "dangerous supplements" of mechanical dolls, a calliope, or human toys. These objects reflect in the narrative the filmic apparatus that crafted Renoir's work as a model of film writing, a "caméra-stylo," or *ciné-écriture*. Use of deep focus and long takes affords diversity and chance. With the narratives, they constitute Renoir's signature, the basis of the concept and practice of the *auteur*.

Renoir's *oeuvre* stands as a monument and a model of cinematography. By summoning the conditions of illusion and artifice of film, it rises out of the massive production of poetic realism of the 1930s in France. He develops a style that is the very tenor of a vehicle studying social contradiction. The films implicitly theorize the limits that cinema confronts in any narrative or documentary depiction of our world.—TOM CONLEY

Resnais, Alain

Nationality *French.* **Born** *Vannes, Brittany, 3 June 1922.* **Education** *St.-François-Xavier, Vannes; studied acting under René Simon, Paris, 1940-42; attended Institut des Hautes Etudes Cinématographiques (IDHEC), Paris, 1943-45.* **Military Service** *Served with occupation army in Germany and Austria.* **Family** *Married Florence Malraux, 1969.* **Career** *Member of travelling theatrical company, Les Arlequins, 1945; directed first feature,* Ouvert pour cause d'inventaire, *in 16mm, 1946; worked as film editor, 1947-58; worked in New York City, 1970-72; directed first film in English,* Providence, *1977.* **Address** *70 rue des Plantes, 75014 Paris, France.*

Films as Director: 1946: *Ouvert pour cause d'inventaire* (short); *Schéma d'une identification* (short). **1947:** *Visite à Lucien Coutaud* (short); *Visite à Félix Labisse* (short); *Visite à Hans Hartung* (short); *Visite à César Domela* (short); *Visite à Oscar Dominguez* (short); *Portrait d'Henri Goetz* (short); *La Bague* (short); *Journée naturelle* (short); *L'Alcool tue* (short) (+ph, ed). **1948:** *Les Jardins de Paris* (short) (+ph, ed); *Châteaux de France* (short) (+sc, ph, ed); *Van Gogh* (short); *Malfray* (short) (co-d); *Van Gogh* (+ed). **1950:** *Gauguin* (short) (+ed); *Guernica* (short) (co-d, ed). **1953:** *Les Statues meurent aussi* (short) (co-d, co-sc, ed). **1955:** *Nuit et brouillard* (Night and Fog) (short). **1956:** *Toute la mémoire du monde* (short) (+ed). **1957:** *Le Mystère de l'Atelier Quinze* (short) (co-d). **1958:** *Le Chant de Styrène* (short) (+ed). **1959:** *Hiroshima mon amour.* **1961:** *L'Année dernière à Marienbad* (Last Year at Marienbad). **1963:** *Muriel, ou le temps d'un retour.* **1966:** *La Guerre est finie* (The War Is Over). **1967:** *Loin du Viêt-Nam* (Far from Vietnam) (co-d). **1968:** *Je t'aime, je t'aime* (+co-sc). **1974:** *Stavisky.* **1977:** *Providence.* **1980:** *Mon Oncle d'Amérique.* **1983:** *La Vie est un roman* (Life Is a Bed of Roses). **1984:** *L'Amour à mort.* **1986:** *Mélo.* **1989:** *I Want to Go Home.* **1991:** *Contre l'oubli.* **1992:** *Gershwin* (video). **1993:** *Smoking; No Smoking.* **1997:** *On connaît le chanson.*

Alain Resnais: *L'Année dernière à Marienbad*

Other Films: 1945: *Le Sommeil d'Albertine* (ed). **1947:** *Paris 1900* (ed). **1948:** *Jean Effel* (ed). **1952:** *Saint-Tropez, devoir de vacances* (ed). **1955:** *La Pointe courte* (ed). **1957:** *L'Oeil du maître* (ed); *Broadway by Light* (ed). **1958:** *Paris à l'automne* (ed).

Alain Resnais is a prominent figure in the modernist narrative film tradition. His emergence as a feature director of international repute is affiliated with the eruption of the French New Wave in the late 1950s. This association was signaled by the fact that his first feature, *Hiroshima mon amour,* premiered at the Cannes Film Festival at the same time as François Truffaut's *Les 400 coups.* However, Resnais had less to do with the group of directors emerging from the context of the *Cahiers du cinéma* than he did with the so-called Left Bank group, including Jean Cayrol, Marguerite Duras, Chris Marker, and Alain Robbe-Grillet. This group provided an intellectual and creative context of shared interest. In the course of his film career Resnais frequently collaborated with members of this group. Marker worked with him on several short films in the 1950s; Cayrol wrote the narration for *Nuit et brouillard* and the script for *Muriel;* Duras scripted *Hiroshima mon amour;* and Robbe-Grillet wrote *L'Année dernière à Marienbad.* All of these people are known as writers and/or filmmakers in their own right; their association with Resnais is indicative of his talent for fruitful creative collaboration.

Resnais began making films as a youth in 8 and 16mm. In the early 1940s he studied acting and filmmaking, and after the war made a number of 16mm films, including a series about artists. His first film in 35mm was the 1948 short, *Van Gogh,* which won a number of international awards. It was produced by Pierre Braunberger, an active supporter of new talent, who continued to finance his work in the short film format through the 1950s. From 1948-58 Resnais made eight short films, of which *Nuit et brouillard* is probably the best known. The film deals with German concentration camps, juxtaposing past and present, exploring the nature of memory and history. To some extent the film's reputation and the sustained interest it has enjoyed is due to its subject matter. However, many of the film's formal strategies and thematic concerns are characteristic of Resnais's work more generally. In particular, the relationship between past and present, and the function of memory as the mechanism of traversing temporal distance, are persistent preoccupations of Resnais's films. Other films from this period similarly reveal familiar themes and traits of Resnais's subsequent work. *Toute la memoire du monde* is a documentary about the Bibliothèque Nationale in Paris. It presents the building, with its processes of cataloguing and preserving all sorts of printed material, as both a monument of cultural memory and as a monstrous, alien being. The film almost succeeds in transforming the documentary film into a branch of science fiction.

Indeed, Resnais has always been interested in science fiction, the fantastic, and pulp adventure stories. If this interest is most overtly expressed in the narrative of *Je t'aime, je t'aime* (in which a human serves as a guinea pig for scientists experimenting with time travel), it also emerges in the play of fantasy/imagination/reality pervading his work, and in many of his unachieved projects (including a remake of *Fantômas* and *The Adventure of Harry Dickson*).

Through editing and an emphasis on formal repetition, Resnais uses the medium to construct the conjunctions of past and present, fantasy and reality, insisting on the convergence of what are usually considered distinct domains of experience. In *Hiroshima mon amour* the quivering hand of the woman's sleeping Japanese lover in the film's present is directly followed by an almost identical image of her nearly-dead German lover during World War II. Tracking shots through the streets of Hiroshima merge with similar shots of Nevers, where the woman lived during the war. In *Stavisky,* the cutting between events in 1933 and a 1934 investigation of those events presents numerous, often conflicting versions of the same thing; one is finally convinced, above all else, of the indeterminacy and contingency of major historical events. And in *Providence,* the central character is an aged writer who spends a troubled night weaving stories about his family, conjoining memory and fantasy, past, present, and future, in an unstable mix.

The past's insistent invasion of the present is expressed in many different ways in Resnais's films. In *Nuit et brouillard,* where the death camps are both present structures and repressed institutions, it is a question of social memory and history; it is an individual and cultural phenomenon in *Hiroshima mon amour,* as a French woman simultaneously confronts her experiences in occupied France and the Japanese experience of the atomic bomb; it is construed in terms of science fiction in *Je t'aime, je t'aime* when the hero is trapped in a broken time-machine and continuously relives moments from his past; and it is a profoundly ambiguous mixture of an individual's real and imagined past in *L'Année dernière à Marienbad* (often considered Resnais's most avant-garde film) as X pursues A with insistence, recalling their love affair and promises of the previous year, in spite of A's denials. In all of these films, as well as Resnais's other work, the past is fraught with uncertainty, anxiety, even terror. If it is more comfortable to ignore, it inevitably erupts in the present through the workings of the psyche, memory traces, or in the form of documentation and artifacts.

In recent years, Resnais' presence on the international film scene barely has been noticed. While serious and provocative in intention, none of his films have measured up to his earlier work. However, in the early 1980s, he did direct two strikingly original films which are outstanding additions to his filmography.

In *Mon Oncle d'Amerique,* Resnais probes human responses and relations by illustrating the theories of Henri Laborit, a French research biologist. The scenario's focus is on the intertwined relationship between three everyday characters: a Catholic farm boy who has become a textile plant manager (Gerard Depardieu); a former young communist who now is an actress (Nicole Garcia); and a conformist (Roger Pierre) who is married to his childhood sweetheart. *La vie est un roman (Life Is a Bed of Roses)* is a bewitching allegory contrasting the accounts of a rich man (Ruggero Raimondi) constructing a "temple of happiness" around the time of World War I, and a seminar on education being held at that location decades later. Resnais' points are that there are no easy answers to complex dilemmas and, most tellingly, that individuals who attempt to dictate to others their concepts of perfection are as equally destructive as those whose actions result in outright chaos.

Resnais's filmic output has been relatively small. He nonetheless stands as a significant figure in modernist cinema. His strategies of fragmented point-of-view and multiple temporality, as well as his use of the medium to convey past/present and fantasy/imagination/reality as equivocal and equivalent modes of experience have amplified our understanding of film's capacity for expression.—M.B. WHITE and ROB EDELMAN

Riefenstahl, Leni

Nationality German. **Born** Helene Berta Amalie Riefenstahl in Berlin, 22 August 1902. **Education** Studied Russian Ballet at the Mary Wigmann School for Dance, Dresden, and

Jutta Klamt School for Dance, Berlin. **Family** *Married Peter Jacob, 1944 (divorced 1946).* **Career** *Dancer, from 1920; appeared in "mountain films" directed by Arnold Franck, from 1936; established own production company, Riefenstahl Films, 1931; first film,* Das blaue Licht, *released, 1932; appointed "film expert to the National Socialist Party" by Hitler, 1933; detained in various prison camps by Allied Forces on charges of pro-Nazi activity, 1945-48; charges dismissed by Berlin court, allowed to work in film industry again, 1952; suffered serious auto accident while working in Africa, 1956; commissioned by* The Times *(London) to photograph the Munich Olympics, 1972; honored at Telluride Film Festival, Colorado (festival picketed by anti-Nazi groups), 1974; was the subject of the documentary* The Wonderful, Horrible Life of Leni Riefenstahl, *directed by Ray Muller, 1993.* **Awards** *Silver Medal, Venice Festival, for* Das Blaue Licht, *1932; Exposition Internationale des Arts et des Techniques, Paris, Diplome de Grand Prix, for* Triumph des Willens, *1937; Polar Prize, Sweden, for* Olympia, *1938.* **Address** *20 Tengstrasse, 8000 Munich 40, Germany.*

Films as Director: 1932: *Das blaue Licht* (*The Blue Light*) (+co-sc, role as Junta). **1933:** *Sieg des Glaubens* (*Victory of the Faith*). **1935:** *Triumph des Willens* (*Triumph of the Will*) (+pr, ed); *Tag der Freiheit: unsere Wermacht* (+ed). **1938:** *Olympia* (*Olympische Spiele 1936*) (+sc, co-ph, ed). **1944:** *Tiefland* (*Lowland*) (+sc, ed, role as Marta) (released 1954).

Films as Actress: 1926: *Der heilige Berg* (Fanck). **1927:** *Der grosse Sprung* (Fanck). **1929:** *Das Schiscksal derer von Hapsburg* (Raffé); *Die weisses Hölle vom Piz Palü* (Fanck). **1930:** *Stürme über dem Montblanc* (Fanck). **1931:** *Der weiss Rausch* (Fanck). **1933:** *S.O.S. Eisberg* (Fanck).

The years 1932 to 1945 define the major filmmaking efforts of Leni Riefenstahl. Because she remained a German citizen making films in Hitler's Third Reich, two at the Fuhrer's request, she and her films were viewed as pro-Nazi. Riefenstahl claims she took no political position and committed no crimes. In 1948, a German court ruled that she was a follower of, not active in, the Nazi Party. Another court in 1952 reconfirmed her innocence of war crimes. But she is destined to remain a politically controversial filmmaker who made two films rated as masterpieces.

She began to learn filmmaking while acting in the mountain films of Arnold Fanck, her mentor. She made a mountain film of her own, *The Blue Light,* using smoke bombs to create "fog." She used a red and green filter on the camera lens, over her cameraman's objections, to obtain a novel magical effect. This film is Riefenstahl's own favorite. She says it is the story of her own life. Hitler admired *The Blue Light* and asked her to photograph the Nazi Party Congress in Nuremburg. She agreed to make *Victory of the Faith,* which was not publicly viewed. Hitler then asked her to film the 1934 Nazi Party rally.

Triumph of the Will, an extraordinary work, shows Hitler arriving by plane to attend the rally. He proceeds through the crowded streets of Nuremburg, addresses speeches to civilians and uniformed troops, and reviews a five-hour parade. The question is: Did Riefenstahl make *Triumph* as pro-Nazi propaganda or not? "Cinematically dazzling and ideologically vicious," is R. M. Barsam's judgment. According to Barsam, three basic critical views of *Triumph* exist: 1) those who cannot appreciate the film at all, 2) those who can appreciate and understand the film, and 3) those who appreciate it in spite of the politics in the film.

Triumph premiered 29 March 1935, was declared a masterpiece, and subsequently earned three awards. *Triumph* poses questions of staging. Was the rally staged so that it could be filmed? Did the filming process shape the rally, give it meaning? Riefenstahl's next film, *Olympia,* posed the question of financing. Did Nazi official-dom pay for the film to be made? Riefenstahl claims the film was made independently of any government support. Other opinions differ.

The improvisatory techniques Riefenstahl used to make *Triumph* were improved and elaborated to make *Olympia*. She and her crew worked sixteen-hour days, seven days a week. *Olympia* opens as *Triumph* does, with aerial scenes. Filmed in two parts, the peak of Olympia I is Jesse Owens's running feat. The peak of Olympia II is the diving scenes. In an interview with Gordon Hitchens in 1964, Riefenstahl revealed her guidelines for making *Olympia*. She decided to make two films instead of one because "the form must excite the content and give it shape. . . . The law of film is architecture, balance. If the image is weak, strengthen the sound, and vice-versa; the total impact on the viewer should be 100 percent." The se-

Leni Riefenstahl

cret of *Olympia*'s success, she affirmed, was its sound—all laboratory-made. Riefenstahl edited the film for a year and a half. It premiered 20 April 1938 and was declared a masterpiece, being awarded four prizes.

Riefenstahl's career after the beginning of World War II is comprised of a dozen unfinished film projects. She began *Penthesilea* in 1939, *Van Gogh* in 1943, and *Tiefland* in 1944, releasing it in 1954. Riefenstahl acted the role of a Spanish girl in it while co-directing with G. W. Pabst this drama of peasant-landowner conflicts. Visiting Africa in 1956, she filmed *Black Cargo*, documenting the slave trade, but her film was ruined by incorrect laboratory procedures. In the 1960s, she lived with and photographed the Mesakin Nuba tribe in Africa.

Riefenstahl's *Triumph of the Will* and *Olympia* are two of the greatest documentaries ever made. That is indisputable. And it also is indisputable that they are among the most notorious and controversial. Each has been lauded for its sheer artistry, yet damned for its content and vision of Adolph Hitler and a German nation poised on the edge of totalitarian barbarism. After years as a name in the cinema history books, Riefenstahl was back in the news in 1992. *Memoirnen,* her autobiography, was first published in English as *The Sieve of Time: The Memoirs of Leni Riefenstahl,* and she was the subject of a documentary, Ray Muller's *The Wonderful, Horrible Life of Leni Riefenstahl.* Clearly, Riefenstahl had written the book and participated in the documentary in an attempt to have the final word regarding the debate over her involvement with Hitler and the Third Reich.

The documentary, which is three hours in length, traces Riefenstahl's undeniably remarkable life, from her success as a dancer and movie actress during the 1920s to her career as a director, her post-World War II censure, and her latter-day exploits as a still photographer. Still very much alive at age ninety-one, Riefenstahl is shown scuba diving, an activity she first took up in her seventies.

Riefenstahl is described at the outset as a "legend with many faces" and "the most influential filmmaker of the Third Reich." The film goes on to serve as an investigation of her life. Was she an opportunist, as she so vehemently denies, or a victim? Was she a "feminist pioneer, or a woman of evil?" Riefenstahl wishes history to view her as she views herself: not as a collaborator but as an artist first and foremost, whose sole fault was to have been alive in the wrong place at the wrong moment in history, and who was exploited by political forces of which she was unaware.

Upon meeting Hitler, she says, "He seemed a modest, private individual." She was "ignorant" of his ideas and politics, and "didn't see the danger of anti-Semitism." She claims to have acquiesced to making *Triumph of the Will* only after Hitler agreed that she would never have to make another film for him. To her, shooting *Triumph* was just a job. She wanted to make a film that was "interesting, one that was not with posed shots. . . . It had to be filmed the way an artist, not a politician, sees it." The same holds true for *Olympia,* which features images of perfectly proportioned, God-like German athletes. When queried regarding the issue of whether these visuals reflect a fascist aesthetic, Riefenstahl refuses to answer directly, replaying again that art and politics are separate entities.

"If an artist dedicates himself totally to his work, he cannot think politically," Riefenstahl says. Even in the late 1930s, she chose not to leave Germany because, as she observes, "I loved my homeland." She claims that she hoped that reports of anti-Semitism were "isolated events." And her image of Hitler was "shattered much too late. . . . My life fell apart because I believed in Hitler. People say of me, 'She doesn't want to know. She'll always be a Nazi.' [But] I was never a Nazi."

"What am I guilty of?" Riefenstahl asks. "I regret [that I was alive during that period]. But I was never anti-Semitic. I never dropped any bombs." Explained director Muller, after a New York Film Festival screening of the film, "She was an emancipated woman before there was even such a term. She has a super ego, which has been trod upon for half a century. . . . [She is] an artist and a perfectionist. I believe that she was purposefully blind not to look in the direction that would get her into trouble."

In this regard, *The Wonderful, Horrible Life of Leni Riefenstahl* ultimately works as a portrait of denial. As Muller so aptly observes, "Any artist has a great responsibility. Anyone who influences the public has this. She is possessed with her art. She says, 'I'm only doing my thing.' I think this is irresponsible. She may be obsessed and possessed, and a genius. But that does not exempt her from responsibility."

In 1995, Riefenstahl briefly resurfaced in Edgar Reitz's *The Night of the Film-Makers,* consisting of interviews with German filmmakers from Frank Beyer to Wim Wenders. Eric Hansen, writing in *Variety,* summed up the essence of her appearance by noting, "Names like the ninety-two-year-old Leni Riefenstahl and young director Detlev Buck are allowed only a few self-glorifying or sarcastic comments."

Perhaps the final word on Riefenstahl is found in Istvan Szabo's *Hanussen,* a 1988 German-Hungarian film. Much of *Hanussen* is set in Germany between the world wars. One of the minor characters is a celebrated, egocentric woman artist, a member of the political

inner circle, who surrounds herself with physical beauty while remaining callously unconcerned with all but her own vanity. Clearly, this character is based on Riefenstahl.
—LOUISE HECK-RABI and ROB EDELMAN

Rivette, Jacques

Nationality French. **Born** *Jacques Pierre Louis Rivette in Rouen, 1 March 1928.* **Education** *Lycée Corneille, Rouen.* **Career** *Moved to Paris, began writing for* Gazette du cinéma, *1950; writer for* Cahiers du cinéma, *from 1952; worked on films in various capacities, 1952-56; directed first film in 35mm,* Le Coup de berger, *1956, co-scripted with Chabrol, and featuring Godard and Truffaut in small roles; first feature,* Paris nous appartient, *released 1961; editor-in-chief,* Cahiers du cinéma, *1963-65; director for French TV, from late 1960s.* **Award** *Berlin Film Award, for* The Gang of Four, *1989.*

Films as Director: 1950: *Aux Quatre Coins; Le Quadrille.* **1952:** *Le Divertissement.* **1956:** *Le Coup de berger* (+co-sc). **1961:** *Paris nous appartient* (*Paris Belongs to Us*) (+role as party guest). **1966:** *La Religieuse* (*Suzanne Simonin, la religieuse de Denis Diderot; The Nun*) (+co-sc); *Jean Renoir, le patron* (for TV). **1968:** *L'Amour fou* (+co-sc). **1971:** *Out 1: noli me tangere* (for TV, never released). **1974:** *Out 1: ombre* (+co-sc); *Céline et Julie vont en bateau* (*Céline and Julie Go Boating*) (+co-sc). **1976:** *Duelle* (*Twilight*) (+co-sc); *Noroît* (*Northwest*) (+co-sc). **1979:** *Merry-Go-Round* (+co-sc) (released 1983). **1981:** *Le Pont du Nord* (*North Bridge*); *Paris s'en va.* **1984:** *L'Amour par terre.* **1985:** *Hurlevent* (*Wuthering Heights*). **1989:** *La Bande des quatre.* **1990:** *La Belle noiseuse* (+sc). **1991:** *La Belle noiseuse divertimento.* **1994:** *Jeanne la Pucelle.* **1995:** *Haut Bas Fragile* (+sc).

Jacques Rivette (left) on the set of *L'Amour par terre.*

Other Films: 1955: *French Cancan* (Renoir) (asst); *Une Visite* (Truffaut) (ph). **1960:** *Chronique d'un été* (*Chronicle of a Summer*) (Morin and Rouch) (role as Marilu's Boyfriend).

In the days when the young lions of the New Wave were busy railing against "Le Cinéma du papa" in magazine articles and attending all-night screenings of Frank Tashlin and Jerry Lewis movies at La Cinémathèque, Jacques Rivette was quite the keenest cinephile of them all. He made a short as early as 1950, worked as an assistant director for Becker and Renoir, and wrote endless essays for *Gazette du cinéma* and *Cahiers du cinéma,* which he would later edit. If his films seem academic and acutely self-reflexive, we must remember that he is somebody who has spent an eternity theorizing about cinema.

Rivette's first feature, *Paris nous appartient,* clocks in at a mere 140 minutes, and takes as its theme the abortive attempt by a group of French actors to mount a production of Shakespeare's *Pericles*. Rivette's fascination with the play-within-the-film, a leitmotif of his work, is given an initial, and not entirely successful, airing here. The film seems stage-bound, literary, and rather earnest, something which Rivette himself would later acknowledge: "I am very unhappy about the dialogue, which I find atrocious."

After his second feature, *La Religieuse,* was briefly banned (although it did make money) on account of its perceived anti-clericalism, Rivette decided to abandon conventional narrative cinema. Unlike Godard, who never managed to fully overcome the cult of personality (even *Tout va bien* and his other post-1968 collaborations with Gorin are inevitably treated as the great Jean-Luc's personal statements), Rivette easily evolved a kind of collective cinema, where the director's role was on a par with that of the actors. He gave his actors the task of improvising his/her dialogue and character and let the narrative stumble into being. A haphazard and risky working method, Rivette found this infinitely preferable to rigidly conforming to a pre-conceived script. As a result, Rivette's films rarely appear polished and finished.

The subject matter of Rivette films is often rehearsal: they explore the process of creation, rather than the finished artefact itself. *L'Amour fou,* an account of a company's attempts to produce Racine's *Andromaque* while the director and his actress-wife have a break-up, stops short of opening night.

In Rivette's monumental work *Out,* which lasts a full thirteen hours but has only ever seen the commercial light of day as *Ombre,* a four-hour shadow of itself, Rivette takes his theory of Direct Cinema as far as it will go. Determined to make a film "which, instead of being predicated on a central character presented as the conscience, reflecting everything that happens in the action, would be about a collective," the director assembled a large cast of actor/characters, amongst them Juliet Berto and Jean-Pierre Leaud. The film opens as a documentary. Only very gradually does Rivette allow a fictional narrative to emerge through the interaction of the cast. He describes *Out* as being "like a game . . . a crossword."

Rivette commissioned Roland Barthes to write for *Cahiers du cinéma*. Rivette share Barthes' well-chronicled suspicion of authors, and he is also a fervent "intertextualist": his films abound in references to other books and films. *The Hunting of the Snark,* Aeschylus, Balzac, Shakespeare, and Edgar Allen Poe are all liable to be thrown into the melting pot. He mixes 16mm and 35mm film stock in *L'Amour fou,* where he actually depicts a television crew filming the same rehearsals that he is filming: a case of Chinese boxes, perhaps, that goes some way to explaining his unpopularity with certain British critics. Harold Hobson in the *Sunday Times* described the director's 1974 film, *Céline et Julie vont en bateau,* as a "ghastly exhibition of incompetent pretentiousness" while David Robinson suggested that *L'Amour par terre* offered the director's "now accustomed fey and onanistic silliness."

It should be noted that both of the films attacked above offered strong parts for women. Rivette, more than most of his New Wave contemporaries, has provided opportunities for actresses. He is hardly the most prolific director, and the length of his films has often counted against him. Nonetheless, his clinical, self-reflexive essays in film form, coupled with the sophisticated games he continues to play within the "house of fiction," reveal him as a cinematic purist whose commitment to the celluloid muse has hardly diminished since the heady days of the 1950s.—G.C. MACNAB

Roeg, Nicolas

Nationality British. *Born* Nicolas Jack Roeg in London, 15 August 1928. *Education* Mercers School. *Family* Married 1) Susan Rennie Stephens; 2) actress Theresa Russell. *Career* Junior at Marylebone Studio, dubbing French films and making tea, from 1947; hired at MGM's Borehamwood Studios as part of camera crew on The Miniver Story, 1950; camera operator, from 1958; directed first feature (with Donald Cammell), Performance, 1970. *Address* c/o Hatton and Baker, 18 Jermyn Street, London SW1Y 6HN, England.

Films as Director: 1970: *Performance* (co-d, +ph). **1971:** *Walkabout* (+ph). **1973:** *Don't Look Now.* **1976:** *The Man Who Fell to Earth.* **1980:** *Bad Timing.* **1981:** *Dallas Through the Looking Glass.* **1982:** *Eureka.* **1985:** *Insignificance.* **1986:** *Castaway.* **1987:** Episode in *Aria.* **1988:** *Track 29.* **1989:** *The Witches; Sweet Bird of Youth* (for TV). **1992:** *Cold Heaven.* **1993:** *Heart of Darkness* (for TV). **1994:** *Two Deaths.* **1995:** *Full Body Massage* (for TV). **1996:** *Samson and Delilah* (for TV).

Nicolas Roeg on the set of *Cold Heaven*.

Other Films: (as camera operator) 1958: *A Woman Possessed* (Max Varnel); *Moment of Indiscretion* (Max Varnel); *The Man Inside* (Gilling). **1959:** *The Great Van Robbery* (Max Varnel); *Passport to Shame* (Rakoff); *The Child and the Killer* (Max Varnel). **1960:** *The Trials of Oscar Wilde* (Hughes); *Jazz Boat* (Hughes). **1961:** *The Sundowners* (Zinnemann); *Information Received* (Lynn). **1962:** *Lawrence of Arabia* (Lean) (2nd unit ph); *Dr. Crippen* (Lynn).

(As lighting cameraman) 1963: *The Caretaker* (Donner); *Just for Fun* (Flemyng); *Nothing But the Best* (Donner). **1964:** *The Masque of the Red Death* (Corman); *The System* (*The Girl Getters*) (Winner); *Every Day's a Holiday* (Hill); *Victim Five* (*Code Seven, Victim Five*) (Lynn). **1965:** *Judith* (Mann) (2nd unit ph). **1966:** *A Funny Thing Happened on the Way to the Forum* (Lester); *Farenheit 451* (Truffaut). **1967:** *Far from the Madding Crowd* (Schlesinger); *Casino Royale* (Huston et al) (some sections only). **1968:** *Petulia* (Lester).

Nicolas Roeg is a visual trickster who plays havoc with conventional screen narratives. Choosing an oblique storytelling formula, he riddles his plots with ambiguous characters, blurred genres, distorted chronologies, and open-ended themes to invite warring interpretations.

Even the most facile Roeg synopsis betrays alienation and incongruity, with characters getting caught in bewildering and hostile situations. His first effort, *Performance* (with co-director Donald Cammell) offers a dark look at the last days of a pursued gangster (James Fox) who undergoes a psychosexual identity change while hiding out with a has-been rock star (Mick Jagger). This psychedelic cornucopia of androgynous sex, violence, and Borges allusions blessed and cursed Roeg with the lingering label "cult director."

We had already been warned of Roeg's charming peculiarities during his cinematographer days. Such notable films as *Far from the Madding Crowd* and *Fahrenheit 451* had odd, even anachronistic looks that sometimes ran contrary to the story proper. In fact, the latter film barely resembles Truffaut at all and looks more Roegish with its dreamy color schemes and chilly atmospherics.

Even Roeg's relatively tame second feature, *Walkabout,* based on a novel by James Vance Marshall, has narrative trap doors. Jarring cross-cuts, sensuous photography, and Edward Bond's enigmatic script are more satisfying to mystics than humanists. Marshall's novel is much more clear in its tale of two Australian children (Jenny Agutter and Lucien John) who get lost in the outback and are saved by an aborigine (David Gumpilil). Roeg's version is a more complex and fatalistic expose of people from separate cultures who have no hope of connecting.

Roeg flaunts a talent for shattering a relatively simple story into heady fragments with his adaptation of Daphne du Maurier's *Don't Look Now.* The tragedy of a couple (Julie Christie and Donald Sutherland) haunted in Venice by a psychic (Hilary Mason) claiming to communicate with their drowned daughter turns into something more than just a proto-Hitchcock thriller. As in most Roegian journeys, we emerge from *Don't Look Now* more discombobulated than we were at the start. Is the psychic a fraud? Is there foul play among the Venetian authorities? Could the occult implications be just a ruse? Roeg operates on a logic that is more visceral than intellectual. Instead of outright clues, we get recurrent shapes, sounds, colors, and gestures that belie a hidden order linking people and events.

Of all Roeg's work, *The Man Who Fell to Earth* is the most accomplished and de-centered. A space alien (David Bowie) arrives on Earth, starts a multi-million dollar enterprise and is later captured by a government-corporate collusion. What threatens to be another trite sci-fi plot becomes, in Roeg's hands, a visually stunning mental conundrum. All the continuity gaffes plaguing many an outer-space movie are here intentionally exacerbated to the point where we doubt that the "visitor" is really an alien at all. We see events mostly through the alien's abstruse viewpoint as days, months, years, even decades transpire sporadically and inconsistently. The story is a sleight-of-hand distraction that forces our attention more onto the transitory mood of loneliness and dissociation.

Unlike a purely experimental director who would flout story-lines altogether, Roeg retains the bare bones of old genres only to disfigure them. His controversial *Bad Timing* could easily have been an updated "Inner Sanctum" spin-off with its pathological lovers (Art Garfunkel and Theresa Russell) and the voyeuristic detective (Harvey Keitel) snooping for foul play. But the film unfolds with vignettes that tell us one thing and show another. Time and motive—the staples of mysteries—are so deviously jumbled that we can only resign ourselves to the Roeg motto that "nothing is what it seems."

Roeg's under-appreciated and least-seen *Eureka* starts out as an adventure about a Yukon prospector (Gene Hackman) who finds gold and becomes one of the world's richest men. But soon the story splinters into soap opera, romance, murder mystery, and even splatter film—a tortuous, visionary, frustrating, and ultimately mad epic.

Since *Eureka*, Roeg has been more skittish about re-entering the labyrinth. Films like *Insignificance* (about a night when the prototypes of Albert Einstein, Marilyn Monroe, Joe DiMaggio, and Joe McCarthy meet) and *Castaway* (based on Lucy Irvine's ordeal with a lover on a deserted island) have shades of the older Roeg films but lack his gift for reckless lust. The "Twilight Zone" teasers reemerge somewhat in *Track 29*, where he teams with absurdist scriptwriter Dennis Potter in a tale about a woman beleaguered by a man her own age who claims to be her illegitimate son. Once more, Roeg treats us to another story about frustrated love and the fragile border between "reality" and hallucination.

The career of Nicolas Roeg has in recent years been in sad decline. By far his best work in this latter period was the made-for-television feature *Heart of Darkness,* a moody, shadowy adaptation of the famed Joseph Conrad novella. *Cold Heaven* is a muddled drama about a husband who may or may not have been killed in a grisly accident just as his wife is set to leave him.

Though a well-intentioned expose of the horror of war, *Two Deaths,* his most recent film, shows no evidence of a return to form. It is set during a bloody conflict. Several aristocratic types sit in a room awaiting the start of a dinner party. They complain about trifling matters, while on the streets around them blood flows like the wine they will enjoy with their meal. All too obviously, before the night is over the violence outside will intrude on their lives, with much moralizing and sermonizing along the way. Roeg beats you over the head with unsubtle symbolism: the guests slurp down oysters while a woman bleeds to death outside, and he even uses the cliched image of a dead dove.—JOSEPH LANZA and ROB EDELMAN

Rohmer, Eric

Nationality *French.* **Born** *Jean-Marie Maurice Scherer in Tulle, 4 April 1920.* **Career** *Literature teacher at lycée, Nancy, 1942-50; film critic, from 1948; founder, with Godard and Rivette,* La Gazette du cinéma, *Paris, 1950; Co-wrote book on Alfred Hitchcock with Claude Chabrol, 1957; editor-in-chief of* Cahiers du cinéma, *1957-63; directed first* *feature,* Le Signe du lion, *1959; made the "Six contes moraux" (Six Moral Tales), 1962-73; with* La Femme de l'aviator, *began new series, "Comédies et proverbes," 1980; began new series, "Tales of the Four Seasons," 1989.* **Awards** *Prix Max Ophüls, for* My Night at Maud's, *1970; Prix Louis Delluc, and Prix Méliès, for* Claire's Knee, *1971; Special Jury Prize, Cannes Festival, for* The Marquise of O . . . , *1976; Silver Bear and share of International Critics Prize, Berlin Festival, for* Pauline at the Beach, *1983; Officier des Arts et des Lettres.* **Address** *26 av. Pierre-1er-de-Serbie, 75116 Paris, France.*

Films as Director and Scriptwriter: **1950:** *Journal d'un scélérat.* **1951:** *Présentation ou Charlotte et son steak* (*Charlotte and Her Steak*). **1952:** *Les Petites Filles modèles* (co-d) (unfinished). **1954:** *Bérénice.* **1956:** *La Sonate à Kreutzer* (*The Kreutzer Sonata*). **1958:** *Véronique et son cancre.* **1959:** *Le Signe du lion* (*Sign of the Lion; The Sign of Leo*). **1963:** *La Boulangerie de Monceau* (first of the "Contes moraux"; following five films identified by "CM" and number assigned by Rohmer); *La Carrière de Suzanne* (*Suzanne's Profession*) (CM no. 2). **1964:** *Nadja à Paris.* **1964-69:** Films for educational television: *Les Cabinets de physique au XVIIIème siècle; Les Métamorphoses du paysage industriel; Perceval; Don Quichotte; Edgar Poë; Pascal; La Bruyère; Mallarmé; La Béton dans la ville; Les Contemplations; Hugo architecte; Louis Lumière.* **1965:** Films for television series "Cinéastes de notre temps": *Carl Dreyer, Le Celluloid et la marbre;* "Place de l'étoile" episode of *Paris vu Par ... (Six in Paris).* **1966:** *Une Étudiante d'aujourd'hui.* **1967:** *La Collectionneuse* (CM no. 4) (+sc); *Fermière à Montfaucon.* **1969:** *Ma Nuit chez Maud* (*My Night at Maud's*) (CM no. 3). **1970:** *Le Genou de Claire* (*Claire's Knee*) (CM no. 5). **1972:** *L'Amour l'après-midi* (*Chloe in the Afternoon*) (CM no. 6). **1976:** *La Marquise d'O ... (The Marquise of O ...).* **1978:** *Perceval le Gaullois.* **1980:** *La Femme de l'aviateur* (*The Aviator's Wife*). **1982:** *Le Beau Mariage* (*The Perfect Marriage*). **1983:** *Loup y es-tu?* (*Wolf, Are You There?*); *Pauline à la plage* (*Pauline at the Beach*). **1984:** *Les Nuits de la pleine lune* (*Full Moon in Paris*). **1986:** *Le Rayon vert* (*The Green Ray*). **1987:** *L'Ami de mon amie* (*My Girlfriend's Boyfriend; Boyfriends and Girlfriends*); *Quatre Aventures de Reinette et Mirabelle* (*Four Adventures of Reinette and Mirabelle*). **1989:** *Conte de printemps* (*A Tale of Springtime*). **1992:** *Conte d'hiver* (*A Tale of*

Eric Rohmer

Winter). **1993:** *L'Arbre, le maire et la mediatheque* (*The Tree, the Mayor, and the Mediatheque*). **1995:** *Les rendez-vous de Paris.* **1996:** *Conte d'été* (*A Summer's Tale*).

Other Films: 1954: *Berenice* (role). **1993:** *Francois Truffaut: portraits voles* (*Francois Truffaut: Stolen Portraits*) (Toubiana, Pascal) (appearance). **1994:** *Citizen Langlois* (appearance).

By virtue of a tenure shared at *Cahiers du Cinéma* during the 1950s and early 1960s, Eric Rohmer is usually classified with Truffaut, Godard, Chabrol, and Rivette as a member of the French New Wave. Yet, except for three early shorts made with Godard, Rohmer's films seem to share more with the traditional values of such directors as Renoir and Bresson than with the youthful flamboyance of his contemporaries. Much of this divergence is owed to an accident of birth. Born Jean-Marie Maurice Scherer in Tulle in 1920, Rohmer was at least ten years older than any of the other critic/filmmakers in the *Cahiers* group. By the time he arrived in Paris in 1948, he was an established teacher of literature at the lycée in Nancy and had published a novel, *Elizabeth* (1946), under the pseudonym Gilbert Cordier. When he joined the *Cahiers* staff in 1951 Rohmer had already spent three years as a film critic with such prestigious journals as *La Revue du cinéma* and Sartre's *Les Temps modernes*. Thus Rohmer's aesthetic preferences were more or less determined before he began writing for *Cahiers*.

Still, the move proved decisive. At *Cahiers* he encountered an environment in which film critics and filmmaking were thought of as merely two aspects of the same activity. Consequently, the critics who wrote for *Cahiers* never doubted that they would become film directors. As it turned out, Rohmer was one of the first to realize this ambition. In 1951 he wrote and directed a short 16mm film called *Charlotte and Her Steak* in which Godard, the sole performer, plays a young man who tries to seduce a pair of offscreen women. Two of his next three films were experiments in literary adaptation. These inaugurated his long association with Barbet Schroeder, who produced or co-produced all of Rohmer's subsequent film projects.

In 1958 filmmaking within the *Cahiers* group was bustling. Rivette, Truffaut, and Chabrol were all shooting features. Rohmer, too, began shooting his first feature, *Sign of the Lion*. The result, however, would not be greeted with the same enthusiasm that was bestowed on Godard and Truffaut. Rohmer has always maintained that his films are not meant for a mass audience but rather for that small group of viewers who appreciate the less spectacular qualities of the film medium. Unfortunately, *Sign of the Lion* failed to find even this elite audience. And while Truffaut's *The 400 Blows* and Godard's *Breathless* were establishing the *Cahiers* group as a legitimate film force, it was not until 1963 that Rohmer was able to secure funding for a film of any length. That same year he ended his association with *Cahiers du Cinéma*. The journal had for some time been moving away from the aesthetic policies of Bazin and towards a more leftist variety of criticism. Rohmer had always been viewed as something of a reactionary and was voted down as co-director. He chose to leave the magazine and devote his entire career to making films. At just this moment Barbet Schroeder was able to find money for a short 16mm film.

While writing the scenario for *Suzanne's Profession,* Rohmer conceived the master plan for a series of fictional films, each a variation on a single theme: a young man, on the verge of committing himself to one woman, by chance meets a second woman whose charms cause him to question his initial choice. As a result of this encounter, his entire way of thinking, willing, desiring, that is to say, the very fabric of his moral life starts to unwind. The young man eventually cleaves to his original choice, his ideal woman against whom he measures all his other moral decisions, but the meeting with the second woman (or, as is the case in *Claire's*

Knee, a trinity of women) creates a breathing space for the young man, a parenthesis in his life for taking stock. The vacillations of the young man, who often functions as the film's narrator, comprise the major action of the six films, known as "Six Moral Tales."

Rohmer recognizes the irony in his use of cinema, a medium which relies on objective, exterior images, to stage his interior moral dramas. But by effecting minute changes in the exterior landscape, he expresses subtle alterations in his protagonist's interior drama. This explains why Rohmer pays such scrupulous attention to rendering surface detail. Each film in the "Six Moral Tales" was shot on the very location and at the exact time of year in which the story is set. Rohmer was forced to postpone the shooting of *My Night at Maud's* for an entire year so that Jean-Louis Trintignant would be available during the Christmas season, the moment when the fiction was scripted to begin. The painter Daniel in *La Collectioneuse* is played by Daniel Pommereulle, a painter in real life. The Marxist historian and the priest who preaches the sermon at the end of *My Night at Maud's* are, in real life, historian and priest. The female novelist of *Claire's Knee* is a novelist and the married couple of *Chloe in the Afternoon* are portrayed by husband and wife. Such attention to detail allowed Rohmer to realize an advance in the art of cinematic adaption with his next two films, *The Marquise of O ...* and *Perceval.*

As he entered the 1980s, Rohmer completed two films of a new series of moral tales which he calls "Parables." In contrast to the "Six Moral Tales," the "Parables" are not played out on the interior landscape of a single character but rather engage an entire social milieu. In *The Aviator's Wife,* a young postal clerk trails his mistress around Paris to spy on her affair with another man. During his peregrinations, he meets a young female student and loses track of his mistress. He decides he prefers the company of the young student, only to discover her in the arms of another man. *The Perfect Marriage* chronicles the attempts of a young Parisian woman to persuade the man whom she had decided will make her a perfect husband that she will, in turn, make him the perfect wife. She discovers, too late, that he has been engaged to another woman all along.

Emerging from the crucible of the French New Wave, Rohmer has forged a style that combines the best qualities of Bresson and Renoir with distinctive traits of the Hollywood masters. And though he was never as flamboyant as Godard or Truffaut, Rohmer's appeal has proved much hardier. The international success that met *My Night at Maud's* and *The Marquise of O ...* built a following that awaited the new set of moral dilemmas limned by each further installment of the "Parables" with eagerness and reverence.

During the 1980s, Rohmer went on to complete his "Comedies and Proverbs" series. His films include: *Pauline at the Beach,* a clever, sharply observed comedy which compares the dishonesty of adult alliances and the forthrightness of adolescence; *Full Moon in Paris,* which details the plight of a willful young woman and her involvement with different men; *Four Adventures of Reinette and Mirabelle,* which insightfully contrasts the lives of two young women, one from the country and the other from the city; and *My Girlfriend's Boyfriend,* which also follows what happens when two very different women begin a friendship and then start playing amorous games with a pair of men. Here, Rohmer proves a master at writing dialogue for characters whose romantic feelings change with the setting sun.

Rohmer then began a new series, called "Tales of the Four Seasons." Its initial entry, *A Tale of Springtime,* is a typically refreshing Rohmer concoction. The filmmaker tells the story of Jeanne, a high school philosophy teacher with time on her hands who meets and befriends a younger woman. The latter's father has a girlfriend her age, whom she despises, so she decides to play cupid for Jeanne and her dad. Rohmer's dialogue is typically casual yet revealing. Beneath what may seem like superficial chatter, much is divulged regarding the characters' wants, needs, and desires. *A Tale of Springtime* is a film about everyday feelings and reactions— and Rohmer transforms these everyday feelings and reactions into art. His characters find themselves in uncomfortable or comic situations that are nonetheless of a real-life quality that can be related to on a universal level.

Rohmer's follow-up, *A Tale of Winter,* is the bittersweet story of a hairdresser who has an affair while on holiday but accidently gives her lover the wrong address when they part. They lose touch, and she has his baby. All that remains of the child's father are some photos and memories, her undying love—and the baby. Two ardent but very different suitors have become her boyfriends, and she cannot decide which one to marry. Rohmer's point, beautifully illustrated, is that one should not settle for second best in love. Follow your heart, and allow it to lead you to your true destiny.

A Tale of Winter is flawed, if only because Rohmer's heroine is far too flaky; she is constantly wavering and unfairly leading on the two suitors in a manner that makes it difficult to sympathize with her plight. Still, Rohmer's thesis is well-taken; even mid-dle-of-the-road Rohmer is far more engaging than the works of most other filmmakers.
—DENNIS NASTAV and ROB EDELMAN

Rosi, Francesco

Nationality *Italian.* **Born** *Naples, 15 November 1922.* **Education** *Studied law, Naples University.* **Military Service** *1942.* **Career** *Radio journalist in Naples, early 1940s; worked in theatre as actor, stage designer, and assistant director, Rome, from 1946; assistant director and script collaborator, through 1956, also dubbing director for Italian versions of foreign films; directed first film,* La sfida, *1957.* **Awards** *Special Jury Prize, Venice Festival, for* La sfida, *1958; Silver Bear for Best Direction, Berlin Festival, for* Salvatore Giuliano, *1963; Golden Lion, Venice Festival, for* Le mani sulla città, *1963.*

Films as Director and Co-Scriptwriter: 1958: *La sfida* (*The Challenge*). **1959:** *I magliari.* **1961:** *Salvatore Giuliano.* **1963:** *Le mani sulla città* (*Hands over the City*). **1965:** *Il momento della verità* (*The Moment of Truth*) (co-d). **1967:** *C'era una volta* (*More than a Miracle*). **1970:** *Uomini contro.* **1972:** *Il caso Mattei* (*The Mattei Affair*). **1973:** *A proposito Lucky Luciano* (*Lucky Luciano*). **1976:** *Cadaveri eccelenti* (*Illustrious Corpses*). **1979:** *Cristo si è fermato a Eboli* (*Christ Stopped at Eboli*). **1981:** *Tre fratelli* (*Three Brothers*). **1984:** *Carmen* (*Bizet's Carmen*). **1988:** *Cronaca di una morte annunciata* (*Chronicle of a Death Foretold*). **1990:** *Dimenticare Palermo* (*To Forget Palermo*). **1993:** *Neapolitan Diary.* **1996:** *La Tregua* (*The Truce*).

Other Films: 1947: *La terra trema* (Visconti) (asst d). **1949:** *La domenica d'agosto* (Emmer) (asst d). **1950:** *Tormento* (Matarazzo) (asst d). **1951:** *I figli di nessuno* (Matarazzo) (asst d); *Parigi e sempre parigi* (Emmer) (asst d, co-sc); *Bellissima* (Visconti) (asst, co-sc). **1952:** *Camicie Rosse* (supervised post-production after director Goffredo Alessandri abandoned project); *I vinti* (Antonioni) (asst d); *Processo alla città* (Zampa) (sc). **1954:** *Carosello Napoletano* (Giannini) (asst d); *Proibito* (Monicelli) (asst d); *Senso* (Visconti) (asst d). **1955:** *Racconti Romani* (Franciolini) (co-sc). **1956:** *Il bigamo* (Emmer) (asst d, co-sc).

The films of Francesco Rosi stand as an urgent riposte to any proposal of aesthetic puritanism as a *sine qua non* of engaged filmmaking. From *Salvatore Giuliano* to *Illustrious*

Corpses and *Chronicle of a Death Foretold,* he uses a mobilisation of the aesthetic potential of the cinema not to decorate his tales of corruption, complicity, and death, but to illuminate and interrogate the reverberations these events cause. If one quality were to be isolated as especially distinctive and characteristic it would have to be the sense of intellectual passion, of direction propelled by an impassioned sense of inquiry. This can be true in a quite literal way in *Salvatore Giuliano,* in which any "suspense" accruing to Giuliano's death is put aside in favour of a search for another kind of knowledge; and *The Mattei Affair,* in which the soundtrack amasses evidence which is presented virtually in opposition to the images before us; or, in a more metaphoric sense, *Christ Stopped at Eboli,* which represents an inquiry into the social conditions of the South of Italy.

Rosi traces the evolution of his style to his early experience as an assistant on Rosselini's *Terra Trema,* where he learnt the value of immediacy, improvisation, and the use of non-professional performers. It was a mode of filmmaking that suited the exploration of concerns found within a particular current in Italian thought. It finds expression in the writings of Carlo Levi and Leonardo Sciascia, both of whom deal with the issue of the South and both of whose work Rosi has adapted for the screen, along with, latterly, that of Primo Levi. It is a current that also finds political expression in the work of Antonio Gamsci. Rosi's films are perhaps above all the films of an industrialising Italy, the Italy of Fiat, that exists dialectically with that of the peasant South.

Throughout his work there is an abiding interest in the social conditions in which individuals live their lives and their expression at the public or civic level, licit or illicit. Concern with organised crime and its social roots—though free from any taint of sociologizing—appears as a major thread through films as diverse as *Salvatore Giuliano, Hands over the City, The Mattei*

Affair, Lucky Luciano, and *Chronicle of a Death Foretold.* Although Rosi uses the appurtenances of the thriller or the gangster film (in *Lucky Luciano,* for instance), his interests, as Michel Ciment has pointed out, are not at all with whodunnit but with what the crime reveals about the social context of individual lives. *Lucky Luciano,* for example, is not (unlike *The Godfather*) in the business of creating monsters but of creating a way of understanding the men who are thus mythologised. It is a tribute to Rosi's virtuosity and commitment that the trajectory he describes is not a whit less exciting.

He may examine the mesh of the individual and his context from the point-of-view of the public sphere (*Illustrious Corpses*) or the private (*Three Brothers* or *Christ Stopped at Eboli*). The issue might be the ruthless mechanics of market forces in *Hands over the City,* or the process whereby the Mafia is set in place in *The Mattei Affair.* But above all Rosi remains a pre-eminent craftsman of the cinema in his acute and responsive relationship with his regular or occasional collaborators, especially with his cinematographers and musicians.

Of recent films, *Forget Palermo* was criticised for superficiality and some awkwardness in its casting of James Belushi. Rosi argues that its initially touristical mode was part of its point. The film follows an American "man of power" to his Sicilian roots. His honeymoon trip cannot be innocent of political implications and the tangled web of drugs and finance is meticulously revealed.

Neapolitan Diary was a more personal exploration of the same theme, taking Rosi himself back to the city of his birth and back to the location for *Hands over the City.* It is harsh and lucid, but never without hope of change, not even in bleak interviews with school-aged drug dealers. The South, urges Rosi, is not other than Italy but the place where the nation's problems outcrop most painfully. Primo Levi's *The Truce,* the subject of Rosi's most recent film, follows the homeward journey of a mixed group of Auschwitz prisoners. In it Rosi has said he sees a foreshadowing of the tensions that have frighteningly emerged in Europe since the fall of the Wall.

If his most recent films may be less wholly satisfying than, say, the urgent definitiveness of *Hands over the City,* or less rigorously aesthetic than *Illustrious Corpses,* they still reveal a rare and vital intellectual commitment to cinema as a platform for debate and testimony—a form, he has said, of active participation in public life.—VERINA GLAESSNER

Rossellini, Roberto

*Nationality Italian. **Born** Rome, 8 May 1906. **Family** Married 1) Marcella de Marquis (marriage annulled), two children; 2) actress Ingrid Bergman, 1950 (divorced), three children, including actress Isabella; 3) screenwriter Somali Das Gupta (divorced), one son. **Career** Worked on films, in dubbing and sound effects, then as editor, from 1934; directed first feature,* La nave bianca, *1940; technical director in official film industry, while simultaneously shooting documentary footage of Italian resistance fighters, 1940-45; accepted offer from Howard Hughes to make films for RKO with Ingrid Bergman in Hollywood, 1946; apparently fell out of public favour over scandal surrounding relationships with Bergman and later Das Gupta; television director of documentaries, 1960s. **Died** 4 June 1977.*

Films as Director: 1936: *Daphne* (+sc). **1938:** *Prelude à l'apres-midi d'une faune* (+sc). **1939:** *Fantasia sottomarina* (+sc); *Il tacchino prepotente* (+sc); *La vispa Teresa* (+sc). **1941:** *Il Ruscello di Ripasottile* (+sc); *La nave bianca* (+co-sc). **1942:** *Un pilota ritorna* (+co-sc); *I tre aquilotta* (uncredited collaboration). **1943:** *L'uomo della croce* (+co-sc); *L'invasore* (+supervised production, sc); *Desiderio* (+co-sc) (confiscated by police and finished by Marcello Pagliero in 1946). **1945:** *Roma, città aperta* (*Rome, Open City*) (+co-sc). **1946:** *Paisà* (*Paisan*) (+co-sc, pr). **1947:** *Germania, anno zero* (*Germany, Year Zero*) (+co-sc) *L'amore* (*Woman, Ways of Love*) (+sc); *Il miracolo* (*The Miracle*) (+co-sc); *La macchina ammazzacattivi* (+co-sc, pr); *Stromboli, terra di dio* (*Stromboli*) (+co-sc, pr). **1950:** *Francesco—giullare di Dio* (*Flowers of St. Francis*) (+co-sc). **1952:** "L'Invidia" episode of *I sette peccati capitali* (*The Seven Deadly Sins*) (+co-sc); *Europa '51* (*The Greatest Love*) (+co-sc). **1953:** *Dov'è la libertà* (+co-sc); *Viaggio in Italia* (*Voyage to Italy, Strangers*); *The Lonely Woman* (+co-sc); "Ingrid Bergman" episode of *Siamo donne*. **1954:** "Napoli '43" episode of *Amori di mezzo secolo* (+sc); *Giovanna d'Arco al rogo* (*Joan of Arc at the Stake*) (+sc); *Die Angst* (*Le Paura; Fear*); *Orient Express* (+sc, production supervision). **1958:** *L'India vista da Rossellini* (ten episodes) (+sc, pr); *India* (+co-sc). **1959:** *Il Generale della Rovere* (+co-sc). **1960:** *Era notte a Roma* (+co-sc); *Viva l'Italia* (+co-sc). **1961:** *Vanina Vanini* (*The Betrayer*) (+co-sc); *Torino nei centi'anni*; *Benito Mussolini* (*Blood on the Balcony*) (+sc, production supervision). **1962:** *Anima nera* (+sc); "Illibatezza" episode of *Rogopag* (+sc). **1966:** *La Prise de pouvoir par Louis XIV* (*The Rise of Louis XIV*). **1967:** *Idea di un'isola* (+pr, sc). **1968:** *Atti degli apostoli* (co-d, co-sc, ed). **1970:** *Socrate* (*Socrates*) (+co-sc, ed). **1972:** *Agostino di Ippona*. **1975:** *Blaise Pascal; Anno uno*. **1978:** *Il Messia* (*The Messiah*) (+co-sc).

Other Films: 1938: *Luciano Serra, pilota* (sc). **1963:** *Le carabiniere* (co-sc). **1964:** *L'eta del ferro* (sc, pr). **1967:** *La lotta dell'uomo per la sua sopravvivenza* (sc, pr).

Roberto Rossellini has been so closely identified with the rise of the postwar Italian style of filmmaking known as neorealism that it would be a simple matter to neatly pigeonhole him as merely a practitioner of that technique and nothing more. So influential has that movement been that the achievement embodied in just three of his films—*Roma, città aperta; Paisà;* and *Germania, anno zero*—would be enough to secure the director a major place in film history. To

Roberto Rossellini (right) directing *Era notte a Roma.*

label Rossellini simply a neorealist, however, is to drastically undervalue his contribution to the thematic aspects of his art.

At its most basic level, Rossellini's dominant concern appears to be a preoccupation with the importance of the individual within various aspects of the social context that emerged from the ashes of World War II. In his early films, which a number of historians have simplistically termed fascist, his concern for the individual was not balanced by an awareness of their social context. Thus, a film like his first feature, *La nave bianca,* while it portrays its sailors and hospital personnel as sensitive and caring, ignores their ideological and political milieu. It is *Roma, città aperta,* despite its carry-over of the director's penchant for melodrama, that is properly considered Rossellini's "rite of passage" into the midst of the complex social issues confronting the individual in postwar Europe. The crude conditions under which it was shot, its authentic appearance, and certain other naturalistic touches lent it an air of newsreel-like veracity, but its raw power was derived almost entirely from the individuals that Rossellini placed within this atmospheric context. With the exception of Anna Magnani and Aldo Fabrizi, the cast was made up of non-professionals who were so convincing that the effect upon viewers was electric. Many were certain that what they were viewing must have been filmed as it was actually occurring.

Despite legends about how Rossellini's neorealistic style arose as a result of the scarcity of resources and adverse shooting conditions that were present immediately after the war, the director had undoubtedly begun to conceive the style as early as his aborted *Desiderio* of 1943, a small-scale forerunner of neorealism which Rossellini dropped in mid-shooting. Certainly, he continued the style in *Paisà* and *Germania, anno zero,* the remaining parts of his war trilogy. In both of these features, he delineates the debilitating effects of war's aftermath on the psyche of modern man. The latter film was a particularly powerful statement on the effect of Nazi ideology on the mind of a young boy, in part because it simultaneously criticizes the failure of traditional social institutions like the church to counter fascism's corrupting influence.

The Rossellini films of the 1950s shed many of the director's neorealistic trappings. In doing so he shifted his emphasis somewhat to the spiritual aspects of man, revealing the instability of life and of human relationships. *Stromboli, Europa '51, Voyage to Italy,* and *La paura* reflect a quest for a transcendent truth akin to the secular saintliness achieved by the priest in *Open City.* In the 1950s films, however, his style floated unobtrusively between involvement and contemplation. This is particularly obvious in his films with Ingrid Bergman, but is best exemplified by *Voyage to Italy* with its leisurely-paced questioning of the very meaning of life. Every character in the film is ultimately in search of his soul. What little action there is has relatively little importance since most of the character development is an outgrowth of spiritual aspirations rather than a reaction to events. In this sense, its structure resembled the kind of neorealism practiced by De Sica in *Umberto D* (without the excessively emotional overtones) and yet reaffirms Rossellini's concern for his fellow men and for Italy. At the same time, through his restriction of incident, he shapes the viewer's empathy for his characters by allowing the viewer to participate in the film only to the extent of being companion to the various characters. The audience is intellectually free to wander away from the story, which it undoubtedly does, only to find its involvement in the character's spiritual development unchanged since its sympathy is not based upon the physical actions of a plot.

Such an intertwining of empathetic involvement of sorts with a contemplative detachment carried over into Rossellini's historical films of the 1960s and 1970s. His deliberately obtrusive use of zoom lenses created in the viewer of such films as *Viva l'Italia* and *Agostino di Ippona* a delicate distancing and a constant but subtle awareness that the director's point of view was inescapable. Such managing of the viewer's consciousness of the historical medium turns his characters into identifiable human beings who, though involving our senses and our emotions, can still be scrutinized from a relatively detached vantage point.

This, then, is the seeming contradiction central to Rossellini's entire body of work. As most precisely exemplified in his early, pure neorealistic films, his camera is relentlessly fixed on the physical aspects of the world around us. Yet, as defined by his later works, which both retain and modify much of this temporal focus, the director is also trying to capture within the same lens an unseen and spiritual landscape. Thus, the one constant within all of his films must inevitably remain his concern for fundamental human values and aspirations, whether they are viewed with the anger and immediacy of a *Roma, città aperta* or the detachment of a *Viaggio in Italia.*—STEPHEN L. HANSON

Rossen, Robert

Nationality American. *Born* Robert Rosen in New York City, 16 March 1908. *Education* Attended New York University. *Family* Married Sue Siegal, 1954, three children. *Career* Staged plays for Washington Square Players, later the Theater Guild, 1920s; actor, stage manager, and director in New York City, 1930-35; writer under contract to Mervyn LeRoy and Warner Bros., 1936-45; member of Communist Party in Hollywood, 1937-45; directed first feature, Johnny O'Clock, 1947; subpoenaed by House Un-American Activities Committee (HUAC), hearing suspended after arrest of Hollywood Ten, 1947; produced first film, 1949; blacklisted after refusing to cooperate when called again to testify before HUAC, 1951-53; allowed to work again after naming names, 1953. *Award* Best Direction, New York Film Critics, for The Hustler, 1961. *Died* 18 February 1966.

Films as Director: 1947: *Johnny O'Clock* (+sc); *Body and Soul.* **1949:** *All the King's Men* (+sc, pr). **1951:** *The Brave Bulls* (+pr). **1955:** *Mambo* (+co-sc). **1956:** *Alexander the Great* (+sc, pr). **1957:** *Island in the Sun.* **1959:** *They Came to Cordura* (+co-sc). **1961:** *The Hustler* (+co-sc, pr). **1964:** *Lilith* (+co-sc, pr).

Other Films: 1937: *Marked Woman* (Bacon) (co-sc); *They Won't Forget* (LeRoy) (co-sc). **1938:** *Racket Busters* (co-sc). **1939:** *Dust Be My Destiny* (sc); *The Roaring Twenties* (Walsh) (co-sc). **1940:** *A Child Is Born* (Bacon) (sc). **1941:** *Blues in the Night* (Litvak) (sc); *The Sea Wolf* (Curtiz) (sc); *Out of the Fog* (Litvak) (co-sc). **1943:** *Edge of Darkness* (Milestone) (sc). **1946:** *A Walk in the Sun* (Milestone) (sc); *The Strange Love of Martha Ivers* (Milestone) (sc). **1947:** *Desert Fury* (sc). **1949:** *The Undercover Man* (pr).

Robert Rossen died as he was beginning to regain a prominent position in the cinema. His premature death left us with a final film which pointed to a new, deepening devotion to the study of deteriorating psychological states.

As a contract writer for Warner Bros. in the late 1930s and early 1940s, Rossen worked on many excellent scripts which showed a strong sympathy for individuals destroyed by or battling "the system." His first produced screenplay, *Marked Woman,* a little-known and highly underrated Bette Davis vehicle, deserves serious attention for its study of prostitution racketeering and its empowerment of women to overthrow corruption. His fifth film, *The Roaring Twenties,* is a thoughtful study of the obsessive drive for power and money amidst the harshness of the post-

World War I period and the beginnings of the Great Depression. While his early scripts occasionally displayed an idealism which bordered on naiveté, Rossen deserves credit for his commitment to the depiction of economic and social injustice.

Robert Rossen

According to Alan Casty in *The Films of Robert Rossen,* Rossen was invited to direct his own screenplay for *Johnny O'Clock,* a tale of murder among gamblers, at the insistence of the film's star, Dick Powell. Rossen followed this poorly received directorial debut with two of his most critically and financially successful films: *Body and Soul* and *All the King's Men,* two male-centered studies of corruption and the drive for success. The first of these films is centered in the boxing ring, the second in the political arena. The success of *Body and Soul* (from a screenplay by Abraham Polonsky) allowed Rossen the financial stability to set up his own company with a financing and releasing contract through Columbia Pictures. As a result, he wrote, directed, and produced *All the King's Men,* which was awarded the Best Picture Oscar in 1949.

These back-to-back successes apparently triggered an unfortunate increase in directorial ego: production accounts of the later films detail Rossen's inability to openly accept collaboration. This paranoia was exacerbated by his deepening involvement in House Un-American Activities Committee (HUAC) proceedings. Despite a 1953 reprieve after providing names of alleged Communists to the committee, he was unable to revive his Hollywood career, although he continued to work. He seemed a particularly unlikely candidate to direct his next three films: the Ponti-DeLaurentis melodrama *Mambo,* the historical epic *Alexander the Great,* and the interracial problem drama, *Island in the Sun.* The last of his 1950s films, *They Came to Cordura,* is an interesting film which should have succeeded. Its failure so obsessed Rossen that he spent many years unsuccessfully trying to re-edit it for re-release.

Rossen's final films, *The Hustler* and *Lilith,* show a return to form, due in great part to the atmospheric cinematography of Eugene Schufftan. Rossen, firmly entrenched in the theatrical values of content through script and performance, had previously worked with strong cinematographers (especially James Wong Howe and Burnett Guffey), but had worked from the conviction that content was the prime area of concern. As he told *Cahiers du Cinéma,* "Technique is nothing compared to content." In *The Hustler,* a moody film about winners and losers set in the world of professional pool-playing, the studied script was strongly enhanced by Schufftan's predominantly claustrophobic framings. Schufftan, long a respected European cameraman (best known for his work on Lang's *Metropolis* and Carné's *Quai des brumes*), had been enthusiastically recommended to Rossen by Jack Garfein, who had brought Schufftan back to America for his *Something Wild.*

Schufftan's working posture was one of giving the director what he asked for, and production notes from the set of *The Hustler* indicate he gave Rossen what he wanted while also achieving results that one feels were beyond Rossen's vision. There was no denying Schufftan's influence in the film's success (it won him an Oscar), and Rossen wisely invited him to work on his next film.

Lilith, an oblique and elliptical film in which a psychiatric worker ends up seeking help, signalled an advance in Rossen's cinematic sensibility. While several of the purely visual passages border on being overly symbolic, one feels that Rossen was beginning to admit the communicative power of the visual. Less idealistic and with less affirmative endings, these last two films showed a deeper sense of social realism, with Rossen striving to portray the effect of the psychological rather than social environment on his characters. Rossen's last project, which went unrealized because of his death, would have allowed him to portray both the social and psychological problems of people living in the vicinity of Cape Canaveral (Cape Kennedy). Such a project would have provided him with a further opportunity to break away from his tradition of dialogue-bound character studies.—DOUG TOMLINSON

Rouch, Jean

*Nationality French. **Born** Jean Pierre Rouch in Paris, 31 May 1917. **Education** Lycée Henri IV, Paris, degree in literature; Ecole nationale des ponts et chaussées, Paris, degree in civil engineering. **Family** Married Jane Margaret Gain, 1952. **Career** Became first to make descent of Niger River by dugout canoe, also began making ethnographic films*

Jean Rouch (left) with David Francis

during trip, 1946-47; director of research at Centre Nationale de la Recherche Scientifique, 1966-86; Sécretaire Général du Comité du Film Ethnographique, 1972; President of La Cinémathéque française, 1987-91. **Awards** *Prize Festival du Film Maudit, Biarritz, for* Initiation à la danse, *1949; Prix du Reportage, Paris Short Film Festival, for* Circoncision, *1950; Critics Prize, Venice Film Festival, for* Les Maîtres fous, *1955; Prix Delluc, for* Moi, un Noir, *1959; Prizes at Cannes, Manheim, and Venice Festivals for* Chronique d'un été, *1961; Golden Lion Prize, Venice, for* La Chasse au lion, *1965.*

Films as Director: 1947: *Au pays des mages noirs* (co-d, sc, ph). **1948:** *Hombori; Les Magiciens de Wanzerbé* (co-d, pr, ph). **1949:** *Initiation à la danse des Possédés; La Circoncision* (+pr, ph). **1950:** *Chasse à l'hippopotame.* **1951:** *Bataille sur le grand fleuve* (+ph); *Cimetière dans la falaise; Yenendi: les Hommes qui font la pluie* (+ph); *Les Gens du mil* (+ph). **1952:** *Les Fils de l'eau* (compilation of earlier films; released 1958). **1953:** *Mammy Water* (+sc, ph). **1954:** *Les Maîtres fous* (+ph, narration). **1957:** *Baby Ghana; Moi, un noir* (+sc, ph). **1958:** *Moro Naba* (+ph); *La royale goumbé* (+ph); *Sakpata* (co-d, +ph). **1961:** *La Pyramide humaine* (+sc, co-ph); *Chronique d'un été* (*Chronicle of a Summer*) (co-d, co-sc); *Les Ballets de Niger.* **1962:** *La Punition* (co-d); *Urbanisme africain* (+sc); *Le Mil; Les Pêcheurs du Niger* (+sc); *Abidjan, port de pêche* (+sc). **1963:** *Le Palmier à l'huile; Les Cocotiers; Monsieur Albert Prophète; Rose et Landry.* **1964:** "Véronique et Marie-France" (also known as "La Fleur de l'âge ou les adolescents") episode of *Les Veuves de quinze ans* (*The Adolescents; That Tender Age*) (+sc); "Gare du nord" episode of *Paris vu par* (*Six in Paris*) (+sc). **1965:** *La Chasse au lion à l'arc* (*The Lion Hunters*) (+sc, ph, narration); *La Goumbe des jeunes noceurs* (+sc, ph) (released 1967); *L'Afrique et la recherche scientifique; Alpha noir; Tambours de pierre; Festival de Dakar; Hampi; Musique et danse des chasseurs Gow; Jackville.* **1966:** *Batteries Dogon—éléments pour une étude des rythmes* (co-d); *Fêtes de novembre à Bregbo; Dongo Horendi; Dongo Yenendi; Koli-Koli; Sigui année zero* (co-d). **1967:** *Jaguar* (+ph); *Daudo Sorko; Sigui: l'enclume de Yougo; Tourou et Bitti.* **1968:** *Pierres chantantes d'Ayorou; Wanzerbe; Sigui 1968—les danseurs de Tyogou* (co-d); *Un Lion nommé l'Américain.* **1969:** *Sigui 1969—la caverne de Bongo.* **1970:** *Yenendi de Yantalla; Mya—la mère; Sigui 1970—Les clameurs d'Amani* (co-d). **1971:** *Petit à petit* (+co-sc, ph); *Porto Novo—la danse des reines* (co-d); *Sigui 1971—la dune d'Idyeli* (co-d); *Architectes Ayorou; Yenendi de Simiri.* **1972:** *Horendi; Sigui 1972—les pagnes de lame* (co-d); *Yenendi de Boukoki; Tanda Singui.* **1973:** *L'Enterrement du Hogon; VW—Voyou; Dongo Hori; Sécheresse à Simiri; Boukoki; Hommage à Marcel Mauss: Taro Okamoto.* **1974:** *Cocorico, Monsieur Poulet* (+co-sc); *Pam Kuso Kar; Sigui 1973—l'auvent de la circoncision; La 504 et les foudroyers* (co-d); *Ambara Dama* (co-d); *Sécheresse à Simiri* (continuation of 1973 film); *Toboy Tobaye.* **1975:** *Souna Kouma; Initiation.* **1976:** *Babatou ou les trois conseils* (+ph); *Médecines et médecins* (co-d); *Rhythme de travail.* **1977:** *Makwayela; Ciné-Portrait de Margaret Head* (*Margaret Head: Portrait of a Friend*); *Ispbahan: Lettre Persane 1977; Fête des Gandyi Bi à Simiri; Le Griot Badye* (co-d); *Hommage à Marcel Mauss: Marcel Levy; Hommage à Marcel Mauss: Germaine Dieterlen.* **1978:** *Simi Siddo Kuma.* **1979:** *Funérailles à Bongo: Le Vieux Anai* (co-d). **1982:** *Yenendi Gengel.* **1983:** *Portrait de Raymond Depardon.* **1984:** *Dionysos.* **1986:** *Folie ordinaire d'une fille de Cham* (*The Ordinary Madness of a Daughter of Cham*). **1987:** *Enigma* (co-d). **1988:** *Brise-Glace* (*Icebreaker*) (co-d); *Boulevards d'Afrique—bac ou mariage.* **1990:** *Cantate pour deux généraux* (doc); *Liberté, egalité, fraternité, et puis après.* **1993:** *Madame l'eau.* **1997:** *Moi fatigué debout, moi couché.*

Other Films: 1953: *Alger—Le Cap* (adviser). **1961:** *Niger, jeune républiquem* (adviser). **1976:** *Chantons sous l'Occupation* (co-ph).

A prolific and innovative ethnographic filmmaker as well as a pioneer of *cinéma vérité* and improvised film psychodrama, Jean Rouch has not only redefined documentary film practice but also stimulated radical developments in fiction film. It was as a civil engineer preferring West Africa to the German occupation that Rouch came to anthropology through observation of Songhay rituals. After the liberation, his untutored enthusiasm found an intellectual framework at the Musée de l'Homme, where he studied social anthropology under Marcel Mauss and ethnography under Marcel Griaule, the initiator of film recording in fieldwork.

It was at Griaule's instigation that in 1946 Rouch descended the Niger in a dugout canoe with a 16mm camera to make the first of over eighty ethnographic films.

Rouch's early films dutifully followed Griaule's lead in providing celluloid records of cultural practice. Typically, the self-effacing camera discreetly captured events which a later commentary interpreted for a posited Western audience. However, inspired by Flaherty's example, Rouch began to incorporate his subjects' perspective (*Cimetière dans la falaise*). Rather than make generalist exotic documentaries, he focused on particular aspects of African culture, sometimes in collaboration with fellow ethnographers. In the early years (1950-52), Rouch worked closely with Roger Rosfelder on migration, while in the period 1966-73, he made eight films with Germaine Dieterlen on the Sigui festivals of the Dogon.

Salient among the subjects covered during five decades of filming are: funeral rituals (*Cimetière dans la falaise; Moro Naba; Funérailles du vieil Anaï; L'Enterrement de Hogon; Souna Kouma; Pam Kusoka; Ambara Dama; Simir Siddo Kuma*), hunting (*La Chasse à l'hippopotame; Musique et danse des chasseurs Gow; La Chasse au lion à l'arc; Un Lion nommé l'Américain, Koli-Koli*), fishing (*Au Pays des mages noires; Bataille sur le grand fleuve; Mammy Water; Abidjan—port de pêche; Les Pêcheurs de Niger*), spiritual practices (*Les Magiciens de Wanzerbe; Monsieur Albert, prophète; Jackville*), possession rituals (*Initiation à la danse des possédés; Les Maîtres fous*), rain-making rituals (*Yenendi; les hommes qui font la pluie; Dongo Yendi; Dauda Sorko; Yenendi de Ganghel, Yenendi de Yantalla; Yenendi de Simiri; Yenendi de Boukoki*), and celebrations (*Baby Ghana; Fêtes de l'indépendance de Niger; La Goumbé des jeunes noceurs*).

Apart from the rituals dealing with possession, rain-making, and funerals, the most celebrated ethnographic films concern the Gow lion-hunters: *La Chasse au lion à l'arc* and *Un lion nommé l'Américain*. Filming over a seven-year period Rouch earned the trust of the tribal hunters to capture not only their techniques but, most importantly, the intimate lion hunt rituals and their meaning for the Gow hunters.

Rouch's evolution as an ethnographic filmmaker and his progressive exploration of subjectivity can be traced through key films. In the possession rituals of *Les Maîtres fous,* participants adopt the personas of their colonial masters. Rouch conveys both collective and personal responses in the self-induced hysteria which culminates in the eating of a sacrificial dog. Inserted satirical images of the British governor break with the tradition of presenting only the pro-filmic event while the commentary indicates the violence as a politically therapeutic act. This combination of socio-political and psychological insights brought a new dimension to the ethnographic film. The powerful exteriorisation of violence and role-play had particular meaning for two creative artists: Peter Brook staging his *Marat/Sade,* and Jean Gênet in his conception of *Les Noirs.*

Rouch's first feature film, *Moi, un Noir,* has thematic links with *Les Maîtres fous.* Observation of the daily lives of migrant workers includes their fantasies as they talk to the camera in the guise of their self-attributed movie-star pseudonyms. Discovering himself through the film's rushes, "Edward G. Robinson" is stimulated to talk openly about his problems and ambitions. The valuable perceptions derived from this participatory technique reinforced the importance of including the subjective conscious alongside objective observation in the ethnographic film.

As a means to gather further insights into issues of racial and cultural difference, Rouch regularly experimented with improvised dramas: *Jaguar; Cocorico, Monsieur Poulet; Les Adolescents; La Punition;* or the indicative *La Pyramide humaine.* In this film Rouch set up the situation of a white girl attempting to integrate with black classmates. With the camera providing the catalyst, pupils developed scenes from their own experiences to create a form of cathartic psychodrama, but the experiment was flawed by the lack of synchronized sound, and efforts to recreate raw emotions for a later sound-track proved difficult.

At the suggestion of the sociologist Edgar Morin, Rouch applied his investigative documentary approach to a group of Parisians questioned about happiness (*Chronique d'un été*). With lightweight sound equipment and a special wide-angled camera developed by fellow cinematographer Michel Brault, Rouch achieved a sense of immediacy and intimacy previously lacking. Despite reservations about the interview sample (mostly Morin's friends) and the *post hoc* shaping implicit in editing twenty-five hours of recording to the ninety-minute feature, *Chronique d'été* was lauded as the new realism, or in Rouch's terms, *cinéma vérité.*

The approach differs from the didacticism or idealism of scripted documentaries and implies a new directness and truthfulness (the term is borrowed from Vertov's *kino-pravda*). Whereas the contemporary "direct" cinema movement maintained the camera's invisibility, *cinéma vérité* foregrounded the technology, insisting that the elicited information is generated by the interview situation itself. The interventionist approach was geared to stimulate spontaneity, and with it, revelation.

The influence of the film was considerable. Radical filmmakers like Jacques Rozier, Chris Marker, and Jean-Luc Godard adapted the approach, so that hand-held cameras, actors addressing the camera, improvisation, or the undisguised directorial voice became staple elements.

The experiment of *Chronique d'un été* was extended in *La punition,* where Rouch also brought into play the techniques of *La Pyramide humaine.* Non-professional actors were wired for sound and left to improvise around the theme of a girl's encounters with three men in Paris. Rouch's aim was to maximise *cinéma vérité* spontaneity and, in order to reduce intervention through editing, filming was conducted in ten-minute takes over a single weekend. This attempt at convergence between film time and narrative time was only partially successful, and Rouch returned to the question in his "real life" drama of a fatal quarrel in *Gare du Nord,* one of the episodes in *Paris vu par. . . .*

In subsequent films Rouch explored cultural issues through folk tales or contemporary African drama. In *Babatou ou les trois conseils,* he draws on war chronicles and a fairy tale to articulate views on slavery, while in *Cocorico, Monsieur Poulet,* a Nigerian tale about a travelling chicken dealer is retold through the collective improvisation of non-professional actors. A stage play is the source both for *Folie ordinaire d'une fille de Cham,* in which two female inmates of a mental institution act out their frustrations born of gender, race, religion, and upbringing, and for *Boulevards d'Afrique,* based on a Senegalese musical comedy, in which a young woman challenges her parent's cultural assumptions about an arranged marriage.

Rouch's most recent work confirms the continuing vitality of his eclectic interests. In the powerful *Cantate pour deux généraux,* he returns to a possession ritual in which Africans perform voodoo rites on Napoleon's grave to release the spirit of a black general. With *Brise-*

Glace, he produced a wordless documentary about a Swedish ice-breaker in the North sea, while his current project, *Madame l'eau* has taken him to Holland.

As a self-tutored ethnographic filmmaker, Rouch pioneered approaches which in turn radicalised several areas of filmmaking in the 1960s. His interactive approach to documentary, which evolved into extemporized psychodramas, brought fresh insights into cultural difference, while the French tradition of scripted documentary (encapsulated in Rouquier's *Farrebique*) was jolted into a new form of directness by *Chronique d'un été*. Latter-day film and TV documetarists as well as radical filmmakers such as Godard attest to his influence in sociological film essays (*Masculin et féminin*). After half a century as a filmmaker, academic, and author, Rouch's commitment to promoting film as an instrument of enthnographical research remains undiminished. In 1978, as a mark of his international standing, he was himself the subject of a TV documentary, *Jean Rouch and His Camera in the Heart of Africa,* but there are no greater monuments to his life's work than the unique corpus of films produced for the Musée de l'Homme and the worldwide host of filmmakers who have followed his stimulating cross-disciplinary approach to filmmaking.—R.F. COUSINS

Russell, Ken

Nationality *British.***Born** *Henry Kenneth Alfred Russell in Southampton, England, 3 July 1927.* **Education** *Attended Pangbourne Nautical College, 1941-44.* **Military Service** *Served in merchant navy, 1945, and in Royal Air Force, 1946-49.* **Family** *Married 1) Shirley Ann Kingdom, 1957 (divorced), four sons, one daughter; 2) Vivian Jolly, 1984,*

Ken Russell directing *The Rainbow*. Photograph by Clive Coote.

one daughter. **Career** *Dancer with Ny Norsk ballet, 1950; actor with Garrick players, from 1951; documentary maker for the BBC's* Monitor, *from 1959; directed first feature,* French Dressing, *1963; TV director for* Omnibus, *from 1966, and for* South Bank Show, *from 1983.* **Address** *Old Tinsleys, Main Road, East Boldre, Brockinhurst, Hampshire SOH2 7WT, England.*

Films as Director (for television): 1959: *Poet's London; Gordon Jacob; Guitar Craze; Variations on a Mechanical Theme,* untitled film on Robert McBryde and Robert Colquhoun; *Portrait of a Goon.* **1960:** *Marie Rambert Remembers; Architecture of Entertainment; Cranks at Work; The Miners' Picnic; Shelagh Delaney's Salford; A House in Bayswater; The Light Fantastic.* **1961:** *Old Battersea House; Portrait of a Soviet Composer; London Moods; Antonio Gaudí.* **1962:** *Pop Goes the Easel; Preservation Man; Mr. Chesher's Traction Engines; Lotte Lenya Sings Kurt Weill* (co-d); *Elgar.* **1963:** *Watch the Birdie.* **1964:** *Lonely Shore; Bartok; The Dotty World of James Lloyd; Diary of a Nobody.* **1965:** *The Debussy Film; Always on Sunday.* **1966:** *Don't Shoot the Composer; Isadora Duncan, the Biggest Dancer in the World.* **1967:** *Dante's Inferno.* **1968:** *Song of Summer.* **1970:** *The Dance of the Seven Veils.* **1978:** *Clouds of Glory, Parts I and II.* **1983:** *Ken Russell's View of the Planets.* **1984:** *Elgar; Vaughan Williams.* **1988:** *Ken Russell's ABC of British Music.* **1989:** *Ken Russell—A British Picture.* **1990:** *Strange Affliction of Anton Bruckner.* **1991:** *Prisoner of Honor.* **1993:** *Lady Chatterly* (+co-sc). **1995:** *Classic Widows.*

(Features as director, unless otherwise indicated)1957: *Amelia and the Angel* (amateur short). **1958:** *Peep Show* (amateur short); *Lourdes* (amateur short). **1963:** *French Dressing.* **1967:** *Billion Dollar Brain.* **1969:** *Women in Love.* **1970:** *The Music Lovers* (+pr). **1971:** *The Devils* (+sc, co-pr); *The Boy Friend* (+pr, sc). **1972:** *Savage Messiah* (+pr). **1974:** *Mahler* (+sc); *Tommy* (+co-pr, sc). **1975:** *Lisztomania* (+sc). **1977:** *Valentino* (+co-sc). **1980:** *Altered States.* **1984:** *Crimes of Passion.* **1986:** *Gothic.* **1987:** Episode in *Aria.* **1988:** *Salome's Last Dance* (+sc); *The Lair of the White Worm* (+sc). **1989:** *The Rainbow* (+co-sc). **1991:** *Whore* (+co-sc). **1994:** *The Insatiable Mrs. Kirsch* (+sc). **1995:** *Mindbender.*

Other Films: 1991: *The Russia House* (Schepisi) (role as Walter).

British director Ken Russell was forty-two when his film of D. H. Lawrence's *Women in Love* placed him in the ranks of movie directors of international stature. For more than a decade before that, however, British television viewers had been treated to a succession of his skilled TV biographies of great artists like Frederick Delius (*Song of Summer*) and Isadora Duncan. Russell has always gravitated toward the past in choosing subjects for filming because, as he says, "topics of the moment pass and change. Besides, we can be more dispassionate and therefore more truthful in dealing with the past. And to see the past from the vantage point of the present is to be able to judge the effect of the past on the present."

His first TV documentaries, like that on Edward Elgar, correspond to what he calls "the accepted textbook idea of what a documentary should be; you were supposed to extol the great artists and their work. Later I turned to showing how great artists transcended their personal problems and weakness in creating great art." But this more realistic approach, exemplified in his telefilm about Richard Strauss (*Dance of the Seven Veils*) and his feature film *The Music Lovers,* about Tchaikovsky, upset some of the members of the audience for both his TV and theatrical films.

As Russell advanced from the small screen to the large in continuing to turn out what have come to be called his biopics, he has almost singlehandedly revolutionized the whole concept of the conventional film biography—to the point where the genre will never be quite the same again. One need only recall the heavily romanticized Hollywood screen biographies on subjects like Cole Porter to grasp how Russell's biopics have come to grips with the problems of an artist's life in relation to his work in a way that makes for much more challenging and entertaining films than the sugar-coated Hollywood screen biographies.

In addition to experimenting with the nature of biographical films, Russell has at the same time been seeking by trial and error to discover in all of his films, biopics or not, to what extent a motion picture can be cut loose from the moorings of conventional storytelling; and his mind-bending science-fiction thriller *Altered States* is an excellent example of this experimentation. If these experiments in narrative technique account for occasional lapses in narrative logic, as in *Lisztomania,* his biopic about Franz Liszt, they also account for the intricate and arresting blend of past and present, fact and fantasy, that characterize his best work.

Among his outstanding films must surely be numbered his screen adaptations of Lawrence's two companion novels, *Women in Love* (1969) and *The Rainbow* (1989), which focus on the personal lives of two sisters as they struggle to carve out their destinies in the modern world. The two films, taken together, represent Russell's finest achievement in the cinema.

Other films of his later career that deserve mention include *The Lair of the White Worm,* based on Bram Stoker's neglected novel about a female vampire who parallels Stoker's male vampire in *Dracula.* Russell turned Stoker's *Lair* into a bloodcurdling horror show. In addition, there is *Whore,* which, like his earlier *Crimes of Passion,* explores with unvarnished realism the grim life of a prostitute. Last but not least, mention must be made of Russell's *Lady Chatterly,* his superb four-hour TV version of Lawrence's controversial novel *Lady Chatterly's Lover,* which depicts a sensational love affair that reaches across the British class barriers. This telefilm, of course, is linked with his two previous Lawrence adaptations and marks another milestone in his career.

Although Russell has often been looked upon as a maverick who makes films that are perhaps more subjective and personal than many directors working today, it is worth noting he is the only British director in history ever to have three films playing first-run engagements in London simultaneously: *The Music Lovers, The Devils,* and *The Boy Friend.* Indeed, this provocative and fascinating director has already assured himself a place in the history of world cinema.—GENE D. PHILLIPS

Sautet, Claude

Nationality French. *Born* Montrouge, Paris, 23 February 1924. *Education* Ecole des Arts Decoratif, entered IDHEC, 1948. *Career* Music critic for newspaper Combat, late 1940s; assistant director to Pierre Montazel, Gut Lefranc, Georges Franju, and Jacques Becker, 1950s; also TV producer; directed first feature, Classe tous risques, 1960.

Films as Director and Scriptwriter: 1951: *Nous n'irons plus au bois* (short). **1956:** *Bonjour sourire* (d only). **1960:** *Classe tous risques* (*The Big Risk*). **1965:** *L'Arme à gauche* (*Guns for the Dictator*). **1970:** *Les Choses de la vie* (*The Things of Life*). **1971:** *Max et les ferrailleurs.* **1972:** *César et Rosalie* (*Cesar and Rosalie*). **1974:** *Vincent, François, Paul . . . et les autres.* **1976:** *Mado.* **1978:** *Une Histoire simple.* **1980:** *Un Mauvais fils* (*A Bad Son*). **1983:** *Garçon.* **1988:** *Quelques jours avec moi.* **1992:** *Un Coeur en hiver* (*A Heart in Winter*) (co-sc). **1995:** *Nelly & Monsieur Arnaud* (*Nelly & Mr. Arnaud*) (co-sc); *Les Enfants de Lumière.*

Other Films: (incomplete listing) 1954: *Touchez pas au Grisbi* (*Grisbi*). **1959:** *Les Yeux sans visages* (*Eyes without a Face*) (Franju) (asst d).

The career of Claude Sautet was slow in getting underway, but by the 1970s he had virtually become the French cinema's official chronicler of bourgeois life. He had made his directing debut with a solidly constructed thriller, *Classe tous risques,* in 1960, but a second film, *L'Arme à gauche,* did not follow until 1965 and was markedly less successful. Despite numerous scriptwriting assignments, his directing career did not really get underway until he completed *Les Choses de la vie* in 1969. This set the pattern for a decade of filmmaking.

The core of any Sautet film is a fairly banal emotional problem—a man caught between two women in *Les Choses de la vie* or a married woman confronted with a former lover in *César et Rosalie.* Around this situation Sautet weaves a rich pattern of bourgeois life: concerns with home and family, with money and possessions, give these films their particular tone. This is a cinema of warm, convincingly depicted characters for whom Sautet clearly has great affection and more than a touch of complicity. Problems and motivations are always explicitly set out, for this is a style of psychological realism in which the individual, not the social, forms the focus of attention.

The director's style is a sober, classical one, built on the model of Hollywood narrative traditions: action, movement, vitality. Though his style can encompass such set pieces as the boxing match in *Vincent, Francois, Paul . . . et les autres,* Sautet is more concerned with the unfolding of a strong and involving narrative line. A key feature of all his work are the confrontation scenes which offer such excellent opportunities for the talented stars and solid character players who people his films.

Sautet's films from the mid-1970s to early 1980s—*Mado, Une Histoire simple,* and *Une Mauvais fils*—are all characterized by a total assurance and a mastery of the medium. This mastery, however, is exercised within very precise limits—not in terms of the subject matter, which widens to take in the problems of affluence, women's independence, and juvenile delinquency, but in the manner in which such issues of the moment are approached. Sautet's classicism of form and ability to communicate directly with his audience is not accompanied by the resonances of social criticism which characterize the best North American cinema. Seeking to move his audience rather than enlighten it, Sautet uses powerful actors cast to type in carefully constructed roles, but any probing of the essential contradictions is avoided by a style of direction which keeps rigidly to the surface of life, the given patterns of bourgeois social behaviour. His approach is therefore condemned to a certain schematism, particularly in the handling of dialogue scenes, but his work gets its sense of vitality from the vigor with which the group scenes—the meals and excursions—and the typical locations of café or railway station are handled. Sautet offers a facsimile of life, a reflection of current problems or issues, but contained within a form calculated not to trouble the spectator after he has left the cinema. This conformism may seem limiting to the contemporary critic, but it will offer future generations a rare insight into the manner in which the French middle classes liked to see themselves in the 1970s.

In his most recent features, the popularly and critically well-received *Un Coeur en hiver* and *Nelly & Monsieur Arnaud*, Sautet continues to offer versions of French middle-class bourgeois life in the 1990s. In keeping with Sautet's thematic and stylistic terrain, *Un Coeur* and *Nelly* both focus on a small group of individuals as they undergo a set of personal and emotional situations. Again, while one senses a touch of Sautet's complicity with the bourgeois world he represents, these films do not simply offer the conservative resolutions that characterize so many of the bourgeois Hollywood productions of the 1980s and 1990s. As we watch *Un Coeur* and *Nelly*, we proceed along the interior, emotional topographies of characters like the remote and ostensibly affectless Stephan in *Un Coeur*. The tension which builds throughout *Un Coeur* as a result of Stephan's unwillingness and/or incapacity to love does not find its release, however, through the union of Stephan and Camille by the film's end: Camille continues her relationship with Maxim, Stephan remains alone. As a result, Sautet powerfully succeeds in having *us* experience the frustration these characters feel, because *Un Coeur* resists consummating a formulaic relationship with its audience via a happy ending as Hollywood films are likely to do.

Nelly & Monsieur Arnaud affects its audience in similar ways. Comparable to *Un Coeur*, *Nelly's* presentation of the emotional firings and mis-firings between Nelly, Arnaud, Vincent, and Jerome draw the viewer into a narrative that resists uncomplicated closure; because of this, the world of *Nelly & Monsieur Arnaud* is more likely to resemble the reality its audience will encounter once the credits role and the lights go up. Derek Elley aptly comments in *Variety* that Sautet, in his films, "is more interested in the what-could-have-happened than the what-actually-has." *Nelly,* he concludes, "will delight those who don't like their T's crossed and I's dotted." While neither a revolutionary cinema nor one which simply gives way to Hollywood narrative conventions, Claude Sautet's films endure as poignant and insightful tales depicting the often beguiling world of human affairs.—ROY ARMES and KEVIN J. COSTA

Sayles, John

Nationality American. *Born* John Thomas Sayles in Schenectady, New York, 28 September 1950. *Education* Williams College, Williamstown, Massachusetts, B.S. in psychology, 1972. *Career* First novel published, 1975; writer for Roger Corman's New World Pictures, from 1977; first film as director, The Return of the Secaucus Seven, 1980; directed own plays New Hope for the Dead and Turnbuckle, Off-Off-Broadway, 1981; writer and director for TV, from 1980; director of promo videos for Bruce Springsteen, including "Born in the U.S.A." and "I'm on Fire."

Films as Director and Scriptwriter: 1980: *The Return of the Secaucus Seven* (+ed, role as Howie). **1981:** *Lianna* (+ed, role as Jerry). **1983:** *Baby, It's You.* **1984:** *The Brother from Another Planet* (+ed, role as bounty hunter). **1987:** *Matewan* (+role as preacher). **1988:** *Eight Men Out* (+role as Ring Lardner). **1991:** *City of Hope* (+ed, song, role as Carl). **1992:** *Passion Fish* (+ed). **1994:** *The Secret of Roan Inish.* **1995:** *Lone Star* (+pr). **1997:** *Men with Guns.*

Other Films: 1978: *Piranha* (Dante) (sc). **1979:** *The Lady in Red* (*Kiss Me and Die; Guns, Sin, and Bathtub Gin*) (Teague) (sc). **1980:** *Battle beyond the Stars* (Murakami) (sc); *The Howling* (Dante) (co-sc); *Alligator* (Teague) (sc). **1982:** *The Challenge* (Frankenheimer) (co-sc). **1984:** *Hard Choices* (King) (role as Don). **1985:** *The Clan of the Cave Bear* (Chapman) (sc); *Enormous Changes at the Last Minute* (Bank, Hovde) (sc). **1987:** *Wild Thing* (Reid) (sc); *Something Wild* (Demme) (role as motorcycle cop). **1989:** *Breaking In* (Forsyth) (sc). **1992:** *Straight Talk* (Kellman) (role as Guy Girardi); *Malcolm X* (Lee) (role as FBI man); *Matinee* (Dante) (role as phoney moral crusader). **1993:** *A Safe Place* (Lang) (sc); *My*

Life's in Turnaround (Schaeffer, Ward) (role as film producer). **1994:** *Men of War* (sc); *Bedlam* (Maclean) (sc). **1995:** *Apollo 13* (Howard) (sc).

No other American director has so successfully straddled both Hollywood and independent filmmaking as John Sayles. While his fellow independents have tended to restrict themselves either in terms of audience (Jim Jarmusch, Henry Jaglom) or creative scope (Woody Allen), Sayles has continued to make highly individual, idiosyncratic films of increasingly ambitious range, aimed firmly at a mainstream audience, without compromising his own socially subversive outlook.

Even before launching out as a director, Sayles had established his reputation both as a novelist and as a provider of witty, literate scripts for genre movies—*Alligator, The Howling, The Lady in Red*—into whose conventions he deftly introduced sharp touches of political allegory. His own films, though, have steered clear of generic formulae, remaining (in subject matter as in treatment) fresh and quirkily unpredictable. The first of them, *The Return of the Secaucus Seven,* observed the reunion of a bunch of ex-1960s radicals with an affection, and a relaxed humour, that Kasdan's glossier treatment in *The Big Chill* never quite matched. "There was a realism there," Roger Corman noted, "which more money might have obscured." The film picked up several awards and rapidly became a cult favourite.

Secaucus, for all its small-scale subject and slightly shaggy charm, established the priorities of all Sayles's work to date: in his own words, "the acting, and believing in the characters and caring about them." His films, situated (as Pat Aufderheide put it) "at the intersection of culture and politics," favour ensemble playing over star performances, communication over sensation, and the exploration of character and ideas over pictorial values or technical bravura. "I don't regard anything I do as art. That's a foreign world to me. I regard it as a conversation. Very often in a conversation, you tell a story to illustrate something you think or feel," Sayles has stated.

Even so, Sayles's work has developed steadily in terms of visual as well as dramatic complexity. His early films, such as *Secaucus* and *Lianna,* a sympathetic account of a married woman awakening to her lesbian nature, were criticised in some quarters for their static camerawork. Sayles, while readily conceding his lack of technical experience, pointed out that "Fluid camera work takes money. Unless it's an action movie, why cut away from good actors?" More recently, however, from *Matewan* onwards, he has adopted a more sophisticated and even elegant shooting style, though never at the expense of the story. The long, intricate tracking shots of *City of Hope* map out social connections and tensions as graphically as anything in Ophuls; while in *Matewan* scenes of nocturnal wood-smoky encampments in the Appalachian foothills, shot by Haskell Wexler in dark, grainy tones, recall elements of late Ford—*Wagonmaster,* say, or *The Horse Soldiers.*

Not that Sayles (unlike his "movie brat" contemporaries) is interested in strewing his pictures with allusive film-buff references. "I want people to leave the theater thinking about their own lives, not about other movies," he noted. His work draws its resonance from his social concerns, from his sense of character as a product of historical and cultural influences, from his acute ear for dialogue and his insight into the political process. The mismatched young couple of *Baby It's You* are no less constrained by the pressures of their class and environment (small-town 1960s New Jersey) than the West Virginian miners of *Matewan,* the baseball professionals of *Eight Men Out,* or the hostile urban factions of *City of Hope.* By contrast, the two women in

Passion Fish, both maimed by life and thrown together in prickly proximity, surmount their backgrounds and prejudices to achieve tentative friendship. Sayles's hope is that we, as viewers, will extrapolate from what we see, grasping its relevance to our own situation. "If storytelling has a positive function, it's to put us in touch with other people's lives, to help us connect and draw strength or knowledge from people we'll never meet, to help us see beyond our own experience."

Sayles's sympathy for his characters can sometimes verge on sentimentality, as in *The Brother from Another Planet,* his least satisfactory though perhaps most likeable film—or in *The Secret of Roan Inish,* a rather too consciously poetic treatment of Celtic legend. His attitude to the movie industry, though, displays a clear-eyed realism, and an integrity which has so far resisted the lure—and the attendant compromises—of Hollywood mega-budgets. In his work as a

John Sayles

director, Sayles has steadily extended and deepened his personal vision of his country's history. If he can sustain the balancing act, funding his own staunchly independent work with lucrative scripting for other people's movies, he looks set to become one of the most original and incisive cinematic interpreters of the American myth.—PHILIP KEMP

Schlesinger, John

Nationality *British.* **Born** *John Richard Schlesinger in London, 16 February 1926.* **Education** *Uppingham School and Balliol College, Oxford, 1945-50.* **Career** *Maker of short films, from 1948; actor with Colchester Repertory Company then Ngaio Marsh's Touring Company, 1950-52; directed 24 short documentaries for BBC TV series* Tonight *and* Monitor, *1956-61; directed first feature,* A Kind of Loving, *1962; associate director, National Theatre, London, from 1973; opera director, 1980s; also director for TV, work includes* Separate Tables, *1982, and* An Englishman Abroad, *1983.* **Awards** *Best Direction, New York Film Critics, for* Darling, *1965; Oscar for Best Director, Best Direction Award, British Film Academy, and Directors Award, Directors Guild of America, for* Midnight Cowboy, *1969; Best Direction Award, British Film Academy, for* Sunday, Bloody Sunday, *1970; Commander of the British Empire, 1970; British Film and TV Academy Award, for* An Englishman Abroad, *1983.* **Agent** *c/o Duncan Heath, 76 Oxford Street, London W1R 1RB, England.*

Films as Director: 1961: *Terminus* (doc) (+sc). **1962:** *A Kind of Loving.* **1963:** *Billy Liar.* **1965:** *Darling* (+sc). **1967:** *Far from the Madding Crowd.* **1969:** *Midnight Cowboy* (+co-pr). **1971:** *Sunday,*

Bloody Sunday. **1972:** "Olympic Marathon" section of *Visions of Eight.* **1975:** *The Day of the Locust.* **1976:** *Marathon Man.* **1979:** *Yanks.* **1980:** *Honky Tonk Freeway.* **1981:** *Privileged* (consultant d only). **1985:** *The Falcon and the Snowman* (+pr). **1987:** *The Believers* (+pr). **1988:** *Madame Sousatzka.* **1990:** *Pacific Heights.* **1991:** *A Question of Attribution.* **1993:** *The Innocent.* **1996:** *Eye for an Eye; Cold Comfort Farm.*

Other Films: 1953: *Single-Handed* (*Sailor of the King*) (Boulting) (role). **1955:** *The Divided Heart* (Crichton) (role as ticket collector). **1956:** *The Last Man to Hang?* (Fisher) (role as Dr. Goldfinger). **1957:** *The Battle of the River Plate* (*Pursuit of the Graf Spee*) (Powell and Pressburger) (role); *Brothers in Law* (Boulting) (role). **1986:** *Fifty Years of Action!* (appearance as himself).

John Schlesinger began his professional career by making short documentaries for the BBC. His first major venture in the cinema was a documentary for British Transport called *Terminus,* about twenty-four hours at Waterloo Station, which won him an award at the Venice Film Festival. Schlesinger's documentaries attracted the attention of producer Joseph Janni; together they formed a creative association which has included several of Schlesinger's British films, beginning with *A Kind of Loving,* which won the Grand Prize at the Berlin Film Festival.

Schlesinger began directing feature films in Britain at the point when the cycle of low-budget, high-quality movies on social themes (called "Kitchen Sink" dramas) was in full swing. Because these films were made outside the large studio system, Schlesinger got used to developing his own film projects. He has continued to do so while directing films in Hollywood, where he has worked with increasing regularity in recent years, starting with his first American film, *Midnight Cowboy.*

"I like the cross-fertilization that comes from making films in both England and America," he explains. "Although I am English and I do like to work in England, I have gotten used to regarding myself more and more as mid-Atlantic." As a matter of fact, foreign directors like Lang

and Hitchcock and Schlesinger, precisely because they are not native Americans, are sometimes able to view American life with a vigilant, perceptive eye for the kind of telling details which home-grown directors might easily overlook or simply take for granted. Indeed, reviews of _Midnight Cowboy_ by and large noted how accurately the British-born Schlesinger had caught the authentic atmosphere not only of New York City, but also of Miami Beach and the Texas Panhandle, as surely as he had captured the atmosphere of a factory town in his native England in _A Kind of Loving._

"Any film that is seriously made will reflect the attitudes and problems of society at large," he says, and consequently possess the potential to appeal to an international audience, as many of his films have. "But it is inevitable that a director's own attitudes will creep into his films. For my part I try in my movies to communicate to the filmgoer a better understanding of other human beings by exploring the hazards of entering into a mutual relationship with another human being, which is the most difficult thing on earth to do, because it involves a voyage of discovery for both parties." Hence his prime concern as a director with examining complex human relationships from a variety of angles—ranging from the social outcasts of _Midnight Cowboy_ to members of the jet set in _Darling._

Among the standout films of his later career are: _Marathon Man,_ a thriller about a young American Jew who finds himself pitted against a Nazi war criminal in New York; _The Falcon and the Snowman,_ the true story of two young Americans who betrayed their country to the Russians; and _Madame Sousatzka,_ which concerns a dedicated, demanding London piano teacher, whose exacting standards threaten to drive her most promising pupil away. Significantly, Schlesinger's acutely observed depiction of the ramshackle old rooming house where Madame lives, with its colorful assortment of diverse tenants, lends to the film an authentic atmosphere that recalls Schlesinger's social ("Kitchen Sink") dramas.

Given the great success of _Marathon Man,_ Schlesinger went on to make a trio of superior thrillers: _Pacific Heights,_ in which a hapless young landlord is victimized by a psychotic tenant; _The Innocent,_ a story of international intrigue about a young English technician sent by British Intelligence to work on a secret operation in Berlin after World War II; and _Eye for an Eye,_ a dark study wherein a vengeful mother vows to bring to justice the brute who raped and murdered her daughter. This trilogy of suspense films clearly established Schlesinger as a worthy successor to Hitchcock in the thriller genre.

In sum, John Schlesinger is a member of the international community of filmmakers who speak to an equally international audience. That is the way the world cinema has been developing, and directors like Schlesinger have helped to lead it there.—GENE D. PHILLIPS

Schlöndorff, Volker

**Nationality** German. **Born** Wiesbaden, 31 March 1939. **Education** Lycée Henri IV, Paris; studied political science and economics; studied film directing at IDHEC, Paris. **Family** Married filmmaker Margarethe von Trotta, 1969. **Career** Assistant to various French directors, 1960-64; returned to Germany, 1965; formed Hallelujah-Film with Peter Fleischmann, went into partnership with German TV stations, 1969; formed Bioskop-Film with Reinhard Hauff, 1973; opera director, from 1974. **Awards** FIPRESCT

Prize, Cannes Festival, for Young Törless, *1966; Oscar for Best Foreign-Language Film, and Best Film, Cannes Festival* (ex aequo), *for* The Tin Drum, *1979.*

Films as Director: 1960: *Wen kümmert's . . . (Who Cares . . .)* (short, unreleased). **1966:** *Der junge Törless (Young Törless)* (+sc). **1967:** *Mord und Totschlag (A Degree of Murder)* (+co-sc). **1969:** *Michael Kohlhaas—Der Rebell (Michael Kohlhaas—The Rebel)* (+co-sc). **1970:** *Baal* (for TV) (+sc); *Ein unheimlicher Moment (An Uneasy Moment)* (short; originally episode of uncompleted feature *Paukenspieler,* filmed 1967); *Der plötzlicher Reichtum der armen Leute von Kombach (The Sudden Fortune of the Poor People of Kombach)* (+co-sc). **1971:** *Die Moral der Ruth Halbfass (The Moral of Ruth Halbfass)* (+co-sc); *Strohfeuer (A Free Woman; Straufire; Summer Lightning* (+co-sc). **1974:** *Übernachtung in Tirol (Overnight Stay in the Tyrol)* (for TV) (+co-sc). **1975:** *Georginas Grunde (Georgina's Reasons)* (for TV); *Die verlorene Ehre der Katharina Blum (The Lost Honor of Katharina Blum)* (co-d, co-sc). **1976:** *Der Fangschuss (Coup de grâce)*. **1977:** *Nur zum Spass—Nur zum Spiel (Only for Fun—Only for Play), Kaleidoskop Valeska Gert (Kaleidoscope Valeska Gert)* (doc) (+sc). **1978:** *Deutschland im Herbst (Germany in Autumn)* (co-d). **1979:** *Die Blechtrommel (The Tin Drum)* (+co-sc). **1980:** *Der Kandidat (The Candidate)* (doc) (+co-sc). **1981:** *Die Fälschung (The Forgery)* (+sc); *Circle of Deceit*. **1983:** *Krieg und Frieden (War and Peace)* (doc). **1984:** *Swann in Love (Un Amour de Swann)*. **1985:** *Death of a Salesman*. **1987:** *Vermischte Nachrichten (Odds and Ends)* (co-d); *A Gathering of Old Men* (for TV). **1990:** *The Handmaid's Tale*. **1991:** *Homo Faber (Voyager)* (+co-sc). **1992:** *The Michael Nyman Songbook; Billy Wilder: wie haben sie's gemacht* (for TV). **1996:** *Der Unhold.*

In discussions of the New German Cinema, Volker Schlöndorff's name generally comes up only after the mention of Fassbinder, Herzog, Wenders, and perhaps Straub, Syberberg, or von Trotta. Though his work certainly merits consideration alongside that of any of his countrymen, there are several reasons why he has stood apart from them.

As a teenager, Schlöndorff moved to France to study, earning academic honors and a university degree in economics and political science. He enrolled at IDHEC with an interest in film directing but chose instead to pursue an active apprenticeship within the French film industry. Eventually he served as assistant director to Jean-Pierre Melville, Alain Resnais, and Louis Malle. Schlöndorff then returned to Germany and scored an immediate triumph with his first feature, *Young Törless*. Like his mentor Louis Malle, then, he ushered in his country's new wave of film artists, but also like Malle, Schlöndorff's eclectic range of projects has defied easy categorization, causing his work to seem less personal than that of almost any other German filmmaker. The thorough professional training received during his decade in France also set Schlöndorff apart. His time there instilled in him an appreciation for the highly-crafted, polished filmmaking that marks his style. (The quality of the photography in his work—both black and white and in color, whether by Sven Nykvist, Franz Rath, or Igor Luther—has been consistently exceptional.) While most of his contemporaries declared their antipathy toward the look and production methods of the declining German film industry of the 1960s, Schlöndorff endeavored successfully to make larger-scaled features. Toward this end he helped form and continues to operate two production companies—Hallelujah-Film and Bioskop-Film—and has regularly obtained financing from German television and a variety of international producers. Yet he has met shooting schedules of just three weeks, and his wide career includes shorts, documentaries, and television films (one is a production of Brecht's *Baal* with Fassbinder in the title role). In the mid-1970s he even turned to directing opera: Janáček's *Katya Kabanova* and a work by Hans Werner Henze.

Intellectual, literate, and fluent in several languages, Schlöndorff has chiefly been attracted to the adaption of literary works—a practice which has yielded mixed results: *Young Törless,* from Robert Musil, remains one of his best films, and there is much to praise in *The Tin*

Drum, the New German Cinema's foremost commercial success, which Günter Grass helped to adapt from his novel. Despite strengths in each, though, the director's adaptations of Kleist's *Michael Kohlhaas* and Marguerite Yourcenar's *Coup de grace* turned out unevenly for quite different reasons. The admirable *Lost Honor of Katharina Blum* comes from a Heinrich Böll story, while the problematic *Circle of Deceit* was based on the novel by Nicolas Born.

Among "original" projects, on the other hand, are *A Degree of Murder,* a failure by all accounts; the fine *A Free Woman*; and the excellent *Sudden Wealth of the Poor People of Kombach.*

Despite the variety of his subjects, Schlöndorff is almost invariably drawn to material that allows him expression as social critic. All the films cited above share this characteristic. Some of his projects have been courageously political: *Katharina Blum* is

Volker Schlöndorff

an undisguised attack on Germany's powerful right-wing, scandal-mongering press, which serves large-scale social repression. As notable are his leading contributions to three collaborative documentaries: *Germany in Autumn,* a response to the authoritarian climate in the country in the wake of the Baader-Meinhof affair; *The Candidate,* a work shot during the election campaign that examines the career of ultra-conservative Christian Social Unionist Franz Josef Strauss; and *War and Peace,* an agit-prop film essay on the deployment of new American nuclear missiles in the Federal Republic.

Schlöndorff's major theme is the temptation toward moral and political equivocation within an ambiguous or malignant social order, and his films are wryly or skeptically realistic about any hoped-for solutions, even courting controversy. *A Free Woman* chastens unbridled feminist idealism; *Circle of Deceit* (made prior to the Israeli invasion of Lebanon) refuses to take sides in the Lebanese conflict.

Margarethe von Trotta, to whom Schlöndorff is married, has performed in a number of her husband's films and is a frequent collaborator on his scripts; interestingly, her own work as director is characterized not only by a polish equal to Schlöndorff's and similar political inspiration but also by a compelling intelligence and power of evocation.

Throughout the 1980s and early 1990s, Schlöndorff has continued directing films based on fine literature. They feature characters in moral conflict who are spooked by their pasts, uncertain of their futures, and unable to control their impulses and their fates.

Swann in Love, based on Marcel Proust's "Remembrance of Things Past," is the elegantly sensual story of a wealthy gentleman (Jeremy Irons) who thrives in the finest circles of high society but risks everything over his erotic obsession with a courtesan. *Death of a Salesman,* superbly adapted from the 1984 Broadway revival of the Arthur Miller play, is the saga of Willy Loman (Dustin Hoffman), the tragic, desperate travelling salesman to whom "attention must be paid." *The Handmaid's Tale,* scripted by Harold Pinter from Margaret Atwood's bestseller, is an intriguing science fiction chiller told from a woman's point of view. It is set in the future, when white women are coerced into birthing babies who will make up a new, "pure" generation. The story focuses on one such female (Natasha Richardson) who must contend with the advances of the powerful "commander" (Robert Duvall). Finally, *Voyager,* based on the Max Frisch book *Homo Faber,* is a pensive drama about two very different romances—one in the past, the other in the present—experienced by Walter Faber (Sam Shepard), a repressed American traveler.—HERBERT REYNOLDS and ROB EDELMAN

Schrader, Paul

Nationality American. *Born* Grand Rapids, Michigan, 22 July 1946. *Education* Educated in Ministry of Christian Reformed religion at Calvin College, Grand Rapids, Michigan, graduated 1968; took summer classes in film at Columbia University, New York; University of California at Los Angeles Film School, M.A., 1970. *Family* Married actress Mary Beth Hurt, 1983, one daughter, one son. *Career* Moved to Los Angeles, 1968; writer for Los Angeles Free Press, then became editor of Cinema magazine; first script to be filmed, The Yakuza, 1974; directed first feature, Blue Collar, 1977. *Award* First Prize, Paris Festival, for Blue Collar, 1978. *Address* Schrader Productions, 1501 Broadway, Suite 1405, New York, New York 10019, U.S.A. *Agent* Jeff Berg, International Creative Management, 8899 Beverly Blvd., Los Angeles, California 90048, U.S.A.

Films as Director and Scriptwriter: 1977: *Blue Collar.* **1978:** *Hardcore.* **1979:** *American Gigolo.* **1981:** *Cat People* (d only). **1985:** *Mishima: A Life in Four Chapters.* **1987:** *Light of Day.* **1988:** *Patty Hearst* (d only). **1990:** *The Comfort of Strangers* (d only). **1992:** *Light Sleeper.* **1994:** *Witch Hunt* (d only). **1997:** *Touch; Affliction.*

Other Films: 1974: *The Yakuza* (Pollack) (co-sc). **1976:** *Taxi Driver* (Scorsese) (sc); *Obsession* (De Palma) (co-sc). **1977:** *Rolling Thunder* (Flynn) (sc); *Close Encounters of the Third Kind* (Spielberg) (co-sc, uncredited). **1978:** *Old Boyfriends* (Tewkesbury) (co-sc, exec pr). **1980:** *Raging Bull* (Scorsese) (co-sc). **1986:** *The Mosquito Coast* (Weir) (sc). **1988:** *The Last Temptation of Christ* (Scorsese) (sc). **1995:** *City Hall* (Becker) (co-sc).

While it is doubtless fanciful and recherché to read Paul Schrader's movies as unmediated reflections of his own life and feelings, it is nonetheless true that the director/screenwriter's "religious fascination with the redeeming hero" echoes his extreme fascination with himself. The incredible urge that his characters have to confess (Schrader frequently resorts to voice-overs and interior monologues), exemplified by Travis Bickle's mutterings in *Taxi Driver,* Christ's musings on the cross during his *Last Temptation,* and Patty Hearst's thoughts about her abduction, suggest that his films are firmly rooted in self-analysis. The recent book *Schrader on Schrader,* and the filmmaker's enthusiasm for the bio-pic (*Mishima, Patty Hearst*), a genre that had been more or less moribund since the time of Paul Muni, testify that he does indeed share the Calvinist urge to account for everything, to make his art out of the introspective inventory of his, or somebody else's, life.

Appropriately, for a confirmed fan of the films of Bresson, the image of the condemned man/woman attempting to escape his/her fate is a leitmotif in Schrader's work. He seems obsessed with prison metaphors, with images of captivity. In *Patty Hearst,* Natasha Richardson is locked up in a cupboard. In *Cat People,* Nastassia Kinski ends up behind bars, in a zoo—a human captive in a panther's body. Richard Gere, in *American Gigolo,* is "framed" (he is "framed" for a murder he did not commit and "framed" as the object of the gaze—the camera seems to love him), and the last time we see him, he is reaching out for Lauren Hutton but is separated from her by the glass panel in the prison interview booth. Christ, predictably, ends up on the cross: he too is trapped. A last, sad image of *Raging Bull* is of Jake La Motta (Robert De Niro) banging his head against his cell wall. Schrader's work abounds in figures cabined, cribbed, and confined.

Paul Schrader

Travis Bickle, that emissary from 1970s America, is a prisoner in the city, a prisoner in his own body, a prisoner behind the wheel of his taxi, a slave to pornography and junk food, and he is trying, in his mildly psychotic way, to free Jodie Foster's child prostitute, who is similarly trapped. Season Hubley in *Hardcore* is whisked away from a Calvinist Convention, kidnapped by a snuff movie producer, and needs an Ahab/John Wayne figure (George C. Scott) from the suburbs to rescue her, to try to reincarcerate her within the family. Even Schrader's Venice in *The Comfort of Strangers,* studio-built and full of interminable dark corridors, seems more like San Quentin than a beautiful European city on water.

An American of Dutch/German extraction, Schrader had a strict religious upbringing in Grand Rapids, Michigan. He did not watch as much TV as one might expect, and when it came to the cinema, he was cruelly deprived: incredibly, he saw his first film, *The Absent-Minded Professor,* when he was seventeen. Then came the revelation of *Wild in the Country,* a lurid Elvis Presley vehicle which gave him his vision on the Road to Damascus: he was captured by the celluloid muse. His Calvinist background combined with his early career as film historian/critic (he was a Pauline Kael protegé, a "Paulette" as he describes it, and it was Kael's influence which got him into the film course at UCLA) make him among the more academically inclined of mainstream Hollywood filmmakers. Few of his contemporaries have been fellows of the American Film Institute or have written ineffably unfathomable monographs on transcendental style in the movies of Ozu, Bresson, and Dreyer. He straddles two mutually exclusive cultures, traditions, discourses. On the one hand, he is the film scholar and expert in European and Japanese cinema. On the other, he is the hack Hollywood director and screenwriter. It is a tension which he seems to enjoy. Is he the artist locked up in a commercial catacomb or is he the popular filmmaker, hampered by his own notions of art? Is he, perhaps, just plain religious freak and show-off? "The reason I put that Bressonian ending onto *American Gigolo* was a kind of outrageous perversity, saying I can make this fashion-conscious, hip Hollywood movie and at the end claim it's really pure; and in *Cat People* I can make this horror movie and say it was about Dante and Beatrice."

Sometimes Schrader seems too clever by half. Kael, attacking *Patty Hearst*, suggested he lacked a basic instinct for moviemaking: "he doesn't reach an audience's emotions." This is probably unfair. His own scripts have a relentless narrative drive, generally toward some kind of judgement day (witness his work with Scorsese). When he is directing another writer's scenario, he can lose that obsessive will to destruction, salvation, damnation. Both *Patty Hearst* and *The Comfort of Strangers*—though it must be taxing for any director to try to animate a Pinter script— lack the momentum, the frenetic desire to tell a story of the films which he wrote himself.

Apparently, he worked with Spielberg on early drafts of *Close Encounters,* but Spielberg elbowed him off the project because Schrader did not share his Capra-like love of the common man and wanted to make the protagonist a crusading religious fruitcake *à la* Travis Bickle. Whatever one's reservations about Schrader's evangelism or his tedious self-obsession, he is undoubtedly one of Hollywood's most formally arresting filmmakers. He pays enormous attention to set design. (He has worked frequently with Scarfiotti, Bertolucci's designer on *The Conformist*.) He seems equally at home with the lush, magical opulence of New Orleans in *Cat People*, the sober, almost drama-doc look of *Patty Hearst*, the glossy, superficial Los Angeles, all hotels, restaurants, and expensive apartments, of *American Gigolo*, or the stagy, elaborate sets on *Mishima*. Edgy, prowling tracks (the opening shot of *The Comfort of Strangers* is a virtuoso effort in camera peripeteia to rival the first few minutes of Welles' *Touch of Evil*), a predilection for high angle shots (humans as bugs), and his discerning use of music (he has worked with Philip Glass and Giorgio Moroder, among others) show him as a filmmaker with a consummate love of his craft.

Yet Schrader thrives on controversy. He was sacked from his job as film critic for the *Los Angeles Free Press* because he gave a debunking review to *Easy Rider*. *American Gigolo* was attacked as being homophobic. *Mishima* provoked an outcry in Japan. *The Last Temptation of Christ* brought the moral majority out to the picket line. Apparently a student radical in the 1960s, Schrader caricatures the Symbionese Liberation Army, Patty Hearst's abductors, as idiotic mouthers of revolutionary platitudes. His films seem to abound in right-wing visionaries (Travis Bickle, George C. Scott in *Hardcore,* Mishima, Christopher Walken in *The Comfort of Strangers*) and, while he does not straightforwardly endorse their viewpoints, he respects their right to be individuals and their struggle for redemption, a struggle which invariably leaves onlookers dead and dying in the crusading hero's wake. Social historians of American culture and politics in the 1970s and 1980s will find rich pickings in the Schrader *oeuvre*.

Schrader continued his cinematic explorations of characters attempting to purge themselves of their excesses and sins in *Light Sleeper,* a knowing, sobering film set amid the strata of the New York City drug culture. Symbolically, its scenario is set during a sanitation strike, allowing the streets to be strewn with garbage. Willem Dafoe plays John LeTour, a forty-year-old ex-junkie and "mid-level drug dealer" whose clientele consists of upscale New Yorkers willing to pay big bucks for top-quality product. Both LeTour and Ann (Susan Sarandon), his boss, are fascinating characters. Within the confines of her world, Ann is a celebrity, a legend: the Mayflower Madam of the drug trade. She dresses like a high-powered business executive, dines in fancy restaurants, and tools around town in a chauffeured limousine. She also is shifting from drug dealing to marketing cosmetics. LeTour, too, yearns to go straight: he is having trouble sleeping, and he fears he has run out of luck. However, his redemption will not come easily, a fact that quickly becomes apparent when he runs into Marianne (Dana Delany), his ex-girlfriend and also a former junkie.

On occasion in *Light Sleeper*, Schrader waxes nostalgic about the "good old days" of drug use, "before crack came," when cocaine was the drug of choice. Otherwise, he graphically depicts the ravages of drugs. His junkies are unromanticized and ultimately pathetic. Despite its top-of-the-line cast, *Light Sleeper* was too unsexy a film to earn the widespread hype enjoyed by many of Schrader's earlier films. For this reason, the name Paul Schrader no longer holds the pull and allure it did back in the days of *Taxi Driver* or *American Gigolo*.—G.C. MACNAB and ROB EDELMAN

Scorsese, Martin

Nationality American. *Born* Flushing, New York, 17 November 1942. *Education* Cardinal Hayes High School, Bronx, 1956-60; New York University, B.A., 1964, M.A., 1966. *Family* Married 1) Laraine Brennan, 1965 (divorced), one daughter; 2) Julia Cameron (divorced), one daughter; 3) Isabella Rossellini, 1979 (divorced 1983); 4) Barbara DeFina, 1985. *Career* Film Instructor, NYU, 1968-70; directed TV commercials in England, and first feature, Who's That Knocking at My Door?, 1968; directed Boxcar Bertha for producer Roger Corman, 1972; directed The Act on Broadway, 1977; director for TV of "Mirror, Mirror" for Amazing Stories, 1985; directed promo video for Michael Jackson's "Bad," 1987. *Awards* Best Director, National Society of Film Critics, and Palme d'Or, Cannes Festival, for Taxi Driver, 1976; Best Director, National Society of Film Critics, for Raging Bull, 1980; Best Director, Cannes Festival, for The Color of Money, 1986; Best Director, National Society of Film Critics, for Goodfellas, 1990.

Films as Director: 1963: *What's a Nice Girl Like You Doing in a Place Like This?* (short) (+sc). **1964:** *It's Not Just You, Murray* (short) (+co-sc). **1967:** *The Big Shave* (short) (+sc). **1968:** *Who's That Knocking at My Door?* (+sc, role as gangster). **1970:** *Street Scenes* (doc). **1972:** *Boxcar Bertha* (+role as client of bordello). **1973:** *Mean Streets* (+co-sc, role as Shorty the Hit Man). **1974:** *Italian-American* (doc) (+co-sc). **1975:** *Alice Doesn't Live Here Anymore* (+role as customer at Mel and Ruby's). **1976:** *Taxi Driver* (+role as passenger). **1977:** *New York, New York*. **1978:** *The Last Waltz* (doc). **1979:** *American Boy* (doc) (+sc). **1980:** *Raging Bull*. **1983:** *The King of Comedy* (+role as assistant). **1985:** *After Hours* (+role as disco patron). **1986:** *The Color of Money*. **1988:** *The Last Temptation of Christ*. **1989:** "Life Lessons" episode in *New York Stories*. **1990:** *Goodfellas* (+sc); *Man in Milan* (doc). **1991:** *Cape Fear*. **1993:** *Age of Innocence* (+sc, role). **1995:** *Casino* (+sc). **1997:** *Kundun*.

Other Films: 1965: *Bring on the Dancing Girls* (sc). **1967:** *I Call First* (sc). **1970:** *Woodstock* (ed, asst d). **1976:** *Cannonball* (Bartel) (role). **1979:** *Hollywood's Wild Angel* (Blackwood) (role); *Medicine Ball Caravan* (assoc pr, post prod spvr). **1981:** *Triple Play* (role). **1982:** *Bonjour Mr. Lewis* (Benayoun) (role). **1990:** *Dreams* (Kurosawa) (role); *The Grifters* (Frears) (pr); *Fear No Evil* (Winkler) (role); *The Crew* (Antonioni) (exec pr); *Mad Dog and Glory* (McNaughton) (exec pr). **1991:** *Guilty by Suspicion* (role as Joe Lesser). **1993:** *Jonas in the Desert* (role). **1994:** *Quiz Show* (Redford) (role as sponsor); *Naked in New York* (exec pr). **1995:** *Search and Destroy* (exec pr, role as accountant); *Clockers* (Lee) (pr).

At present, with regard to the Hollywood cinema of the last fifteen years, two directors appear to stand head-and-shoulders above the rest, and it is possible to make large claims for their work on both formal and thematic grounds: Scorsese and Cimino. The work of each is strongly rooted in the American and Hollywood past, yet is at the same time audacious and

Martin Scorsese

innovative. Cimino's work can be read as at once the culmination of the Ford/Hawks tradition and a radical re-thinking of its premises; Scorsese's involves an equally drastic re-thinking of the Hollywood genres, either combining them in such a way as to foreground their contradictions (western and horror film in *Taxi Driver*) or disconcertingly reversing the expectations they traditionally arouse (the musical in *New York, New York*, the boxing movie and "biopic" in *Raging Bull*). Both directors have further disconcerted audiences and critics alike in their radical deviations from the principles of classical narrative: hence *Heaven's Gate* is received by the American critical establishment with blank incomprehension and self-defensive ridicule, while Scorsese has been accused (by Andrew Sarris, among others) of lacking a sense of structure. Hollywood films are not expected to be innovative, difficult, and challenging, and must suffer the consequences of authentic originality (as opposed to the latest in fashionable *chic* that often passes for it).

The Cimino/Scorsese parallel ends at this shared tension between tradition and innovation. While *Heaven's Gate* can be read as the answer to (and equal of) *Birth of a Nation*, Scorsese has never ventured into the vast fresco of American epic, preferring to explore relatively small, limited subjects (with the exception of *The Last Temptation of Christ*), the wider significance of the films arising from the implications those subjects are made to reveal. He starts always from the concrete and specific—a character, a relationship: the vicissitudes in the careers and love-life of two musicians (*New York, New York*); the violent public and private life of a famous boxer (*Raging Bull*); the crazy aspirations of an obsessed nonentity (*King of Comedy*). In each case, the subject is remorselessly followed through to a point where it reveals and dramatizes the fundamental ideological tensions of our culture.

His early works are divided between self-confessedly personal works related to his own Italian-American background (*Who's That Knocking at my Door?, Mean Streets*) and genre movies (*Boxcar Bertha, Alice Doesn't Live Here Anymore*). The distinction was never absolute, and the later films effectively collapse it, tending to take as their starting point not only a specific character but a specific star: Robert De Niro. The Scorsese/De Niro relationship has proved one of the most fruitful director/star collaborations in the history of the cinema; its ramifications are extremely complex. De Niro's star image is central to this, poised as it is on the borderline between "star" and "actor"—the charismatic personality, the self-effacing impersonator of diverse characters. It is this ambiguity in the De Niro star persona that makes possible the ambiguity in the actor/director relationship: the degree to which Scorsese identifies with the characters De Niro plays, versus the degree to which he distances himself from them. It is this tension (communicated very directly to the spectator) between identification and repudiation that gives the films their uniquely disturbing quality.

Indeed, Scorsese is perhaps the only Hollywood director of consequence who has succeeded in sustaining the radical critique of American culture that developed in the 1970s through the Reagan era of retrenchment and recuperation. Scorsese probes the tensions within and between individuals until they reveal their fundamental, cultural nature. Few films have chronicled so painfully and abrasively as *New York, New York* the impossibility of successful heterosexual relations within a culture built upon sexual inequality. The conflicts arising out of the man's constant need for self-assertion and domination and the woman's bewildered alterations between rebellion and complexity are—owing to the peculiarities of the director/ star/character/spectator relationship—simultaneously experienced and analysed.

Raging Bull goes much further in penetrating to the root causes of masculine aggression and violence, linking socially approved violence in the ring to socially disapproved violence outside it, violence against men to violence against women. It carries to its extreme that reversal of generic expectations so characteristic of Scorsese's work: a boxing melodrama/success story, it is the ultimate anti-*Rocky*; a filmed biography of a person still living, it flouts every unwritten rule of veneration for the protagonist, celebration of his achievements, triumph after tribulation, etc. Ostensibly an account of the life of Jake LaMotta, it amounts to a veritable case history of a paranoiac, and can perhaps only be fully understood through Freud. Most directly relevant to the film is Freud's assertion that every case of paranoia, without exception, has its roots in a repressed homosexual impulse; that the primary homosexual love-objects are likely to be father and brothers; that there are four "principle forms" of paranoia, each of which amounts to a *denial* of homosexual attraction (see the analysis of the Schreber case and its postscript). *Raging Bull* exemplifies all of this with startling (if perhaps largely inadvertent) thoroughness: all four of the "principle forms" are enacted in Scorsese's presentation of LaMotta, especially significant being the paranoid's projection of his repressed desires for men onto the woman he ostensibly loves. The film becomes nothing less than a statement about the disastrous consequences, for men and women alike, of the repression of bisexuality in our culture.

King of Comedy may seem at first sight a slighter work than its two predecessors, but its implications are no less radical and subversive: it is one of the most complete statements about the emotional and spiritual bankruptcy of patriarchal capitalism today that the cinema has given us. The symbolic Father (once incarnated in figures of mythic force, like Abraham Lincoln) is here revealed in his essential emptiness, loneliness, and inadequacy. The "children" (De Niro and Sandra Bernhard) behave in exemplary Oedipal fashion: he wants to *be* the father, she wants to screw the father. The film moves to twin climaxes. First, the father must be reduced to total impotence (to the point of actual immobility) in order to be loved; then Bernhard can croon to him "You're gonna love me/like nobody's loved me," and remove her clothes. Meanwhile, De Niro tapes his TV act which (exclusively concerned with childhood, his parents, self-deprecia- tion) culminates in a joke about throwing up over his father's new shoes, the shoes he is (metaphorically) now standing in. We see ambivalence towards the father, the hatred-in-rivalry of "brother" and "sister," the son's need for paternal recognition (albeit in fantasy) before he can announce himself to the woman he (very dubiously) loves; and the irrelevance of the mother (a mere, intermittently intrusive, off-screen voice) to any "serious"—i.e., Oedipal patriarchal— concerns. Thus *King of Comedy* constitutes one of the most rigorous assaults we have on the structures of the patriarchal nuclear family and the impossible desires, fantasies, frustrations, and violence those structures generate: an assault, that is, on the fundamental premises of our culture.

Since 1990, Scorsese has made four films which, taken together, establish him definitively as the most important director currently working in Hollywood. *Goodfellas, Cape Fear, The Age of Innocence,* and *Casino* reveal an artist in total command of every aspect of his medium—narrative construction, *mise-en-scène,* editing, the direction of actors, set design, sound, music, etc. Obviously, he owes much to the faithful team he has built up over the years, each of whom deserves an individual appreciation; but there can be no doubt of Scorsese's overall control at every level, from the conceptual to the minutiae of execution, informed by his sense of the work as a totality to which every strand, every detail, contributes integrally. If the films continue to raise certain doubts, to prompt certain reservations, it is not on the level of realization, but on moral and philosophical grounds. Let it be said at once, however, that *The Age of Innocence,* which in advance seemed such an improbable project—provoking fears that it would not transcend the solid and worthy but fundamentally dull literary adaptations of James Ivory—is beyond all doubts and reservations a masterpiece of nuance and refinement, alive in its every moment.

The other three films all raise the much-debated issue of the presentation of violence. There seem to be two valid ways of presenting violence (as opposed to the violence as "fun" of *Pulp Fiction,* violence as "aestheticized ballet" of John Woo's films, or violence as "gross out" in the contemporary horror movie). One way is to refuse to show it, always locating it (by a movement of the camera or the actors) just off-screen (Lang in *The Big Heat,* Mizoguchi in *Sansho Dayu),* leaving our imaginations free to experience its horror: a method almost totally absent from modern Hollywood. The other is to make it as explicit, ugly, painful, and disturbing as possible so that it becomes quite impossible for anyone other than an advanced criminal psychotic to enjoy it. The latter is Scorsese's method, and he cannot be faulted for it in the recent work. It was still possible, perhaps, to get a certain "kick" out of the violence in *Taxi Driver,* because of our ambiguous relationship to the central character, but this is no longer true of the violence in *Goodfellas* or *Casino.* An essential characteristic of the later films is the rigorous distance Scorsese constructs between the audience and *all* the characters: identification, if it can be said to exist at all, flickers only sporadically—is always swiftly contradicted or heavily qualified.

Yet herein lies what is at least a potential problem of these films. One can analyze the ways in which this distance is constructed, especially through the increasing fracturing of the narrative line, the splitting of voice-over narration among different characters in both *Goodfellas* and *Casino;* but isn't alienation, for many of us, inherent in the characters themselves and the subject matter? Scorsese has insisted that the characters of *Casino* are "human beings": fair enough. But he seems to imply that if we cannot feel sympathetic to them we are somehow assuming an unwarranted moral superiority. One might retort (to take an extreme case—but the Pesci character is already pretty extreme) that Hitler and Albert Schweitzer were both "human beings": may we not at least discriminate between them? One can feel a certain compassion for the characters (even Joe Pesci) as people caught up in a process they think they can control but which really controls *them;* but can one say more for them than that?

Beyond that, though connected with it, is the films' increasing inflation: not merely their length (*Goodfellas* plays for almost two-and-a-half hours, *Casino* for almost three) but its accompanying sense of grandeur: for Scorsese, apparently, the grandeur of his subjects. One is invited to lament, respectively, the decline of the Mafia and of Las Vegas. But suppose one cannot see them, in the first place, in terms other than those of social disease? The films strike me as too insulated, too enclosed within their subjects and milieux: the Mafia and Las Vegas are never effectively "placed" in a wider social context. Scorsese's worst error seems to be the use in *Casino* of the final chorus from Bach's *St. Matthew Passion:* an error not merely of "tease" but of sense, comparable in its enormity to Cimino's use of the Mahler "Resurrection" symphony at the end of *Year of the Dragon*. If it is possible to lament the decline of Las Vegas, it surely cannot be inflated into the lament of Bach's cheer for the death of Christ on the cross.

One cannot doubt the authenticity of Scorsese's sense of the tragic. Yet it is difficult not to feel that he has not yet found for it (to adopt T. S. Eliot's famous formulation) an adequate "objective correlative."—ROBIN WOOD

Sennett, Mack

Nationality *Canadian.* **Born** *Mikall (Michael) Sinnott in Danville, Quebec, 17 January 1880.* **Career** *Burlesque performer and chorus boy on Broadway, 1902-08; actor in Biograph films, 1908-10; director of Biograph shorts, from 1910, moved to Hollywood; formed Keystone Production Company with Charles Bauman and Adam Kessel, 1912; Keystone absorbed into Triangle Film Corporation with Thomas Ince's and D.W. Griffith's production companies, 1915; formed production company Mack Sennett Comedies following collapse of Triangle, 1917, though films released by Paramount; associated with Pathé, 1923-28, and with Educational Films, 1929-32, also returned to directing; producer and director of shorts for Paramount, from 1932, and experimented with early color process called "Natural Color"; returned to Educational Films, 1935, then retired to Canada; held nominal position at 20th Century-Fox from 1939.* **Award** *Special Oscar for contributions to screen comedy, 1937.* **Died** *1960.*

Films as Director: 1910: *The Lucky Toothache* (+sc, role); *The Masher* (+sc, role). **1911:** *Comrades* (+role); *Priscilla's April Fool Joke; Cured; Priscilla and the Umbrella; Cupid's Joke; Misplaced Jealousy; The Country Lovers; The Manicure Lady* (+role); *Curiosity; A Dutch Gold Mine* (+role); *Dave's Love Affair; Their Fates Sealed; Bearded Youth; The Delayed Proposal; Stubbs' New Servants; The Wonderful Eye; The Jealous Husband; The Ghost; Jinks Joins the Temperance Club; Mr. Peck Goes Calling; The Beautiful Voice; That Dare Devil* (+role); *An Interrupted Game; The Diving Girl; $500,000 Reward* (+role); *The Baron; The Villain Foiled; The Village Hero* (+role); *The Lucky Horseshoe; A Convenient Burglar; When Wifey Holds the Purse Strings; Too Many Burglars; Mr. Bragg, A Fugitive; Trailing the Counterfeit* (+role); *Josh's Suicide; Through His Wife's Picture; The Inventor's Secret; A Victim of Circumstances; Their First Divorce Case* (+role); *Dooley Scheme; Won Through a Medium; Resourceful Lovers; Her Mother Interferes; Why He Gave Up; Abe Gets Even with Father; Taking His Medicine; Her Pet; Caught with the Goods* (+role); *A Mix-up in Raincoats; The Joke on the Joker; Who Got the Reward; Brave and Bold; Did Mother Get Her Wash; With a Kodak; Pants and Pansies; A Near-Tragedy; Lily's Lovers; The Fatal Chocolate* (+role); *Got a Match; A Message from the Moon; Priscilla's Capture; A Spanish Dilemma* (+role); *The Engagement Ring; A Voice from the Deep; Hot Stuff; Oh, Those Eyes; Those Hicksville Boys; Their First Kidnapping Case* (+role); *Help, Help; The Brave Hunter; Won by a Fish; The Leading Man; The Fickle Spaniard; When the Fire Bells Rang; The Furs; A Close Call; Helen's Marriage; Tomboy Bessie; Algy, the Watchman; Katchem Kate; Neighbors; A Dash through the Clouds; The New Baby; Trying to Fool; One Round O'Brien; The Speed Demon; His Own Fault; The Would Be Shriner* (+role); *Willie Becomes an Artist; The Tourists; What the Doctor Ordered; An Interrupted Elopement; The Tragedy of a Dress Suit; Mr. Grouch at the Seashore; Through Dumb Luck.*

1912: *Cohen Collects a Debt* (*Cohen at Coney Island*) (+pr); *The Water Nymph* (+pr); *Riley and Schultz* (+pr); *The New Neighbor* (+pr); *The Beating He Needed* (+pr); *Pedro's Dilemma* (+pr, role); *Stolen Glory*

(+pr, role); *The Ambitious Butler* (+pr, role); *The Flirting Husband* (+pr); *The Grocery Clerk's Romance* (+pr); *At Coney Island* (+pr, role); *Mabel's Lovers* (+pr); *At It Again* (+pr, role); *The Deacon's Troubles* (+pr); *A Temperamental Husband* (+pr); *The Rivals* (+pr, role); *Mr.* (+pr, role); *A Desperate Lover* (+pr); *A Bear Escape* (+pr, role); *Pat's Day Off* (+pr, role); *Brown's Seance* (+pr); *A Family Mixup* (+pr, role); *A Midnight Elopement* (+pr); *Mabel's Adventures* (+pr); *Useful Sheep* (+pr); *Hoffmeyer's Legacy* (+pr); *The Drummer's Vacation* (+pr); *The Duel* (+pr, role); *Mabel's Strategem* (+pr).

1913: *Saving Mabel's Dad* (+pr); *A Double Wedding* (+pr); *The Cure That Failed* (+pr); *How Hiram Won Out* (+pr); *For Lizzie's Sake* (+pr); *Sir Thomas Lipton Out West* (+pr); *The Mistaken Masher* (+pr, role); *The Deacon Outwitted* (+pr); *The Elite Ball* (+pr); *Just Brown's Luck* (+pr); *The Battle of Who Run* (+pr, role); *The Jealous Waiter* (+pr); *The Stolen Purse* (+pr, role); *Mabel's Heroes* (+pr, role); *Her Birthday Present* (+pr); *Heinze's Resurrection* (+pr); *A Landlord's Troubled* (+pr); *Forced Bravery* (+pr); *The Professor's Daughter* (+pr); *A Tangled Affair* (+pr); *A Red Hot Romance* (+pr); *A Doctored Affair* (+pr); *The Sleuth's Last Stand* (+pr, role); *A Deaf Burglar* (+pr); *The Sleuths at the Floral Parade* (+pr, role); *A Rural Third Degree* (+pr); *A Strong Revenge* (+pr, role); *The Two Widows* (+pr); *Foiling Fickle Father* (+pr); *Love and Pain* (+pr); *The Man Next Door* (+pr); *A Wife Wanted* (+pr); *The Rube and the Baron* (+pr, role); *Jenny's Pearls* (+pr); *The Chief's Predicament* (+pr); *At Twelve O'Clock* (+pr); *Her New Beau* (+pr, role); *On His Wedding Day* (+pr); *The Land Salesman* (+pr); *Hide and Seek* (+pr); *Those Good Old Days* (+pr); *A Game of Poker* (+pr); *Father's Choice* (+pr); *A Life in the Balance* (+pr); *Murphy's I.O.U.* (+pr); *A Dollar Did It* (+pr); *Cupid in the Dental Parlor* (+pr); *A Fishy Affair* (+pr); *The Bangville Police* (+pr); *The New Conductor* (+pr); *His Chum, the Baron* (+pr); *That Ragtime Band* (+pr); *Algie on the Force* (+pr); *His Ups and Downs* (+pr); *The Darktown Belle* (+pr); *A Little Hero* (+pr); *Mabel's Awful Mistake* (+pr, role); *The Foreman and the Jury* (+pr); *The Gangster* (+pr); *Barney Oldfield's Race for a Life* (+pr, role); *Passions—He Had Three* (+pr); *Help! Help! Hydrophobia!* (+pr); *The Hansom Driver* (+pr, role); *The Speed Queen* (+pr); *The Waiter's Picnic* (+pr); *The Tale of the Black Eye* (+pr); *Out and In* (+pr); *A Bandit* (+pr); *Peeping Pete* (+pr); *His Crooked Career* (+pr, role); *For Love of Mabel* (+pr); *Safe in Jail* (+pr); *The Telltale Light* (+pr); *Love and Rubbish* (+pr); *A Noise from the Deep* (+pr); *The Peddler* (+pr); *Love and Courage* (+pr); *Professor Bean's Removal* (+pr); *Cohen's Outing* (+pr); *The Firebugs* (+pr); *Baby Day* (+pr); *Mabel's New Hero* (+pr); *Mabel's Dramatic Career* (+pr, role); *The Gypsy Queen* (+pr); *Willie Minds the Dog* (+pr); *When Dreams Come True* (+pr); *Mother's Boy* (+pr); *The Bowling Match* (+pr); *The Speed Kings* (+pr); *Love Sickness at Sea* (+pr, role); *A Muddy Romance* (+pr); *Cohen Saves the Flag* (+pr); *Zuzu the Band Leader* (+pr).

1914: *In the Clutches of the Gang* (+pr); *Mabel's Strange Predicament* (co-d, pr); *Love and Gasoline* (+pr); *Mack at it Again* (+pr, role); *Mabel at the Wheel* (+pr, role); *The Knockout* (+pr); *A New York Girl* (+pr, role); *His Talented Wife* (+pr, role); *Tillie's Punctured Romance* (+pr, feature); *The Fatal Mallet* (co-d with Chaplin, pr, role). **1915:** *Hearts and Planets* (+pr, role); *The Little Teacher* (+pr, role); *My Valet* (+pr, role); *A Favorite Fool* (+pr); *Stolen Magic* (+pr, role). **1921:** *Oh, Mabel Behave* (co-d, pr, role). **1927:** *A Finished Actor* (co-d, pr). **1928:** *The Lion's Roar* (+sc, pr). **1929:** *The Bride's Relation* (+pr); *The Old Barn* (+pr); *Whirls and Girls* (+pr); *Broadway Blues* (+pr); *The Bee's Buzz* (+pr); *Girl Crazy* (+pr); *The Barber's Daughter* (+pr); *Jazz Mamas* (+pr); *The New Bankroll* (+pr); *The Constable* (+pr); *Midnight Daddies* (+pr); *The Lunkhead* (+pr); *The Golfers* (+pr); *A Hollywood Star* (+pr); *Scotch* (+pr); *Sugar Plum Papa* (+pr); *Bulls and Bears* (+pr); *Match Play* (+pr); *Honeymoon Zeppelin* (+pr); *Fat Wives for Thin* (+pr); *Campus Crushes* (+pr); *The Chumps* (+pr); *Goodbye Legs* (+pr); *Average Husband* (+pr); *Vacation Loves* (+pr); *The Bluffer* (+pr); *Grandma's Girl* (+pr); *Divorced Sweethearts* (+pr); *Racket Cheers* (+pr); *Rough Idea of Love* (+pr). **1931:** *A Poor Fish* (+pr); *Dance Hall Marge* (+pr); *The Chiseler* (+pr); *Ghost Parade* (+pr); *Hollywood Happenings* (+pr); *Hold 'er Sheriff* (+pr); *Monkey Business in America* (+pr); *Movie-Town* (+pr, role); *The Albany Bunch* (+pr); *I Surrender Dear* (+pr); *Speed* (+pr); *One More Chance* (+pr). **1932:** *Hypnotized* (+pr, sc). **1935:** *Ye Olde Saw Mill* (+pr, sc); *Flicker Fever* (+pr); *Just Another Murder* (+sc, pr); *The Timid Young Man* (+pr); *Way Up Thar* (+pr).

Other Films: (incomplete list) 1908: *Balked at the Altar* (Griffith) (role); *Father Gets in the Game* (Griffith) (role); *The Song of the Shirt* (Griffith) (role); *Mr. Jones at the Ball* (Griffith) (role). **1909:** *Mr. Jones Has a Card Party* (Griffith) (role); *The Curtain Pole* (Griffith) (role); *The Politician's Love Story* (Griffith) (role); *The Lonely Villa* (Griffith) (role); *The Way of a Man* (Griffith) (role); *The Slave* (Griffith) (role); *Pippa Passes* (Griffith) (role); *The Gibson Goddess* (Griffith) (role); *Nursing a Viper* (Griffith) (role). **1910:** *The Dancing Girl of Butte* (Griffith) (role); *All on Account of the Milk* (Griffith) (role); *The*

Englishman and the Girl (Griffith) (role); *The Newlyweds* (Griffith) (role); *An Affair of Hearts* (Griffith) (role); *Never Again!* (Griffith) (role); *The Call to Arms* (Griffith) (role); *An Arcadian Maid* (Griffith) (role). **1911:** *The Italian Barber* (Griffith) (role); *Paradise Lost* (Griffith) (role); *The White Rose of the Wilds* (Griffith) (role); *The Last Drop of Water* (Griffith) (role). **1912:** *The Brave Hunter* (role).

1913: *Their First Execution* (pr); *Hubby's Job* (pr); *Betwixt Love and Fire* (pr); *Toplitsky and Company* (pr); *Feeding Time* (pr); *Largest Boat Ever Launched Sidewalks* (pr); *Rastus and the Game-Cock* (pr); *Get Rich Quick* (pr); *Just Kids* (pr); *A Game of Pool* (pr); *The Latest in Life Saving* (pr); *A Chip Off the Old Block* (pr); *The Kelp Industry* (pr); *Fatty's Day Off* (pr); *Los Angeles Harbour* (pr); *The New Baby* (pr); *What Father Saw* (pr); *The Faithful Taxicab* (pr); *Billy Dodges Bills* (pr); *Across the Alley* (pr); *The Abalone Industry* (pr); *Schnitz the Tailor* (pr); *Their Husbands* (pr); *A Healthy Neighborhood* (pr); *Two Old Tars* (pr); *A Quiet Little Wedding* (pr); *The Janitor* (pr); *The Making of an Automobile Tire* (pr); *Fatty at San Diego* (pr); *A Small Town Act* (pr); *The Milk We Drink* (pr); *Wine* (pr); *Our Children* (pr); *Fatty Joins the Force* (pr); *The Woman Haters* (pr); *The Rogues' Gallery* (pr); *The San Francisco Celebration* (pr); *A Ride for a Bride* (pr); *The Horse Thief* (pr); *The Gusher* (pr); *Fatty's Flirtation* (pr); *Protecting San Francisco from Fire* (pr); *His Sister's Kids* (pr); *A Bad Game* (pr); *Some Nerve* (pr); *The Champion* (pr); *He Would A Hunting Go* (pr).

1914: *A Misplaced Foot* (pr); *A Glimpse of Los Angeles* (pr); *Love and Dynamite* (pr); *Mabel's Stormy Love Affair* (pr); *The Under Sheriff* (pr); *A Flirt's Mistake* (pr); *How Motion Pictures Are Made* (pr); *Too Many Brides* (pr); *Won in a Closet* (pr); *Rebecca's Wedding Day* (pr); *Little Billy Triumphs* (pr); *Mabel's Bare Escape* (pr); *Making A Living* (pr); *Little Billy's Strategy* (pr); *Kid Auto Races at Venice* (pr); *Olives and their Oil* (pr); *A Robust Romeo* (pr); *Raffles* (pr); *Gentleman Burglar* (pr); *A Thief Catcher* (pr); *Twixt Love and Fire* (pr); *Little Billy's City Cousin* (pr); *Between Showers* (pr); *A Film Johnnie* (pr); *Tango Tangles* (pr); *His Favorite Pastime* (pr); *A Rural Demon* (pr); *The Race (How Villains Are Made)* (pr); *Across the Hall* (pr); *Cruel, Cruel Love* (pr); *Barnyard Flirtations* (pr); *A Back Yard Theater* (pr); *Chicken Chaser* (pr); *The Star Boarder* (pr); *Fatal High* (pr); *The Passing of Izzy* (pr); *A Bathing Beauty (A Bathhouse Beauty)* (pr); *Twenty Minutes of Love* (pr); *Where Hazel Met the Villain* (pr); *Bowery Boys* (pr); *Caught in a Cabaret* (pr); *When Villains Wait* (pr); *Caught in the Rain* (pr); *A Busy Day* (pr); *The Morning Papers* (pr); *A Suspended Ordeal* (pr); *Finnegan's Bomb* (pr); *Mabel's Nerve* (pr); *The Water Dog* (pr); *When Reuben Fooled the Bandits* (pr); *Acres of Alfalfa* (pr); *Our Large Birds* (pr); *The Fatal Flirtation* (pr); *The Alarm* (pr); *The Fatal Mallet* (pr); *Her Friend the Bandit* (pr); *Our Country Cousin* (pr); *Mabel's Busy Day* (pr); *A Gambling Rube* (pr); *A Missing Bride* (pr); *Mabel's Married Life* (pr); *The Eavesdropper* (pr); *Fatty and the Heiress* (pr); *Caught in Tights* (pr); *Fatty's Finish* (pr); *Love and Bullets* (pr); *Row-Boat Romance* (pr); *Laughing Gas* (pr); *Love and Salt Water* (pr); *World's Oldest Living Thing* (pr); *Mabel's New Job* (pr); *The Sky Pirate* (pr); *The Fatal Sweet Tooth* (pr); *Those Happy Days* (pr); *The Great Toe Mystery* (pr); *Soldiers of Misfortune* (pr); *The Property Man* (pr, role); *A Coat's Tale* (pr); *The Face on the Barroom Floor* (pr); *Recreation* (pr); *The Yosemite* (pr); *Such a Cook* (pr); *That Minstrel Man* (pr); *Those Country Kids* (pr); *Caught in a Flue* (pr); *Fatty's Gift* (pr); *The Masquerader* (pr); *Her Last Chance* (pr); *His New Profession* (pr); *The Baggage Smasher* (pr); *A Brand New Hero* (pr); *The Rounders* (pr); *Mabel's Latest Prank* (pr); *Mabel's Blunder* (pr); *All at Sea* (pr); *Bombs and Bangs* (pr); *Lover's Luck* (pr); *He Loved the Ladies* (pr); *The New Janitor* (pr); *Fatty's Debut* (pr); *Hard Cider* (pr); *Killing Hearts* (pr); *Fatty Again* (pr); *Their Ups and Downs* (pr); *Hello Mabel* (pr); *Those Love Pangs* (pr); *The Anglers* (pr); *The High Spots on Broadway* (pr); *Zipp, the Dodger* (pr); *Dash, Love and Splash* (pr); *Santa Catalina Islands* (pr); *The Love Thief* (pr); *Stout Heart But Weak Knees* (pr); *Shot in the Excitement* (pr); *Doug and Dynamite* (pr); *Gentlemen of Nerve* (pr); *Lovers' Post Office* (pr); *Curses! They Remarked* (pr); *His Musical Career* (pr); *His Trysting Place* (pr); *An Incompetent Hero* (pr); *How Heroes Are Made* (pr); *Fatty's Jonah Day* (pr); *The Noise of Bombs* (pr); *Fatty's Wine Party* (pr); *His Taking Ways* (pr); *The Sea Nymphs* (pr); *His Halted Career* (pr); *Among the Mourners* (pr); *Leading Lizzie Astray* (pr); *Shotguns That Kick* (pr); *Getting Acquainted* (pr); *Other People's Business* (pr); *His Prehistoric Past* (pr); *The Plumber* (pr); *Ambrose's First Falsehood* (pr); *Fatty's Magic Pants* (pr); *Hogan's Annual Spree* (pr); *A Colored Girl's Love* (pr); *Wild West Love* (pr); *Fatty and Minnie-He-Haw* (pr); *His Second Childhood* (pr); *Gussle the Golfer* (pr); *Hogan's Wild Oats* (pr); *A Steel Rolling Mill* (pr); *The Knockout* (Chaplin) (role).

1915: *A Dark Lover's Play* (pr); *Hushing the Scandal* (pr); *His Winning Punch* (pr); *U.S. Army in San Francisco* (pr); *Giddy, Gay and Ticklish* (pr); *Only A Farmer's Daughter* (pr); *Rum and Wall Paper* (pr);

Mabel's and Fatty's Wash Day (pr); *Hash House Mashers* (pr); *Love, Speed, and Thrills* (pr); *Mabel and Fatty's Simple Life* (pr); *Hogan's Messy Job* (pr); *Fatty and Mabel at the San Diego Exposition* (pr); *Colored Villainy* (pr); *Mabel, Fatty and the Law* (pr); *Peanuts and Bullets* (pr); *The Home Breakers* (pr); *Fatty's New Role* (pr); *Hogan the Porter* (pr); *Caught in the Park* (pr); *A Bird's a Bird* (pr); *Hogan's Romance Upset* (pr); *Hogan's Aristocratic Dream* (pr); *Ye Olden Grafter* (pr); *A Glimpse of the San Diego Exposition* (pr); *A Lucky Leap* (pr); *That Springtime Fellow* (pr); *Hogan Out West* (pr); *Ambrose's Sour Grapes* (pr); *Wilful Ambrose* (pr); *Fatty's Reckless Fling* (pr); *From Patches to Plenty* (pr); *Fatty's Chance Acquaintance* (pr); *Love in Armor* (pr); *Beating Hearts and Carpets* (pr); *That Little Band of Gold* (pr); *Ambrose's Little Hatchet* (pr); *Fatty's Faithful Fido* (pr); *A One Night Stand* (pr); *Ambrose's Fury* (pr); *Gussie's Day of Rest* (pr); *When Love Took Wings* (pr); *Ambrose's Lofty Perch* (pr); *Droppington's Devilish Dream* (pr); *The Rent Jumpers* (pr); *Droppington's Family Tree* (pr); *The Beauty Bunglers* (pr); *Do-Re-Mi-Fa* (pr); *Ambrose's Nasty Temper* (pr); *Fatty and Mabel Viewing the World's Fair at San Francisco* (pr); *Love, Loot and Crash* (pr); *Gussie Rivals Jonah* (pr); *Their Social Splash* (pr); *A Bear Affair* (pr); *Mabel's Wilful Way* (pr); *Gussie's Backward Way* (pr); *A Human Hound's Triumph* (pr); *Our Dare Devil Chief* (pr); *Crossed Love and Swords* (pr); *Miss Fatty's Seaside Lover* (pr); *He Wouldn't Stay Down* (pr); *For Better—But Worse* (pr); *A Versatile Villain* (pr); *Those College Girls* (pr); *Mabel Lost and Won* (pr); *Those Bitter Sweets* (pr); *The Cannon Ball* (pr); *A Home Breaking Hound* (pr); *Foiled by Fido* (pr); *Court House Crooks* (pr); *When Ambrose Dared Walrus* (pr); *Dirty Work in a Laundry* (pr); *Fido's Tin-Type Tangle* (pr); *A Lover's Lost Control* (pr); *A Rascal of Wolfish Ways* (pr); *The Battle of Ambrose and Walrus* (pr); *Only a Messenger Boy* (pr); *Caught in the Act* (pr); *His Luckless Love* (pr); *Viewing Sherman Institute for Indians at Riverside* (pr); *Wished on Mabel* (pr); *Gussie's Wayward Path* (pr); *Settled at the Seaside* (pr); *Gussie Tied to Trouble* (pr); *A Hash House Fraud* (pr); *Merely a Married Man* (pr); *A Game Old Knight* (pr); *Her Painted Hero* (pr); *Saved by Wireless* (pr); *Fickle Fatty's Fall* (pr); *His Father's Footsteps* (pr); *The Best of Enemies* (pr); *A Janitor's Wife's Temptation* (pr); *A Village Scandal* (pr); *The Great Vacuum Robbery* (pr); *Crooked to the End* (pr); *Fatty and the Broadway Stars* (pr, role); *A Submarine Pirate* (pr); *The Hunt* (pr).

1916: *The Worst of Friends* (pr); *Dizzy Heights and Daring Hearts* (pr); *The Great Pearl Tangle* (pr); *Fatty and Mabel Adrift* (pr); *Because He Loved Her* (pr); *A Modern Enoch Arden* (pr); *Perils of the Park* (pr); *A Movie Star* (pr); *His Hereafter* (pr); *He Did and He Didn't* (*Love and Lobsters*) (pr); *Love Will Conquer* (pr); *His Pride and Shame* (pr); *Fido's Fate* (pr); *Better Late Than Never* (pr); *Bright Lights* (pr); *Cinders of Love* (pr); *Wife and Auto Troubles* (pr); *The Judge* (pr); *A Village Vampire* (pr); *The Village Blacksmith* (pr); *A Love Riot* (pr); *Gipsy Joe* (pr); *By Stork Delivery* (pr); *An Oily Scoundrel* (pr); *A Bathhouse Blunder* (pr); *His Wife's Mistake* (pr); *His Bread and Butter* (pr); *His Last Laugh* (pr); *Bucking Society* (pr); *The Other Man* (pr); *The Snow Cure* (pr); *A Dash Of Courage* (pr); *The Lion and the Girl* (pr); *His Bitter Pill* (pr); *Her Marble Heart* (pr); *Bathtub Perils* (pr); *The Moonshiners* (pr); *Hearts and Sparks* (pr); *His Wild Oats* (pr); *Ambrose's Cup of Woe* (pr); *The Waiter's Ball* (pr); *The Surf Girl* (pr); *A Social Club* (pr); *Vampire Ambrose* (pr); *The Winning Punch* (pr); *His Lying Heart* (pr); *She Loved a Sailor* (pr); *His Auto Ruination* (pr); *Ambrose's Rapid Rise* (pr); *His Busted Trust* (pr); *Tugboat Romeos* (pr); *Sunshine* (pr); *Her Feathered Nest* (pr); *No One to Guide Him* (pr); *Her First Beau* (pr); *His First False Step* (pr); *The Houseboat* (pr); *The Fire Chief* (pr); *Love on Skates* (pr); *His Alibi* (pr); *Love Comet* (pr); *A la Cabaret* (pr); *Haystacks and Steeples* (pr); *A Scoundrel's Toll* (pr); *The Three Slims* (pr); *The Girl Guardian* (pr); *Wings and Wheels* (pr); *Safety First Ambrose* (pr); *Maid Mad* (pr); *The Twins* (pr); *Piles of Perils* (pr); *A Cream Puff Romance* (pr); *The Danger Girl* (pr); *Bombs* (pr); *His Last Scent* (pr); *The Manicurist* (pr).

1917: *The Nick of Time Baby* (pr); *Stars and Bars* (pr); *Maggie's First False Step* (pr); *Villa of the Movies* (pr); *Dodging His Doom* (pr); *Her Circus Knight* (pr); *Her Fame and Shames* (pr); *Pinched in the Finish* (pr); *Her Nature Dance* (pr); *Teddy at the Throttle* (pr); *Secrets of a Beauty Parlor* (pr); *A Maiden's Trust* (pr); *His Naughty Thought* (pr); *Her Torpedoed Love* (pr); *A Royal Rogue* (pr); *Oriental Love* (pr); *Cactus Nell* (pr); *The Betrayal of Maggie* (pr); *Skidding Hearts* (pr); *The Dog Catcher's Love* (pr); *Whose Baby* (pr); *Dangers of a Bride* (pr); *A Clever Dummy* (pr); *She Needed a Doctor* (pr); *Thirst* (pr); *His Uncle Dudley* (pr); *Lost a Cook* (pr); *The Pawnbroker's Heart* (pr); *Two Crooks* (pr); *A Shanghaied Jonah* (pr); *His Precious Life* (pr); *Hula Hula Land* (pr); *The Late Lamented* (pr); *The Sultan's Wife* (pr); *A Bedroom Blunder* (pr); *Roping Her Romeo* (pr); *The Pullman Bride* (pr); *Are Waitresses Safe* (pr); *An International Sneak* (pr); *That Night* (pr); *Taming Target Center* (pr).

1918: *The Kitchen Lady* (pr); *His Hidden Purpose* (pr); *Watch Your Neighbors* (pr); *It Pays to Exercise* (pr); *Sheriff Nell's Tussle* (pr); *Those Athletic Girls* (pr); *Friend Husband* (pr); *Saucy Madeline* (pr); *His Smothered Love* (pr); *The Battle Royal* (pr); *Love Loops the Loop* (pr); *Two Tough Tenderfeet* (pr); *Her Screen Idol* (pr); *Ladies First* (pr); *Her Blighted Love* (pr); *She Loved Him Plenty* (pr); *The Summer Girls* (pr); *Mickey* (pr); *His Wife's Friend* (pr); *Sleuths* (pr); *Beware the Boarders* (pr); *Whose Little Wife Are You* (pr); *Her First Mistake* (pr); *Hide and Seek Detectives* (pr); *The Village Chestnut* (pr).

1919: *Cupid's Day Off* (pr); *Never Too Old* (pr); *Rip & Stitch, Tailors* (pr); *East Lynne with Variations* (pr); *The Village Smithy* (pr); *Reilly's Wash Day* (pr); *The Foolish Age* (pr); *The Little Widow* (pr); *When Love is Blind* (pr); *Love's False Faces* (pr); *Hearts and Flowers* (pr); *No Mother to Guide Him* (pr); *Trying to Get Along* (pr); *Among Those Present* (pr); *Yankee Doodle in Berlin* (pr); *Why Beaches Are Popular* (pr); *Treating 'em Rough* (pr); *A Lady's Tailor* (pr); *Uncle Tom Without the Cabin* (pr); *The Dentist* (pr); *Back to the Kitchen* (pr); *Up in Alf's Place* (pr); *Salome vs. Shenandoah* (pr); *His Last False Step* (pr); *The Speak Easy* (pr). **1920:** *The Star Boarder* (pr); *Ten Dollars or Ten Days* (pr); *Gee Whiz* (pr); *The Gingham Girl* (pr); *Down on the Farm* (pr); *Fresh from the City* (pr); *Let 'er Go* (pr); *By Golly* (pr); *You Wouldn't Believe It* (pr); *Married Life* (pr); *The Quack Doctor* (pr); *Great Scott* (pr); *Don't Weaken* (pr); *It's a Boy* (pr); *Young Man's Fancy* (pr); *His Youthful Fancy* (pr); *My Goodness* (pr); *Movie Fans* (pr); *Fickle Fancy* (pr); *Love, Honor, and Behave* (pr); *A Fireside Brewer* (*Home Brew*) (pr); *Bungalow Troubles* (pr).

1921: *Dabbling in Art* (pr); *An Unhappy Finish* (pr); *On a Summer's Day* (pr); *A Small Town Idol* (pr, sc); *Wedding Bells Out of Tune* (pr); *Officer Cupid* (pr); *Away from the Steerage* (*Astray from the Steerage*) (pr); *Sweetheart Days* (pr); *Home Talent* (pr, sc); *She Sighed by the Seaside* (pr); *Hard Knocks and Love Taps* (pr); *Made in the Kitchen* (pr); *Call a Cop* (pr); *Love's Outcast* (pr); *Molly O* (pr, sc). **1922:** *By Heck* (pr); *Be Reasonable* (pr); *Bright Eyes* (pr); *The Duck Hunter* (pr); *On Patrol* (pr); *Step Forward* (pr); *Gymnasium Jim* (pr); *The Crossroads of New York* (pr, sc); *Oh Daddy!* (pr); *Home-Made Movies* (pr); *Ma and Pa* (pr); *Bow Wow* (pr); *Love and Doughnuts* (pr); *When Summer Comes* (pr).

1923: *Suzanna* (pr); *The Shriek of Araby* (pr, sc); *Where is My Wandering Boy This Evening* (pr); *Nip and Tuck* (pr); *Pitfalls of a Big City* (pr); *Skylarking* (pr); *Down to the Sea in Shoes* (pr); *The Extra Girl* (pr, co-sc); *Asleep at the Switch* (pr); *One Cylinder Love* (pr); *The Dare-Devil* (pr); *Flip Flops* (pr); *Inbad the Sailor* (pr). **1924:** *Ten Dollars or Ten Days* (remake, pr); *One Spooky Night* (pr); *Picking Peaches* (pr); *The Half-Back of Notre Dame* (pr); *Smile Please* (pr); *Scarem Much* (pr); *Shanghaied Ladies* (pr); *The Hollywood Kid* (pr); *Flickering Youth* (pr); *Black Oxfords* (pr); *The Cat's Meow* (pr); *Yukon Jake* (pr); *The Lion and the Souse* (pr); *His New Mama* (pr); *Romeo and Juliet* (pr); *Wall Street Blues* (pr); *The First Hundred Years* (pr); *East of the Water Plug* (pr, sc); *Lizzies of the Field* (pr); *The Luck of the Foolish* (pr); *Three Foolish Wives* (pr); *Little Robinson Corkscrew* (pr); *The Hansom Cabman* (*Be Careful*) (pr); *Riders of the Purple Cows* (pr); *The Reel Virginian* (*The West Virginian*) (pr); *Galloping Bungalows* (pr); *All Night Long* (pr); *Love's Sweet Piffle* (pr); *The Cannon Ball Express* (pr); *Feet of Mud* (pr); *Off His Trolley* (pr); *Bull and Sand* (pr); *Watch Out* (pr); *Over Here* (pr); *The Lady Barber* (pr); *North of 57* (pr); *Love's Intrigue* (pr); *The Stunt Man* (pr).

1925: *The Sea Squaw* (pr); *The Plumber* (pr); *The Wild Goose Chaser* (pr); *Honeymoon Hardships* (pr); *Boobs in the Woods* (pr); *The Beloved Bozo* (pr); *Water Wagons* (pr); *His Marriage Wow* (pr); *The Raspberry Romance* (pr); *Bashful Jim* (pr); *Giddap* (pr); *Plain Clothes* (pr); *Breaking the Ice* (pr); *The Marriage Circus* (pr); *The Lion's Whiskers* (pr); *Remember When* (pr); *He Who Gets Smacked* (pr); *Skinners in Silk* (pr); *Good Morning, Nurse!* (pr); *Super-Hooper-Dyne Lizzies* (pr); *Don't Tell Dad* (pr); *Isn't Love Cuckoo* (pr); *Sneezing Breezes* (pr); *Cupid's Boots* (pr); *Tee for Two* (pr); *The Iron Nag* (pr); *Lucky Stars* (pr); *Cold Turkey* (pr); *Butter Fingers* (pr); *There He Goes* (pr); *Hurry, Doctor* (pr); *A Rainy Knight* (pr); *Love and Kisses* (pr); *Over There-Abouts* (pr); *Good Morning, Madam* (pr); *A Sweet Pickle* (pr); *Dangerous Curves Behind* (pr); *The Soapsuds Lady* (pr); *Take Your Time* (pr); *The Window Dummy* (pr); *From Rags to Britches* (pr); *Hotsy Toty* (pr).

1926: *The Gosh-Darn Mortgage* (pr); *Wide Open Faces* (pr); *Hot Cakes for Two* (pr); *Whispering Whiskers* (pr); *Saturday Afternoon* (pr); *Funnymooners* (pr); *Trimmed in Gold* (pr); *Gooseland* (pr); *Circus Today* (pr); *Meet My Girl* (pr); *Spanking Breezes* (pr); *Wandering Willies* (pr); *Hooked at the Altar* (pr); *A Love Sundae* (pr); *Soldier Man* (pr); *The Ghost of Folly* (pr); *Fight Night* (pr); *Hayfoot, Strawfoot* (pr); *A Yankee Doodle Dude* (pr); *Muscle-Bound Music* (pr); *Oh, Uncle!* (pr); *Puppy Lovetime* (pr); *Ice Cold Cocos* (pr); *A Dinner Jest* (pr); *A Sea Dog's Tale* (pr); *Baby's Pets* (pr); *A Bachelor Butt-in* (pr); *Smith's Baby* (pr); *Alice Be Good* (pr); *When a Man's a Prince* (pr); *Smith's Vacation* (pr); *Hubby's Quiet Little Game* (pr); *Her Actor Friend* (pr); *Hoboken to Hollywood* (pr); *The Prodigal Bridegroom* (pr); *The Perils of Petersboro* (pr); *Smith's Landlord* (pr); *Love's Last Laugh* (pr); *Smith's Visitor* (pr); *Should Husbands Marry* (pr); *Masked Mamas* (pr); *A Harem Knight* (pr); *Smith's Uncle* (pr); *Hesitating Houses* (pr); *The Divorce Dodger* (pr); *A Blonde's Revenge* (pr); *Flirty Four-Flushers* (pr); *Smith's Picnic* (pr).

1927: *Kitty from Killarney* (pr); *Smith's Pets* (pr); *Should Sleepwalkers Marry* (pr); *Pass the Dumpling* (pr); *A Hollywood Hero* (pr); *Smith's Customer* (pr); *Peaches and Plumbers* (pr); *Plumber's Daughter* (pr); *A Small Town Princess* (pr); *A Dozen Socks* (pr); *The Jolly Jilter* (pr); *Smith's Surprise* (pr); *Smith's New Home* (pr); *Broke in China* (pr); *Smith's Kindergarten* (pr); *Crazy to Act* (pr); *Smith Fishing Trip* (pr); *His First Flame* (pr); *Pride of Pickeville* (pr); *Cured in the Excitement* (pr); *Catalina, Here I Come* (pr); *The Pest of Friends* (pr); *Love's Languid Lure* (pr); *College Kiddo* (pr); *Smith's Candy Shop* (pr); *The Golf Nut* (pr); *Smith's Pony* (pr); *A Gold Digger of Weepah* (pr); *Smith's Cook* (pr); *Daddy Boy* (pr); *For Sale a Bungalow* (pr); *Smith's Cousin* (pr); *The Bull Fighter* (pr); *Fiddlesticks* (pr); *Smith's Modiste Shop* (pr); *The Girl from Everywhere* (pr); *Love in a Police Station* (pr); *Hold that Pose* (pr).

1928: *Smith's Holiday* (pr); *Run, Girl, Run* (pr); *The Beach Club* (pr); *Love at First Sight* (pr); *Smith's Army Life* (pr); *The Best Man* (pr); *The Swan Princess* (pr); *Smith's Farm Days* (pr); *The Bicycle Flirt* (pr); *The Girl From Nowhere* (pr); *His Unlucky Night* (pr); *Smith's Restaurant* (pr); *The Good-bye Kiss* (pr); *The Chicken* (pr); *Taxi for Two* (pr); *Caught in the Kitchen* (pr); *A Dumb Waiter* (pr); *The Campus Carmen* (pr); *Motor Boat Mamas* (pr); *The Bargain Hunt* (pr); *Smith's Catalina Rowboat Race* (*Catalina Rowboat Race*) (pr); *A Taxi Scandal* (pr); *Hubby's Latest Alibi* (pr); *A Jim Jam Janitor* (pr); *The Campus Vamp* (pr); *Hubby's Week-end Trip* (pr); *The Burglar* (pr); *Taxi Beauties* (pr); *His New Stenographer* (pr).

1929: *Clunked on the Corner* (pr); *Baby's Birthday* (pr); *Uncle Tom* (pr); *Calling Hubby's Bluff* (pr); *Taxi Spooks* (pr); *Button My Back* (pr); *Ladies Must Eat* (pr); *Foolish Husbands* (pr); *Matchmaking Mamas* (pr); *The Rodeo* (pr); *Pink Pajamas* (pr); *The Night Watchman's Mistake* (pr); *The New Aunt* (pr); *Taxi Dolls* (pr); *Don't Get Jealous* (pr); *Caught in a Taxi* (pr); *A Close Shave* (pr); *The Big Palooka* (pr); *Motoring Mamas* (pr); *Clancy at the Bat* (pr); *The New Half-Back* (pr); *Uppercut O'Brien* (pr). **1930:** *He Trumped Her Ace* (pr); *Radio Kisses* (pr); *Hello Television* (pr); *Take Your Medicine* (pr); *Don't Bite Your Dentist* (pr); *Strange Birds* (pr); *A Hollywood Theme Song* (pr).

1931: *No, No, Lady* (pr); *One Yard to Go* (pr); *The College Vamp* (remake, pr); *The Bride's Mistake* (pr); *The Dog Doctor* (pr); *Just a Bear* (*It's a Bear*) (pr); *Ex-Sweeties* (pr); *In Conference* (pr); *The Cowcatcher's Daughter* (pr); *Slide, Speedy, Slide* (pr); *Fainting Lover* (pr); *Too Many Husbands* (pr); *The Cannonball* (pr); *The Trail of the Swordfish* (pr); *Poker Widows* (pr); *The World Flier* (pr); *Who's Who in the Zoo* (pr); *Taxi Troubles* (pr); *The Great Pie Mystery* (pr); *Wrestling Swordfish* (pr); *All American Kickback* (pr); *Half Holiday* (pr); *The Pottsville Palooka* (pr).

1932: *Playgrounds of the Mammals* (pr); *Dream House* (pr); *The Girl in the Tonneau* (pr); *Shopping with Wife* (pr); *Lady! Please!* (pr); *Heavens! My Husband!* (pr); *The Billboard Girl* (pr); *The Flirty Sleepwalker* (pr); *Speed in the Gay Nineties* (pr); *Man-Eating Sharks* (pr); *Listening In* (pr); *The Spot in the Rug* (pr); *Divorce a la Mode* (pr); *The Boudoir Brothers* (pr); *Freaks of the Deep* (pr); *The Candid Camera* (pr); *Sea Going Birds* (pr); *Hatta Marri* (pr); *Alaska Love* (pr); *For the Love of Ludwig* (pr); *Neighbor Trouble* (pr); *His Royal Shyness* (pr); *Young Onions* (pr); *The Giddy Age* (pr); *Lighthouse Love* (pr); *Hawkins and Watkins* (pr); *The Singing Plumber* (pr); *Courting Trouble* (pr); *False Impressions* (pr); *Bring Back 'em Sober* (pr); *A Hollywood Double* (pr); *The Dentist* (pr); *Doubling in the Quickies* (pr); *The Lion and the House* (pr); *Human Fish* (pr). **1933:** *Blue of the Night* (pr); *The Wrestlers* (*A Wrestler's Bride*) (pr); *Don't Play Bridge with Your Wife* (pr); *The Singing Boxer* (pr); *Too Many Highballs* (pr); *Easy on the Eyes* (pr); *A Fatal Glass of Beer* (pr); *Caliente Love* (pr); *Sing, Bing, Sing* (pr); *The Plumber and the Lady* (pr); *Sweet Cookie* (pr); *The Pharmacist* (pr); *Uncle Jake* (pr); *Dream Stuff* (pr); *Roadhouse Queen* (pr); *See You Tonight* (pr); *Daddy Knows Best* (pr); *Knockout Kisses* (pr); *Husband's Reunion* (pr); *The Big Fibber* (pr); *The Barber Shop* (pr). **1939:** *Hollywood Cavalcade* (role). **1949:** *Down Memory Lane* (role).

Mack Sennett was the outstanding pioneer and primitive of American silent comedy. Although Sennett's name is most commonly associated with the Keystone Company, which he founded in 1912, Sennett's film career began four years earlier with the Biograph Company, the pioneering film company where D.W. Griffith established the principles of film narrative and rhetoric. Sennett and Griffith were colleagues and contemporaries, and Sennett served as actor, writer, and assistant under Griffith in 1908 and 1909. In 1910 he began his career as director of his own films under Griffith's supervision.

Sennett became associated with comic roles and comic films from the beginning under Griffith. In his first major role for Griffith, *The Curtain Pole* in 1908, Sennett played a comically drunk Frenchman who visits chaos upon all he meets in a desperate race through town to replace a broken curtain rod. The film contains several traits that would become associated with the mature Sennett style: the breathless chase, the reduction of human beings to venal stereotypes, the reduction of human society and its physical surroundings to chaotic rubble, and a fondness for games concerning the cinema mechanism itself, manifested in the use of accelerated (by undercranking) and reverse motion. In other roles for Griffith, Sennett consistently played the comic rube or dumb servant—roles that took advantage of Sennett's shambling bulk and oafish facial expressions.

According to legend, Sennett founded the Keystone Company when he conned his bookies, Adam Kessel and Charles Bauman, to go double or nothing on his gambling debts and stake him to a film company. Kessel and Bauman, however, had been out of the bookmaking business and in the moviemaking business for at least five years as owners of Thomas Ince's flourishing New York Motion Picture Company. Between late 1912 and early 1914, Sennett assembled a troupe of the finest raucous physical comedians and burlesque clowns in the film business. From Biograph he brought the pretty Mabel Normand, who was also an extremely agile and athletic physical comedienne, and the loony Ford Sterling, with his big-gesturing burlesque of villainy and lechery. Among the other physical comedians he found in those years were the burly Mack Swain, the tiny Chester Conklin, the round Fatty Arbuckle, and the cross-eyed Ben Turpin. He also discovered such future comic stars as Charles Chaplin, Harold Lloyd, and Harry Langdon, as well as the future director of sound comedies, Frank Capra. Perhaps more important than any artistic contribution was Sennett's managerial ability to spot comic talent and give it the opportunity to display itself.

At the root of Sennett's comic style was the brash, the vulgar, and the burlesque. His films parodied the serious film and stage hits of the day, always turning the serious romance or melodrama into outrageous nonsense. There were no serious moral, psychological, or social issues in Sennett films, simply raucous burlesque of social or emotional material. His short comedies were exuberantly impolite and often made public jokes out of ethnic, sexual, or racial stereotypes. Among the characters around whom he built film series were the Germans Meyer and Heinie, the Jewish Cohen, and the black Rastus. Many of these films were so brashly vulgar in their stereotypical humor that they cannot be shown in public today. As indicators of social attitudes of the 1910s, these films seem to suggest that the still largely immigrant American society of that time was more willing to make and respond to jokes openly based on ethnic and sexist stereotypes than they are today in an era of greater sensitivity to the potential harm of these stereotypes. In defense of Sennett's making sport of ethnic types, it must be said that the method and spirit was consistent with his films' refusal to take any social or psychological matters seriously.

Mack Sennett

Sennett's Keystone films were extremely improvisational; a typical formula was to take a camera, a bucket of whitewash, and four clowns (two male, two female) out to a park and make a movie. Sennett's aesthetic was not so much an art that conceals art but an art that derides art. His many Keystone films reveal the same contempt for orderly, careful, well-crafted art that one can see in the Marx Brothers' Paramount films or W.C. Fields's Universal films two decades later. The one conscious artistic tool which Sennett exploited was speed—keeping the actors, the action, the gags, the machines, and the camera in perpetual speeding motion. The typical Keystone title might be something like *Love, Speed, and Thrills* or *Love, Loot, and Crash*.

Among other Sennett inventions were the Keystone Kops, a burlesque of attempts at social order, and the Bathing Beauties, a burlesque of attempts at pornographic sexuality. Sennett served his apprenticeship in the American burlesque theater, and he brought to the Keystone films that same kind of entertainment which took place at the intersection of vulgar lunacy and comic pornography.

Sennett's most memorable films include a series of domestic films starring Mabel Normand, married either to Fatty Arbuckle or Charlie Chaplin; a series of films pairing the beefy Mack Swain and the diminutive Chester Conklin; a series featuring Ben Turpin as a cross-eyed burlesque of romantic movie stars; a series built around remarkably athletic automobiles and rampaging jungle beasts starring Billy Bevan; and a series of short films featuring the pixieish child-clown Harry Langdon. Sennett also produced and personally directed the first comic feature film produced in America (or anywhere else), *Tillie's Punctured Romance,* starring Chaplin, Normand, and stage comedienne Marie Dressler in her first film role.

Sennett ceased to direct films after 1914, becoming the producer and overseer of every comic film made by his company for the next two decades. Although the Keystone Company folded by the late 1910s, Sennett's immensely long filmography is a testament to the sheer number of comic films he produced, well into the sound era. Sennett's real importance to film history, however, derives from that crucial historical moment between 1912 and 1915, a period when a comic assumption, the evolution of film technique, and a collection of talented physical clowns all came together under Sennett's stewardship to create a unique and memorable type of comedy that has assumed its place not only in the history of cinema, but in the much longer history of comedy itself.—GERALD MAST

Siegel, Don

Nationality *American.* **Born** *Chicago, 26 October 1912.* **Education** *Jesus College, Cambridge University, England; Royal Academy of Dramatic Art, London.* **Family** *Married 1) actress Viveca Lindfors, 1948 (divorced 1953), one son; 2) actress Doe Avedon, 1957 (divorced), four children; 3) Carol Rydall.* **Career** *Actor with the Contemporary Theater, Los Angeles, 1930; joined Warner Bros. as film librarian, 1934, later assistant editor, then joined insert department; set up montage department at Warners, 1939; 2nd unit director for Michael Curtiz, Raoul Walsh, and others, 1940-45; directed first film,* Star in the Night, *1945, and first feature,* The Verdict, *1946; worked for Howard Hughes at RKO, 1948-51; producer and director for TV, from 1961; executive producer for* Trial and Error, *for TV, 1988.* **Awards** *Oscars for Best Short Subject, for* Star in the Night, *and for Best Documentary, for* Hitler Lives?, *1946.* **Died** *Of cancer, after a long illness, 20 April 1991, in Nipoma, California.*

Films as Director: 1945: *Star in the Night; Hitler Lives?.* **1946:** *The Verdict.* **1949:** *Night unto Night; The Big Steal.* **1952:** *No Time for Flowers; Duel at Silver Creek.* **1953:** *Count the Hours (Every Minute Counts); China Venture.* **1954:** *Riot in Cell Block 11; Private Hell 36.* **1955:** *An Annapolis Story (The Blue and the Gold).* **1956:** *Invasion of the Body Snatchers; Crime in the Streets.* **1957:** *Spanish Affair; Baby Face Nelson.* **1958:** *The Gun Runners; The Line-Up.* **1959:** *Edge of Eternity* (+co-pr, role as man at the pool); *Hound Dog Man.* **1960:** *Flaming Star.* **1962:** *Hell Is for Heroes.* **1964:** *The Killers* (+pr, role as short-order cook in diner); *The Hanged Man.* **1967:** *Stranger on the Run.* **1968:** *Madigan.* **1969:** *Coogan's Bluff* (+pr, role as man in elevator); *Death of a Gunfighter* (uncredited co-d). **1970:** *Two Mules for Sister Sara.* **1971:** *The Beguiled* (+pr); *Dirty Harry* (+pr). **1973:** *Charley Varrick* (+pr, role as Murph). **1974:** *The Black Windmill* (+pr). **1976:** *The Shootist.* **1977:** *Telefon.* **1979:** *Escape from Alcatraz* (+pr, role as doctor). **1980:** *Rough Cut.* **1982:** *Jinxed!*

Other Films: 1940: *City for Conquest* (Litvak) (montage d). **1941:** *Blues in the Night* (Litvak) (montage d). **1942:** *Casablanca* (Curtiz) (art d). **1943:** *Edge of Darkness* (Milestone) (set d); *Mission to Moscow* (Curtiz) (art d); *Northern Pursuit* (Walsh) (special effects d). **1944:** *The Adventures of Mark Twain* (Rapper) (ph). **1971:** *Play Misty For Me* (Eastwood) (role as Marty the bartender). **1978:** *Invasion of the Body Snatchers* (Kaufman) (cab driver). **1985:** *Into the Night* (Landis) (role as embarrassed man).

Don Siegel's virtues—tightly constructed narratives and explosive action sequences—have been apparent from the very beginning. Even his B pictures have an enviable ability to pin audiences to their seats through the sheer force and pace of the events they portray. Unlike some action-movie specialists, however, Siegel rarely allows the action to overcome the characterization. The continuing fascination of *Riot in Cell Block 11,* for instance, stems as much from its central character's tensions as from the violent and eventful story. Dunn is a paradigmatic Siegel protagonist, caught between a violent inclination and the strategic need for restraint. Such incipient personal instability animates many Siegel films, finding material expression in the hunts and confrontations which structure their narratives. His people react to an unpleasant world with actions rather than words, often destroying themselves in the process. They rarely survive with dignity.

Siegel's singular distinction, however, lies in his refusal to strike conventional moral postures in relation to this depressing and often sordid material. Though one cannot fail to be involved in and excited by his action-packed stories, there is always a clear sense that he remains outside of them as something of a detached observer. In the 1950s that seeming "objectivity" gave him a minor critical reputation as a socially conscious and "liberal" director,

Don Siegel

though this was a liberalism by implication rather than a direct and paraded commitment. In retrospect the 1950s movies seem best described as individualistic, antagonistic to unthinking social conformity, rather than liberally sentimental after the fashion of "socially concerned" Hollywood movies of the period. These films are generalized warnings, not exercises in breast-beating. Their spirit is that of Kevin McCarthy's cry to his unheeding fellows in Siegel's original ending to *Invasion of the Body Snatchers* (United Artists added an epilogue): "You're next!"

In the 1960s and 1970s Siegel's reputation and his budgets grew. He struck out in new directions with such films as *Two Mules for Sister Sara* and *The Beguiled,* though his major concerns remained with action and with his emotionally crippled "heroes." The three cop movies (*Madigan, Coogan's Bluff,* and *Dirty Harry*) are representative, the latter especially encouraging the critical charge that Siegel had become a law-and-order ideologue. Its "wall-to-wall carpet of violence" (Siegel's description) easily lent itself to a "tough cop against the world" reading. Yet, just as his earlier films cannot be reduced to simple liberal formulae, so the later movies are far more complex than much criticism has suggested. A colleague remarks of Madigan: "For him everything's either right or wrong—there's nothing in between." In exploring his characters' doomed attempts to live by such absolutes Siegel refuses to make their mistake. And though he does not presume to judge them, that does not mean that he approves of their actions. As the less frenetic films like *The Shootist* and *Escape from Alcatraz* make clear, his appreciation of character and morality is far more subtle than that.

More than any other action director of his generation Siegel has avoided the genre's potential for reductive simplification. He has combined entertainment with perception, skilled filmmaking economy with nicely delineated characters, and overall moral detachment with sympathy for his hard-pressed protagonists. His movie world may often seem uncongenial, but its creator has never appeared callous or unconcerned. His films have achieved much-deserved commercial success; his skill and subtlety have deserved rather more in the way of critical attention.—ANDREW TUDOR

Siodmak, Robert

Nationality American/German. *Born* Memphis, Tennessee, 8 August 1900. *Education* University of Marburg, Germany. *Career* Actor with German repertory companies, 1920-21; bank worker, 1921-23; titler for imported American films, 1925; editor for Herbert

Nossen and Seymour Nebenzal, 1926-28; hired by Erich Pommer to scout for writers for UFA, 1928; directed first feature, 1930; following attack by Goebbels on film Brennende Geheimnis, *moved with brother Curt to Paris, 1933; moved to Hollywood, 1940, signed two-year contract with Paramount, then moved to Universal under seven-year contract; after filming* The Crimson Pirate *in England and Spain, remained in Europe, from 1952.* **Died** *In 1973.*

Films as Director: 1929: *Menschen am Sonntag* (*People on Sunday*) (doc) (co-d). **1930:** *Abschied* (*So sind die Menschen*). **1931:** *Der Mann der seinen Mörder sucht* (*Looking for His Murderer*); *Voruntersuchung* (*Inquest*). **1932:** *Stürme der Leidenschaft* (*The Tempest; Storm of Passion*); *Quick* (*Quick—König der Clowns*). **1933:** *Brennende Geheimnis* (*The Burning Secret*) (+pr); *Le Sexe faible*. **1934:** *La Crise est finie* (*The Slump Is Over*). **1936:** *La Vie parisienne; Mister Flow* (*Compliments of Mr. Flow*). **1937:** *Cargaison blanche* (*Le Chemin de Rio; French White Cargo; Traffic in Souls; Woman Racket*). **1938:** *Mollenard* (*Hatred*); *Ultimatum* (co-d; completed for Robert Wiene). **1939:** *Pièges* (*Personal Column*). **1941:** *West Point Widow*. **1942:** *Fly by Night; The Night Before the Divorce; My Heart Belongs to Daddy*. **1943:** *Someone to Remember; Son of Dracula*. **1944:** *Phantom Lady; Cobra Woman; Christmas Holiday*. **1945:** *The Suspect; Uncle Harry* (*The Strange Affair of Uncle Harry; The Zero Murder Case*); *The Spiral Staircase*. **1946:** *The Killers; The Dark Mirror*. **1947:** *Time Out of Mind* (+pr). **1948:** *Cry of the City*. **1949:** *Criss Cross; The Great Sinner*. **1950:** *Thelma Jordan; Deported*. **1951:** *The Whistle at Eaton Falls*. **1952:** *The Crimson Pirate*. **1954:** *Le Grand Jeu* (*Flesh and Woman*). **1955:** *Die Ratten*. **1956:** *Mein Vater der Schauspieler*. **1957:** *Nachts wann der Teufel kam* (*The Devil Strikes at Night*). **1959:** *Dorothea Angermann; The Rough and the Smooth* (*Portrait of a Sinner*). **1960:** *Katya* (*Un Jeune Fille un seul amour, Magnificent Sinner*); *Mein Schulefreund*. **1962:** *L'Affaire Nina B* (*The Nina B Affair*); *Tunnel 28* (*Escape from East Berlin*). **1964:** *Der Schut*. **1965:** *Der Schatz der Azteken; Die Pyramide des Sonnengottes*. **1968:** *Custer of the West* (*A Good Day for Fighting*). **1968/69:** *Der Kampf um Rom* (in two parts).

Other Films: 1936: *Le Grand Refrain* (*Symphonie d'amour*) (Mirande) (supervisor). **1945:** *Conflict* (*Bernhardt*) (co-story).

Robert Siodmak is an example of the UFA-influenced German directors who moved to Hollywood when war threatened Europe. Less well known than his compatriots Billy Wilder and Fritz Lang, Siodmak demonstrated his cinematic skills early in his career with his innovative movie *Menschen am Sonntag,* which featured a non-professional cast, hand-held camera shots, stop motion photography, and the sort of flashbacks that later became associated with his work in America.

Siodmak carried with him to Hollywood the traditions and skills of his German film heritage, and became a major influence in American *film noir* of the 1940s. Deep shadows, claustrophobic compositions, elegant camera movements, and meticulously created settings on a grand scale mark the UFA origins of his work. Such themes as the treachery of love and the prevalence of the murderous impulse in ordinary people recur in his American films. The use of the flashback is a dominant narrative device, reflecting his fatalistic approach to story and character. *The Killers* (1946 version) presents a narrative that includes multiple flashbacks, each one of which is a part of the total story and all of which must be accumulated to understand the opening sequence of the film. This opening, based directly on Ernest Hemingway's famous short story, is a masterful example of film storytelling.

A typical Siodmak film of his *noir* period is *Phantom Lady,* a mini-masterpiece of mood and character that creates intense paranoia through the use of lighting and setting. Two key sequences demonstrate Siodmak's method. In the first, the heroine follows a man into the subway, a simple action that sets off feelings of danger and tension in viewers, feelings that grow

Robert Siodmak.
Photograph by Constantin/Connex.

entirely out of sound, light, cutting, and camera movement. In the second, one of the most famous sequences in *film noir,* Siodmak uses jazz music and cutting to build up a narrative meaning that is implicitly sexual as the leading lady urges a drummer to a faster and faster beat.

Siodmak's work is frequently discussed in comparison with that of Alfred Hitchcock, partly because they shared a producer, Joan Harrison, for a period of time. Harrison produced two Siodmak films for Universal, *The Suspect* and *Uncle Harry.* In both films a seemingly ordinary, innocent man is drawn into a tangled web of murder, while retaining the audience's sympathy. *Criss Cross,* arguably Siodmak's best *noir* work, ably demonstrates his ability to create depth of characterization through music, mood, and action, particularly in a scene in which Burt Lancaster watches his ex-wife, Yvonne DeCarlo, dance with another man. His fatal obsession with his wife and the victim/victimizer nature of their relationship is capably demonstrated through purely visual means.

In later years, Siodmak turned to such action films as *The Crimson Pirate* and *Custer of the West,* the former a celebrated romp that was one of the first truly tongue-in-cheek anti-genre films of its period. Although Siodmak's films were successful both critically and commercially in their day, he has never achieved the recognition which the visual quality of his work should have earned him. An innovative and cinematic director, he explored the criminal or psychotic impulses in his characters through the ambience of his elegant mise-en-scène. The control of all cinematic tools at his command—camera angle, lighting, composition, movement, and design—was used to establish effectively a world of fate, passion, obsession, and compulsion. Although his reputation has been elevated in recent years, his name deserves to be better known.—JEANINE BASINGER

Sirk, Douglas

Nationality *German/American.* **Born** *Claus Detlev Sierk in Skagen, Denmark, 26 April 1900.* **Education** *Studied law, philosophy, and art history in Copenhagen, Munich, Jena, and Hamburg until 1922.* **Career** *Dramaturg for Deutsches Schauspiele, Hamburg, 1921; director for Chemnitz "Kleinez Theater," 1922; artistic director, Bremen Schauspielhaus, 1923-29; director of Altes Theater, Leipzig, 1929-36; directed first film, as Detlef Sierck, for UFA, 1935; head of Leipzig drama school, 1936; left Germany, worked on scripts in Austria and France (notably Renoir's* Partie de campagne, *1937); signed for*

Warners in Hollywood, 1939, but inactive, 1940-41; contract as writer for Columbia, 1942; director for Universal, from 1950; returned to Europe, 1959; active in theatre in Munich and Hamburg, 1960s. **Died** *Of cancer, in Lugano, Switzerland, 14 January 1987.*

Films as Director: (as Detlef Sierck) 1935: *It Was een April* (Dutch version); *April, April* (German version); *Das Madchen vom Moorhof; Stutzen der Gesellschaft.* **1936:** *Schlussakkord* (*Final Accord*) (+co-sc); *Das Hofkonzert* (+co-sc); *La Chanson du souvenir* (*Song of Remembrance*) (co-d) (French version of *Das Hofkonzert*). **1937:** *Zu neuen Ufern* (*To New Shores, Paramatta, Bagne de femmes*) (+co-sc); *La Habanera.* **1939:** *Boefje* (+co-sc).

(As Douglas Sirk) 1943: *Hitler's Madman.* **1944:** *Summer Storm* (+co-sc). **1946:** *A Scandal in Paris.* **1947:** *Lured.* **1948:** *Sleep My Love.* **1949:** *Slightly French; Shockproof.* **1950:** *Mystery Submarine.* **1951:** *The First Legion* (+co-pr); *Thunder on the Hill; The Lady Pays Off; Weekend with Father.* **1952:** *No Room for the Groom; Has Anybody Seen My Gal?; Meet Me at the Fair; Take Me to Town.* **1953:** *All I Desire; Taza, Son of Cochise.* **1954:** *Magnificent Obsession; Sign of the Pagan; Captain Lightfoot.* **1955:** *All That Heaven Allows; There's Always Tomorrow.* **1956:** *Never Say Goodbye* (Hopper) (d uncredited, completed film); *Written on the Wind.* **1957:** *Battle Hymn; Interlude; The Tarnished Angels.* **1958:** *A Time to Love and a Time to Die.* **1959:** *Imitation of Life.*

(For Munich Film School) 1975: *Talk to Me Like the Rain.* **1977:** *Sylvesternacht.* **1979:** *Bourbon Street Blues.*

Other Films: 1937: *Liebling der Matrosen* (Hinrich) (co-sc as Detlef Sierck). **1938:** *Dreiklang* (Hinrich) (story as Detlef Sierck). **1939:** *Accordfinal* (Bay) (supervision, uncredited); *Sehnsucht nach Afrika* (Zoch) (role). **1986:** *My Life for Zarah Leander* (Blackwood) (doc) (role).

Douglas Sirk's critical reputation has almost completely reversed from the time when he was a popular studio director at Universal in the 1950s. He was regarded by contemporary critics as a lightweight director of soap operas who showcased the talents of Universal name stars such as Rock Hudson and Lana Turner. His films often were labelled "women's pictures," with all of the pejorative connotations that term suggested. After his last film, *Imitation of Life,* Sirk retired to Germany, leaving behind a body of work that was seldom discussed, but which was frequently revived on television late shows.

Standard works of film criticism either totally ignored or briefly mentioned him with words such as "not a creative film maker" (quoted from his brief entry in Georges Sadoul's *Dictionary of Film Makers*). In the early 1970s, however, a few American critics began to re-evaluate his works. The most important innovators in Sirk criticism in this period were Jon Halliday, whose lengthy interview in book form, *Sirk on Sirk,* has become a standard work, and Andrew Sarris, whose program notes on the director's films were compiled into the booklet *Douglas Sirk—The Complete American Period.* From the time of these two works, it became more and more appropriate to speak of Sirk in terms of "genius" and "greatness." By 1979, Sirk was even honored by BBC Television with a "Sirk Season" during which his now loyal following was treated to a weekly installment from the Sirk *oeuvre* as it now fashionably could be called.

Critics today see Sirk's films as more than melodramas with glossy photography and upper-middle-class houses. The word "expressionist" is frequently used to describe his technique, an indication not only of the style of Sirk's work in the United States, but also his background in films within the framework of German expressionism in the 1920s and early 1930s.

Douglas Sirk

Sirk, who was born in Denmark, but emigrated to Germany in the teens, began work in the theater, then switched to films in the mid-1930s. Known for his "leftist" leanings, Sirk left Germany with the rise of Nazism, and eventually came to the United States in the early 1940s.

The first part of Sirk's American career was characterized by low-budget films which have faded into oblivion. His first well-known film was *Sleep My Love,* a variation on the *Gaslight* theme starring Don Ameche and Claudette Colbert. Soon he began directing films that starred several of the "hot" new Universal stars, among them Hudson and John Gavin, as well as many of the *grandes dames* of the 1930s and 1940s, such as Barbara Stanwyck, Lana Turner, and Jane Wyman. Although today he is known primarily for his dramas, Sirk did make a few lighter pieces, among them *Has Anybody Seen My Gal?,* a musical comedy set in the 1920s, and remembered by movie buffs as one of the first James Dean movies.

Many critics consider *Written on the Wind* to be Sirk's best film. It was also the one which was best received upon its initial release. All of Sirk's movies deal with relationships which are complicated and often at a dead-end. In *Written on the Wind,* the film's central characters are unhappy despite their wealth and attractiveness. They have little to interest them and seek outlets for their repressed sexuality. One of the four main characters, Kyle Hadley (Robert Stack), has always lived in the shadow of his more virile friend Mitch Wayne (Rock Hudson). He hopes to forget his own feelings of inadequacy by drinking and carousing, but his activities only reinforce his problems. Sexuality, either in its manifestation or repression, is a strongly recurrent theme in all of Sirk's works, but perhaps no where is it more blatantly dramatized than in *Written on the Wind,* where sex is the core of everyone's problems. Mitch is the only truly potent figure in the film, and thus he is the pivotal figure. Hudson's role as Mitch is very similar to that of Ron Kirby in *All That Heaven Allows.* Ron and Mitch both exhibit a strong sense of sexuality that either attracts or repels the other characters and initiates their action.

Kyle's feelings of sexual inadequacy and jealousy of Mitch are interrelated; Mitch is the manly son Kyle's father always wanted and the virile lover his wife Lucy (Lauren Bacall) loves. Kyle admires Mitch, yet hates him at the same time. Similarly, Carey Scott in *All That Heaven Allows* desires the earthy gardener Ron, yet she is shocked at her own sexuality, an apparent rejection of the conventions of her staid upper-middle-class milieu. In *There's Always Tomorrow,* Clifford Groves (Fred MacMurray) is faced with a similar situation. He seeks sexual and psychological freedom from his stifling family with Norma Vail (Barbara Stanwyck), yet his responsibilities and sense of morality prevent him from finding the freedom he seeks.

It is an ironic key to Sirk's popular acclaim now that exactly the same stars whose presence seemed to confirm his films as being "programmers" and "women's pictures" have ultimately added a deeper dimension to his works. By using popular stars of the 1930s through 1950s— stars who often peopled lightweight comedies and unregenerate melodramas, Sirk revealed another dimension of American society. His films often present situations in which the so-called "happy endings" of earlier films are played out to their ultimate (and often more realistic) outcomes by familiar faces. For example, in *There's Always Tomorrow*, Clifford and his wife Marion (Joan Bennett) might very well have been the prototypes for the main characters of a typical 1930s comedy in which "boy gets girl" in the last reel. Yet, in looking at them after almost 20 years of marriage, their lives are shallow. The happy ending of a youthful love has not sustained itself. Similarly, in *All That Heaven Allows,* the attractive middle-aged widow of a "wonderful man" has few things in life to make her happy. Whereas she was once a supposedly happy housewife, the loving spouse of a pillar of the community, her own identity has been suppressed to the point that his death means social ostracism. These two examples epitomize the cynicism of Sirk's view of what was traditionally perceived as the American dream. Most of Sirk's films depict families in which a house, cars, and affluence are present, but in which sexual and emotional fulfillment are not. Many of Sirk's films end on a decidedly unhappy note; the ones that do end optimistically for the main characters are those in which traditions are shattered and the strict societal standards of the time are rejected.—PATRICIA KING HANSON

Sjöberg, Alf

Nationality Swedish. *Born* Stockholm, 21 June 1903. *Education* Studies at the Royal Dramatic Theater. *Career* Stage actor, from 1925; stage director, from 1927 (chief director, Royal Dramatic Theater, from 1930); directed first film, Den starkaste, 1929; returned to filmmaking, 1940. *Award* Best Film (ex aequo), Cannes Festival, for Fröken Julie, 1951. *Died* In Stockholm, 17 April 1980.

Films as Director: 1929: *Den starkaste* (*The Strongest*) (+story). **1940:** *Med livet som insats* (*They Staked Their Lives*) (+co-sc); *Den blomstertid* (*Blossom Time*) (+sc). **1941:** *Hem från Babylon* (*Home from Babylon*) (+co-sc). **1942:** *Himlaspelet* (*The Road to Heaven*) (+co-sc). **1944:** *Hets* (*Torment*); *Kungajakt* (*The Royal Hunt*). **1945:** *Resan bort* (*Journey Out*) (+sc). **1946:** *Iris och löjtnantshjärta* (*Iris and the Lieutenant*) (+sc). **1949:** *Bara en mor* (*Only a Mother*) (+co-sc). **1951:** *Fröken Julie* (*Miss Julie*) (+sc). **1953:** *Barabbas* (+sc). **1954:** *Karin Mansdotter* (+sc). **1955:** *Vildfåglar* (*Wild Birds*) (+co-sc). **1956:** *Sista paret ut* (*Last Pair Out*). **1960:** *Domaren* (*The Judge*) (+co-sc). **1966:** *Ön* (*The Island*). **1969:** *Fadern* (*The Father*).

Along with Sjöström, Stiller, and Bergman, Sjöberg must be counted as one of the most significant directors of the Swedish cinema, and indeed as the most important in that long period between the departure of Sjöström and Stiller for Hollywood and the establishment of Bergman as a mature talent. However, it is hard not to agree with the judgement of Peter Cowie when he states that Sjöberg "is hampered by a want of thematic drive, for he is not preoccupied, like Bergman, with a personal vision. He has not created a world to which one returns with an immediate feeling of recognition and empathy. Each of his films is a solitary achievement, illuminating for a moment the universe of Strindberg, Lagerkvist and others with a cinematic expertise that rarely falters. . . . If one concludes that Sjöberg's most successful accomplishments are founded on the inspiration of others . . . , it is not to deny his impeccable craftsmanship, his

Alf Sjöberg

uncanny grasp of historical period, and his gift for describing his characters compellingly within their environment."

After studying with Greta Garbo at Stockholm's famous Dramatic Theatre School, Sjöberg rapidly made a name for himself as a theatre director, becoming chief director at the Stockholm Theatre by 1930. In the late 1920s he encountered the films of Eisenstein and Pabst, but the chief influence on his early films would appear to be the fatalism and melancholy of French "poetic realism" of the 1930s. However, in his first film, *The Strongest,* an epic tale of the seal hunters of Arctic Norway, the influences would appear to be an intriguing blend of Jack London, Robert Flaherty, the Sjöström of *The Outlaw and His Wife* and, in the remarkably fluidly edited bear-hunt that climaxes the film, *Eisenstein.* All this was too much for a cinema industry preoccupied with feeble studio comedies and light dramas, and Sjöberg was unable to make another film for ten years. Instead he confined his experiments in mise-en-scène to the theatre.

In *They Stake Their Lives,* a sombre story of the underground in an unidentified Baltic totalitarian state, and *The Royal Hunt,* which deals with Russian attempts to overthrow Gustav III of Sweden in the late eighteenth century, there are clear references to the Nazi threat. In more general terms these films deal with the theme of power and domination, one of the threads that runs through much of the director's work. More important, however, is *The Road to Heaven,* a film very much in the Sjöström/Lagerlöf tradition that is generally regarded as one of the finest of the period 1920-1950 and an important milestone in the revival of the Swedish cinema at this time. A sort of Swedish *Pilgrim's Progress,* it draws heavily on the same kind of Swedish peasant art which influenced *The Seventh Seal,* though it is both more nationalistic and more specifically and directly Christian in inspiration than that work. As Forsyth Hardy has pointed out, "it helped to give spiritual structure to the revival of the Swedish cinema."

Frenzy signalled a new departure both for Swedish cinema in general and Sjöberg's work in particular, as well as the arrival of a powerful new talent in the form of its scriptwriter—Ingmar Bergman. In its story of a tyrannical schoolmaster (aptly nicknamed Caligula) who torments one of his students beyond endurance, Sjöberg clearly found a subject close to his heart, one which went beyond the obvious theme of youthful ardour vs. oppressive, reactionary middle and old age. The story allowed him to explore power relationships (with all their distinctly sexual ramifications) in a more general way. Sjöberg created a remarkably claustrophobic and sombre atmosphere to match Bergman's agonised screenplay—there are few sets, less still exterior shots, and the harsh lighting at times recalls the German silent cinema.

One of the themes explored in *Frenzy* is the destructive effect of outdated class divisions, and the evils of class society are also very much to the fore in *Only a Mother*, which is set among the "stataren," rural communities where farm labourers and their families were forced to endure almost serf-like conditions. The social dimension of Sjöberg's work at this time is a reminder that Sweden had recently introduced the full apparatus of a welfare state. At the same time, the director is still much preoccupied with formal matters, experimenting here with deep focus, huge close-ups, and sharply angled interior shots.

Sjöberg's best known film is probably *Miss Julie*, which transforms Strindberg's by then rather outdated condemnation of the class system into a study of power relationships between the sexes. Here the sado-masochistic element comes right to the fore, which earned the film a rather risqué reputation in Anglo-Saxon countries. In addition to instituting considerable modifications to the original story, Sjöberg also experimented with rapid transitions between past and present, often without the aid of cuts, and the film also contains a rare example of the flash-forward. Like *Iris and the Lieutenant* and *Only a Mother*, *Miss Julie* is also an indictment of the position of women under a stern patriarchal order. Strindberg was also the inspiration behind *Karin Mansdotter*, parts of which were based on his play *Erik XIV*. Beginning with a bizarre (and rather out of place) parody of cinematic costume drama, the film is beautifully shot, mostly on location in some of Sweden's most spectacular castles, by Sven Nykvist.

In his later work Sjöberg returned to contemporary Swedish society. The struggle between the sexes is continued in *Wild Birds* and the Bergman-scripted *The Last Pair Out*. At the same time, the director's concern with social injustice is evident in *The Judge*, an indictment of dubious legal activities, and *The Island*, in which the central character urges his apathetic fellow islanders to fight government plans to take away their land and turn it into a gunnery range. It has to be admitted, however, that Sjöberg's later work does not show him at his best; characters too often come across as mere puppets, there are too many wordy passages, and Sjöberg often seems unable to sustain any consistency of mood or refrain from exaggerated melodramatics. Still, his dramatically resonant use of settings, and the way in which he controls his characters' movements within them, remain interesting, reminding one that Sjöberg, at his best, has been compared to Emile Zola.—JULIAN PETLEY

Sjöström, Victor

Nationality *Swedish.* **Born** *Victor David Sjöström in Silbodal, Sweden, 20 September 1879; also known as Victor Seastrom.* **Education** *Attended high school in Uppsala, Sweden.* **Family** *Married 1) Sascha St. Jagoff, 1900 (died 1916); 2) Lili Bech, 1916; 3) actress Edith Erastoff, 1922 (died 1945), two children.* **Career** *Lived in Brooklyn, New York, from 1880; returned to Sweden to live with aunt, 1887; stage actor and director in Sweden and Finland, from 1896; formed own theater company, 1911; film director for Svenska Biograf film studio, Stockholm, from 1912; director for MGM, Hollywood, from 1923; worked under "Americanized" name, "Seastrom"; returned to Sweden as actor, 1930; artistic director, Svensk Filmindustri, 1943-49.* **Died** *In Stockholm, 3 January 1960.*

Films as Director: 1912: *Trädgårrdsmaåstaren (The Gardener) (+role); Ett Hemligt giftermaål (A Secret Marriage); En sommarsaga (A Summer Tale).* **1913:** *Lö jen och tårar (Ridicule and Tears);*

Blodets röst (*Voice of the Blood*) (+sc, role) (released 1923); *Lady Marions sommarflirt* (*Lady Marion's Summer Flirt*); *Äktenskapsbrydån* (*The Marriage Agency*) (+sc); *Livets konflikter* (*Conflicts of Life*) (co-d, role); *Ingeborg Holm* (+sc); *Halvblod* (*Half Breed*); *Miraklet*; *På livets ödesvägar* (*On the Roads of Fate*). **1914:** *Prästen* (*The Priest*); *Det var i Maj* (*It Was in May*) (+sc); *Kärlek starkare än hat* (*Love Stronger Than Hatred*); *Dömen icke* (*Do Not Judge*); *Bra flicka reder sig själv* (*A Clever Girl Takes Care of Herself*) (+sc); *Gatans barn* (*Children of the Street*); *Högfjällets dotter* (*Daughter of the Mountains*) (+sc); *Hjärtan som mötas* (*Meeting Hearts*). **1915:** *Strejken* (*Strike*) (+sc, role); *En av de många* (*One of the Many*) (+sc); *Sonad oskuld* (*Expiated Innocence*) (+co-sc); *Skomakare bliv vid din läst* (*Cobbler Stay at Your Bench*) (+sc). **1916:** *Lankshövdingens dottrar* (*The Governor's Daughters*) (+sc); *Rösen på Tistelön* (*Havsgammar, The Rose of Thistle Island; Sea Eagle*); *I. Prövningens stund* (*Hour of the Trial*) (+sc, role); *Skepp som motas* (*Meeting Ships*); *Hon segrade* (*She Conquered*) (+sc, role); *Therese* (+co-sc). **1917:** *Dödskyssen* (*Kiss of Death*) (+co-sc, role); *Terje Vigen* (*A Man There Was*) (+co-sc, role). **1918:** *Berg-Ejvind och hans hustru* (*The Outlaw and His Wife*) (+co-sc, role); *Tösen från stormyrtorpet* (*The Lass from the Stormy Croft*) (+co-sc). **1919:** *Ingmarsönerna, Parts I and II* (*Sons of Ingmar*) (+sc, role); *Hans nåds testamente* (*The Will of His Grace*). **1920:** *Klostret I Sendomir* (*The Monastery of Sendomir*) (+sc); *Karin Ingmarsdotter* (*Karin, Daughter of Ingmar*) (+co-sc, role); *Mästerman* (*Master Samuel*) (+role). **1921:** *Körkarlen* (*The Phantom Chariot; Thy Soul Shall Bear Witness*) (+sc, role as David Holm). **1922:** *Vem dömer* (*Love's Crucible*) (+co-sc); *Det omringade huset* (*The Surrounded House*) (+co-sc, role). **1923:** *Eld ombord* (*The Tragic Ship*) (+role). **1924:** *Name the Man; He Who Gets Slapped*. **1925:** *Confessions of a Queen; The Tower of Lies*. **1927:** *The Scarlet Letter*. **1928:** *The Divine Woman; The Wind; Masks of the Devil*. **1930:** *A Lady to Love*. **1931:** *Markurells I Wadköping* (+role). **1937:** *Under the Red Robe*.

Other Films: 1912: *Vampyren* (Stiller) (role as Lt. Roberts); *De svarta maskerna* (Stiller) (role as the Lieutenant); *I livets vår* (Garbagni) (role). **1913:** *Nar karlekan dodar* (Stiller) (role as the painter); *Barnet* (Stiller) (role as medical student). **1914:** *För sin kädleks skull* (Stiller) (role as Borgen); *Högfjällets dotter* (Stiller) (role); *Guldspindeln* (Magnusen) (role); *Thomas Graals bästa film* (Stiller) (role as Thomas Graal); *Thomas Graals bästa barn* (Stiller) (role as Thomas Graal). **1934:** *Synnove Solbakken* (T. Ibsen) (role). **1935:** *Valborgsmaässoafton* (Edgren) (role). **1937:** *John Ericsson* (role). **1939:** *Gubben Kommer* (Lindberg) (role); *Mot nya tider* (Wallen) (role). **1941:** *Striden går vidare* (Molander) (role). **1943:** *Det brinner en eld* (Molander) (role); *Ordet* (Molander) (role). **1944:** *Kejsaren av Portugalien* (Molander) (role). **1947:** *Rallare* (Mattson) (role). **1940s:** *Farlig vår* (Mattson) (role). **1950:** *Till Glädje* (Bergman) (role); *Kvartetten som sprängdes* (Molander) (role). **1952:** *Hård klang* (Mattson) (role). **1955:** *Nattens väv* (Mattson) (role). **1957:** *Smultronstället* (*Wild Strawberries*) (Bergman) (role as Professor).

With a career in film that in many ways paralleled that of his close friend Mauritz Stiller, Victor Sjöström entered the Swedish film industry at virtually the same time (1912), primarily as an actor, only to become almost immediately, like Stiller, a film director. Whereas Stiller had spent his youth in Finland, however, Sjöström had spent six formative years as a child in America's Brooklyn. Once back in Sweden after an unhappy childhood, his training for the theater proved fruitful. He became a well-established actor before entering the film industry at the age of 32. "The thing that brought me into filmmaking was a youthful desire for adventure and a curiosity to try this new medium," he once said in an interview. The first films in which he appeared in 1912 were Stiller's *The Black Masks* and *Vampyren*.

Although Sjöström proved excellent as an actor in comedy, his innate seriousness of outlook was reflected in the films he directed. He developed a deep response to nature and the spectacular northern landscape, capturing the expanses of ice, snow, trees, and mountains in all their (to him as to other Scandinavians) mystical force. One of his earliest films was *Ingeborn Holm,* which exposed the cruelties of the forced labor system to which the children of paupers were still subjected. This film was produced partially outdoors; Sjöström's pantheistic response to nature was developed in *Terje Vigen,* his adaptation of Ibsen's ballad poem, with its narrative set in the period of the Napoleonic confrontation with Britain. Sjöström himself played Terje, the bitter Norwegian sailor who had been imprisoned for a while by the British for attempting to break through their blockade at sea in order to bring food through to the starving people, including his wife and son, in his village. He fails in this attempt and they die as a consequence. Terje's obsessive desire for vengeance is later purged as a result of his response to his British captor's child, whom he rescues in a storm.

Sjöström became a prolific director. He completed nearly 30 films between 1912 and 1918, the year he directed *The Outlaw and His Wife*. Of that film, French critic and filmmaker Louis Delluc wrote in 1921: "Here without doubt is the most beautiful film in the world. Victor Sjöström has directed it with a dignity that is beyond words . . . it is the first love duet heard in the cinema. A duet that is entire life. Is it a drama? . . . I don't know. . . . People love each other and live. That is all." In this film a rich widow abandons

Victor Sjöström

her estate to live in the mountains with her outlaw lover until, hounded by his pursuers, they die together in the snow. It is typical of the Swedish film that winter, after the symbolic summer of love, should become the synonym for death.

Sjöström's intense feeling for nature expanded still further in his first adaptation of a novel by Selma Lagerlöf who, as a writer in the grand tradition, became one of the primary inspirers of the Swedish cinema of this period. This adaptation was from *The Lass from the Stormy Croft* and featured a magnificent rustic setting which seems at once to transcend and embody the exigencies of human passion—the frustration of the poor peasant girl with her illegitimate child and the troubles that afflict the son of a landowner (played by Lars Hanson in his first important film role) who tries to befriend her. As Carl Dreyer, who in the same year made *The Parson's Widow* in Sweden, commented, "Selma Lagerlöf's predilection for dreams and supernatural events appealed to Sjöström's own somewhat sombre artistic mind."

Sjöström's most famous film before his departure for Hollywood in 1923 was *The Phantom Chariot* (also known as *Thy Soul Shall Bear Witness*), also based on a novel by Selma Lagerlöf. The legend had it that the phantom chariot came once each year, on New Year's Eve, St. Sylvester's Night, to carry away the souls of sinners. In the film the central character is David Holm, a violent and brutalized man who is brought to relive his evil past on St. Sylvester's Night, especially the ill-treatment he had given his wife, until his conscience is awakened. As Holm recalls his wicked deeds in flashback he is haunted by the approach of the chariot, and is saved just in time through reunion with his wife, whose imminent suicide he prevents. Holm is played brilliantly by Sjöström himself, while Julius Jaenzen's multi-exposure camerawork emphasizes the distinction between body and soul in visuals that surpass virtually all that had been achieved in cinematography by 1920.

In the postwar era, Swedish films, with their comparatively heavy themes, began to prove less popular as exports. Sjöström, like Stiller, left for America on the invitation of Louis B. Mayer at MGM. He was to remain in Hollywood six years, directing nine films under the name of Victor Seastrom. Of these, *The Scarlet Letter,* with Lillian Gish as Hester Prynne and Lars Hanson as the priest, and *The Wind,* also with Lillian Gish and Lars Hanson, are the more significant; the latter now ranks as a masterpiece of the silent cinema. Lillian Gish said of Sjöström that "his direction was a great education for me . . . the Swedish school of acting is one of repression." In *The Wind* she plays a sensitive girl from Kentucky forced into marriage with a coarse cattleman from Texas, a repellent marriage which, along with the harsh Texan environment, finally drives her nearly insane and impels her to kill a male intruder in self-defense. The film, shot in the Mojave region, suffered from re-editing by the studio and the imposition of a sound track.

Sjöström's single attempt to recreate Sweden in America was *The Tower of Lies* (with Lon Chaney and Norma Shearer), an adaptation of Selma Lagerlöf's novel *The Emperor of Portugal,* which at least one American reviewer praised for, "its preservation of the simplicity of treatment in *Thy Soul Shall Bear Witness.*"

Sjöström returned to Sweden in 1928 and directed one good sound film, *Markurells i Wadköping,* in which he starred as a grim man, much like Terje Vigen, who is finally purged of his desire for revenge. Apart from directing a lame period romance in England called *Under the Red Robe,* with Raymond Massey and Conrad Veidt, Sjöström concentrated on his career as an actor, giving at the age of 78 a great performance as the aged professor in Bergman's *Wild Strawberries.*—ROGER MANVELL

Skolimowski, Jerzy

Nationality Polish. *Born* Warsaw, 5 May 1938. *Education* Educated in literature and history at Warsaw University, diploma 1959; Warsaw University and State Superior Film School in Lodz, 1960-64. *Career* Published first collection of poetry, Quelque part près de soi, 1959; directed first feature (as film student), Rysopis, 1964; Rece de gory banned by Polish authorities, left Poland, 1967; moved to United States, 1984. *Awards* Grand Prix for Grand Prize, Bergamo International Film Festival, 1966, for Barrier; Golden Bear, Berlin Film Festival, 1967, for Le Depart; Special Jury Grand Prize, Cannes Festival, 1978, for The Shout; British Film Award and Best Screenplay, Cannes Festival, for Moonlighting, 1982; Special Prize, Venice Film Festival, 1985, for The Lightship.

Films as Director: 1960: *Oko wykol* (*L'Oeil Torve*) (short) (+sc); *Hamles* (*Le Petit Hamlet*) (short) (+sc); *Erotyk* (*L'Érotique*) (short)(+sc). **1961:** *Boks* (*Boxing*) (short) (+sc); *Piednadze albo zycie* (*La Bourse ou la vie*) (short) (+sc); *Akt* (short) (+sc). **1964:** *Rysopis* (*Identification Marks: None*) (+sc, pr, art d, ed, role as Andrzej Leszczyc). **1965:** *Walkower* (*Walkover*) (+sc, co-ed, role as Andrzej Leszczyc). **1966:** *Bariera* (*Barrier*) (+sc). **1967:** *Le Départ* (+co-sc); *Rece do gory* (*Hands Up!*) (+sc, co-art d, role as Andrzej Leszczyc). **1968:** *Dialog* (*Dialogue*) (+sc, art d). **1970:** *The Adventures of Gerard* (+co-sc); *Deep End* (+co-sc). **1971:** *King, Queen, Knave* (+co-sc). **1978:** *The Shout* (+co-sc). **1982:** *Moonlighting* (+sc, co-pr). **1984:** *Success is the Best Revenge* (+pr). **1985:** *The Lightship.* **1989:** *Acque di primavera* (*Torrents of Spring*) (+co-sc, role). **1992:** *Ferdydurke* (*30 Door Key*) (+co-sc).

Other Films: 1959: *Niewinni czardodzieje* (*Innocent Sorcerers*) (Wajda) (co-sc). **1960:** *Noz w wodzie* (*Knife in the Water*) (Polanski) (co-sc); *Przy Jaciel* (*A Friend*) (co-sc). **1981:** *Falschung* (Schlöndorff) (role). **1985:** *White Knights* (Hackford) (role). **1987:** *Big Shots* (role). **1996:** *Mars Attacks!* (role).

Together with Roman Polanski, Jerzy Skolimowski is the most remarkable representative of the second generation of the Polish new wave. Younger than Wajda, Munk, or Kawalerowicz. These two did not share the hope for a new society after World War II. They are more skeptical filmmakers, to the point of cynicism at times. With Polanski, Skolimowski wrote *Knife in the Water,* which deals precisely with the relationship between two generations, after having also collaborated on the script of Wajda's *Innocent Sorcerers,* one of the director's rare attempts at portraying Poland's youth.

A student in ethnography, a poet, an actor, and a boxer, Skolimowski went to the Lodz film school (1960-1964) and graduated with a diploma work that brought world attention to his talent. That film, *Rysopis (Identification Marks: None),* and its totally controlled sequel *Walkover,* reveal an astonishing flexible style as it follows a central character, Andrzej Leszczyc, played by Skolimowski himself. Without resorting to a subjective camera, the director nevertheless makes us see reality through his hero. He refuses dramatic plot twists, filming instead in a manner very much like a jazz musician—all rhythm and improvisation. *Rysopis* tells of the few hours before being called up for military service, while *Walkover* provides an account of the time preceding a boxing match. A limited number of shots (39 and 29, respectively!) give an extraordinary sense of fluidity, of life caught in its most subtle shifts.

Bariera is a much more literary and symbolic work. It offers the same themes and milieu (young people, often students), although with a dreamlike atmosphere. The film's somnambulistic quality reappears later in Skolimowski's work, though integrated into its realistic surface. "Our cynical and indifferent generation still possesses romantic aspirations," says one of the characters, a statement that accurately sums up the filmmaker's ambivalent attitude towards life.

Jerzy Skolimowski (right) with Jeremy Irons on the set of *Moonlighting.*

If *Bariera* was, according to Skolimowski, influenced by Godard's *Pierrot le fou,* his next film, *Le Départ,* shot in Belgium, borrowed two actors, Jean-Pierre Léaud and Catherine Duport, from the French director's *Masculin féminin.* The film deals with a young hairdresser who dreams of becoming a rally driver, and his relationship with a girl. The same sensitive portrait of youth is found again in a more accomplished work, *Deep End,* a brilliant portrayal of a London swimming bath attendant and his tragic love affair.

The titles of Skolimowski's films (*Walkover, Barrier, Departure, Hands Up, Deep End*) suggest the relationship to sports, movement, and physical effort that characterize his nervous and dynamic style. *Hands Up,* banned for fifteen years by the Polish authorities because of its bleak symbolic portrayal of a group of people shut up inside a railway carriage, prompted Skolimowski to work in the West, though he has always returned regularly to his home country. But difficulties associated with an international career appeared quickly with the failure of *The Adventures of Gerard,* a spoof on Conan Doyle's Napoleonic novel, and the more evident one of *King, Queen, Knave,* a film based on Nabokov's novel that was shot in Munich.

However, Skolimowski came back to the forefront of European filmmaking with *The Shout* and *Moonlighting.* The former, adapted from a Robert Graves short story, has a sense of the absurd which verges on creating a surrealistic atmosphere—a classic component of Polish culture. This film, which concerns a love triangle between a kind of sorcerer, the woman he is in love with, and her husband, is an intense, haunting piece of work.

Moonlighting, arguably Skolimowski's best film to date, was written and shot within a few months and looks deceptively simple. The tale of four Polish workers sent from Warsaw to refurbish the house a rich Pole has bought in London gradually reveals layers of meaning, commenting on contacts between East and West and repression in Poland. The nightmare emerges slowly from a close scrutiny of reality, confirming that Skolimowski's materialism and lucidity do not contradict but rather refine his unique poetic sensibility.

Subsequent films included *Success, The Lightship, Torrents of Spring,* and *30 Door Key.* Of these, *The Lightship* was notable for its depiction of a grim power struggle between characters played by Klaus Maria Brandauer and Robert Duvall. *Torrents of Spring,* meanwhile, a visually lavish drama about a nineteenth-century Russian aristocrat and his love for two women, was based on an Ivan Turgenev story.—MICHEL CIMENT

Soderbergh, Steven

Nationality American. *Born* 14 January 1963, in Atlanta, Georgia. *Education* High school graduate, 1980. *Family* Married Betsy Brantley; one daughter. *Career* Did odd jobs while writing scripts and directing short films, 1980-85; directed 90215, a Yes concert film, for MTV, 1986; first feature, sex, lies, and videotape, a surprise international success, 1989. *Awards* Grammy Award for Best Director, 1986, for 90215; Palme d'Or for Best Feature Film, Cannes International Film Festival, 1989, and Independent Spirit awards for Best Feature and Best Director, 1990, for sex, lies, and videotape. *Agent* Pat Dollard, United Talent Agency, 9560 Wilshire Blvd., Beverly Hills, California 90212, U.S.A.

S
.....
FILM DIRECTORS

Films as Director: 1986: *90215* (doc; for TV). **1989:** *sex, lies, and videotape* (+sc, ed). **1991:** *Kafka* (+ed). **1993:** *King of the Hill* (+sc); "The Quiet Room" (episode of TV series *Fallen Angels*). **1995:** *The Underneath* (+co-sc, uncredited). **1996:** *Gray's Anatomy; Schizopolis* (+sc, role).

Other Films: 1993: *Suture* (McGehee and Siegel) (exec pr). **1996:** *The Daytrippers* (Mottola) (co-pr). **1997:** *Nightwatch* (Ornedal) (co-sc). **1998:** *Pleasantville* (Ross) (co-pr).

Steven Soderbergh's work is difficult to characterize as a whole, considering the remarkable variety among his first four features: a contemporary sexual drama/comedy; a fantasy thriller set in Kafka's Prague; a portrait of a child growing up in Depression-era America; and a remake of a classic film noir. Following the sensational success of his first feature, *sex, lies, and videotape,* Soderbergh was often compared to other young independent American filmmakers, notably Jim Jarmusch and Hal Hartley. However, as subsequent films have shown, his film style is much less immediately identifiable (or from a Hollywood viewpoint, less eccentric) than those others'. Overall, one can say that his narrative techniques tend to be concise and polished in ways reminiscent of classic Hollywood rather than European models, yet fresh, with unusual overall structures and surprising turns from scene to scene; his cinematography is always superb, notably in framing and lighting, though extremely varied from film to film to match the subject matter and mood. Unfortunately, Soderbergh has not continued to receive the critical and popular attention awarded to his first feature, or attracted enthusiasts (e.g., Internet fan clubs) as have Hartley and some others; yet he remains in his own way a daring artist whose projects have been far from predictable.

sex, lies, and videotape is more than a highly accomplished debut film—it is quite simply a remarkably accomplished film. In portraying a budding relationship between a man who is impotent, except when watching his own video interviews with women on sexual topics, and a woman who finds that her husband and sister are having an affair behind her back, the writer/director manages to create neither low farce nor soap-operatic psychodrama. Actually, the film is rather touchingly romantic, in a witty, gentle, unsoppy sort of way. Soderbergh deftly introduces the four main characters through a montage of scenes linked by a voiceover of Ann speaking to her therapist; he moves the story forward with some striking closeups and high angle shots, while unobtrusively establishing a world for each character through decor (including Graham's mostly empty spaces). And he brilliantly structures the climactic scene of Ann taking hold of Graham's camera: he postpones the second half of it until later, when her unfaithful but furious husband seizes the tape and begins to watch it, and Soderbergh cuts from the tape itself to a flashback of Ann and Graham making the tape. As for Soderbergh's handling of the actors, one might simply note that the film immeasurably boosted the careers of James Spader and Andie MacDowell and gave Laura San Giacomo a strong debut. If Peter Gallagher's performance is merely solid—perhaps because his character is conceived more as a simple type than the other three—Soderbergh did later provide the actor with one of his best, most subtle screen roles, in *The Underneath*.

Striking into new territory for his eagerly anticipated second feature, Soderbergh created a work uneasily occupying a space between a European art film and a plot-driven Hollywood suspense film. *Kafka* has a script that derives from two different kinds of paranoid world—the literary one of Franz Kafka and the cinematic one of the political-conspiracy thriller—and a visual style inspired by Carol Reed's *The Third Man* (rather more than by Orson Welles's eccentric version of Kafka's *The Trial*), and perhaps too blatantly by Terry Gilliam's *Brazil* in the color sequence inside the Castle. The film does have astonishingly handsome black-and-white

**Steven Soderberg on the set of *The Underneath.*
Photograph by Alan Pappe.**

cinematography, some quite terrifying moments involving a shrieking killer, and some droll slapstick humor in the antics of a pair of office assistants. But there is an awkwardness in having a protagonist who on one level is the "real" Franz Kafka—shown as a drudge in an insurance office who writes agonized letters to his father and also fantastic stories like "Metamorphosis" and others alluded to—but on another level is a reluctant movie hero drawn into uncovering a sinister organization that turns out to be diabolical in a much more conventional way than anything in an actual Kafka story.

King of the Hill has its terrifying moments too, notably in the figure of a snarly bellboy trying to evict the young hero from the hotel room where his father has more or less abandoned him. Indeed, all three of Soderbergh's features following *sex, lies, and videotape* have a single isolated male protagonist trapped in a world out of his control or comprehension. But *King of the Hill* also particularly recalls *sex, lies, and videotape* in its concern with lies and the doubtful knowability of other people. The plot, based upon A. E. Hotchner's memoir, centers upon the efforts of an impoverished twelve-year-old (Jesse Bradford) to pass himself off at school as well-to-do, and upon his need to trust that his suspiciously undemonstrative father (Jeroen Krabbe) will return to him. Overall, the story line is rather dark: the boy not only is exposed as a liar, but loses contact with everyone he loves—in turn, his kid brother, sickly mother, travelling-salesman father, the girl next door, and his roguish best friend—until he is nearly literally reduced to starvation. Yet, in Dickensian fashion, there are also warm and downright comical moments and whole episodes, as well as a number of reunions. Soderbergh manages to balance the bleak and joyful elements skillfully, for the most part, though one might wish the cinematography did not have that hazy golden glow that has become too commonly used for period pieces.

In choosing to remake the classic film noir *Criss Cross,* Soderbergh had a perfect vehicle for continuing his fascination with motifs of lies, trust, and seemingly cosmic entrapment within the conventions of a genre that specializes in such concerns. Most impressively, *The Underneath* has the true noir feel, without aping the black-and-white visuals of the Robert Siodmak original or other 1940s films, or leaning toward parody a la *Body Heat,* or making a slick melodrama with an unambiguously decent protagonist and an upbeat ending (as in the case of Barbet Schroeder's remake of another noir classic, *Kiss of Death,* which opened at the same time as *The Underneath*). Selecting widescreen Panavision with some very unsettling compositions, and constructing a far more complex flashback structure than the original film had, Soderbergh flawlessly plays out the drama of an ex-gambling addict still obsessed with his ex-wife (now married to a gangster) and drawn into an armored car robbery that betrays his kindly mentor. There is a telling moment when Michael's new girlfriend, sensing his mind on other things, remarks, "You're not very present tense": a perfect description of a film noir hero trapped in webs of the past and fearing the future. In the film's fluid flashback structure we indeed see Michael's life fluctuating between three time lines, and we gradually put the puzzle together: his selfish or addictive past (marked by his having a beard); his ethical/familial/sexual entanglements when he returns to his hometown; and (in what may be considered flashforwards) the day of the robbery, marked by bluish lighting and time subtitles, like "6:02 p.m." Only at the violent moment of the robbery, more than an hour into the film, are we fully "caught up" in time; and at this point Soderbergh proceeds to a daring seven minutes of subjective-viewpoint shots as various characters address a delirious Michael in his hospital bed. This is followed by a set piece of suspense, involving a possible assassin, that may derive from the earlier film or the novel but is so superbly gauged that it is a classic in itself.

Receiving mixed reviews and low attendance at its opening, *The Underneath* quickly disappeared from theatres—an undeserved fate for one of the best of the neo-noirs, and perhaps Soderbergh's most accomplished work after *sex, lies, and videotape*. One can only hope that the director will continue to explore his favorite—or obsessive—themes of honesty and (self-) deceit in ways that use Hollywood traditions with a new vigor.—JOSEPH MILICIA

Spielberg, Steven

Nationality American. Born Cincinnati, Ohio, 18 December 1947. Education California State College at Long Beach, B.A. in English, 1970. Family Married 1) actress Amy Irving (divorced 1989), one son, one daughter; 2) actress Kate Capshaw, one daughter.

Steven Spielberg

Career *Won amateur film contest with 40-minute film* Escape to Nowhere, *1960; on strength of film* Amblin', *became TV director for Universal, late 1960s; TV work included episodes of* Marcus Welby, M.D., Columbo, *and* Night Gallery, *and TV films, including* Duel, *then given theatrical release; directed first feature,* The Sugarland Express, *1974; formed own production company, Amblin Productions; produced television series* Amazing Stories, *late 1980s, and* seaQuest DSV *and others, 1990s; formed new Hollywood studio DreamWorks SKG, with David Geffen and Jeffrey Katzenberg, 1995.* ***Awards*** *David Di Donatello Award (Italy) for Best Foreign Director, Kinema Jumpo Award (Japan) for Best Foreign Director, National Society of Film Critics Award for Best Director, and L.A. Film Critics Award for Best Director, for* E.T., *1982; Directors Guild Award for Best Director, and British Academy of Film and Television Arts Award for Best Director, for* The Color Purple, *1985; Irving G. Thalberg Award for body of work, Motion Picture Academy, 1986; D. W. Griffith Award, National Board of Review, for* Empire of the Sun, *1987; Academy Awards for Best Director and Best Film, L.A. Film Critics Best Film, New York Film Critics Circle Best Film, D. W. Griffith Award for Best Film, and National Society of Film Critics Best Film and Director, for* Schindler's List, *1993; Golden Lion for Career Achievement, Venice Film Festival, 1993; Life Achievement Award, American Film Institute, 1995.* ***Agent*** *Jay Moloney, Creative Artists Agency, 9830 Wilshire Boulevard, Beverly Hills, California 90212, U.S.A.* ***Address*** *Amblin Entertainment/Dreamworks SKG, 100 Universal City Plaza, Bungalow 477, Universal City, California 91608-1085, U.S.A.*

Films as Director, Scriptwriter, and Producer: 1969: *Amblin'* (short). **1971:** *Duel* (for TV). **1972:** *Something Evil* (for TV). **1974:** *The Sugarland Express* (+co-story). **1975:** *Jaws.* **1977:** *Close Encounters of the Third Kind* (2nd version released 1980) (+story). **1979:** *1941.* **1981:** *Raiders of the Lost Ark.* **1982:** *E.T.—The Extraterrestrial* (co-pr). **1983:** episode of *The Twilight Zone—The Movie* (co-pr). **1984:** *Indiana Jones and the Temple of Doom.* **1986:** *The Color Purple* (co-pr). **1987:** *Empire of the Sun* (co-pr). **1989:** *Indiana Jones and the Last Crusade.* **1990:** *Always* (co-pr). **1991:** *Hook.* **1993:** *Jurassic Park* (+co-exec pr); *Schindler's List* (+co-exec pr). **1997:** *The Lost World: Jurassic Park; Amistad.* **1998:** *Saving Private Ryan* (+co-pr).

Other Films: 1973: *Ace Eli and Rodger of the Skies* (Erman) (story). **1978:** *I Wanna to Hold Your Hand* (Zemeckis) (pr). **1980:** *Used Cars* (Zemeckis); *The Blues Brothers* (Landis) (role). **1981:** *Continental Divide* (Apted) (co-exec pr). **1982:** *Poltergeist* (Hooper) (co-pr, co-story, co-sc). **1984:** *Gremlins* (Dante) (co-exec pr). **1985:** *Back to the Future* (Zemeckis) (co-exec pr); *Young Sherlock Holmes* (Levinson) (co-exec pr); *Goonies* (Donner) (co-exec pr). **1986:** *The Money Pit* (Benjamin) (co-exec pr); *An American Tail* (Bluth) (co-exec pr); *Innerspace* (Dante) (co-exec pr); **batteries not included* (Matthew Robbins) (co-exec pr). **1988:** *Who Framed Roger Rabbit?* (Zemeckis) (co-exec pr); *The Land Before Time* (Bluth) (co-exec pr). **1989:** *Dad* (Goldberg) (co-exec pr); *Back to the Future, Part II* (Zemeckis) (co-exec pr); *Joe vs. the Volcano* (Shanley) (co-exec pr). **1990:** *Arachnophobia* (Frank Marshall) (co-exec pr); *Back to the Future, Part III* (Zemeckis) (co-exec pr); *Gremlins 2: The New Batch* (Dante) (co-exec pr). **1991:** *Cape Fear* (Scorsese) (exec pr); *An American Tail: Fievel Goes West* (Nibbelink) (co-pr). **1993:** *We're Back: A Dinosaur's Tail* (co-exec pr); *Trail Mix-up* (exec pr). **1994:** *I'm Mad* (exec pr); *The Flintstones* (co-pr). **1995:** *To Wong Foo, Thanks for Everything, Julie Newmar* (Kidron) (co-exec pr); *Balto* (exec pr); *Casper* (exec pr); *The Bridges of Madison County* (Eastwood) (exec pr [uncredited]). **1996:** *Twister* (de Bont) (co-exec pr). **1997:** *Cats* (co-exec pr); *Men in Black* (Sonnenfeld) (exec pr).

Perhaps any discussion of Steven Spielberg must inevitably begin with the consideration that, as of 1996, Spielberg remains the most commercially successful director the world has yet seen—an incredible, if mind-boggling proposition which, in another time, might have immediately made the director's films ineligible for serious critical consideration. Yet the fact that Spielberg's combined films have grossed well over one billion dollars attests to their power in connecting to the mass audience and offers the analyst an immediate conundrum which may take a more distanced generation of critics and filmgoers to answer fully: What does Spielberg know? And why has so much of his work invited such audience approval?

Spielberg has worked in a variety of genres: the television film *Duel* is a thriller; *Jaws* is a horror film; *1941* is a crazy comedy; *Close Encounters of the Third Kind* is a science-fiction film; *Raiders of the Lost Ark* is an adventure film patterned after film serials of the early 1950s; *E.T.—The Extraterrestrial* is a fantasy/family film combining elements from *The Wizard of Oz, Lassie,* and *Peter Pan; The Color Purple* is a social drama; *Empire of the Sun* is an expansive wartime epic. And yet virtually all of Spielberg's films are united by the same distinctive vision: a vision imbued with a sense of wonder which celebrates the magic and mystery that imagination can reveal as an alternative to the humdrum and the everyday. The artistic consistency within Spielberg's work is demonstrated further by his narratives, which are structurally similar. In the typical Spielberg film, an Everyman protagonist has his conception of the world enlarged (often traumatically) as he comes face to face with some extraordinary and generally non-human antagonist who is often hidden from the rest of the world and/or the audience until the narrative's end. In *Duel,* a California businessman named Mann finds himself pitted against the monstrous truck whose driver's face is never shown; in *Jaws,* the water-shy sheriff must face an almost mythological shark whose jaws are not clearly shown until the final reel; in *Close Encounters,* a suburban father responds to the extrasensory messages sent by outer-space creatures who are not revealed until the last sequence of the film; in *Raiders of the Lost Ark,* Indiana Jones quests for the Lost Ark which does not let forth its Pandora's Box of horrors until summoned up by those who would attempt to profit from it; and, of course, in *E.T.,* a small boy whose life is already steeped in imagination keeps secret his adoption of a playful extra-terrestrial (although one could easily argue that the non-human antagonist here is not really the sensitive E.T., but the masked and terrifying government agents who, quietly working behind the scenes throughout the narrative, finally invade the suburban house and crystallize the protagonist's most horrific fears). Structural analysis even reveals that *Poltergeist,* the Spielberg-produced, Tobe Hooper-directed film which relates to Spielberg's career in the same way the Howard Hawks-produced, Christian Nyby-directed *The Thing* related to Hawks's career, is indeed a continuation of the Spielberg canon. In *Poltergeist,* a typical American family ultimately discovers that the antagonists responsible for the mysterious goings-on in their suburban home are the other-worldly ghosts and skeletons not shown until the end of the film, when the narrative also reveals the villainy of the real estate developer who had so cavalierly disposed of the remains from an inconveniently located cemetery.

Technically proficient and dazzling, Spielberg's films are voracious in their synthesis of the popular culture icons which have formed the director's sensibilities: Hitchcock movies, John Wayne, comic books, *Bambi,* suburban homes, fast food, the space program, television. His vision is that of the child-artist—the innocent and profound imagination that can summon up primeval dread from the deep, as well as transcendent wonder from the sky. If Spielberg's films are sometimes attacked for a certain lack of interest in social issues or "adult concerns," they may be defended on the grounds that his films—unlike so many of the "special effects" action films of the 1970s and 1980s—derive from a sensibility which is sincerely felt. A more subtle attack on Spielberg would hold that his interest in objects and mechanical effects (as in *1941* and *Raiders of the Lost Ark*), though provocative, may not always be in perfect balance with his interest in sentiment and human values. Spielberg himself acknowledges his debt to Walt Disney, whose theme "When You Wish upon a Star," a paean to faith and imagination, dictates the spirit of several Spielberg films. And yet certainly if intellectual and persuasive critical constructions be sought to justify our enjoyment of Spielberg's cinema, they can easily be found in the kind of mythic, Jungian criticism which analyzes his very popular work as a kind of direct line to the collective unconscious. *Jaws,* for instance, is related to the primal fear of being eaten as well as to the archetypal initiation rite; *Close Encounters* is constructed according to the archetypal form of the quest and its attendant religious structures of revelation and salvation; and of course *E.T.* has already been widely analyzed as a re-telling of the Christ story—complete with a sacred heart, a ritual death, a resurrection brought about by faith, and an eventual ascension into heaven as E.T. returns home.

If Spielberg is especially notable in any other way, it is perhaps that he represents the most successful example of what has been called the film-school generation, which is increasingly populating the new Hollywood: a generation which has been primarily brought up on television and film, rather than literature, and for whom film seems apparently to have replaced life as a repository of significant experience. And yet if the old Hollywood's studio system is dead, it has been partially replaced by a solid, if informal matrix of friendships and alliances: between Spielberg and a fraternity that includes George Lucas, Francis Ford Coppola, Lawrence Kasdan, John Milius, Bob Zemeckis, Robert Gale, Hal Barwood, Matthew Robbins, Melissa Mathison, and Harrison Ford.

It is noteworthy that Hollywood, though consistently accused of a preference for box-office appeal over critical acclaim, has nevertheless refused (until *Schindler's List* in 1994) to valorize publicly Spielberg's work, despite his popular and critical success. The Academy of Motion Picture Arts and Sciences has consistently chosen to pass over Spielberg's films and direction—in 1975 bypassing *Jaws* in favor of *One Flew over the Cuckoo's Nest* and Milos Forman; in 1977, bypassing *Close Encounters* for *Annie Hall* and Woody Allen; in 1981 bypassing *Raiders of the Lost Ark* for *Chariots of Fire* and Warren Beatty (as director of *Reds*); in 1982 bypassing *E.T.* for *Gandhi* and Richard Attenborough; and in 1985 bypassing *The Color Purple* for *Out of Africa* and Sydney Pollack.

More than requiring an explanatory footnote in film history texts, these "slights" made it clear that the industry of the time had come to hold Spielberg responsible for the juvenilization of the American cinema in the late 1970s and 1980s. If the Coppolas and the Scorseses attempted to remake Hollywood to their own vision of a freer, more European, artistic sensibility (and by and large failed), should Spielberg now be held responsible for betraying earlier victories and turning Hollywood into a Disneyland? And although Spielberg became the richest man in Hollywood, the most commercially savvy, the man everyone most wanted to make a deal with, the most influential, he could not easily become anything at all like its most serious, respected artist. Spielberg's longtime insistence on avoiding adult themes, instead taking refuge in nostalgia, special effects, remakes, and sequels, seemed to be directly responsible for rather perniciously preventing non-Spielberg-like films from being produced. As well, the overwhelming number of Spielberg imitators, many producing films under Spielberg's own auspices, have largely contributed commercially successful hackwork.

Hollywood noted the irony, too, that it was in the Spielberg production of *The Twilight Zone* movie (directed by John Landis) that two children and actor Vic Morrow should have been killed in a clearly avoidable accident in which the children's employment violated child-labor law. *The Color Purple,* although conforming to Spielberg's typical pattern of the hidden antagonist, backed off from an explicit representation of Celie's lesbianism, turning her instead into a cute *E.T.*-like creature. Thus the confrontation of the hidden antagonist (Celie's true nature) became a kind of missing climax in a film which many critics ridiculed. After *The Color Purple,* when receiving the Irving Thalberg award from the Motion Pictures Academy, Spielberg gave a widely quoted speech which seemed surprisingly to admit responsibility for the state of American film culture: "I think in our romance with technology and our excitement at exploring all the possibilities of film and video, I think we have partially lost something. . . . It's time to renew our romance with the word; I'm as culpable as anyone in exalting the image at the expense of the word. . . . Only a generation of readers will spawn a generation of writers." Spielberg's speech was followed by arguably his finest work: from a screenplay by famed dramatist Tom Stoppard, *Empire of the Sun,* set in Asia during World War II, includes some of Spielberg's most startling set-pieces (such as a crowd sequence which rivals Eisenstein's use of montage in "The Odessa Steps" sequence of *Potemkin,* or an unusually expressive evocation of the atomic bombing at Hiroshima), as well as more adult themes relating to war and peace, community integration and disintegration. Nevertheless, when this film was overshadowed in many ways by Bertolucci's Asia epic, *The Last Emperor,* Spielberg seemed to beat a hasty retreat into safer material.

Always, a remake of *A Guy Named Joe* in which Spielberg portrayed adult relationships within a fantasy context including helpful ghosts, was both a critical and financial failure. Even more distressing was the critical failure of the 1991 *Hook,* in which Spielberg's professed appreciation for the word disappeared under the weight of charmless Hollywood juveniles having onscreen food fights amidst special effects gleefully presented by Spielberg as artistic entertainment. Although critics had for years suggested that the source material *Peter Pan* would provide Spielberg his most natural material (a boy not wanting to grow up), many were stunned when Spielberg's version finally arrived: bloated, overlong, overproduced, looking more like a vapid amusement park ride or a multimillion dollar commercial for a new attraction at the Universal Studio Tour than a film. Its artistic message—that its adult Peter Pan should work less and spend more quality time with his children—was in ludicrous contradiction to the herculean effort required by all, including its director, to devote themselves to such a high-budget, effects-heavy project; thus the film emerges as the most cynical, hypocritical attempt to play on audience sentiment to attract box-office in the Spielberg *oeuvre.*

The year 1993 marked a turning point for Spielberg—with the release of two films in the same year that could not have been more different. *Jurassic Park,* a cinefantastique wonder showing dinosaurs wreaking havoc in a contemporary theme park, was a roller-coaster ride which fast became the most commercially successful film of all time, bypassing even Spielberg's own *E.T.* Although the special effects were mostly marvelous and definitely the reason for the film's appeal (can anyone who has seen the film ever forget the startlingly graceful images of apatosaurs grazing in the forest?), many critics were startled by a certain desultoriness in the construction of the narrative: loose ends here and there, scenes which seemed not all to pay off. And indeed, deficiencies may be attributed to Spielberg losing some interest in the project—for the other Spielberg film released in 1993 was the film which would finally, irrevocably answer his critics: a black-and-white film photographed in a radically different camera style, devoid of the famous Spielberg backlighting as well as his traditional over-the-top orchestrations, using virtually unknown actors, and all on the single most unremittingly serious subject of the contemporary world: the Holocaust. Spielberg's *Schindler's List* was his most striking, overwhelming work; with it, he finally won his Academy Awards for film and director, as well as best film awards from the L.A. and New York critics groups, the Board of Review, and the National Society of Film Critics—a startlingly unanimous achievement. For a serious film, *Schindler's List* was also amazingly successful with the public, which was powerfully moved and horrified by the film. Based on the real-life story of Oskar Schindler, a German industrialist who actually saved over a thousand Jews by employing them at his factory, *Schindler's List,* keeping with the Spielberg ethos, emphasized the most hopeful components of the story without minimizing or denying its horrifying components. The film's coda, which showed the actors along with their real-life counterparts who survived because of Schindler visiting the gravesite of the real Schindler, was criticized by some, but this strategy insisted the audience understand the story as historical and gave the film an even greater emotional depth. Although time will tell whether *Schindler's List* will retain its instant reputation as a great, towering achievement comparable to, say, Alain Resnais's short *Night and Fog,* the definitive Holocaust film, the film has—according to his own testimony—altered Spielberg's life, sensibility, and career. The first artistic work that allowed Spielberg directly to explore his Jewish heritage, *Schindler's List* so consumed him that he has since embarked on what he has called his most important life's work: a video project documenting the survivors of the Holocaust for educational purposes. In interviews given before his multiple Academy Award wins, Spielberg has also said that he could no longer imagine going back to directing the kinds of films he made before *Schindler's List.*

On other fronts, Spielberg has continued to consolidate his position in Hollywood as its most powerful man. His company, Amblin, has stepped up television production, either Spielberg and/or Amblin involved in television series as disparate as *Amazing Stories, seaQuest,* the top-rated drama *ER,* and the children's show *The Animaniacs.* Spielberg has continued to help produce the films of others, and at least one of those post-*Schindler* films, *To Wong Foo, Thanks for Everything, Julie Newmar,* though a traditional Hollywood film in its warmth and sentiment, took on a non-traditional subject: homophobia in America. More monumentally, in one of the most publicized entertainment stories of 1994, Spielberg has formed a new Hollywood studio called DreamWorks SKG in partnership with two of the other most powerful men in Hollywood, Jeffrey Katzenberg and David Geffen. As Spielberg moves closer and closer to being a modern-day mogul in the style of Walt Disney or Cecil B. DeMille, will his *Schindler's* conversion continue and he devote himself to serious, revealing, personal projects requiring no apology, or will the lure of big bucks for future installments of Indiana Jones and other popular entertainments prove too great a temptation for DreamWorks to forego? Perhaps Spielberg will find some way of mediating these apparently contradictory goals with enough integrity and skill to retain his popular appeal as well as his newfound critical respectability as a serious artist.—CHARLES DERRY

Stahl, John M.

Nationality American. *Born* New York City, 21 January 1886. *Education* Educated in New York City public schools. *Family* Married Roxana Wray, 1932. *Career* Actor on stage and later in films, from 1901; hired by Vitagraph Studio, Brooklyn, as director, 1914; moved to Hollywood, worked for Louis B. Mayer in independent productions, then at MGM, 1917; vice-president and directorial producer, Tiffany-Stahl Studios, 1928; sold interest in studio and joined Universal, 1930. *Died* 12 January 1950.

Films as Director: (incomplete listing prior to 1918) 1914: *The Boy and the Law* **1917:** *The Lincoln Cycle* (14-reeler distributed in six chapters including *My Mother, My Father, My Self, The Call to Arms*). **1918:** *Scandal Mongers; Wives of Men* (+sc); *Suspicion.* **1919:** *Her Code of Honor; A Woman Under Oath.* **1920:** *Greater Than Love; Women Men Forget; The Woman in His House; Sowing the Wind; The Child Thou Gavest Me* (+pr). **1922:** *The Song of Life; One Clear Call* (+pr); *Suspicious Wives.* **1923:** *The Wanters* (+pr); *The Dangerous Age* (+pr). **1924:** *Why Men Leave Home; Husbands and Lovers* (+pr). **1925:** *Fine Clothes.* **1926:** *Memory Lane* (+pr, co-sc); *The Gay Deceiver.* **1927:** *Lovers?* (+pr); *In Old Kentucky* (+pr). **1930:** *A Lady Surrenders.* **1931:** *Seed; Strictly Dishonorable.* **1932:** *Back Street.* **1933:** *Only Yesterday.* **1934:** *Imitation of Life.* **1935:** *Magnificent Obsession.* **1937:** *Parnell.* **1938:** *Letter of Introduction* (+pr). **1939:** *When Tomorrow Comes* (+pr). **1941:** *Our Wife.* **1942:** *The Immortal Sergeant.* **1943:** *Holy Matrimony.* **1944:** *The Eve of St. Mark; The Keys of the Kingdom.* **1946:** *Leave Her to Heaven.* **1947:** *Forever Amber* (replaced by Otto Preminger); *The Foxes of Harrow.* **1948:** *The Walls of Jericho.* **1949:** *Father Was a Fullback; Oh, You Beautiful Doll.*

John Stahl was a key figure in the development of the Hollywood "women's melodrama" during the 1930s and 1940s, and quite possibly in the 1910s and 1920s as well. Although he began directing in 1914, and apparently made as many films before sound as after, only two of his silents (*Her Code of Honor* and *Suspicious Wives*) seem to have survived. Yet this is hardly the only reason that the ultimate critical and historical significance of his work remains to be established. More pertinent is the critical disrepute of the "tearjerker" genre in which he worked almost exclusively—a genre which had to await the discovery of Douglas Sirk's melodramas and the reworking of the form by R.W. Fassbinder to attract serious critical attention.

Comparisons between Sirk's baroquely aestheticized and Stahl's straightforwardly unadorned treatments of equally improbable plots is somewhat useful, and virtually inevitable, given that Sirk remade three of Stahl's classic 1930s "weepies": *Imitation of Life* (1934/1959), *Magnificent Obsession* (1935/1954), and *When Tomorrow Comes* (1939), which became

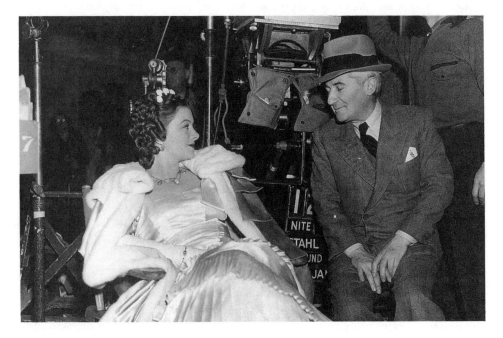

John M. Stahl with Myrna Loy on the set of *Parnell*.

Interlude (1957). In a genre focusing on the problems presented by the social/sexual order for the individual (most frequently, the bourgeois female), Sirk tended to abstract dramatic conflicts in the direction of Brecht, while Stahl chose to emphasize the effects of social rigidities through the emotions of his characters.

Stahl's career seemed to flourish most at Universal in the 1930s with the production of the highly accomplished *Back Street, Only Yesterday,* and the three films Sirk remade, all of which present emotionally similar heroines buffeted by twists of fate which wreak havoc on their socially-determined modes of behavior. In his version of Fannie Hurst's *Back Street* (remade in 1941 and 1961), Stahl encourages sympathy for Irene Dunne, an independent working woman who gives up everything to be "kept" in isolation by the respectable married man she loves. Audacious contradictions emerge from the very simplicity with which Stahl presents outrageous plot twists. Dunne meets the "kept woman" next door to her back street apartment, for example, only when the woman literally catches on fire and must be rescued. Recognizing a sister in shame, Dunne counsels the injured woman against allowing herself to be exploited by the man she loves; yet what seems to be a dawning moment of self-awareness on the part of our heroine is instantly obscured by a romantic haze when her own lover walks through the door in the middle of her diatribe. Similarly powerful contradictions abound in *Imitation of Life* (based on another Hurst novel), where best friends Claudette Colbert and Louise Beavers find themselves incapable, despite their best intentions, of breaking the social conventions which keep the black woman subservient to the white, even when the former is responsible for the latter's wealth and success.

Given material such as the Fannie Hurst novels, the "inspirational" message of Lloyd C. Douglas's *Magnificent Obsession,* and the hopelessly romantic *Only Yesterday* (virtually remade as Max Ophüls' *Letter from an Unknown Woman*), and considering the period during which Stahl worked, the point of reference seems not to be Sirk so much as Stahl's better-appreciated contemporary Frank Borzage. It is Borzage's unrelenting romanticism which is usually assumed to characterize the "weepies" of the 1920s and 1930s; yet Stahl's work offers another perspective. While he clearly encourages emotional identification with his heroines, Stahl seems more interested in exposing their romantic illusions than in relishing them. In fact, his meditative restraint in such situations has prompted George Morris to suggest that "it is Carl Th. Dreyer whom Stahl resembles more than directors like Sirk or Borzage."

Yet ultimately, Stahl's visual style seems largely dependent upon studio and cinematographer, a fact most clearly demonstrated by *Leave Her to Heaven,* a preposterously plotted drama of a psychotically duplicitous woman shot in Technicolor by Leon Shamroy on the modernesque sets of 20th Century-Fox, where the director's mise-en-scène emerges as florid and baroque as Sirk in his heyday—and a full decade earlier.

It seems that Stahl's films represent something of a missing link between Borzage's romanticism and Sirk. Certainly, an examination of his work expands an understanding of the variety of Hollywood's strategies in personalizing overtly ideological questions of sex, status, and money. In fact, if film scholars are serious about studying the melodrama in any depth, then the films of John Stahl remain a top and current priority.—ED LOWRY

Stevens, George

Nationality *American.* **Born** *George Cooper Stevens in Oakland, California, 18 December 1904.* **Family** *Married Joan (Stevens) (divorced), one son.* **Military Service** *Joined U.S. Army Signal Corps, became head of Special Motion Pictures Unit assigned to photograph activities of 6th Army, 1943; Unit awarded citation from General Eisenhower, 1945.* **Career** *Actor and stage manager for father's theatrical company, 1920-21; moved to Hollywood, 1921, worked as assistant and 2nd cameraman, then cameraman; joined Hal Roach as cameraman for Laurel and Hardy shorts, 1927; director of two-reel shorts for Roach, from 1930, and for RKO and Universal, from 1932; directed first feature,* The Cohens and Kellys in Trouble, *1933; also producer, from 1938; resumed career after military service during World War II.* **Awards** *Oscars for Best Director, for* A Place in the Sun, *1951, and* Giant, *1956; Irving G. Thalberg Award, Academy of Motion Picture Arts and Sciences, 1953.* **Died** *In Paris, 9 March 1975.*

Films as Director: 1930: *Ladies Past.* **1931:** *Call a Cop !; High Gear; The Kick-Off; Mama Loves Papa.* **1932:** *The Finishing Touch; Boys Will Be Boys; Family Troubles.* **1933:** *Should Crooners Marry; Hunting Trouble; Rock-a-bye Cowboy; Room Mates; A Divorce Courtship; Flirting in the Park; Quiet Please; Grin and Bear It; The Cohens and the Kellys in Trouble.* **1934:** *Bridal Bail; Ocean Swells; Bachelor Bait; Kentucky Kernels.* **1935:** *Laddie; The Nitwits; Alice Adams; Annie Oakley.* **1936:** *Swing Time.* **1937:** *Quality Street; A Damsel in Distress.* **1938:** *Vivacious Lady* (+pr). **1939:** *Gunga Din* (+pr). **1940:** *Vigil in the Night* (+pr). **1941:** *Penny Serenade* (+pr). **1942:** *Woman of the Year; The Talk of the Town* (+pr). **1943:** *The More the Merrier* (+pr). **1948:** *I Remember Mama* (+co-pr). **1951:** *A Place in the Sun* (+pr). **1952:** *Something to Live For* (+pr). **1953:** *Shane* (+pr). **1956:** *Giant* (co-pr). **1959:** *The Diary of Anne Frank* (+pr). **1965:** *The Greatest Story Ever Told* (+pr). **1970:** *The Only Game in Town.*

George Stevens (right) with Warren Beatty on the set of *The Only Game in Town.*

Other Films: (partial list) 1924: *The White Sheep* (cameraman); *The Battling Oriole* (cameraman). **1925:** *Black Cyclone* (cameraman). **1926:** *The Devil Horse* (cameraman); *The Desert's Toll* (cameraman); *Putting Pants on Philip* (cameraman). **1927:** *No Man's Law* (cameraman); *The Valley of Hell* (cameraman); *Lightning* (cameraman); *The Battle of the Century* (cameraman). **1928:** *Leave 'em Laughing* (cameraman); *Two Tars* (McCarey) (cameraman); *Unaccustomed as We Are* (cameraman). **1929:** *Big Business* (cameraman).

Katharine Hepburn had originally been responsible for bringing George Stevens to the attention of those in the front office. He had directed a great many two-reelers for Hal Roach, and was just entering films as a director of features when Hepburn met him, liked him, and asked that he be assigned as director to her next film, *Alice Adams*. It was a giant step forward for Stevens, but *Alice Adams,* from the Booth Tarkington novel, was a project right up his alley.

Two years later Stevens directed Hepburn again in a charming version of Barrie's play, *Quality Street,* and then in 1941 Hepburn again got him over to MGM to direct her and Spencer Tracy in *Woman of the Year,* the first film the two actors did together.

In the first half of his film career Stevens directed a Barbara Stanwyck feature, *Annie Oakley,* one of the best Astaire-Rogers dancing romances, *Swing Time,* and a delightful Ginger Rogers feature, *Vivacious Lady.* Astaire was never more debonair than in the adaption of Wodehouse's novel *A Damsel in Distress,* with George Burns and Gracie Allen. Stevens then really hit his stride as director of *Gunga Din,* a Kiplingesque glorification of romantic derring-do that featured Cary Grant, Victor McLaglen, and Douglas Fairbanks Jr. Two romances, *Vigil in the Night,* starring Carole Lombard, and *Penny Serenade,* co-starring Irene Dunne with Cary Grant, added to his reputation as an ideal director for romance, especially the weepy sort. His final feature before departing for wartime Europe was one of his best. *The More the Merrier* was a very funny comedy concerning the wartime housing situation in the nation's capital.

After the war, Stevens decided that he would like to produce and direct something that glorified America's past, preferably a comedy. Fortunately, Stevens had been named by Irene Dunne as one of those she would like to work for as the projected star of *I Remember Mama.*

The film was in production for six months and went far over schedule and budget. Stevens was a perfectionist who was determined not to be caught short of any piece of film he needed when making his first cut. He shot a master scene fully, with moving camera, and then shot and kept shooting the same scene from every conceivable angle. For a montage sequence involving Sir Cedric Hardwicke, Stevens spent nearly ten days shooting footage of Sir Cedric reading aloud while the family listened. He overshot, and it was expensive, but the end result was as nearly perfect as any movie could be. Because of the excessive production cost (over $3 million), *I Remember Mama* did not realize the profit it might have earned, although it premiered and played five continuous weeks at Radio Music City Hall, gathering rave notices and honors for all concerned.

Stevens had proved that he was back in form and at the top. He moved over to Paramount, where he made two of his best pictures—*A Place in the Sun,* from Theodore Dreiser's American classic, and *An American Tragedy,* with three perfectly-cast players: Montgomery Clift, Elizabeth Taylor, and Shelly Winters. He then served as the producer-director of one of the most remarkable westerns ever filmed, *Shane.* Told through the eyes of a young boy, the film has a disarming innocence in spite of its violence.

Stevens moved over to Warner Bros. to film *Giant,* Edna Ferber's novel about Texas. *Giant* featured Elizabeth Taylor, Rock Hudson, and James Dean. It was Dean's final credit, for he was killed in an auto crash directly after the shooting of his scenes was finished. Stevens' last three features—*The Diary of Anne Frank, The Greatest Story Ever Told,* and *The Only Game in Town*—were released by 20th Century-Fox. The last one, the best of the three, was virtually sloughed off in its release. When asked what the story was about, Stevens replied, "It's about an aging hooker and a losing gambler, if you think the world is ready for that." He had become embittered. The climate had changed in Hollywood, and it was difficult to get a first-class release for a picture made with the kind of extravagance Stevens was accustomed to.—DeWITT BODEEN

Stiller, Mauritz

Nationality *Swedish/Russian (became citizen of Sweden, 1921).* **Born** *Mosche Stiller in Helsinki, Finland, 17 July 1883.* **Career** *Actor in Finland, from 1899; moved to Sweden to avoid Russian military draft, worked as actor in Sweden, from 1904; manager of avant-garde theatre Lilla Teatern, Stockholm, 1911; hired as film director (also writer and actor) for newly-formed Svenska Biograf film studio, Stockholm, 1912; began collaboration with Greta Gustafsson (Greta Garbo), 1923; moved to Hollywood under contract to MGM, 1925; fired by MGM before completing a film, hired by Erich Pommer at Paramount to direct* Hotel Imperial, *then returned to Sweden, 1927.* **Died** *8 November 1928.*

Films as Director: **1912:** *Mor och dotter* (*Mother and Daughter*) (+sc, role as Count Raoul de Saligny); *När svärmor regerar* (*When the Mother-in-Law Reigns*) (+sc, role as the pastor); *Vampyren* (*Vampire*) (+sc); *Barnet* (*The Child*); *De svarta maskerna* (*The Black Masks*) (+co-sc); *Den tyranniske fästmannen* (*The Tyrannical Fiancée*) (+sc, role as Elias Petterson). **1913:** *När kärleken dödar* (*When Love Kills*) (+co-sc); *När larmklockan ljuder* (*When the Alarm Bell Rings*); *Den okända* (*The Unknown Woman*) (+sc); *Bröderna* (*Brothers*) (+co-sc); *Den moderna suffragetten* (*The Suffragette*) (+sc); *Pålivets ödesväger* (*The Smugglers*); *Mannekägen* (*The Model*) (+sc); *För sin kärleks skull* (*The Stockbroker*) (+sc); *Gränsfolken* (*The Border Feud*); *Livets konflikter* (*Conflicts of Life*) (+sc); *Kammarjunkaren* (*Gentleman of the Room*) (+sc). **1914:** *Lekkamraterna* (*The Playmates*) (+sc); *Stormfågeln* (*The Stormy Petrel*); *Det röda tornet* (*The Master*) (+co-sc); *Skottet* (*The Shot*); *När konstnärer älska* (*When Artists Love*). **1915:** *Hans hustrus förflutna* (*His Wife's Past*); *Hämnaren* (*The Avenger*); *Madame de Thèbes* (*The Son of Destiny*); *Mästertjuven* (*The Son of Fate*); *Hans bröllopsnatt* (*His Wedding Night*); *Minlotsen* (*The Mine Pilot*); *Dolken* (*The Dagger*) (+co-sc); *Lyckonälen* (*The Motorcar Apaches*) (+co-sc). **1916:** *Balettprimadonnan* (*Anjuta, the Dancer*); *Kärlek och journalistik* (*Love and Journalism*); *Kampen om hans hjärta* (*The Struggle for His Heart*); *Vingarne* (*The Wings*) (+co-sc). **1917:** *Thomas Graals bästa film* (*Thomas Graal's Best Picture*); *Alexander den Store* (*Alexander the Great*) (+sc). **1918:** *Thomas Graals bästa barn* (*Thomas Graal's First Child*) (+co-sc); *Sången om den eldröda blomman* (*Song of the Scarlet Flower, The Flame of Life*). **1919:** *Fiskebyn* (*The Fishing Village*); *Herr Arnes Pengar* (*Sir Arne's Treasure*) (+co-sc). **1920:** *Erotikon* (*Bonds That Chafe*) (+co-sc); *Johan* (+sc). **1921:** *De Landsflyktige* (*The Exiles*) (+co-sc). **1922:** *Gunnar Hedes saga* (*Gunnar Hede's Saga, The Old Mansion*) (+sc). **1923:** *Gösta Berlings saga* (*The Story of Gösta Berling, The Atonement of Gösta Berling*) (+co-sc). **1926:** *The Temptress* (finished by Fred Niblo) (+sc). **1927:** *Hotel Imperial* (+co-sc); *The Woman on Trial; Barbed Wire* (finished by Rowland Lee) (+sc). **1928:** *The Street of Sin* (finished by Ludvig Berger) (+sc).

Like the other two distinguished pioneers of the early Swedish cinema, Sjöström and Sjöberg, Mauritz Stiller had an essentially theatrical background. But it must be remembered that he was reared in Finland of Russian-Jewish stock, did not emigrate to Sweden until he was 27, and remained there only 15 years before going to Hollywood. He responded relatively late to the

Mauritz Stiller

Swedish cultural tradition, so heavily influenced by the country's extreme northern climate and landscape, and by the fatalistic, puritanical literary and dramatic aura exerted most notably by the Swedish dramatist Strindberg and the Nobel prize-winning novelist Selma Lagerlöf. The latter's works—*Herr Arne's Treasure, Gunnar Hede's Saga,* and *Gösta Berlings Saga*—were inspired by tradition and legend, and were all to be adapted by Stiller for the silent screen.

After establishing himself as a talented stage actor, Stiller's work on film began in 1912. He immediately proved to be a meticulous craftsman, with a strong visual instinct and a polished sense of timing and rhythm. His early work showed how much he had learned technically from the considerable number of D.W. Griffith's short narrative films shown in Sweden. For example, *The Black Masks,* made in 1912, is noted by Forsyth Hardy as having, "over a hundred scenes, a constantly changing combination of interiors and exteriors, close-ups and panoramic shots." In 1913 Stiller even made a film based on the activities of Mrs. Pankhurst called *Den moderna suffragetten,* reflecting his reputation in the theater for avant-garde subjects.

Stiller also proved adept at comedy, as his films *Love and Journalism, Thomas Graal's Best Film*—one of the earliest films about filmmaking—and *Thomas Graal's First Child* reveal, with their skirmishing and coquetry that characterize the relationship of the sexes. Stiller insisted, however, on restraint in acting style; he was an autocratic perfectionist, and Emil Jannings, Germany's leading actor, termed him "the Stanislavski of the cinema." The second of these films had a complex structure, full of flashbacks and daydreams; the director Victor Sjöström starred in all three, as well as in other of Stiller's films. In some of his earliest efforts, Stiller made appearances himself.

The climax to Stiller's career in the production of elegant and graceful comedies of sex manners was *Erotikon;* though better known, because of its alluring title, than its predecessors, it is somewhat less accomplished. Elaborately staged and full of sexual by-play—the wife of a preoccupied professor has two lovers in hot pursuit, a young sculptor and an elderly baron—it includes a specially commissioned ballet performed by the opera in Stockholm. These sophisticated silent films rank alongside the early comedies of Lubitsch, whose work in this genre in Germany in fact succeeded them. Lubitsch readily acknowledged his debt to Stiller.

Again like Lubitsch (with whose career Stiller's can best be compared at this stage), Stiller also worked on epic-style, historical subjects. He took over the adaptation of Selma Lagerlöf's novel *Sir Arne's Treasure* from Sjöström, its original director. This was essentially an eighteenth-century story of escape and pursuit—three Scottish mercenaries in the service of King John III are imprisoned for conspiracy. They abscond in the depths of winter, undertaking a desperate journey overland to flee the country. In the process they become increasingly violent and menacing until they come upon Arne's mansion. They steal his treasure, burn his house, and slaughter its inhabitants except for an orphan girl. The orphan Elsalill, who survives the massacre, is a haunted figure half-attracted to the leader of the Scottish renegades. But she eventually betrays him and dies in the final confrontation in which the Scots are recaptured. The long, snake-like column of black-robed women moving over the icy waste in the girl's funeral procession is Stiller's concluding panoramic scene; one of the best-known spectacular shots in early cinema, it still appears in most history books. The film illustrates grandly the response of the early Swedish filmmakers to the menacing magnificence of the northern winter landscape.

After completing *Erotikon* Stiller moved on to *Johan,* a dark and satiric study of the triangular relationship of husband, wife, and the visitant, stranger-lover. Set in the desolate expanse of the countryside, the film includes a climax worthy of Griffith as the guilty couple, chased by the husband, ride the rapids in a small boat. Stiller then crowned his career in Sweden with two further adaptations of Lagerlöf's work: *Gunnar Hedes Saga* and *Gösta Berlings Saga.* In the former—in every way an outstanding film of its period in its immixture of dream and actuality—the hero, the violinist Nils (Einar Hansson), is inspired to emulate his father, who made a fortune by driving a vast herd of reindeer south from the Arctic circle. Nils's adventure in realizing this dream only leads to severe injury resulting in amnesia; back home in the forests of the south he experiences hallucinations from which the girl who loves him finally liberates him. The film's duality is striking: the realism of the trek with the reindeer, which involved panoramic shots of the great herds and brilliant tracking shots of the catastrophic stampede which leads to Nils's accident, is in marked contrast to the twilit world of his hallucinations.

Gösta Berling's Saga, on the other hand, though famous for its revelation of the star quality of the young drama student, Greta Garbo, and its melodramatic story of the defrocked priest (Lars Hanson) fatally in love with Garbo's Italian girl, is clumsy in structure compared with *Gunnar Hede's Saga,* and was later destructively cut for export to half its original length of four hours.

Stiller travelled in 1925 to America at the invitation of Louis B. Mayer of MGM on the strength of his reputation as a sophisticated European director, but mostly (it would seem) because he was Garbo's Svengali-like and obsessive mentor. He very soon fell out with Mayer, who endured him because he wanted Garbo as a contract player. All but mesmerized by Stiller, Garbo insisted that he direct her in *The Temptress;* the inevitable difficulties arose and he was withdrawn from the film.

Stiller's best film in America was made at Paramount. *Hotel Imperial,* which starred Pola Negri, concerned a wartime love affair between a hotel servant and an Austrian officer and was notable for its spectacular, composite hotel set over which the camera hung suspended from an overhead rail. After finishing a second film with Negri, *The Woman on Trial,* Stiller never managed to complete another film; the respiratory illness that was undermining his health forced him to part from Garbo and return to Sweden, where he died in 1928 at the age of 45.

—ROGER MANVELL

Stone, Oliver

Nationality American. *Born* New York City, 1946. *Education* Studied at Yale University, dropped out, 1965; studied filmmaking under Martin Scorsese, New York University, B.F.A., 1971. *Military Service* Volunteered for 25th Infantry Division, U.S. Army, 1967, awarded Bronze Star for Valor, and the Purple Heart with Oak Leaf Cluster. *Family* Married 1) Majwa Sarkis, 1971 (divorced 1977); 2) Elizabeth Burkit Cox, 1981 (divorced). *Career* Teacher at Free Pacific Institute, Cholon, Vietnam, 1965; joined U.S. Merchant Marine, 1966; taxi driver in New York City, 1971; directed first film, Seizure, 1974. *Awards* Oscar for Best Screenplay Adaptation, and Writers Guild Award, for Midnight Express, 1979; Directors Guild of America Award, Oscar for Best Director, and Golden Globe Award for Best Director, for Platoon, 1987, and for Born on the Fourth of July, 1989.

Films as Director and Scriptwriter: 1974: *Seizure.* **1981:** *The Hand.* **1986:** *Salvador* (+pr, co-sc); *Platoon.* **1987:** *Wall Street* (co-sc). **1988:** *Talk Radio* (co-sc). **1989:** *Born on the Fourth of July* (co-sc). **1991:** *The Doors* (co-sc, +uncredited role as film professor); *JFK* (+pr). **1993:** *Heaven and Earth* (+pr). **1994:** *Natural Born Killers.* **1995:** *Nixon* (+pr). **1997:** *U-Turn.*

Other Films: 1978: *Midnight Express* (Parker) (sc). **1982:** *Conan the Barbarian* (Milius) (co-sc). **1983:** *Scarface* (De Palma) (sc). **1985:** *Year of the Dragon* (Cimino) (sc). **1986:** *8 Million Ways to Die* (Ashby) (co-sc). **1991:** *The Iron Maze* (Yoshida) (exec pr). **1992:** *South Central* (Anderson) (exec pr); *Zebrahead* (Drazan) (exec pr). **1993:** *Dave* (Reitman) (role as himself); *The Last Party* (Benjamin and Levin) (role as himself); *The Joy Luck Club* (Wang) (exec pr); *Wild Palms* (for TV) (exec pr). **1994:** *The New Age* (exec pr). **1995:** *Indictment: The McMartin Trial* (for TV) (Jackson) (exec pr); *Killer: A Journal of Murder* (Metcalfe) (exec pr). **1996:** *The People vs. Larry Flynt* (Forman) (co-pr); *Freeway* (Bright) (exec pr). **1997:** *Savior* (Antonijevic) (co-pr).

Anyone attempting with any degree of success, both artistic and commercial, to make overtly political movies that sustain a left-wing position within the Hollywood cinema of the 1980s and 1990s deserves at least our respectful attention. In fact, Oliver Stone's work dramatizes, in a particularly extreme and urgent form, the quandary of the American left-wing intellectual.

Platoon and *Wall Street* provide a useful starting point, as they share the same basic structure. A young man (Charlie Sheen, in both films) has to choose in terms of values between the Good Father (Willem Dafoe, Martin Sheen) and the Bad Father (Tom Berenger, Michael Douglas); he learns to choose the Good Father and destroy the Bad. The opposition is very similar in both cases: the Good Father is a liberal with a conscience, aware of the impossibility of changing or radically affecting the general situation but committed to the preservation of his personal integrity; the Bad Father has no conscience and no integrity to preserve, and this, combined with a total ruthlessness, is what equips him to survive (until the dénouement) and makes him an insidiously seductive figure. The Bad Father is completely adapted to a system that the Good Father can protest against but do nothing to change. The young man can exact a kind of individual justice by destroying the Bad Father, but the system remains intact.

Platoon and *Wall Street* do not represent Stone's work at its best: their targets are a bit too obvious, the characteristic rage comes too easily, tinged with self-righteousness, so that the alienating aspects of his manner—the heavy stylistic rhetoric, the emotional bludgeoning—are felt at their most obtrusive. But the two films encapsulate the quandary—one might say the *blockage*—that is treated more complexly elsewhere: what does one fight for within a system one perceives as totally corrupt but in which the only alternative to capitulation is impotence?

The fashionable buzz-phrase "structuring absence" becomes resonant when applied to Stone's films: in the most literal sense, his work so far is structured precisely on the absence of an available political alternative, which could only be a commitment to what is most deeply and hysterically taboo in American culture, a form of Marxist socialism. There is a curious paradox here which Americans seem reluctant to notice: Lincoln's famous formula, supposedly one of the foundations of American political ideology, "Government of the people, by the people and for the people," could only be realized in a system dubbed, above all else, "un-American" (American capitalism, as Stone sees very clearly, is government *by* the rich and

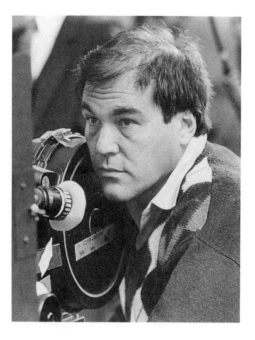

Oliver Stone directing *Wall Street*.
Photograph by Andy Schwartz.

powerful *for* the rich and powerful). In both *Salvador* and *Born on the Fourth of July* the protagonist declares, at a key point in the development, "I am an American, I love America," and we must assume he is speaking for Stone. But we must ask, *which* America does he love, since the American actuality is presented in both films as unambiguously and uniformly hateful? What is being appealed to here is clearly a *myth* of America, but the films seem, implicitly and with profound unease, to recognize that the myth cannot possibly be realized, that capitalism *must* take the forms it has historically taken. Hence the sense one takes from the films of a just but impotent rage: without the availability of the alternative there is no way out.

This is nowhere clearer than in *Salvador,* one of Stone's strongest, least flawed works and a gesture of great courage within its social-political context. While in American capitalist democracy it is still possible to make a film like *Salvador* (the equivalent in Stalinist Russia would have been unthinkable), it is not possible for the film to go further than it does, to take the necessary, logical step. Impotent rage is permissible, the promotion of a constructive alternative is not. Stone's films can be acceptable, even popular, even canonized by Academy Awards precisely because their ultimate effect, beyond the rage, is to suggest that things *cannot* be changed (as indeed they cannot, while one remains within the system). *Salvador* offers a lucid and cogent analysis of the political situation, a vivid dramatization of historical events (the death of Romero, the rape and murder of the visiting Nicaraguan nuns), and an outspoken denunciation of American intervention. Neither does it chicken out at the end: the final scene, where the protagonist at last gets his lover and her two children over the border into the "land of the free," to have them abruptly and brutally sent back by American security officers, is as chilling as anything that modern Hollywood cinema has to offer. But the film's attitude to the concept of a specifically *socialist* revolution (as opposed to a vague notion of people "fighting for their freedom") is thoroughly cagy and equivocal. Nothing is done to demystify the habitual American conflation of socialism and Marxism with Stalinism.

All the film can say is that the threat of a general "Communist" takeover is either imaginary or grossly exaggerated (if it were not, presumably the horrors we are shown would all be justified or at least pardonable), that the Salvadoreans, like good Americans, just want their liberty, and that America, in its own interests, has betrayed its founding principles by intervening on the wrong side.

Born on the Fourth of July recapitulates the earlier film's force, rage, and outspokenness, and also its impasse. It seems to be weakened, however, by its final construction of its protagonist as a redeemer-hero. Ron Kovic, by the end of the film, in realizing (with whatever irony) his mother's dream that he would one day speak before thousands of people saying wonderful things, at once regains his full personal integrity and sense of self-worth and offers an apparent political escape by revealing the "truth." But recent history has shown many times that the revelation of truth can be very readily mythified and absorbed into the system (the Oscar awards and nominations for Stone's movies represent an exact equivalent).

Talk Radio received no such accolades and seems generally regarded as a minor, marginal work. On the contrary, it is arguably Stone's most completely successful film to date and absolutely central to his work, to the point of being confessional. It has been taken as more an Eric Bogosian movie than a Stone movie. We can credit Stone with firmer personal integrity and higher ambitions than are evidenced by Barry Champlain (Bogosian's character), but, that allowance made, Stone has found here the perfect "objective correlative" for his own position, his own quandary. Champlain's rage, toppling over into hysteria, parallels the tone of much of Stone's work and identifies one of its sources, the frustration of grasping that no one really listens, no one understands, no one *wants* to understand; the sense of addressing a people kept in a state of mystification so complete, by a system so powerful and pervasive, that no formal brainwashing could improve on it (this "reading" of the American public is resumed in *Born on the Fourth of July*). The film is indeed revelatory, and very impressive in its honesty and nakedness.

In the 1990s, Stone's career entered a new phase as the director became even more commercially successful while raising the ante of political controversy. His earlier films, especially *Platoon,* had successfully exploited classic realist techniques—especially the device of a likeable main character—to arouse audience sympathy for a radical point of view: that the system deals in death, not life, and counts as enemies all who oppose it, including "good" Americans. Classic realism, however, leads the spectator toward emotional catharses that blunt the point of such political perceptions; furthermore, the narrative closure required in such texts suggests a victory for the protagonists of good will even as the political problems so tellingly enunciated are transcended. Of Stone's recent films, only *Heaven and Earth,* which completes his Vietnam trilogy, remains more or less within the regime of classic realism. Based on the autobiographical novels of Le Ly Hayslip, *Heaven and Earth* also offers a main character—a young Vietnamese woman—who is both sympathetic and socially typical, who offers, in short, an ideal emotional and narrative vantage point for the representation—poignant if not objective or detailed—of Vietnamese history since 1953. Le Ly is abused and manipulated by the successive regimes in her village—French, South Vietnamese, Viet Cong—only to be "rescued" by a burned-out GI who takes her to an America concerned only with materialism and its own comfort. This ambitious film never individualizes, hardly humanizes its main character (who heroically resists Americanization by an entrepreneurship that allows her to live alone and return to Vietnam). With its startling visual stylization, artful use of disorienting editing, and expressionistic mise-en-scène, *Heaven and Earth* treats its subject with an operatic grandeur. The abandonment of realism (with its carefully restrained stylization) for expressionism is also evident in *The Doors,* which takes as its subject yet another—for Stone—heroic rebel of the 1960s, musician/poet Jim Morrison. Here visual and aural stylizations are motivated by Stone's desire to pay homage to the psychodelism of the period, even as they "express" the artistic rebellion of Morrison's music. As in *Heaven and Earth,* the film is less about a character than a *zeitgeist,* but many reviewers and spectators were disappointed by Stone's lack of emphasis on narrative and complex character.

A further, though never complete rejection of realism is to be found in the three Stone films that have found the most commercial success, even as they have aroused the greatest political controversy (making Stone a frequent guest on TV talk shows to defend his latest work and simultaneously plug it). *Natural Born Killers,* though ostensibly set in the 1990s, actually constructs its own, nightmarish version of American reality. Following Brecht, Stone here revives an American myth—the outlaw couple a la Bonnie and Clyde—but empties the outrageously violent attack on family and society perpetrated by Mickey and Mallory of all emotional content through two defamiliarizing techniques: a fragmentary, Eisensteinian montage that prevents any scene from achieving a reality effect; and acting that avoids naturalism at all costs. If *Platoon* uses the violence of war for melodramatic effect, *Natural Born Killers* eschews emotion of any kind to make a political point: the murderous connection between the deep-seated pathology of American family life and the reprehensible tendency for the media to exploit the desire of the abused and battered to find some kind of identity and self-worth. The result is the most intellectually profound and cerebral contemplation of violence in American life since Peckinpah's *The Wild Bunch.*

Stone, however, has not been satisfied to transcend the historical through mythopoeia and stylistic virtuosity (in the manner of, say, Jim Morrison). His conception of the film director's social role is the most enlarged since the time of D. W. Griffith, whose career his own has in part mirrored. What the Civil War was for Griffith's generation, the Kennedy assassination has been for Stone's: a defining historical event, seen rightly or wrongly as the source of subsequent developments. *JFK* is Stone's attempt to argue that case: not simply to advance yet another conspiracy theory, but to identify the death of Kennedy as the beginning of a deterioration in American life that has not yet come to an end. Like Griffith, Stone attempted a paradoxical recreation of history: a film that, he argues, is "true" to the facts and yet, making use of dramatic license, creates its own facts as an interpretation, a possible version of history. Like Griffith, Stone has been much attacked for so doing, even as his film has reopened interest in an event and its aftermath for a new generation. *JFK* uneasily joins two stylistic regimes: a classic realist narrative (the pursuit of the truth by a sympathetically presented main character, district attorney Jim Garrison) and a highly rhetorical, expressionistic recreation of the events under investigation. Of course, Garrison, like Stone's other heroes, fails to do more than the right thing: the vaguely evoked fascistic cabal of southern businessmen and loose cannon Cubans emerges unscathed after pinning the rap on hapless Lee Harvey Oswald. Like *Heaven and Earth, JFK* ultimately turns nostalgically toward a past as yet unspoiled by the fall into political violence. *Nixon,* in contrast, is less oriented toward an event and an era than toward political biography. In the extensively annotated published screenplay, Stone answers his expected critics by pointing to the historical record as a source for the film's material. In that book, Stone insists that his story of Nixon is a classically tragic tale of the essentially good man who overreaches and thereby dooms himself to disgrace. The resulting film, however, is disappointingly simplistic. Nixon becomes a bumbling, foul-mouthed fool whose physical and political gaffes define his relations with others (their constant disapproval is evoked by numerous reaction shots). This interpretation is very much at odds with the substance of the political record and does nothing to explain the shifting tides of popular sentiment that swept Nixon into office and returned him for a second term. Choosing a subject for which he could feel little sympathy, Stone reveals in *Nixon* the limits of his political vision, which, like Griffith's, depends too much on the melodramatic opposition of heroes to villains.—ROBIN WOOD and R. BARTON PALMER

Sturges, Preston

Nationality American. *Born* Edmund P. Biden in Chicago, 29 August 1898; adopted by mother's second husband, Solomon Sturges. *Education* Educated in Chicago (Coulter School); Lycée Janson, Paris; Ecole des Roches, France; Villa Lausanne, Switzerland; and in Berlin and Dresden. *Family* Married 1) Estelle Mudge (divorced 1928); 2) Eleanor Post Hutton, 1932 (annulled 1932); 3) Louise Sergeant Tervis (divorced); 4) actress Anna Nagle (known professionally as Sandy Mellen), three sons. *Career* Managed mother's cosmetic shop in Deauville, then New York, early 1910s; runner for Wall Street brokerage firm, 1914; enlisted in Air Corps, attended School of Military Aeronautics, Austin, Texas, 1917; returned to cosmetic business in New York, invented kissproof lipstick, 1919; turned business over to mother, worked in various jobs and as inventor; playwright, from 1927; The Guinea Pig ran 16 weeks on Broadway, 1929; scriptwriter from 1930, moved to Hollywood, 1932; directed own screenplays, from 1940; also manager of Sturges Engineering Company, producing diesel engines; began association with Howard Hughes, 1944; moved to Paris, 1949. *Awards* Oscar for Best Original Screenplay, for The Great McGinty, 1940; Laurel Award for Achievement (posthumously), Writers Guild of America, 1974. *Died* At the Algonquin Hotel, New York, 6 August 1959.

Films as Director and Scriptwriter: 1940: *The Great McGinty; Christmas in July.* **1941:** *The Lady Eve; Sullivan's Travels.* **1942:** *The Palm Beach Story.* **1944:** *Hail the Conquering Hero; The Miracle of Morgan's Creek; The Great Moment.* **1947:** *Mad Wednesday* (+pr). **1948:** *Unfaithfully Yours* (+pr). **1949:** *The Beautiful Blonde from Bashful Bend* (+pr). **1951:** *Vendetta* (co-d with Ferrer, uncredited). **1957:** *Les Carnets du Major Thompson* (*The French, They Are a Funny Race*).

Other Films: 1930: *The Big Pond* (Henley) (co-sc, co-dialogue); *Fast and Loose* (Newmeyer) (sc, dialogue). **1931:** *Strictly Dishonorable* (Stahl) (sc, play basis). **1933:** *The Power and the Glory* (Howard) (sc); *Child of Manhattan* (Buzzell) (sc, play basis). **1934:** *Thirty Day Princess* (Gering) (co-sc); *We Live Again* (Mamoulian) (co-sc); *Imitation of Life* (Stahl) (co-sc, uncredited). **1935:** *The Good Fairy* (Wyler) (sc); *Diamond Jim* (Sutherland) (co-sc). **1936:** *Next Time We Love* (Edward Griffith) (co-sc, uncredited); *One Rainy Afternoon* (Lee) (lyrics for "Secret Rendezvous"). **1937:** *Hotel Haywire* (Archainbaud) (sc); *Easy Living* (Leisen) (sc). **1938:** *Port of Seven Seas* (Whale) (sc); *If I Were King* (Lloyd) (sc). **1940:** *Remember the Night* (Leisen) (sc). **1947:** *I'll Be Yours* (Seiter) (screenplay basis). **1951:** *Strictly Dishonorable* (Frank and Panama) (play basis). **1956:** *The Birds and the Bees* (Taurog) (screenplay basis). **1958:** *Rock-a-bye Baby* (Tashlin) (screenplay basis); *Paris Holiday* (Oswald) (role as Serge Vitry).

As a screenwriter, Preston Sturges stands out for his narrative inventiveness. All of the amazing coincidences and obvious repetitions in such comedies as *Easy Living* and *The Good*

Fairy show Sturges's mastery of the standard narrative form, as well as his ability to exaggerate it and shape it to his own needs. Moreover, in *The Power and the Glory* (an early model for *Citizen Kane*), Sturges pioneered the use of voice-over narration to advance a story.

Along with John Huston, Sturges was one of the first of the sound-era screenwriters to become a director, and those films that he made from his own screenplays take even further the narrative experiments he began as a writer in the 1930s. He continued making comedies, but often he combined them with elements that more properly belonged to social dramas in the Warner Brothers tradition, even though Sturges himself worked primarily for Paramount. *The Great McGinty,* for instance, deals with big-city political corruption. *Christmas in July,* despite its happy end, analyzes an American dream perverted by dishonesty and commercial hype.

Preston Sturges

And *Sullivan's Travels,* even as it mixes aspects of *It Happened One Night* and *I Am a Fugitive From a Chain Gang,* examines the uses of comedy in a society burdened by poverty and social injustice.

With *The Palm Beach Story* and *The Lady Eve,* Sturges goes from combining genres to parodying the standard narrative form. Traditionally, in the classical narrative, elements repeat from scene to scene, but with slight differences each time. The story, then, becomes a series of episodes that are similar, but not obviously so. *The Palm Beach Story,* however (although we cannot be sure of this until the end), deals with two sets of twins, one pair male and the other female, and Sturges takes full advantage of a practically infinite number of possibilities for doubling and repetition.

In *The Lady Eve,* there are no twins to call our attention to how Sturges exaggerates the typical narrative. But the central female character, Jean, changes her identity and becomes Eve Harrington, an English aristocrat, so she can double-cross the man who jilted her when he found out she made her living as a con artist. So in this film, too, Sturges provides us with some obvious doubling. In fact, *The Lady Eve* divides neatly into two very similar parts: the shipboard romance of Charles and Jean, and then the romance, on land, of Charles and Jean-as-Eve. In this second half, the film virtually turns into a screwball comedy version of *Vertigo.* Charles falls in love with a woman who looks exactly like another woman he had loved and lost, and who, indeed, really is that woman.

The Lady Eve is most interesting in the way that it stands narrative convention on its head. Charles Pike, a wealthy ale heir, looks for snakes on the Amazon, but as soon as he leaves the jungle and heads back to civilization, the hunter becomes the hunted. This inversion itself is hardly remarkable, either in literature or the cinema. What does stand out as unusual is that the predators are all women. Pike boards a luxury liner steaming back to the United States, and every unmarried woman on board decides to end the voyage engaged to him, to "catch" him just as Charles had been trying to capture reptiles. Few films from this period feature such active, aggressive female characters.

Sturges works out the notion of feminine entrapment not only in his script but also through his visual style. On board, Jean plots to get Charles, and Sturges shows us her predatory skill by letting her capture Pike's image. In the dining room, Jean watches as various women attempt to attract Pike's attention. She does not want him to see her staring, so she turns away from Pike's table and holds a mirror to her face, as if she were giving a quick re-arrangement to her makeup. But instead she uses the mirror to watch Charles. Sturges cuts to a close-up of the mirror, and so we share Jean's point of view. As spectators, we are used to an appreciative male gaze, and are accustomed to a woman as the subject of that gaze. But here, once again, Sturges reverses our expectations. In his tale it is the woman who plays the voyeur. As an added show of her strength, it is Jean who apparently controls the images through her possession of the mirror. She thus captures an unknowing Charles within the frame of a looking-glass.

Sturges's most interesting achievement may be his 1948 film, *Unfaithfully Yours*. Here, he shows the same event three times. While fairly common in literature, this sort of narrative construction is extremely rare in the cinema. But even in literature, the repeated event almost always comes to us from the points of view of different characters. In Sturges's films, we see the event the first and second time through the eyes of the same man: an orchestra conductor plots revenge on his wife, whom he suspects of infidelity, and he imagines two different ways of accomplishing his goal. Then, the next repetition, rather than being imaginary, actually depicts the conductor's attempts to murder his wife. So, since the conductor acts once again as the main character, even this last repetition comes to us from his point of view. The film stands out, then, as a remarkable case study of the thoughts and actions of a single character, and as one more of Sturges's experiments in narrative repetition.

During the early and mid-1940s, critics hailed Sturges as a comic genius. But after *Unfaithfully Yours,* over the last eleven years of his life, Sturges made only two more films. Upon leaving Paramount, he set out to make films for Howard Hughes, but the attempt was an ill-fated one, and Sturges's standing in the critical community declined rapidly. For several years, though, a reevaluation has been underway. Sturges's sophisticated handling of sexual relations (which the heiress in *The Palm Beach Story* refers to as "Topic A") make his films seem remarkably contemporary. And there can be no doubting Sturges's screenwriting abilities. But only recently have critics come to appreciate Sturges's consummate skills as a filmmaker.—ERIC SMOODIN

Tanner, Alain

Nationality *Swiss.* **Born** *Geneva, 6 December 1929.* **Education** *Educated in economic sciences, Calvin College, Geneva.* **Career** *Shipping clerk, early 1950s; moved to London, worked at British Film Institute, 1955; assistant producer for the BBC, 1958; returned to Switzerland, 1960; co-founder, Association Suisse des Réalisateurs, early 1960s; director for Swiss French TV, 1964-69; began collaboration with writer John Berger on* Une Ville à Chandigarh, *1966; co-founder, Groupe 5, 1968.* **Awards** *Experimental Film Prize, Venice Festival, for* Nice Time, *1957; Best Screenplay (with Berger), National Society of Film Critics, for* Jonah Who Will Be 25 in the Year 2000, *1976; Special Jury Prize, Cannes Festival, for* Les Années lumière, *1981.*

Films as Director: 1957: *Nice Time* (short) (co-d). **1959:** *Ramuz, passage d'un poète* (short). **1962:** *L'Ecole* (sponsored film). **1964:** *Les Apprentis* (doc feature). **1966:** *Une Ville à Chandigarh.* **1969:** *Charles, mort ou vif* (*Charles, Dead or Alive*) (+sc). **1971:** *Le Salamandre* (*The Salamander*) (+co-sc). **1973:** *Le Retour d'Afrique.* **1974:** *Le Milieu du monde* (*The Middle of the World*) (+co-sc). **1976:** *Jonah qui aura 25 ans en l'année 2000* (*Jonah Who Will Be 25 in the Year 2000*) (+co-sc). **1978:** *Messidor* (+sc). **1981:** *Les Années lumière* (*Light Years Away*) (+co-sc). **1983:** *Dans la ville blanche* (*In the White City*) (+pr, sc). **1985:** *No Man's Land* (+sc). **1986:** *François Simon—La présence.* **1987:** *Une Flamme dans mon coeur* (*A Flame in My Heart*) (+co-sc); *La Vallée Fantôme* (+sc, pr). **1989:** *La Femme de Rose Hill* (*The Woman of Rose Hill*) (+sc, pr). **1992:** *L'Homme que a perdu son ombre* (*The Man Who Lost His Shadow*) (+pr, sc). **1993:** *Le Journal de Lady M* (*The Diary of Lady M*) (+pr). **1995:** *Les Hommes du port* (+sc). **1996:** *Fourbi* (+co-sc, pr).

Alain Tanner's involvement with film began during his college years. While attending Geneva's Calvin College, he and Claude Goretta formed Geneva's first film society. It was during this time that Tanner developed an admiration for the ethnographic documentaries of Jean Rouch and fellow Swiss Henry Brandt, an influence that continued throughout his career. After a brief stint with the Swiss merchant marine, Tanner spent a year in London as an apprentice at the BFI, where, with Goretta, he completed an experimental documentary, *Nice Time,* which chronicled the night life of Piccadilly Circus. While in London he participated in the Free Cinema Movement, along with Karel Reisz, Tony Richardson, and Lindsay Anderson. Through Anderson, Tanner made the acquaintance of novelist and art critic John Berger, who would later write the scenarios for *Le Salamandre, Middle of the World, Jonah Who Will Be 25 in the Year 2000,* and *Le Retour d'Afrique.*

Upon returning to Switzerland in 1960, Tanner completed some forty documentaries for television. Among these were: *Les Apprentis,* which concerned the lives of teenagers (and created using the methods of Rouch's direct cinema); *Une Ville à Chandigarh,* on the architecture designed by Le Corbusier for the Punjab capital (the narration for this film was assembled by John Berger); and newsreel coverage of the events of May 1968 in Paris. This last project provided the ammunition for Tanner (once again with Goretta) to form Groupe 5, a collective of Swiss filmmakers. They proposed an idea to Swiss TV for the funding of full-length narrative features to be shot in 16-millimeter and then blown-up to 35-millimeter for release. The plan enabled Tanner to make his first feature, *Charles, Dead or Alive,* which won first prize at Locarno in 1969.

The film tells of a middle-aged industrialist who, on the eve of receiving an award as the foremost business personality of the year, discovers his disaffection for the institution-laden society in which he finds himself. Following an innate sense of anarchism that Tanner posits as universal, he attempts to reject this lifestyle. His retreat into madness is blocked by his family and friends, who compel him, by appealing to his sense of duty, to resume his responsibilities.

All Tanner's films follow a similar scenario: individuals or a group become alienated from society; rejecting it, they try to forge a new society answerable to themselves alone, only to be defeated by the relentless pressures of traditional society's institutions, whose commerce they never cease to require. This theme receives its fullest and most moving expression in *Jonah Who Will Be 25 in the Year 2000.* Here the failure of the collective and the survivors of 1968, who

Alain Tanner (left) on the set of *Messidor*.

come together at Marguerite's farm outside Geneva, is not viewed as a defeat so much as one generation's attempt to keep the hope of radical social change alive by passing on the fruits of its mistakes, that is, its education or its lore, to the succeeding generation.

Tanner's style is a blend of documentary and fable. He uses techniques such as one scene/one shot, a staple of cinéma-vérité documentary, to portray a fable or folk-story. This tension between fact and fiction, documentary and fable, receives its most exacting treatment in *Le Salamandre*. Rosemonde's indomitable, rebellious vitality repeatedly defeats the efforts of the two journalists to harness it in a pliable narrative form. After *Jonah,* Tanner introduces a darker vision in *Messidor, Light Years Away,* and *Dans la ville blanche.* The possibility of escaping society by returning to nature is explored and shown to be equally provisional. The tyranny of physical need is portrayed as being just as oppressive and compromising as that of the social world.—DENNIS NASTAV

Tarantino, Quentin

Nationality *American.* **Born** *Quentin Jerome Tarantino in Knoxville, Tennessee, 27 March 1963; grew up in Los Angeles.* **Education** *Studied acting.* **Career** *Worked at Video Archives with Roger Avary; did telephone sales for Imperial Entertainment; began writing scripts for Cinetel; formed production company, A Band Apart, with Lawrence Bender.* **Awards** *Palme d'Or, Cannes Film Festival, and Academy Award, Best Original Screenplay, for* Pulp Fiction, *1994.* **Address** *A Band Apart Productions, 6525 Sunset Blvd. #G-12, Los Angeles, California 90028, U.S.A.*

Quentin Tarantino (left) on the set of *Reservoir Dogs.*

Films as Director, Screenwriter, and Actor: 1992: *Reservoir Dogs.* **1994:** *Pulp Fiction.* **1995:** "Man from Hollywood" episode of *Four Rooms* (+ex pr); "Motherhood" episode of *ER* (for TV) (d only). **1997:** *Jackie Brown* (+pr).

Other Films: 1992: *Past Midnight* (Eliasberg) (assoc pr, sc). **1993:** *Natural Born Killers* (Stone) (sc); *True Romance* (Tony Scott) (sc); *Eddie Presley* (role as hospital orderly). **1994:** *Killing Zoe* (Avary) (sc, exec pr); *Sleep with Me* (role as Sid); *The Coriolis Effect* (short) (role as radio disc jockey); *Somebody to Love* (role as bartender); *Destiny Turns on the Radio* (role as Johnny Destiny); *It's Pat* (Bernstein) (co-sc, uncredited). **1995:** *Desperado* (Rodriguez) (role as pick-up guy); *Crimson Tide* (Scott) (co-sc, uncredited). **1996:** *From Dusk till Dawn* (Rodriguez) (sc, co-exec pr, role as Richard Gecko); *Girl 6* (Lee) (role); *Red Rain* (Hijningen) (pr); *Curdled* (Braddock) (ex pr); *The Rock* (Bay) (co-sc, uncredited); *The Typewriter, the Rifle and the Movie Camera* (Simon) (appearance). **1997:** *Full Tilt Boogie* (Kelly) (appearance).

Quentin Tarantino's meteoric rise to fame with the phenomenal critical and popular success of *Pulp Fiction,* his second feature, is not only the result of his considerable talent but of two forces operating within contemporary Hollywood: first, an economic mini-crisis brought on by the box-office and critical failures of many recent high-budget blockbuster productions (*Waterworld* is perhaps the most remarkable example) that has opened the door, as in the past, for young directors who are able to make successful films on small budgets (made for $8 million, *Pulp Fiction* earned almost $64 million at the box office, not counting video sales and rentals); second, the continuing popularity of neo-noir films, a popularity not limited to its most thriving sub-genre, the erotic thriller. If Hollywood's economic hard times have given Tarantino (and others) a chance, it is the director's personal obsessions, so much in tune with what contemporary audiences want to see, that have made him popular.

The widely read and very cineliterate Tarantino has an obvious liking for classic hardboiled pulp fiction (evidently Jim Thompson and W. R. Burnett in particular) and classic film noir (Huston's *Asphalt Jungle* probably served as a model for *Reservoir Dogs*). But like several of the prominent directors of the Hollywood Renaissance in the middle 1970s (especially Martin Scorsese and Paul Schrader), Tarantino also owes a substantial debt to French film noir, especially the work of Jean Pierre Melville and Jean Luc Godard. Godard's modernist refiguration of noir themes and conventions (*Alphaville* is the classic example), however, would hardly please the mass audience Tarantino has in mind. The most substantial contribution of nouvelle vague anti-realism in Tarantino's films can be seen in their creative use of achronicities, disorderings in the storytelling process that make the narratives intriguing puzzles even as they uncover interesting ironies for the spectator, who must take an active role in the deciphering of the plot. The anti-Aristotelianism of this procedure, its disruption of emotional identification with the characters' plight, allows Tarantino to concentrate on thematic elements, especially the role violence plays in American culture.

Like the gang in *Asphalt Jungle,* the crooks in *Reservoir Dogs* assembled to pull a heist (itself never represented) are shown participating in what is simply a "left-handed form of endeavor." If Huston endeavors to demonstrate that criminals too have an ordinary life (households to run, relationships to pursue, bills to pay), Tarantino, in contrast, is more interested in moral dilemmas and conflict, especially as these are brought to life by situations of extraordinary danger and threat. In fact, the central conflicts of *Reservoir Dogs* carry a substantial moral charge and significance, even if, in the end, as the all-knowing spectator alone recognizes, the characters are destroyed no matter if they are sociopaths with a yen for torture or men of good will who stand by their friends even at the cost of their own lives. And yet Tarantino obviously sympathizes with those who despise *mauvaise foi* and make the difficult choices that confront them. A Sartrean and Camusian moralism pervades this film.

Much the same can be said of the similar characters in *Pulp Fiction,* whose existential plights and difficult choices are here examined from a serio-comic perspective. A torpedo working for a drug dealer is given the assignment of looking after the boss's flirtatious wife. He tries to resist her various come-ons, only to be faced with a sudden, more demanding test: she overdoses on heroin, goes into a near-fatal coma from which he can arouse her only by jabbing a harpoon-sized needle into her heart. Amazingly, she recovers, and Tarantino finishes this sequence with a comic leave-taking scene that ends their "date." Once again, in *Pulp Fiction* difficult moral questions are raised. A boxer in the same drug dealer's pay refuses out of personal integrity to throw a fight as ordered. Fleeing town, he meets his boss by accident on a city street. Their confrontation, however, opens unexpectedly onto another moral plane. Both men wind up the prisoners of local sadists, who plan to sodomize, torture, and kill them. The boxer escapes, and, feeling the pang of conscience, goes back to free his erstwhile boss, who forgives the man's earlier betrayal before exacting a terrible vengeance on his torturers, one of whom is a policeman.

With their philosophical dimensions, unremitting representations of venality and depravity among the criminal under and over class, art cinema narrational complexities, and black humor, Tarantino's first two films are strikingly original contributions to an American cinema struggling to rebound from the artistic doldrums of the 1980s. As a screenwriter, he has been no less successful. Written for former video shop co-worker Roger Avary, *Killing Zoe* offers a romantic twist on the themes examined in Tarantino's own directorial efforts. In this case, a somewhat naive and easily swayed young criminal must make a moral stand against his lifelong friend to save the life of a prostitute he has come to care for; the gesture is reciprocated, and the two rescue themselves from a nightmarish world of self-destructive violence and addiction. Similarly, *True Romance* and *Natural Born Killers* offer outlaw couples on the run whose loyalty to each other is rewarded in the end by their escape from a corrupt and disfiguring America that attempts to destroy them.—R. BARTON PALMER

Tarkovsky, Andrei

Nationality *Soviet Russian.* **Born** *Moscow, 4 April 1932.* **Education** *Institute of Oriental Languages, graduated 1954; All-Union State Cinematography Institute (VGIK), graduated 1960.* **Family** *Married twice (two children by first marriage, one son by second marriage).* **Career** *Geological prospector in Siberia, 1954-56; on diploma work* The Steamroller and the Violin, *began collaboration with cameraman Yadim Yusov and Vyacheslav Ovchinnikov, 1960; directed opera* Boris Godunov *at Covent Garden, 1983; made last film,* The Sacrifice, *in Sweden, 1986.* **Awards** *Lion of St. Mark for Best Film, Venice Festival, for* Ivan's Childhood, *1962; International Critics Award, Cannes Festival, for* Andrei Rublev, *1969; Special Jury Prize, Cannes Festival, for* Solaris, *1972; Merited Artistic Worker of the RSFSR, 1974; Grand Prix, Cannes Festival, for* The Sacrifice, *1986.* **Died** *Of cancer, in Paris, 29 December 1986.*

Films as Director: 1959: *There Will Be No Leave Today* (short). **1960:** *Katok i skripka* (*The Steamroller and the Violin*) (+co-sc). **1962:** *Ivanovo detstvo* (*Ivan's Childhood*). **1969:** *Andrei Rublev* (+co-sc).

1971: *Solyaris* (*Solaris*) (+co-sc). **1975:** *Zerkalo* (*The Mirror*) (+co-sc). **1979:** *Stalker*. **1983:** *Nostalghia* (*Nostalgia*). **1986:** *Offret* (*The Sacrifice*).

"Tarkovsky is the greatest of them all. He moves with such naturalness in the room of dreams. He doesn't explain. What should he explain anyhow?" Thus Ingmar Bergman, in his autobiography *The Magic Lantern,* bows down before the Russian director while also hinting at what makes Tarkovsky's work so awkward to critics: it can verge on the inscrutable. Too opaque to yield concrete meaning, it offers itself as sacral art, demanding a rapt, and even religious, response from its audiences. His 1979 film *Stalker,* for instance, features a place called the Zone where all "desires come true." Rather like the land of Oz, this mysterious outland promises to reveal the secret of things to any intrepid travellers who prospect it to its core. But there are no cowardly lions or tin men to ease the journey, no yellow brick road to follow. The Zone is an austere realm—typical Tarkovsky territory—of bleak landscapes populated by characters laden with a peculiarly Russian gloom.

Watching Tarkovsky's films, his "sculptures in time," spectators can find themselves on a journey every bit as arduous as that undertaken by the pilgrims who headed toward the Zone. The son of a poet, the director treated film as a medium in which he could express himself in the first person. His six years at the Moscow State Film School, during which he received a thorough grounding in film technique from such Soviet luminaries as Mikhail Romm, did nothing to disabuse him of the notion that cinema was a "high art." He felt he could tap the same vein of poetic intimacy that his father sought in lyric verse. The necessary intrusion of camera crews and actors, and the logistical problems of exhibition and distribution, worried him not a jot. Although all his films are self-reflexive, he does not draw attention to the camera for radical Brechtian reasons. He is not trying to subvert bourgeois narrative codes. He is not even assaulting the tenets of Socialist Realism, a doctrine he found every bit as unappealing as Western mass culture aimed at the consumer (although his ex-partner, Konchalovsky, ended up in Hollywood directing Sylvester Stallone vehicles). What his constant use of tracking shots, slow motion, and never-ending pans—indeed his entire visual rhetoric—seems to emphasize is that he is moulding the images. He is a virtuoso, and he wants us to be aware of the fact.

Tarkovsky's first two feature length projects, *Ivan's Childhood* and *Andrei Rublev,* mark a curious collision between the personal and the political. On one level, the former is a propaganda piece, telling yet again the great Soviet story of the defeat of the Nazi scourge during World War II. But Tarkovsky destabilizes the film with dream sequences. The "big questions" that are ostensibly being addressed turn out to be peripheral: the director is more concerned with the poetic rekindling of childhood than with a triumphal narrative of Russian resilience. Similarly, *Rublev,* an epic three-hour biography of a medieval icon painter, is, in spite of the specificity and grandeur of its locations, a rigorous account of the role of the artist in society, as applicable to the 1960s as to the 1300s.

As if to display his versatility, Tarkovsky skipped genres, moving from the distant past to the distant future for his third feature, *Solaris,* a rather ponderous sci-fi movie taken from a novel by the Polish writer Stanislaw Lem. The harsh, Kubrick-like spaceship interiors suit the director far less than his customary wet and muddy landscapes. The musings on love and immortality engaged in by the cosmonauts as they hover above a sea of liquid gas—for a filmmaker with such a flair for images, Tarkovsky resorts to portentous dialogue with surprising frequency—weigh the story down. Still, *Solaris* works on a more intimate level when it explores a man's attempts to come to terms with the death of his wife.

Mirror is quintessential Tarkovsky; ravishing to look at, full of classical music, and so narratively dense as to be almost unfathomable on a first viewing. There are only 200 or so shots in it, and it is a film that fell into shape, almost by accident, late in the editing stage, but it is Tarkovsky's richest and most resonant work. The narrative flits between the present and the past, between the "adult" mentality of the narrator and the memory of his childhood. Moreover, the wide open spaces of the countryside where Tarkovsky spent his earliest years are contrasted with the constricting rooms of city apartments. Poems by the director's father, Arseny, appear on the soundtrack. Complementing these, Tarkovsky is at his most elemental in this film: the wind rustling the trees, fire, and water are constant motifs.

Andrei Tarkovsky

Tarkovsky went to enormous lengths to recreate the landscape of his infancy, planting buckwheat a year before shooting started, and constructing, from memory and old photographs, the bungalow where he had lived. There is a humour and warmth in *Mirror* sometimes absent in his work as a whole. (This may have something to do with the fact that it is his only film to have a woman protagonist. Margarita Terekova, who ranks with Anatoli Solonitzine as Tarkovsky's favourite actor, plays both the narrator's wife and his mother.) Generally, Tarkovsky terrain is desolate, ravaged by war, or threatened with catastrophe, as in *The Sacrifice*. In *Mirror,* however, the forests and rivers and fields are nurturing and colourful. Accused by the authorities of being narratively obscure, Tarkovsky testified that he received many letters from viewers who had seen their own childhoods miraculously crystallize as they watched the film.

Nostalgia was his first film in exile after his defection to the West. Shot in Italy, it showed the Russian pining for his homeland. He wouldn't live to see it again.

The Sacrifice is a typically saturnine final testament from a filmmaker overly aware of his own reputation. Tarkovsky believed that "modern mass culture, aimed at the consumer . . . is crippling people's souls." A self-conscious exercise in spiritual plumbing, his last work before his premature death from cancer in 1987 is weighed down by its own gravitas. Shot by Sven Nykvist, who used natural light for the interior scenes, and full of intricate pans, the film has the formal beauty that one has come to associate with the director. But its endless and wordy metaphysical surmising stops it from tugging at memory and emotion in the way of the best of his work, most notably *Mirror*.—G.C. MACNAB

Tashlin, Frank

Nationality American. *Born* Weehawken, New Jersey, 19 February 1913. *Education* Educated in public school, Astoria, Long Island. *Family* Married Mary Costa. *Career* Errand boy for Max Fleischer, 1928; worked on Aesop's Fables *cartoons at RKO, from 1930, became animator; sold cartoons to magazines under pseudonym "Tish-Tash," until 1936; moved to Hollywood, worked at Vitaphone Corp. on* Merrie Melodies *and* Looney Tunes, *1933; comic strip* Van Boring *syndicated, 1934-36; gagman at Hal Roach Studios, 1935, then director and scriptwriter for* Looney Tunes; *story director at Disney studios for* Mickey Mouse *and* Donald Duck *series, 1939-40; executive producer, Columbia's Screen Gems Cartoon Studios, 1941; returned to* Merrie Melodies *and* Looney Tunes, *1942, also directed first* Private Snafu *cartoon for Frank Capra's Army Signal Corps Unit; first non-animated film credit as co-scriptwriter for* Delightfully Dangerous, *1944; gag writer at Paramount, 1945; writer for Eddie Bracken's CBS radio shows, 1946; took over direction of* The Lemon Drop Kid *at request of Bob Hope, 1950; writer, producer and director for television, from 1952.* *Died* In Hollywood, 5 May 1972.

Films as Director: 1950: *The Lemon Drop Kid* (co-d, uncredited, +co-sc). **1951:** *The First Time* (+co-sc); *Son of Paleface* (+co-sc). **1953:** *Marry Me Again* (+sc); *Susan Slept Here* (+co-sc uncredited). **1955:** *Artists and Models* (+co-sc); *The Lieutenant Wore Skirts* (+co-sc). **1956:** *Hollywood or Bust* (+co-sc uncredited); *The Girl Can't Help It* (+pr, co-sc). **1957:** *Will Success Spoil Rock Hunter?* (+sc, pr). **1958:** *Rock-a-Bye Baby* (+sc); *The Geisha Boy* (+sc). **1959:** *Say One for Me* (+co-sc uncredited, pr). **1960:** *Cinderfella* (+sc). **1962:** *Bachelor Flat* (+co-sc). **1963:** *It's Only Money* (+co-sc); *The Man from The Diner's Club*; *Who's Minding the Store?* (+co-sc). **1964:** *The Disorderly Orderly* (+sc). **1965:** *The*

Frank Tashlin: *The Girl Can't Help It*

Alphabet Murders. **1966:** *The Glass Bottom Boat; Caprice* (+co-sc). **1968:** *The Private Navy of Sergeant O'Farrell* (+sc).

Other Films: 1944: *Delightfully Dangerous* (Lubin) (sc). **1947:** *Variety Girl* (Marshall) (co-sc); *The Paleface* (McLeod) (co-sc); *The Fuller Brush Man* (*That Mad Mr Jones*) (Simon) (co-sc). **1948:** *One Touch of Venus* (Seiter) (co-sc); *Love Happy* (Miller) (co-sc). **1949:** *Miss Grant Takes Richmond* (*Innocence Is Bliss*) (Bacon) (co-sc); *Kill the Umpire* (Bacon) (sc); *The Good Humor Man* (Bacon) (sc). **1950:** *The Fuller Brush Girl* (*The Affairs of Sally*) (Bacon) (sc). **1956:** *The Scarlet Hour* (Curtiz) (co-sc).

Frank Tashlin had achieved recognition as a children's writer when he entered the film industry to work in the animation units at Disney and Warner Bros. Both of these early careers would have decisive import for the major films that Tashlin would direct in the 1950s. This early experience allowed Tashlin to see everyday life as a visually surreal experience, as a kind of cartoon itself, and gave him a faith in the potential for natural experience to resist the increased mechanization of everyday life. Tashlin's films of the 1950s are great displays of cinematic technique, particularly as it developed in a TV-fearing Hollywood. They featured a wide-screen sensibility, radiant color, frenetic editing, and a deliberate recognition of film as film. Tashlin's films often resemble live versions of the Warners cartoons. Jerry Lewis, who acted in many of Tashlin's films, seemed perfect for such a visual universe with his reversions to a primal animality, his deformations of physicality, and his sheer irrationality.

Tashlin's films are also concerned with the ways the modern world is becoming more and more artificial; the films are often filled with icons of the new mass culture (rock and roll, comic books, television, muscle men, Jayne Mansfield, Hollywood) and are quite explicit about the ways such icons are mechanically produced within a consumer society. For example, in *Will Success Spoil Rock Hunter?,* the successful romance of Rita Marlow (Jayne Mansfield) causes other women to engage in dangerous bust-expanding exercises to the point of nervous exhaustion. Yet the very critique of mass culture by an artist working in a commercial industry creates the central contradiction of Tashlin's cinema: if the danger of modern life is its increasing threat of mechanization, then what is the critical potential of an art based on mechanization? Significantly, Tashlin's films can be viewed as a critique of the ostentatious vulgarity of the new plastic age while they simultaneously seem to revel in creating ever better and more spectacular displays of sheer technique to call attention to that age. *The Girl Can't Help It,* for instance, chronicles the making of a non-talent (Jayne Mansfield) into a star, viewing the process with a certain cynicism but at the same time participating in that process. These films are vehicles for Mansfield as Mansfield, and are thus somewhat biographical.

As with Jerry Lewis, serious treatment of Tashlin began in France, especially in the pages of *Positif,* which has always had an attraction to the comic film as an investigator of the Absurd. Anglo-American criticism tended to dismiss Tashlin; for example, Andrew Sarris in *American Cinema* called him "vulgar". In such a context, Claire Johnston and Paul Willemen's *Frank Tashlin* had the force of a breakthrough, providing translations from French journals and analyses of the cinematic and ideological implications of Tashlin's work.—DANA B. POLAN

Tati, Jacques

Nationality *French.* **Born** *Jacques Tatischeff in Le Pecq, France, 9 October 1908.* **Education** *Attended Lycée de St.-Germain-en-Laye; also attended a college of arts and engineering, 1924.* **Family** *Married Micheline Winter, 1944; children: Sophie and Pierre.*

Career *Rugby player with Racing Club de Paris, 1925-30; worked as pantomimist/ impressionist, from 1930; recorded one of his stage routines, "Oscar, champion de tennis," on film, 1932; toured European music halls and circuses, from 1935; served in French Army, 1939-45; directed himself in short film,* L'Ecole des facteurs, *1946; directed and starred in first feature,* Jour de fête, *1949; offered American television series of 15-minute programs, refused, 1950s; made* Parade *for Swedish television, 1973.* ***Awards*** *Best Scenario, Venice Festival, for* Jour de fête, *1949; Max Linder Prize (France) for* L'Ecole des facteurs, *1949; Prix Louis Delluc, for* Les Vacances de M. Hulot, *1953; Special Prize, Cannes Festival, for* Mon Oncle, *1958; Grand Prix National des Arts et des Lettres, 1979; Commandeur des Arts et des Lettres.* ***Died*** *5 November 1982.*

Films as Director: 1947: *L'Ecole des facteurs* (+sc, role). **1949:** *Jour de fête* (+co-sc, role as François the postman). **1953:** *Les Vacances de Monsieur Hulot* (*Mr. Hulot's Holiday*) (+co-sc, role as M. Hulot). **1958:** *Mon Oncle* (+co-sc, role as M. Hulot). **1967:** *Playtime* (+sc, role as M. Hulot). **1971:** *Trafic* (*Traffic*) (+co-sc, role as M. Hulot). **1973:** *Parade* (+sc, role as M. Loyal).

Other Films: 1932: *Oscar, champion de tennis* (sc, role). **1934:** *On demande une brute* (Barrois) (co-sc, role). **1935:** *Gai Dimanche* (Berry) (co-sc, role). **1936:** *Soigne ton gauche* (Clément) (role). **1938:** *Retour à la terre* (pr, sc, role). **1945:** *Sylvie et le fantôme* (Autant-Lara) (role as ghost). **1946:** *Le Diable au corps* (Autant-Lara) (role as soldier).

Jacques Tati's father was disappointed that his son didn't enter the family business, the restoration and framing of old paintings. In Jacques Tati's films, however, the art of framing—of selecting borders and playing on the limits of the image—achieved new expressive heights. Instead of restoring old paintings, Tati restored the art of visual comedy, bringing out a new density and brilliance of detail, a new clarity of composition. He is one of the handful of film

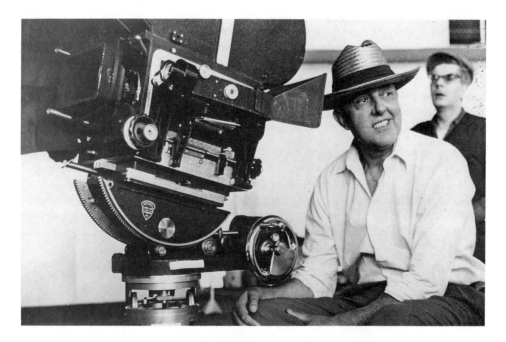

artists—the others would include Griffith, Eisenstein, Murnau, Bresson—who can be said to have transformed the medium at its most basic level, to have found a new way of seeing.

After a short career as a rugby player, Tati entered the French music hall circuit of the early 1930s; his act consisted of pantomime parodies of the sports stars of the era. Several of his routines were filmed as shorts in the 1930s (and he appeared as a supporting actor in two films by Claude Autant-Lara), but he did not return to direction until after the war, with the 1947 short *L'Ecole des facteurs*. Two years later, the short was expanded into a feature, *Jour de fête*. Here Tati plays a village postman who, struck by the "modern, efficient" methods he sees in a short film on the American postal system, decides to streamline his own operations. The satiric theme that runs through all of Tati's work—the coldness of modern technology—is already well developed, but more importantly, so is his visual style. Many of the gags in *Jour de fête* depend on the use of framelines and foreground objects to obscure the comic event—not to punch home the gag, but to hide it and purify it, to force the spectator to intuit, and sometimes invent, the joke for himself.

Tati took four years to make his next film, *Les Vacances de Monsieur Hulot (Mr. Hulot's Holiday)*, which introduced the character he was to play for the rest of his career—a gently eccentric Frenchman whose tall, reedy figure was perpetually bent forward as if by the weight of the pipe he always kept clamped in his mouth. The warmth of the characterization, plus the radiant inventiveness of the sight gags, made *Mr. Hulot* an international success, yet the film already suggests Tati's dissatisfaction with the traditional idea of the comic star. Hulot is not a comedian, in the sense of being the source and focus of the humor; he is, rather, an attitude, a signpost, a perspective that reveals the humor in the world around him.

Mon Oncle is a transitional film: though Hulot had abdicated his star status, he is still singled out among the characters—prominent, but strangely marginal. With *Playtime,* released after nine years of expensive, painstaking production, Tati's intentions become clear. Hulot was now merely one figure among many, weaving in and out of the action much like the Mackintosh Man in Joyce's *Ulysses*. And just as Tati the actor refuses to use his character to guide the audience through the film, so does Tati the director refuse to use close-ups, emphatic camera angles, or montage to guide the audience to the humor in the images. *Playtime* is composed almost entirely of long-shot tableaux that leave the viewer free to wander through the frame, picking up the gags that may be occurring in the foreground, the background, or off to one side. The film returns an innocence of vision to the spectator; no value judgements or hierarchies of interest have been made for us. We are given a clear field, left to respond freely to an environment that has not been polluted with prejudices.

Audiences used to being told what to see, however, found the freedom of *Playtime* oppressive. The film (released in several versions, from a 70mm stereo cut that ran over three hours to an absurdly truncated American version of 93 minutes) was a commercial failure. It plunged Tati deep into personal debt.

Tati's last theatrical film, the 1971 *Traffic,* would have seemed a masterpiece from anyone else, but for Tati it was clearly a protective return to a more traditional style. Tati's final project, a 60-minute television film titled *Parade,* has never been shown in America. Five films in 25 years is not an impressive record in a medium where stature is often measured by prolificacy, but *Playtime* alone is a lifetime's achievement—a film that liberates and revitalizes the act of looking at the world.—DAVE KEHR

Tavernier, Bertrand

Nationality French. *Born* Lyons, 25 April 1941. *Education* Studied law for one year. *Family* Married writer Colo O'Hagan (separated); two children. *Career* Film critic for Positif *and* Cahiers du Cinema, *Paris, early 1960s; press agent for producer Georges de Beauregard, 1962; freelance press agent, associated with Pierre Rissient, 1965; directed first film,* L'Horloger de St. Paul, *1974.* *Awards* Prix Louis Delluc, for L'Horloger de St. Paul, *1974; Cesar Awards for Best Director and Best Original Screenplay (with Jean Aurenche), for* Que la fête commence, *1975; European Film Festival Special Prize, for* La Vie et rien d'autre, *1989.*

Films as Director and Co-Scriptwriter: 1964: "Une Chance explosive" episode of *La Chance et l'amour.* **1965:** "Le Baiser de Judas" episode of *Les Baisers.* **1974:** *L'Horloger de Saint-Paul (The Clockmaker of St. Paul).* **1975:** *Que la fête commence (Let Joy Reign Supreme).* **1976:** *Le Juge et l'assassin (The Judge and the Assassin).* **1977:** *Des enfants gâtés (Spoiled Children).* **1979:** *Femmes Fatales.* **1980:** *La Mort en direct (Deathwatch)* (+co-pr). **1981:** *Une Semaine de vacances (A Week's Vacation).* **1982:** *Coup de torchon (Clean Slate); Philippe Soupault et le surréalisme* (doc). **1983:** *Mississippi Blues (Pays d'Octobre)* (co-d, +pr). **1984:** *Un Dimanche à la campagne (A Sunday in the Country)* (+pr). **1986:** *Round Midnight (Autour de minuit).* **1987:** *Le Passion Béatrice (The Passion of Beatrice).* **1988:** *Lyon, le regard intérieur* (doc for TV). **1989:** *La Vie et rien d'autre (Life and Nothing But).* **1990:** *Daddy Nostalgie (These Foolish Things).* **1991:** *La guerre sans non (The Undeclared War); Contre l'oubli (Against Oblivion).* **1992:** *L.627.* **1994:** *Le fille de D'Artagnan (The Daughter of D'Artagnan); Anywhere But Here.* **1995:** *L'appat (Fresh Bait).* **1996:** *Capitaine Conan (Captain Conan).*

Other Films: 1963: *La Boulangère de Monceau (The Baker of Monceau)* (Rohmer) (role, uncredited). **1967:** *Coplan ouverte le feu à Mexico* (Freda) (sc). **1968:** *Capitaine Singrid* (Leduc) (sc). **1977:** *Le Question* (Heynemann) (pr). **1978:** *Cosi come sei (Stay As You Are)* (Lattuada) (pr). **1979:** *Rue du pied de Grue* (Grandjouan) (pr); *Le Mors aux dents* (Heynemann) (pr). **1983:** *La Trace* (Faure) (assoc pr, co-sc). **1986:** *Les Mois d'avril sont meurtriers* (Heynemann) (co-sc). **1993:** *Des demoiselles ont en 25 ans (The Young Girls Turn 25)* (Varda) (appearance); *Francois Truffaut: portraits voles (Francois Truffaut: Stolen Portraits)* (Toubiana, Pascal) (appearance); *Jean Renoir* (Thompson) (appearance). **1994:** *Troubles We've Seen: A History of Journalism in Wartime* (pr). **1995:** *The World of Jacques Demy* (Varda) (appearance); *American Cinema* (role). **1997:** *Cannes. . .les 400 coups* (Nadeau) (for TV) (appearance); *Fred* (Jolivet) (ex pr).

It is significant that Bertrand Tavernier's films have been paid little attention by the more important contemporary film critics/theorists: his work is resolutely "realist," and realism is under attack in critical quarters. Realism has frequently been a cover for the reproduction and reinforcement of dominant ideological assumptions, and to this extent that attack is salutary. Yet Tavernier's cinema demonstrates effectively that the blanket rejection of realism rests on very unstable foundations. Realism has been seen as the bourgeoisie's way of talking to itself. It does not necessarily follow that its only motive for talking to itself is the desire for reassurance; nor need we assume that the only position realist fiction constructs for the reader/viewer is one of helpless passivity (Tavernier's films clearly postulate an alert audience ready to reflect and analyze critically).

Three of Tavernier's films, *Death Watch, Coup de torchon,* and *A Week's Vacation,* while they may not unambiguously answer the attacks on realism, strongly attest to the inadequacy of their formulation. For a start, the films' range of form, tone, and address provides a useful reminder of the potential for variety that the term "classical realist text" tends to obliterate. To place beside the strictly realist *A Week's Vacation* the futurist fantasy of *Death Watch* on the one hand and the scathing, all-encompassing caricatural satire and irony of *Coup de torchon* on the other is to illustrate not merely a range of subject-matter but a range of strategy. Each film constructs for the viewer a quite distinct relationship to the action and to the protagonist, analyzable in terms of varying degrees of identification and detachment which may also shift *within* each film. Nor should the description of *A Week's Vacation* as "strictly realist" be taken to suggest some kind of simulated cinéma-vérité: the film's stylistic poise and lucid articulation, its continual play between looking *with* the protagonist and looking *at* her, consistently encourage an analytical distance.

Bertrand Tavernier

Through all his films, certainly, the bourgeoisie "talks to itself," but the voice that articulates is never reassuring, and bourgeois institutions and assumptions are everywhere rendered visible and opened to question. Revolutionary positions are allowed a voice and are listened to respectfully. This was clear from Tavernier's first film, *The Clockmaker,* among the screen's most intelligent uses of Simenon. Under Tavernier, the original project is effectively transformed by introducing the political issues that Simenon totally represses, and by changing the crime from a meaningless, quasi-existentialist *acte gratuit* to a gesture of radical protest. But Tavernier's protagonists are always bourgeois: troubled, questioning, caught up in social institutions but not necessarily rendered impotent by them, capable of growth and awareness. The films, while basically committed to a well-left-of-center liberalism, are sufficiently open, intelligent, and disturbed to be readily accessible to more radical positions than they are actually willing to adopt.

Despite the difference in mode of address, the three films share common thematic concerns (most obviously, the fear of conformism and dehumanization, the impulse towards protest and revolt, the difficulties of effectively realizing such a protest in action). They also have in common a desire to engage, more or less explicitly, with interrelated social, political, and aesthetic issues. The caustic analysis of the imperialist mentality and the kind of personal rebellion it provokes (itself corrupt, brutalized, and ultimately futile) in *Coup de torchon* is the most obvious instance of direct political engagement. *Death Watch,* within its science fiction format, is fascinatingly involved with contemporary inquiries into the construction of narrative and the objectification of women. Its protagonist (Harvey Keitel) attempts to create a narrative around an unsuspecting woman (Romy Schneider) by means of the miniature television camera surgically implanted behind his eyes. The implicit feminist concern here becomes the structuring principle of *A Week's Vacation.* Without explicitly raising feminist issues, the film's theme is the focusing of a contemporary bourgeois female consciousness, the consciousness of an intelligent and sensitive woman whose identity is not defined by her relationship with men, who is actively engaged with social problems (she is a schoolteacher), and whose fears (of loneliness, old age, death) are consistently presented in relation to contemporary social realities rather than simplistically defined in terms of "the human condition."

In Tavernier's films through the early 1990s, he has covered a wide variety of moods, styles and settings, with the most representative of these works linked by a common contemplative quality. His concerns are the passage of time and its effect on human relationships and the individual soul. In particular, he is interested in characters who are aged and ill, or have seen too much of the seamier aspects of human behavior. These latter works investigate how they come to terms with loved ones—especially their children.

A Sunday in the Country, set at the turn of the twentieth century, is the story of an elderly painter who resides in the country and is visited one Sunday by his reserved son and daughter-in-law, their three children, and his free-spirited daughter. The film is a pensive, poignant tale of old age and the choices people make in their lives. There is much drama and emotion in *Life and Nothing But,* a thoughtful war film which in fact takes place at a time when there is no fighting and bloodshed. Set after the conclusion of a war, the film concerns a soldier (Tavernier regular Philippe Noiret) who is assigned to chronicle his country's war casualties. Meanwhile, a couple of women have set out in search of their lovers, who are missing in action.

In *Round Midnight,* Tavernier caringly recreates the community of black jazz artists in exile in France. The film is a character study of an aged, alcoholic tenor sax legend, a composite of Bud Powell and Lester Young (and played by Dexter Gordon, himself a jazz great). He settles in Paris in 1959 and plays nightly at a famed jazz club; at the core of the story is his friendship with a young, adoring Frenchman, a dedicated jazz fan. Finally, in *Daddy Nostalgia,* the filmmaker examines the complex alliance between a father (Dirk Bogarde) and daughter (Jane Birkin). He is seriously ill; she visits him for an extended stay and attempts to understand their relationship, and his life.

Interestingly, in Tavernier's more recent films he has abandoned weighty themes for entertaining exercises in genre. *The Daughter of D'Artagnan* is a lightly likable comic swash-buckler, while *L.627* is a gritty police thriller.

We should not celebrate the resurgence of "bourgeois realism" in Tavernier's films (and they do not stand alone) without qualification or misgivings. Certainly, one regrets the failure of contemporary cinema to substantially follow up the radical experimentation with narrative that characterized the most interesting European films of the 1960s and 1970s. Nonetheless, Tavernier's work testifies to the continuing vitality and validity of a tradition many theorists have rejected as moribund.—ROBIN WOOD and ROB EDELMAN

Tourneur, Jacques

Nationality American/French. Born Paris, 12 November 1904, son of director Maurice Tourneur; became U.S. citizen, 1919. Education Attended Hollywood High School. Family Married actress Christianne (died). Career Moved to United States with family, 1914; office boy at MGM, 1924, later actor; script clerk for father's last six American films; moved to Paris, edited father's films, 1928; directed first film, in France, 1931; 2nd unit director for MGM, Hollywood, 1935; directed shorts, then B features, from 1939; director for producer Val Lewton at RKO, from 1942; television director, from late 1950s. **Died** *In Bergerac, 19 December 1977.*

Films as Director: 1931: *Un vieux garçon; Tout ça ne vaut pas l'amour.* **1933:** *La Fusée; Toto; Pour être aimée.* **1934:** *Les Filles de la concierge.* **1939:** *They All Came Out; Nick Carter, Master Detective.* **1940:** *Phantom Raiders.* **1941:** *Doctors Don't Tell.* **1942:** *Cat People.* **1943:** *I Walked with a Zombie; The Leopard Man.* **1944:** *Days of Glory; Experiment Perilous.* **1946:** *Canyon Passage.* **1947:** *Out of the Past (Build My Gallows High).* **1948:** *Berlin Express.* **1949:** *Easy Living.* **1950:** *The Flame and the Arrow; Stars in My Crown.* **1951:** *Circle of Danger; Anne of the Indies.* **1952:** *Way of a Gaucho.* **1953:** *Appointment in Honduras.* **1955:** *Stranger on Horseback; Wichita.* **1956:** *Great Day in the Morning.* **1957:** *Nightfall; Night of the Demon (Curse of the Demon).* **1958:** *The Fearmakers.* **1959:** *Timbuktu; La battaglia di Maratona (The Battle of Marathon); Frontier Rangers* (originally for TV). **1963:** *The Comedy of Terrors.* **1965:** *War Gods of the Deep (City Under the Sea).*

Other Films: 1923: *Scaramouche* (Ingram) (role). **1927:** *The Fair Co-ed* (Wood) (role); *Love* (Goulding) (role). **1929:** *The Trail of '98* (Brown) (role).

The first director Val Lewton hired for his RKO unit was Jacques Tourneur, and the first picture made by that unit was *Cat People,* an original screenplay by DeWitt Bodeen.

When Tourneur's father, Maurice, returned to Paris after a number of years in America, Jacques had gone with him, working as assistant director and editor for his father. In 1933, he made a few directorial solos in the French language and then returned to Hollywood, where he became an assistant director at MGM. It was at this time that he first met Val Lewton, and the two young men worked as special unit directors for Jack Conway on *A Tale of Two Cities;* it was Lewton and Tourneur who staged the storming of the Bastille sequence for that film.

Tourneur remained at MGM, directing over 20 short subjects, and Lewton eventually went on to become David O. Selznick's story editor. When Lewton left Selznick to head his own

Jacques Tourneur with Patricia Roc on the set of *Circle of Danger.*

production unit at RKO, he had already made up his mind that Tourneur would direct his first production. Tourneur came to RKO, where he served as director for Lewton's first three films—*Cat People, I Walked With a Zombie,* and *The Leopard Man.* The front office held his work in such esteem that he was given the "A" treatment—solo direction of a high-budget film called *Days of Glory,* which was Gregory Peck's first starring film. It was not held against him that *Days of Glory* bombed. Tourneur immediately turned to another high budget picture at RKO—*Experiment Perilous,* starring Hedy Lamarr with Paul Lukas and George Brent. Under Tourneur's skillful direction, it became a suspenseful mood period film, certainly one of his and Hedy Lamarr's best.

Tourneur stayed on at RKO to direct Robert Mitchum in one of his finest pictures, *Out of the Past* (aka *Build My Gallows High*), as well as an excellent melodrama, *Berlin Express,* starring Merle Oberon and Robert Ryan with Paul Lukas. Filmed partially in Berlin, the work was the first Hollywood picture to be made in Germany since the end of the war.

Tourneur then directed three excellent westerns for his friend Joel McCrea—*Stars in My Crown, Stranger on Horseback,* and *Wichita,* which featured McCrea as Wyatt Earp. He also directed *The Flame and the Arrow,* starring Burt Lancaster, and *Great Day in the Morning,* another RKO western with Robert Stack and Virginia Mayo. He then went back to make another horror picture in England, *Night of the Demon,* with Dana Andrews. This film is rated as highly as those he made for Lewton.

Television direction occupied the greater part of Tourneur's time for the next decade, but he retired in 1966 and returned to his native country, where he died in Bergerac on December 19, 1977. The best pictures which he directed were those of suspense and genuine terror, though he also did well with those that had a great deal of action. He wisely resisted scenes with long patches of dialogue. When confronted with such scenes, he typically frowned and said, "It sounds so corny."—DeWITT BODEEN

Tourneur, Maurice

Nationality French/American. **Born** *Maurice Thomas in Paris, 2 February 1876; became U.S. citizen, 1921.* **Education** *Educated at Lycée Condorcet.* **Military Service** *Military service in artillery, late 1890s.* **Family** *Married Fernande Petit (stage name Van Doren), 1904 (separated 1927), son Jacques Tourneur.* **Career** *Illustrator and graphic and interior designer, from 1894; assistant to Auguste Rodin and Puvis de Chavannes; actor, then stage director, from 1900; actor, then director for Eclair films, from 1912; moved to United States, 1914; production head of Paragon studio, 1915; contracted to Jesse Lasky for three Olga Petrova vehicles, 1917; formed own production company, 1918; moved to California, contracted to Paramount, formed Associated Producers Inc. with Thomas Ince and others 1919, (failed 1921); moved to Universal, 1920; quit direction of* The Mysterious Island, *returned to France, 1926; son Jacques edited films, 1928.* **Died** *1961.*

Films as Director: 1912: *Le Friquet* (+sc); *Jean la poudre* (+sc); *Le Système du Docteur Goudron et du Professeur Plume; Figures de cire.* **1913:** *Le Dernier Pardon* (+sc); *Le Puits mitoyen; Le Camée; Sœurette* (+sc); *Le Corso rouge; Mademoiselle 100 millions; Les Gaîtes de l'escadron* (+sc); *La Dame de*

Montsoreau (+sc). **1914:** *Monsieur Lecocq* (+sc); *Rouletabille I: Le Mystère de la chambre jaune* (+sc); *Rouletabille II: La Dernière Incarnation de Larson* (+sc); *Mother* (+sc); *The Man of the Hour* (+sc); *The Wishing Ring* (+sc); *The Pit.* **1915:** *Alias Jimmy Valentine* (+sc); *The Cub; Trilby* (+sc); *The Ivory Snuff Box* (+sc); *A Butterfly on the Wheel; Human Driftwood.* **1916:** *The Pawn of Fate; The Hand of Peril* (+sc); *The Closed Road* (+sc); *The Rail Rider; The Velvet Paw.* **1917:** *A Girl's Folly; The Whip; The Undying Flame; Exile; The Law of the Land* (+sc); *The Pride of the Clan; The Poor Little Rich Girl; Barbary Sheep; The Rise of Jennie Cushing.* **1918:** *Rose of the World; A Doll's House; The Blue Bird; Prunella; Woman; Sporting Life.* **1919:** *The White Heather; The Life Line; Victory; The Broken Butterfly* (+co-sc). **1920:** *My Lady's Garter; The County Fair; Treasure Island; The White Circle; Deep Waters; The Last of the Mohicans.* **1921:** *The Bait; The Foolish Matrons.* **1922:** *Lorna Doone.* **1923:** *While Paris Sleeps* (made in 1920); *The Christian; The Isle of Lost Ships; The Brass Bottle; Jealous Husbands.* **1924:** *Torment* (+co-sc); *The White Moth.* **1925:** *Never the Twain Shall Meet; Sporting Life* (+sc) (remake); *Clothes Make the Pirate.* **1926:** *Aloma of the South Seas; Old Loves and New; The Mysterious Island* (co-d, sc). **1927:** *L'Equipage* (+co-sc). **1929:** *Das Schiff der verlorene Menschen* (*Le Navire des hommes perdus*). **1930:** *Accusée, levez-vous.* **1931:** *Maison de danses; Partir ... (Partir!).* **1932:** *Au nom de la loi; Les Gaîtes de la escadron* (+co-sc); *L'Idoire* (+co-sc). **1933:** *Les Deux Orphelines* (+co-sc); *L'Homme mysterieux* (*Obsession*). **1934:** *Le Voleur.* **1935:** *Justin de Marseille.* **1936:** *Konigsmark; Samson; Avec le sourire.* **1938:** *Le Patriote; Katia.* **1940:** *Volpone.* **1941:** *Péchés de jeunesse; Mam'zelle Bonaparte.* **1942:** *La Main du diable.* **1943:** *Le Val d'enfer; Cecile est morte.* **1947:** *Après l'amour.* **1948:** *L'Impasse des deux anges.*

Other Films: 1920: *The Great Redeemer* (Brown) (supervisor).

Maurice Tourneur is one of the greatest pictorialists of the cinema, deriving his aesthetic from his early associations with Rodin and Puvis de Chavannes. Having worked for André Antoine as an actor and producer, he joined the Eclair Film Company in 1912 and travelled to their American Studios at Fort Lee, New Jersey, in 1914. There he directed films based on successful stage plays. In *The Wishing Ring* it is possible to see the charm and visual beauty he brought to his work. His team consisted of John van der Broek, the cameraman who later tragically drowned during one of Tourneur's productions; Ben Carré, the art director; and Clarence Brown, his editor, who would later achieve fame as Garbo's favorite director.

Tourneur was most literate in his pronouncements on the cinema, individualistic and iconoclastic at times. He saw the cinema in perspective and would not concede it a status equal to the other arts. He stated: "To speak of the future development of the art of the cinema is futile. It cannot be. It costs a great deal of money to produce a motion picture. The only way the financial backer can get his money back, to say nothing of a profit, is to appeal to the great masses. And the thing that satisfies millions cannot be good. As Ibsen once wrote, it is the minority which is always right." In practice, however, Tourneur's own work belied this statement. To everything he did he brought a sense of beauty and great responsibility to his audiences.

Tourneur directed Clara Kimball Young in *Trilby,* Mary Pickford in *Pride of the Clan* and *Poor Little Rich Girl,* the latter a very successful film. He made three films with Olga Petrova. In 1918 five memorable films came from his hand: Elsie Ferguson appeared in his *The Doll's House;* two other stage plays, *The Bluebird* by Maeterlinck and *Prunella* by Granville Barker, gave Tourneur full scope for his visual style; *Woman* was a series of episodes that dealt with Adam and Eve, Claudius and Messalina, Heloise and Abelard, a Breton fisherman and a mermaid, and a Civil War story; and *Sporting Life* was significant for its absence of stars and its depiction of a fog-ridden London, anticipating Griffith's *Broken Blossoms* of the following year.

In 1919 Tourneur made Joseph Conrad's *Victory* for Paramount. A year later, he unveiled a delightful *Treasure Island* with Shirley Mason (as Jim Hawkins) and Lon Chaney, who also

Maurice Tourneur

starred in *While Paris Sleeps.* For Associated Producers he made *The Last of the Mohicans,* which many consider to be his masterpiece, although Clarence Brown took over direction when Tourneur fell ill during production.

Tourneur's remaining Hollywood films included *Lorna Doone, The Christian, The Isle of Lost Ships, The Brass Bottle, The White Moth, Never the Twain Shall Meet,* and *Aloma of The South Seas.* During the production of *The Mysterious Island* for MGM, however, Tourneur grew resentful of a producer's interference. He walked off the set and returned to France. He continued to work in films in Europe, his first being *L'Equipage.* In 1929 he made *Das Schiff der Verlorene* in Germany with Marlene Dietrich. This was his last silent film, but he accepted the coming of sound and, before his death in 1961, he had made over 20 sound films. The most important of these were *Les Deux Orphelines,* the delightful *Katia* with Danielle Darieux, *Volpone* with Harry Baur and Louis Jouvet, *La Main du diable,* made from a story by Gerard de Nerval and featuring Pierre Fresnay, and his last film, *L'Impasse des deux anges.*

Tourneur was a man who had no illusions about working in films. He realized the limitations of Hollywood and the films he was given to direct. However, he brought his considerable talent as a designer to bear on his work, and did not hesitate to experiment. He stylized his sets and was influenced by new movements in the theater, but he also used the effects of nature to heighten his dramas. His awareness of the potentialities of the camera was profound, giving strength to his images.—LIAM O'LEARY

Truffaut, François

*Nationality French. **Born** Paris, 6 February 1932. **Education** Attended Lycée Rollin, Paris. **Military Service** Enlisted in army, but deserted on eve of departure for Indochina, 1951; later released for "instability of character." **Family** Married Madeleine Morgenstern, 1957 (divorced), two daughters. **Career** Founded own cine-club in Paris, lack of funds caused closing, was jailed for inability to pay debts, released with help of André Bazin, 1947; with Godard, Rivette, and Chabrol, member of Ciné-club du Quartier Latin, 1949; briefly employed by the Service Cinématographique of the Ministry of Agriculture, 1953; writer on film for* Cahiers du cinéma, *then* Arts, *from 1953, including seminal article, "Une Certain Tendance du cinéma français," in 1954; with Rivette and Resnais, made short 16mm film, 1955; assistant to Roberto Rossellini, 1956-58; directed first feature,* Les Quatre Cents Coups, *and wrote script for Godard's* A bout de souffle, *1959; published* Le*

Cinéma selon Hitchcock, *1966; instigated shutting down of 1968 Cannes Festival in wake of May uprisings.* **Awards** *Best Director, Cannes Festival, for* Les Quatres Cents Coup, *1959; Prix Louis Delluc, and Best Director, National Society of Film Critics, for* Stolen Kisses, *1969; Acedemy Award for Best Foreign-Language Film, Best Director, National Society of Film Critics, Best Direction, New York Film Critics, and British Academy Award for Best Direction, for* Day for Night, *1973.* **Died** *Of cancer, in Paris, 21 October 1984.*

Films as Director: 1955: *Une Visite* (+sc, co-ed). **1957:** *Les Mistons* (+co-sc). **1958:** *Une Histoire d'eau.* **1959:** *Les Quatre Cents Coups* (*The Four Hundred Blows*) (+sc). **1960:** *Tirez sur le pianist* (*Shoot the Piano Player*) (+co-sc). **1961:** *Jules et Jim* (*Jules and Jim*) (+co-sc). **1962:** "Antoine et Colette" episode of *L'Amour a vingt ans* (*Love at Twenty*) (+sc, role). **1964:** *La Peau douce* (*The Soft Skin*) (+co-sc). **1966:** *Fahrenheit 451* (+co-sc). **1967:** *La Mariée était en noir* (*The Bride Wore Black*) (+co-sc). **1968:** *Baisers volés* (*Stolen Kisses*) (+co-sc). **1969:** *La Sirène du Mississippi* (*Mississippi Mermaid*) (+sc); *L'Enfant sauvage* (*The Wild Child*) (+co-sc, role as Dr. Jean Itard). **1970:** *Domicile conjugal* (*Bed and Board*) (+co-sc). **1971:** *Les Deux Anglaises et le continent* (*Two English Girls*) (+co-sc). **1972:** *Une Belle Fille comme moi* (*Such a Gorgeous Kid Like Me*) (+co-sc). **1973:** *La Nuit américaine* (*Day for Night*) (+co-sc, role as Ferrand). **1975:** *L'Histoire d'Adèle H.* (*The Story of Adele H.*) (+co-sc). **1976:** *L'Argent de poche* (*Small Change*) (+co-sc). **1977:** *L'Homme qui aimait les femmes* (*The Man Who Loved Women*) (+co-sc). **1978:** *La Chambre verte* (*The Green Room*) (+co-sc, role as Julien Davenne). **1979:** *L'Amour en fuite* (*Love on the Run*) (+co-sc). **1980:** *Le Dernier Metro* (*The Last Metro*) (+sc). **1981:** *La Femme d'à côté* (*The Woman Next Door*). **1984:** *Vivement dimanche!* (*Finally Sunday*).

Other Films: 1977: *Close Encounters of the Third Kind* (Spielberg) (role as French scientist).

François Truffaut was one of five young French film critics, writing for André Bazin's *Cahiers du cinéma* in the early 1950s, who became the leading French filmmakers of their generation. It was Truffaut who first formulated the *politique des auteurs,* a view of film history and film art that defended those directors who were "true men of the cinema"—Renoir, Vigo,

François Truffaut directing *Jules et Jim.*

and Tati in France; Hawks, Ford, and Welles in America—rather than those more literary, script-oriented film directors and writers associated with the French "tradition of quality." Truffaut's original term and distinctions were subsequently borrowed and translated by later generations of Anglo-American film critics, including Andrew Sarris, Robin Wood, V.F. Perkins, and Dave Kehr. When Truffaut made his first feature in 1959, *Les Quatre Cent Coups,* he put his ideas of cinema spontaneity into practice with the study of an adolescent, Antoine Doinel, who breaks free from the constrictions of French society to face an uncertain but open future. Since that debut, Truffaut's career has been dominated by an exploration of the Doinel character's future (five films) and by the actor (Jean-Pierre Léaud) whom Truffaut discovered to play him. In Truffaut's 25 years of making films, the director, the Doinel character, and Léaud all grew up together.

The rebellious teenager of *Les Quatre Cent Coups* becomes a tentative, shy, sexually clumsy suitor in the "Antoine et Colette" episode of *Love at Twenty.* In *Baisers volés,* Antoine is older but not much wiser at either love or money making. In *Domicile conjugal,* Antoine has married but is still on the run toward something else—the exotic lure of other sexual adventures. And in *L'Amour en fuite,* Antoine is still running (running became the essential metaphor for the Doinel character's existence, beginning with the lengthy running sequence that concludes *Les Quatre Cent Coups*). Although Antoine is now divorced, the novel which he has finally completed has made his literary reputation. That novel, it turns out, is his life itself, the entire Doinel saga as filmed by Truffaut, and Truffaut fills his films with film clips that are both visual and mental recollections of the entire Doinel cycle. Truffaut deliberately collapses the distinction between written fiction and filmed fiction, between the real life of humans and the fictional life of characters. The collapse seems warranted by the personal and professional connections between Truffaut the director, Doinel the character, and Léaud the actor.

Many of Truffaut's non-Doinel films are style pieces that similarly explore the boundaries between art and life, film and fiction. The main character of *Tirez sur le pianist* tries to turn himself into a fictional character, as does Catherine in *Jules et Jim.* Both find it difficult to maintain the consistency of fictional characters when faced with the demanding exigencies of real life. *La Mariée etait en noir* was Truffaut's elegy to Hitchcock, a deliberate style piece in the Hitchcock manner, while *Fahrenheit 451,* his adaption of Ray Bradbury's novel, explores the lack of freedom in a society in which books—especially works of fiction—are burned. Adele H in *L'Histoire d'Adele H* attempts to convert her passion into a book (her diary), but life can neither requite nor equal her passion; instead, it drives her to madness and a total withdrawal from life into the fantasy of her romantic fiction. In *L'Homme qui aimait les femmes,* an incurable womanizer translates his desire into a successful novel, but the existence of that work in no way diffuses, alleviates, or sublimates the desire that vivified it. *The Green Room* is Truffaut's homage to fiction and the novelist's craft—a careful, stylish adaption of a Henry James story.

Given his conscious commitment to film and fiction, it is not surprising that Truffaut devoted one of his films to the subject of filmmaking itself. *La Nuit américaine* is one of the most loving and revealing films about the business of making films, an exuberant illustration of the ways in which films use artifice to capture and convey the illusion of life. This film, in which Truffaut himself plays a film director, is a comically energetic defense of the joys and pains of filmmaking, a deliberate response to the more tortured visions of Fellini's *8½* or Bergman's *Persona.*

Those Truffaut films not concerned with the subject of art are frequently about education. *L'Enfant sauvage* explores the beneficial power and effects of civilization on the savage passions of a child who grew up in the forest, apparently raised by beasts. Truffaut again plays a major role in the film (dedicated to Jean-Pierre Léaud), playing a patient scientist who effects the boy's conversion from savagery to humanity. Like the director he played in *La Nuit américaine,* Truffaut is the wise and dedicated patriarch, responsible for the well-being of a much larger enterprise. *L'Argent de poche* examines the child's life at school and the child's relationships with adults and other children. As opposed to the imprisoning restrictions which confined children in the world of *Les Quarte Cent Coups,* the now adult Truffaut realizes that adults—parents and teachers—treat children with far more care, love, and devotion than the children (like the younger, rebellious Truffaut himself) are able to see.

Unlike his friend and contemporary Jean-Luc Godard, Truffaut remained consistently committed to his highly formal themes of art and life, film and fiction, youth and education, and art and education, rather than venturing into radical political critiques of film forms and film imagery. Truffaut seems to state his position in *Le Dernier Métro,* his most political film, which examines a theater troupe in Nazified Paris. The film director seems to confess that, like those actors in that period, he can only continue to make art the way he knows how, that his commitment to formal artistic excellence will eventually serve the political purposes that powerful art always serves, and that for him to betray his own artistic powers for political, programmatic purposes would perhaps lead to his making bad art and bad political statements. In this rededication to artistic form, Truffaut is probably restating his affinity with the Jean Renoir he wrote about for *Cahiers du cinéma.* Renoir, like Truffaut, progressed from making more rebellious black-and-white films in his youth to more accepting color films in his maturity; Renoir, like Truffaut, played major roles in several of his own films; Renoir, like Truffaut, believed that conflicting human choices could not be condemned according to facile moral or political formulae; and Renoir, like Truffaut, saw the creation of art (and film art) as a genuinely humane and meaningful response to the potentially chaotic disorder of formless reality. Renoir, however, lived much longer than Truffaut, who died of cancer in 1984 at the height of his powers.—GERALD MAST

Ulmer, Edgar

Nationality *Austrian.* **Born** *Edgar Georg Ulmer in Vienna, 17 September 1904.* **Education** *Studied architecture at Academy of Arts and Sciences, Vienna; studied stage design at Burgteater, Vienna.* **Family** *Married Shirley Castle, one daughter.* **Career** *Designer for Decla-Bioscope film company, 1918; designer for Max Reinhardt, Vienna, 1919-22; designer for Universal in New York, 1923; returned to Germany as assistant to Murnau, 1924; returned to United States, art director and production assistant at Universal, from 1925; co-directed first film, with Robert Siodmak, 1929; art director at MGM and stage designer for Philadelphia Grand Opera Co., 1930-33; made public health documentaries for minority groups, New York, mid-1930s; director and writer for Producers' Releasing Corporation (PRC), Hollywood, 1942-46; worked in United States, Mexico, Italy, Germany, and Spain, through 1950s.* **Died** *In Woodland Hills, California, 30 September 1972.*

Films as Director: (claimed to have directed 128 films; following titles are reported in current filmographies): 1929: *Menschen am Sonntag (People on Sunday)* (co-d, co-sc). **1933:** *Damaged Lives* (+co-sc); *Mr. Broadway.* **1934:** *The Black Cat* (+co-sc); *Thunder over Texas* (d as "John Warner"). **1937:** *Green Fields* (co-d). **1938:** *Natalka Poltavka* (+sc, assoc pr); *The Singing Blacksmith* (+pr); *Zaporosch Sa Dunayem* (*Cossacks in Exile; The Cossacks Across the Danube*). **1939:** *Die Tlatsche* (*The Light Ahead*) (original title: *Fishe da Krin*) (+pr); *Moon Over Harlem; Americaner Schadchen* (*The Marriage Broker, American Matchmaker*); *Let My People Live.* **1940:** *Cloud in the Sky.* **1941:** *Another to Conquer.* **1942:** *Tomorrow We Live.* **1943:** *My Son, the Hero* (+co-sc); *Girls in Chains* (+story); *Isle of Forgotten Sins* (+story); *Jive Junction.* **1944:** *Bluebeard.* **1945:** *Strange Illusion* (*Out of the Night*); *Club Havana; Detour.* **1946:** *The Wife of Monte Cristo* (+co-sc); *Her Sister's Secret; The Strange Woman.* **1947:** *Carnegie Hall.* **1948:** *Ruthless.* **1949:** *I pirati de Capri* (*Pirates of Capri*). **1951:** *St. Benny the Dip; The Man from Planet X.* **1952:** *Babes in Bagdad.* **1955:** *Naked Dawn; Murder Is My Beat* (*Dynamite Anchorage*). **1957:** *The Daughter of Dr. Jekyll; The Perjurer.* **1960:** *Hannibal; The Amazing Transparent Man; Beyond the Time Barrier; L'Atlantide* (*Antinea, L'amante della città Sepolta*); *Journey Beneath the Desert*) (co-d). **1964:** *Sette contro la morte* (*Neunzing Nächte und ein Tag*). **1965:** *The Cavern.*

Other Films: 1927: *Sunrise* (Murnau) (asst prod des). **1934:** *Little Man, What Now?* (set design). **1942:** *Prisoner of Japan* (story). **1943:** *Corregidor* (co-sc); *Danger! Women at Work* (co-story).

The films of Edgar G. Ulmer have generally been classified as "B" pictures. However, it might be more appropriate to reclassify some of these films as "Z" pictures. On an average, Ulmer's pictures were filmed on a six-day shooting schedule with budgets as small as $20,000. He often worked without a decent script, adequate sets, or convincing actors. But these hardships did not prevent Ulmer from creating an individual style within his films.

Part of the look of Ulmer's films was, naturally, a result of their meager budgets. The cast was kept to a minimum., the sets were few and simple, and stock footage helped to keep costs down (even when it did not quite match the rest of the film). The length of the scripts was also kept to a minimum. Most of Ulmer's films ran only 60 to 70 minutes, and it was not uncommon for his pictures to open upon characters who were not formally introduced. Ulmer often plunged his audience into the middle of the action, which would add to their suspense as the story finally did unfold.

Characters in Ulmer's films commonly found themselves in strange and distant surroundings. This plight is especially true for the title character of *The Man from Planet X*. This curious being is stranded on earth (which from his point of view is an alien world) and is at the mercy of the strangers around him. In another example, the Allisons, a young couple on their honeymoon in *The Black Cat,* find themselves trapped in the futuristic home of the bizarre Mr. Poelzig. They are held against their will with all avenues of escape blocked off. Many of Ulmer's characters find that they are prisoners. Some of them are innocent, but many times they live in prisons of their own making.

Another theme that is prevalent in Ulmer's films is fate. His characters rarely have control over their own destiny, an idea verbalized by Al Roberts in *Detour,* who says, "whichever way you turn, Fate sticks out its foot to trip you." In *The Amazing Transparent Man,* a scientist who

Edgar Ulmer: *The Black Cat*

has been forced to work against his will on experiments with nuclear material explains that he "didn't do anything by choice." The Allisons in *The Black Cat* have no control over their destiny, either—their fate will be determined by the outcome of a game of chess. In most cases the characters in Ulmer's films find themselves swept away in a series of circumstances that they are unable to stop.

The critical recognition of Ulmer's work has been a fairly recent "discovery." Initial reviews of Ulmer's films (and not all of his films received reviews) were far from complimentary. Part of the reason for their dismissal may have been their exploitative nature. Titles like *Girls in Chains* and *Babes in Bagdad* could conceivably have some difficulty finding a respectable niche in the film world. Taken as a whole, however, the work of Edgar Ulmer reveals a personal vision that is, at the very least, different and distinctive from the mainstream of film directors.
—LINDA OBALIL

Varda, Agnès

Nationality Belgian. Born Brussels, 30 May 1928. Education Studied literature and psychology at the Sorbonne, Paris; studied art history at the Ecole du Louvre; studied photography at night school. Family Married director Jacques Demy, one son, one daughter. Career Stage photographer for Theatre Festival of Avignon, then for Theatre National Populaire, Paris, Jean Vilar; directed first film, 1954; accompanied Chris Marker to China as advisor for Dimanche à Pekin, 1955; directed two shorts in U.S., 1968; founded production company Ciné-Tamaris, 1977. Awards Prix Méliès for Cléo de 5 à 7, 1961; Bronze Lion, Venice Festival, for Salut les Cubains, 1964; Prix Louis Delluc, David Selznick Award, and Silver Bear, Berlin Festival, for Le Bonheur, 1966; First Prize, Oberhausen, for Black Panthers, 1968; Grand Prix, Taormina, for L'Une chante, l'autre pas, 1977; Cesar Award, for Ulysse, 1984; Golden Lion, Venice Festival, Prix Melies, and Best Foreign Film, Los Angeles Film Critics Association, for Vagabond, 1985; Commander des Arts et des Lettres, Chevalier Legion d'honneur. Address c/o Cine-Tamaris, 86 rue Daguerre, 75014 Paris, France.

Films as Director: 1954: *La Pointe courte* (+pr, sc). **1957:** *O saisons, o châteaux* (doc short). **1958:** *L'Opéra-Mouffe* (short); *Du côté de la Côte* (short). **1961:** *Cléo de cinq à sept (Cleo from 5 to 7)* (+sc). **1963:** *Salut les Cubains (Salute to Cuba)* (+text) (doc short). **1965:** *Le Bonheur (Happiness)* (+sc). **1966:** *Les Créatures* (+sc). **1967:** *Uncle Yanco;* episode of *Loin du Vietnam (Far from Vietnam).* **1968:** *Black Panthers (Huey)* (doc). **1969:** *Lion's Love* (+pr, sc, role). **1970:** *Nausicaa* (for TV). **1975:** *Daguerrotypes* (+pr); *Réponses de femmes* (8mm). **1977:** *L'Une chante l'autre pas (One Sings, the Other Doesn't).* **1980:** *Mur Murs (Wall Walls; Mural Murals)* (+pr, sc). **1981:** *Documenteur: An Emotion Picture* (+pr, sc). **1983:** *Ulysse.* **1984:** *Les Dites cariatides; Sept P., Cuis., S. de B., . . . a saisir.* **1986:** *Vagabonde (Sans Toit ni loi,; Vagabond)* (+sc, ed). **1988:** *Kung Fu Master (Don't Say It)* (+co-sc); *Jane B. par Agnès V.* (doc) (+sc, ed, appearance). **1991:** *Jacquot de Nantes* (+pr, sc). **1993:** *Des demoiselles ont en 25 ans (The Young Girls Turn 25)* (doc) (+sc). **1995:** *Les cent et une nuits (A Hundred and One Nights)* (+sc); *L'universe de Jacques Demy (The World of Jacques Demy)* (doc).

Other Films: 1971: *Last Tango in Paris* (Bertolucci) (co-dialogue). **1978:** *Lady Oscar* (Demy) (pr). **1995:** *Kulonbozo helyek (Different Places)* (Fesos) (appearance).

Agnès Varda's startlingly individualistic films have earned her the title "grandmother of the New Wave" of French filmmaking. Her statement that a filmmaker must exercise as much freedom as a novelist became a mandate for New Wave directors, especially Chris Marker and Alain Resnais. Varda's first film, *La Pointe courte,* edited by Resnais, is regarded, as Georges Sadoul affirms, as "the first film of the French *nouvelle vuage.* Its interplay between conscience, emotions, and the real world make it a direct antecedent of *Hiroshima, mon amour."*

The use of doubling, and twin story lines; the personification of objects; the artistic determination of cinematic composition, color, texture, form, and time; and the correlation of individual subjectivity to societal objectivity to depict socio-political issues are denominators of Varda's films, which she writes, produces, and directs.

After *La Pointe courte* Varda made three documentaries in 1957-58. The best of these was *L'Opéra-Mouffe,* portraying the Mouffetard district of Paris. Segments of the

Agnès Varda.
Photograph by Stephane Fefer.

film are prefaced by handwritten intertitles, a literary element Varda is fond of using. In 1961-62, Varda began but did not complete two film projects: *La Cocotte d'azur* and *Melangite.* Her next film, *Cléo de cinq à sept,* records the time a pop singer waits for results of her exam for cancer. Varda used physical time in *Cleo:* events happening at the same tempo as they would in actual life. The film is divided into chapters, using Tarot cards which symbolize fate. Varda next photographed 4,000 still photos of Castro's revolution-in-progress, resulting in *Salute to Cuba.*

Le Bonheur is considered Varda's most stunning and controversial achievement. Critics were puzzled and pleased. Of her first color film, Varda says it was "essentially a pursuit of the palette. . . . Psychology takes first place." A young carpenter lives with his wife and children. Then he takes a mistress; when his wife drowns, his mistress takes her place. The film was commended for its superb visual beauties, the use of narrative in *le nouveau roman* literary pattern, and its tonal contrasts and spatial configurations. Critics continue to debate the film's theme.

Elsa is an essay portraying authors Elsa Triolet and her husband Louis Aragon. *Les Créatures* uses a black and white with red color scheme in a fantasy-thriller utilizing an inside-outside plot that mingles real and unreal events. As in *La Pointe courte,* a young couple retreat to a rural locale. The pregnant wife is mute, due to an accident. Her husband is writing a book. He meets a recluse who operates a machine forcing people to behave as his or her subconscious would dictate. The wife gives birth, regaining her speech.

Visiting the United States, Varda and her husband Jacques Demy each made a film. Varda honored her *Uncle Janco* in the film so named. *The Black Panthers* (or *Huey*) followed. Both documentaries were shown at the London Film Festival in 1968. She next directed a segment of the antiwar short *Far from Vietnam.*

Using an American setting and an English-speaking cast, including the co-authors of the musical *Hair,* Varda made *Lions Love* in Hollywood. This jigsaw-puzzle work includes a fake suicide and images of a TV set reporting Robert Kennedy's assassination. G. Roy Levin declared that it was hard to distinguish between the actual and the invented film realities. *Nausicaa* deals with Greeks living in France. Made for television, it was not shown, Varda says, because it was against military-ruled Greece.

In 1971, Varda helped write the script for *Last Tango in Paris.* Varda's involvement in the women's movement began about 1972; a film dealing with feminist issues, *Réponses de femmes,* has yet to be shown. Made for German television, *Daguerreotypes* has no cast. Varda filmed the residents and shops of the Rue Daguerre, a tribute to L. J. M. Daguerre.

In 1977, Varda made *One Sings, the Other Doesn't* and established her own company, Ciné-Tamaris, to finance it. This "family" of workers created the film. Chronicling the friendship of two women over fifteen years, it earned mixed reviews, some referring to it as feminist propaganda or as sentimental syrup. But Varda, narrating the film and writing the song lyrics, does not impose her views. In *One Sings,* she wanted to portray the happiness of being a woman, she says.

Easily Varda's most potent film of the 1980s, and one of the best of her career, is *Vagabond,* an evocative drama about the death and life of a young woman, Mona (Sandrine Bonnaire). She is an ex-secretary who has chosen to become a drifter, and her fate is apparent at the outset. As the film begins, Mona has died. Her frost-bitten corpse is seen in a ditch. Her body is claimed by no one, and she is laid to rest in a potter's field. As *Vagabond* unfolds, Varda explores Mona's identity as she wanders through the rural French countryside hitching rides and begging for the necessities that will sustain her. The scenario also spotlights the manner in which she impacts on those she meets: truck drivers; a gas station owner and his son; a vineyard worker; a professor-researcher; and other, fellow drifters. Varda constructs the film as a series of sequences, some comprised of a single shot lasting several seconds, in which Mona passes through the lives of these people. The result is an eloquent film about one average, ill-fated young woman and the choices she makes, as well as a meditation on chance meetings and missed opportunities. On a much broader level, the film serves as an allegory of the travails a woman must face if she desires to completely liberate herself from the shackles of society.

Varda's most notable recent films have been valentines to her late husband, filmmaker Jacques Demy. *The Young Girls Turn 25* is a nostalgia piece about the filming of Demy's *The Young Girls of Rochefort; The World of Jacques Demy* is an up-close-and-personal documentary-biography consisting of interviews and clips from Demy's films.

A third title, *Jacquot de Nantes,* was the most widely seen. It is an exquisite film: a penetrating, heart-rending account of the measure of a man's life, with Varda moving between sequences of Demy in conversation, filmed in extreme close-up; clips from his films; and a re-creation of his childhood in Nantes and the manner in which he developed a passion for cinema. Varda illustrates how Demy's life and world view impacted on his films; for example, his hatred of violence, which is ever so apparent in his films, was forged by his memories of Nantes being bombed during World War II. But *Jacquot de Nantes* (which was conceived prior to Demy's death) is most effective as a tender love letter from one life partner to another. Varda visually evokes her feeling towards her departed mate in one of the film's opening shots. She pans her camera across a watercolor, whose composition is that of a nude woman and man who are holding hands. With over three decades of filmmaking experience, Varda's reputation as a filmmaker dazzles and endures.—LOUISE HECK-RABI and ROB EDELMAN

Vidor, King

Nationality *American.* **Born** *King Wallis Vidor in Galveston, Texas, 8 February 1894.* **Education** *Attended Peacock Military Academy, San Antonio, Texas.* **Family** *Married 1) actress Florence Arto, 1915 (divorced 1924), one daughter; 2) actress Eleanor Boardman, 1926 (divorced 1932); 3) Elizabeth Hall, 1932 (died 1973).* **Career** *Ticket-taker and part-time projectionist in Galveston's first movie house, 1909-10; amateur newsreel photographer, 1910-15; drove to Hollywood in Model T, financed trip by shooting footage for Ford's advertising newsreel, 1915; worked at various jobs in film industry, then directed first feature,* The Turn in the Road, *1919; hired by 1st National, built studio called Vidor Village, 1920 (shut down, 1922); director for Goldwyn Studios, 1923, later absorbed by MGM; taught graduate course in cinema, University of California, Los Angeles, 1960s.* **Awards** *Best Direction, Venice Festival, for* Wedding Night, *1935; Special Prize, Edinburgh Festival, 1964; Honorary Academy Award, 1978.* **Died** *Of heart failure, in California, 1 November 1982.*

Films as Director: 1919: *The Turn in the Road* (+sc); *Better Times* (+sc); *The Other Half* (+sc); *Poor Relations* (+sc). **1920:** *The Jack Knife Man* (+pr, co-sc); *The Family Honor* (+co-pr). **1921:** *The Sky Pilot; Love Never Dies* (+co-pr). **1922:** *Conquering the Woman* (+pr); *Woman, Wake Up* (+pr); *The Real Adventure* (+pr); *Dusk to Dawn* (+pr). **1923:** *Peg-O-My-Heart; The Woman of Bronze; Three Wise Fools* (+co-sc). **1924:** *Wild Oranges* (+co-sc); *Happiness; Wine of Youth; His Hour.* **1925:** *Wife of the Centaur; Proud Flesh; The Big Parade.* **1926:** *La Bohème* (+pr); *Bardelys, The Magnificent* (+pr). **1928:** *The Crowd* (+co-sc); *The Patsy; Show People.* **1929:** *Hallelujah.* **1930:** *Not So Dumb; Billy the Kid.* **1931:** *Street Scene; The Champ.* **1932:** *Bird of Paradise; Cynara.* **1933:** *Stranger's Return.* **1934:** *Our Daily Bread* (+pr, co-sc). **1935:** *Wedding Night; So Red the Rose.* **1936:** *The Texas Rangers* (+pr, co-sc). **1937:** *Stella Dallas.* **1938:** *The Citadel* (+pr). **1940:** *Northwest Passage* (+pr); *Comrade X* (+pr). **1941:** *H.M. Pulham, Esq.* (+pr, co-sc). **1944:** *American Romance* (+pr, co-sc). **1946:** *Duel in the Sun.* **1949:** *The Fountainhead; Beyond the Forest.* **1951:** *Lightning Strikes Twice.* **1952:** *Ruby Gentry* (+co-pr). **1955:** *Man Without a Star.* **1956:** *War and Peace* (+co-sc). **1959:** *Solomon and Sheba.*

King Vidor began work in Hollywood as a company clerk for Universal, submitting original scripts under the pseudonym Charles K. Wallis. (Universal employees weren't allowed to submit original work to the studio.) Vidor eventually confessed his wrongdoing and was fired as a clerk, only to be rehired as a comedy writer. Within days, he lost this job as well when Universal discontinued comedy production.

Vidor next worked as the director of a series of short dramatic films detailing the reform work of Salt Lake City Judge Willis Brown, a Father Flanagan-type. Vidor tried to parlay this experience into a job as a feature director with a major studio but was unsuccessful. He did manage, however, to find financial backing from nine doctors for his first feature, a picture with a Christian Science theme titled *The Turn in the Road.* Vidor spent the next year working on three more features for the newly-christened Brentwood Company, including the comedy *Better Times,* starring his own discovery, Zasu Pitts.

King Vidor

In 1920 Vidor accepted an offer from First National and a check for $75,000. He persuaded his father to sell his business in order that he might build and manage "Vidor Village," a small studio which mirrored similar projects by Chaplin, Sennett, Griffith, Ince, and others. Vidor directed eight pictures at Vidor Village, but was forced to close down in 1922. The following year, he was hired by Louis B. Mayer at Metro to direct aging stage star Laurette Taylor in *Peg-O-My-Heart.* Soon after, he went to work for Samuel Goldwyn, attracted by Goldwyn's artistic and literary aspirations. In 1924 Vidor returned to Metro as a result of a studio merger that resulted in MGM. He would continue to work there for the next 20 years, initially entrusted with molding the careers of rising stars John Gilbert and Eleanor Boardman, soon to be Vidor's second wife.

The Big Parade changed Vidor's status from contract director to courted screen artist. Produced by Irving Thalberg, the film grew from a minor studio production into one of MGM's two biggest hits of 1926, grossing $18 million. *The Big Parade* satisfied Vidor's desire to make a picture with lasting value and extended exhibition. It was the first of three films he wanted to make on the topics of "wheat, steel, and war." Vidor went on to direct Gilbert and Lillian Gish, a new studio acquisition, in *La Bohème.*

Encouraged by the popularity of German films of the period and their concern with urban life, Vidor made *The Crowd,* "*The Big Parade* of peace." It starred unknown actor James Murray, whose life would end in an alcoholic suicide. (Murray inspired one of Vidor's later projects, an unproduced picture titled *The Actor.*) Like *The Big Parade, The Crowd* presented the reactions of an everyman, this time to the anonymity of the city and the rigors of urban survival. Vidor's silent career then continued with two of Marion Davies' comedies, *The Patsy* and *Show People.* His career extended into "talkies" with a third comedy, *Not So Dumb.* Though only moderately successful, Vidor became a favorite in William Randolph Hearst's entourage.

Vidor was in Europe when the industry announced its conversion to sound. He quickly returned to propose *Hallelujah,* with an all-black cast. Although considered a politically-astute director for Hollywood, the film exposes Vidor's political shortcomings in its paternalistic attitude toward blacks. With similar political naiveté, Vidor's next great film, the pseudo-socialist agricultural drama *Our Daily Bread,* was derived from a *Reader's Digest* article.

By this point in his career, Vidor's thematics were fairly intact. Informing most of his lasting work is the struggle of Man against Destiny and Nature. In his great silent pictures, *The Big Parade* and *The Crowd,* the hero wanders through an anonymous and malevolent environment, war-torn Europe and the American city, respectively. In his later sound films, *The Citadel, Northwest Passage, Duel in the Sun,* and *The Fountainhead* various forms of industry operate as a vehicle of Man's battle to subdue Nature. Unlike the optimism in the films of Ford and Capra, Vidor's films follow a Job-like pattern in which victory comes, if at all, with a great deal of personal sacrifice. Underlying all of Vidor's great work are the biblical resonances of a Christian Scientist, where Nature is ultimately independent from and disinterested in Man, who always remains subordinate in the struggle against its forces.

Following *Our Daily Bread,* Vidor continued to alternate between films that explored this personal thematic and projects seemingly less suited to his interests. In more than 50 features, Vidor worked for several producers, directing *Wedding Night* and *Stella Dallas* for Samuel Goldwyn; *The Citadel, Northwest Passage,* and *Comrade X* for MGM; *Bird of Paradise,* where he met his third wife Elizabeth Hill, and *Duel in the Sun* for David O. Selznick; *The Fountainhead, Beyond the Forest,* and *Lightning Strikes Twice* for Warner Brothers; and late in his career, *War and Peace* for Dino De Laurentiis. Vidor exercised more control on his films after *Our Daily Bread,* often serving as producer, but his projects continued to fluctuate between intense metaphysical drama and lightweight comedy and romance.

In the 1950s Vidor's only notable film was *Ruby Gentry,* and his filmmaking career ended on a less-than-praiseworthy note with *Solomon and Sheba.* In the 1960s he made two short documentaries, *Truth and Illusion* and *Metaphor,* about his friend Andrew Wyeth. Vidor wrote a highly praised autobiography in 1953, *A Tree is a Tree.* In 1979 he received an honorary Oscar (he was nominated as best director five times). In the last years of his life, he was honored in his hometown of Galveston with an annual King Vidor film festival.—MICHAEL SELIG

Vigo, Jean

Nationality French. **Born** Paris, 26 April 1905, son of anarchist Miguel Alemreyda (Eugène Bonaventure de Vigo). **Education** Attended a number of schools, including the Boys School of St. Cloud, until 1917; following death of father, attended boarding school in Nîmes, under the name Jean Sales. **Family** Married Elizabeth Lozinska, 1929, child: Luce. Father found dead under mysterious circumstances in jail cell, 1917; mother confined to a hospital, 1923. **Career** Experienced health problems, entered clinic in Montpellier, then moved to Nice because of his tuberculosis, 1929; directed first film, À propos de Nice, 1930, then returned to live in Paris, 1932; Zéro de conduite removed from circulation by censors because of perceived "anti-France" content; became seriously ill with leukemia, 1933. **Died** 5 October 1934.

Films as Director: 1930: À propos de Nice. **1931:** Taris (Taris roi de l'eau; Jean Taris champion de natation). **1933:** Zéro de conduite. **1934:** L'Atalante.

It is difficult to think of another director who made so few films and yet had such a profound influence on other filmmakers. Jean Vigo's *À propos de Nice,* his first film, is his contribution to the French surrealist movement. The film itself is a direct descendant of Vertov's *Man with a Movie Camera.* Certainly, his films make political statements similar to those seen in Vertov's work. Vertov's documentary celebrates a people's revolution, while Vigo's chastises the bourgeois vacationers in a French resort town. Even more importantly, both films revel in the pyrotechnics of the camera and the editing room. They are filled with dizzying movement, fast cutting, and the juxtaposition, from frame to frame, of objects that normally have little relation to

Jean Vigo: *L'Atalante*

each other. In yet another link between the two directors, Vertov's brother photographed *À propos de Nice,* as well as Vigo's other three films.

À propos de Nice provides a look at a reality beyond the prosaic, common variety that so many films give us. The movie attempts nothing less than the restructuring of our perception of the world by presenting it to us not so much through a seamless, logical narrative, but rather through a fast-paced collection of only tangentially related shots.

After *À propos de Nice,* Vigo began combining his brand of surrealism with the poetic realism that would later be so important to a generation of French directors, such as Jean Renoir and Marcel Carné. For his second film, he made another documentary, *Taris,* about France's champion swimmer. Here Vigo takes his camera underwater as Taris clowns at the bottom of a pool and blows at the lens. *Taris* certainly has some striking images, but it is only eleven minutes long. Indeed, if Vigo had died in 1931, after finishing *Taris,* instead of in 1934 (and given the constantly precarious state of his health, this would not have been at all unlikely), he would have been remembered, if at all, as a director who had shown great potential, yet who could hardly be considered a major talent.

Vigo's third film, however, secured his place in film history. *Zéro de conduite* stands out as one of the cinema's most influential works. Along with films such as Sagan's *Mädchen in Uniform* and Wyler's *These Three,* it forms one of the more interesting and least studied genres of the 1930s—the children's boarding school film. Although it is Vigo's first fiction film, it continues the work he began with *À propos de Nice.* That first movie good-naturedly condemns the bourgeoisie, showing the rich as absolutely useless, their primary sin being banality rather than greed or cruelty. In *Zéro de conduite,* teachers, and not tourists, are the representatives of the bourgeoisie. But like the Nice vacationers, they are not so much malicious as they are simply inadequate; they instruct their schoolboys in nothing important and prize the school's suffocating regulations above all else. Vigo lets the schoolboys rebel against this sort of mindless monotony. They engage in an apocalyptic pillow fight, and then bombard their teachers with fruit during a stately school ceremony. The film's anarchic spirit led to its being banned in France until 1945. But during the 1950s, it became one of the inspirations for the French New Wave directors. In subject matter, it somewhat resembles Truffaut's *400 Blows.* But it is the film's style—the mixture of classical Hollywood visuals with the dreamlike illogic of slow motion, fast action, and quick cutting—that particularly influenced a new generation of filmmakers.

Vigo's last film, *L'Atalante,* is his masterpiece. It is a love story that takes place on a barge, with Vigo once again combining surrealism with poetic realism. The settings are naturalistic and the characters lower-class, and so bring to mind Renoir's poetic realist films such as *Toni* and *Les*

Bas-Fonds. There is also an emphasis on the imagination and on the near-sacredness of banal objects that places the film strongly in the tradition of such surrealist classics as *Un Chien andalou.* After Juliette leaves Jean, the barge captain, Jean jumps into the river and sees his wife's image everywhere around him. The underwater sequence not only makes the viewer think of *Taris,* but also makes us aware that we are sharing Jean's obsession with him. This dreamy visualization of a character's thoughts brings to mind the priority that the surrealists gave to all mental processes. The surrealists prized, too, some of the more mundane aspects of everyday life, and Vigo's film is full of ordinary objects that take on (for Juliette) a magical status. They are only puppets, or fans, or gramophones piled in a heap in the room of Père Jules, Jean's old assistant, but Juliette has spent her entire life in a small town, and for her, these trinkets represent the mysteries of faraway places. They take on a special status, the banal being raised to the level of the exotic.

Despite the movie's links to two film movements, *L'Atalante* defies categorization. It is a masterpiece of mood and characterization, and, along with *Zéro de conduite,* it guarantees Vigo's status as a great director. But he was not granted that status by the critical community until years after his death. Because of the vagaries of film exhibition and censorship, Vigo was little known while he was making films. He received nowhere near the acclaim given to his contemporaries Jean Renoir and René Clair.—ERIC SMOODIN

Visconti, Luchino

Nationality *Italian.* **Born** *Count Don Luchino Visconti di Modrone in Milan, 2 November 1906.* **Education** *Educated at private schools in Milan and Como; also attended boarding school of the Calasanzian Order, 1924-36.* **Military Service** *Served in Reggimento Savoia Cavalleria, 1926-28.* **Career** *Stage actor and set designer, 1928-29; moved to Paris, assistant to Jean Renoir, 1936-37; returned to Italy to assist Renoir on* La Tosca, *1939; directed first film,* Ossessione, *1942; directed first play, Cocteau's* Parenti terrible, *Rome, 1945; directed first opera,* La vestale, *Milan, 1954; also ballet director, 1956-57.* **Awards** *International Prize, Venice Festival, for* La terra trema, *1948; 25th Anniversary Award, Cannes Festival, 1971.* **Died** *17 March 1976.*

Films as Director: 1942: *Ossessione* (+co-sc). **1947:** *La terra trema* (+sc). **1951:** *Bellissima* (+co-sc); *Appunti su un fatto di cronaca* (second in series *Documento mensile*). **1953:** "We, the Women" episode of *Siamo donne* (+co-sc). **1954:** *Senso* (+co-sc). **1957:** *Le notti bianche* (*White Nights*) (+co-sc). **1960:** *Rocco e i suoi fratelli* (*Rocco and His Brothers*) (+co-sc). **1962:** "Il lavoro (The Job)" episode of *Boccaccio '70* (+co-sc). **1963:** *Il gattopardo* (*The Leopard*) (+co-sc). **1965:** *Vaghe stelle dell'orsa* (*Of A Thousand Delights; Sandra*) (+co-sc). **1967:** "Le strega bruciata viva" episode of *Le streghe; Lo straniero* (*L'Etranger*) (+co-sc). **1969:** *La caduta degli dei* (*The Damned; Götterdämmerung*) (+co-sc). **1970:** *Alla ricerca di Tadzio.* **1971:** *Morte a Venezia* (*Death in Venice*) (+pr, co-sc). **1973:** *Ludwig* (+co-sc). **1974:** *Gruppo di famiglia in un interno* (+co-sc). **1976:** *L'innocente* (*The Innocent*) (+co-sc).

Other Films: 1936: *Les Bas-fonds* (Renoir) (asst d). **1937:** *Une Partie de campagne* (Renoir) (asst d) (released 1946). **1940:** *La Tosca* (Renoir) (asst d). **1945:** *Giorni di gloria* (De Santis) (asst d).

The films of Luchino Visconti are among the most stylistically and intellectually influential of postwar Italian cinema. Born a scion of ancient nobility, Visconti integrated the most heterogeneous elements of aristocratic sensibility and taste with a committed Marxist political

Luchino Visconti

consciousness, backed by a firm knowledge of Italian class structure. Stylistically, his career follows a trajectory from a uniquely cinematic realism to an operatic theatricalism, from the simple quotidian eloquence of modeled actuality to the heightened effect of lavishly appointed historical melodramas. His career fuses these interests into a mode of expression uniquely Viscontian, prescribing a potent, double-headed realism. Visconti turned out films steadily but rather slowly from 1942 to 1976. His obsessive care with narrative and filmic materials is apparent in the majority of his films.

Whether or not we choose to view the wartime *Ossessione* as a precursor or a determinant of neorealism, or merely as a continuation of elements already present in Fascist period cinema, it is clear that the film remarkably applies a realist mise-en-scène to the formulaic constraints of the genre film. With major emendations, the film is, following a then-contemporary interest in American fiction of the 1930s, a treatment (the second and best) of James M. Cain's *The Postman Always Rings Twice*. In it the director begins to explore the potential of a long-take style, undoubtedly influenced by Jean Renoir, for whom Visconti had worked as assistant. Having met with the disapproval of the Fascist censors for its depiction of the shabbiness and desperation of Italian provincial life, *Ossessione* was banned from exhibition.

For *La terra trema*, Visconti further developed those documentary-like attributes of story and style generally associated with neorealism. Taken from Verga's late nineteenth-century masterpiece *I malavoglia*, the film was shot entirely on location in Sicily and employed the people of the locale, speaking in their native dialect, as actors. Through them, Visconti explores the problems of class exploitation and the tragedy of family dissolution under economic pressure. Again, a mature long-shot/long-take style is coupled with diverse, extensive camera movements and well-planned actor movements to enhance the sense of a world faithfully captured in the multiplicity of its activities. The extant film was to have become the first episode of a trilogy on peasant life, but the other two parts were never filmed.

Rocco e i suoi fratelli, however, made over a dozen years later, continues the story of this Sicilian family, or at least one very much like it. Newly arrived in Milan from the South, the Parandis must deal with the economic realities of their poverty as well as survive the sexual rivalries threatening the solidarity of their family unit. The film is episodic in nature, affording time to each brother's story (in the original version), but special attention is given to Rocco, the forebearing and protective brother who strives at all costs to keep the group together, and Simone, the physically powerful and crudely brutal one, who is unable to control his personal fears, insecurities, and moral weakness. Unable to find other work, they both drift into prize fighting, viewed here as class exploitation. Jealousy over the prostitute Nadia causes Simone to turn his fists against his brother, then to murder the woman. But Rocco, impelled by strong traditional ties, would still act to save Simone from the police. Finally, the latter is betrayed to the law by Ciro, the fourth youngest and a factory worker who has managed to transfer some of his familial loyalty to a social plane and the labor union. Coming full circle from *La terra trema,* Luca, the youngest, dreams of a day when he will be able to return to the Southern place of his birth. *Rocco* is perhaps Visconti's greatest contribution to modern tragedy, crafted along the lines of Arthur Miller and Tennessee Williams (whose plays he directed in Italy). The Viscontian tragedy is saturated with melodramatic intensity, a stylization incurring more than a suggestion of decadent sexuality and misogyny. There is also, as in other Visconti works, a rather ambiguous intimation of homosexuality (here between Simone and his manager.)

By *Senso* Visconti had achieved the maturity of style that would characterize his subsequent work. With encompassing camera movements—like the opening shot, which moves from the stage of an opera house across the audience, taking in each tier of seats where the protest against the Austrians will soon erupt—and with a melodramatic rendering of historical fact, Visconti begins to mix cinematic realism with compositional elegance and lavish romanticism. Against the colorful background of the Risorgimento, he paints the betrayal by an Austrian lieutenant of his aristocratic Italian mistress who, in order to save him, has compromised the partisans. The love story parallels the approaching betrayal of the revolution by the bourgeois political powers.

Like Gramsci, who often returned to the contradictions of the Risorgimento as a key to the social problems of the modern Italian state, Visconti explores that period once more in *Il gattopardo,* from the Lampedusa novel. An aristocratic Sicilian family undergoes transformation as a result of intermarriage with the middle-class at the same time that the Mezzogiorno is undergoing unification with the North. The bourgeoisie, now ready and able to take over from the dying aristocracy, usurps Garibaldi's revolution; in this period of *transformismo,* the revolutionary process will be assimilated into the dominant political structure and defused.

Still another film that focuses on the family unit as a barometer of history and changing society is *La caduta degli dei.* This treatment of a German munitions industry family (much like Krupp) and its decline into betrayal and murder in the interests of personal gain and the Nazi state intensifies and brings up-to-date an examination of the social questions of the last mentioned films. Here again a meticulous, mobile camera technique sets forth and stylistically typifies a decadent, death-surfeited culture.

Vaghe stelle dell'orsa removes the critique of the family from the social to the psychoanalytic plane. While death or absence of the father and the presence of an uprising surrogate is a thematic consideration in several Visconti films, here he explores it in conjunction with Freudian theory in this deliberate yet entirely transmuted re-telling of the Elektra myth. We are never completely aware of the extent of the relationship between Sandra and her brother, and the possibility of past incest remains distinct. Both despise their stepfather Gilardini, whom they accuse of having seduced their mother and having denounced their father, a Jew, to the Fascists. Sandra's love for and sense of solidarity with her brother follows upon a racial solidarity with her father and race, but Gianni's love, on the other hand, is underpinned by a desire for his mother, transferred to Sandra. Nevertheless, dramatic confrontation propels the dialectical investigations of the individual's position with respect to the social even in this, Visconti's most densely psychoanalytic film.

Three films marking a further removal from social themes and observation of the individual, all literary adaptations, are generally felt to be his weakest: *Le notte bianche* from Dostoevski's *White Nights* sets a rather fanciful tale of a lonely man's hopes to win over a despairing woman's love against a decor that refutes, in its obvious, studio-bound staginess, Visconti's concern with realism and material verisimilitude. The clear inadequacy of this Livornian setting, dominated by a footbridge upon which the two meet and the unusually claustrophobic spatiality that results, locate the world of individual romance severed from large social and historical concerns in an inert, artificial perspective that borders on the hallucinatory. He achieves similar results with location shooting in *Lo straniero*, where—despite alterations of the original Camus—he perfectly captures the difficult tensions and tones of individual alienation by utilizing the telephoto lens pervasively. Rather than provide a suitable Viscontian dramatic space rendered in depth, it reduces Mersault to the status of a Kafkaesque insect-man observed under a microscope. Finally, *Morte a Venezia*, based on the fiction of Thomas Mann, while among Visconti's most formally beautiful productions, is one of his least critically successful. The baroque elaboration of mise-en-scène and camera work does not rise above self-pity and self-indulgence, and is cut off from social context irretrievably.—JOEL KANOFF

von Sternberg, Josef

Nationality Austrian. *Born* Jonas Sternberg in Vienna, 19 May 1894. *Education* Educated briefly at Jamaica High School, Queens, New York, returned to Vienna to finish education. *Family* Married 1) Riza Royce, 1926 (divorced 1930); 2) Jeanne Annette McBride, 1943, two children. *Career* Film patcher for World Film Co. in Fort Lee, New

Josef von Sternberg and Marlene Dietrich on the set of *Dishonored.*

Jersey, 1911; joined U.S. Army Signal Corps to make training films, 1917; scenarist and assistant for several directors, 1918-24; attached "von" to his name at suggestion of actor Elliot Dexter, 1924; directed first film, The Salvation Hunters, *then signed eight-picture contract with MGM (terminated after two abortive projects), 1925; directed* The Sea Gull *for Charlie Chaplin (Chaplin did not release it), 1926; director for Paramount, 1926-35; began collaboration with Marlene Dietrich on* Der blaue Engel, *made for UFA in Berlin, 1930; attempted to direct* I, Claudius *for Alexander Korda in England, 1937 (not completed); made documentary* The Town *for U.S. Office of War Information, 1941; taught class in film direction, University of Southern California, 1947.* **Awards** *George Eastman House Medal of Honor, 1957; honorary member, Akademie der Künste, Berlin, 1960.* **Died** *22 December 1969.*

Films as Director: 1925: *The Salvation Hunters* (+pr, sc); *The Exquisite Sinner* (+co-sc) (remade by Phil Rosen); *The Masked Bride* (remade by Christy Cabanne). **1926:** *The Sea Gull* (*Woman of the Sea*) (+sc). **1927:** *Children of Divorce* (d add'l scenes only); *Underworld.* **1928:** *The Last Command* (+sc); *The Drag Net; The Docks of New York.* **1929:** *The Case of Lena Smith; Thunderbolt.* **1930:** *Der blaue Engel* (*The Blue Angel*); *Morocco.* **1931:** *Dishonored; An American Tragedy.* **1932:** *Shanghai Express; Blonde Venus* (+co-sc); *I Take This Woman.* **1934:** *The Scarlet Empress.* **1935:** *The Devil Is a Woman* (+co-ph); *Crime and Punishment.* **1936:** *The King Steps Out; New York Cinderella* (remade by Frank Borzage and W.S. Van Dyke). **1941:** *The Shanghai Gesture* (+co-sc). **1943-44:** *The Town.* **1946:** *Duel in the Sun* (d several scenes only). **1951:** *Macao* (re-shot almost entirely by Nicholas Ray). **1953:** *Anatahan* (*The Saga of Anatahan*) (+sc, ph). **1957:** *Jet Pilot* (completed 1950).

Other Films: (partial list) 1919: *The Mystery of the Yellow Room* (asst d); *By Divine Right* (asst d, sc, ph); *Vanity's Price* (asst d).

There is a sense in which Josef von Sternberg never grew up. In his personality, the twin urges of the disturbed adolescent towards self-advertisement and self-effacement fuse with a brilliant visual imagination to create an artistic vision unparalleled in the cinema. But von Sternberg lacked the cultivation of Murnau, the sophistication of his mentor von Stroheim, the humanity of Griffith, or the ruthlessness of Chaplin. His imagination remained immature, and his personality was malicious and obsessive. His films reflect a schoolboy's fascination with sensuality and heroics. That they are sublime visual adventures from an artist who contributed substantially to the sum of cinema technique is one paradox to add to the stock that make up his career.

Much of von Sternberg's public utterance, and in particular his autobiography, was calculated to confuse; the disguise of his real Christian name under the diminutive "Jo" is typical. Despite his claims to have done so, he did not "write" all his films, though he did *re*-write the work of some skilled collaborators, notably Jules Furthman and Ben Hecht. While his eye for art and design was highly developed, he never designed sets; he merely "improved" them with props, veils, nets, posters, scribbles, but above all with light. Of this last he was a natural master, the only director of his day to earn membership in the American Society of Cinematographers. Given a set, a face, a camera, and some lights, he could create a mobile portrait of breathtaking beauty.

Marlene Dietrich was his greatest model. He dressed her like a doll, in a variety of costumes that included feathers and sequins, a gorilla suit, a tuxedo, and a succession of gowns by Paramount's master of couture, Travis Banton. She submitted to his every demand with the skill and complaisance of a great courtesan. No other actress provided him with such malleable material. With Betty Compson, Gene Tierney, and Akemi Negishi he fitfully achieved the same "spiritual power," as he called the mood of yearning melancholy which was his ideal, but the effect never equalled that of the seven Dietrich melodramas.

Von Sternberg was born too early for the movies. The studio system constrained his fractious temperament; the formula picture stifled his urge to primp and polish. He battled with MGM, which offered him a lucrative contract after the success of his von Stroheim-esque expressionist drama *The Salvation Hunters,* fell out with Chaplin, producer of the still-suppressed *Woman of the Sea,* and fought constantly with Paramount until Ernst Lubitsch, acting studio head, "liquidated" him for his intransigence; the later suppression of his last Paramount film, *The Devil Is a Woman,* in a political dispute with Spain merely served to increase von Sternberg's alienation.

For the rest of his career, von Sternberg wandered from studio to studio and country to country, always lacking the facilities he needed to achieve his best work. Even Korda's lavish *I Claudius,* dogged by disaster and finally terminated in a cost-cutting exercise, shows in its surviving footage only occasional flashes of von Sternbergian brilliance. By World War II, he had already achieved his best work, though he lived for another 30 years.

Von Sternberg alarmed a studio establishment whose executives thought in terms of social and sexual stereotypes, formula plotting, and stock happy endings; their narrative ideal was a *Saturday Evening Post* novelette. No storyteller, von Sternberg derided plot; "the best source for a film is an anecdote," he said. From a single coincidence and a handful of characters, edifices of visual poetry could be constructed. His films leap years in the telling to follow a moral decline or growth of an obsession.

The most important film of von Sternberg's life was one he never made. After the humiliation of the war years, when he produced only the propaganda short *The Town,* and the nadir of his career, as close-up advisor to King Vidor on *Duel in the Sun,* he wrote *The Seven Bad Years,* a script that would, he said, "demonstrate the adult insistence to follow the pattern inflicted on a child in its first seven helpless years, from which a man could extricate himself were he to realize that an irresponsible child was leading him into trouble." He was never to make this work of self-analysis, nor any film which reflected a mature understanding of his contradictory personality.

Von Sternberg's theories of cinema were not especially profound, deriving largely from the work of Reinhardt, but they represented a quantum jump in an industry where questions of lighting and design were dealt with by experts who jealously guarded this prerogative. In planning his films not around dialogue but around the performers' "dramatic encounter with light," in insisting that the "dead space" between the camera and subject be filled and enlivened, and above all in seeing every story in terms of "spiritual power" rather than star quality, he established a concept of personal cinema which presaged the *politique des auteurs* and the Movie Brat generation.

In retrospect, von Sternberg's contentious personality—manifested in the self-conscious affecting of uniforms and costumes on the set and an epigrammatic style of communicating with performers that drove many of them to frenzy—all reveal themselves as reactions against the banality of his chosen profession. Von Sternberg was asked late in life if he had a hobby. "Yes. Chinese philately." Why that? "I wanted," he replied in the familiar weary, uninflected voice, "a subject I could not exhaust."—JOHN BAXTER

von Stroheim, Erich

Nationality *Austrian.* **Born** *Erich Oswald Stroheim in Vienna, 22 September 1885; became U.S. citizen, 1926.* **Education** *According to von Stroheim he attended Mariahilfe Military Academy, though several biographers doubt this.* **Military Service** *Served briefly in the Austro-Hungarian Army.* **Family** *Married 1) Margaret Knox, 1914 (died 1915); 2) May Jones, 1916 (divorced 1918), one son; 3) Valerie Germonprez, 1918 (separated), one son.* **Career** *Moved to America and worked as salesman, railroad worker, short story writer, and travel agent, 1909-14; actor, assistant and military adviser for D.W. Griffith, 1914-15; assistant director, military adviser, and set designer for director John Emerson, 1915-17; became known as "The Man You Love to Hate" after role as Prussian officer in* For France, *1917; directed* Blind Husbands *for Carl Laemmle at Universal, 1918 (terminated contract with Universal, 1922); directed* Greed *for Goldwyn Co., his version cut to ten reels by studio, 1924; moved to France, 1945.* **Died** *12 May 1957.*

Films as Director: 1918: *Blind Husbands* (+sc, art d, role as Lieutenant von Steuben). **1919:** *The Devil's Passkey* (+sc, art d). **1921:** *Foolish Wives* (+sc, co-art d, co-costume, role as Count Wladislas Serge Karamazin). **1922:** *Merry-Go-Round* (+sc, co-art d, co-costume) (completed by Rupert Julian). **1924:** *Greed* (+sc, co-art d). **1925:** *The Merry Widow* (+sc, co-art d, co-costume). **1927:** *The Wedding March* (+sc, co-art d, co-costume, role as Prince Nicki). **1928:** *The Honeymoon* (+sc, role as Prince Nicki—part two of *The Wedding March* and not released in United States); *Queen Kelly* (+sc, co-art d) (completed by others). **1933:** *Walking Down Broadway* (+sc) (mostly reshot by Alfred Werker and Edwin Burke and released as *Hello Sister*).

Other Films: 1914: *Captain McLean* (Conway) (role). **1915:** *Old Heidelberg* (Emerson) (asst d, military advisor, role as Lutz); *Ghosts* (Emerson) (role); *The Birth of a Nation* (Griffith) (role). **1916:** *Intolerance* (Griffith) (asst d, role as second Pharisee); *The Social Secretary* (Emerson) (asst d, role as a reporter); *Macbeth* (Emerson) (asst d, role); *Less Than the Dust* (Emerson) (asst d, role); *His Picture in the Papers* (Emerson) (asst d, role as the traitor). **1917:** *Panthea* (Dwan) (asst d, role as Russian policeman); *Sylvia of the Secret Service* (Fitzmaurice) (asst d, role); *In Again—Out Again* (Emerson) (asst d, art d, role as Russian officer); *For France* (Ruggles) (role as Prussian officer). **1918:** *Hearts of the World* (Griffith) (asst d, military advisor, role as German officer); *The Unbeliever* (Crosland) (role as German officer); *The Hun Within* (Cabanne) (role as German officer). **1927:** *The Tempest* (sc). **1929:** *The Great Gabbo* (Cruze) (role as Gabbo). **1930:** *Three Faces East* (del Ruth) (role). **1931:** *Friends and Lovers* (Schertzinger) (role); *As You Desire Me* (Fitzmaurice) (role). **1932:** *The Lost Squadron* (Archimbaud and Sloane) (role); *As You Desire Me* (Fitzmaurice) (role). **1934:** *Crimson Romance* (Howard) (military advisor, role as German pilot); *Fugitive Road* (sc/co-sc, military advisor). **1935:** *The Crime of Dr. Crespi* (Auer) (role as Dr. Crespi); *Anna Karenina* (Brown) (military advisor). **1936:** *Devil Doll* (Browning) (sc/co-sc); *San Francisco* (Van Dyke) (sc/co-sc); *Marthe Richard* (Bernard) (role as German officer). **1937:** *Between Two Women* (sc/co-sc); *La Grande Illusion* (Renoir) (role as von Rauffenstein); *Mademoiselle Docteur* (Gréville) (role as Col. Mathesius); *L'Alibi* (Chenal) (role as Winkler). **1938:** *Les Pirates du rail* (Christian-Jaque) (role as Tschou-Kin); *L'Affaire Lafarge* (Chenal) (role as Denis); *Les Disparus de Saint-Agil* (Christian-Jaque) (role as German professor); *Ultimatum* (Wiene and Siodmak) (role as Général Simovic); *Gibraltar* (role as Marson) (*It Happened in Gibraltar*); *Derrière la façade* (Lacombe) (role as Eric). **1939:** *Menaces* (Gréville) (role as Hoffman); *Rappel immédiat* (Mathot) (role as Stanley Wells); *Pièges* (Siodmak) (role as Pears); *Tempête sur Paris* (Bernard-Deschamps) (role as Kohrlick); *La Révolte des vivants* (Pottier) (role as Emile Lasser); *Macao l'enfer* (Delannoy) (role as Knall); *Paris—New York* (Heymann and Mirande) (role). **1940:** *I Was an Adventuress* (Ratoff) (role); *So Ends Our Night* (Cromwell) (role). **1943:** *Five Graves to Cairo* (Wilder) (role as Field Marshall Rommel); *The North Star* (Milestone) (role as German medic). **1944:** *The Lady and the Monster* (Sherman) (role); *Storm over Lisbon* (Sherman) (role). **1945:** *The Great Flamarion* (Mann) (role as Flamarion); *Scotland Yard Investigation* (Blair) (role); *The Mask of Dijon* (Landers) (role as Dijon). **1946:** *On ne meurt pas comme* *ça* (Boyer) (role as Eric von Berg). **1947:** *La Danse de mort* (Cravenne) (co-adapt, co-dialogue, role as Edgar). **1948:** *Le Signal rouge* (Neubach) (role). **1949:** *Portrait d'un assassin* (Bernard-Roland) (role). **1950:** *Sunset Boulevard* (Wilder) (role as Max). **1952:** *Minuit, quai de Bercy* (Stengel) (role); *Alraune* (*La Mandragore*) (Rabenalt) (role). **1953:** *L'Envers du paradis* (Gréville) (role as O'Hara); *Alerte au sud* (Devaivre) (role). **1954:** *Napoléon* (Guitry) (role as Beethoven). **1955:** *Série noire* (Foucaud) (role); *La Madone des sleepings* (Diamant-Berger) (role).

Erich von Stroheim had two complementary careers in cinema, that of actor-director, primarily during the silent period, and that of distinguished character actor when his career as a director was frustrated as a result of his inability to bring his genius to terms with the American film industry.

After edging his way into the industry in the humblest capacities, von Stroheim's lengthy experience as bit player and assistant to Griffith paid off. His acceptance during the pioneer period of American cinema as Prussian "military adviser," and his bullet-headed physical resemblance to the traditional monocled image of the tight-uniformed Hun officer, enabled him to create a more established acting career and star in his own films. With his first personal film, *Blind Husbands,* he became the prime creator in Hollywood of witty, risqué, European-like sex-triangle comedy-dramas. His initial successes in the early 1920s were characterized by subtle acting touches and a marked sophistication of subject that impressed American audiences of the period as essentially European and fascinatingly decadent. *Blind Husbands* was followed by other films in the same genre, the 12-reel *The Devil's Pass Key* and the critically successful *Foolish Wives*. In all three works, women spectators could easily identify with the common character of the lonely wife, whose seduction by attractively wicked Germanic officers and gentlemen (usually played by von Stroheim, now publicized as "the man you love to hate") provided the essential thrill. Von Stroheim also cunningly included beautiful but excitingly unprincipled women characters in both *The Devil's Pass Key* and *Foolish Wives,* played by Maude George and Mae Busch. Details of bathing, dressing, and the ministration of servants in the preparation of masters or mistresses in boudoir or dressing room were recurrent, and the von Stroheim scene always included elaborate banquets, receptions, and social ceremonies.

Von Stroheim's losing battle with the film industry began in his clashes with Irving Thalberg at Universal. His obsessive perfectionism over points of detail in setting and costume had pushed the budget for *Foolish Wives* to the million dollar mark. Though the publicists boasted of von Stroheim's extravagance, the front office preferred hard profits to such self-indulgent expenditures. Thalberg also refused von Stroheim's demands that his films should be of any length he determined, and *Foolish Wives* (intended to be in two parts) was finally taken out of his hands and cut from 18-20 to some 12-14 reels. Although a critical success, the film lost money.

Foolish Wives was von Stroheim's most discussed film before *Greed*. In it he played a bogus aristocratic officer, in reality a swindler and multi-seducer. His brilliant, sardonic acting "touches" brought a similar psychological verisimilitude to this grimly satiric comedy of manners as Lubitsch was to establish in his *Kammerspielfilme* (intimate films). He also specialized in decor, photographic composition, and lighting. The latticed light and shadow in one sequence, when the seducer in full uniform visits the counterfeiter's underworld den with hope of ravishing the old man's mentally defective daughter, is unforgettable.

Greed, von Stroheim's most important film, was based meticulously on Norris's Zolaesque novel, *McTeague*. Von Stroheim's masterpiece, it was eventually mutilated by the studio because of its unwieldy length; it was reduced over von Stroheim's protests from 42 reels to 24 (between 5 and 6 hours), and then finally cut to 10 reels by the studio. Von Stroheim's emphasis on the ugly and bizarre in human nature emerged in this psychologically naturalistic study of avarice and degradation seen in a mismatched couple—McTeague, the impulsive, primitive (but bird-loving) lower-class dentist, and Trina, the pathologically avaricious spinster member of a German-Swiss immigrant family and winner of a $5,000 lottery. After their marriage, Trina hoards her money as their circumstances decline to the point where the husband becomes drunk and brutal, and the wife mad. After he murders her and becomes a fugitive, McTeague ends up in the isolated wastes of Death Valley, handcuffed to Marcus, his former friend whom he has killed. Using the streets of San Francisco and the house where the actual murder that had inspired Norris had taken place, von Stroheim anticipated Rossellini in his use of such locations. But his insistence on

Erich von Stroheim

achieving an incongruous and stylized realism, which starts with McTeague's courtship of Trina sitting on a sewerpipe and culminates in the macabre sequence in Death Valley, goes beyond that straight neorealism of the future. Joel W. Finler, in his book *Stroheim,* analyzes the wholesale cutting in the 10-reel version, exposing the grave losses that render the action and motivation of the film unclear. But the superb performances of Zasu Pitts and Gibson Gowland compensate, and the grotesque Sieppe family provide a macabre background, enhanced by von Stroheim's constant reminder of San Francisco's "mean streets." The film was held to be his masterpiece by many, but also condemned as a "vile epic of the sewer."

Von Stroheim was to work as director on only five more films: the Ruritanian *Merry Widow* (adapted from the operetta), *The Wedding March* (in two parts, and again severely cut), the erotic *Queen Kelly* (directed for Gloria Swanson, but never completed by von Stroheim, though released by Swanson with her own additions), and the sound films *Walking Down Broadway* (released as *Hello, Sister;* it was never released in von Stroheim's original version), and *The Emperor's Candlesticks,* on which it appears he collaborated only in direction. The silent films portray the same degenerate Imperial Viennese society von Stroheim favored. Half-romantic and half-grotesque fantasy, the films once again presented von Stroheim's meticulous attention to detail in decor and characterization. *The Wedding March* (in spite of studio intervention) is the high point in von Stroheim's career as a director after *Greed.* Subsequently he remained content to star or appear in films made by others, making some 50 appearances between 1929 and 1955. His most notable acting performances during this period were in Renoir's *La Grande Illusion* and Wilder's *Five Graves to Cairo* and *Sunset Boulevard,* in which his past as a director is almost ghoulishly recalled.—ROGER MANVELL

von Trotta, Margarethe

Nationality German. **Born** Berlin, 21 February, 1942. **Education** Universities of Munich and Paris; studied acting in Munich. **Family** Married director Volker Schlöndorff (divorced). **Career** Actress in theatres in Dinkelsbül, Stuttgart, and Frankfurt, 1960s; worked only in TV and film, from 1969; directed first film, Die verlorene Ehre der Katharina Blum, 1975. **Award** Golden Lion, Venice Festival, for Die Bleierne Zeit, 1981.

Films as Director: 1975: Die verlorene Ehre der Katherina Blum (The Lost Honor of Katharina Blum) (co-d, co-sc). **1977:** Das zweite Erwachen der Christa Klages (The Second Awakening of Christa Klages) (+sc). **1979:** Schwestern oder Die Balance des Glücks (Sisters, or The Balance of Happiness) (+sc). **1981:** Die Bleierne Zeit (Leaden Times; Marianne and Julianne; The German Sisters) (+sc). **1983:** Heller Wahn (Sheer Madness) (+sc). **1986:** Rosa Luxemburg (+sc). **1987:** episode of Felix. **1988:** Paura e amore (Three Sisters/Love and Fear) (+co-sc). **1990:** Die Rückkehr (Return; L'Africana; The African Woman). **1993:** Il lungo silenzio (The Long Silence). **1994:** Das versprechen (The Promise) (+co-sc).

Other Films: 1968: Schräge Vögel (Ehmck) (role). **1969:** Brandstifter (Lemke) (role); Götter der Pest (Fassbinder) (role as Margarethe). **1970:** Baal (Schlöndorff) (role as Sophie); Der amerikanische Soldat (Fassbinder) (role as maid). **1971:** Der plötzliche Reichtum der armen Leute von Kombach (Schlöndorff) (co-sc, role as Heinrich's woman); Die Moral der Ruth Halbfass (Schlöndorff) (role as Doris Vogelsang). **1972:** Strohfeuer (Schlöndorff) (role as Elisabeth, co-sc). **1973:** Desaster (Hauff) (role); Übernachtung in Tirol (Schlöndorff) (role as Katja). **1974:** Invitation à la chasse (Chabrol) (for TV) (role as Paulette); Georgina's Gründe (Schlöndorff) (for TV) (role as Kate Theory). **1975:** Das andechser Gefühl (Achternbusch) (role as film actress). **1976:** Der Fangschuss (Schlöndorff) (co-sc, role as Sophie von Reval). **1984:** Blaubart (Bluebeard) (Zanussi) (role); Unerreichbare Nahe (Hirtz) (sc).

An important aspect of Margarethe von Trotta's filmmaking, which affects not only the content but also the representation of that content, is her emphasis on women and the relationships that can develop between them. For example, von Trotta chose as the central theme in two of her films (Sisters, or The Balance of Happiness and Marianne and Juliane) one of the most intense and complex relationships that can exist between two women, that of sisters. Whether von Trotta is dealing with overtly political themes as in The Second Awakening of Christa Klages (based on the true story of a woman who robs a bank in order to subsidize a daycare center) and Marianne and Juliane (based on the experiences of Christine Ensslin and her "terrorist" sister) or with the lives of ordinary women as in Sisters or the Balance of Happiness or Sheer Madness, von Trotta shows the political nature of relationships between women. By paying close attention to these relationships, von Trotta brings into question the social and political systems which either sustain them or do not allow them to exist.

Although the essence of von Trotta's films is political and critical of the status quo, their structures are quite conventional. Her films are expensively made and highly subsidized by the film production company Bioskop, which was started by her husband Volker Schlöndorff and Reinhard Hauff, both filmmakers. Von Trotta joined the company when she started making her own films. She did not go through the complicated system of incentives and grants available to independent filmmakers in Germany. Rather, she began working for Schlöndorff as an actress and then as a scriptwriter, and finally on her own as a director and co-owner in the production company which subsidizes their films.

Von Trotta has been criticized by some feminists for working too closely within the system and for creating characters and structures which are too conventional to be of any political value.

Other critics find that a feminist aesthetic can be found in her choice of themes. For although von Trotta uses conventional women characters, she does not represent them in traditional fashion. Nor does she describe them with stereotyped, sexist clichés; instead, she allows her characters to develop on screen through gestures, glances, and nuances. Great importance is given to the psychological and subconscious delineation of her characters, for von Trotta pays constant attention to dreams, visions, flashbacks, and personal obsessions. In this way, her work can be seen as inspired by the films of Bresson and Bergman, filmmakers who also use the film medium to portray psychological depth.

"The unconscious and subconscious behavior of the characters is more important to me than what they do," says von Trotta. For this reason, von Trotta spends a great deal of time with her actors and actresses to be sure that they really understand the emotions and motivations of the characters which they portray. This aspect of her filmmaking caused her to separate her work from that of her husband, Volker Schlöndorff. During their joint direction of *The Lost Honor of Katharina Blum,* it became apparent that Schlöndorff's manner of directing, which focused on action shots, did not mix with his wife's predilections for exploring the internal motivation of the characters. Her films are often criticized for paying too much attention to the psychological, and thus becoming too personal and inaccessible.

Margarethe von Trotta

Von Trotta has caused much controversy within the feminist movement and outside of it. Nevertheless, her films have won several awards not only in her native Germany but also internationally, drawing large, diverse audiences. Her importance cannot be minimized. Although she employs the commonly used and accepted structures of popular filmmakers, her message is quite different. Her main characters are women and her films treat them in a serious and innovative fashion. Such treatment of women within a traditional form has in the past been undervalued or ignored. Her presentation of women has opened up possibilities for the development of the image of women on screen and contributed to the development of film itself.

Von Trotta's films have continued to express other concerns that were central to her earlier work as well. These include examinations of German identity and the impact of recent German history on the present; the view of historical events through the perceptions of the individuals those events affect; the personal risks that individuals take when speaking the truth or exposing the hypocrisy of those in power; and, in particular, the strengths of women and the manner in which they relate to each other and evolve as their own individual selves.

Rosa Luxemburg is a highly intelligent, multi-faceted biopic of the idealistic, politically committed, but ill-fated humanist and democratic socialist who had such a high profile on the

German political scene near the beginning of the twentieth century. *Love and Fear,* loosely based on Chekhov's *The Three Sisters,* is an absorbing (if sometimes overdone) allegory about how life is forever in transition. It focuses on a trio of sisters, each with a different personality. The senior sibling is a scholarly type who is too cognizant of how quickly time goes by; the middle one lives an aimless life, and is ruled by her feelings; the junior in the group is a fervent, optimistic pre-med student.

The Long Silence is the story of a judge whose life is in danger because of his prosecution of corrupt government officials. After his murder—an unavoidable occurrence, given the circumstances—his gynecologist wife perseveres in continuing his work. *The Promise,* which reflects on the downfall of Communism and the demise of the Berlin Wall, tells of two lovers who are separated in 1961 during a failed attempt to escape from East to West. With the exception of a brief reunion in Prague in 1968, they are held apart until 1989 and the death of Communism in East Germany.—GRETCHEN ELSNER-SOMMER and ROB EDELMAN

Walsh, Raoul

Nationality *American.* **Born** *New York City, 11 March 1887 (some sources say 1892).* **Education** *Attended Public School 93, New York; also attended Seton Hall College.* **Family** *Married 1) Miriam Cooper, 1916 (divorced 1927); 2) Mary Edna Simpson, 1941.* **Career** *Sailed to Cuba on uncle's trading ship, 1903; horse wrangler in Mexico, 1903-04; worked in variety of jobs in United States, including surgeon's assistant and undertaker, 1904-10; cowboy actor in films for Pathé Studio, New Jersey, then for Biograph, from 1910; actor and assistant to D.W Griffith, then director at Biograph, Hollywood, from 1912; director for William Fox, from 1916; lost eye in auto accident, 1928; introduced John Wayne as feature actor in* The Big Trail, *1930; director for various studios, then retired to ranch, 1964.* **Died** *In California, 31 December 1980.*

Films as Director: 1912: *The Life of General Villa* (co-d, role as young Villa); *Outlaw's Revenge.* **1913:** *The Double Knot* (+pr, sc, role); *The Mystery of the Hindu Image* (+pr, sc); *The Gunman* (+pr, sc; credit contested). **1914:** *The Final Verdict* (+pr, sc, role); *The Bowery.* **1915:** *The Regeneration* (+co-sc); *Carmen* (+pr, sc); *The Death Dice* (+pr, sc; credit contested); *His Return* (+pr); *The Greaser* (+pr, sc, role); *The Fencing Master* (+pr, sc); *A Man for All That* (+pr, sc, role); *11:30 P.M.* (+pr, sc); *The Buried Hand* (+pr, sc); *The Celestial Code* (+pr, sc); *A Bad Man and Others* (+pr, sc); *Home from the Sea; The Lone Cowboy* (+co-sc). **1916:** *Blue Blood and Red* (+pr, sc); *The Serpent* (+pr, sc); *Pillars of Society.* **1917:** *The Honor System; The Silent Lie; The Innocent Sinner* (+sc); *Betrayed* (+sc); *The Conqueror* (+sc); *This Is the Life.* **1918:** *Pride of New York* (+sc); *The Woman and the Law* (+sc); *The Prussian Cur* (+sc); *On the Jump* (+sc); *I'll Say So.* **1919:** *Should a Husband Forgive* (+sc); *Evangeline* (+sc); *Every Mother's Son* (+sc). **1920:** *The Strongest* (+sc); *The Deep Purple; From Now On.* **1921:** *The Oath* (+pr, sc); *Serenade* (+pr). **1923:** *Lost and Found on a South Sea Island* (*Passions of the Sea*); *Kindred of the Dust* (+pr, sc). **1924:** *The Thief of Bagdad.* **1925:** *East of Suez* (+pr); *The Spaniard* (+co-pr); *The Wanderer* (+co-pr). **1926:** *The Lucky Lady* (+co-pr); *The Lady of the Harem; What Price Glory.* **1927:** *The Monkey Talks* (+pr); *The Loves of Carmen* (+sc). **1928:** *Sadie Thompson* (*Rain*) (+co-sc, role); *The Red Dance; Me Gangster* (+co-sc). **1929:** *In Old Arizona* (co-d); *The Cock-eyed World* (+co-sc); *Hot for Paris* (+co-sc). **1930:** *The Big Trail.* **1931:** *The Man Who Came Back; Women of all Nations; The Yellow Ticket.* **1932:** *Wild Girl; Me and My Gal.* **1933:** *Sailor's Luck; The Bowery; Going Hollywood.* **1935:** *Under Pressure; Baby Face Harrington; Every Night at Night.* **1936:** *Klondike Annie; Big Brown*

Eyes (+co-sc); *Spendthrift*. **1937:** *O.H.M.S.* (*You're in the Army Now*); *When Thief Meets Thief*; *Artists and Models*; *Hitting a New High*. **1938:** *College Swing*. **1939:** *St. Louis Blues*; *The Roaring Twenties*. **1940:** *The Dark Command* (+pr); *They Drive by Night*. **1941:** *High Sierra*; *The Strawberry Blonde*; *Manpower*; *They Died With Their Boots On*. **1942:** *Desperate Journey*; *Gentleman Jim*. **1943:** *Background to Danger*; *Northern Pursuit*. **1944:** *Uncertain Glory*; *San Antonio* (uncredited co-d); *Salty O'Rourke*; *The Horn Blows at Midnight*. **1946:** *The Man I Love*. **1947:** *Pursued*; *Cheyenne*; *Stallion Road* (uncredited co-d). **1948:** *Silver River*; *Fighter Squadron*; *One Sunday Afternoon*. **1949:** *Colorado Territory*; *White Heat*. **1950:** *The Enforcer* (uncredited co-d); *Montana* (uncredited co-d). **1951:** *Along the Great Divide*; *Captain Horatio Hornblower*; *Distant Drums*. **1952:** *The World in His Arms*; *The Lawless Breed*; *Blackbeard the Pirate*. **1953:** *Sea Devils*; *A Lion in the Streets*; *Gun Fury*. **1954:** *Saskatchewan*. **1955:** *Battle Cry*; *The Tall Men*. **1956:** *The Revolt of Mamie Stover*; *The King and Four Queens*. **1957:** *Band of Angels*. **1958:** *The Naked and the Dead*; *The Sheriff of Fractured Jaw*. **1959:** *A Private's Affair*. **1960:** *Esther and the King* (+pr, sc). **1961:** *Marines, Let's Go* (+pr, sc). **1964:** *A Distant Trumpet*.

Other Films: 1910: *The Banker's Daughter* (Griffith) (role as bank clerk); *A Mother's Love* (role as young man); *Paul Revere's Ride* (Emile Cocteau) (role as Paul Revere). **1915:** *Birth of a Nation* (Griffith) (role as John Wilkes Booth).

Raoul Walsh's extraordinary career spanned the history of the American motion picture industry from its emergence, through its glory years in the 1930s and 1940s, and into the television era. Like his colleagues Alan Dwan, King Vidor, John Ford, and Henry King, whose careers also covered 50 years, Walsh continuously turned out popular fare, including several extraordinary hits. Movie fans have long appreciated the work of this director's director. But only when auteurists began to closely examine his films was Walsh "discovered," first by the French (in the 1960s), and then by American and British critics (in the 1970s). To these critics Walsh's action films come to represent a unified view, put forth by means of a simple, straightforward technique. Raoul Walsh is now accepted as an example of a master Hollywood craftsman who worked with naive skill and an animal energy, a director who was both frustrated and buoyed by the studio system.

Unfortunately, this view neglects Walsh's important place in the silent cinema. Raoul Walsh began his career with an industry still centered in and around New York City, the director's birthplace. He started as an actor in Pathé westerns filmed in New Jersey, and then journeyed to California to be with D.W. Griffith's Fine Arts production company. Walsh apprenticed with Griffith as an actor, appearing in his most famous role as John Wilkes Booth in *Birth of a Nation*.

Walsh then turned to directing, first for the fledgling Fox Film Company. For the next five years (interrupted by World War I service experience) Walsh would master the craft of filmmaking, absorbing lessons which would serve him for more than forty years. His apprenticeship led to major assignments, and his greatest financial successes came in the 1920s. Douglas Fairbanks's *The Thief of Bagdad* was directed by Walsh at the height of that famous star's career.

Walsh took advantage of this acclaim by moving for a time to the top studio of that era, Paramount, and then signed a lucrative long-term contract with Fox. At that point Fox began expanding into a major studio. Walsh contributed to that success with hits like *What Price Glory?* and *The Cockeyed World*. The introduction of new sound-on-film technology, through its Movietone Newsreels, helped Fox's ascent. Consequently, when Fox was about to convert to all-sound features, corporate chieftains turned to Walsh to direct *In Old Arizona*, in 1929. (It was on location for that film that Walsh lost his eye.) Because of its experience with newsreel shooting, Fox was the only studio at the time that could film and record quality sound on location. Walsh's next film used the 70mm "Grandeur" process on a western, *The Big Trail*. The film did well but could not save the company from succumbing to the Great Depression.

Walsh's career stagnated during the 1930s. He and Fox never achieved the heights of the late 1920s. When Darryl F. Zanuck came aboard with the Twentieth Century merger in 1935, Walsh moved on, freelancing until he signed with Warners in 1939. For slightly more than a decade, Walsh functioned as a contract director at Warners, turning out two or three films a year. Walsh never established the degree of control he had enjoyed over the silent film projects, but he seemed to thrive in the restrictive Warners environment. Walsh's first three films at Warners fit into that studio's mode of crime melodramas: *The Roaring Twenties, They Drive By Night,* and *High Sierra. The Roaring Twenties* was not a classic gangster film, like Warners' *Little Caesar* and *Public Enemy,* but

Raoul Walsh

a realistic portrait of the socio-economic environment in the United States after World War I. *High Sierra* looked ahead to the film noir of the 1940s. In that film the gangster became a sympathetic character trapped by forces he did not understand. During the World War II era Walsh turned to war films with a textbook example of what a war action film ought to be. Walsh continued making crime melodramas and war films in the late 1940s and early 1950s. *Battle Cry, The Naked and the Dead,* and *Marines, Let's Go* proved that he could adapt to changing tastes within familiar genres.

Arguably Walsh's best film of the post-war era was *White Heat,* made for Warners in 1949. The James Cagney character is portrayed against type: we see the gangster hiding and running, trying to escape his past and his social, economic, and psychological background. *White Heat* was the apex of Walsh's work at Warners, for it simultaneously fit into an accepted mode and transcended the formula. *White Heat* has come to symbolize the tough Raoul Walsh action film. Certainly that same sort of style can also be seen in his westerns at Warners, *They Died With Their Boots On, Pursued,* and a remake of *High Sierra* called *Colorado Territory*. But there are other sides of the Walsh oeuvre, usually overlooked by critics, or at most awkwardly positioned among the action films. *The Strawberry Blonde* is a warm, affectionate, turn-of-the-century tale of small town America. *Gentleman Jim* of 1942 also swims in sentimentality. These films indicate that Walsh, though known as an action director, certainly had a soft touch when required. Indeed, when his works are closely examined, it is clear that Walsh had the ability to adapt to many different themes and points of view.

The 1950s seemed to pass Walsh by. Freed from the confines of the rigid studio system, Walsh's output became less interesting. But he was a survivor. He completed his final feature, a cavalry film for Warners called *A Distant Trumpet,* in 1964. By then Raoul Walsh had truly become a Hollywood legend, having reached two career peaks in a more than fifty-year career. To carefully examine the career of Raoul Walsh is to study the history of the American film in toto, for the two are nearly the same length and inexorably intertwined.—DOUGLAS GOMERY

Walters, Charles

Nationality American. *Born* Pasadena, California, 17 November 1911. *Education* Attended University of Southern California. *Career* Broadway debut as actor and dancer in New Faces, *1934; began choreographing on Broadway with* Sing Out the News, *1938; first film appearance, 1942; began as choreographer on* DuBarry Was a Lady, *1943; shot and staged "Brazilian Boogie" number, in* Broadway Rhythm, *1944; directed first feature,* Good News, *for Arthur Freed, 1947.* *Died* In Malibu, California, 13 August 1982.

Films as Director: 1942: *Spreadin' the Jam* (short). **1947:** *Good News.* **1948:** *Easter Parade.* **1949:** *The Barkleys of Broadway.* **1950:** *Summer Stock* (*If You Feel Like Singing*) (+choreo). **1951:** *Three Guys Named Mike; Texas Carnival.* **1952:** *The Belle of New York.* **1953:** *Lili* (+choreo, role); *Dangerous When Wet; Torch Song* (+choreo, role); *Easy to Love.* **1955:** *The Glass Slipper; The Tender Trap.* **1956:** *Don't Go Near the Water.* **1957:** *High Society* (+choreo). **1959:** *Ask Any Girl.* **1960:** *Please Don't Eat the Daisies.* **1961:** *Two Loves* (*Spinster*). **1962:** *Billy Rose's Jumbo.* **1964:** *The Unsinkable Molly Brown.* **1966:** *Walk, Don't Run.*

Other Films: 1942: *Seven Days Leave* (Whelan) (choreo, role/dancer). **1943:** *DuBarry Was a Lady* (Del Ruth) (choreo); *Presenting Lily Mars* (Taurog) (co-choreo, role/dancer); *Best Foot Forward* (Buzzell) (choreo); *Girl Crazy* (Taurog) (choreo, role/dancer). **1944:** *Broadway Rhythm* (Del Ruth) (co-choreo); *Three Men in White* (Goldbeck) (choreo); *Meet Me in St. Louis* (Minnelli) (choreo). **1945:** *Thrill of a Romance* (Thorpe) (choreo); *Her Highness and the Bellboy* (Thorpe) (choreo); *Weekend at the Waldorf* (Leonard) (choreo); *The Harvey Girls* (Sidney) (choreo); *Abbott & Costello in Hollywood* (Simon) (choreo). **1946:** *Ziegfeld Follies* (Minnelli and others) (choreo Judy Garland's "An Interview" sequence). **1962:** *Summer Holiday* (Yates) (choreo).

Before going to Hollywood Charles Walters spent about eight years on Broadway. For the most part he was a dancer, but in 1938 he choreographed his first show. A few years later Robert Altman introduced him to MGM and he began to stage routines for the screen. He worked with Gene Kelly on a number for *Du Barry Was A Lady,* then began staging musical numbers for some of Metro's leading ladies such as June Allyson, Gloria De Haven, Lucille Ball, and Judy Garland. Garland became a great friend and he worked on a number of her films, sometimes dancing with her. His first effort at directing was Lena Horne's "Brazilian Boogie" number in *Broadway Rhythm.* The following year he directed a short film called *Spreadin' the Jam,* but it was not until 1947 that he made his first feature, *Good News.*

As a dancer, movement was very much on Walters' mind. As a director he moved not only the performers but also the camera, making full use of tracking shots, pans, and crane shots. The studio was impressed with his work and gave him *Easter Parade* with Astaire and Garland. The budget was twice that of his first film, and notable for the "Couple of Swells" number—which Walters danced with Garland when she did her memorable show at the Palace a few years later. *The Barkleys of Broadway* should have starred Astaire and Garland again, but Garland was ill and Ginger Rogers returned to the screen in her stead.

These first three films were made under Walters' original contract as a choreographer, and at the same fee. But after proving himself with those projects, he was recognized as a director of musicals ready to follow into the footsteps of other MGM stalwarts like Stanley Donen and Vincente Minnelli. *Summer Stock* began with the pleasantly relaxed number "If You Feel Like Singing," as the camera moved through the window into the shower and followed Garland into the dressing-room. But the rest of the filming was far from relaxed, for Walters had to cope with Garland's nerves and weight problems. The final song, "Get Happy," was staged by Walters after the film was finished because they needed a good number for the climax, and Judy's loss of weight was quite noticeable.

In 1951 Walters directed his first straight picture, *Three Guys Named Mike*, a passable romantic comedy. His least favourite film, *The Belle of New York*, was followed by his favorite, *Lili*. In this light, whimsical piece he drew a charming performance from Leslie Caron and received an Oscar nomination. *Dangerous When Wet* was one of three films

Charles Walters

he made with Esther Williams. Walters staged the lively opening number with each character taking up the song, and "Ain't Nature Grand," with Charlotte Greenwood showing great vitality in her high kicks. In the dramatic musical *Torch Song* Walters was the first to direct Joan Crawford in a color film. He got to know her well, and put a lot of the real Joan Crawford into the character of Jenny. His careful handling of Frank Sinatra in *The Tender Trap* was most opportune. After a string of dramatic roles, this film confirmed Sinatra's talent as a comedy actor. In 1957 he was reunited with Sinatra for what is arguably his best film, *High Society*. Every number in this film is significant, yet they are all completely different. One of the high spots was Crosby and Sinatra's "Well, Did You Evah," which Walters himself had introduced years before with Betty Grable. It took place in two rooms and was shot without a single cut. In the early 1960s he made *The Unsinkable Molly Brown* and *Billy Rose's Jumbo,* the latter by far the better of the two.

Walters was a sincere director whose musicals had a style of their own. He was equally at home with a field full of dancers as he was with soloist or a group on a bandstand. He not only moved his cameras and his performers, but staged many numbers on moving vehicles—a car, a carriage, a coach, a trolley, a boat, and even a tractor. His use of color and his sudden cuts produced striking effects, and the energy and spirit of his work contributed greatly to the Hollywood musical.—COLIN WILLIAMS

Welles, Orson

Nationality *American.* **Born** *Kenosha, Wisconsin, 6 May 1916.* **Education** *Attended Todd School in Woodstock, Illinois, 1926-31.* **Family** *Married 1) Virginia Nicholson, 1934 (divorced 1939), one son; 2) Rita Hayworth, 1943 (divorced 1947), one daughter;*

Orson Welles as he appeared in *Citizen Kane*.

3) Paola Mori, 1955, one daughter. **Career** *Actor and director at the Gate Theatre, Dublin, 1931-34; debut on Broadway with Katherine Cornell's road company, also co-directed first film, 1934; collaborated with John Houseman for the Phoenix Theatre Group, 1935, later producer and director for Federal Theater Project; co-founder, with Houseman, Mercury Theatre Group, 1937; moved into radio with "Mercury Theatre on the Air," 1938, including famous dramatization of H. G. Wells's* War of the Worlds, *Halloween, 1938; given contract by RKO, 1939; directed feature debut,* Citizen Kane, *1941; began documentary* It's All True, *1942, then Welles and his staff were removed from RKO; directed* The Lady *from Shanghai* for Columbia Studios, 1947; directed *Macbeth for Republic Pictures, 1948; moved to Europe, 1949; completed only one more film in United States,* Touch of Evil, *1958; appeared in advertisements, and continued to act, from 1960s.* **Awards** *20th Anniversary Tribute, Cannes Festival, 1966; Honorary Academy Award, for "Superlative artistry and versatility in the creation of motion pictures," 1970; Life Achievement Award, American Film Institute, 1975; Fellowship of the British Film Institute, 1983.* **Died** *In Hollywood, 10 October 1985.*

Films as Director: 1934: *The Hearts of Age* (16mm short) (co-d). **1938:** *Too Much Johnson* (+co-pr, sc) (unedited, not shown publicly, destroyed in 1970 fire). **1941:** *Citizen Kane* (+pr, co-sc, role as Charles Foster Kane). **1942:** *The Magnificent Ambersons* (+pr, sc); *It's All True* (+pr, co-sc) (not completed and never shown). **1943:** *Journey into Fear* (co-d, uncredited, pr, co-sc, role as Colonel Haki). **1946:** *The Stranger* (+co-sc, uncredited, role as Franz Kindler, alias Professor Charles Rankin). **1948:** *The Lady from Shanghai* (+sc, role as Michael O'Hara) (produced in 1946); *Macbeth* (+pr, sc, co-costumes, role as Macbeth). **1952:** *Othello* (+pr, sc, role as Othello and narration). **1955:** *Mr. Arkadin* (*Confidential Report*) (+sc, art d, costumes, role as Gregory Arkadin and narration); *Don Quixote* (+co-pr, sc, asst ph, role as himself and narration) (not completed). **1958:** *Touch of Evil* (+sc, role as Hank Quinlan). **1962:** *Le Procès* (*The Trial*) (+sc, role as Hastler and narration). **1966:** *Chimes at Midnight* (*Falstaff*) (+sc, costumes, role as Sir John Falstaff). **1968:** *The Immortal Story* (+sc, role as Mr. Clay). **1970:** *The Deep* (+sc, role as Russ Brewer). **1972:** *The Other Side of the Wind* (+sc) (filming begun in 1972, uncompleted). **1975:** *F for Fake* (+sc).

Other Films: 1937: *The Spanish Earth* (Ivens) (original narration). **1940:** *Swiss Family Robinson* (Ludwig) (off-screen narration). **1943:** *Jane Eyre* (R. Stevenson) (role as Edward Rochester). **1944:** *Follow the Boys* (Sutherland) (revue appearance with Marlene Dietrich). **1945:** *Tomorrow is Forever* (Pichel) (role as John McDonald). **1946:** *Duel in the Sun* (Vidor) (off-screen narration). **1947:** *Black Magic* (Ratoff) (role as Cagliostro). **1948:** *Prince of Foxes* (role as Cesare Borgia). **1949:** *The Third Man* (Reed) (role as Harry Lime). **1950:** *The Black Rose* (Hathaway) (role as General Bayan). **1951:** *Return to Glennascaul* (Edwards) (role as himself). **1953:** *Trent's Last Case* (Wilcox) (role as Sigsbee Manderson); *Si Versailles m'était conté* (Guitry) (role as Benjamin Franklin); *L'uomo, la bestia e la virtu* (Steno) (role as the beast). **1954:** *Napoléon* (Guitry) (role as Hudson Lowe); "Lord Mountdrago" segment of *Three Cases of Murder* (O'Ferrall) (role as Lord Mountdrago). **1955:** *Trouble in the Glen* (Wilcox) (role as Samin Cejador y Mengues); *Out of Darkness* (documentary) (narrator). **1956:** *Moby Dick* (Huston) (role as Father Mapple). **1957:** *Pay the Devil* (Arnold) (role as Virgil Renckler); *The Long Hot Summer* (Ritt) (role as Will Varner). **1958:** *The Roots of Heaven* (Huston) (role as Cy Sedgwick); *Les Seigneurs de la forêt* (Sielman and Brandt) (off-screen narration); *The Vikings* (Fleischer) (narration). **1959:** *David e Golia* (Pottier and Baldi) (role as Saul); *Compulsion* (Fleischer) (role as Jonathan Wilk); *Ferry to Hong Kong* (Gilbert) (role as Captain Hart); *High Journey* (Baylis) (off-screen narration); *South Sea Adventure* (Dudley) (off-screen narration). **1960:** *Austerlitz* (Gance) (role as Fulton); *Crack in the Mirror* (Fleischer) (role as Hagolin/Lamorcière); *I tartari* (Thorpe) (role as Barundai). **1961:** *Lafayette* (Dréville) (role as Benjamin Franklin); *King of Kings* (Ray) (off-screen narration); *Désordre* (short) (role). **1962:** *Der grosse Atlantik* (documentary) (narrator). **1963:** *The V.I.P.s* (Asquith) (role as Max Buda); *Rogopag* (Pasolini) (role as the film director). **1964:** *L'Echiquier de Dieu* (*La Fabuleuse Aventure de Marco Polo*) (de la Patellière) (role as Ackermann); *The Finest Hours* (Baylis) (narrator). **1965:** *The Island of Treasure* (J. Franco) (role); *A King's Story* (Booth) (narrator). **1966:** *Is Paris Burning?*

(Clément) (role); *A Man for All Seasons* (Zinnemann) (role as Cardinal Wolsey). **1967:** *Casino Royale* (Huston and others) (role); *The Sailor from Gibralter* (Richardson) (role); *I'll Never Forget Whatshisname* (Winner) (role). **1968:** *Oedipus the King* (Saville) (role as Tiresias); *Kampf um Rom* (role as Emperor Justinian); *The Southern Star* (Hayers) (role). **1969:** *Tepepa* (role); *Barbed Water* (documentary) (narrator); *Una su 13* (role); *Michael the Brave* (role); *House of Cards* (Guillermin) (role). **1970:** *Catch-22* (Nichols) (role as General Dweedle); *Battle of Neretva* (Bulajia) (role); *Start the Revolution Without Me* (Yorkin) (narrator); *The Kremlin Letter* (Huston) (role); *Waterloo* (Bondarchuk) (role as King Louis XVIII). **1971:** *Directed by John Ford* (Bogdanovich) (narrator); *Sentinels of Silence* (narrator); *A Safe Place* (Jaglom) (role). **1972:** *La Decade prodigieuse* (role); *Malpertuis* (role); *I racconti di Canterbury* (Pasolini) (role); *Treasure Island* (Hough) (role as Long John Silver); *Get to Know Your Rabbit* (De Palma) (role). **1973:** *Necromancy* (Gordon) (role). **1975:** *Bugs Bunny Superstar* (Jones) (narrator). **1976:** *Challenge of Greatness* (documentary) (narrator); *Voyage of the Damned* (Rosenberg) (role). **1977:** *It Happened One Christmas* (Thomas) (for TV) (role). **1979:** *The Late Great Planet Earth* (on-camera narrator); *The Muppet Movie* (Frawley) (role as J.P. Morgan); *Tesla* (role as Yug). **1981:** *Butterfly* (Cimber) (role as the judge); *The Man Who Saw Tomorrow* (Guenette) (role). **1984:** *Where is Parsifal?* (Helman) (role); *Almonds and Raisins* (Karel) (narrator). **1985:** *Genocide* (Schwartzman) (narrator). **1987:** *Someone to Love* (Jaglom) (role).

References to Orson Welles as one of America's most influential directors and *Citizen Kane* as one of the great American films have become a simplistic way to encapsulate Welles's unique contribution to cinema. It is a contribution which seems obvious but is difficult to adequately summarize without examining his complex career.

Welles began as an actor in Ireland at Dublin's famous Gate Theater, bluffing his way into the theater's acting troupe by claiming to be well-known on the Broadway stage. He began directing plays in New York, and worked with John Houseman in various theatrical groups. At one point they attempted to stage Marc Blitzstein's leftist, pro-labor *The Cradle Will Rock* for the Federal Theatre Project, but government agents blocked the opening night's production. Performers and audience subsequently moved to another theater, and the events surrounding the performance became one of Broadway's most famous episodes. The incident led to Houseman being fired and Welles's resignation from the Project.

Houseman and Welles then formed the Mercury Theatre Group, armed with a manifesto written by Houseman declaring their intention to foster new talent, experiment with new types of plays, and appeal to the same audiences that frequented the Federal Theater plays. Welles's work on the New York stage was generally leftist in its political orientation, and, inspired by the expressionist theater of the 1920s, prefigured the look of his films.

Welles and his Mercury Theater Group expanded into radio as the Mercury Theater on the Air. In contrast to most theater-oriented shows on radio, which consisted merely of plays read aloud, the Mercury group adapted their works in a more natural, personal manner: most of the plays were narrated in the first person. Shrewd imitations of news announcements and technical breakdowns heightened the realism of his 1938 Halloween *War of the Worlds* broadcast to such a degree that the show has become famous for the panic it caused among its American listeners, a number of which thought that New Jersey was actually being invaded by Martians. This event itself has become a pop culture legend, shrouded in exaggeration and half-truths.

RKO studios hired Welles in 1939, hoping he could repeat the success on film for them that he had enjoyed on stage and in radio. Welles, according to most sources, accepted the job because his Mercury Theater needed money to produce an elaborate production called *5 Kings,* an anthology of several of Shakespeare's plays. Whatever the reason, his contract with RKO began an erratic and rocky relationship with the Hollywood industry that would, time and again, end in bitter disappointment for Welles. The situation eventually led him to begin a self-imposed exile in Europe.

The film on which Welles enjoyed the most creative freedom was his first and most famous, *Citizen Kane*. At the time the film created a controversy over both its subject matter and style. Loosely based on the life of newspaper magnate William Randolph Hearst, the film supposedly upset Hearst to such a degree that he attempted to stop the production, and then the distribution and exhibition. In the end, his anger was manifested in the scathing reviews critics gave the film in all his newspapers. The film's innovative structure, which included flashbacks from the differing points-of-view of the various characters, in addition to other formal devices so different from the classic Hollywood cinema, also contributed to *Kane*'s financial failure and commercial downfall, though critics other than those employed at Hearst's papers generally gave the film positive reviews.

Other controversies surrounded the film as well, including one over scriptwriting credit. Originally, Welles claimed solo credit for writing the film, but the Writer's Guild forced him to acknowledge Herman Mankiewicz as co-author. Each writer's *exact* contributions remain unknown, but the controversy was revived during the early 1970s by critic Pauline Kael, who attempted to prove that Mankiewicz was most responsible for the script. Whatever the case, the argument becomes unimportant and even ludicrous given the unique direction which shapes the material, and which is undeniably Welles's.

Due to the failure of *Kane*, Welles was supervised quite closely on his next film, *The Magnificent Ambersons*. After shooting was completed, Welles went to South America to begin work on a documentary, *It's All True*, designed to help dispel Nazi propaganda in Latin America. He took a rough cut of *Ambersons* with him, hoping to coordinate cutting with editor Robert Wise. A sneak preview of Welles's *Ambersons* proved disastrous, however, and the studio cut his 140-minute-plus version to eighty-eight minutes and added a "happy ending." The film was a critical and commercial failure, and the entire Mercury staff was removed from the RKO lot.

Welles spent the remainder of his Hollywood career sparring with various producers or studios over the completed versions of his films and his uncredited direction on films in which he starred. For example, *Journey Into Fear* was begun by Welles but finished by Norman Foster, though Welles claims he made contributions and suggestions throughout. *Jane Eyre,* which made Welles a popular star, was directed by Robert Stevenson, but the gothic overtones, the mise-en-scène, and other stylistic devices suggest a Wellesian contribution. With *The Stranger,* directed for Sam Spiegel, he adhered closely to the script and a preplanned editing schedule, evidently determined to prove that he could turn out a Hollywood product on time and on budget. Welles, though, subsequently referred to *The Stranger* as "the worst of my films," and several Welles scholars agree.

Welles directed one of his best films, *The Lady from Shanghai,* for Harry Cohn of Columbia. The film, a loose, confusing, noirish tale of double-crosses and corrupted innocence, starred Welles's wife at the time, Rita Hayworth. Cohn, who was supposedly already dissatisfied with their marriage because he felt it would reduce Hayworth's box-office value, was furious at Welles for the image she presented in *Shanghai*. The film, shot mostly on location, was made under stressful circumstances, with Welles often re-writing during the shooting. It was edited several times and finally released two years after its completion, but failed commercially and critically. His final Hollywood project, a version of *Macbeth* for Republic Studios, was also considered a commercial flop.

Disenchanted with Hollywood, Welles left for Europe, where he began the practice of acting in other directors' films in order to finance his own projects. His portrayal of Harry Lime in Carol Reed's *The Third Man* is considered his finest work from this period, and Welles continued to create villainous antagonists who are often more interesting, complex, or exciting than the protagonists of the films. In the roles of Col. Haki in *Journey Into Fear,* Will Varner in Martin Ritt's *The Long Hot Summer,* Quinlan in *Touch of Evil,* and in *Mr. Arkadin,* Welles created a sinister persona for which he has become as famous as for his direction of *Citizen Kane.* His last roles were often caricatures of that persona, as in Marlo Thomas's *It Happened One Christmas,* or parodies as in *The Muppet Movie.*

Welles's European ventures include his *Othello,* shot over a period of years between acting assignments, often under chaotic circumstances. The difficulties of the film's production are often described as though they were the madcap adventures of a roguish artist, but in reality it must have been an extreme hardship to assemble and reassemble the cast over the course of the film's shooting. At one point, he "borrowed" equipment under cover of night from the set of Henry King's *The Black Rose* (in which Welles was starring) to quickly shoot a few scenes. Welles later obtained enough financial backing to make *Mr. Arkadin,* a *Kane*-like story of a powerful man who made his fortune as a white slaver, and *Chimes at Midnight.*

Welles returned to America in the late 1950s to direct *Touch of Evil,* starring Charlton Heston. Originally approached only to star in the film, Welles mistakenly thought he was also to direct. Heston intervened and insisted he be allowed to do so. Welles immediately threw out the original script, rewriting it without reading the book, *Badge of Evil,* upon which the script was based. Welles's last works include *The Immortal Story,* a one-hour film made for French television, and *F for Fake,* a strange combination of documentary footage shot by another director, some Welles footage from earlier ventures, and Welles's own narration.

Welles's outsider status in connection with the American film industry is an interesting part of cinema history in itself, but his importance as a director is due to the innovations he introduced through his films and the influence they have had on filmmaking and film theory. Considering the turbulent relationship Welles experienced with Hollywood and the circumstances under which his films were made in Europe, it is surprising there is any thematic and stylistic consistency in his work at all.

The central character in many of his films is often a powerful, egotistical man who lives outside or above the law and society. Kane, Arkadin, and Mr. Clay (*The Immortal Story*) are enabled to do so by their wealth and position; Quinlan (*Touch of Evil*) by his job as a law enforcer, which allows him to commit injustices to suit his own purposes. Even George Minafer (*Ambersons*) becomes an outsider as a modern, industrialized society supersedes his aristocratic, nineteenth-century way of life. These characters are never innocent, but seem to be haunted by an innocence they have lost. *Kane's* "Rosebud," the emblem of childhood that he clings to, is the classic example, but this theme can also be found in *Mr. Arkadin,* where Arkadin is desperate to keep his daughter from discovering his sordid past. Many parallels between the two films have been drawn, including the fact that the title characters are both wealthy and powerful men whose past lives are being investigated by a stranger. Interestingly, just as Kane whispers "rosebud" on his deathbed, Arkadin speaks his daughter's name at the moment of his death.

Quinlan, in *Touch of Evil,* is confronted with his memories and his past when he runs into Tanya, now a prostitute in a whorehouse. The ornaments and mementoes in her room (some of them from Welles's personal collection), seem to jog his memory of a time when he was not a corrupt law official. In *Shanghai,* it is interesting to note that Welles does not portray the egotist, Bannister, but instead the "innocent" Michael O'Hara, who is soiled by his dealings with Bannister's wife. That the corrupt antagonist is doomed is often indicated by a prologue or introductory sequence which foreshadows his destruction—the newsreel sequence in *Kane*; the opening montage of *Ambersons,* which condenses eighteen years of George Minafer's life into ten minutes to hint that George will get his "comeuppance" in the end; the opening funeral scene of *Othello*; and the detailing of Mr. Clay's sordid past in *The Immortal Story.* The themes of lost innocence and inescapable fate often shroud Welles's films with a sense of melancholy, which serves to make these characters worthy of sympathy.

Much has been made of Welles's use of deep-focus photography, particularly in *Kane* and *Ambersons.* Though a directorial presence is often suggested in the cinema through the use of editing, with Welles it is through mise-en-scène, particularly in these two films. Many Welles scholars discuss the ambiguous nature of long-shot/deep-focus photography, where the viewer is allowed to sift through the details of a scene and make some of his own choices about what is important to the narrative, plot development, and so on. However, Welles's arrangement of actors in specific patterns; his practice of shooting from unusual angles; and his use of wide-angle lenses, which distort the figures closest to them, are all intended to convey meaning. For example, the exaggerated perspective of the scene where Thatcher gives young Charles Kane a sled makes Thatcher appear to tower over the boy, visually suggesting his unnatural and menacing hold on him (at least from young Kane's point of view).

Welles also employed rather complex sound tracks in *Kane* and *Ambersons,* perhaps a result of his radio experience. The party sequence of *Ambersons,* for example, makes use of overlapping dialogue as the camera tracks along the ballroom, as though one were passing by, catching bits of conversation.

Welles's visual style becomes less outrageous and less concerned with effects as his career continued. There seems to be an increasing concentration on the acting in his latter works, particularly in the Shakespeare films. Welles had a lifelong interest in Shakespeare and his plays, and is well known for his unique handling and interpretations of the material. *Macbeth,* for example, was greatly simplified, with much dialogue omitted and scenes shifted around. A primitive feel is reflected by badly synchronized sound, and much of the impact of the spoken word is lost. *Othello,* shot in Italy and Morocco, makes use of outdoor locations in contrast to the staginess of *Macbeth.* Again, Welles was quite free with interpretation: Iago's motives, for example, are suggested to be the result of sexual impotency. His most successful adaptation of Shakespeare is *Chimes at Midnight,* an interpretation of the Falstaff story with parts taken from *Henry IV,* parts one and two, *Henry V, Merry Wives of Windsor,* and *Richard II.* In *Chimes,* Falstaff, as with many of Welles's central characters, is imprisoned by the past. Like George Minafer, he straddles two ages, one medieval and the other modern. Falstaff is destroyed not only by the aging process but also by the problems of being forced into a new world, as is Minafer (and perhaps Kane). Again Welles is quite individualistic in his presentation of the material, making Falstaff a true friend to the king and an innocent, almost childlike, victim of a new order.

In the years before he died, Welles became known for his appearances in television commercials and on talk shows, playing the part of the celebrity to its maximum. His last role was as a narrator on an innovative episode of the television detective series *Moonlighting,* starring Bruce Willis and Cybill Shepherd. It is unfortunate that his latter-day persona as a *bon vivant* often overshadows his contributions to the cinema.—SUSAN DOLL

Wellman, William

Nationality *American.* **Born** *William Augustus Wellman in Brookline, Massachusetts, 29 February 1896.* **Education** *Attended Newton High School, Newton Highlands, Massachusetts, 1910-14.* **Military Service** *Joined volunteer ambulance corps destined for France, 1917, then joined French Foreign Legion, where he learnt to fly planes; when United States entered World War I, became part of Lafayette Flying Corps, an arm of the Lafayette Escadrille.* **Family** *Married 1) Helene Chadwick, 1918 (divorced 1920); three other marriages 1920-33; 5) Dorothy Coonan, 1933, seven children.* **Career** *Professional ice hockey player for minor league team, 1914; film actor, United States, from 1919; messenger for Goldwyn Pictures, then directed first film, 1920; director for 20th Century-Fox, 1923; signed by Paramount, 1927.* **Awards** *Oscar for* Wings, *1927; Oscar for Best Writing (Original Story) for* A Star is Born *(shared with Robert Carson), 1937.* **Died** *9 December 1975.*

Films as Director: **1920:** *The Twins from Suffering Creek.* **1923:** *The Man Who Won; 2nd Hand Love; Big Dan; Cupid's Fireman.* **1924:** *The Vagabond Trail; Not a Drum Was Heard; The Circus Cowboy.* **1925:** *When Husbands Flirt.* **1926:** *The Boob; The Cat's Pajamas; You Never Know Women.* **1927:** *Wings.* **1928:** *The Legion of the Condemned; Ladies of the Mob; Beggars of Life.* **1929:** *Chinatown Nights; The Man I Love; Woman Trap.* **1930:** *Dangerous Paradise; Young Eagles; Maybe It's Love.* **1931:** *Other Men's Women; The Public Enemy; Night Nurse; Star Witness; Safe in Hell.* **1932:** *The Hatchet Man; So Big; Love is a Racket; The Purchase Price; The Conquerors.* **1933:** *Frisco Jenny; Central Airport; Lily Turner; Midnight Mary; Heroes for Sale; Wild Boys of the Road; College Coach.* **1934:** *Looking for Trouble; Stingaree; The President Vanishes.* **1935:** *The Call of the Wild.* **1936:** *The Robin Hood of Eldorado* (+co-sc); *Small Town Girl.* **1937:** *A Star is Born* (+co-sc); *Nothing Sacred.* **1938:** *Men with Wings* (+pr). **1939:** *Beau Geste* (+pr); *The Light That Failed* (+pr). **1941:** *Reaching for the Sun* (+pr). **1942:** *Roxie Hart; The Great Man's Lady* (+pr); *Thunder Birds.* **1943:** *The Ox-Bow Incident; The Lady of Burlesque.* **1944:** *Buffalo Bill.* **1945:** *This Man's Navy; The Story of G.I. Joe.* **1946:** *Gallant Journey* (+pr, co-sc). **1947:** *Magic Town.* **1948:** *Iron Curtain.* **1949:** *Yellow Sky; Battleground.* **1950:** *The Next Voice You Hear.* **1951:** *Across the Wide Missouri.* **1952:** *Westward the Women; It's a Big Country* (co-d); *My Man and I.* **1953:** *Island in the Sky.* **1954:** *The High and the Mighty; Track of the Cat.* **1955:** *Blood Alley.* **1958:** *Darby's Rangers; Lafayette Escadrille* (+pr, co-sc).

Other Film: **1919:** *Knickerbocker Buckaroo* (Parker) (role).

William Wellman's critical reputation is in many respects still in a state of flux long after re-evaluations and recent screenings of his major films should have established some consensus of opinion regarding his place in the pantheon of film directors. While there is some tentative agreement that he is, if nothing else, a competent journeyman director capable of producing entertaining male-dominated action films, other opinions reflect a wide range of artistic evaluations, ranging from comparisons to D.W. Griffith to outright condemnations of his films as clumsy and uninspired. His own preferred niche, as indicated by his flamboyant personality and his predilection for browbeating and intimidating his performers, would probably be in the same general class as highly masculine filmmakers like Howard Hawks, John Ford, and Raoul Walsh. While those three enjoy a distinct _auteur_ status, a similar designation for Wellman is not so easily arrived at since much of his early work for Warner Bros. in the late 1930s is, at first glance, not easily distinguishable from the rest of the studio's output of sociological problem films and exposés of organized crime. In addition, his later films do not compare favorably, in many scholars' opinions, to treatments of similar themes (often employing the same actors and locales) by both Ford and Hawks.

It might be argued, however, that Wellman actually developed what has come to be regarded as the Warner Bros. style to a greater degree than did the studio's other directors. His 1931 _The Public Enemy,_ for example, stands above most of the other gangster films of the era in its creative blend of highly vivid images and in the subtle

William Wellman

manner in which it created a heightened impression of violence and brutality by giving only hints of it on the screen. Exhibiting similar subtlety, Wellman's depiction of a gangster, beginning with his childhood, graphically alluded to the sociological roots of organized crime. While many of his more typical treatments of men in adversity, like 1927's Academy Award-winning _Wings,_ were sometimes artificial, everything worked in _Public Enemy._

In Wellman's later films like _The Ox-Bow Incident, The Story of G.I. Joe,_ and _Battleground,_ the interactions of men in various groupings are shaped in such a way as to determine the direction and thematic force of each story. In others, like _Track of the Cat,_ the emphasis shifts instead to one individual and his battle with forces of nature beyond his control. Yet in all cases, the issue is one of survival, a concept that manifests itself in some manner in all of Wellman's films. It is overt and recognizable in war dramas like _Battleground_ or in a disaster film like _The High and the Mighty,_ but it is reflected at least as much in the psychological tensions of _Public Enemy_ as it is in the violence. It becomes even more abstract in a complex picture like _Track of the Cat_ when the issue concerns the family unit and the insecurity of its internal relationships. In the more heavy-handed propaganda films such as _The Iron Curtain_ and _Blood Alley,_ the theme centers on the threat to democratic forms of government, and finally, in the _Ox-Bow Incident,_ the issue is the very fragility of society itself in the hands of a mob.

Wellman's supporters feel that these concerns arise from the latent cynicism of a disappointed romantic but are expressed by an instinctive artist with a keen awareness of the intellectual force of images conveyed with the raw power of many of those in _Public Enemy._ Yet it is the inconsistency of these images and a corresponding lack of inspiration in his work overall that clouds his stature as an _auteur_ of the first rank. While, ultimately, it is true that Wellman's films cannot be easily separated from the man behind them, his best works are those that sprang from his emotional and psychological experiences. His lesser ones have been overshadowed by the cult of his personality and are best remembered for the behind-the-scenes fistfights, parties, and wild stunts, all of which detracted from the production. Perhaps he never got the chance to make the one indisputable masterpiece that would thematically support all of the seemingly irreconcilable aspects of his personality and firmly establish him as a director of the first magnitude.—STEPHEN L. HANSON

Wenders, Wim

Nationality *German.* **Born** *Wilhelm Wenders in Düsseldorf, 14 August 1945.* **Education** *Studied medicine and philosophy; studied at Hochschule für Fernsehen und Film, Munich, 1967-70.* **Family** *Married Ronee Blakley, 1979 (divorced 1981).* **Career** *Film critic in Munich for* Süddeutsche Zeitung *and* Filmkritik, *late 1960s; professional filmmaker, from 1971.* **Awards** *Golden Lion, Venice Festival, for* The State of Things, *1982; Best Director, Cannes Festival, for* Wings of Desire, *1987.* **Agent** *c/o Gary Salt, The Paul Kohner Agency, 9169 Sunset Blvd., Los Angeles, California 90069, U.S.A.*

Films as Director: 1967: *Schauplätze* (*Locations*) (+pr, sc, ed) (short); *Same Player Shoots Again* (short) (+pr, sc, ed). **1968:** *Silver City* (short) (+pr, sc, ed); *Victor I* (short). **1969:** *Alabama—2,000 Light Years* (short) (+sc, ed); *Drei amerikanische LPs* (*Three American LPs*) (short). **1970:** *Polizeifilm* (*Police Film*) (short) (+co-sc); *Summer in the City* (*Dedicated to the Kinks*) (diploma film) (+sc, role). **1971:** *Die Angst des Tormanns beim Elfmeter* (*The Goalie's Anxiety at the Penalty Kick*) (+co-sc). **1972:** *Der scharlachrote Buchstabe* (*The Scarlet Letter*) (+co-sc). **1973:** *Alice in den Städten* (*Alice in the Cities*) (+co-sc, role). **1974:** *Aus der Familie der Panzerechsen* (*From the Family of the Crocodilia*) (short, for TV); *Die Insel* (*The Island*) (short, for TV); *Falsche Bewegung* (*Wrong Movement*). **1976:** *Im Lauf der Zeit* (*Kings of the Road*) (+sc); *In the Course of Time.* **1977:** *Der amerikanische Freund* (*The American Friend*) (+co-sc, role). **1981:** *Lightning Over Water* (*Nick's Film*) (+co-sc). **1982:** *Hammett; Der Stand der Dinge* (*The State of Things*) (+co-sc). **1984:** *Paris, Texas; Room 666* (doc). **1985:** *Tokyo-Ga* (doc) (+sc). **1987:** *Der Himmel über Berlin* (*Wings of Desire*) (+co-sc). **1989:** *Aufzeichnungen zu Kleidern und Städten* (*Notebook on Cities and Clothes*) (doc). **1991:** *Bis ans Ende der Welt* (*Until the End of the World*) (+co-sc). **1993:** *In weiter Ferne, so nah!* (*Faraway, So Close*) (+co-sc). **1994:** *Arisha, der Bär und der steinerne Ring* (*Arisha, the Bear and the Stone Ring*) (+pr, sc, role as Santa Claus). **1995:** *Lisbon Story* (+co-pr, sc); *Par-delà les nuages* (*Beyond the Clouds*) (co-d with Antonioni, +co-sc); *Lumière et compagnie* (*Lumière and Company*) (co-d); *Die Gebrüder Skladanowsy* (*The Brothers Skladanowsky*). **1997:** *The End of Violence* (+co-sc). **1998:** *The Million Dollars Hotel* (+co-sc).

Other Films: 1978: *Long Shot* (Hatton) (role). **1985:** *I Played it For You* (Blakley) (role). **1987:** *Helsinki Napoli: All Night Long* (Mika Kaurismaki); *Yer Demir, Gok Bakir* (Livaneli) (pr). **1990:** *Isabelle Eberhardt* (Pringle) (pr).

Of the three young German filmmakers who achieved the greatest international fame in the 1970s as the vanguard of a German New Wave, Wim Wenders had perhaps a less radical though no less distinctive film style than his compatriots R. W. Fassbinder and Werner Herzog. Though critics typically cite American influences upon Wenders's "road trilogy" of the mid-1970s, there is a greater affinity with the modernist tradition of the European "art film" exemplified by the Antonioni of *L'avventura* and *Red Desert*—dramas of alienation in which restless, unrooted individuals wander through haunted, sterile, but bleakly beautiful landscapes within a free-floating narrative structure. (It is most appropriate that Wenders has directed the "frame" sections for some short pieces by the aged Italian master.) True, the *ennui* in these films shades into *angst* and American Beat gestures, and the alienation has strong roots in the spiritual

yearning, the love of loneliness and wandering, of German Romanticism. Romanticism
seems too to be at the root of Wenders's
conception of himself (well articulated in
numerous interviews) as an artist: one who
evolves spiritually with each work, or reaches dead ends (as he has called *The State of
Things*) from which he must break out; and
who sees each new work as an adventure,
not to be mapped out too much in advance.

A crucial observation about Wenders's
art is found in cinematographer Ed Lachman's
remark that "light and landscape are actors"
in his films. Wenders's characters are typically revealed against urban or rural landscapes,
upon which the camera frequently lingers as
the actors pass from the frame. Most of the
films take place predominantly out-of-doors
(the studio sets of *Hammett* making that film
all the more of an anomaly), or offer striking
views from high-rise windows and moving
vehicles. The urban views most often sug-

Wim Wenders. *Photograph Stephane Fefer.*

gest sterility but have a certain grandeur, sharing with his views of desert (*Paris, Texas*) or sea
(*The State of Things*) that vastness the Romantics called "sublime." The climactic scene in the
peep-show booth in *Paris, Texas* is all the more powerful and inventive in the context of the epic
vistas of the rest of the film. And the urban scene finally becomes the central "actor" in *Wings of
Desire/Himmel über Berlin,* indeed a "Symphony of a Great City," in which the Wall is no barrier
to the gliding camera or the angelic inhabitants.

Wenders's films are dialectical: they structure contrasts not as simple polarities but as rich
ongoing dialogue, and the later films seem to be in dialogue with the earlier ones. Among the
central concerns from film to film are American versus European culture, the creation of mood
versus tight narrative, a sense of "home" versus rootless "freedom," and even black-and-white
versus color photography.

Wenders's ambivalent fascination with America has been a favorite topic for critics. None
of his films is without interest in this regard, but *Alice in the Cities* is the first to be shot partially in
America—a world of boardwalks, motels, neon, and skyscrapers, though still not so different
from the urban, industrial Europe of the second half; it is also his first feature to make extensive
use of American music, including the Chuck Berry concert in Wuppertal. *The American Friend* is
a dizzying vortex of allusiveness, with its gangsters and cowboys, iconographic presences of
Nicholas Ray and Dennis Hopper, miniature Statue of Liberty in Paris, Ripley's digs in Hamburg,
hints of an allegory of the American film industry in Germany (the pornographers seducing the
hapless framemaker), and a narrative derived from a novel by an expatriate American and
strongly echoing *Strangers on a Train*. Wenders's "American period" from *Hammett* through
Paris, Texas is of course of central interest here, with a whimsically mystical and lyrical

embracing of humanity and the particulars of physical life that recalls Walt Whitman. Wenders still calls his production company "Road Movies" (in English).

The mid-1970s films may owe much to the American "road movie" of a few years earlier (themselves echoing Kerouac's *On the Road*), but the classical Hollywood cinema is defined by its tight narrative structures, and Wenders can be felt to be wrestling with such a structure in *The American Friend*. He has said of *Paris, Texas*, in a *Film Quarterly* interview, "For once I was making a movie that wasn't meandering all over the place. That's what Sam [Shepard] brought to this movie of mine as an American writer: forward movement, which is very American in a way." Still, *Paris, Texas* is very unlike a classical Hollywood film, though the problematic *Hammett,* ironically enough, *is* like one; and the later *Wings of Desire* is much more a fantasia upon a great city than a classical symphony. (*Tokyo-Ga* too meanders through a great city rather than being a tight documentary on Yasujiro Ozu.)

Also explored dialectically are the concepts of home and homelessness, omni-present concerns in Wenders's films. *Alice in the Cities, Kings of the Road,* and *Until the End of the World* could all have as epigraph a Barbara Stanwyck line from *Clash by Night* quoted by Wenders in a piece on Fritz Lang: "Home is where you get when you run out of places." *The State of Things* is perhaps Wenders's most bleak portrayal of homelessness, while *Paris, Texas* expresses the greatest yearning for home, and *Until the End of the World* portrays home as a trap (both womblike and filled with scientific gadgetry) of obligations to parents—a place the viewers too are trapped for the second half of a long film. *Wings of Desire* features an angel wishing he could "come home like Philip Marlowe and feed the cat;" an acrobat who has always felt "alone" and unattached, but now, in love, can feel "loneliness," which means "I am finally whole;" and a conclusion in which the former angel muses, "I found Home . . . instead of forever hovering above"—like Wenders's camera in this film. Obviously the issues of home/homelessness shade into the other prominent Wenders theme of aloneness versus tentative human bonds, explored especially in terms of adult-child friendships, unstable male bondings (see *Faraway, So Close* for its treatments of both of these), and in *Wings,* the angelic/mortal possibilities of adult heterosexual love.

Until the End of the World, Wenders's most ambitious project to date, indeed a would-be magnum opus, is quintessentially Wenders in its fascination with home and the road, memory and dream, the mundane and the sublime; yet it disappoints, despite its fine moments. Its early scenes splendidly evoke a future world through decor, a few striking process shots, and multiple uses of video and computer screens; yet the film is flawed in its vague and inconsistent notions of science in the second half, the amateurish handling of the few action scenes, the implausibility of some of the heroine's motives, and above all in the lack of enough meaningful connections between the "dance around the world" of the first half and the Australian home-as-science-lab second half. The Australian landscapes, and the European ones of the very beginning, are hauntingly resonant, like so many in other Wenders films, though the hopscotch around the continents in the first half seems to turn the beauties of Lisbon and rural Japan into mere postcards, an effect seemingly unintended. Perhaps the film succeeds best in its use of various video or computer-generated images to suggest the working—and inseparability—of dreams, memories, and desires. *Faraway, So Close,* the sequel to *Wings of Desire* in which Damiel's angel partner Cassiel too becomes a mortal but finds it much harder to adjust to a world of time, suffers artistically from an attempt to include too many plot strands, to work farcical gangsters and daring rescue attempts into an otherwise private, meditative film. Wenders seems at his best when his stories are starkly simple, with complexity coming from the textures of the films' environments.

Wenders once claimed, with some relish of paradox, or perhaps recollection of *The Wizard of Oz,* that black-and-white was suited to realism, color to fantasy. Hence those stylized tales of murder *The Goalie's Anxiety* and *The American Friend,* as well as the science-fiction *Until the End of the World,* were in color, and the "road trilogy" not, with *Kings of the Road* immediately declaring itself "a Wim Wenders film in black/white." He further claimed himself to be incapable of making a documentary in color—though he was soon to make more than one. Once again *Wings of Desire* seems a synthesis of previous concerns, if not a downright reversal, with the angels seeing the spiritual essence of things in black-and-white but humans perceiving the particularities of mortal life in color. Such inconsistency—or rather, willingness to change perspective—may be taken as representative of the exploratory nature of Wenders's film work as a whole.—JOSEPH MILICIA

Whale, James

Nationality British. Born Dudley, England, 22 July 1889 (some sources state 1896). Military Service Held in prisoner-of-war camp, World War I. Career Cartoonist for The Bystander, from 1910; actor and set designer for Birmingham Repertory Theatre, 1917-25; actor on London stage, from 1925; directed Journey's End on London stage, 1929; moved to Hollywood to direct film version, 1930; director for Universal, mostly of horror films, 1931-41; retired from film to pursue painting, 1941; attempted comeback Hello Out There failed, 1949; occasional stage director, from 1949. Died 30 May 1957.

Films as Director: 1930: *Journey's End.* **1931:** *Waterloo Bridge; Frankenstein.* **1932:** *The Impatient Maiden; The Old Dark House.* **1933:** *The Kiss Before the Mirror; The Invisible Man.* **1934:** *By Candlelight; One More River.* **1935:** *The Bride of Frankenstein; Remember Last Night.* **1936:** *Showboat.* **1937:** *The Road Back; The Great Garrick.* **1938:** *The Port of Seven Seas; Sinners in Paradise; Wives Under Suspicion.* **1939:** *The Man in the Iron Mask.* **1940:** *Green Hell.* **1941:** *They Dare Not Love.*

Although he is primarily remembered as the director of the cult horror films *Frankenstein, The Old Dark House, The Invisible Man,* and *The Bride of Frankenstein,* James Whale contributed much more to the cinema. He also handled such stylish and elegant productions as *Waterloo Bridge* and *One More River,* which had little critical impact when they were first released and are, unfortunately, largely unknown today.

A quite, introspective man, James Whale's background was the stage, notably the original London and New York productions of R.C. Sheriff's pacifist play *Journey's End.* Aside from some work assisting Howard Hughes with the direction of *Hell's Angels* (work which is both negligible and best forgotten), James Whale made his directorial debut with *Journey's End,* a film which illustrates many of the qualities which were to mark Whale's later work: close attention to acting and dialogue, a striving for authenticity in settings, and a thoughtful use of camera (here somewhat hampered by the limits imposed on early talkies).

From 1930 through 1937, while Whale was under contract to Universal and under the patronage of studio production head Carl Laemmle Jr., the director was able to turn out a group of literate and accomplished features. Among his varied productions was the First World War

James Whale

melodrama *Waterloo Bridge,* later remade in a gaudy Hollywood fashion by Mervyn LeRoy, but in this version noteworthy for its honest approach to its leading character's prostitution and a stunning performance by Mae Clarke (a favorite Whale actress). Both *The Invisible Man* and *The Bride of Frankenstein* are influenced by the director's earlier *Frankenstein,* but both contain an element of black humor which lifts them above the common horror film genre. *The Kiss Before the Mirror* and *By Candlelight* possess an intangible charm, while *One More River* is simply one of Hollywood's best depictions of upper-class British life, memorable for the ensemble playing of its cast, headed by Diana Wynyard, and the one-liners from Mrs. Patrick Campbell. *Show Boat* demonstrates that Whale could handle a musical as easily as a romantic drama and is, without question, the finest screen version of the Jerome Kern-Oscar Hammerstein hit.

All of Whale's Universal features were well received with the exception of his last, *The Road Back,* based on an Erich Maria Remarque novel and intended as a sequel to *All Quiet on the Western Front. The Road Back* today appears badly constructed, a problem created in part by the studio's interference with the production out of concern that the German government might find the film unacceptable.

Whale's final films after leaving Universal are uniformly without interest, and contemporary response to them was lukewarm at best. The director simply grew tired of the hassles of filmmaking and retired. It has been suggested that Whale's homosexuality may have been unacceptable in Hollywood and helped to end his career, but he was a very private man who kept his personal life to himself, and it seems unlikely that his sexual preference created any problem for him or his employees; certainly Whale's homosexuality is not evident from his films, unless it be in the casting of the delightfully "camp" Ernest Thesiger in *The Old Dark House* and *The Bride of Frankenstein.*—ANTHONY SLIDE

Wilder, Billy

Nationality American. Born Samuel Wilder in Sucha, Austria (now part of Poland), 22 June 1906; became U.S. citizen, 1934. Family Married Audrey Young. Military Service Served in U.S. Army as colonel in Psychological Warfare Division of the Occupational Government, Berlin, 1945. Career Journalist in Vienna, then in Berlin, from 1926; collaborated with Robert and Kurt Siodmak, Edgar Ulmer, Fred Zinnemann, and Eugen Schüfftan on Menschen am Sonntag, 1929; scriptwriter, mainly for UFA studios, 1929-33;

moved to Paris, co-directed Mauvaise graine, *first directorial effort, then moved to Hollywood, 1933; hired by script department at Columbia, then 20th Century-Fox; hired by Paramount, began collaboration with Charles Brackett on* Bluebeard's Eighth Wife, *1937; directed first American film,* The Major and the Minor, *1942; began making films as independent producer/director with* The Seven Year Itch, *1955; began collaboration with writer I. A. L. Diamond on* Love in the Afternoon, *1957; directed* The Front Page *for Universal, 1974.* **Awards** *Oscars for Best Direction and Best Screenplay (with Charles Brackett), and Best Direction Award, New York Film Critics, for* The Lost Weekend, *1945; Oscar for Best Story and Screenplay (with Charles Brackett), for* Sunset Boulevard, *1950; Oscars for Best Direction and Best Screenplay (with I. A. L. Diamond), Best Direction Award and Best Writing Award (with Diamond), New York Film Critics, for* The Apartment, *1960; American Film Institute Lifetime Achievement Award, 1985; Irving G. Thalberg Award, 1988; Kennedy Center Award, 1990; National Medal of Arts, 1993.* **Address** *c/o Equitable Investment Corporation, P.O. Box 93877, Hollywood, California 90093, U.S.A.*

Films as Director: 1933: *Mauvaise graine* (co-d). **1942:** *The Major and the Minor* (+co-sc). **1943:** *Five Graves to Cairo* (+co-sc). **1944:** *Double Indemnity* (+co-sc). **1945:** *The Lost Weekend* (+co-sc). **1948:** *The Emperor Waltz* (+co-sc); *Foreign Affair* (+co-sc). **1950:** *Sunset Boulevard* (+co-sc). **1951:** *Ace in the Hole* (*The Big Carnival*) (+co-pr, co-sc). **1953:** *Stalag 17* (+pr, co-sc). **1954:** *Sabrina* (+pr, co-sc). **1955:** *The Seven Year Itch* (+co-pr, co-sc). **1957:** *The Spirit of St. Louis* (+co-sc); *Love in the Afternoon* (+co-sc, pr). **1958:** *Witness for the Prosecution* (+co-sc). **1959:** *Some Like It Hot* (+co-sc, pr). **1960:** *The Apartment* (+co-sc, pr). **1961:** *One, Two, Three* (+co-sc, pr). **1963:** *Irma La Douce* (+co-sc, pr). **1964:** *Kiss Me, Stupid* (+co-sc, pr). **1966:** *The Fortune Cookie* (+co-sc, pr). **1970:** *The Private Life of Sherlock Holmes* (+co-sc, pr). **1972:** *Avanti!* (+co-sc, pr). **1974:** *The Front Page* (+co-sc). **1978:** *Fedora* (+co-pr, co-sc). **1981:** *Buddy Buddy* (+co-sc).

Other Films: (in Germany) 1929: *Menschen am Sonntag* (*People on Sunday*) (Siodmak) (co-sc); *Der Teufelsreporter* (co-sc). **1930:** *Seitensprünge* (story). **1931:** *Ihre Hoheit befiehlt* (co-sc); *Der falsche Ehemann* (co-sc); *Emil und die Detektive* (*Emil and the Detectives*) (sc); *Der Mann der seinen Mörder sucht* (*Looking for his Murderer*) (Siodmak) (co-sc). **1932:** *Es war einmal ein Walzer* (co-sc); *Ein blonder Traum* (co-sc); *Scampolo, ein Kind der Strasse* (co-sc); *Das Blaue von Himmel* (co-sc). **1933:** *Madame wünscht keine Kinder* (co-sc); *Was Frauen träumen* (co-sc).

(In the United States) 1933: *Adorable* (Dieterle) (co-story, based on *Ihre Hoheit befiehlt*). **1934:** *Music in the Air* (co-sc); *One Exciting Adventure* (co-story). **1935:** *Lottery Lover* (co-sc). **1937:** *Champagne Waltz* (Sutherland) (co-story). **1938:** *Bluebeard's Eighth Wife* (Lubitsch) (co-sc). **1939:** *Midnight* (Leisen) (co-sc); *What a Life* (co-sc); *Ninotchka* (Lubitsch) (co-sc). **1940:** *Arise My Love* (Leisen) (co-sc). **1941:** *Hold Back the Dawn* (Leisen) (co-sc); *Ball of Fire* (Hawks) (co-sc).

During the course of his directorial career, Billy Wilder succeeded in offending just about everybody. He offended the public, who shunned several of his movies as decisively as they flocked to others; he offended the press with *Ace in the Hole,* the U.S. Congress with *A Foreign Affair,* the Hollywood establishment with *Sunset Boulevard* ("This Wilder should be horsewhipped!" fumed Louis B. Mayer), and religious leaders with *Kiss Me, Stupid;* he offended the critics, both those who found him too cynical and those who found him not cynical enough. And he himself, in the end, seems to have taken offence at the lukewarm reception of his last two films, and retired into morose silence.

Billy Wilder on the set of *Sunset Boulevard*.

Still, if Wilder gave offence, it was never less than intentional. "Bad taste," the tweaking or flouting of social taboos, is a key tactic throughout his work. His first film as director, *The Major and the Minor,* hints slyly at pedophilia, and several other Wilder movies toy with offbeat sexual permutations: transvestism in *Some Like It Hot,* spouse-swapping in *Kiss Me, Stupid,* an ageing woman buying herself a young man in *Sunset Boulevard,* the reverse in *Love in the Afternoon.* Even when depicting straightforward romantic love, as in *The Emperor Waltz,* Wilder cannot resist counterpointing it with the eager ruttings of a pair of dogs.

He also relishes emphasising the more squalid of human motives. *Stalag 17* mocks prison-camp mythology by making a mercenary fixer the only hero on offer, and *Double Indemnity* replays *The Postman Always Rings Twice* with greed replacing honest lust. In *The Apartment* Jack Lemmon avidly demeans himself to achieve professional advancement (symbolised by the key to a lavatory door), and virtually everybody in *Ace in the Hole,* perhaps the most acerbic film ever made in Hollywood, furthers personal ends at the expense of a poor dupe dying trapped in an underground crevice. Wilder presents a disillusioned world, one (as Joan Didion put it) "seen at dawn through a hangover, a world of cheap *double entendres* and stale smoke . . . the true country of despair."

Themes of impersonation and deception, especially emotional deception, pervade Wilder's work. People disguise themselves as others, or feign passions they do not feel, to gain some ulterior end. Frequently, though—all too frequently, perhaps—the counterfeit turns genuine, masquerade love conveniently developing into the real thing. For all his much-flaunted cynicism, Wilder often seems to lose the courage of his own disenchantment, resorting to unconvincing changes of heart to bring about a slick last-reel resolution. Some critics have seen this as blatant opportunism. "Billy Wilder," Andrew Sarris remarked, "is too cynical to believe even his own cynicism." Others have detected a sentimental undertow, one which surfaces in the unexpectedly mellow, almost benign late films like *Avanti!* and *The Private Life of Sherlock Holmes.*

But although, by comparison with a true moral subversive like Buñuel, Wilder can seem shallow and even facile, the best of his work retains a wit and astringent bite that sets it refreshingly off from the pieties of the Hollywood mainstream. When it comes to black comedy, he ranks at least the equal of his mentor, Lubitsch, whose audacity in wringing laughs out of concentration camps (*To Be or Not To Be*) is matched by Wilder's in pivoting *Some Like It Hot* around the St. Valentine's Day Massacre.

The consistency of Wilder's sardonic vision allows him to operate with assurance across genre boundaries. *Sunset Boulevard*—"full of exactness, cleverness, mastery and pleasure, a gnawing, haunting and ruthless film with a dank smell of corrosive delusion hanging over it," wrote Axel Madsen—has yet to be surpassed among Hollywood-on-Hollywood movies. In its cold fatality, *Double Indemnity* qualifies as archetypal *noir,* yet the same sense of characters trapped helplessly in the rat-runs of their own nature underlies both the erotic farce of *The Seven Year Itch* and the autumnal melancholy of *Sherlock Holmes.* Acclamation, though, falls beyond Wilder's scope: his Lindbergh film, *The Spirit of St. Louis,* is respectful, impersonal, and dull.

By his own admission, Wilder became a director only to protect his scripts, and his shooting style is essentially functional. But though short on intricate camerawork and stunning compositions, his films are by no means visually drab. Several of them contain scenes that lodge indelibly in the mind: Swanson as the deranged Norma Desmond, regally descending her final staircase; Jack Lemmon dwarfed by the monstrous perspectives of a vast open-plan office; Ray Milland (*The Lost Weekend*) trudging the parched length of Third Avenue in search of an open pawn-shop; Lemmon again, tangoing deliriously with Joe E. Brown, in full drag with a rose between his teeth. No filmmaker capable of creating images as potent—and as cinematic—as these can readily be written off.—PHILIP KEMP

Wiseman, Frederick

Nationality American. *Born* Boston, 1 January 1930. *Education* Williams College, B.A., 1951; Yale Law School, L.L.B., 1954; Harvard University. *Family* Married Zipporah Batshaw, 29 May 1955, two sons. *Military Service* Served in U.S. Army, 1954-56. *Career* Practiced law in Paris, and began experimental filmmaking, 1956-58; taught at Boston University Law School, 1958-61; bought rights to The Cool World by Warren Miller, and produced documentary version directed by Shirley Clarke; directed first film, Titicut Follies, 1966; received foundation grant to do High School, 1967; directed three films funded in part by PBS and WNET Channel 13 in New York, 1968-71; contracted to make documentaries for WNET, 1971-81; continued to make films for PBS, through 1980s; also theatre director, late 1980s. *Awards* Emmy Award, Best Documentary Direction, for Hospital, 1970; Peabody Award; Career Achievement Award, International Documentary Association. *Address* Zipporah Films, Inc., 1 Richdale Avenue, Suite 4, Cambridge, Massachusetts 02140, U.S.A.

Films as Director, Producer, and Editor: 1967: *Titicut Follies.* **1968:** *High School.* **1969:** *Law and Order.* **1970:** *Hospital.* **1971:** *Basic Training.* **1972:** *Essene.* **1973:** *Juvenile Court.* **1974:** *Primate.* **1975:** *Welfare; Meat.* **1977:** *Canal Zone.* **1979:** *Sinai Field Mission.* **1980:** *Manoeuvre.* **1981:** *Model.* **1982:** *Seraphita's Diary* (+sc). **1983:** *The Store.* **1985:** *Racetrack.* **1986:** *Deaf; Blind; Multi-Handicapped; Adjustment and Work.* **1988:** *Missile.* **1989:** *Near Death.* **1990:** *Central Park.* **1991:** *Aspen.* **1993:** *Zoo.* **1994:** *High School II.* **1995:** *Ballet.*

Other Films: 1964: *The Cool World* (Clarke) (pr). **1968:** *The Thomas Crown Affair* (Jewison) (sc, uncredited).

In the context of their times, Wiseman's classic documentaries of the 1960s and 1970s are comprehensively anti-traditional. They feature no commentary and no music; their soundtracks carry no more than the sounds Wiseman's recorder encounters; they are long, in some cases over three hours; and, until recent years, they were monochrome. Following the Drew/Leacock "direct cinema" filmmakers, Wiseman developed a shooting technique using lightweight equipment and high-speed film to explore worlds previously inaccessible. In direct cinema the aim was to achieve what they considered to be more honest reportage. Wiseman's insight, however, was to recognise that there is no pure documentary, and that all filmmaking is a process of imposing order on the filmed materials.

For this reason he prefers to call his films "reality fictions." Though he shoots in direct cinema fashion (operating the sound system, in his finest achievements in tandem with cameraman William Brayne), the crucial stage is the imposition of structure during editing. As much as forty hours of film may be reduced to one hour of finished product, an activity he has likened to that of a writer structuring a book. This does not mean that Wiseman's films "tell a story" in any conventional sense. The pattern and meaning of Wiseman's movies seem slowly to emerge from events as if somehow contained within them. Only after seeing the film, perhaps more than once, do the pieces fall into place, their significance becoming clear as part of the whole system of relations that forms the movie. Thus, to take a simple example, the opening shots of the school building in *High School* make it look like a factory, yet it is only at the end when the school's principal reads out a letter from a former pupil in Vietnam that the significance of the image becomes clear. The soldier is, he says, "only a body doing a job," and the school a factory for producing just such expendable bodies.

Wiseman is not an open polemicist; his films do not appear didactic. But as we are taken from one social encounter to the next, as we are caught up in the leisurely rhythms of public ritual, we steadily become aware of the theme uniting all the films. In exploring American institutions, at home and

Frederick Wiseman

abroad, Wiseman shows us social order rendered precarious. As he has put it, he demonstrates that "there is a gap between formal and actual practice, between the rules and the way they are applied." What emerges is a powerful vision of people trapped by the ramifications and unanticipated consequences of their own social institutions.

Some critics, while recognising Wiseman's undoubted skill and intelligence, attack him for lack of passion, for not propagandising more overtly. They argue that when he shows us police violence (*Law and Order*), army indoctrination (*Basic Training*), collapsing welfare services (*Welfare*), or animal experiments (*Primate*) he should be more willing to apportion blame and make his commitments clear. But this is to misunderstand his project. Wiseman avoids the easy taking of sides for he is committed to the view that our institutions over-run us in more complex ways than we might imagine. By forcing us to piece together the jigsaw that he offers, he ensures that we understand more profoundly how it is that our institutions can go so terribly wrong. To do that at all is a remarkable achievement. To do it so uncompromisingly over so many years is quite unique.

In the 1980s he sought to broaden his enterprise somewhat. In 1982, for instance, he turned briefly to "fiction," though *Seraphita's Diary* is hardly orthodox and it is an intelligible extension of his interests. The subsequent documentaries, still produced at regular intervals, have perhaps not had quite the same force as his 1970s work. *Central Park,* for instance, is hypnotic in the rhythms of daily life that it invokes, but lacks the sheer power of the earlier films, which focused on the often ferocious tensions found in the collision between social institutions and people at the end of their tethers. Nevertheless, he has had a huge influence on the shape of modern documentary filmmaking, and, with *Welfare* his most compelling achievement, he remains the most sophisticated and intelligent documentarist of postwar cinema.—ANDREW TUDOR

Wyler, William

Nationality American. *Born* Willy Wyler in Mulhouse (Mülhausen), Alsace-Lorraine, 1 July 1902; became U.S. citizen, 1928. *Family* Married 1) Margaret Sullavan, 1934 (divorced 1936); 2) Margaret Tallichet, 1938, four children. *Military Service* U.S. Army Air Corps, 1942-45; major. *Career* Travelled to America at invitation of cousin Carl Laemmle, 1920; worked in publicity department for Universal in New York, then transferred to Universal City, Hollywood, 1921; assistant director at Universal, from 1924; directed first film, Crook Buster, 1925, and first feature, Lazy Lightning, 1926; signed contract with Samuel Goldwyn, 1936; helped to found Committee for the First Amendment to counteract Hollywood investigations by House Un-American Activities Committee, 1947; "Hommage à William Wyler" organized by Henri Langlois at the Cinémathèque française, 1966; retired from directing, 1972. *Awards* Oscar for Best Direction, for Mrs. Miniver, 1942; Oscar for Best Direction and New York Film Critics Award for Best Direction, for The Best Years of Our Lives, 1946; Oscar for Best Direction, for Ben Hur, 1959; Irving G. Thalberg Award, 1965; American Film Institute Lifetime Achievement Award, 1976. *Died* 29 July 1981.

Films as Director: 1925: *Crook Buster.* **1926:** *The Gunless Bad Man; Ridin' for Love; Fire Barrier; Don't Shoot; The Pinnacle Rider; Martin of the Mounted; Lazy Lightning; Stolen Ranch.* **1927:** *Two Fister; Kelly Gets His Man; Tenderfoot Courage; The Silent Partner; Galloping Justice; The Haunted Homestead; The Lone Star; The Ore Riders; The Home Trail; Gun Justice; Phantom Outlaw; Square Shooter; The Horse Trader; Daze in the West; Blazing Days; Hard Fists; The Border Cavalier; Straight Shootin'; Desert Dust.* **1928:** *Thunder Riders; Anybody Here Seen Kelly.* **1929:** *The Shakedown; The Love Trap.* **1930:** *Hell's Heroes; The Storm.* **1931:** *A House Divided.* **1932:** *Tom Brown of Culver.* **1933:** *Her First Mate; Counselor at Law.* **1934:** *Glamour; The Gay Deception.* **1936:** *These Three; Dodsworth; Come and Get It.* **1937:** *Dead End.* **1938:** *Jezebel.* **1939:** *Wuthering Heights.* **1940:** *The Westerner; The Letter.* **1941:** *The Little Foxes.* **1942:** *Mrs. Miniver.* **1944:** *Memphis Belle.* **1946:** *The Best Years of Our Lives.* **1947:** *Thunder-Bolt.* **1949:** *The Heiress.* **1951:** *Detective Story.* **1952:** *Carrie.* **1953:** *Roman Holiday.* **1955:** *The Desperate Hours.* **1956:** *Friendly Persuasion.* **1958:** *The Big Country.* **1959:** *Ben-Hur.* **1962:** *The Children's Hour.* **1965:** *The Collector.* **1966:** *How to Steal a Million.* **1968:** *Funny Girl.* **1970:** *The Liberation of L.B. Jones.*

William Wyler's career is an excellent argument for nepotism. Wyler went to work for "Uncle" Carl Laemmle, the head of Universal, and learned the movie business as assistant director and then director of programmers, mainly westerns. One of his first important features, *A House Divided,* demonstrates many of the qualities that mark his films through the next decades. A transparent imitation of Eugene O'Neill's *Desire under the Elms,* it contains evidence of the staging strategies that identify Wyler's distinctive mise-en-scène. The film's premise holds particular appeal for a director who sees drama in claustrophobic interiors, the actors held in expressive tension by their shifting spatial relationships to each other, the decor, and the camera. In *A House Divided* Wyler extracts that tension from the dynamics implicit in the film's principal set: the downstairs room that confines the crippled father (Walter Huston) and the stairs leading to the landing between the rooms of the son (Kent Douglass) and the young stepmother (Helen Chandler). The stairway configuration is favored by Wyler for the opportunity it gives him to stack the agents of the drama and to fill the frame both vertically and in depth. When he later collaborates with cinematographer Gregg Toland, the potential of that depth and height is enhanced through the use of varying degrees of hard and soft focus. (Many critics, who are certainly unfamiliar with Wyler's early work, have unjustly credited Toland for the depth of staging that characterizes the partnership.)

The implications of focus in Wyler's stylistics go far beyond lighting procedures, lenses, or even staging itself. Focus directs the viewer's attention to varieties of information within the field, whatever its shape or extent. Focus gives simultaneous access to discordant planes, characters, and objects that challenge us to achieve a full, fluctuating reading of phenomena. André Bazin, in his important essay on Wyler in the French edition of _What Is Cinema?,_ speaks of the director's "democratic" vision, his way of taking in the wholeness of a field in the unbroken time and space of the _plan-séquence,_ a shot whose duration and complexity of staging goes far beyond the measure of the conventional shot. Bazin opposes this to the analytic montage of Soviet editing. In doing so he

William Wyler directing _Funny Girl._

perhaps underestimates the kind of control that Wyler's deep field staging exerts upon the viewer, but he does suggest the richness of the visual text in Wyler's major films.

Counselor At Law is a significant test of Wyler's staging. The Broadway origins of the property are not disguised in the film; instead, they are made into a virtue. The movement through the law firm's outer office, reception room, and private spaces reflects a fluidity that is a function of the camera's mobility and a challenge to the fixed frame of the proscenium. Wyler's _tour de force_ rivals that of the film's star, John Barrymore. Director and actor animate the attorney's personal and professional activities in a hectic, ongoing present, sweeping freely through the sharply delineated (and therefore sharply perceived) vectors of the cinematic/theatrical space.

Wyler's meticulousness and Samuel Goldwyn's insistence on quality productions resulted in the series of films, often adaptations of prestigious plays, that most fully represent the director's method. In _Dodsworth,_ the erosion of a marriage is captured in the opening of the bedroom door that separates husband and wife; the staircase of _These Three_ delimits the public and private spaces of a film about rumor and intimacy; the elaborate street set of _Dead End_ is examined from a dizzying variety of camera angles that create a geometry of urban life; the intensity of _The Little Foxes_ is sustained through the focal distances that chart the shape of family ties and hatreds.

After the war, the partnership of Wyler and Toland is crowned by _The Best Years of Our Lives,_ a film whose subject (the situation of returning servicemen) is particularly pertinent, and whose structure and staging are the most personal in the director's canon.

In his tireless search for the perfect shot, Wyler was known as the scourge of performers, pushing them through countless retakes and repetitions of the same gesture. Since performance in his films is *not* pieced together in the editing room but is developed in complex blockings and shots of long duration, Wyler required a high degree of concentration on the part of the actors. Laurence Olivier, who was disdainful of the medium prior to his work in *Wuthering Heights,* credits Wyler for having revealed to him the possibilities of the movies. But it is Bette Davis who defines the place of the star actor in a Wyler film. The three projects she did with Wyler demonstrate how her particular energies both organize the highly controlled mise-en-scène and are contained within it. For *Jezebel* she won her second Academy Award. In *The Letter,* an exercise in directorial tyranny over the placement of seemingly every element in its highly charged frames, the viewer senses a total correspondence between the focus exercised by director and performer.

During the last decades of Wyler's career, many of the director's gifts, which flourished in contexts of extreme dramatic tension and the exigencies of studio shooting, were dissipated in excessively grandiose properties and "locations." There were, however, exceptions. Wyler's presence is strongly felt in the narrow staircase of *The Heiress* and the dingy station house of *Detective Story.* He even manages to make the final shootout of *The Big Country* adhere to the narrowest of gulches, thereby reducing the dimensions of the title to his familiar focal points. But the epic scope of *Ben Hur* and the ego of Barbra Streisand (in *Funny Girl*) escape the compact economies of the director's boxed-in stackings and plane juxtapositions. Only in *The Collector,* a film that seems to define enclosure (a woman is kept prisoner in a cellar for most of its duration) does Wyler find a congenial property. In it he proves again that the real expanse of cinema is measured by its frames.—CHARLES AFFRON

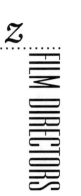

Zhang Yi-Mou

*Nationality Chinese. **Born** Zhang Yi-Mou in Xian, Shaanxi Province, China, 1950. **Education** Beijing Film Academy. **Family** Married 1) Hua Xie (divorced); 2) Xiao Hu in 1982 (separated in 1991), daughter Zhang Mo. **Career** Forced to work for ten years as a field laborer during the Cultural Revolution (1968-78); photographer and artist; camera operator; cinematographer, actor, and director as one of the "Fifth Generation" Chinese filmmakers (so-called because the students in 1982 were only the fifth class to be graduated from the Beijing Film Academy since its establishment in the early 1950s). **Awards** Golden Bear, Berlin Film Festival, 1988, for* Red Sorghum; *Silver Lion, Venice Film Festival, 1991, for* To Live.

Films as Director: 1987: *Hong Gao Liang* (*Red Sorghum*) (+role). **1989:** *Daihao Meizhoubao* (*Operation Cougar, Codename Cougar*). **1990:** *Ju Dou.* **1991:** *Da Hong Deng Long Gao Gao Gua* (*Raise the Red Lantern*). **1992:** *Qiu Ju Da Guan Si* (*The Story of Qiu Ju*). **1994:** *Huozhe* (*To Live, Living, Lifetimes*). **1995:** *Yao a yao yao dao waipo yiao* (*Shanghai Triad*); *Lumière et compagnie* (*Lumiere and Company*). **1997:** *Keep Cool.*

Other Films: 1983: *Yi Ge He Ba Ge* (*One and Eight*) (ph). **1984:** *Huang Tu Di* (*Yellow Earth*) (Chen Kaige) (ph). **1986:** *Lao Jing* (*Old Well*) (ph, role); *Da Yue Bing* (*The Big Parade*) (Chen Kaige) (ph). **1989:** *Qin Yong* (*The Terracotta Warrior*) (role).

With a handful of international film awards and two Academy Award nominations for best foreign film (*Ju Dou* in 1990, and *Raise the Red Lantern* in 1991), Zhang Yi-Mou has emerged as the most distinguished and celebrated of mainland China filmmakers. This success is particularly admirable in view of the fact that, following a promising early education, Zhang was tragically forced to work for ten years as a field laborer during China's notorious Cultural Revolution and was not admitted to the Beijing Film Academy until he was twenty-seven. It was Zhang's sheer will to survive that carried him through the tortuous (and, he claims above all, excruciatingly boring) years of the Cultural Revolution.

Zhang Yi-Mou:
The Story of Qiu Ju

Given the decade he spent as a laborer, it comes as little surprise that Zhang Yi-Mou's films are rich, colorful, epic, dramatic tributes to the forbearance and integrity of everyday Chinese people, both contemporary and historic. The Chinese peasants in particular provide him with inspiration, and he manages to massage elements of Jacobean tragedy and Aesopian allegory into all of his narratives, often resulting in a not-so-subtle, unflattering deconstruction of Chinese politics. Following the flood of stultifying, social-realist films made in the Communist era, Zhang and his "Fifth-Generation" colleagues have vowed, as he told interviewer Lawrence Chua in the *Village Voice* (2 April 1991), "never to make films that go backwards."

But Zhang is also a cinematographer's director, a result of the painterly eye he secretly developed during his years of forced labor. *Red Sorghum, Raise the Red Lantern,* and *Ju Dou,* for example, are probably best remembered in the West for their sheer beauty—their striking use of China's beloved and redolent reds, from lanterns and silks to sorghum wine and blood. When coupled with his formalized and always-controlled interiors, his scenes become emblematic of the juxtaposition of order and desire—the often Homeric, usually erotic, and seemingly uncontrollable sweep of life, love, pride, politics, and death that engulfs his simple characters.

Red Sorghum was at first hailed in China (and internationally) as a masterpiece. It received seven Golden Rooster Awards in China, and the Golden Bear Award at the Berlin Film Festival in 1988. That same year, it closed the prestigious New York Film Festival and played to sold-out audiences at Cannes. Based on a semi-autobiographical short story by writer Mo Yan, *Red Sorghum* is the story of a proud young girl (actress Gong Li) who has been promised to a lecherous old wine-merchant in exchange for a mule. A series of abductions, a murder and a birth—all amidst fields of sometimes-tall, sometimes-crushed red sorghum—suggest life's arbitrary "lifting of veils." Slavery becomes mastery, and harvest an ode to death—all of which seemed to temporarily blind the conservative Chinese government to Zhang's portrayal of the lead couple's adultery.

Zhang's second feature, *Operation Cougar,* also won considerable acclaim for its portrayal of cooperation between Taiwanese and mainland-Chinese anti-terrorist teams in thwarting an airline hijacking (ironic because no such cooperation has ever been documented). But after the Tiananmen Square massacre in 1989, the Chinese government banned his movies in China and has even refused to allow them to be entered in foreign competitions, unwittingly legitimizing his dramatic vision.

It was only a matter of time before more dogmatic Chinese moviegoers branded *Red Sorghum* as a salacious attempt to downgrade Chinese moral and cultural norms and an attempt to capture the prurient interest of Western audiences. Disapproval spread quickly, and Zhang's third and fourth directorial efforts—*Ju Dou* and *Raise the Red Lantern*—were quickly withdrawn from foreign competition with the ineffectual excuse that they had not been—and were not about to be—released in China. The director has routinely been enjoined from attending ceremonies around the world where his films have been shown and nominated for awards, prompting in many instances the ceremonial placing of an empty chair on the stage as a symbolic international gesture of protest.

There is little doubt that the triumph of rebellion against tradition and authority is what draws the most ire from the government. Moreover, in Zhang's vision, this rebelliousness is being initiated by women, for centuries deemed second-class citizens in Chinese culture. The notion that a resolute woman will lead a modern China out of the fray—toward a youthful future and away from a withering gerontocracy—is a central theme in Zhang's oeuvre. In *Ju Dou,* a self-willed woman (Gong Li) is sold into a slavish marriage, routinely beaten for not bearing her elderly husband a child, and triumphantly flaunts an affair with her husband's nephew in an attempt to carve her way out of her mental and cultural entrapment. In *Raise the Red Lantern,* Zhang's heroine is not quite so successful, falling victim to madness after a vain but glorious attempt to thwart her husband's habit of sleeping round-robin with four caged-bird concubines—at once feeding their pride and placing them in cutthroat competition with each other. In *The Story of Qiu-Ju,* Zhang appears to concede to authorities with a flattering (if unrealistic) portrayal of the efficiency and compassion of the bureaucracy but at the same time centers a stubborn search for justice in the actions of a determined peasant woman. And in *Shanghai Triad,* the director parallels contemporary China's obsession with material goods—and comments on how violence affects human relations—by examining the relationship between a teenage boy and a 1930s mob mistress with a (small) heart of gold.

With the completion of *Keep Cool* (1997)—likewise banned, honored, and used as an excuse to keep Zhang from attending ceremonies at Cannes—Zhang admits to being somewhat worn down by the powers that be. The film is said to be a complete departure from earlier works, a "comedy" about a man who falls in love with a woman and is summarily beaten up by her business partners. And even though there are fewer subtexts and complexities here, Zhang's power to move an audience and elicit strong emotional responses with just his cinematic eye remains unmatchable. His abilities as an innovator and chronicler of an ever-evolving Chinese culture continues unchallenged, even as his hands remain tied at home.

And as art imitates life, Zhang's career increasingly pantomimes the trapped struggles for justice symbolized by his characters. As punishment for *Keep Cool,* Chinese authorities have dictated that all his future films be entirely produced and financed in China, a restriction that would surely prompt a less-dedicated filmmaker to entertain thoughts of emigration. Yet, Zhang fears that leaving China would render his films too abstract—separate him too definitively from empathy for the Chinese people and their plight. "To survive is to win," he has told several interviewers over the years, a sentiment bred in his own hardships and translated to his films with a sure belief in the eventuality of justice.—JEROME SZYMCZAK

Zinnemann, Fred

Nationality *Austrian/American.* **Born** *Vienna, 29 April 1907.* **Education** *Educated in law, University of Vienna, degree 1927; studied one year at the Ecole Technique de Photographie et Cinématographie, Paris.* **Family** *Married Renée Bartlett, 1936, one son.* **Career** *Assistant cameraman in Paris and Berlin, then with Billy Wilder, Eugen Schüfftan, and Robert Siodmak, made* Menschen am Sonntag, *1928; moved to Hollywood, became assistant cameraman and cutter for Berthold Viertel, 1929; worked with Robert Flaherty on unrealized documentary project, Berlin, 1931; worked in Mexico with Paul Strand on* Los Redes, *1934-35; hired by MGM to direct short subjects, 1937; directed first feature, 1942; vice-president, Directors Guild of America, 1961-64.* **Awards** *Oscars for Best Short Subject, for* That Mothers Might Live, *1938, and* Benjy, *1951; Best Direction, New York Film Critics, for* High Noon, *1952; Oscar for Best Director, and Director Award, Directors Guild of America, for* From Here to Eternity, *1953; Best Direction, New York Film Critics, for* The Nun's Story, *1959; Oscar for Best Director, Best Direction, New York Film Critics, and Director Award, Directors Guild of America, for* A Man for All Seasons, *1966; D. W. Griffith Award, 1971; Order of Arts and Letters, France, 1982; U.S. Congressional Lifetime Achievement Award, 1987; John Huston Award, Artists Rights Foundation, 1994.* **Died** *14 March 1997.*

Films as Director: 1934-35: *Los Redes* (*The Wave*). **1938:** *A Friend Indeed* (short for MGM); *The Story of Dr. Carver* (short for MGM); *That Mothers Might Live* (short for MGM); *Tracking the Sleeping Death* (short for MGM); *They Live Again* (short for MGM). **1939:** *Weather Wizards* (short for MGM); *While America Sleeps* (short for MGM); *Help Wanted!* (short for MGM); *One Against the World* (short for MGM); *The Ash Can Fleet* (short for MGM); *Forgotten Victory* (short for MGM). **1940:** *The Old South* (short for MGM); *Stuffie* (short for MGM); *The Way in the Wilderness* (short for MGM); *The Great Meddler* (short for MGM). **1941:** *Forbidden Passage* (short for MGM); *Your Last Act* (short for MGM). **1942:** *The Lady or the Tiger?* (short for MGM); *The Kid Glove Killer; Eyes in the Night.* **1944:** *The Seventh Cross.* **1945:** *Little Mr. Jim.* **1946:** *My Brother Talks to Horses.* **1947:** *The Search.* **1948:** *Act of Violence.* **1950:** *The Men.* **1951:** *Teresa; Benjy* (short). **1952:** *High Noon; The Member of the Wedding.* **1953:** *From Here to Eternity.* **1955:** *Oklahoma.* **1957:** *A Hatful of Rain.* **1958:** *The Nun's Story.* **1960:** *The Sundowners* (+pr). **1963:** *Behold a Pale Horse* (+pr). **1966:** *A Man for All Seasons* (+pr). **1973:** *The Day of the Jackal* (+pr). **1977:** *Julia* (+pr). **1982:** *Five Days One Summer* (+pr) (re-edited version released 1988).

Other Films: 1927: *La Marche des machines* (Deslaw) (asst cameraman). **1929:** *Ich Küsse Ihre Hand, Madame* (Land) (asst cameraman); *Sprengbagger 1010* (Achaz-Duisberg) (asst cameraman); *Menschen am Sonntag* (*People on Sunday*) (Siodmak) (asst cameraman). **1930:** *Man Trouble* (asst d to Berthold Viertel); *All Quiet on the Western Front* (Milestone) (bit role). **1931:** *The Spy* (asst d to Viertel). **1932:** *The Wiser Sex* (asst d to Viertel); *The Man from Yesterday* (asst d to Viertel); *The Kid from Spain* (asst to Busby Berkeley). **1989:** *Stand Under the Dark Clock* (doc) (Walker) (role).

In 1928 Fred Zinnemann worked as assistant to cinematographer Eugene Schüfftan on Robert Siodmak's *Menschen am Sonntag (People on Sunday),* along with Edgar Ulmer and Billy Wilder, who wrote the scenario for this semi-documentary silent feature made in the tradition of Flaherty and Vertov. Having been strongly influenced by realistic filmmaking, particularly the work of Erich von Stroheim, King Vidor, and Robert Flaherty, Zinnemann immigrated to the United States in 1930 and worked with Berthold Viertel, Flaherty ("probably the greatest single influence on my work as a filmmaker," he later stated), and the New York photographer-documentarist Paul Strand on *Los Redes,* the first of a proposed series intended to document everyday Mexican life. *Los Redes* told the story of the struggle of impoverished fishermen to organize themselves against economic exploitation. The film was shot in Vera Cruz, and Zinnemann was responsible for directing the actors.

Zinnemann's documentary training and background developed his style as a "social realist" in a number of early pictures (several shorts he directed, for example, in MGM's *Crime Does Not Pay* and *The Passing Parade* series) during the years 1937-42. His medical short *That Mother Might Live* won an Academy Award and enabled Zinnemann to direct feature films. His first feature at MGM was a thriller, *The Kid Glove Killer*, with Van Heflin and Marsha Hunt. *The Seventh Cross* was adapted from Anna Segher's anti-fascist World War II novel. Starring Spencer Tracy, the film was notable for its atmosphere and documentary style. *The Search,* shot on loca-

Fred Zinnemann on the set of *Julia*.

tion in Europe in 1948, with Montgomery Clift, gave a realistic portrayal of children who had been displaced by the turmoil of World War II and was a critical as well as a commercial success. *The Men* was the first of a three-picture contract Zinnemann signed with Stanley Kramer and dealt with the problem of paraplegic war veterans, marking Marlon Brando's debut as a film actor. Zinnemann filmed *The Men* on location at the Birmingham Veteran's Hospital and used a number of patients there as actors.

Zinnemann's next film for Kramer, *High Noon,* was significant because of the way Zinnemann's realistic style turned the genre of the Western upside down. It featured Gary Cooper in an Oscar-winning performance as Will Kane, a retired marshal who has taken a Quaker bride (Grace Kelly), but whose marriage is complicated by the anticipated return of paroled desperado Frank Miller, expected on the noon train. Zinnemann treated his "hero" as an ordinary man beset with doubts and fears in an existential struggle to protect himself and the community of Haddleyville, a town that proves to be undeserving of his heroism and bravery. Zinnemann created a tense drama by coordinating screen time to approximate real time, which is extended only when the fateful train arrives, bearing its dangerous passenger. Working against the stylized and mythic traditions that had come to dominate the genre, *High Noon* established the trend of the "psychological" Western and represents one of Zinnemann's finest accomplishments.

Zinnemann's last Kramer picture was *The Member of the Wedding*, a Carson McCullers novel that had been adapted into a popular Broadway production by McCullers herself. The film utilized the same cast that had made the stage production successful (Julie Harris, Brandon de Wilde, and Ethel Waters) but created cinematically an effective atmosphere of entrapment. *Member of the Wedding* is a model of effective theatrical adaption. Zinnemann went on to adapt the 1955 movie version of the Rodgers and Hammerstein classic *Oklahoma!*, removing the exclamation point, as one wit noted, in a spacious and lyrical, but also rather perfunctory, effort.

In 1953 Zinnemann moved to Columbia Pictures to direct the adaption of the popular James Jones novel *From Here to Eternity,* a huge popular success starring Montgomery Clift, Frank Sinatra, and Ernest Borgnine that won Zinnemann an Academy Award for Best Director. Zinnemann's approach effectively utilized newsreel footage of the Japanese attack on Pearl Harbor, and his realistic style both tightened and dramatized the narrative. *A Hatful of Rain* applied Zinnemann's documentary approach to the problem of drug addiction in New York. *The Nun's Story* (with Audrey Hepburn and Peter Finch) has been linked to *A Man For All Seasons* in that both reflect conflicts of conscience, a recurring motif in Zinnemann's films. *A Man for All Seasons,* adapted from Robert Bolt's play, won Paul Scofield an Academy Award for his portrayal of St. Thomas More.

Among Zinnemann's political films are *Behold a Pale Horse,* starring Gregory Peck and set during the Spanish Civil War, a picture that also incorporated newsreel authenticity, and *The Day of the Jackal,* a story about an assassin's attempt on the life of Charles de Gaulle, shot on location "like a newsreel." A later and in many ways impressive political film involving a conflict of conscience was Zinnemann's *Julia,* adapted by Alvin Sargent from Lillian Hellman's *Pentimento,* concerning Hellman's love affair with the writer Dashiell Hammett (Jason Robards) and her long-standing friendship with the mysterious Julia (Vanessa Redgrave), the daughter of a wealthy family who becomes a socialist-intellectual politicized by events in Germany under the Nazi regime. *Julia* is a perfect Zinnemann vehicle, impressive in its authenticity and historical reconstruction, and also psychologically tense, particularly in the way Zinnemann films Hellman's suspense-laden journey from Paris to Moscow via Berlin. It demonstrates the director's sense of psychological realism and his apparent determination to make worthwhile pictures that are nevertheless highly entertaining.—JAMES M. WELSH

Affron, Charles Professor of French, New York University, since 1965. Author of *Star Acting: Gish, Garbo, Davis,* 1977; *Cinema and Sentiment,* 1982; *Divine Garbo,* 1985; and *Fellini's 8½,* 1987. General editor of Rutgers Film in Print Series. **Essays:** Capra; Lean; Wyler.

Andrew, Dudley Angelo Bertocci Professor of Critical Studies and director of the Institute for Cinema and Culture, University of Iowa (joined faculty, 1969). Author of *Major Film Theories,* 1976; *André Bazin,* 1978; *Kenji Mizoguchi: A Guide to References and Resources* (co-author), 1981; *Concepts in Film Theory,* 1984; and *Film in the Aura of Art,* 1984. **Essays:** Astruc; Becker; Clément; Clouzot; Grémillion; Mizoguchi.

Armes, Roy Reader in film and television, Middlesex Polytechnic, London. Author of *French Cinema since 1946,* 1966, 1970; *The Cinema of Alain Resnais,* 1968; *French Film,* 1970; *Patterns of Realism,* 1972, 1983; *Film and Reality,* 1974; *The Ambiguous Image,* 1976; *A Critical History of British Cinema,* 1978; *The Films of Alain Robbe-Grillet,* 1981; *French Cinema,* 1985; *Third World Filmmaking and the West,* 1987; *On Video,* 1988; and *Studies in Arab and African Film,* 1991. **Essays:** Carné; Cocteau; Feuillade; Gance; Melville; Sautet.

Basinger, Jeanine Professor of film, Wesleyan University, Middletown, Connecticut, since 1969. Trustee, American Film Institute, National Center for Film and Video Preservation.

Member of Advisory Board, Foundation for Independent Video and Film. Author of *Working with Kazan,* 1973; *Shirley Temple,* 1975; *Gene Kelly,* 1976; *Lana Turner,* 1977; *Anthony Mann: A Critical Analysis,* 1979; *The World War II Combat Book: Anatomy of a Genre,* 1986; *The "It's a Wonderful Life" Book,* 1986; and numerous articles. **Essay:** Siodmak.

Baxter, John Novelist, screenwriter, TV producer, and film historian. Visiting lecturer, Hollins College, Virginia, 1974-75; broadcaster with BBC Radio and Television, 1976-91. Author of six novels, two anthologies of science fiction (editor), various screenplays for documentary films and features, and works of film criticism including: *Hollywood in the Thirties,* 1968; *The Australian Cinema,* 1970; *Science Fiction in the Cinema,* 1970; *The Gangster Film,* 1970; *The Cinema of Josef von Sternberg,* 1971; *The Cinema of John Ford,* 1971; *Hollywood in the Sixties,* 1972; *Sixty Years of Hollywood,* 1973; *An Appalling Talent: Ken Russell,* 1973; *Stunt,* 1974; *The Hollywood Exiles,* 1976; *King Vidor,* 1976; with Brian Norris, *The Video Handbook,* 1982; and *Filmstruck,* 1989. **Essays:** Bogdanovich; Ford; Frankenheimer; Malle; von Sternberg.

Bock, Audie Free-lance author and lecturer. Visiting lecturer at Harvard, Yale, University of California, and others, 1975-83. Assistant producer of the international version of Kurosawa's *Kagemusha,* 1980. Author of *Japanese Film Directors,* 1978, 1985; and *Mikio Naruse: un maitre du cinéma japonais,* 1983; translator of *Something Like an Autobiography* by Kurosawa, 1982. **Essay:** Kurosawa.

Bodeen, DeWitt Screenwriter and film critic. Author of screenplays for *Cat People*, 1942; *Seventh Victim*, 1943; *Curse of the Cat People*, 1944; *The Yellow Canary*, 1944; *The Enchanted Cottage*, 1945; *Night Song*, 1947; *I Remember Mama*, 1948; *Mrs. Mike*, 1959; *Billy Budd*, 1962; and numerous teleplays, 1950-68. Also author of *Ladies in the Footlights; The Films of Cecil B. DeMille; Chevalier; From Hollywood; More from Hollywood; 13 Castle Walk* (novel); editor of *Who Wrote the Movie and What Else Did He Write?* Died 1988. **Essays:** Borzage; Guitry; Korda; Murnau; Stevens; Jacques Tourneur.

Bordwell, David Professor of film, University of Wisconsin—Madison, since 1973. Author of *Filmguide to La Passion de Jeanne d'Arc*, 1973; *Film Art: An Introduction*, with Kristin Thompson, 1979; *French Impressionist Cinema*, 1980; *The Films of Carl-Theodor Dreyer*, 1981; *The Classical Hollywood Cinema: Film Style and Mode of Production to 1960*, with Janet Staiger and Kristin Thompson, 1984; *Narration in the Fiction Film*, 1985; *Ozu and the Poetics of Cinema*, 1988; and *Making Meaning: Inference and Rhetoric in the Interpretation of Cinema*, 1990. **Essay:** Ozu.

Bowles, Stephen E. Associate professor of film, University of Miami, since 1976. Author of *An Approach to Film Study*, 1974; *Index to Critical Reviews from British and American Film Periodicals 1930-71*, 3 volumes, 1974-75; *Sidney Lumet: A Guide to References and Resources*, 1979; and *Index to Critical Film Reviews: Supplement I, 1971-76*, 1983. **Essay:** Lumet.

Burgoyne, Robert Associate professor of English, Wayne State University, Detroit. Contributor to *Film Quarterly, Screen,* and *October.* Author of *Bertolucci's 1900: A Narrative and Historical Analysis*, 1991; and *Imaging Nation: Changing Perspectives on Nation and History in Contemporary American Film*, 1997. Co-author of *New Vocabularies in Film Semiotics*, 1992. **Essay:** Bertolucci.

Ciment, Michel Associate professor in American Studies, University of Paris. Member of the editorial board of *Positif.* Author of *Erich von Stroheim*, 1967; *Kazan by Kazan*, 1973; *Le Dossier Rosi*, 1976; *Le Livre de Losey*, 1979;

Kubrick, 1980; *Les Conquérants d'un nouveau monde*, 1981; *Elia Kazan: An Outsider*, 1982; *All about Mankiewicz*, 1983; *Boorman*, 1985; *Francesco Rosi: Chronique d'un film annoncé*, 1987; and *Passport pour Hollywood*, 1987. **Essays:** Angelopoulos; Skolimowski.

Conley, Tom Professor of French and comparative literature, University of Minnesota. Former editor, *Enclitic;* and contributor to *Theater Journal, MLN, Hors Cadre, Revue des Lettres Modernes,* and *Littérature.* **Essay:** Renoir.

Costa, Kevin J. B.A. in English and Film Studies and M.A. in English, Rhode Island College. Adjunct instructor of writing, Rhode Island College. Pursuing graduate studies in English at State University of New York at Buffalo. **Essay:** Sautet.

Cousins, R.F. Lecturer in French, University of Birmingham. Author of *Zola's Thérèsa Raquin*, 1991. Contributor to *University Vision* and *Literature/Film Quarterly.* Executive member of British Universities Film and Video Council. **Essays:** Lumière; Rouch.

D'Arpino, Tony Free-lance writer. Author of *The Tree Worshipper*, 1983; and *Untitled Zodial*, 1984. **Essay:** Pasolini.

Derry, Charles Ph.D. in Film, Northwestern University. Coordinator of Film Studies, Wright State University, Dayton, Ohio, from 1978. Author of *Dark Dreams: A Psychological History of the Modern Horror Film*, 1977. Co-author, with Jack Ellis and Sharon Kern, of the reference work *The Film Book Bibliography: 1940-1975*, 1979. Director of the short films *Cerebral Accident* and *Joan Crawford Died for Your Sins.* Fiction has appeared in *Reclaiming the Heartland: Gay and Lesbian Voices from the Midwest*, 1996. **Essays:** Altman; Chabrol; Lee; Mulligan; Preminger; Spielberg.

Doll, Susan M. Instructor in film at Oakton Community College and at the School of the Art Institute of Chicago. Author of *Marilyn: Her Life and Legend*, 1990, and *The Films of Elvis Presley*, 1991. **Essay:** Welles.

Durgnat, Raymond Visiting professor of film, Wright State University, Dayton, Ohio. Author of numerous publications on film, including *Durgnat on Film*, 1975; *King Vidor—American*, 1988; and *Michael Powell and the English Genius*, 1991. **Essays:** Clayton; Makavejev.

Edelman, Rob Author of *Great Baseball Films,* 1994. Co-author of *Angela Lansbury: A Life on Stage and Screen,* 1996. Contributing editor of *Leonard Maltin's Movie and Video Guide* and *Leonard Maltin's Movie Encyclopedia.* Director of programming of *Home Film Festival.* Contributor to *The Political Companion to American Film* and *The Whole Film Sourcebook.* Film critic/columnist, *New Haven Register* and *Gazette Newspapers.* Former adjunct instructor, The School of Visual Arts, Iona College, Sacred Heart University. **Essays:** Armstrong; Benton; Bergman; Blier; Burnett; Campion; Costa-Gavras; Dassin; Demme; Demy; Dovzhenko; Erice; Fellini; Forman; Forsyth; Frankenheimer; Godard; Greenaway; Ivory; Jarmusch; Kaurismaki; Kurosawa; Kusturica; Leconte; Loach; Malle; Maysles; Moretti; Marcel Ophuls; Polonsky; Pudovkin; Resnais; Riefenstahl; Roeg; Rohmer; Schlöndorff; Schrader; Tavernier; Varda; Von Trotta.

Ellis, Jack C. Professor of film and former chair of the Department of Radio/Television/Film at Northwestern University, Evanston, Illinois. Also taught at UCLA, New York University, and the University of Texas at Austin. Author of *A History of Film,* 1979, third edition 1990; *John Grierson: A Guide to References and Resources,* 1986; and *The Documentary Idea,* 1989. Founding member and past president of Society for Cinema Studies; editor of society's journal, *Cinema Journal,* 1976-82. **Essay:** Marker.

Elsner-Sommer, Gretchen Film critic and director of Foreign Images distribution company. Formerly asssociate editor of *Jump Cut.* **Essay:** von Trotta.

Erens, Patricia Associate professor, Rosary College, River Forest, Illinois, since 1977. Author of *Akira Kurosawa: A Guide to References and Resources,* 1979; and *The Jew in American Cinema,* 1984; editor of *Sexual Stratagems: The World of Women in Film,* 1979. **Essays:** Ichikawa; Pollack.

Estrin, Mark W. Professor of English and film studies, Rhode Island College, Providence, since 1966. Has published widely on film, dramatic literature, and theatre. Author of books including *Conversations with Eugene O'Neill,* 1990, and *Critical Essays on Lillian Hellman,* 1989. **Essays:** Allen; Nichols.

Faller, Greg S. Associate professor in film, Towson State University, Baltimore, since 1986. Taught at Northwestern University, 1984-86. Assistant/associate editor of *The International Dictionary of Films and Filmmakers,* first edition, volumes 3, 4, and 5; and of *Journal of Film and Video,* 1985-87. Editor of *Film Reader 6,* 1985. **Essays:** Lewis; Lubitsch.

Farnsworth, Rodney Ph.D., Indiana University, 1980. Associate professor of comparative studies, Indiana University-Purdue University, Fort Wayne. Has published internationally in scholarly publications, including *Literature/Film Quarterly.* **Essay:** Herzog.

Felleman, Susan Art historian and author of numerous essays on modern art. Has taught at Hampshire College, the College of Staten Island, and the School of Visual Arts. Author of *Botticelli in Hollywood: Albert Lewin, Director,* 1997. Contributor of articles on film to *Camera Obscura, Iris,* and *Film History.* **Essay:** Lewin.

Felperin, Leslie Graduate student in Film, University of Kent, Canterbury. **Essay:** Armstrong.

Foreman, Alexa Account executive, Video Duplications, Atlanta, since 1986. Formerly theatre manager, American Film Institute. Author of *Women in Motion,* 1983. **Essay:** Malick.

Frampton, Saul Graduate student at the University of Oxford. Contributor to *Time Out* and *20/20.* **Essays:** Davies; Greenaway.

Glaessner, Verina Free-lance critic and lecturer, London. Contributor to *Sight and Sound.* **Essays:** Chen Kaige; Rosi.

Gomery, Douglas Professor, Department of Radio/Television/Film, University of Maryland, and senior researcher, Media Studies Project, Woodrow Wilson Center for International Scholars, Washington, D.C. Author of *High Sierra: Screenplay and Analysis,* 1979; *Film History: Theory and Practice* (co-author), 1985; *The Hollywood Studio System,* 1986; *The Will Hays Papers,* 1987; *American Media* (co-author), 1989; and *Movie History: A Survey,* 1991. **Essays:** Benton; Curtiz; Walsh.

Hanson, Patricia King Executive editor, American Film Institute, Los Angeles, since 1983. Film critic, *Screen International,* since 1986. Associate editor, Salem Press, 1978-83. Editor of *American Film Institute Catalog of Feature*

Films 1911-1920 and *1931-1940.* Co-editor of *Film Review Index,* vols. 1 and 2, 1986-87; and of *Source Book for the Performing Arts,* 1988. **Essays:** Mamoulian; Sirk.

Hanson, Stephen L. Humanities biographer, University of Southern California, Los Angeles, since 1969. Film critic, *Screen International,* since 1986. Associate editor, Salem Press, 1978-83. Co-editor of *Film Review Index,* vols. 1 and 2, 1986-87, and of *Source Book for the Performing Arts,* 1988. **Essays:** Fellini; La Cava; Powell and Pressburger; Rossellini; Wellman.

Heck-Rabi, Louise Formerly free-lance writer, author of *Women Filmmakers: A Critical Reception,* 1984, and producer and co-writer of *Video Slow Reader,* 1991. Died 1995. **Essays:** Riefenstahl; Varda.

Holdstein, Deborah Assistant professor of English, Illinois Institute of Technology, Chicago, since 1980. **Essay:** Pakula.

Hong, Guo-Juin M.A. in Cinema Studies, San Francisco State University. Teacher of courses in Chinese Cinema, Third World Cinema, and Asian American Cinema at San Francisco State University and the University of California, Santa Cruz. Independent documentary filmmaker of projects in affiliation with the Oral History Project of the Gay and Lesbian Historical Society of Northern California. **Essay:** Marker.

Kaminsky, Stuart M. Professor of film, Northwestern University, Evanston, Illinois. Author of *Don Siegel, Director,* 1973; *Clint Eastwood,* 1974; *American Film Genres,* 1977; *John Huston, Maker of Magic,* 1978; *Coop: The Life and Legend of Gary Cooper,* 1980; *Basic Filmmaking* (co-author), 1981; *American Television Genres,* 1985; and *Writing for Television,* 1988. Editor of *Ingmar Bergman: Essays in Criticism,* 1975. Also a novelist; works include *Murder on the Yellow Brick Road,* 1978; *He Done Her Wrong,* 1983; *A Cold, Red Sunrise,* 1988; and *Buried Caesars,* 1989. **Essays:** Huston; Leone.

Kanoff, Joel Lecturer in the visual arts, Princeton University, New Jersey, since 1983. **Essays:** De Sica; Visconti.

Kehr, Dave Film critic, *Chicago Tribune,* since 1986. **Essays:** Edwards; Tati.

Kemp, Philip London-based free-lance reviewer and film historian. Contributor to *Sight and Sound, Variety,* and *Film Comment.* Author of *Lethal Innocence: The Cinema of Alexander Mackendrick,* 1991, and of a forthcoming biography of Michael Balcon. **Essays:** Clair; Mackendrick; Penn; Nicholas Ray; Sayles; Wilder.

Khanna, Satti Research associate, Center for South and Southeast Asia Studies, University of California, Berkeley, since 1976. Author of *Indian Cinema and Indian Life,* 1980. **Essay:** Satyajit Ray.

Kupferberg, Audrey E. Film historian and archivist. Co-author of *Angela Lansbury: A Life on Stage and Screen,* 1996. Former director, Yale University Film Study Center; former assistant director, The National Center for Film and Video Preservation at the American Film Institute; former project director, The American Film Institute Catalog. Former adjunct instructor, University of Bridgeport. **Essay:** Edwards.

Lanza, Joseph Free-lance writer. Author of *Fragile Geometry: The Films, Philosophy and Misadventures of Nicolas Roeg,* 1989. Contributor to *Kirkus Reviews, Performing Arts Journal, ReSearch,* and *Forum.* **Essay:** Roeg.

Lockhart, Kimball Member of the faculty, Department of Romance Studies, Cornell University, Ithaca, New York. Founding editor, *Enclitic,* 1977-80, and member of editorial board, *Diacritics,* since 1978. **Essay:** Antonioni.

Lorenz, Janet E. Associate editor and film critic, *Z Channel Magazine,* since 1984. Assistant supervisor, University of Southern California Cinema Research Library, Los Angeles, 1979-82; and film critic, *SelecTV Magazine,* 1980-84. **Essay:** Losey.

Lowry, Ed Formerly assistant professor of film studies, Southern Illinois University at Carbondale. Contributor to various film periodicals. Died 1987. **Essays:** Aldrich; Minnelli; Stahl.

Macnab, G.C. Free-lance writer, researcher, and filmmaker, London. Author of *J. Arthur Rank and the British Film Industry.* **Essays:** Marcel Ophuls; Rivette; Schrader; Tarkovsky.

Mancini, Elaine Has taught film at the College of Staten Island, and at St. John's University, New York. Author of *The Films of Luchino*

Visconti: A Reference Guide, and *The Struggles of the Italian Film Industry during Fascism.* **Essay:** Lattuada.

Manvell, Roger Formerly professor of film, Boston University. Director, British Film Academy, London, 1947-59; governor and head of Department of Film History, London Film School, until 1974; Bingham Professor of the Humanities, University of Louisville, 1973. Author of numerous novels, biographies, and books on film, including: *Film,* 1944; *The Animated Film,* 1954; *The Living Screen,* 1961; *New Cinema in Britain,* 1969; *Films and the Second World War,* 1975; *Ingmar Bergman,* 1980; and *Images of Madness: The Portrayal of Insanity in the Feature Film,* with Michael Fleming, 1985. Died 1987. **Essays:** Bergman; Méliès; Sjöström; Stiller; von Stroheim.

Marchetti, Gina Associate professor, Comparative Literature Program, University of Maryland, College Park. Author of *Romance and the "Yellow Peril": Race, Sex, and Discursive Strategies in Hollywood Fiction.* **Essay:** Makavejev.

Mast, Gerald Formerly professor of English and general studies in the Humanities, University of Chicago. Author of numerous books on film, including: *A Short History of the Movies,* 1971, third edition, 1981; *The Comic Mind: Comedy and the Movies,* 1974, 1979; *Film/Cinema/Movie: A Theory of Experience,* 1977, 1982; and *Howard Hawks: Storyteller,* 1982. Died 1987. **Essays:** Chaplin; Hawks; Keaton; Sennett; Truffaut.

McCarty, John Free-lance writer, East Greenbush, New York. Host, narrator, and writer of television series *The Fearmakers: The Screen's Directorial Masters of Suspense and Terror,* 1996, based on his 1994 book of the same name. Author of *Splatter Movies: Breaking the Last Taboo of the Screen,* 1984; *John McCarty's Official Splatter Movie Guide, Volume 1,* 1989, and *Volume 2,* 1992; *Movie Psychos and Madmen: Film Psychopaths from Jekyll and Hyde to Hannibal Lecter,* 1993; *Thrillers: Seven Decades of Classic Film Suspense,* 1992; *The Modern Horror Film: Fifty Contemporary Classics,* 1990; *The Complete Films of John Huston,* 1992; *Alfred Hitchcock Presents: The Ten-Year Television Career of the Master of Suspense,* 1985; and the horror novel *Deadly Resurrection,* 1990. **Essays:** Lumet; Lynch; Polanski; Pollack.

Merritt, Russell Professor, University of Wisconsin—Madison. **Essay:** Griffith.

Michaels, Lloyd Professor of English, Allegheny College, Meadville, Pennsylvania. Editor of *Film Criticism* since 1977. Author of *Elia Kazan: A Guide to References and Resources,* 1983. **Essay:** Kazan.

Milicia, Joseph Has taught at Colgate University, Stevens Institute, Northwestern University, and the University of Wisconsin—Sheboygan. Has published articles on science fiction film. Also contributor to the *International Dictionary of Films and Filmmakers—Volume 1: Films, Volume 3: Actors and Actresses,* and *Volume 4: Writers and Production Artists.* **Essays:** Hartley; Soderbergh; Wenders.

Miller, Norman Journalist and author, London. Author of *Toontown: Cartoons, Comedy, and Creativity,* and contributor to a variety of periodicals. **Essay:** Demme.

Monty, Ib Director of Det Danske Filmmuseum, Copenhagen, since 1960. Literary and film critic for newspaper *Morgenavisen Jyllands-Posten,* since 1958. Editor in chief of the film periodical *Kosmorama,* 1960-67. Author of *Leonardo da Vinci,* 1953. Editor of *Se-det-er film I-III* (anthology of articles on film), with Morten Piil, 1964-66; and of *TV Broadcasts on Films and Filmmakers,* 1972. **Essay:** Dreyer.

Morrison, James E. Lecturer, English Department, North Carolina State University, Raleigh. Contributor to *New Orleans Review, Centennial Review,* and *Film Criticism.* **Essay:** Ivory.

Murphy, William T. Chief, Motion Picture, Sound, and Video Branch, National Archives, Washington, D.C., since 1976. Author of *Robert Flaherty: A Guide to References and Resources,* 1978. **Essay:** Flaherty.

Nastav, Dennis Critic and documentary filmmaker. **Essays:** Pagnol; Rohmer; Tanner.

Newman, Kim Free-lance writer and broadcaster. Author of *Nightmare Movies,* 1988, and *Wild West Movies,* 1990. Contributor to *Sight and Sound, Empire, New Musical Express,* and other periodicals. Film critic for *Box Office,* Channel 4, London. **Essay:** Lynch.

Obalil, Linda J. Assistant, Special Effects Unit, Dreamscape, Bruce Cohn Cutris Productions/Bella Productions, since 1983. **Essay:** Ulmer.

O'Brien, Daniel Free-lance writer, London. B.A. in Film Studies and Theology, 1988, and M.A. in Film Studies, 1990, University of Kent. Author of *The Hutchinson Encyclopedia*, ninth edition. Contributor to *Robert Altman—Hollywood Survivor*, 1995, and *Clint Eastwood—Filmmaker*, 1996. **Essay:** Lester.

O'Kane, John Film critic and historian, Minneapolis. **Essay:** Fassbinder.

O'Leary, Liam Film viewer, Radio Telefis Eireann, Dublin, 1966-86. Director, Liam O'Leary Film Archives, Dublin, since 1976. Producer, Abbey Theatre, 1944. Director of the Film History Cycle at the National Film Archive, London, 1953-66; co-founder, 1936, and honorary secretary, 1936-44, Irish Film Society. Director of the films *Our Country*, 1948; *Mr. Careless*, 1950; and *Portrait of Dublin*, 1951. Author of *Invitation to the Film*, 1945; *The Silent Cinema*, 1965; and *Rex Ingram, Master of the Silent Cinema*, 1980. **Essays:** Pabst; Paradzhanov; Maurice Tourneur.

Palmer, R. Barton Professor of English, Clemson University; formerly professor of English, Georgia State University. Author of *Studies in the Literary Imagination*. **Essays:** Bogdanovich; Coen; Malick; Mazursky; Pakula; Stone; Tarantino.

Petley, Julian Lecturer in communications at Brunel University. Contributor to *Sight and Sound, Monthly Film Bulletin*, and *Broadcast*. **Essays:** Loach; Sjöberg.

Petrie, Duncan J. Research officer at the British Film Institute, London. Author of *Creativity and Constraint in the British Film Industry*, 1991. **Essay:** Forsyth.

Phillips, Gene D., S.J. Professor of English, Loyola University, Chicago, (joined faculty, 1970). Contributing editor, *Literature/Film Quarterly*, since 1977. Author of several books, including *Hemingway and Film*, 1980; *George Cukor*, 1982; *Alfred Hitchcock*, 1984; *Fiction, Film, and F. Scott Fitzgerald*, 1986; *Fiction, Film, and Faulkner*, 1988; *Major Film Directors of the American and British Cinema*, 1990; and *Conrad and Cinema*, 1995. **Essays:** Coppola; Cukor; Kubrick; Reed; Russell; Schlesinger.

Polan, Dana B. Professor of English, University of Pittsburgh. **Essays:** Fuller; Tashlin.

Reynolds, Herbert Historian and project coordinator, Museum of Modern Art Department of Film, New York City, since 1981. Consultant, American Federation of Arts Film Program, since 1982. **Essay:** Schlöndorff.

Rubenstein, E. Formerly coordinator of the Program in Cinema Studies, College of Staten Island, City University of New York. Author of *Filmguide to "The General,"* 1973. Died 1988. **Essay:** Buñuel.

Saeli, Marie Adjunct faculty in English and the Humanities, Triton Community College, River Grove, Illinois, since 1983. Free-lance film reviewer. Contributor to the *International Dictionary of Films and Filmmakers—Volume 1: Films*. **Essays:** Anderson; Lucas.

Schiff, Lillian Free-lance film critic and consultant, New York. Author of *Getting Started in Filmmaking*, 1978. **Essays:** Akerman; Maysles.

Schuth, H. Wayne Professor in the Department of Drama and Communications at the University of New Orleans. B.S. and M.A. degrees in Radio, Television, and Film from Northwestern University, Evanston, Illinois; Ph.D. in Communications from Ohio State University. Author of *Mike Nichols*, 1978. Contributor of numerous articles to scholarly journals and film books. Member of board of trustees, University Film and Video Foundation, since 1988. **Essay:** Nichols.

Selig, Michael Assistant professor, University of Vermont, since 1983. Contributor to *Film Reader, Jump Cut*, and *Journal of Popular Film and Television*. **Essay:** Vidor.

Shipman, David Film historian and critic, London. Author of many books, including *Brando*, 1974; *The Story of Cinema: From the Beginnings to Gone with the Wind*, 1982; *The Story of Cinema: From Citizen Kane to the Present Day*, 1984; *A Pictorial History of Science Fiction Films*, 1985; *Marlon Brando*, 1989; and *The Great Movie Stars: The Independent Years*, 1991. **Essay:** Naruse.

Silet, Charles L.P. Teacher of film and contemporary culture and literature at Iowa State University. Has written widely on a variety of authors and directors, as well as on topics in film and television. **Essay:** Lang.

Simmon, Scott Film programmer, Mary Pickford Theatre, Library of Congress, Washington, D.C., since 1983. Contributor to *Film Comment, Journal of Popular Film and Video,* and *Literature/Film Quarterly;* and co-author of *King Vidor—American,* 1989. **Essay:** Boetticher.

Sitney, P. Adams Lecturer, Princeton University. Former director of Library and Publications, Anthology Film Archives. Author of *Film Culture Reader, Essential Cinema, The Avant-Garde Film,* and *Visionary Film.* **Essays:** Bresson; Mekas; Olmi.

Skvorecký, Josef Professor of English and Film, University of Toronto, Canada, since 1969. Author of *All the Bright Young Men and Women: A Personal History of the Czech Cinema,* 1972; and *Jiri Menzel and the History of "Closely Watched Trains,"* 1982. Works as novelist include *Miss Silver's Past,* 1975; *The Bass Saxophone,* 1977; *The Engineer of Human Souls,* 1984; and *The Miracle Game,* 1990. **Essay:** Forman.

Slide, Anthony Free-lance writer. Associate film archivist, American Film Institute, 1972-75; resident film historian, Academy of Motion Picture Arts and Sciences, 1975-80. Author of many books, including *Early American Cinema,* 1970; *The Griffith Actresses,* 1973; *The Idols of Silence,* 1976; *The Big V: A History of the Vitagraph Company,* 1976; *Early Woman Directors,* 1977; *Aspects of American Film History Prior to 1920,* 1978; *Fifty Great American Silent Films 1912-20,* with Edward Wagenknecht, 1980; *The Vaudevillians,* 1981; *A Collector's Guide to Movie Memorabilia,* 1983; *Fifty Classic British Films 1932-1982,* 1985; *The American Film Industry: A Historical Dictionary,* 1986; and *The International Film Industry: A Historical Dictionary,* 1989. Editor of seven-volume *Selected Film Criticism, 1896-1950,* and Scarecrow Press Filmmakers Series. **Essays:** Browning; Whale.

Smoodin, Eric Lecturer, Department of Literature, American University, Washington, D.C. Contributor to *Film Studies Annual* and *Journal of the University Film and Video Association.* **Essays:** De Mille; Mankiewicz; Sturges; Vigo.

Szymczak, Jerome Researcher and writer, Alameda, California. **Essays:** Cameron; Zhang Yi-Mou.

Taylor, Richard Senior lecturer in politics and Russian studies at the University College of Swansea. Author of *The Politics of Soviet Cinema, 1917-29,* 1979; *Film Propaganda: Soviet Russia and Nazi Germany,* 1979; *The Film Factory: Russian and Soviet Cinema in Documents, 1896-1939* (co-editor), 1988; and editor of English-language edition of Eisenstein's *Selected Works,* 1988 onwards. **Essays:** Eisenstein.

Telotte, J. P. Associate professor of English, Georgia Institute of Technology. Author of *Dreams of Darkness: Fantasy and the Films of Val Lewton,* and *Voices in the Dark: The Narrative Patterns of Film Noir.* Member of *Film Criticism* and *Literature/Film Quarterly* editorial boards; and co-editor, *Post Script.* **Essay:** Polanski.

Tomlinson, Doug Associate professor of film studies, Montclair State College, New Jersey. Principal researcher for *Voices of Film Experience,* edited by Jay Leyda, 1977; and editor of *Actors on Acting for the Screen,* 1989. **Essays:** Berkeley; Rossen.

Tudor, Andrew Reader in sociology, University of York, England; previously taught sociology at the University of Essex. Film critic for the magazine *New Society* for seven years. Author of *Theories of Film, Image, and Influence: Studies in the Sociology of Film,* and *Monsters and Mad Scientists: A Cultural History of the Horror Movie,* as well as numerous articles on aspects of the cinema. **Essays:** Boorman; Eastwood; Peckinpah; Siegel; Wiseman.

Tyrkus, Michael J. Award-winning independent filmmaker; co-writer and director of over a dozen short films. Writer and editor specializing in biographical and critical reference sources in literature and the cinema. Contributor to *International Dictionary of Films and Filmmakers, vol 1: Films.* Editor of *Gay & Lesbian Biography* and co-editor of *Outstanding Lives: Profiles of Lesbians and Gay Men.* In-house project editor for *St. James Film Directors Encyclopedia.* **Essays:** Chronology of Film History; Cronenberg.

Urgošíková, Blažena Film historian, Czechoslovakian Film Archives, Prague. Author of *History of Science Fiction Films.* **Essay:** Kieślowski.

Vincendeau, Ginette Lecturer in film studies, University of Warwick. Co-editor of *French Film: Texts and Contexts,* 1989. **Essay:** Pialat.

Welsh, James M. Associate professor of English, Salisbury State University, Maryland. Editor, *Literature/Film Quarterly*. Author of *His Majesty the American: The Films of Douglas Fairbanks Sr.,* 1977; *Abel Gance,* 1978; *Peter Watkins: A Guide to References and Resources,* 1986; and *Abel Gance and the Seventh Art.* **Essays:** Levinson; Zinnemann.

White, M. B. Assistant professor, Department of Radio/TV/Film, Northwestern University, Evanston, Illinois. Contributor to *Enclitic;* and other periodicals. **Essays:** Autant-Lara; Duras; Resnais.

Williams, Colin Researcher and writer, London. **Essay:** Walters.

Wine, Bill Assistant professor of communications, LaSalle College, Philadelphia, since 1981. Film, theater, and television critic, *Camden Courier-Post,* 1974-81. **Essay:** Cassavetes.

Winning, Rob Author and film scholar, Pittsburgh. **Essay:** Jarmusch.

Wood, Robin Professor of film study, Department of Fine Arts, Atkinson College, York University, Toronto, 1977-90. Member of the film studies Department, Queen's University, Kingston, Ontario, 1969-72, and University of Warwick, England, 1973-77. Member of the editorial board, *CineAction!* Author of *Hitchcock's Films,* 1965; *Arthur Penn,* 1968; *Ingmar Bergman,* 1969; *Antonioni* (co-author), 1970; *Claude Chabrol* (co-author), 1971; *The Apu Trilogy of Satyajit Ray,* 1971; *Personal Views: Explorations in Film,* 1976; *Howard Hawks,* 1977; *The American Nightmare: Essays on the Horror Film* (co-author), 1979; *Hollywood from Vietnam to Reagan,* 1985; and *Hitchcock's Films Revisited,* 1989. Took early retirement to devote himself to fiction, 1990. Novels include *That Last and Fatal Time,* 1990; and *I Remember . . . ,* 1991. **Essays:** Burton; Demy; Franju; Godard; Hitchcock; Mann; McCarey; Max Ophüls; Scorsese; Stone; Tavernier.

nationality index

American
Aldrich, Robert
Allen, Woody
Altman, Robert
Benton, Robert
Berkeley, Busby
Boetticher, Budd
Bogdanovich, Peter
Borzage, Frank
Browning, Tod
Burnett, Charles
Burton, Tim
Capra, Frank
Cassavetes, John
Coen, Joel
Coppola, Francis Ford
Cukor, George
Dassin, Jules
De Mille, Cecil B.
Demme, Jonathan
Eastwood, Clint
Edwards, Blake
Flaherty, Robert
Ford, John
Frankenheimer, John
Fuller, Samuel
Griffith, D.W.
Hartley, Hal
Hawks, Howard
Huston, John
Ivory, James
Jarmusch, Jim
Kazan, Elia
Keaton, Buster
Kubrick, Stanley
La Cava, Gregory

Lang, Fritz
Lee, Spike
Lester, Richard
Levinson, Barry
Lewin, Albert
Lewis, Joseph H.
Losey, Joseph
Lubitsch, Ernst
Lucas, George
Lumet, Sidney
Lynch, David
Malick, Terrence
Mamoulian, Rouben
Mankiewicz, Joseph L.
Mann, Anthony
Maysles, Albert and
    David Paul
Mazursky, Paul
McCarey, Leo
Minnelli, Vincente
Mulligan, Robert
Nichols, Mike
Ophuls, Marcel
Pakula, Alan J.
Peckinpah, Sam
Penn, Arthur
Pollack, Sydney
Polonsky, Abraham
Preminger, Otto
Ray, Nicholas
Renoir, Jean
Rossen, Robert
Sayles, John
Schrader, Paul
Scorsese, Martin
Siegel, Don

Siodmak, Robert
Sirk, Douglas
Soderbergh, Steven
Spielberg, Steven
Stahl, John M.
Stevens, George
Stone, Oliver
Sturges, Preston
Tarantino, Quentin
Tashlin, Frank
Tourneur, Jacques
Tourneur, Maurice
Vidor, King
Walsh, Raoul
Walters, Charles
Welles, Orson
Wellman, William
Wilder, Billy
Wiseman, Frederick
Wyler, William
Zinnemann, Fred

Australian
Armstrong, Gillian

Austrian
Pabst, G.W.
Ulmer, Edgar
von Sternberg, Josef
von Stroheim, Erich
Zinnemann, Fred

Belgian
Akerman, Chantal
Varda, Agnès

Bosnian
Kusturica, Emir
Makavejev, Dušan

British
Anderson, Lindsay
Boorman, John
Chaplin, Charles
    (Charlie)
Clayton, Jack
Davies, Terence
Greenaway, Peter
Hitchcock, Alfred
Korda, Alexander
Lean, David
Loach, Ken
Powell, Michael
Pressburger, Emeric
Reed, Carol
Roeg, Nicolas
Russell, Ken
Schlesinger, John
Whale, James

Canadian
Cameron, James
Cronenberg, David
Sennett, Mack

Chinese
Chen Kaige
Zhang Yi-Mou

Czech
Forman, Milos

583 . . . .

The *St. James Film Directors Encyclopedia* Index includes page references for all film directors entries, as well as all film titles listed in the Films as Director sections. Also included are cross-references for alternative or translation titles. The name in parentheses after a title refers to the film's director.

W